Crime and Justice in America
A Human Perspective, Sixth Edition

The most experienced author team of any introduction to criminal justice textbook brings the world of criminal justice to life in *Crime and Justice in America: A Human Perspective*, Sixth Edition. Reflecting the authors' decades of experience as police officers, police administrators, correctional administrators, trial attorneys, trainers, scholars, and educators, *Crime and Justice in America* takes students inside the real world of the criminal justice system. The authors combine their first-rate scholarship with their first-hand knowledge to provide students with an authoritative, relevant, and thought-provoking introduction to the everyday functions of the police, the courts, and the correctional system in the United States.

EXPERIENCE MATTERS

Crime and Justice in America: A Human Perspective, Sixth Edition features the most experienced authors of any introductory text on the market:

Leonard Territo—Former Chief Deputy Sheriff, patrol officer, homicide detective, jail administrator, trainer

Jim Halsted—Former prosecuting attorney and defense counsel, member of the bar of the Texas Supreme Court

Max Bromley—Former Assistant Police Chief, probation officer, and crime prevention specialist

Crime and Justice in America: A Human Perspective, Sixth Edition balances theory and practice—In addition to their practical experience, the authors are recognized scholars, have written dozens of scholarly articles and books, and have received numerous prestigious awards for outstanding teaching and research.

THE BEST BOOK IS NOW TEAMED WITH THE BEST PUBLISHER

The sixth edition of *Crime and Justice in America: A Human Perspective* is the first edition to be published by Prentice Hall, the leader in college criminal justice publishing.

Crime and Justice in America: A Human Perspective, Sixth Edition has been completely redesigned and features a new clear, streamlined 4-color design that eliminates excess clutter and distractions from the flow of the main text.

Crime and Justice in America: A Human Perspective, Sixth Edition also features a new complete multimedia supplements package—including PowerPoint, a Companion Website, WebCT, Blackboard and CourseCompass content, and access to the Research Navigator online research engine.

COMPLETELY UPDATED

Crime and Justice in America: A Human Perspective, Sixth Edition is the most up-to-date text available for your introduction to criminal justice course. It includes coverage of the CJ system's response to the ongoing threat of domestic terrorism, the recent corporate crime scandals, and the DC-area sniper as well as updated statistics, court cases, and examples throughout.

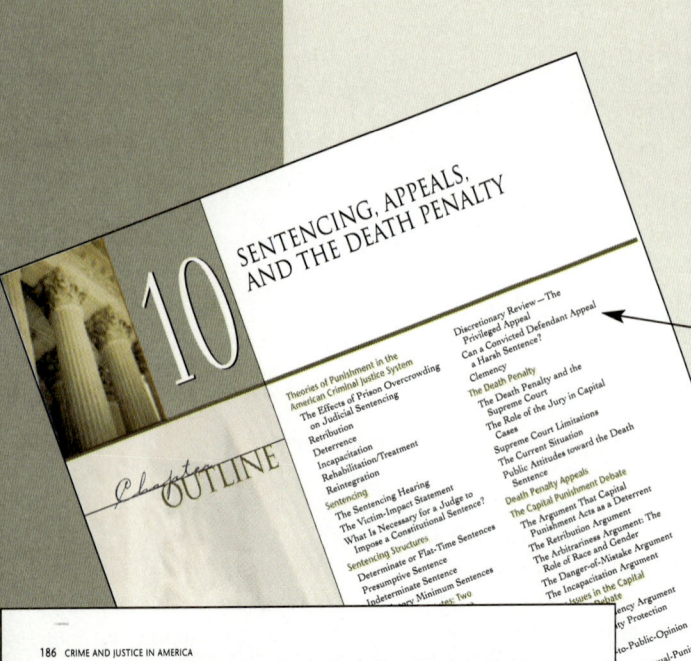

CRIME AND JUSTICE IN AMERICA:
A HUMAN PERSPECTIVE

Explore the features of the Sixth Edition

CHAPTER OUTLINES AND KEY TERMS
Open each chapter to maximize the learning benefits in each lesson.

CRITICAL THINKING QUESTIONS (CTQs)
Ensure students stop and think about the materials presented, invigorating the learning process and applying newly acquired knowledge.

IN THE NEWS
Feature boxes appear in each chapter and use current news stories to illustrate key points discussed in the text.

IN THE WORKPLACE
Each chapter contains a brief job description of various careers in the criminal justice field. Students discover how to take their knowledge from the classroom to career and beyond.

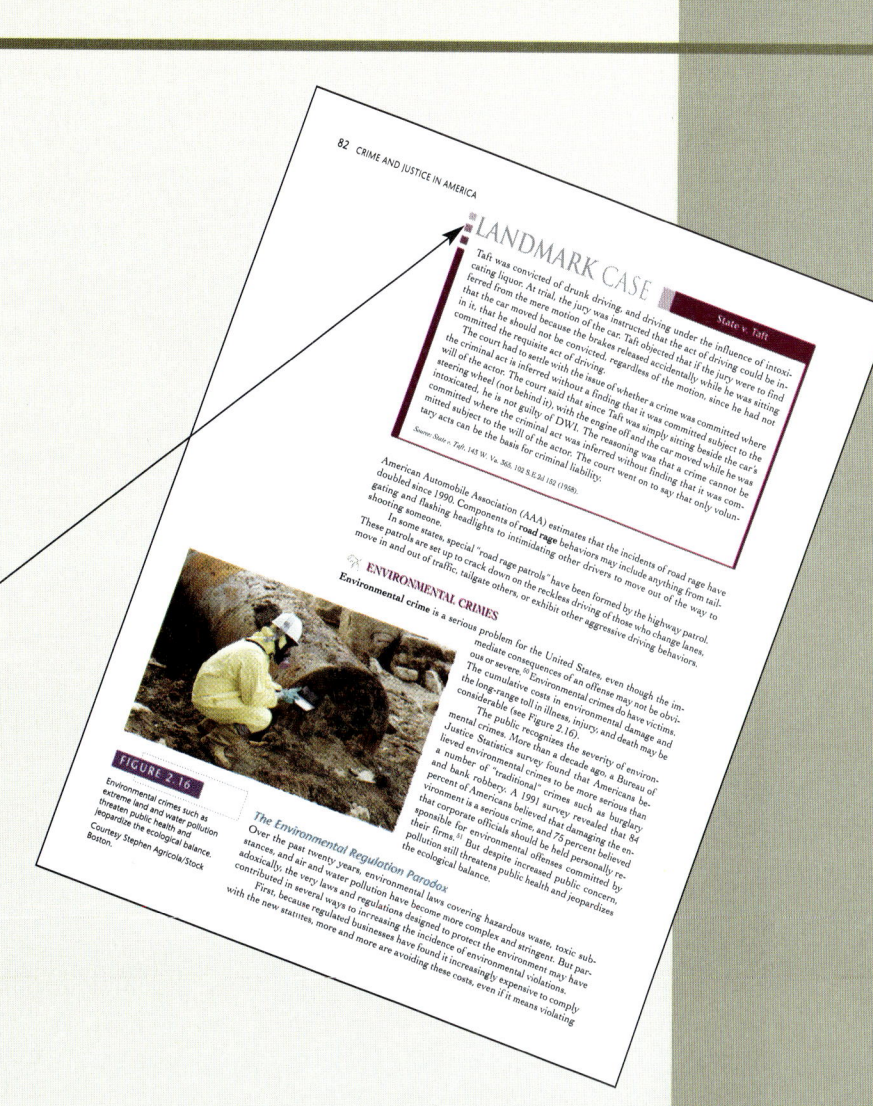

LANDMARK CASES

Significant legal cases are highlighted with every legal discussion addressed throughout the text. Students experience the principles of law and the maneuvering of our criminal courts system.

WEBSITE REFERENCES

Numerous website references are available for specific topics and discussions. These will assist students by providing more in-depth information for research.

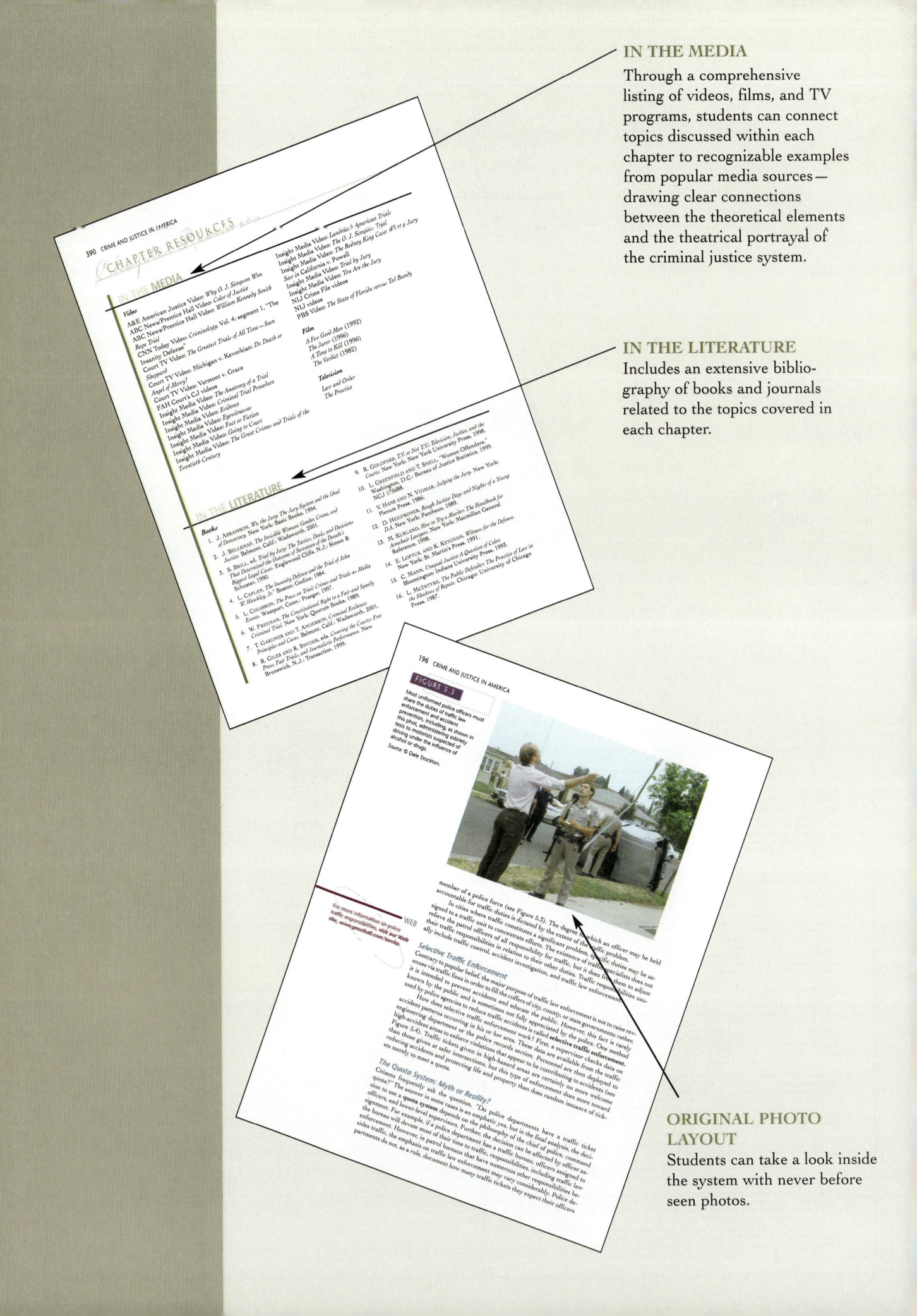

IN THE MEDIA
Through a comprehensive listing of videos, films, and TV programs, students can connect topics discussed within each chapter to recognizable examples from popular media sources—drawing clear connections between the theoretical elements and the theatrical portrayal of the criminal justice system.

IN THE LITERATURE
Includes an extensive bibliography of books and journals related to the topics covered in each chapter.

ORIGINAL PHOTO LAYOUT
Students can take a look inside the system with never before seen photos.

ANNOTATED INSTRUCTOR'S EDITION

Sixth Edition

CRIME AND JUSTICE IN AMERICA
A Human Perspective

LEONARD TERRITO
University of South Florida

JAMES B. HALSTED
University of South Florida

MAX L. BROMLEY
University of South Florida

PEARSON
Prentice Hall

Upper Saddle River, New Jersey 07458

Library of Congress Cataloging-in-Publication Data
Territo, Leonard.
   Crime and justice in America : a human perspective / Leonard Territo, James B. Halsted, Max L. Bromley.—6th ed.
     p. cm.
   Includes bibliographical references and index.
   ISBN 0-13-098168-0   ISBN 0-13-143346-6 (Instructor's edition)
   1. Criminal justice, Administration of—United States. 2. Crime—United States. I. Halsted, James. II. Bromley, Max. III. Title.

HV9950.T47 2004
364.973—dc21

2003051189

Editor-in-Chief: Stephen Helba
Director of Production and Manufacturing: Bruce Johnson
Executive Editor: Frank Mortimer, Jr.
Assistant Editor: Korrine Dorsey
Development Editor: Susan Beauchamp
Editorial Assistant: Barbara Rosenberg
Marketing Manager: Tim Peyton
Managing Editor—Production: Mary Carnis
Manufacturing Buyer: Cathleen Petersen
Production Liaison: Denise Brown
Full Service Production: Ann Mohan/WordCrafters Editorial Services, Inc.
Director, Image Resource Center: Melinda Reo
Manager, Rights and Permissions: Zina Arabia
Interior Image Specialist: Beth Brenzel
Cover Image Specialist: Karen Sanatar
Image Permission Coordinator: Nancy Seise
Photo Researcher: Sheila Norman
Composition: Carlisle Communications, Ltd.
Design Director: Cheryl Asherman
Senior Design Coordinator: Miguel Ortiz
Cover and Interior Design: Donna Wickes
Cover Image: Doug Armand/Stone/GettyImages
Cover Printer: Phoenix Color
Printer/Binder: RR Donnelley & Sons/Willard, OH

Credits and acknowledgments borrowed from other sources and reproduced, with permission, in this textbook appear on appropriate page within text.

Copyright 2004 by Pearson Education, Inc., Upper Saddle River, New Jersey, 07458.
Previous editions published by Butterworth-Heinemann.
Pearson Prentice Hall. All rights reserved. Printed in the United States of America. This publication is protected by Copyright and permission should be obtained from the publisher prior to any prohibited reproduction, storage in a retrieval system, or transmission in any form or by any means, electronic, mechanical, photocopying, recording, or likewise. For information regarding permission(s), write to: Rights and Permissions Department.

Pearson Prentice Hall™ is a trademark of Pearson Education, Inc.
Pearson® is a registered trademark of Pearson plc.
Prentice Hall® is a registered trademark of Pearson Education, Inc.

Pearson Education LTD.
Pearson Education Singapore, Pte. Ltd.
Pearson Education, Canada, Ltd.
Pearson Education–Japan
Pearson Education Australia PTY, Limited
Pearson Education North Asia Ltd.
Pearson Educaçion de Mexico, S.A. de C.V
Pearson Education Malaysia, Pte. Ltd.

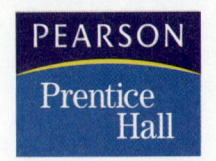

10 9 8 7 6 5 4 3 2 1
ISBN 0-13-143346-6

To
> *My daughter, Lorraine*

and my grandchildren,
> *Matthew and Branden*

—LT

To
> *My wife, Amy*

my children,
> *Richard, Stephanie, and Ashley*

—JBH

To
> *My wife, Debbie*

our children,
> *Jeffrey and Melissa*

—MLB

BRIEF CONTENTS

- **CHAPTER 1** Crime and Justice in America 2
- **CHAPTER 2** The Substantive Criminal Law 36
- **CHAPTER 3** The Law of Criminal Procedure and the Rights of the Criminally Accused 88
- **CHAPTER 4** The Nature and Distribution of Crime and Its Victims 142
- **CHAPTER 5** Police Operations 176
- **CHAPTER 6** Issues and Trends in Policing 216
- **CHAPTER 7** The Dynamics of the Criminal Court 254
- **CHAPTER 8** Pretrial Procedures: Bail, Pretrial Hearings, and Plea Bargaining 312
- **CHAPTER 9** The Criminal Trial 356
- **CHAPTER 10** Sentencing, Appeals, and the Death Penalty 394
- **CHAPTER 11** Jails and Detention 444
- **CHAPTER 12** Correctional Institutions 474
- **CHAPTER 13** Probation, Parole, and Community Corrections 516
- **CHAPTER 14** Juvenile Justice 542
- **CHAPTER 15** Drugs, Crime, and the Criminal Justice System 580

CONTENTS

About the Authors XXVIII
Preface XXIX
Acknowledgments XXXI

1 CRIME AND JUSTICE IN AMERICA 2

CRIME IN AMERICAN HISTORY 4
THE PSYCHOLOGICAL AND SOCIAL IMPACTS OF CRIME 5
DEFINING AND CLASSIFYING CRIMES 6
  Conventional Crime 6
  Economic Crime 7
  Telecommunication Crime 10
    Hacking 10 * *Illegal Bulletin Boards* 11 * *Misuse of Telephone Systems* 11
  Syndicated (Organized) Crime 13
    The Future of Organized Crime 15
  Terrorist Crime 16
    Counterterrorism for Emergency Responders 16 * *A New Kind of Terrorism* 19
DRUGS AND CRIME 19
THE ADMINISTRATION OF JUSTICE 21
RACE, CRIME, AND THE ADMINISTRATION OF JUSTICE 25
  Patterns of Crime Victimization 25
  Stereotypes and Criminal Profiles 26
  Disparities in Conviction Rates 27
  Strengthening Diversity within the Criminal Justice System 28
DECLINE IN VIOLENT CRIMES 28
  Decline in the Proportion of Young Males 29
  Tougher Sentencing 29
  Changes in the Drug Market 30
  A Moderate Unemployment Rate 30
  Community Policing and Other Law-Enforcement-Related Factors 30
FUTURE CRIME WAVE 30
SUMMARY 31

2 THE SUBSTANTIVE CRIMINAL LAW 36

CRIMINAL LAW VERSUS CIVIL LAW 39
NORMS AND SOCIALIZATION 42
  Social Sanctions 42
  Normative Variations 42

Social Values and Law 43
The Value Consensus and Value Conflict Models 43
The Value Divergence Model 43
Deviance 44

SUBSTANTIVE CRIMINAL LAW 46
Sources of American Substantive Criminal Law 46

The Common Law of England 46 ❖ The U.S. Constitution 47 ❖ Common Law as Interpreted by American Statutes 47 ❖ American Administrative Law 47 ❖ American Case Law and Stare Decisis 47

The Classification of Crime 49

CRIMINAL RESPONSIBILITY 49
Actus Reus 49

Mens Rea 49

Concurrence of *Actus Reus* and *Mens Rea* 50

Absence of Attendant Circumstances That Would Otherwise Negate Criminal Liability 50

The Criminal Act That Must Have Caused the Illegal Harm 51

THE MAJOR INDIVIDUAL CRIMES OF AMERICAN SUBSTANTIVE CRIMINAL LAW 51

HOMICIDE 52
Murder 52

Voluntary Manslaughter 53

Involuntary Manslaughter 56

CRIMES AGAINST PERSONS 56
Battery 56

Hate Crimes 61

Assault 61

Rape 62

Consent Usually Negates Rape 62 ❖ The Mens Rea of Rape 62 ❖ Statutory Rape 63 ❖ Sexually Neutral Offenses 63 ❖ Date Rape 63

Sexual Harassment Is Not a Crime 64

False Imprisonment 65

Kidnapping 65

CRIMES AGAINST HABITATION 66
Burglary 66

How the Elements of Common-Law Burglary Have Been Modified by Modern American Criminal Statutes 66

Arson 67

How the Elements of Common-Law Arson Have Been Modified by Modern American Criminal Statutes 67

CRIMES AGAINST PROPERTY—THE ACQUISITION OFFENSES 68
Larceny 68

How the Elements of Common-Law Larceny Have Been Modified by Modern American Criminal Statutes 69

Robbery 69

How the Elements of Common-Law Robbery Have Been Modified by Modern American Criminal Statutes 70

Embezzlement 70

How the Elements of Common-Law Embezzlement Have Been Modified by Modern American Criminal Statutes 71

Obtaining Property by False Pretense or Fraud 71

Extortion (Blackmail) 72

Receiving Stolen Property 72

CONSENSUAL CRIMES 73

CRIMES AGAINST MORALITY 74

Historical Roots 74

Fornication 75

Adultery 75

Illicit Cohabitation 75

Bigamy 75

Incest 75

Sodomy 75

Prostitution 76

MODERN CRIMES 77

Computer Crime 77

Internal Computer Crime 77 ❖ *Trojan Horses 77* ❖ *Salami Technique 78* ❖ *Trap Doors 78* ❖ *Logic Bombs 78*

Identity Theft 78

Stalking 78

TRAFFIC OFFENSES THAT ARE CRIMES 80

Racing 80

Reckless Driving 81

Hit and Run 81

Vehicular Homicide 81

DUI/DWI 81

Multiple Offenses, Classified as "Road Rage" 81

ENVIRONMENTAL CRIMES 82

The Environmental Regulation Paradox 82

SUMMARY 83

3 THE LAW OF CRIMINAL PROCEDURE AND THE RIGHTS OF THE CRIMINALLY ACCUSED 88

THE LAW OF CRIMINAL PROCEDURE VERSUS SUBSTANTIVE CRIMINAL LAW 90

THE BILL OF RIGHTS IS INEXTRICABLY TIED TO THE LAW OF CRIMINAL PROCEDURE 91

Constitutional Rights as Possible Constraints on Efficient Law Enforcement 92

THE CONSTITUTION AND THE BILL OF RIGHTS 92

A Historical Overview of Their Rationale 92

The Doctrine of Selective Incorporation 93

The Supreme Court's Power of Judicial Review 95

THE FOURTEENTH AMENDMENT'S DUE PROCESS CLAUSE 95

THE FOURTH AMENDMENT RIGHTS ON ARREST, SEARCH, AND SEIZURE 98

Evidentiary Standards of the Degrees of Certainty Used throughout the Various Phases of the Criminal Justice System 99

THE RIGHT TO A CONSTITUTIONAL ARREST 99

Can a Citizen Make an Arrest? 99

The Requirements for an Arrest Warrant 100

When Can an Officer Use Deadly Force to Make an Arrest? 102

ARRESTS THAT ARE NOT REALLY ARRESTS—"STOPS" AND "DETENTIONS": WHEN ARE THEY CONSTITUTIONAL? 103

Limited Detention—Stop and Frisk 103

Use of Excessive Force When Effecting an Arrest 104

Expanding the Permissible Scope of "Stops" and "Detentions" 105

THE RIGHT AGAINST UNREASONABLE SEARCHES AND SEIZURES 105

Government Conduct 106

Reasonable Expectation of Privacy 106

*Standing 106 * Items Held Out to be Public 107*

SEARCHES CONDUCTED PURSUANT TO A WARRANT 107

The General-Warrant Requirement 107

The Reasonableness Requirement 109

The Neutral-and-Detached-Magistrate Requirement 110

The Probable-Cause Requirement 110

Constitutional Execution of a Search Warrant 110

THE SIX RECOGNIZED EXCEPTIONS TO THE SEARCH WARRANT REQUIREMENT 111

A Search Incident to a Lawful Arrest 111

The Automobile Exception 112

The Consent Exception 113

The Plain-View Exception 115

The Stop-and-Frisk Exception 116

Exigent Circumstances 116

THE EXCLUSIONARY RULE 117

The Defendant's Right to a Suppression Hearing 118

THE EXPANDED EXCEPTIONS TO THE EXCLUSIONARY RULE 118

The Recently Recognized Additional Seven Exceptions to the Exclusionary Rule 120

Criticism of the Exclusionary Rule 121

THE FIFTH AMENDMENT PRIVILEGE AGAINST SELF-INCRIMINATION 122

A Constitutional Confession 124

THE SIXTH AMENDMENT RIGHT TO COUNSEL AND OTHER TRIAL RIGHTS 126

The Right to Counsel 126

*Cases in Which the Right to Counsel Exists 127 * May a Defendant Represent Himself or Herself? 127 * Does an Indigent Defendant Have the Right to a Particular Lawyer? 128*

The Right to a Speedy Trial 129

*What Happens When a Person's Right to a Speedy Trial Is Violated? 129 * When Does a Speedy Trial Attach? 129 * What Is the Standard for Determining an Unreasonable Delay? 130*

The Right to a Public Trial 130

The Right to a Jury Trial 130

The Right to Confront Witnesses Testifying against the Defendant 131

The Right to a Compulsory Process for Obtaining Witnesses in the Defendant's Favor 132

THE FIFTH AMENDMENT RIGHT PROHIBITING DOUBLE JEOPARDY 133

Exceptions to the Double Jeopardy Prohibition 133

Mistrials 133 ❖ Dismissals 133 ❖ Appeals 133

Jeopardy as a Bar to Prosecution for the Same Offense 134

THE FIFTH AMENDMENT RIGHT TO SUBSTANTIVE DUE PROCESS 134

THE EIGHTH AMENDMENT RIGHTS AGAINST EXCESSIVE BAIL AND CRUEL AND UNUSUAL PUNISHMENT 134

Excessive Bail 134

Cruel and Unusual Punishment 134

TOWARD EQUAL JUSTICE 135

SUMMARY 136

4 THE NATURE AND DISTRIBUTION OF CRIME AND ITS VICTIMS 142

THE UNIFORM CRIME REPORTING PROGRAM 144

INDEX CRIMES 145

Violent Crimes 145

Murder and Nonnegligent Manslaughter 145 ❖ Forcible Rape 146 ❖ Robbery 147 ❖ Aggravated Assault 148

Crimes against Property 149

Burglary 149 ❖ Larceny-Theft 149 ❖ Motor Vehicle Theft 150 ❖ Arson 150

Hate Crime 151

Limits to National Crime Data 152

CRITICISMS OF THE UCR PROGRAM 152

Crime Data Manipulation 152

Nonmandatory Nature of the Program 152

Incomplete Crime Categories 152

UCR Hierarchy Rule 153

Lack of Information on Part II Crimes 153

FUTURE OF THE UCR PROGRAM 153

COLLECTION OF CAMPUS CRIME DATA 154

WHAT CRIME DOES TO VICTIMS AND SOCIETY 155

The Victim in Historical Perspective 155

Talion Law 155

Victim Compensation 155

GOVERNMENT PROGRAMS FOR VICTIMS 155

Compensable Crimes 156

Eligibility Requirements for Victims 156

Restitution 156

Victim and Witness Intimidation Issues and Responses 157

Intimidation Prevention and Control 157 ❖ Cooperation with the Judiciary 158 ❖ Targets of Victim and Witness Intimidation 158

VICTIMIZATION STUDIES 158

NATIONAL CRIME DATA COLLECTION 159

National Crime Victimization Survey 159

Comparing UCR and NCVS 159
Race and Victims of Violence 160
Issues with Victim Surveys 160

SPECIAL CATEGORIES OF VICTIMS 160
Intimate-Partner Violence 160

Handling Cases of Domestic Violence 161 ❋ *The Violence against Women Act 163* ❋ *Need for a Theoretical Framework 164* ❋ *Innovations Suggest a Direction 164*

Children as Victims 165

Assistance for Child Victims 167 ❋ *The Cycle of Violence 167*

Victims of Drunk-Driving Accidents 168
Older People as Victims 168
Sexual and Physical Violence against College Women 169
Victims of Workplace Violence 170

VICTIM SPECIAL-INTEREST GROUPS 170
COSTS OF CRIME VICTIMIZATION 171
Number of Victimizations 171
Costs and Other Consequences 172
Implications 172

UNRESOLVED VICTIM–CRIMINAL JUSTICE SYSTEM ISSUES 172
SUMMARY 172

5 POLICE OPERATIONS 176

POLICE DEPARTMENTS IN THE UNITED STATES 178
POLICE OFFICER SELECTION AND TRAINING 179
A Snapshot of Local Police Departments and Sheriffs' Offices in the United States 179
Local Police Department Characteristics 179
Sheriff's Office Characteristics 179
Smaller Law Enforcement Agencies 180

THE EVOLUTION OF POLICING IN AMERICA 181
Influence of Robert Peel 181
Creating City Police Forces in the United States 182
The Emergence of County, State, and Federal Law Enforcement Agencies 182

County Law Enforcement 183 ❋ *State Law Enforcement 183* ❋ *Federal Law Enforcement 183*

PATROL OPERATIONS 184
Patrol Division Assignments 184
Activities of Patrol Officers 186

Noncrime Calls for Service 187 ❋ *Attendance at Public Gatherings 187* ❋ *Benevolent and Community Services 187* ❋ *Preliminary Investigations 187* ❋ *Arrests 188* ❋ *Traffic Direction and Traffic Law Enforcement 188* ❋ *Court Testimony 189*

CHANGING PATROL STRATEGY 190
Kansas City Preventive Patrol Experiment 190
Nontraditional Patrol 190
Flint, Michigan, Foot Patrol 191
Directed Patrol 193
Crackdowns 193

ZERO-TOLERANCE ENFORCEMENT 193
POLICE TRAFFIC RESPONSIBILITIES 194
    Selective Traffic Enforcement 196
    The Quota System: Myth or Reality? 196
    Who Gets the Money? 197
RURAL POLICING 197
CAMPUS POLICE 198
THE DETECTIVE ROLE 199
    The Media Stereotype 199
    The Historical Stereotype 199
    The Critical Stereotype 200
    Activities of Detectives 200

Incident Report and Preliminary Investigation 200 ❖ *Evidence Collection and Processing 201* ❖ *Screening and Case Assignment 201* ❖ *Follow-Up (Latent) Investigation 201* ❖ *Clearance and Arrest 202* ❖ *File Maintenance 202*

MAJOR STUDIES OF THE INVESTIGATOR'S ROLE 202
    The Rand Criminal Investigation Study 202

The Study Design 202 ❖ *Policy Recommendations 203*

    The PERF Study: Solving Crimes 203

THE NCIC NETWORK IN INVESTIGATIONS 204
EVOLUTION IN POLICING: COP AND POP 205
    Community Policing and the Office of the Sheriff 207
    Trends in Community Policing 207
    The Problem-Oriented Approach to Policing 210
    The Future of Community-Oriented Policing and Problem Solving (COPPS) 211

SUMMARY 213

6 ISSUES AND TRENDS IN POLICING 216

PROFESSIONALISM 218
LAW ENFORCEMENT AGENCY ACCREDITATION 218
    Benefits of Accreditation 218
HIGHER EDUCATION AND LAW ENFORCEMENT 219
    The Rationale for Collegiate Standards 219
    Educational Upgrading: A Second Rationale 219
POLICE MISCONDUCT 220
EMPLOYMENT OF MINORITIES AND WOMEN IN POLICING 223
    Recruitment of Minorities 223
    Innovative Minority Recruiting 223
    Recruitment of Women 224
    Research on Women on Patrol 225
    The Current Status of Women in Policing 225
OFFICER HEALTH 225
    Job Stress 226
    Stress and Female Police Officers 227
    Alcoholism 227
    Police Department Drug Testing 228

Suicide 229
Coping with Health Problems 229
POLICE CONTACT WITH THE PUBLIC 230
USE OF DEADLY FORCE 230
Managing the Use of Force 230
Shooting-Control Techniques 232
Research on Use of Force by Police 233
Violence-Prone Police Officers 233
Evaluating the Use of Pepper Spray as an Alternative to Deadly Force 233
POLICE-PROSECUTOR COOPERATION 233
PRIVATE SECURITY AND LAW ENFORCEMENT: PARTNERS FOR THE FUTURE 234
TECHNOLOGICAL TRENDS IN POLICING 234
Computer-Aided Dispatch 234
Fingerprint Automation 235
Police Use of Laptop Computers 237
Future Applications of Computers 237
DNA Profiling 238
Geographical Information Systems 238
POLICE/CITIZEN ROLES IN CRIME PREVENTION 239
Citizen Responsibility in Crime Prevention 239
Neighborhood Watch Programs 240
Fear of Crime and Police Response 240
Evaluating Crime-Prevention Programs 241
CRIME PREVENTION THROUGH ENVIRONMENTAL DESIGN 243
Applications of CPTED 243
Convenience Stores 244 ❖ *Safe Neighborhoods* 244
Combining CPTED and Community-Policing Strategies 244
What Police and Residents Can Do 244
Specific Crime-Prevention Activities 245
Security in Parks 245 ❖ *Building Regulations* 245 ❖ *Civil Remedies* 245
CITIZEN INVOLVEMENT IN CRIME PREVENTION 245
The McGruff Campaign 245
The CAT Program 246
The Watch Your Car Program 246
Campus Crime Prevention 246
Community Anti-drug Efforts 246
SUMMARY 249

7 THE DYNAMICS OF THE CRIMINAL COURT 254

WHAT IS A COURT? 256
What Is a Court's Jurisdiction? 257
THE DUAL COURT SYSTEM 259
The Federal Court System 260
State and Local Court Systems 260
THE U.S. SUPREME COURT 262

How Supreme Court Case Law Comes into Being 264
State Courts of Last Resort 265

STATE AND FEDERAL INTERMEDIATE APPELLATE COURTS 265
FEDERAL AND STATE TRIAL COURTS 267
STATE AND FEDERAL LOWER COURTS 269
SPECIALTY COURTS 270
Drug Courts: A Blend of Treatment and Coercion through Judicial Sanctions 270
Military Tribunals in the Age of Terrorism 272

COURT ADMINISTRATIVE PERSONNEL 274
The Law Clerk 274
The Judicial Assistant 274
The Bailiff 275
The Court Reporter 275
The Court Clerk 275
The Court Administrator 276
Courthouse Regulars 277
Special-Service Court Employees 277
The Chief Judge 278

THE EFFECT OF COURTROOM CONGESTION ON CASE PROCESSING TIME 278
AMERICAN CRIMINAL COURTS 279
PROSECUTORS AND DEFENSE LAWYERS—ADVERSARIES IN THE CRIMINAL COURT 279
The Adversary System 280
The Prevalence of Guilty Pleas in the American Criminal Justice System 281
The Adversarial Model of the Criminal Trial versus the Reality of Plea Bargaining 281

THE DYNAMICS OF THE CRIMINAL COURT 282
THE PROSECUTOR 283
The Prosecutor's Specific Function 283
Step by Step—The Prosecutor's Role 283
The Prosecutor's Public Image 285
Division of Prosecutorial Duties 286
The Decision to Prosecute 286
The Power of Prosecutorial Discretion 287
Unethical Procedures and Wrongful Conviction 288
The Prosecutor's Constitutional Duty to Disclose Evidence Favorable to the Defendant 289
Prosecutorial Diversion 289
Adjudication Deferred/Withheld Adjudication 289
Too Many Cases, Too Few Prosecutors 289

THE CRIMINAL DEFENSE LAWYER 290
The Role of the Criminal Defense Lawyer 290
Privately Retained Counsel 292

LEGAL SERVICES FOR THE POOR 293
The Public-Defender System 293
The Assigned-Counsel System 295
The Contract System 296

THE JUDICIARY 296
    The Selection of Judges 296
    The Election of Judges 297
    The Appointment of Judges 297
    Modified Appointment of Judges 298
    Which Is the Best System for Selecting Judges? 298
    Judges at Work 299
    Female Judges and Justices 299

COURTHOUSE CULTURE AND THE SOCIALIZATION OF JUDGES 300
    Job Stress and the Judiciary 301

THE CONSEQUENCES OF COURT CONGESTION, DELAY, AND BACKLOG 304
SUMMARY 306

8 PRETRIAL PROCEDURES: BAIL, PRETRIAL HEARINGS, AND PLEA BARGAINING 312

INITIATING PROSECUTION IN MISDEMEANOR CASES 314
    Pretrial Detention 314
    The Complaint 315
    The Three Types of Preliminary Hearings 316

BAIL OR JAIL? 317
    The Time and the Criteria for the Bail Decision 318
    Drug Testing to Reduce Pretrial Misconduct 318

TYPES AND AMOUNTS OF BAIL 318
    Commercial Bail 318
    The Bail Schedule 319
    State Bail Statutes 320
    Conditions of Bail 320
    Alternatives to Bail 320
    Forfeiture of Bail 323
    Defects in the Bail System: Commercialization of Bail Bondspeople, Bounty Hunters, and Bail Jumpers 324

DENIAL OF BAIL 325
    Reforms in the Bail System 328
    The Effects of Preventive Detention 320
    May a Convicted Defendant Be Out on Bail While Awaiting an Appeal? 331

MISDEMEANOR TRIALS 331
INITIATING FELONY PROSECUTION 332
THE PRELIMINARY HEARING (THE BINDOVER HEARING) 332
THE GRAND JURY 334
    The Grand Jury Today 334
    True Bills and Presentments 335
    The Special Investigative Grand Jury 335

FORMAL FELONY CHARGING 335
    Constitutional Requirements of a Prosecutor's Information 336
    Showups, Lineups, and Other Pretrial Identification Procedures During the Prearrest, Postarrest, and After the Formal Felony Charging 338
    Constitutional Requirements and Identification Procedures 339

THE ARRAIGNMENT 339
PRETRIAL MOTIONS 340
    The Motion to Dismiss 340
    The Motion for Discovery 341
    The Motion for a Change of Venue 341
    The Motion of Intention to Provide Alibi 341
    The Motion for Severance 341
    The Motion to Determine Competency 342
    The Constitutional Right of Being Competent to Stand Trial 342
    The Motion for a Bill of Particulars 343
THE SUPPRESSION HEARING 343
    The Motion to Suppress 343
    The Right to a Suppression Hearing 344
PLEA NEGOTIATIONS 344
    Justification for Plea Bargaining 345
    The Prevalence of Guilty Pleas 345
    Entering a Constitutional Guilty Plea 346
    The Plea Process 346
    The Victim and Plea Bargaining 347
FACTORS IN PLEA NEGOTIATION 349
    Evaluating Plea Bargaining 350
    How Can a Defendant Successfully Appeal a Guilty Plea? 350
PRETRIAL DIVERSION AS AN ALTERNATIVE TO PLEA BARGAINING 351
SUMMARY 352

9 THE CRIMINAL TRIAL 356

THE QUESTION OF GUILT DISPOSED OF BY THE CRIMINAL TRIAL 358
THE PHILOSOPHICAL FOUNDATIONS OF THE CRIMINAL TRIAL 358
    The Defendant Is Presumed Innocent 359
    The State Has the Burden of Proof 359
    The State Must Prove the Defendant Guilty beyond a Reasonable Doubt 359
THE CRIMINAL TRIAL'S FIRST STEP—IMPANELING A FAIR AND IMPARTIAL JURY 360
    The Press in the Courtroom 360
    The Problem of Pretrial Publicity 361
    The Social and Political Baggage Juries Bring to Trial 362
    The Jury Selection Process 362
        Scientific Jury Selection 366 ❖ *The Use of Jury Consultants 366* ❖ *The Relationship between Quality Jury Selection and the Outcome of the Trial 366*
THE RULES OF EVIDENCE 366
    Requirements for Admissible Evidence—It Must Be Relevant, Material, and Competent 367
    Testimonial Evidence 368
    Real Evidence 368
    Opinion Evidence Offered by an Expert Witness 369
    A Limitation—Evidence of Privileged or Confidential Communications 370

Another Limitation—Hearsay Evidence 371
Some Exceptions to the Hearsay Rule 371

THE PROCEDURAL ORDER OF A CRIMINAL TRIAL 372
OPENING STATEMENTS 374
PRESENTATION OF THE STATE'S EVIDENCE 374
PRESENTATION OF THE DEFENSE'S CASE 376
THE AFFIRMATIVE DEFENSES 377
The Defense of Infancy 377
The Insanity Defense 377
The Legal Definition of Insanity 378
Self-Defense 379
The Defense of Ignorance or Mistake of Fact 381
The Defense of Protection of Property 381
The Defense of the Use of Force to Effect an Arrest 382
The Battered-Spouse Defense 383

REBUTTAL AND SURREBUTTAL 385
CLOSING ARGUMENTS 385
THE TRIAL JUDGE'S CHARGE TO THE JURY 385
THE JURY'S DELIBERATIONS 386
THE JURY'S VERDICT 386
A Hung Jury 386
Polling the Jury 386
Jury Nullification 386
Postverdict Motions 387

SUMMARY 388

10 SENTENCING, APPEALS, AND THE DEATH PENALTY 394

THEORIES OF PUNISHMENT IN THE AMERICAN CRIMINAL JUSTICE SYSTEM 396
The Effects of Prison Overcrowding on Judicial Sentencing 397
Retribution 398
Deterrence 399
Incapacitation 400
Rehabilitation/Treatment 400
Reintegration 401

SENTENCING 401
The Sentencing Hearing 402
The Structure and Procedures Used in the Sentencing Hearing 404 ❋ Constitutional Rights Afforded during a Sentencing Hearing 404 ❋ The Effect of the Presentence Report in the Sentence Imposition 404
The Victim-Impact Statement 405
What Is Necessary for a Judge to Impose a Constitutional Sentence? 405

SENTENCING STRUCTURES 407
Determinate or Flat-Time Sentences 408
Presumptive Sentences 408
Indeterminate Sentences 409
Mandatory Minimum Sentences 409

ENHANCEMENT STATUTES—TWO PUNISHMENTS FOR ONE CRIME 409
Habitual-Criminal Statutes 412
Hate Crimes 413
The New Sentencing Structures of the Twenty-First Century 413

TRADITIONAL SENTENCING DISPARITIES 413
Sentencing Guidelines—An Attempt to Resolve the Problem of Sentencing Disparities 415
Gain Time, Good Time, and Actual Time Served 416

THE APPEAL PROCESS 417
Postconviction Relief—A Hidden Form of Appeal 419
Discretionary Review—The Privileged Appeal 419
Can a Convicted Defendant Appeal a Harsh Sentence? 419
Clemency 420

THE DEATH PENALTY 420
The Death Penalty and the Supreme Court 423
The Role of the Jury in Capital Cases 423
Supreme Court Limitations 423
Competency to Stand Trial at the Time of Execution 424
The Current Situation 424
Public Attitudes toward the Death Sentence 427

DEATH PENALTY APPEALS 428

THE CAPITAL PUNISHMENT DEBATE 429
The Argument That Capital Punishment Acts as a Deterrent 429
The Retribution Argument 431
The Arbitrariness Argument: The Role of Race and Gender 431
The Danger-of-Mistake Argument 434
DNA and the Death Penalty 434
The Incapacitation Argument 435

MINOR ISSUES IN THE CAPITAL PUNISHMENT DEBATE 437
The Cost-Efficiency Argument 437
The Community Protection Argument 437
The Appeal-to-Public-Opinion Argument 438
The Cruel-and-Unusual-Punishment Argument 438
The Brutalization Argument 438

SUMMARY 438

11 JAILS AND DETENTION 444

A BRIEF HISTORY OF JAILS 446
THE PURPOSE OF JAILS 447
JAIL CROWDING 449
Looking at the Local Justice System 450
How System Decision Makers Can Affect Jail Crowding 450

Law Enforcement 450 ❖ Jail Administrators 451 ❖ Prosecutors 451 ❖ Pretrial Services 451 ❖ Judiciary 451 ❖ Defense 452 ❖ Probation and Parole 452 ❖ Outside the Local Level 452 ❖ Outside the System 452

DIRECT SUPERVISION 452
Personnel Issues 453

Effective Management 454
Improved Staff Morale 454
Reduced Sick Leave 454
Improved Working Conditions 454
Staffing Level 455
Safe Working Environment 455

SPECIAL-MANAGEMENT INMATES 455
Physically Ill Inmates 456
Alcoholics 456
Inmates with Disabilities 456
Aggressive and Assaultive Inmates 456
Vulnerable Inmates 456
Mentally Ill Inmates 457
Drug Addicts 457
Sex Offenders 458

SUICIDE IN JAIL 458
Precipitating Factors of Suicidal Behavior 462
Identifying the Suicidal Inmate 462
Key Components of a Suicide Prevention Program 463

TREATMENT PROGRAMS 464

JAIL SECURITY 466
Counts 466
Shakedowns 467
Frisks 467
Tool Control 467
Key Control 467
Cutlery Control 468
Narcotics Control 469
Visitation Control 469

SUMMARY 470

12 CORRECTIONAL INSTITUTIONS 474

HISTORICAL PERSPECTIVE 476
MAXIMUM-SECURITY PRISONS 477
The History of Administrative Segregation 478
New Maximum-Security Prisons 480

Federal Prison at Marion, Illinois 480 ❋ *Federal Prison at Florence, Colorado 481* ❋
Minnesota Correctional Facility at Oak Park Heights 484

MEDIUM-SECURITY PRISONS 485
MINIMUM-SECURITY PRISONS 486
RECEPTION AND CLASSIFICATION CENTERS 486
PRISON OVERCROWDING 487
Alternative Approaches to Relieving Prison Crowding 488

RIOTS AND DISTURBANCES IN CORRECTIONAL INSTITUTIONS 489
Inmate Groups Prone to Causing Problems 491

Antisocial Inmates 491 ❋ *Inmates with Mental Problems 491* ❋ *Racial/Ethnic Minorities 491* ❋ *Radical/Revolutionary Organizations 491*

GANGS IN PRISON 491
  Becoming a Gang Member 491
    Classes of Membership 492 ❖ Knowledge of Other Members 493 ❖ Structure of the Gang: Leadership 493 ❖ Hierarchy 493 ❖ Longevity of Current Leadership 493 ❖ Replacement of Leader 493 ❖ Moving Up in Rank 493 ❖ Operation of the Gang: Prescribed Behavior for Members 493 ❖ Maintaining Order, Loyalty, and Obedience 494 ❖ Gang Values 494 ❖ Noncriminal Activities 494
  Leaving the Gang 494
INSTITUTIONAL PROGRAMS AND SERVICES 495
  Educational Programs 495
    Adult Basic Education and Literacy Programs 495 ❖ GED Programs 495 ❖ Life Skills Programs 496 ❖ Vocational Education Programs 496
  Prison Work Programs 496
    Prison Maintenance Programs 496 ❖ Agricultural, Forestry, and Road Work Activities 497
  Recreational Programs 497
  Treatment Programs 497
    Mental Health Programs 497 ❖ Treatment for the Seriously Mentally Ill 498 ❖ Drug Treatment 498
  Religious Programs 498
ELDERLY MALE PRISONERS 498
SEXUALITY IN PRISONS 499
HIV AND AIDS IN PRISON 500
  Prevention 500
WOMEN IN PRISON 501
  Early Punishments and Places of Confinement 501
  Reformatories for Women 502
  Women's Prisons Today 504
  Women's Criminal Activity 505
  Women's Adaptation to Imprisonment 505
    Involvement in Pseudofamilies 505
  The Nature and Amount of Homosexuality 506
  Programs for Women 506
  Sexual Contact between Staff and Inmates 506
PRIVATE PRISONS 506
  Arguments for Privatization 507
  Arguments against Privatization 508
SUMMARY 509

13 PROBATION, PAROLE, AND COMMUNITY CORRECTIONS 516

PROBATION 518
  The Suspended Sentence: Birthplace of Probation 518
  John Augustus: Father of Probation 519
  Imposing Probation 519
    Probation without Adjudication 519 ❖ Presentence Investigation Reports 520 ❖ Conditions of Probation and Parole 520

XXIII

Restructuring Probation as an Intermediate Sanction 521
Intensive-Supervision Probation (ISP) Programs 521
Massachusetts Courts Project 521 ❖ *ISP in New Jersey* 521 ❖ *ISP in Three California Counties* 522
Revocation of Probation 522

INNOVATIONS IN PROBATION 523
House Arrest 523
Advantages of House Arrest 523
Social Benefits 523 ❖ *Responsiveness to Local and Offender Needs* 524 ❖ *Implementation Ease and Timeliness* 524 ❖ *Cost-Effectiveness* 524
Electronically Monitored Home Confinement 524
Disadvantages of House Arrest 525
House Arrest May Not Punish the Crime 525 ❖ *House Arrest Focuses Primarily on Offender Surveillance* 525 ❖ *Class and Income Bias May Enter into Participant Selection* 526 ❖ *House Arrest Compromises Public Safety* 526

PAROLE 526
Origins of the American System of Parole 526
Transportation to America 526 ❖ *Maconochie and Norfolk Island* 527 ❖ *Crofton and the Irish System* 527 ❖ *Developments in the United States* 528 ❖ *Elmira Reformatory* 528
Modern Parole 529
Parole Selection 529 ❖ *Conditions of Parole* 530
Enhancing Parole Prediction 531
The Salient Factor Score 532 ❖ *Other Prediction Efforts* 533 ❖ *Critiques and Justifications* 534

INNOVATIONS IN PAROLE 535
Shock Incarceration Programs 535
Community Correctional Centers 535
Halfway Houses 536
Work Release 537
Educational Release 537
Furloughs 537

COMMUNITY SERVICE 537
Objectives of Community Service 538
Types of Programs 538
Issues in Community Service 538

SUMMARY 539

14 JUVENILE JUSTICE 542

THE CREATION OF DELINQUENCY 544
DEVELOPMENT OF THE JUVENILE COURT 547
The First Juvenile Courts: 1899–1967 547
Where We Are Today 547

LANGUAGE OF THE COURTS 548
Teen Courts 548

PREVENTION AND DIVERSION 548
The Police 549

Intake and the Courts 549
Programs Outside the Juvenile Justice System 550

EDUCATIONAL PROGRAMS 550
Drug Abuse Resistance Education (DARE) 550
Community Policing and DARE 550 ❖ *Criticism of DARE* 550
Education in the Law 551

HANDLING JUVENILES IN THE SYSTEM 551
Dependent and Abused Children 551
Delinquent Children 551
Police Contact 552
Juvenile Intake 554
Removing Juveniles from Adult Jails 555

JUVENILE DETENTION CENTERS 556
Research on Juveniles in Detention 556

DEINSTITUTIONALIZATION OF STATUS OFFENDERS 556

POSTADJUDICATION DISPOSITIONS 557
Juvenile Restitution Programs 557
Community-Based Programs 557
Residential Programs 557
Wilderness Programs 558
Nonresidential Programs 558

LONG-TERM INSTITUTIONAL FACILITIES 559

EVALUATING JUVENILE BOOT CAMPS 559

COMMUNITY SUPERVISION 559
Juvenile Probation 560
Juvenile Aftercare 560
The Quality of Supervision 561
Revocation 561

RUNAWAY AND MISSING CHILDREN 561
Characteristics of the Runaway 562
The System's Response to Runaway Youth 562

JUVENILE CURFEWS 563
Representative Curfew Programs 563

SERIOUS AND VIOLENT JUVENILE OFFENDERS 564
SVJ Offenders—A Distinct Group 564
Predictors of SVJ Offending 565
Interventions to Prevent SVJ Offending 565

CRIME IN SCHOOLS 566
Nonfatal Student Victimization—Student Reports 566
Violence and Crime at School—Public School Principal/Disciplinarian Reports 566
School Environment 566
The School Resource Officer (SRO) 569

THE SECRET SERVICE SAFE SCHOOL INITIATIVE 569
Background 569
Method 570
Incident Characteristics 570

Preliminary Findings 571
Implications 571
YOUTH GANGS 571
Scope of the Problem 571
Why Do Youth Join Gangs? 572
Conclusion 572
CHILDREN WHO KILL THEIR PARENTS 573
Youths at Risk 573
JUVENILE JUSTICE IN THE NEW CENTURY 574
Objectives of an Effective Juvenile Justice System 574
Elements of an Effective Juvenile Justice System 574
SUMMARY 575

15 DRUGS, CRIME, AND THE CRIMINAL JUSTICE SYSTEM 580

WHAT IS DRUG ADDICTION? 582
Narcotics 582
Depressants 586
Psychedelics 586
Ketamine 588 ❖ *MDMA 588*
Stimulants 589
Cocaine 589 ❖ *Methamphetamine 589* ❖ *Crystal Meth 590* ❖ *Methcathinone 590*
DRUG-FACILITATED SEXUAL ASSAULT 590
Drugs of Choice 591
Other Date-Rape Drugs 593
EMERGING DRUG TRENDS 593
REDUCING THE DEMAND FOR ILLICIT DRUGS 595
Reducing Demand through Treatment 595
Managed Care and State Health Care Reform 595 ❖ *Linking Criminal Justice and Treatment 595* ❖ *Drug Courts 596* ❖ *Treatment Research 596*
Reducing Demand through Prevention 596
Alcohol Abuse by Minors 596 ❖ *Safe and Drug-Free Schools 596*
COMMUNITY COLLABORATION WITH LAW ENFORCEMENT 597
Antidrug Coalitions and Partnerships 597
Drug-Free Workplace Programs 598
Faith Community Involvement 598
National Service Programs 598
Prevention Research 598
THE ARGUMENTS FOR AND AGAINST THE LEGALIZATION OF DRUGS 598
Arguments for Legalization 598
The Punitive Model for Regulating Drug Use Has Proved a Historical Failure 599 ❖ *Drugs Vary Substantially in Their Effects, Health Consequences, and Addictive Potential 599* ❖ *The Costs of Criminal Enforcement, Processing, and Confinement of Drug Offenders Are Exceedingly High 599* ❖ *Criminalization of Recreational and Limited Use of Drugs Does Not Conform to Many Americans' Moral Values and Breeds Cynicism about the Law 599* ❖ *Drug Use Is a Social Health Issue, Not a Crime Issue 599* ❖ *The Illegality of Drugs Gives Rise to*

Additional Problems Associated with the Underground Economy Resulting from Illegal Drug Distribution 599 ❖ Basic Constitutional Guarantees Are Threatened by Overzealous Enforcement 599 ❖ If Drugs Were Legalized, Crime and the Violence Associated with Drug Use Would Decrease 600

Arguments against Legalization 600

Increased Acceptance of Drugs Leads to Increased Levels of Drug Use 600 ❖ Increased Drug Availability and Use Will Worsen Our Crime Problem 600 ❖ Increased Drug Use Has Terrible Consequences for Our Citizens 601 ❖ Legalization of Dangerous Substances Sends a Conflicting Message to the Youth of America 601 ❖ Unsuccessful Experiments 601

SUMMARY 602

INDEX 606

ABOUT THE AUTHORS

Leonard Territo is a Professor of Criminology at the University of South Florida, Tampa. He was previously the Chief Deputy (Undersheriff) of the Leon County Sheriff's Office in Tallahassee, Florida. Part of his responsibilities included administration of the jail. Within this capacity he was actively involved in creating new programs, as well as selecting, training, promoting, and supervising correctional officers. He has served for more than twenty years as an expert witness in jail- and prison-related litigation focusing primarily on security matters, jail suicides, and inmate health issues. He has qualified as an expert in both federal and state courts in numerous states. He has also served for nine years with the Tampa, Florida, Police Department as a patrol officer, motorcycle officer, and homicide detective. He is the former Chairperson of the Department of Police Administration and Director of the Florida Institute for Law Enforcement at St. Petersburg Junior College, St. Petersburg, Florida. In addition to writing numerous articles, book chapters, and technical reports, he has authored and co-authored nine books, including *Criminal Investigation*, which is in its eighth edition; *Police Administration*, which is in its sixth edition; *Police Civil Liability*; *College Crime Prevention and Personal Safety Awareness*; and *Stress Management in Law Enforcement*. His books have been used in more than a thousand colleges and universities in all fifty states. His books and other writings have been used and referenced by both academic and police departments in fourteen countries: Australia, Barbados, Canada, Chile, Czechoslavokia, England, France, Germany, Israel, the Netherlands, Poland, Saudi Arabia, South Korea, and Spain.

His teaching awards include being selected from among two hundred criminal justice educators from the state of Florida as the Outstanding Criminal Justice Educator of the Year, and as the Outstanding Teacher of the Year by the College of Social and Behavioral Sciences at the University of South Florida. He has been given awards by both the Florida Police Chiefs Association and the Tampa Police Academy for his years of teaching and meritorious service and has been selected for inclusion in *Who's Who in American Law Enforcement*. His academic credentials include an A.A. in Police Administration from St. Petersburg Junior College, a B.A. in Interdisciplinary Social Sciences from the University of South Florida, an M.A. in Political Science from the University of South Florida, and a Doctor of Education degree from Nova Southeastern University.

James B. Halsted received a bachelor of arts degree from Southern Methodist University in Dallas, Texas. He graduated magna cum laude, with departmental distinction, and was elected to Phi Beta Kappa. He holds a Juris Doctor degree from Southern Methodist University and a Ph.D. in Humanities from Florida State University. He is licensed to practice law in Texas and is a member of the bar of the Texas Supreme Court. He has served as a federal prosecuting attorney in the Judge Advocate General's office as well as defense counsel. Presently, he is a Professor in the Department of Criminology at the University of South Florida and a Professor of the University's Honors College. He has published more than thirty scholarly articles in the fields of criminal law, the humanities, and the criminal justice system. Also a distinguished teacher, Dr. Halsted has won nine teaching awards while at the University of South Florida, including the College of Social and Behavioral Science's Outstanding Teacher Award, culminating in his being named by the senior class as the University of South Florida's Outstanding Professor. Dr. Halsted continues to practice criminal law while teaching at the University of South Florida. He has served as the executive secretary of the Phi Beta Kappa Alumni Association of the Greater Tampa Bay Area since the organization's inception.

Max L. Bromley is an Associate Professor in the Department of Criminology at the University of South Florida. He has previously served as the Associate Director of Public Safety at the University of South Florida and worked in the criminal justice field for almost twenty-five years. In addition to his many years of policing experience, Dr. Bromley also worked as a juvenile probation officer early in his career, which provided him with an understanding and appreciation of this critical part of the criminal justice system. He received his B.S. and M.S. in Criminology from Florida State University and has a doctorate in Higher Education with an emphasis in Criminal Justice from Nova University. He has co-edited a volume entitled *Hospital and College Security Liability* and was the senior co-author of *College Crime Prevention and Personal Safety Awareness*. In addition, he has written dozens of scholarly articles and technical documents on a variety of campus crime and campus policing issues. Recently Dr. Bromley has been involved in research on community policing. His articles have appeared in *Policing*, *Police Quarterly*, *Criminal Justice Policy Review*, and *Journal of Contemporary Criminal Justice*. Dr. Bromley also wrote *Department Self-Study: A Guide for Campus Law Enforcement Administrators*, used at more than a thousand institutions of higher education.

PREFACE

In this book, first published more than twenty years ago, we have consistently sought to focus on the human dimension within the major components of the criminal justice system—namely the police, courts, and corrections. We have done this in part because we know that students who are majoring in criminal justice and criminology often have little or no experience within the criminal justice system, and relevant examples help to illuminate and illustrate what may be abstract or perhaps even esoteric material. We have also attempted to provide information that is interesting, informative, and thought-provoking. We have added much new material to this book and believe it will make this edition our most interesting and relevant to date.

To accomplish our objective of focusing on the human dimension, we have drawn heavily from the current print media and scholarly journals, as well as our criminal justice experience as correctional administrators, police administrators, trainers, trial attorneys, and educators. Because of our longtime affiliation with both police departments and correctional facilities, we have been able to obtain many original photographs never before seen in any criminal justice book.

In Chapter 1 we have added a new section on terrorist crime and discussed some of the major terrorist crimes that have occurred against the United States in the last fifteen years, including the destruction of the World Trade Center on September 11, 2001, as well as the sniper killings in Maryland, Virginia, and Washington, D.C,. in October 2002. A new section has also been added on the topic of race crime and the administration of justice, a topic that has been given considerable attention by the social science community. Within this context we have also discussed racial profiling.

Chapter 2 has a new section on the legal and moral concept of criminal responsibility. We have also expanded the discussion of crimes to include the substantive criminal law, which is the foundation of crimes. Also, we have updated information on how common-law crimes have been modified by modern American criminal statutes. Additional crimes against morality and a variety of modern computer crimes have been added to this chapter. The twenty-first-century crimes of identity theft and stalking have been added, as well as an update on traffic crimes.

In Chapter 3 we have added a section on the Supreme Court's power of judicial review and its significance to criminal procedure. Likewise, we have added an additional dimension to the book by analyzing the constitutionality of every American's rights, including the right to a constitutional arrest and the right to a constitutional stop and detention, by including a discussion on whether these rights have been afforded to detainees after September 11, 2001. We have expanded the Supreme Court's exceptions to the exclusionary rule and have articulated the fundamental requirements for the admissibility of a Constitutional confession. In addition, we have updated the information on every American's right to be afforded a Constitutionally speedy trial, public trial, and jury trial, as well as the constitutional basis supporting every American's right to confront witnesses and the right to a compulsory process of obtaining witnesses. Finally, we have expanded our analyses of the Constitutional right against double jeopardy and the right to substantive due process.

Chapter 4 includes new information on the collection of campus crime data, an area of growing national concern about which little historically has been known. Recent data regarding the relationship between race and violent victimization have also been added. New sections have been included on intimate-partner violence and violence against women on campus. We feel that students can benefit from these units in particular. We also describe and discuss in some detail various victims of violence in the workplace.

Chapter 5 also has significant additions in this new edition. For example, a new segment has been included on police selection and training. The policing strategy based on the "zero tolerance" approach has been added. This strategy has been adapted by various police agencies and has its basis in the "broken windows" theory of crime, first mentioned by George Kelling and James Q. Wilson. The recent technological enhancements in the National Crime Information Center 2000 network are described with respect to police operations. Our discussion regarding community-oriented policing has been expanded, including a section on the future of this evolving police strategy.

Chapter 6 has been revised to reflect numerous current-interest items and recent scholarly contributions to the police field. Given the public's concern about the use of violence by police officers, we have included information on violence-prone officers as well as a section on the use of the less-than-lethal weapon — pepper spray. Science and technology are continuing to enhance policing. We have added discussions on DNA and geographic information systems (GIS) as examples of these enhancements. This chapter continues to highlight trends with respect to citizen-police efforts. It also has an expanded discussion of community anti-drug programs that have been popular in some locations.

In Chapter 7 we have expanded our discussion of courts to include the specialty courts, specifically, drug courts and the new military tribunals in the age of terrorism. We have enriched the human perspective in our presentation of the nature of the professions of the criminal courts' administrative personnel. Also, we have included a new section on the romanticism of the adversarial criminal trial versus the reality of plea bargaining. Furthermore, we have taken a new look at prosecutors who use unethical procedures to obtain lawful convictions and discuss the controversial practice of privately retained counsel who defraud their clients by the "bleed 'em and plead 'em" scheme. Finally, we have looked at how criminal court judges work from a human perspective by examining job stress, courthouse culturalization, and the socialization of judges.

In Chapter 8 we have expanded our investigation of pretrial detention, including drug testing to reduce pretrial misconduct. Our discussion on the American bail system now includes critical analysis of the commercialization of bail bondspeople and the availability of bail after conviction while waiting on appeal. An expanded section has been added on the investigative grand jury and how it has become an effective tool of law enforcement. We have updated the Constitutional requirements necessary for drafting the prosecutor's information, conducting a lineup, and pretrial police identification procedures. In our section on pretrial motions, we have doubled the number of motions we discuss. We have looked at the Constitutional requirements necessary for a constitutional guilty plea.

In Chapter 9 we have added an analysis of the philosophical foundations of the criminal trial and expanded our discussion of the functions of the rules of evidence during a criminal trial. In addition, we have looked at eight of the traditional affirmative defenses that are used by defense counsel during the criminal trial. Finally, we have added a special human dimension to our discussion of the advocates' closing arguments.

In Chapter 10 we have expanded our discussion on the effects of prison overcrowding on judicial sentencing. We have included a new look at the dialectical relationship between the presentence report and the victim-impact statement, and how these relate to the sentencing hearing. We have added a new section on what is necessary for a judge to make a constitutional sentence on a guilty defendant. We also have expanded the chapter by looking at various enhancement statutes such as "three strikes and you're out," as well as their effect on negating judicial discretion. There is an additional section on how one appeals a harsh sentence and a discussion on gubernatorial clemency. Finally, in the death penalty section, we have expanded our discussion on the capital punishment debate between the four most competent arguments on both sides. Finally, we have added a section on the constitutional requirement of mental capacity now necessary before a condemned prisoner can be executed by the government.

In Chapter 11, we provide one of the most comprehensive discussions in any criminal justice book today as it relates to understanding jails and the differences between jails and prisons. We have expanded our discussion of suicides in jails to include the key components of suicide-prevention programs, and we have added a section that deals with the full range of treatment programs in jails, including substance-abuse programs, therapy, counseling, educational programs, religious programs, and therapeutic communities.

In Chapter 12, we have added a section on institutional programs and services, including educational programs, prison work programs, recreational programs, treatment programs, drug treatment programs, and religious programs. We have also added a section in which we address the problem of elderly male prisoners, whose numbers have rapidly increased over the past decade due, in part, to longer sentences. A new section addresses the problems of HIV- and AIDS-infected persons in prisons and the controversial techniques that can be employed to minimize the transmission of the disease from one inmate to another. We have also greatly expanded our discussion of women in prison.

In Chapter 13, we have expanded our discussion of community correctional centers to include halfway houses, correctional facilities that provide a residence for convicted offenders who do not require the secure custody of prison; work release, a program that can be operated out of both jails and prisons; educational release programs, an effort to ensure future employability and a smooth transition back to society for parolees; and furloughs, which involve short periods of release from custody without supervision.

In Chapter 14, a major discussion of serious and violent juvenile offenders has been included. Likewise, given the country's concern about crime and violence in our schools, this unit has been completely redone and updated. A complete description of the Secret Service's Safe School Initiative has been added, as well as a projection of the possible juvenile justice system that is evolving in the twenty-first century.

In Chapter 15 we have expanded our discussion of newer drugs that have become major problems for law enforcement in recent years. These include drugs associated with the all-night parties known as "raves," where large crowds of young people listen to music and dance for six to eight hours at a time. Also included in this chapter is a discussion of two drugs that are commonly used by sex offenders to commit drug-facilitated sexual assault: Rohypnol and gamma hydroxybuterate (GHB). Finally, we have updated our section on emerging drug trends, especially as they relate to drug use among young people; discussed various treatment programs; and suggested ways to deal with the problematic aspect of drugs in American social life.

ACKNOWLEDGMENTS

Writing a book is a solitary endeavor. However, as a process writing is highly interactive; anything that makes the transition from an idea to a published work requires considerable goodwill and support from families, friends, colleagues, reviewers, editors, and production staff. Although it is insufficient compensation, we wish to recognize those organizations and individuals who helped to sustain us in our writing endeavors.

We wish to give extraordinarily special recognition to Elena Ruiz, who is responsible for the modernization of this edition. She singlehandedly integrated all the pedagogical material and reformatted the book to Prentice Hall standards. Her expertise and work ethic, as well as her talent, were indispensable in actualizing the manuscript in its present form and in the quality of its content. Dr. Thomas Mieczkowski and Dr. Richard Dembo, our good friends and colleagues at the University of South Florida, contributed much material and wrote sections for our discussion of drugs in various chapters. We thank them for assisting us in keeping this important topic current. Our colleague Dr. Kathleen Heide, who has become a nationally recognized expert on children who kill their parents, contributed excellent information on the topic of juvenile justice; Dr. Ira Silverman, who is a virtual walking encyclopedia on the topic of corrections, generously provided us with material from his personal research files, which we incorporated into our corrections chapter. Dr. Sergei Paromchik, our colleague and former law enforcement official in the former Soviet Union, provided new material on the operation of Russia's organized crime in the United States. Dr. Mary Cuadrado and Dr. Kim Lersch also contributed to our police chapters. We would also like to thank our colleague Lisa Landis for providing us with the "In the Workplace" descriptions.

Dr. Jim Sewell, Florida Department of Law Enforcement, allowed us to use the results of his research for inclusion in our discussion of police stress. Other individuals who made significant contributions to the police chapters included Darrel W. Stephens, former executive director of the Police Executive Research Forum, and John E. Eck and Gerard Murphy, also with the Police Executive Research Forum.

Photos were provided by Sergeant Richard T. Bailey, Pinellas County Sheriff's Office, Largo, Florida; Mike Davies, Orange County Corrections Department, Orlando, Florida; Lt. Richard E. Hohl, Jr., Polk County Sheriff's Office, Bartow, Florida; and Sgt. Dale Stockton, Carlsbad, California, Police Department.

We would also like to acknowledge our graduate and undergraduate student assistants who researched various chapters: Mandy Healy and Terrance Ford. Heather Traschel and Paunece Ramage provided excellent assistance in revising numerous chapters in our Instructor's Manual. Our colleague, Frank Devine, who shared some of his research results, is greatly appreciated, as is David Wickham for his support in our research efforts. Dr. Halsted's legal clients Kirk Isenhour, Walter Nixon, and Art Norman provided valuable insights, and we appreciate their granting us permission to discuss their cases. Attorneys Samantha Ward and Julie Holt were also most helpful in sharing their legal research. We are deeply indebted to David Gillispie for his assistance in researching the death penalty. We also thank our highly respected colleague Professor Ronald Akers, director of the Center for Studies in Criminology and Law, University of Florida, Gainesville, who was kind enough to share his seminal work on social learning theory.

Typing and other clerical services were provided by a number of people who made innumerable contributions. Many thanks to Carole Rennick for the long hours she devoted to typing drafts of our chapters. A special thanks to Marianne Bell of the University of South Florida Information Processing Center, who not only assisted us in typing the drafts of our chapters but also typed in its entirety the enormous Instructor's Manual that has proven so valuable to faculty members who use this book in their classes.

We also wish to thank Maryellin Territo, who devoted so many hours to researching professional journals, news magazines, and newspapers to be certain we had the most current criminal justice-related information.

Susan Beauchamp, Korrine Dorsey, Denise Brown, and Ann Mohan deserve many thanks for their patience and encouragement throughout the duration of this comprehensive textbook revision process. We also wish to thank our executive editor Frank I. Mortimer, Jr., for his willingness to put the full resources of Prentice Hall behind the production of this book. With his encouragement, support, and guidance we were able to make this sixth edition more user-friendly for students and a more attractive teaching tool for instructors. For his confidence and support we will be forever grateful.

And finally, we want to express our appreciation for the valuable insights provided by the professionals who reviewed the manuscript for this edition: James David Ballard, Grand Valley State University, Grand Rapids, MI; Paul Becker, University of Dayton, Dayton, OH; Robert Bing, University of Texas, Arlington, TX; James Black, University of Tennessee, Knoxville, TN; Stephen Brodt, Ball State University, Muncie, IN; Jon Cella, Central Texas College, Killeen, TX; Kim Davies, Augusta State University, Augusta, GA; Alex del Carmen, University of Texas, Arlington, TX; Shaun Gabbidon, Penn State University, Middletown, PA; James P. Heuser, Portland State University, Portland, OR; Arthur, J. Jipson, University of Dayton, Dayton, OH; Peter Kraska, Eastern Kentucky University, Richmond, KY; Donna Nicholson, Manchester Community College, Manchester, CT; Charles Ousley, Seminole State College, Seminole, OH; Matthew Robinson, Appalachian State University, Boone, NC; Stanley L. Swart, University of North Florida, Jacksonville, FL.

LT   JBH   MLB

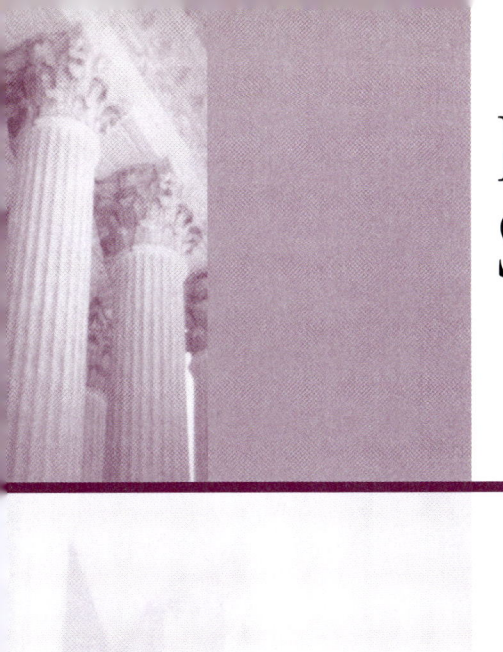

INSTRUCTOR'S SECTION

1 CRIME AND JUSTICE IN AMERICA

CHAPTER LEARNING OBJECTIVES

After reading this chapter the student should be able to:

1. Know which types of crimes are most feared.
2. Differentiate between crimes against the person and crimes against property.
3. Identify Sutherland's four categories of white collar/economic crimes.
4. List the major types of telecommunication crimes.
5. Discuss the decline of the American Mafia and describe the future of organized crime.
6. Define terrorism.
7. List examples of "victimless" crimes.
8. List the eighteen steps of the criminal justice system.
9. Explain why there is evidence of a mistrust of the criminal justice system by people of color.
10. Describe the general patterns of criminal victimization relative to race/ethnicity in the United States.
11. Discuss the results of racial profiling when used in traffic stops.
12. Describe the data with respect to racial disparities in conviction rates.
13. List explanations for the recent decline in serious crimes.
14. Explain the ramifications for the criminal justice system of 39 million youths entering their teen years in the twenty-first century.
15. Have an appreciation of the criminal justice system in America.

KEY TERMS

abuses of trust
anthrax
business crimes
community policing
computer bulletin board
con games
crimes against the person
crimes against property
criminal justice system
economic crimes
felony
hacking
loan-sharking
misdemeanor
organized crime
parole
personal crimes
preponderance of the evidence
probation
psychotropic drugs
telecommunications crimes
terrorist crime
white collar crime

CHAPTER OVERVIEW

Note to Instructor: The following provides you with a summary of key points made throughout the chapter.

Crime in American society is not new. However, attitudes toward crime and the treatment of criminals have varied over the years. There were times when punishment and torture were the order of the day and other times when spirited redemption was thought to be the best way to reform criminals. However, although attitudes and treatments change, crime persists. Certain psychological and social effects of crime can have a profound effect on people. Interestingly, most people fear the crimes that occur less frequently—namely, criminal homicide, forcible rape, and aggravated assault. These crimes are often perpetrated by a family member, close friend, or personal acquaintance. To a great extent, the public fear of crime is directly related to the coverage given to it by the media, especially for high-profile crimes committed by strangers.

In this chapter we discuss a full range of crimes, including conventional crimes (criminal homicide, forcible rape, robbery, aggravated assault, burglary, larceny theft, motor vehicle theft, and arson), economic crime, telecommunications crimes (hacking), illegal bulletin boards, and misuse of telephone systems.

Organized crime (also known as syndicated crime) is a business that provides illegal but desirable goods and serves the noncriminal public. Traditionally, when one thought of organized crime it meant the Italian-American Mafia that emerged during Prohibition. However, there is considerable evidence that the Mafia is in decline, in part because of its conservatism, action by the federal government that resulted in the arrest and conviction of high-ranking Mafia chieftains, and inter-Mafia warfare that has resulted in the murder of well-known Mafia figures. The void left by the Mafia is now being filled by new ethnic groups in the United States, mostly from eastern Asia. Russian organized crime has attracted increased concern and attention of law enforcement agencies, the mass media, and the public in general around the world.

Terrorism has clearly dominated the attention of law enforcement agencies and the public since the destruction of the New York City World Trade Center Twin Towers and partial destruction of the Pentagon in 2001. Terrorism includes both violent acts and threats of violence. It lumps together acts committed by criminal psychotics, self-proclaimed patriots with extreme ideological views.

In this chapter we also discuss the relationship between drugs and crime. Specifically, we examine the mood- and mind-altering (psychotropic) drugs and why for more than a century the American criminal justice system has, for better or worse, been at the center of drug control efforts.

Structurally, the criminal justice system can be described in terms of its component agencies, namely, the police, courts, and corrections. Functionally, the components of this system work well together, although at times they are in conflict. It is generally agreed among scholars that there are eighteen steps to the criminal justice process: reporting the crime; prearrest investigation; arrest; booking; postarrest investigation; decisions to charge; filing the complaint; first appearance; preliminary hearing; grand jury view; filing the indictment or information; arraignment on the information or the indictment; pretrial motions; criminal trial; sentencing; appeals; postconviction remedies; and parole or parole revocation hearing.

We also address the issue of race, crime, and the administration of justice—which includes the patterns of crime victimization, stereotypes, and criminal profiles of disparities and conviction rates—and the ways in which the criminal justice system can strengthen itself through diversity.

The crime statistics of the most serious crimes have dropped dramatically, and a number of explanations have been provided, including a decline in the proportion of young males, tougher sentencing, changes in the drug market, a moderate unemployment rate, community policing, and other law-enforcement-related factors. Finally, we discuss the possibilities of a future crime wave: thirty-nine million youngsters entering their teen years in the late 1900s and early 2000s. Criminologists suggest that this does not bode well for the future since this is the age group that is most crime prone. Only time will tell whether this will indeed be the result.

CRITICAL THINKING QUESTIONS

Note to Instructor: These questions appear throughout the chapter as "CTQs." They can be used to stimulate class discussion.

1. Do you think criminal behavior today is viewed as a result of individual flaws or societal failure? How does this compare, in your opinion, to the way it has been viewed in the past?
2. What are the ways that criminals have been punished over the centuries? Do you think any of these were rationally justified or were they perhaps a result of societal pressures looking to stamp out the imminent fears publicized crime creates?
3. What types of crimes do you most fear? Why? Which crimes do you believe you are least likely to become a victim of? Why?
4. What can people do to protect themselves against violent crime?
5. Why do you think offenses not commonly thought of as violent crimes have a potential for violence? Do you believe property offenses should carry stiffer penalties?
6. Do you believe economic crimes are as devastating to its victims as crimes against a person? If so, how?
7. Do you think cybercrime units are adequately prepared to handle the mass influx of cybercrimes in the early 2000s, a trend that is growing in tandem with the widespread access to and popularity of the Internet? Why or why not?
8. Do you think all bulletin boards should be made illegal to prevent their use for future criminal purposes? How do you think bulletin boards should be regulated, if at all?
9. Do you believe there will be an increase in the number of telecommunication crimes due to the growing popularity, access, and availability of cell phones to larger segments of the population (in particular, youngsters)?
10. Compare and contrast the basic motives and methods of white-collar crime and organized crime.
11. Why is it so difficult to eliminate organized crime in the United States?

12. How do terrorism and the attacks of September 11th on the World Trade Center pose a new challenge to law enforcement agencies?
13. What type of additional training do you believe emergency responders should have in view of the growing trends in foreign and domestic terrorism? Do you think such training should be extended to all law enforcement agencies? Why or why not?
14. Why is drug abuse among young people so prevalent in our society?
15. Most people of all ethnic and racial groups are never convicted of a crime, but stereotypes can work to brand all members of some groups with suspicion. Why do you think this occurs?
16. In what ways do you believe the criminal justice system has become more diversified? In what ways less diversified?
17. What reason has been suggested by one criminologist as to why teenagers are more violent today? Do you agree or disagree?

IN THE MEDIA

Video

ABC News Video: *Criminal Injustice*
ABC News Video: *Guns*
A&E Videos: *American Justice*
CNN Today Video: *Corrections*, Vol.1: segment 9, "Overcoming Crime Generative Factors"
CNN Today Video: *Criminology*, Vol. 4: segment 9, "Restorative Justice"
CNN Today Video: *Introduction to Criminal Justice*, Vol. 3: segment 4, "Driving While Black"
FHH Video: *Racial Profiling and Law Enforcement*
NIJ Video: *Drugs: Military Interdiction*
NIJ Video: *Gun Control*
NIJ Video: *Jobs and Crime*
NIJ Video: *Predicting Criminality*

Films

Arlington Road (1999)
City Hall (1996)
Copy Cat (1995)
Entrapment (1999)
A Few Good Men (1999)
The General's Daughter (1999)
Heat (1995)
The Insider (1999)
Mississippi Burning (1988)
Murder at 1600 (1997)
The Negotiator (1999)
Pulp Fiction (1996)
The Pelican Brief (1993)
Seven (1995)
The Siege (1998)
The Spanish Prisoner (1998)
A Time to Kill (1996)
True Crimes (1998)
U.S. Marshals (1998)
The Usual Suspects (1995)
The Verdict (1982)
Witness (1985)

IN THE LITERATURE

Note to Instructor: These sources can be integrated throughout the chapter as additional sources of information for the students.

Books

C. Beccaria, *Crimes and Punishment*. Indianapolis: Bobbs Merrill, 1993.

J. Einstein and H. Jacob, *Felony Justice*. Boston: Little, Brown, 1977.

Federal Bureau of Investigation, *Crime in the United States*. Washington D.C.: U.S. Government Printing Office, 1993.

R. Flemming and P. Nardulli, *The Craft of Justice*. Philadelphia: University of Pennsylvania Press, 1992.

P. Herbert, *The Limits of the Criminal Sanction*. Stanford, Calif.: Stanford University Press, 1975.

J. Inciardi, *The War on Drugs III: The Continuing Saga of the Mysteries and Miseries of Intoxication, Addiction, Crime, and Public Policy*. Needham Heights, Mass.: Allyn and Bacon, 2002.

V. Kappeler, G. Potter, and M. Victor, *The Mythology of Crime and Criminal Justice*. Prospect Heights, Ill.: Waveland, 1993.

S. Walker, *Popular Justice*. New York: Oxford University Press.

S. Walker, *Sense and Nonsense About Crime and Drug Policy*, 3rd ed. Belmont, Calif.: Wadsworth Publishing, 1994.

J. Wilson and J. Petersilia, eds., *Crime*. San Francisco: Institute for Contemporary Studies Press, 1995.

K. Wright, *The Great American Crime Myth*. Westport, Conn.: Greenwood Press, 1987.

F. Ziring and G. Hawkins, *Crime Is Not the Problem: Lethal Violence in America*. New York: Oxford University Press, 1997.

2. THE SUBSTANTIVE CRIMINAL LAW

CHAPTER LEARNING OBJECTIVES

After reading this chapter the student should be able to:

1. Define substantive criminal law.
2. List the major sources of criminal law.
3. Identify the characteristics of criminal law that distinguish it from other rules governing human conduct.
4. Differentiate between civil law and criminal law.
5. Discuss how felonies are different from misdemeanors.
6. Describe the "law of precedent."
7. List three kinds of homicide.
8. Identify the elements of murder, voluntary manslaughter, and involuntary manslaughter.
9. Distinguish among assault, battery, and false imprisonment.
10. List the crimes against habitation and their elements.
11. Identify what distinguishes larceny from robbery.
12. Describe crimes against morality and their origin in American criminal codes.
13. Discuss strict liability crimes.
14. Describe the doctrine of *stare decisis*.
15. Identify and discuss four sources of American criminal law.

KEY TERMS

actus reus
adequate provocation
administrative law
adultery
aggravated battery
arson
assault
battery
bigamy
burglary
capital felony
carnal knowledge
causation
civil law
common law
consensual crimes
conversion
crime

crimes against habitation
criminal infraction
criminal law
criminal procedure
criminal responsibility
criminally negligent homicide
date rape
deviance
domestic violence
ecclesiastical crimes
elements
embezzlement
environmental crime
extortion
false imprisonment
false pretense
felony
felony murder

fornication
harassment
hate crime
hit and run
homicide
identity theft
illicit cohabitation
incest
intent to commit a felony
intent to inflict great bodily injury
intent to kill
involuntary manslaughter
kidnapping
larceny
malice aforethought
mens rea
misdemeanor
misdemeanor manslaughter

CHAPTER 2 THE SUBSTANTIVE CRIMINAL LAW XXXIX

murder	recklessness	stalking
norms	road rage	*stare decisis*
prostitute	robbery	statutory rape
racing	sexual harassment	strict-liability offenses
rape	sexually neutral offenses	substantive criminal law
rape shield statutes	social sanctions	value conflict model
reasonable provocation	socialization	value consensus model
receiving stolen property	sodomy	value divergence model
reckless driving		

CHAPTER OVERVIEW

Note to Instructor: The following provides you with a summary of key points made throughout the chapter.

To understand the problem of crime, one must examine the broader issue of deviance from societal norms. Society's attempts to contain deviance through controls (sanctions) range from informal disapproval to the use of the police powers of the state. Studies of antisocial attitudes, eccentricities, and various kinds of atypical behavior may all have potential value in helping to illuminate the factors involved in criminal conduct. All criminal acts are deviant, but not all deviant acts are criminal. Thus, only those deviant acts that legislative bodies have defined by statute as criminal may legitimately be considered crimes.

American criminal law, as analyzed in this chapter, combines the features of two systems: The common law, which developed in England, was transported to America, and is based on interpretation of judicial decisions; and statutory law, which is based on specific codes that are written and legislated. These two sources are continually being transformed by American case law, which analyzes the meaning and significance of legislative statutes in the common law tradition. These systems are the basis of substantive criminal law, laws that define necessary elements of crimes and specify the penalties for their commission.

Depending on the punishment, offenses are classified as felony, misdemeanor, *malum in se*, or *malum prohibitum* crimes. Felonies are punishable by death or imprisonment for one or more years. Misdemeanors are punishable by fines and less than one year in jail. There are several classifications of substantive crimes within the criminal justice system. Several crimes constitute the law of homicide; more than eight crimes fit into the category of crimes against persons; arson and burglary are the crimes against habitation; while as many as ten separate crimes constitute the acquisition offenses. Other groupings of crimes constitute the general categories of crimes against property and crimes against morality. American prosecutors are devoting extraordinary resources and energy prosecuting acts which were not even considered criminal until the 1960s. Fighting environmental crime, for example, requires the coordination of many governmental and private agencies to achieve success.

In this chapter we study each crime by defining the particular elements that, as a whole, constitute a particular criminal offense. The significance of studying each crime in the American criminal justice system by the composition of its respective elements is for proof. The burden of proof is on the government to prove the defendant guilty beyond a reasonable doubt. What this means in reality is that the government has the burden of proving beyond a reasonable doubt each and every element making up the crimes with which the defendant is charged. Thus, if a defendant is charged with a crime like burglary, which has seven elements, and if the government proves six of these elements beyond a reasonable doubt but the jury has a reasonable doubt as to the seventh element, the jury must find the defendant "not guilty" of burglary.

CRITICAL THINKING QUESTIONS

Note to Instructor: These questions appear throughout the chapter as "CTQs." They can be used to stimulate class discussion.

1. What is the difference between a criminal act and a morally unethical act?
2. What types of behavior does your society label *criminal* that you believe should be considered *deviant*?
3. What types of behavior does your society label *deviant* that you believe should be legally defined as *criminal*?
4. Compare and contrast civil law and criminal law.
5. List five different crimes for which the victim of the crime could also sue the perpetrator in civil court. Explain why.
6. Can you explain the two seemingly inconsistent verdicts in the O. J. Simpson criminal trial and the O. J. Simpson civil trial? How are they reconcilable by understanding the differences between civil law and criminal law?
7. Some people claim that the social values that eventually make their way into law are social values of the

powerful, which may be completely opposite of the social values of the unprivileged and subcultures. Do you believe this is true?

8. Is a deviant act always a criminal act? Why or why not? Is a criminal act always a deviant act? Why or why not?
9. Before going any further, do you believe that you can name at least five sources of American substantive criminal law?
10. Most jurors agree that American substantive criminal law is fundamentally based in the legal definitions of English common law. Can you explain why this is the case?
11. Since there is only one crime in the U.S. Constitution (treason), how can the Constitution be a source of criminal law?
12. Almost all the texts used in law school to train our future lawyers require the students to read only case law for their acquisition of knowledge of the law. Does this seem odd to you? Why?
13. If the prosecution has already proved that a defendant committed a crime, why does our system of justice insist that the state also prove that the defendant was criminally responsible for the act? Should the doctrine be modified? Why or why not?
14. Are strict-liability crimes consistent with our notion of fundamental fairness and due process? Why or why not?
15. Explain the difference between the state proving that the defendant committed the criminal act versus proving each and every one of the elements of the crime beyond a reasonable doubt.
16. Why does the criminal law define a fetus as a human for homicide purposes, while at the same time abortion laws refuse to recognize the personhood of the fetus after abortion, in which the fetus also dies?
17. Does the fact that the *mens rea* of murder has four total and complete definitions that are not logically connected to each other make it more difficult to understand the reasoning for the definition of malice aforethought?
18. A lot of people who kill do so in a state of rage. Likewise, many murderers commit their killings in a state of rage, but their cases are not reduced to voluntary manslaughter. What is the difference between killing in a state of rage, which makes it voluntary manslaughter, and rage that keeps the crime a murder?
19. Why should we allow a person who kills another human being with equal hatred, malice, and with the same intent to kill as that of a premeditated, cold-blooded murder to be exposed to a far less severe criminal sentence because at the time of the killing, this type of killer was "out of control, in a full state of rage" as a result of being provoked?
20. Have you ever experienced a person in the throes of road rage while on the highway? What percentage of these people do you think are potential killers?
21. Do you believe that a foster care parent who is so overburdened with the number of children that he or she has, and as a result negligently lets one die, should be held responsible under criminal homicide statutes for negligence?
22. Most people consider an assault a battery, but they are two entirely different crimes. Can you explain the differences in the crimes of assault and battery?
23. Most police officers and prosecutors shy away from becoming involved with violence against the family, since the victims often change their mind about pressing charges. What strategies can we use outside the criminal justice system to help reduce the massive violence occurring within the American household?
24. Since a hate crime attaches to an enhancement statute (as shown in Chapter 10, ("Sentencing, Appeals, and the Death Penalty"), it adds an extra 25 years in addition to years received for the crime committed), do you believe it's fair to add that many years on to a sentence based on the politically incorrect motive of the offender?
25. When a woman has consented to intercourse while she was drunk, but states that she would not have consented had she not been so intoxicated, the man can be charged with rape. Do you think this legal doctrine is fair and should be kept as part of our laws?
26. Do you believe that the *mens rea* of rape should be defined to include cases in which the defendant did not know that the victim was not consenting—or should it use a more general standard that a reasonable person would have known the victim was not consenting, even though the defendant, in fact, did not know she was consenting?
27. Considering that boys and girls are developing sexually at a much younger age than before, do you think that age 16 is the proper age of consent in the twenty-first century, or should it be lowered?
28. Compare and contrast date rape with forcible rape.
29. Many states have passed laws allowing a smaller maximum sentence for the kidnapper if the victim is safely returned. Are you in favor of reducing the punishment for such an act, or should all kidnappers be punished equally?
30. An everyday experience of homeowners in America is that they come home to see their house ransacked and scream, "We have been robbed!" Why is this statement a total legal mischaracterization of the situation?
31. Is it possible for a college student who has a roommate sharing an apartment to be a victim of a burglary by that roommate if the roommate comes into a mutually shared room and steals the student's watch?

32. Since arson criminalizes only the burning of the dwelling of another, does this mean that there is no crime committed when one intentionally and maliciously burns down his or her own home?
33. Almost all states require that the *mens rea* of arson of structure is the intent to burn the structure; however, in the new crime of woods arson, the defendant could be convicted if the burning occurred only through negligence. Do you believe this disparity of intents is justified?
34. It is generally agreed that crimes against property constitute 60 percent of all criminal offenses. Why do you think they are so seldom glamorized in television and film compared to crimes of violence and sexual misconduct?
35. Have you or any of your friends ever been guilty of shoplifting? How do you think this crime incurs such a fascination for kids between ages 12 and 17?
36. Robbery and extortion are often confused. Can you differentiate between the two crimes?
37. Why would a bad pickpocket be guilty of robbery, while a good pickpocket would only be guilty of larceny?
38. Do you think people who steal from people who trust them with their money (embezzlement) should be punished more severely than people who commit larceny?
39. Many victims of false pretense are elderly people, who are scammed into purchasing items or sending money by enticements over the telephone. Do you believe that when the victims are elderly, the punishments should be more severe since they are more vulnerable?
40. One legal commentator said that extortion is the "sleaziest of all crimes" because the victim cannot charge his or her accuser without exposing that which the victim most definitely does not want to be made public—and hence, the victim wrestles with the decision whether to legally prosecute or not. Do you agree with the "sleazy" characterization of extortion?
41. How can you be certain that any items in your wardrobe or music collection that were given to you as gifts by friends were not stolen property? If they were, are you guilty of receiving stolen property?
42. Which consensual crimes do you believe are victimless crimes and which do you believe are not victimless crimes? Explain why.
43. What do you think would be the consequences of reinstating ecclesiastical crimes to the jurisdiction of American churches and allowing them to punish members for what they consider to be crimes (sins) instead of the courts doing so?
44. Since most surveys indicate that the vast majority of Americans are sexually active by the time they are 22, which necessarily means that they committed the crime of fornication, do you consider these people to be criminals? Why or why not?
45. In the 2000 census, the results indicated that more than 50 percent of people living together were not married. Is half of our population committing the crime of illicit cohabitation? If so, why are they not being arrested?
46. Prostitution is legalized and controlled in certain counties in Nevada. Do you think this should be a nationwide practice? Why or why not?
47. Can the criminal law keep up with the rapid pace of technology in computers by making changes that identify misconduct on a computer as crimes?
48. What is the difference between aggressively, romantically pursuing a love interest and stalking a love interest?
49. Which of the six following traffic crimes do you believe should be reduced from a misdemeanor to a traffic infraction? Which do you believe should be raised from a misdemeanor to a felony? Racing, reckless driving, hit and run, vehicular homicide, DUI/DWI, multiple offenses ("road rage").
50. What laws need to be passed in order to alleviate the environmental paradox?

IN THE MEDIA

Television

Court TV: "Cabey v. Goetz, Vigilante Justice: The Civil Trial of Bernhard Goetz"°—Darrel Cabey, paralyzed in 1984 when he and several friends were panhandling and asked the defendant for money, sues subway vigilante Bernhard Goetz.

Court TV: "Florida v. Smith"—William Kennedy Smith is accused of rape in the Kennedy family compound in West Palm Beach, Florida.

Court TV: "Massachusetts v. Louise Woodward: Child Killer or Child Lover?°—British au pair Louise Woodward is charged with murdering eight-month-old Matthew Eappen.

Court TV: "New York v. Nelson"°—Lermrick Nelson, an African American teen, is charged with the stabbing death of a Hasidic Jewish scholar during a riot in the Crown Heights section of Brooklyn, New York.

Video

ABC Videos

A&E American Justice Videos

Anatomy of a Murder (1959)

"Can Rules Define Morality?"°°

"Censorship and Content Control on the Internet"°°

CNN Crime File Videos

COURT TV Videos

FFH Videos

"Law and the Legal System"**

"Legislation Morality: There Ought to Be a Law!"**

NIJ Crime File Video: "The Three Strikes Law"

NIJ Crime File Videos

PBS Videos

"Sources of Law"**

"The Internet: Cyber-Hate and Freedom of Speech"**

"The Rule of Law"**

*Free Court TV videos. Policy on the number of free videos available to each adaptor is based on adoption size.

**These expensive videos are part of the *Legal Studies Video Collection* by Insight Media. Your department/educational institution can purchase these videos by calling Insight Media at 1-800-233-9910.

IN THE LITERATURE

Note to Instructor: These sources can be integrated throughout the chapter as additional sources of information for the students.

Books

G. Barak, ed., *Crimes by the Capitalist State: An Introduction to State Criminality.* New York: State University of New York Press, 1991.

D. Bodenhamer, *Fair Trial: Rights of the Accused in American History.* New York: Oxford, 1991.

J. Calvi and S. Coleman, *American Law and Legal Systems.* Upper Saddle River, N.J.: Prentice Hall, 1989.

L. Carter, *Reason in the Law.* Glenview, Ill.: Scott, Foresman and Company, 1988.

M. Clinard and R. Quinney, *Criminal Behavior Systems : A Typology.* Cincinnati: Anderson, 1994.

D. Close and N. Meier, *Morality in Criminal Justice: An Introduction to Ethics.* Belmont, Calif.: Wadsworth, 1995.

J. Coleman, *The Criminal Elite: The Sociology of White Collar Crime,* 2nd ed. New York: St. Martin's, 1989.

N. Crowell and A. Burgess, eds., *Understanding Violence Against Women.* Washington, D.C.: National Academy Press, 1996.

A. Dershowitz, *The Advocate's Devil.* New York: Warner Books, Mass Market Paperbacks, 1995.

A. Dershowitz, *Taking Liberties: A Decade of Hard Cases, Bad Laws, and Bum Raps.* Chicago: Contemporary Books, 1988.

L. Friedman, *Crime and Punishment in American History.* New York: Basic Books, 1993.

T. Gardner and T. Anderson, *Criminal Law,* 7th ed. Belmont, Calif.: Wadsworth, 2000.

B. Lofferda, *Losing Matt Shepard: Life and Politics in the Aftermath of Anti-Gay Murder.* New York: Columbia University Press, 2000.

R. Meier, ed., *Major Forms of Crime.* Beverly Hills, Calif.: Sage, 1984.

N. Morris, *Madness and the Criminal Law.* Chicago: University of Chicago Press, 1982.

National Crime Prevention Council, *New Ways of Working with Local laws to Prevent Crime.* Amsterdam, New York: Author, 1996.

S. Parker, *Popular Justice: A History of American Criminal Justice.* New York: Oxford University Press, 1980.

T. Plucket, *A Concise History of the Common Law.* Boston: Little, Brown, 1956.

J. Pollock, *Ethics in Crime and Justice: Dilemmas and Decisions,* 2nd ed. Belmont, Calif.: Wadsworth, 1994.

J. Reiman, *The Rich Get Richer and the Poor Get Prison: Ideology, Class, and Criminal Justice.* New York: John Wiley & Sons, 1979.

O. Robinson, *The Criminal Law of Ancient Rome.* Baltimore: Johns Hopkins University Press, 1996.

J. Samaha, *Criminal Law,* 6th ed. Belmont, Calif.: Wadsworth, 1999.

R. Schopp, *Justification Defenses and Just Convictions.* Cambridge, England: Cambridge University Press, 1998.

D. Simon and D. Eitzen, *Elite Deviance,* 3rd ed. Boston: Allyn and Bacon, 1990.

S. Stephen et. al., eds., *Actions and Value in Criminal Law.* New York: Oxford University Press, 1996.

Articles

M. Dubber, "Reforming American Penal Law," *Journal of Criminal Law and Criminology,* vol. 90 (1999), p. 49.

H. Hart, "The Aims of Criminal Law," *Law and Contemporary Problems,* vol. 23 (1956), p. 402.

S. Kadish, "Criminal Law and Society: A Symposium," *California Law Review,* vol. 87 (1999), p. 943.

S. Martin, "Investigating Hate Crimes: Case Characteristics and Law Enforcement Responses," *Justice Quarterly,* vol. 13 (1996), pp. 455–480.

C. Smith, "The Forms of Judicial Policymaking: Civil Liability and Criminal Justice Policy," *Justice System Journal,* vol. 19 (1997), pp. 341–354.

T. Smith, "Legislative and Legal Developments in Criminal Justice," *Journal of Criminal Justice,* vol. 5 (1991), pp. 36–37.

3. THE LAW OF CRIMINAL PROCEDURE AND THE RIGHTS OF THE CRIMINALLY ACCUSED

LEARNING OBJECTIVES

After reading this chapter the student should be able to:

1. Discuss how constitutional rights may act as a constraint on efficient law enforcement.
2. Describe when a citizen can make an arrest that is constitutional.
3. Identify the circumstances wherein a police officer can use deadly force to effect an arrest.
4. List three exceptions to the search warrant requirement.
5. Discuss the exclusionary rule and pertinent court decisions.
6. Describe the constitutional significance of *Miranda v. Arizona*.
7. List the four hurdles the prosecution must clear in order to have a defendant's confession used in a criminal trial.
8. Explain the meaning and importance of the concept of probable cause.
9. Discuss when a police officer can lawfully search an automobile.
10. Define the plain view doctrine.
11. Discuss the significance of *Mapp v. Ohio* for police.
12. List the criteria for a constitutional stop and frisk as established in *Terry v. Ohio*.
13. Differentiate between a stop and frisk and a search based on probable cause.
14. Describe when a police officer may make an arrest without a warrant.
15. Identify the two most common exceptions to the search warrant requirement.

KEY TERMS

affidavit
arrest warrant
Bill of Rights
confession
crime control model
deadly force
doctrine of selective incorporation
due process of law

due process model
evanescent evidence
exclusionary rule
frisk
fruit of the poisonous tree
investigatory stop
jeopardy

judicial review
law of criminal procedure
manifest necessity
probable cause
search
search warrant
seizure

CHAPTER OVERVIEW

Note to Instructor: The following provides you with a summary of key points made throughout the chapter.

Criminal procedural law is founded on the United States Constitution. Based on "fundamental fairness" and "due process," the criminal procedural law focuses on how the criminal law is enforced, how evidence is collected, and what rights are guaranteed to persons accused of crimes. Contrary to popular belief, the Bill of Rights of the United States Constitution has not always provided such guarantees to people tried in state courts. Indeed, not until the "due-process revolution of the 1960s" were rights embodied in the Fourth, Fifth, Sixth, and Eighth Amendments made applicable to the states and given as rights to citizens being tried in those states as a matter of Constitutional guarantee. Such rights included the right to a constitutional arrest, the protection against unreasonable searches and seizures, the privilege against self-incrimination, and the right to counsel. Generally, a warrant is required for police to conduct a "reasonable" search; however, the Supreme Court has noted several exceptions. These are: searches incident to a lawful arrest, the automobile exception, the consent exception, the plain view exception, the stop and frisk exception, and the exigent circumstances exception. In addition, the exclusionary rule was created to protect individuals from police misconduct that resulted in unconstitutional searches and seizures. The exclusionary rule is a judicially enforced rule that requires any illegally obtained evidence to be excluded. As such, it is inadmissible against an accused at his or her trial. Other trial rights, such as speedy trial, public trial, the right to an impartial jury, and the right to confront witnesses and compel witnesses to testify on your behalf, were not afforded to all defendants in state courts until the early 1970s.

During the appointment periods of presidents Richard Nixon, Ronald Reagan, George H. W. Bush, and now George W. Bush, more conservative justices maintained power on the Supreme Court. As a consequence, many of the rights that seemed to have expanded during the 1960s are considered to have been significantly retracted during the 1970s, 1980s, and early 1990s.

CRITICAL THINKING QUESTIONS

Note to Instructor: These questions appear throughout the chapter as "CTQs." They can be used to stimulate class discussion.

1. What is the current philosophical orientation of the U.S. Supreme Court regarding criminal justice issues?
2. Is it in the public's interest to protect officers' lives and to expend greater efforts in doing so than the efforts expended to save the lives of ordinary citizens?
3. If you were a Supreme Court justice, which of these two conflicting goals would you choose to give priority to—the due process model or the crime control model?
4. Discuss the relationship between the U.S. Constitution and the Bill of Rights. What particular provisions does the incorporation theory involve?
5. Is the Supreme Court conservative or liberal when it comes to controlling police power? What factors will come into play in the court in the first decade of the twenty-first century? Do you see an increase or decrease in civil liberties during this decade?
6. What do you think the framers of the Constitution meant when they coined the term "due process of the law"?
7. How does the "due process clause" differ from "the law of the land"?
8. Have "criminals" been given too many rights? Should courts become more concerned with the rights of the victims or the rights of the offenders?
9. Why do you believe the Supreme Court has not selectively incorporated every right contained within the Bill of Rights?
10. Why do you think that the rights that were not selected were in fact not selected?
11. Did the opinions supporting crime control in the 1970s, 1980s, 1990s, and the first decade of the twenty-first century make the United States a better or worse place in which to live?
12. What is the paramount goal of the Supreme Court at this time? Is its legal philosophy control of crime, public safety, or protection of civil liberties?
13. Is it possible for a person to be legally under arrest without an officer indicating that he or she is in fact under arrest? Explain.
14. Can you be arrested without doing anything?
15. Should police be personally liable if they violate a person's constitutional rights? How might this influence their investigations?
16. Some students carry identification, some do not. Do the police have the right to arrest a student if they stop him or her and the student fails to provide identification?
17. What are the differences between police investigative powers and police arrest powers?
18. Which Fourth Amendment search warrant requirement is the most important? Should "particularity" really be necessary for search warrants?
19. Which is a more just and fair test of informants' information—the two-pronged test (two set standards that are always legally required) or the totality-of-circumstances test? If you are very cynical, who would you say wrote the anonymous letter in *Illinois v. Gates*?
20. Why would anyone ever consent to a police search conducted at their own home?
21. Suppose a police officer stops a person who looks different from most people in the neighborhood and who certainly acts more strangely. The officer decides to frisk him. During the pat down he feels no weapon, but a soft bulge in the pockets. He retrieves it to find that the contents are cocaine. Would an arrest for cocaine possession hold up in court? Why or why not?
22. Does the exclusionary rule effectively deter police conduct that violates others' constitutional rights?
23. What is the purpose of the *Miranda* warnings? Have rights granted to suspects in the *Miranda* decision been eroded by subsequent decisions? Is this a desirable or an undesirable process? Why has the Court ruled in this manner?
24. When police officers violate the "rules of fair play," which apply administratively to criminal investiga-

tions, is it unusual for guilty people to go free? Can you think of another way of enticing officers to obey the law without necessarily having them arrest someone?

IN THE MEDIA

Video

"The American Constitution: The Road from Runnymede"°

"Bill of Rights: Bill of Responsibilities"°

"The Bill of Rights: A Living Document"°

CNN Today Video- *Introduction to Criminal Justice* vol. 13, seg. 1, "Miranda Rights"

Court TV, *The Greatest Trials of All Time (The Scottsborough Boys)*

"Criminal Procedure"°

FFA Custom CJ Video: *The Courtroom Process; The Public Defendant*

FFH Video: *Amendment 4 & Amendments 5–8*

FFH Video: *Unreasonable Searches and Seizures*

"Interpreting the Law: The Role of the Supreme Court"°

NIJ Video: *Exclusionary Rule*

NIJ Video: *Search and Seizure*

"Profile Stops"°

"Profiling Criminal Violators"°

"Rights of the Accused"°

"The Scales of Justice: Our Court System"°

"Supreme Court Decisions That Changed the Nation"°

°These videos are part of the *Legal Studies* video collection by Internet Media. Your educational institution should purchase these for the class, since they are fairly expensive, by calling Internet Media at 1-800-233-9100.

Films

Double Jeopardy

Gideon's Trumpet

The Insider

The Juror

Mr. Smith Goes to Washington

The Thin Blue Line (1988) Documents key moments in the twenty-month investigation of a young drifter named Randall Adams, who was wrongfully convicted of murdering a Dallas police officer in 1976.

Twelve Angry Men

Television

A&E *American Justice series*

CNN Today

Court TV

First Monday (an absolute must)

The West Wing

IN THE LITERATURE

Books

American Bar Association, *Standards Relating to Electronic Surveillance*, 2nd ed., New York: Institute of Judicial Administration, 1980.

R. V. Del Carmen, *Criminal Procedure for Law Enforcement Personnel*. Monterey, Calif.: Brooks/Cole Publishing Company, 1987.

R. A. Leo, et al., eds., *The Miranda Debate: Law, Justice, and Policing*, Boston, Mass: Northeastern University Press, 1998.

A. Lewis, *Gideon's Trumpet*, New York: Vantage Books, 1989.

D. A. McWhirter, *Search, Seizure, and Privacy: Exploring the Constitution*, Phoenix, Ariz.: Oryx Press, 1994.

Articles

D. Bayley and J. Garofalo, "The Management of Violence by Police Patrol Officers," *Criminology* vol. 27 (1989), pp. 1–27.

D. Dripps, "Is Miranda Case Law Inconsistent? A First Amendment Synthesis," *Constitutional Community*, vol. 17 (2000), p. 19.

J. Fyfe, "The Use of Deadly Force: Research and Reform," *Justice Quarterly* vol. 5 (1998), pp. 165–205.

M. Gardner, "Sixth Amendment Right to Council and Its Underlying Values," *Journal of Criminal Law and Criminology*, vol. 90 (2000), p. 393.

G. Kelder and A. J. Statman, "The Protective Sweep Doctrine: Recurrent Questions Regarding the Propriety of Searches Conducted Contemporaneously with an Arrest on or Near Private Premises," *Syracuse Law Review*, vol. 30 (1979), pp. 973–1092.

R. Leo, "Miranda Revisited," *Journal of Criminal Law and Criminology*, vol. 86 (1996), p. 621.

W. Lippman, "Miranda v. Arizona—Twenty Years Later," *Criminal Justice Journal* (1987), p. 241.

J. Nestlerode, "Distinguishing the Exclusionary *Rule Exceptions*." *Journal of National Association of District Attorneys* vol. 24 (1991), pp. 29–35.

J. Riggs, "Excluding Automobile Passengers from the Fourth Amendment," *Journal of Law and Criminology*, vol. 88 (1998), p. 55.

G. Thomas, "The End of the Road for Miranda Arguers," *American Criminal Law Review*, vol. 37 (2000), p. 1.

J. Wasowiz, "Future of the Exclusionary Rule," *Trial Magazine* vol. 34, p. 79.

4. THE NATURE AND DISTRIBUTION OF CRIME AND ITS VICTIMS

CHAPTER LEARNING OBJECTIVES

After reading this chapter the student should be able to:

1. Identify the two categories that encompass the eight index crimes.
2. Discuss why the clearance rate for murder is higher than the clearance rate for other index crimes.
3. List reasons why rape is one of the most underreported violent crimes.
4. Describe the difference between robbery and larceny.
5. Identify the three categories of motor vehicle theft.
6. List the traditional criticisms of the Uniform Crime Report (UCR) system.
7. Discuss the major differences between the National Crime Survey (NCS) and the UCR.
8. Describe what is involved in the concept "victim eligibility" for compensation.
9. Discuss victimization surveys and why they are useful.
10. List ways in which crime victims may receive callous or insensitive treatment by the criminal justice system.
11. Describe the Minneapolis domestic violence experiment and its results.
12. List three recommendations that have been made to assist prosecution when the victims are children.
13. Describe the two ways victims and witnesses can be intimidated.
14. Discuss the implications of the results from a recent study of costs of crime victimization.
15. Describe the results of recent research on violence against college women.

KEY TERMS

aggravated assault
arson
burglary
clearance rate
compensation
crime data manipulation
crime rate
criminal homicide
domestic crisis intervention unit

FBI Uniform Crime Reports (UCR)
forcible rape
hate crime
larceny-theft
Mothers Against Drunk Driving (MADD)
motor vehicle theft
National Crime Victimization Survey (NCVS)
National Incident-Based Reporting System (NIBRS)

National Organization for Victim Assistance (NOVA)
restitution
robbery
victim impact statement
victim special-interest groups
waiver of prosecution

CHAPTER OVERVIEW

Note to Instructor: The following provides you with a summary of key points made throughout the chapter.

In this chapter we want to accomplish a number of objectives. First, we introduce why crime data are collected and which departments of the federal government publish the information. Next, we attempt to familiarize the reader with the crime reporting system in the United States. The Uniform Crime Reporting program is a voluntary system established in 1930 by the International Association of Chiefs of Police, with the FBI serving as the national clearinghouse. With crime statistics voluntarily contributed by over sixteen thousand law enforcement agencies throughout the country, the UCR program provides periodic assessments of crime in the United States. Data from the program are widely used by criminal justice professionals, legislators, and scholars who have an interest in the crime problem. We also discuss the collection of campus crime data.

Another objective of this chapter is to discuss some of the problems related to gathering crime data and some of the changes that have been implemented for the UCR. We also discuss the National Crime Victimization Survey (NCVS) and how it differs from the UCR.

In addition to discussing crime data, we want to provide the reader with some insights into the effects of crime on both the victim and society. The findings of victimization surveys are discussed as well as the response by the criminal justice system. We also describe various special categories of victims, as well as discussing both the tangible and intangible costs associated with crime victimization.

CRITICAL THINKING QUESTIONS

Note to Instructor: These questions appear throughout the chapter as "CTQs." They can be used to stimulate class discussion.

1. Why is it important to know the crime rate of a city as opposed to simply the number of crimes?
2. Do you think the classification of violent crimes such as murder and nonnegligent manslaughter should be based solely on police investigation, as it is now, or should other criminal justice entities partake in the classification process?
3. What factors do you believe are most responsible for the underreported nature of the crime of rape by victims?
4. Is it good public policy to have a "waiver of prosecution?" Why or why not?
5. Why do you think larcenies are the crimes most frequently reported to the UCR?
6. Is enough being done on the part of government officials to label hate crimes as serious criminal offenses, on par with aggravated assault and other crimes?
7. Are there any disparities in how the media report and represent hate crimes and the actual statistical evidence shown in the Uniform Crime Reports? If so, explain.
8. What should be done to police officials who are guilty of manipulating crime data?
9. Should the reporting of crime data on the part of law enforcement agencies be made mandatory in order to improve the overall accuracy of the UCR system? If so, would there be any disadvantages to this? Why or why not?
10. If you could change the UCR system, which Part II Crimes would you add to the crime index? Justify your response.
11. What improvements would you suggest be made to the UCR method of collecting and reporting crime data?
12. Why is it important to collect campus crime data separately from the UCR?
13. Why do you suppose the American criminal justice system has until recently largely ignored the victims of crime?
14. Do you think state victim compensation programs should extend the basic core of criminal offenses for which a victim can apply for compensation? If so, what types of crimes do you believe would also warrant victim compensation?
15. To what extent do you think victim and witness intimidation undermines the functionality of the criminal justice system?
16. Why do you think that people who live in urban centers are more vulnerable to crime victimization than those who live in nonurban areas such as suburbs?
17. What factors do you believe would best explain the marked differences between the victimization rates of whites and those of minority groups?
18. Do you think that intimate-partner violence should be treated more seriously by justice officials due to the likelihood of future violence, or should mediation be promoted as a way to resolve domestic disputes?
19. What role do you believe the Violence against Women Act played in reforming the criminal justice system's response to the problem of domestic violence?
20. Do you believe community policing is an effective results-oriented approach to reducing violence against women?
21. How is the crime of stalking perceived in society? In the media? Do you believe stalking deserves more attention on the part of criminal justice officials due to its potential for future violence? If so, explain why in brief.
22. Do you agree with the statistic that victimization costs society an average of $450 billion annually? Do you think this should be higher, considering long-term costs such as pain and suffering?

IN THE MEDIA

Video

ABC NEWS Video: *America's Fastest Growing Crime: Rape*

ABC NEWS Video: *Blacks and the Criminal Justice System*

CNN Today Video: *Corrections, vol. 1:* "Crime Statistics"

FHH Custom Video: *Crime in American Society*

NIJ Video: *Violent Crime Rates*

IN THE LITERATURE

Note to Instructor: These sources can be integrated throughout the chapter as additional sources of information for the students.

Books

J. Bachman, L. Johnston, and P. O'Malley, *Monitoring the Future*, Ann Arbor, Mich.: Institute for Social Research, 1991.

C. Beccaria, *On Crimes and Punishment*, 6th ed., Indianapolis; Ind.: Bobbs-Merrill, 1977.

A. Biderman and J. Lynch, *Understanding Crime Statistics: Why the UCR Diverges from the NCS*, New York: Springer-Verlag, 1991.

F. Butterfield, *All God's Children: The Basket Family and the American Tradition of Violence*, New York: Avon, 1996.

R. Clarck, *Situational Crime Prevention*, Albany, N.Y.: Harrow and Heston, 1992.

Federal Bureau of Investigation, *Crime in the United States*, Washington D.C.: U.S. Government Printing Office, 1991.

S. Flaherty and A. Sarat, eds., *Victim's Rights*, New York: Chelsea House Publishers, 1998.

D. Friedrichs, *Trusted Criminals: White Collar Crime in Contemporary Society*, Belmont, Calif.: Wadsworth Publishing, 1996.

F. Heidensohn, *Women and Crime*, New York: New York University Press, 1985.

Jason, *The Complete Book of Victim's Rights*, Highlands Ranch, Colo.: Prose Associates, 1996.

J. Katz, *Seductions of Crime: Moral and Sensual Attractions of Doing Evil*, New York: Basic Books, 1988.

G. Lafree, *Rape and Criminal Justice*, Belmont, Calif.: Wadsworth Publishing, 1989.

S. Messner, *Crime and the American Dream*, Belmont, Calif.: Wadsworth Publishing, 1994.

Pierce and J. Fox, *Recent Trends in Violent Crime: A Closer Look*, Boston: NCAP, Northeastern University Press, 1992.

E. M. Wietekamp and H. Kerner, *Cross National Longitudinal Research on Human Development and Criminal Behavior*, The Netherlands: Kluwer, 1994.

E. Wish, *Drug Use Forecasting 1990*, Washington D.C: National Institute of Justice, 1991.

Articles

Blumstein, J. Cohen, and R. Rosenfeld, "Trend and Deviation in Crime Rates: A Comparison of UCR and NCS Data for Burglary and Robbery," *Criminology*, vol. 29 (1991), pp. 237–263.

E. Currie, "Radical Criminology or Just Criminology—Then, and Now," *Social Justice*, vol. 26 (Summer 1999), p. 16.

A. Dunkers, "Factors Affecting Support After Criminal Victimization: Needed and Received Support from the Partner, the Social Network and Distant Support Providers," *Journal of Social Psychology*, vol. 139 (1999), p. 121.

D. Fishbeing, "Biological Perspectives in Criminology," *Criminology*, vol. 28 (1990), pp. 27–72.

J. Freedman, "Violence in the Mass Media and Violence in Society: The Link Is Unproven," *Harvard Mental Health Letter*, vol. 12 (1996), p. 4.

D. Gorman-Smith, P. Tolan, and D. Henry, "Relation of Family Problems to Patterns of Delinquent Involvement Among Urban Youth," *Journal of Abnormal Child Psychology*, vol. 26 (1998), p. 339.

R. Lotspeich, "Crime in Transitional Economies," *Europe-Asia Studies*, vol. 47 (1995), p. 555.

K. McCabe and S. Gregory, "Elderly Victimization: An Examination Beyond the FBI's Index Crimes," *Research on Aging*, vol. 20 (1998), pp. 363–373.

B. Miller, W. Downs, and D. Gondoli, "Delinquency, Childhood Violence, and the Development of Alcoholism in Women," *Crime and Delinquency*, vol. 35 (1989), pp. 94–108.

A. Roy, "Recent Trends in Official Male and Female Crime Rates: The Convergence Controversy," *Journal of Criminal Justice*, vol. 21 (1993), pp. 447–466.

D. Schwartz, S. Mcfaden, K. Dodge, G. Pettit, and J. Bates, "Early Behavior Problems as Predictor of Later Peer Group Victimization: Moderators and Mediators in the Pathways of Social Risk," *Journal of Abnormal Child Psychology*, vol. 27 (1999), p. 191.

S. Singer, "Homogenous Victim-Offender Populations: A Review and Some Research Implications," *Journal of Criminal Law and Criminology*, vol. 72 (1981), pp. 779–799.

S. Singer, "Rethinking Subcultural Theories of Delinquency and the Cultural Resources of Youth." (Paper presented at the annual meeting of the American Society of Criminology, Phoenix, Ariz., November 1993.)

E. Staub, "The Psychology of Bystanders, Perpetrators, and Heroic Helpers," *International Journal of Intercultural Relations*, vol. 17 (1993), pp. 315–341.

O. Yu and L. Zangh, "Crime Crackdown Continues as Statistics Increase," *CJ International*, vol. 12 (1996), p. 8.

5 POLICE OPERATIONS

CHAPTER LEARNING OBJECTIVES

After reading this chapter the student should be able to:

1. Describe the differences between rural/small town police agencies and their urban/suburban counterparts.
2. List Sir Robert Peel's principles for effective policing and discuss their relevance today.
3. Describe the emergence of state police in the United States.
4. Discuss the role of the field training officer.
5. Describe the roles of the FBI and the DEA.
6. List the tasks performed during a preliminary investigation by the first officer responding to the scene.
7. Discuss the findings and implications of the Kansas City Patrol Experiment.
8. List common activities of a patrol division.
9. Name and discuss four types of nontraditional patrol.
10. Discuss zero-tolerance enforcement and its relationship to the "Broken Windows" perspective.
11. Describe how the role of campus police has evolved over the last few decades.
12. List some of the common activities of detectives.
13. Discuss the policy recommendations made based on the findings of the Rand Criminal Investigation Study.
14. Describe the three eras of American policing.
15. Discuss problem-oriented policing and the SARA model.

KEY TERMS

community-oriented policing (COP)
crackdowns
crime analysis
evidence technician
field interview files
field training officer (FTO)
National Crime Information Center
nontraditional patrol
Police Executive Research Forum (PERF)
proactive beats
proactive crime prevention
problem-oriented policing (POP)
professional officer track
professional police management track
quota system
reactive beats
selective traffic enforcement
special-purpose police
zero-tolerance policing

CHAPTER OVERVIEW

Note to Instructor: The following provides you with a summary of key points made throughout the chapter.

This chapter serves a number of varied purposes in introducing police operations. In order to better understand why police departments operate the way they do today, we find it useful not only to provide a current profile of police departments but also to discuss how policing evolved in America. For example, we spend some time describing the early policing efforts in Boston and New York City. We think it is also useful to provide an overview of smaller police departments in the United States, since the majority of communities are served by this type of agency.

In addition, considerable time is spent in this chapter describing the role and functions of uniformed patrol officers who comprise the majority of personnel in any law enforcement agency. We find it useful to briefly discuss some of the activities that are performed by a patrol officer in a typical police department. Later in this section, we discuss how patrol strategies have changed as a result of police research conducted during the last two decades.

L CRIME AND JUSTICE IN AMERICA

One of the most frequently criticized but least understood functions performed by police officers relates to their traffic responsibilities. Therefore, we try to provide some insight in this chapter regarding these important duties. In addition, we discuss both rural and campus policing to offer our readers information that is often missing from standard textbooks.

Following the discussion of rural and campus policing, the role of the detective or investigator is described. In addition, we spend some time relating research that has been conducted regarding the detective role. Research conducted by the Rand Corporation and the Police Executive Research Forum (PERF) is discussed in some detail.

We also include an overview of the computerized criminal history information, specifically, the use of the National Crime Information Center (NCIC and NCIC 2000) by law enforcement agencies. In the final portion of this chapter, we describe an evolution occurring in modern-day policing that involves a change in philosophy and operational approaches. We highlight some of the elements in community-oriented policing (COP) and problem-oriented policing (POP). We also discuss community policing within the context of an elected sheriff's office. Questions regarding the future of COP and POP are also discussed.

CRITICAL THINKING QUESTIONS

Note to Instructor: These questions appear throughout the chapter as "CTQs." They can be used to stimulate class discussion.

1. In your opinion, what role do the media play in how members of the public form their opinions about police departments in the United States?
2. Do you believe that proactive crime-prevention activities can also be viably implemented in larger, urban police departments? Why or why not?
3. Which of Sir Robert Peel's principles for effective policing do you believe are most visible in today's law enforcement agencies?
4. Do you believe there should be a standard, mandatory time requirement for rookies to spend with an FTO, irrespective of the policy of the organization or the pace at which the new officer masters certain skills? Briefly explain your answer.
5. Do you think a two-track dual-career system is an adequate response to the built-in promotional limitations in police departments across the United States?
6. Should patrol officers be expected to perform nonpolice functions as part of their jobs? Do you believe this type of interactive community involvement constitutes good police work, or do such tasks do nothing to enhance the image of the officers in the eyes of the public?
7. Considering the findings of the Kansas City experiment, do you believe that higher visibility of patrol officers would deter the commission of certain types of crime (such as burglary) in your community? Why or why not?
8. What are the advantages and disadvantages of zero-tolerance policing?
9. The "broken windows theory of crime" suggests that if petty crimes or disorder are ignored by police, this will encourage criminals to commit more serious crimes. Do you agree or disagree with this statement? Explain briefly.
10. In your opinion, is the quota system, which requires officers to write a specified number of traffic tickets in a given time, an effective method of curtailing the number of accidents in a given area?
11. What are some of the differences between urban and rural styles of policing? Do you think some of the practices arising from those differences (such as the upkeep of detailed written records) warrant administrative reform?
12. What factors do you most attribute to the increased role of campus police as professional law enforcement officers? Would the same factors apply to campuses with less than 2,500 students?
13. Which stereotype do you believe to be the most responsible for the misunderstanding of the detective role in actuality: the media stereotype, the historical stereotype, or the critical stereotype?
14. Is the role of the detective held in high regard by the public today? Why or why not?
15. Should the follow-up investigative procedures, in your opinion, be the responsibility of the first responding officer or that of the detective? Briefly explain your answer.
16. Do you think that increased usage and availability of computerized criminal information for both large and small police departments will lead to a higher number of arrests being made as a result of the automation of criminal justice information?
17. Do you believe that the increasing amount of personal information being collected by the government for criminal databases poses potential risks to an individual's right to privacy? If so, briefly explain why.
18. Should police officers be primarily "crime fighters" or community-oriented in their approach to policing? Support your answer.
19. What is unique about the office of the sheriff today? Do you believe that sheriffs' offices would be more or less responsive to community needs when compared to city police agencies? Justify your response.
20. In your opinion, what types of crime problems would best be addressed by applying the strategy known as problem-oriented policing? Support your answer.

IN THE LITERATURE

Note to Instructor: These sources can be integrated throughout the chapter as additional sources of information for the students.

Books

D. Bayley, *Policing for the Future*, New York: Oxford University Press, 1944.

W. Geller, *Police Leadership in America*, New York: Praeger, 1985.

H. Goldstein, *Problem-Oriented Policing*, New York: McGraw Hill, 1990.

J. Greene, *Community Policing: Rhetoric or Reality?* New York: Praeger, 1988.

P. Manning, *Police Work*, Cambridge, Mass.: MIT Press, 1977.

J. Skolnick, *Justice without Trial: Law Enforcement in a Democratic Society*, New York: Wiley, 1986.

M. Tonry and N. Morris, eds., *Modern Policing*, Chicago: University of Chicago Press, 1992.

J. Wilson, *Varieties of Police Behavior*, Cambridge, Mass.: Harvard University Press, 1968.

Articles

J. Harpold, "Medical Model for Community Policing," *FBI Law Enforcement Bulletin*, vol. 69 (June 2000), p. 23.

H. Kuntz, "Battered Women, Reluctant Police," *Washington Post*, February 28, 1988.

R. Lane, "Urban Police and Crime in Nineteenth Century America." In N. Morris and M. Tonry, eds., *Crime and Justice*, vol. 2, Chicago: University of Chicago Press, 1980.

W. Miller, "The Good, the Bad, and the Ugly: Policing America," *History Today*, vol. 50 (August 2000), p. 29.

B. Reaves, "State and Local Police Departments," Washington, D.C.: Bureau of Justice Statistics.

J. Wilson and G. Kelling, "Broken Windows," *Atlantic Monthly*, vol. 29 (March 1982), pp. 29–38.

6 ISSUES AND TRENDS IN POLICING

CHAPTER LEARNING OBJECTIVES

After reading this chapter the student should be able to:

1. Discuss the principal motivation for police administrators and officers wanting to achieve the status of professional.
2. List the major benefits of attaining law enforcement accreditation.
3. Explain why the widespread availability of illicit drugs has increased police corruption.
4. Describe the relationship between higher education and law enforcement today.
5. Discuss the results of the Bloch and Anderson study on the effectiveness of female officers on patrol.
6. Identify four categories of stress in law enforcement.
7. Describe the results of studies of stress among female officers.
8. List the benefits the Denver police derive from their alcohol abuse program.
9. Discuss what can be done to help police officers reduce stress or learn to cope with it.
10. Identify examples of shooting-control techniques that can be used by police departments.
11. Describe the significance of *Tennessee v. Garner*.
12. Discuss how DNA profiling may be used to identify or eliminate potential suspects.
13. List applications of geographical information systems (GIS) in law enforcement.
14. Identify some of the "signs of crime" associated with higher levels of citizen fear.
15. List the types of programs that have been initiated by police to reduce fear of crime and crime itself.

KEY TERMS

campus crime-prevention programs
Combat Auto Theft (CAT) program
Commission on Accreditation for Law Enforcement Agencies
Computer-aided dispatch (CAD)
Crime Prevention through Environmental Design (CPTED)
deadly force
DNA profiling
fingerprint automation
geographical information system (GIS)
International Association of Chiefs of Police (IACP)
job stress
Law Enforcement Critical Life Events Scale
McGruff campaign
National Organization of Black Law Enforcement Executives (NOBLE)
National Sheriff's Association (NSA)
Neighborhood Watch
Police Executive Research Forum (PERF)
police misconduct
shooting-control techniques
signs of crime

CHAPTER OVERVIEW

Note to Instructor: The following provides you with a summary of key points made throughout the chapter.

This chapter focuses on issues deserving of special attention in the last decade: professionalization of the police; police misconduct; affirmative action and equal opportunities in law enforcement; police officer stress; police use of deadly force; law enforcement's response to violence in America; the emergence of private security in this country and its interactive role with public law enforcement; and, finally, technological trends designed to assist police agencies now and in the future.

In addition, in this chapter we discuss the history and evolution of crime prevention. Our focus is on the role played by citizens and police as well as some of the innovative programs now being used to prevent crime in our communities. Evaluations of crime prevention and community anti-drug efforts are also included in this chapter.

CRITICAL THINKING QUESTIONS

Note to Instructor: These questions appear throughout the chapter as "CTQs." They can be used to stimulate class discussion.

1. Why would some police agencies not pursue law enforcement accreditation?
2. If you were the police chief of a department of fifty personnel in a city of 25,000 citizens, what minimum education level would you establish for your new police officers? Justify your response.
3. Should police departments increase the recruitment of college-educated officers? Why or why not?
4. Should police officers who engage in illegal misconduct be punished more or less severely than their civilian counterparts? Do you agree that ethics course trainings are the best preventive way to deal with police misconduct?
5. As a police chief, what programs would you implement to hire and retain more minorities and women for your department?
6. What administrative strategies would you find most useful for increasing the recruitment of women officers?
7. What factors do you believe contribute most to officer stress? Which contribute least? Why?
8. What administrative measures do you believe should be taken by police departments to curb alcoholism among officers? Do you agree with the statement that police work is especially conductive to alcoholism, or does that hold true for a number of other high-stress jobs?
9. Do you think it is important to have a drug-screening policy for police officers? Why or why not? If you were chief, what would you do with an officer who was found to be using illegal drugs?
10. Do you believe that the use of deadly force by a police officer is ever justified? If so, under what conditions?
11. Considering previous research findings, do you think the use of pepper spray is an effective alternative to more violent methods for subduing criminals? Why or why not?
12. What problems do you believe could be associated with private policing? What are some of the benefits?
13. In what ways do you think technological trends affect policing practices in America?
14. Some authorities have suggested that despite the improvements in the use of technology, policing remains primarily a "people" profession. Do you agree? Why or why not?
15. What constitutional concerns might the establishment of a DNA databank composed of samples from non-convicted offenders have?
16. How do you think civic responsibility for crime prevention is viewed in your community today?
17. Why do think low-income communities have a more difficult time maintaining community-based prevention programs than middle-class communities?
18. What signs of crime can you identify in your community? Do any of these contribute significantly to your fear of crime? Why or why not?
19. Do you agree with the statement that proper design and effective use of the physical environment can produce behavioral effects that will reduce the incidence and fear of crime? Why or why not?
20. If you were a campus law enforcement official or administrator, what educational programs would you implement in your college or university to stress community participation in the prevention of campus crime?
21. What role can the police play in assisting residents with community anti-drug efforts?

IN THE MEDIA

Video

CNN Today Video: *Introduction to Criminal Justice*, vol. 2: seg. 7, "Culture and Violence"

CNN Today Video: *Introduction to Criminal Justice*, vol. 3: seg. 4, "Officer Stopped Verdict"

CNN Today Video: *Introduction to Criminal Justice*, vol. 1: seg. 4, "Parting the Blue Curtain"

NIJ Crime File Video: *Deadly Force*

FHH Video: *The Tarnished Shield: When Cops Go Bad*

FHH *Custom CJ* Video, Seg. 4: "Suicide and the Police Officer"

Films

Angel Eyes (Fox Entertainment, 2001)

The Fugitive, (Paramount Pictures, 1993)

Training Day (Columbia Tri-Star, 2001)

Television

The District (CBS)

Law and Order (NBC)

NYPD Blue (NBC)

IN THE LITERATURE

Note to Instructor: These sources can be integrated throughout the chapter as additional sources of information for the students.

Books

Human Rights Watch, *Shielded from Justice: Police Brutality and Accountability in the United States,* Washington, D.C.: Human Rights Watch, 1998.

J. Greene, and S. Mastrofsky, eds., *Community Policing: Rhetoric or Reality?* New York: Praeger, 1988.

H. Goldstein, *Police Corruption: A Perspective on Its Nature and Control,* Washington, D.C.: The Police Foundation, 1975.

A. Reiss, *Police and the Public,* New Haven, Conn.: Yale University Press, 1971.

C. Shearing, and P. Stenning, eds., *Private Policing,* Newbury Park, Calif.: Sage Publications, 1987.

J. Skolnich and J. Fyfe, *Above the Law: Police and the Excessive Use of Force,* New York: Free Press, 1993.

S. Smith, G. Steadman, T. Minton, and M. Townsend, *Criminal Victimization and Perceptions of Community Safety in 12 Cities,* Washington, D.C.: Bureau of Justice Statistics, May 1999.

Articles

L. Gelhaus, "Civil Suits Against Police Change Domestic Violence Response," *Trial,* vol. 35 (September 1999), p. 103.

D. Griswold, "Complaints Against the Police: Predicting Dispositions," *Journal of Criminal Justice,* vol. 22 (1994), pp. 215–224. J. McCormick, "On a High-Tech Firing Line: Simulators That Shoot Back Are Helping Cops Learn How to Use Deadly Force," *Newsweek* (6 December 1999).

W. King and B. Sanders, "Nice Guys Finish Last: A Critical Review of Police Officers Killed in the Line of Duty," *Policing,* vol. 20 (1997), pp. 392–408.

J. McCormick, "On a High-Tech Firing Line: Simulators That Shoot Back Are Helping Cops Learn How to Use Deadly Force," *Newsweek* (6 December 1999).

C. Miller, "In the Line of Fire: Learning from Assaults on Law Enforcement Officers," *FBI Law Enforcement Bulletin,* vol. 67 (1998), pp. 15–24.

M. Vaughn, "Police Civil Liability for Abandonment in High-Crime Areas and Other High-Risk Situations," *Journal of Criminal Justice,* vol. 22 (1994), pp. 407–424.

M. Vaughn, "Police Sexual Violence: Civil Liability Under State Tort Law," *Crime and Delinquency,* vol. 45 (1999), pp. 334–357.

7 THE DYNAMICS OF THE CRIMINAL COURT

❧ CHAPTER LEARNING OBJECTIVES

After reading this chapter the student should be able to:

1. Discuss why state supreme courts are sometimes called courts of last resort.
2. Identify the principle areas of jurisdiction of the U.S. Superior Court.
3. List the areas of jurisdiction for the U.S. District Courts.
4. Describe the functions and duties of the trial judge.
5. Discuss the most serious problem facing the courts today.
6. Identify six prosecutorial functions during a case.
7. List the major functions of a criminal defense attorney.
8. List the types of criminal defense systems in the United States.
9. Describe the nature of the contractual counsel system and how it functions.
10. Describe the nature of the assigned counsel system and how it functions.
11. Discuss the percentage of guilty pleas in criminal cases and what would happen if this rate were not maintained.
12. Describe the function of the three-tiered federal court system.
13. List three ways in which one may become a judge.
14. Identify the stages in the occupational socialization of judges.
15. Describe the parallels between the state and federal court systems.

❧ KEY TERMS

adversary system
appellate court
assigned-counsel system
bailiff
chief judge
contract system
court
court administrator
court clerk
court reporter
defense attorney
de novo
deferred adjudication
dual court system
en banc
judge
judicial assistant
jurisdiction
justice
law clerk
magistrate
pro se
prosecuting attorney
public defender
writ of *certiorari*
writ of *habeas corpus*

❧ CHAPTER OVERVIEW

Note to Instructor: The following provides you with a summary of key points made throughout the chapter.

The American judicial system is extremely complex. It is more accurate, in fact, to speak of the American judicial systems. This is because there are courts at the federal, state, county, and municipal levels of jurisdiction, all of which are making independent decisions. The state operates trial courts, intermediate appellate courts, and courts of last resort (i.e., the highest tribunals to which cases can be appealed). This pattern is repeated at the federal level. Federal appellate courts, however, can rule on state cases and have greater power to change state decisions than state courts have to change federal decisions. The United States Supreme Court is the court of last resort for all cases involving constitutional issues that are decided in the United

LV

States, regardless of whether they are decided initially in federal court or in state trial court.

Our system of criminal justice is based upon the adversary system—the presentation of opposing views in vigorous debate as a prelude to decision making. The system is not designed to discover the ultimate truth in the absolute sense, but rather to protect the people against the abuse of governmental power and to ensure that no innocent person is found guilty of a crime he or she did not commit. Cross-examination is used to determine the facts and historically has proven to be the most effective means of exposing false testimony and inaccuracies in testimony. Our system also rejects the practice of torture and other inhuman practices incompatible with the values of free people. In summary, the adversary system seeks to accomplish justice by eliciting provable facts under fixed rules of procedure.

In America, prosecutors represent the executive branch of the government. Their powers are formidable, and they exert considerable influence upon and within the criminal justice system. Their power to institute criminal prosecution vests in them an authority in the administration of criminal justice as large as, if not greater than, the authority of the judge who presides in criminal cases. They may initiate criminal charges, stop the charging process, or request that the court dismiss the charges. Thus, the power within the prosecutor's office in this country is indeed quite formidable.

On the opposing side is the defense counsel. The courts have mandated that counsel be provided at both the state and federal levels in all cases in which the defendant is threatened with loss of liberty, whether the accused is charged with a misdemeanor or felony. Legal assistance may be provided by privately retained counsel, public defenders, counsel assigned by the courts, or counsel under contract. Each alternative has its strengths and weaknesses. For example, hiring a private attorney does not guarantee competent or interested representation. The best criminal lawyers are expensive, and frequently there is a direct correlation between the defendant's ability to pay and the quality of representation received.

Direct supervision of the courts is the responsibility of the judiciary. Judges are either appointed or elected, or attain office on a modified appointment plan (the Missouri Plan). As public officials, they are involved in the political issues and controversies that are an inseparable feature of public life. Coming from a variety of backgrounds and experiences, newcomers to the bench undergo a process of learning that gradually accommodates them to the role of judge. The human side of judging is nowhere more clearly revealed than in the job-related stresses that affect members of the judiciary. This stress seems particularly evident when judges are campaigning for reelection. Other members of the judicial staff include the bailiff, court clerk, court reporter, chief judge, and court administrator. These members of the judicial team provide expert assistance and counsel, without which the judicial process would barely function. The court administrator, in particular, is beginning to emerge as the focal figure in easing the administrative and management burden, especially for the chief judge. Still, court congestion and delay in the courtroom may be the most serious problems facing the courts. These phenomena have engulfed the state and county court systems throughout the nation, with few exceptions. While reformers and patrons acknowledge the existence of these problems, few efforts appear to have any impact on the immediate problems.

CRITICAL THINKING QUESTIONS

Note to Instructor: These questions appear throughout the chapter as "CTQs." They can be used to stimulate class discussion.

1. What is the jurisdictional dilemma between the state and federal courts in high-profile cases, and how might it be resolved?
2. What is the dual court system in America? Could the drive toward court unification eventually lead to a monolithic court system? Would such a system be effective?
3. What type of restructuring would be most efficient to unify the state court systems?
4. What types of cases fall under the jurisdiction of the U.S. Supreme Court?
5. What effect does the Supreme Court's refusal to issue a writ of *certiorari* have on the lower court's decisions?
6. What is meant when one calls the Supreme Court the court of last resort?
7. What are the major problems found in the lower courts, and how might these be remedied?
8. What is the best solution for reducing the number of drug cases in the American court system?
9. "The primary adversarial relationship in the courts is not between the plaintiff (prosecutor, or state) and the defendant, but rather between the ideal of justice and the reality of bureaucratic limitations." Explain why you either disagree or agree with this statement.
10. Is it true that there is no concern for truth in our adversarial system of justice?
11. Should the prosecutor's office be an elected or an appointed position? Is it possible to separate politics from the prosecutor's office?
12. Does the prosecutor have too much power over the criminal justice process? What is his or her most powerful tool of controlling the criminal justice process?
13. Comparing the roles of the police and the prosecutors, who has more discretion, and who has greater potential for abuse of their discretion? Why?

14. Why are public prosecutors considered to be the most dominant figures in the American criminal justice system?
15. What, if any, are some of the judicial restraints put on prosecutorial discretion? What are some of the system factors and case factors that affect the prosecutor's decision-making process?
16. What is "prosecutorial vindictiveness" and what have the courts done to control it?
17. What is the primary duty of the prosecutor in your opinion? Is it to seek justice, or is it merely to secure a conviction?
18. Do defense attorneys have an obligation to defend a client who they know is guilty of committing the criminal act? Why or why not?
19. Should criminal defense attorneys disclose information given to them by their clients concerning their participation in earlier unsolved crimes?
20. Should defense attorneys cooperate with prosecutors if it means that it dramatically increases the chances that their clients will go to jail?
21. Does the assigned-counsel system present an inherent conflict of interest because these types of indigent-criminal defense attorneys are hired and paid by the institutions (usually the court) and not by the clients they represent?
22. What qualities should a judge have? Should judgeship be a lifetime appointment or should a judge's record on the judiciary be reviewed periodically?
23. Should it be legally required that all judges be licensed attorneys? When can people with no legal training be a benefit to the court system while acting in the judicial role?
24. What are the benefits and drawbacks of holding judicial elections?
25. What are some of the various functions undertaken by a criminal court judge during a jury trial?
26. Do rapid trials lead to "less justice"?

IN THE MEDIA

Films

A Few Good Men
A Time to Kill
Body Heat
Murder in the First
Night Falls on Manhattan
Silkwood
To Kill a Mockingbird

The Devil's Advocate
The Firm
The Verdict

Television

Law and Order
The Practice

IN THE LITERATURE

Note to Instructor: These sources can be integrated throughout the chapter as additional sources of information for the students.

Books

L. Alpert, *Learning About Trial Judging: The Association of State Trial Judges, Courts, and Judges*, ed. A. Cramer, Beverly Hills, Calif.: Sage Publishing., 1981.

N. Chamelin, V. Fox, and P. Whisenand, *Introduction to Criminal Justice*, Upper Saddle River, N.J.: Prentice Hall, 1979.

K. Davis, *Discretionary Justice*, Baton Rouge, La.: Louisiana State University Press, 1969.

H. Glick and K. Vines, *State Court Systems*, Upper Saddle River, N.J.: Prentice Hall, 1973.

I. Janis and L. Mann, *Decision Making*, New York: The Free Press, 1977.

J. Jennings, *Evaluation of the Manhattan Criminal Court's Master Calendar Project*, New York: Rand Corporation, 1972.

Y. Kamisar, W. LaFave, and G. Israel, *Basic Criminal Procedure*, 9th ed., St. Paul, Minn.: West Publishing, 1999.

H. Levinson, *Executive Stress*, New York: Harper & Row, 1970.

M. Lewis, W. Bundy, and J. Hague, *An Introduction to the Courts and Judicial Process*, Upper Saddle River, N.J.: Prentice Hall, 1978.

D. Neubauer, *America's Courts and the Criminal Justice System*, Pacific Grove, Calif.: Brooks/Cole Publishing, 1992.

J. Ryan, A. Ashman, B. Sales, and S. Dubow, *American Trial Judges*, New York: The Free Press, 1980.

W. Seymour, *Why Justice Fails*, New York: William Morrow & Company, 1973.

A. Smith and H. Pollack, *Criminal Justice and Mass Society*, New York: Holt, Rinehart and Winston Publishing, 1972.

P. Wice, *Criminal Lawyers: An Endangered Species*, Beverly Hills, Calif.: Sage Publications, 1978.

Articles

R. Burke, "Occupational Stresses and Job Satisfaction," *Journal of Social Psychology*, vol. 100 (1976).

A. Alschuler, "The Prosecutor's Role in Plea Bargaining," *University of Chicago Law Review*, vol. 76 (1968).

P. Annin, A. Murr, and M. Liu, "An Irresistible Case," *Newsweek* (14 August, 1995).

G. Cole, "The Decision to Prosecute," *Law and Society Review*, vol. 3 (1983).

R. Ginsberg, J. Howard, N. Hon, A. Robinson, C. Russell, and R. Wheeler, "On Becoming a Judge: Socialization to the Judicial Role," *Judicature*, vol. 69 (1985).

J. Goldcamp, "Judicial Responsibility for Pretrial Release Decision-Making and the Information Role of Pretrial Services." *Federal Probation*, vol. 57 (1993).

P. Houlden and S. Balkin. "Quality and Cost Comparisons of Private Bar Indigent Defense Systems: Contract vs. Ordered Assigned Counsel." *Journal of Criminal Law and Criminology*, vol. 76 (1985).

J.W. Howard, "The Freshman Years." *Judicature*, vol. 69 (1985).

G. Kessel, "Adversarial Experiences in the American Criminal Trial," *Notre Dame Law Review*, vol. 67 (1992). p. 402.

P. Marcotte, "Federalism and the Rise of State Courts." *ABA Journal* (1 April 1987).

J. Nijboer, "The American Adversary System in Criminal Cases: Between Ideology and Reality," *Journal of International and Criminal Law* (Spring 1997). p. 74.

8 PRETRIAL PROCEDURES: BAIL, PRETRIAL HEARINGS, AND PLEA BARGAINING

CHAPTER LEARNING OBJECTIVES

After reading this chapter the student should be able to:

1. Identify five forms of pretrial release mechanisms.
2. Discuss the bail schedule and how it works.
3. Describe some of the major inequities of the bail system.
4. List the four questions a prosecutor must ask in determining whether a criminal complaint should be prepared.
5. Identify the alternatives to bail.
6. Discuss the concept of preventive detention.
7. Describe the purpose of a preliminary hearing.
8. Discuss the concept of pretrial discussion.
9. Identify the major functions of the grand jury.
10. Describe the ways one can be charged with a felony in jurisdictions throughout the United States.
11. Discuss pretrial motions and how they can be advantageous to the defense.
12. List the five factors influencing plea negotiations as described by Mather.
13. Discuss the roles of the prosecutor, defense attorney, judge, and victim in the plea-bargaining process.
14. List three forms of concessions in plea bargaining.
15. Identify the six concepts that a judge must ensure that a criminal defendant understands before a guilty plea can be accepted.

KEY TERMS

arraignment
bail
bail bondsperson
change of venue
citation
complaint
forfeiture
grand jury
indictment
initial appearance
motion for discovery
nolle prosequi
plea colloquy
presentment
pretrial diversion program
pretrial misconduct
pretrial motion
probable cause
summary trial
true bill
victim-impact statement

CHAPTER OVERVIEW

Note to Instructor: The following provides you with a summary of key points made throughout the chapter.

Since the due process revolution in the 1960s, the Supreme Court has recognized that the Constitution and the rights it affords manifest themselves from the period of custodial interrogation of an accused to the accused's arrest and pretrial hearings and motions. This pretrial period is the time when many important decisions are made about what will happen to the defendant. If the grand jury proceeding or preliminary hearing (two procedures by which either citizens or magistrates determine whether or not there is probable cause to bind the defendant over and charge him or her with a felony) results in sufficient evidence to charge the individual with a felony, then the defendant will be arraigned. At the initial appearance, the defendant is informed of his or her constitutional rights, particularly the right to representation by counsel. Next, the judge places the accused in confinement, frees the accused on bail, or releases the accused on his or her own recognizance. Prior to trial, many pretrial motions by defense counsel are made on the defendant's behalf in order to try to dismiss charges or to exclude evidence before trial begins.

The two critical issues that most significantly affect a defendant during the pretrial period both involve discretion by one or two of the central agencies in the criminal justice system. The first of these involves the discretion of the judge. Every defendant makes a motion for pretrial release. It is generally considered true that a defendant who is detained in jail suffers adverse consequences from the experience. However, his or her individual plight has to be weighed against the possibility that release will result in further danger to society or the possibility of escape. The second act of discretion is performed by the district attorney's office. This is in the area of plea negotiation. Because the criminal justice system is so overcrowded, it lacks the resources to try even 10 percent of those accused of a crime. As a consequence, the practice of plea negotiation, despite its critics and detractors, is essential, and it is the most common element in the administrative disposition of the largest percentage of criminal cases processed through the American criminal justice system.

CRITICAL THINKING QUESTIONS

Note to Instructor: These questions appear throughout the chapter as "CTQs." They can be used to stimulate class discussion.

1. What is case attrition?
2. Is it possible for an expert to give a scientific opinion on the question of whether or not a particular human being has a proclivity toward future violence?
3. What is the purpose of bail versus the purpose of preventive detention?
4. What purpose does the grand jury or preliminary hearing have in the adjudication of felony cases?
5. What is the distinction between a preliminary hearing and an initial appearance?
6. Should due process be extended to include grand jury proceedings?
7. Does the grand jury play too large a role in the criminal justice system? Is the weight of its special investigative power justified?
8. If the grand jury indicts in almost every case that it hears, then why do we have the grand jury?
9. Research has shown that plea bargaining is the key in the ability of players in the criminal justice system to manage their caseloads. If it were eliminated, what would happen to the functioning of the system is well as to criminal justice in America besides the extraordinary financial strain and the strain on efficient administration of the criminal justice system?
10. What are the legal issues in plea bargaining?
11. Should a criminal be allowed to bargain for a reduced sentence in exchange for a guilty plea?
12. Do most criminals, including those who are innocent, "cop a plea" to a charge because the reduction of the charge is so significant that they cannot afford not to due to the risk involved?
13. In 2002–2003, criminal justice research revealed a shockingly large number of inmates who later were conclusively proven innocent (usually by DNA evidence) but who often had confessed and even more often had pleaded guilty to crimes they did not commit. What policy implications do these revelations suggest about the whole plea-bargaining process in the American criminal justice system? What practical remedies do you believe can be taken to correct these unconscionable situations?
14. Should the judge participate in the court's plea bargaining, since 90 percent of the cases brought before the court are disposed of in that manner?
15. Will the now allowable and required participation of victims during the plea bargaining process offer them a more important sense of their own significance and a sense of well-being?

IN THE MEDIA

Video

A&E *American Justice* series

CNN Today Videos: *Introduction to CJ Today*, vol. 2, seg. "Jail and Bail"

Court TV videos of the judicial system

FFH collection videos: *Pretrial Process*

FHH CJ custom videos: *Plea Bargaining* and *Dealing with Justice*

Films for Humanity

NIJ *Crime Mob* video

NIJ Videos: *Introduction to CJ*, vol. 2, seg. 9: "Grand Jury"

Films

Inherit the Wind

And Justice for All

IN THE LITERATURE

Note to Instructor: These sources can be integrated throughout the chapter as additional sources of information for the students.

Books

Amnesty International, *Judges and Human Rights* [electronic book] available from http://www.amnesty.org.

Bureau of Justice Assistance, *Pretrial Services Program*, Washington, D.C.: U.S. Government Printing Office, 1990.

B. Burton, *Bail Enforcer: The Advanced Bounty Hunter*, Boulder, Colo.: Palma Springs, 1990.

D. Emmerson, *Grand Jury Reform: A Review of Key Issues*, Washington, D.C.: National Institute of Justice, 1983.

G. Fuller, *Plea Bargaining Triumph*, London, U.K.: Yale, 2000.

M. Heumann, *Plea Bargaining: The Experiences of Prosecutors, Judges, and Defense Attorneys*, (reprint ed.), Chicago: University of Chicago Press, 1991.

H. Jones, *Public Defender for the People*, New York: Longstar Books, 1991.

S. Kennedy, and K. Carlson, *Pretrial Release and Detention: The Bail Reform Act of 1984*, Washington, D.C: Bureau of Justice Statistics, 1988.

W. McDonald, *Plea Bargaining: Critical Issues and Common Practices*, Washington, D.C.: U.S. Government Printing Office, 1985.

K. Segebarth, *Pretrial Services and Practices in the 1990s*, Washington, D.C.: Pretrial Resource Center, 1990.

Articles

D. Henry and B. Beaudin, "Bail Bondsmen," *American Jails* vol. 4 (1990); pp. 8–16.

J. River, "When Men Hunt Man: The Rights and Duties of the Bounty Hunter in the American Criminal Justice System," *Houston Law Review*, vol. 33 (1966); pp. 731–793.

9 THE CRIMINAL TRIAL

CHAPTER LEARNING OBJECTIVES

After reading this chapter the student should be able to:

1. Discuss how the question of guilt is disposed by a criminal trial.
2. Describe how excessive pretrial publicity can endanger a defendant's Sixth Amendment right to a fair and impartial jury.
3. List the three significant foundations of the American criminal trial.
4. Discuss the distinctions among real, testimonial, and circumstantial evidence.
5. Describe the differences among competent, relevant, and material evidence.
6. Distinguish between privileged communication and confidential communication.
7. Discuss the difference between the "guilt beyond a reasonable doubt" standard and the "preponderance of evidence" standard.
8. Distinguish between direct examination and cross-examination.
9. List the elements of self-defense.
10. Define the following terms: *jury deliberation, jury nullification, charging the jury,* and *jury verdict*.
11. Identify in order the formal steps in a trial.
12. Distinguish between "challenges for cause" and "pre-emptory challenges."
13. List the affirmative defenses recognized in American criminal trials.
14. Identify the areas to be covered in the judge's instructions to the jury.
15. Discuss the role of the expert witness in a criminal trial.

KEY TERMS

adversary proceeding
challenge for cause
circumstantial evidence
direct evidence
factual guilt
hearsay

jury consultants
legal guilt
M'Naghten Test of Insanity
peremptory challenge
preponderance of evidence

real evidence
reasonable doubt
testimonial evidence
venire
voir dire

CHAPTER OVERVIEW

Note to Instructor: The following provides you with a summary of key points made throughout the chapter.

Compared with the total volume of cases entering the criminal justice system, relatively few cases are disposed of by trial. Nevertheless, the criminal trial is an indispensable feature of our system. The accused is brought to trial under a presumption of innocence; it is the task of the prosecution to prove beyond a reasonable doubt that the defendant is guilty of the crime for which he or she is charged. The burden of proof, however, beginning in the conservative 1980s and 1990s, has shifted somewhat. For example, should the defendant plead insanity, in many courts the burden of proof is on the defendant to prove either by clear and convincing evidence or by a preponderance of the evidence that he or she was insane at the time of committing the crime.

The adversary concept of criminal justice is most clearly exhibited at trial. The prosecutor uses the authority and resources of the state to gather enough evidence to convince a court and jury of the defendant's guilt. The defense counsel attacks the weaknesses of the prosecution's case, seeks to impeach the testimony of state witnesses, questions the validity and reliability of the prosecution's evidence, and is alert to any tactics of the opposing counsel that might violate the constitutional rights of the defendant.

An extremely important aspect of the trial is the selection of people to serve on the jury. Jurors are chosen by a procedure called *voir dire*, which assigns the prosecution and the defense challenges for cause (a stated reason or reasons why a particular person is unfit to serve on a jury) and a number of peremptory challenges (challenges for which no reasons need be given, except in the case of discrimination based on race). In recent years, there have been noteworthy attempts to use the methods of the social scientist to pick jurors who have been inclined to favor the defendant. This process of scientific jury selection has been attacked as "jury stacking" and defended as a guarantor of fairness. Whatever its defects or merits, however, the expenses involved will probably keep it from becoming a routine procedure in criminal trials.

Trials are governed by rules of evidence and the rules of criminal procedure that have evolved over a period of many years and have been articulated by judges and in criminal statutes. These rules are enforced by the judge during the trial, who acts as a decision-maker, arbitrator, and referee as to what the proper procedure will be and how the case will move forward. The jury can only discern the facts of a case based on competent, reliable, and relevant evidence presented to them by both sides. A series of rules have evolved concerning the inadmissibility of evidence that might somehow be relevant to the case but has been excluded based on its nature as either hearsay, confidential, or opinion evidence.

The order of the criminal trial may vary somewhat from one jurisdiction to another, but it generally conforms to a standard pattern. After the reading of the formal charges against the defendant, the prosecution presents its case by making an opening statement and then introducing evidence and witnesses whose testimony is subject to cross-examination by the defense. At the conclusion of the prosecution's case, the defense presents its case, including evidence and testimony. Often the defendant asserts his or her defense by attacking the state's case as failing to meet its burden of proof and thus resting, declaring there was no wrongdoing, or by putting on a defense in which the defendant admits he or she is guilty of the crime charged but is not criminally responsible for the act under one of the legal justifications of the particular affirmative defenses that the defendant asserts. This approach requires the defendant to admit that he or she is guilty of the crime charged, but asserts that the defendant ultimately is not culpable for the crime because of the attending circumstances surrounding the act. Examples of such include the defense of infancy, the battered woman syndrome, the defense of insanity, self-defense, and the defense of mistake of fact. The defense may call the defendant to testify on his or her own behalf or may choose not to do so. Following the presentation of evidence, both counsel present closing arguments to the jury. Next, the judge instructs the jury on the specific law applicable to the particular case. Finally, the jury is sequestered and deliberates until it subsequently announces its verdict in open court. Sometimes the jury is hopelessly deadlocked in a case and cannot reach a unanimous verdict. This is called a "hung" jury, and it causes a mistrial, requiring that the entire process be reinitiated. If a verdict is reached, often the lawyers poll the jury. This procedure requires each individual juror to stand up and convey his or her verdict to the open court. Also, a little known procedure is *jury nullification*. Jury nullification occurs when the trial judge lessens the jury's verdict and finds the defendant not guilty or guilty of a lesser-included offense as a matter of law. Hence, a judge can indeed change or nullify a jury verdict, but only in favor of the defendant.

CRITICAL THINKING QUESTIONS

Note to Instructor: These questions appear throughout the chapter as "CTQs." They can be used to stimulate class discussion.

1. Should prosecutors have more or less control over the life, liberty, and property of defendants than they presently have, which is more than any other public officer?
2. If a defendant waives his or her right to a jury trial, what type of trial takes place?
3. Does the jury trial live up to its exalted reputation of maintaining the defendant's presumption of innocence?
4. Why is there a higher standard of proof in a criminal trial than for a civil trial?
5. "The burden of proof in a criminal trial to show that the defendant is guilty beyond a reasonable doubt by the government is at the heart of the adversarial system of criminal justice." Explain the meaning of this statement.
6. The Sixth Amendment guarantees a jury drawn from a cross-section of the defendant's geographical area; yet, recent studies have shown that juries come from the low end of the social, economic, and intellectual spectrum of society. Does this satisfy the right to a fair and impartial jury of one's peers?
7. What are the pros and cons of the jury trial versus a bench trial?
8. Describe the necessary conditions for a defendant to receive a fair and impartial trial in a trial by jury in the age of technology.

9. In what ways may negative pretrial publicity possibly damage the objective outcome of a criminal trial?
10. What do you think is the greatest concern for jury selection when the objective is to empound a fair and impartial jury so that the defendant will have the best opportunity to receive a just verdict?
11. Given the roles of the defense counsel and the prosecution, is the deliberate seeking of biased jurors either legal or ethical?
12. Explain the jury selection process. Is the process fundamentally fair? Is it really "jury selection" or "jury nonselection"? Why?
13. Describe how the *voir dire* process is different between challenges for cause and peremptory challenges.
14. Why is the phenomenon of jury science not significant for most criminal defendants?
15. Does the fact that the rich can hire a jury consultant and the poor cannot violate the equal protection clause of the Fourteenth Amendment, which provides that no citizen should be at an advantage or a disadvantage based upon poverty or wealth?
16. How does our jury system serve or not serve individual rights and public order needs and, especially, render respected justice?
17. What is the relationship between the structured rules of evidence and the real facts of the case?
18. Explain the difference between testimonial evidence and real evidence, between lay witnesses and expert witnesses, and between direct and circumstantial evidence.
19. Under what circumstances can evidence be inadmissable?
20. When an adversary presents testimonial evidence through a witness, should the jury receive a judicial instruction that eyewitness testimony is inherently unreliable and the jury should consider such evidence with caution before basing any conclusions upon it?
21. Do new technology and scientific evidence, such as video and hyperspecialized cameras, DNA, and computers, dramatically affect the trustworthiness that jurors give such evidence in criminal trials, in much the same way that the advent of the fingerprint did?
22. Since expert witnesses can cost the criminal defendant up to $20,000 for their testimony, does not the availability of expert witnesses to the rich and its nonavailability to the poor discriminate in criminal trials?
23. Since expert witnesses are known to testify for both sides, is it fair to say that their testimony is available to the highest bidder?
24. Is it socially worthwhile to allow all of these privileged communications to exist within our society, knowing that if they were revealed, many more people would be convicted?
25. Most of us base a majority of our significant opinions in life on hearsay evidence. Therefore, is it just to have hearsay evidence inadmissible in a criminal trial?
26. If you could create exceptions to the hearsay rule, what would they be?
27. Is the philosophical basis for allowing certain exceptions to the hearsay rule—trustworthiness and reliability—an objective standard?
28. Why do most courts believe that a person who is about to die is likely to tell the truth? Do you believe this?
29. Is not the terror of a child having to face the molesting defendant in court justification enough to allow an out-of-court testimony by the child victim to come in as hearsay, rather than to victimize the child again through the trauma of the courtroom experience?
30. Should there be any differences in the arrangement of steps in the criminal trial, other than the ones that are listed here that have been that way for a century?
31. Should the formal process of the litigated felony case be more flexible and allow for experimentation to seek a more reliable way of ascertaining the truth?
32. What dangers lie in the defense attorney's disputing a prosecutor's opening statement when the defense gives his or her opening statement?
33. Since most of the prosecution witnesses in a criminal trial are paid a salary by the state (e.g., the police), which also is the same entity that is prosecuting the defendant, is their testimony reliable?
34. If during the cross-examination of a state's witness, he or she is caught in a lie, should the state subsequently prosecute him or her for perjury?
35. Is it ever wise for the defense not to present a case, but rather to close and base its case on the argument that the prosecution has failed to meet the burden of proof (beyond a reasonable doubt) required to convict?
36. Since the core of an affirmative defense is the defendant's admission that he or she in fact committed the acts that constituted the crime, isn't this tantamount to the defendant getting off on a legal technicality?
37. Would there ever be a case in which the defense attorney would not want to put the defendant on the stand during an affirmative defense, since the defendant admitted to committing the act that he or she is being charged with committing?
38. Is it fair that the burden of proof of most affirmative defenses is on the defendant, rather than requiring the prosecution to prove that the affirmative defense does not exist beyond a reasonable doubt?
39. At what age do you think a child is too young to possibly be held criminally responsible for his or her acts?
40. Some states have required that the defendant prove by clear and convincing evidence that he or she was insane in order for the insanity defense to work, rather

than the traditional practice of requiring the state to prove that the defendant was not insane beyond a reasonable doubt. Is this new requirement just?

41. In what ways do changes and developments in the insanity defense reflect the shifting conception of how to balance individual rights with the need to punish wrongdoers?

42. Are the four elements of self-defense too rigid in applying self-defense to negate criminal liability? Should they be more relaxed?

43. Do you think the concept of self-defense should be extended to using defensive threats?

44. Are the two limitations on self-defense valid, when someone is in fear of his or her life or serious bodily harm? When such is the case, should there be no limitations on when one should defend oneself?

45. How is the defense of ignorance or mistake of fact reconciled to the legal cliché "ignorance of the law is no excuse"?

46. Can you make an argument for the fact that many Americans believe that anytime one finds an intruder in one's home, one has the right to use deadly force against them?

47. In the last thirty years, police shooting suspects have been the cause of many urban riots and the loss of life, infliction of personal injury, and millions of dollars in property damage to the entire community. Does this counterbalance the officer's right to use deadly force to effect an arrest in terms of the overall social good?

48. Since the battered-spouse defense is based on the concept of self-defense, does not the fact that when the defendant killed there was no immediate threat to her life negate the legal principle upon which the defense is based?

49. Many argue that battered children and spouses can just flee from the threat posed by their abusers. If this is so, why are they allowed to use these defenses?

50. Presently, under the rules of evidence, the prosecution does not have to advise the defense of the availability of or existence of any of their rebuttal witnesses. Is this nondisclosure essentially consistent with a fair trial?

51. Practicing criminal trial lawyers generally agree that the most important part of their case is their closing argument. Why do you think they consistently believe this to be the case?

52. What is the major problem with the judge's instruction to the jury, and the fact that the judge is not present during jury deliberations?

53. Should the jury have a written copy of the judge's instructions during their deliberations so they can refer to what the law actually states?

54. Presently, jurors are prohibited from discussing with attorneys the manner in which they deliberated, even though attorneys believe it would be most helpful to know this information. Should attorneys be given access to jurors to discuss the full nature of their deliberations?

55. As we enter the twenty-first century, how can we make the jury system more workable?

56. Some people argue that the way to eliminate a hung jury is to allow nonunanimous verdicts. Do you agree with this assessment?

57. What can we do to correct the two aspects of jury nullification? Should they be corrected?

58. Should the judge have the power to enter a verdict of not guilty after a jury of one's peers has found the defendant guilty beyond a reasonable doubt?

IN THE MEDIA

Video

A&E American Justice video: *Why O.J. Simpson Won*

ABC News/Prentice Hall: *Color of Justice*

ABC News/Prentice Hall: *William Kennedy Smith Rape Trial*

The Anatomy of a Trial

CNN Today video: *Criminology* no. 4, seg. 1, "The Insanity Defense"

Court TV video: *The Greatest Trials of All Time: Sam Shepard*

"Criminal Trial Procedure"

"Evidence"°

"Eyewitnesses"°

"Fact or Fiction"°

"Going to Court"°

"The Great Crimes and Trials of the Twentieth Century"

"Landmark American Trials"°

Michigan v. Kevorkian: *Dr. Death or Angel of Mercy?*

"The O.J. Simpson Trial"°

PBS video: *The State of Florida versus Ted Bundy*

"The Rodney King Case: What a Jury Saw in California v. Powell"°

"Trial by Jury"°

Vermont v. Grace: *Battered Woman's Syndrome***

"You Are the Jury"°

ABC videos

A&E and American Justice videos

CNN TODAY videos

°These videos are part of the *Legal Study* video collection by Inside Media. Your educational institution can purchase these expensive videos for your class by calling 1-800-233-9100.

**Free Court TV video policy on the number of free videos available to each adopter is based on the adoption size.

LXVI CRIME AND JUSTICE IN AMERICA

Court TV videos
FAH Court's CJ videos
FHA videos
NIJ Crime File videos
NIJ videos

Films

A Few Good Men
The Juror
A Time to Kill
The Verdict

Television

Law and Order
The Practice

IN THE LITERATURE

Note to Instructor: These sources can be integrated throughout the chapter as additional sources of information for the students.

Books

J. Abramson, *We, the Jury: The Jury System and the Ideal of Democracy*, New York: Basic Books, 1994.

J. Bellknap, *The Invisible Woman: Gender, Crime, and Justice*, Belmont, Calif.: Wadsworth, 2001.

S. Brill, ed., *Trial by Jury: The Tactics, Deals, and Decisions That Determined the Outcomes of Seventeen of the Decade's Biggest Legal Cases*, Upper Saddle River, N.J.: Simon & Schuster, 1990.

L. Caplan, *The Insanity Defense and the Trial of John. W. Hinkley Jr.*, Boston: D. R. Godine, 1984.

L. Chiason, *The Press on Trial: The Crimes of Trials as Media Events*, Westport, Conn.: Praeger, 1997.

W. Freeman, *The Constitutional Right to a Fair and Speedy Criminal Trial*, New York: Quorum Books, 1989.

G. Gilbert and L. Vienen, *Crimes of the Century*, Evanston, Ill.: Northwestern University Press, 1998.

T. Garder and T. Anderson, *Criminal Evidence: Principles and Cases*, Belmont, Calif.: Wadsworth, 2001.

R. Goldfarb, *T.V or not T.V: Television, Justice, and the Courts*, New York: New York University Press, 1998.

R. Gillies and R. Snyder, eds., *Covering the Courts: Free Press, Fair Trial, and the Journalistic Performance* New Brunswick, N.J.: Transaction Publishers, 1999.

L. Greenfield and T. Smell, *Women Offenders*, Washington, D.C.: Bureau of Justice Statistics, 1999. (NCJ 175688).

V. Hans and V. Neil, *Judging the Jury*, New York: Plenum, 1986.

D. Heilvroner, *Rough Justice: Days and Nights of a Young D.A.*, New York: Pantheon, 1989.

H. Kalvin and Z. Hans, *The American Jury*, Boston, Little, Brown, 1966.

M. Kurland, *How to Try a Murder: The Handbook for Armchair Lawyers*, New York: Macmillan General Reference, 1998.

E. Loftus and K. Ketcham, *Witness for the Defense*, New York: St. Martin's Press, 1991.

C. Mann, *Unequal Justice: A Question of Color*, Bloomington, Ind.: Indiana University Press, 1993.

McIntyre, *The Public Defender: The Practice of Law in the Shadows of the Repute*, Chicago: University of Chicago Press, 1987.

K. Miller and M. Radlelet, *Executing the Mentally Ill: The Criminal Justice System and the Case of Alvin Ford*, Newbery Park, Calif.: Sage, 1993.

L. Morris, *The Brothel Boy and Other Parables of the Law*, New York: Oxford University Press, 1992.

G. Munsterman, P. Hannaford, and G. Whitehead, eds., *Jury Trial Innovations*, Williamsburg, Va.: National Center for State Courts, 1997.

National Institute of Justice, *Eyewitness Evidence: A Guide for Law Enforcement*, Washington, D.C.: U.S. Department of Justice, 1999.

R. Satter, *Doing Justice: A Trial Judge at Work*, New York: Simon & Schuster, 1990.

R. Simon, *The Jury and the Defense of Insanity*, 2nd ed., Boston: Little Brown, 1998.

R. Simon and J. Landis, *The Crimes Women Commit, the Punishments They Receive*, New York: Lexington Books, 1991.

S. Walker, C. Stohn, and M. DeLone, *The Color of Justice*, 2nd ed., Belmont, Calif.: Wadsworth, 2000.

Articles

J. Backstrand, D. Gibbons, and J. Jones, "Who Is in Jail: An Examination of the Rapid Hypothesis," *Journal of Crime and Delinquency*, vol. 38 (1992), pp. 219–220.

R. Boatright, "The 21st Century American Jury: Reflections from the CANTIGNY Conference," *Judicature*, vol. 83 (2000), pp. 288–297.

R. Bonnie, N. Poythriess, and S. Shoge, "Decision Making and Criminal Defense: An Empirical Study of Insanity Pleas and the Impact of Doubted Client Confidence," *Journal of Criminal Law and Criminology*, vol. 87 (1996), pp. 48–76.

D. Broadye, "Balancing Jury Secrecy and the Rule of Law: Second Circuit's Guide to Nullifying Jurors," *Justice System Journal*, vol. 20 (1998), pp. 113–120.

L. Cao, A. Adams, and V. Jensen, "A Tale of a Black Subculture and Violence Thesis: Research Methods," *Criminology*, vol. 34 (1997), pp. 367–379.

J. Dunaway, F. Collins, V. Burton, and T. Evans, "The Myth of Social Class and Crime Revisited: An Examination of Class and Adult Criminality," *Criminology*, vol. 38 (2000), pp. 589–613.

H. Fahringer, "The Peremptory Challenge: An Endangered Species?" *Criminal Law Bulletin* (1995), pp. 400–463.

J. Hillwize, "Religion Based Peremptory Challenges Are Unconstitutional," *Trial Magazine*, vol. 35 (1999), p. 15.

T. Hogan, G. Mise, and K. Clark, "How to Improve the American Jury," *World and I*, vol. 13 (1998), p. 64.

I. Horowitz and T. Wilging, "Changing Views on Jury Power: The Nullification Debate 1787–1998," *Journal of Law and Human Behavior*, vol. 15 (1991), p. 165.

P. Jenkins and B. Davidson, "Battered Women and the Criminal Justice System: Analysis of Gender Stereotypes," *Behavioral Sciences and the Law*, vol. 8 (1990), pp. 161–170.

L. Krohman, "Constituting Power and Sexual Assault Cases: Prosecutorial Strategies for Victim Management," *Journal of Social Problems*, vol. 45 (1998), pp. 393–427.

G. LaFrey and K. Russel, "The Argument for Studying Race and Crime," *Journal of Criminal Justice Education*, vol. 4 (1993), pp. 273–289.

K. Vernette, "Letting Focus Groups Work for You," *Trial*, vol. 35 (1999), p. 74.

N. Wonders, " Women's Work? A Contradictory Implication of the Courses on Women and the Criminal Justice System" *Journal of Criminal Justice Education*, vol. 4 (1993), pp. 79–100.

E. Zakaria, "The Role of Juries and the Justice System," *Contemporary View*, vol. 274 (1999), p. 277.

10 SENTENCING, APPEALS, AND THE DEATH PENALTY

CHAPTER LEARNING OBJECTIVES

After reading this chapter the student should be able to:

1. Explain incapacitation as a theory of punishment and describe its impact on the crime rate.
2. Discuss the rehabilitation/treatment philosophy of punishment.
3. Describe reintegration as a theory of punishment.
4. Explain how sentencing structures influence judges' discretion.
5. Discuss the role of the presentence investigation report.
6. Describe what habitual criminal statutes are used for and how the Supreme Court has acted to limit their use.
7. Discuss the effect prison overcrowding has on the validity of the theoretical justifications for punishment in the United States.
8. Explain the retribution theory of punishment and how it may be used to justify correctional punishment.
9. Discuss the studies of the deterrent effect of capital punishment on crime.
10. Distinguish between general and specific deterrence.
11. Explain the difference between a presumptive sentence and a flat time sentence.
12. Compare an indeterminate sentence with a mandatory minimum sentence.
13. Discuss the concept of appellate review.
14. Explain sentencing guidelines and how they function as a practical matter.
15. Describe the five major issues in the capital punishment debate.

KEY TERMS

appellate review
bifurcated trial
clemency
determinate or flat-time sentences
deterrence
discretionary review
enhancement statutes
general deterrence
habeas corpus
hate crimes
incapacitation
retribution
retribution argument
reversible error
sentencing
sentencing disparity
specific deterrence

CHAPTER OVERVIEW

Note to Instructor: The following provides you with a summary of key points made throughout the chapter.

Sentencing is perhaps the most important phase of the criminal process, for it is in this stage that the disposition of the criminal offender is decided. In earlier periods, offenders were subject to retaliation and physical abuse as a punishment for wrongdoing. Contemporary criminal justice is still punitive in its orientation, but its punitive procedures are justified on several theoretical grounds, including retribution, deterrence, incapacitation, rehabilitation, and reintegration.

Until recent years, the goals of rehabilitation and reintegration were important parts of the punitive decision. However, since the advent of the new conservatism of the 1980s, tremendous popular support has grown for the position that retribution ("the law of just desserts") is the most important objective of sentencing.

Traditional sentencing dispositions include fines, probation, and imprisonment. Probation is the most common choice. The American sentencing structures themselves have been riddled with disparity and problems. Also, due to massive prison overcrowding, citizens have become frustrated with the criminal courts' convicting defendants and then sentencing them to long terms in prison, and then finding out that they have served but a fraction of the sentence imposed on them. In response, the federal and a few state legislators have either introduced sentencing guidelines or formulated sentencing councils and/or sentencing commissions to rethink the whole sentencing process. One of the most significant features of the sentencing of a criminal defendant after his or her criminal trial is the process of its tripod structure, involving the legislature, a judge, and a correctional agency. The actions of each of these parties affect the type and length of sentence imposed on the offender. The consequence of sentencing, as it operates in the criminal justice system, often results in sentence disparities in which the court seeks to fit the sentence to the individual offender rather than to the crime.

Regardless of an accused's sentence, certain appeals are granted to him or her based on the sentence, as well as postconviction remedies. Historically, only on rare occasions have sentences imposed by the court been overturned for being excessive. Recently, however, under the sentencing guidelines, if trial judges choose to go outside the guidelines when sentencing defendants, their sentences are subject to automatic review by appellate courts and are often reversed.

The most serious sentence imposed by American criminal courts is the death penalty. Once thought no longer to be part of American law, the death penalty is gaining strength at an astonishing rate. Over 80 percent of Americans support the use of the death penalty. Yet, for the state to take a life, such action must be theoretically justified.

The justification for capital punishment has been hotly debated. Proponents argue that capital punishment acts as a deterrent of the individual as well as for other potential murderers. Furthermore, capital punishment, they say, is the only satisfactory retribution that society can gain as a result of experiencing such a heinous act against society as premeditated murder. Opponents argue, to the contrary, that sentences are imposed arbitrarily, often based on the race of the victim. Opponents also point out that there are many instances in American history in which the death penalty mistakenly has been imposed on the wrong person. Such a mistake, these opponents argue, justifies the elimination of the death penalty altogether.

Finally, they point out that all of the empirical studies on the subject have failed to prove that the death penalty acts as a deterrent. In fact, they argue, it may even have a brutalizing effect. Other minor issues in the capital punishment debate have also come forward. These include the cost of capital punishment and the execution of special populations.

CRITICAL THINKING QUESTIONS

Note to Instructor: These questions appear throughout the chapter as "CTQs." They can be used to stimulate class discussion.

1. Which of the goals of criminal sentencing do you think individual-rights advocates would most likely find attractive? Which ones would crime-control advocates find attractive? Why?
2. Do you believe that too many people are now being sentenced to prison? Would the current "get tough" approach create an extremely large pool of ex-offenders who are at risk for further crimes?
3. Should vengeance be accepted as a rationale for punishment?
4. Most scholars agree that the sentencing based on justice evaluates the weight of a criminal act, not the needs of the defendant or the community. Is this a fair measure to determine a sentencing philosophy?
5. How is the principle of willful wrongdoing central to the idea of retribution, and what does it connote for criminal sentencing in America?
6. Is justice served when a punishment is designed to prevent future law violations, even though there is an overwhelming likelihood that the person may never again violate the law?
7. Which is more important to achieve in criminal sentencing, general deterrence or specific deterrence? Defend your answer with specific examples.
8. The indeterminate sentence is at the heart of the rehabilitation perspective of justice because offenders may be released after a relatively short prison stay if they convince correctional authorities that they can curb their criminal career. Is this rehabilitative view of salvageable offenders a realistic view of what rehabilitative efforts go on inside the prison walls?
9. How do the elements contained in the presentence report reflect our assumption about the causes of criminal behavior?
10. How does a presentence investigation report to the judge affect the sentencing decision? How does determinate sentencing affect the importance of the influence of the presentence investigation?
11. Discuss the role of the presentence investigation report on the process of judicial sentencing. What value do you consider appropriate for the judge to place on the report?
12. Would you be in favor of a constitutional amendment setting forth victims' rights as a criminal proceeding? If so, what kind of rights would this involve?

13. Presently, victim-impact evidence is not permitted in death penalty cases. Do you believe this is appropriate?
14. Would convicted offenders be more likely to favor determinate or indeterminate sentences? Why?
15. Do you believe the additional new forms of punishment compounding the original sentence given in the trial court will have a deterrent influence on the crime rate?
16. Would a person who favors indeterminate sentences over determinate sentences be likely to believe in deterrence, retribution, or incapacitation as being the main goal of punishment? Why?
17. Although crime-control advocates applaud determinate and mandatory sentencing structures, critics fear they will swell prison populations, costing taxpayers additional billions of dollars and taking away from other needs such as higher education, health care, and social security. Which of the two opposing positions do you support? Why?
18. Do you think three-strikes laws serve a useful purpose? If so, what is that purpose? Might other sentencing arrangements be met for the same purposes? What arrangements might those be?
19. How will three-strikes laws affect state and federal spending on the criminal justice system? Do you think that these shifts in spending can be justified? If so, how?
20. Discuss the constitutional implications of habitual-criminal laws.
21. Many jurists believe that a certain amount of discretion in sentencing is inevitable. Is this true, and should we accept it as an inevitable process of sentencing?
22. Should we have judicial discretion in sentencing, or should judges be able to exercise unlimited discretion?
23. Explain how the limitations on judicial discretion under sentencing guidelines have increased the prosecution's discretionary authority on the sentencing decision.
24. *Douglas v. California* gave indigent defendants the right to free counsel on their first automatic appeal, yet *Ross v. Moffitt* did not give them a free lawyer to the court of last resort in their state or to the United States Supreme Court. Can you explain the discrepancy in the philosophy supporting the conclusion of these two cases? Do you believe that these cases render fair justice?
25. Presently, the Supreme Court has denied indigent defendants the right to an attorney to assist them in filing a *habeas corpus* petition, even though *habeas corpus* is the oldest form of due process protection in the Anglo-American system. Is this denial of the right to an attorney to help a defendant with this petition consistent with your notion of justice? Why or why not?
26. Why do you think the Supreme Court takes so few criminal cases on appeal each year?
27. Should it be constitutionally required that all states allow prisoners to appeal a harsh sentence? Why or why not?
28. Explain the difference between the Supreme Court rulings in the cases of *Furman v. Georgia* (1976) and *Gregg v. Georgia* (1976).
29. The movement toward abolition of the death penalty in the United States is encouraged by the fact that so many other nations have abandoned it. Should we model our own system of punishment on those of other nations, or is our criminal problem so unique that it requires the use of capital punishment?
30. Which method of execution do you consider the most humane? Which method do you consider the most cruel and unusual?
31. Can you explain why public opinion was so negative toward the death penalty thirty years ago and is so overwhelmingly in favor of it now? What happened to change all of this?
32. When you compare and contrast the value of punishment for those who deserve it for a wicked crime versus the value of the sacredness of life, which is more important in your morality scheme?
33. Many death sentence appeals are being overturned and people are being released because they are found innocent after spending years in prison on death row. Is that reason alone enough to eliminate the practice of the death penalty?
34. In your opinion, does capital punishment serve as a deterrent?
35. In your own life, has the threat of future punishment deterred you from committing a potential criminal act? At some point in time, the majority of people would say that this threat has had that effect. If this is true, then why doesn't the death penalty deter future would-be killers?
36. If you are in favor of the death penalty, what is your opinion about the fact that only 1 out of every 1,000 people convicted of murder receives the death penalty? Do you believe this part of the system needs to be fixed? Why?
37. Do you think the fact that only 14 percent of Americans are African American and yet 43 percent of the people on death row are African American signals any bias with regard to race in the death penalty? Why or why not?
38. Since more than ninety-eight people have been freed from death row because they were there by mistake, does this number seem too high to make the death penalty an acceptable risk? Should this not cause those who are in favor to reconsider their opinion?

CHAPTER 10 SENTENCING, APPEALS, AND THE DEATH PENALTY

✑ IN THE MEDIA

Video

CNN Today video: *Introduction to Criminal Justice*

"Criminal Justice: From Murder to Execution"°

"The Death Penalty"°

°These videos are part of the *Legal Study* video collection by Inside Media. Your educational institution can purchase these expensive videos by calling 1-800-233-9100.

ABC videos

A&E and American Justice videos

CNN TODAY videos

Court TV videos

FAH Court's CJ videos

NIJ videos

NIJ Crime File videos

The following videos are available from ABC/News Prentice Hall:

Why Not Wilbert Rideau?

Crime and Punishment

Three Strikes: Is It Working?

Victim Impact Statements

Capital Punishment: Judgment at Midnight

Films

The Shawshank Redemption

Criminal Justice

An Innocent Man

Double Jeopardy

Dead Man Walking

The Chamber

Just Cause

True Crime

✑ IN THE LITERATURE

Note to Instructor: These sources can be integrated throughout the chapter as additional sources of information for the students.

Books

J. Austin and J. Irwin, *It's About Time: America's Imprisonment Binge,* Belmont, Calif.: Wadsworth, 2001.

H. Bedau, ed., *The Death Penalty in America,* 3rd ed., London, U.K.: Oxford Press, 1982.

W. Bowers, G. Pierce, and J. McDevitt, *Legal Homicide: Death as Punishment in America, 1864–1982,* Boston: Northeastern University Press, 1984.

J. Caulkins, C. P. Randall, W. Schwabe, and J. Chisea, *Mandatory Drug Sentences: Throwing Away the Key or the Taxpayers' Money?* Santa Monica, Calif.: Rand, 1997.

K. Hass and J. Inciardi, eds., *Challenging Capital Punishment: Legal and Social Science Approaches,* Newbury Park, Calif.: Sage Publications, 1988.

R. Johnson, *Condemned to Die: Life under Sentence of Death,* Prospect Heights, Ill.: Waveland Press, 1989.

D. Neubauer, *America's Courts and the Criminal Justice System,* 5th ed., Pacific Grove, Calif.: Brooks/Cole, 2002.

R. Paternoster, *Capital Punishment in America,* New York: Lexington, 1991.

Articles

N. Alonze and C.W. Johnson, "Probing Limits of the Female Advantage in Criminal Processing: Pretrial Diversion of Drug Offenders in an Urban County," *Justice System,* vol. 21 (2000), pp. 239–259.

K. Doyle, "No Defense," *U.S. Catholic,* vol. 64 (1999), p. 18.

P. Glynn, "Conscience and the Public Square," *Brookings Review,* vol. 17 (1999), p. 24.

S. Grant, "A Dialogue of the Deaf? New International Attitudes and the Death Penalty in America," *Criminal Justice Ethics,* vol. 17 (1998), p. 19.

M. Higgins, "Is Capital Punishment for Killers Only?" *ABA Journal,* vol. 83 (August, 1997), pp. 30–31.

K. Kempf-Leonard and L. Sample, "Disparity Based on Sex: Is Gender-Specific Treatment Warranted?" *Justice Quarterly,* vol. 17 (2000), pp. 89–128.

M. Males, D. Macallair, and K. Taqi-Eddin "Striking Out: The Failure of California's 'Three Strikes and You're Out' Law," *Stanford Law and Policy Review* (Fall 1999).

W. Manning and J. Rhoden-Trader, "Rethinking the Death Penalty," *Corrections Today,* vol. 62 (2000), p. 22.

J. Marquart and J. Sorensen, "Institutional and Postrelease Behavior of Furman-Committed Inmates in Texas," *Criminology,* vol. 26, (November, 1988), pp. 677–693.

C. Moorehead, "Tinkering with Death" *World Press Review,* vol. 42 (1995), p. 38.

11 JAILS AND DETENTION

CHAPTER LEARNING OBJECTIVES

After reading this chapter the student should be able to:

1. Explain the difference between jails and prisons.
2. Discuss the three types of jails in the United States.
3. Describe the role the Quakers played in the early jail system in Philadelphia.
4. List and discuss the three main purposes of jails.
5. Describe the impact jail crowding may have on various components of the criminal justice system.
6. Explain how criminal justice decision makers can affect jail crowding.
7. Describe the major features of direct-supervision jails.
8. Discuss the findings of a survey of jail administrators who manage direct-supervision facilities with regard to improvements in personnel areas.
9. List the types of jail inmates who are considered special-management inmates.
10. Describe the precipitating factors associated with jail suicides.
11. List the key components of a jail suicide prevention program.
12. Discuss the various treatment programs in a jail that may be available to convicted inmates.
13. Explain why jail security is given a higher priority than rehabilitation.
14. Identify typical jail recreation programs.
15. Define the term *shakedown*.

KEY TERMS

alcoholics
combination facility
contact visit
count
cutlery control
direct-supervision jail
frisks
jail crowding
jail security
key control
narcotics control
pretrial detention facility
sentenced facility
sex offenders
shakedown
special-management inmates
"The State of Prisons"
tool control
treatment programs
visitation control
Walnut Street Jail

CHAPTER OVERVIEW

Note to Instructor: The following provides you with a summary of key points made throughout the chapter.

Jails are the intake point of our entire criminal justice system and are the most prevalent type of correctional institution. There has been a tendency for laypeople and even practitioners in the criminal justice system to use the terms *jails* and *prisons* synonymously. However, they are quite different.

They are primarily a function of local government and are as diverse in size, physical condition, and efficiency as the units of government that operate them. The three types of jails are pretrial detention facilities for persons awaiting trial, sentenced facilities for persons serving sentences, and combination facilities for pretrial detentions and some convicted persons.

Many jails in the United States are quite old and in need of extensive repair. In addition, many pose health hazards because of noxious odors, dirty lavatories, dirty floors, stained walls, and vermin. Many jail facilities also contain fire hazards that endanger both inmates and correctional staff. In all fairness, however, it must be noted that there are also many jails that are clean and well maintained. Often, the major differences between a poorly run and poorly kept jail and one that is well maintained are the attitude, philosophy, and priorities of the local sheriff or jail administrator.

Some consequences of jail crowding are well known: increased victimization and fear, decreased public confidence that dangerous persons can be locked up, lawsuits, court-imposed limits on the number of prisoners, and damage to facilities and equipment. Crowding increases both tension in the institution and the strain on correctional budgets.

Officials in a growing number of jurisdictions have concluded that if each part of the local justice system does what it can to ease crowding, the sum of all these solutions has a notable cumulative effect. Thus, the separate decisions of law enforcement, judicial prosecution, defense, pretrial services, probation, corrections, and other officials can interact to influence the number of jail admissions and the length of confinement.

Jails with direct supervision stand in sharp contrast to traditional jails. This concept encourages direct interaction between staff and inmates to prevent negative inmate behavior, and it groups inmates into living units of approximately fifty cells, which can be managed effectively by one officer. Rather than separating staff from inmates by security barriers, as is usual, the new approach places officers in direct contact with prisoners at all times. This new concept combines the principles of human behavior and facility design to create detention environments that enhance the officers' effectiveness.

Special-management inmates who present problems for the jailer include physically ill inmates, alcoholics, disabled inmates, aggressive and assaultive inmates, vulnerable inmates, mentally ill inmates, drug addicts, sex offenders, and suicidal inmates. Jail personnel must be properly trained to recognize and supervise such prisoners, and, when necessary, to provide them with special care.

When hard choices must be made between security and rehabilitation in the jail, security is always given priority. This is not surprising, considering that jail administrators can be fired and sheriffs defeated at election time if a dangerous or infamous prisoner escapes. To ensure the integrity of prison security, several measures are employed: counts; shakedowns, which involve a thorough search of a jail or any part thereof for contraband; regular frisking of inmates, especially when they are moved from one part of the jail to another; tool control; key control; cutlery control; narcotics control; and visitation control.

In spite of the bleak picture often presented of American jails, evidence suggests that the quality of jail personnel and jail facilities has improved steadily over the past 15 years. This has occurred in part because of public pressure about jail crowding, unsanitary conditions, poor health care, and physical abuse. Other improvements will occur because the states are now taking a more active role in requiring minimum qualifications and providing training for jail personnel. Finally, there is reason to believe that the chief administrators of our local jails, whether they are sheriffs or civilian administrators, are better educated, better trained, and generally more professional than their predecessors.

CRITICAL THINKING QUESTIONS

Note to Instructor: These questions appear throughout the chapter as "CTQs." They can be used to stimulate class discussion.

1. What characteristics of prisons make them different from other institutions?
2. How do modern prisons differ from those in the past?
3. Do politics ever play a role in the administration of regional correctional facilities? If so, do you think this is a drawback, or can it ever be advantageous for either the inmates or the community into which some will be released?
4. What can be done to ensure that the professional competency and philosophy of the sheriff are consistent with good jail management?
5. What explanations might be given for the increased use of incarceration during the past two decades?
6. What steps can a jail administrator take to ensure successful facility and inmate management?
7. What factors contribute to effective management outcomes on the parts of staff and administrators who work in direct-supervision jails?
8. Is it fair to conclude that the reduced sick leave is entirely attributed to direct-supervision management techniques, or are there additional factors?
9. In what areas are new-generation jails traditionally viewed as requiring more staffing? In what areas do they not require more staffing? How does the varying degree of staffing affect the level of efficiency at which personnel operate?
10. What can be done to convince governmental officials and the public that direct-supervision jails are the most cost-effective and do not "coddle" criminals?
11. What are some of the management problems associated with special offender populations, such as those who are elderly or disabled or who have contracted HIV/AIDS?
12. What steps do jail officials take in the management and containment of physically ill inmates? Why is there such a disproportionately large number of physically ill inmates in comparison to the general population?
13. Why are inmates suffering from mental illnesses often the most difficult for jail personnel to manage? In

what ways can the behavior of the mentally ill confuse jail officials and delay the diagnosis of a disorder?
14. What should be done to ensure that jail personnel are trained to adequately handle special-management inmates?
15. Why are treatment programs in jails cost-effective if they work?
16. Why is jail security given a higher priority than rehabilitation among jail administrators?

IN THE MEDIA

Video

A&E American Justice series video: *Cruel and Unusual*

CNN Today video: *Introduction to Criminal Justice*, vol. 2: Seg. 15, "Prison Guard Abuse"

FHH video: *Diverting the Mentally Ill from Jail*

FHH video: *The Second City: Inside the World's Largest Jail*

NIJ video: *Prison Crowding*

Films

The Chamber

Criminal Justice

Dead Man Walking

Double Jeopardy

An Innocent Man

Just Cause

The Last Castle

True Crime

The Shawshank Redemption

IN THE LITERATURE

Note to Instructor: These sources can be integrated throughout the chapter as additional sources of information for the students.

Books

J. Dilulio, *Governing Prisons*, New York: The Free Press, 1987.

R. Goldfarb, *Jails: The Ultimate Ghetto of the Criminal Justice System*, Garden City, N.Y.: Doubleday, 1976.

L. Goodstein and D. MacKenzie, eds., *The American Prison: Issues in Research and Policy*, New York: Plenum Press, 1989.

J. Irwin, *The Jail: Managing the Underclass in American Society*, Berkeley, Calif.: University of California Press, 1985.

J. Jacobs, *Stateville*, Chicago: University of Chicago Press, 1977.

R. Johnson, *Hard Time: Understanding and Reforming the Prison*, 2nd ed., Belmont, Calif.: Wadsworth, 1996.

K. Kauffman, *Prison Officers and Their World*, Cambridge, Mass.: Harvard University Press, 1988.

K. Kerle, *American Jails: Looking to the Future*, Boston: Butterworth-Heinemann, 1998.

E. Monkkonen, *Crime and Justice in American History: Prisons and Jails*, New York: K.G. Saur, 1992.

J.M. Moynahan and E.K. Stewart, *The American Jail: Its Development and Growth*, Chicago: Nelson-Hall, 1980.

J. Thompson and L. Mays, eds., *American Jails: Public Policy Issues*, Chicago: Nelson-Hall, 1991.

Articles

K. Adams, "The Bull Market in Corrections," *Prison Journal*, vol. 76 (December 1996), p. 461.

P. Finn, "No Frills Prisons and Jails: A Movement in Flux," *Federal Probation*, vol. 60 (1996), pp. 35–49.

L. Hayes, "Suicide in Adult Correctional Facilities: Key Ingredients to Prevention and Overcoming the Obstacles," *Journal of Law, Medicine & Ethics*, vol. 27 (Fall 1999), p. 260.

M. Tonry, "Why Are U.S. Incarceration Rates So High?" *Crime and Delinquency*, vol. 45 (1999), pp. 419–438.

12 CORRECTIONAL INSTITUTIONS

CHAPTER LEARNING OBJECTIVES

After reading this chapter the student should be able to:

1. Explain the difference between the Pennsylvania and the Auburn corrections systems.
2. Discuss the characteristics of maximum-security prisons.
3. Describe the derivation of the concept of administrative segregation.
4. Discuss the characteristics of medium-security correctional centers.
5. Explain the major purpose of a reception and classification center.
6. Describe the three approaches to dealing with prison overcrowding.
7. Describe the viewpoints of the behavioral scientist, the revolutionary, the media, and the correctional administrator with regard to a prison riot.
8. Identify and discuss the inmate groups prone to causing problems.
9. List the factors that are most significant in becoming a gang member in prison.
10. Discuss the administrative problems associated with elderly male prisoners.
11. Describe how the heterosexual convict image of machismo is chronically overplayed.
12. Identify the four factors that led to the women's prison movement.
13. List the five categories of programs for women in prison.
14. Identify various service programs provided in prisons by private firms.
15. Compare the arguments for privatization of prisons to the arguments against privatization.

KEY TERMS

AIDS
Aryan Brotherhood
Auburn system
Black Guerilla Family
El Rukns
gallows
general equivalency diploma (GED) programs
Great Law of Pennsylvania

Latin Disciples
Latin Kings
maxi-maxi prisons
maximum-security prisons
medium-security prisons
Mexican Mafia
minimum-security prisons
Nuestra Familia
peer tutoring

Pennsylvania system
pillory
prisonization
prison work programs
reception and classification centers
stocks
Texas Syndicate
Therapeutic Recreation
Vice Lords

CHAPTER OVERVIEW

Note to Instructor: The following provides you with a summary of key points made throughout the chapter.

The North American colonists brought with them the harsh penal codes of their homelands. Not until the late 1600s did William Penn take the initial steps that would eventually lead to more humane penal practices and eliminate capital and corporal punishment as sanctions for major crimes.

The monumental penitentiaries still common today in the United States got their start in the first three decades of the nineteenth century. The social planners who designed these prisons had three goals in mind: to remove bad influences; to teach the offender the value of labor and work skills; and to teach the offender about the Scriptures and the principles of right and wrong. The two systems that emerged for meeting these goals were the Pennsylvania system and New York's Auburn system. The Pennsylvania system was based on solitary confinement, with bench labor within the offender's cell. The Auburn system housed inmates in small cells but confined them only during nonworking hours and on the Sabbath. During working hours, inmates labored in factory-like shops. The Auburn system ultimately prevailed in the United States.

Today, the major classifications of correctional institutions are maxi-maxi security, maximum-security, medium-security, and minimum-security. Maxi-maxi institutions house hardcore, violent, and incorrigible prisoners. Most have high perimeter security, high internal security, and operating regulations that curtail movement and maximize control. Maximum-security institutions employ full supervision, control, and surveillance of inmates. Security is the highest priority, as reflected by the architectural design and the types of work and vocational programs available. Medium-security institutions, on the other hand, embody most of the ideals and characteristics of early attempts to reform offenders. Although the top priority in such facilities is still security, intensive rehabilitative efforts are made. Minimum-security facilities, although quite diverse in purpose and location, have two common features: they are relatively open, and they house inmates who are considered nonviolent in their actions and present a low risk for escape.

Reception and classification centers are relatively recent additions to the correctional scene. Some are part of larger facilities, and some are completely separate. Most are maximum-security facilities because the propensity of new inmates for escape or violence is generally unknown. The diagnostic procedures in reception centers included medical examinations, psychological testing, and interviews by caseworkers.

Overcrowded prisons may be one of the most urgent problems facing the criminal justice system today. There are basically three approaches that might be used for dealing with overcrowding: providing more capacity; diverting convicted people to sentences other than prison; and shortening the time served by those who go there.

Riots and disturbances in correctional institutions are a constant and recurring problem today. The prison riot can be viewed in a number of ways. To behavioral scientists, a riot may be a form of communication or expression used after less drastic means have proven unsuccessful. To the revolutionary, a riot may be a form of social protest and a tool for radical change. To the media, it's a rare opportunity to portray real-life drama that rivals the best of fiction. To the correctional administrator, however, a prison riot is a challenge to authority and an insurrection that threatens the delicate balance of power in an institution, as well as the lives of those who live and work there. Typically, the inmate groups most prone to causing problems are antisocial inmates, inmates with mental problems, racial/ethnic minorities, radical/revolutionary organizations, and prison gangs.

The phenomenon of prison gangs has become a sensational part of public awareness. Close-knit, disruptive groups of prison inmates, gangs may vary from loosely to tightly structured, and their direction may range from informal word-of-mouth slogans and rules to formal and written creeds and regulations. These groups are normally clandestine and exclusive; their purposes range from mutual caretaking of members to large profit-making criminal enterprises. Prison gangs are often organized along racial or ethnic lines and deal principally in extortion, drugs, homosexual prostitution, gambling, and protection. Almost without exception, administrators say that gangs are responsible for the majority of drug trafficking in institutions.

As shown by the discussion in this chapter of the quality and quantity of institutional programming services, prisons can do much to assist an inmate in making a successful transition into the free world and reduce the possibility of becoming a repeat offender. The various institutional programs and services include educational programs, prison work programs, recreational programs, treatment programs, drug treatment programs, and religious programs.

The proportion of elderly prisoners in the nation's institutions is rapidly increasing, in part due to tougher long-term sentences inherent in the "get tough on crime" stance, but it is also partly due to the aging of the general population in America. Elderly inmates are most likely to have committed crimes such as homicide and manslaughter as well as sexual offenses, but they are less likely to be in prison for robbery and burglary. Because of their significantly longer sentences, elderly inmates may be concentrated in prisons well beyond their proportion in the civilian population, which will pose problems for them as well as prison administrators.

Homosexuality is a fact of life in every prison in the United States. Typically, there is a convict sexual code that distinguishes dominant partners and submissive partners. The "marked" men who succumb to this sexual pressure are tolerated, because by conforming to the role of women they protect and enhance the masculine role of the men with whom they have sex.

One of the hazards associated with homosexuality in prisons is the potential for contracting HIV and AIDS. AIDS is a communicable disease that occurs when the human immune defenses are broken down by the HIV virus and the body becomes unable to combat infections. The virus is transmitted by semen through sexual intercourse and contaminated blood, primarily through needle-sharing related to intravenous drug use. In most prisons educational programs do not inform staff and inmates about the disease and the ways in which it is spread. Several observers have suggested that condoms be available to prisoners so if they do engage in homosexual activity, their behavior will be protected. Advocates of condom distribution assert that homosexual behavior is a fact of life in many institutions and officials should give inmates access to these devices as a means of protecting them from disease.

Critics of condom distribution note that sexual activity is prohibited within the institutions and that many states have statutes that criminalize homosexual behavior. They argue that this step would imply tacit approval of such conduct by correctional administrators.

Because women have long been thought to hold a special place in society, deviant women have been treated differently not only from their more law-abiding sisters but also from their male counterparts. This is reflected in the kinds of violations for which women have traditionally been institutionalized, as well as the administration of the institutions they are confined in. There are, however, a number of factors that contributed to the women's prison movement. First, there was an apparent rise in female criminality during the 1860s, owing to increased prostitution and abortion associated with the Civil War. Second was women's Civil War social service experience. Third was the development of the charities organization movement and of a prison reform movement that emphasized the investigation of criminality and the reformatory ideal. Last, an embryonic feminist analysis of women's place in U.S. society began.

Something dramatic started happening in women's prisons in the 1980s. During that decade the number of women in U.S. prisons jumped dramatically. In 1980 there were just over 12,000 women in U.S. state and federal prisons. By 1997 the number had increased to almost 80,000. In about a decade and a half the number of women incarcerated in the nation's prisons had increased six-fold.

With the advent of correctional administrators' integrating male staff into female facilities, there was a dramatic increase in illegal activity resulting in prosecutions of staff for sexual assaults as well as lawsuits by female inmates claiming a violation of their Eighth Amendment rights by failure to protect them from sexual assaults. Clear care in the selection, training, and supervision of staff is essential in dealing with such claims and avoiding potential liability.

The United States has more than two million people in prison. This constitutes more persons behind bars than in any other industrialized nation. This has precipitated a serious overcrowding problem, with federal and state prisons currently operating well beyond capacity. Conventional efforts appear insufficient to cope with the increasing shortage of beds or inadequate rehabilitation services. One of the bold solutions recommended is to privatize correctional institutions. In this chapter we discuss the pros and cons of privatization.

CRITICAL THINKING QUESTIONS

Note to Instructor: These questions appear throughout the chapter as "CTQ." They can be used to stimulate class discussion.

1. Do you believe that if any of the early punishments were meted out to inmates today, it would serve as a deterrent to them and others in committing future crimes?
2. What was the effect of the progressive reform movement in the 1800s? How did this movement change penal practices in America, and has its impact been negated in modern times?
3. Which prison system do you think was most effective in terms of deterrence and rehabilitation: the Auburn system or the Pennsylvania system?
4. What style of management would you use if you were a warden of a large maximum-security prison? Why? How would those tactics differ from those used in a medium-security prison?
5. Can American prisons better achieve the correctional goal of deterrence with their current punitive outlook? Should confinement in prison become more harsh and cruel in order to deter future criminality?
6. Do you believe that maxi-maxi prisons constitute cruel and unusual punishment?
7. Do you believe that minimum-security correctional centers are too soft on criminals?
8. Why should prison officials even concern themselves about prison overcrowding?
9. Do you believe that if prisoners were given fewer rights, kept under tight control, and worked longer hours, riots would still occur?
10. Which of the inmate groups identified and discussed as prone to causing problems would you believe to be the most difficult for prison officials to control?
11. Is it possible for prison officials to eliminate the influence of gangs in prisons?
12. Are so many prison inmates deficient in academic skills because they lacked the motivation to develop these skills before they were in prison, or are their deficiencies the result of environmental factors beyond their control?
13. Do you believe that incarcerated repeat offenders should be required to do hard manual labor as punishment for their repeat offenses, or should they be given the opportunity to develop job skills for when they are eventually released?
14. Should nonviolent drug abusers be confined to prison, or do you believe that other, less punitive and less expensive alternatives should be employed?
15. What else would you do administratively to deal with the problems of elderly male prisoners?
16. How can prison officials best protect inmates from sexual exploitation?
17. Should inmates who have been identified as being HIV-positive or as having AIDS be isolated from the

general prison population and kept together, or should they be kept in with the general prison population?

18. Do you believe that all inmates should be given condoms on request?

19. Do you believe that types of crimes women commit today are different from the ones that they might commit in the future, and will they more closely resemble those committed by men?

20. How do female homosexuals in prison differ from male homosexuals in prison?

21. If only female correctional officers were permitted to supervise female prisoners, would that eliminate or reduce sexual contact between staff and inmates?

22. Will we ever reach the point where most prisons in the United States are run by private organizations?

23. Which of the two arguments presented do you believe is more persuasive in the privatization-of-jail debate?

IN THE MEDIA

Video

CNN Today video: *Corrections*, vol. 1, "Hi-Tech Prison"

CNN Today video: *Corrections*, vol. 1, seg. 8, "Life . . . and Death"

CNN Today video: *Corrections*, vol. 1: seg. 3, "Women Behind Bars"

CNN Today video: *Introduction to Criminal Justice*, vol. 3, seg. 12, "Parole Housing"

Court TV video: *Maximum Security*

FHH custom video: *The History of Corrections*

FHH video: *Life after Prison: Success on the Outside*

FHH custom video: *Prison Security*

NIJ video: *Prison Crowding*

NIJ video: *Private Prisons*

Films

The Big House

Birdman of Alcatraz

Brubaker

Chained Heat

Cool Hand Luke

Escape from Alcatraz

The Green Mile

The Longest Yard

The Rock

The Shawshank Redemption

IN THE LITERATURE

Note to Instructor: These sources can be integrated throughout the chapter as additional sources of information for the students.

Books

P. Baunach, *Mothers in Prison*, New Brunswick, N.J.: Transaction Books, 1985.

C. Blinn, ed., *Maternal Ties: A Selection of Programs for Female Offenders*, Lanham, Md.: American Correctional Association, 1997.

M. Braly, *False Starts: A Memoir of San Quentin and Other Prisons*, New York: Penguin Books, 1976.

R. Burns and M. Manchini, *I Am a Fugitive from a Georgia Chain Gang!* Athens, Ga.: University of Georgia Press, 1997.

D. Burton-Rose et al., eds., *The Celling of America: An Inside Look at the U.S. Prison Industry*, Monroe, Me.: Common Courage Press, 1998.

J. Dilulio, *Governing Prisons*, New York: The Free Press, 1987.

P. Earley, *The Hot House: Life inside Leavenworth Prison*, New York: Bantam Books, 1992.

J. Gondles, *Female Offenders: Meeting the Needs of a Neglected Population*, Latham, Md.: American Correctional Association, 1992.

L. Goodstein and D. L. MacKenzie, eds., *The American Prison: Issues in Research and Policy*, New York: Plenum Press, 1989.

V. Hassine, *Life without Parole: Living in Prison Today*, 2nd ed., Los Angeles: Roxbury Publishing Company, 1999.

E. Heffernan, *Making It in Prison*, New York: Wiley, 1972.

J. Irwin and J. Austin, *It's About Time: America's Imprisonment Binge*, Belmont, Calif.: Wadsworth, 1994.

J. Jacobs, *B. Stateville*, Chicago: University of Chicago Press, 1977.

R. Johnson, *Hard Time: Understanding and Reforming the Prison*, 2nd ed., Belmont, Calif.: Wadsworth, 1996.

K. Kauffman, *Prison Officers and Their World*, Cambridge, Mass.: Harvard University Press, 1988.

D. Lockwood, *Prison Sexual Violence*, New York: Elsevier, 1980.

S. Martin and S. Ekland-Olson, *Texas Prisons: The Walls Came Tumbling Down*, Austin: Texas Monthly Press, 1987.

N. Morris, *The Future of Imprisonment*, Chicago: University of Chicago Press, 1974.

J. Petersilia, ed., *Community Corrections: Probation, Parole, and Intermediate Sanctions*, New York: Oxford University Press, 1997.

J. M. Pollock-Byrne, *Women, Prison, and Crime*, Belmont, Calif.: Wadsworth, 1990.

H. Rafter, *Partial Justice: Women in State Prisons, 1800–1935*. Boston: Northeastern University Press, 1985.

D. Schichor, *Punishment for Profit: Private Prisons/Public Concerns*, Thousand Oaks, Calif.: Sage, 1995.

K. Watterson, *Women in Prison: Inside the Concrete Womb*, Boston: Northeastern University Press, 1996.

R.A. Wright, *In Defense of Prisons*, Westport, Conn.: Greenwood Press, 1994.

H. Zehr, ed., *Doing Life: Reflections of Men and Women Serving Life Sentences*, Intercourse, Pa.: Good Books, 1996.

L. Zimmer, *Women Guarding Men*, Chicago: Chicago University Press, 1986.

F. E. Zimring and G. Hawkins, *The Scale of Imprisonment*, Chicago: University of Chicago Press, 1991.

Articles

M. Chesney-Lind, "Vengeful Equity: Sentencing Women to Prison," *The Female Offender: Girls, Women and Crime*. Thousand Oaks, Calif.: Sage, 1997, pp. 1–27.

B. Crouch, "Looking Back to See the Future of Corrections," *Prison Journal*, vol. 76 (1996), p. 468.

S. Donohue and A. Greloch, "Keeping It Simple," *Corrections Today*, vol. 59 (1997), p. 90.

H. Sands and A. Hohnson, "Visitation in Absentia: New Technology Allows Inmates to Receive Visitors without Leaving Cells," *Corrections Today*, vol. 59 (1997), p. 96.

I. Soonachan, "The Future of Corrections: Technological Developments Are Turning Science Fiction into Science Fact," *Corrections Today*, vol. 62 (2000), pp. 64–66.

W. Toller and B. Tsagaris, Managing Institutional Gangs: A Practical Approach Combining Security and Human Services," *Corrections Today*, vol. 58 (1996), p. 110.

13. PROBATION, PAROLE, AND COMMUNITY CORRECTIONS

CHAPTER LEARNING OBJECTIVES

After reading this chapter the student should be able to:

1. Differentiate between probation and a suspended sentence.
2. List the three ways probation may be imposed.
3. Describe a presentence investigation report.
4. Compare traditional and intensive probation.
5. Identify the advantages of house arrest.
6. List the disadvantages of house arrest.
7. Discuss the types of persons transported to Colonial America from England.
8. Discuss the goal of incapacitation as a sentencing strategy.
9. Describe shock incarceration programs.
10. Identify some of the major problems in parole decision-making.
11. List the U.S. Parole Commission's Salient Factor Score items.
12. Identify four examples of common community correctional centers.
13. Discuss the three obstacles faced by virtually every halfway house in the United States.
14. List the objectives of community service.
15. Describe the concept of a furlough.

KEY TERMS

community service
control programs
educational release
electronic monitoring
furloughs
halfway house
house arrest
intensive-supervision probation (ISP)
parole
parole board
Penal Servitude Act
presentence reports
probation
programmed contact devices
Salient Factor Score
selective incapacitation
shock incarceration programs
suspended sentence
work release programs

CHAPTER OVERVIEW

Note to Instructor: The following provides you with a summary of key points made throughout the chapter.

In this chapter we examine some of the more traditional alternatives to confinement, as well as some of the newer ones. Certainly one of the older and more common alternatives is probation, which can be implemented in three ways. First, the law may allow the trial judge to suspend the execution of sentence and place the offender on conditional probation. Second, a state statute may require sentencing but may permit suspension. Third, sentencing and probation may be left to the discretion of the trial judge. If a probationer violates the condition of his or her probation, the trial judge usually orders the execution of the sentence that was originally imposed. If a judge has suspended sentencing, a probation violation might result in a stiffer prison sentence than would have been imposed earlier.

In order to determine which offenders are good candidates for probation, sentencing judges rely heavily upon presentence investigation (PSI) reports. The primary purpose of the PSI is not to determine the guilt or innocence of defendants, but rather to give insights into their personalities and lives. Such reports should include a description of the offense, including statements of codefendants, the defendant's own version of the offense, prior records, family and marital histories, a description of the neighborhood in which the defendant was raised, and facts about the defendant's education, religion, interests, mental and physical health, employment history, and military service.

Certainly one of the most interesting innovations in probation during the past decade has been the concept of house arrest. The concept has been cited for both its advantages and disadvantages. Those in favor of it believe that house arrest is socially cost-effective because if offenders have jobs before they are convicted, they may keep those jobs during house arrest. By preventing the breakup of the family and family networks, house arrest can also prevent psychological and physical disruptions that may have lifelong effects on offenders, their spouses, children, and even the next generation. House arrest is advantageous because it is also flexible and uses a sole sanction as part of the package of sentencing. It can be used at almost any point in the criminal justice process: as a diversion before the offender experiences any jail time; after a short term in jail; after prison term (usually joined with a work release program); or as a condition for probation or parole. In addition, the need to reduce prison crowding is immediate. Jurisdictions are looking for alternatives that can be developed quickly. Because house-arrest sentencing requires no new facilities and can use existing probation personnel, it is one of the easiest programs to implement. It has also been cited as being cost-effective.

Some critics of house arrest argue that a sentence of house arrest is not sufficiently severe to constitute an appropriate punishment for many crimes. Others argue that house arrest, particularly if implemented with electronic devices, will deal the final blow to the rehabilitative ideal. Some have argued that programs discriminate against the young and the poor because to qualify for most house-arrest programs, a person must generally pay a supervision fee every month. Electronic monitors are used for which the offender needs to have a home and a telephone. Other critics have questioned whether house arrest can adequately protect the public, recognizing that it is sometimes difficult to refrain criminals from committing further crimes if allowed to remain free in their homes.

We also discuss parole in this chapter. Parole is the conditional, supervised release of offenders from correctional institutions after they have served part of their sentences. It is the way in which the majority of incarcerated felons are released from prison each year. Parole differs from probation because it implies that the offender has served time. Administratively, parole is a function of the executive branch of government, whereas probation is a judicial act of the court. Selection and supervision regulations, revocation, and release procedures are similar for parole and probation, however, and the two kinds of release are often confused by the public.

Considerable research has been conducted to improve the ability to predict which offenders are good candidates for parole. One of these is the Salient Factor Score, which was developed several years ago by the U.S. Parole Commission to assess prisoners' likelihood of recidivism. This scale is similar to the actuarial tables developed by insurance companies and includes the offender's prior criminal convictions; the offender's prior criminal convictions for longer than thirty days; the offender's age at the time of the offense; how long the offender was at liberty since the last commitment; whether the prisoner went on probation, parole, or escape status as of the time of the most recent offense; and whether the prisoner has a record of heroin dependence.

A number of other alternative forms of incarceration have been developed in recent years. For example, shock incarceration programs (also known as boot camps) have been around since 1983 and have enjoyed considerable popular support. By and large, the boot camp programs have been designed for young male offenders who have committed nonviolent offenses. Community correctional sentences are another alternative means of sentencing. Falling in this category are halfway houses, which provide a residence for convicted offenders, do not require for the secure custody of a prisoner, and work as a transitional setting for prisoners being released from a correctional institution. Halfway houses have several problems, including difficulty in finding suitable locations, staffing the facilities, and often having to depend upon a number of public and private sources.

Finally, we discuss restitution and community service. These two alternatives to incarceration have seen enormous growth since the 1970s. Some types of community service programs include ordering offenders to clean up graffiti, to work in community parks or recreation programs, to clean up government offices, and to wash government vehicles such as police cars or firetrucks. Other community service programs may include requiring offenders to work in emergency rooms or facilities such as clinics, libraries, senior citizen centers, and schools. The objective is for the offender to develop a degree of accountability to the community and to see how the community has been harmed by his or her criminal action.

CRITICAL THINKING QUESTIONS

Note to Instructor: These questions appear throughout the chapter as "CTQs." They can be used to stimulate class discussion.

1. What is meant by the contention that probation is a combination of treatment and punishment? Can such a combination be expected to work?

2. Are there any disadvantages of probation without adjudication?

3. Would you add any additional conditions to intensive supervision to make it more effective?

4. Do you believe probation should be abolished for all but the most minor offenses?
5. Does house arrest have the same deterrence effect on recidivism as imprisonment?
6. Would you be in favor of implementing any features of the system developed by Maconchie and Crofton in today's correctional facilities?
7. Would it be better for prisoner morale if those who realistically will not be considered for parole not be regularly scheduled for parole hearings?
8. Why should a prisoner's past record be considered at his or her parole hearing?
9. Do you believe that the Salient Factor Score is an accurate and fair device for predicting recidivism?
10. What do you believe are the advantages and disadvantages of shock incarceration programs?
11. What recommendations would you make to deal with the three problems facing halfway houses?
12. What are the major features of work release programs and educational release programs? Which do you think is more effective?
13. What can be done to ensure that halfway house residents receive a proper education so that they are employable when they are released from the facility?
14. Why are community service programs sometimes not a realistic and viable alternative to incarceration?

IN THE MEDIA

Video

CNN TODAY video: *Corrections*, vol. 1, seg. 3, "Female Boot Camp"

CNN TODAY video: *Criminology*, vol. 4, seg. 9, "Restorative Justice"

CNN TODAY video: *Introduction to Criminal Justice*, vol. 2, seg. 13, "House Arrest"

CNN TODAY video: *Introduction to Criminal Justice*, vol. 3, seg. 12, "Parole Housing"

NIJ video: *Probation*, vol. 2

NIJ video: *Restitution and Community Service*

IN THE LITERATURE

Note to Instructor: These sources can be integrated throughout the chapter as additional sources of information for the students.

Books

J. Byrne, A. Lurigio, and M. Mahoney, *Smart Sentencing: The Emergence of Intermediate Sanctions*, Newbury Park, Calif.: Sage, 1992.

G. Cole, B. Mahoney, M. Thorton, and R. Hanson, *The Practices and Attitudes of Trial Court Judges Regarding Fines as a Criminal Sanction*, Washington D.C.: U.S. Government Printing Office, 1987.

J. Dilulio, *Governing Prison: A Comparative Study of Correctional Management*, New York: The Free Press, 1997.

D. Duffee, *Corrections, Practice and Policy*, New York: Random House, 1989.

B. Fletcher, L. Dixon, and D. Moon, *Women Prisoners: A Forgotten Population*, Westport, Conn.: Praeger, 1995.

N. Morris and M. Tonry, *Between Prison and Probation: Intermediate Punishments in a Rational Sentencing System*, New York: Oxford University Press, 1990.

J. Petersilia and S. Turner, *Intensive Supervision for High Risk Probationers*, Santa Monica, Calif.: Rand Corporation, 1990.

H. Toch, *Living in Prison*, New York: Free Press, 1977.

Articles

R. Gagliardo, "Parole-Centered Counseling: Motivating Inmates by Addressing Their Primary Concerns," *Corrections Today*, vol. 26 (2000), p. 16.

P. Gendreau, T. Little, and C. Goggin, "An Analysis of the Predictors of Adult Offender Recidivism: What Works?" *Criminology* vol. 34 (1996), pp. 575–607.

J. Kaden, "Therapy for Convicted Sex Offenders: Pursuing Rehabilitation Without Incarceration," *Journal of Law and Criminology*, vol. 89 (1998), p. 347.

R. Lawrence, "Reexamining Community Corrections Models," *Crime and Delinquency*, vol. 37 (1991), pp. 449–464.

B. McKay and B. Paris, "Forging a Police-Probation Alliance," *FBI Law Enforcement Bulletin*, vol. 67 (1998), p. 27.

R. Mercer, M. Brooks, and P. Bryant, "Global Positioning Satellite System: Tracking Offenders in Real Time," *Corrections Today*, vol. 62 (2000), pp. 76–79.

14 JUVENILE JUSTICE

CHAPTER LEARNING OBJECTIVES

After reading this chapter the student should be able to:

1. Describe the development of the juvenile court.
2. Discuss the principle objectives of the child-saving movement.
3. Describe the concept of "individualized justice" and the role it played in the emergence of the juvenile court.
4. Explain the implications of the Gault case for the juvenile justice system.
5. Distinguish between status offenses and crimes.
6. Discuss some of the criticisms of the DARE program.
7. Describe the alternatives available to the police and intake workers in handling juvenile cases.
8. Explain the problems associated with placing juveniles in adult jails or lockups.
9. Discuss the postadjudication alternatives available to the court in the disposition of juvenile cases.
10. List the four categories of missing children.
11. Describe the essential elements of effective community supervision of delinquent youngsters.
12. List common elements of juvenile probation programs.
13. Identify predictors of serious violent juvenile (SVJ) offending.
14. Discuss why some youths join gangs.
15. Liste Heide's five factors that can be used to target youths who are at higher risk of slaying a parent.

KEY TERMS

aftercare
deinstitutionalization of status offenders (DSO)
delinquent
dependent children
disposition
diversion
intake
Juvenile Justice and Delinquency Prevention (JDDP) Act
juvenile
juvenile justice system
juvenile probation
matricide
parens patriae
patricide
restitution
runaways
school resource officer (SRO)
status offenses
serious and violent juvenile (SVJ)

CHAPTER OVERVIEW

Note to Instructor: The following provides you with a summary of key points made throughout the chapter.

The juvenile justice system evolved as an attempt to deal constructively with the problems of dependent, neglected, and delinquent youngsters within an informal, nonadversarial setting. The first juvenile courts operated as a blend of the social casework agency and the criminal court. However, the procedural informality of these courts often resulted in the denial to juveniles of rights guaranteed to adults under the Constitution. Thus, in a series of important decisions in the 1960s, the U.S. Supreme Court eventually extended due process and equal protection rights to juveniles. In this chapter we discuss the federal mandate to remove juveniles from jails.

The police and the courts make a strong effort to divert as many youths as possible from the juvenile justice system. Once a juvenile is adjudicated delinquent, a variety of postadjudication alternatives are available to the court in the form of residential and nonresidential programs. As many delinquents as possible are handled in community-based correctional programs, but the training school continues to house many adjudicated delinquents. Release from training school may allow a youngster to remain in the community under aftercare supervision, a status that roughly corresponds to parole for adult offenders. The private sector is also becoming involved in juvenile justice.

The deinstitutionalization of status offenders is highlighted in this chapter. The issues of missing and exploited children will continue to receive a great deal of attention on the part of the juvenile justice system and the public in general. These issues are also discussed.

Many cities and even smaller towns are experiencing a resurgence of youth gang violence. Juveniles who participate in gang activity often belong to the category of "lifestyle violent juveniles"—youths born and reared in a subculture that reinforces exploitative aggression. Thus far, the juvenile justice system has been unable to deal effectively with these offenders. Many juvenile offenders are shuttled in and out of the system until they become the responsibility of the adult criminal courts. The problem associated with violence in local schools is also a topic in this chapter. Tactics such as utilizing juvenile curfew laws and juvenile boot camps are also reviewed.

Some critics of the current juvenile justice system call for additional reforms that would make the system more closely parallel to the adult process. In this chapter we provide a possible view of the juvenile justice system in the twenty-first century.

CRITICAL THINKING QUESTIONS

Note to Instructor: These questions appear throughout the chapter as "CTQs." They can be used to stimulate class discussion.

1. In your opinion, which has the greatest influence with respect to juvenile delinquency: biology or environment? Justify your response.
2. Does a system of "individualized" justice for juveniles seem as necessary today as when it was first established? Why or why not?
3. Should we return to the historical philosophy of *parens patriae* for juveniles, or should we continue to grant them due process protections during the juvenile adjudication process?
4. Should diversion be used in all offenses involving juveniles? Why or why not?
5. What factors do you believe to be responsible behind the criticism that the DARE program is not effective in reducing future student drug use?
6. How should status offenses be dealt with by the police and the courts?
7. Should the police have many alternatives available to them in disposing of juvenile cases? Why or why not?
8. Do you think the practice of diverting youth offenders in any way compromises the level of safety in their community? Why or why not?
9. Would it be feasible or useful to have a juvenile "bail" system, as is in the adult criminal justice system? Justify your response.
10. Given the research findings linking drug use and juvenile delinquency, should juvenile justice officials do more to curb illicit drug use by minors?
11. Under what circumstances might it be appropriate to place a status offender in juvenile detention?
12. Which of the postadjudication program alternatives do you find most appropriate for first-time juvenile offenders? Which do you find most appropriate for chronic juvenile offenders? Why?
13. Should boot camps be used more often as alternatives to institutionalization? Why or why not?
14. In your opinion, should the juvenile justice system play a greater role in trying to improve the public understanding of runaways? Why or why not?
15. Do you personally know anyone who as a juvenile was a runaway? What happened to him or her short and long term? Did the system help the youth short or long term?
16. What is the best way to deal with SVJ offenders? Justify your response.
17. How should school administrators and school resource officers deal with students who are thought to be a potential risk for targeted violence?
18. What factors do you believe contribute most to the reasons why youth join gangs?
19. What can society do to deal with children who kill their parents?

IN THE MEDIA

Video

ABC custom video: *Girls in the Hood*

ABC custom video: *Reports of Child Abuse and Neglect* (Show TM39)

ABC News Library video: *This Week with David Brinkley*

ABC News video: *Young Criminals, Adult Punishments*

A&E *American Justice* videos

NIJ Crime File videos: *Juvenile Offenders*

Films

Bad Boys

Colors

Television

The Guardian (CBS)

IN THE LITERATURE

Note to Instructor: These sources can be integrated throughout the chapter as additional sources of information for the students.

Books

T. Bernard, *The Cycle of Juvenile Justice*, New York: Oxford University Press, 1992.

M. Clement, *The Juvenile Justice System: Law and Process,* Boston: Butterworth-Heinemann, 1996.

D. Hawkins, *Delinquency and Crime: Current Theories,* New York: Cambridge University Press, 1996.

M. Jacobs, *Screwing the System and Making It Work: Juvenile Justice in the No-Fault Society,* Chicago: University of Chicago Press, 1990.

M. Knox, *Gangsta in the House,* Troy, MI: Momento Books, 1995.

B. Krisberg, and J. Austin, *Reinventing Juvenile Justice,* 2nd ed., Newbury Park, Calif.: Sage, 1993.

A. Platt, *The Child Savers: The Invention of Delinquency,* Chicago: University of Chicago Press, 1969.

J. Rodriguez, *East Side Stories: Gang Life in East L.A.,* New York: PowerHouse Cultural Entertainment, 1998.

I. Schwartz, *(In)Justice for Juveniles: Rethinking the Best Interest of the Child,* Lexington, Mass.: Lexington Books, 1989.

A. Williams, *A Kind and Just Parent: The Children on Juvenile Court,* Boston: Beacon Press, 1997.

Articles

B. Field, "Abolish the Juvenile Court: Youthfulness, Criminal Responsibility, and Sentencing Policy," *Journal of Criminal Law and Criminology,* vol. 88 (1997), pp. 68–136.

S. Morse, "Immaturity and Irresponsibility," *Journal of Criminal Law and Criminology,* vol. 88 (1997), pp. 15–67.

S. Rosenbaum, "Civil Rights Issues in Juvenile Detention and Correctional Systems," *Corrections Today,* vol. 61 (1999), p. 148.

R. Shelden, J. Horvath, and S. Tracy, "Do Status Offenders Get Worse? Some Clarifications on the Question of Escalation," *Crime and Delinquency,* vol. 35 (April 1989), pp. 202–216.

M. Sickmund, H. Snyder, and E. Poe-Yamagata, "Juvenile Offenders and Victims: A 1997 Update on Violence," U.S. Department of Justice, Office of Juvenile Justice and Delinquency Prevention, (Washington D.C., 1996), p. 33.

15 DRUGS, CRIME, AND THE CRIMINAL JUSTICE SYSTEM

CHAPTER LEARNING OBJECTIVES

After reading this chapter the student should be able to:

1. Explain what is meant by drug addiction.
2. Describe the mesolimbic reward system.
3. Identify the narcotic drugs that may be derived from the opium poppy.
4. Discuss the effects of narcotics.
5. List the types of drugs that fall into the category of psychedelics.
6. Describe the effects of psychedelics.
7. Identify the legitimate medical uses of amphetamines.
8. Discuss some of the behavioral signs that indicate someone may be under the influence of MDMA (Ecstasy) and the effects of an overdose.
9. Identify illegal drugs that are often used to facilitate sexual assault and their physical side effects.
10. List some of the potential consequences of youth substance abuse.
11. Discuss the effects of stimulants such as cocaine.
12. List the various categories of people who have used amphetamines in abusive quantities.
13. Discuss the concept of a drug-free workplace program.
14. List the arguments for the decriminalization of drugs.
15. List the major arguments against drug legalization.

KEY TERMS

analgesia
barbiturates
cocaine
codeine
freebasing
gamma hydroxybuterate (GHB)
heroin

hypnotic
ketamine
lysergic acid diethylamide (LSD)
marijuana
mescaline (peyote)
mesolimbic reward system
methamphetamine

morphine
opium
phencyclide (PCP)
psilocybe mushrooms
raves
Rohypnol

CHAPTER OVERVIEW

Note to Instructor: The following provides you with a summary of key points made throughout the chapter.

We live in a drug-saturated society. The drugs available in this country number in the hundreds, the takers number in the millions, and the doses every year number in the billions. Most of these uses of drugs are legitimate uses of legitimate substances that have positive social functions and are often used to alleviate both physical and mental illness. They can also be life-saving. However, a significant amount of drug use in the United States is not legitimate. It is deviant, violates laws and social mores, and is disapproved of by most of the public. There is a litany of drug-related problems and damage to persons in our society.

In this chapter we review the major types of drugs that are abused, highlighting their distinctive attributes and effects. The categories of drugs examined include narcotics, depressants, psychedelics, and stimulants. We also discuss drug-facilitated sexual assault and provide the reader with specific information dealing with the two primary drugs used in drug-facilitated sexual assault: Rohypnol and gamma hydroxybuterate (GHB).

We also examine in detail the emerging drug trends in the United States, especially as they relate to illicit drug use by young people, and we discuss the best way to reduce overall demand for illicit drugs. In order to accomplish this, communities, jails, and prisons must provide more effective drug treatment. The current drug treatment capacity, however, falls well below the level of resources needed to address the problem of chronic, hard-core drug use. We also discuss the linking of criminal justice and treatment, the role of drug courts, treatment research, reduction of demand through prevention, alcohol abuse by minors, and safe and drug-free schools. Finally, we discuss the arguments for and against the legalization of drugs.

CRITICAL THINKING QUESTIONS

Note to Instructor: These questions appear throughout the chapter as "CTQs." They can be used to stimulate class discussion.

1. Do you believe that drug addiction is a brain disease or a matter of individual character flaws and weaknesses? What evidence do you have for your answer?
2. Do you believe that by increasing law enforcement resources, importation of drugs can be eliminated?
3. Do you believe that prescription drugs like OxyContin should be more strictly regulated by the government? How will this affect patients with legitimate uses for the drug?
4. Why is alcohol considered a drug?
5. Do you believe that marijuana use in the United States is a problem? Why or why not?
6. Why do you suppose MDMA/Ecstacy has experienced such a marked increase in popularity among youths and college students?
7. Are there any circumstances in which the use of amphetamines is beneficial? Should these instances be more tightly controlled to reduce their availability?
8. Of the various categories of drugs discussed, including narcotics, depressants, psychedelics, and stimulants, which do you believe are most dangerous and present the greatest problem to law enforcement?
9. How can potential victims of drug-facilitated date rape protect themselves against the seemingly undetectable properties of date-rape drugs?
10. Why do you think a demand for more synthetic and designer drugs has emerged in the drug market?
11. What can potential victims do to protect themselves against drug-facilitated sexual assaults?
12. Do you believe that if treatment programs were more readily available to the drug-using population, a subsequent drop in illicit drug use would result?
13. Do you believe that drug courts are an effective way of managing the problem of drug offenders saturating the criminal justice system?
14. Are you in favor of preventive measures for controlling illicit drug use, or do you believe that a punitive approach would deter future drug use for potential users?
15. What types of programs do you believe should be implemented in schools to reinforce early or primary programs in drug prevention?
16. Are there any steps that you would take to reduce the demand for illicit drugs if you had the power to do so?
17. Which arguments are more persuasive: those in favor of drug legalization or those opposed to drug legalization?

IN THE MEDIA

Videos

Beat the Street

The Cocaine Monkey

Drugs on the Net

Ecstasy: When the Party Is Over

Let's Party

Methamphetamine: Deciding to Live

Rave Clubs: What Every Parent Should Know

Relapse

Stolen Lives: Children of Addicts

Street Drugs

Films

Blow

Drugstore Cowboy

Fear and Loathing in Las Vegas

Lady Sings the Blues

Lenny

Panic in Needle Park

Requiem for a Dream

Rush

Traffic

Trainspotting

Television

America's Most Wanted

Chasing the Dragon

Conflicting Signals

Cory Feldman: The E! True Hollywood Story

ER

Gia

Go Ask Alice

Oprah Winfrey Show (October 11, 1994), "High Class Drug Problem"

Queer as Folk

The Sopranos

IN THE LITERATURE

Note to Instructor: These sources can be integrated throughout the chapter as additional sources of information for the students.

Books

J. Friedman and M. Alicea, *Surviving Heroin*, Gainesville, Fla.: University Press of Florida, 2001.

J. Inciardi and D. Lockwood, *Women and Crack-Cocaine*, New York: Macmillan, 1993.

M. Landry, *Understanding Drugs of Abuse: The Processes of Addiction, Treatment, and Recovery*, Washington, D.C. American Psychiatric Press, 1994.

J. Langone, *Tough Choices: A Book About Substance Abuse*, Boston: Little, Brown, 1995.

T. Miller, *The Hippies and American Values*, Knoxville: University of Tennessee Press, 1991.

J. Platt, *Cocaine Addiction*, Cambridge, Mass.: Harvard University Press, 1997.

G. Rosenwald and R. Ochberg, *Storied Lives*, New Haven: Yale University Press, 1992.

D. Spungen, *And I Don't Want to Live This Life*, New York: Random House, 1983.

P. Stares, *Global Habit: The Drug Problem in a Borderless World*, Washington, D.C.: Brookings Institution, 1996.

R. Stephens, *The Street Addict Role*, Albany: State University of New York Press, 1991.

C. Sterk, *Fast Lives: Women Who Use Crack Cocaine*, Philadelphia: Temple University Press, 1999.

Articles

T. D'Aunno and T. Vaughn, "Variations in Methadone Treatment Practices," *Journal of the American Medical Association*, vol. 267, no. 2 (1992), pp. 253–258.

S. Aziz and A. Shah, "Home Environment and Peer Relations of Addicted and Nonaddicted University Students," *Journal of Psychology*, vol. 129, no. 3 (1995), pp. 122–238.

V. Dole and H. Joseph, "Long-term Outcomes of Patients Treated with Methadone Maintenance," *Annals of the New York Academy of Sciences*, vol. 311, pp. 181–189.

P. Emmelkamp and H. Heeres, "Drug Addiction and Parental Rearing Style," *The International Journal of the Addictions*, vol. 23, pp. 207–216.

R. Granfield and W. Cloud, "The Elephant That No One Sees," *Journal of Drug Issues*, vol. 26, pp. 45–61.

P. Morgan and K. Joe, "Citizens and Outlaws," *Journal of Drug Issues*, vol. 26, pp. 135–142.

E. Preble and J. Casey, "Taking Care of Business," *The International Journal of the Addictions*, vol. 4, pp. 1–24.

C. Sterk-Elifson, "Just for Fun? Cocaine Use Among Middle-Class Women," *Journal of Drug Issues*, vol. 26, pp. 63–76.

A. Sutter, "The World of the Righteous Dope Fiend," *Issues in Criminology*, vol. 2, pp. 177–222.

Sixth Edition

CRIME AND JUSTICE IN AMERICA
A Human Perspective

1 CRIME AND JUSTICE IN AMERICA

Chapter Outline

Crime in American History
The Psychological and Social Impacts of Crime
Defining and Classifying Crimes
   Conventional Crime
   Economic Crime
   Telecommunication Crime
   Syndicated (Organized) Crime
   Terrorist Crime
Drugs and Crime
The Administration of Justice
Race, Crime, and the Administration of Justice
   Patterns of Crime Victimization
   Stereotypes and Criminal Profiles
   Disparities in Conviction Rates
   Strengthening Diversity within the Criminal Justice System

Decline in Violent Crimes
   Decline in the Proportion of Young Males
   Tougher Sentencing
   Changes in the Drug Market
   A Moderate Unemployment Rate
   Community Policing and Other Law-Enforcement-Related Factors
Future Crime Wave
Summary

Key TERMS

abuses of trust, p. 7
anthrax, p. 19
business crimes, p. 8
community policing, p. 30
computer bulletin board, p. 11
con games, p. 8
crimes against the person, p. 6
crimes against property, p. 6
criminal justice system, p. 21
economic crimes, p. 7
felony, p. 6
hacking, p. 10

loan-sharking, p. 14
misdemeanor, p. 6
organized crime, p. 13
parole, p. 24
personal crimes, p. 7
preponderance of the evidence, p. 24
probation, p. 24
psychotropic drugs, p. 19
telecommunication crimes, p. 10
terrorist crime, p. 16
white-collar crime, p. 7

© Dale Stockton.

Courtesy Daniel Portnoy/AP/Wide World Photos.

Courtesy John Neubauer/PhotoEdit.

The problems of crime and how to cope with crime rank as a national priority in the United States. Although early trends in our history may have been more lawless and violent than today, crime is still a major concern for many people. To a great extent, the public's concern with crime rises and falls in lockstep with media reporting of the issue. High-profile crimes, especially those that are particularly brutal, create sensational news coverage as well as considerable public fear.

In this chapter, we will discuss a full range of crimes, including conventional crimes, which most people are familiar with (such as criminal homicide, forcible rape, robbery, aggravated assault, burglary, larceny, and theft) as well as economic crimes, which are illegal acts committed by nonphysical means and by concealment or guile to obtain money or property.

The growing problem of telecommunication crime and law enforcement's reaction to it will also be addressed. Losses as a result of this type of crime have run into billions of dollars.

Syndicated (organized) crime is also addressed. It continues to be a problem, except that organized crime, as it has traditionally been known, has changed, and new ethnic groups are now gaining control.

Terrorism has emerged as a major problem for the criminal justice system in the United States. The country has been struck by both domestic and foreign terrorists, and this will likely be a recurring problem for many years that will create tremendous challenges for the entire criminal justice system.

The problems of drugs and crime have an enormous impact on all facets of the criminal justice system—specifically, the police, courts, and corrections. This is especially true of the mood- and mind-altering (psychotropic) drugs, which are considered the most dangerous and threatening.

To help the reader better understand the various components of the criminal justice system (police, courts, and corrections) and how they are interrelated, we have created a "road map" of eighteen steps that discuss every major phase, starting with reporting the crime and ending with parole and probation revocation hearings.

The relationship between race, crime, and the administration of justice has been given considerable attention by the social science community, and this is especially true of racial profiling. In this chapter we will examine patterns of crime victimization and how they differ among various ethnic groups, as well as stereotypes and criminal profiling. We will also examine the extent to which the law enforcement community uses racial profiling. We will discuss the disparities in conviction rates among the various racial and ethnic groups, and how by strengthening diversity within the criminal justice system we might possibly mitigate racial and ethnic disparities in all areas.

In the past ten years the United States has experienced a dramatic decrease in the crime rate. In this chapter we will provide a number of explanations that have been suggested for this phenomenon. Lastly, we will also discuss a possible future crime wave.

CRIME IN AMERICAN HISTORY

People have been apprehensive about crime in every period of American history. Riots and mob violence erupted in American cities during the Civil War. Rival gangster mobs battled in the streets in the Roaring Twenties. The bank-robbing exploits of Bonnie and Clyde marked the Great Depression. In fact, "crime waves" and "the crime problem" are nothing new. As the President's Commission on Law Enforcement and Administration of Justice noted:

> A hundred years ago contemporary accounts of San Francisco told of extensive areas where "no decent man was in safety to walk to the streets after dark; while at all hours, his property was jeopardized by incendiarism and burglary." Teenage gangs gave rise to the word "hoodlum"; while in one central New York City area, near Broadway, the police entered "only in pairs, and never unarmed. . . ." "Alarming" increases in robbery and violent crimes were reported through the country prior to the Revolution. And in 1910 one author declared that "crime, especially in its more violent forms, and among the young is increasing steadily and is threatening to bankrupt the Nation."[1]

Still, attitudes toward crime and the treatment of criminals have varied over the years. Crime has been viewed as a sin, as an illness, as a result of individual flaws, and as a consequence of societal failure. Over the centuries criminals have been banished, beheaded, impaled, burned, flogged, mutilated, chained to oars as galley slaves, pressed into military service, exiled, and imprisoned. The intent was usually to punish the offender. However, as the ideas of sin and crime came together in Western religion, punishment took on a new dimension: penance. No longer was punishment meted out solely to get even with the offender; rather, through the punishment, the offender was to find a path to reformation and redemption.

Spiritual redemption as an approach to the reform of the criminal was a dominant theme in corrections during the colonial period and in the first two decades of the nineteenth century. It was abandoned when it proved incapable of producing desired changes in people. Its decline was hastened by the growing urbanization and industrialization of the United States in the early and middle 1800s. For all practical purposes, spiritual re-

FIGURE 1.1

An armed gunman robbing a victim at gunpoint as she was about to get into her car in a school yard. The fear on the victim's face is quite apparent. Such incidents often escalate into assaults that result in serious injuries and in some cases even murder.

Courtesy Michael Newman/PhotoEdit.

form for the criminal was largely discarded by the 1850s, although some of its influence has endured to this day within corrections. Although penitentiaries have not been very successful in reforming criminals, imprisonment has persisted as a punishment.

In the twentieth century, yet another approach to criminal reform evolved: rehabilitation was redefined as a medical or psychiatric problem. As a result, people convicted of crimes have been operated on, given drugs, trained for jobs, counseled in groups or as individuals, conditioned, counterconditioned, and otherwise "treated" in attempts to modify their mental states or behavior.

Although attitudes and treatments change, crime persists. Crime may have been as frequent around the time of the American Revolution as it is today. In the nineteenth century, both the cities and the frontier were dangerous, and immigrants were frequently blamed for increases in crime. From 1900 to the 1930s, violent crime soared, with labor battles and racial violence contributing to the toll. Then, from about 1933 until the early 1960s, "the United States, perhaps for the first time in its history, enjoyed a period in which crime rates were either stable or declining and in which fear of crime was relatively low."[2] This domestic peace contrasts with America's past and its future.

Thus, crime is not a new, and not a peculiarly American, problem: Crime is timeless and universal. But it is not crime in foreign countries that Americans fear; it is crime in their own communities. The concern is not whether crime is more prevalent or less prevalent than it was in some earlier period; people are afraid of crime right now. The perceived social reality is largely determined by what a society believes about itself. If the members of a society believe they are unsafe in their homes, workplaces, and public areas, apprehension and insecurity become an important part of that reality (Figure 1.1).

THE PSYCHOLOGICAL AND SOCIAL IMPACTS OF CRIME

Measuring the impact of crime in terms of economic factors is somewhat analogous to assessing the seriousness of an accident based on the total medical bill. Tangible possessions such as money and property can be replaced, even though their loss may impose a

CTQ

Do you think criminal behavior today is viewed as a result of individual flaws or societal failure? How does this compare, in your opinion, to the way sin has been viewed in the past?

CTQ

What are the ways that criminals have been punished over the centuries? Do you think any of these were rationally justified, or were they perhaps a result of societal pressures looking to stamp out the imminent fears that publicized crime creates?

WEB

For more information on the psychological impacts of crime, visit http://dir.yahoo.com/Society_and_Culture/Crime/Outlaws/, and http://www.healthmatters.org.uk/stories/keithley.html.

CTQ

What types of crimes do you most fear? Why? Which crimes do you believe you are least likely to become a victim of? Why?

CTQ

What can people do to protect themselves against violent crime?

WEB

For more information on fear and its social consequences, visit http://www.worldbank.org/poverty/scapital/topic/crime1.htm.

WEB

For more information on the classification of crimes, visit http://www.infoplease.com/ce6/society/A0857629.html, http://www.infoplease.com/ce6/society/A0857628.html, and http://www.tryoung.com/lectures/050techcrm6.htm.

---

crushing burden. But the psychological and social costs of crime, because they involve subjective factors and intangibles, can constitute a far more serious problem.

Fear is a basic ingredient of any psychological or social reaction to crime. It is a gut reaction that produces marked changes in individual behavior. The most intensely feared crimes are the ones least likely to occur: murder, assault, and forcible rape. Ironically, the perpetrator in such crimes is often a family member, close friend, or personal acquaintance. Nevertheless, what people fear most is violence at the hands of a stranger. Fear of an unknown assailant is prominent in both individual and collective responses to crime. Fear of strangers generalizes to fear of strange places, and people eventually can consider even public streets unsafe. When such fear of public places peaks, people avoid areas they perceive to be potentially hazardous. Consequently, normal activity is interrupted in these areas, removing one deterrent to criminal activity. Areas thus avoided are then increasingly frequented by persons bent upon crime.

And the greater the news coverage, the larger the proportion of Americans who cite crime as the most important problem facing the country. Public concern with crime follows news coverage of crimes with an exactness that proves the importance of the media in shaping public opinion.

Another reason for the public's heightened concern about crime is the expansion of the middle-aged population. People in the huge baby boom generation, now age 31 to 49, are more concerned than younger adults about crime. Baby boomers are also more active in protecting themselves from crime: They are more likely than those younger or older to have installed special locks, to have a dog for protection, to have bought a gun, to carry a weapon, or to have a burglar alarm. Middle-aged Americans are struggling to protect their homes, careers, financial assets, and especially their children. No wonder crime is one of their top concerns.

DEFINING AND CLASSIFYING CRIMES

In colonial America, religious offenses such as blasphemy were punished as crimes. In the 1920s, it was a crime to drink Scotch. Today, it is illegal in Wisconsin to sing in a bar; in Louisiana, it is illegal to appear drunk at a meeting of a literary society. Thus, crime is not synonymous with evil or deviance. A society may punish for many kinds of wrong or abnormal behavior by informal sanctions—disapproval, verbal abuse, or ostracism (casting the offender out of the group). Crimes, however, are acts that violate laws (formal, official, written statements of norms). No matter how reprehensible an act or the omission of an act may be, a crime has not been committed unless a specific law has been violated. Moreover, the violation must be either intentional or negligent.

Laws vary greatly with time, place, and circumstance, but they are remarkably similar in their definition of the most serious crimes—felonies. A **felony** is an offense serious enough to merit strong punishment; in the United States, felonies are punishable by one year or more in prison. Criminal homicide, forcible rape, burglary, and aggravated assault—to name just a few—are felonies. Lesser offenses are called **misdemeanors**, generally defined in the United States as crimes for which the sentence is confinement in a county jail for less than one year; a fine may also be assessed. For example, drunk driving, disorders of the peace, and small-scale gambling are misdemeanors.

Conventional Crime

The most serious felonies are **crimes against the person:** criminal homicide, forcible rape, robbery, and aggravated assault. These four crimes arouse the greatest public emotion and concern. They are the "headline" crimes that create fear and incite demands for tougher and more vigorous law enforcement. However, most felonies are directed not against persons, but against property. **Crimes against property**—burglary, larceny-theft, motor vehicle theft, arson—exclude crimes of violence.

Other offenses not commonly thought of as violent crimes or crimes against the person have the potential for violence. For example, an act of shoplifting can result in physical injury if a store employee tries to restrain the shoplifter and is attacked. Similarly, a homeowner who is awakened by a burglar may end up as a murder victim rather than a victim of breaking and entering. An arson may turn into a crime against the person if a security guard is injured or killed when a building is set on fire. Thus, what starts out as a crime against property may, as a consequence of circumstances, become a different crime—a crime against the person. Nevertheless, in recent years property offenses have made up the bulk of the millions of crimes reported annually.

The government collects data on eight offenses that make up the FBI's crime index: criminal homicide, forcible rape, robbery, aggravated assault, burglary, larceny-theft, motor vehicle theft, and arson. As will be discussed in Chapter 4, "The Nature and Distribution of Crime and Its Victims," the crime index provides information on "crime in the streets"; however, it fails to provide adequate coverage of "crime in the suites" (the highly profitable, large-scale property crimes perpetrated by corporations and businesses). Official statistics also fail to report accurately on "workplace crimes"—the auto mechanic who performs unneeded repairs or the microwave repairer who replaces a transistor and charges for a new mag tube. Annual losses from these offenses dwarf by comparison losses from conventional crimes such as shoplifting and burglary.

Economic Crime

Criminologist Edwin Sutherland introduced the idea of white-collar crime to direct attention to crimes of the "upper world," in contrast to conventional crimes committed by the lower classes. He defined **white-collar crime** as offenses committed by people of respectability and high social status in the course of their occupations.

Other criminologists find Sutherland's definition too narrow. For one thing, many so-called white-collar crimes are committed by people outside their occupations—for example, when people file fraudulent claims for unemployment insurance or falsify income tax returns. For another, Sutherland's definition fails to account for businesses in which crime is the central activity—businesses such as fraudulent land-sale companies, pyramid clubs, and bogus home-improvement companies.

Today, Sutherland's white-collar crimes are often considered part of a broader category—economic crimes (see Figure 1.2). **Economic crimes** are illegal acts "committed by nonphysical means and by concealment or guile, to obtain money or property, or to obtain business or personal advantage."[3] these crimes include the following:

1. **Personal crimes.** Crimes committed by persons operating on an individual, ad hoc basis (credit purchases with no intention to pay; individual income tax violations; credit card fraud; bankruptcy fraud; Social Security fraud).
2. **Abuses of trust.** Crimes committed in the course of their occupations by workers operating inside business, government, or other establishments, in violation of their duty of loyalty or fidelity to employer or client (commercial bribery and kickbacks; insider trading; fraudulent bookkeeping practices, embezzlement; securities fraud; employee theft and padding of payroll and expense accounts).

CTQ

Why do you think offenses not commonly thought of as violent crimes have a potential for violence? Do you believe property offenses should carry stiffer penalties?

WEB

For more information on conventional crime, visit http://www.ojp.usdoj.gov/bjs/.

WEB

For more information on the economic impacts of crime, visit http://www.doc.state.ok.us/DOCS/OCJRC/Ocjrc96/Ocjrc55.htm and http://economics.about.com/library/weekly/aa041300.htm.

FIGURE 1.2

Charles H. Keating, Jr., who headed the troubled Lincoln Savings and Loan Association in California, is depicted here arriving at the U.S. District Court in Washington. In 1984 Keating bought Lincoln Savings and Loan with junk bonds and then proceeded to fire senior staff and hire a crew of salespeople to push his worthless bonds on elderly southern Californians. He falsely claimed his bonds were guaranteed by the federal government and instructed his sales staff to focus on "weak, meek, and ignorant" targets. When Lincoln Savings and Loan crashed in 1989, it lost $230 million that had been invested in the bonds by some 23,000 people, most of them seniors. By the time regulators finally seized Lincoln in 1989, the bailout cost taxpayers $2.5 billion. Keating was subsequently sentenced to 10 years in prison.

Courtesy Ron Edmonds/AP/Wide World Photos.

IN THE NEWS

A HUMAN PERSPECTIVE

FEDERAL AUTHORITIES ARREST FIVE IN ADELPHIA COMMUNICATIONS CASE
by Jerry Zremske

The Bush administration initiated its criminal crackdown on corporate America on Wednesday by leading three members of the Rigas family—including the owner of the Buffalo Sabres—off in handcuffs.

Two other former Adelphia Communications Corp. executives were arrested as well, and civil charges were filed against Adelphia, which employs 1,700 in Buffalo. Federal authorities said the charges stem from "one of the most extensive frauds to ever take place at a public company."

Sabres owner John J. Rigas, 78, and two of his sons looted Adelphia of at least $1 billion and cost investors $60 billion, federal officials said in detailing a case that goes far beyond the off-the-books loans that drew Adelphia into bankruptcy last month.

Now Rigas and four other former cable company executives stand accused of constructing fraudulent deals and cooking the books to make Adelphia look more profitable than it was. In addition, Adelphia's new executives filed a racketeering suit against the Rigases, accusing them of conspiring to use company funds for their own benefit. If convicted, each man faces a sentence of up to 100 years in federal prison.

The court papers shed no light on the future or financial condition of the Rigas-owned Sabers, which are now being operated by the National Hockey League and are up for sale.

President Bush praised the arrests, and in effect, so did Wall Street. After a massive two-week slump, the Dow Jones industrial average gained 488 points, and analysts attributed the gains, in part, to the Adelphia crackdown.

The arrests marked the first concrete action of Bush's Corporate Fraud Task Force, which was formed only two weeks ago and quickly came to oversee an investigation that the Justice Department and Securities and Exchange Commission had been working on for several months.

"This government will investigate, will arrest and will prosecute corporate executives who break the law, and the Justice Department took action today," Bush told reporters after meeting with Democratic lawmakers. "Today was a day of action and a day of accomplishment in Washington, D.C."

John Rigas | Courtesy Reuters NewMedia/Corbis.

It was also a day of high drama spanning two states and the District of Columbia, and a day of unusually tough rhetoric from federal officials.

It began with federal agents summoning John J. Rigas and sons Timothy J. and Michael J. from their Manhattan apartment at about 6 a.m. Meanwhile, in Coudersport, Pa., where Adelphia is headquartered, agents arrested James R. Brown, formerly Adelphia's vice president of finance, and Michael C. Mulcahey, director of internal reporting.

The arrests surprised criminal law experts, who said federal authorities typically wait for a grand jury to indict suspected corporate criminals.

"I think it's unusual" for arrests to be made in such cases, said former U.S. Attorney General Benjamin Civiletti. "It may have been done for good and sufficient reasons, or it may have been done for symbolic reasons."

After the arrests came another unusual event: a Justice Department news conference in Washington to detail charges filed in U.S. District Court in Manhattan.

"Together with their co-conspirators in senior management, the complaint alleges that the Rigas family that controlled Adelphia systematically looted the corporation," said Larry Thompson, deputy attorney general and head of the Corporate Fraud Task Force.

Fifteen months after Buffalo-area leaders named John J. Rigas the city's most effective and powerful business leader in a Buffalo News survey, Thompson accused him of taking part in a series of "brazen thefts." Thompson added that the investigation is continuing, and other arrests are possible.

According to the criminal complaint, the Rigas family used more than $252 million in Adelphia funds to pay off loans that they had taken out to buy company stock.

In addition, authorities said John Rigas took at least $67 million in unauthorized loans from Adelphia, along with secret cash payments of $1 million a month from early 2001 to early 2002.

Timothy Rigas, Adelphia's chief financial officer at the time, limited that payment to $1 million a month after telling

(continued)

3. **Business crimes.** Crimes incidental to, and in furtherance of, business operations, but that are not the central purpose of the business (antitrust violations; tax violations; food and drug violations; commercial espionage; deceptive advertising).
4. **Con games.** White-collar crime committed as a business or as the central activity of a business (medical and health fraud; phony contests; diploma mills; charity and religious fraud; insurance fraud; coupon redemption fraud).

After many years of neglect (since the 1940s, when Sutherland coined the phrase *white-collar crime*), economic crime is now receiving the attention it is due from the criminal justice system. Those of the most recent interest are the huge corporate scandals in-

(continued)

Mulcahey that his father "had been spending unacceptably large amounts of Adelphia finds," the court papers said.

In addition, John Rigas stands accused of using $13 million in company funds to build a golf course on land he owns. But John Rigas was by no means the only member of the Rigas family to abuse company funds, according to the court papers. The Rigas family used company funds to buy luxury condominiums in Colorado, Mexico and New York, and frequently used company planes for personal purposes. In fact, authorities said, Timothy Rigas used a company plane to take an African safari in August 2000.

All told, the Rigases "looted Adelphia on a massive scale, using the company as the Rigas family's personal piggy bank, at the expense of public investors and creditors," said Thomas F.X. Feeney, a U.S. postal inspector, in the criminal complaint.

The court papers also allege that the Rigases fraudulently moved more than $2.3 billion in loans off the books.

That's the move that started the company's tailspin when the company finally revealed the loans in late March. But the legal papers filed Wednesday claim that those off-the-books loans were only one part of a web of deceit that concealed the company's true financial state since at least 1999.

Prosecutors accused the Rigases of concocting sham transactions—involving mysterious "fees" paid to Adelphia—that incorrectly boosted the company's earnings by $160 million in 2000 and $210 million in 2001.

In addition, the Rigases stand accused of concocting a sham sale of 525,000 cable converter boxes in order to reduce Adelphia's capital expenditures by $100 million in the third quarter of last year.

The Rigases and Brown also exaggerated Adelphia's number of cable subscribers by including subscribers in cable systems in Brazil and Venezuela—even though Adelphia only had a minority interest in those foreign systems. Investigators said Adelphia exaggerated its number of Internet service subscribers, too.

Authorities said the abuses continued until May, when the Rigases gave up control of the company.

And while the complaint centers on the past three years, it also indicates that Adelphia's problems may have begun far earlier. The complaint cites a conversation in which Timothy Rigas discussed fraudulent adjustments of financial data with a company employee in 1992.

Adding it all up, Steven Cutler, director of the Securities and Exchange Commission's Enforcement Division, said Adelphia's executives "perpetrated an egregious, multi-faced fraud on the company's investors."

SEC seeks restitution

In addition to the criminal charges, the SEC filed a civil lawsuit against John Rigas and all three of his sons—including James, another former Adelphia executive who was not named in the criminal complaint. Brown and Mulcahey are parties to the lawsuit as well, as is Adelphia itself

The SEC asked a federal court to order the Rigases to return all "ill-gotten gains," including all the compensation they received from Adelphia during the time of the fraud. The agency also seeks unidentified civil penalties and a ban on the men ever again serving as an officer or director of a public company.

Adelphia itself also might face a financial penalty stemming from the lawsuit, but the SEC didn't specify what the penalty might be.

In a news release, Adelphia said it supports the criminal action against its former executives but said it was disappointed that the federal government decided to sue the company.

"This action will only have the effect of further penalizing the company's stakeholders, who were victims of the Rigases' improper conduct," the statement said.

As for John, Timothy and Michael Rigas, they appeared in U.S. District Court in Manhattan and were freed on $10 million bail apiece, secured by cash, plus land and other property.

Peter Fleming, a lawyer for John Rigas, called his client "an extremely decent man. . . . He has never sold a share of Adelphia stock and therefore never profited from the sale of Adelphia stock."

And Jeremy Temkin, a lawyer for Timothy Rigas, said, "Timothy Rigas intends to defend himself against the charges vigorously, and he will defend himself against the charges in court."

Meanwhile, a few blocks away on Wall Street, the stock market opened Wednesday with a slight drop, but rallied at the news that the Rigases had been arrested. Analysts said the arrests showed that the government is serious about cleaning up corporate America.

Source: Reprinted with permission. *The Buffalo News*, Knight Ridder Business News, July 25, 2002.

---

volving Enron, WorldCom, and Adelphia, which have led to indictments, arrests, and imprisonment (see "In the News: Federal Authorities Arrest Five in Adelphia Communications Case").

In addition, continuing revelations of abuses of political morality (such as irregularities and illegal practices in campaign funding) have prompted a closer scrutiny of possibly collusive relationships between political leaders and leaders of business and industry (see Figures 1.3 and 1.4). Henceforth, we may witness a closer examination of the political-industrial connection. Concern is already growing over inappropriate appointments to federal regulatory agencies and over the propriety of high-level appointees leaving government to assume positions of responsibility in businesses and industries they once regulated.

FIGURE 1.3

Senator Robert G. Torricelli of New Jersey, as a result of the allegations made against him of accepting illegal campaign contributions from David Chang, a wealthy Korean businessman, withdrew from the 2002 New Jersey U.S. Senate campaign. Attorneys representing the Senator say he is totally innocent and deny the allegations he used his influence to facilitate the business interests of Chang in return for the substantial campaign contributions.

Courtesy Mark Reinstein/Index Stock Imagery.

FIGURE 1.4

David Chang, right, a wealthy Korean businessman, was accused by federal prosecutors of having multiple passports, simultaneous marriages, and murky funding sources for business enterprises. Chang is a central cooperating witness in the long-running Justice Department probe of New Jersey Senator Robert G. Torricelli's 1996 campaign. Chang told prosecutors he did far more for Torricelli than simply serve as a steady source of campaign donations. He says he gave Senator Torricell antiques, Italian suits, a Rolex watch, and even cash, none of which was reported on Torricelli's financial disclosure forms. Chang pled guilty to making $53,700 in illegal donations to Torricelli's campaign by funneling contributions through four other donors who were then reimbursed.

Courtesy AP/Wide World Photos.

CTQ

Do you believe that economic crimes are as devastating to their victims as crimes against a person? If so, how?

Advocates of ecology and environmental protection have contributed greatly to increasing public awareness of economic crime. Ever since the offshore oil spills that blackened the beaches of California and Alaska, organizations like the Sierra Club and Common Cause have pressured the government relentlessly for the passage of legislation—or for the effective enforcement of existing legislation—to prevent further despoliation of irreplaceable natural resources. These efforts have focused on the concept of corporate accountability.

Telecommunication Crime

The major types of **telecommunication crimes** are hacking, illegal bulletin boards, and misuse of telephone systems.[4] The loss due to the combination of cellular fraud, toll fraud, cable TV fraud, PBX and voice-mail fraud, and fraudulent access to computers and data systems is estimated at more than $9 billion per year and is projected to increase approximately 15 percent per year.[5]

Hacking **Hacking** is unauthorized entry into a computer system. For perhaps 99 percent of those who do it, the "hack," or getting in, is the thrill. The remaining 1 percent do things that range from mild pranks to the destruction of theft of data. To be able to hack, you have to get a password. People are often careless with their passwords, writing them down and leaving them in obvious places in their offices. Passwords can also be generated by using a special software program called a "hacker's dictionary." A common hacker's tool, the dictionary generates millions of combinations of letters and numbers until it finds a combination that matches a password—and the hacker is in. Prime targets for hackers are secure sites on independent bulletin board systems and the Internet. Because of its massive size and its connection to international systems, the Internet offers seemingly endless possibilities for hackers.

Several years ago a case involving the National Weather Service's network of more than 120 computers demonstrated how hackers operate.[6] The computer manager for the weather system located in Camp Springs, Maryland, saw signs that hackers were at work. These signs included the attempted use of passwords for former employees, passwords being changed without authorization, and mysterious slowdowns. The intrusions were tracked to a Massachusetts Institute of Technology (MIT) computer on the Internet. Aware of the problem, the computer manager began tracking the progress of the intruders and trying to find out who they were. Fortunately, the hackers stumbled and left their dictionary in one of the National Weather Service's computers. From this dictionary, investigators learned that while only thirty files belonging to the National Weather Service had been entered, the hackers had been into numerous other networks on the Internet and were using passwords stolen from South America and Europe. After continued investigation, police in Denmark arrested the seven hackers, who used such cyberspace nicknames as "Dixie" and "Zepher." (Hackers also use less benign names such as "The Black Baron," "Major Theft," "The Plague," and "Killerette.") The stake in catching these hackers was substantial, as they were creeping closer to controlling the system used to make national weather forecasts. Without such forecasts there are no airline flights, and millions of dollars or more would have been lost.

See "In the News: Federal Cybercrime Unit Hunts for Hackers" for a description of how the federal government is fighting computer criminals.

CTQ

Do you think cybercrime units are adequately prepared to handle the mass influx of cybercrimes in the early 2000s, a trend that is growing in tandem with the widespread access and popularity of the Internet? Why or why not?

Illegal Bulletin Boards Illegal **computer bulletin boards,** which store information for retrieval by someone dialing into the system, represent another vehicle for advancing illegal schemes. There are approximately 16,000 bulletin boards in this country, roughly 10 percent of which are involved in illegal activities.[7] Examples of illegal activities are unlicensed distribution or sale of copyrighted software, distribution of stolen telephone calling numbers and credit card numbers, distribution of pornographic material, and exchange of sexually explicit messages.

An international ring of hackers operating out of Majorca, Spain, stole 140,000 telephone credit card numbers and sold them to bulletin boards in Europe and the United States.[8] Those acquiring the numbers made $140 million worth of long-distance calls. This loss was shared by MCI, AT&T, GTE, and Bell Atlantic, among others. *Playboy* magazine sued half a dozen bulletin boards in two years in the early 1990s for unauthorized use of its pictures.

In a variation on using illegal bulletin boards, hackers "park" illegal materials within computer systems used for legitimate purposes. A vast amount of hacker "loot" was found in Florida State University's computer system, including proprietary software, test versions of new software that had not yet been released to the public, and a variety of hacker programs. Officials of the Lawrence Livermore National Laboratory in California pulled one of its public-access computers offline when they discovered that a hacker had placed a thousand pictures of naked women in the system and the lab was unwittingly distributing them.[9] The administrators of a server used for anonymous Internet access for sexual-abuse survivors had to shut down their system for two days when a hacker started distributing what should have been confidential information through their computers. The subsequent investigation led to the hackers' being expelled from the university they had been attending, whose systems they had been using to reach the survivors' server.

CTQ

Do you think all bulletin boards should be made illegal to prevent their use for future criminality? How do you think bulletin boards should be regulated, if at all?

Misuse of Telephone Systems Telephone "phreakers" are people who trick telephone systems into believing that long-distance and air time are being legitimately purchased. Several years ago, a thousand hackers and phreakers gathered in the Hackers on Planet Earth Conference in New York City to attend seminars and exchange tips on their

IN THE NEWS

A HUMAN PERSPECTIVE

FEDERAL CYBERCRIME UNIT HUNTS FOR HACKERS
by Matt Richtel

Raids by agents of the Federal Bureau of Investigation last week against several suspected computer hackers are part of a new Government cybercrime unit's crackdown against illegal tampering with computer networks and Web sites, a Federal prosecutor said Tuesday.

The raids prompted a counteroffensive in which disparate hacker groups took responsibility for bringing down additional corporate and Government sites, including the FBI's public information site.

The events escalated a longstanding game of tit-for-tat between pranksters using personal computers and a newly galvanized Federal police force stung by recent attacks on some of the Government's high-level Web sites. Paul E. Coggins, the United States Attorney in Dallas who is overseeing the effort, said yesterday that Federal prosecutors had issued 16 warrants in 12 jurisdictions after a year-long investigation, but had not yet charged anyone with a crime.

The investigation is part of the Government's new, Dallas-based cybercrime task force, which includes the FBI, the Secret Service, the United States Attorney's Office and the Defense Department, Coggins said.

"It's probably the most far-reaching investigation of its kind," he said. "It's an investigation with national and international implications." Coggins declined to elaborate or to say whether the targets of the investigation were considered to be part of a conspiracy.

Don K. Clark, a special FBI agent in Houston, said the activities under investigation included stealing and misusing credit card numbers and computer passwords.

Two of those who were raided by the Bureau's agents last Wednesday said one connection between some of the targets was that they knew one another from various discussion groups in an Internet chat forum called Internet Relay Chat. The participants said that the talk sometimes revolved around hacking techniques but that they were not involved in any general hacking conspiracy with other members of the discussion groups.

"I have never defaced any Web pages or taken out any major sites," said Paul Maidman, 18, of Waldwick, N.J., one of those who were raided.

Referring to proprietary computer systems, he said: "I got into other servers. I'd look around, read some E-mail, and that would be it."

Maidman said he was awakened last Wednesday morning by five or six armed F.B.I. agents surrounding a living room couch where he slept. He said the agents confiscated his computer, some diskettes, CD-ROM's and other computer paraphernalia.

Two Internet service providers have also received requests for documentation in connection with the case. The requests, parts of which have been posted on the Internet, seek information about dozens of hackers, hacker groups and software used by hackers.

John Vranesevich, who operates the Anti-Online Web site, which chronicles hacker activity, said the information requested from Internet service providers involved software tools, computer files and aliases pertaining to hacker activities.

Vranesevich said several of the aliases actually represented software programs called "bots," which are posted in chat rooms as automated monitors but may have been mistaken by FBI agents for human participants.

"Anything that has to do with hackers they're going after," he said. "I'm not going to call this a witch hunt, but it's an uninformed investigation."

Meanwhile, hacker groups continued attacks on corporate and Government computers, in some cases making sites inaccessible, and, in others, taking over sites with their own messages, some of them profane. The FBI site, taken down last week, remained inaccessible yesterday.

One hacker group, which calls itself "F0rpaxe," says it is based in Portugal and takes responsibility for "massive attacks" on various Web sites, sent a statement to Anti-Online saying, "If the FBI doesn't stop we won't, and we can start destroying."

Source: The New York Times, June 2, 1999. Reprinted with permission.

"hobby."[10] The interest of phreakers also extends to related areas, such as trying to break the code on magnetic subway cards for free rides and to decode the magnetic strips that are found on the back of some state driver's licenses.[11]

In one phreaker case, a company employee figured out how to avoid the internal tracking system for long-distance charges and then sold time cheaply to friends to make telephone calls, which resulted in a $108,000 loss.[12] Cellular phones are also subject to attack by phreakers, using one of two common counterfeit cloning fraud methods: cloning and tumbling.[13]

Cellular phones have two numbers: a mobile identification number (MIN) and an electronic serial number (ESN). Every time a call is made, the microchip in a cellular phone transmits both numbers to the local switching office for verification and billing. *Cloning* involves using a personal computer to change the microchip in one cellular phone so that it matches a legitimate MIN and ESN from numbers "hacked" from a phone company, bought from a telephone company insider, acquired from a cellular phone whose theft will not be quickly discovered, or "plucked" from the airways by a portable device — about the size of a notebook — that can be plugged into a car's lighter receptacle.

The user with the cloned numbers can simply use them until service is cut off and then change the MIN and ESN and start all over again. The use of cellular phones with cloned numbers is popular with criminals, particularly those dealing in drugs, who may lease them for up to $750 per day. In a related scam, a person leased a cloned cellular phone for a day and then sold international call time cheaply to immigrants or illegal aliens.

Tumbling requires the use of a personal computer to alter a cellular phone's microchip so that its MIN and ESN numbers change after each call, making detection more difficult. One of the newest trends in cellular phone fraud is to use a combination *tumbler-clone*, which affords the fraudulent user the untraceability of a tumbled phone combined with the free service of the cloned phone. There are two other types of cellular phone fraud: *subscription fraud*, in which free service is obtained through theft or forgery of subscriber information or through employee collusion, and *network fraud*, in which weaknesses in the cellular network's technology are exploited to defraud the cellular service provider.

Syndicated (Organized) Crime

Organization is the keynote of syndicated crime. In fact, **organized crime** is the more familiar expression for the illegal activities of syndicate criminals. Syndicated crime is a continuing and self-perpetuating conspiracy that relies heavily on fear and corruption. The roots of syndicated crime reach far back into our national history, with almost every nationality and ethnic group having been represented in its ranks at one time or another. For example, the Italian-American Mafia emerged during Prohibition as the wealthier and more violent successor to local Irish and Jewish city gangs involved in prostitution and gambling (Figure 1.5). Today, however, the Mafia has been almost extinguished as a major actor in the U.S. criminal world. The Mafia's decline is the result of its conservatism, actions by the federal government that have resulted in the arrest and conviction of high-ranking Mafia chieftains (Figure 1.6), and inter-Mafia warfare that has resulted in the murder of high-ranking Mafia figures.

Initially, the American Mafia was a prominent supplier of bootlegged liquor. That required good connections with the local police department and political machine. Paying

CTQ

Do you believe there will be an increase in the number of telecommunication crimes due to the growing popularity and availability of cell phones to larger segments of the population (in particular, youngsters)?

CTQ

Compare and contrast the basic motives and methods of white-collar crime and organized crime.

FIGURE 1.5

The Italian-American Mafia, which emerged during the Prohibition era in the 1920s as the more violent successors to the Irish and Jewish gangs, still captures the imagination of the public today. The highly acclaimed and award-winning series *The Sopranos* attests to this. In this photo, actor James Gandolfini is seen portraying the Mafia capo Tony Soprano; the other actors represent members of his "gang."

Courtesy Anthony Neste/TimePix.

FIGURE 1.6

Convicted mob boss John Gotti is shown in the New York Supreme Court listening to opening arguments in his trial. Gotti, nicknamed the "Teflon Don" because none of the charges brought against him would stick, was subsequently convicted in the early 1990s on a RICO (Racketeering Influenced, and Corrupt Organization) case. He was sentenced to federal prison for life and died of cancer in the Springfield, Missouri, federal prison hospital on June 10, 2002.

Courtesy AP/Wide World Photos.

off a single beat officer on a particular shift protected a speakeasy from the police only during that shift. In order to maximize this protection, it was often most efficient to buy off the whole department, if it was for sale. In many cities it was. Frequently, that also meant that it was necessary to have connections with the urban political machine.[14]

At the same time, the Mafia acquired control of many unions, largely through direct intimidation of members. By 1929, when John Landesco carried out his classic study of organized crime in Chicago, he could already list a dozen local industries that the Mafia dominated through the unions. Prices were fixed or territories were allocated, with the threat of union strikes or picketing of customers as the enforcement mechanism. The Depression, which created a demand for cartel-organizing services later met by various New Deal agencies (such as the Reconstruction Financing Administration), added a few more industries (fur manufacturing, for example) to the list of Mafia-controlled industries, particularly in New York.

By the 1960s, the Mafia had mostly shifted from direct provision of illegal services, such as bookmaking or **loan-sharking,** to selling services to bookmakers, loan sharks, and other criminal entrepreneurs. The organization's reputation for being able to deliver on threats was good enough that it could, in effect, sell these entrepreneurs contract insurance and dispute-settlement services. A bookmaker could insure himself against extortion by other gangsters or customer welshing by making regular payments to some Mafioso. The organization's reputation, painstakingly and bloodily acquired earlier, was now the principal asset.

As noted earlier, however, there is considerable evidence today of the Mafia's decline. For example, during a Senate committee meeting several years ago in which a hearing was held to investigate international fraud and organized crime, the American Mafia went unmentioned. Further, when the Department of Justice recently listed its principal targets for drug enforcement, no Mafia leaders were mentioned.

The Mafia has failed to maintain control of the New York City heroin market, the home of perhaps one-third of the nation's heroin addicts, and has been only a marginal player in the cocaine business elsewhere. When Mexican-source heroin became available in the early 1970s, the Mafia was never able to prevent its distribution in New York City. Its earlier control of the market had apparently rested on its domination of the New York docks through the longshoremen's union as well as its connections with southern European drug processors. Mexican imports evaded that bottleneck. By the late 1980s, the traditional circuitous route for Southeast Asian heroin, through Sicily, southern Italy, or France, had primarily been replaced by direct importation via the West Coast by Chinese and Vietnamese entrepreneurs. The Mafia proved helpless to deal with any of these incursions on its traditional territories.

Asian drug distributors have major advantages as heroin importers and domestic wholesalers. In most of the source countries for heroin, they can more easily establish their credibility as buyers and exporters. They have also demonstrated their ability to corrupt local officials and transportation executives. Moreover, in the United States, these gangs have better natural cover. Even creative and entrepreneurial drug-enforcement organizations have had difficulty developing informants and intelligence about Asian distributors. Few agents speak the relevant languages, and even fewer are of Asian heritage. It is difficult for enforcement agents to blend into the community, which, reflecting its recent immigration and cultural distinctiveness, is generally distrustful of police agencies.

The Mafia's failure to play a role in the cocaine market is particularly striking. Most reasonable estimates suggest that it constitutes the largest single illegal market, in terms of gross sales, in recent times and perhaps ever. Credible estimates of revenues from cocaine in the United States alone are approximately $40 billion, with as much as $10 billion going to higher-level distributors. No list of the major dealers has ever included any senior Mafiosi. Perhaps the failure of the Mafia to participate directly in this market can be partly explained by the very high legal risk associated with drug trafficking.[15]

The Future of Organized Crime   New ethnic groups in the United States, mostly from eastern Asia, have become wealthy through their control of large-scale illicit drug-distribution systems. Chinese and Vietnamese importers have come to dominate the importation of drugs into New York and Los Angeles.

They are also effective extortionists of their own communities. Chinese gangs have long been able to intimidate small businesses in traditional Chinatowns; the expansion of these communities, with new migration and economic mobility, does not seem to have reduced that capacity (Figure 1.7). Like their predecessor migrant populations, Asians have been unwilling to complain to the police about local intimidation. Police departments have made only modest recruiting efforts in Asian communities, with little success.

Yet these gangs have not been able to diversify, as the Mafia did, into control of mainstream political and social institutions outside their communities. The leading Chinese organized crime groups lack the name recognition of Mafia families in a non-Asian community. In fact, Asian-Americans are only just now producing the first generation of prominent local politicians, reflecting, in many cases, the lack of an active political tradition in their native countries. The Mafia's path to success in American urban politics does not seem to be the path that the Asian gangs will follow.[16]

Russian organized crime (ROC) has unfortunately been largely ignored outside the former USSR until recently. However, ROC has attracted increasing concern and attention around the world from law enforcement agencies, the mass media, and the public in general. As ROC spread beyond the borders of Russia, many countries in the world became targets. The United States, the most democratic and highly developed economy in the world, has become one of the most attractive targets of all.

According to the U.S. Immigration and Naturalization Service, during the 1970s and 1980s approximately 200,000 Soviet citizens, some of them Russian-Jewish refugees, immigrated to the United States. Some scholars believe that under this guise the Ministry of Internal Affairs (MVD) and KGB emptied their prisons of hard-core criminals. There is some evidence to support this supposition. By 1984 there were 30,000 new Russian immigrants living in the Brighton Beach area of New York. They came to the United States schooled in crime as one of the essential ingredients of the Soviet mode

FIGURE 1.7

Asian gangs have emerged as major forces in American organized crime and now control a great number of the large-scale illicit drug distribution centers in New York and Los Angeles.

Courtesy A. Ramey/PhotoEdit.

of life. It was therefore not by chance that the Brighton Beach area of New York became the center of ROC in the United States at least for a time.

ROC organizations in the United States make special use of the American democratic system, having been schooled in criminal activity in a totalitarian state. Many members of ROC groups are well educated and multilingual; they are very violent when it's required to achieve their criminal aims; they have the ability to establish good contacts with criminal organizations of other nationalities and ethnic groups; and—very important—they have no fear of the American penal system and no fear of incarceration in an American prison. It's not even possible to compare the conditions of an American prison with those in Russia or any other former Soviet prison.

According to former FBI director Louis J. Freeh, Russian organized crime groups may now operate in much of the United States. In his statement before the House Committee on International Relations at the Hearings on Russian Organized Crime several years ago, he said there is documented evidence that organized crime activity from Russia and the former Soviet republics is expanding and will continue to expand in the United States (Figure 1.8). One of the specific issues of great concern is the theft and diversion of nuclear materials and the potential theft of nuclear weapons. The movement into nuclear materials smuggling represents a dangerous expansion of traditional involvement in extortion, drug trafficking, prostitution, auto theft, money laundering, loan-sharking, fuel scams, telecommunications fraud, and medical insurance fraud.[17]

CTQ
Why is it so difficult to eliminate organized crime in the United States?

WEB
For more information on syndicated (organized) crime, visit http://organizedcrime.about.com/.

CTQ
How do terrorism and the attacks of September 11 pose a new challenge to law enforcement agencies?

Terrorist Crime

Terrorist crime includes both violent acts and threats of violence. It lumps together acts committed by criminal psychotics, self-proclaimed patriots, and others with extreme ideological views. It makes no distinction between acts carried out by individuals, groups, or even governments. It encompasses the capture of airliners and their passengers, such as the case involving the destruction of the New York City World Trade Center towers; the explosion of a bomb in a crowded office building or shopping center; the murder of a prominent person or government official; and seizure of a public building and its occupants. Such actions are carried out to focus attention on a cause or grievance; to accomplish this aim, little heed is given to the terrorist act. Victims may be carefully selected according to a plan or be simply caught in the path of random violence. Incidents of terrorist violence and horror may be directed at only a limited number of people, but can nonetheless have a tremendous psychological impact on millions. Terrorist acts prompt costly and sometimes disruptive security precautions and can lead to oppressive retaliation and erosion of civil rights. Some even challenge the accepted international order among sovereign nations.

Counterterrorism for Emergency Responders On the domestic front, the bombing of the federal building in Oklahoma City, an antigovernment attack, was in retaliation for the federal government's actions in Waco, Texas, and Ruby Ridge, Idaho. David Koresh and members of his Branch Davidian organization were killed in Waco during a confrontation with federal agents, after a siege in which Branch Davidians resisted the agents' attempts to serve warrants at their compound. In another incident on August 12, 1992, federal marshals attempted to arrest Randy Weaver, a white supremacist, in Ruby Ridge for agreeing to buy sawed-off shotguns from an undercover agent for the Bureau of Alcohol, Tobacco, and Firearms (ATF). Weaver's wife and 13-year-old son were killed in the confrontation, along with a U.S. marshal. Weaver

FIGURE 1.8

Recently Russian organized crime has attracted increasing concern and attention around the world from law enforcement agencies, the mass media, and the public in general. Dr. Sergei Paromchik (center), an internationally recognized expert in Russian organized crime, is seen with members of the Polk Country Sheriff's Office.

Courtesy Polk County, Florida, Sheriff's office and Sergei Paromchik, Ph.D.

was later cleared of the charges. The incidents at Waco and Ruby Ridge have become rallying points for many domestic militia and radical antigovernment groups around the country.[18]

For seventeen years, the Unabomber baffled law enforcement officials and spread terror throughout the United States. Some of the bombs were sent through the mail in packages, while others were planted at target facilities. Eight of the bombings occurred on the West Coast, five in the Chicago area, two each on the East Coast and in the Salt Lake City area, and one in Nashville, Tennessee. Primary bombing targets were universities, corporate and government facilities, and their personnel. Devices constructed by the Unabomber were carefully crafted pipe bombs. Pipe bombs can be very unsophisticated devices; many books and Internet sources give step-by-step instructions for making these and other terrorist devices, and component parts for pipe bombs can be purchased at many local hardware stores.

On February 26, 1993, at 12:18 P.M., international terrorism struck the World Trade Center in New York City for the first time when it was bombed by Islamic fundamentalists (Figure 1.9). The World Trade Center at that time was composed of two high-rise towers. Each tower was 110 stories tall, with several other buildings completing the complex. When fully occupied, there could be more than 150,000 people in the buildings. Prior to the September 11, 2001, attack, which resulted in the complete destruction of the World Trade Center, the 1993 bombing was considered the worst terrorist attack ever conducted on American soil. The apparent motive was to weaken U.S. support of Israel. This bombing was intended to send a message to all Americans that terrorism could happen at any time and anywhere in the United States.

As bad as the outcome was, it was far short of the terrorists' goal of reducing the twin towers to a pile of rubble containing the mass grave of thousands, something they would unfortunately accomplish eight years later.

During the 1996 Olympics, Atlanta, Georgia, became the next site of domestic terrorism in the United States on July 27, 1996 at 1:25 A.M. In spite of heavy security and enormous preparations for the possibility of a terrorist attack, a pipe bomb exploded in Olympic Park, killing 2 people and injuring 111, including 10 emergency responders. It was the worst attack at the Olympics since the Munich games in 1972, where eleven Israeli athletes were killed by Palestinian guerrillas. Atlanta police were warned of the device by a call from a pay phone near the scene of the blast at 12:58 A.M. The caller, believed to be a "white male with an indistinguishable accent" and American, stated that "There is a bomb in Centennial Park. You have 30 minutes." (The bomb actually exploded ten minutes earlier than the time given by the caller.) A partial evacuation of the park occurred, but only because police already on duty in the park had happened upon the unattended knapsack that held the bomb. The device was an unsophisticated pipe bomb placed in a satchel near the concert stage in Olympic Park. Nails and screws were loaded into the bomb to create shrapnel to harm people. Police saw three pipes, but did not know if they were three separate bombs or were all hooked together. Experts do not think that international terrorists were involved because of the primitive type of explosive device used in the attack.

On January 12, 1997, in the Atlanta, Georgia, suburb of Sandy Springs, two bombs went off at Northside Family Planning Services. The first bomb did not cause any injuries. However, the second bomb apparently was timed to kill or injure emergency responders. Thirteen emergency responders including three federal agents were injured, though not seriously, by the second blast. A little over a month later, another pair of bombs went off at an Atlanta nightclub called the Otherside Lounge, which caters to gay clientele. Five people were injured, one seriously, by the first blast. Police found a third bomb outside by the curb that was again set for emergency responders. The bomb exploded while a robot tried to disarm it. However, precautions were taken and no one was injured by the blast. The day after the second attack, letters were sent claiming responsibility for both of the bombing incidents. A group calling themselves "The Army of God" indicated they had declared and would wage a total war against agents of the so-called federal government. The author(s) of the letter indicated that they were violent opponents of abortion and homosexuality.

From January to May 1997, acts of violence, including the use of incendiary devices and bombs, occurred against abortion clinics in Tulsa, Oklahoma; Falls Church,

FIGURE 1.9

View of the 1993 World Trade Center bombing, the first assault by international terrorists on U.S. soil.

Courtesy Mike Segar/CORBIS.

Virginia; North Hollywood, California; Bozeman, Montana; Yakima, Washington; and Portland, Oregon. On January 30, 1998, a bomb exploded at an abortion clinic in Birmingham, Alabama. The blast killed an off-duty police officer who was moonlighting as a security guard at the facility and critically injured the clinic counselor. In May 1998, attacks involving butyric acid occurred at eight abortion clinics in Florida. This was the first report of the use of butyric acid against abortion clinics in over four years. From 1992 through May 1998 there had been 99 reports of "noxious" chemical attacks on abortion clinics. Butyric acid is a colorless organic acid with a penetrating obnoxious odor. It is a strong irritant to skin and tissue and can cause severe burns. The most significant problem with butyric acid is removing the odor. With little exception, anything the acid comes into contact with will have to be replaced. As a result, the attacks have caused over $800,000 in damage since 1992.

Federal investigators have determined that the bombings in Olympic Park, the Sandy Springs abortion clinic, the Otherside Lounge, and the abortion clinic in Birmingham are all connected and may have been carried out by the same person(s). Tests performed by ATF and FBI laboratories in Washington, D.C., have discovered that some of the bomb components from the clinic and the Atlanta nightclub are identical. Shrapnel parts found at the bombing sites came from the same foundry. Federal agents feel that the bombings were carried out by a single person or a small group. In February 1998, Eric Rudolph, a 32-year-old resident of Murphy, North Carolina, was charged with bombing the New Woman All Women Health Center in Birmingham, Alabama. On October 14, 1998, Rudolph was also charged with the bombings in Olympic Park and the abortion clinic and nightclub in Atlanta. A $1,000,000 reward has been offered for his arrest and he has been added to the FBI's Ten Most Wanted list of fugitives.

The single greatest attack in the United States was the destruction of the World Trade Center towers in New York City on September 11, 2001 (Figure 1.10) along with the partial destruction of the Pentagon in Washington, D.C. The Islamic extremist group al-Qaeda was responsible for these attacks. The leader of this group, Osama bin Laden, is the son of a billionaire Saudi construction magnate. Bin Laden has an estimated worth

FIGURE 1.10

Site of the World Trade Center Twin Towers, destroyed by terrorists who crashed two commercial airliners into them on September 11, 2001.

Courtesy Louis Lanzano, AP/Wide World Photos.

of hundreds of millions of dollars; this money funded various terrorist operations directed toward the United States and other Western countries. Al-Qaeda was also linked to the 2000 suicide bombing of the destroyer USS *Cole* in Yemen and the 1998 bombing of the American embassy in Nairobi, Kenya. Shortly after the September 11 attacks, numerous cases of anthrax[19] were found around the United States, with the mail service being the principal source of delivery and contamination. **Anthrax** is caused by a bacterium found in soil that normally affects livestock, including cattle and sheep. The disease is rarely contagious; infection requires direct contact with spores, yet if the spores are inhaled, fever, difficulty breathing, and death can occur within days. The treatment of anthrax includes antibiotics and vaccine. Terrorism authorities agree that such attacks will continue in the future; in addition to using biological weapons, terrorists may deploy chemical, perhaps even nuclear, weapons.

A New Kind of Terrorism   Thus far we have discussed what can be loosely described as more traditional acts of terrorism. However, from October 2, 2002, to October 22, 2002, the United States experienced a new kind of terrorism. During this twenty-day period, thirteen Americans—young, old, male, female, white, and black—were gunned down in the Maryland, Virginia, and Washington, D.C., areas. Ten of the shooting victims died, but three survived their severe injuries. The killings simultaneously mesmerized and terrified millions of Americans, especially those in the areas where the killings were occurring. Eventually two sniper suspects were arrested and were identified as John Allen Muhammed, (previously known as John Williams, before changing his name), age 41, and John Lee Malvo, age 17. The arrests resulted from information provided by the public as well as help, sometimes unwittingly, by the snipers themselves. The two men were also linked to murders and assaults in other parts of the country. See "In the News: With Each New Killing a Stronger Dose of Terror" for a discussion of this series of murders.

> **CTQ**
>
> What type of additional training do you believe emergency responders should have, in view of the growing trends in foreign and domestic terrorism? Do you think such training should be extended to all law enforcement agencies? Why or why not?

DRUGS AND CRIME

In the late nineteenth century, American society began regulating the use and distribution of **psychotropic drugs**—narcotics and other consciousness-altering drugs. Since that strategic decision of more than a century ago, both state and federal governments have enacted drug-control legislation, and the American criminal justice system has, for better or worse, been at the center of drug-control efforts. A more detailed discussion of the effects of psychotropic drugs and emerging drug trends can be found in Chapter 15, "Drugs, Crime, and the Criminal Justice System".

Clearly, many kinds of controversial behaviors occur in a complex society, and it is equally true that not all controversial or even morally repugnant or distasteful behaviors become illegal. So why has the use of psychotropic drugs been deemed illegal? As a generalization, we can say that they have appeared to the general public as sufficiently dangerous and threatening to merit legal restriction. The ways in which these behaviors are defined as dangerous include the following:

- Historically, the use of these substances has been seen as generally socially dangerous and injurious. People abandon social and personal responsibilities in lieu of activities centered around drug use. In addition to the social pathology attached to chronic drug abuse, there are physical morbidity and mortality costs. Drugs themselves may cause illness or death or may promote a lifestyle that enhances the likelihood of illness or premature death.
- It is believed that these substances, in a variety of ways, facilitate or increase the occurrence of conventional types of crime such as burglary, robbery, and assault.
- By making these substances, through the law, illegal, society "constructs" a unique form of criminality that is not attached as a status to the use of the substance.[20] This registers social opinion on the behavior and, in theory, creates a condition that will deter drug use. Thus criminalization of drugs is believed to deter at least some people from using or trafficking in them. (Arguments for and

IN THE NEWS

A HUMAN PERSPECTIVE

WITH EACH NEW KILLING A STRONGER DOSE OF TERROR
by Neely Tucker, Serge F. Kovalesk, and Sewell Chan

The first shot and the last came out of clumps of roadside brush and bramble, one blast at dusk and the other before dawn, one harmless and the other deadly. In the long 22-day ordeal, 10 people were killed, three were critically wounded and 5 million people in two states and the nation's capital wondered if someone was aiming at them in the fading light of late autumn.

The killer liked trigger spots in public parking lots and the hideaways of the homeless and the destitute that lie alongside them. Shots could be fired from an old Chevrolet Caprice, evidence gathered yesterday shows, but the gunman often preferred to step over the curb, one-two-three, and duck into the unkempt hedges that offer a place of shadows for those who need them.

Cold-blooded and calculated, the attacks seem to write a new chapter in the annals of American serial murders. "Sometimes it is a historian's sad duty to confess that history is no guide," said Roger Lane, a criminal justice historian at Haverford College and the author of "Murder in America."

"I can think of no similar shooting or murder pattern in American history. This was not a true serial killer, spree killer or mass murderer. It is more akin to a kidnaping, with ransom notes, than simple murder."

The terror began on Wednesday evening three weeks ago with a seemingly incomprehensible rampage in which single rifle blasts fired in no coherent order found their target and blew away the sense of security of suburban Montgomery County. Six people were fatally shot in just over 24 hours, five in Maryland, one in the District, four men and two women of different ethnic backgrounds. None knew the other. No witness saw the shootings. The killer seemed to move like a vicious ghost, silent, efficient, and deadly.

Forensic psychologist Harley Stock said this bloody string of violence occurred so quickly it did not rattle the public's faith in the police to protect them. But two particular attacks changed that.

Days after police assured parents that it was safe to take their children to school, the target was a 13-year-old boy who was shot and critically wounded as he arrived at Benjamin Tasker Middle School in Bowie. Left at the scene was a tarot card with a note stating "I am God," a chilling declaration of omnipotence. Montgomery County Police Chief Charles A.

Courtesy Jahi Chikwen/CORBIS.

Courtesy Reuters/Brendan McL/CORBIS.

John Allen Muhammed (previously known as John Williams) (top) was arrested and charged with a 20-day shooting spree that resulted in 13 Americans, young, old, male, female, white, and black, being gunned down in Maryland, Virginia, and Washington, D.C., in 2002. In his criminal acts he was accompanied by John Lee Malvo, aged 17.

Moose was brought to tears on television, saying the sniper was getting "really personal" and had "crossed the line."

"The tarot card was their way of saying, 'We'll give you just enough to make sure that you're confused,'" said Brian H. Levin, a professor of criminal justice at California State University at San Bernardino and a former New York City police officer. "This was designated to enhance the terror and firmly establish that they were doing the shooting and that they were in control of the situation."

The terror took on a deep resonance the next day when a belligerent letter was found after a shooting almost 90 miles away in Ashland, VA. After a demand of $10 million; the postscript threatened that no children were safe anywhere at any time, and now the specter of more child shootings swept through the region.

What investigators may not have calculated at the time was the probability that two people could be behind the shootings, taunts and demands. Criminal justice analysts not involved with the case said yesterday that this team scenario gives more credence to the possibility extortion was behind the attacks. Eric W. Hickey, a professor of criminal psychology at California State University at Fresno and author of "Serial Murderers and their Victims," said that the assailants may have used the initial round of killings as a brutal means of establishing their credibility.

But the hubris in their letter and calls, designed to make them appear more powerful, may have proved to be their undoing, initial reports from the investigation show.

A caller's demands and an angry burst in which he told police to "check with people" in Montgomery, Ala., to confirm his murderous capabilities, led investigators to John Allen Muhammed and John Lee Malvo.

Jack Levin, director of the Brudnick Center on Violence and Conflict at Northeastern University in Boston, said the sniper's decision to shoot his victims from a significant distance suggested he had more than just a swift, undetected getaway in mind.

"Most serial killers are sexual sadists who enjoy using their own hands to make their victims suffer," Levin said. "Most of these killers who are up close and personal with their victims are sociopaths. But these killers may not have been sociopaths. They created distance between themselves and their victims, and they apparently wanted to make a lot of money—$10 million." "For

(continued)

(continued)

them, killing may have been a means to an end," Levin said. "whereas for most serial killers, murder is an end in itself."

The attacks expanded south, eventually reaching the suburbs of Richmond. Single shots were again shot from tree lines, or from parking lots, as the shooter seemed to play a murderous version of tick-tack-toe, moving from town, to city, to county, to state.

The killer shot his oldest victim, at 72, and then his youngest, at 13. After the first two slayings, he alternated shooting targets between race and gender each time. He also used cruel variations on this theme.

He looked down the barrel at a married couple leaving a Home Depot in Fairfax County on the night of Oct. 14 and shot the wife, leaving her husband to scramble for help. Five days and a few dozen miles down Interstate 95 later, he looked down the barrel at another married couple, this time emerging from dinner at a Ponderosa steakhouse in Ashland. He shot the husband and left the wife to scream.

"There was selectivity in the victims," Clinton Van Zandt, a former FBI profiler, said of the gunman. "He wanted his group of victims to represent America, and he succeeded in doing that." Because they targeted any man, they really targeted every man. Therefore every one of us was a potential victim."

A report of a white van leaving the scene of the shooting at Leisure World in Silver Spring on the second day was a huge and unexpected break for the suspects, analysts said.

That erroneous account afforded them "the equivalent of a disguise," said Gary L. Wells, a professor of psychology at Iowa State University who researches eyewitness identification.

Now, when witnesses heard a shot, Wells said, they likely turned to see a much publicized white van, perhaps skipping right past the suspects' car. And as the investigation broadened, most experts relied on statistical histories [that] the killers were most likely foreign terrorists or white males. No expert suggested that a pair of black males, a middle-aged man and a teenager, might be suspects. "The whole situation was so heavily stacked against the ability of an eyewitness to be able to come away with any good, reliable information," Wells said. "That accounts for why, repeatedly, no one really had much of anything reliable in the way of eyewitnesses."

The last killing came before dawn on Tuesday, less than a mile from the parking lot where the terror campaign started. While the moon shone in the pre-dawn chill, the killer hid in a heavily wooded section of a public park and looked down the barrel at a 35-year-old bus driver.

"The purpose of true terror is to psychologically destabilize the population and make people lose faith in the government's ability to protect them," Stock, the foreign psychologist, said in summing up the region's deadly October. "They absolutely succeeded."

Source: *The Washington Post*, October 25, 2002. © **2002, The Washington Post. Reprinted with permission.**

against the legalization of drug use are discussed in Chapter 15, "Drugs, Crime, and the Criminal Justice System.")

- The law makes the distribution and use of these substances a crime. Thus peculiar crimes emerge out of the activities associated with buying, selling, manufacturing, and importing these substances. This extends criminality beyond the scope of simply sanctioning the use and sanctions the sale as well. Further crimes arise out of trafficking that cannot be attributed to the drug user directly, since data show that traffickers may not use the substances they sell. They are motivated by a desire to make a profit and thus are most accurately classified as distinctively economic criminals.

THE ADMINISTRATION OF JUSTICE

As one studies the **criminal justice system**, it can be described in terms of its component agencies, namely, the police, courts, and corrections. However, in order to better understand the system it is useful to provide a road map that illustrates from beginning to end how cases are processed. Analysis of case processing within the system provides a useful guide and "road map" to the criminal justice system itself. Figure 1.11 illustrates the criminal justice process.[21]

Most scholars agree that processing crime all the way through the criminal justice system requires eighteen steps or processes. These are listed and explored in order next. However, each will be discussed in much greater detail in later chapters.

    Step 1.   *Reporting the Crime.* In this process the police receive information concerning the possible commission of a crime from reports of citizens or from their own observation.

CTQ

Why is drug abuse among young people so prevalent in our society?

WEB

For more information on drugs, **visit** http://www.drugwatch.org/.

WEB

For more information on the administration of justice, **visit** http://www.criminal-justice-system.gov.uk/home.html, http://www.jrsa.org/pubs/reports/handbook1.html, and http://www.ncvc.org/infolink/info11.htm.

22 CRIME AND JUSTICE IN AMERICA

1 Reporting the Crime	→	2 Prearrest Investigation	→	3 Arrest	→	4 Booking	→	5 Postarrest Investigation	→
6 Decision to Charge	→	7 Filing the Complaint	→	8 First Appearance	→	9 Preliminary Hearing	→	10 Grand Jury Review	→
11 Filing the Indictment or the Information	→	12 Arraignment on the Information or Indictment	→	13 Pretrial Motions	→	14 Criminal Trial	→	15 Sentencing	→
16 Appeals	→	17 Postconviction Remedies	→	18 Parole or Probation Revocation Hearing						

FIGURE 1.11

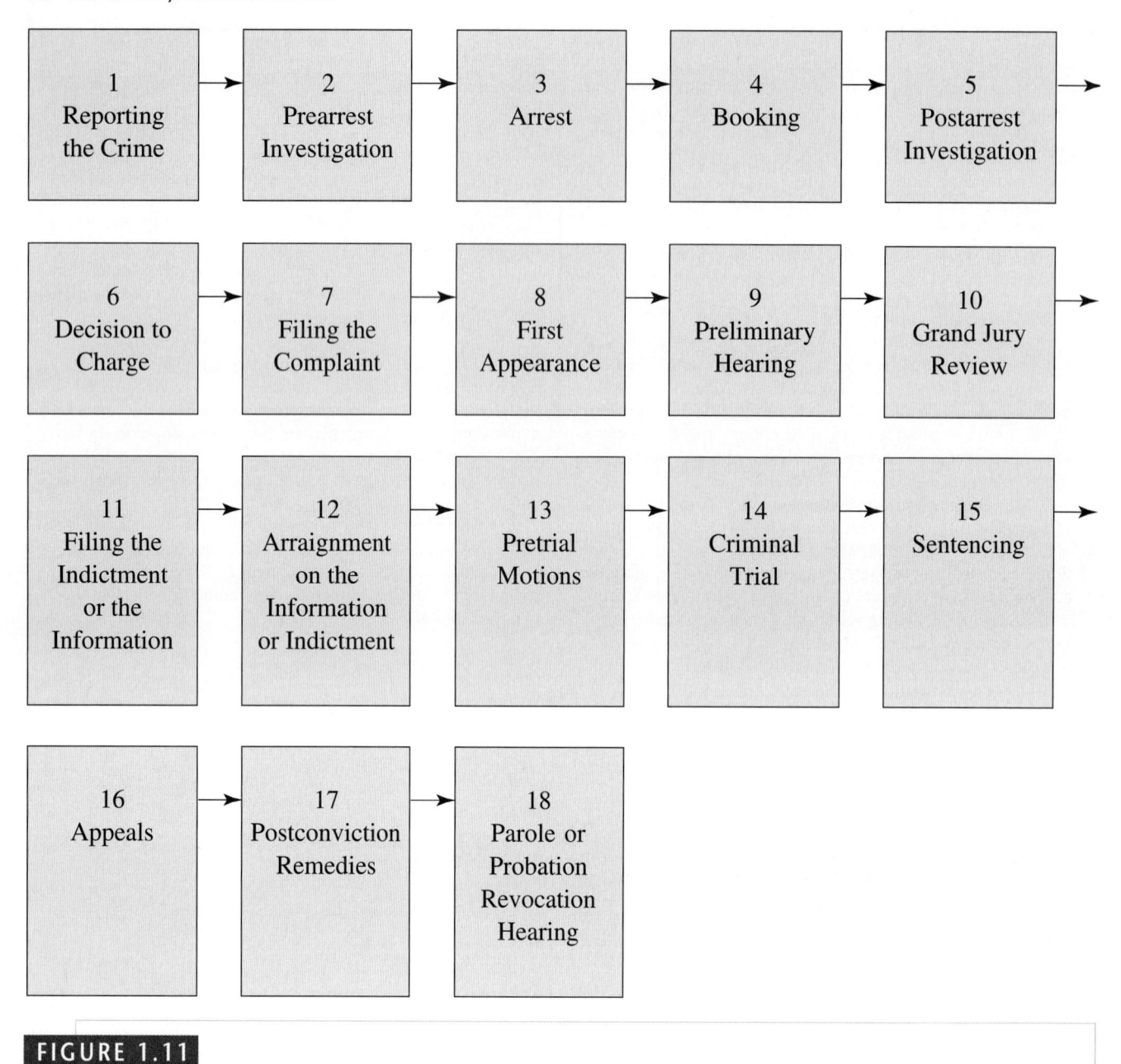

The Eighteen Steps in the Criminal Justice Process

Step 2. *Prearrest Investigation.* During this step, law enforcement investigators must determine whether a crime actually was committed and whether there is information pointing to the guilt of a particular person. This step is designed to answer these questions and to collect evidence to establish guilt at trial. Prearrest investigations include the following procedures: questioning the suspect, asking for identification, asking the suspect to respond to the accusation, interviewing potential witnesses, investigating the crime scene, collecting physical evidence, contacting informants, and, in some investigations, wiretapping.

Step 3. *Arrest.* An arrest occurs when a suspect is taken into custody for the purpose of transporting the suspect to the station and charging him or her with a crime. Most arrests are made on the officer's own initiative rather than on the order of judicially issued warrants.

Step 4. *Booking.* The suspect is transferred to a holding facility. Upon arrival, the arrestee's name and the offenses with which the arrestee is currently being charged are logged. The arrestee will be photographed, fingerprinted, informed of the charge, and allowed to make one telephone call. Minor offenders will be able to make "stationhouse bail," although serious offenders must to appear before a magistrate before bail can be set. These arrestees will be kept in "lockup" until a more through search and inventory of personal belongings is made.

Step 5. *Postarrest Investigation.* This procedure varies with the situation. When an arrestee is caught "red-handed," little has to be done. The police will use many of the prearrest investigative procedures. In postarrest investigation, the arrestee is available for such things as lineups, providing handwriting samples or DNA samples, and lengthy questioning about the crime.

Step 6. *Decision to Charge.* The police officer fills out an arrest warrant that is reviewed by a higher-ranking officer. This officer decides whether charges will be brought or whether the charges will be reduced. A second review by the prosecuting attorney occurs sometime after charges are filed.

Step 7. *Filing the Complaint.* The initial charging instrument is called a *complaint*. In misdemeanor cases it will serve as a charging instrument throughout the proceedings; in a felony case, it sets forth the charges only before the magistrate court. The complaint includes a brief description of the offense and is sworn to by a complainant, either the victim or the investigating officer.

Step 8. *First Appearance.* In this step the arrestee is now formally a defendant. The first appearance is also called the *initial appearance* or *arraignment on the preliminary presentation* in some jurisdictions. The defendant is presented before a magistrate. The magistrate makes certain that the person before him or her is the person in the complaint. The defendant is informed of the charges, his or her various rights, and other proceedings that will follow. Most jurisdictions provide the right to counsel for indigents at the first appearance. In felony cases, the magistrate advises the defendant about the next step, the preliminary hearing. The magistrate sets the date for the hearing unless the defendant waives it. The final function of the magistrate at this point is to set bail.

Step 9. *Preliminary Hearing.* A substantial portion of felony cases are disposed of between the first appearance and the preliminary hearing. A defendant may waive his or her right to a preliminary hearing. Preliminary hearings provide a screening of the decision to charge by a neutral body, the magistrate. This procedure provides the defendant with an adversary proceeding. If the magistrate decides that the evidence presented establishes probable cause (i.e., a reasonable belief that a crime has been committed and the person sought to be arrested committed the crime), he or she will bind over the case to the next stage. If the magistrate finds that probable cause supports a misdemeanor but not a felony, he or she will reject the felony charge and allow the prosecutor to submit a lower charge. If the magistrate finds that the evidence does not support the charge, he or she will order the defendant released.

Step 10. *Grand Jury Review.* The federal system and about one-third of the states currently require grand jury indictments of felony prosecutions, unless waived by the defendant. The grand jury can reject prosecution or reinstate prosecution; it is not bound by the magistrate's decision. Composed of a group of private citizens selected to review cases presented over a term ranging from one to several months, the grand jury's primary function is to determine whether there is significant evidence to justify a trial on the charge sought by the prosecution. The grand jury meets in closed session and hears only evidence presented by the prosecution.

Step 11. *Filing the Indictment or the Information.* If an indictment is issued, it replaces the complaint as the accusatory instrument in the case and is filed with the general trial court. Where the grand jury is not required or has been waived, an information is filed with the general trial court. The information is a charging instrument that replaces the complaint, but it is issued by the prosecutor rather than the grand jury.

Step 12. *Arraignment on the Information or Indictment.* This is also a pretrial procedure. A defendant is brought before a court, informed of the charges before him or her, and asked to enter a plea of guilty, not guilty, or, in some circumstances, *nolo contendere* (no contest).

Step 13. *Pretrial Motions.* During this stage, broad ranges of objections must be raised by pretrial motions. It is quite common during this stage for the defendant's attorney to challenge the prosecution's information and the sufficiency of the charging instrument. Requests for discovery of the prosecution's evidence and requests for suppression of the evidence are also made during this stage. This is the last of the pretrial procedures.

Step 14. *Criminal Trial.* In the trial, the defendant has the right to a jury for all felonies and for misdemeanors punishable by more than six months' imprisonment. Several distinguishing factors in American criminal trials are (a) the presumption of the defendant's innocence, (b) the requirement of proof beyond a reasonable doubt, (c) the right of the defendant not to take the stand, (d) the exclusion of evidence obtained by police through unconstitutional procedures, and (e) the more frequent use of incriminating statements by the defendant.

Step 15. *Sentencing.* Sentencing occurs if a defendant pleads guilty or is found guilty at trial. In either instance, the judge enters a judgment of conviction and sets the date for sentencing. Usually, the sentencing hearing takes place a significant length of time after a conviction. The structure of the sentence and the discretion of the judge are controlled by statute.

Step 16. *Appeals.* In felony cases, the initial case is taken to an intermediate appellate court or the state supreme court. Appeals are filed predominantly by those defendants who are sentenced to imprisonment.

Step 17. *Postconviction Remedies.* Federal postconviction remedies allow state as well as federal prisoners to challenge their convictions in federal court on certain constitutional grounds. Federal district courts receive roughly 15,000 postconviction applications every year. A writ of habeas corpus is the most common form of postconviction remedy.

Step 18. *Parole or Probation Revocation Hearing.* This step occurs when a defendant has been found guilty and sentenced to probation or has been sent to prison and subsequently released on parole. **Probation** is a form of sentencing that allows the offender to remain free in the community under supervision and subject to conditions set by the court; violation of these conditions may lead to revocation. **Parole,** on the other hand, is supervision of offenders in the community before the expiration of their sentences. If parole conditions are violated, parole may be revoked and the offender may be returned to the institution for the remainder of the sentence. This hearing is initiated when the convict's probation or parole officers issue a warrant declaring that the probationer or parolee has violated a condition or conditions of his or her probation or parole. These violations are not necessarily criminal, but are regulatory. During this last stage the convict has an opportunity to deny violations of the charges. The state is required to prove that the probationer or parolee committed the violation only by a preponderance of the evidence. A **preponderance of the evidence** is an amount of persuasiveness of the evidence presented by one side that is slightly greater than 50 percent of that presented by the other side; if this is the case, then the first side has proved its case by a preponderance of the evidence.

RACE, CRIME, AND THE ADMINISTRATION OF JUSTICE

Each of us knows about race, crime, and the administration of justice in many ways: from our own experience, through stories we hear, and from our various understandings of history. We may also retain a current statistic or two, especially if we have stumbled on one that reinforces what we already believe. But what does the subject of race, crime, and justice look like if approached empirically, and with reference to all of what we refer to today as racial groups?[22]

At the most general level, we know that many people of color—Native Americans, Asian Americans, Hispanic Americans, black Americans—do not trust the justice system. For example, a study of Hispanic Texans found that fewer than 30 percent rated the job performance of their local police as good.[23] A Gallup poll taken several years ago found that more than half of black Americans believed that the justice system was biased against them. Moreover, two-thirds of black Americans in that same Gallup poll said that police racism against blacks is common across the country, and a majority of white Americans (52 percent) agreed.[24]

Social scientists usually explain this broad distrust in two ways: historical experience and present-day practice. The historical experience with the justice system among Native Americans, Asian immigrants, black Americans, and Hispanic Americans is more than enough to provoke distrust, and some people today believe that this historical perception is being reinforced by current practice. The following important questions must be addressed in examining these issues. First, how does the pattern of crime and victimization keep us from living as one America? Second, how do stereotypes work to cause people of some races and ethnic groups to be unfairly suspected of crime? Third, how and when does the justice system itself treat defendants and offenders differently on the basis of race or ethnicity? Fourth, does a lack of diversity in the justice system add to distrust?

Social science research has shed some light on each of these concerns, but our empirical knowledge is uneven. We know a lot about some of these issues, but there are great gaps in what we know through research. We know much less about discrimination in judicial decisions regarding Asian American defendants, for example, than we do about "black and white" discrimination. And we know much more about reported index crimes (homicide, robbery, rape, burglary, aggravated assault, larceny, auto theft, and arson) than we do about other criminal conduct. The lack of data and good research on the experience of Asian Americans and Native Americans in particular is a problem.

CTQ

Most people of all ethnic and racial groups are never convicted of a crime, but stereotypes can work to brand all members of some groups with suspicion. Why do you think this occurs?

Patterns of Crime Victimization

First let us look at the pattern of crime victimization. In general, whites have the lowest victimization rates, followed by Asians, Native Americans, Hispanics, and blacks. But the differences are dramatic. For example, recent crime statistics have shown that there are 5.1 homicide victims per 100,000 non-Hispanic white males. The homicide rate for Asian American males was more than one and a half times that, at 8.3 per 100,000. But the homicide rate for Native American males was three times than the white rate; the rate for Hispanics was almost five times the white rate; and the rate for blacks was ten times the white rate.[25]

This pattern changes somewhat for different crimes. For more common violent crimes, such as robbery, the relative position of the groups is the same, but the differences are not as great. For household crimes, such as burglary, Hispanics report the highest rates of victimization in the annual victimization surveys conducted by the Census Bureau for the Justice Department.[26]

Why the differences? The crudest analyses focus on the offenders, telling us that most crime is intraracial. More than 80 percent of homicides where we know the race of the killer are either white-on-white or black-on-black. Research among the Vietnamese and Chinese in California has also shown that most crime there is intraracial.[27]

These groups with high victimization rates also have high offending rates, but several explanations have been provided. First, it is essential to remember that because whites still constitute the majority of the population in the United States, higher numbers of total crimes are committed by whites. However, their offending rates are low because of their proportionally much higher number in the total population.

Second, the chances that a young adult has ever committed a violent offense is roughly equal across races. This is what social scientists call the "ever prevalence rate," and it is the percentage of people who, by a certain age, have at least once in their lifetime committed a certain act. The "ever prevalence rate" for committing a violent crime is roughly the same for blacks and whites. The difference in violent crime rates among these two groups is a function of the greater number of offenses committed each year by those in certain groups and their persistence in such behavior over time.[28]

Third, community conditions seem to be the reason that crime falls so heavily on some groups. The more sophisticated analyses today focus on neighborhoods, and they show us that the differences in victimization and offending rates between groups may have more to do with neighborhood and community conditions than with race itself. Where people live in neighborhoods of concentrated disadvantage, victimization and offending rates are high. When researchers compare similar neighborhoods of different races, the racial differences seem to disappear.[29]

Stereotypes and Criminal Profiles

Most people of all races and ethnic groups are never convicted of a crime, but stereotypes can work to brand all members of some groups with suspicion. These stereotypes may have their roots in past biases, but they also can be reinforced through broadcast news and newspaper reports. A team of researchers at the University of California at Los Angeles has found that blacks and Hispanics are overrepresented in TV news depictions of violent crime, while whites are overrepresented in stories involving nonviolent crime.[30] Unfortunately, these stereotypes work their way into law enforcement through the use of criminal profiles, putting an undue burden on innocent members of these groups (Figure 1.12). A particularly clear example of this phenomenon is found in a study of Maryland state troopers and the searches they made of motorists on Interstate 95 several years ago. On this particular stretch of highway, motorists were found to be speeding equally across races. Black motorists, for example, constituted 17 percent of the motorists and 17.5 percent of the speed-

FIGURE 1.12

A clear example of criminal profiling is the practice of searching a disproportionate number of black motorists stopped for traffic offenses.

© Dale Stockton

IN THE NEWS

A HUMAN PERSPECTIVE

N.J. REPORT ADMITS RACIAL PROFILING

Complaints that state troopers target blacks and Hispanics along the heavily traveled New Jersey Turnpike are "real, not imagined," according to a report issued by the state's attorney general.

The report, released Tuesday, concludes that even though the state police have no policy condoning the practice known as racial profiling, it does exist—and was fostered in part by ambiguous rules.

"There is no question racial profiling exists at some level," Gov. Christie Whitman said. "These findings are distressing and disturbing. Minorities deserve the assurance they will be treated no differently than any other motorist."

The report, commissioned by state Attorney General Peter Verniero, stresses "the great majority of state troopers are honest, dedicated professionals."

But the force's command structure needs to institute policy changes to end a culture that encourages using race as a reason to stop motorists, the report says.

While six out of 10 motorists stopped are white, minorities are far more likely to be subjected to searches and aggressive treatment by troopers, the report said. Statistics show that 77.2 percent of motorist searches were of blacks or Hispanics, and only 21.4 percent were of white motorists.

"Minority motorists have been treated differently than non-minority motorists during the course of traffic stops on the New Jersey Turnpike," the report says. "We conclude the problem of disparate treatment is real—not imagined."

The U.S. Justice Department also has been investigating racial profiling allegations against New Jersey's state police. Similar accusations have been made in Florida, Maryland, Connecticut and elsewhere along the Interstate 95 corridor. The findings in the report confirm what many civil rights activists said they have known for years.

"We do not believe that any reasonable person in New Jersey is surprised at all today to hear this acknowledgment," said the Rev. Reginald Rackson, executive director of the Black Ministers Council of New Jersey. "Now, however, comes the hard and difficult part, and that is the process of ending racial profiling."

Source: *The New York Times*, April 21, 1999. Reprinted with permission of The Associated Press.

---

ers. But black motorists were the subject of 409 of the 533 searches made by the police looking for contraband.[31]

The police might justify such practices on the ground that blacks are more likely to be carrying contraband. And the statistics show this to be true: The police found contraband in 33 percent of the searches of black motorists and in 22 percent of the searches of white motorists. However, blacks had a 50 percent higher chance of being found with contraband, but were searched more than 400 percent more often. The result is that 274 innocent black motorists were searched, while only 76 innocent white motorists were searched. The New Jersey State Police were also accused of racial profiling and the governor admitted that it was occurring (see "In the News: N.J. Report Admits Racial Profiling").

Disparities in Conviction Rates

The combination of higher crime rates and higher levels of police attention produce disproportionate numbers of arrests among some groups. Arrest rates for violent crimes among Asian Americans are about half of that among white Americans. Rates for Native Americans are about one and a half times higher than for whites, and rates for blacks are about five times higher than for whites. Again, as with crime, the arrest rate for whites may be low, but there are so many whites that they account for 55 percent of all arrests for violent crime.[32]

But then what happens? Here is the problem that has attracted more research than any other area under discussion today. Black Americans account for fewer than half of the arrests for violent crimes, but they account for just over half of the convictions and approximately 60 percent of the prison admissions.[33] In 2000, the chance that a black male born in the United States would go to prison in his lifetime—not reform school, not a few days or weeks in jail, but state or federal prison following conviction of a felony and a sentence of more than a year—was more than 28.5 percent. The corresponding chance for a Hispanic male was 16 percent, and for a white male, 4.4 percent.[34]

A similar pattern of disproportionate representation of black and Hispanic Americans appears in juvenile detention facilities, where, in 1994, 43 percent of juveniles were black, 19 percent were Hispanic, and 35 percent were white.[35] These are national figures, but in many individual juvenile and adult institutions the figures are even more stark, as geography and classification systems increase the segregation and concentration of minority inmates. How has this happened? Is this simply the result of fair-minded prosecutors and courts applying the law to disproportionate arrests, or is there bias at work at these later stages of the justice process?

Researchers have looked carefully for evidence of bias, reaching different conclusions. Some of the disparity we see when we visit these institutions is clearly explained by differences in arrest charges, and much more is explained by differences in the prior records of those convicted.

There is no evidence of disparity that stretches across the justice system as a whole when we consider index crimes. But studies of individual jurisdictions and specific parts of the court process do find some evidence of race bias in a significant number of cases. The most we can say is that when crime type and prior record are taken into account, black defendants in some jurisdictions are more likely to receive prison sentences than are white defendants. In addition, there is some evidence that race influences detention and placement decisions in juvenile justice processing.[36] The problems we encounter in this research were illustrated in a recent study of sentencing disparity of Native Americans in Arizona. After accounting for prior felony records and other factors, researchers found that Native Americans received longer sentences than whites only for robbery and burglary, while whites received significantly longer sentences for homicide than did Native Americans.[37]

Finally, in considering the work of the justice system itself, the special case of drug offenses needs to be considered separately. Asian-American youth report very low drug use compared with other groups. Black youth consistently report lower rates of drug use than whites; Hispanic youth report more use than black youth, but less than white youth.[38] Yet police activity, new criminal legislation, special courts, and longer sentences were all brought to bear in the late 1980s against the use and sale of drugs, particularly crack cocaine. Whatever one believes about the rationality of the decision to create special, harsher penalties for crack cocaine, the concentration of these sentences on black defendants is striking. For example, of the drug defendants sentenced for powdered cocaine use in U.S. district courts during the 1995 federal fiscal year, 35 percent were black, 37 percent were Hispanic, and 21 percent were white. In contrast, of those sentenced for crack cocaine use, 86 percent were black, 9 percent were Hispanic, and fewer than 5 percent were white.[39]

Strengthening Diversity within the Criminal Justice System

If these biases were eliminated from the justice system, would we still have a problem? If the police abandoned the use of offensive stereotypes, if the remnants of institutional bias were driven from the courts, would the justice system deserve and win respect across lines of race and ethnicity? Or is the sheer volume of black and Hispanic prisoners in America a problem in its own right?

There is little empirical evidence on this, but it is a question worth considering. Respect for the justice system can be won or lost not just in its decisions, but in who is making them. Slow but real progress has been made in strengthening diversity within the entire criminal justice system, with more minority members now serving as police officers, judges, prosecutors, and correctional officers throughout the United States (see Figure 1.13).

CTQ
In what ways do you believe the criminal justice system has become more diversified? In what ways is it less diversified?

DECLINE IN VIOLENT CRIMES

The incidence of violent crime plummeted nearly 15 percent in 2000, the steepest one-year drop since the federal government began keeping track in 1973. That translated into

FIGURE 1.13

An African American judge is researching the law for an upcoming criminal trial. Racial and ethnic diversity in the criminal justice system is important because it provides greater assurance to minority defendants they will be treated with equal justice under the law.

Courtesy Elena Rooraid/PhotoEdit.

one million fewer violent crimes in 2000 and in 1999, according to the department's National Crime Victimization Survey.

Property crime, which comprises three-fourths of all offenses, dropped 10 percent according to the Bureau of Statistics. Data for 2000 indicate that the homicide rate dropped 1.1 percent from 1999—down from 15,533 to 15,362.

From 1993 to 2000, rapes dropped 60 percent, aggravated assaults fell 52.5 percent, and motor vehicle theft dropped 52.4 percent. As for those victimized, the racial group that saw the biggest drop from 1993 to 2000 was Hispanics (down an average of 5.6 percent per year); in terms of gender, the number of males who were victims of violent crime dropped an average of 4.6 percent per year.

Decreases affected nearly every demographic group in the survey—males, females, whites, blacks, Hispanics, non-Hispanics, and 12- to 24-year-olds. The only groups not seeing significant drops in violence were people of "other races" for whom there was no measurable change, and people with annual household incomes of at least $75,000, which dropped only slightly.

Although two-thirds of the violent crimes (67 percent) involved a weapon, rape and sexual assault victims were least likely to be threatened or harmed by an armed assailant.[40]

Decline in the Proportion of Young Males

During the period of the late 1980s and early 1990s there was a dramatic decline in the proportion of young males—age 15 to 24—in the general population. This is a very important factor because this group is most inclined to commit violent crimes. In addition, during the mid-1980s and continuing into the early 1990s the weapons involved in settling young people's disputes shifted dramatically from fists and knives to handguns. The growth in homicide of young people, which accounted for the entire growth of homicide during this entire period, was all due to handguns.

Tougher Sentencing

The advent of tougher sentencing guidelines results in getting more felons off the streets and keeping them off the streets longer. Over a period of time a relatively small population of repeat offenders is responsible for a disproportionate share of crimes. Many

WEB

For more information on declining crime rates, visit
http://www.cnn.com/2001/LAW/06/13/crime.report/index.html.

states now require inmates to serve as much as 85 percent of their sentence before being eligible for parole; many others have passed habitual criminal statutes that require people who have been convicted of and served time for multiple felony offenses to receive enhanced punishment for the current crime or mandatory life terms without hope of parole. These stiffer sentences essentially keep the individuals in prison well into a chronological age at which they are statistically less inclined to commit violent crimes if and when they are released.

Changes in the Drug Market

Explanations of recent homicide trends that emphasize the role changes in drug markets are promising for several reasons. First, they are essentially symmetrical: They count for both increases and declines in violence. Rates of serious violence, including homicide, went up during the rise of the crack epidemic and have been dropping during the decline. As the crack epidemic spread in the mid- to late 1980s, so did the danger around inner-city drug markets, driving up the incentive for more youths to arm themselves in an increasingly threatening environment and leading to a general diffusion of guns among young people. As the crack epidemic began to abate early in the 1990s and as police became more aggressive about confiscating youths' guns, firearms violence fell as well.[41]

A Moderate Unemployment Rate

Some of the recent declines of the homicide rate also appear to be related to economic expansion starting in the early 1990s, which has resulted in employment opportunities for racial minorities, teenagers, and high school dropouts—groups that participated disproportionately in the rise of crack markets and criminal violence during the growth period.[42] However, with the economic downturn these past few years, this trend could possibly be reversed. Only time will tell.

Community Policing and Other Law-Enforcement-Related Factors

Starting in the mid-1990s, the concept of **community policing** started to become the dominant philosophy of many police departments. This concept, which is discussed in much greater detail in Chapter 5, "Police Operations," is one in which the police department establishes a closer working relationship with its citizens. The only problem is that cities that have incorporated this philosophy as well as those that have not have both seen dramatic decreases in violent crime. It has also been suggested that a combination of many other factors are at work, including more police officers, common-sense laws requiring background checks on gun purchases, legislation banning assault weapons, practical partnership between law enforcement and the communities they serve, crime prevention programs, and a host of effective comprehensive crime strategies.[43]

All of these factors no doubt contributed in some way to the dramatic decrease in violent crimes. However, some people suggest that we may just be enjoying a lull and that a future crime wave is possible.

FUTURE CRIME WAVE

Thirty-nine million youngsters started entering their teenage years in the late 1990s and early 2000s—and these individuals are the most crime-prone. One noted criminologist, James Allen Fox, has suggested several reasons why teenagers are more violent today, including access to weapons, lack of parental supervision, and the brutal aspects of American society: "We have a culture that glorifies violence."

Videotapes have made it easier for children to view violence. The rating system for television and the incorporation of the V-chip (a device that can block out adult-oriented programming) provide incentives for producers to include more gratuitous scenes to achieve higher ratings. Fox comments, "It's a myth that we'll be able to tune this stuff out," arguing that parents would not know how to manage the technology. He further suggests that threats of severe violence will not stem the coming tide: "Many kids face violence and death in the classroom by their peers." As far as they are concerned, the criminal justice system might as well take a number and stand in line with all the other people who want to get them. "It might make us feel better that an offender is getting a hard sentence," he continues, "but that's not accomplishing anything. We want to put him in an environment that is therapeutic." Given that many working parents cannot afford child care, Fox thinks government and corporations should develop programs that keep teens engaged rather than try to hold parents responsible for their children's crimes.[44]

WEB

For more information on theories of a possible future crime wave, visit http://www.ncvc.org/Infolink/info11.htm, http://www.ncpa.org/~ncpa/studies/s219/s219c.html#reduce, http://www.ncpa.org/~ncpa/studies/s229/s229.htm, http://www.newswise.com/articles/2002/3/Crime.asa.html, and http://www.urban.org/crime/module/butts/youth-crime-drop.html.

SUMMARY

Crime in American society is not new. However, attitudes toward crime and the treatment of criminals have varied over the years. There were times when punishment and torture were the order of the day, and other times when spirited redemption was considered the best way to reform criminals. However, although attitudes and treatments change, crime is still present. Certain psychological and social effects of crime can have a profound effect on people. Interestingly, most people fear crimes that occur less frequently—namely, homicide, forcible rape, and aggravated assault. Victims of such crimes are often attacked by a family member, close friend, or personal acquaintance. To a great extent, the public fear of crime is directly related to the coverage given to it by the media, especially for high-profile crimes committed by strangers.

In this chapter we have also discussed a full range of crimes, including conventional crimes (criminal homicide, forcible rape, robbery, aggravated assault, burglary, larceny theft, motor vehicle theft, and arson), economic crimes, telecommunications crimes (hacking), illegal bulletin boards, and misuse of telephone systems.

Organized crime (also known as syndicated crime) is a business that provides illegal but desirable goods and serves the noncriminal public. Traditionally, organized crime meant the Italian-American Mafia, which emerged during Prohibition. However, there is considerable evidence that the Mafia is in decline, in part because of its conservatism, action by the federal government that resulted in the arrest and conviction of high-ranking Mafia chieftains, and inter-Mafia warfare that has resulted in the murder of high-ranking Mafia figures. The void left by the Mafia is now being filled by new ethnic groups in the United States, mostly from eastern Asia. Russian organized crime has attracted increased concern and attention around the world from law enforcement agencies, the mass media, and the public in general.

Terrorist crime has clearly dominated the attention of law enforcement and the public since the terrorist attacks of September 11, 2001. Terrorism includes both violent acts and threats of violence. It lumps together acts committed by criminal psychotics, self-proclaimed patriots, and others with extreme ideological views.

In this chapter we have also discussed the relationship between drugs and crime. Specifically, we have examined mood- and mind-altering (psychotropic) drugs and why for more than a century the American criminal justice system has for better or worse been at the center of drug-control efforts.

Structurally, the criminal justice system can be described in terms of its component agencies, namely the police, courts, and corrections. Functionally, the compo-

CTQ

What reason has been suggested by one criminologist as to why teenagers are more violent today? Do you agree or disagree?

nents of this system usually work well together, at other times they are in conflict. Nevertheless, it is generally agreed among scholars that there are eighteen steps to the criminal justice system process: reporting the crime, prearrest investigation, arrest, booking, postarrest investigation, decision to charge, filing the complaint, first appearance, preliminary hearing, grand jury review, filing the indictment or information, arraignment on the information or the indictment, pretrial motions, criminal trial, sentencing, appeals, postconviction remedies, and parole or parole revocation hearing.

We have also addressed the issues of race, crime, and the administration of justice, which include the patterns of crime victimization, stereotypes and criminal profiles, disparities in conviction rates, and the ways in which the criminal justice system can strengthen itself through diversity.

The incidence rates of the most serious crimes have dropped dramatically, and a number of explanations have been provided, including a decline in the proportion of young males, tougher sentencing, changes in the drug market, a moderate unemployment rate, community policing, and other law-enforcement-related factors. Lastly, we discussed the possibilities of a future crime wave: Thirty-nine million youngsters entered their teen years in the late 1900s and early 2000s. Criminologists suggest that this does not bode well for the future, since this is the age group which is most crime-prone. However, only time will tell if this will indeed be the result.

DISCUSSION AND REVIEW

1. Is violent crime more prevalent today than a hundred years ago?
2. Which types of crimes are most intensely feared?
3. Which conventional crimes are considered crimes against the person and which are considered crimes against property?
4. Discuss Sutherland's fourfold classification of white-collar and economic crimes.
5. What are the major types of telecommunication crimes?
6. What are the functions of federal cybercrime units?
7. What evidence is there of the Mafia's decline?
8. What does the future of organized crime look like?
9. What is terrorism? What group has been identified responsible for the terrorist attacks of September 11, 2001?
10. Who is the leader of the group responsible for the September 11 attacks and what is the source of his money?
11. Why has most psychotropic drug use become legally defined as a criminal act?
12. What are the eighteen steps of the criminal justice system?
13. How do social scientists explain the growing mistrust in the criminal justice system by people of color?
14. In general, what do the patterns of crime victimization in the United States look like?
15. What are the results of racial profiling when used in stopping traffic motorists?
16. What two state police agencies were specifically discussed as they relate to racial profiling in stopping motorists, and what was learned as a result?
17. What do available statistics show regarding racial disparities in conviction rates?
18. The incidence rates for the most serious crimes have dropped dramatically in the past few years. What explanations for this have been provided?
19. What are the implications of having 39 million youngsters enter their teen years in the late 1990s and early 2000s?

CHAPTER RESOURCES

IN THE MEDIA

Video

ABC News Video: *Criminal Injustice*
A&E Videos: *American Justice*
ABC News Video: *Guns*
CNN Today Video: *Corrections*, Vol. 1: segment 9, "Overcoming Crime-Generative Factors"
CNN Today Video: *Criminology*, Vol. 4: segment 9, "Restorative Justice"
CNN Today Video: *Introduction to Criminal Justice*, Vol. 3: segment 4, "Driving While Black"
FHH Video: *Racial Profiling and Law Enforcement*
NIJ Video: *Drugs: Military Interdiction*
NIJ Video: *Gun Control*
NIJ Video: *Jobs and Crime*
NIJ Video: *Predicting Criminality*

Film

Arlington Road (1999)
City Hall (1996)
Copycat (1995)
Entrapment (1999)
A Few Good Men (1999)
The General's Daughter (1999)
Heat (1995)
The Insider (1999)
Mississippi Burning (1988)
Murder at 1600 (1997)
The Negotiator (1999)
The Pelican Brief (1993)
Pulp Fiction (1996)
Seven (1995)
The Siege (1998)
The Spanish Prisoner (1998)
A Time to Kill (1996)
True Crimes (1998)
U.S. Marshals (1998)
The Usual Suspects (1995)
The Verdict (1982)
Witness (1985)

Television

The Agency
The American Embassy
American Justice
America's Most Wanted
Boomtown
Cold Cases
COPS
Crossing Jordan
CSI
The District
Exhibit A
Fastlane
First Monday
The Fugitive
JAG
Judging Amy
Law and Order
The New Detectives
NYPD Blue
The Practice
The Verdict

IN THE LITERATURE

Books

C. BECCARIA, *Crimes and Punishment*. Indianapolis, Ind.: Bobbs-Merrill, 1993.

J. EINSTEIN AND H. JACOB, *Felony Justice*. Boston: Little, Brown, 1977.

FEDERAL BUREAU OF INVESTIGATION, *Crime in the United States*. Washington, D.C.: U.S. Government Printing Office, 1993.

R. FLEMMING AND P. NARDULLI, *The Craft of Justice*. Philadelphia: University of Pennsylvania Press, 1992.

P. HERBERT, *The Limits of the Criminal Sanction*. Stanford, Calif.: Stanford University Press, 1975.

J. INCIARDI, *The War on Drugs III: The Continuing Saga of the Mysteries and Miseries of Intoxication, Addiction, Crime, and Public Policy*. Needham, Mass.: Allyn & Bacon, 2002.

V. KAPPELER, G. POTTER, AND M. VICTOR, *The Mythology of Crime and Criminal Justice*. Prospect Heights, Ill.: Waveland, 1993.

S. WALKER, *Popular Justice*. New York: Oxford University Press, 1998.

S. WALKER, *Sense and Nonsense about Crime and Drug Policy*, 3rd ed. Belmont, Calif.: Wadsworth, 1994.

J. WILSON AND J. PETERSILIA, eds., *Crime*. San Francisco: Institute for Contemporary Studies Press, 1995.

K. WRIGHT, *The Great American Crime Myth*. Westport, Conn.: Greenwood Press, 1987.

F. ZIRING AND G. HAWKINS, *Crime Is Not the Problem: Lethal Violence in America*. New York: Oxford University Press, 1997.

ENDNOTES

1. President's Commission on Law Enforcement and Administration of Justice, *The Challenge of Crime in a Free Society*. Washington, D.C.: U.S. Government Printing Office, 1967, p. 22.

2. C. Silberman, *Criminal Violence, Criminal Justice*. New York: Random House, 1978, p. 30.

3. H. Edelherts, *The Nature, Impact, and Prosecution of White-Collar Crime*. Washington, D.C.: U.S. Government Printing Office, 1970, p.3.

4. Jerry Zremske, *The Buffalo News*, Knight-Ridder Business News, July 25, 2002.

5. R. Taylor, "Computer Crimes." In C. R. Swanson, N. C. Chamelin, and L. Territo, *Criminal Investigation*. New York: McGraw-Hill, 2002, p. 518.

6. Telecommunication Advisors, Inc., *Toll Fraud and Tele-abuse*. Richardson, Tex.: AT&T Wireless Service, 1998, Chapter 2.

7. J. Fialka, "The Latest Flurries at Weather Bureau: Scattered Hacking," *The Wall Street Journal*, October 10, 1994, pp. A1, A17.

8. *The New York Times*, June 2, 1999.

9. M. Meyer and A. Underwood, "Crimes of the Net," *Newsweek*, November 14, 1994, p. 47.

10. Ibid.

11. C. Buress, "On-Line Nudes Exposed at Livermore Lab," *San Francisco Chronicle*, July 12. 1994, p. A3.

12. J. Steinhauer, "Phreakers Take a Swipe at Turnstiles and Nynex," *The New York Times*, August 15, 1994, p. B3.

13. Ibid.

14. C. Conly and T. McEwen, "Computer Crime," *NIJ Reports*, no. 218 (January–February 1990), p. 3.

15. W. Flanagan and B. McMenamin, "Why Cybercrooks Love Cellular," *Forbes*, December 21, 1992, p. 189.

16. P. Reuter, "The Decline of the American Mafia," *Public Interest*, Summer 1995, pp. 88–89.

17. Ibid.

18. Reprinted with permission from *Counterterrorism for Emergency Responders* by Robert Burke, 2000. Copyright CRC Press, Boca Raton, Florida.

19. S. Paromchick, "Russian Organized Crime in Russia and the United States," 2002.

20. R. Burke, *Counter Terrorism for Emergency Responders*. Boca Raton, Fla.: Lewis Publishers, 2000. Much of this discussion on terrorism was adapted with permission from this source, pp. 18–33.

21. Anthrax is caused by a bacteria found in soil that normally infects livestock, including cattle and sheep. It is rarely contagious; infection requires direct contact with spores. If these spores are inhaled, fever, difficulty breathing and death occurs within days. The treatment for this is antibiotics or vaccine.

22. C. Stone, "Race, Crime and the Administration of Justice," *National Institute of Justice Journal*, April 1999, pp. 26–32. This discussion was adapted from a paper presented to President Clinton's Advisory Board on Race on May 19, 1998, at George Washington University in Washington, D.C., for the board's discussion of race, crime, and the administration of justice. The presentation was commissioned to provide a brief overview of the issues and available facts.

23. D. Carter, "Hispanic Perception of Police Performance: An Empirical Assessment," *Journal of Criminal Justice*, vol. 13 (1985), pp. 487–500.

24. *Gallup Poll Monthly*, October 1995.

25. C. Stone, analysis of various data provided by the U.S. Department of Justice, Bureau of Justice Statistics.

26. Bureau of Justice Statistics, *Criminal Victimization Rates in the United States, 1994*. Washington, D.C.: U.S. Department of Justice, Bureau of Justice Statistics, May 1997.

27. J. Song, "Attitudes of Chinese Immigrant and Vietnamese Refugees toward Law Enforcement in the United States," *Justice Quarterly*, vol. 9, no. 4 (1992), pp. 703–719 (NCJ 143561).

28. D. Elliot, "Serious Violent Offenders: Onset, Developmental Course, and Termination—The American Society of Criminology 1993 Presidential Address," *Criminology*, vol. 32, no. 1 (1994), p. 8.

29. R. Sampson, W. Raudenbush, and F. Earls, "Neighborhoods and Violent Crime: A Multilevel Study of Collective Efficacy," *Science*, vol. 277 (August 15, 1997), p. 2 (NCJ 173119).

30. F. Gilliam, Jr., D. Iyengar, A. Simon, and O. Wrights, "Crime in Black and White: The Violent Scary World of Local News," *Press/Politics*, vol. 1, no. 3 (1996), pp. 6–23.

31. This discussion of stops by Maryland state troopers is based on statistics published in Katheryn K. Russell, *The Color of Crime* (New York: New York University Press, 1998), pp. 41–42. Since the presentation, additional data from this study shows that black motorists were no more likely to be found with contraband than white motorists, indicating that the burden of this enforcement practice falls disproportionately on innocent motorists.

32. Federal Bureau of Investigation, *Uniform Crime Reports*. Washington, D.C.: U.S. Department of Justice, Federal Bureau of Investigation, 1996.

33. C. Stone, analysis of various data provided by the U.S. Department of Justice, Bureau of Justice Statistics.

34. T. Bonczar and A. J. Beck, *Lifetime Likelihood of Going to State or Federal Prison*. Washington, D.C.: U.S. Department of Justice, Office of Justice Programs, March 1997 (NCT 160092).

35. M. Roscoe and R. Mortin, *Disproportionate Minority Confinement*. Washington, D.C.: U.S. Department of Justice, Office of Juvenile Justice and Delinquency Prevention, April 1994.

36. R. Sampson and J. L. Lauritsen, "Racial and Ethnic Disparities in Crime and Criminal Justice in the United States." In Michael Tonry, ed., *Ethnicity, Crime, and Immigration: Comparative and Cross-National Perspectives*. Chicago: University of Chicago Press, 1997, p. 335 (NCJ 165176).

37. A. Alvarez and R. D. Bachman, "American Indians and Sentencing Disparity: An Arizona Test," *Journal of Criminal Justice*, vol. 24 (1996), pp. 549–561.

38. Sampson and Lauritsen, op. cit.

39. National Institute on Drug Abuse, *Drug Use among Racial/Ethnic Minorities*. Washington, D.C.: U.S. Department of Health and Human Services, National Institute on Drug Abuse, 1995 (Pub. No. 95-30008).

40. "U.S. reports Steepest Annual Violent Crime Drop," CNN.com Law Center, June 14, 2001. Available online at http://www.cnn.com/2001/LAW/06/13/crime.report/index.html.

41. Ibid.

42. Ibid.

43. *Law Enforcement News* (June 30, 1999), pp. 1, 6.

44. P. Yam, "Catching a Coming Crime Wave," *Scientific American*, vol. 274 (June 6, 1996), pp. 40–44.

2

THE SUBSTANTIVE CRIMINAL LAW

Chapter Outline

Criminal Law versus Civil Law
Norms and Socialization
  Social Sanctions
  Normative Variations
  Social Values and Law
  The Value Consensus and Value Conflict Models
  The Value Divergence Model
  Deviance
Substantive Criminal Law
  Sources of American Substantive Criminal Law
  The Classification of Crime
Criminal Responsibility
  Actus Reus
  Mens Rea
  Concurrence of *Actus Reus* and *Mens Rea*
  Absence of Attendant Circumstances That Would Otherwise Negate Criminal Liability
  The Criminal Act That Must Have Caused the Illegal Harm
The Major Individual Crimes of American Substantive Criminal Law
Homicide
  Murder
  Voluntary Manslaughter
  Involuntary Manslaughter
Crimes against Persons
  Battery
  Hate Crimes
  Assault
  Rape
  Sexual Harassment Is Not a Crime
  False Imprisonment
  Kidnapping

Crimes against Habitation
  Burglary
  Arson
Crimes against Property—The Acquisition Offenses
  Larceny
  Robbery
  Embezzlement
  Obtaining Property by False Pretense or Fraud
  Extortion (Blackmail)
  Receiving Stolen Property
Consensual Crimes
Crimes against Morality
  Historical Roots
  Fornication
  Adultery
  Illicit Cohabitation
  Bigamy
  Incest
  Sodomy
  Prostitution
Modern Crimes
  Computer Crime
  Identity Theft
  Stalking
Traffic Offenses That Are Crimes
  Racing
  Reckless Driving
  Hit and Run
  Vehicular Homicide
  DUI/DWI
  Multiple Offenses, Classified as "Road Rage"
Environmental Crimes
  The Environmental Regulation Paradox
Summary

Key TERMS

actus reus, p. 49
adequate provocation, p. 53
administrative law, p. 47
adultery, p. 75
aggravated battery, p. 57
arson, p. 67
assault, p. 62
battery, p. 56
bigamy, p. 75
burglary, p. 66
capital felony, p. 49
carnal knowledge, p. 63
causation, p. 51
civil law, p. 39
common law, p. 46
consensual crimes, p. 73
conversion, p. 70
crime, p. 38
crimes against habitation, p. 66
criminal infraction, p. 49
criminal law, p. 39
criminal procedure, p. 46
criminal responsibility, p. 46
criminally negligent homicide, p. 56
date rape, p. 63
deviance, p. 44
domestic violence, p. 57
ecclesiastical crimes, p. 74
elements, p. 51
embezzlement, p. 70
environmental crime, p. 82
extortion, p. 72
false imprisonment, p. 65
false pretense, p. 71
felony, p. 49
felony murder rule, p. 53
fornication, p. 75
harassment, p. 78
hate crime, p. 61
hit and run, p. 81

homicide, p. 52
identity theft, p. 78
illicit cohabitation, p. 75
incest, p. 75
intent to commit a felony, p. 53
intent to inflict great bodily injury, p. 53
intent to kill, p. 53
involuntary manslaughter, p. 56
kidnapping, p. 65
larceny, p. 68
malice aforethought, p. 53
mens rea, p. 49
misdemeanor, p. 49
misdemeanor manslaughter, p. 56
murder, p. 52
norms, p. 42
prostitute, p. 76
racing, p. 80
rape, p. 62
rape shield statutes, p. 63
reasonable provocation, p. 53
receiving stolen property, p. 72
reckless driving, p. 81
recklessness, p. 53
road rage, p. 82
robbery, p. 69
sexual harassment, p. 64
sexually neutral offenses, p. 63
social sanctions, p. 42
socialization, p. 42
sodomy, p. 75
stalking, p. 78
stare decisis, p. 47
statutory rape, p. 63
strict-liability offenses, p. 50
substantive criminal law, p. 46
value conflict model, p. 43
value consensus model, p. 43
value divergence model, p. 43

Courtesy Anthony Redpath/CORBIS.

Legal scholars define a **crime** as "an act or an omission that is prohibited by law for the protection of the general public, the violation of which is prosecuted by the State in its own name, and is punishable by death, incarceration, fine, restriction on liberty, or some combination of these."[1] Criminal justice authorities and criminologists, however, are likely to find fault with such a definition. For one thing, crime is relative. That is, behaviors covered by laws and statutes are not fixed and unchanging but vary according to time, place, and circumstance. What the law says is illegal today may not be the same as what the law said was illegal yesterday—or what it may say is illegal tomorrow. Moreover, legal definitions of crimes would be unduly restrictive because they would limit the study of criminal behavior to that of people who have been officially adjudicated (judged) "criminal" or "delinquent"; hence, much behavior that may be relevant to understanding and explaining criminal behavior might never be examined.

A significant point to understand here is that the definition of criminal behavior is derived from the social process and has little to do with the individual criminal. While recognizing the need on legal grounds to deal with crime as law-violating behavior, criminal justice professionals and criminologists find it worthwhile to consider criminal conduct as part of a much broader spectrum of "deviant behavior." Deviance involves behavior that varies or diverges from social norms—the rules that regulate conduct within a group or society. Most people tend to be "socially invisible" within their communities; deviance means, among other things, that an individual or group becomes visible to the majority when the deviant behavior elicits a societal reaction. The motivation of an individual or group explains how they can transcend the moral barrier of becoming a lawbreaker and the fear of possible punishment.

CRIMINAL LAW VERSUS CIVIL LAW

Criminal law, as opposed to noncriminal law, administrative law, or civil law, is the branch of jurisprudence that deals with offenses committed against the safety and order of the state. As such, criminal law relates to actions that are considered so dangerous, or potentially so, that they threaten the welfare of society as a whole. It is for this reason that the government brings an action against the accused in criminal cases.

In addition to criminal law, another body of law regulates the conduct of individuals and groups. When one individual commits a private wrong against another, civil law offers certain remedies. The state declares itself a victim less often in civil cases than it does in criminal cases. **Civil law** concerns include torts, breaches of contracts, contested wills, trusts, worker's compensation, insurance claims, property contests, and divorces. In a civil law violation, one individual sues another individual or organizational entity. The person bringing the action is called the plaintiff; the individual being sued is called the defendant. Unlike in criminal law, where the state determines whether to go forward with a case, in civil law the plaintiff can choose to drop the suit at any time. Civil law is also unlike criminal law in that the consequence for a defendant who has been successfully sued normally is that he or she incurs only the loss of money. In contrast, whenever a defendant is convicted in criminal law, one major consequence is the deprivation of personal liberty by imprisonment. See Figure 2.1 for a comparison of criminal and civil law.

In many jurisdictions throughout the United States, the same court hears both criminal law and civil law cases. Some scholars suggest that this is a primary cause of courtroom overcrowding and of delays in the litigations of both criminal and civil cases. The increase in the number of civil lawsuits filed in the United States in the past thirty years certainly lends credence to this suggestion.

In many instances the civil law and the criminal law overlap each other. Hence, certain actions taken by one party against another can be litigated in both civil court and criminal court. One example of such behavior is assault and battery. For example, suppose that during a dance at a university club, a fight over a woman breaks out between two college seniors. The senior who initiates the fight knocks the other's teeth out and also breaks his arm. The remedies for the victim here lay in both the criminal law and civil law. The purposes of both of these two types of laws is expressed in Table 2.1.

CTQ
What is the difference between a criminal act and a morally unethical act?

WEB
For more information on criminal law, **visit our Web site,** www.prenhall.com/territo.

WEB
For more information and a concise summary on criminal law, **visit our Web site,** www.prenhall.com/territo.

CTQ
What types of behavior does your society label *criminal* that you believe should be considered *deviant*?

CTQ
What types of behavior does your society label *deviant* that you believe should be legally defined as *criminal*?

FIGURE 2.1

Similarities and Differences in Criminal Law versus Civil Law

SIMILARITIES
- Both criminal law and civil law seek to control behavior
- Both impose sanctions against the defendant
- Similar areas of legal action exist, such as personal battery and environmental offenses

DIFFERENCES

Criminal Law
- A crime is an offense against the general public
- Sanctions associated with criminal law are deprivation of liberty, incarceration, and death
- The right to go forward in litigating or to drop a case belongs exclusively to the state
- The state must prove its case "beyond a reasonable doubt"
- If fines are imposed, they go to the state treasury

Civil Law
- Civil law involves litigation against another person for a private wrong
- The damages associated with civil infractions are exclusively monetary
- The individual alone has the choice whether to bring forth litigation and may drop it at any time
- The plaintiff upon victory receives only monetary damages as compensation for the harm done to him or her
- The burden of proof is "a preponderance of the evidence"

TABLE 2.1 — What Does Law Do? The Purposes of the Law

Laws maintain order in society	Laws promote orderly social change
Laws regulate human interaction	Laws sustain individual rights
Laws enforce moral beliefs	Laws redress wrongs
Laws define the economic environment	Laws identify evildoers
Laws support the powerful	Laws mandate punishment and retribution

CTQ Compare and contrast civil law and criminal law.

CTQ List five different crimes for which the victim of the crime could also sue the perpetrator in civil court. Explain why.

CTQ Can you explain the two seemingly inconsistent verdicts in the O. J. Simpson criminal trial and the O. J. Simpson civil trial? How are they reconcilable by understanding the differences between civil law and criminal law?

In criminal law, hypothetically, the college senior who was injured could have his attacker prosecuted by the state on charges of aggravated battery and possibly mayhem. In civil law, he could personally sue his attacker for compensatory damages for reimbursement of his medical expenses, his loss of wages, and his pain and suffering. Also, in the civil action, the defendant may have to pay a significant sum of money for punitive damages because of the intentional act he perpetrated. Thus, whenever the civil law and criminal law overlap, victims may receive the satisfaction of having their attackers incarcerated as well as possibly being awarded money damages by a jury to compensate them for their injuries. Likewise, the plaintiff requires significantly less proof (a *preponderance of the evidence*, or the burden to persuade the jury with 50.001 percent certainty that the defendant committed the behavior charged) to win a civil case. On the other hand, if the state is to win a criminal case it must submit stronger evidence that proves the defendant committed the crime *beyond a reasonable doubt* (which means that the state's evidence must persuade a jury to more than a 90 percent certainty of the defendant's guilt). Litigating the same case in these two different forms often yield opposite results.

The O. J. Simpson criminal and civil trials (which rendered apparently opposite verdicts) are the best example that illustrates this overlap (See "In the News: Simpson Remake"). For a comparison of the two trials, see Table 2.2.

TABLE 2.2 — A Comparison of the Two O. J. Simpson Trials, Criminal and Civil

Jurors
Criminal 10 women, 2 men; 9 black, 2 white, 1 Hispanic
Civil 7 women, 5 men; 9 white, 1 black, 1 Hispanic, 1 black and Asian

Days of Testimony
Criminal Prosecution 99, defense 34
Civil Plaintiffs 29, defense 14

Witnesses
Criminal Prosecution, 72, defense 54
Civil Plaintiffs 73, defense 39

The criminal trial's witness list included Detective Mark Fuhrman, but not Simpson. It was the reverse in the civil trial. The civil trial included Fred Goldman, father of one of the victims.

Most Time on the Stand
Criminal Lakshmanan Sathyavagiswaran, Los Angeles County coroner, and Dennis Fung, criminalist, 9 days each
Civil O. J. Simpson, 4 days

Trial Exhibits
Criminal 857
Civil about 700

Both trials featured crime scene photos, blood drops, and a bloody glove. Pivotal evidence not in the criminal proceeding but in the civil case were 31 photographs that purportedly showed Simpson wearing shoes similar to those worn by the killer.

Estimated Cost
Criminal Prosecution, $9 million; defense, $3 million to $6 million
Civil Plaintiffs, more than $1 million; defense, $2 million

IN THE WORKPLACE

CRIMINAL JUSTICE EDUCATOR

Responsible for teaching undergraduate/graduate criminal justice courses. Candidates are typically sought for tenure-track position at the rank of assistant professor. Minimum qualifications are as follows: Ph.D. in criminal justice or criminology; qualified ABDs (those who have completed all their course requirements but not the dissertation) close to completion will be considered.

IN THE NEWS

A HUMAN PERSPECTIVE

SIMPSON REMAKE
by E. Gleick

Los Angeles Superior Court Judge Hiroshi Fujisaki ruled that no cameras will be allowed in his courtroom for the O. J. Simpson wrongful-death lawsuit. Not only that, but the attorneys in this civil case—unlike their loose-lipped counterparts who starred in the criminal proceedings—have been muzzled by a strict gag order. Courtroom sketch artists will be permitted to ply their trade, sort of: They must produce their sketches from memory after leaving court each day. "History will repeat itself," Fujisaki noted in a written order, "unless the court acts to prevent it."

Still, despite the judge's best efforts, much about the Sequel of the Century seemed like *déjà vu*. John Q. Kelley and Daniel M. Petrocelli were the lead lawyers for the families of murder victims Nicole Brown Simpson and Ronald Goldman; this legal team defeated O.J. Simpson in the civil case against him, making Simpson momentarily liable for the deaths. Nearly 350 witnesses were called, including Kato Kaelin and Mark Fuhrman, though the judge has ruled that Marcia Clark and Christopher Darden could not testify. It took four months to try the case. Simpson's criminal case lasted nine months. This trial's main event was the testimony of Simpson himself, because under civil rules he was obliged to take the stand. The former football star had underwent a grueling nine days of depositions, enduring 248 questions in a row about how he cut his hand in his Chicago hotel room the night of the murders. Though Simpson made no obvious missteps, he was not a model witness.

Fred Goldman, father of the murdered Ronald, said the civil trial is less about money than it is about "a search for justice." That's a good thing, for though the plaintiffs were victorious, Simpson has an IRS lien on his Rockingham estate and unpaid legal bills from the first trial. Thus, he won't be able to pay much in monetary damages. Also, a civil trial has a more relaxed standard for a guilty verdict—jurors need find only that a "preponderance" of the evidence points to guilt, and only nine of 12 jurors need agree.

Meanwhile, Simpson continues to live in a purgatory of presumptive guilt, heckled when he goes out, unable to make a living and fighting to retrieve a semblance of family life.

UPDATE
At the civil trial, a jury found Simpson "liable" for the deaths of Nicole Brown Simpson and Ron Goldman. However, the plaintiffs only had to prove Simpson was the killer by a "preponderance of the evidence" (persuading the jury by a 50.001 percent level of certainty), whereas in the criminal case the prosecution had to prove Simpson was the killer "beyond a reasonable doubt" (requiring the state to persuade a jury to more than a 90 percent level of certainty of this fact). Therefore, these two verdicts are *not* at all inconsistent with each other, as many commentators have suggested to the contrary. Specifically, if after reviewing approximately the same facts, for example, of both the civil case and the criminal case, a jury was 60 percent certain that Simpson was "the killer," then, due to the vast differences in the two burdens of proof in a civil trial versus a criminal trial, both of the Simpson verdicts—*liable* in the civil trial and *not guilty* in the criminal trial—are correct, legal, and, most important, consistent with each other.

Source: E. Gleick, "A Simpson Remake," *Time*, 23 September 1996, 57. © 1996 TIME Inc. Reprinted by permission.

Although one's rights of action in criminal law and civil law often overlap, most often victims of crime do not also sue their attackers. This is primarily because such a lawsuit would be a waste of time. Unlike O. J. Simpson, most criminal defendants are indigent; hence, although suing the criminal defendant might render a big jury award, there is usually no source of funds from which to collect the award. Furthermore, no debtor prisons have existed since colonial times for incarcerating indigent defendants who have lost civil lawsuits.

NORMS AND SOCIALIZATION

The **norms** of a society may be simple or elaborate, but their purpose is the same: they are rules of behavior used to protect the society against disruption and to safeguard its basic structure and values. Members of a society internalize its norms through a complex process of social learning known as **socialization.**

The principal agency of socialization, and the basic unit of society, is the family. Much of a culture is transmitted to children by informal learning within the family. Speech patterns, customs, and social values are acquired through communication between the generations. As an individual develops and matures, peer-group associations assume increasing importance in socialization, often becoming a source of sharp conflict with parental norms (especially during the adolescent years).

Informal learning from interactions with family and peer-group members is augmented by formal school learning. As agents of socialization, schools rank almost as high as the family and peer groups as a medium of societal perpetuation.

Social Sanctions

Norms are acquired and maintained by a system of reward and punishment. When parents approve of their children's actions, they reward them with a smile, a caress, a murmur of praise, or a tangible reward such as candy, cookies, or money. When children misbehave, parents mete out punishment ranging from scolding to physical chastisement.

The rewards and punishments that are incorporated into the normative structure are called **social sanctions.** Social sanctions may contain proscriptive or prescriptive elements. *Proscriptions* are statements of forbidden behavior (such as murder, rape, kidnapping, treason, and other rebellions against group authority). *Prescriptions* are statements of encouraged or reinforced behavior (such as getting married, raising children, holding down a steady job, paying taxes, and other forms of conduct that foster the common welfare).

Social sanctions promote "proper" behavior. Behavior is controlled by social norms called *folkways*. These social rules are usually enforced by mild disapproval (a cold stare, raised eyebrows, a reproving glance) or mild encouragement (a smile, applause, an approving glance). Behavior that threatens the existence of the group or is seen as necessary to the perpetuation of the group is controlled by a set of stronger norms called *mores*. Mores are enforced by more rigorous or severe expressions of social disapproval (verbal abuse, beatings, temporary ostracism) or by greater encouragement (momentary rewards, praise, testimonials, promotions).

Behavior that is not only socially unacceptable but also significantly threatens the social order and the existence of the group is controlled by criminal law. As will be discussed throughout the rest of this textbook, criminal law is enforced by the criminal justice system, which, throughout each stage of the system—be it sentencing, incarceration, probation, or parole—dramatically discourages the kinds of behavior that society has deemed criminal.

Normative Variations

Norms do not set forth a blueprint for behavior; at best, they provide a rough sketch. The institutionalized norms of social conduct never fully define concrete action. A norm is a standard (not necessarily explicit) for the course that actions *should* follow, not a description of the action that actually occurs. Norms are general; the situations within which behavior occur are specific. Hence, behavior can vary considerably around a standard.

One American subculture whose behavior varies from the institutionalized norms and social conduct of the majority are the Amish. This diversity always has been acceptable within America's norms and mores. However, even an accepted subculture such as the Amish still is held responsible when its actions conflict with society's strong mores as they are articulated in its criminal law.

Note also that modern societies are composed of diverse subcultures with different norms and standards. Some behavior that deviates from presumably general or universal norms often is considered acceptable—approved and valued within certain subcultures. A problematic example of this deviant behavior throughout the 1990s and continuing into the twenty-first century was the emerging perception within certain urban subcultures of drug dealers as heroes. Situations in which subcultural norms deviate from universal norms are considered subcultural conflicts.

Social Values and Law

In primitive or preliterate societies, rules governing normative behavior are perpetuated by word of mouth and passed from leader to leader. Eventually, normative expectations evolve into formal statements of proper behavior that are written and codified as laws. These formal statements usually express the most important societal values of the time. As statements of criminal law evolved from primitive societies, they reflected societal values that disapproved of certain forms of behavior, considering them totally unacceptable and, as a consequence, not to be tolerated within the society.

> **CTQ**
>
> Some people claim that the social values that eventually make their way into law are social values of the powerful, which may be completely opposite of the social values of the unprivileged and subcultures. Do you believe this is true?

The Value Consensus and Value Conflict Models

The relationship between social values and law has been interpreted in two sharply differing ways: the value consensus model and the value conflict model. The basic premise of the **value consensus model** is that the criminal law reflects societal values that extend beyond the interests of particular individuals or groups and can therefore be considered an expression of the social consciousness of the entire society. According to this perspective, law develops through the efforts of a unified society to preserve and protect social values. Toward this purpose, the law relies on the deliberations and rational decisions of governing bodies (such as congresses or parliaments) that incorporate the principal authority of the society.[2]

In contrast, the **value conflict model** sees dissension rather than consensus, diversity rather than homogeneity—and perennial struggle for power. Economic power bestows political power, a fact related in this wry twist on the Golden Rule: "Them that has the gold makes the rules." According to the value conflict model, "the rules" (that is, the law) become a tool used by the dominant class to maintain and enhance its power over the weak. Law is used by the state and its elitist government to promote and protect itself.[3] According to this model, through criminal law the government controls enforcement so that certain groups are singled out and labeled as "criminals" and "members of the dangerous classes."

It is difficult to accept either the value consensus model or the value conflict model as an exclusively accurate characterization of the social process underlying the development of criminal law. Despite assertions that the standards for what ought to be considered criminal conduct are a reflection of various group and class definitions, it appears that a consensus on crimes against the person (such as murder, aggravated battery, rape, and kidnapping) cuts across class lines in our society. Disagreement is more likely to be found with regard to laws proscribing gambling, abortion, prostitution, personal consumption of drugs, and homosexual behavior between consenting adults—the offenses often designated as victimless crimes.

The Value Divergence Model

A third position, called the **value divergence model,** recognizes the contributions of both the value conflict and value consensus models. It emphasizes that the United States is not a cultural monolith, but a mosaic of diverse subcultures held together by shared beliefs and social values. It further maintains that the aggregate is stronger than the forces of individuals. Yet seldom in our pluralistic society can anybody of stature claim the support and allegiance of a majority of social groups.

Makielski deals with the processes by which an interest group—"a collection of more than two people who interact on the basis of a commonly shared concern"[4]—is transformed into a pressure group that turns to the political system to press its demands. He defines interests as "the cement that binds a group together and the motivating power which impels a group into politics."[5] These economic, social, or ideological interests are the bases for structuring the policy concerns that characterize various groups. More important, the various ways in which pressure groups gain access through persuasion, mutual interest, established relationships, domination, or outright purchase provide the key to how such groups influence legislative activity initiating statutory changes in the law.

The abortion debate of the 1990s is a clear example of how pressure groups operate within the scope of criminal law. Most legal scholars thought the abortion debate ended in 1973 after the Supreme Court announced its decision that a woman's reasonable expectation of privacy gave her a constitutional right to terminate her pregnancy during the first two trimesters.[6] However, with the leadership of presidents Ronald Reagan, George Bush, and George W. Bush, the pro-life movement became revitalized, and its proponents protested in the streets of America. The debate over the recriminalization of abortion has become one of the central political/criminal law issues facing most legislators, decision makers, and judges in the first decade of the twenty-first century.

Deviance

Deviance is not a fundamental property of human behavior; rather, it is an attribute of certain kinds of conduct. It is a discretionary term in that it can be ascribed to almost any behavior departing from customary standards or expectations. The deviance of an act or an individual is relative, changeable, and a matter of degree, depending on the public's perception of, and response to, the behavior.

It has been suggested that the term *deviance* refers to conduct that the people of a group consider so dangerous or embarrassing or irritating that they bring special sanctions against people who exhibit it.[7] The problem is that, at first glance, certain behaviors seem to be obviously deviant. When facts are finally unveiled, however, the behavior seems more understandable. (See "In the News: Is Tarring and Feathering a Deviant Act?")

Another theory is that deviance is not the quality of an act a person commits, but rather a consequence of the application by others of rules and sanctions to an "offender." The deviant is one to whom that label has successfully been applied; deviant behavior is behavior that people so label.[8]

Schur seems to concur with this theory when he states that human behavior is deviant "to the extent that it comes to be viewed as involving a personally discreditable departure from a group's normative expectation and elicits interpersonal or collective reactions that serve to isolate, treat, correct, or punish individuals engaged in such behavior."[9] This definition asserts that a deviant's behavior is regarded negatively by others and that the response to the behavior has the effect of either changing or suppressing the behavior or punishing the person who exhibits it. It also identifies possible reactions of individuals or groups to those who engage in deviant behavior. Reactions vary according to how serious a threat to basic social values the deviance is perceived as being, whether the

> **CTQ**
> Is a deviant act always a criminal act? Why or why not? Is a criminal act always a deviant act? Why or why not?

IN THE NEWS

A HUMAN PERSPECTIVE

IS TARRING AND FEATHERING A DEVIANT ACT?

Two women charged in Town Creek, Alabama, of tarring and feathering another woman acted in a deviant manner. The facts behind this seemingly deviant behavior are as follows: Mary had been married to John (a physician) for about twenty-five years, but was unable to have children. Due to other marital problems, she obtained a divorce from John. Two years later, John showed up at her Alabama home wanting a reconciliation. Noting that her ex-husband was facing severe financial problems, Mary welcomed him into her house and tried to rescue the relationship. Mary never believed that her marriage was truly over because, as her Roman Catholic upbringing had taught her, those married in the church always remain married. This renewed relationship between Mary and John ended when John announced his engagement to Liz about a year after he had moved in with his former wife. To exacerbate things to an even greater degree, John announced that he and Liz were getting married the next day.

Although John had committed no crime, Mary could not tolerate the humiliation. Acting on a whimsical suggestion of her sister—"in the old days when some trampy women outside the town came in and took men away, we used to tar and feather them and send them out of town on a rail"—Mary became purposeful. She got a bucket of basement sealant from her sister's house, took a feather pillow, and went to the trailer where John and Liz were living. Once inside she asked Liz to strip to the waist (except for her undergarments). Mary then smeared tar over Liz's body and the top of her head, which had been cropped, and then sprinkled feathers all over her. Liz eventually was taken outside of town and told to sit on a garbage dump.

Mary was charged with kidnapping and aggravated battery for tarring and feathering Liz. Although kidnapping was criminally sanctioned for a minimum of two years in Alabama, the trial judge imposed only a probated sentence on Mary.

Does this tarring-and-feathering case suggest that certain behaviors might be considered criminal and deviant, yet understandable under certain circumstances?

Source: Based on a criminal case defended by author James B. Halsted.

IN THE NEWS

A HUMAN PERSPECTIVE

BIKER GANGS AND RACKETEERING

They traded women as property, and one defendant purchased a 15-year-old girl, a federal prosecutor says. A chapter president was beaten to a pulp by his boss to underscore a demotion to vice president. "This is not a bunch of good old boys riding motorcycles with their hair blowing in the wind trying to be different," Assistant United States Attorney Stephen Kunz said, during opening statements in the racketeering trial of 16 purported Outlaw motorcycle gang members. The one-time 15-year-old sex slave is among witnesses expected to provide a rare glimpse into the lifestyles of a group who call themselves the "One Percenters," after their decision to turn their backs on the remaining 99 percent of society and its rules and values.

"The Outlaws" are a highly-organized and disciplined group dedicated to committing crime and getting away with it through intimidation and brutality, Kunz said. The bike gang went as far as trying to chase law-abiding motorcycle clubs from Florida [see Figure 2.2]. A group of recovering alcoholics who tried to form a club will testify they were beaten, robbed and threatened with death if they told, he said. The prosecutor's comments contrasted sharply with those of defense lawyers, who portrayed their clients as hard-partying rebels targeted by the government for entrapment in agent-supervised drug transactions.

Kunz promised jurors a journey into the world of "The Outlaws." "There will be much testimony concerning the treatment of women, or to be more accurate the mistreatment," he said. Biker girlfriends, known as "old ladies," were verbally humiliated, beaten, forced to support their men by working as topless dancers and made to wear vests with the words "Property of the Outlaws" emblazoned across the backs, he said. "The Outlaws'" clubhouses in the Florida cities of Tampa, St. Petersburg and Daytona were armed camps where "patched" members who wore the gang's insignia of a skull over crossed engine pistons were required to attend "church meetings" to discuss ongoing criminal activities, the prosecutor said. The bikers adorned their bodies with tattoos of gang slogans such as "God Forgives, Outlaws Don't" and "All Hell's Angels Must Die."

Four of the men are charged with firebombing a Warlocks clubhouse in Orlando and plotting to bomb another clubhouse. The bombing occurred after the bulk of the defendants were arrested in September. Kunz said agents were able to infiltrate the Outlaws because a man associated with the Daytona chapter came forward in 1999 and offered to introduce officers to gang members. At the same time, a sheriff's office detective was able to infiltrate the St. Petersburg chapter by posing as a thief who could provide motorcycle parts in exchange for guns and drugs, Kunz said.

Source: "Trial Opens with Look into Outlaws' Bloody History," Copyright *Tampa Tribune,* 25 June 1995, B1. Reprinted with permission of the *Tampa Tribune,* all rights reserved.

---

deviance is viewed as voluntary or something beyond the doer's control, and whether the behavior ceases to be objectionable to a large minority, or even a majority, of people in the society. During the 1960s and 1970s, for example, alcoholism came to be viewed by both the courts and the general public as a disease. Although public drunkenness continued to be subject to criminal sanctions, the movement of alcoholism from the category of criminality to that of illness allowed people to be treated rather than punished. Other acts, such as participation in labor unions, divorce, and doing business on Sunday, had undergone a shift from condemnation to tolerance and finally public approval.

In the first decade of the twenty-first century, one particular deviant group has captured the attention of not only sociologists but criminologists as well: skinheads. Although their appearance may be considered a degree of deviance, it is their activities, such as extreme violence and heavy use of drugs, that are deviant beyond debate.

Deviance is also a matter of degree: Cheating on an income tax return and committing armed robbery are both viewed as deviant behavior, but the robber is much more likely to be condemned and punished than the tax violator. Normative violations do not have equally adverse effects on an individual's identity. Large sectors of society are tolerant of, or even sympathetic toward, tax violators, but robbery is universally condemned as a violent crime. People who commit such crimes are apt to be scarred for the rest of their lives.

Deviance and criminality have their most integrated and visible expressions perhaps in the customs, social mannerisms, and exclusiveness in the dynamics of rapid lawbreaking in biker gangs (see Figure 2.2 and "In the News: Biker Gangs and Racketeering").

FIGURE 2.2

The code of honor of biker gangs, including valuing violence and heavy use of drugs, are examples of values that deviate from the conventional morality of most American citizens.

Courtesy Getty Images/EyeWire.

SUBSTANTIVE CRIMINAL LAW

Substantive criminal law is concerned with acts, mental states, and accompanying circumstances or consequences that constitute the necessary features of crimes (a crime was defined in the first paragraph of this chapter). It identifies particular kinds of behavior (acts or omissions) as wrongs against society or the state and prescribes punishments to be imposed for such conduct. Any references in this book to "criminal law" are actually in fact and in law references to "substantive criminal law."

Criminal procedure (discussed fully in Chapter 3, "The Law of Criminal Procedure and the Rights of the Criminally Accused") sets forth the rules that direct the application and enforcement of substantive criminal law. That is, criminal procedure lays the steps that officials—police, prosecutors, judges, corrections personnel, and others—must take in the proper administration of justice, from arrest to conviction and beyond.

For a particular act to legally be considered a crime, the perpetrator must not only have committed an intentional violation of the law, but must also be deemed under American legal principles to be legally responsible, considering the circumstances attendant to the commission of the act. **Criminal responsibility** requires that criminal acts be committed without defense, excuse, or justification. The doctrine of criminal responsibility incorporates several defenses that mitigate or excuse an individual's guilt for a criminal offense (see Chapter 9, "The Criminal Trial," for a discussion of these defenses). Hence, if a person committed a criminal act, but did so while legally insane, or did so because of a mistake of fact, or did so because he or she was under duress, the doctrine of criminal responsibility excuses the person from being held criminally liable and accountable for his or her behavior. Likewise, if one was entrapped, or underage at the time the offense was committed, or acting in self-defense, then the doctrine of criminal responsibility, which is the seminal foundation of American criminal jurisprudence, declares that such a person is not to be held criminally responsible for the offense and therefore cannot be punished for it.

Sources of American Substantive Criminal Law

Several sets of legal systems have had at least some impact on the formation of what today is the American substantive criminal law.

The Common Law of England   American law is deeply indebted to the English common law. Laws began to be written in England as early as 680 A.D. Eventually, English law became a combination of tribal rules, Roman law, and the customs of invaders from northern France, Scandinavia, and what was later to become modern Germany.

When the Normans from France invaded England in the eleventh century, they found among the defeated Anglo-Saxons a well-developed and workable system of laws for maintaining public order and administering justice. The system had evolved over a lengthy period and was based on a body of common law derived from the customs of collective experience of Anglo-Saxon society. A principal feature was its reliance on precedents to continually refine and develop suitable legal responses to meet the needs of a growing and dynamic society.

In 1066 the Norman ruler William the Conqueror imposed his own representatives on the existing system to consolidate his power and authority. Under the royal justices appointed by William, state law became common law—called such because it originated in the customary practices of the realm and was common to all of England. Common law was embedded firmly in custom and tradition; however, it nonetheless continued to evolve through the process of judicial decision making.

Common law is judge-made law, molded, refined, examined, and changed in a collection of actual decisions handed down from generation to generation in the form of reported cases. Judges drew their decisions from existing principles of law (a process known as *stare decisis*) that reflected the living values, attitudes, and ethical ideals of the English people. In practice, these judges relied on their own past actions, which they modified under the pressure of changing times and changing patterns of litigation.[10]

WEB

For more information on some of the various questions raised in criminal laws and procedures, **visit the American Civil Liberties Union link at our Web site, www.prenhall.com/territo.**

CTQ

Before going any further, do you believe that you can name at least five sources of American substantive criminal law?

Common law forms the basis of much of our modern statutory and case law. It has often been called *the* major source of modern criminal law.

Common law refers to a traditional body of unwritten legal precedents created through everyday practice and supported by court decisions during the Middle Ages in English society. As novel situations arose and were dealt with by British justices, their declarations became the start for any similar future deliberation. These decisions generally incorporated the customs of society as it operated at the time.

Eventually, court decisions were recorded and made available to barristers (the English word for trial lawyers) and judges. As Abadinsky says, "Common law involved the transformation of community rules into a national legal system. The controlling element (was) precedent."[11]

The U.S. Constitution Constitutional law (see Figure 2.3) is another source of American criminal law, not because it defines new crimes (the only crime defined in the U.S. Constitution is treason), but because it sets limitations on other laws by determining them to be unconstitutional. The furor in the first decade of the twenty-first century about making burning the American flag a criminal offense exemplifies well how the Constitution both influences and is a source of American criminal law. In two separate cases, the Supreme Court declared statutes that prohibited burning the American flag unconstitutional because they violated the individual's First Amendment right to freedom of expression.

Common Law as Interpreted by American Statutes American criminal law combines features of both civil and common law in that it includes both written codes and judge-made law based on precedents. Statutory law—that is, statutes enacted by state legislatures and Congress—is a major source of criminal law in the United States. These laws are usually compiled in codes that sort or classify statutes under separate headings. State codes are usually subject to revision at annual legislative sessions. The criminal laws of any state are found in the state penal code.

American Administrative Law As an offshoot of statutory law, **administrative law** comprises rulings, regulations, and specific procedures created by the government to dictate an agency's manner of operation and function at the federal, state, and local levels. The legislative or executive branch invests a body, such as a board of health, with the authority to establish regulations governing specific policy areas (such as social problems or safety and health standards). Although much administrative law is not targeted directly at criminal behavior, direct violations of the rules of certain governmental agencies are dealt with in criminal courts. For example, the scheduling of drugs (determining how stringently a drug should be controlled) by the Drug Enforcement Administration is governed by a set of administrative rules. These have been adopted into many criminal statutes in federal government as well as in several states.

American Case Law and* Stare Decisis** The meaning and intent of criminal statutes are tested and interpreted within the context of specific cases. The courts are generally bound to follow the criminal law as it has been jurisdictionally determined in prior cases. This is one of the principal components of criminal law and is referred to as the *law of precedent*. Thus, criminal law can be created by judges in their rulings on statutory laws. Known as case law, this kind of law is heavily influenced by the principle of ***stare decisis (literally, "let the decision stand")—the rule that requires judges to follow precedent in judicial interpretations. The legal principles of *case precedent* and *stare decisis* promote stability and certainty in the process of making legal decisions. Without these principles, "the defendant in a civil or criminal case would never know whether or not his activities were lawful."[12] Nevertheless, prior decisions are sometimes overruled by the higher authority of a court of appeals, thus reversing or modifying existing case law.

CTQ

Most jurors agree that American substantive criminal law is fundamentally based in the legal definitions of English common law. Can you explain why this is the case?

WEB

For more information on the U.S. Constitution, **visit our Web site,** www.prenhall.com/territo.

CTQ

Since there is only one crime in the U.S. Constitution (treason), how can the Constitution be a source of criminal law?

WEB

For more information on state criminal codes, **visit our web site,** www.prenhall.com/territo.

CTQ

Almost all the texts used in law school to train future lawyers require the students to read only case law for their acquisition of knowledge of the law. Does this seem odd to you? Why or why not?

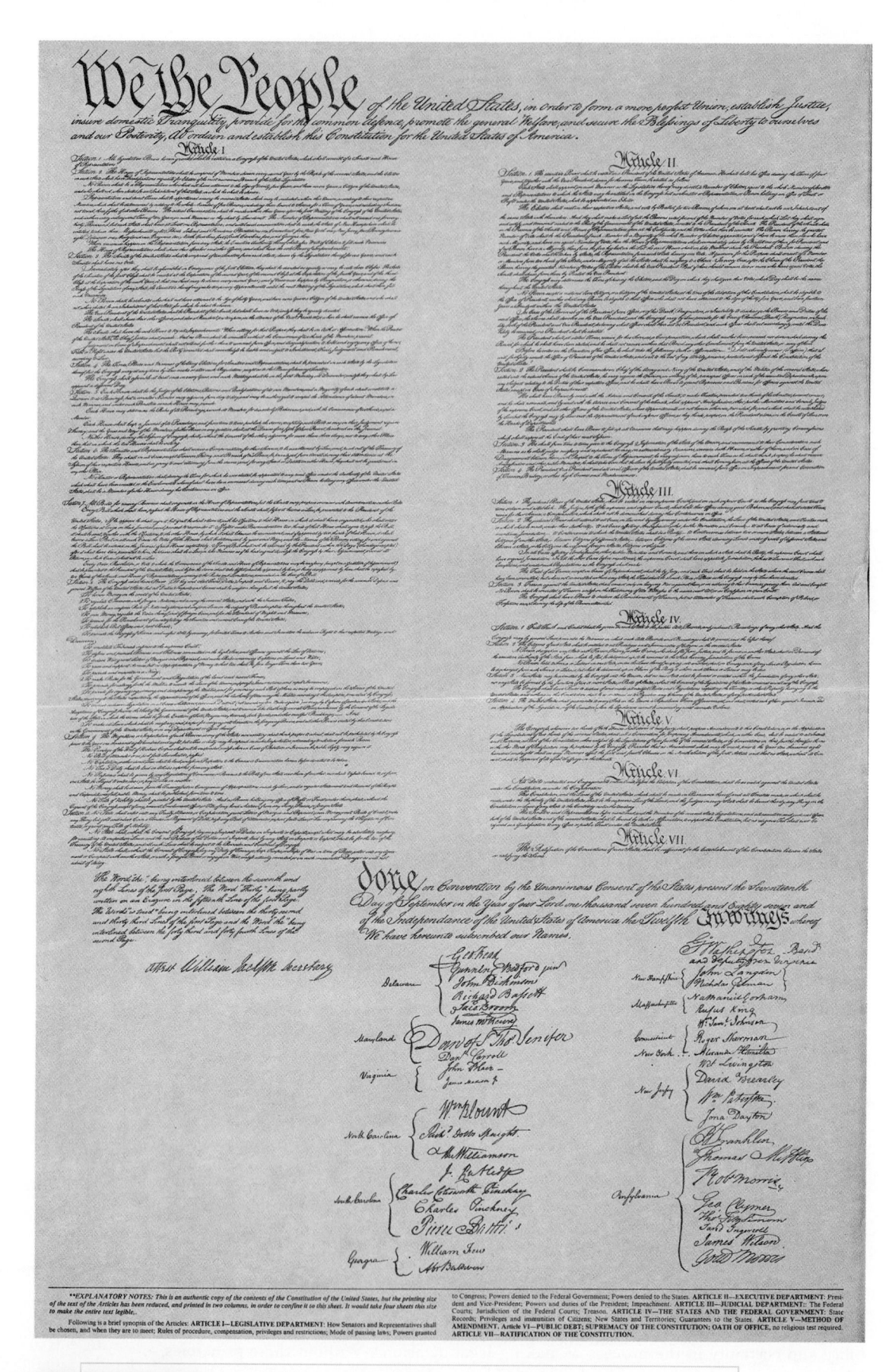

FIGURE 2.3

The Constitution of the United States.
Source: Courtesy Library of Congress.

IN THE WORKPLACE

STATE LEGISLATOR

Responsible for analyzing and voting on policy issues affecting the state, including budget. Age requirement varies for House and Senate and from state to state but the minimum age is 18; must be a registered voter, U.S. citizen, and resident of the district.

The Classification of Crime

Crimes are legally classified as felonies, misdemeanors, or treason. In general, a **felony** is a more serious crime and is punishable by incarceration of a year or more in state prison. Some states have established another kind of felony, also defined by the maximum penalty its violation might impose. A **capital felony,** or sometimes a *life felony*, is a felony in which the maximum sentence authorized for the offense is either death or life imprisonment.

A **misdemeanor** is a less serious crime, punishable by fines usually not exceeding one thousand dollars or by, in certain circumstances, a term of up to one year in city or county jail. A few states provide a fourth classification for certain offenses—*high misdemeanors*. In terms of seriousness, these offenses lie between felonies and misdemeanors. Although still technically misdemeanors, they often provide a maximum sentence in excess of one year's incarceration. Some states, such as North Carolina, have a two-year maximum penalty for the commission of misdemeanors. A **criminal infraction** is still another kind of criminal offense for which the maximum punishment does not include incarceration.

CRIMINAL RESPONSIBILITY

Anglo-American criminal law is founded on five basic interlocking principles traditionally observed by legislatures and the courts in formulating and interpreting substantive criminal law. Substantive criminal law recognizes the existence of the same essential five elements that are necessary for every crime. Thus, for a particular behavior to be considered criminal and, as such, to be penalized by the state, all of these five principles must be present: (1) *actus reus*; (2) *mens rea*; (3) concurrence of *actus reus* and *mens rea*; (4) absence of attendant circumstances that would otherwise negate criminal liability; and (5) the criminal act that must have caused the illegal harm.

Actus Reus

Actus reus, which means the "guilty act," refers to the forbidden act itself. Criminal law uses this term to describe the physical crime and/or the commission of the criminal act. Thoughts alone do not constitute a crime. One can legally wish an enemy dead, fantasize about rape, or harbor thoughts about income tax evasion—as long as the thoughts do not result in an action *(actus reus)* to bring about the desired result.

One of the most enduring principles supporting the doctrine of *actus reus* is that the actor and the actor alone is criminally responsible for his or her crimes. Hence, an employer is not responsible for the crimes of an employee, although the employer may be civilly liable under the doctrine of vicarious liability for the acts of an employee. Similarly, a person who is in control of another person traditionally has not been subject to prosecution for the criminal acts of the person over whom he or she was in control. Recently, however, this firmly rooted doctrine seems to have been modified.

Mens Rea

A further requirement of criminal conduct is the presence of the "guilty mind" *(**mens rea**)* of the accused. This requirement is also called the criminal intent of the crime. For the

WEB

For more information on criminal responsibility, **visit our Web site,** www.prenhall.com/territo.

CTQ

If the prosecution has already proved that a defendant committed a crime, why does our system of justice insist on the state also proving that the defendant was criminally responsible for the act? Should the doctrine be modified? Why or why not?

prosecution, proving criminal intent is more complex than proving *actus reus* because it demands an evaluation of the psychology, motives, and intent of the defendant. For example, a bus driver who fails to stop at an intersection and causes a collision with an automobile entering from a cross street would not be charged with a crime if it could be proven that he was unaware his brakes were defective—and he had done everything he could to avert the accident. Similarly, a person who unknowingly buys stolen goods from a local merchant is not guilty of the criminal offense of receiving stolen property because the element of intent is missing. On the other hand, a person who drives a sports car at ninety miles an hour in a residential area and kills a young child may well be convicted of manslaughter, because the behavior constitutes a reckless disregard for associated risks.

The fundamental principle of criminal responsibility is intricately interwoven with the criminal law concept of *mens rea*. The concept of *mens rea* is based on the assumption that people have the capacity to control their behavior and the ability to choose between alternative courses of conduct. Traditionally, the *mens rea* of the crime means the defendant intended to commit the prohibited act. In addition, states of mind such as malice, criminal knowledge, recklessness, negligence, and criminal purpose are considered the *mens rea* of certain crimes. Whenever a defendant is perceived as not having criminal intent, but the criminal justice system imputes criminal responsibility on the defendant anyway, passionate controversy almost always arises.

Offenses that involve no mental element but consist of only forbidden acts or omissions are classified as **strict-liability offenses.** Thus, a statute may simply indicate that someone who does or omits a certain act, or who brings about a certain result, is guilty of a crime. Historically, statutory rape was considered a strict-liability crime whose elements required only that a man have sexual intercourse with a female under age 16. In every instance the sexual intercourse was with her consent. There was no *mens rea* requirement. Therefore, if the defendant believed in good faith that the victim was over 16, as would all reasonable people in the same situation, that mental belief is irrelevant to his conviction since statutory rape is a strict-liability crime. Such statutes are justified on the grounds that although there is a need to control the behavior in question, convictions would be difficult to obtain if the prosecution had to prove fault. Examples of laws imposing liability without fault include statutory liquor and narcotics laws, pure-food laws, and traffic laws. Since these offenses require no *mens rea*, even an accidental violation of statute is proscribed. Accordingly, the accused cannot claim in court that he or she made an "innocent mistake."

The law recognizes that some groups of people are unable to attain the requisite mental state for crime. Children, mentally handicapped people, and, in some cases, those diagnosed as insane are exempt from criminal responsibility because they are unable to appreciate the nature and quality of their behavior. *Mens rea* is also considered lacking when people act under coercion or defend themselves or others; act under statutory authority (for example, a the police officer acting in the line of duty); act under a reasonable mistake of fact; or cause a genuine accident.

Concurrence of Actus Reus and Mens Rea

Another basic premise of criminal law is that the act and the mental state must concur in time for a crime to have been committed. The act and the mental state are not concurrent if they are separated by a considerable gap in time. A lack of concurrence in time between mental state and act is a strong argument that the mental state did not activate or cause the act.

Absence of Attendant Circumstances That Would Otherwise Negate Criminal Liability

The fourth general element of all crimes requires an omission. This proposes that certain circumstances exist, and if these circumstances are present—such as self-defense, insanity, mistake, or infancy—they decriminalize actions and intents that would normally be a crime. However, the absence of these attendant circumstances must be shown in order for criminal liability to exist.

CTQ

Are strict-liability crimes consistent with our notion of fundamental fairness and due process? Why or why not?

WEB

For more information on some of the defenses that can be raised to avoid criminal liability, **visit our Web site, www.prenhall.com/territo.**

The Criminal Act That Must Have Caused the Illegal Harm

Causation relates to crimes that require that a defendant's conduct produce a given result. Crimes such as perjury or forgery are defined so that the crime consists of both the act itself and the intent to cause the harmful result—without regard to whether the result in fact occurs. On the other hand, offenses such as murder and battery require a specific result. In such cases, but for the defendant's conduct the result never would have happened; furthermore, the harm that actually occurs must be similar enough to the intended result that the defendant can be held responsible.

In many instances, it is difficult for the prosecution to prove a causal connection between intent and harm. For example, if A, with the intent to kill, drives a knife into the heart of B, a prosecutor would have no particular difficulty demonstrating that A's action was the cause of B's death. However, the matter of intended harm varies according to person, manner, and type of harm. For example, who is responsible when A shoots B and—believing B is dead—leaves B's body on the interstate? If B is killed when C—who doesn't see B lying on the road—runs over her, will A be convicted of B's murder? There will be a conviction only if it can be demonstrated that A's conduct was a substantial factor in bringing about B's death or that what happened to B was a foreseeable consequence of A's behavior.

THE MAJOR INDIVIDUAL CRIMES OF AMERICAN SUBSTANTIVE CRIMINAL LAW

The definition and legal significance of every separate crime in the criminal justice system, whether it was derived from common law or was created by statutes, consists of a certain number of unique **elements** that are applicable to one and only one crime in our legal system. One crime may have but three elements, while another may have six, another four, and still another nine. It is essential to understand that in order to legally convict someone of any crime charged in the American system of criminal justice, the state has the burden of proof for each and every one of these elements separately and must prove them beyond a reasonable doubt.

Thus, the common-law tradition of defining a crime by the totality of all the elements assigned to it has been assimilated completely by American substantive criminal law. The significance of this cannot be overstated; its single consequence is that being accused of a crime is essentially being accused of every element of a crime. Since in an American criminal trial the burden of proof is on the prosecution to prove the defendant guilty beyond a reasonable doubt of the crime charged, the prosecution therefore must prove each and every one of these elements.

For example, if the state has proved seven elements of a crime beyond a reasonable doubt, but at the same time the jury finds reasonable doubt as to whether the seventh element existed, the jury must find the defendant not guilty of the crime charged.

Generally, since the development of common law and up until modern times, all crimes defined in American substantive criminal law have consisted of two general elements: (1) the physical act or omission (which usually constitutes the majority of the elements within a particular crime) and (2) a mental requirement known as the *mens rea*, or the criminal intent or purpose.

In the following study of the various substantive crimes in the American criminal justice system, each crime examined will be initially defined in terms of each of its separate physical and mental elements. Next, we will examine the specific definitions and legal issues embodied in each of these elements. This pedagogical approach is essential, because the state must prove each and every one of these elements beyond a reasonable doubt in order to gain a guilty verdict in our system. Conversely, finding an evidentiary flaw in one of the elements that constitute the crime charged is a fundamental strategy for the defense to obtain a not guilty verdict.

When studying the major crimes of substantive criminal law, it is essential to know the name, definition, and significance of every element of every crime. Successful litigations to determine whether a defendant committed a particular crime can occur in but one and only one way in our system. This requirement is that the state prove each and every one of the particular crime's elements beyond a reasonable doubt. If the jury has a

---

CTQ

Explain the difference between the state proving that the defendant committed the criminal act versus proving each and every one of the elements of the crime beyond a reasonable doubt.

reasonable doubt about one element in a seven-element crime, it must give a verdict of not guilty to the charge.

The major crimes of substantive criminal law, which will be presented in this chapter, have been organized into general categories: (1) homicide, (2) crimes against persons, (3) crimes against habitation, (4) crimes against property—the acquisition offenses, (5) crimes against morality, (6) modern crimes, (7) traffic offenses, and (8) environmental crimes. The crimes embodied in these major categories also constitute "traditional" common-law crimes. They also constitute the majority of crimes prosecuted annually (90 percent) in American courtrooms.[13] Certain newer crimes that were unheard of during the common-law period are still seldom prosecuted. Since the crimes studied in this chapter constitute the vast majority of crimes being perpetrated and prosecuted in America, they will be defined by their common-law elements. This rendering best represents the most comprehensive and general overview of American substantive criminal law throughout the United States.

Crimes much newer than those traditional common-law crimes in fact do exist in substantive criminal law. They are also being violated and prosecuted in American courtrooms. Unfortunately, even though every state generally has adopted the common-law crimes as its major substantive crimes, states often have modified the elements of the crime and in some instances even changed the names of the common-law crime. These changes vary from jurisdiction to jurisdiction. For example, the criminal behavior described in *The Uniform Crime Reports* (see Chapter 4, "The Nature and Distribution of Crime and Its Victims") describes certain behavior as "aggravated assault." This same violent behavior has been defined as "aggravated battery" throughout the last five hundred years in the common law. Inconsistencies like these tend to confuse not only criminal justice students but professors of criminal justice as well. Hence, the following presentation of the major common-law crimes is not absolutely precise and consistent in every jurisdiction. However, the authors propose that this general presentation is the one that best prepares the criminal justice student and provides the necessary foundation of knowledge of American substantive criminal law.

The last section of this chapter focuses on certain modern crimes that are presently being committed and prosecuted with alarming frequency. The focus here will be on environmental, electronic, consensual, and computer crimes as well as stalking and identity theft.

HOMICIDE

The most serious crime punished in the American criminal justice system is homicide. A **homicide** is the killing of one human being by another human being. In common law, homicides are classified as criminal, justifiable, and excusable. Killings commanded or authorized by law are justifiable; excusable homicides are those in which the killer is not necessarily without fault, but where circumstances do not justify the infliction of normal punishment. Killings are lawful if they are justifiable or excusable. Police who kill in the line of duty, executioners, National Guard members ordered to kill by the governor, and military personnel who kill during declared or undeclared wars commit justifiable homicides. An example of an excusable homicide is a killing in self-defense or by mistake. Killings without justification or excuse are criminal homicides.

Murder

The study of criminal homicide should begin with the definition of murder. **Murder** is defined in the following elements: (1) the unlawful (2) killing (3) of another human being (4) with malice aforethought.

A killing requires that the victim of the homicide be dead. Under traditional common-law rules, death does not occur until the heartbeat and respiration stop. However, under some statutes death occurs when the brain ceases to function. The victim of a homicide must be a living human being. In common law, a fetus was not a human being until fully brought from the mother with an independent circulation. Some states have broadened homicide statutes to include a criminal charge of *fetal homicide* if (1) the

TABLE 2.3	The Four Separate States of Mind That Constitute Malice Aforethought—The *Mens Rea* of Murder

(1) Intent to kill
(2) Intent to inflict great bodily injury
(3) Intent to commit a felony
(4) Acting out of extreme recklessness

---

attack on the mother was so severe that had it killed the mother, the attacker would have been charged with the murder of the mother and (2) the attacker kills the fetus. Other states will bring a charge of fetal homicide if the perpetrator willfully, intentionally, knowingly, purposefully, and through design attacks the mother's uterus in a manner consistent with an intent to kill the fetus. He or she is then guilty of fetal homicide.

The most significant and difficult element of the crime of murder is **malice aforethought**. Malice aforethought is the *mens rea* of murder and refers to any of four fully developed but different mental states (discussed shortly). It does not necessarily refer to the killer's motive. A killer may have numerous motives—like the Columbine killers, whose motives are still being studied by a multitude of experts (see "In the News: From Way Cool to Out of Control"). Any motive will suffice to make a killing murder (see Table 2.3).

The first of the four mental states that reflect malice aforethought is **intent to kill,** which can be inferred from the defendant's conduct or from the intentional use of a deadly weapon. The second mental state is **intent to inflict great bodily injury.** In this instance, the defendant does not intend to kill but merely intends to hurt the victim. If the victim dies anyway, the crime is murder. The third mental state is **intent to commit a felony.** Generally, any killing that is caused with intent to commit a felony is murder. Specifically, if one commits a felony, and during the perpetration of this felony another person dies (for example, a person has a heart attack, is shot by a resisting victim, or is run over by a pursuing police car), the perpetrator is guilty of murder even though he or she never meant to kill or physically harm anyone (see the Landmark Case *People v. Patterson*).

The fourth mental state in malice aforethought is "acting out of extreme recklessness." **Recklessness** is defined as engaging in a course of conduct that is so dangerous that a reasonable person could foresee that such conduct has a strong probability of resulting in either death or infliction of great bodily harm to another. (see "In the News: Rock Thrown off Interstate Bridge Kills College Professor" for a case demonstrating recklessness, which constitutes the mental state for murder.) The perpetrator is guilty of the murder in spite of the fact that he or she did not intend to (1) kill or (2) injure the victim, or (3) commit a felony. The **felony murder rule** requires that when a death occurs during the defendant's perpetration of another felony, where the defendant intended to commit the other felony but did not intend to kill or harm the victim, he or she is completely criminally responsible for the murder of that victim and will be charged with murder. Recently, in the United States, the courts have tended to limit the scope of the felony murder rule.[14] It has been eliminated altogether in England.[15]

Voluntary Manslaughter

Voluntary manslaughter is a lesser degree of murder. Voluntary manslaughter is a killing that would otherwise be murder but was committed in response to **adequate provocation** (see Table 2.4); one of the elements of adequate provocation is **reasonable provocation.** Often, it has been said that voluntary manslaughter is a "crime of passion and rage." Courts have defined reasonable provocation as that which would cause an average, reasonable person to act rashly, without deliberation, and from passion rather than judgment. The provocation must itself be reasonable, meaning that a reasonable person could be provoked by such an event. Examples of such inflammatory provocations are adultery, violent and painful blows, and mutual combat. The courts have held that words

---

CTQ

Why does criminal law define a fetus as human for homicide purposes, while at the same time abortion laws refuse to recognize the personhood of the fetus after abortion, in which the fetus also dies?

CTQ

Does the fact that the *mens rea* of murder has four total and complete definitions that are not logically connected to each other make it more difficult to understand the reasoning for the definition of malice aforethought?

IN THE NEWS

A HUMAN PERSPECTIVE

FROM WAY COOL TO OUT OF CONTROL
by B. Koerner

It was the oldest form of high school enmity. Eric Harris and Dylan Klebold were self-styled outcasts who ate their lunch beneath the stairs and endured the social elite's ruthless gibes—until something pushed them over the edge.

What's new, though, is the shape of the greater cultural environment that nurtured their growing dissatisfaction. Bits and pieces of several subcultures, most of them familiar to typical American school kids, fed their hardhearted nihilism. And while it is now a cliche to speak of the violence in popular culture, it is nonetheless true that children and teenagers today have access and exposure to a bewildering—often disturbing—array of imagery and information that would have been unimaginable even 20 years ago.

Most puzzling to adults is the glee with which many young people approach depictions of violence. That strange fascination is most evident in the teen world's blood-drenched video games—like Doom, a favorite of Harris and Klebold. In the game, players take on the character of a marine, walking around a maze blowing away beasts with a vast array of high-tech cannons, growing mesmerized by the thrill of staring down a digitized gun barrel, or snaking around corners in search of fire-hurling beasts, waiting for their blood to be splattered upon the walls.

Groping for answers last week, some observers looked also to Harris and Klebold's affection for the grim posturings of popular German music groups Rammstein and KMFDM, whose name translates to "No pity for the majority." Their "industrial" sound is influenced by the cold clangings of factory floors, and their lyrics question life's meaning with images of violent resistance to the status quo and intense self-loathing.

Dylan Klebold   Eric Harris
Courtesy AP/Wide World Photos.

GOTHIC REVIVAL
Along with their comrades in the "Trench Coat Mafia," the pair also favored black clothes and unkempt hair; some boys in the clique occasionally added gender-bending touches, such as fingernail polish or pancake makeup, opening them up to jock barbs challenging their sexual orientation. To many students, however, the look screamed "Goth," or Gothic, an umbrella term for a culture whose adherents' fashion senses resemble that of Morticia Addams. Taking their cue from claustrophobic verse of Baudelaire and Poe, Goths are united by a fascination with death and a love for morbid, introspective music. "Goth is about the transgressive, very much the embracing of the decadent," says Clifford Low, 28, a New Yorker who has been on the scene for 12 years. "Its nihilism is purgative. People are in it to feel release from tension and anxiety."

But Goths say that violence plays no part in their culture. Goths are quiet and introspective, much preferring a good horror novel to a bare-knuckle fight. Indeed, most children and teenagers who temporarily become obsessed with violence, whether it be in pulp novels, films, or video games, do not act on violent fantasies.

RACIST LEANINGS
Harris and Klebold were interested in something far more ominous, of course: the fashion and beliefs of racist skinheads, whose violence has cast a shadow over Denver recently. In November, 1997, two such shaved-headed youths allegedly murdered a West-African immigrant, after cruelly asking, "Are you ready to die for being a n-----?"

The negative publicity surrounding the murder did not deter Harris and Klebold from adorning their coats with swastikas or wearing the steel-boot combat boots (for maximum damage when kicking enemies) with red shoe laces—a symbol of blood shed for the "master race"—favored by racist skinheads. Their dark belief system and fascination with all things German, from the language of World War II insignias, are hallmarks of a large band of racist skins who boast of being "soldiers of the Fourth Reich."

It's the kind of attraction that may only get more prevalent. William Damon, director of Stanford University's Center on Adolescence, blames a lack of community structure for pushing kids towards the odious. "Without the connectedness of real community, there's no checks on the cynicism." Typical teenage angst, in other words, can turn ugly. "Fascination with death is normal, but this Satanic celebration of death is sick," says Damon. "The culture is much more toxic today."

Source: B. Koerner, "From Way Cool to Out of Control, "*U.S. News & World Report*, 3 May 1999. Copyright 1999 U.S. News & World Report, L. P. Reprinted with permission.

CHAPTER 2 THE SUBSTANTIVE CRIMINAL LAW   55

TABLE 2.4	The Four Conditions Necessary to Establish Adequate Provocation and Reduce a Murder Charge to Voluntary Manslaughter

(1) The event must provoke a reasonable person to act from passion rather than reason.
(2) The defendant must have killed in the heat of passion.
(3) The time between the provocation and the killing was insufficient for a reasonable person to cool down.
(4) The defendant did not cool down between the time of the provocation and the time of the killing.

CTQ

A lot of people who kill do so in a state of rage. Likewise, many murderers commit their killings in a state of rage, but their cases are not reduced to voluntary manslaughter. What is the difference between killing in a state of rage, which makes it voluntary manslaughter, and rage that keeps the crime a murder?

LANDMARK CASE — People v. Patterson

Patterson was convicted of second-degree murder based on the felony murder rule. Patterson sold cocaine to a friend, in violation of California drug laws. The friend subsequently died from a drug overdose that she inflicted upon herself by voluntarily taking the drug. Patterson had no intent for her to overdose, nor did he want her to. Patterson contends his conviction was illegal, since the exchange of recreational drugs does not carry a high probability of death.

The ruling of the California Supreme Court stated that "violation of a law prohibiting the sale of cocaine may lead to felony-murder liability if selling cocaine carries a high probability of death," and also called the sale of cocaine "inherently dangerous in this context."

Source: People v. Patterson, 262 Cal. 3d 615 (1989).

IN THE NEWS — A HUMAN PERSPECTIVE

ROCK THROWN OFF INTERSTATE BRIDGE KILLS COLLEGE PROFESSOR

A poignant example of recklessness, essential for malice aforethought, occurred in Florida in the spring of 1999 on Interstate 75. While on spring break, a young professor from the University of Alabama was driving south on the interstate, on her way to see her mother, when several young teenagers poised on top of an overpass were throwing large rocks at passing motorists below.

The juveniles later stated that "for kicks" they would stand on the top of a bridge throwing boulders at cars as they passed under the bridge. One such throw hit the college professor's car, killing her. The juveniles were convicted of murder. The court, in upholding the murder conviction, stated that even though the juveniles had no intention of either killing or injuring anyone inside the automobile by throwing the rocks, their behavior was of such "extreme recklessness" that a reasonable person could have foreseen that such behavior involved a strong probability of causing either death or great bodily injury to passengers in the automobiles below. As a result of these acts of recklessness, all of the teenagers were convicted of the murder of the college professor, even though they had no intent to kill her.

Source: WELA News Channel 8 report, 6:00 P.M. News, Tampa, Fla., March 20, 1999.

alone are never enough to provoke a reasonable person. Also, to be convicted of voluntary manslaughter instead of murder, the defendant must have been actually provoked. Hence, he or she must have killed "in the heat of passion." The courts have required further that there must be an absence of time for a reasonable person to "cool off," and that the defendant in fact did not cool off before he or she killed the victim. (See the Landmark Case *Reynolds v. State*.)

LANDMARK CASE — Reynolds v. State

In the mid-1970s, Reynolds attended a party in which he met his estranged wife in the company of another man. During the evening he engaged in drunken horseplay, firing his pistol into the air. On the third shot, the bullet hit his wife, killing her. After placing the body in the car, Reynolds drove away; he was later stopped by a patrol car. The sheriff noticed the dead body in the back of the car. Reynolds was charged with first-degree murder. At the trial, the state introduced evidence that Reynolds had quarreled with his wife over her boyfriend the night before. Reynolds's defense attorney introduced evidence at the trial that when Reynolds fired his pistol, his hand was struck by a spectator, causing his wife to be shot. Although charged with first-degree murder, Reynolds was convicted of voluntary manslaughter, and appealed, requesting an instruction that his conduct only involved involuntary manslaughter.

Source: *Reynolds v. State*, 617 P.2d 1352 (Okla. Crim. App. 1979).

CTQ — Why should we allow a person who kills another human being with equal hatred, malice, and with the same intent to kill as that of a premeditated, cold-blooded murder to be exposed to a far less severe criminal sentence because at the time of the killing, this type of killer was "out of control, in a full state of rage" as a result of being provoked?

Involuntary Manslaughter

Involuntary manslaughter is a third type of common-law homicide. **Criminally negligent homicide** (see the Landmark Case *People v. Ochoa*) is one kind of involuntary manslaughter. It consists of an (1) unintentional killing (2) caused by the commission of any act (3) in a criminally negligent manner. (See "In the News: The Crisis of Foster Care.") The other kind of involuntary manslaughter is called **misdemeanor manslaughter.** It operates similarly to the felony murder rule. If someone is perpetrating a misdemeanor and during the course of that misdemeanor someone dies, even though the death is unintended by the misdemeanant, the perpetrator has committed misdemeanor manslaughter (see the Landmark Case *Comber v. United States*).

CRIMES AGAINST PERSONS

In substantive criminal law, homicide is the first set of general crimes usually examined. Other crimes of violence include assault and battery and other crimes against persons. Within the last decade, one of the more famous cases was the media-sensation event of two top Olympic figure skaters, Tonya Harding and Nancy Kerrigan. Harding was convicted of conspiracy in the attack on Kerrigan. The state's theory of the case was that Harding was attempting to eliminate Kerrigan as a competitor in the upcoming Olympic games. The assault, however, was a failure, since Kerrigan recuperated from the injury and skated to a silver medal, while Harding's lackluster performance placed her out of contention for any medal.[16]

CTQ — Have you ever observed a person in the throes of road rage while on the highway? What percentage of these people do you think are potential killers?

The FBI has measured the frequency of four of the major crimes against persons (all violent crimes). Figure 2.4 reveals a sobering picture of an almost constant and perpetual perpetration of one violent act after another within a twenty-four-hour period in the United States.

Battery

CTQ — Do you believe that a foster parent who is so overburdened with the number of children that he or she has, and as a result negligently lets one die, should be held responsible under criminal homicide statutes for negligence?

The elements of the crime of **battery** are (1) unlawful (2) application of force (3) by a person (4) on another. The *mens rea* of battery usually is "the intent to batter." However, the courts have indicated that mere negligence will satisfy the *mens rea* requirement of battery. Traditionally, in order to batter someone or commit the crime of battery, no mark need be left on the victim. All that is required is the application of force. A punch, slap, kick, push, or shove will suffice for this crime. More often these days, states are requiring that the victim experience some form of bodily injury. However, if the victim consents to the battery, no crime is committed.

LANDMARK CASE — People v. Ochoa

Ochoa drank heavily at a Sunday picnic, and then began driving back to his home after only a few hours of sleep. On the freeway, he was driving above the speed limit, where he made a sudden lane change, hitting another car and killing the two occupants. Ochoa failed a series of field coordination tests, and was arrested for driving under the influence. He was convicted of negligent homicide—gross negligence under the state statute. Ochoa appealed the decision successfully; the court ruled that the evidence showed that while Ochoa drove at high speeds while intoxicated, his conduct amounted only to simple negligence. The question before the court was whether gross negligence can be shown from all the relevant circumstances to determine if the defendant acted with a conscious disregard of the consequences rather than mere inadvertence to conduct. The court stated that gross negligence is an objective test, and is the exercise of so slight a degree of care as to raise a presumption of conscious indifference to the consequence.

Source: *People v. Ochoa*, 6 Cal. 4th 1199, 26 Cal. Rptr. 2d 23 (1993).

LANDMARK CASE — Comber v. United States

Comber punched a victim who was substantially heavier a couple of times in the face. The victim, who was drunk at the time, later lapsed into unconsciousness and died. The court found Comber guilty of involuntary manslaughter. Comber appealed the decision on the ground that simple assault was not an inherently dangerous misdemeanor. The court upheld the involuntary manslaughter conviction, stating that the misdemeanor of a fistfight would be dangerous under the circumstances if its commission entails a reasonably foreseeable risk of physical injury, such as in the present case. The ruling was upheld.

Source: Comber v. United States, 584 A.2d 26 (D.C. Cir. 1995).

The most commonly used weapons in the perpetration of aggravated battery are illustrated in Figures 2.5 and 2.6. **Aggravated battery** is battery whose nature is such that it is classified as felony battery; the two traditional ways a defendant can be charged with aggravated battery are (1) if he or she used a "deadly weapon" in the perpetration of the battery or (2) if, as the result of the battery, the victim received serious bodily injuries. However, aggravated battery still exists when less violent conduct is committed. One commits aggravated battery, for example, in certain states, whenever one touches a senior citizen, a law enforcement officer, or a public schoolteacher.

Domestic violence (the battery of an intimate) is probably the most common form of battery in the United States today. Domestic

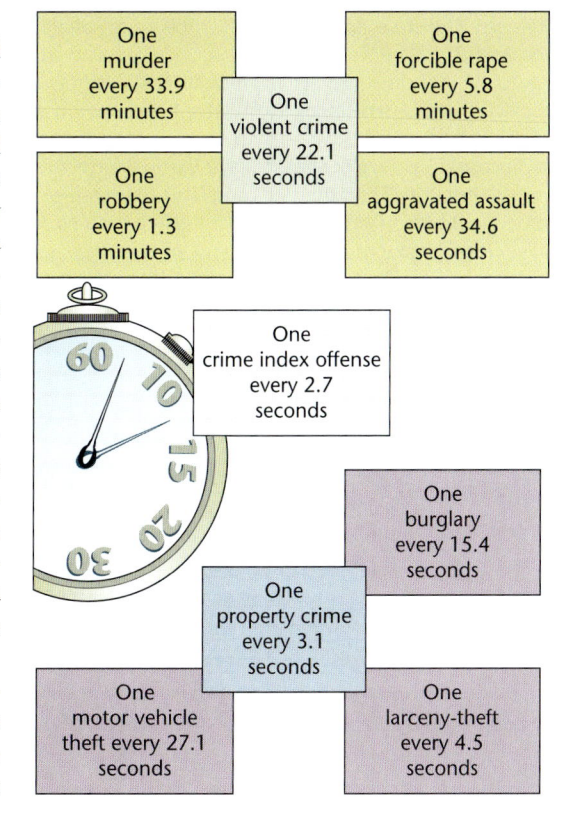

FIGURE 2.4

The FBI Crime Clock, Showing the Frequency of Major Crime Commission in 2000.

Source: Adapted from Federal Bureau of Investigation, *Crime in the United States, 2000* (Washington, D.C.: U.S. Government Printing Office, 2001).

- One murder every 33.9 minutes
- One forcible rape every 5.8 minutes
- One violent crime every 22.1 seconds
- One robbery every 1.3 minutes
- One aggravated assault every 34.6 seconds
- One crime index offense every 2.7 seconds
- One burglary every 15.4 seconds
- One property crime every 3.1 seconds
- One motor vehicle theft every 27.1 seconds
- One larceny-theft every 4.5 seconds

CTQ

Most people consider an assault a battery, but they are two entirely different crimes. Can you explain the differences in the crimes of assault and battery?

IN THE NEWS
A HUMAN PERSPECTIVE

THE CRISIS OF FOSTER CARE
by T. Roche

The autopsy photo shows a little boy who looks relieved to be dead. His eyes are closed. A hospital tube protrudes from his broken nose. He has deep cuts above his right ear and dark linear scars on his forehead. The bruises on his back are a succession of yellows, greens, and blues. On the bottom of his tiny feet are unhealed third-degree burns. He had been battered and tortured. He had been tied with panty hose and belts to a banister by the woman who had become his foster grandmother. The state of Georgia had taken him away from his mother, then abandoned him in the woman's care. Little Terrell Peterson had so many injuries that the medical examiner gave up counting them. The child was six years old. He weighed only 29 lbs. This foster care system is not working in Atlanta.

It costs at least $7 billion a year, or about $13,000 a child, to care for America's foster kids. The problem is not a single black hole but a series—each state affected with its own distinct problems. A year-long investigation by *Time* has found the crisis mounting in at least 20 states as lawyers file class actions asking judges to take over the control of entire agencies and Governors to appoint task forces to review child-welfare programs. Three states in particular—Georgia, Alabama, and California—show the severity of the crisis.

Terrell Peterson was young and black, like 50% of the foster-care population. He was a victim of the crack epidemic that spawned not only a generation of addicts but also a generation of lost children, most of whom have found their way into the foster care system. His mother was addicted to crack. He had two siblings with different fathers. The state opened eight files on his family in five years, and 21 different caseworkers from five offices were involved in the cases. Social workers, faithful to policy trend of placing kids with family members, sent Terrell to the home of a woman who was the paternal grandmother of one of his siblings. Technically she was not a blood relative, but she was close enough. Then they apparently closed his case file and forgot about him. "Terrell Peterson should not have happened," says Georgia governor Roy Barnes. Earlier this year, he ordered a sweeping criminal investigation into the suspicious deaths of Terrell and 12 other foster children around the state. The boy's foster grandmother, Pharina Peterson, has been charged with murder, along with his foster aunt Terri Lynn Peterson and her boyfriend, Calvin Pittman. The Georgia bureau of investigation has spent much of this year trying to determine whether negligence of social workers made them accomplices in the children's deaths. Bureau agents seized more than 30,000 documents last January when raiding state welfare offices to investigate the deaths. They believe some files may have been conveniently lost or perhaps pilfered by people with secrets to hide.

The stories of the children and their deaths fill seven cardboard boxes. Among the dead is Octavius Sims, whose family's suspected negligence had been reported over and over to social workers before he was starved, immersed in boiling water, and beaten to death three days before his first birthday. Another is Raymond Ellis, 16, paralyzed in a car accident as a toddler and needed constant care. For years doctors had begged caseworkers to remove him from his mother's care. No one did. Raymond died of a preventable infection and pneumonia.

The files, obtained by *Time*, show a pattern of inadequate monitoring, poor record keeping and bad decisions. In the case of Terrell, the records show that social workers skipped home visits, missed a crucial court hearing and lied in reports that supervisors signed but did not read.

As appalling as is Terrell's death, the fact is that Georgia took steps years ago to keep such a tragedy from happening. After the death of a little girl named Kathy Joe in 1997, Georgia lawmakers vowed reform. Panic over foster care produced regulations designed to save children's lives. Until Terrell's death, however, no one had checked to make sure that the changes were enforced. "I am not here to defend this system," says Barnes, who this year pushed for a children's advocate and laws to increase caseworker accountability. "We have not made this a high enough priority."

Source: T. Roche, "The Crisis of Foster Care," *Time*, November 13, 2000, 73. © 2000 TIME Inc. Reprinted by permission.

WEB
For more information on domestic violence, **visit our Web site,** www.prenhall.com/territo.

violence is a form of violent personal crime and can be defined as activities of physically aggressive nature occurring among members of a family, current or former spouses or lovers, and others in close relationships, as a result of conflicts in personal relations. Domestic violence typically occurs in the home, but it can also take place at the house of another family member (see Figure 2.7) or a neighbor, at the victim's place of employment, at a commercial establishment, or even in public. The victim and offender are most often opposite sexes, although they may be the same sex.

The scope of domestic violence is quite broad and includes a wide range of behavioral patterns and offense categories. There is battering by spouses and lovers, which is a consistent pattern of behavior that seeks to establish dominance and control over another through the use or threat of force or violence. There is also abuse, which may be psychological or economic in nature, involving ridicule, threats, and harassment. Other forms of domestic violence include marital and date rape, elder abuse, and child neglect and abuse.

FIGURE 2.5

The Tools of Aggravated Battery. This array of guns, knives, brass knuckles, and other weapons confiscated on school grounds was displayed as Leon County, Florida, teacher Judith Birtman, who was severely beaten by a student, commented at a news conference in Tallahassee in 1996.

Courtesy AP/Wide World Photos.

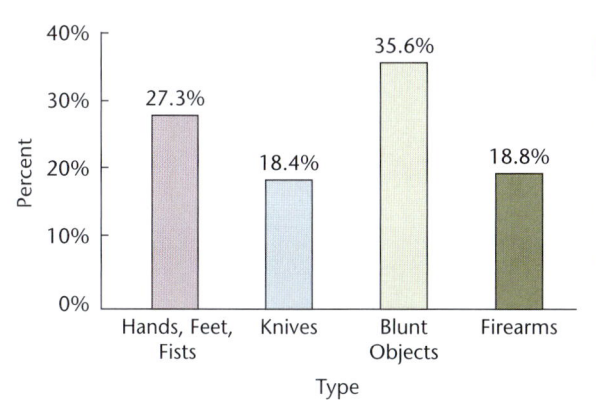

FIGURE 2.6

Aggravated Battery—Weapons Used, 1998.

Source: Federal Bureau of Investigation, *Crime in the United States 1998* (Washington, D.C.: U.S. Government Printing Office, 1999).

- Hands, Feet, Fists: 27.3%
- Knives: 18.4%
- Blunt Objects: 35.6%
- Firearms: 18.8%

FIGURE 2.7

Some of the most disturbing crimes against persons are perpetrated on children. Barbara Atkinson locked her minor children in a closet for weeks on end without providing hardly any food. When they were rescued, her 8-year-old daughter weighed only 25 pounds.

Courtesy Milton Hinnant/*The Dallas Morning News.*

These, however, are broad categories. The actual criminal statutes involved include murder and manslaughter, assault, rape, incest, harassment, and stalking, to name just a few.

Domestic violence has occurred throughout human history. In many cultures men were legally and socially permitted to punish their wives and children for disobedience or disloyalty. Moreover, much of what is now referred to as domestic violence was once considered a legitimate means by which men could maintain control over the family.[17] (See Figure 2.8.)

An important aspect of domestic violence is the relationship between the victim and the offender. This suggests that a large portion of such behavior is well beyond the control of law enforcement. In the case of murder, for example, the majority of offenses occur between people who know each other. Of the 15,878 murders reported during 1996, 5.6 percent of the victims were spouses, 7.2 percent of the murders involved other family members, and 37.9 percent included neighbors or other close acquaintances.[18] In the remaining cases of domestic violence, the majority of killings involved "romantic triangles," quarrels over money or property, or other arguments.

Although official statistics on assaults are not as complete as those on criminal homicide, this crime, too, reflects the growing incidence of domestic violence. Random street muggings do indeed occur, but nearly two-thirds of all known aggravated batteries result from domestic arguments, altercations, jealousies, and arguments over money and property. Further, victim-offender relationships are typically intimate, close, and frequent, primarily involving family members and close acquaintances. (See the Landmark Case *State v. Tripp*.)

Child abuse, or domestic violence directed against children (also termed *battered child syndrome*), is a form of personal violence that has received widespread attention only during recent years. Studies suggest that offenders are typically parents or guardians, and the abuse is an enduring pattern provoked by behaviors that are typical of children—persistent crying, failure to use the toilet, aggression toward siblings, breaking toys or household items, or disobedience.[19]

WEB

For more information on how the courts handle domestic violence, visit our Web site, www.prenhall.com/territo.

CTQ

Most police officers and prosecutors are reluctant to become involved with violence against the family, since the victims often change their mind about pressing charges. What strategies can we use outside the criminal justice system to help reduce the massive violence occurring within the American household?

LANDMARK CASE — State v. Tripp

Burke testified that that she and Tripp had lived together for several months in a house located on Onaha St., and although Burke had listed her grandfather's residence on Gardenia St. as her permanent residence, she resided at the Onaha St. residence for the purposes of watching the property on behalf of the owner, who was away. Likewise, Tripp testified that his permanent residence was at his sister's home on Anianiku St. However, Tripp kept his clothes at the Onaha St. address, did his laundry there, ate his meals there, and slept there on a continuous basis. While they were living together, Burke became pregnant. While Burke was in the hospital to deliver her child by cesarean section, Tripp punched her several times, inflicting several injuries. Tripp was found guilty of unlawfully abusing a family or household member. The relevant section of the HRS statute defines "family or household member" to include people "jointly residing or formerly residing in the same dwelling unit." Tripp appealed, claiming that the statute was vague and overbroad in its definition of family and household members.

The Hawaii Supreme Court had to determine whether this particular penal statute was void for vagueness, questioning whether it provided sufficient notice of the type of conduct prohibited and proved fixed standards for adjudging guilt by stating with reasonable clarity the activity it proscribes. The court held that no, the penal statute was not void for vagueness or overbreadth. The court went on to say that due process of law requires that a penal statute give a person of ordinary intelligence a reasonable opportunity to know what conduct is prohibited so that he or she may make a proper choice between lawful and unlawful conduct. Here the statute was clear when it defined "family and household member" to include people residing jointly in the same dwelling house.

Source: State v. Tripp, 71 Haw. 479, 795 P.2d 280 (1990).

Another form of abuse is child molestation, which is most frequently manifested as parent-child incest, sexual fondling of a child, or persuasion or coercion of a child to engage in other kinds of sexual acts with a parent, sibling, or guardian. Recently, the use of cocaine during pregnancy has been defined as child abuse.[20]

Contrary to popular belief, women are not the only victims of domestic violence and men are not the only offenders. Although men are the offenders in most domestic violence situations, studies have found that men are at risk as well and hence, there is also a *battered husband syndrome*.[21]

Hate Crimes

A **hate crime** can be defined as an offense motivated by hatred against a victim because of his or her race, ethnicity, religion, sexual orientation, handicap, or national origin. Also referred to as *bias-motivated crimes*, hate crimes are often difficult to identify, primarily because criminal acts motivated by bias can easily be confused with forms of expression that are protected by the U.S. Constitution.

From the Romans' persecution of the Christians almost two thousand years ago and the Nazis' "final solution" for the Jews during World War II, to the "ethnic cleansing" in Bosnia and the genocide in Rwanda during the 1990s, hate crimes have shaped and sometimes defined world history. In the United States, most hate crimes have been inspired by racial and religious biases. During the nation's early history, Native Americans became the targets of bias-motivated intimidation of violence. Later, there were lynchings of African Americans, followed by hate crimes directed against Chinese laborers. More current examples of hate crimes include assaults on gays, the painting of swastikas on Jewish synagogues, and cross burnings intended to drive black families out of predominantly white neighborhoods.[22]

According to the FBI's Uniform Crime Reports, 8,063 bias-motivated criminal incidents were reported in 2000. According to the data collected, 53.8 percent were motivated by racial bias, 18.3 percent by religious bias, 16.1 percent by sexual-orientation bias, 11.3 percent by ethnicity/national origin bias, and 0.5 percent by disability and multiple biases.[23] (See Figure 2.9.)

Victims of hate crimes in the United States are most often African Americans, followed by Jews, gays, Muslims, and increasingly, Asian Americans.[24] Although the Ku Klux Klan and Nazi skinhead groups are the most visible perpetrators of hate crimes, the majority of offenses are committed by individuals rather than groups.

Assault

An unfortunate development in American substantive criminal law is the interchanging of the two historical common-law crimes of assault and battery. For example, in

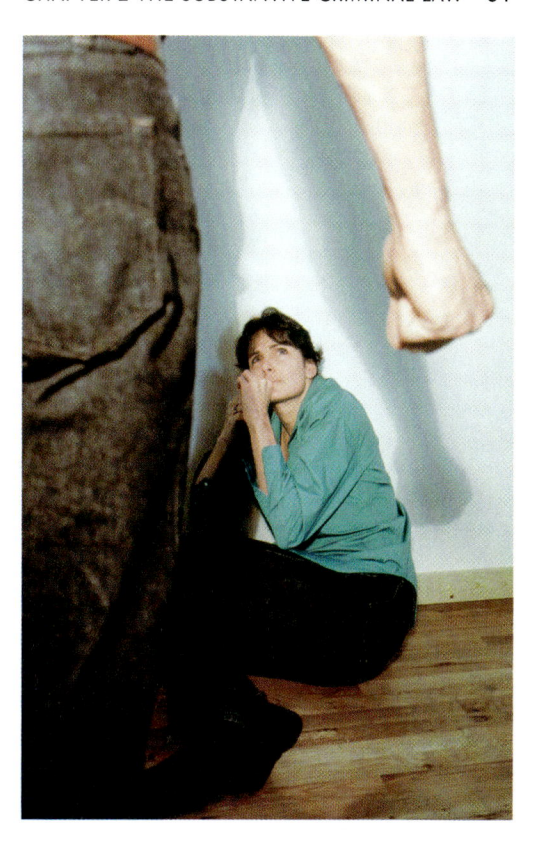

FIGURE 2.8

Victims of domestic violence often feel an extreme sense of helplessness when trapped in the violent home.

Courtesy Roy Morsch/CORBIS.

CTQ

Since a hate crime attaches to an enhancement statute (as discussed in Chapter 10 ("Sentencing, Appeals, and The Death Penalty"), it adds an extra 25 years in addition to years received for the crime committed), do you believe it's fair to add that many years on to a sentence based on the politically incorrect motive of the offender?

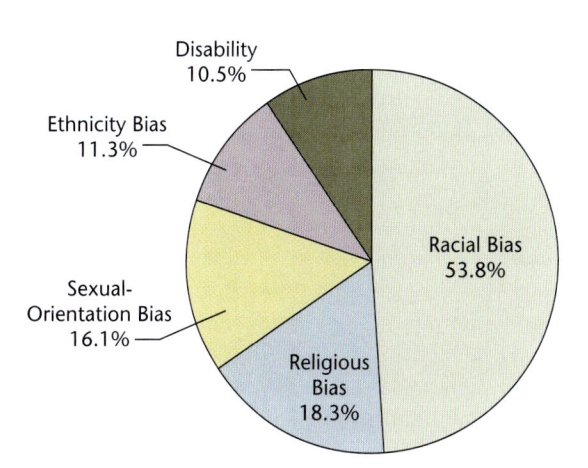

FIGURE 2.9

Hate Crimes by Motivating Factor, 1998–1999.

Source: Federal Bureau of Investigation, *Crime in the United States 1999* (Washington, D.C.: U.S. Government Printing Office, 2000).

WEB

For more information on hate crimes, **visit our Web site,** www.prenhall.com/territo.

Pie chart data:
- Racial Bias 53.8%
- Religious Bias 18.3%
- Sexual-Orientation Bias 16.1%
- Ethnicity Bias 11.3%
- Disability 10.5%

many states and in the federal government, the exact same behavior that has been designated as the crime of battery in common-law jurisdictions is instead designated as the crime of assault in other jurisdictions. The most flagrant example of this unfortunate interchange, as discussed in Chapter 4 ("The Nature and Distribution of Crime and Its Victims"), is in the *Uniform Crime Reports*, published by the FBI. Listed as one of the four violent crimes in the crime index of offenses is the crime of *aggravated assault*. This is a total interchange of the common-law crime of *aggravated battery*. The FBI's definition of aggravated assault is identical to the four-hundred-year-old definition of aggravated battery presented earlier. Most state statutes define separate crimes of battery and assault using the traditional common-law definitions.

The common-law crime of **assault** involves two different kinds of behavior, and they are often confused. The first type of an assault is an *attempted battery*. The elements necessary to commit this first type of assault are (1) engagement in conduct that comes reasonably close to committing a battery, (2) having the present ability to succeed in committing the battery, and (3) intending to commit the battery. If one swings and misses, or throws a knife and misses, or shoots a gun and misses, each of these acts are all examples of this first type of an assault. The second type of assault is *intentionally placing another in fear*. This second type of assault is defined by the following elements: (1) the placing of another person (2) in fear (3) that he or she will receive an immediate battery; (4) the victim must be in fact apprehensive; (5) the conduct must be sufficient so as to create apprehension in a reasonable person; and (6) the defendant had the intent to cause apprehension.

Rape

The crime of rape is also a crime against the person. In the common law **rape** is defined as (1) unlawful (2) sexual intercourse (3) with a female (4) without her consent (5) with the intent to rape. In most states, a rape must be forceful, and in many states, when a man has sexual intercourse with a female and the only resistance he has from her is her saying "no," her verbal objection alone is often considered legally insufficient to negate consent.

Under common law, the defendant must have compelled an act of sexual intercourse with a woman other than his wife without her consent. The slightest penetration of the female sexual organs suffices for the *actus reus*. Although a husband traditionally could not commit rape against his wife, modern statutes in forty-nine states now allow the prosecution of a husband for raping his wife. Furthermore, modern statutes have criminalized the forcible rape of a male by a female. Although the consent of the victim is usually a defense to a rape charge, if the consent was obtained from an intoxicated, mentally retarded, or insane victim, the consent is invalid.

Consent Usually Negates Rape All rapes must be without the consent of the victim. Often, the victim appears to give consent, but this consent will not preclude conviction. Examples of such type of illegal consent include consent that was obtained by serious or immediate bodily harm; consent that was given by a victim lacking the capacity, due to her intoxication, mental deficiency, or insanity; and consent that was obtained by deceiving the victim about the nature of the act. For example, if a gynecologist gains consent to penetrate with medical instruments and in fact sexually penetrates the patient, this is consent by fraud. Finally, consent is invalidated if the defendant has deceived the victim into believing she was married to him. But other types of fraud will not invalidate consent. This means that if a woman consents based on a lie told to her by the perpetrator, the act is not rape.

The* Mens Rea *of Rape It is unclear exactly what the *mens rea* of rape is. Traditionally, it is the intent to rape. Some states require that the rapist *must know* that the victim is not consenting; if he doesn't know that, there is no rape. Other states require that if a reasonable person would know the victim was not consenting, then the courts will hold the same standard to the defendant. This was the standard used in the rape case of Mike Tyson, former world heavyweight boxing champion. Another famous rape case in the

---

CTQ

When a woman has consented to intercourse while she was drunk, but states that she would not have consented had she not been so intoxicated, the man can be charged with rape. Do you think this legal doctrine is fair and should be kept as part of our laws?

news is that of William Kennedy Smith, where the *mens rea* of rape was an issue in the jury decision.

Traditionally, the defendant was allowed to introduce the rape victim's prior sexual promiscuity as evidence to show that she consented to the act. However, due to the initiative of women's movements across the country, most states now have **rape shield statutes**[25] that disallow evidence of any prior sexual activities by the victim—even evidence that the victim was a prostitute.

Statutory Rape Rape is often confused with **statutory rape.** There are two major differences between these crimes. Rape is *forcible* sexual intercourse in which the victim *never consents*; statutory rape is *unlawful* sexual intercourse in which the victim *is definitely consenting*. Statutory rape is defined as (1) sexual intercourse with a female (2) who is too young to give legally effective consent. The age of consent is set by state statutes. Some statutes set the age of consent as young as 14. Others require that the child be 18. Statutory rape is a strict-liability crime. Hence, the defendant's awareness of the victim's age or his reasonable mistaken belief that she was older is irrelevant under this general rule.

Sexually Neutral Offenses A number of jurisdictions have replaced the crime of rape with a new offense called *sexual assault*, or criminal sexual conduct that is designed to be sexually neutral. Under these new statutes, the victim can be of either sex—the offense need not involve a female victim, but rather covers consensual sexual behavior (see the Landmark Case *State v. Walden*). Furthermore, the offenses have been extended to cover not only the traditional vaginal penetration necessary for the crime of rape, but also nonconsensual cunnilingus, anal intercourse, fellatio, any intrusions into any cavity by objects, and intentional touching of the victim's genital parts for the purpose of sexual gratification.

Some states do not require penetration, but instead define rape as "carnal knowledge of the woman." **Carnal knowledge** is defined as having sexual bodily connection. Under many statutes, there is carnal knowledge if there is slight penetration of the sexual organs of the woman, and often it is not necessary that the vaginal canal be entered. Sexual contact without penetration is generally referred to as carnal knowledge. Most states have expanded their definitions of rape; for example, Michigan criminalizes **sexually neutral offenses.** Under these statutes, assaults other than vaginal penetration, including forced sodomy, are criminalized. Likewise, penetration of an unconsenting male is punished under these statutes.[26]

Date Rape The nationally publicized trials of socialite William Kennedy Smith and heavyweight boxer Mike Tyson introduced the public to another element of intimate violence: **date rape** and date battering. Date rape has the exact same elements as the traditional crime of rape; each of these elements must be proven beyond a reasonable doubt.

> **CTQ**
>
> Do you believe that the *mens rea* of rape should be defined to include cases in which the defendant did not know that the victim was not consenting—or should it use a more general standard that a reasonable person would have known the victim was not consenting, even though the defendant, in fact, did not know she was consenting?

> **CTQ**
>
> Considering that boys and girls today are developing sexually at a much younger age than before, do you think that age 16 is the proper age of consent in the twenty-first century, or should it be lowered?

LANDMARK CASE — State v. Walden

Walden allegedly forced an acquaintance to engage in oral sexual intercourse by holding him in a headlock position. When convicted of second-degree rape, Walden alleged in appeal that the trial court should have instructed the jury on fourth-degree assault because the elements of fourth-degree assault are all necessary elements of second-degree rape and because the evidence supported an inference that he committed fourth-degree assault. The issue before the court was, does rape criminalize nonconsensual sexual intercourse regardless of criminal intent or knowledge? The court ruled that yes, it does criminalize it. The court went on to say that fourth-degree assault is not an inherent characteristic of second-degree rape such that the latter cannot be committed without also committing fourth-degree assault. The crime of assault requires proof of intent; rape does not.

Source: State v. Walden, 67 Wash. App. 891, 841 P.2d 81 (1992).

IN THE WORKPLACE

CRISIS INTERVENTION COUNSELOR

Responsible for providing crisis counseling and supportive listening to clients, by phone and in person. Performs a variety of duties, including the following: act as rape counselor when necessary, provide follow-up, provide advocacy, assist in statistical data compilation and file maintenance, assist in training and evaluation of volunteer counselors, and assist in community educational initiatives. Minimum requirements are as follows: associate of arts degree, or must be a degree-seeking student in a mental-health-related field; one year crisis intervention training and experience.

However, sociological factors differentiate date rape from stranger rape": (1) the victim always knows the suspect, and (2) in many instances the victim has voluntarily engaged in some forms of moderate sexual activity with the defendant before she refuses to consent to his efforts to initiate sexual intercourse. Despite their prevalence, less than one in ten date rapes may be reported to police.[27] Some victims fail to report date rapes because they do not view their experiences as "real rape," which they believe involves a strange man jumping out of the bushes; others are embarrassed and frightened.

CTQ
Compare and contrast date rape with forcible rape.

Many date rapes occur on college campuses, in dormitories and fraternity houses. Demeaning hazing rituals and antifemale attitudes support a climate in which date rape and gang rape are common. To fight back, some campus women's groups have taken to writing the names of the men accused of date rape and sexual assault on bathroom walls so that women can avoid these predators. Unfortunately, agents of the criminal justice system have not responded as vigorously to intimate violence as they have to stranger assaults.

Sexual Harassment Is Not a Crime

Ever since Clarence Thomas, a Supreme Court Justice nominee, was accused by a former subordinate, Anita Hill, of sexually harassing her, the law of sexual harassment has come to the forefront of acts considered deviant by the American public. Several state, federal, and local regulations control **sexual harassment** at job sites, which is essentially defined as (1) creating a hostile atmosphere that is sexually charged and makes it unpleasant to work in because of the atmosphere, or (2) what is called *quid pro quo sexual harassment*, in which advancement and benefits are offered in exchange for submitting to sexual advances. Some cases receive national attention because they involve famous defendants.

The Supreme Court ruled in 1986 that workers could sue for sexual harassment, but until 1998 it failed to define the term. In three 1998 cases, the Supreme Court established new parameters for behavior in both schools and workplaces (see Table 2.5 for

TABLE 2.5 Sexual Harassment Issues That the Supreme Court Has Changed

Issue	Old Rule	New Rule
What is harassment?	To prove harassment, a worker has to show that because she resisted sexual advances she was punished in terms of salary, assignments, or promotions.	It can count as harassment even if an employee is otherwise treated well.
Is ignorance a defense?	If a manager isn't informed that one of his or her employees is harassing other workers, the supervisor probably is not responsible for the harasser's actions.	The manager can be held responsible for a harasser's actions—unless a company has a strong system of dealing with problems.
Whom do you inform?	Tell someone if you have been harassed.	Tell a person with decision-making power if you have been harassed.

IN THE NEWS

A HUMAN PERSPECTIVE

HARASSED OR HAZED?
By J. Cloud

WHY THE SUPREME COURT RULED THAT MEN CAN SUE MEN FOR SEXUAL HARASSMENT

Little more than a decade ago, the Supreme Court had said nothing yet about sexual harassment, and a Court stuffed with Ronald Reagan's and George Bush's appointees might have been expected to maintain the silence. But since 1986, the Court has ruled three times on the issue, and every time, feminists have rejoiced. Last week that happy chorus was joined by men and women alike who feel harassers and their victims aren't always members of the opposite sex.

In a unanimous decision written by one of the most conservative Justices, Antonin Scalia, the Court said men who sexually harass other men (and women who harass women) are discriminating against them and thus breaking a law, the 1964 Civil Rights Act. It was only 12 years ago that the Court ruled for the first time that sexual harassment amounted to discrimination. The decision was seen as an advance for women suffering abuse from lecherous bosses and co-workers. But Scalia pointed out that the law has always been gender-blind: "Sexual harassment of any kind," he wrote, is illegal.

The ruling reinstates the case of oil-rig worker Joseph Oncale—earlier thrown out by an appeals court—against Sundowner Offshore Services, a Houston firm that drills for oil in the Gulf of Mexico. Oncale claims that three male co-workers held him down in a shower and shoved a bar of soap between his buttocks. One of them threatened rape, he says. He quit and later was found to have posttraumatic stress.

Brutal, yes. But illegal sexual harassment? Even after the Supreme Court's ruling, Oncale might not convince a jury that Sundowner and its men discriminated against him. Scalia's brief opinion merely allows the possibility for the first time. Sundowner attorney Harry Reasoner says his clients deny the shower incident. They admit to roughhousing with Oncale, but they didn't single him out for special abuse, Reasoner says. "All males who go onto an offshore platform are subject to a kind of hazing." Reasoner also points out that Oncale could have brought state assault charges against the men but went for a federal suit that could yield a fatter award.

Oncale will have to convince a jury that he was discriminated against "because of" his gender. That's what the Civil Rights Act says. Scalia noted that behavior with mere "sexual content" isn't necessarily illegal. There's no law against acting like a sex-crazed boor—so long as one acts that way to men and women alike. The Court isn't creating any "general civility code," Scalia noted.

The Oncale decision is the first of four sexual harassment cases before the Court. In two of the cases, the Court will determine the extent to which employers are liable for harassment perpetrated by non-management employees. In another case, the Court will decide whether a woman threatened with retaliation for refusing a sexual advance—but never actually punished—can go ahead with her lawsuit.

Source: J. Cloud, "Harassed or Hazed?" *Time*, 16 March 1998. © 1998 TIME Inc. Reprinted by permission.

---

a summary of the Supreme Court changes in sexual harassment laws). Finally, the Court said in 1998 that men could sue other men for sexual harassment (see "In the News: Harassed or Hazed?").

False Imprisonment

Still another crime against the person is **false imprisonment.** The elements of false imprisonment are (1) intentional, (2) unlawful (3) confinement or restraint (4) of another (5) with the intent to confine. There is no false imprisonment when the defendant was acting under legal authority, such as the actions of a police officer. The victim must be compelled by the defendant's use of force or his or her threats of the use of force to remain somewhere the victim doesn't want to be or to go somewhere the victim doesn't want to go.

Kidnapping

Kidnapping is aggravated false imprisonment. The elements of kidnapping are (1) confinement and movement of the victim (also called *abduction*), (2) plus an aggravating factor(s) (including confinement in a secret place, confinement by deadly force or threats thereof, or confinement for the purposes of extortion, ransom, or sexual abuse), (3) intent to abduct, and (4) intent to perform one of the aggravating factors. Kidnapping is usually punished as a felony in most states and is punished severely. However, some statutes authorize a reduction in the penalty when the defendant releases the victim in a safe condition.

CTQ

Many states have passed laws allowing a smaller maximum sentence for the kidnapper if the victim is safely returned. Are you in favor of reducing the punishment for such an act, or should all kidnappers be punished equally?

CRIMES AGAINST HABITATION

The third general classification of crimes in the common law are **crimes against habitation.** These crimes are against the place where a citizen sleeps regularly (his or her dwelling house). These crimes include burglary and arson.

Burglary

Burglary is legally defined as having the following elements: (1) the breaking (2) and entering (3) of the dwelling house (4) of another (5) in the nighttime (6) with the intent to commit a felony (7) therein. For a burglary to be committed, the "break-in" must be accomplished by the use of force to create an unconsensual opening of the structure where none previously existed. The use of force is not necessarily required to satisfy the element of breaking. Breaking also may be accomplished by fraud, threats, or collusion with someone already inside. The second element of burglary, entry, can be either actual entry or constructive entry into the structure. *Actual entry* into a structure requires only the slightest human physical intrusion into the structure to occur. *Constructive entry* is accomplished when the defendant sends an innocent agent (a child or someone who is mentally retarded) into the structure to effect the offender's felonious design. The third element, *dwelling house*, in common law means a place where one regularly sleeps; for example, in a residence or domicile. The fourth element of burglary, *of another*, simply means that one cannot burglarize his or her own dwelling. The common-law courts have stated that the determining factor in deciding whether a given dwelling belongs to one person or another is to determine who has the "superior right to habitation to the dwelling house." Therefore, ownership of the dwelling house is not determinative. Hence, a landlord (who may own the house) still can burglarize his own home that is presently being leased by a tenant, because the lease agreement gives the tenant a superior right to habitation over the landlord. The fifth common-law element of burglary is that it must be perpetrated in the nighttime. This element was created because at the time of the writing of the common law, there was no electricity. Hence, intrusions into a home during the night were cause for great alarm, as they still are today, since one simply cannot see who is in the home late at night.

> **CTQ**
> An everyday experience of homeowners in America is that they come home to see their house ransacked and scream, "We have been robbed!" Why is this statement a total legal mischaracterization of the situation?

The *mens rea* element of burglary is satisfied if, at the time that the defendant breaks and enters into the dwelling, he or she has the intent to commit a felony upon the moment of entry. The *mens rea* for burglary is the intent to commit a felony inside. It can be any felony. But the courts insist that the intent to commit a felony must be fully formed at the time of the breaking and entering. If the felonious intent comes a short time afterward, there is no burglary.

Most career burglars' motive for breaking and entering into someone else's structure is the intent to steal. Often, laypeople think of someone who has been burglarized as a theft victim or even sometimes a robbery victim. However, this is a crime against habitation, not a crime against the person or a crime against property; if one breaks and enters into a structure with the intent to rape, rob, kidnap, or commit any other felony, the crime is still burglary. However, if the burglar commits the more serious crime, he or she will be charged with that crime as well.

> **CTQ**
> Is it possible for a college student who has a roommate sharing an apartment to be a victim of a burglary by that roommate if the roommate comes into a mutually shared room and steals the student's watch?

How the Elements of Common-Law Burglary Have Been Modified by Modern American Criminal Statutes Modern statutes have significantly modified the crime of burglary. The following changes are typical. In many states, the element of breaking is not required. Often, the requirement that entry be accomplished by breaking has been eliminated. As a result, any entry, however accomplished, is sufficient.[28]

Another change is that the structure need not be a "dwelling house"; structures other than dwellings can now be subject to burglary. Some modern statutes also extend the crime to the entry of motor vehicles. The California Penal Code illustrates how expansive the element of burglary of a dwelling house has become; it covers the entry of a house, room, apartment, shop, warehouse, store, mill, barn, stable, outhouse, other building, tent, railroad car, trailer coach, vehicle, aircraft, or mine.[29] However, the common-law definition of "dwelling house" has maintained its integrity in the fact that most states penalize burglarizing a dwelling house more severely than burglarizing an uninhabited structure. "In the nighttime" is another element that has all but practically dissipated. All fifty states recognize daytime burglaries. However, like the element of "dwelling house," "nighttime" has maintained some of its common-law power through punishment; in most states, burglary in the nighttime is punished more severely than other forms of burglary. The *mens rea* of burglary has also expanded. The intent element of burglary is frequently broadened to include the intent to commit a felony "or any theft," whether a felony or not. The Model Penal Code [30] allows the intent "to commit any crime."

Arson

The other common-law crime against habitation is arson. The common-law elements of **arson** are as follows: (1) the malicious (2) burning (3) of a dwelling house (4) of another. The legal definitions of "dwelling house" and "of another" are the same as in the crime of burglary. The distinguishing element of common-law arson is "burning." In order to be guilty of arson, one must burn some part of the structure. This means that the structure itself must be physically damaged by fire. This effect is called "slight charring." However, if the structure is merely discolored by heat or smoke there is no arson. The *mens rea* of arson is twofold. First, the defendant must have intended to burn the structure. However, case law has articulated that if a defendant did not intend to burn the structure but intentionally and without justification or excuse created an obvious fire hazard to the structure, this state of mind is also sufficiently blameworthy to create the *mens rea* necessary for arson (see Figure 2.10).

CTQ

Since arson criminalizes only the burning of the dwelling of another, does this mean that there is no crime committed when one intentionally and maliciously burns down his or her own home?

How the Elements of Common-Law Arson Have Been Modified by Modern American Criminal Statutes Modern statutes tend to expand somewhat on the common-law crime of arson. Common modifications are as follows. Modern statutes allow the burning of structures other than just dwellings. The burning of many structures is often punished as arson. The California Penal Code[31] makes it arson to burn any structure "for slander or property."

The element of "another" has been modified by modern arson statutes, which sometimes prohibit the burning of structures without regard to ownership or occupancy. Thus, arson can be committed by burning a structure that the defendant owns and occupies. Unbelievably, some statutes have eliminated the element of "burning." With the problems of the common-law concept of "burning" (scorching versus charring), lawmakers attempted to eliminate it by requiring that the defendant start a fire with the intent of damaging or destroying the structure concerned without a fire actually starting.[32] The common-law element of "dwelling house" has also expanded; some states have broadened arson to include the burning of another's personal property (clothes, backpacks, and so on). This type of arson is punished less severely than arson involving the destruction of a structure.

A spin-off of the crime of arson is the crime of *arson with the intent to defraud the insurer*, or intentional burning for the purpose of collecting insurance, which is frequently made a separate but related crime to the crime of arson. Some states go further, prohibiting starting a fire with the intent to damage property and collect the insurance for it. Finally, arson, unlike many of the common-law crimes, is a felony in all fifty states, regardless of the insignificance of the property that was burned.

FIGURE 2.10

Contrary to popular belief, the substantive criminal law of arson requires only a partial combustive burning of a structure rather than total destruction by fire.

Courtesy Pearson Education/PH College.

CRIMES AGAINST PROPERTY—THE ACQUISITION OFFENSES

The fourth general classification of crimes after homicide, crimes against persons, and crimes against habitation is crimes against property, or *acquisition offenses*. These property crimes include larceny, robbery, embezzlement, false pretense, extortion, receiving stolen property, and all forms of theft.

Larceny

Larceny is the most clearly defined crime in common law. Larceny is a crime against another's "possessory interest" in property. Larceny's elements are (1) taking (2) and carrying away (3) the personal property (4) of another (5) with the intent to permanently deprive the owner of the property.

In order for the state to prove that the defendant took the property, it merely needs to show that the defendant has acquired "dominion and control" over the property. Courts have said this means that the defendant could gain physical possession over the property should he or she so desire.

Some defendants who steal know no social or economic boundaries. In order to prove the element of "carrying away," the state must present evidence that the defendant in fact carried the property away (see Figure 2.11). What is necessary to satisfy this element? Restated, how far must the property be carried away? The courts have continually stated that the "slightest movement in a carrying away motion" is sufficient. In common law, the word *property* within the context of the larceny law referred only to tangible personal property. Hence, other property such as realty, fixtures, tame and wild animals, intangibles, intellectual property, and services could not be subject to larceny. Above all, if the property that was taken was in fact tangible personal property, another requirement still exists to convict; the state must prove that the property was a "thing of value" (see the Landmark Case *People v. Home Insurance Co.*).

Consent is a defense to larceny. This is because the taking element of larceny must be a "trespassory taking"; that is, the taking must have been accomplished without the victim's effective consent. As was the case with burglary, the larceny element "of another" usually means that a person cannot commit the crime of larceny against himself or herself. However, the principle of law is well received in certain cases; one can steal from oneself, especially if the person you take your property from has a "superior right to possession" than you do. For example, suppose a college student takes his car into a repair shop, but when he returns to pick up the car, he finds it in worse shape than when he originally brought it in. Thinking to himself, "I'm not going to pay money on an inadequate job," he enters the car, starting it with a spare key, and proceeds to drive away.

FIGURE 2.11

So-called "shoplifting" is the most frequent type of larceny committed in the United States.

Courtesy David Young-Wolff/Getty Images Inc.

WEB

For more information on how the elements of these common-law crimes have been modified by your own state's code, **visit our Web site, www.prenhall.com/territo.**

CTQ

Almost all states require that the *mens rea* of arson of a structure is the intent to burn the structure; however, in the new crime of woods arson, the defendant could be convicted if the burning occurred only through negligence. Do you believe that this disparity of intents is justified?

CTQ

It is generally agreed that crimes against property constitute 60 percent of all criminal offenses. Why do you think they are so seldom glamorized in television and film, compared to crimes of violence and sexual misconduct?

LANDMARK CASE — People v. Home Insurance Co.

Agents of the Home Insurance Company were charged with theft for procuring confidential medical records of two Denver hospital patients. The trial court granted a motion to dismiss, declaring that confidentiality records were not a thing of value, therefore not subject to theft. The state appealed.

In answering the issue of whether confidentiality of a medical record is a thing of value, the appellate court of Colorado stated that no, it is not. The language of the ruling states that intangible personal property generally is property representative of value such as stocks and bonds, and there is no statutory basis for expanding the meaning of this to cover confidentiality of medical records. The court admitted that although this was an invasion of medical records, and may give rise to civil liability, the confidentiality lost due to the procurement of such records is not a thing of value, and hence is not subject to prosecution for theft.

Source: People v. Home Insurance Co., 197 Colo. 261, 251 P.2d 1063 (1979).

Subsequently, he could be prosecuted for larceny of his own car. The legal principle here is that the garage owner, after working on the car, had a mechanic's lien on the car because he had put his own labor into it. The person with the lien has the superior right to possession, and the owner does not regain the superior right to possession until the lien has been removed, which usually means that the labor has been paid for. Hence, if someone has a lien on another's property and the owner of the property takes the property away from the lien holder, he or she commits an act of larceny.

The *mens rea* of larceny is that the defendant must have intended to permanently deprive the victim of his or her property. If he or she intends to temporarily deprive the owner of property (for example, joyriding in someone else's automobile), the defendant commits the crime of *wrongful appropriation*. The courts have also stated that whenever someone takes another person's property without the intent to permanently deprive, but in the course of the taking of the property he or she creates a substantial risk of permanent loss of the property, this state of mind also satisfies the *mens rea* of the crime of larceny.

The crime of shoplifting is a type of larceny that is perpetrated probably more than any other type of larceny. Many suggest indeed that it is the most common form of larceny.

How the Elements of Common-Law Larceny Have Been Modified by Modern American Criminal Statutes Modern statutes have significantly refined the five elements of common-law larceny. For example, most statutes define larceny-type crimes as ones of taking or conducting an "exercise of control" over the property. Accordingly, it is likely that the traditional common-law analysis of taking will still be applied in its purest form. Modern statutes have made larceny one type of theft, often dispensing with the requirement of "taking away" entirely. The Model Penal Code[33] requires only an exercise of control over property, and not the "carrying away." This is often found in shoplifting cases; when the shoplifter only conceals an item, even though he or she is still in the store and has not taken it away, he or she is at that moment guilty of shoplifting. Personal property, an element of larceny, has changed dramatically. Modern jurisdictions have expanded the definition of property to include electronically processed store data and either tangible or intangible data while in transit; although such items were not included in common law, larceny now includes the theft of gas, services, pets, and intangibles as well as real property. Modern statutes have changed the *mens rea* of larceny to a degree—from the intent to permanently deprive to the specific intent to deprive the owner of his or her property. This includes withholding property for an extended period of time, or withholding property with the intent to restore only upon payment of a reward, or disposing of property in such a way as to make it unlikely that the owner would recover it.

Robbery

Robbery is aggravated larceny. The first five elements of robbery are identical with the first five elements of larceny. However, the crux of robbery is in the final two additional elements. It is general knowledge that anyone who becomes involved in or is in the general vicinity of an ongoing armed robbery has placed himself or herself in one of the most dangerous situations and crime scenes in America. Why do people take the risks associated with committing the incredibly dangerous crime of armed robbery? Table 2.6 gives us an additional understanding which we might not have otherwise.

The common-law elements of robbery are (1) taking (2) and carrying away (3) the personal property (4) of another (5) with the intent to permanently deprive the owner of the property, and (6) taking the property in the presence of the victim (7) by the means of either violence or intimidation, or both. Therefore, if the state proves that the taking was a larceny, then the prosecution merely needs to prove the two additional elements to gain a robbery conviction.

The sixth element of robbery is "taking in the presence of the victim," defined as taking property while it is on the victim's person, or is close enough to the victim that he or she could have prevented the taking had the defendant not used violence or intimidation.

Taking by the use of violence or intimidation (the seventh element of robbery) is legally defined as the use of any force applied to overcome the victim's immediate

CTQ

Have you or any of your friends ever been guilty of shoplifting? Why do you think this crime holds such a fascination for kids between ages 12 and 17?

CTQ

Robbery and extortion are often confused. Can you differentiate between the two crimes?

TABLE 2.6 Motivation for Robbery

Motivation	Percent
Money	57%
For drugs	17
For food and shelter	8
For other specific items	16
General desire for money	16
Other Than Money	24%
Excitement	6
Anger	6
Impress friends	6
Not sure; drunk or on drugs	6
Not Really a Robber	19%
Recover money owed	5
Interrupted burglary	4
Fight turned into a robbery	4
Partner started robbery	6

Source: President's Commission on Law Enforcement and Administration of Justice, *Crime and Its Impact: An Assessment* (Washington, D.C.: U.S. Government Printing Office).

resistance. If someone commits a battery to steal, this is referred to as *strong-armed robbery*. Threats (in the law of robbery, they are referred to as "intimidation") also can be used to satisfy the seventh element of robbery. The courts require that these intimidations must be made toward the victim, or toward someone in his or her family, or toward someone (who may be a total stranger) in his or her presence. Traditionally, the robbery threat or intimidation threatens great bodily harm or immediate death.

CTQ
Why would a bad pickpocket be guilty of robbery, while a good pickpocket would only be guilty of larceny?

How the Elements of Common-Law Robbery Have Been Modified by Modern American Criminal Statutes Practically the only change carried out by the modern penal code was dispensing with the former requirement that the intent to steal and the taking and carrying away with violence and intimidation must occur at the exact same time.[34]

Embezzlement

If larceny is a crime against possession, **embezzlement** is a crime against ownership. The six elements of embezzlement are (1) fraudulent (2) conversion (3) of the property (4) of another (5) by one who is already in lawful possession thereof (6) with the intent to defraud the victim. As always, the burden of proof is on the state to prove each and every one of these six elements beyond a reasonable doubt. If the jury has a reasonable doubt on just one of the six elements, it must acquit the defendant.

Embezzlers have been trusted employees charged with taking care of the owner's property. Well-respected citizens within our community such as accountants, lawyers, store managers, and treasurers ironically typify the kinds of people who are indicted for embezzlement. Quite often these types of professionals already have the money in hand, a financial problem arises which they do not have the money to cover, and thinking that they are only "temporarily" borrowing the money that they are in charge of, they take it with the intent to return it once their financial position restabilizes. They are subsequently audited and charged with embezzlement.

CTQ
Do you think people who steal from people who trust them with their money (embezzlement) should be punished more severely than people who commit larceny?

The most distinguishing element in the crime of embezzlement is the element of conversion. **Conversion** requires a thief to make a serious act of interference with the owner's rights. Simple movement of the property without anything more is not enough. The conversion must be accompanied by the defendant's intent to defraud the victim (see Figure 2.12). The totality of the circumstances is used to see if a conversion took place. Normally, juries look at the limits with which the owner has permitted the defendant to

FIGURE 2.12

Embezzlement is often considered a white-collar crime—sometimes committed by some of America's wealthiest citizens, such as oil conglomerate Enron's accused chief executive officer Kenneth Lay.

Courtesy Paul Hosefros/New York Times Pictures.

freely use his property or money. If this limit is breached, conversion has occurred. Essentially, this means that if property has been used in some authorized manner beyond the scope of the owner's permission, then the property has been converted. (See the Landmark Case *United States v. Wilson*.)

How the Elements of Common-Law Embezzlement Have Been Modified by Modern American Criminal Statutes Embezzlement was not a common-law crime. It was created by the British Parliament in 1798 to close some of the loopholes in the larceny law. Hence, for the most part, the elements have remained unscathed by modern statutes.

Obtaining Property by False Pretense or Fraud

False pretense is acquiring someone else's property through the use of deception, trick, beguile, lying, or outright fraud. Often, this is referred to as fraudulent theft. Generally, the crime of false pretense is defined by the following elements: (1) obtaining title (2) to the property of another (3) by means of a material false representation (4) with intent to defraud the victim (5) knowing that the material false representation was false.

LANDMARK CASE — United States v. Wilson

Wilson was employed by a division of the U.S. department of Health, Education, and Welfare, which was abolished and reorganized. Wilson was subsequently employed by another government agency, yet in the interim remained with his old agency payroll. He simply had no work to do during this period, but did not avoid any assignments. It was at this time he asked his secretary, who was in the same situation of inactivity, to type some reports for a private woodworking business that he was going to start after his retirement. She agreed to do so, while on government time and property. Wilson was convicted of embezzlement of government property and using a secretarial service for personal use.

On appeal the issue before the court was, does the element of conversion occur only if its control is knowingly exercised over the property to such an extent that it seriously interferes with the rights of the owner? The court agreed that yes, it does, stating the rule that in this case, there is no evidence that Wilson failed to perform government work instead of private activity, or that he concealed the use of the labor work of his secretary. As a result, the government failed to show beyond a reasonable doubt that Wilson converted government property. Wilson's conviction was reversed.

Source: United States v. Wilson, 636 F.2d 225 (1980).

False pretense is the crime of the con artist. The critical element of this acquisition offense is the element of the *material false misrepresentation*, which simply means that the property was acquired as a result of the lies, trickery, foolery, deceit, or scam of the defendant. The nature of the misrepresentation or lies must concern only past facts or present fact. If a con artist lies about future facts, he or she does not commit false pretense. The common-law requirement that the defendant obtain the title to the property simply meant that the scam was so complete that the victim did not just give temporary possession of his or her goods or money to the thief. Rather, the victim gave up all his or her property as a result of the scam.

There is a double *mens rea* to the crime of false pretense. The defendant must (1) know that the misrepresentation is false (the defendant knows he or she is lying), and (2) must have intended to defraud the victim. That is, there is no false pretense if the defendant believed the property was his or her own or if he or she intended to restore it.

Extortion (Blackmail)

Extortion is extremely similar to robbery. The elements of extortion (often called blackmail) are (1) obtaining (2) property (3) by the use of threats (4) with the intent to obtain the property. The extortion threats used by blackmailers consist of four different types (1) threats to injure or kill a person, (2) threats to accuse a person of a crime, (3) threats to expose a person's personal secret, and (4) threats to expose an individual's disgrace or deformity. Regardless of the amount of property gained from the extortion threat, even though it may be an unusually small amount of money, under modern statutes the crime of extortion is usually punished as a felony.

Receiving Stolen Property

Receiving stolen property generally consists of four elements: (1) receiving (2) stolen property, (3) knowing it was stolen, (4) with the intent to deprive the owner of the property. Property that has been recovered by the police acting on the owner's behalf is no longer "stolen." (See the Landmark Case *People v. Rojas*.)

Also, the defendant is not guilty of a crime if he or she subsequently acquires the recovered property. Furthermore, the property must in fact have been stolen at the time the defendant received it. Normally, this means that property was obtained by robbery, burglary, or larceny. However, some statutes fail to cover property obtained by embezzlement or false pretense.

The defendant's "knowledge" of the stolen nature of the property can be inferred by circumstantial evidence. Usually, this consists of the nature of the shady character from whom the property was acquired, or the criminal-like circumstances in which the property was acquired. Also, the courts look very strictly at whether the property was ac-

---

CTQ

Many victims of false pretense are elderly people, who are scammed into purchasing items or sending money by enticements over the telephone. Do you believe that when the victims are elderly, the punishment should be more severe since they are more vulnerable?

CTQ

One legal commentator said that extortion is the "sleaziest of all crimes" because the victim cannot charge his or her accuser without exposing that which the victim most definitely does not want to be made public—and hence, the victim wrestles with the decision whether to legally prosecute or not. Do you agree with the "sleazy" characterization of extortion?

CTQ

How can you be certain that any items in your wardrobe or music collection that were given to you as gifts by friends were not stolen property? If they were, are you guilty of receiving stolen property?

LANDMARK CASE — People v. Rojas

Hall had arranged with Rojas to sell him all the electric conduit he could steal. After stealing $4,500 worth, Hall was caught with the conduit by the police. Thereupon he arranged with the police to sell the recaptured goods to Rojas. Immediately upon making the purchase Rojas was arrested and convicted of receiving stolen property. On appeal the court looked at the issue of whether these goods were actually stolen, since the crime was completed and the goods had already been recovered by the police. The court held that no, these were not stolen goods, saying that goods, once recovered by the police, lose their status as stolen goods, and anyone who subsequently receives them cannot be convicted of receiving stolen property.

Source: People v. Rojas, 55 Cal. 2d 252 (1961).

quired at an extraordinarily disproportionately low purchase price. These three circumstantial facts allow the jury to infer that that the defendant knew the property was stolen.

CONSENSUAL CRIMES

Organized crime is profitable because many people are willing, even eager to buy illegal goods and services. The buyers, too, are breaking the law. Who are the victims of organized crime? Gambling, prostitution, and deviant drug use are also illegal, but it is often difficult to pinpoint the victims. Thus, these activities are often called **consensual crimes** or victimless crimes—illegal acts in which all parties choose to be involved. Other victimless crimes include some types of pornography and deviant sexual acts among consenting adults.

Some people argue that these crimes are *not* victimless crimes, that they in fact harm a broad range of people and society in general. Because social norms are violated, the offenses might instead be called *public-order* offenses. At any rate, many people question whether these acts—even if they are shameful, immoral, or harmful—should be defined as crimes (see Table 2.7). Two arguments are often made for decriminalizing activities such as marijuana use, pornography, and prostitution. First, critics argue that criminal sanctions against these activities constitute an unwarranted intrusion into individual privacy and an indefensible extension of the government's authority. In other words, is it the government's business what sexual activities consenting adults engage in, or whether they gamble? Second, some critics claim that enforcing laws against these activities overburdens the police, the courts, and the prisons and increases congestion problems in the criminal justice system.

Although some consensual crimes are not considered serious by most criminal justice students, there are certainly cases of these particular kinds of crime every day. See the Landmark Cases of *State v. Peery* and *Smith v. California* for examples.

CTQ

Which consensual crimes do you believe are victimless crimes and which do you believe are not victimless crimes? Explain why.

WEB

For more information on each of the fifty states' criminal classifications of particular consensual offenses, **visit our Web site, www.prenhall.com/ territo.**

TABLE 2.7 Fifteen Consensual and Nonconsensual Sex Offenses

Fornication	Sexual intercourse between two unmarried people or between one married person and one unmarried person.
Adultery	Sexual intercourse between a man and a woman, at least one of whom is married to someone else.
Incest	Sexual intercourse between any two people who are too closely related to each other by either law or marriage, according to state statute.
Sodomy	Certain consensual sexual acts, including *fellatio* (oral contact with the male sex organ), *cunnilingus* (oral contact with the female sex organ), *buggery* (penetration of the anus), *homosexuality* (sexual relations between members of the same sex), and *bestiality* (sexual intercourse with an animal).
Indecent exposure	(Exhibitionism) Exposing one's own sexual organs to others in a public place.
Lewdness	Degenerate sexual behavior that is so well known that it may result in the corruption of public decency.
Obscenity	A display of an apparently prurient sexual act that is offensive to the morality of the general public living in the area where it occurred.
Pornography	Literature, art, film, and articles whose subject matter is of an extreme, sexually explicit nature to such an extent that it is considered obscene by a community's moral standards.
Bigamy	The act of marrying another person while still married to someone else; often a strict-liability crime.
Prostitution	Offering to have sexual relations with another person in exchange for monetary or other gain as payment for the sexual acts.
Child molestation	(In some cases) Handling, fondling, or making other lewd contact of a sexual nature with a child.
Exhibitionism	Engaging in public sexual acts in front of others, or disrobing in front of others to achieve sexual gratification.
Forcible rape	Having sexual intercourse with another person without his or her consent; usually accomplished through the use of threat of force or fear of violence.
Statutory rape	Sexual intercourse by a male with a female who is under the age of statutory consent. The age is set by each state (usually 16 or 18, but sometimes 14). In each instance of statutory rape, the victim is consenting to the intercourse.
Seduction	Gaining a woman's consent to have sexual intercourse with the defendant based on the promise that he will marry her, having sexual intercourse with her, and then retracting the promise.

LANDMARK CASE — State v. Peery

Peery, a student, lived in a college dormitory. He was an army veteran, and a professor testified that he was a man with a good reputation and of high standing in his class. However, the state charged him with indecent exposure. Some witnesses observed Peery standing in front of or near his window in the dormitory exposed to view and he was entirely unclothed. There was no evidence that he called to the witnesses or otherwise tried to attract their attention. Peery testified that he did not intentionally expose himself.

The issue before the court centered on whether one can expose himself or herself without the intent to do so in order to be indecent or lewd. The Minnesota Supreme Court said no, declaring that before one can be found guilty of indecent exposure it must be shown that the misconduct complained of was committed with the deliberate intent of being indecent or lewd.

Source: State v. Peery, 224 Minn. 346, 28 N.W.2d 851 (1947).

CRIMES AGAINST MORALITY

Of particular interest to criminal justice scholars are the crimes against morality. These crimes were unknown in common law and not punished by common-law courts. Instead, they were **ecclesiastical crimes,** tried and punished by the Church of England. Such a situation was impossible in the United States because of our religious pluralism (that is, what may be an act of righteousness in one church denomination may be a sin in another). Hence, giving each church the power to enforce criminally what it believes to be a crime against that particular church's morality would be disastrous. England had only one church, the Anglican church, and so there the system worked fine.

Historical Roots

In the early part of American history, one particular religious group (the Puritans) made a concerted effort to ensure that all the offenses against morality were criminalized by the state legislatures. For the most part, they were remarkably successful. Every state

> **CTQ**
> What do you think would be the consequences of reinstating ecclesiastical crimes to the jurisdiction of American churches and allowing them to punish members for what they consider to be crimes (sins) instead of the courts doing so?

LANDMARK CASE — Smith v. California

Smith was convicted under a Los Angeles strict-liability ordinance for having an obscene book in his shop. Guilt under the statute does not depend on knowledge of the obscene nature of the book; knowledge is imputed per se from the possession. On appeal, Smith challenged the use of strict-liability cases as placing an unacceptable burden on his First Amendment freedom of expression. The U.S. Supreme Court in 1959 answered the issue of whether a person may be held criminally responsible on a strict-liability basis even though such application of strict liability would tend to infringe First Amendment rights. Justice Brennan said no. The Court held that the state power to create strict-liability crimes is limited by constitutional guarantees of the First Amendment and the Bill of Rights. While the requirement of *mens rea* is the rule rather than the exception, strict-liability definitions are permissible where they do not otherwise conflict with the general limitations on criminal law or the Constitution. Where they do so conflict, as in this case, such strict-liability statutes, even though they are intended with the high-minded reason to regulate obscene literature, nonetheless place an unnecessary burden on the citizen's right to exercise his freedom of expression in nonobscene literature (by intimidation). The law was deemed unconstitutional.

Source: Smith v. California, 361 U.S. 147 (1959).

has at least one, if not all, of the following five crimes against morality: fornication, adultery, illicit cohabitation, bigamy, and incest.

Fornication

The crime of **fornication** is defined as (1) illicit (2) sexual intercourse (3) between people who are not married to each other. This crime consists, essentially, of engaging in premarital sex. Anyone who has engaged in sexual intercourse without being married has committed the crime of fornication.

Adultery

The crime of **adultery** is defined as (1) sexual intercourse (2) by a married person (3) with some person other than his or her spouse. In some states, a single person can be convicted of adultery if his or her partner is married. In other states, the crime of adultery is applicable only to married citizens. Adultery came to the forefront in the late 1990s with the case of the first female B-52 bomber who later was kicked out of the Air Force for adultery.

Illicit Cohabitation

The third crime against morality is **illicit cohabitation.** The elements of illicit cohabitation are (1) living together (2) in adultery (3) or fornication. This crime is committed on many college campuses by students who "live with each other," but are not yet married. Indeed, in the 2000 census, well over one-quarter of the couples interviewed were living together illicitly (CNN, *Headline News*, October 5, 2001). Cohabitation has been defined as liberally as a one-night stand in a hotel room.

Bigamy

Bigamy is the fourth crime against morality. It is committed by marrying another person while one's spouse is still living. Traditionally, this was a strict-liability crime (meaning that if you believed that you had a valid divorce or that your spouse was dead, such a belief was no defense for the crime). Most statutes have changed the strict-liability feature of bigamy.

Incest

The final crime against morality is **incest.** This crime is committed when two people either marry or have sexual relations when they are so closely related that the statute prohibits marriage or sexual relations. Some states declare that sexual intercourse between fourth cousins is incest. Other states, like Florida, define sexual intercourse between first cousins as nonincestuous.

Sodomy

As was stated earlier, illicit cohabitation as well as the other four crimes against morality were normally prosecuted in the church of England. However, with the advent of the Puritans, the many so-called sex crimes that were the five ecclesiastical crimes became criminalized as well other sex crimes at an alarming rate. One of these sex crimes in particular needs studying: the crime of **sodomy,** or "unnatural intercourse." Scientifically, this term applied only to the insertion of the penis into the rectum of another person. However, laws in most states have included the following activities under sodomy as well: oral-genital acts between two people, oral-anal intercourse between two people, and bestiality. Other states have defined sodomy to include *buggery* (penetration of the anus), *necrophilia*, (sexual intercourse with a dead body), *pederasty* (unnatural intercourse between a man and a boy), *cunnilingus* (oral contact with the female sex organ), *fellatio* (oral contact with the male sex organ), and *homosexuality* (sexual relations between members of the same sex). Sodomy is a wide topic, and in more than thirty states, one act of sodomy, including the ten different acts described previously, yields the maximum prison sentence of 15 years. The law of sodomy was challenged in the U.S. Supreme Court, using the argument that the law violates our constitutional right to privacy to do private acts in the private area of our own bedroom. However, in *Bowers v. Hardwick* [35] the Court declared sodomy law to be constitutional. Figure 2.13 shows which states have sodomy laws.

CTQ

Since most surveys indicate that the vast majority of Americans are sexually active by the time they are 22, which necessarily means that they committed the crime of fornication, do you consider these people to be criminals? Why or why not?

CTQ

In the 2000 census, the results indicated that more than 50 percent of people living together were not married. Is half of our population committing the crime of illicit cohabitation? If so, why are they not being arrested?

FIGURE 2.13

Sodomy Laws in the United States.

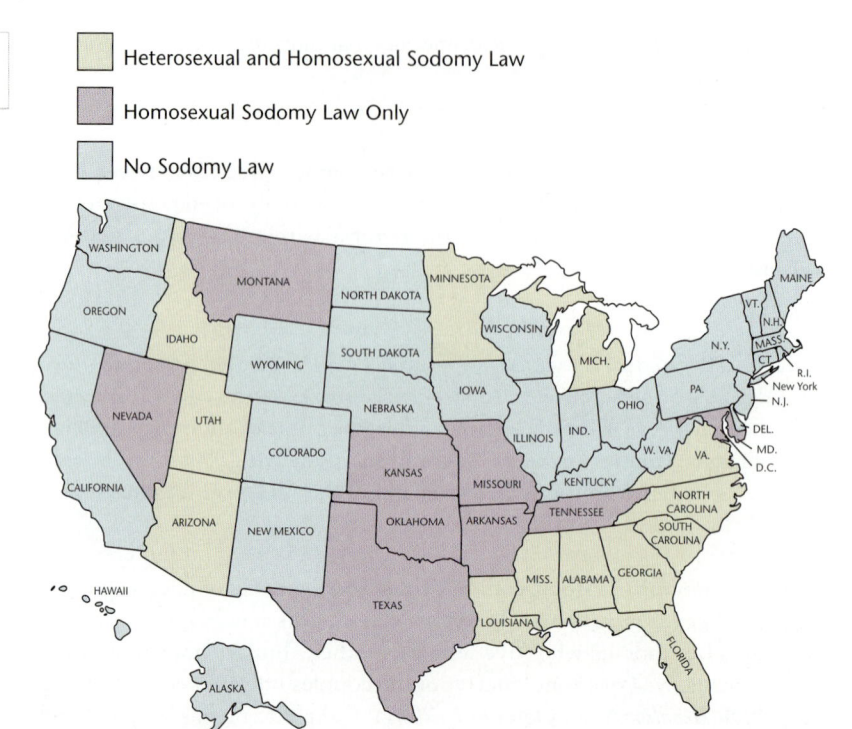

- Heterosexual and Homosexual Sodomy Law
- Homosexual Sodomy Law Only
- No Sodomy Law

FIGURE 2.14

A prostitute is one who indulges in indiscriminate sexual actions for hire.

Courtesy Michael Goldman/Getty Images, Inc.

CTQ

Prostitution is legalized and controlled in certain counties in Nevada. Do you think this should be a nationwide practice? Why or why not?

Prostitution

Although prostitution was not an original crime against morality, statutes proscribing prostitution have been part of the laws directed against public immorality since the early history of the United States.[36] A **prostitute** is a person who indulges in indiscriminate sexual activity for hire (see Figure 2.14). Today prostitution is illegal in all states except Nevada, where it exists by local option in some counties, although it is strictly regulated by law.[37] Historically, statutes prohibiting prostitution have been directed at females who have sexual intercourse with males for compensation, but in recent years, as prostitution by males has increased, enforcement has come to be directed at males as well.

Previously, enforcement was directed almost exclusively at the prostitute. Newer statutes, however, provide for conviction of customers as well as prostitutes. (See "In the News: Prostitutes Will Get Treatment, Not Jail.") This is legal because under the law of accomplice liability, even though the "johns" did not solicit the act, they are still criminally liable for their acts as an accomplice. Indeed, if the statutes are not so construed, they may be vulnerable to constitutional attack as a denial of equal protection of the law.

Lawmakers have officially deplored the existence of prostitution, and law enforcement authorities have long linked the activity with vice, narcotics offenses, and the exploitation of women. In addition to making prostitution an offense, most states make it an offense to solicit for a prostitute or to live off the earnings of a person engaged in prostitution. Statutes also commonly declare brothels and houses of prostitution as public nuisances.

Texas statutes provide that a person who offers or agrees to engage, or engages in sexual conduct for a fee, or who solicits another in a public place to engage in such conduct commits the misdemeanor offense of prostitution.[38] Texas also makes promotion of prostitution a misdemeanor offense,[39] and makes it a serious felony for a person to cause another by force, threat, or fraud to commit prostitution or to cause by any means a person younger than age 17 to commit prostitution.[40]

Prostitution has been dealt with primarily at the state and local level, but the federal government has also shown an interest in coping with the problem. The Mann Act[41] prohibits interstate transportation of an individual for purposes of prostitution or with the intent to compel an individual to become a prostitute or to engage in any other im-

A HUMAN PERSPECTIVE

PROSTITUTES WILL GET TREATMENT, NOT JAIL
by L. Minai

State lawmakers in St. Petersburg have passed a two-year pilot program offering prostitutes in Pinellas and Hillsborough counties drug treatment instead of jail. The law also increases penalties statewide for repeat offenders. The bill (HB415) is before Gov. Jeb Bush for his signature. "The old school used to be throw them in jail," said Rep. Frank Farkas, R–St. Petersburg, the bill's co-sponsor. "When we know that 90 percent of these prostitutes have substance abuse addiction, we know that jail is not the answer. We need treatment."

While the state considers new initiatives, the city of St. Petersburg is thinking of a way to crack down on prostitution. A task force met for the first time this week. "It's a revolving door," said Ginny Lomagno, a task force member and president of the Fourth Street Business Association. "Police arrest the prostitute and before the ink is dry on the paperwork, they're back on the streets."

A misdemeanor, prostitution arrests in St. Petersburg have increased steadily since 1998. Across the country, states and municipalities are trying nontraditional methods to reduce prostitution, a crime often fueled by addiction.

The two-year pilot project in Pinellas and Hillsborough counties is called "Project HOPE" for Healthy Operations Promoting Esteem. The state has allocated $100,000 for each county in the fiscal year 2002–2003.

Prostitutes in Pinellas and Hillsborough who are convicted twice or more can get screened for drugs and enter a treatment program. Hillsborough County Sheriff Cal Henderson likes the project. "Any drug treatment that we can give is positive," he said. Farkas, the bill's sponsor, originally wanted the drug treatment for prostitutes statewide. But the state did not have the money. The pilot project has also a component for people who solicit prostitutes. Someone convicted for the first or second time can attend a rehabilitative program and pay a $350 fine. The bill also amends the law for repeat offenders. Anyone arrested a third time for selling or soliciting sex will be charged with a third degree felony. Repeat solicitors could also get their license revoked for at least one year.

Source: L. Minai, "Prostitutes Will Get Treatment, Not Jail," *St. Petersburg Times*, March 22, 2002. Copyright *St. Petersburg Times*, 2002. Reprinted by permission.

---

moral practice. The Supreme Court has held that the act applies to transporting a person for immoral purposes even if commercial vice is not involved.[42]

MODERN CRIMES

Although more than 90 percent of all crimes prosecuted in American criminal courtrooms are common-law crimes,[43] we have included other crimes as part of the substantive criminal law chapter as well. For the most part, the sources of the substantive law of these crimes may be derived either from state statutes and the judicial case precedent attached to them, or from the federal statutes in the case precedent attached to them. More than ten thousand new statutory crimes have been enacted by Congress or state legislatures.[44] We call these crimes "modern crimes." Clearly, it is impossible to discuss every faction of them. The modern crimes presented next were selected because the authors of this book believe that college and university students might find them the most interesting.

Computer Crime

Although we have had a glimpse at some of the more exotic computer crimes in Chapter 1, this section concerns itself with new computer crimes and prosecution.

Internal Computer Crime Internal computer crimes are alterations to computer programs that result in the performance of unauthorized functions, such as deletion or manipulation of data in a computer program. Because these unauthorized functions have been around for years, they have acquired colorful names like *Trojan horse, salami technique, trap door,* and *logic bomb*.

Trojan Horses Two notable Trojan horses involved efforts to get the passwords of individual computer users on networks. In the first case, a hacker got inside a system and put out an instruction for everyone to change his or her password. When the users

CTQ

Can the criminal law keep up with the rapid pace of technology in computers by making changes that identify misconduct on a computer as crimes?

complied, the new passwords were conveniently recorded by the hacker's program. Later he recovered and used them. In the second case, in New York City in 1991, Panix Public Access—an online service—had to shut down operations for three days when a Trojan horse was found recording users' passwords in a secret file.

Salami Technique Typically, the salami technique is a money crime; it is an automated means of stealing assets from a large number of accounts. In the round-down salami technique, the program rounds down to the nearest dollar on the amount in many accounts and transfers this amount to an account controlled by the perpetrator.

Trap Doors When developing large programs and computer operating systems, programmers often use debugging aids that provide breaks in the code called trap doors. Most of the time, these breaks are removed. However, their removal may be overlooked or they may be left to provide easy maintenance of the program in the future. However, once hackers or unscrupulous programmers find a trap door, they have the means to commit internal computer crimes with little likelihood of detection.

Logic Bombs Logic bombs are illegal program instructions that operate at a specific time or periodically. A logic bomb may be executed based on a specific date or time or other instructions. For example, if a specific Social Security number is entered, all records pertaining to that person are erased.[45]

Identity Theft

Identity theft is a "crime of the 1990s and the first decade of the 21st Century."[46] It occurs when a person uses the personal identification—name, address, Social Security number, date of birth, mother's maiden name and so forth—of another to use or open new credit card and bank accounts; apply for a driver's license, a new Social Security card, or a passport; lease cars and apartments; and apply for loans. The victims are then left to deal with calls from collection agencies and creditors, paperwork, and the anxiety of wondering if other illegal accounts exist. The poor marks on credit reports can also be devastating, particularly when it affects individuals' abilities to get loans, apply for jobs, and get apartments.

It is difficult for individuals to protect themselves from identity theft, because offenders may obtain personal information about their victims in a number of ways. Data have been obtained from the Internet, locations in the workplace, mailboxes, and application forms. Most victims are also typically unaware of the fact that they are victims until they receive a call from a creditor or bill collector or apply for a loan or credit (see "In the News: Stolen Identity").

Stalking

Until 1990, when the California legislature adopted antistalking legislation, stalking was not recognized as a crime, because there were no legal means for law enforcement and criminal justice personnel to protect people who had been threatened.

Following California's lead, forty-eight states and the District of Columbia adopted legislation that criminalized stalking; however, with each legislative body defining the crime, there were broad and varying definitions, and many states found their antistalking laws challenged as being unconstitutionally vague. **Stalking** is when one willfully and maliciously and repeatedly follows, harasses, or makes a credible threat to another with the intent of placing the other in fear of death or bodily injury.[47] Essentially, stalking is behavior that reminds the victim, "I am still here . . . I am watching you." (See Figure 2.15)

Stalking is difficult to prove because often there is no physical evidence, and the legal standard for convictions was not based on the defendant's intent to commit the crime, but rather was based on how his or her pattern of behavior affected the victim. Antistalking statutes often contain the language "maliciously," "willfully and repeatedly," "harass," "credible threat," and "reasonable fear." (See the Landmark Case *Commonwealth v. Matsos*.) **Harassment,** for the purposes of the crime of stalking, means to

IN THE NEWS

A HUMAN PERSPECTIVE

STOLEN IDENTITY
by M. Manix

When Jessica Grant and her husband went to the bank in December to refinance their home, they thought it would be routine. After all, the couple, who live in Sun Prairie, Wis., were refinancing with their existing mortgage lender, and they prided themselves on their credit history. So it was quite a shock when the bank officer turned them down, pointing to their credit report, which listed numerous accounts in arrears.

It turns out that a woman in Texas had applied for credit 19 times using Grant's name and Social Security number. In all, she had made purchases totaling $60,000, leaving a trail of unpaid debt that Grant was desperately trying to prove was not hers: a $25,000 loan for a mobile home, two car loans, credit card bills, and charges for a cellular phone and other services. "She torched my credit to the point where even *she* was denied," says Grant.

Grant is a victim of a crime of the 1990's and the first decade of the 21st century: identity theft. It happens when one individual uses another's personal identification—name, address, Social Security number, date of birth, mother's maiden name—to take over or open new credit card and bank accounts, apply for car and house loans, lease cars and apartments, even take out insurance. The perpetrators don't make the payments, and the victim is left to deal with the damage—calls from collection agencies and creditors, the endless paperwork that results from trying to expunge fraudulent accounts from credit record, the agony if waiting to see if more phony accounts pop up. Meanwhile, the proliferation of black marks on a credit report can be devastating. Victims of identity theft are often unable to get loans; some run into trouble applying for a job. A few have even been arrested after the thief committed a crime in the victim's name. Many identity thieves use stolen personal information to obtain a driver's license or birth certificate, making it easier to obtain credit. Even the victims do not know how the criminal pulled it off; data have been stolen from desk drawers in the workplace, mailboxes, job application forms, and the Internet. False identification cloaks a thief in anonymity, and the impostor can often use the alias for a prolonged period of time; thieves typically have the bills sent to an address that is not the victim's, concealing the scheme for months, even years. Most victims aren't aware that their credit has taken a nose-dive until, like Grant, they apply for credit themselves or receive a call from a bill collector.

That's evident in a soon-to-be-released U.S. General Accounting Office report. While no single agency tracks identity fraud, statistics collected by the GAO point to a growing problem. Trans Union, for example, one of the three major credit bureaus, says two thirds of all consumer inquiries relate to identity fraud. Those inquiries numbered 35,235 in 1992; last year there were 522,922. "The cost of identity fraud can be very high," states the report: The Secret Service says losses to victims and institutions in its identity-fraud investigations were $745 million in 1997, up from $442 million in 1995.

Identity fraud is a relatively new phenomenon, and it's not a crime, except in a handful of states like Arizona and California that have recently made it so. (Legislation is pending to make it a federal crime.) Most victims call the police. But in states with no statute, some police departments refuse to take a report because the law sees the victim in a case of identity fraud as the party that granted the credit (the bank or merchant, for example), not the person impersonated. "That's frustrating to the victims because they often need a report to prove they are not the bad guys."

Source: M. Manix, "Stolen Identity," *U.S. News & World Report*, June 1, 1998. Copyright 1998 U.S. News & World Report, L. P. Reprinted with permission.

FIGURE 2.15

(a) Internationally famous singer and dancer Madonna also was a victim of a stalker who was repeatedly followed by and received threatening letters and phone messages from an obsessed fan. (b) Madonna's stalker, Robert Dewey Hoskins (left), was sentenced to ten years in prison for terrorizing the pop star.

(a) Courtesy Reuters/Jonathan Evans/Getty Images, Inc.

(b) Courtesy AP/Wide World Photos.

LANDMARK CASE — Commonwealth v. Matsos

Matsos began following the victim, an officer with the Salem police department, and writing her letters filled with sexual references. After filing a complaint against Matsos for stalking, the victim learned that Matsos had sent a signed document to her employer alleging that she had used drugs with him. While the allegations prompted an extensive internal affairs investigation, including drug testing of the victim, the police department ultimately concluded that the allegations were unfounded. Matsos was convicted of the crime of stalking and appealed the decision, stating that the stalking statute was unconstitutionally vague because it left unclear whether one must engage repeatedly in a pattern of conduct, a series of acts over a period of time, to be guilty of harassment. The appeals court reversed the lower court's decision, arguing that the crime of stalking closely approximates the common-law definition of the crime of assault, and may be found wherever the defendant makes threats placing another in imminent fear of death, imminent injury, or unreasonable apprehension that force may be used. Matsos's actions clearly fell within the scope of conduct prohibited by the harassment portion of the statute, even though the statute is interpreted as requiring the defendant to engage repeatedly in patterns of conduct of a series of acts that would cause a reasonable person to suffer substantial emotional distress. The court went on to say that the jury was made aware of more than forty letters sent by Matsos over a ten-month period. The facts established that Matsos's campaign of harassment involved distinctive and repetitive patterns of conduct that poisoned the victim's personal and professional life. The statute gave him fair notice, said the court, that his repeated, obsessive behavior was indeed prohibited.

Source: Commonwealth v. Matsos, 421 Mass. 391, 697 N.E.2d 264 (1995).

CTQ
What is the difference between aggressively, romantically pursuing a love interest and stalking a love interest?

CTQ
Which of the six traffic crimes in the following discussion do you believe should be reduced from a misdemeanor to a traffic infraction? Which do you believe should be raised from a misdemeanor to a felony?

WEB
For more information on topics ranging from blood alcohol levels to vehicular homicide, visit our Web site, www.prenhall.com/territo.

engage in a course of action directed toward a specific person that causes substantial emotional strain.[48]

In 1992, Congress directed the Justice Department to construct an antistalking code that was both constitutional (did not violate individuals' right to free speech or their reasonable expectation to privacy) and enforceable. The Justice Department contracted with the National Criminal Justice Administration and the National Institute of Justice to study the various antistalking statutes in each state and, from this information, develop a model antistalking code. The model penal code for antistalking laws required prosecutors to prove a "course of conduct directed at a specific person that would cause a reasonable person to fear" and to prove that the stalker "had knowledge or should have had knowledge" that the victim would be in fear as a consequence of his or her behavior.[49]

TRAFFIC OFFENSES THAT ARE CRIMES

Although local traffic laws existed before the advent of the automobile to govern the speed and conduct of those using horses and buggies and even bicycles, not until the introduction of the automobile did it became necessary to introduce laws that were uniform throughout the country. In 1926, the first Uniform Vehicle Code was written. This code has been adopted by every state, although many modifications are made to meet local needs.

Racing

In the past few decades, traffic offenses have taken new forms. For example, in the case of "racing," life imitates art, and what may be a game in the movies is, in real life, a criminal act with potentially fatal consequences. The Uniform Vehicle Code defines **racing** as one or more vehicles that attempt to (1) out-gain or (2) out-distance each other, (3) prevent another vehicle from passing, (4) arrive first at a given point, or (5) test the stamina of the drivers. Although the drivers of the vehicles do not have to be exceeding the legal speed limit, any competitive conduct of the drivers will define their actions as racing.

Reckless Driving

Reckless behavior is defined as intentionally engaging in behavior with potentially harmful consequences. This definition also applies to the traffic offense of reckless driving, with the emphasis being that the conduct is intentional. Although driving while intoxicated or speeding could be seen as reckless behaviors, they do not necessarily meet the definition of reckless driving. For instance, a person who drives thirty miles per hour over the speed limit is not necessarily reckless, unless that person intentionally drives at that rate of speed through a crowded school zone, as this displays an obvious disregard for the safety of others.

The Uniform Vehicle Code defines **reckless driving** as "driving any vehicle in willful or wanton disregard for the safety of persons or property." This definition could apply to people with medical conditions or under medication that would hamper their ability to drive, who voluntarily get behind the wheel of a car, presenting themselves as a safety hazard to themselves or others. Reckless driving also applies to drivers who intentionally exceed the speed limit when weather conditions such as rain, snow, or dense fog would dictate that driving at a high rate of speed could be hazardous to others.

Hit and Run

In compliance with the Uniform Vehicle Code, all drivers involved in accidents are required to immediately report the incident to the authorities, call for medical help, and assist the victims if necessary. Drivers are not to leave the scene of an accident. If the driver must leave to report the accident or to seek medical assistance, she or he must immediately return to the accident.

If the accident involves another car, a pedestrian, or even a person occupying the vehicle one is driving, leaving the scene of an accident would be a violation of the Uniform Vehicle Code and classified as a **hit and run.**

Vehicular Homicide

Vehicular homicide is another relatively modern traffic offense. To find a person guilty of vehicular homicide, the issue of causation must be resolved. It is not sufficient for a murder charge for someone merely to be in control of a vehicle that kills someone else; it must be proven that the operator of the vehicle acted in a reckless and negligent manner—in other words, that the individual failed to demonstrate due care with respect to the standard traffic laws and the safety of others, resulting in the death of another as a direct consequence of that person's actions.

Because many prosecutors do not prosecute vehicular homicide under general homicide statutes due to the penalties that homicide convictions carry (life in prison, death), many states allow prosecution of vehicular homicide under a lesser degree of murder or even manslaughter.

DUI/DWI

Like many other laws, DUI laws are written to deter people from driving while they are impaired by the use of alcohol or drugs. The key concept in DUI laws is the condition or impairment of the driver, rather than how the driver was operating the car.

Three criteria must be met for someone to be charged with DUI: (1) The person must have been under the influence of alcohol or drugs; (2) a vehicle must exist; and (3) the person, if not actually driving the vehicle, must have been in physical control of it (see the Landmark Case *State v. Taft*). To determine if a person is DUI, most states have adopted statutes to prohibit driving with an unlawful blood-alcohol level (DUBAL). Many states have set the limit of alcohol in the blood at 0.10 percent, making it unlawful for a person whose blood contains 0.10 percent or more alcohol to operate a vehicle. As the focus on the damage and cost to society by impaired drivers has increased, some states have responded by reducing their legal blood-alcohol level to 0.08 percent. Many law enforcement agencies, insurance groups, and anti–drunk driving organizations are lobbying for even stricter legislation.

WEB

For more information on DUI/DWI, visit Mothers Against Drunk Driving via our Web site, www.prenhall.com/territo

Multiple Offenses, Classified as "Road Rage"

The 1990s officially had their own psychological traffic condition known as "road rage," a condition that turns ordinary people into angry, vindictive, and revengeful drivers. The

LANDMARK CASE — State v. Taft

Taft was convicted of drunk driving, and driving under the influence of intoxicating liquor. At trial, the jury was instructed that the act of driving could be inferred from the mere motion of the car. Taft objected that if the jury were to find that the car moved because the brakes released accidentally while he was sitting in it, that he should not be convicted, regardless of the motion, since he had not committed the requisite act of driving.

The court had to settle with the issue of whether a crime was committed where the criminal act is inferred without a finding that it was committed subject to the will of the actor. The court said that since Taft was simply sitting beside the car's steering wheel (not behind it), with the engine off and the car moved while he was intoxicated, he is not guilty of DWI. The reasoning was that a crime cannot be committed where the criminal act was inferred without finding that it was committed subject to the will of the actor. The court went on to say that only voluntary acts can be the basis for criminal liability.

Source: State v. Taft, 143 W. Va. 365, 102 S.E.2d 152 (1958).

American Automobile Association (AAA) estimates that the incidents of road rage have doubled since 1990. Components of **road rage** behaviors may include anything from tailgating and flashing headlights to intimidating other drivers to move out of the way to shooting someone.

In some states, special "road rage patrols" have been formed by the highway patrol. These patrols are set up to crack down on the reckless driving of those who change lanes, move in and out of traffic, tailgate others, or exhibit other aggressive driving behaviors.

ENVIRONMENTAL CRIMES

Environmental crime is a serious problem for the United States, even though the immediate consequences of an offense may not be obvious or severe.[50] Environmental crimes do have victims. The cumulative costs in environmental damage and the long-range toll in illness, injury, and death may be considerable (see Figure 2.16).

The public recognizes the severity of environmental crimes. More than a decade ago, a Bureau of Justice Statistics survey found that Americans believed environmental crimes to be more serious than a number of "traditional" crimes such as burglary and bank robbery. A 1991 survey revealed that 84 percent of Americans believed that damaging the environment is a serious crime, and 75 percent believed that corporate officials should be held personally responsible for environmental offenses committed by their firms.[51] But despite increased public concern, pollution still threatens public health and jeopardizes the ecological balance.

The Environmental Regulation Paradox

Over the past twenty years, environmental laws covering hazardous waste, toxic substances, and air and water pollution have become more complex and stringent. But paradoxically, the very laws and regulations designed to protect the environment may have contributed in several ways to increasing the incidence of environmental violations.

First, because regulated businesses have found it increasingly expensive to comply with the new statutes, more and more are avoiding these costs, even if it means violating

FIGURE 2.16

Environmental crimes such as extreme land and water pollution threaten public health and jeopardize the ecological balance.

Courtesy Stephen Agricola/Stock Boston.

the law. Although there are still numerous instances of "midnight dumping" (randomly dumping hazardous materials or waste by the roadside or in vacant lots), increasing numbers of businesses are consciously and systematically violating environmental laws to save money and increase profit margins.

Second, environmental offenders and their defense counsel are becoming more sophisticated in their methods. For example, a large number of firms have learned to shield their involvement in illegal activities through the use of intermediaries and dummy corporations, and many environmental defense attorneys are former prosecutors who know the laws and are adept at using procedural techniques to protect their clients.

Such actions show that regulation alone is not always enough to protect the public and the environment. The stigma of criminal indictment and the threat of criminal penalties, including incarceration, are increasingly viewed as necessary deterrents to environmental criminals.

Passage of criminal penalties for environmental offenses has made local prosecutors equal partners with the regulatory agencies that had been primarily responsible for enforcement. In a handful of jurisdictions, prosecutors, investigators, and environmental regulators have forged innovative and effective strategies for identifying and punishing environmental offenders. One of the first local programs to create a team approach to environmental crime prosecution was the Los Angeles County Environmental Crimes Strike Force. Under the leadership of the office of the district attorney, the Strike Force has sent a clear message to polluters that their acts will no longer be tolerated and that, unlike much administrative and civil enforcement, criminal prosecution really hurts. As a result of the personal and institutional relationships fostered by the Strike Force, member regulatory agencies, previously reluctant to refer matters for criminal prosecution, have themselves become strong advocates of criminal enforcement.[52]

> **CTQ**
>
> What laws need to be passed in order to alleviate the environmental paradox?

SUMMARY

To understand the problem of crime, one must examine the broader issue of deviance from societal norms. Society's attempts to contain deviance through controls (sanctions) range from informal disapproval to the use of the police powers of the state. Studies of antisocial attitudes, eccentricities, and various kinds of atypical behavior may all have potential value in helping to illuminate the factors involved in criminal conduct. All criminal acts are deviant, but not all deviant acts are criminal. Thus, only those deviant acts that legislative bodies have defined by statute as criminal may be legitimately considered crimes.

American criminal law as analyzed in this chapter combines the features of two systems: the common law, which developed in England, was transported to America, and is based on interpretation of judicial decisions; and statutory law, which is based on specific codes that are written and legislated. These two sources are continually being transformed by American case law, which analyzes the meaning and significance of legislative statutes in the common law tradition. These systems are the basis of substantive criminal law, laws that define necessary elements of crimes and specify the penalties for the commission.

In this chapter we initially have studied each crime by defining its particular elements that, as a whole, constitute a particular criminal offense. The significance of studying each crime in the American criminal justice system by the composition of its respective elements is for proof. The burden of proof is on the government to prove the defendant guilty beyond a reasonable doubt; what this means in reality is that the government has the burden of proving beyond a reasonable doubt each and every element making up the crime with which the defendant is charged. This means that if a defendant is charged with burglary, which has seven elements, and if the government proves six of these elements beyond a reasonable doubt but the jury has a reasonable doubt as to the seventh element, the jury must find the defendant not guilty.

Depending on the punishment, offenses are classified as felony and misdemeanor crimes. Felonies are punishable by death or imprisonment for at least one year. Misdemeanors are punishable by fines and less than one year in jail.

There are several classifications of substantive crimes within the criminal justice system. Several crimes constitute the law of homicide; more than eight crimes fit into the category of crimes against the person; arson and burglary are the crimes against habitation, while as many as ten separate crimes constitute the acquisition offenses. Other groupings of crimes constitute the general categories of crimes against property and crimes against morality. American prosecutors are devoting extraordinary resources and energy to prosecuting acts that were not even considered criminal until the 1960s, including computer crimes, identity theft, stalking, and new forms of traffic offenses. Fighting environmental crime requires the coordination of many governmental and private agencies to achieve success.

DISCUSSION AND REVIEW QUESTIONS

1. Define and discuss substantive criminal law. What are the major sources of criminal law?
2. What four characteristics of criminal law distinguish it from other rules governing human conduct?
3. What is the difference between criminal law and civil law?
4. What are felonies and how do they differ from misdemeanors? Why is the distinction important in the administration of justice?
5. What is the "law of precedent"?
6. What is the paradox between the laws and regulations designed to protect the environment?
7. What are three kinds of homicide?
8. What are the elements of murder, voluntary manslaughter, and involuntary manslaughter?
9. Name five crimes against the person.
10. Distinguish between rape, statutory rape, and date rape.
11. What is the difference between assault and battery and false imprisonment?
12. What are the crimes against habitation and what are their elements?
13. Name the acquisition offenses. What distinguishes larceny from robbery?
14. What distinguishes false pretense from embezzlement?
15. What are the crimes against morality and what is the origin of their placement in the American criminal codes?
16. What are strict-liability crimes?
17. Identify the categories of *mens rea* and provide examples of each category.
18. Discuss the degrees of murder in terms of differentiating intent.
19. Describe the legal doctrine of *stare decisis*.
20. Provide two examples of acts of commission and acts of omission that are crimes.
21. Identify four sources of American criminal law and discuss their influence on the American criminal justice system.
22. What constitutes a hate crime?
23. What is common law? How did it influence the development of criminal law in the United States?
24. What is criminal responsibility?
25. Discuss the various kinds of crime classification. How are they distinguishable?
26. To what type of situation would each of the following defenses apply: entrapment, age, intoxication, and self-defense.
27. What is a criminal act? What is a criminal state of mind? When are individuals criminally responsible for their actions?

28. What are the specific aims and purposes of criminal law? To what extent does criminal law control behavior?
29. Distinguish between criminal law and civil law, including their similarities and their differences.

CHAPTER RESOURCES

IN THE MEDIA

Video

A&E American Justice Videos
ABC Videos
CNN Crime File Videos
Court TV Videos
FFH Videos
Insight Media Video: *Can Rules Define Morality?***
Insight Media Video: *Censorship and Content Control on the Internet***
Insight Media Video: *The Internet: Cyber-Hate and Freedom of Speech***
Insight Media Video: *Law and the Legal System***
Insight Media Video: *Legislation Morality: There Ought to Be a Law!***
Insight Media Video: *The Rule of Law***

Insight Media Video: *Sources of Law***
NIJ Crime File Video: "The Three Strikes Law"
PBS Videos

Film

Anatomy of a Murder (1959)

Television

Court TV: "*Cabey v. Goetz*, Vigilante Justice: The Civil Trial of Bernhard Goetz"°
Court TV: "*Florida v. Smith*"
Court TV: "*Massachusetts v. Louise Woodward*: Child Killer or Child Lover?"°
Court TV: "*New York v. Nelson*"°

IN THE LITERATURE

Books

G. Barak, ed., *Crimes by the Capitalist State: An Introduction to State Criminality* New York: State University of New York Press, 1991.

D. Bodenhamer, *Fair Trial: Rights of the Accused in American History.* New York: Oxford, 1991.

C. Brinton, J. Christopher, and R. Wolff, *A History of Civilization*, Vol. 1, 3rd ed. Englewood Cliffs, N.J.: Prentice Hall, 1967.

E. Burns, *Western Civilization*, 7th ed. New York: Norton, 1969.

J. Calvi and S. Coleman, *American Law and Legal Systems* Englewood Cliffs, N.J.: Prentice Hall, 1989.

L. Carter, *Reason in Law*, Glenview, Ill.: Scott, Foresman, 1988.

M. Clinard and R. Quinney, *Criminal Behavior Systems: A Typology.* Cincinnati, Ohio: Anderson, 1994.

D. Close and N. Meier, *Morality in Criminal Justice: An Introduction to Ethics*, (Belmont, Calif.: Wadsworth, 1995.

J. Coleman, *The Criminal Elite: The Sociology of White-Collar Crime*, 2nd ed. New York: St. Martin's Press, 1989.

N. Crowell and A. Burgess, eds., *Understanding Violence against Women*, Washington, D.C.: National Academy Press, 1996.

A. Dershowitz, *Taking Liberties: A Decade of Hard Cases, Bad Laws, and Bum Raps*. Chicago: Contemporary Books, 1988.

A. Dershowitz, *The Advocate's Devil.* New York: Warner Books, 1995.

L. Friedman, *Crime and Punishment in American History.* New York: Basic Books, 1993.

T. Gardner and T. Anderson, *Criminal Law*, 7th ed. Belmont, Calif.: Wadsworth, 2000.

J. Inciardi, *Criminal Justice*, 7th ed. Ft. Worth, Texas: Harcourt College Publishers, 2002.

B. Lofferda, *Losing Matt Shepard: Life and Politics in the Aftermath of Anti-Gay Murder.* New York: Columbia University Press, 2000.

R. Meier, ed., *Major Forms of Crime.* Beverly Hills, Calif.: Sage, 1984.

N. Morris, *Madness and the Criminal Law*. Chicago: University of Chicago Press, 1982.

National Crime Prevention Council, *New Ways of Working with Local Laws to Prevent Crime.* New York, Amsterdam: NCPC, 1996.

S. PARKER, *Popular Justice: A History of American Criminal Justice.* New York: Oxford University Press, 1980.

T. PLUCKET, *A Concise History of the Common Law.* Boston: Little, Brown, 1956.

J. POLLOCK, *Ethics in Crime and Justice: Dilemmas and Decisions.* 2nd ed. Belmont, Calif.: Wadsworth, 1994.

J. REIMAN, *The Rich Get Richer and the Poor Get Prison: Ideology, Class, and Criminal Justice.* New York: Wiley, 1979.

O. ROBINSON, *The Criminal Law of Ancient Rome.* Baltimore: Johns Hopkins University Press, 1996.

J. SAMAHA, *Criminal Law,* 6th ed. Belmont, Calif.: Wadsworth, 1999.

R. SCHOPP, *Justification Defenses and Just Convictions.* Cambridge, England: Cambridge University Press, 1998.

D. SIMON and D. EITZEN, *Elite Deviance,* 3rd ed. Boston: Allyn & Bacon, 1990.

S. STEPHEN et al., eds., *Actions and Value in Criminal Law.* New York: Oxford University Press, 1996.

Articles

W. COOK, "Mad Driver's Disease," *U.S. News & World Report,* November 11, 1996.

"Cruising to Dodge a Royal Bruising," *U.S. News & World Report,* August 9, 1999, p. 12.

"Death for McVeigh," *St. Petersburg (Fla.) Times,* June 14, 1997, p. 1A.

M. DUBBER, "Reforming American Penal Law," *Journal of Criminal Law and Criminology,* vol. 90 (1999), p. 49.

H. HART, "The Aims of Criminal Law," *Law and Contemporary Problems,* vol. 23 (1956), p. 402.

N. HENTOFF, 1993. Letting loose the hate crime police. *Village Voice,* 13 July.

G. HERIOT, 1996. An essay on the civil-criminal distinction with special reference to punitive damages. *Journal of Contemporary Legal Issues* 7: 43.

S. KADISH, "Criminal Law and Society: A Symposium," *California Law Review,* vol. 87 (1999), p. 943.

S. MARTIN, "Investigating Hate Crimes: Case Characteristics and Law Enforcement Responses," *Justice Quarterly,* vol. 13 (1996), pp. 455–480.

C. SMITH, "The Forms of Judicial Policymaking: Civil Liability and Criminal Justice Policy," *Justice System Journal,* vol. 19 (1997), pp. 341–354.

T. SMITH, "Legislative and Legal Developments in Criminal Justice," *Journal of Criminal Justice,* vol. 5 (1991), pp. 36–37.

"Witch Faces Jail for Sex with Minor," *Philadelphia Inquirer,* October 13, 1996, p. 14A.

Government Publications

Bureau of Justice Statistics, *Sourcebook of Criminal Justice Statistics, 1992.* Washington, D.C.: U.S. Department of Justice, 1993.

Bureau of Justice Statistics, *The Criminal Justice and Community Response to Rape.* Rockville, Md.: National Criminal Justice Reference Service, 1994.

Bureau of Justice Statistics, *Violent Crime in the United States.* Washington, D.C.: Bureau of Justice Statistics, 1996.

Federal Bureau of Investigation, *Hate Crimes—1999.* Washington, D.C.: U.S. Department of Justice, 2000.

Federal Bureau of Investigation, *Crime in the United States, 1998.* Washington, D.C.: U.S. Government Printing Office, 1999.

T. M. HAMMETT and J. EPSTEIN, *Prosecuting Environmental Crime: Los Angeles County.* Washington, D.C.: U.S. Department of Justice, National Institute of Justice, 1993.

Hate Crime Statistics for the United States, 2000. Available online at http://www.fbi.gov/ucr/ucr.htm.

W. LOGAN, L. STELLWAGEN, and P. LAGEN, *Felony Laws of the Fifty States and the District of Columbia.* Washington, D.C.: Bureau of Justice Statistics, 1987.

Uniform Crime Reports for the United States, 2000. Available online at http://www.fbi.gov/ucr/ucr.htm.

National Institute of Justice, *Research Update Project to Develop an Anti-Stalking Statute.* Washington, D.C.: U.S. Department of Justice, 1994.

STATUTES

18 U.S.C.A. §2421 *et seq.*
Cal. Penal Code, §§ 450, 459
Homicide Act, 1957, 5 & 6 Eliz. 2, ch. 11, § 1 (Eng.)
Fl. Stat. ch. 784.045 (1–4)
Mich. Stat. Ann. § 750.520A *et seq*

Model Penal Code, §§ 1.014, 221, 223.2, 2221(1)
Nev. Rev. Stat. §§ 201.380, 201.430, 201.440
Tex. Penal Code Ann. §§ 28.02, 43.03–43.04
Tex. Penal Code Ann. art. 43.02, 43.05

CASES

Bowers v. Hardwick, 478 U.S. 186 (1986)
Cleveland v. United States, 329 U.S. 14 (1946)
Comber v. United States, 584 A.2d 26 (D.C. Cir. 1995)
Commonwealth v. King, 372 N.E.2d 196 (Mass. 1977)

Commonwealth v. Matchett, 436 N.E.2d 400 (Mass. 1982)
Commonwealth v. Matsos, 421 Mass. 391, 697 N.E.2d 264 (1995)
People v. Home Insurance Co., 197 Colo. 261, 251 P.2d 1063 (1979)
People v. Ochoa, 6 Cal. 4th 1199, 26 Cal. Rptr. 2d 23 (1993)

People v. Patterson, 262 Cal. 3d 615 (1989)
People v. Rojas, 55 Cal. 2d 252 (1961)
Reynolds v. State, 617 P.2d 1352 (Okla. Crim. App. 1979)
Roe v. Wade, 410 U.S. 113 (1973)
Smith v. California, 361 U.S. 147 (1959)

State v. Peery, 224 Minn. 346, 28 N.W.2d 851 (1947)
State v. Taft, 143 W. Va. 365, 102 S.E.2d 152 (1958)
State v. Tripp, 71 Haw. 479, 795 P.2d 280 (1990)
State v. Walden, 67 Wash. App. 891, 841 P.2d 81 (1992)
United States v. Wilson, 636 F.2d 225 (1980)

ENDNOTES

1. Model Penal Code, § 1.014.
2. J. Hall, *General Principles of Criminal Law*. Indianapolis, Ind.: Bobbs-Merrill, 1947.
3. I. Taylor, *The New Criminology—For a Social Theory of Deviance*. New York: Harper & Row, 1973.
4. S. Makielski, *Pressure Politics in America*. Landham, Md.: University Press of America, 1980, p. 17.
5. Ibid, p. 21.
6. *Roe v. Wade*, 410 U.S. 113 (1973).
7. K. Erikson, *Wayward Puritans: A Study of the Sociology of Deviance*. New York: Wiley, 1966.
8. H. Becker, *Outsiders: Studies in the Sociology of Deviance*. New York: Free Press, 1963, p. 24.
9. E. Schur, *Labeling Deviant Behavior: Its Sociological Implications*. New York: Harper & Row, 1971.
10. L. Friedman, *A History of American Law*. New York: Simon & Schuster, 1973.
11. H. Abadinsky, *Law and Justice*. Chicago: Nelson-Hall, 1988, p. 6.
12. E. Eldefonso and A. Coffey, *Criminal Law: History, Philosophy, and Enforcement*. New York: Harper & Row, 1981, p. 36.
13. Bureau of Justice Statistics, *Sourcebook of Criminal Justice Statistics, 1992*. Washington, D.C.: U.S. Department of Justice, 1993.
14. *Commonwealth v. Matchett*, 436 N.E.2d 400 (Mass. 1982).
15. Homicide Act, 1957, 5 & 6 Eliz. 2, ch. 11, § 1 (Eng.).
16. Uniform Crime Reports for the United States, 2000. Available online at http://www.fbi.gov/ucr/ucr.htm.
17. E. Buzawa and C. Buzawa, *Domestic Violence: The Criminal Justice Response*. Thousand Oaks, Calif.: Sage, 1996.
18. Bureau of Justice Statistics, *Violent Crime in the Unites States*. Washington, D.C.: Bureau of Justice Statistics, 1996.
19. C. Mariani, *Domestic Violence: A Survival Guide*. Flushing, N.Y.: Looseleaf, 1996.
20. W. Logan, L. Stellwagen, and P. Lagen, *Felony Laws of the Fifty States and the District of Columbia*. Washington, D.C.: Bureau of Justice Statistics, 1987.
21. M. Strauss, "Physical Assaults by Wives: A Major Social Problem." In R. Gelles and D. Loske, eds., *Current Controversies in Family Violence*. Newbury Park, Calif.: Sage, 1993.
22. Federal Bureau of Investigation, *Hate Crime—1999*. Washington, D.C.: U.S. Department of Justice, 2000.
23. Hate Crime Statistics for the United States, 2000. Available online at http://www.fbi.gov/ucr/ucr.htm.
24. N. Hentoff, "Letting Loose the Hate Crime Police," *Village Voice*, July 13, 1993.
25. Bureau of Justice Statistics, *The Criminal Justice and Community Response to Rape*. Rockville, Md.: National Criminal Justice Reference Service, 1994.
26. Mich. Stat. Ann. § 750.520A *et seq.*
27. Study: Rape Vastly Underreported," *Fayetteville (N.C.) Observer-Times*, April 26, 1992, P. 16A.
28. Model Penal Code, § 221.1.
29. Cal. Penal Code, § 459.
30. Model Penal Code, § 221.
31. Cal. Penal Code, § 450.
32. Tex. Penal Code Ann., § 28.02.
33. Model Penal Code, § 223.2.
34. Model Penal Code, § 2221(1).
35. *Bowers v. Hardwick*, 478 U.S. 186 (1986).
36. *Commonwealth v. King*, 372 N.E.2d 196 (Mass. 1977).
37. See Nev. Rev. Stat. §§ 201.380, 201.430, 201.440.
38. Tex. Penal Code Ann. art. 43.02.
39. Tex. Penal Code Ann. §§ 43.03–43.04.
40. Tex. Penal Code Ann. art. 43.05.
41. 18 U.S.C.A. § 2421 *et seq.*
42. *Cleveland v. United States*, 329 U.S. 14 (1946).
43. Federal Bureau of Investigation, *Crime in the United States, 1998*. Washington, D.C.: U.S. Government Printing Office, 1999.
44. Ibid.
45. M. Meyer and A. Underwood, "Crimes on the Net," *Newsweek*, November 14, 1994, p. 4A.
46. M. Manix, "Stolen Identity," *U.S. News & World Report*, June 1, 1998.
47. Fla. Stat. ch. 784.045 (1–4).
48. Ibid.
49. National Institute of Justice, *Research Update Project to Develop an Anti-Stalking Statute*. Washington, D.C.: U.S. Department of Justice, 1994.
50. T. M. Hammett and J. Epstein, *Prosecuting Environmental Crime: Los Angeles County*. Washington, D.C.: U.S. Department of Justice, National Institute of Justice, 1993.
51. Ibid.
52. Ibid.

3

THE LAW OF CRIMINAL PROCEDURE AND THE RIGHTS OF THE CRIMINALLY ACCUSED

Chapter OUTLINE

The Law of Criminal Procedure versus Substantive Criminal Law

The Bill of Rights Is Inextricably Tied to the Law of Criminal Procedure
- Constitutional Rights as Possible Constraints on Efficient Law Enforcement

The Constitution and the Bill of Rights
- A Historical Overview of Their Rationale
- The Doctrine of Selective Incorporation
- The Supreme Court's Power of Judicial Review

The Fourteenth Amendment's Due Process Clause

The Fourth Amendment Rights on Arrest, Search, and Seizure
- Evidentiary Standards of the Degrees of Certainty Used throughout the Various Phases of the Criminal Justice System

The Right to a Constitutional Arrest
- Can a Citizen Make an Arrest?
- The Requirements for an Arrest Warrant
- When Can an Officer Use Deadly Force to Make an Arrest?

Arrests That Are Not Really Arrests— "Stops" and "Detentions": When Are They Constitutional?
- Limited Detention—Stop and Frisk
- Use of Excessive Force When Effecting an Arrest
- Expanding the Permissible Scope of "Stops" and "Detentions"

The Right against Unreasonable Searches and Seizures
- Government Conduct
- Reasonable Expectation of Privacy

Searches Conducted Pursuant to a Warrant
- The General-Warrant Requirement
- The Reasonableness Requirement
- The Neutral-and-Detached-Magistrate Requirement
- The Probable-Cause Requirement
- Constitutional Execution of a Search Warrant

The Six Recognized Exceptions to the Search Warrant Requirement
- A Search Incident to a Lawful Arrest
- The Automobile Exception
- The Consent Exception
- The Plain-View Exception
- The Stop-and-Frisk Exception
- Exigent Circumstances

The Exclusionary Rule
- The Defendant's Right to a Suppression Hearing

The Expanded Exceptions to the Exclusionary Rule
- The Recently Recognized Additional Seven Exceptions to the Exclusionary Rule
- Criticism of the Exclusionary Rule

The Fifth Amendment Privilege against Self-Incrimination
- A Constitutional Confession

The Sixth Amendment Right to Counsel and Other Trial Rights
- The Right to Counsel
- The Right to a Speedy Trial
- The Right to a Public Trial
- The Right to a Jury Trial
- The Right to Confront Witnesses Testifying against the Defendant
- The Right to a Compulsory Process for Obtaining Witnesses in the Defendant's Favor

The Fifth Amendment Right Prohibiting Double Jeopardy
- Exceptions to the Double Jeopardy Prohibition
- Jeopardy as a Bar to Prosecution for the Same Offense

The Fifth Amendment Right to Substantive Due Process

The Eighth Amendment Rights against Excessive Bail and Cruel and Unusual Punishment
- Excessive Bail
- Cruel and Unusual Punishment

Toward Equal Justice

Summary

Key TERMS

affidavit, p. 100
arrest warrant, p. 100
Bill of Rights, p. 91
confession, p. 119
crime control model, p. 92
deadly force, p. 102
doctrine of selective incorporation, p. 95
due process of law, p. 91
due process model, p. 92
evanescent evidence, p. 117
exclusionary rule, p. 117
frisk, p. 103
fruit of the poisonous tree, p. 118
investigatory stop, p. 103
jeopardy, p. 133
judicial review, p. 95
law of criminal procedure, p. 91
manifest necessity, p. 133
probable cause, p. 98
search, p. 98
search warrant, p. 107
seizure, p. 98

Courtesy Jeff Hunter/Getty Images Inc.

The study of criminal procedure requires balancing society's need for law and order against the individual's right to due process and fundamental fairness in criminal proceedings. This balancing occupies the constant attention of courts, the legislature, scholars, and candidates for public office. Unlike other more esoteric branches of law, the criminal process is the subject of scrutiny by the press and voters in almost every election. Nearly all issues in criminal procedure ultimately involve deciding how to balance the need for efficient crime control with society's desire to ensure that no innocent person is swept away into the net of the criminal justice system.

The past few decades have witnessed a dramatic upsurge in the amount of constitutional litigation about the criminal process. Beginning in the early 1960s, the U. S. Supreme Court expressed concern that the real world of crime control bore little relation to the constitutional ideal. Throughout the 1960s, the Warren Court attempted to realign the real and the ideal in a series of decisions substantially expanding federally protected constitutional rights for state criminal defendants. The Court federalized the criminal process by systematically applying the provisions of the Bill of Rights to state criminal cases. As the number of constitutional rights increased, the Court simultaneously increased access of state prisoners to federal courts for the vindication of these newly created rights by broadening the scope of the writ of habeas corpus.

While constitutional status for criminal procedure remains an enduring legacy of the Warren years, the Burger and Rehnquist Courts, beginning in the 1970s, reduced both the scope of the state criminal defendant's federally protected rights and the defendant's access to federal courts to overturn state court convictions. However, it would be a mistake to see the decisions of the Warren, Burger, or Rehnquist Court as uniformly heading in a single direction. The Warren Court produced decisions quite favorable to the state, such as those limiting the judicial role in overseeing the conduct of grand juries, permitting investigative detention without probable cause, and denying Fifth Amendment protection to the seizure of incriminatory real or physical evidence.

The Burger and Rehnquist Courts, while generally accommodating what were perceived as legitimate law enforcement needs, produced real expansions of defendants' rights in decisions mandating selection of juries from pools representing a fair cross-section of the community—requiring appointment of counsel for indigent misdemeanants who receive jail sentences, mandating warrants before police may make a nonemergency arrest or search of a person in his or her own home, and reaffirming the individual privilege against self-incrimination under the Fifth Amendment.

Some fairly consistent themes emerged during the Burger Court since 1970 and have been generally continued with the Rehnquist Court:

- *The Court has created a hierarchy among the provisions of the Bill of Rights*. Not all rights receive the same scrutiny by the Supreme Court. The hierarchy is based on a single criterion: How much positive impact does the right in question have on the ultimate mission of the criminal justice system, namely, convicting the guilty and acquitting the innocent? Rights such as the right to counsel and the right to jury trial, which have a direct bearing on the guilt-determination process, have received more favorable attention from the Court than rights such as the Fourth Amendment's right to be free from unreasonable searches and seizures which, when coupled with its remedy of the exclusionary rule, may have a negative impact on truth determination at trial.

- *The Court has become more accommodating to law enforcement needs*. The Supreme Court has usually sought to accommodate law enforcement's investigative needs. Thus, the Court has refused to adopt rules or procedures it views as unduly restrictive of effective law enforcement. The justices refused, for example, to require a *Miranda*-type set of warnings about the person's right to refuse consent to a warrantless search. Similarly, the Court held that the reasonableness of a police officer's stopping a car should be viewed against the whole picture as it would be seen by trained law enforcement.

- *The Court has enacted procedures that dramatically limits individual access to federal courts*. The Supreme Court in recent years has shifted power to interpret the meaning of the Constitution in state criminal cases back to the state judiciary by substantially curtailing the opportunity of state prisoners to relitigate constitutional claims in federal *habeas corpus* proceedings. The Court has also substantially narrowed the access to federal courts for those who fail to assert their Constitutional claims in state court.

WEB
For the latest statistics on the criminal justice system, **visit the Bureau of Justice Statistics link on our Web site, www.prenhall.com/territo**

This analysis is not meant to suggest a diametrical opposition of the Burger and Rehnquist Courts to the Warren Court. The point is that the Supreme Court in recent years has been generally reluctant to elevate the interest of the individual over that of the state in its oversight of the criminal justice system. The difference in emphasis between the Courts shows that diverging approaches exist not only on the central issue of criminal procedure, but also on how best to protect the rights of the accused while providing full and effective enforcement of the law.

THE LAW OF CRIMINAL PROCEDURE VERSUS SUBSTANTIVE CRIMINAL LAW

The influence of the Supreme Court in criminal procedural law is felt whenever the Court has established basic constitutional principles that apply to criminal defendants. For example, the Supreme Court has established that defendants must not be tried through the use of an arbitrary procedure, but according to due process of law. In the United States, criminal procedural **due process of law** means that an accused person in criminal cases must be afforded certain rights and protections in keeping with the adversarial nature of the proceedings, and that he or she will be tried according to these legally established procedures. This due process model of criminal procedure is based on the premise that Americans believe their freedom is so valuable that government efforts must be made to prevent erroneous court decisions that would result in innocent people being deprived of their freedom. The government may act against accused people only when it follows the criminal procedure of due process, thus ensuring that the rights of all are maintained.

Like substantive criminal law, which we examined in Chapter 2, the law of criminal procedure is derived from many sources: the U.S. Constitution, all state constitutions, federal and state statutes, and judicial opinions for both federal courts and state courts. Among all of these sources, the Bill of Rights—the first ten amendments to the U.S. Constitution—holds a primary position. The **law of criminal procedure** may best be described as a set of rules governing the balance of the conflicting governmental functions of maintaining law and order while at the same time protecting the rights of individual citizens. These functions, which are common to every government (except those that are anarchistic or authoritarian), are not necessarily conflicting. Throughout the history of the United States, political emphasis has shifted, either supporting a procedure that maintains law and order (and thus allows an acceptable intrusion on individual rights) or allowing the pendulum to swing in the other direction toward the due process model. When the focus has not been on law and order, citizens have sought procedures that preserve individual rights, knowing that such efforts are sometimes counterproductive; they may cause a destabilization in law and order and arouse citizen antipathy toward law enforcement personnel. The focus of criminal procedure is to harbor a set of rules that justly balances the twin goals of preserving individual rights and guaranteeing law and order. This occurs when people feel secure in their homes and communities and believe that the integrity of their privacy and rights will not be intruded upon by the state unnecessarily.

During America's first Congress in June 1789, two years after the signing of the Constitution, James Madison (Figure 3.1) who later would become the fourth president of the United States, proposed a dozen constitutional amendments. Congress approved ten of these amendments in September 1791. They took effect on December 15 of that year. After ratification by the requisite number of states, these first ten amendments to the Constitution became known as the **Bill of Rights.**

THE BILL OF RIGHTS IS INEXTRICABLY TIED TO THE LAW OF CRIMINAL PROCEDURE

The Bill of Rights is inextricably tied to the law of criminal procedure. The Fourth, Fifth, Sixth, and Eighth Amendments to the Constitution are aimed directly at specific rights that individuals receive when they are subject to either a criminal investigation or a criminal trial, or at criminal sentencing hearings. The major significance of the Bill of Rights is that it restricts the activities of government and government organizations, rather than individuals and private groups. Specifically, these four amendments are precisely what give profound uncompromising authority to the rules and provisions of criminal procedure, as will be explained and examined in detail later in this chapter.

Criminal procedure requires a balancing act and is obviously difficult. Naturally, it is the constant target of criticism. The nature of American criminal procedure thereby causes the criminal justice system to reflect often on its own competency. Most often when these reflections are made, a certain stability arises. Because the earliest American collective perception of justice was formed in part as a reaction to abuses perpetrated by British authorities on Americans' individual rights, our form of government has had a strong commitment to criminal procedure that guarantees the protection of individual rights from government abuse. This commitment also was embodied in the original Constitution of 1787 and in the Bill of Rights, which was adopted shortly thereafter.

WEB

For more information on the National Center for Policy Analysis, an advocacy group often associated with the crime control model of criminal justice, **visit our Web site, www.prenhall.com/territo.**

WEB

To view the original copy of the Bill of Rights, **visit the National Records and Archive Administration link on our Web site, www.prenhall.com/territo.**

CTQ

What is the current philosophical orientation of the U.S. Supreme Court regarding criminal justice issues?

FIGURE 3.1

James Madison not only was the fourth president of the United States, but more important, he drafted a dozen constitutional amendments. Congress approved ten of these, and they became known as the Bill of Rights.

Courtesy Getty Images Inc.

TABLE 3.1 The Due Process Model and the Crime Control Model Compared

	Goal	Value	Process	Major Decision Point	Basis of Decision Making
Due process model	Preserve individual liberties	Reliability	Adversarial	Courtroom	Law
Crime control model	Repress crime	Efficiency	Administrative	Police, pretrial processes	Discretion

WEB
For more information on the rights embodied in the Fourth Amendment, **visit our Web site,** www.prenhall.com/territo.

WEB
To view historical documents such as the U. S. Constitution, **visit our Web site,** www.prenhall.com/territo.

CTQ
Is it in the public's interest to protect police officers' lives and to expend greater efforts in doing so than the efforts expended to save the lives of ordinary citizens?

CTQ
If you were a Supreme Court justice, which of these two conflicting goals would you choose to give priority to—the due process model or the crime control model?

Constitutional Rights as Possible Constraints on Efficient Law Enforcement

The aims and goals of criminal law, when juxtaposed with those of American constitutional law, create a legal dynamic tension. This is furthered by the adversary model of due process and equal protection, both of which come under attack frequently. American critics assert that it hinders law enforcement and, consequently, crime prevention and control. Frequently, reference is made to the conflict between what noted scholar Herbert L. Packer called the "crime control model of criminal justice" and "the due process model."[1]

The goal of the **crime control model** is quick and efficient processing of people who violate the law. In contrast, placing priority on the dignity, autonomy, and individual rights of the accused is the aim of the **due process model.** The crime control model, according to many legal scholars, is similar to an assembly line; the due process model of criminal justice is a constitutional theory that gives priority to the preservation of individual liberties when a person is being processed throughout the various stages of the criminal justice system. The goal of due process is to ensure that the administration of the laws pertaining to a defendant's case do not violate the sacredness of either the Constitution or the defendant's private rights. Within criminal justice systems, support for the due process model comes mainly from the courts and defense attorneys, whereas the main support for the crime control model comes from the prosecution and the police.[2] This tension is rendered in Table 3.1.

Laws may not specify everything that is prohibited; they must be flexible. Fifth Amendment due process requires that the behavior intended to be prohibited by the criminal law must be clearly articulated in the statute and easily understood by citizens. A statute should not encompass other activities that constitute an exercise of other constitutional rights. Hence, criminal laws may not be too broad or too vague. Hence, in order to avoid being held unconstitutional due to vagueness, statutory crimes must meet at least three criteria: (1) They must give notice or warning to all who are subject to them; (2) they must protect against discriminatory enforcement; and (3) they must not unreasonably deny other rights, such as the First Amendment rights of free speech and religion.

What may be expected to continue into the twenty-first century is the conflict between the legitimate concern of governments to maintain peace and control and the rights of citizens to be free from unreasonable governmental interference. Throughout this text, examples of these problems are highlighted in sections on the human perspective on issues within criminal justice systems.

THE CONSTITUTION AND THE BILL OF RIGHTS
A Historical Overview of Their Rationale

The U.S. Constitution continues to play a critical role in the development of criminal procedure used in the criminal justice system. The forerunner of the Constitution was the Articles of Confederation, adopted by the Continental Congress in 1781. The articles were generally inadequate as a foundation for effective government because they did not create a proper balance of power between the states and the central government. As a result, in 1787, the Congress of the Confederation adopted a resolution calling for a convention of delegates from the original states. Meeting in Philadelphia, the delegates' express purpose was to revise the Articles of Confederation. However, the work of that convention culminated in the drafting of the U.S. Constitution. It was ratified by the states in 1788 and put into effect in 1789.

In its original form, the Constitution of the United States (herein after referred to as the Constitution) consisted of a preamble and seven articles. The Constitution divided the powers of government into three independent but equal parts: the executive, legislative, and judicial branches. The purpose of the separation of powers was to ensure that no single branch of the government could usurp power for itself and institute a dictatorship. The measures and procedures initiated by the framers of the Constitution have developed over time into our present form of government.

How does the Constitution, with its formal set of rights and privileges, affect the operations of the criminal justice system? One way is to guarantee that no one branch of government determines the fate of a man or a woman accused of crime. The workings of the criminal justice process illustrate this principle. Suppose a sheriff, who represents the executive branch of the government, makes an arrest based on a law passed by the legislative branch that criminalizes "having an obscene bumper sticker" on the back of one's car. The accused is subsequently tried by the judiciary and found guilty, However, his conviction is subsequently reversed by the appeals court on the grounds that the law is unconstitutional, it is overly broad and vague and violates the First and Fifth Amendments—the right to free speech (First Amendment) and the right to specificity of a crime (Fifth Amendment due process clause). Thus, citizens are protected from the arbitrary abuse of power by any single element of the law.

In addition to providing protection by ensuring separation of powers within the government, the Constitution also controls the operations of the criminal justice system by simultaneously guaranteeing the individual freedoms in the ten amendments added to it on December 15, 1791, which are collectively known as the Bill of Rights[3] (see Table 3.2). The Bill of Rights was adopted only to protect individual liberties from being abused by the national government; however, it is significantly more important to remember that these rights did not apply to the actions of state or local officials, law enforcement officers, prosecutors, or judges. Over the last four decades, however, the U.S. Supreme Court's interpretation of the Constitution has served as the basis of the legal rights of the accused. The principles that govern criminal procedure are outlined by the U.S. Constitution's Bill of Rights. The particular rights in the Bill of Rights that are of primary concern to the law of criminal procedure are the Fourth, Fifth, Sixth, and Eighth Amendments. These four amendments embody fifteen criminal procedural rights that limit and control the manner in which the federal government operates the justice system. The due process clause of the Fourteenth Amendment, often also referred to as the procedural due process clause, has had the historical effect of limiting governmental actions against the accused on a state level. These key amendments furnish the basis for the law of criminal procedure as it operates within the criminal justice system.

While only a very few rights were specified in the articles of the Constitution when it was adopted in 1787, the Constitution has served as the basis of the government of the United States for most of our country's history as an independent nation. Paradoxically, the Constitution was drafted when there were only thirteen states. At that time, most citizens lived in rural locations. Yet regardless of any historical circumstance, the Constitution has proved a viable, stable, and durable document despite enormous social, political, economic, and military changes.

The Doctrine of Selective Incorporation

Throughout most of our history, the Bill of Rights had no meaningful consequences in the criminal justice system; the Fourth, Fifth, Sixth, and Eighth Amendments protected

TABLE 3.2 The Bill of Rights

Amendment I
Congress shall make no law respecting an establishment of religion, or prohibiting the free exercise thereof; or abridging the freedom of speech, or of the press; or the right of the people peaceably to assemble, and to petition the government for a redress of grievances.

Amendment II
A well regulated militia, being necessary to the security of a free state, the right of the people to keep and bear arms, shall not be infringed.

Amendment III
No soldier shall, in time of peace be quartered in any house without the consent of the owner, nor in time of war, but in a manner to be prescribed by law.

Amendment IV
The right of the people to be secure in their persons, houses, papers, and effects, against unreasonable searches and seizures, shall not be violated, and no warrants shall issue, but upon probable cause, supported by oath or affirmation, and particularly describing the place to be searched, and the persons or things to be seized.

Amendment V
No person shall be held to answer for a capital, or otherwise infamous crime, unless on a presentment or indictment of a grand jury, except in cases arising in the land or naval forces, or in the militia, when in actual service in time of war or public danger; nor shall any person be subject for the same offense to be twice put in jeopardy of life or limb; nor shall be compelled in any criminal case to be a witness against himself, nor be deprived of life, liberty, or property, without due process of law; nor shall private property be taken for public use, without just compensation.

Amendment VI
In all criminal prosecutions, the accused shall enjoy the right to a speedy and public trial, by an impartial jury of the state and district wherein the crime shall have been committed, which district shall have been previously ascertained by law, and to be informed of the nature and cause of the accusation; to be confronted with the witnesses against him; to have compulsory process for obtaining witnesses in his favor, and to have the assistance of counsel for his defense.

Amendment VII
In suits at common law, where the value in controversy shall exceed twenty dollars, the right of trial by jury shall be preserved, and no fact tried by a jury, shall be otherwise reexamined in any court of the United States, than according to the rules of the common law.

Amendment VIII
Excessive bail shall not be required, nor excessive fines imposed, nor cruel and unusual punishment inflicted.

Amendment IX
The enumeration in the Constitution, of certain rights shall not be construed to deny or disparage others retained by the people.

Amendment X
The powers not delegated to the United States by the Constitution, nor prohibited by it to the states, are reserved to the states respectively, or to the people.

CTQ
Discuss the relationship between the U.S. Constitution and the Bill of Rights. What particular provisions does the incorporation theory involve?

CTQ
Is the Supreme Court conservative or liberal when it comes to controlling police power? What factors will come into play in the court of the first decade of the twenty-first century? Do you see an increase or decrease in civil liberties during this decade?

the criminally accused only if they were prosecuted in federal courts and not state courts during the country's first 150 years. This is particularly significant when one considers that today nine out of every ten criminal defendants in this country are being tried in state courts, not federal courts.[4]

In 1868, the Fourteenth Amendment was added to the Constitution. It provides that "*no state* [emphasis added] shall deprive any person of life, liberty, or property without due process of law." Yet sixty-seven years would pass before the Fourteenth Amendment's due process clause was interpreted by the Supreme Court to mean "without abridgement of certain rights guaranteed by the Bill of Rights."[5] Thus, only in 1925 did the Supreme Court start to recognize that the rights enumerated in the Bill of Rights should be granted to every individual who was being processed by a state criminal justice system.

The Supreme Court has *never* ruled that *all* of the criminal procedural rights embodied in the Fourth, Fifth, Sixth, and Eighth Amendments are to be afforded to every individual processed through an individual state's criminal justice system. However, the Court has declared that certain fundamental concepts of fairness within the

Bill of Rights are so fundamental to liberty, fairness, and the American system of justice that they must be recognized as part of the due process law and made applicable to the individual state courts as well as the federal courts.[6] This recognition process and subsequent requirement that the states adopt these rights through the power of the due process clause of the Fourteenth Amendment is known as the **doctrine of selective incorporation.**

Upon the selective incorporation of a right, the Supreme Court makes each right, along with its "constitutional baggage" (this includes each and every Supreme Court case and federal case that has rendered a decision interpreting the meaning, significance, and applicability of each and every particular aspect embodied within the right) completely applicable to every state's administration, laws, and procedures as it processes an individual through the criminal justice system.

For the most part, however, selective incorporation did not begin when the Fourteenth Amendment was passed in the 1860s; it was only in the Warren Court's opinions, which were rendered during the 1960s, that the major rights contained in the Fourth, Fifth, Sixth, and Eighth Amendments were afforded to every criminal defendant being processed through a state criminal justice system. However, by the end of the 1970s, most of the Bill of Rights had been integrated into every executive, judicial, and legislative branch affecting the nature of every state's criminal justice system.

Most American citizens are unaware that as recently as 1961, for example, in the state of Florida and many other states, an indigent person accused of a noncapital felony did not have the Sixth Amendment right to counsel under state law in a circuit court. Indigent defendants were required to defend themselves if they wished to have counsel at trial. Yet in 1961, this was precisely the situation with Clarence Earl Gideon, a defendant charged with burglary at a pool hall in Pensacola, Florida. Although for 170 years the Sixth Amendment had guaranteed as a fundamental right that criminal defendants could have counsel to represent them in federal and state courts, this right was limited to those who could afford to hire a lawyer. Gideon was too poor to afford counsel. Hence, he was forced to defend himself. Gideon's trial, conviction, and appeals, and the Supreme Court's decision in *Gideon v. Wainwright* (discussed later in this chapter), represent the paradigm of the doctrine of selective incorporation. (see Table 3.3).

The Supreme Court's Power of Judicial Review

The most fundamental function of the Supreme Court is **judicial review,** the power of the Supreme Court to review the constitutionality of all acts, laws, statutes, and case opinions, both federal and state, in the American legal system. If in exercising the power of judicial review, the Supreme Court determines that a certain statute or case opinion is unconstitutional, then the Court has the absolute power to void the statute or the opinion. Thus Americans are guaranteed that all laws are in accordance with the highest law of the land, the U. S. Constitution. There is no higher authority over state legislation, federal legislation, state court opinions, and federal court opinions than the power of judicial review of the Supreme Court of the United States. The Court's decision is final and stands as inevitable and supreme.[7]

THE FOURTEENTH AMENDMENT'S DUE PROCESS CLAUSE

The Fourteenth Amendment declares, in part, that "no state shall make or enforce any law which shall abridge the privileges or immunities of citizens of the United States, nor shall any state deprive any person of life, liberty, or property, without due process of law; nor deny any person within its jurisdiction the equal protection of the laws...." Together with the Thirteenth and Fifteenth Amendments, which were passed just after the Civil War, the Fourteenth Amendment extended citizenship to former slaves and guaranteed them the same protections of law as were previously provided for other particular citizens governed by the Constitution. Unfortunately, the due process and equal protection clauses of the Fourteenth Amendment were not immediately interpreted as quickly as they should have been by incorporating the Bill of Rights to be applicable to state governments. Instead, as late as the 1940s, state courts and the Supreme Court began to employ Fourteenth Amendment rights primarily to protect business corporations from government regulations.

The Supreme Court has never clearly established the exact meaning of what constitutes due process. Both the definition and significance of due process seem to be flexible and continually changing. One thing seems certain: procedural due process of law in the beginning of the twenty-first century has meant, at least, that all people accused in criminal cases in both state and federal courts in the United States must be afforded certain rights to ensure that they receive a fair trial.

During 1961 to 1969—a period often referred to as the "due process revolution"—the Supreme Court took an activist role, becoming a giver of the law rather than just an interpreter. Under Chief Justice Earl Warren, the Court expanded the meaning of the due process requirement; it moved from the old policy that a state must afford "fundamental fairness" to an accused toward insisting on absolute compliance by state and local officials with a vast majority of the provisions in the Bill of Rights. Some statistics illustrate the magnitude of the revolution.

Today, the Supreme Court normally writes about 115 opinions in any term. During the 1938–1939 term, only five cases appeared under the heading of criminal law; three decades later, however, during the height of the due process revolution, about one-fourth of all decisions related to criminal law. Yet the key Supreme Court decisions during the due process revolution focused on the rights stated in the Fourth, Fifth, Sixth, and Eighth Amendments to the Constitution. Collectively, the multitude of these cases delivered during the 1960s constitute a watershed period in the administration of criminal justice in the United States.

Table 3.3 provides a list of cases that illustrate how and when the Supreme Court has decided whether a particular right embodied in the Bill of Rights was so fundamental to the concept of "ordered liberty" that it required all state courts and state criminal justice system agencies to apply the right to criminal procedure used in state courts. When the Supreme Court selectively incorporated these rights as fundamental requirements of the due process clause, not only did it require that states adopt the rights immediately within their criminal rules and procedures, but it also required them to adopt all previous and subsequent Supreme Court cases that have interpreted the particular constitutional right being incorporated as an additional "package" of the states' own rules of criminal procedure.

As mentioned in the introduction to this chapter, the debate concerning the application of the due process model continued in the mid-1970s. Conservative political leaders emphasized that the crime control model, rather than protection of an accused's individual liberties, created the greater social good. When Chief Justice Earl Warren retired in 1969, President Richard Nixon appointed Warren Burger as the fifteenth Chief Justice of the United States. Subsequently, the resignations of liberal justices Black and Harlan (who were replaced by conservative justice Lewis Powell and ultraconservative justice William Rehnquist in 1971) began to alter the direction and the strength of the due process revolution. Subsequent additional changes, when exclusively Republican presidents appointed new conservative justices, transformed the Supreme Court from a liberal Court to a moderate Court and, by 1982, to a definitely conservative Court that totally adopted the crime control model of justice.

WEB

For more information on due process visit our Web site, www.prenhall.com/territo.

CTQ

What do you think the framers of the Constitution meant when they coined the term "due process of law"?

WEB

For more information on Supreme Court decisions on issues of criminal procedure, visit Cornell's Legal Information Institute link on our Web site, www.prenhall.com/territo.

CTQ

How does "due process of law" differ from "the law of the land"?

CTQ

Have "criminals" been given too many rights? Should courts become more concerned with the rights of the victims or the rights of the offenders?

WEB

For information on the American Civil Liberties Union (ACLU), an advocacy group of the due process model of the criminal justice system, visit our Web site, www.prenhall.com/territo.

IN THE WORKPLACE

APPELLATE COURT JUDGE

Responsible for all elements of arbitration. Performs a variety of duties including the following: arbitrates disputes; advises counsel, jury, litigants, and court personnel; administers judicial system. Appellate court judge has mandatory jurisdiction in civil, noncapital criminal, administrative agency, juvenile, original proceeding, and interlocutory decision cases. Minimum requirements are as follows: must be a state resident; must not have reached the maximum age of 70; must have at least ten years with the state bar.

TABLE 3.3 The Selected Incorporation of the Bill of Rights

Most provisions of the Bill of Rights have been held applicable to individual states under the Fourteenth Amendment due process clause:

Amendment	Incorporated Right	Case and Date
Fourth Amendment	(1) The prohibition against unreasonable searches and seizures (2) The exclusionary rule, which prohibits the use of items obtained as a result of an unreasonable search and seizure as evidence against a criminal defendant	*Wolf v. Colorado* (1949) *Mapp v. Ohio* (1961)
Fifth Amendment	(1) The bar against double jeopardy (2) The privilege against forced self-incrimination	*Benton v. Maryland* (1969) *Malloy v. Hogan* (1964)
Sixth Amendment	(1) The right to a jury trial (2) The right to a public trial (3) The right to a speedy trial (4) The right to confront witnesses (5) The right to compulsory process to obtain witnesses (6) The right to the assistance of an attorney in felony cases (7) The right to the assistance of an attorney in misdemeanor cases in which a prison term is imposed	*Duncan v. Louisiana* (1968) *In re Oliver* (1948) *Klopfer v. North Carolina* (1967) *Pointer v. Texas* (1965) *Washington v. Texas* (1967) *Gideon v. Wainwright* (1963) *Argersinger v. Hamlin* (1972); *Scott v. Illinois* (1979)
Eighth Amendment	(1) The prohibition against cruel and unusual punishment	*Robinson v. California* (1962)

Two provisions of the Bill of Rights have not been held applicable to individual states:

Amendment	Nonincorporated Right	Case and Date
Fifth Amendment	(1) The Fifth Amendment right to indictment by a grand jury for capital and infamous crimes has been held not binding on the states. Many states do not use grand juries as a regular part of the charging process. Where grand jury indictment is not used or the defendant waives the right to grand jury action, the state charges by information—a formal charging instrument drawn up by the prosecutor or by a preliminary hearing judge.	*Hurtado v. California* (1884)
Eighth Amendment	(1) The prohibition of the Eighth Amendment against excessive bail is not binding on the states. Most state constitutions, however, create a right to bail and prohibit excessive bail. Note that Supreme Court decisions are the minimum stardards for citizens' rights—states can give their citizens more rights, but they cannot take away rights.	*United States v. Salerno* (1987)

Constitutional expert Yale Kamisar writes,

> A Warren Court admirer probably would say that the new Court did retreat on any number of search and seizure fronts but that it held firm on others and even advanced on some. In the confession area, again viewed from the perspective of a Warren Court supporter, the Burger Court did inflict substantial damage, especially in earlier years, but much less than it had been threatening to do.[8]

The Burger Court of the 1970s and 1980s and the Rehnquist Court of the 1990s and the beginning of the twenty-first century have interpreted the meaning of the due process clause in a far more conservative manner than did the Warren Court. Any examination of the Bill of Rights from a criminal justice perspective must include both the due process revolution of the Warren Court and the somewhat conservative retreat of the Burger and Rehnquist Courts. Remaining through all of these changes and interpretations, however, are the Fourth, Fifth, Sixth, and Eighth Amendments' guarantees of specific rights and the historical interpretations attached to them. The personality and philosophical changes of the new and returning justices over the years have had a great impact in determining what the Court's overall legal direction will become.

CTQ

Why do you believe the Supreme Court has not selectively incorporated every right contained within the Bill of Rights?

CTQ

Why do you think that the rights that were not selected were in fact not selected?

CTQ

Did the opinions supporting crime control in the 1970s, 1980s, 1990s, and the first decade of the twenty-first century make the United States a better or worse place in which to live?

THE FOURTH AMENDMENT RIGHTS ON ARREST, SEARCH, AND SEIZURE

The Fourth Amendment prohibits the government from conducting unreasonable searches and seizures. The Fourth Amendment states, "The right of the people to be secure in their persons, houses, papers, and effects, against unreasonable searches and seizures, shall not be violated, and no warrants shall issue, but upon probable cause, supported by oath or affirmation, and particularly describing the place to be searched, and the persons or things to be seized." For the purposes of the Fourth Amendment, a **search** can be defined as any governmental intrusion upon a person's reasonable and justifiable expectation of privacy; **seizure** can be defined as the exercise of control by the government over a person or thing.

Whether or not an intrusion is a "reasonable intrusion" depends on the definition of reasonableness. Whether a search or seizure is reasonable under the Fourth Amendment depends on the scope of the seizure (is it an arrest, or merely a stop?) and the strength of the suspicion prompting the seizure (an arrest requires probable cause, whereas an investigatory stop requires only a reasonable suspicion).

Since an arrest is a seizure, all arrests must satisfy the constitutional requirements of the Fourth Amendment. Hence, the question comes up, what is a constitutional arrest? In order for an arrest to be constitutional, the police must take a person into custody against his or her will for the purposes of criminal prosecution or interrogation. This requires a physical application of force by the police officer or a submission to the officer's show of force.[9] The arrestee must not be free to leave of his or her own volition. It is not relevant whether the act is termed an arrest under state law.[10] Finally, mere words (for example, "Stop in the name of the law!") do not normally constitute an arrest. Furthermore, there is no arrest when an officer simply approaches a person in a public place and asks him or her if he or she is willing to answer questions, as long as the person is not involuntarily detained.[11] A police officer's pursuit of an individual constitutes a seizure only when a reasonable person would have believed that he or she was not free to leave.[12]

The Constitution requires that an arrest, with or without an arrest warrant, be based on **probable cause.** This requirement is satisfied when, at the time of the arrest, the facts and circumstances within the officer's knowledge are based on reasonably trustworthy information, and these facts and circumstances are sufficient to warrant a prudent person to believe that the suspect has committed or was committing an offense.[13]

As a general rule, the Fourth Amendment requires all U. S. law enforcement officers to obtain warrants before conducting searches and seizures. Indeed, warrantless searches are permissible, but they happen seldom and they must conform to specific Supreme Court guidelines. However, the Fourth Amendment requirement that searches and seizures be reasonable does not mean that a warrant must be obtained before making an arrest.[14] In *United States v. Watson*, the Court held that the police need not obtain a warrant before arresting a person in a public place, even if there is time and opportunity to do so. In fact, most arrests are made without warrants. The only time that an arrest warrant is almost always required is when the government wants to arrest a private citizen in his or her home.

Finally, the framers of the Constitution were greatly concerned about the power of the central government to interfere in personal matters. After all, the Constitution's authors had just engineered a revolution against a government they viewed as tyrannical and opposed to individual freedom. In addition, the predominant philosophical movement of the time, known today as the Enlightenment, stressed limitations on the state's power to interfere with the rights of its citizens. Such issues as liberty and privacy were of central concern when the Bill of Rights was formulated. Considering these goals, it is not surprising that the Fourth Amendment was designed to protect citizens from unnecessary intrusions by the government into their private affairs. Hence, the Fourth Amendment is especially important for the criminal justice system because it means that police officers cannot indiscriminately use their authority to investigate a possible crime or arrest a suspect unless both actions are justified by the law and the facts of the case. Stopping, questioning, or searching an individual without legal justification represents a serious violation of the Fourth Amendment right to personal privacy.[15]

CTQ

What is the paramount goal of the Supreme Court at this time? Is its legal philosophy control of crime and public safety, or protection of civil liberties?

CTQ

Is it possible for a person to be legally under arrest without an officer indicating that he or she is in fact under arrest? Explain.

CTQ

Can you be arrested without doing anything?

WEB

For more information on specific decisions announced by the Supreme Court, visit the National Criminal Justice Reference Service link on our Web site, www.prenhall.com/territo.

TABLE 3.4 Evidentiary Standards of the Degrees of the Certainty Used Throughout the Various Phases of the Criminal Justice System

Level of Certainty	As Applied to the Criminal Justice System	Percentage of Certainty Required
Beyond a reasonable doubt	The level of certainty necessary to find a defendant guilty at criminal trial.	93%
Clear and convincing evidence	The level of certainty a judge must have in order to deny bail to a criminal defendant.	75%
Preponderance of the evidence	The standard of proof in civil law. It is also the standard of proof necessary to win suppression hearings at a criminal trial to exclude evidence obtained from unconstitutional acts by the police such as an illegal search or a forced confession.	50.0001%
Probable cause	The level of certainty necessary to make an arrest or conduct a constitutional search.	33.3 %
Reasonable suspicion	The level of certainty necessary to stop and frisk someone who is acting unusually.	25%
Hunch	*Not* a legally recognized level of certainty, but most good police work is done with it.	Below 20%

Evidentiary Standards of the Degrees of the Certainty Used throughout the Various Phases of the Criminal Justice System

In this text, we will mention constitutional concepts such as *probable cause, reasonable suspicion,* and *beyond a reasonable doubt*. These and other legal concepts represent evidentiary standards of proof that law enforcement officers or state prosecutors must present to obtain a search or arrest warrant or a guilty verdict.

Some of these standards require far less certainty of the truth (to allow a law enforcement officer's actions) than do others. Indeed, in the criminal justice system, there are five different degrees of certainty that must be met and correlated with the standard of proof that is involved. Table 3.4 illustrates this hierarchy of certainty for each of the specific constitutional standards listed on the left hand side of the column. For educational purposes, the author has suggested an approximate "percentage of certainty" that the author believes necessary to meet each burden of proof, based on thirty years of experience practicing criminal law. This numerical "percentage of certainty" is in no way a Constitutional right, nor has it been articulated in cases.

THE RIGHT TO A CONSTITUTIONAL ARREST

The Fourth Amendment protects individual citizens from unreasonable searches and seizures. The Supreme Court has determined that a seizure of the body is the placement of an individual under arrest by an agent of the state. Hence, the Fourth Amendment gives individual citizens constitutional rights regarding the manner in which they are arrested. Recall that a constitutional arrest is the taking of a person into custody against his or her will for criminal prosecution; it deprives a person of liberty by legal authority; the person must be restricted by the law enforcement officer to the extent that the person does not feel free to leave on his or her own volition; and the arrest must be based on probable cause.

Can a Citizen Make an Arrest?

The right of a citizen to make an arrest is not a constitutional question, but is based on a state-by-state determination. For example, the Idaho Code of Criminal Procedure states that a private person may make an arrest of another:

1. for a public offense committed in the citizen's presence
2. when the person arrested has committed a felony, although not in his presence
3. when the felony has been committed and he has reasonable cause for believing the person arrested to have committed it.[16]

It must be remembered, however, that in most jurisdictions the specific statutes governing arrest are quite specific and quite different from each other. Furthermore, the circumstances under which a citizen can and cannot make an arrest are very specific.

However, there is a category of person that falls halfway between being a citizen and a police officer, and this is the private security police officer. The central issue raised with regard to private security police officers is related to their authority to make arrests.

Private security police have the same rights as any other citizen to make an arrest and hold a suspect until the police arrive. Some states have afforded private police additional powers (e.g., to conduct a "pat-down search"), but for the most part their authority is the same as any citizen, unless additional authority is provided by state statute.

The following four steps for making an arrest apply to private security police and citizens. First, the party must see the crime being committed. If the suspect is found not guilty in a court of law, the party may be sued for false arrest charges regardless of how many witnesses say they observed the incident. Second, the party cannot detain the suspect and conduct a search or on-the-spot investigation. Nor can the party physically bring the suspect to the police precinct. The party may hold the suspect until the police arrive. Third, the party must tell the suspect why he or she is being arrested; the accused has a right to know. Fourth, if the suspect resists arrest, the party may only use such force as is necessary to hold the suspect. Since local laws vary on the amount of force a citizen may use, the party must be aware of what the limitations are before making a citizen's arrest.

The Requirements for an Arrest Warrant

If a defendant is to be arrested pursuant to an **arrest warrant** (see Figure 3.2), the warrant is valid only if it is based on a sworn complaint that sets forth facts showing the commission of an offense and the accused's responsibility for it. Generally, a complaint is in the form of an **affidavit,** which is a sworn written statement by a police officer.

The sufficiency of the complaint is determined by federal constitutional standards; that is, probable cause must be demonstrated before a valid arrest warrant may be issued by a judicial officer. The requirements for obtaining a constitutional arrest warrant are as follows: The complaint is a written statement of the central fact containing the offense; the complaint is made before a magistrate; it appears from the complaint that there is probable cause to believe that an offense has been committed and the defendant committed it; a warrant may be issued to any officer authorized by law to execute it; probable cause may be based on hearsay evidence; the warrant should be signed by the magistrate, and should contain the name of the defendant or his or her description, which will allow him or her to be identified with reasonable certainty; the warrant shall describe the offense charged and shall command the defendant to be arrested and brought before the magistrate; the warrant shall be executed by the arrest of the defendant, and the officer need not have the warrant in his possession at the time of arrest; and the officer executing the warrant shall return it to the magistrate.

CTQ

Should police be personally liable if they violate a person's constitutional rights? How might this influence their investigations?

LANDMARK CASE — Payton v. New York

Having cause to believe Payton had murdered a gas station manager, the police entered his apartment to effect a routine felony arrest. Although he was not at home, the police found a 30-caliber shell casing in plain sight in the apartment and seized it for ultimate use as evidence. Payton's motion to suppress the evidence was denied and he was convicted of murder. On appeal he argued that the statute authorizing warrantless entries into a routine felony arrest violated the Fourth Amendment. The Court considered the question of whether, under normal circumstances, it is constitutional for the police to make a warrantless, nonconsensual entry into a private residence to effect a routine felony arrest. The holding of the Supreme Court was that the police must have an arrest warrant before they can enter a suspect's home to arrest the suspect. The Court also stated that absent exigent circumstances, the police may not make a warrantless, nonconsensual entry into a private residence to make a felony arrest and should instead obtain a warrant.

Source: Payton v. New York, 445 U.S. 573 (1980).

FIGURE 3.2

Arrest Warrant

United States District Court

_______________ DISTRICT OF _______________

UNITED STATES OF AMERICA
V.

WARRANT FOR ARREST

CASE NUMBER:

To: The United States Marshal
and any Authorized United States Officer

YOU ARE HEREBY COMMANDED to arrest _______________
Name

and bring him or her forthwith to the nearest magistrate to answer a(n)

☐ Indictment ☐ Information ☐ Complaint ☐ Order of court ☐ Violation Notice ☐ Probation Violation Petition

charging him or her with (brief description of offense)

in violation of Title _______ United States Code, Section(s) _______________

Name of Issuing Officer | Title of Issuing Officer

Signature of Issuing Officer | Date and Location

Bail fixed at $ by _______________
Name of Judicial Officer

RETURN

This warrant was received and executed with the arrest of the above-named defendant at _______________

DATE RECEIVED	NAME AND TITLE OF ARRESTING OFFICER	SIGNATURE OF ARRESTING OFFICER
DATE OF ARREST		

Police officers must have an arrest warrant to enter a person's home or arrest him or her, absent emergency circumstances or consent. The government bears the burden of proof of demonstrating exigent circumstances.[17] (see the Landmark Case *Payton v. New York*). However, there are some exceptions to the law that prohibits a home arrest without an arrest warrant. The first is what is referred to as the *hot pursuit exception*. Under this exception, if police officers have probable cause to arrest a person who retreats into his or her home, a warrantless entry into the person's home is permissible if necessary for the police to act quickly to prevent the suspect's escape or the destruction of evidence (see Figure 3.3). The next logical question that arises about home arrests is whether the police are required to announce their presence. The answer is generally, yes. There are announcement requirements, but there are exceptions to these. One such exception is referred to as the "*no knock rule*." Under federal statutes and many state laws, police officers must announce their authority and purpose before using force to enter a home to make an arrest. Generally, failure to make such an announcement renders the arrest unlawful, although most jurisdictions recognize exceptions to this requirement. Some of these exceptions include the officer's reasonable belief that the announcement would endanger him or her, prompt a suspect's escape, or permit the destruction of evidence.

WEB

For more information on government intrusion in personal communications, **visit our Web site, www.prenhall.com/territo**.

FIGURE 3.3

Payton v. New York required that the police have an arrest warrant before entering a suspect's home. However, if, after announcing their presence and purpose, they still are not admitted to the home, they may use whatever force is necessary to gain entry.

© Dale Stockton

As a general rule, the police make arrests without warrants; the person arrested must ordinarily be brought before a magistrate promptly for a probable-cause hearing. The U.S. Supreme Court dealt with the meaning of promptness in 1991.[18] The Court said that the police could detain an individual arrested without a warrant for up to forty-eight hours without a court deciding whether the arrest was justified. The decision takes into account the state's interest in taking suspects into custody and an individual's concern about prolonged custody affecting employment and family relations.

When Can an Officer Use Deadly Force to Make an Arrest?

An area of increasing interest in the beginning of the twenty-first century is under what circumstances police are allowed to use **deadly force** in order to arrest a fleeing felon. In *Tennessee v. Garner*, the Court announced that using deadly force to apprehend a suspect constitutes a seizure and is therefore protected under the Fourth Amendment. Hence, the Court concluded that the use of deadly force must be reasonable. The Court stated that deadly force is reasonable only when (1) it is necessary to prevent the felon's escape, and (2) the felon threatens death or serious bodily harm during the escape itself—not at the time of the commission of the felony. (See the Landmark Case *Tennessee v. Garner.*)

LANDMARK CASE — Tennessee v. Garner

Garner was shot and killed by a Tennessee police officer while fleeing the scene of a felony. The officer saw that Garner was unarmed, but shot him to prevent escape. Garner's father sued, contending that the use of deadly force in this situation, pursuant to a Tennessee statute, was unconstitutional. The Supreme Court looked at the issue of whether deadly force may be used to prevent the escape of an unarmed, nonviolent felon and declared that deadly force cannot be used to effect an arrest unless (1) it is necessary to prevent escape and (2) the officer harbors a good-faith belief that the suspect poses a significant threat of death or serious injury to the officer or to others.

Source: Tennessee v. Garner, 471 U.S. 1 (1985).

IN THE NEWS

A HUMAN PERSPECTIVE

CAN A COP SEARCH YOU AND YOUR CAR DURING A ROUTINE TRAFFIC STOP?
by Marissa Melton

The U.S. Supreme Court ruled in an Iowa case that police may no longer routinely search cars stopped for minor traffic violations unless they suspect criminal behavior or have already made an arrest. The ruling handed a victory to civil rights advocates, and worried traffic cops; it also raised some questions about what a motorist's legal rights really are. Here's what the legal experts say you should know: If you have been stopped for a traffic violation such as speeding, police officers may require you or your passengers to get out of the car. If the officer reasonably suspects you are dangerous and have a weapon, he can still, despite last week's ruling, superficially search your car or frisk you without your permission. He may detain you for a brief period, but no more than about 15 minutes. Most important, says Prof. Susan Herman of Brooklyn Law School, you should remember that in matters of search and seizure, the justice system favors law enforcement.

Source: Marissa Melton, "Can a Cop Search You and Your Car during a Routine Traffic Stop?" *U.S. News & World Report,* 21 December 1998. Copyright 1998 U.S. News & World Report, L.P. Reprinted with permission.

ARRESTS THAT ARE NOT REALLY ARRESTS–"STOPS" AND "DETENTIONS": WHEN ARE THEY CONSTITUTIONAL?

The Fourth Amendment protects citizens who are unreasonably arrested by stating that if officers do not have probable cause to believe that a crime has been committed or do not have probable cause to believe that an individual committed it, then the arrest is unconstitutional (see "In the News: Can a Cop Search You and Your Car during a Routine Traffic Stop?"). However, the Supreme Court has carved out exceptions to the general probable-cause arrest rule that allow police to stop and detain citizens without first having Fourth Amendment probable cause on their side. The Court has suggested that under certain circumstances it might be permissible to require a person to go to the police station for investigatory purposes without probable cause for an arrest under certain conditions. When the police require the suspect to make a trip to the station, they can do so only for the limited purposes of gathering evidence for "identification procedures." Hence, one can be taken to the station (1) to stand in a lineup,[19] (2) to give a hair sample,[20] (3) to give a voice sample,[21] or (4) to be photographed.[22] However, a police officer must have full probable cause to bring a suspect into the station for questioning[23] or for fingerprinting.[24]

The Court has also specified that detention during a search is permissible. It announced that when executing a search warrant, the police may detain people who are present on the premises while the search is being conducted.

Limited Detention—Stop and Frisk

The Supreme Court has allowed another form of limited detention that police can use on citizens that also falls short of probable cause. One type of limited detention is called a "stop and frisk" situation. In 1968, the Supreme Court announced that the police have the authority to detain a person briefly for questioning even without having probable cause to believe the person has committed a crime.[25] Such **investigatory stops** do not constitute an arrest and are permissible if prompted by three factors: (1) the observation of unusual conduct (2) leading the officer to have reasonable suspicion "that criminal activity may be afoot," and (3) the officer has the ability to articulate specific facts to justify that suspicion. The Court stated that investigatory stops must be temporary and no longer than necessary to effect their purpose. Once a person is stopped, the police also may frisk him or her. A **frisk** is a limited pat-down of the person's outer clothing to check for instruments of assault. An officer can frisk anyone who he or she reasonably suspects "places the officer in danger." The Supreme Court has stated that the totality of the circumstances—the whole picture—must be taken into account. The detaining officer must

LANDMARK CASE — Terry v. Ohio

A police officer observed Terry and two other men engaged in behavior that led him to believe that they were about commit a robbery and that they were armed. The officer stopped the men and "frisked" them—patted down their clothing for weapons—although at the time he had no probable cause to arrest them. When he discovered that Terry and one of his companions were carrying revolvers, he placed all three under arrest. Terry claimed that the stop and frisk was an unreasonable search and seizure and thus violated the First and Fourteenth Amendments. The Supreme Court looked at the following issue: If there is no probable cause to arrest, may the police nonetheless stop a suspect and pat down the outer clothing for weapons, if the officer reasonably believes that the suspect is armed and dangerous. The Court held that yes they can. The ruling in the case was that a stop and frisk is constitutionally authorized when the officer has reasonable grounds to believe that the suspect is armed and dangerous and that the search, therefore, is necessary for the protection of the officer and others. The officer need not have enough evidence to establish probable cause for arrest, but must base his or her conclusion on specific inferences drawn from the factual observations, interpreted in the light of his or her experience as a police officer. That is, the officer may not stop and frisk a person for weapons on mere suspicion or a hunch. In this case, the police officer related detailed facts and circumstances that reasonably led him to believe that Terry was armed and dangerous. The officer conducted a pat-down search of Terry's outer clothing only to determine if he was carrying a weapon. The search, then, even though it was made without a warrant and with no probable cause for arrest, was reasonable in accordance with the Fourth Amendment.

Source: Terry v. Ohio, 392 U.S. 1 (1968).

---

have particularized objectives as a basis for suspecting a particular person stopped for criminal activity. (See the Landmark Case *Terry v. Ohio*.)

In addition to stop and frisks, the Supreme Court has recognized that not all arrests need to be supported by probable cause. Other limited stops and detentions may justify a lesser showing.

The Supreme Court has held that police may not stop a single vehicle for the sole purpose of checking the driver's license and vehicle registration unless the officer has a reasonable and articulable suspicion, as required by *Terry v. Ohio*, that a traffic law has been violated. However, in *Brower v. Inyo County*, the Supreme Court announced that stopping a person at a roadblock is a seizure for purposes of the Fourth Amendment;[26] however, the Court suggested that even in the absence of articulable suspicion it would be constitutional to set up a roadblock to check every car that passed, or certain cars, according to some neutral articulable standard (such as every fifth car). Furthermore, the Court allowed roadblocks near the national border, in which every car that passes a roadblock is stopped to search for undocumented aliens.

In an extraordinarily controversial case, especially from the point of view of college students, the Supreme Court upheld the use of roadblocks to check sobriety of all drivers passing by. The Court found that the intrusion on privacy was slight and was outweighed by the state's interest in preventing drunk driving. In this particular case, the police officer stayed outside the only exit from a bar that was very popular among college students.[27]

Use of Excessive Force When Effecting an Arrest

In the absence of excessive or unnecessary force by an arresting officer, a person may not use force to resist an arrest by one who he or she knows or has good reason to believe is an authorized police officer, engaged in the performance of his or her duties, re-

---

CTQ

Some students carry identification, some do not. Do the police have the right to arrest a student if they stop him or her and the student fails to provide identification?

WEB

The ACLU provides information on what to do if you are stopped by the police. To view this information, **visit our Web site, www.prenhall.com/territo**

gardless of whether the arrest was unlawful. But if an officer uses excessive or unnecessary force to subdue the arrestee, regardless of whether the arrest is lawful or unlawful, the arrestee may defend himself or herself by employing such force as reasonably appears to be necessary[28] (see Figure 3.4).

"Unlawful" or "false" arrests can have several consequences. First, evidence seized as an outgrowth of an unlawful arrest is inadmissible in court. Similarly, any conviction resulting from an illegal arrest may be overturned. Typically, however, if it is clear in the early stages of the criminal justice process that the arrest was indeed unlawful, it is likely that the charges against the suspect will be dropped before adversary proceedings follow their full course. Second, in most jurisdictions, a citizen who has been wrongly taken into custody can institute a civil suit against the officer and the police department that initiated or authorized the arrest (although such suits are seldom won).

A number of issues associated with wrongful arrest vary greatly from one state to another. Under Tennessee law, for example, as early as 1860 and as recently as the 1970s, numerous court decisions have declared that if the officer acts at his or her peril, if he or she has no right to make an arrest without a warrant, or if his or her warrant is not valid, the officer is a trespasser. Under such circumstances, the police officer is liable for money damages. However, where the arrest would have been proper without a warrant, it is immaterial whether the warrant was good or bad.

In Tennessee, Alabama, and numerous other jurisdictions, case law has dictated that every person has a right to resist an unlawful arrest and that "in preventing such illegal restraint of his liberty he may use such force as may be necessary." In Idaho, by contrast, the suspect has no such right. Further, in jurisdictions where resistance to wrongful arrest is lawful, the means or amount of resistance cannot be disproportionate to the effort of the police officer to make the arrest.

Finally, virtually all states place no liability for wrongful arrest on police officers if the arrest was made on the basis of a valid warrant or probable cause, but a verdict of not guilty was returned. Thus, an acquittal is not tantamount to a finding of no reasonable grounds for arrest. However, in 1986, the Supreme Court ruled in *Malley v. Briggs* that a police officer could be held liable for damages if an arrest was made *without* probable cause—*even if* he or she had obtained an arrest warrant.[29]

In addition to limiting the powers of the police regarding when they can arrest, stop, and detain American citizens, the Fourth Amendment also articulates under what conditions the police are and are not allowed to conduct searches of people, places, their homes, and their effects.

Expanding the Permissible Scope of "Stops" and "Detentions"

A citizen may not be certain whether he or she has been "stopped" by the police or arrested. In both instances, the police officer's behavior is identical. However, the conservative justices of the last thirty years have allowed "stops" or "detentions," which incorporate every single feature of a custodial arrest except for the fact that they're not called arrests, to become constitutional—thus allowing the constitutionality of stops and detentions to atrophy the right to a constitutional arrest. We have already mentioned those stops and detentions that are now constitutional. We will restate them quickly: automobile stops for ordinary traffic tickets, random roadblocks with no probable cause and no reasonable suspicion,[30] sobriety checkpoints,[31] undocumented aliens,[32] detentions during lawful searches,[33] and police station investigatory purpose stops without probable cause.[34]

THE RIGHT AGAINST UNREASONABLE SEARCHES AND SEIZURES

The Fourth Amendment is an expression of a philosophy that grew out of offensive British practices prior to the American Revolution.[35] It was written into the fundamental law of the land by the framers of the Constitution, who hoped to assure that our government would respect the sanctity, dignity, and privacy of its citizens. The Fourth Amendment recognizes the right to privacy, but the application of this protection to the

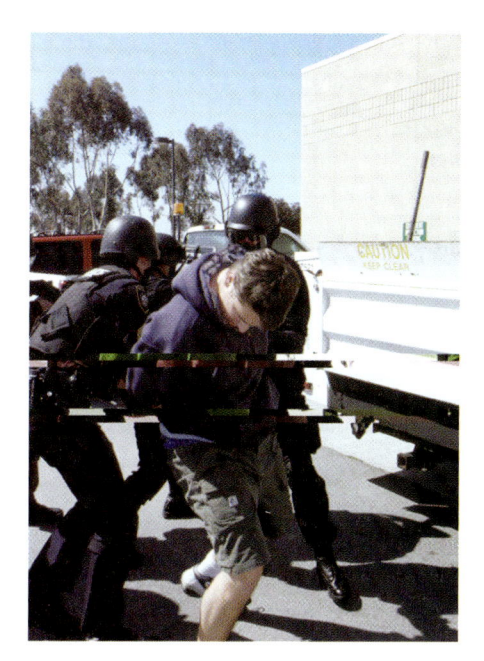

FIGURE 3.4

When effecting an arrest of a physically resisting suspect, it is constitutionally permissible for the police to use whatever force is necessary, including extreme force, to subdue the suspect.

© Dale Stockton

daily operations of the criminal justice system has caused problems. First, not all searches are prohibited, only those that are unreasonable. Second is the problem of what to do with evidence that is illegally obtained. Should murderers be set free because a vital piece of evidence was seized without a search warrant? The ambiguity of these portions of the amendment and the complexity of some arrest and investigation incidents have created difficulties. Like arrests, evidentiary searches and seizures are covered by the Fourth Amendment. The Fourth Amendment prohibits the government from conducting unreasonable searches (intrusions on a person's privacy) and seizures (control of the government over a person or a thing). Reasonableness here requires that the warrant be obtained before a search can be commenced.

Provided the search is reasonable, the police may search for the following: (1) The instrumentalities of crime (such as burglary tools); (2) the fruits of the crime (such as stolen goods); (3) contraband (such as illegal drugs); and (4) the mere evidence of crime, as long as probable cause exists to believe that the item is connected to criminal activity (such as a suspect's bloodstained clothing).

Government Conduct

Generally, the Fourth Amendment prohibits only against government conduct—not searches conducted by private persons.[36] Government agents include the following types of people:(1) publicly paid police; (2) private persons acting at police direction; (3) privately paid police (such as security guards); (4) deputized members of the public police force; and (5) public school officials.

Reasonable Expectation of Privacy

In addition to the government conduct requirement (above), the Fourth Amendment requires a reasonable expectation of privacy before it will protect citizens from unconstitutional searches. Ordinarily, the Supreme Court determined the applicability of the Fourth Amendment to searches almost entirely on the basis of whether the place searched was a place protected by the Fourth Amendment. In 1967, however, the Court departed from this approach in *Katz v. United States*, holding that the "Fourth Amendment protects people, not places."[37] Since *Katz*, the Supreme Court has held that a search falls within the protections of the Fourth Amendment when government actions intrude into an area where a person has a reasonable and justifiable expectation of privacy. This approach, however, does not expand the Fourth Amendment protection as greatly as it might first appear. First of all, there can be no reasonable expectation of privacy if the defendant doesn't have *standing* in the place to be searched or the thing to be seized. Second, there can be no reasonable and justifiable expectation of privacy in *items held out to be public*.

Standing The Supreme Court also limits the scope of Fourth Amendment protection by requiring *standing*, which is what a person with an expectation of privacy has in the place being searched or item being seized so that he or she might challenge the search. To have standing to challenge a search under the Fourth Amendment, a person must have a legitimate expectation of privacy.[38] Whether a person has standing is determined on a case-by-case basis, assessing the claimant's reasonable expectation of privacy under the totality of the circumstances. Nevertheless, the Supreme Court has held that a person has standing to raise a Fourth Amendment claim whenever (1) the person owned or had the right to possession of the place being searched; (2) the place being searched was in fact the person's home whether or not the person owned or had the right to possession (for example, a granddaughter living in the house with her grandfather); or (3) the person was an overnight guest of the owner of the place being searched.

However, the Court has put the following limitations on automatic standing. First of all, the Court has said that standing does not apply to a person who was harmed through an introduction of evidence obtained from an illegally unconstitutional search of a third person's property. Thus, passengers in automobiles who have no claim in relation to the automobile or to the property seized do not have standing simply because they were legitimately on the premises at the time of the search. Furthermore, the Court has said that ownership of the property seized is not necessarily enough for standing[39]; the totality of

FIGURE 3.5

Examples of Items Held Out to Be Public

A person's handwriting [41]

The sound of a person's voice [42]

Telephone numbers dialed [43]

Bank records [44]

Paint on the outside of a car [45]

Magazines offered for sale [46]

Open fields (areas outside the home that are held to be public) [47]

Garbage left outside [48]

Buildings outside the curtilage (an area of land surrounding the house that can be fenced in) [49]

Buildings close to the dwelling where a plane may fly over and view contraband that is impossible to see from the street,[50] or buildings viewed by a four-hundred-foot flyover by a helicopter[51]

Items viewed with the aid of vision-enhancing cameras (the Supreme Court has even allowed the use of a powerful camera to take photographs from the air, as long as the cameras are generally allowable to the public and the plane is legitimate[52])

---

the circumstances must be evaluated to determine whether the individual had a reasonable expectation of privacy, considering not only such factors as ownership of the property seized but also the location of the property at the time of the search. Finally, the Court said that where government intrusions only reveal possession of a controlled substance (a sniff test by a trained narcotics dog or a cocaine field test does not have any legitimate interest in privacy[40]), the defendant has no standing under a Fourth Amendment violation.

Items Held Out to be Public Recall that a search consists of government conduct that violates a person's reasonable and justifiable expectation of privacy. A person's reasonable and justifiable expectation to privacy exists only if the person has standing to object to the place being searched or the item being seized, and if the item being seized is not an item held out to be public. The Supreme Court recently has held that several items that appear to be items of privacy are instead items held out to be public, and hence are not protected by the Fourth Amendment. This means the police do not need probable cause, reasonable suspicion, or a search warrant to seize these items. (See Figure 3.5 for a list of examples of items held out to be public.) In a surprising decision in June 2001, the Supreme Court, by a 5–4 vote, rejected a form of high-tech search called thermal imaging, which is used to try to discover whether marijuana is growing inside a private residence.[53] By using this imaging, police could view the people walking about the house, which the Court held to be an invasion of privacy.

SEARCHES CONDUCTED PURSUANT TO A WARRANT

Generally, all searches are presumed unreasonable unless they are pursuant to a **search warrant** (see Figure 3.6) A warrant is required before the search and seizure of property is conducted. This requirement is central to the Fourth Amendment protection against unreasonable searches and seizures. Searches conducted without a search warrant are unconstitutional unless they qualify as one of the six exceptions to the search warrant requirement,[54] which are discussed later in this chapter.

The General-Warrant Requirement

If and when a warrant is issued it must (1) be based on probable cause, (2) be supported by an oath or an affirmation, and (3) particularly describe that which is to be searched. The warrant must be based on probable cause. Probable cause exists for a search when an officer presents to a magistrate sufficient underlying facts and circumstances such that a reasonable person would conclude that seizable evidence would be found on the premises to be searched. Information is provided to the magistrate by affidavit or sworn

CTQ

What are the differences between police investigative powers and police arrest powers?

CTQ

Which Fourth Amendment search warrant requirement is the most important? Should "particularity" really be necessary for search warrants?

testimony. This information must enable the magistrate to make an independent evaluation as to whether probable cause is present.[55] A warrant may be based on affidavits that consist entirely of hearsay. The affidavit must show by a totality of the circumstances that there is a fair probability that contraband or evidence of the crime can be found in a particular place. Among considerations are whether the warrant information given by the affiant (the officer who swears out the affidavit) comes from a reliable informant and whether the informant has a sound basis for his or her knowledge.

The validity of the warrant based on an informant's tip is determined by the totality-of-the-circumstances test, according to the Supreme Court. It is not always unconstitutional to issue a warrant based on a tip when the reliability and credibility cannot be established. All that is required is that the affidavit be based in part on a tip—that is, the allegation and the affidavit together permit the magistrate to make a common sense case of probable cause. However, this was precisely the opposite of the case in the 1960s. In the 1960s, the "Aguilar/Spinelli test" required two considerations, both of which had to be shown if a search was to be based on an informant's tip:

1. The officer's affidavit shows the reliability of the informant.
2. The affidavit shows that the informant had a sound basis for his or her knowledge of the information.

See the Landmark Case *Illinois v. Gates*, in which the informant wrote an anonymous letter. Generally, the informant's identity does not have to be revealed.[56] The reason for this

LANDMARK CASE — Illinois v. Gates

The Gateses, husband and wife, were charged with conducting illegal purchases and sales of marijuana following the receipt by the local police of an anonymous informant's letter. The letter described the Gateses' *modus operandi*, whereby Mrs. Gates would drive the car from their Bloomingdale, Illinois, condominium to Florida and load the car with drugs, and then Mr. Gates would drive the car home. Mr. Gates would fly to Florida and pick up the car, and Mrs. Gates would fly home. The letter gave specific dates and details of the next trip. The Bloomingdale police investigated the tip and found out that Gates did indeed have a plane reservation on the dates predicted. Federal drug enforcement agents observed the activities in Florida. Upon the Gateses return home, the Bloomingdale police searched their car and home and found marijuana, weapons, and other contraband. The Gateses made a motion to suppress the search because it lacked probable cause and was based on an anonymous tip. The case went to the Supreme Court, which had to determine whether probable cause existed to issue a search warrant when the reliability of the source that provided the information was totally unproven. The Court, rejecting the Aguilar/Spinelli test, said yes, this was sufficient, stating a new test. Justice Rehnquist wrote that under the totality-of-the-circumstances analysis, the magistrate need only decide whether, given all the circumstances set forth in the affidavit, there is a fair probability that contraband or evidence of a crime will be found in a particular place. Here, the anonymous letter, standing alone, was not sufficient to show probable cause on which to base a search warrant. Alone, the letter contained nothing to support the informant's reliability and gave no basis for the informant's predictions. The lower courts, while correctly examining the informant's veracity and reliability and basis of knowledge, should have not looked at these elements entirely separately. These elements are intertwined and must be considered in their totality to reach a common-sense decision as to the existence of probable cause. Here, the letter contained detailed information regarding travel and future plans of third parties. The information was independently corroborated by police observation. It was enough that there appeared to be a fair probability of accuracy, the police observation corroborated the letter's predictions and provided just probability. Hence, the search was legal.

Source: Illinois v. Gates, 103 S. Ct. 2317 (1983).

is that once we start revealing the identity of informants they will be discouraged, out of fear, to continue to cooperate with the police.

The Reasonableness Requirement

Since 1968, the Supreme Court has tried in several rulings to define "reasonable" in the context of the search-and-seizure provisions of the Fourth Amendment. Its conclusion seems to be that a personal search that is incident to a lawful arrest is reasonable. But even if it is not incident to an arrest, a search is sometimes legally justified when an officer believes that a suspect is armed or when there is concern about the officer's or the public's safety. The extension of a search to the area surrounding an arrest has been restricted to situations in which the suspect may reasonably be expected to obtain a weapon or destroy evidence.[57]

In addition to these two questions, others also are problematic. The language of the Fourth Amendment leaves several critical questions unanswered. Perhaps most important, the amendment does not tell us when a search or seizure is "unreasonable." Can a search or seizure be reasonable if it is not authorized by a warrant? Can a search or seizure be reasonable if it is not based on probable cause? These and similar questions have plagued the Supreme Court in its efforts to construe the Fourth Amendment and to

CTQ

Which is a more just and fair test of informants' information—the two-pronged test (two set standards that are always legally required) or the totality-of-circumstances test? If you are very cynical, who would you say wrote the anonymous letter in *Illinois v. Gates*?

FIGURE 3.6

Search Warrant

United States District Court

____________ DISTRICT OF ____________

In the Matter of the Search of
(Name, address or brief description of person or property to be searched)

SEARCH WARRANT

CASE NUMBER:

TO:____________ and any Authorized Officer of the United States

Affidavit(s) having been made before me by ____________ who has reason to
Affiant

believe that ☐ on the person of or ☐ on the premises known as (name, description and/or location)

in the ____________ District of ____________ there is now concealed a certain person or property, namely (describe the person or property)

I am satisfied that the affidavit(s) and any recorder testimony establish probable cause to believe that the person or property so described is now concealed on the person or premises above-described and establish grounds for the issuance of this warrant.

YOU ARE HEREBY COMMANDED to search on or before ____________
Date

(not to exceed 10 days) the person or place named above for the person or property specified, serving this warrant and making the search (in the daytime — 6:00 A.M. to 10:00 P.M.) (at any time in the day or night as I find reasonable cause has been established) and if the person or property be found there to seize same, leaving a copy of this warrant and receipt for the person or property taken, and prepare a written inventory of the person or property seized and promply return this warrant to ____________
as required by law. U.S. Judge or Magistrate

____________ at ____________
Date and Time Issued City and State

____________ ____________
Name and Title of Judicial Officer Signature of Judicial Officer

strike an appropriate balance between society's legitimate interest in effective law enforcement and its often competing interest in preserving the privacy, integrity, and dignity of its citizens.

The question of whether the police need a warrant as a precondition to a reasonable search or seizure has played a central role in the Court's interpretation of the Fourth Amendment. Over time, the justices have taken two very distinct positions on the issue. Some justices have concluded that the ultimate issue under the Fourth Amendment is the reasonableness of police conduct. These justices emphasize that the critical considerations in the reasonableness determination—whether the search was conducted in a reasonable manner—can be resolved after the search or seizure takes place. Thus, for these justices, the presence or absence of a warrant is merely one of several factors to be considered in each case in deciding whether the particular search or seizure was reasonable.

Other justices have concluded that failure to obtain a warrant is presumptively unreasonable except in extraordinary circumstances. These justices emphasize that the Fourth Amendment is designed not merely to remedy unreasonable searches and seizures after the fact but to prevent them from occurring at all. Thus, for these justices, a warrantless search or seizure is reasonable only if the officer can demonstrate that the failure to obtain a warrant was justified by exigent circumstances.

The Neutral-and-Detached-Magistrate Requirement

With some exceptions, searches may not be made until the police secure a search warrant from a neutral and detached magistrate. According to the Court, the point of the Fourth Amendment, which often is not grasped by zealous officers, is not that it denies law enforcement the support of the usual inferences that reasonable people draw from evidence. Its protection consists in requiring that those inferences be drawn by a neutral and detached magistrate instead of being judged by the officer engaged in the often competitive enterprise of flushing out crime. When the right of privacy must reasonably yield to the right of search is, as a rule, to be decided by a judicial officer, not by a police officer or government agent.[58]

The Probable-Cause Requirement

The Fourth Amendment requires that a warrant shall not be issued except upon a finding of probable cause. Probable cause is required for the police to conduct a search. To constitute a probable cause for a search, totality of the circumstances must be such that, upon hearing the facts and circumstances, a reasonable person would conclude that (1) certain seizable items (fruits of the crime, instrumentalities of the crime, relevant evidence of the crime, or contraband) exist, and (2) the seizable items exist in the area designated to be searched.

Constitutional Execution of a Search Warrant

In addition to the probable-cause requirement, the Constitution also requires other rules about warrant execution. Seven rules that govern the serving of a constitutional warrant: (1) the police-execution requirement, (2) the announcement requirement, (3) the search-specification requirement, (4) detention during search, (5) the time-of-service requirement, (6) the scope-of-search requirement, and (7) the search of third-party premises to execute an arrest warrant.

The first of these is that only the police may execute a warrant; private citizens are not permitted to do so.

Second, an officer executing a search warrant must knock and announce his or her authority for the purpose and be refused admittance before using force to enter the place to be searched. In cases of true emergencies, "no knock" entries are permitted if the police have a reasonable belief that notice will lead to destruction of items sought or endanger the officers.[59]

Third, the search warrant does not authorize the police to search people found on the premises who are not named in the warrant. The police are allowed to search only that which the warrant specifies.

Fourth, when executing a search warrant, the police may detain those people who are present while the search is being conducted. They are free to leave only after the search is over.

Fifth, a search warrant must be executed without unreasonable delay. Furthermore, statutes often require that searches be executed during daylight hours, unless nighttime searches are specifically authorized (see Figure 3.7).

Sixth, the scope of the search may not exceed the premises described on the warrant, and the search is limited to the items described in the warrant. However, when executing a warrant, the police may generally seize any contraband or fruits or instrumentalities of a crime they discover, whether or not such items are specified in the warrant. Furthermore, if the police officer makes an objective, reasonable mistake when executing the warrant, the evidence obtained is still admissible. For example, if the police have a warrant to search an apartment and mistakenly search an adjoining apartment and discover evidence of criminal activity, the evidence is admissible in spite of the error. As long as the mistake was objectively reasonable, the evidence may not be excluded.[60]

Seventh, absent consent or exigent circumstances, a search warrant is required before the police can enter a third party's home in order to arrest a person named in an arrest warrant who is presently in that home.

One of American citizens' most cherished rights is the Fourth Amendment's prohibition against unreasonable searches and seizures. As one Supreme Court justice put it, this is the right "to be left alone" by government officials.

FIGURE 3.7

Once a constitutional search warrant has been issued by a magistrate authorizing a search of a suspect's home for a small item (e.g., contraband diamonds), the police can take all the time necessary to search the house, including destroying property (e.g., pillows, the back panel of a television set), in an attempt to seize what they are looking for. And they are not required to clean up.

© Dale Stockton

THE SIX RECOGNIZED EXCEPTIONS TO THE SEARCH WARRANT REQUIREMENT

As previously stated, it is a well established principle of constitutional law that in order for the government to search a citizen, it must obtain a search warrant. All searches conducted without a search warrant are unconstitutional unless they fall under one of the six exceptions to the search warrant requirement: (1) a search incident to a lawful arrest, (2) the automobile exception, (3) the plain-view exception, (4) the stop-and-frisk exception, (5) the consent exception, and (6) exigent circumstances.

A Search Incident to a Lawful Arrest

The first commonly invoked exception to the search warrant requirement involves searches "incident to arrest." Under this doctrine, when an individual is lawfully arrested, the police may automatically—without obtaining either a search or arrest warrant—search the individual for weapons and evidence of crime. The Court has justified this doctrine on a number of grounds: the need to protect the arresting officers, the need to prevent the arrestee from destroying evidence in his or her possession, the intrusiveness of the lawful arrest already being so great that the incidental search is of minor consequence, and the fact that the individual could in any event be subjected to an inventory search at the stationhouse. Because of this, it is not unreasonable to search him or her at the time of arrest itself (see Figure 3.8).

There are limits to this exception, however. Suppose, for example, an individual is arrested in his or her home. May the police search the entire home incident to arrest? Although at one time the Court allowed this, more recently it has limited these searches to

FIGURE 3.8

When police are constitutionally authorized to either search or arrest an individual, they also are authorized to do a full and complete search of the person's bag, clothes, body, and body cavities, if what they are looking for might be hidden there.

© Dale Stockton

FIGURE 3.9

Implications of *Chimel v. California* (1969)

1. Arresting officers may search the defendant and the physical area within easy reach of the defendant.
2. Valid reasons for conducting a search include protecting the arresting officers, preventing evidence from being destroyed, and keeping the defendant from escaping.
3. A search becomes illegal when it goes beyond the defendant and the area within the defendant's immediate control and when it is conducted for other than a valid reason.

the area within the arrestee's immediate control—the area from which he or she might gain possession of a weapon or destructible evidence.[61] (see Figure 3.9.)

The most controversial search-and-seizure issue pertains to the search of body cavities. Some searches are permitted, but there are limitations on the type, time, place, and method of search. Body cavity searches may be conducted at U.S. borders whenever customs officials have reason to believe a person is smuggling contraband by carrying the contraband, usually illegal drugs, therein. This crime is referred to as *alimentary canal smuggling*. Probable cause is not required for the search of body cavities in these cases; customs officials need only have a reasonable suspicion that a traveler is committing the crime of alimentary canal smuggling to conduct the search.

The Automobile Exception

In *Carroll v. United States*, the Court held that when police stop an automobile and have probable cause to believe it contains contraband, it is not unreasonable to search that vehicle without a search warrant[62] (see Figure 3.10). However, the Court did not deal with the scope of that permissible search. The Court held that a search warrant is not necessary "where there is probable cause to search an automobile stopped on the highway; the car is mobile; the occupants are alerted; and the car's contents may never be found again if a warrant must be obtained."[63] Each case must be judged on its facts, for the Court has made it clear that not all warrantless car searches are lawful.

In 1991, the Court held that when police stopped a car for proceeding erratically, smelled marijuana smoke as the door was opened, searched the car, and found two packages wrapped in opaque plastic, they went beyond the scope of a legitimate search without a warrant when they opened the packages.[64] One year later the Court reconsidered its position by examining the extent to which police officers who have stopped an automobile legitimately and who have probable cause to believe that contraband is concealed somewhere within it may conduct a probing search of compartments and containers within the vehicle whose contents are not in plain view.[65] "We hold that they may conduct a search of the vehicle that is as thorough as a magistrate could authorize in a war-

FIGURE 3.10

When police are authorized to search an automobile they are authorized to search not only its interior but also inside the engine compartment and other mechanical parts when what they are seeking to seize might be hidden there. And they are not required to clean up.

© Dale Stockton.

LANDMARK CASE: Wyoming v. Houghton

The Wyoming Highway Patrol stopped a car for speeding and discovered that the driver had a syringe in his pocket and admitted to the use of drugs. The officer then searched the passenger compartment of the car for contraband. On the backseat, he found a purse that belonged to Sandra Houghton, the driver's girlfriend, who was the passenger of the car. Drug paraphernalia and methamphetamines were found in the purse, and fresh needle marks were found on Houghton's arms. Houghton was placed under arrest and she was charged with felony possession of methamphetamines. After hearing the trial court deny the motion to suppress the evidence obtained from the purse as a fruit of the violation of the Fourth and Fourteenth Amendments, she was convicted and appealed to the Wyoming supreme court. The state supreme court held that the search of her purse violated the Fourth and Fourteenth Amendments because the officer should have known the purse did not belong to the driver but to one of the passengers, and because there was no probable cause to search the passenger's personal effects and no reason to believe that the contraband had been placed within the purse. The state appealed and the U.S. Supreme Court granted certiorari. The question that the Supreme Court had to deal with was, may a police officer with probable cause search a car and inspect passengers' belongings found in the car that are capable of concealing an object of search? Justice Scalia, writing for the Court, answered yes, stating that police, with probable cause to search a car, when the passengers themselves are under no suspicion, may inspect any passenger's belongings found in the car that are capable of concealing objects for search.

Source: Wyoming v. Houghton, 526 U.S. 295 (1999).

---

rant 'particularly describing the place to be searched.'" The Court emphasized that such searches must be based on probable cause.[66]

Before beginning any search at all, under the automobile exception, the police must have probable cause to believe that the moving vehicle or a vehicle that has been temporarily stopped contains fruits or instrumentalities of a crime, evidence of a crime, or contraband. However, probable cause to search may develop as a result of observation after stopping a car. As long as the stopping of the automobile was lawful, what the police observe can ripen into probable cause to believe that the car contains fruits and instrumentalities of crime and contraband sufficient to justify a full warrantless search. (See the Landmark Case *Wyoming v. Houghton.*)

The exigency requirement of the automobile's mobility excuses the failure to secure a warrant and justifies the warrantless search for the entire automobile (interior compartment and trunk). Also, the Supreme Court announced that there is a lower expectation of privacy in an automobile.[67] The Court stated that the police may not use probable cause plus exigent circumstances to justify a warrantless entry to search a person's home. The automobile exception applies only to automobiles and mobile recreational vehicles (motorhomes, boats, airplanes); the Supreme Court has held that citizens in such situations have a lesser expectation of privacy (as compared to their homes, offices, and personal property).

The Consent Exception

Another common exception to the search warrant requirement involves the doctrine of consent. Just as individuals may waive other constitutional rights, such as the right to jury trial or the right to counsel, they may also waive the right to be "secure against unreasonable searches and seizures." Thus, valid consent will legitimate a search and seizure that otherwise would be constitutionally prohibited.

There are three elements to the consent doctrine. First, to be valid, the consent must be voluntary—it must not be the product of duress, coercion, or "show of authority" by the police. On the other hand, the Court has held that the police are under no obligation to warn individuals of their right to withhold consent and, moreover, that consent is valid even if individuals do not know that they have a right to withhold consent.[68] The Court explained that it "would be thoroughly impractical to impose on the normal consent search the detailed requirements of an effective warning," and that a requirement that the government prove that the consenting person was aware of this right would "create serious doubt whether consent searches could continue to be conducted" in light of the difficulty in proving such awareness. The Court thus concluded that the "voluntariness" standard represented an appropriate accommodation of the competing interests.

The second element of the consent doctrine involves the problem of third-party consent. Suppose two people share an apartment. Can one consent to a search of the common area? Of the other's bedroom? The Court held that an individual who shared a bedroom with the defendant could validly consent to a search of the room.[69] The Court explained that it is reasonable to recognize that any of the co-inhabitants has the right to permit the inspection in his or her own right and that the others have assumed the risk that one of their roommates might permit the common area to be searched. Any person with equal right to use or occupy property may consent to a search, and any evidence found may be used against the other owners or the occupants. However, a landlord does not have the authority to give effective consent to a search of a tenant's premises. Similarly, a hotel clerk cannot consent to a search of a guest's room.[70]

Third, consent is valid as long as the police reasonably believe that the person giving the consent had equal rights to occupy the searched premises. It does not matter if the person, in fact, did not have such right. Thus, a search was upheld when a defendant's girlfriend gave police consent to search his apartment, where the police erroneously but reasonably believed that she lived (where in fact she had not lived for weeks and had just come back to get her stuff), based on the fact that she had a key to the apartment and referred to it as "our apartment." In fact, she was an infrequent visitor. (see the Landmark Case *Illinois v. Rodriguez*).

> **CTQ**
>
> Why would anyone ever consent to a police search conducted in their own home?

LANDMARK CASE — Illinois v. Rodriguez

Ms. Fischer, Rodriguez's former girlfriend, authorized the police to conduct a warrantless search of Rodriguez's apartment after he had apparently assaulted her. Prior to entering the apartment, Fischer had referred to it as "our" apartment, and she had told police that she had personal belongings there. Subsequently, after Fischer opened the apartment with a key and gave the police permission to search it, the police found drugs and related paraphernalia, whereupon Rodriguez was arrested. At the criminal proceedings Illinois brought against Rodriguez for possession of a controlled substance with intent to deliver, Rodriguez moved to suppress all evidence seized at the time of his arrest, claiming that Fischer had vacated the apartment several weeks earlier and had no authority to consent to the entry. On the other hand, Illinois argued that even if Fischer had no authority to consent to the entry, since the police reasonably believed that she did, then their entry was permissible. Notwithstanding Illinois's argument, the trial court granted Rodriguez's motion, which was affirmed on appeal to the Illinois supreme court. Illinois appealed. The issue the U.S. Supreme Court had to decide is, where a third party agrees to allow officers to search certain premises over which they reasonably believe that the former has common authority, is their subsequent warrantless search of the premises reasonable under the Fourth Amendment? Justice Scalia said yes.

Source: *Illinois v. Rodriguez*, 497 U.S. 177 (1990).

Today, consent searches have additional significance because of their use in drug control programs. On June 20, 1991, in *Florida v. Bostick*, the Supreme Court upheld the police drug interaction technique (known as the bus sweep) of boarding buses and, without suspicion of illegal activity, questioning passengers, asking for identification, and requesting permission to search luggage.[71] In the *Bostick* case, police boarded a bus bound from Miami to Atlanta during a stopover in Fort Lauderdale. Without suspicion, let alone probable cause, that Bostick had contraband in his luggage, the officers nonetheless picked out the defendant and asked to inspect his ticket and identification. After identifying themselves as narcotics officers looking for illegal drugs, they asked to inspect the defendant's luggage. Although there was some uncertainty about whether the defendant consented to the search in which contraband was found and whether he was informed of his right to refuse to consent to the search, the defendant was convicted.

The Supreme Court was faced with deciding whether consent was freely given or the nature of the bus sweep search negated the defendant's consent. Justice Sandra Day O'Connor, writing for the majority, said that police may approach individuals without any suspicion and that asking questions and requesting to search luggage does not constitute a "seizure" in every instance.[72] In other words, drug enforcement officers, after obtaining consent, may search luggage on a crowded bus without meeting the Fourth Amendment requirements for a search warrant or probable cause.

These are only a few of the many issues arising under the Fourth Amendment. They do not address such important questions as remedies for violations of the amendment or invasions of privacy by means that do not constitute conventional searches or seizures, such as wiretapping or the use of undercover agents. But they do offer some glimpse of the central Fourth Amendment inquiry: How does a free and democratic society preserve the privacy, dignity, and integrity of its citizens while at the same time assuring efficient and effective enforcement of its criminal laws?

The Plain-View Exception

The fourth exception to the Fourth Amendment warrant requirement concerns the seizure of objects in plain view. Warrantless seizures by the police are justified when the police are legitimately on the premises, discover objects and have probable cause to believe that the objects are contraband or fruits or instrumentalities of a crime, and inadvertently observe such evidence in plain view.[73]

Typically, plain-view searches occur when the police are conducting a search pursuant to a search warrant and come across contraband or instrumentalities they did not expect to see. The other common situation occurs when the police enter the house in hot pursuit to arrest a suspect and instrumentalities or contraband come into plain view. For the plain-view exception, an officer does not normally have the right to seize evidence on private property merely because it's in plain view; there must be some particular prior justification for the officer's presence on the property. Hence, if the officer is walking down a public sidewalk and sees an object through the window of someone's home, the officer cannot cross the threshold of the home to seize the object; he or she must obtain a warrant. However, when an officer in the process of investigating a loud-party complaint comes to the defendant's door and the defendant opens the door, the officer may seize contraband lying in plain view on a table.

Even when police illegally enter private property and evidence is initially discovered during that illegal entry, it may be admissible if it is later discovered during a valid search that is wholly unrelated to the entering.[74] Finally, certain knowledge that incriminating evidence is in plain view is not necessary. For example, an officer saw, in what he declared to be in plain view, a tied-off, opaque balloon that he suspected, based on experience and knowledge, contained illegal drugs, even though he could not see any. The Supreme Court said this evidence was admissible because what the officer saw was based on his experience.[75]

The Court has expanded the ability of police to spy on criminal offenders. In one case, the police received a tip that marijuana was growing in the defendant's backyard. The yard was surrounded by fences, one of which was ten feet high.[76] The officers flew over the yard in a private plane at an altitude of one thousand feet to ascertain that it contained marijuana plants. One the basis of this information, a search warrant was obtained and executed, and, using the evidence, the defendant was convicted on drug charges. On appeal, the Supreme Court found that the defendant's privacy had not been violated because the contraband was in plain view.

This holding was expanded in 1989 when the Court held that police do not need a search warrant to conduct even low-altitude helicopter searches of private property.[77] The Court allowed Florida prosecutors to use evidence obtained by a police helicopter that flew four hundred feet over a greenhouse in which defendants were growing marijuana plants. The Court said the search was constitutionally permissible because the flight was within airspace legally available to helicopters under federal regulations. Here, too, the contraband was considered to be in plain view.

The Stop-and-Frisk Exception

The stop-and-frisk exception permits an officer to detain a suspect without a warrant, if the officer reasonably believes that the suspect is engaging in criminal activity. The officer's reasonable suspicion does not need to be based on personal knowledge. Reasonable suspicion may be based on informants, wanted flyers, computers, and so on.[78] Furthermore, reasonable suspicion is determined by the totality of the circumstances.[79] The officer may question the suspect if s/he believes the suspect may be dangerous; the officer is also permitted to pat down the suspect's outer garments and reach into the garments if s/he feels a weapon.

For a stop and frisk to be constitutional, it must meet the following three criteria established in *Terry v. Ohio*:

1. The officer must observe unusual conduct; the officer must define what the unusual conduct was, define what made it unusual, and specify the totality of the circumstances that the situation brought about. The Supreme Court has not outlined what "unusual" means, but has acknowledged that experienced officers, by definition, have sufficient knowledge and instincts about criminal activity to make this determination.

2. The officer must have reasonable suspicion to believe that criminal activity is afoot; based on experience and knowledge, as well as the fact that the suspect's unusual activity continued, the officer must develop a reasonable suspicion that there may be criminal activity. The Supreme Court has not yet defined reasonable suspicion, but we do know that its standard is less than probable cause, but more than vague suspicion.

3. The officer must be able to point to specific and articulable facts that would lead a prudent person to the same conclusion when presented with these facts. Essentially, this means that an officer must be able to clearly articulate how and why he or she believed that the suspect was engaged in unusual conduct related to criminal activity. This also implies that a stop and frisk is a limited arrest—the suspect can only be held long enough to dispel the officer's reasonable suspicion.

When stopping for a traffic violation, officers may search the passenger compartment and the person therein as long as there is reasonable suspicion to believe that the person is dangerous. Moreover, the Supreme Court has also ruled that police officers may search an automobile by allowing the police officers to "frisk" the passenger's personal belongings during a traffic stop (see "In the News: Score One for the Cops").

Exigent Circumstances

The exigent-circumstances exception to the search warrant requirement states that if an officer, in good faith, cannot obtain a warrant quickly enough and needs to conduct an immediate search, under certain specified exigent circumstances, then he or she need not obtain a warrant in order to conduct the search. Typical examples of these searches have been special emergencies, such as burning fires, contaminated food, or children in trouble.

The application of hot pursuit to the exception of the search warrant requirement is such that when an officer is in hot pursuit of a dangerous suspect, he or she may scope the suspect's home as far as reasonably necessary to make sure that the person

---

CTQ

Suppose a police officer stops a person who looks different from most people in the neighborhood and who certainly acts more strangely. The officer decides to frisk him. During the pat down he feels no weapon, but a soft bulge in the pockets. He retrieves it to find that the contents are cocaine. Would an arrest for cocaine possession hold up in court? Why or why not?

IN THE NEWS

A HUMAN PERSPECTIVE

SCORE ONE FOR THE COPS: A NEW EXPANSION OF POLICE SEARCH RIGHTS
by A. Cannon

The U.S. Supreme Court has handed cops another big win. Last week's 6–3 ruling gives police the green light to dig through passengers' personal belongings during traffic stops. The decision continues a 20-year trend that has seen the court rule in favor of enhanced police power. "The court is focused on giving law enforcement every possible tool and every degree of power out there to apprehend, seek out, and find criminals and contraband," says David Harris, a University of Toledo law professor.

Police and prosecutors applaud the decision, saying it will make it easier for them to do their jobs. But civil libertarians say it tramples on personal freedom. "People should not have to forfeit their privacy merely because they are riding in the car of a person the police might search," says Steven Shapiro of the American Civil Liberties Union.

The ruling overturns an earlier decision in Wyoming, where a judge threw out drug evidence he found was obtained illegally. State troopers discovered two syringes containing methamphetamine in the purse of Sandra Houghton, a passenger in a car they stopped in 1995. "The court is saying police officers shouldn't have to study opinions and split hairs like lawyers," says Ronald Bretz of the Thomas Cooley Law School in Lansing, Michigan. "They are out there fighting crime."

Source: A. Cannon, "Score One for the Cops," *U.S. News & World Report*, 19 April 1999. Copyright 1999 *U.S. News & World Report*, L. P. Reprinted with permission.

---

does not resist or escape. This also applies when the individual moves from a public to a private place.

Evanescent evidence, or evidence that dissipates quickly over time, also falls under the emergency exception to the search warrant requirement. Because the evidence will disappear quickly, the officer risks losing it if s/he leaves to obtain a search warrant. Examples of evanescent evidence include alcohol content in blood and fingernail scrapings that can be scraped away by the suspect.

THE EXCLUSIONARY RULE

In 1914, in *Weeks v. United States*, the Supreme Court established the exclusionary rule to govern the operation of the federal courts.[80] According to the **exclusionary rule,** evidence obtained as a result of an unreasonable or illegal search is not admissible in a federal criminal prosecution. In *Weeks*, the Court argued that the government must not be encouraged to commit illegal acts by gaining a conviction from illegally seized evidence. The Court suggested that without this rule, the police would not be deterred from conducting unconstitutional searches and seizures against private citizens.

The exclusionary rule curbed, but did not eliminate, abuse of the Fourth Amendment. Evidence obtained illegally by *state* law enforcement officers continued to find its way into federal prosecutions on the grounds that no *federal* official had participated in violating the defendant's rights. This type of federal-versus-state search and seizure became known as the *silver platter doctrine*, a name that originated in Justice Frankfurter's 1949 decision. in *Lustig v. United States*.[81] Frankfurter held that "the crux of that doctrine is that a search is a search by a federal official if he had a hand in it; it is not a search by a federal official if evidence secured by state authorities is turned over to the federal authorities on a silver platter." The Supreme Court condemned this practice with regard to criminal investigations.[82] Writing for the majority, Justice Stewart held that the silver platter doctrine constituted an "inducement to subterfuge and evasion."[83]

In *Mapp v. Ohio*, the exclusionary rule was extended to the state courts,[84] a reversal of the 1949 decision of *Wolf v. Colorado*,[85] which permitted the states to establish their own procedural safeguards against unreasonable search. On May 23, 1957, Cleveland police officers entered the home of Doll Ree Mapp (see Figure 3.11) without a search warrant, saying that they were looking for a suspect in a recent bombing. The police claimed they thought he was hiding in Mapp's house. She demanded to see a search warrant. One of the officers held up a piece of paper (later it turned out not to be a search warrant), whereupon Mapp grabbed it and tucked it into her blouse. A struggle ensued and the officer recovered the paper. Then Mapp was handcuffed and led to her bedroom while the officers searched the other rooms in her home. Finally, they went into the basement where they found some obscene material in a trunk. At trial, no search warrant was produced, yet the Ohio supreme court upheld the conviction because the evidence was not taken from the defendant's person by the use of coercion or offensive physical force. Mapp successfully appealed her case to the U. S. Supreme Court, which held that:

> . . . all evidence obtained by searches and seizures in violation of the Constitution is, by that same authority, inadmissible in a state court. Since the Fourth Amendment's right of privacy has been declared enforceable against the States through the Due Process Clause of the Fourteenth Amendment, it is enforceable against them by the same sanction of exclusion as is used against the Federal Government . . .[86]

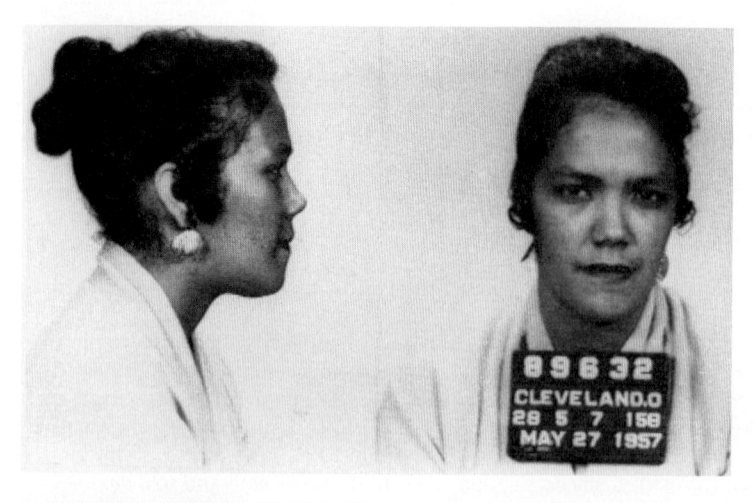

FIGURE 3.11

Doll Ree Mapp, the woman whose rights were violated when the police conducted an unconstitutional search of her home, took the case to the U.S. Supreme Court, which rendered the opinion that the exclusionary rule was a constitutional due process right and thereby required all states to follow it.

Courtesy AP/Wide World Photos.

WEB

To hear oral arguments of *Mapp v. Ohio,* **visit our Web site, www.prenhall.com/territo.**

An even broader extension of the exclusionary rule is the doctrine known as the **fruit of the poisonous tree,** which prohibits the admission of evidence obtained as a result of an "illegal or initially 'tainted' admission, confession, or search."[87] Assume, for example, that the police employ coercive methods to extract a confession from a suspect who names a second party as an accomplice in the illegal sale of narcotics. Using a properly executed search warrant, the police search the residence occupied by the second party and confiscate a quantity of heroin. In this case, the fact that the search was authorized by a legal warrant does not validate the admission of the heroin as evidence, because the police obtained the information leading to the search and seizure in an unauthorized, or "tainted," manner. The "fruit of the poisonous tree" doctrine originally had one exception—"if the fruit was so attenuated so as to dissipate the taint." This means that a significant number of steps from the original illegal search were taken until the final piece of evidence was found, but it was so far removed from the original illegal search that it was considered admissible. This was the only exception to the exclusionary rule throughout the 1960s.

The Defendant's Right to a Suppression Hearing

The defendant has a right to a suppression hearing outside the jury's presence, at which time a judge decides whether the evidence or confession is admissible.[88] If the judge decides that the evidence or the confession is admissible, the jury may consider it. The defendant may present to the jury much of the same evidence presented at the suppression hearing in an attempt to persuade the jury not to believe the confession. Finally, the defendant has no right to a specific finding of fact on the factual question.

During the suppression hearing, the defendant has the right to testify. If the defendant does testify, his or her testimony may *not* be used against him or her at trial, specifically on the issue of guilt.[89] During the suppression hearing the government bears the burden of proof to establish the admissibility of the evidence of the confession or other fruit of the poisonous tree by a preponderance of the evidence.

THE EXPANDED EXCEPTIONS TO THE EXCLUSIONARY RULE

During the Warren Court era, the exclusionary rule's scope was wide. The "fruits of the poisonous tree", except those that were far removed in time and place, were the only exception to the exclusionary rule. However, in the 1970s, 1980s and 1990s, the scope of the exclusionary rule was narrowed extraordinarily, in two different ways. The first way is by using the 1960s language of "dissipated taint." The Supreme Court found six new ways whereby taint can be dissipated, other than being removed by time and distance, from the original unconstitutional act. The second way the Court created additional exceptions was literally to name eight specific exceptions to the exclusionary rule. Hence, if the exception is "dissipated taint", then it was never considered eligible for the exclusionary rule in the first place. But in these eight exceptions, the Supreme Court has carved out situations in which evidence should ordinarily be suppressed. However, these kinds of evidence, which would have been excluded in the 1960s, are now admissible to the jury for consideration even though each clearly is evidence that is immediate "fruit of the poisonous tree."

All evidence that has been illegally obtained must be included in the general scope of suppressing the evidence demanded by the exclusionary rule, or at least so in the 1960s. In addition, the Supreme Court seems to indicate that the use of other evidence that has been acquired directly or indirectly, as the result of an illegal search or an arrest, or as "fruit of the poisonous tree," is not allowed.[90]

In contradiction to this general rule about the general scope of the exclusionary rule, in the past four decades, several Supreme Court cases have diluted it in two different ways. The first is by calling a situation an exception to the exclusionary rule and another is by calling the exceptions "dissipated taint."

The Court argues that evidence otherwise not admissible may be allowed if the prosecution demonstrates that the taint has been removed. This may be accomplished in three major ways and three minor ways. The first major way that the taint may be dissipated is through the *doctrine of inevitable discovery*: if the police would have discovered the evidence, regardless of their illegal action, the evidence would be admissible. In this exception the prosecution must show "inevitable discovery by a preponderance of the evidence" and *need not* prove the absence of "bad faith" by government officers responsible for the constitutional violation.[91] The second major way that the taint may be dissipated is through the *independent source doctrine*,[92] in which the Court declared that if police obtained evidence from an independent source, not connected to the illegal search or seizure, the evidence was admissible. For example, the police initially discovered evidence during an illegal search of a warehouse, but subsequently discovered the same evidence during a valid search. The Court declared the second discovery of evidence to be admissible.[93]

The third major way that the taint may be dissipated is if there is a weak link between the illegal conduct of the police and the challenged evidence, especially if that evidence is a **confession.** The Court argued that the purpose of the exclusionary rule is to deter police misconduct (specifically illegal arrests that would result if the police were allowed to use evidence obtained from such conduct). The Court went on to argue that if the link between the misconduct and the evidence is weak, the application of the exclusionary rule serves little purpose, since the police would not rely on the illegal conduct to explain the evidence. In *Payton v. New York* (which appeared as a Landmark Case earlier in this chapter), the police had probable cause to arrest Payton for murder. They went to his home without a warrant and arrested him, which violates the Fourth Amendment. Payton confessed in his home and when the police took him to the station, he confessed again. The Supreme Court held that the first confession must be suppressed as fruit of the illegal arrest, but the second confession is admissible because it was not a fruit of the unlawful arrest. The Court reasoned that because the police had probable cause to arrest the defendant they did not gain anything by the illegal arrest—they could have arrested him the moment he stepped outside of his house and then brought him to the station for the confession. Hence, they stated that the subsequent statement was not an exploitation of the illegal entry. (Most defendants this author is familiar with believe that once they have confessed to the police the cat is out of the bag, and they never try to retract a confession a second time but try to use it to make a deal.)

The first type of subset of confessions came into existence when the Supreme Court said that a witness's in-court identification of the defendant will not be excluded as the fruit of an illegal detention of the defendant when he was originally identified.[94] The second type

WEB

For more information on the inevitable-discovery exception to the exclusionary rule, **visit the FBI link on our Web site, www.prenhall.com/territo.**

involving this dissipation was announced in a case in which an illegal search enabled the police to locate a witness.[95] The third type involves a witness's statements, which, according to the Court, will be less readily excluded as fruit of the illegal conduct; a more direct link would be required for the exclusion to be allowed. The Court stated that the factors the court will consider include to the extent to which the witness is willing to testify and the extent to which not allowing the witness to testify could defer future police conduct. Essentially, what the police said is that the "fruit of the poisonous tree" doctrine was violated because a witness was discovered after the unconstitutional act. Regardless of how close to the unconstitutional act of the police in identifying the witness was, if the witness can identify the defendant in court, the identification is admissible, and even if this is not the case, if the witness is willing to testify in court, he or she will be allowed to testify.

The Recently Recognized Additional Seven Exceptions to the Exclusionary Rule

The first exception to the exclusionary rule is the *impeachment exception*. Illegally seized evidence may be used to impeach the credibility of a defendant who testifies in his or her own behalf. For example, if during an unconstitutional confession, a defendant said X, and then later took the stand and declared Not X, the prosecution has the option of showing the entire confession to the jury to demonstrate that Not X was inconsistent with the X claimed during the confession. The jury will not be influenced by the fact that the original statement was a confession because the judge will instruct them to ignore the value of the confession in terms of the jury's determination of guilt or innocence and to use the confession only to evaluate the credibility of the defendant.

The second exception is a postconviction federal *habeas corpus* proceeding. The Supreme Court stated that regardless of the egregious ruling on the exclusionary rule by the trial court, a defendant cannot challenge a state conviction in a later federal *habeas corpus* proceeding on the ground that the evidence against him or her was a product of an illegal search.[96]

The third exception is the *private party exception*. The courts will not exclude illegally obtained evidence by a private party acting independently of the police.[97] However, if the police request or encourage a private party to engage in an illegal search, the exclusionary rule applies.

The fourth exception is the *civil proceedings exception*. The exclusionary rule does not bar the use of illegally seized evidence in the civil proceedings of another.[98] In the most famous criminal/civil case of the past decade (the O. J. Simpson criminal and civil cases), evidence that was excluded at the criminal trial because it violated the Constitution was admissible at the civil trial under this exception.

The fifth exception, and probably the most controversial, is a rather recent one: the police good-faith exception. The Supreme Court declared that the exclusionary rule does not apply when the police relied in good faith on case law later changed by another judicial opinion or on a facially valid statute or ordinance that existed—even though it later was declared unconstitutional by the court decision. Moreover, the exclusionary rule does not apply to a search warrant that was unconstitutional because it was lacking in probable cause or violated the preciseness requirement but nonetheless was signed by a judge.

The controversial part of the good-faith exception involves the cases of *United States v. Leon* and *Massachusetts v. Sheppard*. In *Leon*, the police searched and found tainted goods, based on a search warrant. Every judicial review that looked at that warrant declared it to be an illegal search warrant, because it lacked probable cause. However, since the police did not know that it lacked probable cause, they acted in good faith. The incompetence of the judge allowed the evidence to be admitted (see the Landmark Case *United States v. Leon*). In *Massachusetts v. Sheppard*, police acted in good faith on a defective search warrant that allowed the police to look only for drugs, but instead they were searching Sheppard's car for evidence of dead bodies, murder weapons, and bloody clothes.

The sixth exception is the *grand jury exception*. This exception means that grand jury witnesses may not refuse to answer questions based on illegally seized evidence.[99] The seventh exception is the *agency rule exception*. The Court said that a search did not violate

LANDMARK CASE: United States v. Leon

The federal court of appeals held that evidence seized pursuant to a facially invalid warrant (not supported by probable cause) must be suppressed because the evidence discovered was "fruit of the poisonous tree." The facts of the case center on the nature of the warrant. All areas of judicial review stated that the warrant issued by a neutral magistrate subsequently found to be based on an affidavit that, as a matter of law, did not sufficiently establish probable cause, was nonetheless used by the police to search the residence of the defendant. However, the lower court declared that the evidence should be excluded. The Supreme Court, in accepting the case, answered the issue of whether the Fourth Amendment requires the exclusion of evidence seized pursuant to a facially valid warrant, where the warrant was in fact lacking probable cause but the police acted in their search in good faith. The Supreme Court said no, and that the evidence was admissible. The Court went on to state that the exclusionary rule applied only in cases where it would be consistent with its rationale. The rule is imposed to punish illegal police conduct that collects evidence in an unconstitutional manner by excluding that evidence from trial. Where the police act in good faith, under the authorization of a neutral magistrate, the deterrent purposes do not apply. As a result, the rule should not be applied. The case was reversed.

Source: United States v. Leon, 468 U.S. 897 (1984).

the Constitution or a federal statute, but only the internal workings of the searching agency (in this case the agents were investigative officers of the Internal Revenue Service); therefore, the defendant is not entitled to have it excluded.[100]

Many types of searches that were once unconstitutional have become constitutional; the number is growing at an alarming rate as the effectiveness of the exclusionary rule becomes trivialized, and hence seemingly every search is permissible.

Criticism of the Exclusionary Rule

Conservatives, mainly law enforcement officers, believe that the exclusionary rule subverts justice and lets criminals go free on technicalities. Also, these conservatives maintain that the chief purpose of the exclusionary rule is to punish police misconduct involving disregard of the Fourth Amendment. Although no one defends the proposition that police officers should be free to disregard the Constitution in pursuit of a conviction, it is argued that the exclusionary rule punishes good-faith mistakes made by honest, conscientious officers. Such mistakes include writing the wrong address on an affidavit on a warrant or writing an incomplete description of the premises to be searched.

Criticisms of the exclusionary rule commonly take three forms: (1) The rule is not an effective deterrent of unlawful searches and seizures; (2) the rule is morally bankrupt and corrupts the administration of justice; and (3) the rule does not rest on the Constitution and is therefore beyond the constitutional authority of the courts to establish.

Many observers of law enforcement have noted, however, that arrests rather than convictions are the primary measure of success in police work. According to its critics, then, the exclusionary rule is well tailored to affect the judge, the prosecutor, and the criminal defendant, but it has no teeth when it comes to disciplining the police.

Many critics of the exclusionary rule find it unjust that reliable incriminating evidence cannot be used in a trial simply because of the manner in which it was obtained. Justice Benjamin Cardozo once expressed astonishment that "the criminal is to go free because the constable has blundered." The argument made by critics of the rule to back up Cardozo's sentiment is this: Rules of criminal procedure are meant to provide for conviction and punishment of the guilty while protecting the innocent. If two offenses have been committed—one by the defendant and one by the police officer—then both

WEB

For more information on the exclusionary rule, **visit the ACLU and National Association of Criminal Defense Lawyers links on our Web site, www.prenhall.com/territo.**

CTQ

Does the exclusionary rule effectively deter police misconduct that violates others' constitutional rights?

should be punished. The exclusionary rule departs from the truth-finding process of a trial by suppressing proof of guilt, and it does nothing to punish the police officer who broke the law. Thus criminals often walk free while the ends of justice go unserved.

Another criticism of the exclusionary rule goes beyond a critique of its existence to a critique of its creator—the Supreme Court. According to this view, the role of the courts is to interpret the law, not to make it. If the courts have authority to apply an exclusionary rule, it must be because the Constitution requires them to do so or because a legislature has created such a rule. The exclusionary rule, say its constitutional critics, is based neither on the Constitution nor on legislation but only on judicial mandate.[101]

First, the Fourth Amendment is silent about how it should be enforced. Second, the ideal of judicial integrity is not well served by a rule that suppresses incriminating evidence; it is in any case an ideal not firmly rooted in any Constitutional provision. Third, deterrence of unlawful police behavior is the domain of legislative and executive action, not of the judiciary acting as a legislature.

THE FIFTH AMENDMENT PRIVILEGE AGAINST SELF-INCRIMINATION

Among the provisions of the Fifth Amendment is the right of protection against self-incrimination: "No person . . . shall be compelled in any criminal case to be a witness against himself . . . ." This right goes to the very heart of the adversary system of criminal justice because it implies that the state must prove the guilt of the accused. It has its greatest relevance in the matter of interrogation and how confessions are elicited from suspects. The Supreme Court ruled that confessions secured by physical abuse were inadmissible in state courts.[102] The Court added that to secure the validity of confessions, suspects must be notified of their right against self-incrimination and of their right to representation by counsel during an interrogation.[103] The Fifth Amendment has had its greatest relevance in the matter of stationhouse interrogations and how confessions can be elicited from suspects.

In March 1963, Ernesto Miranda (see Figure 3.12) was arrested in Arizona for kidnapping and rape. After being identified by the victim and questioned by police for several hours, Miranda signed a confession that included a statement that his confession was made voluntarily. Over the objections of his attorney, the confession was admitted into evidence and Miranda was found guilty. The Arizona supreme court affirmed the conviction and held that Miranda's constitutional rights had not been violated in obtaining the conviction; the court said its decision was in accordance with the earlier *Escobedo* ruling because Miranda had not specifically requested counsel. The U.S. Supreme Court, in reversing the Arizona decision, attempted to clarify its intent in the *Escobedo* case by spelling out specific guidelines to be followed by police before interrogating people in custody and using their statements as evidence. The guidelines require that after a suspect is taken into custody for an offense and prior to any questioning by law enforcement officers, the suspect must be advised of certain rights if there is intent to use his or her statements in court. (See the Landmark Case *Miranda v. Arizona*.) These guidelines, as they have been incorporated into the *Miranda* warning, have become familiar to many Americans by their frequent reiteration on police shows on television. A copy of the warning, reproduced from a card carried by urban law enforcement officers, is shown in Figure 3.13.

The Miranda story had a violent ending. On the night of Saturday, January 13, 1976, Miranda became involved in a fight over a card game in a skid row bar in Phoenix, Arizona. He was stabbed twice by one of the men he had beaten—an illegal alien from Mexico named Fernando Zamora Rodriguez—and was dead on arrival at the hospital. One assumes that the police officer who arrested Rodriguez remembered to read him his *Miranda* rights!

The Supreme Court has declared that the right to counsel is violated if the defendant was questioned by police, without a lawyer, in an adversarial judicial proceeding (such as an indictment). For this reason, any subsequent confession that was made should be excluded.[104]

The right to counsel is violated even if the defendant was not explicitly questioned, as long as incriminating information was actively secured from the defendant without the

FIGURE 3.12

Ernesto Miranda confessed to rape without the police first advising him of his rights. When the Supreme Court reversed his conviction, it announced that the Fifth Amendment requires state police to read suspects their "Miranda rights." If not, any subsequent confessions will be excluded from evidence at trial.

Courtesy AP/Wide World Photos.

LANDMARK CASE — Miranda v. Arizona

Ernesto Miranda was arrested, taken into custody, and transported to the police station, where officers questioned him for two hours. They did not give him any warning of his rights. He signed a confession. The top of the typed statement said that his statement was made voluntarily and with full knowledge of his legal rights. The confession was submitted against Miranda's objection. He was found guilty of rape and kidnapping. The Arizona supreme court confirmed. The U.S. Supreme Court took up the issue of whether, whenever a person is taken into police custody, it is necessary that his legal rights (to remain silent and to have an attorney) be explained to him. The Court declared yes. Its reasoning was that the Fifth Amendment privilege against self-incrimination is jeopardized when a person is taken into custody or otherwise deprived of his or her freedom. To protect this privilege, the following warnings must be given:

1. That the suspect has the right to remain silent
2. That anything the suspect says may be used against him or her in a court of law
3. That the suspect has the right to have the presence of attorney
4. That if the suspect cannot afford an attorney, he or she has the right to have one appointed

Once these warnings have been given, the person may knowingly and intelligently waive these rights and agree to answer questions or make a statement. But unless the prosecution demonstrates such warnings and waiver at trial, no evidence obtained as a result of the interrogation can be used against the person. Also, the person is always free to exercise these rights; if at any time during the questioning the person indicates a desire to remain silent or have his or her attorney present, the interrogation must cease or wait until the attorney is present. The admissibility of volunteered confessions or statements is not affected by this decision. Statements given freely, without compelling influence, are not protected by the Fifth Amendment and are admissible.

Source: Miranda v. Arizona, 384 U.S. 436 (1966).

FIGURE 3.13

As a result of Supreme Court decisions, arrested persons are handed a copy of this card. The police officer also asks the accused person whether he or she understands the rights and, having these rights in mind, wishes to talk to the police.

DEFENDANT	LOCATION

SPECIFIC WARNING REGARDING INTERROGATIONS

1. YOU HAVE THE RIGHT TO REMAIN SILENT.
2. ANYTHING YOU SAY CAN AND WILL BE USED AGAINST YOU IN A COURT OF LAW.
3. YOU HAVE THE RIGHT TO TALK TO A LAWYER AND HAVE HIM PRESENT WITH YOU WHILE YOU ARE BEING QUESTIONED.
4. IF YOU CANNOT AFFORD TO HIRE A LAWYER ONE WILL BE APPOINTED TO REPRESENT YOU BEFORE ANY QUESTIONING, IF YOU WISH ONE.

SIGNATURE OF DEFENDANT	DATE
WITNESS	TIME

☐ REFUSED SIGNATURE

WEB

For more information on the *Miranda* case, **visit our Web site,** www.prenhall.com/territo.

presence of counsel.[105] In *United States v. Henry*, the defendant's cellmate initiated a conversation with the defendant from which incriminating evidence was obtained. Furthermore, the Court declared that a defendant's Sixth Amendment right to counsel was violated again when the police arranged to record a conversation between the defendant and a co-defendant, who was a government informant, at a meeting in which both defendants, without counsel, planned to discuss defense strategy.[106]

> **WEB**
>
> For more information on the dissenting opinion in *Miranda*, visit our Web site, www.prenhall.com/territo.

In *Kuhlman v. Wilson*, the Court declared that it is not a violation merely to place an informer in a defendant's cell, unless the informant takes some action beyond mere listening and the action is designed deliberately to elicit incriminating remarks.[107]

The Court has looked carefully at confessions from defendants who have obtained lawyers when the police do not allow the attorney to assist in the interrogation. When the police promise the attorney that no questioning will take place, any confession obtained after questioning, unless Sixth Amendment rights were clearly waived by the defendant, are inadmissible.[108]

The Sixth Amendment right to counsel is "offense-specific." Thus, a defendant who makes a Sixth Amendment request for counsel for one charge must make another request if he or she is subsequently charged with a separate unrelated crime. Finally, the right to counsel enters the confession realm under the famous *Escobedo* case, which occurred two years before *Miranda v. Arizona*. In *Escobedo v. Illinois*, the Supreme Court held that a confession obtained from a defendant was inadmissible when the investigation focused on the suspect; he had been taken into custody, had requested and been denied the opportunity to speak with a lawyer, and the lawyer was present and available to consult with him—even though there was no prior adversarial judicial proceeding.[109] *Escobedo* is famous because it is the first time the Fourth, Fifth, or Sixth Amendment had been afforded to a suspect before the adversarial proceeding began.

A Constitutional Confession

A review of Supreme Court cases on the Fifth, Sixth, and Fourteenth Amendment rights against involuntary confessions demonstrates that four hurdles must be made by the prosecution before any self-incriminating statement (in the form of either a confession or an admission) may be introduced as evidence against a defendant at his or her trial.

First, the state must demonstrate that the confession was *voluntary*. How is the confession voluntary? Statements made by a defendant may not be offered into evidence for any purposes at any time if they violate the voluntariness requirement of the due process clause of the Fifth and Fourteenth Amendments. They are voluntary if the confession was the product of an essentially free and unconstrained choice by its maker. A judge must determine by the weight of the evidence whether the defendant's statement was voluntarily made; if the court concludes that it was not, admission of the statement into evidence is subject to reversible error and the conviction must be set aside.

> **CTQ**
>
> What is the purpose of the *Miranda* warnings? Have rights granted to suspects in the *Miranda* decision been eroded by subsequent decisions? Is this a desirable or an undesirable process? Why has the Court ruled in this manner?

Second, the courts have also said that even though the defendant's confession is voluntary, it may still be inadmissible because it occurred under conditions that violated the accused's Sixth Amendment *right to counsel*. Generally, the defendant may not be interrogated without counsel after an adversary judicial proceeding (indictment or preliminary hearing) has been initiated against him or her. The right to counsel may also be violated for confession purposes when the defendant is not explicitly questioned by a police officer but a statement is secured without counsel or when the defendant's attorney is not present at the interrogation.

Third, the defendant must have been informed of his or her Fifth Amendment *privilege against self-incrimination*. Most confession claims arise under the Fifth Amendment's self-incrimination clause as interpreted by *Miranda*, which essentially gives the defendant the right not to have a statement used against him or her in a federal or state court if his or her statement was made in response to a custodial interrogation without required warnings being given to him or her.

Most police departments now direct officers to follow the warnings almost precisely as provided in *Miranda*. In some cases, however, warnings are not exactly given and may still comply with *Miranda*. The Supreme Court has held that if the defendant is given adequate information with respect to the right to have an attorney present and a right to remain silent, *Miranda* has not been violated. (This means that two out of the four required warnings are sufficient.) In a 1987 case, the Supreme Court announced even further that the defendant does not have to be informed of the particular crime for which he or she is being investigated.[110] Generally, *Miranda* still has a certain amount of potency. If the warnings are not given, the statement of the defendant will not be admissible at trial, even if the defendant's Sixth Amendment right to counsel was not violated (hurdle two) and even if in traditional terms the confession was voluntarily given (hurdle one).

The *Miranda* warnings were intended to offset the coercive nature of a police-dominated interrogation. Therefore, *Miranda* warnings need not be given before interrogation by someone whom the defendant does not know to be a police officer. The court stated that *Miranda* warnings do not need to be given before questioning by a passive cellmate working for the police.[111]

Miranda warnings are not necessary unless the suspect is in custody and is being interrogated by a government official. Therefore, it is necessary to examine Supreme Court decisions regarding the definitions of (1) being in custody, (2) being interrogated, and (3) who is a government official. Since all three are required before *Miranda* warnings must be given, they must be examined one at a time.

First, the defendant is in custody if freedom of movement has been limited by the police. Thus, custody can occur in a defendant's home, if the defendant believes he or she is not free to go, or if the defendant in is jail on an unrelated charge. The key question is whether the defendant's freedom of movement has been limited. Thus, even if the investigation has been focused on the defendant, the custody requirement may not have been met unless the defendant is unable to leave afterward. The Supreme Court declared that no custody took place during an IRS investigation of the defendant when he was already the target of the investigation.[112]

Second, the defendant's statement is subject to *Miranda* only if it is given in response to interrogation. Hence, volunteered remarks (spontaneous remarks not made in response to questioning) are not covered by *Miranda*. Interrogation, however, is not limited to any particular type of questioning. Police should know that their actions are reasonably likely to elicit an incriminating response from the suspect.

Third, a government agent must be interrogating the suspect. Examples of government agents include publicly paid police, private people acting on police direction, privately paid police (such as security guards), deputized members of the public police force, public school officials, and heads of government-based agencies.

Many commentators believe the death blow to *Miranda* began in 1999 in the case of *Dickerson v. United States*. Dickerson's non-Mirandized confession was suppressed at the trial court, but the prosecution stopped the case and appealed (called an interlocutory

LANDMARK CASE — Dickerson v. United States

Dickerson was indicted for bank robbery and conspiracy to commit bank robbery. Before the trial he moved to suppress a statement he made at the FBI office, on the grounds that he had not received *Miranda* warnings before being interrogated. The district court granted the motion and the government took an interlocutory appeal to the court of appeals, which reversed, stating that Section 3501 of the Omnibus Crime Control and Safe Streets Act was satisfied since the statement was made voluntarily. Dickerson appealed the case to the U.S. Supreme Court.

The Supreme Court granted certiorari. Legal commentators remarked that the procedural facts of this case gave the Supreme Court the opportunity to attack *Miranda* that eleven previous cases had failed to offer. The conservatives on the Supreme Court, for the first time since 1966, were presented with the opportunity to overrule a *Miranda* decision and thereby make its legal effect null and void. Many legal scholars believed that this precisely was what they would do.

Yet when the Court rendered its opinion, it let *Miranda* keep its status quo. The Supreme Court overruled the federal circuit court of appeals not so much for any love or respect for the *Miranda* decision, but because of the disdain it felt toward the lower court. A Supreme Court decision interpreting the Constitution or a federally mandated legislative statute overrules Congressional statutes interpreting the Constitution. The Supreme Court felt that the lower court had violated the power of judicial review (discussed earlier in this chapter).

Source: Dickerson v. United States, 120 S.Ct. 2326 (2000).

appeal) to the federal court of appeals. The court of appeals reversed the federal district courts, that had suppressed Dickerson's confession because he had not received the Miranda warnings before being interrogated, citing a statute from the 1968 Omnibus Crime Control and Safe Streets Act that requires the prosecutor to prove only that the confession was voluntary in order for it to be admissible.

Essentially, this case represented a direct challenge to the validity of *Miranda;* when the Supreme Court voted to consider the case, many wondered about *Miranda*'s fate. The issue the Court was required to resolve was, where a decision of the court involves interpreting a Supreme Court application of the Constitution versus a statute that Congress passed concerning the same principle of law, should the Court supercede the congressional statute? The Supreme Court said yes; the decisions of the Supreme Court always supersede congressional statutes. Justice Rehnquist held that where a decision in court involves an interpretation and application of the Constitution, Congress does not legislate to supersede the decision. *Miranda* and its progeny govern the admissibility of statements during custodial interrogations in both state and federal courts. The statute in question was enacted two years after *Miranda* decision and was intended by Congress to overrule the Court's decision in the case. The issue is whether Congress has the constitutional authority to do so. While Congress retains the ultimate authority to modify or set aside any judicially created rules of evidence and procedure that are not required by the Constitution, it may not legislatively supersede a Court's decision that interprets and applies the Constitution. (See the Landmark Case *Dickerson v. United States*).

The fourth criterion for a constitutional confession is that it must not violate the defendant's Fourteenth Amendment rights, which ensure that if a defendant confesses, the confession must be both voluntary and intelligent. Hence, even if the defendant was afforded his or her complete Sixth Amendment rights (right to counsel), Fifth Amendment rights (privilege against incrimination, as interpreted by *Miranda*), and Fourteenth Amendment rights (right of voluntariness, as interpreted by due process), still the prosecution may not use the confession against the defendant at trial, unless the state demonstrates that the defendant knowingly and intelligently waived his or her rights. This demonstration, or failure to demonstrate, will be determined by the judge at the suppression hearing.

There are two exceptions to these general rules. One, if the defendant responds to questions the police ask because of their reasonable concern for public safety, and they fail to read the defendant's *Miranda* rights, the confession may be admitted into evidence.[113] Two, *Miranda* rights do not apply when the defendant gives a statement in response to a nongovernment official, such as a personal friend or someone not associated with the government. This is true unless the government arranged the situation, or the confession was given to an undercover agent posing as an inmate talking to the accused in jail.[114]

To recap, accused people do not have the right to be read their *Miranda* rights unless they are actually in custody. The Supreme Court has declared that defendants are in custody when their freedom of movement is limited by police. Also, defendants' statements are subject to *Miranda* only if they were in response to police interrogation. Police interrogation is often more than just questioning. The test for interrogation is whether the police should have known that their actions were reasonably likely to elicit an incriminating response.

THE SIXTH AMENDMENT RIGHT TO COUNSEL AND OTHER TRIAL RIGHTS

The Right to Counsel

No prison is without its share of "jailhouse lawyers," men and women who have become familiar with the law from firsthand experience. In the days when the right to an attorney was not available in court, much less behind the jailhouse walls, these jailhouse lawyers helped put cases together for appellate review. With time on their hands and great personal interest in their cases, these men and women paved the way for the prisoners of today. Perhaps the most famous appeal was made by Clarence Earl Gideon, an indigent prisoner in Florida State Prison at Raiford. Gideon's case was of such national significance that it was described in Anthony Lewis's best-selling book *Gideon's Trumpet*

WEB

To read the full opinion of the Supreme Court in *Dickerson v. United States,* visit the Supreme Court link on our Web site, www.prenhall.com/territo.

CTQ

When police officers violate the "rules of fair play," which apply administratively to criminal investigations, is it unusual for guilty people to go free? Can you think of another way of enticing officers to obey the law without necessarily having them arrest someone?

LANDMARK CASE — Gideon v. Wainwright

Gideon was charged in state court with breaking and entering a poolroom with the intent to commit a misdemeanor. This offense is a felony. He appeared in court without funds and asked for court-appointed counsel. The request was denied. Therefore, Gideon represented himself. He was convicted and sentenced to five years in state prison. He filed a petition for *habeas corpus*, which was denied by the state supreme court but accepted by the U.S. Supreme Court. The single issue before the Supreme Court was the question, does an indigent defendant charged in state court with a noncapital felony offense have a right to court-appointed counsel? In a unanimous decision, the Supreme Court answered yes, reasoning that this provision of the Bill of Rights, which is so fundamental and essential to a fair trial, is protected in the state courts by the Fourteenth Amendment. The Court had previously held that the right to counsel was not fundamental and hence is not required in state court. However, the Court overruled its previous decision, and stated that Gideon should have had court-appointed counsel. The case was reversed and remanded. To support its decision, the Court noted that the government hires lawyers to prosecute defendants. Lawyers are necessities, not luxuries, in criminal actions.

Source: Gideon v. Wainwright, 372 U.S. 335 (1963).

(later made into a movie starring Henry Fonda). (See the Landmark Case *Gideon v. Wainwright*).

Cases in Which the Right to Counsel Exists   The right to counsel exists in criminal prosecutions if actual imprisonment, however short, is actually imposed.[115] Defendants in many criminal trials are entitled to an appointed lawyer, regardless of their ability to pay. Few courts have set out specific standards with respect to indigency. In most courts, however, it is not necessary to establish total destitution.

Many jurisdictions specifically give the judge the discretion to provide assistance other than counsel, such as medical experts and investigators. In federal courts, by statute, the defendant may obtain investigative experts and other services necessary for an adequate defense. More broadly, due process may require such services.

Defendants in a joint trial may have their own attorneys appointed or, in many cases, share the services of one lawyer. If, however, the appointed attorney advises the trial court that a conflict of interest exists, the trial court must give separate counsel.

Furthermore, the defendant is entitled to the assistance of counsel at any critical stage of the proceeding, when the absence of counsel "might derogate from his right to a fair trial." This includes certain pretrial proceedings. The constitutional right to counsel arises upon the initiation of an adversarial proceeding. Defendants are entitled to counsel in the following situations: post–adversary proceeding lineups,[116] custodial interrogations,[117] psychiatric examinations,[118] pretrial arraignments,[119] preliminary hearings,[120] sentencing hearings,[121] and during his or her first automatic appeal.[122] However, the defendant is not entitled to counsel in probation and parole revocation proceedings where the trial is already completed and the sentence determined, or at discretionary appeals (state supreme courts and the U.S. Supreme Court, where the courts do not even have to consider the appeal).[123]

May a Defendant Represent Himself or Herself?   The defendant may waive the right to counsel and represent himself or herself at trial. The right of self-representation is not "inferior to the right of assistance of counsel."[124] A defendant may also waive his or her right to counsel prior to trial. This often occurs after indictment, when a defendant may agree to respond to police questioning without the presence of an attorney.

In order to waive the right to counsel, the defendant must be advised of his or her rights and be competent to intelligently and voluntarily abandon the right. If these requirements are met, the court must allow the defendant to proceed without counsel.

WEB

For more on the Sixth Amendment right to counsel, **visit our Web site, www.prenhall.com/territo**.

WEB

To listen to the oral argument in Gideon, **visit Northwestern University's Oyez Project link on our Web site, www.prenhall.com/territo**.

IN THE WORKPLACE

ATTORNEY AT LAW

Responsible for conducting criminal and civil lawsuits; draws up legal documents and practices other phases of law. Performs a variety of duties, including the following: advises clients as to legal rights; gathers evidence; conducts research; interviews clients and witnesses; handles details for trial preparation; prepares legal briefs; prepares arguments and testimony for case presentation; files briefs with court clerk; interprets laws, rulings, and regulations for individuals and businesses; confers with colleagues with specialty in area of lawsuit; may act as trustee, guardian, or executor; may draft wills, trusts, transfer of assets, and gifts; may supervise and coordinate activities of subordinate legal personnel; may prepare business contracts, settle labor disputes, or teach college courses in law. Minimum requirements are as follows: a four-year college degree, three years of law school, and successful completion of a written bar exam.

LANDMARK CASE — Wheat v. United States

Wheat was arrested along with Gomez Varajas and Bravo on drug conspiracy charges. Arrandale, an attorney, represented all three defendants. Bravo pleaded guilty; Gomez Varajas was acquitted. He was scheduled to be tried on a separate charge; however, he pleaded guilty, pursuant to a plea bargain. After this agreement was made, before it was accepted by the court, Wheat sought to have Arrandale represent him. The government moved to disqualify Arrandale on the basis that such representation would require cross-examination of his previous clients and thus present a conflict of interest. The court denied Wheat's request to have Arrandale represent him, rejecting Wheat's contention that the denial violated his constitutional right to counsel. Wheat was convicted and appealed. The Supreme Court looked at the issue of whether a criminal defendant is entitled to have counsel of his or her own, where such representation would create an inherent conflict. Justice Rehnquist, writing for the Court, answered no. The right to counsel does not always include the right to counsel of choice. In this case, the representation of all three co-conspirators incurably compromised the counsel's ability to represent all of his clients. As a result, the representation was properly denied.

Source: Wheat v. United States, 486 U.S. 153 (1998).

Does an Indigent Defendant Have the Right to a Particular Lawyer? A defendant is not entitled to a particular lawyer of his or her own choosing. The question is whether a lawyer can render effective assistance. Unless the relationship between the lawyer and the defendant is so strained that they cannot cooperate, the trial court is not required to appoint any particular attorney.[125] (See the Landmark Case *Wheat v. United States*.) Nor does the Sixth Amendment guarantee a "meaningful relationship" between counsel and defendant. There is no requirement that the defendant develop a certain kind of rapport with the attorney.[126]

Furthermore, the defendant is entitled only to have a lawyer represent him or her. Even in cases where the defendant would prefer that someone such as an accountant handle the matter, only the presence of a lawyer is required.[127]

In addition to guaranteeing the accused the assistance of counsel, the Sixth Amendment also guarantees an accused person five additional rights during his or her criminal trial: (1) the right to a speedy trial, (2) the right to a public trial, (3) the right to be tried by an impartial jury, (4) the right to confront witnesses testifying against the defendant, and (5) the right to a compulsory process for obtaining witnesses in the defendant's favor.

LANDMARK CASE: Barker v. Wingo

On July 20, 1958, an elderly couple was murdered. Shortly afterward, Silas Manning and Willie Barker were arrested as suspects. On September 15, they were indicted; counsel was appointed on September 17; and Barker's trial was set for October 21. However, Barker was not brought to trial for more than five years after his arrest due to numerous continuances by the prosecution. Initially, the continuances were for the purpose of convicting Manning, against whom the state had a stronger case, to assure his testimony against Barker. However, Manning was not convicted until 1962. Afterward, Barker's trial was delayed another seven months due to the illness of the investigating officer. During these continuances, Barker was free for all but ten months in jail, and made no objections for the first four years of the delay. However, Barker did object to the last few continuances, and, at his trial he moved for dismissal based on the Sixth Amendment right to a speedy trial. The motion was denied and Barker was convicted of murder. This case went to the Supreme Court, which considered the issue of whether a delay of five years between arrest and trial of a defendant is a violation of the Sixth Amendment right to a speedy trial. The Court held that no, it was not reasoning that the determination of whether a defendant was being deprived of the Sixth Amendment right to a speedy trial must be made on a case-by-case basis by balancing the following four factors: (1) the length of the delay, (2) the reason for the delay, (3) the defendant's assertion of his or her right, and (4) the prejudice to the defendant.

Source: Barker v. Wingo, 407 U.S. 514 (1972).

The Right to a Speedy Trial

The Sixth Amendment, applicable to federal courts and selectively incorporated to apply to the states, provides that in all criminal prosecutions, the accused shall enjoy a right to a speedy trial.[128] The purposes of the constitutional guarantee to a speedy trial, according to the Supreme Court, are twofold.[129] The first purpose is to relieve the defendant of unnecessary consequences of being accused of a crime. These consequences include oppressive pretrial incarceration (which disrupts employment, drains financial resources, and separates family). Also, being accused often has the consequence of subjecting the defendant to public scorn and personal anxiety, which impairs his or her defense. The second purpose is to promote society's interest in disposing of charges so as to enhance proper administration of justice. (See the Landmark Case *Barker v. Wingo*.)

What Happens When a Person's Right to a Speedy Trial Is Violated? The sole remedy for the violation of the right to a speedy trial is the dismissal of the charges. This dismissal bars all future prosecutions for the offense. Courts are, therefore, reluctant to find violations of this right. The Supreme Court has held that the dismissal remedy should be used sparingly. The Court will often overturn a lower court's decision with prejudice, especially if it's based on a claim of "nonchalant government attitude."

When Does a Speedy Trial Attach? The right to a speedy trial attaches (begins to be calculated) only after a person has become accused. A person is accused when either an indictment or an information processed has been issued against him or her, or when the person has been taken into custody under a judicially signed warrant. Therefore, once arrested on a judicially signed warrant, a person is deemed accused and is entitled to a speedy trial, even if he or she is released thereafter and not indicted for a substantial period of time.[130] Hence, the right is not violated by delaying the filing of charges, although such a delay may violate other rights.

However, the speedy-trial clause is *not* violated on delay between dismissal of charges and reindictment for the same offense.[131] Furthermore, the speedy-trial clause attaches even when the defendant does not know about the charges against him or her and is not being restrained in any way.

What Is the Standard for Determining an Unreasonable Delay? Whether a case must be dismissed for lack of a speedy trial requires a balancing test. The conduct of both the prosecution and the defendant is weighed; such factors as length of delay, reason for delay, defendant's assertion or nonassertion of the right, and prejudice to the defendant are also considered. In terms of what constitutes a "length of delay," the court has said that a length of delay alone does not establish the violation of speedy trial, unless the defendant can show that the delay is prejudicial. However, the reasons for the delay are another story. A deliberate attempt by the prosecution to delay the trial so as to receive an advantage weighs heavily toward violation of speedy trial. Therefore, the Court has reasoned that if a justifiable reason for a delay (missing witness or illness of the party) may be determined, there is no constitutional violation.

If the delay is attributable to a willful delay by a accused, he or she is deemed to have waived his or her right to a speedy trial.[132] However, the mere fact that the accused is serving a jail sentence in another jurisdiction does *not* justify the delay of his or her trial on a pending charge. The prosecution must attempt to have the other jurisdiction temporarily cede custody for purposes of the pending charge. As stated previously, once arrested, the accused is entitled to a speedy trial, even if he or she is released thereafter and not indicted for a substantial period of time.

The Right to a Public Trial

The Sixth Amendment provides that in "all criminal prosecutions, the accused shall enjoy the right to a public trial . . . ." The right to a public trial is rooted in traditional Anglo-American distrust of secret trials. Its purpose is to safeguard against any attempt to employ the courts as instruments of persecution and to inform the public of government actions against citizens. However, there are certain instances where the trial may be a closed proceeding.

The issues surrounding closed trial proceedings involve two groups: (1) spectators in the courtroom, and (2) the media. In limited situations, if the need arises, the judge has the discretion to exclude members of the public from a trial. This is particularly relevant in sexual assault cases. In 1990, during the famous New York case of the investment banker–jogger who was mugged and raped by a gang of teenage boys, spectators were excluded from the courtroom during the victim's testimony, and her name was never allowed to be printed in the media. The Court held that a judge could properly exclude certain people if it was shown that they were likely to intimidate a witness.[133] (Note: After newly discovered DNA evidence in 2002, the confessions by these teenagers have come into question as to whether or not they were coerced by the New York Police Department.)

One of the major areas of concern is whether a judge can exclude the media from a trial. The courts have said that even if the government, the defendant, and the judge all agree to a closed hearing, Fifth, Sixth, and First Amendment concerns may be raised by members of the media. Rules have been laid down with respect to when the media can and cannot attend a trial. The media does not have a First Amendment right to attend a pretrial hearing in a criminal case.[134] However, the media does have a First Amendment right to attend a criminal trial.[135]

Preliminary hearings (mini-trials conducted by judges to determine whether probable cause exists in felony cases) are presumptively open to the public and the press. Furthermore, the Sixth Amendment right to a public trial also extends to pretrial suppression hearings. Public hearings may not be closed to the public except in one of the following four situations: (1) The party seeking closure shows an overriding interest likely to prejudice a public hearing; (2) the closure is broader than necessary to protect such interests; (3) reasonable alternatives to closure have been considered; or (4) adequate findings to support closure are entered by the trial court.

The Right to a Jury Trial

The right to a trial by jury is guaranteed by Article II, Section 2 of the Constitution. The right is also guaranteed by the Sixth and Fourteenth Amendments, which state that "in all criminal prosecutions, the accused shall enjoy the right to a trial by an impartial jury."

The Sixth Amendment's right to a jury trial has been applied to the states on the basis of the Fourteenth Amendment. In *Duncan v. Louisiana*, the Supreme Court held that the right to a jury trial was fundamental to the proper administration of justice.[136] Juries serve several purposes in our criminal justice system. Primarily, juries serve as a check against arbitrary vindictive law enforcement. The Supreme Court has recognized that juries also improve the fact-finding process. In addition, juries provide public participation in the criminal justice system, which is essential in a democratic society. (See Figure 3.14.)

The right to a jury trial applies only to serious offenses. For the purposes of a jury trial, a serious offense is one in which more than six months' imprisonment is authorized. The Supreme Court held that there is no right to a trial by jury in juvenile delinquency proceedings.[137] The Court reasoned that juries would materially disrupt both the nature and purpose of the state's separate juvenile justice system. Particularly, juries would undercut the confidentiality of the juvenile justice system.

The requirements regarding the size of the jury and whether a unanimous decision is required depend on whether the case is in federal or state court. In federal court, a twelve-person jury is required, and the verdict must be unanimous. Because the Supreme Court considers the twelve-person jury the result of a "historical accident," the Court has declined to impose this requirement on the states.

The Supreme Court upheld Florida's jury system, which permitted a six-person jury in noncapital cases.[138] The Court reasoned that the size of the jury had little impact on the ability to buffer between the accused and the state, nor did the size of the jury diminish community participation or the function of juries. The only limitation on jury size is that the jury must be large enough to ensure group deliberation and provide a possibility of a representative cross-section of the community. However, the Court said that a five-person jury was unconstitutional because it would not provide effective group discussion.[139]

The right to a unanimous jury verdict is not absolute, but may depend on the size of the jury. The Supreme Court, indeed, has approved nonunanimous verdicts in state criminal cases. For example, the Court has upheld 11–1, 10–2, and 9–3 verdicts against due process and Sixth Amendment challenges that the dissenting votes on the jury established a reasonable doubt, thus violating the requirement that guilt be proven beyond a reasonable doubt.[140] However, a six-member jury must be unanimous. (For more information on a defendant's right to a fair cross-section on the jury, please refer to Chapter 9.)

Finally, a defendant may waive the right to a trial by jury, as long the waiver is voluntary and intelligently made. The government can require that the waiver be approved by the prosecution and the court.

The Right to Confront Witnesses Testifying against the Defendant

The purpose of the Sixth Amendment confrontation clause is threefold: First, it ensures the reliability of the witness's testimony by means of administering an oath; second, it exposes the witness to the probative effects of cross-examination; third, it permits the trier of fact—either the judge or the jury—to weigh the demeanor of the witness in determining credibility.[141]

The right of confrontation is a trial-based right; it does not necessarily apply in pretrial situations. For example, the confrontation clause is not violated by the defendant's exclusion from a pretrial hearing to determine the competency of too-young child witnesses. Nor does the confrontation clause give the defendant the right to obtain investigative reports made by the state agency investigating cases of sexual abuse.

In federal and state prosecutions, the right to confront witnesses against the defendant is deemed a fundamental right and hence is applicable to the states under the due process clause of the Fourteenth Amendment.[142] It includes the right of the accused to

FIGURE 3.14

The right of a criminal defendant to a trial by jury is the only trial right embedded in three provisions of the Constitution (Article II, Section 2; the Sixth Amendment; and the Fourteenth Amendment).

Courtesy John Neubauer/PhotoEdit.

be physically present during the course of the trial. However, the right to be present may be waived as a result of improper conduct of the accused. For example, if an accused is present at the start of a trial but voluntarily absents himself or herself, most jurisdictions hold that the trial may continue in his or her absence (that is, this is his or her waiver of the right to be present[143]).

A defendant who persists, after warning, in disorderly, disrespectful conduct in the courtroom may be held to have waived his or her right to be present and may be excluded from the trial. Methods of dealing with disruptive behavior at trial are (1) holding the defendant in contempt, (2) binding and gagging the defendant in the courtroom, and (3) removing the defendant altogether.

Finally, the state may not place a burden on this right by requiring the defendant to appear in court in prison clothing. The right also includes the right to identify prosecution witnesses, including their true names and addresses. They cannot take the stand anonymously. Furthermore, the Sixth Amendment generally includes the right to a face-to-face encounter between the defendant and a witness testifying against him or her. However, the absence of a face-to-face encounter does not necessarily violate the Sixth Amendment. The right to a face-to-face encounter is denied when preventing such confrontation serves an important public purpose, such as the reliability of the witness's testimony is otherwise assured.

The right to confront witnesses is essentially the right to cross-examine witnesses. In the U. S. criminal justice system, the accused has the right to lead and impeach witnesses (to make their testimony less believable; see Chapter 9) who are called by the prosecution, as well as witnesses who are defense witnesses but give damaging testimony on the witness stand. In these situations, traditional rules of evidence against impeaching "one's own witness" give way to the constitutional right of confrontation. While the scope of permissible cross-examination must be wide enough to be effective, the accused must be allowed to show any and all matters that would reflect a witness's possible bias in testifying against him or her. In one instance, the defendant was permitted to show that the prosecution witness was on probation as a juvenile delinquent, and any state interest protecting the anonymity of juvenile offenders must give way to his or her right to confrontation.[144]

Finally, hearsay rules limiting the use of out-of-court statements in the confrontation clause are generally designed to deal with the problems that stem from the same roots; however, the overlap is not too complete. The constitutional question is not whether the out-of-court statement falls within the hearsay exception, but whether it violates the Sixth Amendment.[145]

The Right to a Compulsory Process for Obtaining Witnesses in the Defendant's Favor

The Sixth Amendment expressly provides that an accused in any criminal prosecution shall have the right to a compulsory process for obtaining witnesses in his or her favor. In conjunction with the due process clause, this means that the defendant has the same right as the prosecutor to present witnesses in state and federal proceedings. The scope of this right means more than just the power to subpoena witnesses. It encompasses the right to present a defense that includes the right of the accused to present his or her own witnesses and version of the facts.

The Supreme Court has said that where a trial judge makes threatening remarks to the only defense witness, which effectively drives that witness off the stand, the accused is deprived of the right to present a defense.[146] Furthermore, exclusion by the trial judge of evidence that is crucial to the defense and bears a substantial assurance of trustworthiness impairs the right of the accused to present a defense, even where the evidence offered is technically inadmissible under appropriate local rules. In one case, the defendant offered evidence of an oral confession of the crime by a person other than the defendant. The trial court excluded the evidence because it was inadmissible as hearsay under the local rules of evidence. The Supreme Court reversed, holding that the evidence for substantial assurance of trustworthiness and the local rules could not be allowed to impair the accused's right to present a defense.[147]

Finally, the Sixth Amendment right to compulsory process is relevant whenever the government deports a witness or a would-be defense witness. The defendant has a constitutional claim if the deported witness would have been material and favorable to the defendant's defense. If the witness is judged not so material and favorable, then the compulsory process right has not been violated.

THE FIFTH AMENDMENT RIGHT PROHIBITING DOUBLE JEOPARDY

The Fifth Amendment to the Constitution provides that "[no person shall] be subject for the same offense to be twice put in **jeopardy.**" The Fifth Amendment applies only to federal prosecutions, but double jeopardy prohibition is so fundamental to the constitutional heritage of the United States that it has been incorporated by the due process clause of the Fourteenth Amendment, therefore binding the states as well.[148] The basic principle supporting double jeopardy is that a person who has committed a single criminal offense can be subjected to only one prosecution or punishment for that offense. Accordingly, when the defendant has been prosecuted for a criminal offense and the prosecution resulted in either a conviction or acquittal—or proceedings reached the point where the dismissal is tantamount to a termination of the proceeding based on the innocence of the accused—any further prosecution or punishment for the same offense is barred.

The prohibition against double jeopardy is designed to ensure that the defendant will not be forced to live in a continuing state of anxiety and insecurity over the possibility of repeated prosecutions.

Jeopardy attaches at a defendant's trial when the jury is empaneled or, in a nonjury case, when the first witness is sworn in. The trial needs to go no further to a judgment of conviction or acquittal for example.[149] Once this threshold has been passed (subject to the following exceptions), the defendant cannot be retried for the same crime.

Exceptions to the Double Jeopardy Prohibition

Even if jeopardy attaches, the prohibition on double jeopardy may be removed or waived in any of the following three situations: (1) mistrials, (2) dismissals, or (3) appeals.

Mistrials Where a mistrial is ordered on the motion of the defendant or otherwise with the defendant's consent, the bar to jeopardy is usually waived and the defendant may be retried for the same offense.[150] Retrial is barred, however, if bad-faith conduct of the judge or the prosecutor is intended to goad the defendant into seeking a mistrial and thereby giving the prosecution a more favorable opportunity to convict.[151]

When the defendant objects to the mistrial, double jeopardy bars any retrial. The two exceptions to this rule are (1) there was a "manifest necessity" for granting a mistrial and (2) retrial is dictated by the "ends of public justice."[152] **Manifest necessity** will be found where a scrupulous exercise of judicial discretion leads to the conclusion that the ends of public justice would not be served by continuation of the trial.

Dismissals If a dismissal occurs before trial, the defendant can be reindicted and prosecuted for the offense. However, if a dismissal occurs after jeopardy is attached, but before the conviction, it does not preclude the prosecution from reindicting the defendant if the dismissal is at the defendant's request and is for some reason unrelated to guilt or innocence.[153] Finally, if the dismissal occurs after the conviction, the prosecution can attempt to reinstate the conviction by appeal, since no further trial would be required.[154]

Appeals If the defendant appeals his or her conviction and the case is reversed because of an error at trial, the general rule is that the defendant can be retried because of the errors committed during the trial. Here, there has not been "one fair opportunity" to litigate guilt or innocence, and the defendant has waived his or her double jeopardy claim by appealing.[155]

Jeopardy as a Bar to Prosecution for the Same Offense

Once jeopardy has attached, the defendant cannot normally be prosecuted a second time for the same offense involved in the first trial, nor can he or she receive more than one punishment for the same offense. Two crimes are considered the same offense unless each crime requires proof of an additional element that the other crime does not. This is called the *Blockburger test* for the definition of "same offense." If the offense charged in the second trial is the same in law or fact as the offense charged in the first trial, the double jeopardy clause prohibits successive trials. Normally, lesser included offenses (for example, "voluntary manslaughter" is a lesser included offense of the crime of murder; see Chapter 2) from the original offense charged are considered the same offense. Finally, there is an instance when the same act may be a crime and tried in two different courtrooms—both under federal and state law, in two different states,[156] or in federal court and state court.[157]

THE FIFTH AMENDMENT RIGHT TO SUBSTANTIVE DUE PROCESS

Substantive due process refers to the content or subject matter of a law. This right protects people against unreasonably capricious or arbitrary laws or acts by all branches of the government. In the criminal justice process, the major right under Fifth Amendment due process is defined by the *void-for-vagueness doctrine*. Under this Fifth Amendment due process right, the Constitution requires that laws must not be so vague and uncertain that people of common intelligence must necessarily guess at their meaning and differ as to their application.[158] The Supreme Court, when using this clause of the Fifth Amendment, strikes down criminal statutes and local ordinances. Examples of unduly vague laws include those that prohibit a person from wandering the street at night without lawful business or from willfully obstructing public passages (see the Landmark Case *Chicago v. Morales*). Also, a statute prohibiting the contemptuous treatment of the American flag is declared to be in violation of substantive due process.

EIGHTH AMENDMENT RIGHTS AGAINST EXCESSIVE BAIL AND CRUEL AND UNUSUAL PUNISHMENT

Excessive Bail

Bail is a guarantee in return for being released from jail. The accused guarantees his or her future appearance by posting funds or some other form of security with the court. When the defendant's appearance in court is completed, the security is returned. If the defendant fails to appear, the security is forfeited. The Eighth Amendment states that "excessive bail shall not be required, nor excessive fines imposed, nor cruel and unusual punishment inflicted." The right to bail is one of the rights in the Bill of Rights that the Supreme Court has not declared to be a due process right. Hence, defendants prosecuted in state courts do not have a constitutional right to bail. However, every state has some type of law that assures state defendants of the right to bail in certain cases.

In 1987, the Supreme Court ruled that an accused facing a future trial in federal court may be denied bail if the prosecution demonstrates by clear and convincing evidence that his or her release on bail would present a risk and danger to the public. Critics argue that this decision delivers a "crushing blow" to the presumption of innocence enjoyed in the United States for two centuries.[159]

Cruel and Unusual Punishment

The cruel and unusual punishment clause in the Eighth Amendment has been used throughout the years to prevent the use of torture and excessive physical punishment on prisoners, which was common in early European history and still is common today in many parts of the world (for example, Iraq's torture chambers discovered in 2003). In addition, at one time in American history this clause was interpreted to overturn the legality of the death penalty,[160] only to have the courts restore it later. Many laws affecting the regulation of prisons, including the elimination of isolation and segregation, have been enacted under this provision. Indeed, most prisoners' rights, including the right to moderate discipline and to express their grievances, have come from litigation based on this clause (see "In the News: Castration Agreement Challenged as Cruel and Unusual Punishment").

WEB

For more information on Eighth Amendment rights, **visit our Web site, www.prenhall.com/territo**.

LANDMARK CASE: Chicago v. Morales

Because of an epidemic of gang violence, Chicago passed the Gang Congregation Ordinance in 1997. Under the ordinance, if a police officer observed a person whom he or she believes to be a gang member loitering in a public place with one or more people, the officer could order them to disperse; failure to do so was a violation of the ordinance and grounds for arrest. The ordinance also limited officers' enforcement discretion by confining arrest authority to designated officers, establishing criteria for defining street gangs and their membership, and providing for designated enforcement areas. In 1998, after a number of arrests of gang members by the police, the Illinois Supreme Court found that the statute violated due process of law because it was vague and an arbitrary restriction on personal liberty. In a 6–3 decision, the U.S. Supreme Court affirmed the Illinois court's decision and ruled that the ordinance's broad sweep violated the requirement that the legislature establish minimal guidelines to govern law enforcement activities. The Court said the ordinance encompassed too much harmless behavior. State courts had interpreted the statutory language "to remain in any one place with no apparent purpose" as giving officers absolute discretion to determine what activities constitute loitering. They ruled that the three features of the ordinance that limit the officer's discretion—it does not permit issuance of a dispersal order to anyone who is moving along or who has an apparent purpose; it does not permit an arrest if individuals obey a dispersal order; and no order can be issued unless the officer reasonably believes that one of the loiterers is a gang member—were insufficient to limit police discretion.

This case reinforces the constitutional principle that criminal laws with unlimited discretion and vagueness will be struck down. The problem with the statute was that it covered a broad range of innocent conduct and delegated too much discretion to the police. On the other hand, the Court said that the statute could be "made Constitutional by requiring that loiterers have some harmful purpose before being arrested, or making it clear that only gang members could be arrested rather than people standing nearby." This language has been taken by legal scholars as a cue that a properly drafted ordinance could be constitutional.

Source: Chicago v. Morales, 119 S.Ct. 246 (1999).

TOWARD EQUAL JUSTICE

The police may take a variety of actions to fulfill their missions of providing services, maintaining order, and enforcing the criminal law. Rarely do most of these, particularly actions taken to provide services and many to maintain order, evoke comment. However, when the police initiate certain actions not necessarily to enforce the criminal law but sometimes to maintain order, it is quite a different story. These frequently unwanted invasions of liberty and privacy provoke controversy. Most actions taken to enforce the criminal law arise out of the need for information. These information-seeking actions—including surveillance, stop-and-frisk, arrest, search, interrogation, and identification procedures—require an objective basis in fact. Mere suspicion will not suffice. The greater the government invasion, the more facts the law requires to back it up. The objective-basis requirement limits, but does not remove, police discretion in enforcing the criminal law.

The Constitution balances the government need for enough power to enforce the law with the privacy and liberty of innocent, suspected, and guilty individuals. These limits fall mainly under the Fourth, Fifth, Sixth, Eighth, and Fourteenth Amendments to the U. S. Constitution and similar provisions in state constitutions. The key terms in understanding the Fourth Amendment are "unreasonable," "searches," and "seizures"; the Fifth Amendment, "compelled," "self-incrimination," "double jeopardy," and "substantive due process"; the Sixth Amendment, "confrontation of witnesses," "the right to a trial

IN THE NEWS

A HUMAN PERSPECTIVE

CASTRATION CHALLENGED AS CRUEL AND UNUSUAL PUNISHMENT

Civil liberties groups were protesting a decision in Texas to castrate a child molester in lieu of a jail sentence, but they seemed unable to halt the action. Texas State District Judge Mike McSpadden approved a request by Steven Allen Butler, 27, facing trial in the rape of a 13-year-old girl. Conviction on the charges carries a maximum life sentence. "The problem is, who is to say who should make the choice between life in prison and this sort of penalty if it isn't the person who is affected by it," said Ira Glasser, executive national director of the American Civil Liberties Union. Also objecting were state NAACP officials, who said that the idea could lead to the castration of thousands of black males. Butler is black, and Texas NAACP officials want McSpadden to resign.

The date for the surgery wasn't announced, but legal experts said that it was unlikely the decision could be blocked. Both the prosecutor and the victim's family agreed to the plan.

"All of the parties that have (legal) standing to complain about it have no complaints . . . so it isn't likely to be tested," said Monroe Freedman, who teaches legal ethics at Hofstra Law School in New York. Freedman said the next question is the ethics of "that doctor removing a healthy part of a human being."

Pauline Bart, a sociologist at the University of Illinois–Chicago and author of several books on rape, said the sentence will spare the victim—already traumatized by the rape—from the ordeal of a trial. The "downside of it is that sex is also in your head and not just in your hormones," Bart said. "Even with the castration he could continue molesting with an erection, with objects, or with his hands." [Castration, regardless, continues to be a sentencing option in many U.S. states.]

Source: "Castration Challenged as Cruel and Unusual Punishment," *USA Today,* 3 September 1992. Copyright 1992, USA Today. Reprinted with permission.

IN THE WORKPLACE

RESOURCE COORDINATOR/COURT ANALYST

Responsible for reviewing and recommending alternative sentence plans; provides ongoing information and technical assistance to staff on program issues; oversees submission of required reports; serves as liaison among judge, courtroom staff, attorneys, victim advocates, service providers, and the public; participates in program planning and development; works on research; conducts confidential analysis of issues relating to personnel of the court. Minimum qualifications are as follows: one year as a court analyst or a bachelor's degree from an accredited college or university and two years of relevant experience; or a master's degree in public or business administration, criminal justice, or social work and one year of relevant experience.

by jury," and "the right to counsel"; the Eighth Amendment, "cruel or unusual punishment"; the Fourteenth Amendment, "due process clause" and "deprivation of life, liberty, and property." The history of the law of criminal procedure shows the gradual application of formal rules to the discretionary judgments of officials in proceedings before and after criminal trials. During the 1960s, the Supreme Court tried to balance discretionary judgments with formal rules in the day-to-day encounters between police officers and individuals both in police stations and on the street. Today the Court seems bound and determined to manifest precisely the opposite quality of encounters and relationships.

SUMMARY

Criminal procedural law is founded on the U. S. Constitution. Based on "fundamental fairness" and "due process," the law of criminal procedure focuses on how the criminal law is enforced, how evidence is collected, and what rights are guaranteed to people accused of crimes. Contrary to popular belief, the Bill of Rights has not always provided such guarantees to people tried in state courts. Indeed, not until the due process revolution of the 1960s were rights embodied in the Fourth, Fifth, Sixth, and Eighth Amendments made applicable to the states and given as rights to citizens being tried in the states as a matter of constitutional guarantee. Such rights included the right to a constitutional arrest, protection against unreasonable searches and seizures, the privilege against self-incrimination, and the right to counsel. Generally, a warrant is required for police to conduct a "reasonable" search; however, the Supreme Court has noted several exceptions: searches incident to a lawful arrest, the automobile exception, the consent exception, the plain-view exception, the stop-and-frisk exception, and exigent circumstances. Additionally, the exclusionary rule was created to protect individuals from police misconduct that resulted in unconstitutional searches and seizures. The exclusionary rule is a judicially enforced rule that requires any illegally obtained evidence to be excluded. As such, it is inadmissible against an accused at trial. Other trial rights, such as a speedy trial, public trial, the right to an impartial jury, the right to confront witnesses, and the right to compel witnesses to testify on one's behalf, were not afforded to all defendants in state courts until the early 1970s.

During the appointment periods of presidents Richard Nixon, Ronald Reagan, George H. W. Bush, and George W. Bush, more conservative justices maintained power on the Supreme Court. As a consequence, many of the rights that seemed to have expanded during the 1960s are considered to have been significantly retracted during the 1970s, 1980s, 1990s, and the first decade of the twenty-first century.

DISCUSSION AND REVIEW

1. How do constitutional rights act as a constraint on efficient law enforcement?
2. Briefly describe police activities that appear to be an arrest (a stop and detention) but do not require probable cause.
3. When does a citizen have the power to arrest another?
4. What are the minimal requirements necessary for a constitutional search?
5. When can police use deadly force to effect an arrest?
6. What is the constitutional basis for police to search and seize a private citizen?
7. What type of search always requires a search warrant? What are the thresholds to obtain such a warrant? What are some of the requirements while using such a warrant?
8. Name and justify at least three exceptions to the search warrant requirement.
9. What is the exclusionary rule? What are its exceptions?
10. What is the constitutional significance of *Miranda v. Arizona* in the 1960s and at the beginning of the twenty-first century?
11. What was the significance of the U. S. Supreme Court's decision in *Gideon v. Wainwright*?
12. What are the four hurdles necessary for the prosecution to clear in order to admit defendants' confessions as evidence against them in a criminal trial?
13. List and explain five of an accused's constitutional rights at trial under the Sixth Amendment.
14. Explain the meaning of *unreasonable* as used in the Fourth Amendment to the U. S. Constitution.
15. Explain the meaning of probable cause and indicate why it is an important concept.
16. When can a police officer search an automobile? What part or parts of an automobile can a police officer search lawfully?
17. What is meant by the plain-view doctrine?
18. When do the *Miranda* warnings have to be given to a suspect?
19. What is the significance of *Mapp v. Ohio* for law enforcement officers in the United States?

20. Outline the facts of *Terry v. Ohio* and describe its implications for law enforcement.
21. Differentiate between a stop and frisk and a search based on probable cause.
22. When may a law enforcement officer make a warrantless arrest?
23. Under what circumstances must a police officer knock and announce his or her identity and purpose before entering a dwelling in order to execute an arrest warrant?
24. Identify the two most frequent exceptions to the search warrant requirement, and describe the procedure whereby those exceptions apply.
25. Describe the exclusionary rule and how it applies to illegally seized evidence and confessions as per Supreme Court rulings.

CHAPTER RESOURCES

IN THE MEDIA

Video

CNN Today Video: *Introduction to Criminal Justice*, Vol. 13: Segment 1, "Miranda Rights"
Court TV Video: *The Greatest Trials of All Time (The Scottsborough Boys)*
FFA Custom CJ Video: *The Courtroom Process: The Public Defendant*
FFH Video: *Amendment 4 and Amendments 5–8*
FFH Video: *Unreasonable Searches and Seizure*
Insight Media Video: *The American Constitution: The Road from Runnymede*
Insight Media Video: *Bill of Rights: Bill of Responsibilities*
Insight Media Video: *The Bill of Rights: A Living Document*
Insight Media Video: *Criminal Procedure*
Insight Media Video: *Interpreting the Law: The Role of the Supreme Court*
Insight Media Video: *Profile Stops*
Insight Media Video: *Profiling Criminal Violators*
Insight Media Video: *Rights of the Accused*
Insight Media Video: *The Scales of Justice: Our Court System*
Insight Media Video: *Supreme Court Decisions That Changed the Nation*
NIJ Video: *Exclusionary Rule*
NIJ Video: *Search and Seizure*

Film

Double Jeopardy (1999)
Gideon's Trumpet (1980)
The Insider (1999)
The Juror (1996)
Mr. Smith Goes to Washington (1939)
The Thin Blue Line (1988)
Twelve Angry Men (1957)

Television

American Justice
CNN Today
Court TV
First Monday (An absolute must)
The West Wing

IN THE LITERATURE

Books

AMERICAN BAR ASSOCIATION, "*Standards Relating to Electronic Surveillance*, 2nd ed. New York: Institute of Judicial Administration, 1980.

R. V. DEL CARMEN, *Criminal Procedure for Law Enforcement Personnel*. Monterey, Calif.: Brooks/Cole, 1987.

G. FLETCHER, *With Justice for Some—Victims' Rights in Criminal Trials*. New York: Addison-Wesley, 1995.

R. A. LEO et al., eds., *The Miranda Debate: Law, Justice, and Policing*. Boston: Northeastern University Press, 1998.

A. LEWIS, *Gideon's Trumpet*, New York: Vantage Books, 1989.

D. A. MCWHIRTER, *Search, Seizure, and Privacy: Exploring the Constitution*, Phoenix, Ariz.: Oryx Press, 1994.

Articles

D. BAYLEY, AND J. GAROFALO, "The Management of Violence by Police Patrol Officers," *Criminology*, vol. 27, (1989), pp. 1–27.

D. DRIPPS, "Is *Miranda* Case Law Inconsistent? A Fifth Amendment Synthesis," *Constitutional Community*, vol. 17 (2000), p. 19.

J. FYFE, "The Use of Deadly Force: Research and Reform," *Justice Quarterly*, vol. 5 (1998), pp. 165–205.

M. GARDNER, "Sixth Amendment Right to Counsel and Its Underlying Values," *Journal of Criminal Law and Criminology*, vol. 90 (2000), p. 393.

G. KELDER AND A. J. STATMAN, "The Protective Sweep Doctrine: Recurrent Questions Regarding the Propriety of Searches Conducted Contemporaneously with an Arrest on or near Private Premises," *Syracuse Law Review*, vol. 30 (1979), pp. 973–1092.

R. Leo, "*Miranda* Revisited," *Journal of Criminal Law and Criminology*, vol. 86 (1996), p. 621.

J. Nestlerode, "Distinguishing the Exclusionary Rule Exceptions," *Journal of National Association of District Attorneys*, vol. 24 (1991), pp. 29–35.

J. Riggs, "Excluding Automobile Passengers from the Fourth Amendment," *Journal of Law and Criminology*, vol. 88 (1998), p. 55.

G. Thomas, "The End of the Road for Miranda Arguers," *American Criminal Law Review*, vol. 37 (2000), p. 1.

J. Wasowiz, "Future of the Exclusionary Rule," *Trial Magazine*, vol. 34, p. 79.

CASES

Barron v. Baltimore, 7 PET 243 (1833)
Brewer v. Williams, 430 U.S. 387 (1977)
Massachusetts v. Sheppard, 468 U.S. 981 (1984)
United States v. Cortez, 449 U.S. 411 (1981)

ENDNOTES

1. H. Packer, "The Courts, the Police and the Rest of Us," *Journal of Criminal Law, Criminology, and Police Science*, vol. 57, pp. 238–243.
2. Ibid.
3. M. Zalman and L. Siegel, *Criminal Procedure—Constitution and Society*. Belmont, Calif.: West/Wadsworth, 1997.
4. G. Fletcher, *With Justice for Some—Victims' Rights in Criminal Trials*. New York: Addison-Wesley, 1995.
5. *Getlow v. New York*, 268 U.S. 650 (1925).
6. *Duncan v. Louisiana*, 391 U.S. 145 (1968).
7. *Marbury v. Madison*, 1 Cranch 137 (U.S. 1803).
8. Y. Kamisar, "The Warren Court (Was It Really So Defense-Minded?), the Burger Court (Is It Really So Prosecution-Oriented?) and the Policy Investigation Practices." In V. Blasi, ed., *The Burger Court*, New Haven, Conn.: Yale University Press, 1990.
9. *California v. Hodari D.*, 499 U.S. 621 (1991).
10. *Dunaway v. New York*, 442 U.S. 200 (1979).
11. *Florida v. Royer*, 460 U.S. 491 (1983).
12. *Michigan v. Chestnut*, 486 U.S. 567 (1988).
13. *Beck v. Ohio*, 379 U.S. 89 (1964).
14. *United States v. Watson*, 423 U.S. 411 (1976).
15. J. Senna and L. Siegel *Introduction to Criminal Justice*, 7th ed. St. Paul, Minn.: West, 1996, p. 164.
16. Idaho Code § 19–604.
17. *Payton v. New York*, 445 U.S. 573 (1980).
18. *Riverside County v. McLaughlin*, 500 U.S. 44 (1991).
19. *Kirby v. Illinois*, 406 U.S. 682 (1972).
20. *Schmerber v. California*, 384 U.S. 757 (1966).
21. *United States v. Mandujano*, 425 U.S. 564 (1976).
22. *United States v. Wade*, 388 U.S. 218 (1967).
23. *Dunaway v. New York*, 442 U.S. 200 (1979).
24. *Hayes v. Florida*, 470 U.S. 1811 (1985).
25. *Terry v. Ohio*, 392 U.S. 1 (1968).
26. *Brower v. Inyo County*, 489 U.S. 593 (1989).
27. *Michigan Department of State Police v. Sitz*, 496 U.S. 444 (1990).
28. *Commonwealth v. Moreira*, Massachusetts Supreme Judicial Court, 33 CrL 2078 (1983).
29. *Malley v. Briggs*, 475 U.S. 335 (1986).
30. *United States v. Martinez-Fuerte*, 428 U.S. 543 (1976).
31. *Michigan Department of State Police v. Sitz*, 496 U.S. 444 (1990).
32. *Brower v. Inyo County*, 489 U.S. 593 (1989).
33. *Michigan v. Summers*, 452 U.S. 692 (1981).
34. *Davis v. Mississippi*, 394 U.S. 721 (1969).
35. G. Stone, *Search and Seizure*. National Institute of Justice Crime File Series. Washington, D.C.: U.S. Department of Justice, 1990.
36. *Burdeau v. McDowell*, 256 U.S. 465 (1921).
37. *Katz v. United States*, 389 U.S. 347 (1967).
38. *Rakas v. Illinois*, 439 U.S. 128 (1978).
39. *Rawlings v. Kentucky*, 448 U.S. 98 (1980).
40. *United States v. Place*, 462 U.S. 696 (1983).
41. *United States v. Mara*, 410 U.S. 19 (1973).
42. *United States v. Dionisio*, 410 U.S. 1 (1973).
43. *Smith v. Maryland*, 442 U.S. 735 (1979).
44. *Fisher v. United States*, 425 U.S. 391 (1976).
45. *Cardwell v. Lewis*, 417 U.S. 593 (1974).
46. *Maryland v. Macon*, 472 U.S. 163 (1985).
47. *United States v. Oliver*, 466 U.S. 170 (1984).
48. *California v. Greenwood*, 486 U.S. 35 (1988).
49. *United States v. Dunn*, 480 U.S. 294 (1987).
50. *California v. Ciraolo*, 476 U.S. 207 (1986).
51. *Florida v. Riley*, 488 U.S. 445 (1989).

52. *Dow Chemical Company v. United States*, 476 U.S. 227 (1986).
53. *Kyllo v. United States*, 121 S.Ct. 2038 (2001).
54. *Michigan v. Barlow*, 436 U.S. 499 (1978).
55. *United States v. Ventresca*, 380 U.S. 102 (1965).
56. *McCray v. Illinois*, 386 U.S. 300 (1967).
57. G. F. Cole, *The American System of Criminal Justice*, 7th ed. Belmont, Calif.: Wadsworth, 1995, p. 118.
58. *John v. United States*, 333 U.S. 10 (1948).
59. *Wilson v. Arkansas*, 115 S.Ct. 1914 (1995).
60. *Maryland v. Garrison*, 480 U.S. 79 (1987).
61. *Chimel v. California*, 395 U.S. 752 (1969).
62. *Carroll v. United States*, 267 U.S. 132 (1925).
63. *Chambers v. Maroney*, 399 U.S. 42 (1970).
64. *Robbins v. California*, 453 U.S. 420 (1982).
65. *United States v. Ross*, 456 U.S. 798 (1982).
66. Ibid.
67. *United States v. Chadwick*, 433 U.S. 1 (1976).
68. *Scheckloth v. Bustamonte*, 412 U.S. 218 (1973).
69. *United States v. Matlock*, 415 U.S. 164 (1974).
70. *Stoner v. California*, 376 U.S. 483 (1964).
71. *Florida v. Bostick*, 501 U.S. 429 (1991).
72. J. Cronin, "Working the Busses: Leave the Searching to Us," *Suffolk University Law School Journal*, vol. 22 (1991), pp. 31–37.
73. *Arizona v. Hicks*, 480 U.S. 321 (1987).
74. *Murray v. United States*, 487 U.S. 533 (1988).
75. *Texas v. Brown*, 460 U.S. 730 (1983).
76. *California v. Ciraolo*, 476 U.S. 207 (1986).
77. *Florida v. Riley*, 488 U.S. 445 (1989).
78. *United States v. Hensley*, 469 U.S. 221 (1985).
79. *United States v. Cortez*, 449 U.S. 411 (1981).
80. *Weeks v. United States*, 232 U.S. 383 (1914).
81. *Lustig v. United States*, 338 U.S. 74 (1949).
82. *Elkins v. United States*, 364 U.S. 206 (1960).
83. Ibid., p. 222.
84. *Mapp v. Ohio*, 367 U.S. 643 (1961).
85. *Wolf v. Colorado*, 338 U.S. 25 (1949).
86. *Mapp v. Ohio*, 367 U.S. 643 (1961).
87. *Wong Sun v. United States*, 371 U.S. 471 (1963).
88. *Jackson v. Denno*, 378 U.S 368 (1964).
89. *Simmons v. United States*, 390 U.S. 377 (1968).
90. *Wong Sun v. United States*, 371 U.S. 471 (1963).
91. *Nix v. Williams*, 467 U.S. 431 (1984).
92. *United States v. Crews*, 445 U.S. 463 (1980).
93. *Murray v. United States*, 487 U.S. 533 (1988).
94. *United States v. Crews*, 445 U.S. 463 (1980).
95. *United States v. Ceccolini*, 435 U.S. 268 (1978).
96. *Stone v. Powell*, 428 U.S. 465 (1976).
97. *Burdeau v. McDowell*, 256 U.S. 465 (1921).
98. *United States v. Janis*, 428 U.S. 433 (1976).
99. *United States v. Calandra*, 414 U.S. 338 (1974).
100. *United States v. Caceres*, 440 U.S. 741 (1979).
101. B. Wilson, *The Exclusionary Rule*. National Institute of Justice Crime File Series, Washington, D.C.: U.S. Department of Justice, 1990.
102. *Brown v. Mississippi*, 297 U.S. 278 (1936).
103. *Miranda v. Arizona*, 384 U.S. 436 (1966).
104. *Massiah v. United States*, 377 U.S. 201 (1964).
105. *United States v. Henry*, 447 U.S. 264 (1980).
106. *Maine v. Moulton*, 474 U.S. 159 (1995).
107. *Kuhlman v. Wilson*, 447 U.S. 436 (1986).
108. *Brewer v. Williams*, 430 U.S. 387 (1977).
109. *Escobedo v. Illinois*, 378 U.S. 478 (1964).
110. *Colorado v. Spring*, 479 U.S. 564 (1987).
111. *United States v. Henry*, 447 U.S. 264 (1980).
112. *Oregon v. Mathiason*, 429 U.S. 492 (1977).
113. *New York v. Quarles*, 467 U.S. 649 (1984).
114. *Illinois v. Perkins*, 496 U.S. 292 (1990).
115. *Argersinger v. Hamlin*, 407 U.S. 25 (1972); *Scott v. Illinois*, 440 U.S. 367 (1979).
116. *Kirby v. Illinois*, 406 U.S. 682 (1972).
117. *Miranda v. Arizona*, 384 U.S. 436 (1966).
118. *Estelle v. Smith*, 451 U.S. 454 (1981).
119. *Hamilton v. Alabama*, 368 U.S. 52 (1961).
120. *Coleman v. Alabama*, 399 U.S. 1 (1970).
121. *Mempa v. Rhay*, 389 U.S. 128 (1967).
122. *Douglas v. California*, 372 U.S. 355 (1963).
123. *Ross v. Moffitt*, 417 U.S. 600 (1974).
124. *Faretta v. California*, 422 U.S. 802 (1975).
125. *Brown v. Craven*, 424 F.2d 1166 (9th Cir. 1970).
126. *Morris v. Slappey*, 461 U.S. 1 (1983).
127. *United States v. Whitesel*, 543 F.2d 1176 (6th Cir. 1976).
128. *Klopfer v. North Carolina*, 386 U.S. 213 (1967).
129. *Barker v. Wingo*, 407 U.S. 514 (1972).
130. *Dillingham v. United States*, 423 U.S. 64 (1975).
131. *United States v. MacDonald*, 456 U.S. 1 (1982).
132. *Strunk v. United States*, 412 U.S. 434 (1973).
133. *Unites States v. Harold*, 368 F.2d 187 (1985).
134. *Gannett Company v. DiPesquale*, 443 U.S. 368 (1979).
135. *Richmond Newspapers, Inc. v. Virginia*, 448 U.S. 555 (1980).
136. *Duncan v. Louisiana*, 391 U.S. 145 (1968).
137. *McKeever v. Pennsylvania*, 402 U.S. 528 (1971).

138. *Williams v. Florida*, 399 U.S. 78 (1970).
139. *Ballew v. Georgia*, 435 U.S. 223 (1978).
140. *Apodaca v. Oregon*, 406 U.S. 404 (1972).
141. *California v. Greene*, 399 U.S. 149 (1970).
142. *Pointer v. Texas*, 380 U.S. 400 (1965).
143. *Taylor v. United States*, 414 U.S. 17 (1973).
144. *Davis v. Alaska*, 415 U.S. 308 (1974).
145. *Dutton v. Evans*, 400 U.S. 74 (1970).
146. *Webb v. Texas*, 409 U.S. 95 (1972).
147. *Chambers v. Mississippi*, 410 U.S. 284 (1973).
148. *Benton v. Maryland*, 395 U.S. 784 (1969).
149. *Crist v. Bretz*, 437 U.S. 28 (1978).
150. *United States v. Dinitz*, 424 U.S. 600 (1976).
151. *Oregon v. Kennedy*, 456 U.S. 667 (1982).
152. *Illinois v. Somerville*, 410 U.S. 458 (1973).
153. *United States v. Scott*, 437 U.S. 82 (1978).
154. *Unites States v. Wilson*, 420 U.S. 332 (1975).
155. *Burks v. United States*, 437 U.S. 1 (1978).
156. *Heath v. Alabama*, 474 U.S. 82 (1985).
157. *Bartkus v. Illinois*, 359 U.S. 121 (1959)
158. P. Lewis and K. Peoples, *The Supreme Court and the Criminal Process—Cases and Comments*. Philadelphia: W. B. Saunders, 1978.
159. *Unites States v. Salerno*, 481 U.S. 739 (1987).
160. *Furman v. Georgia*, 408 U.S. 238 (1972).

4

THE NATURE AND DISTRIBUTION OF CRIME AND ITS VICTIMS

Chapter Outline

The Uniform Crime Reporting Program
Index Crimes
  Violent Crimes
  Crimes against Property
  Hate Crime
  Limits to National Crime Data
Criticisms of the UCR Program
  Crime Data Manipulation
  Nonmandatory Nature of the Program
  Incomplete Crime Categories
  UCR Hierarchy Rule
  Lack of Information on Part II Crimes
Future of the UCR Program
Collection of Campus Crime Data
What Crime Does to Victims and Society
  The Victim in Historical Perspective
  Talion Law
  Victim Compensation
Government Programs for Victims
  Compensable Crimes
  Eligibility Requirements for Victims
  Restitution
  Victim and Witness Intimidation Issues and Responses

Victimization Studies
National Crime Data Collection
  National Crime Victimization Survey
  Comparing UCR and NCVS
  Race and Victims of Violence
  Issues with Victim Surveys
Special Categories of Victims
  Intimate-Partner Violence
  Children as Victims
  Victims of Drunk-Driving Accidents
  Older People as Victims
  Sexual and Physical Violence against College Women
  Victims of Workplace Violence
Victim Special-Interest Groups
Costs of Crime Victimization
  Number of Victimizations
  Costs and Other Consequences
  Implications
Unresolved Victim–Criminal Justice System Issues
Summary

Key TERMS

aggravated assault, p. 148
arson, p. 150
burglary, p. 149
clearance rate, p. 146
compensation, p. 156
crime data manipulation, p. 152
crime rate, p. 144
criminal homicide, p. 144
domestic crisis intervention unit, p. 162
FBI Uniform Crime Reports (UCR), p. 144
forcible rape, p. 146
hate crime, p. 151
larceny-theft, p. 149
Mothers Against Drunk Driving (MADD), p. 168
motor vehicle theft, p. 150
National Crime Victimization Survey (NCVS), p. 159
National Incident-Based Reporting System (NIBRS), p. 154
National Organization for Victim Assistance (NOVA), p. 171
restitution, p. 156
robbery, p. 147
victim impact statement, p. 156
victim special-interest groups, p. 170
waiver of prosecution, p. 148

Courtesy Getty Images, Inc.

For some time in the United States, there has been significant interest in crime data and issues related to that information. Groups such as criminal justice practitioners, legislators, the media, and everyday citizens are keenly interested in crime data. Common questions raised by these groups often include the following: How much crime is there, when and where do crimes occur, who is most often victimized, what types of crimes are most frequently committed, who gets arrested, and what happens to those people after the arrest?

A variety of federal government agencies collect crime-related data and ultimately publish the information in order to respond to these and other pertinent questions. For example, the Department of Justice, the FBI, the National Institute of Justice, the Office of Juvenile Justice and Delinquency Prevention, the Bureau of Justice Statistics, and the Bureau of Prisons each collect and publish data relevant to the study of crime in the United States.

For purposes of this chapter, we will narrow the focus of attention on crime data to reports most commonly depicted in the media, which are of general interest to most members of our society. In addition, we will discuss the impact crime has on its victims, characteristics of victims, and responses to victims by the criminal justice system.

The average citizen, by listening to the radio, viewing television, or reading the daily newspaper, is frequently exposed to reports about the community crime rate. Yet few people realize that news reports about the crime rate refer to only eight categories of crime: murder and nonnegligent manslaughter (**criminal homicide**); forcible rape; robbery; aggravated assault; burglary; larceny-theft; motor vehicle theft; and arson. The **crime rate** in an area is defined as the number of these offenses that occur per 100,000 inhabitants.

Crimes reported to the police extend beyond these eight categories, but only these eight are included in the crime rate or crime index reported in the **FBI Uniform Crime Reports.** The solution of crimes involving these eight offenses is an index by which the public and media can evaluate the efficiency of police departments; other indices can be used to evaluate policy efficiency, but for better or for worse, this one is used most often by the media in news reports.

This chapter discusses the crime reporting system in the United States, examines each of the eight index crimes, and defines and describes the elements of these crimes. The accuracy of offenses reported to the FBI by local police is examined, and the problems of underreporting by victims and the manipulation of statistics by police are discussed. We also examine recommendations for changes in the Uniform Crime Reporting Program that address these and other criticisms of the system. Additionally, we compare the National Crime Victimization Survey (NCVS), conducted by the Bureau of Justice Statistics, with the Uniform Crime Reporting Program. Later in this chapter we will look at what crime does to victims and to society and will discuss the price of crime for victims as individuals and for the nation as a whole. The results of victimization surveys, system responses to victims, and special categories of victims such as those involved in domestic violence and acquaintance rape will be discussed.

THE UNIFORM CRIME REPORTING PROGRAM

Using crime statistics contributed by more than 17,000 law enforcement agencies across the United States, the Uniform Crime Reporting (UCR) Program provides periodic assessments of crime in the nation as measured by offenses that come to the attention of law enforcement agencies. The program's primary goal is to generate reliable criminal statistics for use in law enforcement administration, operation, and management. However, data from the program are also used by other criminal justice professionals, legislators, and scholars who have an interest in the crime problem. In addition, the statistics furnish the general public with an indication of fluctuations in crime levels.[1]

The Committee on Uniform Crime Records of the International Association of Chiefs of Police (IACP) initiated the voluntary national data collection effort in 1930. That same year, Congress appointed the FBI as the national clearinghouse for statistical information on crime. Since then, a large volume of data based on uniform classifications and reporting procedures has been obtained from the nation's law enforcement agencies.

To provide a more complete picture of crime in the United States, the Committee on Uniform Crime Records of the IACP chose to use data on offenses coming to the attention of law enforcement agencies; these data are more readily available than any other reportable crime information. Because of their seriousness, frequency of occurrence, and likelihood of being reported to police, seven offenses were initially selected to compute an index for evaluating fluctuations in crime volume. These crimes, known as the *index offenses*, were murder and nonnegligent manslaughter, forcible rape, robbery, aggravated assault, burglary, larceny-theft, and motor vehicle theft. By congressional mandate, arson was added as the eighth index offense in late 1979.

To provide nationwide uniformity in the reporting of data, standard definitions have been adopted for all offenses. Standardization is needed to eliminate variations in the definitions of offenses in different parts of the country. Without regard for local statutes, reporting agencies are required to submit data in accordance with the UCR definitions. Because punishment for some offenses varies among the state codes, the program does not distinguish between felonies and misdemeanors.

CTQ

Why is it important to know the crime rate of a city as opposed to simply the number of crimes?

WEB

For more information on the UCR program, **visit our Web site,** www.prenhall.com/territo.

The IACP's Committee on Uniform Crime Records still serves in an advisory capacity to the FBI on the operation of the UCR program. In this connection, the IACP, through surveys of law enforcement records and crime reporting systems, has an active role in the program. In June 1966, the National Sheriffs' Association (NSA) established a Committee on Uniform Crime Reporting to serve in an advisory role to the NSA membership and to the national UCR program. This committee actively encourages sheriffs throughout the country to fully participate in the program. Committees on uniform crime reporting within state law enforcement associations are also active in promoting interest in the UCR program. These committees foster widespread and more intelligent use of uniform crime statistics and assist the agencies that contribute data.

Contributors to the UCR program compile and submit their data in one of two ways: directly to the FBI or through state UCR programs. Contributors that submit directly to the FBI are provided with continuing guidance and support from the national program. At present, there are forty-one operational state-level UCR programs; these programs have increased the coverage of agencies by instituting mandatory state reporting requirements, by providing more direct and frequent service to participating agencies, and by making information readily available at the state level. Thus, state programs have greatly increased the efficiency of operations at the national level.

When a state develops a UCR program, the FBI ceases to collect data directly from individual law enforcement agencies within the state. Instead, information from within the state is forwarded to the national program by the state collection agency. The state systems are developed to ensure the consistency and comparability of data submitted to the national program and to provide for regular and timely reporting of national crime data.

INDEX CRIMES

The eight index crimes are frequently divided into two categories: violent crimes and crimes against property. The distribution of these crimes is depicted in Figure 4.1.

Violent Crimes

The violent crimes among the index crimes are murder and nonnegligent manslaughter, aggravated assault, forcible rape, and robbery.

Murder and Nonnegligent Manslaughter   Murder and nonnegligent manslaughter are defined in the UCR program as the willful (nonnegligent) killing of one human being by another. The classification of these offenses, as in all index offenses, is based solely on police investigation—as opposed to determination by a court, medical examiner, coroner's jury, or other judicial body. Not included under this classification are deaths caused by

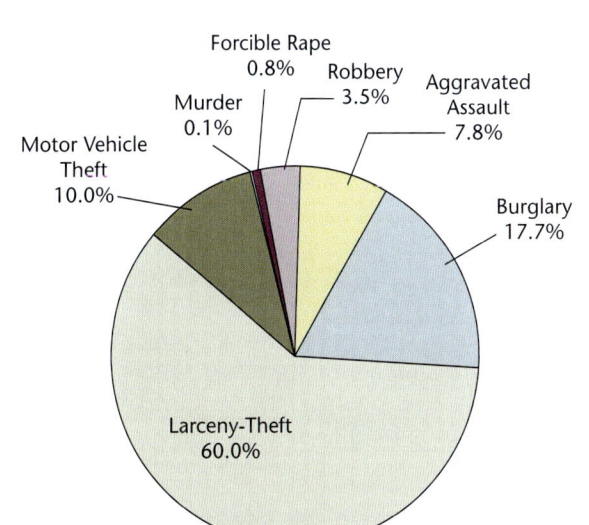

FIGURE 4.1

Crimes Percent Distribution, 2000*

Source: Data from Federal Bureau of Investigation, *Crime in the United States,* FBI Uniform Crime Reports (Washington, D.C.: U.S. Government Printing Office, 2001), p. 9.

- Forcible Rape 0.8%
- Robbery 3.5%
- Aggravated Assault 7.8%
- Murder 0.1%
- Motor Vehicle Theft 10.0%
- Burglary 17.7%
- Larceny-Theft 60.0%

*Due to rounding, the percentages do not add to 100.0 percent.

IN THE WORKPLACE

SENIOR CRIME DATA SPECIALIST

Responsible for the training and supervision of assigned staff. Performs technical support work utilizing automated law enforcement systems and software to provide crime data for police officers and management to use in the identification and apprehension of criminal offenders, the deployment of officers, and the improvement of public safety. Minimum qualifications usually include a combination of training and experience equivalent to the following: high school diploma or equivalent, two years of supervisory experience utilizing software and multiple automated police information systems.

TABLE 4.1 Clearance Rates of Index Crimes

Index Crime	Clearance Rate
Murder/nonnegligent manslaughter	63%
Forcible rape	47%
Robbery	25%
Aggravated assault	51%
Burglary	13%
Larceny-theft	18%
Motor vehicle theft	14%
Arson	29%

Source: FBI *Uniform Crime Reports,* 2001.

WEB

For more information on murder and nonnegligent manslaughter, visit our Web site, www.prenhall.com/territo.

CTQ

Do you think the classification of violent crimes such as murder and nonnegligent manslaughter should be based solely on police investigation, as it is now, or should other criminal justice entities partake in the classification process?

WEB

For more information on forcible rape, visit our Web site, www.prenhall.com/territo.

---

negligence, suicide, or accident; justifiable homicides (the killing of felons by law enforcement officers in the line of duty or by private citizens); and attempted murder or assault with the intent to murder (classified as aggravated assaults).

The rate of murders per 100,000 in 2000 was 5.5, the lowest since 1965. Murder consistently has the highest solution rate, or **clearance rate** (63 percent), of the eight index crimes. See Table 4.1 for the clearance rates of the index crimes. Based on supplemental homicide data, the racial correlation of murder victims to murder offenders is usually intraracial. In almost half of all murders, the victims either knew their assailant or were related to them. Handguns were the weapon of choice in approximately 57 percent of all murders.

"In the News: The Deadly Parking Place" gives an example of acquaintance homicide. This case illustrates that—although tragic—murders involving acquaintances are rarely difficult to solve and almost impossible to prevent.

Forcible Rape **Forcible rape** is defined in the UCR program as carnal knowledge of a female, forcibly and against her will. Assault or attempts to commit rape by force or threat of force are included in this category, but statutory rape (without force) and other sex offenses are not.

It is widely accepted that rape is one of the most underreported violent crimes. As victimization studies reveal, victims have specific reasons for not reporting rapes:[2]

1. Lack of belief in the ability of the police to apprehend the suspect.
2. Concern that they would receive unsympathetic treatment from the police and would have to go through discomfiting procedures.

IN THE NEWS

A HUMAN PERSPECTIVE

THE DEADLY PARKING PLACE

Bill and Lonnie were next-door neighbors and regularly argued about the parking places in the street in front of their homes. Each man lived in his own single-family home, and each usually parked his car on the city street directly in front of his home when the parking place was vacant. Lonnie usually got home from work earlier than Bill, and if the parking place in front of his own home was taken, he would park in front of Bill's home. Bill's parking place was on the city street, so neither man had a legal right to the spot.

One evening Lonnie returned home from work, found the parking place in front of his home taken, and parked in the vacant spot in front of Bill's home. When Bill arrived home and saw that Lonnie had once again parked in front of his home, he went directly to Lonnie and confronted him. Bill was verbally abusive and profane, and threatened to "beat Lonnie's ass" if he didn't move his car. Lonnie agreed to move it, and both men then walked toward the car. When they reached it, Bill punched Lonnie in the face, knocking him to the pavement. He told Lonnie never to park in his spot again. Lonnie got up, got into his car, and drove away. The assault was witnessed by both families, including the children. (Bill was six feet four inches tall and weighed 225 pounds, Lonnie was five feet four inches tall and weighed 140 pounds.)

The following morning as Bill was exiting his home, Lonnie approached him with a razor-sharp pocketknife that he had opened but concealed in his pocket. Lonnie told Bill he should not have hit him the evening before, then pulled the knife out of his pocket and cut Bill's throat. Bill fell to the pavement and bled to death. This assault was witnessed by both families, as well as by some neighbors seated on their porches. After the attack, Lonnie fled on foot. He was arrested several hours later in a nearby saloon after police were advised by neighbors that the saloon was his regular hangout.

---

3. Desire to avoid the embarrassment of publicity.
4. Fear of reprisal by the rapist.
5. Apprehension, based on television programs or newspaper reports, that they would be further "victimized" by court proceedings.

Unfortunately, some complaints about the treatment of rape victims are justified; efforts are being made to correct these deficiencies in the system. For example, victim advocacy groups are working with local police departments to educate the public about the crime of rape and to correct misinformation presented in television programs and the news media.

The failure of victims to report rapes seriously diminishes the ability of the police to protect other women. In an effort to combat the problems of rape and the nonreporting of rape, many police departments have implemented rape prevention programs. One hazard of such programs is that if they are successful there could be an initial increase in the number of rapes reported to the police—thus conveying an impression that the program has failed. Therefore, prior to launching a rape prevention program, a police department should make the public and the news media aware of the possibility of increased reporting. There will be more discussion of victims of acquaintance rape later in this chapter.

Robbery **Robbery** is the taking, or the attempt to take, anything of value from the care, custody, or control of a person or persons by force, by threat of violence, by violence, or by putting the victim in fear. Because of the face-to-face confrontation between perpetrator and victim, the potential for violence is always present in a robbery; when violence does occur, injuries can range from minor harm to loss of life. Because of its personal and often violent nature, robbery is feared greatly by the public; this fear may well be heightened by perceptions of police inability to deal effectively with the offense (only one in every four reported robberies is solved). In 2000, robberies accounted for about 3.5 percent of all crimes reported to UCR. Firearms were used in 41 percent of all robberies; robberies committed on the streets and highways accounted for 46 percent of the total.

In addition, the force or threat of force in robbery must precede or accompany the taking. Force applied after the taking does not constitute robbery. Thus, victims who, realizing that their property has been stolen, encounter force when attempting to recover

> **CTQ**
> What factors do you believe are most responsible for the underreported nature of the crime of rape by victims?

that property, are not robbery victims if their property was originally taken without force. When force is not used but a threat to the physical well-being of the victim is substituted, it is not necessary that the victim be frightened to the point of panic. It is enough that he or she is reasonably apprehensive and aware of the potential for injury.

Robbery has a low clearance rate for several reasons: Physical evidence may not be found; the on-scene time of perpetrators is limited; and witnesses are usually so shaken that their information runs the gamut from minimal to completely erroneous. Physical descriptions are the most common evidence in robbery, but the descriptions are of limited use because the robbers are usually some distance away by the time the police arrive.[3]

Aggravated Assault **Aggravated assault** is an unlawful attack by one person upon another for the purpose of inflicting severe or aggravated bodily injury. This type of assault is usually accompanied by the use of a weapon or by means likely to produce death or great bodily harm. Attempts are included in this category, since it is not necessary that an injury result when a gun, knife, or other weapon is used that could and probably would result in serious personal injury if the crime were successfully completed.

Aggravated assaults are the most frequent type of violent crime, accounting for almost 8 percent of all UCR crimes. The most common weapon used is a blunt object or other dangerous weapon (not including firearms).

Often victims and assailants in aggravated assaults are known to one another, just as for victims and assailants in criminal homicides. It is not uncommon for assault victims to be uncooperative with the police, for one of the following reasons:[4]

1. The assailant is a husband or boyfriend who is the breadwinner of the family or is a wife or girlfriend who cares for the disputant's children. An arrest would undo an arrangement that benefits the victim.
2. The victim considers the offense to be a personal matter and wants to settle the dispute privately.
3. The victim believes that he or she got what he or she deserved, and therefore does not want the assailant to be punished.
4. The victim fears revenge if charges are pursued.

An uncooperative victim creates both legal and investigative difficulties. All states consider felony assaults to be crimes against the people of the state; thus, the state is legally the aggrieved party. Technically, the victim has no legal right to decide whether an assailant will be prosecuted. Rather, the decision is made by the prosecutor; many prosecutors are reluctant to pursue prosecution in felony assaults involving uncooperative victims. This is especially true when a victim's injuries are not critical and when the parties involved are related.

Faced with an uncooperative victim, an officer's job is to get that victim to provide facts about the crime. This can be done, but the victim generally has to be convinced that no legal action will be taken against the assailant. The laws vary from state to state, but in many jurisdictions informal arrangements have been worked out between the prosecutor's office, the courts, and the police department to give police the authority (under carefully controlled conditions) to have a victim sign a **waiver of prosecution.** A waiver includes the name of the assailant, a statement of the victim's total satisfaction with the investigation by the police, and a statement of the victim's desire not to have the state prosecute.

Some people object strenuously to the practice of using waivers, because they believe that nonprosecution tends to encourage assaults. This position assumes that persons who commit assaults and are not punished are encouraged to commit similar assaults in the future. Nevertheless, overcrowded court dockets and the difficulties associated with prosecuting cases with reluctant victims obviate any preventive or punitive benefits that might be derived from the prosecution of all assaults.

Many state and local governments have statutes and ordinances that make it unlawful to intentionally withhold information relating to a crime or to provide false and misleading information about the crime. A victim who is uncooperative or who is sus-

---

CTQ

Is it good public policy to have a waiver of prosecution? Why or why not?

pected of not being completely truthful is usually advised of such laws and the penalties associated with them.

Crimes against Property

Among the eight index crimes, the four crimes against property are burglary, larceny-theft, motor vehicle theft, and arson.

Burglary **Burglary** is the unlawful entry of a structure to commit a felony or theft. The use of force is not required to classify an offense as a burglary. Burglary is divided into three classifications in the UCR: forcible entry, unlawful entry where no force is used, and attempted forcible entry.

According to the 2001 UCR, daytime burglaries comprised 55 percent of the total; 45 percent occurred during the night. Two out of every three burglaries were residential in nature.

Although burglars tend to come from lower socioeconomic classes and are often not well educated, there have been notable exceptions. Burglaries have been committed by professors, probation officers, and psychiatrists. Burglars can be classified according to several variables, such as preferences for premises to be attacked and types of property they will or will not take. But the most useful classification is skill. Burglars range from the amateur to the professional, but most are unskilled at their crime.

Professional burglars may commit only four or five offenses each year. Despite the infrequency of their acts, however, they are important to the police because of the large value of cash or property taken and their intimate knowledge of sophisticated fencing systems. In addition to the "big score," the hallmark of the professional is thorough planning preceding each burglary. Professionals refuse to place themselves in jeopardy for anything other than sizable gain, and they do so only after weeks or months of painstaking study of a target. Because they know exactly what they want in advance, professionals do not ransack premises. Thus, a stolen article may not be missed for some time. Working nationally—or, at the highest professional level, internationally—the professional burglar often operates for a long time without being arrested.

Larceny-Theft **Larceny-theft** is the unlawful taking, carrying, leading, or riding away of property from the possession or constructive possession of another without the use of force or fear. It includes crimes such as theft from motor vehicles, shoplifting, theft of parts and accessories for motor vehicles, pocket picking, purse snatching, and bicycle theft. Thefts from motor vehicles accounted for one-quarter of all thefts, followed by shoplifting. Figure 4.2 shows the types of larcenies by percentage distribution.

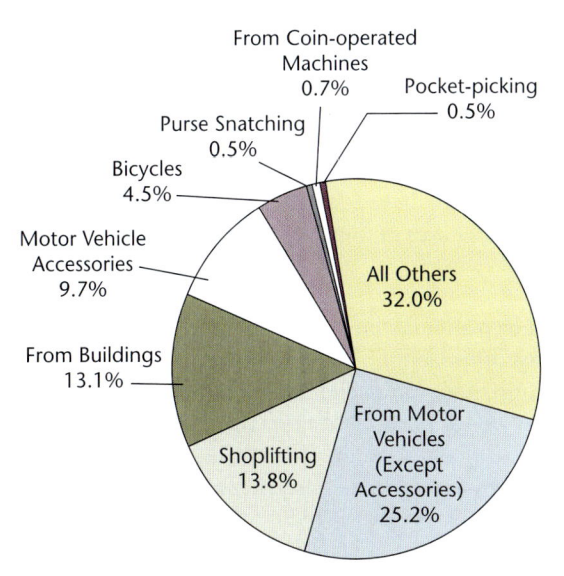

FIGURE 4.2

Percentage Breakdown of Larceny, 2000

Source: Data from Federal Bureau of Investigation, *Crime in the United States.* FBI Uniform Crime Reports (Washington, D.C.: U.S. Government Printing Office, 2001), p. 50.

- From Coin-operated Machines 0.7%
- Pocket-picking 0.5%
- Purse Snatching 0.5%
- Bicycles 4.5%
- Motor Vehicle Accessories 9.7%
- From Buildings 13.1%
- Shoplifting 13.8%
- From Motor Vehicles (Except Accessories) 25.2%
- All Others 32.0%

Larcenies are the most frequently reported UCR crime; they comprised approximately 60 percent of the index crimes in the 2001 report. Studies indicate that many offenses in this category, particularly when the value of stolen goods is low, never come to the attention of the police because victims do not report the thefts.

Motor Vehicle Theft **Motor vehicle theft** is the theft or attempted theft of a motor vehicle, including the theft of automobiles, trucks, buses, motorcycles, motor scooters, snowmobiles, and so on. This definition excludes the taking of a motor vehicle for temporary use by someone with lawful access. The 2001 report included 1.2 million motor vehicle thefts, accounting for 10 percent of all index crimes. Total value of the motor vehicles stolen was $7.8 billion, with an average loss of $6,682. These thefts are generally grouped into three categories: joyriding, professional thefts, and fraud.[5]

- *Joyriding:* Car thefts for joyriding constitute the majority of motor vehicle thefts. The perpetrators are usually teenagers—15 to 19 years old—who steal a car on a dare, as initiation into a gang, or for parts and accessories. Youths arrested for car theft are often repeat offenders.
- *Professional Theft:* The professional auto thief steals with the specific intent of making a profit, either by dismantling the vehicle for parts or by altering it for resale. An example of international professional auto theft follows, in the section "International Trends."
- *Fraud:* Although certain types of theft involve fraud perpetrated on innocent purchasers, the major category of vehicle fraud as described here does not actually involve the theft of vehicles by professionals, or even strangers. These various types of crimes are generally committed by the owner or someone acting on behalf of the owner, and the underlying purpose is to profit at the expense of an insurance company. For example, the owner of an expensive car may file a false police report regarding the theft of the vehicle and then file an insurance claim.

CTQ
Why do you think larcenies are the crimes most frequently reported to the UCR?

The emerging international character of the vehicle theft trade contributes to this increase of American cars being stolen for resale in other nations, especially in areas with access to large port facilities.[6] The practice of selling stolen vehicles overseas, where eager buyers will often pay double the original purchase price for a quality automobile, is rapidly changing the domestic auto-theft trade. Increasingly, vehicles stolen in the United States are being shipped out of the country, where potential profits are far greater. As international trade increases and shipping terminals around the country are expanded, auto-theft rings will have greater access to foreign ports.

While stolen cars were once painted, transported across state lines, and delivered to either unsuspecting or unscrupulous used-car dealerships, shipping stolen vehicles out of the country for sale is quickly emerging as the method of choice among car-theft rings. The United States is becoming a supplier of stolen vehicles to third-world countries. While auto theft has long been a problem for law enforcement, the emerging international character of auto-theft rings increases the threat of this crime, especially in areas near overseas shipping terminals. As international trade increases, new ports are constructed, existing ports are expanded, and more cities obtain access to international shipping lines. Unfortunately, this also enhances opportunities for auto theft rings to export their illegal cargo out of the country. Cooperation between federal, state, and local agencies that have jurisdiction over the different phases of the illegal vehicle trade is the best way to combat this growing problem.

Arson **Arson** is defined as any willful or malicious burning or attempt to burn—with or without intent to defraud—a dwelling, house, public building, motor vehicle, aircraft, or personal property of another (see Figure 4.3). Only fires determined through investigation to have been willfully or maliciously set are classified as arsons. Fires of suspicious or unknown origin are excluded. Because arson was not added to the list of index offenses until 1979, limited historical data are available for the crime. Some limited data are shown in Table 4.2.

FIGURE 4.3

The occurrence of hate crimes can be very disturbing. Racial hatred was the suspected motivation behind the arson of this African American church.

Courtesy AP/Wide World Photos.

TABLE 4.2 Targets of Arsonists

Type of Target	Percentage
Structures	44%
Motor vehicles trailers	31%
Other property (crops, timber, etc.)	25%

Note: Based on 78,280 arsons reported to police.
Source: FBI *Uniform Crime Reports* 2001.

Hate Crime

A **hate crime,** also known as a bias crime, is a criminal offense committed against a person, property, or society that is motivated, in whole or in part, by the offender's bias against a race, religion, disability, sexual orientation, or ethnicity/national origin.

In response to growing concern about hate crimes, Congress enacted the Hate Crime Statistics Act of 1990. The Attorney General designated the UCR Program to develop a hate crime data collection system that would include data "about crimes that manifest evidence of prejudice based on race, religion, sexual orientation, or ethnicity." In September 1994, the Violent Crime Control and Law Enforcement Act amended the Hate Crime Statistics Act to add disabilities, both physical and mental, as factors that could be considered a basis for hate crimes. The disability bias data collection began in January 1997.

Hate crimes are not separate, distinct crimes, but rather traditional offenses motivated by the offender's bias; therefore, hate crime data can be collected by capturing additional information about offenses currently being reported to the UCR Program. Included are the offenses of murder and nonnegligent manslaughter; forcible rape; aggravated assault, simple assault, and intimidation; robbery; burglary; larceny-theft; motor vehicle theft; arson; and destruction, damage, or vandalism of property.

FIGURE 4.4

Percentage Distribution of Hate Crimes, 2000*

Source: Data from Federal Bureau of Investigation, *Crime in the United States.* FBI Uniform Crime Reports (Washington, D.C.: U.S. Government Printing Office, 2001), p. 62.

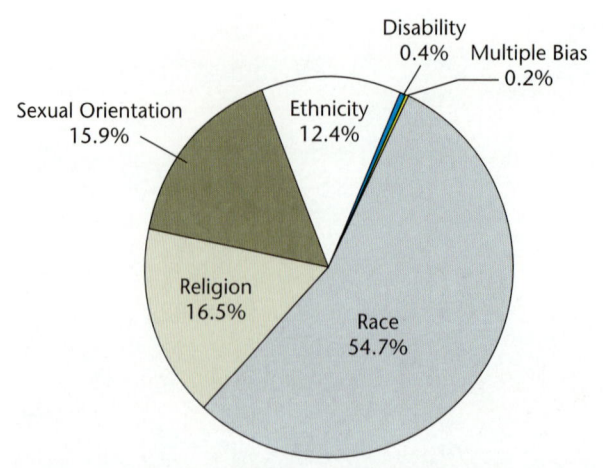

- Disability 0.4%
- Multiple Bias 0.2%
- Ethnicity 12.4%
- Sexual Orientation 15.9%
- Religion 16.5%
- Race 54.7%

*Due to rounding, the percentages do not add to 100.0.

The statistics given in Figure 4.4, which shows the percent distribution of hate crimes by category, represent data received from law enforcement agencies that provided one to twelve months of hate crime reports during 2000. More detailed information concerning characteristics of hate crime can be found in the UCR annual publication *Hate Crime Statistics*.

Limits to National Crime Data

Although the total number of crimes occurring throughout the nation is unknown, information about those reported to law enforcement gives a reliable indication of criminal activity. In reviewing any crime data in the UCR, it must be remembered, that many factors can cause the volume and type of crime to vary from place to place. For example, even though population is used in computing crime rates, many communities are affected to some degree by seasonal or transient populations. Since counts of current, permanent population are used in their construction, crime rates do not account for short-term population variables, such as an influx of day workers, tourists, shoppers, and so on.

National UCR data can serve as a guide for criminal justice administrators in analyzing the local crime count as well as the performance of the jurisdiction's agencies. Only through an appraisal of local conditions can a clear picture of the community crime problem or the effectiveness of the criminal justice system be created.

CRITICISMS OF THE UCR PROGRAM

Crime Data Manipulation

Although most police departments report crimes accurately to the FBI, **crime data manipulation** does sometimes occur—and for various reasons. For example, a police chief may want to convey the impression to citizens and superiors that everything is under control and that the police department is doing an effective job.

One technique used by police departments to manipulate crime data is a practice referred to as *clearing the books*. This procedure involves getting people already charged with a crime to confess to crimes they did not commit, thus improving police clearance rates (see "In the News: Clearing The Books").

Nonmandatory Nature of the Program

Historically, law enforcement agencies' contributions to the UCR system of crime data gathering have been voluntary. Therefore, almost by definition, the UCR system does not reflect all crimes reported to police agencies in the United States.

Incomplete Crime Categories

Critics argue that although the current categories of violent crimes and crimes against property may still be relevant for the most part in the twenty-first century, shouldn't crimes such as major drug activities, white-collar violations, serial murder, and domestic terrorism be added to the index?

WEB

For more information on hate crime, visit our Web site, www.prenhall.com/territo.

CTQ

Is enough being done on the part of government officials to label hate crimes as serious criminal offenses, on par with aggravated assault and other crimes?

CTQ

Are there any disparities in how the media reports and represents hate crimes and the actual statistical evidence shown in the Uniform Crime Reports? If so, explain.

CTQ

What should be done to police officials who are guilty of manipulating crime data?

CTQ

Should the reporting of crime data on the part of law enforcement agencies be made mandatory in order to improve the overall accuracy of the UCR system? If so, would there be any disadvantages to this? Why or why not?

IN THE NEWS

A HUMAN PERSPECTIVE

CLEARING THE BOOKS

Frank, a 26-year-old previously convicted burglar, was arrested by police inside an appliance store he had broken into. There was little doubt in Frank's mind that he was going to be convicted and sent back to prison. The detectives who interrogated him realized his desperate plight and seized the opportunity to improve their own difficulties with a dramatically increasing burglary rate.

The detectives approached Frank with a "deal" that they described as mutually beneficial. If Frank would accept responsibility for approximately fifty unsolved burglaries, they would put in a "good word" for him with the local prosecutor, judge, and parole and probation officer who would eventually be doing his presentence investigation. Frank, of course, would only be charged with the crime he actually committed. Frank agreed, and as the detectives promised, they put in a "good word" with the appropriate people. In turn for his help in "clearing the books," Frank was given a lighter sentence than he might normally have received.

UCR Hierarchy Rule

When a crime is recorded for UCR purposes, only the most serious crime appearing in the UCR hierarchy is scored. For example, if an individual broke into a person's home, raped a woman, and stole jewelry, only the most serious crime in the UCR hierarchy (rape) would be scored for UCR purposes. Many critics argue that, because of this rule, UCR information on the actual level of criminal activity is incomplete at best.

Lack of Information on Part II Crimes

The nation's crime rate, as defined by the FBI Uniform Crime Reports, includes only the eight "index" or Part I offenses. Unfortunately, Part II crimes, or "other" offenses, are recorded for UCR purposes only when an arrest is made. Some examples of Part II crimes are simple assault; forgery; fraud; embezzlement; buying, receiving, or possessing stolen goods; vandalism; sex offenses; violation of narcotic drug laws; gambling; and driving under the influence. Critics suggest that some of the Part II offenses should be elevated to the status of index offenses—including some police officials who devote resources to combat these crimes.

FUTURE OF THE UCR PROGRAM

Although UCR data have been widely used by law enforcement agencies, researchers, government policymakers, and the media, many criticisms of the program have arisen from the same sources. Many think the system needs to be expanded to cover a wider range of offenses and provide more detailed information on the nature of criminal incidents. Some indicate that the system needs to provide greater analytic flexibility, while others suggest that published reports should have more analysis and interpretation. Many question the accuracy of UCR data; UCR statistics appear to disagree in some ways with those of related sources, such as the National Crime Survey, but the form of UCR data prevents meaningful comparison or reconciliation between different crime series. At the same time, the data processing capabilities of state programs and large police and sheriffs' agencies have begun to outpace the antiquated methods of the national UCR program.

Based on the extensive criticism and the rapidly changing data processing environment, the IACP three times called for a review of the UCR program. In response, the Bureau of Justice Statistics and the Federal Bureau of Investigation formed a joint task force, which in 1982 contracted with Abt Associates, Inc., to determine what, if any, changes should be made to the current national UCR program.[7] The study encompassed all aspects of the program, including its objectives and intended user audience, data items, reporting mechanisms, quality control, publications and user services, and relationships with other criminal justice data systems.

CTQ

If you could change the UCR system, which Part II crimes would you add to the crime index? Justify your response.

The redesigned UCR program is called the **National Incident-Based Reporting System (NIBRS).** NIBRS collects data on each single incident and arrest in twenty-two categories. For each offense known to police within these categories, incident, victim, property, offender, and arrestee information are gathered when available. The goal of the redesign is to modernize crime information by collecting data presently maintained in law enforcement records; the enhanced UCR program is, therefore, a by-product of current records systems. The implementation of NIBRS is occurring at a pace commensurate with the resources, abilities, and limitations of the contributing law enforcement agencies. The UCR's long-running statistical series integrity will, of course, be maintained.

> **CTQ**
> What improvements would you suggest be made to the UCR method of collecting and reporting crime data?

COLLECTION OF CAMPUS CRIME DATA

The federal government has recently shown much interest in the extent and nature of campus crime. Its interest has manifested into a clear commitment to ensure that victim services, especially sexual victimization services, are available to the campus community, and that this availability is communicated to the campus community. Its interest and actions will have a lasting impact on the roles and functions of campus law enforcement.[8] Following the on-campus murder of Jeanne Clery, a Lehigh University (Pa.) student, her family was successful in pushing for state and federal laws regarding campus crime data and related issues. Congress passed the Student Right-to-Know and Campus Security Act and President Bush signed it into law in 1990. The act and its subsequent amendments require all higher-education institutions, both public and private, that participate in federal Title IV financial aid programs to publicly disclose their respective campus crime statistics, security policy, and victim services. The act states that schools must "prepare, publish, and distribute, through appropriate publications or mailings, to all current students and employees, and to any applicant for enrollment or employment upon request, an annual security report" containing campus security policies and campus crime statistics for that institution (see 20 U.S.C. § 1092[f][1]). The original law required schools to publish statistics for murder, rape, robbery, aggravated assault, burglary, and motor vehicle theft. In addition, schools had to publish arrests for liquor-law, drug-law, and weapons-law violations. The law was amended by the Higher Education Act of 1992 to require schools to replace rape statistics with data for forcible and nonforcible sex offenses.

The Student Right-to-Know and Campus Security Act was the first federal mandate to require colleges and universities to publicly report their crime statistics. Prior to the passage of the act, there was no requirement for schools to report any crime to the FBI for inclusion in the UCR. Since 1972, when the FBI began including colleges and universities in the UCR, very few schools reported to it. In 1991, for example, only 12 percent of all colleges and universities in the United States reported their crime statistics to the UCR. As a result, little was actually known about what and how many crimes were known to campus police.

In 1991, Congress amended the act to include the Campus Sexual Assault Victims' Bill of Rights, which requires colleges and universities to develop and publish, as part of their annual security report, policies regarding the awareness and prevention of sexual assaults and to afford basic rights to sexual assault victims. The requirements are as follows: (1) The "accuser and accused must have the same opportunity to have others present (at the disciplinary hearing), (2) both parties shall be informed of the outcome of any disciplinary proceeding, (3) victims shall be informed of their options to notify law enforcement, (4) victims shall be notified of counseling services, and (5) victims shall be notified of options for changing academic and living situations." In addition to counseling services, victims must also be informed of medical and legal assistance.

The act was amended again in 1998 to include additional reporting obligations (such as for manslaughter and arson), extensive campus security-related provisions, and the requirement of keeping a daily public crime log for the first time. The 1998 amendments officially changed the name of the Act to the Jeanne Clery Disclosure of Campus Sex Policy and Campus Crime Statistics Act (20 U.S.C. § 1092).

In the fall of 1999, the U.S. Justice Department awarded $8.1 million to twenty-one colleges and universities to develop, implement, and improve campus-based programs and services for victims of sexual assault, domestic violence, and stalking. The universities and colleges receiving these funds must train campus police about responding to sexual assault, domestic violence, and stalking, and must establish a mandatory prevention and education program on violence against women for all incoming students. Many of these schools are developing comprehensive victim response systems that include the campus police, faculty, student organizations, health and counseling services, and local law enforcement.

WHAT CRIME DOES TO VICTIMS AND SOCIETY

There is always a danger when studying aggregate data on crime to overlook the tragic impact it has on individual victims and society. Victims are too often lumped into a "victim profile," where they become part of a "crime trend." People who study crime should never lose sight of the fact that crime has tragic effects on people and their families and an equally important and profound effect on the way we live and interact as a society. The remainder of this chapter provides valuable insight into this aspect of crime.

The Victim in Historical Perspective

Redress of injury was once the responsibility of the victims themselves, their immediate families, or others bound to them by blood or tribal loyalties. Thus, the beginnings of social control are apparent in the transition from the individual quest for retaliation to the identification of injuries sustained by the victim with the interests of the victim's family or social group. This idea of familial or blood relationships is central to the concept of the "blood feud." Consanguinity implied a responsibility on the part of the individual's relatives to act on his or her behalf in seeking compensation or vengeance for injuries sustained as the result of a criminal act.

With the increase in population and the growth of the organs of social control, however, it became necessary for the rest of society to set limits on the blood feud. An obvious problem with the private vendetta was the lack of effective means to bring a particular dispute to conclusion. Once started, vendettas tended to become perpetual; each injury spawned a search for vengeance in the form of a counterinjury, and an endless cycle of retaliation and counterretaliation was thus inflicted on society.

Talion Law

Talion law (*lex talionis*) represented an early effort by society to constrain the widening circle of damage caused by the blood feud. Central to this law was the concept of "equivalent retaliation." An individual who had suffered injury or loss of property was entitled to a fair and just recompense—one that did not exceed the original injury or loss. Thus, talion law was an effort toward social defense (that is, toward the imposition of curbs upon parties to the vendetta to protect and maintain the social organization of the tribe or clan).

Victim Compensation

With the establishment of the king as a strong central authority, the conception of crime changed, as did the methods used to deal with lawbreakers. A crime was defined as an offense against the king's peace and was consequently dealt with by public authority. The dominant way of handling offenders shifted away from compensation and restitution to various methods of corporal punishment and, more recently, to incarceration.

By the middle of the twentieth century, interest in the idea of compensation to crime victims had been renewed. This phenomenon, which may be seen as part of a more general concern for civil rights and the rights of minorities, has led to a renewed emphasis by criminologists on the victim's role in the criminal justice system.

GOVERNMENT PROGRAMS FOR VICTIMS

Crime victims can hardly be blamed for feeling that the American system of criminal justice has historically neglected them in its concern for the rights of offenders. Not only do victims suffer financial losses, but they are also often forced to pay for the treatment of

---

WEB

For more information on the collection of crime data, **visit our Web site, www.prenhall.com/territo**.

CTQ

Why is it important to collect campus crime data separately from the UCR?

WEB

For more information on what crime does to victims and society, **visit our Web site, www.prenhall.com/territo**.

WEB

For more information on victim compensation, **visit our web site, www.prenhall.com/territo**.

CTQ
Why do you suppose the American criminal justice system has until recently largely ignored the victims of crime?

their injuries. In contrast, the criminal in custody receives free medical attention. Public funds pay for the prosecution, and if the criminal has no money, public funds also pay for the defense.

Further, victims may be threatened with reprisal by defendants who are freed on bail or on their own recognizance. Victims can be intimidated by domineering defense attorneys and forced to take days off from work to appear as witnesses in hearings that are postponed again and again. Rarely are they notified of court dates, and no one bothers to keep them posted about the results of plea bargaining. Months may pass before they are able to recover stolen property being held as evidence.

Crime victims may often receive insensitive or callous treatment from the criminal justice system:

- There may be insensitive questioning.
- There may be innuendos that the victim was somehow at fault. (There is a dilemma here—often the police do not know who was at fault and whether the apparent victim was the aggressor or somehow provoked the offender; aggressive questioning may be a necessary investigative technique.)
- The victim may have difficulty learning what is happening with the case.
- Property may be kept as evidence for a long time or may never be returned.[9]

Some state legislation regarding victims of crimes now allows for the introduction of **victim impact statements** at the sentencing stage of the criminal justice process. These statements are used to inform the sentencing judge of the physical, financial, and emotional impact of the crime on the victim or the victim's survivors.

Compensable Crimes

Claimants' eligibility for **compensation** depends on the type of crime in which they were injured. About three-fourths of the statutes define compensable crimes in broad language, similar to the Uniform Crime Victims Reparations Act:[10]

Criminally injurious conduct means conduct that (1) occurs or is attempted in this State, (2) poses a substantial threat of personal injury or death, and (3) is punishable by fine, imprisonment, or death. . . .

Eligibility Requirements for Victims

Eligibility requirements are a cornerstone of state victim compensation programs. Eligibility requirements have undergone substantial change, reflecting important shifts in public values on criminal victimization. Eligibility is a broad concept, involving who was victimized, the type of crime that occurred, the type and amount of loss sustained, and claimants' meeting certain procedural requirements in filing claims.

WEB
For more information on eligibility requirements for victims, visit our Web site, www.prenhall.com/territo.

Although state victim compensation programs differ in the specific crimes compensated, most include a basic core of offenses that can result in substantial physical harm. The following crimes are those for which compensation is most commonly available:

- Fatalities and injuries due to drunk drivers
- Homicide
- Rape
- Robbery
- Aggravated assault (including domestic and all other assaults)
- Child abuse (combining sexual and physical abuse)

CTQ
Do you think state victim compensation programs should extend the basic core of criminal offenses for which a victim can apply for compensation? If so, what types of crimes do you believe would also warrant victim compensation?

Restitution

Restitution sometimes involves partial or complete payments voluntarily offered by adult criminal offenders—particularly for white-collar crimes—to allay prosecution or to mitigate the sentence. More commonly, however, it involves offender-restitution-to-the-victim schemes that consider both punishment and offender rehabilitation.

Restitution by adult offenders, either as a condition of probation or voluntarily offered, has been largely limited to cases of fraud, embezzlement, forgery, and other

IN THE WORKPLACE

RAPE COUNSELOR

Responsible for providing phone and face-to-face counseling to victims of rape, sexual assault, or abuse. Performs a variety of duties, including the following: provide information and referrals, document contacts and statistics, receive training in counseling and advocacy skills, and provide community education services. Minimum qualifications generally are as follows: high school diploma or equivalent; 20 years old; and ability to demonstrate skills in interpersonal communications, therapeutic techniques, and management.

---

white-collar offenses. In cases involving vandalism by juvenile offenders against schools, churches, and public property, there is usually little relationship between the amount of restitution—usually paid in services rather than in money—and the actual extent of damage.

Victim and Witness Intimidation Issues and Responses

Intimidation of victims and witnesses undermines the functioning of the justice system by denying critical evidence to police and prosecutors. This long-standing problem also erodes confidence in the government's ability to protect citizens. Victim and witness intimidation has usually been associated with organized-crime and domestic violence cases. But this form of intimidation is developing new characteristics as its occurrence increases in urban drug- and gang-related violent crime.[11]

Intimidation can be characterized as follows:

- Case-specific—threats or violence intended to dissuade a victim or witness from testifying in a specific case.
- Community-wide—acts by gangs or drug-selling groups intended to foster a general atmosphere of fear and noncooperation within a neighborhood or community.

Intimidation Prevention and Control Prosecutors, law enforcement, and the judiciary have critical roles to play in any program to prevent victim and witness intimidation. Law enforcement officers are better positioned than prosecutors to foresee and prevent intimidation at the street level. Law enforcement officers can inform prosecutors about repeat offenders and potential intimidators, alert prosecutors to potential witnesses who are being intimidated, and reduce gang income and intimidation by disrupting gang operations with intensive policing tactics. In one small jurisdiction, community police officers found it effective to visit the families of potential intimidators and explain the laws concerning obstruction of justice. In another community where intimidation was severe, police officers reassured tenants in gang-dominated housing projects by establishing field precincts in empty apartments and storefronts, or by bringing in a mobile precinct, in order to decrease response time. In one jurisdiction where a comprehensive witness

WEB
For more information on restitution, visit our Web site, www.prenhall.com/territo.

CTQ
To what extent do you think victim and witness intimidation undermines the functionality of the criminal justice system?

IN THE WORKPLACE

VICTIM ADVOCATE

Responsible for review and assessment of violent crime reports to assist victims and witnesses of all crime categories. Performs a variety of assignments, including the following: assist victims of crimes, serve as liaison between the court system and victims of crimes who are going through the court process, act as an advocate for victims of crime, and assist in volunteer training. Minimum qualifications generally are as follows: high school diploma or equivalent, some work-related experience in the criminal justice system, and knowledge of police terminology.

security program was being established by the prosecutor's office, police reported approximately two hundred violent gang- and drug-related crimes that had not been presented to the prosecutor due to witness intimidation. With better communication between police and prosecutors, these witnesses might have been persuaded to enter the new witness security program and testify.

Cooperation with the Judiciary   In jurisdictions where the judiciary takes threats against victims and witnesses seriously, prosecutors were much more confident in their ability to deter intimidation and secure witness testimony. Prosecutors and police suggested that gang-related victim and witness intimidation could be reduced in court when judges were knowledgeable about gang characteristics and were willing to exclude from the courtroom people who wore identifying colors or made threatening hand signs. In some jurisdictions, additional judicial resources were provided to expedite cases where victim and witness intimidation had become a factor.

Targets of Victim and Witness Intimidation   No typical victim of intimidation exists, but interview respondents and working-group participants pointed to four factors that increase the chance that a victim or witness will be intimidated:

- The violent nature of the initial crime
- A previous personal connection to the defendant
- Geographic proximity to the defendant
- Cultural vulnerability—that is, membership in an easily victimized group, such as the elderly, children, or recent or illegal immigrants

Residents of gang-dominated neighborhoods are likely to fall into more than one of these categories, greatly increasing their exposure to intimidation.

Most nonviolent crimes (such as drug sales or use, burglaries, or white-collar crimes) rarely involve victim and witness intimidation. By contrast, victims and witnesses in violent crime cases (such as rape, murder, and gang assaults), where more severe penalties may be imposed, are at higher risk of experiencing intimidation.

In general, victims and witnesses who have no previous relationship and share no community ties with the defendant or suspect are better insulated from intimidation. Victims and witnesses who have been—and stay—relocated and are able to keep their home and work addresses secret are also generally immune to intimidation. Prosecutors and police consider it extremely rare for a defendant or associate to leave his or her own community or socioeconomic milieu to intimidate a victim or witness in another jurisdiction.

VICTIMIZATION STUDIES

The official counting of crimes is susceptible to many errors. A major reason for inaccuracy in official crime statistics is that people are reluctant, for a variety of reasons, to report that they have been victimized. Fortunately, victimization studies provide supplemental crime data. Victimization studies and investigations ask people to indicate the frequency and types of crimes that have been perpetrated against them. In addition to gathering information on selected crimes of violence and theft, these surveys also collect data on the characteristics of victims and the circumstances surrounding criminal acts—including victim-offender relationships, characteristics of offenders, victim self-protection, extent of victim injuries, time and place of occurrence, economic consequences to victims, use of weapons, whether the police were called, and reasons advanced for not calling the police.

In general, victimization surveys confirm that groups disproportionately involved in the perpetration of crimes—the young, males, the poor, and African Americans—are also the groups most likely to be victimized (both by crimes against the person and crimes against property). In addition, residents of the central city—our urban ghettos—are much more vulnerable to crime victimization than people who live in nonmetropolitan areas or suburbs. Among commercial victims, retail stores suffer the highest rates of burglary and robbery.

Fear of crime in America is often related to concern about being the victim of a violent crime committed by a stranger. Many surveys have shown, however, that friends, acquaintances, or relatives are more often the ones involved in the commission of violent crimes against persons.

NATIONAL CRIME DATA COLLECTION

The U.S. Department of Justice administers two statistical programs to measure the magnitude, nature, and impact of crime in the nation: the Uniform Crime Reporting (UCR) Program, described earlier, and the **National Crime Victimization Survey (NCVS).** Each of these programs produces valuable information about aspects of the nation's crime problem. Because the UCR and NCVS programs are conducted for different purposes, use different methods, and focus on somewhat different aspects of crime, the information they produce together provides a more comprehensive panorama of the nation's crime problem than either could produce alone.[12]

National Crime Victimization Survey

The Bureau of Justice Statistics' NCVS, which began in 1973, provides a detailed picture of crime incidents, victims, and trends. U.S. Bureau of the Census personnel interview all household members at least 12 years old in a nationally representative sample of approximately 50,000 households. Households stay in the sample for three years and are interviewed at six-month intervals.

The NCVS collects information on crimes suffered by individuals and households, whether or not those crimes were reported to law enforcement. It estimates the proportion of each crime type reported to law enforcement, and it summarizes the reasons that victims give for reporting or not reporting.

The survey provides data or both the offenders and the crimes. Questions also cover the experiences of victims with the criminal justice system, self-protective measures used by victims, and possible substance abuse by offenders.

Comparing UCR and NCVS

Because the NCVS was designed to complement the UCR Program, the two programs share many similarities. As much as their different collection methods permit, the two measure many of the same serious crimes, defined alike. Both programs cover rape, robbery, aggravated assault, burglary, theft, and motor vehicle theft.

There are also significant differences between the two programs. First, the two programs were created to serve different purposes. The UCR Program's primary objective is to provide a reliable set of criminal justice statistics for law enforcement administration, operation, and management. The NCVS was established to provide previously unavailable information about crime (including crime not reported to police), victims, and offenders.

Second, the two programs measure an overlapping but nonidentical set of crimes. The NCVS includes crimes both reported and not reported to law enforcement.

Third, because of methodology, the NCVS and UCR definitions of some crimes differ. For example, the UCR defines burglary as the unlawful entry or attempted entry of a structure to commit a felony or theft. The NCVS, not wanting to ask victims to ascertain offender motives, defines burglary as the entry or attempted entry of a residence by a person who had no right to be there.

Fourth, for property crimes (burglary, theft, and motor vehicle theft), the two programs calculate crime rates using different bases. The UCR rates for these crimes are per capita (number of crimes per 100,000 persons), whereas the NCVS rates for these crimes are per household (number of crimes per 1,000 households).

By understanding the strengths and limitations of each program, it is possible to use the UCR and NCVS to achieve a greater understanding of crime trends and the nature of crime in the United States. For example, changes in police procedures, shifting attitudes toward crime and police, and other societal changes can affect the extent to which people report and law enforcement agencies record crime. NCVS and UCR data can be used in concert to explore why trends in self-reported and police-reported crime may differ.

CTQ

Why do you think, that people who live in urban centers are more vulnerable to crime victimization than those who live in nonurban areas such as suburbs?

WEB

For more information on the National Crime Victimization Survey (NCVS) data, go to **http://www.ojp.usdoj.gov/bjs/**.

Race and Victims of Violence

Data drawn from the NCVS have consistently underscored the differences between the victimization rates of whites and members of minority groups. For example, African Americans experience higher rates of household and violent crimes than whites. NCVS data have demonstrated over the years that certain population groups (the poor, central-city residents, males, and younger people) have typically had higher victimization rates. Because proportionately more minorities are associated with some of the population groups, it is not altogether surprising to see a higher victimization rate.

Data published by the Bureau of Justice Statistics in 2001 report that Native Americans have the highest per-capita rate of violent victimizations, while Asians have the lowest rate of violent victimization. African Americans were disproportionately represented among homicide victims.[13]

Issues with Victim Surveys

The value of information obtained from victimization studies depends on the accuracy and reliability of the survey techniques. A key issue is the adequacy of the sample on which the results are based. Other factors include the fallibility of memory of crime victims and the truthfulness—or lack of it—that characterizes survey responses.

Early victimization studies (those conducted for the President's Commission on Law Enforcement and Administration of Justice in 1967) were criticized because approximately one-quarter of the people who were approached refused to be interviewed, thus introducing an immediate bias into the sample. The National Opinion Research Center's study was challenged because only one available adult in each household was questioned—a method that produced an overrepresentation of women and older people (the people most likely to be at home during the day). These problems were overcome in later surveys, in which everyone over age 12 in a household was interviewed; these surveys obtained nearly 100 percent participation of eligible people and eliminated the excessive reliance on the responses of a single individual in a household.

Victims do not always remember crimes that were perpetrated against them during a given period. In some cases, they may not even be aware that they were victims (for example, in such offenses as fraud, embezzlement, and buying stolen property). It is also possible that victimization figures are inflated by respondents who give false reports to justify illegal tax deductions or spurious insurance claims. Unfortunately, there is no easy way to gauge the extent of such overreporting.

SPECIAL CATEGORIES OF VICTIMS

In recent years much attention has been drawn to specific categories of criminal victimization. Each category is significant enough to merit recognition and a response from the public at large and from practitioners within the criminal justice system.

Intimate-Partner Violence

Recent estimates from the National Crime Victimization Survey (NCVS) indicate that about one million violent crimes were committed against people by their current or former spouses, boyfriends, or girlfriends. Such crimes, termed *intimate-partner violence*, are committed primarily against women. About 85 percent of victimizations by intimate partners were against women. Other results reported by the Bureau of Justice Statistics in 2000 include the following:[14]

- Intimate-partner violence made up 22 percent of violent crimes against women. By contrast, intimate partners committed 3 percent of the violence against men.
- The percentage of female murder victims killed by intimate partners has remained at about 30 percent since 1976.
- Considered by age category, women age 16 to 24 experienced the highest per-capita rates of intimate-partner violence.
- About half of the intimate-partner violence against women was reported to police; African American women were more likely than other women to report such violence.

- About four of ten female victims of intimate-partner violence lived in households with children under age 12. Population estimates suggest that 27 percent of U.S. households were home to children under 12.
- Half of female victims of intimate-partner violence reported a physical injury. About four in ten of these victims sought professional medical treatment.

Handling Cases of Domestic Violence   Nationwide, many homicides and serious assaults result from domestic disputes (see Figure 4.5). Minor violence, which usually precedes serious injuries, is far more pervasive. Although it is hard to measure, family violence is probably the most widespread form of violence in the country and can occur in all social classes and income groups. Most of the cases to which police are called involve poor people. Whether this is because lower-income people are likelier to call the police, because lower-income people are likelier to be victims of family violence, or because of other factors is unclear. In a study in Minneapolis (discussed in more detail below), a city with about 5 percent unemployment, about 60 percent of the males in the households to which police were called were unemployed.[15]

Handling a violent domestic incident has never been an easy matter for police, and for years arrest was unusual as long as the police themselves were not assaulted or insulted. In the late 1960s the police became more involved in the conflict itself and tried to act as mediators or counselors. The U.S. Department of Justice provided funds to police departments to support training for police officers in techniques of counseling and mediation.

By the mid-1970s, however, the innovative mediation approaches came under criticism because, it was argued, they did not provide sufficient punishment for spouse abusers or child abusers. Advocates of victims demanded that police arrest offenders, and they filed lawsuits in New York City and elsewhere to enforce their demand. Although these suits had some impact, in 1984 a survey of big-city police departments found that only 10 percent encouraged officers to make arrests in domestic violence cases, while 40 percent still encouraged mediation and 50 percent had no policy at all.

There are many possible explanations why traditionally the police have not arrested assailants in domestic violence cases. One of the most important is that in the past, the police had legal authority to make an arrest only if they witnessed the incident or if they had obtained an arrest warrant from a judge. This is because the law treats much domestic violence as a misdemeanor, a less serious offense. Traditionally only for felonies, the more serious offenses, may an arrest be made without a warrant or without witnessing the alleged criminal conduct.

Even where the police are permitted to make arrests on their own authority, they are often afraid the arrest will backfire and produce more violence rather than less. They may even decide not to make an arrest out of fear that the offender will return to the victim and inflict even more harm.

In explaining why arrests in domestic violence cases are not more common, police also cite the frequent change of heart victims have the day after the assault and their refusal to cooperate with a criminal prosecution—both reasons for dropping the charges. Police argue that it is pointless to make an arrest if there will be no court-imposed punishment to produce a deterrent effect, and it is very difficult to obtain court-imposed punishment unless the victim cooperates.

Many police also consider the risk of injury to themselves if they make an arrest. Academies have taught, and most police believe, that domestic "disturbance" calls are among the most dangerous tasks police face.

A major experiment was conducted in the mid-1980s by the Police Foundation in Minneapolis to determine whether mediation, separation, or arrest works best at reducing subsequent violence against the victim. The premise was that police practice should be guided by knowledge about the actual effects of using one policy instead of another.

The experiment was conducted by police officers who agreed to give up their discretion in domestic assault cases and to take whatever action was dictated by a random system of employing arrest in some cases, mediation in others, and separation. This method attempts to ensure that those arrested, those advised, and those ordered out of the house were roughly comparable in average age, education, income, rate of offending, percentage who were black or white, and whether they were intoxicated. Otherwise, the police would have arrested only

WEB

For more information on intimate-partner violence, **visit our Web site, www.prenhall.com/territo**.

CTQ

Do you think that intimate-partner violence should be treated more seriously by justice officials due to the likelihood of future violence, or should mediation be promoted as a way to resolve domestic disputes?

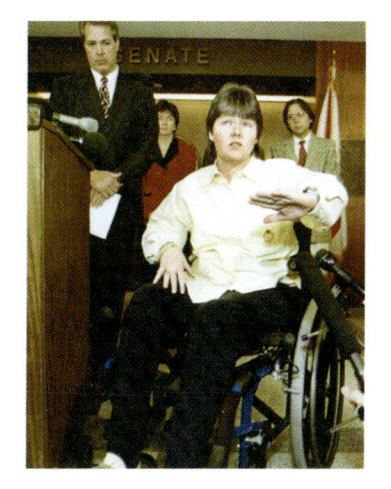

FIGURE 4.5

Victims of domestic violence may suffer emotional and physical disabilities. This victim has spoken to a group of legislators in an effort to seek additional funding to support other victims of domestic violence.

Courtesy Don Edgar/AP/Wide World Photos.

WEB

For more information on handling domestic violence, **visit our Web site, www.prenhall.com/territo.**

the most "serious" offenders, who might then have had the highest rate of repeat violence—not because they were arrested, but because they were unusually violent people.

After the police completed their work on a case, Police Foundation researchers contacted the victims and attempted to interview them every two weeks for the next six months. The main focus of the interviews was to discover whether the offenders had repeated their assault. Repeat violence was also measured by tracking, for six months, all of the official records of repeat contacts between police and offenders (or victims). Under both methods of measurement, the arrested offenders were about half as likely to commit repeat violence as the nonarrested offenders. The official records showed that about 18 percent of all offenders repeated their violence, while only 10 percent of the arrested offenders repeated it. Findings from the interviews with victims were similar. The researchers note that their findings should not generalize to all locations and in all cases.

In some cities domestic violence cases are handled differently than in Minneapolis. For example, some departments employ a special unit, the **domestic crisis intervention unit,** to handle domestic violence calls. Police working in this unit receive extensive training in mediation and use it in most simple assault cases, although they may make an arrest if it seems appropriate.

One strength of this type of program is the provision for longer-term treatment through a network of social service agencies working together. Social workers play an important role in the program, particularly in follow-up treatment. Referrals for treatment of offenders may come through court orders after arrest. See Figure 4.6 for an example of a form used by police in domestic violence cases.

FIGURE 4.6

Domestic Violence Victim Information Form

Domestic Violence Checklist
Initial Investigative Checklist

Report Number _____

	Yes	No
1. Written Statement of the Victim	☐	☐
2. Taped Statement of the Victim	☐	☐
3. Oral Statement of the Victim	☐	☐
4. Photos of the Victim	☐	☐
5. Photos of the Defendant	☐	☐
6. Crime Scene Photos	☐	☐
7. Witnesses (Other Family Present)	☐	☐
8. Witnesses (Nonfamily)	☐	☐
9. Victim Taken to Hospital	☐	☐
a. Hospital Records?	☐	☐
b. Name of Doctor	☐	☐
10. Paramedic Records/Statements?	☐	☐
11. Crime Scene Description (Damage, etc.)	☐	☐
12. Weapons Seized	☐	☐
13. Lab Reports	☐	☐
14. 9-1-1 Tape or Wav File	☐	☐
15. Police Department Call-in Tape (If Different)	☐	☐
16. Statements/Admission by Defendant	☐	☐
17. Other Evidence (Torn Clothes, etc.)	☐	☐
18. Domestic Violence Brochure Issued	☐	☐
19. Witness Card Issued	☐	☐
20. Does Report Indicate Why No Arrest Was Made?	☐	☐

Postinvestigation Stage

	Yes	No
1. Does Victim Wish to Prosecute*	☐	☐
2. Photo Taken (Injuries More Developed)	☐	☐
3. Statement Consistent with Police Report	☐	☐
4. Past Violence	☐	☐
5. Injunction	☐	☐
6. Visible Injuries Noted	☐	☐
7. Contact Person Listed in Report	☐	☐
8. Impact Statement	☐	☐
9. Was Report Sent to Domestic Violence Center?	☐	☐

*If no prosecution desired state reasons:

Source: Courtesy of Chief Tony Velong, Temple Terrace, Florida, Police Department.

"In the News: Transitions: Responding to the Needs of Domestic Violence Victims" describes how one police agency has dealt with victims of domestic violence.

The Violence against Women Act The Violence against Women Act (VAWA) created a federal initiative to encourage—indeed, to require—the coming together of various professions and perspectives to forge partnerships in responding to violence against women

IN THE NEWS

A HUMAN PERSPECTIVE

TRANSITIONS: RESPONDING TO THE NEEDS OF DOMESTIC VIOLENCE VICTIMS
by Cheryl Rucinski

Over the years, various crimes have demanded law enforcement attention. Drugs, violent crime, and domestic violence all have pulled the focus of police departments, law makers, and society alike. In many cases, the law enforcement response to these types of crimes has changed.

Just as many police departments have done, the Cheektowaga, New York, Police Department identified domestic violence as a priority. The department developed a proarrest policy and provided extensive training to its 125-officer force. Yet, 10 years later, a significant number of officers misunderstood the department's domestic violence initiatives. In fact, the department seemed to have developed a culture that remained unresponsive to the needs of the victims and families of domestic violence. Discovering this through surveys, training evaluations, and verbal feedback from the officers, the department immediately set out to improve the officers' understanding, attitudes, and behavior.

MISUNDERSTANDING THE NATURE OF DOMESTIC VIOLENCE
In a home fractured by domestic violence, offenders seek power and control over their victims. Thus, when an officer exhibits biased or hostile attitudes or controlling behavior, whether intentional or not, victims can view the officer's behavior as no different than that of the offender. Some victims withdraw under these circumstances; others become highly emotional. No one's needs are served in a discourse of this nature. The department does not develop sufficient information to prosecute the offender. The victim feels further victimized and becomes less likely to report future incidents of violence. When attitude problems become a barrier to the effective delivery of services to the victim, the cycle of violence continues.

MAKING THE TRANSITION
To address these concerns, the Cheektowaga Police Department entered into a joint endeavor with Haven House, the local battered women's shelter, and the National Conference, a human relations organization dedicated to recognizing diversity and combating prejudice. Because of its dual roles of moving the department to a new way of responding to domestic violence and helping victims transcend their abusers, the project was christened Transitions. Its objectives included:

- Dispelling invalid myths about victims of domestic violence that officers may harbor
- Increasing the interpersonal and communication skills of responding officers
- Reducing bias and discrimination by officers toward victims
- Increasing officers' ability to recognize the violent human dynamics in domestic scenarios
- Developing data identifying areas for growth and improvement.

In light of these objectives, the partners decided to focus the majority of the training on addressing attitude issues and the misconceptions held by the officers because these seemed to be the root cause of some of the communication problems between officers and domestic violence victims. Training was offered to all of the department's officers, emergency dispatchers, and civilian personnel, as well as to police officers from other local agencies. In all, 300 public safety employees attended the Transitions conference.

SEEING RESULTS
Following the training, officers completed a written survey to provide feedback. Several officers stated that it was the best training session they had attended in their careers. They learned how their prejudices, words, and actions had affected interaction with domestic violence partners and took away concrete ideas on how to improve their respect to both offenders and victims. Many officers made suggestions for follow-up programs. Moreover, in months following the Transitions training, domestic violence victims praised the department's responsiveness to their needs.

CONCLUSION
Domestic violence is a complicated issue, and responding officers no longer can afford to give offenders time to cool off or tell couples to kiss and make up. Both offenders and victims may need a variety of interventions to help them break the cycle of violence. The police represent their first step on the road to recovery. Yet, myths and misconceptions can block that route, as the Cheektowaga Police Department discovered, paying attention to its officers' attitudes and behaviors.

Source: C. Rucinski. "Transitions: Responding to the Needs of Domestic Violence Victims." *FBI Law Enforcement Bulletin.* April 1998, pp. 15–18.

in all its forms.[16] In framing the legislation, Congress heeded the advice of advocates, practitioners, and service providers at the local level who know from their own experience that a coordinated, community-wide response is the best response.

Looking at the issue from a historical perspective reveals how far the system has evolved. Twenty years ago, most criminal justice practitioners thought it inappropriate even to allow victims a voice in criminal proceedings. Shelters for battered women were rare, and the latest reform in policing was the idea that officers should be trained to respond to family disputes by serving as mediators and counselors and to use arrest only as a last resort.

Over the past two decades, research has produced some valuable findings that have shaped the development of the criminal justice system's response to the problem of violence against women. The National Institute of Justice has had a major role in some of that research, with one area of particular note—our study of the effects of mandatory arrest in cases of spouse assault. The first path-breaking study, conducted more than fifteen years ago in Minneapolis, found that when police officers made an arrest, the person charged was less likely to recidivate than if they took another course of action (removing the suspect from the home or providing counseling and mediation).

In subsequent studies the results were not as definitive as in the original. In some cities the Minneapolis findings were confirmed; in others the findings were mixed, with reduced violence observed among men who were arrested, but only among those who were employed. By contrast, unemployed men were just as likely to engage in violence again whether or not they had been arrested for the initial incident.

These findings are consistent with the notion that people who are less invested in society are more prone to criminal behavior. But again, what should be the policy implications? To many, it is obvious that the cities with mixed results could hardly have mandated arrest for employed men and allowed police discretion for unemployed men. In this situation, a different overriding value must be preserved—that of equal enforcement of the law.

Need for a Theoretical Framework While in the process of implementing the Violence against Women Act, law enforcement agencies need to answer a number of questions: Will the type of coordinated response required in VAWA ensure greater safety for women? Will it deter violent behavior? Will it break the cycle of violence within the family?

In considering these questions, we should also push the limits of belief in the appropriateness of the criminal justice response in these cases. Should domestic violence be treated just as severely as (or even more severely than) violence committed against strangers? Does a belief in a criminal justice response mean we advocate domestic-violence versions of preventive-detention statutes, shock incarceration (boot camps), and three-strikes laws? And if not, why not?

These multiple questions suggest the need for a theoretical framework for shaping an "ideal" response to domestic violence. In shaping that framework, we should look to innovations happening elsewhere that can provide guidance, while still taking into account the uniqueness of this type of criminal behavior.

Innovations Suggest a Direction In conceptualizing a new theoretical framework, two innovations can inform our thinking. The first is found in community policing, whose philosophy is grounded in the twin notions of problem solving and partnership with the community. The police, in concert with the community, identify a problem involving crime or disorder, define a strategy for responding, and subsequently evaluate the effectiveness of the response. Few crime problems lend themselves as well to this pragmatic, results-oriented approach as does violence in the family. From this perspective, the mission of the police becomes not just to enforce the law but also to solve the problem. And solving the problem means reducing violence.

Creative police departments are experimenting with a number of strategies—location histories that record all responses to a particular residence, home visits to violent households by police officers and victim advocates explaining mandatory-arrest policies

---

WEB

For more information on the Violence against Women Act, visit our Web site, www.prenhall.com/territo.

CTQ

What role do you believe the Violence against Women Act played in reforming the criminal justice system's response to the problem of domestic violence?

and offering service referrals, emergency orders of protection to provide immediate safety, transportation to battered women's shelters, and personal call buttons that enable victims to activate 911. These strategies are all premised on the notion that the police are responsible not just for enforcement of the law but also for preventing the next crime.

A second innovation is the domestic violence court of Dade County, Florida, where judges mix criminal and civil jurisdictions and keep a case on their calendar long enough to determine whether the attitude and behavior of the defendant are changing. Counseling and other services are offered to the men, women, and, interestingly, children, who are silent victims of this violence. An entire community has been mobilized to support this court—including resident psychiatrists who provide *pro bono* service and school counselors who note changes in children's behavior in the classroom.

As in the community policing model (discussed in Chapter 5), this court focuses on problem solving. Traditional measures of judicial efficiency are discarded as judges keep cases on their calendars for long periods. Traditional notions of adversarial procedure are set aside as public defenders acquiesce in extended state control over their clients during periods of drug treatment and other therapies, and prosecutors forgo convictions and prison sentences in favor of therapeutic outcomes.

These relatively new approaches demonstrate that in seeking to build a framework for dealing with violence against women, we need more than simply a better-coordinated system of law enforcement and criminal justice. Criminal justice can make a difference, but for that to happen the system needs re-engineering that matches flexible governmental responses to this unique form of criminal behavior.

Another type of crime that often involves women as victims is stalking. "In the News: Stalking—Investigation Strategies" describes a stalking case and police efforts to deal with this crime.

Children as Victims

It is a sad commentary on modern society that children, like adults, become victims of crime. Any crime that can be committed against an adult can be perpetrated as easily (if not more so) upon a child. What is perhaps even more appalling is the fact that so little is known about the incidence and types of crimes committed against children. We do not even know the true magnitude of the problem.[17]

There is no single data source to consult for statistics on crimes committed against children. Although several sources provide partial information, attempts to develop a composite are confounded by variations in definitions and reporting practices. For example, sources define the end of childhood at different ages, varying from 12 to 16 to 18 to 21. Some sources provide only "snapshot" views of crimes occurring during a brief period and have not been routinely updated. Existing sources are also limited in the types of crimes for which they collect data on child victims. Admittedly, the available data are sketchy, but they do suggest that children become victims of crime more often than some may care to believe.

The FBI's Uniform Crime Reports (UCR) publishes crime statistics contributed by law enforcement agencies covering 97 percent of the American population. Although the UCR offers the most comprehensive picture of reported crime in the United States, it provides almost no information on crimes against children. With the exception of murder, UCR statistics are not reported by victim age.

No one knows the proportion of crimes against children that is reported to law enforcement or child protection authorities. Indeed, even the child's most trusted confidant may be unaware that something has happened. Very young children may simply lack the verbal capacity to report or the knowledge that an incident is inappropriate or criminal. Older children may be embarrassed. Many child victims are threatened into silence. When they do confide in trusted adults, their reports may be dismissed as fantasy or outright lies.

There are several reasons why some child sexual abuse cases, particularly intrafamilial cases, do not result in criminal prosecution. Cases that involve juvenile perpetrators are typically pursued in juvenile court. Some offenders are "diverted" into a supervised treatment program, and prosecution is deferred pending its outcome. Sometimes

CTQ

Do you believe community policing is an effective results-oriented approach to reducing violence against women?

CTQ

How is the crime of stalking perceived in society? In the media? Do you believe stalking deserves more attention on the part of criminal justice officials due to its potential for future violence? If so, explain why in brief.

IN THE NEWS
A HUMAN PERSPECTIVE

STALKING—INVESTIGATION STRATEGIES
by George E. Wattendorf, J.D.

On a warm summer evening some years ago, an officer received a call that shots had been fired at a residence. When the officer arrived at the home, a woman, crying and shaking, opened the door. The officer noticed blood trickling from the woman's head. She told the officer that she thought her ex-husband had broken into her house and fired a gun at her while she was sleeping. After investigating, the officer found a single .38 caliber round of ammunition embedded in the mattress near a pillow where the woman had been sleeping.

The woman explained to the officer that her divorce had been finalized just the week before. She also advised that her ex-husband had threatened her, saying, "If I can't have you, no one will." She described letters she had received from her ex-husband and the feeling that he had been watching her (i.e., he could recite her daily routine and who she had been with at a particular time). She said that she had not reported the incidents to the police because she did not think her ex-husband had committed a crime. Upon further investigation, officers learned that her ex-husband suddenly had quit his job and sold his car and other possessions, and he had not been to his residence in another state for weeks. Additionally, evidence showed that the ex-husband had started drinking again after a long period of sobriety.

Despite the danger, the woman chose not to stay at a shelter until the police could apprehend her ex-husband. A few days later, the ex-husband waited for her at work. He shot her, emptying his .38 caliber revolver into her body at close range. He then committed suicide by driving his car into a large boulder.

Unfortunately for the victim in this real-life incident, her state had not yet enacted stalking laws. But if this tragic incident had occurred several years later, this woman might have reported her ex-husband's conduct to the police before the initial shooting. Moreover, if she had known what actions to take to protect herself, she might still be alive.

Stalking cases present unique challenges to law enforcement. Offenders do not adhere to predictable stalking patterns; therefore, no one knows what stalkers will do next or how far they will go. In some instances, stalkers limit harassment to annoying phone calls and letters, but other cases can escalate to assault or homicide.

CATEGORIZING STALKERS

Most stalking cases involve a male offender and a female victim who had some type of prior intimate relationship with each other. Although not as common, other types of stalking cases include acquaintance stalking, where the stalker and the victim may know each other casually (e.g., co-workers or neighbors), and stranger stalking, where the stalker and the victim do not know each other at all (e.g., victims who are celebrities or public figures). Often, acquaintance and stranger stalkers have a mental disorder such as erotomania—a delusional belief that the victim loves them.

CONCLUSION

At one time, the behavior associated with stalking was not considered a crime. Today, however, most jurisdictions have criminalized stalking. Moreover, greater awareness has led to the ability to charge offenders under such statutes as harassment or trespass. This capability often hinges on the investigator's ability to collect evidence and protect the victim.

Investigators should provide victims with the support they need to gather evidence and keep themselves safe. Victims should document and report every incident, save proof of the offender's behavior, and, most important, take safety precautions. Community service organizations can provide a lifeline for victims in this regard.

Stalking represents a crime that can leave victims psychologically traumatized, physically injured or even dead. For the sake of these victims, members of the criminal justice community need to take stalking threats seriously and work together to pursue, arrest, and prosecute stalkers.

Source: G. E. Wattendorf. "Stalking—Investigation Strategies." *FBI Law Enforcement Bulletin.* March 2000, pp. 10–14.

---

prosecutors and families choose not to subject a child to the perceived trauma of the criminal justice process.

From the prosecutor's perspective, victim and offense characteristics are perfectly sound reasons to decline a case. But what happens to the children when their cases are not prosecuted? Victims of stranger abuse may feel that no one believed them, and they may fear being victimized again. These children are sometimes at an advantage; with counseling and a supportive family, they may overcome some of the long-range effects of victimization. Victims of intrafamily abuse, however, may not fare as well. When their cases are not prosecuted in the criminal courts, the best they can hope for is a favorable outcome of juvenile court intervention. Perhaps the offender will obey a no-contact order. Perhaps he or she will be amenable to treatment. But in many cases, removing child victims from their homes and placing them in foster care is nec-

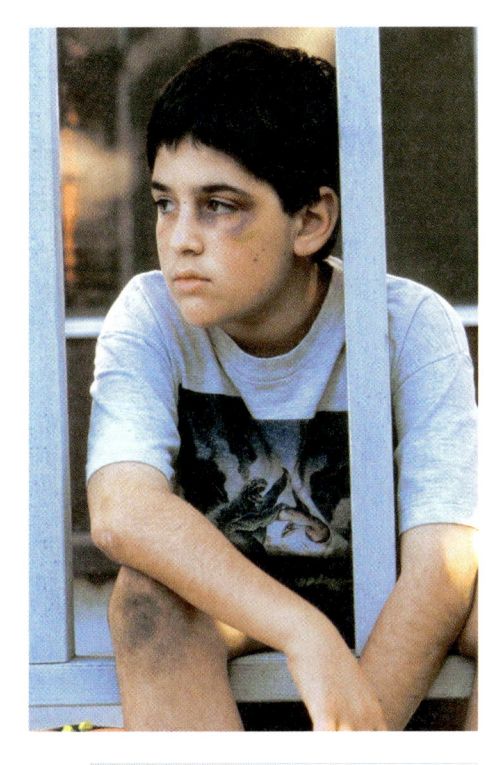

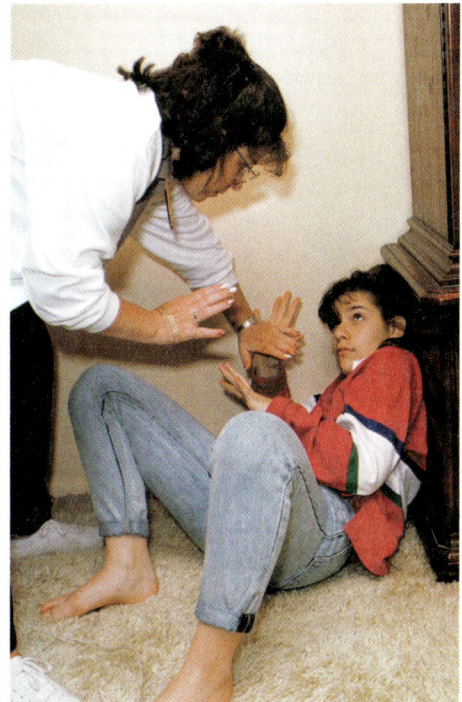

FIGURE 4.7

Existing data sources on crimes committed against children are somewhat sketchy. Children such as the one shown are often reluctant to report their victimization.

Courtesy Bill Aron/PhotoEdit.

FIGURE 4.8

The harmful results of child abuse may be both long and short term for the victim. Some research has found that childhood abuse and neglect increase the odds of future criminality.

Courtesy Robert Brenner/PhotoEdit.

essary as a last resort of the juvenile courts. Figures 4.7 and 4.8 show the results of child victimization.

Assistance for Child Victims The U.S. Department of Justice has made the following recommendations for assisting child victims in prosecution:[18]

- *Aids to communication.* By now most prosecutors should be familiar with the anatomically complete dolls that therapists use to help child victims explain what happened to them. And every prosecutor should be conscious of the need to scale down his or her vocabulary to meet the child's level.
- *Modifying the physical environment.* Providing a smaller chair for child witnesses, sitting at their level, and wearing business clothes rather than formal courtroom attire are simple things judges have done to help child witnesses feel more at ease.
- *Preparing the child.* Many prosecutors and victim advocates spend a great deal of time preparing child witnesses for the experience of testifying. They brief children on the roles of people in the courtroom and the range of possible outcomes. They introduce them to a judge. They take them for a tour of the courtroom, show them where their support person and the defendant will be, and let them sit on the witness chair and speak into the microphone. They explain the proceedings and let the children ask questions—this may be the only opportunity to find out what worries each child as an individual.

The Cycle of Violence In one of the most detailed studies of the issue to date, research sponsored by the National Institute of Justice (NIJ) found that childhood abuse and neglect increased the odds of future delinquency and adult criminality overall by 29 percent.[19] The study followed 1,575 cases from childhood through young adulthood, comparing the arrest records of two groups:

- A study group of 908 substantiated cases of childhood abuse or neglect processed by the courts from 1967 through 1971 and tracked through official criminal records over approximately 25 years
- A comparison group of 667 children, not officially recorded as abused or neglected, matched to the study group according to sex, age, race, and approximate family socioeconomic status

Although many individuals in both groups had no juvenile or adult criminal record, being abused or neglected as a child increased the likelihood of arrest as a juvenile by 59 percent, as an adult by 28 percent, and for a violent crime by 30 percent.

The cycle-of-violence hypothesis suggests that a childhood history of physical abuse predisposes the survivor to violence in later years. This study reveals that victims of neglect are also likely to develop later violent criminal behavior. If violence is begotten by not only violence, but also by neglect, far more attention needs to be devoted to the families of children who are abandoned and severely malnourished.

Childhood victimization represents a widespread, serious social problem. General delinquency research shows that childhood abuse (physical and sexual) is often associated with delinquency and that the early onset of maltreatment may increase the variety, seriousness, and duration of problems. It is also widely suggested that violence begets violence—that today's abused children become tomorrow's violent offenders. Further, children who suffer from neglect—not physical abuse—are also at risk.

Victims of Drunk-Driving Accidents

Drunk driving is one of the most serious public health and safety problems facing the American people and their policymakers. In a typical two-year period, 50,000 Americans die as a result of drunk driving—almost as many American lives as were lost in the entire ten years of the Vietnam War. Conservative estimates place the annual economic loss from drunk-driving accidents at billions of dollars for property damage alone.[20]

In the past, state laws dealing with drunk driving ran the gamut of sanctions from release with warning, through moderate to heavy fines, to suspension and revocation of licenses and—rarely—incarceration. Enforcement, too, varied considerably from one jurisdiction to the next.

Citizens groups such as **Mothers Against Drunk Driving (MADD)** have become very active and persuasive in the victims' advocacy movement regarding drunk-driving accidents. Groups such as MADD state that, just as the offender has the right to a fair trial and suitable defense, so should victims, as law-abiding citizens, have equal or enhanced rights. MADD, whose goal is to enact state bills of rights that will not reduce the rights guaranteed defendants but will assure the rights of victims, maintains that these rights should be afforded the victims of alcohol-impaired crashes. They encourage citizen groups to contact government representatives as advocates for nonexistent victims' rights in these cases.

Older People as Victims

Older people are the victims of both property and violent crimes and are often very fearful of such occurrences. Individuals over age 60 constitute a significant segment of our population. A generally higher standard of living in this country, the control of many diseases in younger people, advancements in medical technology, and better overall health care all are likely to lead to continued increases in the numbers of this age-specific group (see Figure 4.9).

Older Americans as potential victims of crimes create additional challenges for the criminal justice system. For example, some criminals seem to specialize in the following categories of crimes against older people:[21]

WEB

For more information on victims of drunk driving, **visit our Web site, www.prenhall.com/territo.**

- *Home-improvement con artists.* These criminals offer home repairs at a very low price without a written estimate. Frequently, they use inferior materials and provide poor workmanship at a price much higher than the verbal quote. The older person is left with no choice but to pay.
- *Mail fraud.* Older citizens receive notice that they have won a prize or receive letters offering miracle cures for diseases. The actual "prize" or "cure" is not legitimate, yet the victims find out only after parting with their cash.
- *Insurance fraud.* A bogus insurance agent contacts the victim and requires jewelry to be turned over for reappraisal due to increasing insurance rates. The jewelry is never seen again or is replaced with fakes.
- *Mail theft.* Thieves know when monthly pension checks are to arrive and raid mailboxes.

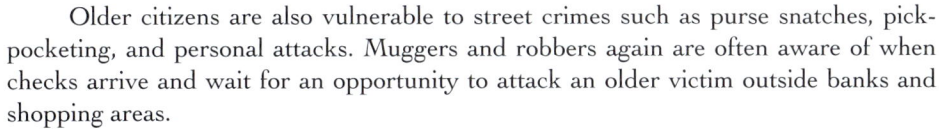

Older citizens are also vulnerable to street crimes such as purse snatches, pickpocketing, and personal attacks. Muggers and robbers again are often aware of when checks arrive and wait for an opportunity to attack an older victim outside banks and shopping areas.

Once an elderly person has been victimized, emotional and psychological support may be necessary. This is of particular importance if the older person lives alone or does not have other family nearby. The financial losses that an older victim might suffer may represent a significant portion of his or her total income or monthly allotment.

It is important to look beyond crime statistics in order to better understand the problems of violence against the elderly. They indicate that the seriousness of the problems of crime against the elderly may not have been recognized, given that the official statistics do not reflect an exact number of elderly victimizations. For a variety of reasons, as noted in this chapter, crime statistics can be misleading. In order to clarify the issues relative to crimes against the elderly, more research will be necessary on issues such as the quality of life for older people, the actual number of victimizations, and the relationship between victimization and fear of crime.

At present, the criminal justice system is not adequately prepared to meet the specific needs of older victims of crimes. As this particular segment of American society grows, it can only be a matter of time until more adequate resources are allocated toward preventing crimes against the elderly and assisting after a victimization has occurred.

Sexual and Physical Violence against College Women

Some research suggests that college women are at a higher risk for rape and other forms of sexual assault than women in the general population. For example, one study reported that in its sample, on-campus rape and sexual assault rates for women age 20 to 24 were 3.3 and 3.1 times higher, respectively, than for the same crimes in the National Crime Victimization Survey.[22]

A recent national study of college women in the United States who were enrolled in two-year and four-year colleges and universities with 1,000 or more students sheds some more light on the incidence of sexual victimization among college women. Bonnie Fisher and Francis Cullen reported that 11 percent of their sample experienced some form of sexual victimization during the 1996–1997 academic year. Further, they estimated that 2 percent of their sample had experienced rape (completed and attempted) on campus during the same academic year. If a school has 5,000 female students enrolled, this means that 100 of the female students would be raped on campus during the school year—an estimate that would alarm any school administrator.

FIGURE 4.9

Older people often are the victims of property crimes and violent crimes. Street criminals look for vulnerable targets such as the older woman in this photo who had just used an automated teller machine.

Courtesy Bart Geerligs/Getty Images, Inc.

Other researchers have also reported that the incidence of physical violence—hitting, slapping, kicking, or beating—against college women is frequent, especially against women who are in a dating or intimate relationship. Studies on violence in dating relationships have reported that about three out of five college women know someone who has experienced violence in a dating relationship, and about one in five college women have experienced such violence.

Violence in college dating relationships was also the subject of an inquiry by Christine Sellers and Max Bromley. In their study, conducted at a large urban university, they found that approximately 22 percent of their respondents had been the victim of either physical or sexual aggression in their relationship. The majority of violent behaviors involved pushing, grabbing, shoving, and slapping. Although these victimizations may involve low-level violence, they are important from the standpoint of providing interventions to prevent more serious victimizations, as Sellers and Bromley also found that the use of violence increased with the length of the relationship.

Victims of Workplace Violence

Data from the National Crime Victimization Survey (NCVS) indicate that on average, each year U.S. residents experience more than two million violent victimizations while they are working or on duty. The most common type of workplace violent crime is simple assault, with an estimated average of 1.5 million victimizations occurring each year. While at work U.S. residents also suffered 396,000 aggravated assaults, 51,000 rapes and sexual assaults, 84,000 robberies, and 1,000 homicides.[23]

Workplace violence is defined as violent acts against a person at work or on duty, including physical assaults (rape, sexual assault, and aggravated and simple assault) and robbery. Attempts are included with completed victimizations.[24]

- More than 1,000 workplace homicides occurred annually.
- The most common type of workplace victimization was simple assault; about 84,000 robberies occurred at work.
- Annually, more than 230,000 police officers became victims of a nonfatal violent crime while they were working or off duty.
- About 40 percent of victims of nonfatal violence in the workplace reported that they knew their offenders.
- Women were more likely than men to be victimized by someone they knew.
- Approximately 12 percent of the nonfatal violent workplace crimes resulted in an injury to the victim. Of those injured, about half received medical treatment.
- Intimates (current and former spouses, boyfriends, and girlfriends) were identified by the victims as the perpetrators of about 1 percent of all workplace violent crimes.

Among people victimized while working or on duty, male victims outnumber females by about two to one. Nearly nine in ten of victims of workplace violence were white. Fewer than 10 percent of the workplace violence victims were black. About 70 percent of the victims were between ages 25 and 49, and fewer than 10 percent of the victims were over age 50.

While females made up the majority of rape/sexual assault victims (83 percent); males were more likely than females to be victims of robbery and simple and aggravated assault. More than half of the violent crime victimizations happened to individuals who worked for a private employer. While government employees make up approximately 16 percent of the U.S. workforce, about 37 percent of the victims of workplace violence were employed by a federal, state, or county government organization. The victimization of law enforcement officers accounts for the overrepresentation of government employees as workplace violence victims.

VICTIM SPECIAL-INTEREST GROUPS

Several **victim special-interest groups** have become troubled by the psychological and financial burdens that crime imposes on its victims. Women's groups particularly are concerned about the double trauma of rape victims, who are first assaulted by the rapist

---

WEB

For more information on victims of workplace violence, **visit our Web site, www.prenhall.com/territo**.

and then are often handled insensitively by the criminal justice system. In 1975 and 1976, social service providers and criminal justice personnel organized the **National Organization for Victim Assistance (NOVA)** to promote a victim-oriented perspective in the administration of criminal justice (see Figure 4.10). NOVA is a private, nonprofit, membership organization committed to the recognition of victim rights.

Advocacy groups such as NOVA and MADD do not seek to reduce the protection afforded the defendant by the courts, nor do they attempt to pressure law enforcement officers, prosecutors, and judges to "bend the rules." Rather, they work to improve the treatment of victims and witnesses in order to create a balance between the consideration shown to them and the attention paid to defendants.

FIGURE 4.10

Over the last 20 years numerous improvements have been made with respect to the criminal justice system's response to victims of traumatic crimes. In this photo a victim advocate is providing counseling to a rape victim.

Courtesy Richard T. Nowitz/CORBIS.

COSTS OF CRIME VICTIMIZATION

Crime exacts a heavy toll—on governments, on society at large, and especially on its victims (see Figure 4.11). The cost of crime has two dimensions: a dollar amount calculated by adding up property losses, productivity losses, and medical bills, and an amount less easily quantifiable because it takes the forms of pain, emotional trauma, and risk of death from victimization. Just how much social resources are drained has been uncertain; previous studies have been able to estimate some of the short-term costs attendant on victimization, but long-term estimates have been incomplete.

In recent research conducted by the U.S. Department of Justice[25] on the tangible and intangible costs to crime victims researchers found that victimizations generate $105 billion annually in property and productivity losses and outlays for medical expenses. This amounts to an annual "crime tax" of roughly $425 per man, woman, and child in the United States. When the values of pain, long-term emotional trauma, disability, and risk of death are put in dollar terms, the costs rise to $450 billion annually (or $1,800 per person).

CTQ

Do you agree with the statistic that victimization costs society an average of $450 billion annually? Do you think this should be higher, considering long-term costs such as pain and suffering?

Number of Victimizations

For counts of crime, researchers in the Department of Justice study used the UCR and the NCVS, supplemented by data from other nationally representative surveys. For the most part, only street crime and domestic crime were counted and their costs calculated. Certain categories were excluded, among them crimes against business and government, personal fraud, white-collar crime, child neglect, and most "victimless" crimes.

FIGURE 4.11

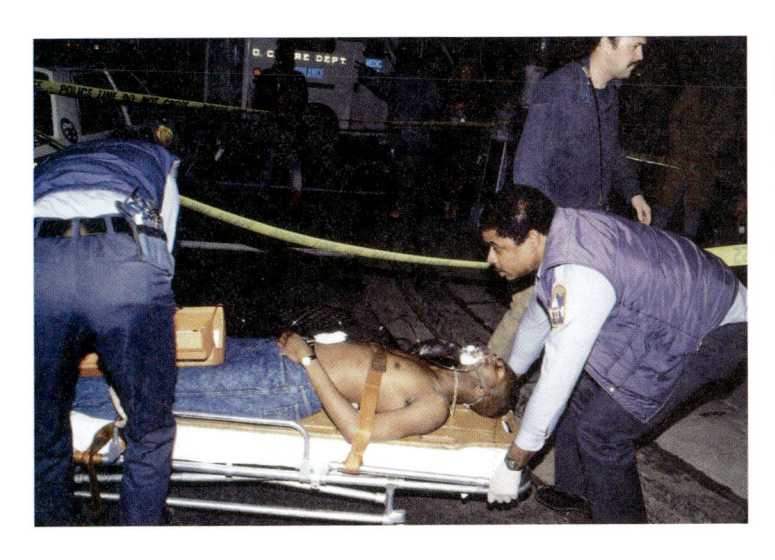

The costs associated with crimes are considerable. The victim in this photo will not only suffer physical pain, but also economic loss as a result of not being able to work due to his injuries.

Courtesy M. Reinstein/The Image Works.

Costs and Other Consequences

Both intangible and tangible costs were calculated. This study focused on victim-related costs, not costs to operate the criminal justice system. In the aggregate, tangible losses amounted to $105 billion annually, but intangibles were much higher at $345 billion. Overall, rape is the costliest crime: With annual victim costs at $127 billion, it exacts a higher price than murder. The calculations shed new light on domestic violence against adults, revealing the aggregate costs of crimes in this category to be $67 billion per year. Losses due to violence against children, some 40 percent of which is domestic violence, exceed $164 billion.

Implications

The study findings make clear that when quality-of-life factors are included in calculating the cost of crime, the burden of the "crime tax" is higher than other measures suggest. Behind the dollar figures lies the reality of the social toll exacted by crime. This social cost consists of adverse emotional and psychological effects, which can have far-reaching consequences for the victims. Translating them into dollar figures borrows from the approach of the civil law damage suit and helps illustrate just how profound these effects can be. By taking these factors into account in assessing the effects of crime, the study can serve as a starting point for recognizing the full consequences for victims. That in turn can affect public policy toward victims, including expansion of the concept of victim compensation.

The findings have the potential to affect programs and strategies aimed at reducing crime and criminal behavior. Analysts who evaluate the effectiveness of such programs and strategies may want to include a calculation of the social cost to victims. Early-release programs are an example. When offenders are kept in prison, there is no cost to individual victims during the incapacitation period. By contrast, when an offender who is released early (to avoid the high cost of incarceration) commits a crime, the costs are shifted to the victim. The high cost the victim must pay highlights the importance of ensuring public safety in designing early-release programs.

The information brought to light by the study might also be used as the basis of a standard that can be applied in calculating the effectiveness of prevention programs and the need for fuller victim compensation. But the value of the study may be greatest on another level: creating a fuller recognition of the burden that crime victims bear.

UNRESOLVED VICTIM–CRIMINAL JUSTICE SYSTEM ISSUES

As this discussion has shown, more services for victims are becoming available, and victims are playing a larger role in the American criminal justice system as a result of the research that has led to many of today's innovations in the treatment of victims. But much remains to be learned about ways to make these reforms as effective and as efficient as possible.[26] Areas of justice research might include an evaluation of the effect of service programs—counseling, police, or court-related—on victims; more research is also needed about the role of the victim in the criminal justice system. Current research on victim impact statements will yield important information on the administrative effects of such statements. Surveys of victims will need to be conducted regarding their perceptions of the usefulness of the victim impact statements. These and perhaps other significant victim assistance issues remain to be reviewed in the future.

SUMMARY

In this chapter we wanted to accomplish a number of objectives. First, we introduced why crime data are collected and which departments of the federal government publish the information. Next, we attempted to familiarize the reader with the crime reporting system in the United States. The Uniform Crime Reporting Program is a voluntary system established in 1930 by the International Association of Chiefs of Police, with the

FBI serving as the national clearinghouse. With crime statistics voluntarily contributed by more than 17,000 law enforcement agencies throughout the country, the UCR program provides periodic assessments of crime in the United States. Data from the program are widely used by criminal justice professionals, legislators, and scholars who have an interest in the crime problem. All index crimes and hate crimes were discussed in detail.

Another objective of this chapter was to discuss some of the problems related to gathering crime data and some of the changes that have been implemented for the UCR. We also discussed the National Crime Victimization Survey (NCVS) and how it differs from the UCR. The recent requirement to collect college crime data is also discussed.

In addition to discussing crime data we wanted to provide the reader with some insights into the effects of crime on both the victim and society. The findings of victimization surveys were discussed, as well as the response by the criminal justice system. In addition we described various special categories of victims, as well as discussing both the tangible and intangible costs associated with crime victimization.

DISCUSSION AND REVIEW

1. What two categories encompass the eight index crimes?
2. Why is the clearance rate for murder higher than the clearance rate for the other index crimes?
3. Why is the clearance rate for aggravated assault lower than the clearance rate for murder, even though both crimes often involve close relationships between victims and assailants?
4. Why is rape one of the most underreported violent crimes?
5. What is the difference between robbery and larceny?
6. What are the three categories of motor vehicle theft?
7. Why would a law enforcement agency manipulate crime data?
8. What are some of the traditional criticisms of the UCR system?
9. Briefly discuss the difference between the National Crime Victimization Survey (NCVS) and the Uniform Crime Reports (UCR).
10. Briefly describe what is involved in the concept of victim "eligibility" for compensation.
11. Discuss why victim compensation program staff often find domestic violence cases troubling.
12. How did early societies attempt to provide compensation or restitution to the victims of crime?
13. What are victimization surveys and why are they important?
14. List and describe ways in which crime victims may receive insensitive or callous treatment from the criminal justice system.
15. Discuss the Police Foundation experiment conducted in Minneapolis regarding the handling of domestic violence cases. What were the results?
16. List and discuss three recommendations that have been made to assist in the prosecution of cases when the victims are children.
17. Describe recent research on crimes of violence against college women.
18. Describe the two ways victims and witness intimidation can be characterized.
19. Briefly discuss two innovations that may aid in conceptualizing a theoretical framework for dealing with domestic violence.
20. Discuss the implications of the results from a recent study of costs of crime victimization.

CHAPTER RESOURCES

IN THE MEDIA

Video

ABC Custom Video: *America's Fastest Growing Crime: Rape*
ABC Custom Video: *Blacks and the Criminal Justice System*
CNN Today Video: *Criminal Justice Series: Index II Crimes*
Court TV Video: *Victims of Rape*

Television

America's Most Wanted
COPS
Crime and Punishment
The District
LAPD: Life on the Beat
Law and Order
Law and Order: Special Victims Unit

IN THE LITERATURE

Books

A. BIDERMAN AND J. LYNCH, *Understanding Crime Statistics: Why the UCR Diverges from the NCS*. New York: Springer-Verlag, 1991.

R. CLARK, *Situational Crime Prevention*. Albany, N.Y.: Harrow and Heston, 1992.

S. FAHERTY AND A. SARAT, eds., *Victims and Victims' Rights*. New York: Chelsea House, 1998.

G. LAFREE, *Rape and Criminal Justice*. Belmont, Calif.: Wadsworth, 1989.

S. MESSNER AND R. ROSENFELD, *Crime and the American Dream*. Belmont, Calif.: Wadsworth, 1994.

G. PIERCE AND J. FOX, *Recent Trends in Violent Crime: A Closer Look*. Boston: Northeastern University Press, 1992

D. WILSON, *The Complete Book of Victims' Rights*. Highlands Ranch, Colo.: ProSe Associates, 1996.

Articles

A. BLUMSTEIN, J. COHEN, AND R. ROSENFELD, "Trend and Deviation in Crime Rates: A Comparison of UCR and NCS Data for Burglary and Robbery," *Criminology*, vol. 29 (1991), pp. 237–263.

A. DUNKERS, "Factors Affecting Support after Criminal Victimization: Needed and Received Support from the Partner, the Social Network, and Distant Support Providers," *Journal of Social Psychology*, vol. 139 (1999), p. 191.

D. GORMAN-SMITH, P. TOLAN, AND D. HENRY, "Relation of Family Problems to Patterns of Delinquent Involvement among Urban Youth," *Journal of Abnormal Child Psychology*, vol. 26 (1998), p. 319.

S. MALINOWSKI, "Battling an Emergency Crime Problem," *CJ International*, vol. 12 (1993), p. 3.

B. MILLER, W. DOWNS, AND D. GONDOLI, "Delinquency, Childhood Violence, and the Development of Alcoholism in Women," *Crime and Delinquency*, vol. 35 (1989), pp. 94–108.

A. ROY, "Recent Trends in Official Male and Female Crime Rates: The Convergence Controversy," *Journal of Criminal Justice*, vol. 21 (1993) pp. 447–446.

S. SINGER, "Homogeneous Victim-Offender Populations: A Review and Some Research Implications," *Journal of Criminal Law and Criminology*, vol. 72 (1981) pp. 779–799.

W. WILSON, "Inner City Dislocations," *Society*, vol. 35 (January-February 1998), p. 270.

ENDNOTES

1. The discussion of UCR classifications of crimes against property and violent crimes and their related data was adapted from Federal Bureau of Investigation, *Crime in the United States*, FBI Uniform Crime Reports. Washington, D.C.: U.S. Government Printing Office, 2001, pp. 1–56.

2. C. R. Swanson, N. C. Chamelin, and L. Territo, *Criminal Investigation*, 8th ed. New York: McGraw-Hill, 2003, p. 352. This source also provided information on uncooperative victims in assault cases.

3. Ibid., pp. 435–439.

4. Ibid., p. 324.

5. Ibid., pp. 535, 536.

6. This section is adapted from M. E. Beekman and M. R. Daly, "Motor Vehicle Theft Investigations: Emerging International Trends," *FBI Law Enforcement Bulletin* (September 1990), 14/014193/, pp. 14–17.

7. The discussion of future trends in the UCR program was adapted from Eugene C. Poggio et al., *Blueprint for the Future of the Uniform Crime Reporting Program*. Washington, D.C.: U.S. Department of Justice, Bureau of Justice

Statistics, Federal Bureau of Investigation, 1985, pp. 1–3.

8. Adapted from M. Bromley and B. Fisher, "Campus Policing and Victim Services." In L. Moriarity, ed., *Police and Crime Victims*. Upper Saddle River, N.J.: Prentice Hall, 2002, pp. 141–142.

9. P. Finn, *Crime File Study Guide—Victims*, Washington, D.C.: U.S. Department of Justice, National Institute of Justice, 1987.

10. Ibid., p. 3.

11. The discussion of victim intimidation was adapted from K. Healey, *Victim and Witness Intimidation*. Washington, D.C.: U.S. Department of Justice, 1995, pp. 1–4.

12. The comparison of the UCR and NCVS programs was adapted from Federal Bureau of Investigation, *Crime in the United States*, FBI Uniform Crime Reports. Washington, D.C.: U.S. Government Printing Office, 1999, pp. 407–408.

13. C. Rennison, "Violent Victimization and Race." Bureau of Justice Statistics Special Report. U.S. Department of Justice, Office of Justice Programs, March 2001, p. 1.

14. C. M. Rennison and S. Welchans, "Intimate Partner Violence." Bureau of Justice Statistics Special Report. U.S. Department of Justice, Office of Justice Programs, May 2000, p. 1.

15. The information regarding the victims of domestic violence was adapted from L. Sherman, *Crime File Study Guide—Domestic Violence*. Washington, D.C.: U.S. Department of Justice, National Institute of Justice, 1987, pp. 1–3.

16. The Violence against Women Act discussion was adapted from J. Travis, *Violence against Women: Reflections on NIJ's Research Agenda*. Washington, D.C.: U.S. Department of Justice, 1996.

17. The discussion of children as victims and the recommended responses by the criminal justice system was adapted from D. Whitcomb, E. R. Shapiro, and L. D. Stellwagen, *When the Victim Is a Child: Issues for Judges and Prosecutors*. Washington, D.C.: U.S. Department of Justice, National Institute of Justice, Office of Development, Testing and Dissemination, 1985, pp. 1, 4, 5, 6, 111, 112, 115.

18. Ibid., p. 116.

19. C. S. Widom and M. G. Maxfield, "An Update on the 'Cycle of Violence.'" National Institute of Justice, Research in Brief, February 2001, pp. 1–2.

20. The discussion of the vast number of drunk-driving accidents in the United States and victims' rights in alcohol-related accidents was adapted from National Institute of Justice, *Jailing Drunk Drivers Impact on the Criminal Justice System*. Washington, D.C.: U.S. Department of Justice, 1984, p. 1, and Mothers Against Drunk Driving, *Victims' Rights in Alcohol Impaired Crashes*. Hurst, Texas: Mothers Against Drunk Driving, 1985. The following individuals on the National Institute of Justice staff contributed to the NIJ document: Fred Heinzelmann, Ph.D.; W. Robert Burkhart; Bernard A. Gropper, Ph.D.; Cheryl V. Martorana; Louis Felson Mock; Maureen O'Connor; and Walter Philip Travers. Permission was obtained from MADD for use of their materials.

21. Much of the information regarding categories of crimes committed against older people was provided courtesy of the Florida Attorney General's Help Stop Crime program. For a detailed discussion of crimes against the elderly, see the text cited in note 2, Swanson, Chamelin, & Territo.

22. For a more complete discussion of this topic, see Bromley and Fisher, "Campus Policing and Victim Services," p. 146. See also B. Fisher, J. Sloan, F. Cullen, and L. Lu, "Crime in the Ivory Tower: The Level and Sources of Student Victimization," *Criminology*, vol. 36, no. 3 (1998), pp. 671–710; A. Burgess and N. Crowell, "Understanding Violence Against Women." Washington, D.C.: National Academy Press, 1996; C. Sellers and M. Bromley, "Violent Behavior in College Student Dating Relationships: Implications for Campus Service Providers," *Journal of Contemporary Criminal Justice*, vol. 12, no. 1 (1996), pp. 1–27.

23. The issue of workplace violence was adapted from G. Warchol, *Workplace Violence, 1992–96*. Washington, D.C.: Bureau of Justice Statistics, U.S. Department of Justice, 1998, pp. 1–5.

24. Ibid, pp. 4–68.

25. Adapted from *The Extent and Costs of Crime Victimization: A New Look*. Washington, D.C.: U.S. Department of Justice, 1996, pp. 1–2.

26. The discussion of additional unresolved victims' issues was adapted from R. C. Davis, *Crime Victims: Learning How to Help Them*. Washington, D.C.: U.S. Department of Justice, National Institute of Justice, 1987, p. 6.

5

POLICE OPERATIONS

Chapter OUTLINE

Police Departments in the United States
Police Officer Selection and Training
  A Snapshot of Local Police Departments and Sheriffs' Offices in the United States
  Local Police Department Characteristics
  Sheriff's Office Characteristics
  Smaller Law Enforcement Agencies
The Evolution of Policing in America
  Influence of Robert Peel
  Creating City Police Forces in the United States
  The Emergence of County, State, and Federal Law Enforcement Agencies
Patrol Operations
  Patrol Division Assignments
  Activities of Patrol Officers
Changing Patrol Strategy
  Kansas City Preventive Patrol Experiment
  Nontraditional Patrol
  Flint, Michigan, Foot Patrol
  Directed Patrol
  Crackdowns
Zero-Tolerance Enforcement

Police Traffic Responsibilities
  Selective Traffic Enforcement
  The Quota System: Myth or Reality?
  Who Gets the Money?
Rural Policing
Campus Police
The Detective Role
  The Media Stereotype
  The Historical Stereotype
  The Critical Stereotype
  Activities of Detectives
Major Studies of the Investigator's Role
  The Rand Criminal Investigation Study
  The PERF Study: Solving Crimes
The NCIC Network in Investigations
Evolution in Policing: COP and POP
  Community Policing and the Office of the Sheriff
  Trends in Community Policing
  The Problem-Oriented Approach to Policing
  The Future of Community-Oriented Policing and Problem Solving (COPPS)
Summary

Key Terms

community-oriented policing (COP), p. 205
crackdowns, p. 193
crime analysis, p. 193
evidence technician, p. 201
field interview files, p. 202
field training officer (FTO), p. 179
National Crime Information Center (NCIC), p. 204
nontraditional patrol, p. 191
Police Executive Research Forum (PERF), p. 203
proactive beats, p. 190
proactive crime prevention, p. 180
problem-oriented policing (POP), p. 205
professional officer track, p. 186
professional police management track, p. 186
quota system, p. 196
reactive beats, p. 190
selective traffic enforcement, p. 196
special-purpose police, p. 178
zero-tolerance policing, p. 194

Courtesy Jack Kurtz/The Image Works.

This chapter begins with a brief descriptive profile of police departments in the United States, including a discussion of smaller police departments. Next we review policing from a historical perspective.

Considerable time is spent describing police patrol, traffic, and investigative functions. The findings of experimental research are described as they relate to changes in contemporary police patrol and criminal investigations. Strategies such as directed patrol, crackdowns, and selective enforcement are described. A section on zero-tolerance enforcement has been added. Rural and campus policing are reviewed. Following this discussion is information regarding computerized police files including the National Crime Information Center (NCIC) network and its uses. The chapter concludes with a discussion regarding what many feel to be an evolution in contemporary policing: community-oriented policing (COP) and problem-oriented policing (POP). Finally, a new module on community policing in sheriffs' offices has been included.

POLICE DEPARTMENTS IN THE UNITED STATES

Members of the public often form their opinions about police agencies in the United States by watching the electronic news media or reading national newspaper headlines. Popular television police shows also play a significant part in shaping citizen beliefs about the size, operation, and functions of police departments across the country. To many individuals, the Los Angeles, New York, and Chicago police departments are the models that come to mind when they think of the police "role."

In reality there is no single "model" police agency in the United States. Instead, the thousands of police departments in existence vary widely. Most police agencies are somewhat small in number of personnel (fewer than twenty), are not highly specialized in terms of officer assignments (patrol, detective, crime scene technician), and may perform functions the public does not readily associate with law enforcement (serving eviction notices, providing money escorts, delivering minutes of town council meetings, and so forth).

> **CTQ**
>
> In your opinion, what role do the media play in how members of the public form their opinions about police departments in the United States?

There are also numerous types of law enforcement agencies, at various levels of government. For example, on the federal level there are agencies such as the Federal Bureau of Investigation, the Secret Service, and the Drug Enforcement Administration. Each of these federal agencies operates under mandates set forth in federal legislation and is responsible for enforcing specific federal laws and performing duties that range from investigating bank robberies (FBI) to protecting the president (Secret Service).

Some states have state police (responsible for general policing and investigations), highway patrol (responsible for enforcing motorist-related laws), or state investigation bureaus. Such state investigation bureaus usually do not employ uniformed officers but investigate major crimes as required by statute or when requested by local agencies.

Local governments may have township police, city police, county sheriffs' departments, or some combination of agencies that are responsible for enforcing local ordinances and laws. Some small towns or municipalities may "contract" for law enforcement services with the local sheriff's department or the state police. This practice can be very cost-effective if the local government tax base is too small to support its own law enforcement agency. Some small localities may employ a police officer during certain hours of the day or night and rely on the county sheriff's department or state police to provide after-hours assistance and law enforcement service.

In many areas of the country, a category of **special-purpose police** agency may exist. Some examples of special-purpose police agencies include university police, airport police, harbor police, park police, transit authority police, housing authority police, and school system police. All such agencies were established to provide special-purpose law enforcement services for unique communities or constituents. For example, the emergence of university police departments reflects the desire of legislative bodies, campus trustees, or similar governing groups to have professional police services within a campus setting, without having to rely on city or country agencies exclusively.

The jurisdiction of most special-purpose police agencies is limited to specific geographic boundaries, which may in fact fall within a larger overall jurisdiction. For example, a public housing project within a city or an airport within a county may have its own police agency. Generally, there is an operating agreement or "mutual aid pact" between the smaller special-purpose agency and the larger municipal/county police department; the agreement establishes which agency is responsible for handling various kinds of investigations and incidents.

Despite the wide variety of police agencies across the country, some general statements apply to most municipal or county departments: they serve law enforcement and order-maintenance functions; officers must meet required formal training standards; the majority of personnel working in police agencies are sworn officers as opposed to civilians; and the largest percentage of sworn personnel are assigned to the uniformed patrol bureau.

POLICE OFFICER SELECTION AND TRAINING

Given the fact that there are thousands of state and local police agencies in the United States, it is difficult to generalize about their selection and training requirements. Most police officers are employed by local police departments. According to the Bureau of Justice Statistics, some typical selection techniques and the percentages of use by police agencies are as follows:[1]

Criminal-record checks	99%
Background investigations	98%
Driving-record checks	98%
Medical exams	97%
Psychological tests	91%
Aptitude tests	84%
Physical-agility tests	78%

After they are hired, most police officers are required to complete academy training. In the police academy, new officers are trained in areas such as the law, constitutional issues, criminal investigation, pursuit driving, use of force, community policing, and first aid. Upon successful completion of the academy, rookie officers will be assigned to a **field training officer (FTO).** The FTO is an experienced officer who teaches rookie officers how to apply what they learned in the academy as well as how to follow departmental procedures. The FTO also evaluates the performance of the new officers while on probation. Rookie officers serve in a probationary status for six to twelve months in most departments.

A Snapshot of Local Police Departments and Sheriffs' Offices in the United States

Two recent nationwide reports published by the Bureau of Justice Statistics documented current information regarding local police departments and sheriff's offices.[2] Some of the highlights are discussed next.

Local Police Department Characteristics

There are approximately 13,000 local police departments in the United States. In 1999, local police departments had an estimated 556,631 full-time employees. About 436,000 full-time local police department employees (78 percent) were sworn officers. Nationwide, 573 local police departments (4 percent) employed at least 100 sworn personnel. This included 46 departments with 1,000 or more officers. In contrast, an estimated 7,095 departments (52 percent) employed fewer than ten sworn personnel, including nearly 800 departments with just one officer.

Although 77 percent of local police departments served fewer than 10,000 residents, these agencies employed just 15 percent of all local police officers. About half of all officers served a jurisdiction with 100,000 or more residents, including nearly a fourth in jurisdictions with one million or more residents.

Overall, 89 percent of sworn personnel worked in field operations (primarily patrol officers). Officers working in the field operations area, but not assigned to respond to calls, often performed supervisory or investigative duties.

All local police departments provided patrol services, and all used automobiles for at least some of their routine patrol units. About half used foot patrol units, including nearly all departments serving a population of one million or more. Departments with routine foot patrol employed about three-fourths of all officers.

Sheriff's Office Characteristics

Except for a small number of appointees, sheriffs are elected officials. To better reflect this status, the term *office* is used universally. Sheriffs' offices typically serve counties and independent cities. Although sheriffs' offices may have countywide jail- and court-related responsibilities, their law enforcement jurisdiction may exclude county areas served by

IN THE WORKPLACE

SHERIFF'S DEPUTY

Responsible for patrolling unincorporated areas to prevent crime, enforce laws, and render aid or intervention where needed. Performs a variety of duties, including the following: responding to calls for service, conducting investigations. Minimum qualifications are as follows: high school diploma or equivalent, no felony convictions, valid driver's license, successful completion of academy.

a local police department. In some counties, municipalities contract with the sheriff's office for law enforcement services. In counties and independent cities with a separate police department, the sheriff's office may not have any primary law enforcement jurisdiction.

In 1999, there were approximately 3,100 sheriffs' offices throughout the country. These offices employed an estimated 290,767 full-time employees, including about 186,000 sworn personnel. About half of all sworn personnel were assigned to law enforcement field operations.

Overall, approximately 66,000 deputies had regularly assigned duties that included responding to calls for service. About a third of all sworn personnel worked in jail-related positions, and about one in ten performed court-related duties such as providing court security or serving civil process.

Nearly all sheriffs' offices had responsibility for court-related functions such as executing arrest warrants (98 percent), serving civil process (98 percent), and providing court security (94 percent). About four-fifths operated at least one jail.

Nationwide, 408 sheriffs' offices (13 percent) employed at least 100 sworn personnel. This included seventeen agencies with 1,000 or more officers. An estimated 815 agencies (26 percent) employed fewer than ten sworn personnel.

Smaller Law Enforcement Agencies

As noted in the previous section, most police departments and sheriffs' offices in America are small. Law enforcement agencies in small towns or rural areas play an extremely important role in addressing the public safety needs of their communities. While the frequency of violent acts or other serious crimes may be less than that of their urban counterparts, these smaller law enforcement agencies must deal with the full range of demands for service.

At the same time, policing in small communities is generally more personalized than in large cities or counties. Police officers in small towns are usually well known and are easily accessible to their citizens. Many officers in small communities are usually involved in **proactive crime prevention** activities and other non–law enforcement duties that seek to involve community members as partners in enhancing public safety.

Recently, populations have been shifting out of large cities and into smaller towns or rural areas as well as to traditional suburbs. If this trend continues, smaller law enforcement agencies may need to modify the ways in which they have traditionally operated. Unfortunately, little research data is available to describe the current state of small law enforcement departments. There are many unanswered questions regarding the differences and similarities of smaller departments and their urban and suburban counterparts. Victor Sims notes the following differences between small and large town police agencies, based upon the limited data available:[3]

- *Salary.* Rural and small-town police officers are paid significantly less than their urban counterparts. There is a direct relationship between the size of the police agency and the average annual salary of its individual officers. The larger the agency, the larger the salary; the smaller the agency, the smaller the salary.

- *Education.* There is a direct correlation between the size of the police agency and the average education of its officers. The larger the police agency, the more years of education the average individual officer is likely to have. Perhaps the best explanation for this is the attractive salaries the larger agencies offer beginning officers who have just completed some college study.
- *Training.* The same relationship is found in regard to training. The larger the agency, the more police training the average officer is likely to have had. Officers in smaller police departments do not receive as much basic academy training or training by a field training officer, roll-call training, specialized training, or inservice training as do officers employed by suburban or big-city police departments. Limited budgets, resources, and staff seem to be the most frequent explanations for the limited training. Training efforts, like federal monies, go to those who ask and demand. Larger police agencies are more likely to have the sophistication and expertise required to ask and demand.
- *Age.* Police officers employed by rural and small-town police departments are on average older than urban officers. There is a definite negative relationship between the size of the police agency and the average age of its officers. Although there is evidence to indicate that this gap between the ages of rural police officers and urban police officers is narrowing, it does still exist. Perhaps the lower turnover rate and longer tenure of rural and small-town police officers account for the older ages.

CTQ

Do you believe that proactive crime-prevention activities can also be viably implemented in larger, urban police departments? Why or why not?

THE EVOLUTION OF POLICING IN AMERICA

The early colonial American settlements relied heavily on self-policing to assure the peace. Communal pressure, rather than formal policing, was the backbone of law enforcement. The colonists were of similar background, most held similar religious beliefs, and there was actually little worth stealing.[4]

Many features of British law enforcement were present in early American colonial settlements. In New England, where people depended on commerce and industry, the night watchman or constable served as protector of public order. In the South, where agriculture played a dominant role, the office of sheriff was established as a means of area law enforcement. Most watchmen and sheriffs were volunteers, but many were paid to serve in the place of others who were supposed to patrol as a civic duty.

Many different types of law enforcement were tried in many different parts of the country. Almost all used some kind of night watch system, with little or no protection during the day. As might be expected, the fastest-growing municipalities were the first to organize legal forces.

Influence of Robert Peel

Many of the roots of modern American policing may be found in the model established by Sir Robert Peel in 1829, when the British Parliament agreed to the formation of a metropolitan police force in London. Many of Peel's principles of effective policing, such as organizing police along military lines, distributing crime news to the public, training police officers, and hiring them on a probationary basis, still exist in today's law enforcement agencies in the United States.

The following is a list of the principles that Sir Robert Peel used as the foundation for the London Metropolitan Police Department:

1. The police must be stable, efficient, and militarily organized under government control.
2. The absence of crime will best prove the efficiency of the police.
3. Crime news must be widely distributed.
4. Territorial distribution of the force by hours and shifts must be accomplished.
5. No quality is more indispensable to an officer than a perfect command of temper; a quiet, determined manner has more effect than violent action.

6. Good appearance commands respect.
7. Proper securing and training of personnel lies at the root of police efficiency.
8. Public safety requires that every policeman be given a number.
9. Police headquarters should be centrally located and easily accessible to all the people.
10. Policemen should be appointed on the probation basis.
11. Police records are necessary for the correct distribution of police strength.
12. The best way to select men is to "size them up" and then find out what their neighbors think of them.[5]

These principles are important in gaining an understanding of the evolution of policing in America. Many relate directly to community policing as discussed later in this chapter.

CTQ
Which of Sir Robert Peel's principles for effective policing do you believe are most visible in today's law enforcement agencies?

Creating City Police Forces in the United States

The establishment of police forces as we view them today took considerable time in the United States. Until the early 1800s, volunteer citizens often served as night watchmen to protect their small communities.[6] The watch systems were often ineffective, as some watchmen were actually convicted criminals serving sentences. Other watchmen were hired to serve in the place of citizens who did not want to serve their watch.

A brief summary of efforts in two of the largest cities in the United States (Boston and New York) to develop police protection is shown in Table 5.1.

According to Henry Wrobleski and Karen Hess, the evolution of policing would continue throughout the nineteenth century:

> The Civil War brought new problems of social control. Municipal forces tried to meet these problems by organizing new divisions and specializing the force. As centers of population became increasingly urbanized and fringe areas became incorporated suburbs of the hub city, a trend developed to add individual police organizations rather than to centralize or consolidate them. Consequently, newly developed fringe cities had their own forces, which fostered complex, uncoordinated relationships, compartmentalization, and inefficiency.[7]

The Emergence of County, State, and Federal Law Enforcement Agencies

Perhaps the best way to describe the various types of police agencies in the United States is to consider the various levels of government. For each level of government there is a specific type of law enforcement agency. A brief description of each is provided in the following sections.

TABLE 5.1 Timeline for the Evolution of the Police in Boston and New York

Boston
1631	Six-man force established to guard the city sunset to sunup. First night watch in America.
1735	Watchmen were required to call out the time of day and the weather.
1801	First city in the United States to have a permanent night watch.
1838	Day force created to supplement the night watch.

New York
1694	First uniformed police officers replaced the night watch.
Mid-1700s	Heavy reliance on volunteer watchmen for city protection.
1844	First paid day watch created with 16 officers; separate from the night watch (1,100 watchmen). The officers were paid and the department was modeled after the London Metropolitan Police Department.

IN THE WORKPLACE

HIGHWAY PATROL OFFICER/STATE TROOPER

Responsible for enforcing criminal and motor vehicle laws for the state. Performs a variety of duties, including the following: arresting criminals statewide and patrolling highways, issuing traffic citations, directing traffic at accident scenes, determining the cause of accidents, and rendering assistance to other law enforcement agencies. Minimum qualifications are as follows: age 20, U.S. citizen, high school diploma or equivalent, valid driver's license, and satisfactory driving record.

County Law Enforcement   At the county level of government, police services are usually provided by a sheriff's office; the sheriff is typically an elected official. There is considerable variation across the country regarding the responsibilities of the sheriff. In some states the sheriff is primarily an officer of the court, while in others the sheriff operates the county jail. Finally, most notably in the South and West, the sheriff's office has responsibility for court functions, jail management, and general policing— primarily in unincorporated areas of the county. In some parts of the United States where city and county governments have been consolidated, an agency called the *county police* may exist.

State Law Enforcement   Historically, state police agencies have been created in order to respond to circumstances that went beyond the capabilities or authority of city and county law enforcement agencies. For example, according to V. L. Folley, the Texas Rangers were established in 1835 to patrol the borders and to apprehend cattle rustlers.[8] Likewise, the Pennsylvania State Police was formed in 1905 to deal with the violence associated with coal miner strikes and to provide assistance to rural police agencies. The Pennsylvania State Police is considered the first modern state police agency and is the model other states often followed. In some states, such as Florida and California, state highway patrols were established primarily to deal with traffic problems on state-maintained highways.

Federal Law Enforcement   Federal law enforcement agencies are too numerous to describe here. However, a few should be mentioned given their notoriety and the importance of their roles. Federal law enforcement agencies are established by Congress to meet specific national needs. The majority of federal agencies report to the Department of Justice, which is headed by the U.S. Attorney General. An example would be the Federal Bureau of Investigation (FBI), which has wide-ranging responsibilities including the investigation of approximately 260 federal crimes, many key antiterrorism duties, management of the National Crime Information Center (NCIC), and publication of the Uniform Crime Report (UCR). The Drug Enforcement Administration (DEA) also reports to the attorney general. The DEA, as its name implies, is responsible for investigating the sources of illegal drugs and arresting federal drug law violators. Given the international nature of illegal drug manufacturing and sales, DEA agents operate both in the United States and in numerous foreign embassies. A third example of a federal law enforcement agency that reports to the attorney general is the U.S. Marshals Service. This agency has various responsibilities relating to federal courts, prisoners, and witnesses.

The Department of the Treasury, headed by the Secretary of the Treasury, also encompasses numerous federal law enforcement agencies. One example is the Secret Service, formed in 1865 to combat the problem of counterfeit currency following the Civil War. After President McKinley was assassinated in 1901, the secret service was also authorized to protect the president. The Bureau of Customs focuses on stopping smuggling of merchandise and drugs or other contraband into or out of the United States. A final

IN THE WORKPLACE

FBI AGENT

Responsible for enforcing more than 260 federal statutes and conducting sensitive national security investigations. Performs a variety of duties, including the following: investigating organized crime, white-collar crime, public corruption, financial crime, government fraud, bribery, copyright matters, civil rights violations, bank robbery, extortion, kidnapping, air piracy, terrorism, foreign counterintelligence, interstate criminal activity, fugitive and drug-trafficking matters, and other violations of federal statutes. Minimum qualifications are as follows: age 23, must not have reached 37th birthday upon appointment, U.S. citizen, must pass color vision test, excellent health and physical condition, valid driver's license, and four-year degree from an accredited college.

---

example is the Bureau of Alcohol, Tobacco, and Firearms (ATF), which, among other responsibilities, enforces the various federal firearms laws and investigates bombings such as the 1995 bombing of a federal building in Oklahoma City.

PATROL OPERATIONS

The first assignment for almost all new police officers, regardless of the size of the agency, is with the patrol division. This assignment is the foundation upon which all other police experiences are formed. As previously mentioned, the rookie officer is usually assigned to work directly under the supervision and direction of a field training officer (FTO) or coach. These senior officers are often very influential in the professional development of the new officers placed under their tutelage. The amount of time a rookie and a senior officer spend together is dictated by the policy of the organization, the pace at which the new officer masters certain skills, and the needs of the organization.

One of the earliest, if not the first formally recognized, field training programs was established in the San Jose (California) Police Department. The program was developed as a result of an incident in which an inadequately trained new officer negligently operated a police vehicle, causing the death of a citizen. Today the San Jose field training program is held in high regard and is widely emulated throughout the country.

CTQ

Do you believe there should be a standard, mandatory time requirement for rookies to spend with an FTO, irrespective of the policy of the organization or the pace at which the new officer masters certain skills? Briefly explain your answer.

Patrol Division Assignments

The part of a community to which a new officer is assigned depends on the personnel needs of the patrol division and the philosophy of the chief administrator or division commander. For example, one administrator might favor assigning rookie officers to high-crime areas to accelerate their experience and to allow an assessment of their ability to function under stress. This type of intensive exposure to crime problems might also reduce the time a new officer has to spend under the direct supervision of a senior partner.

IN THE WORKPLACE

SECRET SERVICE AGENT

Responsible for protecting our nation's leaders and conducting criminal investigations of crimes against the currency. Performs a variety of duties, including the following: protecting the president and vice-president, their immediate families, former presidents and their spouses, widows, and minor children of former presidents, minor presidential and vice-presidential candidates and their spouses, and visiting foreign heads of state. Minimum qualifications are as follows: age 21, U.S. citizen, bachelor's degree from an accredited college or two years of work experience in criminal investigation or law enforcement, excellent health and physical condition, must pass Treasury Department enforcement agent exam and background investigation.

IN THE WORKPLACE

PATROL OFFICER

Responsible for patrolling assigned areas to inspect, interrogate suspicious people, and monitor suspected criminal activities. Also responsible for the following: investigating incidents that are in violation of civil and criminal laws; apprehending and arresting law violators; preserving evidence; enforcing traffic laws; and providing information, assistance, and counseling to members of the public. Minimum qualifications are as follows: age 19–21, depending on the state; high school diploma or equivalent; U.S. citizen; valid driver's license; and law enforcement certification.

Other administrators assign rookie officers to areas with few serious crime problems, allowing the officers to gain experience at a slower rate and in a less volatile environment.

Most patrol divisions contain some interesting organizational contradictions that can have a negative impact on operations. For example, chief administrators frequently espouse the position that the patrol bureau is the "backbone" of the agency, but they then proceed to transfer the best and brightest officers away from that bureau to other assignments, such as the detective bureau, vice squad, or training academy. This practice, which is common to many police departments, can create serious personnel problems. If continued with regularity, the practice guarantees that the "backbone" of the police department will be composed primarily of inexperienced officers and those who are average, or even below average, in ability and motivation.

Why would a police administrator employ a policy that depletes a primary operating unit of its finest people? There are several answers to this question. First, an administrator may not really believe in the importance of the patrol division. Second, he or she may not believe that the patrol division is sufficiently stimulating, rewarding, or challenging to keep the best, brightest, and most able officers satisfied. Such officers are therefore provided with higher status and more challenging positions to keep them from resigning or becoming dissatisfied and bored with their patrol assignments. A chief of police who clings to these beliefs probably has instituted policies that do indeed make an assignment to the patrol bureau unchallenging and lacking in status. For instance, if a police chief believes that patrol officers should have little or no responsibility for investigating even the most routine criminal offenses and that all segments of an investigation should be conducted by a detective, then that chief has eliminated for the patrol officer one of the most interesting and challenging functions of police work—namely, criminal investigation.

Another problem in patrol divisions is that many officers wish to be transferred to other units. The environment of most patrol division probably contributes to this situation. By necessity, patrol divisions operate twenty-four hours a day, every day of the year; because of this schedule, officers assigned to patrol must work more weekends, nights, and holidays than many of their counterparts in other units. This work schedule increases the possibility that days off will be spent making court appearances, and shift-related problems may be particularly troublesome to officers whose spouses work at regular daytime jobs with weekends off.

The normal working day of a patrol officer is not filled with glamorous and exciting crime-fighting activities like those depicted on popular television programs. Instead, days are spent on routine patrol or performing noncriminal services for the public. However, in spite of this routine, the patrol officer's job is often far more dangerous than most people imagine. Patrol officers are the ones who are called to respond to crimes in progress or crimes that have just been committed. Such assignments increase the possibility that a criminal will still be at the scene of the crime or in the immediate area, thereby increasing the potential for physical and armed confrontation. Thus, the job of the patrol officer has often been described as one consisting of both hours of boredom (especially on the midnight shift) and moments of terror.

Patrol officers also routinely come in contact with individuals who have little respect for social norms or authority. They have to deal with intoxicated individuals who have soiled themselves but who still must be searched before being transported to jail; with teenage gang members who are arrogant, disrespectful, and openly contemptuous; with prostitutes, pimps, and petty thugs; and with child abusers. Patrol officers are called upon to intercede in domestic disputes in which combating couples often turn on the officers trying to settle the dispute peacefully. With all of these problems—on top of the incredible number of written reports that patrol officers must complete—a job in the patrol division can be highly stressful, both physically and psychologically. Thus, in spite of efforts by many progressive administrators to improve supervision and working conditions and to give greater recognition to patrol division officers, the ambition of many of these officers is first to become a detective and later to move into management, with its higher status, better hours, and higher pay.

Patrol officers know that the financial rewards and professional status in most police departments are reserved for managers. Those who serve as patrol officers for twenty years and then retire are frequently considered "not very successful" by their peers, regardless of their accomplishments. This is a serious problem, because the organization of most police departments makes it impossible for more than 10 to 20 percent of all officers to rise above the rank of patrol officer. Thus, because of the built-in limitations of organizations, the expectations and ambitions of many officers cannot be met.

One can find among the ranks of any police department many individuals who have neither the interest nor the aptitude to become managers, yet these individuals feel compelled to pursue supervisory and managerial positions because such positions offer the only route for achieving some degree of professional stature and monetary reward. It is apparent that new organizational models must be considered to provide realistic and cost-effective alternatives. One possibility is a dual-career system that allows police officers to follow either a nonmanagerial, **professional officer track** or a **professional police management track.**

A two-track system could provide a realistic and workable alternative to management. An officer could remain within the patrol ranks in a nonmanagerial role, yet still enjoy some of the professional and monetary rewards of the organization. For each track, specific training and educational components can be built into the system to assure individual development along with quality control. Thus, all police officers would know precisely what they must do to move up the professional police officer track or the professional police management track. This dual-track model may not be appropriate in its present form to meet the needs of some police departments, but it does provide a conceptual framework within which alternative models can be developed.

Activities of Patrol Officers

No two patrol divisions perform identical tasks, although some tasks are basic to all, regardless of size. In general, patrol duties are not spelled out in great detail, except when

CTQ
Do you think a two-track dual-career system is an adequate response to the built-in promotional limitations in police departments across the United States?

IN THE WORKPLACE

PATROL SERGEANT

Responsible for planning, organizing, directing, and supervising work on an assigned shift or unit within the police department and instructing and assisting subordinates in performance of their assigned duties. Performs a variety of duties, including the following: recommending and assisting in implementation of unit goals and objectives; instructing officers in the enforcement of laws and ordinances; participating in budget preparation and implementation; supervising crime scenes; and supervising the gathering, handling, and preserving of evidence. Minimum qualifications are as follows: valid driver's license, high school diploma or equivalent, two to five years of law enforcement experience (depending on education level), and understanding of the principles of supervision, training, methods and techniques of law enforcement.

patrol officers are assigned to a specific call for police service. Thus, the catchall phrase "routine patrol and observation" is interpreted in different ways by individual departments, supervisors, and patrol officers. For example, some patrol officers on the day shift who do not have a specific assignment might decide to concentrate on traffic enforcement; others might decide to patrol a residential area that has had a recent rash of daytime burglaries. The same variations in preference may also exist in the evening and midnight shifts; some officers might patrol a main street or business district to prevent robberies, and others might patrol a warehouse district to prevent burglaries.

Ideally, the type of routine patrol and observation engaged in by patrol officers should be the result of a collaborative effort between the patrol supervisor and the patrol officer, based on the crime data for a given patrol area. Some innovative police departments have developed programs in which patrol officers who work days and are not on a call are encouraged to conduct crime-prevention checks of homes and businesses in their districts that are susceptible to burglaries and robberies. Such efforts usually result in more productive use of patrol time. Further examples of innovative patrol practices are discussed later in this chapter.

Noncrime Calls for Service In many departments it is estimated that between 80 and 90 percent of all calls for police service are of a noncriminal nature. Many of these calls involve possession and repossession of property, landlord-tenant disputes, property-line arguments, animal control, and noise complaints. Thus, patrol officers must be knowledgeable about the civil law as well as the criminal law. Even calls for service that are clearly civil in nature must be handled promptly and tactfully because they can quickly escalate into violent confrontation between disputants or between a disputant and an officer.

Attendance at Public Gatherings Patrol officers are frequently assigned to work at large public gatherings such as political rallies and sporting events. Their presence is needed to assure peaceful assembly and to provide protection for those wishing to exercise their rights to peaceful assembly and free speech. Sometimes arrests are made at events. An officer's presence may also prevent unlawful activity on the part of individuals or the crowd as a whole. A recent trend is for sponsors of an event to hire off-duty patrol officers, especially if the sponsors are private enterprises or individuals. For example, many sports authorities and convention centers now employ off-duty officers to work the interior and exterior of their facilities during special events and to control traffic into and out of parking areas.

Benevolent and Community Services Patrol officers are frequently called upon to perform tasks not in their job descriptions. They are called upon to deliver babies, to give advice to families about marital problems and problems with adolescent children, to help people who have lost the keys to their homes or automobiles, to inform people about accidents and deaths, and to deliver blood from one hospital to another. Some patrol officers feel that they should not have to perform so many nonpolice functions; such tasks do nothing to enhance the image of officers in the eyes of the public or in the eyes of the officers themselves. In more service-oriented departments these duties are accepted and embraced as part of good police work. However, in some locations the expectations of local government leaders regarding what constitutes police work is questionable. "In the News: Community Service or City Hall Interference?" illustrates that point.

Preliminary Investigations The patrol officer is on duty and available for all incidents that call for police service, including crimes and accidents. A patrol bureau that is adequately staffed and has properly trained its officers is in the best position to handle the preliminary investigation of all types of crimes. As the first police officer to arrive at the scene of a crime, the patrol officer must care for any injured people and must apprehend the criminal if he or she is still in the immediate area. The patrol officer takes immediate steps to preserve the crime scene, then establishes communication with the dispatcher to broadcast a description of the wanted person and to request additional assistance if needed.

CTQ

Should patrol officers be expected to perform nonpolice functions as part of their jobs? Do you believe this type of interactive community involvement constitutes good police work, or do such tasks do nothing to enhance the image of the officers in the eyes of the public?

IN THE NEWS
A HUMAN PERSPECTIVE

COMMUNITY SERVICE OR CITY HALL INTERFERENCE?

In one city, the head librarian of the public library contacted the city manager and asked for police assistance in recovering overdue books. The city manager agreed to help and ordered the police chief to have patrol officers go to the homes of violators (children, in some cases) and pick up books. If no one was at home, the officers were to leave a written warning on the door that arrest for larceny could result if the books were not returned immediately. Needless to say, the patrol officers were not thrilled with this task; some were, in fact, quite embarrassed by it.

In another city, officers were instructed to turn on (at dusk) the Christmas tree lights in front of the homes of several influential citizens. The lights were also to be turned off at sunrise.

FIGURE 5.1

After an arrest, in most cases, the arrestee is taken to jail, booked, and (as in this photo) fingerprinted. The arrestee is then given the opportunity to post bail.

© Dale Stockton.

Because he or she has been on the scene from the beginning, the patrol officer usually continues with the initial investigation—collecting evidence, cataloging and filing it, and preparing the necessary reports. When all leads are exhausted and further investigation would take the officer out of his or her assigned district for a long period of time, the follow-up work is usually taken over by an investigator and other specialists.

However, many small departments cannot afford the expense of employing full-time investigators to conduct follow-up investigations. Therefore, in these departments a more experienced patrol officer or supervisor will usually assume the role of investigator. Likewise, many small agencies allow their patrol officers to conduct most investigations in their entirety, which makes the job more challenging, interesting, and rewarding.

Arrests Another of the many duties of the patrol officer is to arrest those who violate the law. This activity is one of the officer's primary objectives at the crime scene. Once an officer makes an arrest, several methods may be used to introduce the arrestee into the criminal justice system. These methods are defined by the laws, the courts, and the procedural manuals of various agencies. In most cases the arrestee is taken to jail and "booked" or processed and then given an opportunity to post bail to assure his or her appearance in court at a later date.[9] (see Figure 5.1.)

Traffic Direction and Traffic Law Enforcement Safe and efficient movement of pedestrians and vehicles through a community is the patrol officer's responsibility even if another division of the police department exists strictly for traffic control.

Traffic law enforcement is an important task for agencies that provide full-service policing to a local community. While traffic law enforcement is often misunderstood by members of the public, its primary objectives are to help assure public compliance with traffic laws and to promote motorist safety. Given the high volume of traffic in and around many urbanized areas, this is no easy task for the police.

As noted in an earlier chapter, the practice of racial profiling has damaged the public's confidence in many police departments. "In the News: Professional Police Traffic Stops" illustrates how police agencies can implement an effective, legal traffic law enforcement program based on professional standards to reduce the likelihood of allegations and actual instances of racial profiling.

A HUMAN PERSPECTIVE

PROFESSIONAL POLICE TRAFFIC STOPS
by Grady Carrick

The phenomenon of targeting "people of color" in traffic enforcement as a pretext to further investigation or search describes the term *racial profiling.* To professional law enforcement officers and the public, racial profiling is blatantly objectionable and indefensible. Basically, it amounts to the improper practice of selecting potential criminal suspects because of their race or ethnicity.

The law enforcement response to racial profiling, termed *professional police traffic stops,* can ensure that officers base their behavior on sound legal reason, safety for officers and citizens, and the accepted standards of modern policing. The reason for the stop and any enforcement action of the officer must be legally and morally defensible. The mechanical elements of executing a professional police traffic stop aside, agencies need a comprehensive strategy for success. To implement professional police traffic stops, agencies must adopt a three-dimensional approach. Organizational policy, officer training, and data collection represent the essential ingredients of a comprehensive agency strategy.

AGENCY POLICY
Policy formation is the process of establishing a new direction for agency philosophy or employee conduct. Agencies must develop a well-structured policy concerning professional traffic stops, outlining the conduct of officers and prohibition of discriminatory practices. Managers, supervisors, and the entire workforce must embrace and employ the policy.

OFFICER TRAINING
Integrating discussion about racial profiling into diversity and refresher training proves beneficial. Agencies may not need to create an additional forum for the issue, provided they adequately can infuse it into an existing program. Nationally, the Police Officer Standards and Training Commission should evaluate the topic for inclusion in current diversity training programs required for all officers. Moreover the discussion of racial profiling is appropriate for both entry-level and in-service officer training.

Raising sensitivity to the issue, as well as reinforcing the agency's position, stands as the objective of the training. Agencies must ensure that a clear message is delivered to all employees—racial profiling is not an acceptable law enforcement practice and will not be tolerated.

DATA COLLECTION
Agencies must offer a skeptical public more than rhetoric concerning their stance on the issue. Statistics comparing traffic stop demographics with population demographics can assure the public that an agency does not practice racial profiling. In short, agencies must collect information that shows that they do not stop a disproportionate number of minorities. Data should include:

- reason for the stop;
- race, sex, approximate age, and ethnicity of the individual stopped;
- type of search conducted, if any;
- rationale for the search;
- nature of contraband recovered, if any; and
- enforcement action taken during the stop (e.g., ticket issued or warning given).

While traffic citation data can prove useful, critics argue that many stops do not result in the issuance of a citation. Notably, the "questionable stops" that are predicated on no articulatable reason cannot result in enforcement action because they were not the result of a violation occurring. Officers who use profiling tactics typically do not "give paper" to individuals they stop who subsequently turn out not to be criminals. Therefore, agencies may find traffic ticket or other statistical information a good starting point, but may need a more comprehensive data set to provide insight into their use or nonuse of profiles.

To obtain complete data, agencies may need to modify their traffic citation, written warning, or field interview forms. An alternative to these changes may include having officers complete a separate form that captures the desired information. Either way, a snapshot of who officers are stopping is needed. Policy should require officers to document each traffic stop they initiate. By requiring data collection on all stops, agencies obtain a complete data set and an accurate depiction of officer actions. Complete data collection on all stops also minimizes the ability of unethical officers to hide improper conduct.

The highly visible function of police patrol and traffic enforcement mandates professionalism in traffic stops. By implementing a strategy that addresses racial profiling, agencies move closer to professionalism. Moreover, implementing a program for professional police traffic stops can protect and strengthen the bond of trust between the public and the police.

Source: G. Carrick, "Professional Police Traffic Stops," *FBI Law Enforcement Bulletin,* Washington, D.C., vol. 69, no. 11 (2000), pp. 8–11.

Court Testimony Testifying in court is the patrol officer's final step in the investigative process. When an officer receives a call, he or she responds, then conducts the investigation, arrests the offender, processes the evidence, completes reports, and presents evidence and testimony in court.

CHANGING PATROL STRATEGY

Traditional police patrol strategies have been based on two assumptions: first, that highly visible patrol cars deter crime; second, that the presence of these patrol vehicles makes citizens feel safer. Over the last thirty years police patrol strategies and philosophies have changed. In order to better understand contemporary police patrol efforts it is useful to discuss some of the early research on patrol practices, as well as various patrol practices that evolved in the last quarter of the twentieth century. The first test of these assumptions was the now-famous Kansas City Preventive Patrol Experiment conducted in 1972.[10] The experiment and its findings are described next.

Kansas City Preventive Patrol Experiment

The study was conducted within fifteen beats in a thirty-two-square-mile area with a 1970 resident population of 148,395. (*Beats* are limited geographical areas that are ordinarily patrolled by marked vehicles operated by one or two uniformed officers.) The beats were designated as reactive, proactive, or control areas. **Reactive beats** did not have preventive patrols; officers entered these areas only upon a citizen's request for service. When not responding to calls, officers in reactive units patrolled adjacent proactive beats or the boundaries of their own beats. In **proactive beats,** routine preventive patrol was intensified to two to three times its usual level.

A normal amount of patrolling was conducted in *control beats*. The following trends were noted in the evaluation of the experiment:

1. The amount of reported crime in reactive, control, and proactive beats showed only one significant statistical variation: The number of incidents in the category of "other sex crimes," which excludes rape and includes such offenses as exhibitionism and molestation, was higher in reactive areas than in control areas. However, project evaluators felt that this statistical significance was probably random.
2. No statistically significant differences were found among the three types of areas with regard to fluctuations in crimes that were not officially reported to the police.
3. There was no statistically significant difference in arrests among the three types of beats.
4. Citizen fear of crime was not significantly altered by changes in the level of routine preventive patrol.
5. Variations in the level of patrolling did not significantly alter the security measures taken by citizens or businesses.
6. Little correlation was found between the level of patrol and the attitudes of citizens and businesspeople toward the policing.
7. The time taken by police to answer calls was not significantly altered by variations in the level of routine preventive patrol.
8. Level of patrol had no significant effect on the incidence of traffic accidents.

The interpretations and findings of the Kansas City Preventive Patrol Experiment were highly controversial at the time. Upon learning of the study, some local leaders felt that further increases in police personnel were not warranted and that decreases might even be justified. However, such leaders failed to consider that just because the prevailing method of preventing crime—routine preventive patrol—was not effective, it did not follow that no strategy of prevention would work. The findings do suggest that administrators might be able to test alternative patrol strategies—diverting significant blocks of time from routine patrol to community interface—without increasing the crime rate. The following section describes some of the patrol alternative strategies used since the Kansas City study.

Nontraditional Patrol

For the last thirty years, the majority of police officers assigned to the patrol division conducted their business out of patrol cars. Although there is little doubt that the ability to

---

CTQ

Considering the findings of the Kansas City experiment, do you believe that higher visibility of patrol officers would deter the commission of certain types of crime (such as burglary) in your community? Why or why not?

cover large geographic areas has been enhanced by motorized police vehicles, there is a growing concern among law enforcement officials that too much emphasis has been placed on officers themselves being in the cars.

What seems to be missing in many towns and cities is face-to-face interaction between police officers and their communities. If officers are required to respond to calls for service, take appropriate action, and return immediately to their cars to continue "patrol," there is little opportunity for officers and citizens to get to know one another. Furthermore, the patrol officer has virtually no opportunity to learn what has gone on prior to his or her response and even less chance to be empathetic.

In an effort to develop more positive police-community interaction and to reduce the overdependence on vehicular patrol, some police departments have used forms of **nontraditional patrol,** such as the following:

1. *Park and walk.* Officers are assigned to specific geographic areas and are required to park their patrol cars several times a day and conduct foot patrol for a period of time.
2. *Bicycle patrol.* Officers are provided with bicycles and assigned to a geographic zone for patrol purposes (see Figure 5.2). Officers respond to calls for service and provide a conspicuous presence in areas that cannot be accessed by cars. (See "In the News: Bike Patrol.")
3. *Golf cart patrol.* Officers are assigned to patrol (usually) business districts or parking lots in golf carts, which allow officers to interact readily with the public and to be available for calls for service.
4. *Horse patrol.* Some cities have gone back to purchasing horses for use in patrol by select officers. The officers are highly visible and can interact quite easily with the community. (See "In the News: Police on Horseback.")

Flint, Michigan, Foot Patrol

Municipalities have also recognized the positive value of assigning some officers in certain geographic locations to foot patrol for their entire shift. They find that an officer on foot patrol is able to improve communications through frequent, positive contact and develop meaningful linkages between the community and its government. The use of officers on foot patrol, with a broadened role is part of the community-oriented policing philosophy discussed later in this chapter.

For example, in the Flint (Michigan) Police Department, a specific program of foot patrol was implemented and evaluated.[11] In Flint, foot patrol officers were expected to serve as a catalyst for community crime-prevention programs and were seen as the

FIGURE 5.2

To enhance face-to-face interaction between police and the community many police departments have instituted nontraditional forms of patrol such as the bicycle patrol. These officers can make their presence felt in areas not accessible to patrol cars and get to know and be known by the residents of the neighborhoods they serve.

Courtesy Bob Daemmrich/Stock Boston.

IN THE NEWS

A HUMAN PERSPECTIVE

BIKE PATROL: OFFICERS IN ACTION

While on bicycle patrol, Officers William Campbell and Pete Rangel of the Gilbert, Arizona, Police Department detected an odor of smoke. Checking the area, they traced the source of the smoke to a fire at a nearby residence. The officers entered the home, located the source of the fire, and proceeded to evacuate the occupants, one adult and three children, who were unaware of the emergency. As the officers led the occupants to safety, an explosion sent flames 20 feet into the air. After calling for backup patrol units and the fire department, Officers Campbell and Rangel then alerted and evacuated the occupants of surrounding residences. Due to the officers' decisive actions and teamwork, no one was injured during the evacuation, despite two large explosions. Fire department officials later credited the officers' actions with helping to prevent the fire from spreading to other residences.

Source: FBI Law Enforcement Bulletin, vol. 66, no. 7 (1997), p. 32.

IN THE NEWS

A HUMAN PERSPECTIVE

POLICE ON HORSEBACK: A NEW CONCEPT FOR AN OLD IDEA
by John C. Fine

Modern policing emphasizes constructive interaction between law enforcement officers and members of the public. Community policing initiatives have served as a basis for a number of enforcement innovations designed to increase the patrol officer's personal contact with citizens. In an effort to get officers out of their patrol cars, some departments have either initiated, expanded or reinvigorated equestrian units to enhance community policing efforts. An officer on horseback invites constructive community contact in its own unique way.

BACKGROUND

Folklore of the frontier lawman on horseback in the American old west evokes an image of peace and justice. These peace officers on horseback ensured their townspeople security from exploitation and banditry. The sheriff or marshal had a vast territory to cover with few people to rely on for assistance. The horse not only served as a constant companion for the peace officer, but also as an ally.

ONE DEPARTMENT'S EXPERIENCE

Rockland County, New York is a 172-square-mile suburban area 16 miles north of New York City, with a population of approximately 300,000. The Rockland County Sheriff's Office currently has 67 sworn full-time deputies in the police patrol division, including six full-time mounted deputies.

The unit helps locate and apprehend criminal suspects; manage crowds; assist with major event security; attend special public appearances; and promote neighborhood watch and area school programs. The high vantage point of the rider, coupled with how quickly and easily the horses allow them to negotiate difficult areas, such as crowded streets, proves their value as an operational asset to the department. A few horses can move a large crowd that normally would require 10 times the number of officers on foot.

Mounted units prove successful in crime prevention as well. The fact that a deputy on horseback has better view than a deputy on foot can provide a helpful edge in many situations. Horses with mounted deputies often exceed 10 feet in height and their presence alone often can bring calm to an unruly or violent situation or even prevent crimes from occurring. In their recent routine patrols, mounted deputies in Rockland County have participated actively in a variety of calls ranging from stolen vehicles and DWIs to disorderly conduct and domestic issues. The mounted deputies carry portable radios and mobile telephones to ensure coordination and team policing and to remain in contact with their patrol supervisor and dispatchers. The deputies must rely on cooperation from other officers and coordination between agencies for the mounted patrols to remain successful.

In addition to routine patrols, the increased rapport with the public constitutes an added benefit of mounted deputies from an agency's public relations aspect. Mounted units in parades, at public events, or even while on patrol serve as excellent ways for citizens to meet and appreciate their local law enforcement. Mounted deputies can visit elementary schools and provide scheduled tours of the stables to interested groups.

In Rockland County, mounted patrols have become an integral part of community policing. Citizens often approach mounted deputies to touch and talk about the patrol horses. This curiosity that draws citizens toward the horses allows the mounted deputies to help establish liaison, and contact with the community. Mounted units effectively can handle crowd control and public relations activities, as well as perform many traditional policing duties (e.g., apprehending criminal suspects). The mere presence of mounted officers also can deter crime, even more so than a marked police car patrolling a neighborhood.

The concept of police on horseback has changed very little since the days of the western lawman. Mounted sheriffs continue to recognize residents by name and offer citizens reassurance by patrolling the streets. Today, enhanced with modern practices, communication, and technology, officers on horseback symbolize the original concept of American law enforcement—they provide protection, denote authority, and strengthen community involvement.

Source: John C. Fine, "Police on Horseback: A New Concept for an Old Idea," *FBI Law Enforcement Bulletin*, vol. 70, no. 7 (2001), pp. 6–8.

WEB

For more information on foot patrol, visit our Web site, www.prenhall.com/territo.

"link" to governmental services for neighborhood residents. These officers routinely conducted public-education programs on crime prevention, developed community newsletters with crime-prevention tips, and made house or business visits to encourage good crime-prevention techniques.

The Flint foot patrol program was generally successful. Among the indicators of success were the fact that crime was down; that residents surveyed responded positively to foot patrol; that residents reported feeling safer in their neighborhoods; and that police-community relations appear to have improved. These findings were useful in providing a foundation for community-oriented policing, described later in this chapter.

Directed Patrol

Since the Kansas City Preventive Patrol Experiment, police administrators have reviewed numerous ways to improve the overall productivity of their patrol officers. One technique, frequently called *directed patrol*, attempts to define priorities for patrol officers and to encourage the productive use of uncommitted, random patrol time. The details of this operational concept are as follows.[12]

Two operational mechanisms have been combined to greatly enhance the value of visible patrol. First, **crime analysis** has been used to specify carefully the time and locations of directed-patrol so that police visibility is concentrated in areas of high criminal activity. In most cases, patrols have focused on areas where the suppressible crimes of robbery, burglary, auto theft, and larceny, as well as traffic accidents, vandalism, and order maintenance constitute significant problems.

A second but no less significant factor has been the high priority given to directed patrol. Directed-patrol assignments take precedence over all other patrol activities except emergency calls, which represent 10 to 15 percent of the entire patrol call workload in most departments. The high priority assigned to directed patrol ensures that officers will have an opportunity to plan and complete these patrols. Perhaps the principal achievement of directed patrol is that it has enabled departments to achieve a level of patrol without increasing the number of personnel assigned to patrol operations.

It is safe to say that police operations have benefitted from techniques such as directed patrol, which developed as a result of research such as the Kansas City Preventive Patrol Experiment. Many of today's community policing efforts (discussed later) are a direct result of the changing patrol strategies.

Crackdowns

Given the overall scarcity of police patrol resources, some experts believe it is important to rotate patrol plans to meet changing community law enforcement priorities. Some refer to these changing patrol strategies as **crackdowns.** Specifically, crackdowns are defined as "increases in either the certainty or the severity of police reaction to a specific crime or all crime in a specific area."[13] Crimes such as drunk driving, domestic violence, and public drug sales have all drawn significant police attention over the last several years. (See "In the News: Examples of Police Crackdowns.")

ZERO-TOLERANCE ENFORCEMENT

Over the last two decades many criminal justice researchers and practitioners have become increasingly concerned with the quality of life of many citizens living largely in urban areas. In many of these regions signs of blight and physical decay are ever-present. In their now-classic article published in *Atlantic Monthly* in 1982, James Q. Wilson and George Kelling emphasized the connection between signs of minor disorder and ultimately serious community crime. They argued that if one broken window in a building was left unfixed, it would only be a matter of time before all the windows would be broken. The following statement by Kelling and Wilson best summarizes this notion:

> A stable neighborhood of families who care for their homes, mind each other's children, and confidently frown on unwanted intruders can change, in a few years or even a few months, to an inhospitable and frightening jungle. A piece of property is abandoned, weeds grow up, a window is smashed. Adults stop scolding rowdy children; the children, emboldened, become more rowdy. Families move out, unattached adults move in. Teenagers gather in front of the corner store. The merchant asks them to move; they refuse. Fights occur. Litter accumulates. People start drinking in front of the grocers; in time, an inebriate slumps to the sidewalk and is allowed to sleep it off. Pedestrians are approached by panhandlers.[14]

Eventually, this school of thought would be coined the "broken windows theory of crime." By analogy, if petty crimes of disorder are ignored by police, this will encourage criminals to commit more serious crimes. Many police departments have changed their

WEB

For more information on directed patrol, **visit our Web site,** www.prenhall.com/territo.

WEB

For more information on crackdowns, **visit our Web site,** www.prenhall.com/territo.

IN THE NEWS
A HUMAN PERSPECTIVE

EXAMPLES OF POLICE CRACKDOWNS
by Larry Sherman

Police crackdowns can target specific neighborhoods or specific offenses, and their duration can range from a few weeks to several years. The following, selected from the 18 case studies reviewed for this article, illustrate this range. Initial and residual deterrent effects varied, sometimes based on factors outside the scope of the crackdowns themselves.

- Drug crackdown, Washington, D.C. A massive police presence—60 police officers per day and a parked police trailer—in the Hanover Place neighborhood open-air drug market provided an effective initial deterrent.
- Lynn, Massachusetts, open-air heroin market. A 4-year crackdown using four to six police officers led to 140 drug arrests in the first 10 months and increased demand for drug treatment.
- Operation Clean Sweep, Washington, D.C. The city allocated 100 to 200 officers—many on overtime—to 59 drug markets, making 60 arrests a day. Tactics included roadblocks, observation of open-air markets, "reverse buy" sell-and-bust by undercover officers, and seizure of cars.
- Repeat Call Address Policing (RECAP) Experiment, Minneapolis. A special unit of five police officers attempted to reduce calls for service from 125 residential addresses, increasing their presence with landlords and tenants. This short-term targeting of resources led to a 15 percent drop in calls from these addresses, compared to 125 control addresses.
- Nashville, Tennessee, patrol experiment. A sharp increase in moving patrol at speeds under 20 miles per hour in four high-crime neighborhoods netted a measurable decrease in Part I Index crime during two short crackdowns (11 days and 15 days).
- Disorder crackdown in Washington, D.C. Massive publicity accompanied a crackdown on illegal parking and disorder that was attracting street crime to the Georgetown area of the city. Police raised their weekend manpower 30 percent and installed a trailer at a key intersection to book arrestees.
- New York City subway crackdown. This massive crackdown involved increasing the number of police officers from 1,200 to 3,100, virtually guaranteeing an officer for every train and every station. Crime fell during the first 2 years of the crackdown but rose again during the following six years.
- Cheshire, England, drunk driving crackdowns. During two short-term crackdowns, one accompanied by continuing publicity, police increased breathalyzer tests up to sixfold between 10:00 P.M. and 2:00 A.M. Significant deterrent effects continued up to 6 months after the crackdowns ceased.
- London prostitution crackdown. Stepped up arrests of prostitutes, pimps, and brothel keepers—combined with cautions of their customers—succeeded in reducing "curb-crawling," with no displacement.
- New Zealand drunk driving crackdowns. Deterrent effects of two short-term crackdowns were felt even before they began, because of intensive publicity about the impending crackdowns and stepped-up administration of breathalyzer tests.

Source: L. Sherman, "Police Crackdowns," *NIJ Reports* (Washington, D.C.: U.S. Department of Justice, 1990), p. 3.

CTQ
What are the advantages and disadvantages of zero-tolerance policing?

CTQ
The "broken windows theory of crime" suggests that if petty crimes or disorder are ignored by police, this will encourage criminals to commit more serious crimes. Do you agree or disagree with this statement? Explain briefly.

---

tactics over the recent years by paying more direct attention to petty crimes such as panhandling, loitering, and disorderly conduct.[15] Making arrests for these less serious crimes has become more commonplace in cities such as Seattle, San Francisco, Boston, and Baltimore. Some have argued that combating these crimes of disorder has reduced the numbers of serious felonies in recent years.

In the early 1990s, New York City implemented **zero-tolerance policing,** an approach in which officers were encouraged to clean up the streets by making arrests for minor offenses. "In the News: Zero Tolerance in a Small Town" illustrates how the zero-tolerance approach may be useful in smaller communities as well. Albert J. McCarthy, chief of police in Kennett Square, Pennsylvania, describes his experience.

POLICE TRAFFIC RESPONSIBILITIES

Traffic is one of the most pervasive problems confronting police agencies. Every person who drives and every vehicle on the street is part of the problem. Because the responsibility for congestion control, traffic law enforcement, and accident prevention cannot be fixed on any single unit, traffic duty must be shared to some degree by every uniformed

A HUMAN PERSPECTIVE

ZERO TOLERANCE IN A SMALL TOWN
by Albert J. McCarthy

The Kennett Square, Pennsylvania, Police Department and the New York City Police Department (NYPD) have one thing in common—both are law enforcement agencies. Beyond that, similarities can be hard to find. With a police force of over 38,000 sworn personnel, New York City has more than six times as many police officers as Kennett Square has citizens. Yet, in recent years, this small community of 5,600, located 25 miles southwest of Philadelphia, has suffered many of the plagues normally associated with big cities—including increased assaults, heightened levels of public drunkenness and disorderly conduct, prostitution, and a flourishing open-air drug market operating around the clock.

The combined effects of these and other factors fueled an appreciable decline in the quality of life in Kennett Square. Throughout the early 1990s, Part I crime-per-capita figures increased. In 1993, the once-placid community experienced four homicides. In 1994, *Philadelphia Magazine* ranked the borough as one of the 10 least safe communities in the Philadelphia metropolitan area.[a]

The growing crime problem did not reflect a lack of resourcefulness on the part of the police department. High clearance rates for Part I and Part II crimes—50 percent and 65 percent, respectively—demonstrated the effectiveness of the 12-member police force.[b] Periodic drug sweeps conducted with the assistance of the state police yielded numerous convictions and helped to dismantle organized trafficking rings. Residents of Kennett Square consistently expressed confidence and satisfaction with their police department. But, the overall quality of life continued to decline. The question remained: What could be done to reverse this trend?

ADAPTING THE NEW YORK MODEL
When I began reading articles about New York City's zero tolerance approach, I was intrigued by the reduction in all types of criminal activity it yielded. The approach itself seemed to reflect a fundamental perception regarding the nature and effects of criminal activity: Citizens in industrialized societies have come to understand and accept that major crimes are going to occur, and they generally are satisfied with the law enforcement response to these types of crimes. However, the approach adopted by New York City addressed the types of miscreant activity and minor crimes that have an even greater impact on communities. When the police began to target *those* kinds of problems, crime rates in all classifications dropped.

RESULTS
In the three-month period of June through August 1995, the year before the zero tolerance approach was adopted, the Kennett Square Police Department made 39 arrests for public nuisance offenses. During the first year of the policy, officers made 220 such arrests. During the three summer months of 1997, as the department continued its proactive community-wide focus on maintaining order, officers made 89 such arrests, indicating a general decline in disorderly activity throughout the borough.

Close cooperation with the district justice (district attorney) has resulted in a very high conviction rate for offenders charged with summary offenses. In fact, most offenders plead guilty rather than contest the charges. At the same time, the police department's focus on defensible arrests has helped to limit public criticism of the department's zero tolerance orientation. During the first year of the policy, only one formal complaint was filed against the department, despite the increased number of arrests.[c] Minority groups who feared that the police department's zero tolerance approach might give officers an excuse to harass innocent people instead have found that they are among the primary beneficiaries of the policy. Minorities had been the targets in a large percentage of the crimes that occurred in the borough.

As the prevalence of minor criminal activity began to fade and the quality of life began to improve throughout the community, police officers in Kennett Square began to experience something their counterparts in New York City had by now grown accustomed to: Citizens began stopping officers to thank them for helping to reclaim their neighborhoods. The enhanced citizen support and involvement, in turn, has helped officers respond even more effectively to problems that do occur. Also as in New York City, Kennett Square's focus on maintaining order and addressing minor criminal activity has resulted in a significant decline in serious (Part I) crime throughout the community. Although criminologists and sociologists might debate the specific causal factors, it would be difficult to dismiss the correlation between an emphasis on enforcing quality-of-life ordinances and resulting declines in serious crime.

CONCLUSION
Today, more than two years after the police department adopted a zero tolerance policy, the open-air drug markets have closed down and have not relocated to other areas of the community. Incidents of disorderly conduct have fallen sharply. The din of car stereos blaring through the night has subsided. Come this summer, residents of Kennett Square will be hoping for mild weather—they look forward to sleeping through cool summer evenings with the windows open.

Source: A. J. McCarthy, "Zero Tolerance in a Small Town," *FBI Law Enforcement Bulletin*, vol. 67, no. 1 (1998), pp 6–10.
[a] Larry Platt, "In My Little Town," *Philadelphia Magazine* (November 1994).
[b] Internal crime data, Kennett Square (Pennsylvania) Police Department.
[c] Christina Asquith, "Kennett Square Tries Zero Tolerance," *Philadelphia Inquirer* (September 10, 1997).

FIGURE 5.3

Most uniformed police officers must share the duties of traffic law enforcement and accident prevention, including, as shown in this photo, administering sobriety tests to motorists suspected of driving under the influence of alcohol or drugs.

© Dale Stockton.

WEB

For more information on police traffic responsibilities, visit our Web site, www.prenhall.com/territo.

member of a police force (see Figure 5.3). The degree to which an officer may be held accountable for traffic duties is dictated by the extent of the traffic problem.

In cities where traffic constitutes a significant problem, specific duties may be assigned to a traffic unit to concentrate efforts. The existence of traffic specialists does not relieve the patrol officers of all responsibility for traffic, but it does free them to adjust their traffic responsibilities in relation to their other duties. Traffic responsibilities usually include traffic control, accident investigation, and traffic law enforcement.

Selective Traffic Enforcement

Contrary to popular belief, the major purpose of traffic law enforcement is not to raise revenues via traffic fines in order to fill the coffers of city, county, or state governments; rather, it is intended to prevent accidents and educate the public. However, this fact is rarely known by the public and is sometimes not fully appreciated by the police. One method used by police agencies to reduce traffic accidents is called **selective traffic enforcement.**

How does selective traffic enforcement work? First, a supervisor checks data on accident patterns occurring in his or her area. These data are available from the traffic engineering department or the police records section. Personnel are then deployed to high-accident areas to enforce violations that appear to be contributing to accidents (see Figure 5.4). Traffic tickets given in high-hazard areas are certainly no more welcome than those given at safer intersections, but this type of enforcement does more toward reducing accidents and protecting life and property than does random issuance of tickets merely to meet a quota.

The Quota System: Myth or Reality?

Citizens frequently ask the question, "Do police departments have a traffic ticket quota?" The answer in some cases is an emphatic yes, but in the final analysis, the decision to use a **quota system** depends on the philosophy of the chief of police, command officers, and lower-level supervisors. Further, the decision can be affected by officer assignment. For example, if a police department has a traffic bureau, officers assigned to the bureau will devote most of their time to traffic responsibilities, including traffic law enforcement. However, in patrol bureaus that have numerous other responsibilities besides traffic, the emphasis on traffic law enforcement may vary considerably. Police departments do not, as a rule, document how many traffic tickets they expect their officers

FIGURE 5.4

Traffic law enforcement is an important function in many communities. This officer is using a speed gun to track motorists passing by.

© Dale Stockton.

to write, but the expected number is rarely zero. Most officers are fully aware, often by way of informal channels, what is expected of them by their departments or supervisors.

Who Gets the Money?

In most cases, money derived from traffic fines does not go to the agencies that enforce the traffic laws; rather, it goes into a general fund at the city, county, or state level. On occasion, a small surcharge (one or two dollars) imposed along with a regular fine is diverted to the police department for training purposes. However, contrary to popular belief, law enforcement agencies that issue traffic citations rarely derive much financial benefit from their activities. The fee system that was common in this country about fifty years ago—in which officers got a percentage of fines—is virtually nonexistent today.

RURAL POLICING

Police practices vary from one area to another, and studying the varieties of police behavior can yield important insights into the role of law enforcement officers in a community. Most studies of variations in police behavior have been conducted in urban settings. Neglecting rural policing and rural crime might be justifiable if there is nothing about policing, crime, or the community in rural environments that precludes directly applying knowledge from urban areas. It is evident, however, that rural environments are distinct from urban environments in ways that affect policing, crime, and public policy.[16]

Given the differences between rural and urban crime and culture, it should be expected that police in rural and urban areas would approach police work differently. Styles of policing are partly a reflection of the relationship between police and the community. In interviews with officers from one rural department and several urban departments, researchers found that officers in rural and urban departments had many similar concerns, but differed in several interesting respects. Urban officers thought they were less respected by citizens. At the same time, police in rural communities felt more public support for being tough, particularly with juveniles. Consistent with the greater informality of rural areas, rural and urban officers believed they were given public respect for different reasons. In urban areas, respect went to the position, and it was believed that a good way to improve public respect was through professionalizing the department. In contrast, respect was thought to be given to rural officers as individuals, who had to prove that respect was deserved. This was often done by establishing a reputation for toughness early in their career.

CTQ

In your opinion, is the quota system, which requires officers to write a specified number of traffic tickets in a given time, an effective method of curtailing the number of accidents in a given area?

WEB

For more information on rural policing, **visit our Web site,** www.prenhall.com/territo.

Given the nature of rural culture and of social interactions in rural areas, police-community relations will likely be very different in rural and urban departments. In rural areas, officers are likely to know offenders and their families, just as the officer and his family will be known by the community (see Figure 5.5). Rural officers are also more likely to know and appreciate the history and culture of an area and to use that information in their work.

Given the closer social ties between police and their community, it should be expected that rural officers will use policing styles that are more responsive to citizens in their area and that, in turn, local residents would be more supportive of the police.

The same features of rural policing that compel officers to be more responsive to the public also mean that rural police have relatively less discretion. An explanation for the high degree of police discretion found in urban areas compared to rural areas is the low visibility of police actions. The actions of police officers in smaller communities are known to most of the population because of the effective informal communication networks that are more highly visible. Small-town police have less latitude in deviating from dominant community values as a result.

The less-formal nature of rural life, along with the small size of many rural departments, makes complex bureaucratic procedures less necessary for day-to-day operations. Thus, rural departments are less likely to have detailed written policies in a variety of areas, a situation that can place them in a legally vulnerable position should a civil lawsuit arise from an allegation of negligence or misconduct.[17]

FIGURE 5.5

Many police departments today use mounted officers on a routine basis. These officers perform patrol and community policing duties.

© Dale Stockton.

CTQ

What are some of the differences between urban and rural styles of policing? Do you think some of the practices arising from those differences (such as the upkeep of detailed written records) warrant administrative reform?

CAMPUS POLICE

The role of campus police has evolved over the last few decades from rule enforcement and property protection to professional law enforcement. Over the last few decades, college campuses have grown in population and size; many now have crime-related problems that require the presence of a full-service campus police department.[18] Baseline research reveals the many similarities between local law enforcement agencies and their counterparts on colleges and universities with 2,500 or more students. Consider the following highlights of research conducted by the Bureau of Justice Statistics:

- During 1995 about three-fourths of the campus law enforcement agencies serving U.S. four-year colleges and universities with 2,500 or more students employed sworn police officers with general arrest powers granted by a state or local government. The remainder relied on nonsworn security personnel.
- Larger institutions and those under public control were the most likely to use sworn officers.
- Most sworn campus police officers were armed, and 64 percent of all agencies used armed officers. Most agencies serving 20,000 or more students used armed officers, compared to less than half of those serving 2,500 to 4,999 students.
- Nearly all agencies with sworn personnel (98 percent) conducted background investigations and criminal record checks of applicants for sworn positions.
- Combined field and classroom training requirements for new officers ranged from an average of more than 900 hours on campuses of 20,000 or more students to less than 400 hours on the smallest campuses.
- About 30 percent of all agencies required new officers to have some college education. About a fourth required a degree, including 11 percent with a four-year-degree requirement.
- All agencies reported that they provided routine patrol services.
- Nearly all agencies used automobile patrol, about three-fourths used officers on foot patrol, and about a third used bicycle patrol. A majority of the agencies serving a campus with 25,000 or more students had bike patrol units.
- About three in five agencies had primary responsibility for homicide investigations, and three in four investigated other serious violent crimes such as rape, rob-

bery, and assault. About four in five investigated major property crimes such as burglary and motor vehicle theft.[19]

THE DETECTIVE ROLE

Three common stereotypes influence the public's perception of investigative effectiveness: the media stereotype, the historical stereotype, and the critical stereotype.[20]

The Media Stereotype

The media image of working detectives—an image pervasive on television—is that of clever, imaginative, persevering, streetwise cops who consort with glamorous women or handsome men and duel with crafty criminals. They and their partners roam cities for days or weeks trying to break a single case that is ultimately solved by means of the investigator's deductive powers. This is the image that many investigators prefer—although perhaps with some concessions. Most investigators concede that criminals are rarely as crafty or diabolical as depicted in the media, but they may not quarrel with the media portrayal of their own capabilities. Some current investigative practices are used mainly to preserve a medialike image or to give victims the services they expect because of that image. For example, sometimes activities such as dusting for fingerprints, showing mug shots, or questioning people are conducted without any hope of developing leads; rather, they are done simply for public relations.

The Historical Stereotype

The historical stereotype is the image held by older police administrators of the special status of detectives in earlier times. Not so many years ago, various illicit activities such as vice, gambling, prostitution, and speakeasies were openly tolerated by city governments. These illegal, but accepted, enterprises created problems for the city police. How could they control such institutions without driving them completely out of business?

Police dealings with illegal institutions were frequently handled by detectives. The detectives ensured that the businesses were run in an orderly fashion and that "undesirables" were driven out. By maintaining this delicate balance the detectives often won the favor of the business leaders and politicians involved in the illegal activities. Such political connections elevated the detective to a position of respect and influence.

The police in general also benefited by allowing these illegal enterprises to continue. When serious crimes occurred or when the public pressured the police to deal with a particular problem, illegal activities provided a valuable source of information for detectives. Not surprisingly, thieves and con artists were often the customers of the vice and gambling operations, or at least had close contact with the people engaged in these businesses. If the police wanted information on a particular criminal activity, they could solicit information as a favor or extort it by threatening the safety of the illegal operations. Thus, the "effectiveness" of detective operations frequently depended on close contacts with a select group of potential informers.

CTQ

What factors do you most attribute to the increased role of campus police as professional law enforcement officers? Would the same factors apply to campuses with less than 2,500 students?

WEB

For more information on campus police, **visit our Web site,** www.prenhall.com/territo.

WEB

For more information on the role of the detective, **visit our Web site,** www.prenhall.com/territo.

IN THE WORKPLACE

DETECTIVE

Responsible for apprehending offenders eluding arrest and investigating incidents and offenses such as death cases, sex offenses, violent felony offenses, burglary and stolen-property offenses, gambling, and controlled-substance offenses. Performs a variety of duties, including the following: maintaining the evidence and property room, controlling all crime scenes, conducting interviews, examining records, observing activities of suspects, and participating in raids or arrests. Minimum qualifications are as follows: associate degree in police science or other related field, two to four years experience in law enforcement, and training that includes criminal investigation, forensic science procedures, and criminology.

Another role played by detectives of the past was that of dispensers of street-corner justice. Good cops were expected to maintain order without resorting to the courts. They did this by persuasion, by making threats, and, if necessary, by using physical force. Only when it was clear that their presence alone would not deter crime did the police bring a suspect in for criminal proceedings. Detectives played this role because they were less visible than uniformed patrol officers. Because of their experience, they were expected to be more diplomatic in handling these incidents (part of the detective's basic working knowledge was an understanding of which individuals could be treated roughly without getting the department into trouble). Detectives who could handle delicate situations without causing a commotion were highly valued by police and city administrators.

Another method once available to detectives was the third degree, which included the use of physical force or extended interrogation. However, this type of activity has been limited by the Supreme Court decision on interrogations in *Miranda v. Arizona*—which increased the enforcement of civil liberties—and by the rise of community review boards. It is no longer acceptable for detectives to arbitrarily arrest suspects and keep them in custody for extended periods of time simply for investigative purposes. Neither is it permissible to use physical or psychological force to extort a confession or to get information about other suspects in a case.

The Critical Stereotype

The critical stereotype of investigative effectiveness is expressed in several studies that analyze how detectives go about their work. One of the earliest critics of investigative practices and detectives was Raymond Fosdick.[21] After visiting police departments in all of the major cities of the United States, he criticized detectives for lack of civil-service standards in selection; lack of training; poor coordination with patrol operation; lack of effective supervision; and lack of ordinary "business systems" for handling administrative work.

Uncomplimentary views of detectives have also been espoused by progressive police chiefs who have seen reforms and new initiatives in every other area of policing except the detective bureau. In such departments, an appointment to the detective bureau is no longer viewed as the best path to promotion. In other departments, independent detective bureaus no longer exist, and investigators are assigned directly to local operations commanders. Many progressive police chiefs are candidly critical of the old, freewheeling style of detective work. They see detectives as trying to preserve the freedom and prerequisites of their jobs without making any effort to adapt to the shifting community and legal climate in which they work.

CTQ
Which stereotype do you believe to be the most responsible for the misunderstanding of the detective role in actuality: the media stereotype, the historical stereotype, or the critical stereotype?

Activities of Detectives

A realistic view of investigative activities can be conveyed by describing how a typical case is handled, variations that frequently occur in the typical pattern, departmental policies that govern how cases are handled, and the supporting activities police perform to increase the likelihood of identification and apprehension.

CTQ
Is the role of the detective held in high regard by the public today? Why or why not?

Incident Report and Preliminary Investigation Most cases involving the discovery of major felonies are initiated by a citizen who calls the police to report the crime or by a police patrol unit that responds to evidence that a crime is in progress. In either case, the first police representative on the scene is usually a uniformed patrol officer. The patrol officer's duties are to aid the victim, to secure the crime scene for later investigation, and to document the facts of the crime. In a few departments, investigators may be dispatched simultaneously with the patrol unit to begin an investigation of the crime, but in most departments, investigation by detectives does not take place until after a patrol officer files a report. The patrol officer's initial report usually contains the basic facts of the crime—the identity of the victim, a description of the suspect, the identity and location of any potential witnesses, a description of the crime scene, and any pertinent statements by witnesses or the victim. This report is passed on to the detective unit, which then continues the investigation.

Patrol units are generally under considerable pressure to cut short their investigations and get back on patrol. Thus, detectives, rather than patrol officers, are usually responsible for developing potential leads and continuing an investigation. In some departments, however, patrol officers are encouraged to use their own initiative to continue an investigation, perhaps by conducting house-to-house checks or using other means to track down suspects.

Evidence Collection and Processing   Studies show that many crime scenes contain physical evidence linking a suspect with the crime. To collect this evidence (such as fingerprints, DNA evidence, firearms evidence, etc.), many departments use trained **evidence technicians** whose sole task is to process crime scenes. Technicians may be dispatched at the time of the crime report, or they may be sent out following the initial report if the responding patrol officer feels that usable evidence might be found. Their job is to examine the crime scene, collect and preserve any physical evidence, and submit a report of their results to the responsible unit.

Screening and Case Assignment   Every morning, incident reports are assembled from the previous day and distributed to the appropriate investigative unit. The assignment of an investigator to a case is determined by the organizational pattern of the department; for example, assignments might be made by crime specialty (such as homicide, robbery, burglary, or sex offenses) or by geographic area. Specialization might be so detailed that assignment personnel can direct an incident report to the specific investigator who will handle that case. Otherwise, the report goes to a unit supervisor who assigns the case to a detective in his or her unit, based on previous assignments or individual workloads. Each detective usually receives one or two new cases a day. Caseloads are generally lower for detectives who handle crimes against the person than for those detectives who handle minor property crimes.

In some departments, formal "solvability factors" and the judgment of the unit supervisor are used to determine whether a specific case should be followed up by an investigator or suspended until new facts develop. Generally, however, every case is assigned to a responsible investigator, with some minimal attempt at follow-up expected. This minimal effort is usually an attempt to contact the victim to obtain facts in addition to those recorded in the incident report. Although investigators may have as many as twenty or thirty open cases at any one time, only two or three cases are really considered active. Workload data shows that most cases are closed within the first day of activity, and very few remain active after two or three days.

Follow-Up (Latent) Investigation   New cases assigned to an investigator generally fall into one of three categories. Cases that receive first priority are those in which the investigative steps are obvious, based on the facts in the incident report. These are the cases in which the victim names a suspect, gives a license number, identifies where the suspect can be found, or indicates additional witnesses who were not interviewed by the responding patrol officer.

Second in priority are cases that require attention not because of obvious leads, but because of the seriousness of the offense or its notoriety in the press or in the community. Investigators want to avoid charges by the community that they are not doing their job, and they may simply be outraged by an offense and want to help the victim.

Cases of the lowest priority are routine cases that offer no additional leads. In all departments, these cases are given only perfunctory treatment.

The first task of investigators when they come to work is to plan their activities for the day. Part of the morning is usually devoted to reviewing new cases, finishing paperwork, and making required court appearances. Late morning and afternoon are usually free for conducting interviews or other follow-up activities. The use of this "free" time is

CTQ

Should the follow-up investigative procedures, in your opinion, be the responsibility of the first responding officer or that of the detective? Briefly explain your answer.

WEB

For more information on evidence collection and processing, **visit our Web site, www.prenhall.com/territo**.

WEB

For more information on the case assignments and workload of detectives, **visit our Web site, www.prenhall.com/territo**.

usually determined by a detective's own judgment; this judgment is based on a sense of priority about each case, the difficulty or attractiveness of conducting various interviews, and the activities of fellow investigators.

Clearance and Arrest   A major demand on an investigator's time occurs when a suspect is taken into custody—usually as a consequence of patrol activity. When an arrest occurs, an effort is often made to clear other crimes similar to the one for which the suspect was arrested. Such is the responsibility of the investigator. If the suspect is willing, the investigator may talk to him or her about similar offenses; if the suspect is not willing to talk, investigators may use their own judgment about whether the suspect might be involved in other cases. If a suspect has been identified by a victim (as often occurs in sex crimes or robberies), previous victims may be brought in to view the suspect in a lineup.

All results of a follow-up investigation are conveyed to the prosecutor in written reports. In many jurisdictions, prosecutors require investigators to consult them about the facts of a case at the time of filing. If an investigator helps solve a case, he or she may also have to testify in court.

File Maintenance   In addition to regular investigative activities, most departments expend resources to develop leads or identify suspects by alternative means. For example, all departments maintain a variety of information files or computerized databanks that serve as sources of investigative leads. These files may include a file of crimes by type, location, or time period; a file of the addresses, descriptions, and *modus operandi* of known offenders; files of mug shots (usually organized by crime type and basic descriptors); files containing the fingerprints of all past arrestees; intelligence files with the names of individuals suspected of particular criminal activity; files of stolen or pawned property; and **field interview files** that indicate where and why certain individuals or vehicles were stopped, along with a description of the person and his or her vehicle. In addition, an increasing number of police agencies have highly developed crime analysis units that provide valuable information to investigators to help them narrow and focus their efforts.

In some departments, special details or strike forces are operated to provide investigative leads that never come through in normal incident reports. The most common example of such activity is a pawnshop detail that routinely inspects items taken in by pawnshops and compares them with lists of stolen property. Another type of strike force—typically called a *sting operation*—uses investigators to buy stolen property in an attempt to identify fences and burglars. In other cases, investigators are assigned temporarily as decoys in high-crime areas.

MAJOR STUDIES OF THE INVESTIGATOR'S ROLE

There have been very few major scientific studies of the role of the detective. Two of these studies are described in the passages that follow.

The Rand Criminal Investigation Study

The Rand Corporation was awarded a grant by the National Institute of Law Enforcement and Criminal Justice in 1978 to undertake a nationwide study of criminal investigations in major metropolitan police agencies. The purposes of the study were to describe how police investigations were organized and managed and to assess the contribution of various activities to overall police effectiveness. Prior to the Rand study, police investigators had not been subject to the type of scrutiny that was being focused on other types of police activity. Most police administrators knew little about the effectiveness of the day-to-day activities of their investigative units and even less about the practices of other departments.[22]

The Study Design   The Rand study concentrated on the investigation of index offenses—serious crimes against unwilling victims—as opposed to vice, narcotics, gambling, or traffic offenses. Information on current practices was obtained by a national survey of all municipal and county police agencies employing more than 150 officers or serving jurisdictions with a population in excess of 100,000. Interviews and observations were conducted in more than twenty-five departments selected to represent different investigative styles. Data on the outcome of investigations were obtained from FBI Uniform Crime Report tapes; from samples of completed cases, which were coded for the study; and from internal evaluations or statistics compiled by individual departments. Data on the allocation of investigative efforts were obtained from a computerized workload file maintained by the Kansas City Police Department.

Data from the national survey and the Uniform Crime Reports were combined for the purpose of analyzing relationships between departmental characteristics and apprehension effectiveness. Case samples were analyzed to determine how specific cases were solved. Recommendations made at the conclusion of these analyses follow.

Policy Recommendations The first recommendation of the Rand study was that postarrest investigation activities be coordinated more directly with prosecutors—either by assigning investigators to prosecutors' offices or by allowing prosecutors to exert more guidance over the policies and practices of investigators. The purpose of the recommendation was to increase the percentage of cases that could be prosecuted.

The second suggestion was that patrol officers be given a larger role in conducting preliminary investigations, both to provide an adequate basis for case screening and to eliminate redundant efforts by an investigator. Most cases can be closed on the basis of the preliminary investigation, and patrol officers can be trained to conduct such investigations adequately. Expanding the role of the patrol officer is consistent with other trends toward geographic decentralization and job enrichment. A third recommendation was that additional resources be devoted to processing latent prints and that improved systems be developed for organizing and searching print files.

Finally, the study recommended that, with regard to follow-up investigations for cases that a department elected to pursue, a distinction should be drawn between cases that require only routine clerical processing and those that require special investigative or legal skills. The former could be handled by lower-level clerical personnel, the latter by a separate bureau.

The PERF Study: Solving Crimes

In 1983 the **Police Executive Research Forum (PERF)** conducted a study of the roles played by patrol officers and detectives in the investigation of robbery and burglary cases. Some of the findings and implications of that study are reviewed in the following paragraphs.[23]

Police detectives and patrol officers contribute equally to the solution of robbery and burglary cases. But the investigation of such cases rarely consumes more than four hours, spread over as many days, and three-quarters of the investigations are suspended within two days for lack of leads. In the remainder of cases, the follow-up work by detectives is a major factor in determining whether suspects will be identified and arrested. However, detectives and patrol officers alike rely too heavily on victims, who seldom provide information leading to an arrest, and make too little use of sources of information most likely to lead to arrest—witnesses, informants, their own colleagues, and police records.

Those were the major findings of PERF's two-year study of criminal investigations of burglary and robbery in three jurisdictions: DeKalb County, Georgia; St. Petersburg, Florida; and Wichita, Kansas. The findings demonstrate that investigations are not necessarily as wasteful or mismanaged as earlier studies suggested, perhaps because those studies stimulated management improvements. The findings show in addition that follow-up investigations by detectives are more valuable in identifying and arresting suspects than earlier research suggested. Finally, PERF's research points the way toward a series of management changes.

WEB

For more information about the PERF study, **visit our Web site,** www.prenhall.com/territo.

The major difference between PERF's findings and those of earlier researchers concerns the role of detectives and the value of follow-up investigations. Earlier studies tended to emphasize the importance of patrol officers and preliminary investigations while downgrading the worth of follow-up investigations. The PERF study reaches the quite different conclusion that patrol officers and detectives contribute equally important work toward the solution of cases.

THE NCIC NETWORK IN INVESTIGATIONS

An innovation in law enforcement investigations that has been critical to the efficiency and effectiveness of police operations has been the development of computerized criminal information. Large and small police departments have come to rely heavily on computerized information that now includes such items as a person's wanted status, whether a vehicle or other property has been stolen, prior criminal history on persons, and the like. For example, officers making a routine traffic stop are aware of the types of information that the **National Crime Information Center (NCIC)** makes available and further coordinates with parallel state crime computer systems.[24]

The NCIC is a nationwide computerized information system established in 1967 to make an automated file of documented criminal justice information available to criminal justice agencies throughout the country. The NCIC computer equipment is located at FBI headquarters in Washington, D.C. Connecting terminals are located throughout the United States, Canada, Puerto Rico, and the U.S. Virgin Islands, in police departments, sheriffs' offices, state police facilities, federal law enforcement agencies, and other criminal justice agencies. The system provides virtually uninterrupted service twenty-four hours a day, seven days a week. Types of information in the NCIC system include wanted persons, missing persons, stolen vehicles, stolen license plates, stolen guns, stolen boats, stolen securities, stolen articles, and unidentified persons.

For three decades, NCIC has efficiently and reliably aided the criminal justice community effort to apprehend criminals. However, it has long since outlived its intended technological life. Thus, the FBI implemented the new generation of NCIC 2000 in July 1999 with powerful new computers and software technology. Through enhancements to existing systems and newly created capabilities, NCIC 2000 facilitates information exchange between agencies, better equips members of the law enforcement community to perform their duties, and increases police officer safety.[25]

NCIC 2000 performs all of the functions of the legacy system augmented with impressive new capabilities. These include the addition of image processing (such as mugshots, signatures, and identifying marks); automated single-finger fingerprint matching; and information linking, which provides the ability to associate logically related records across NCIC files for the same criminal or the same crime. For example, an inquiry on a gun also could retrieve a wanted person, a stolen vehicle, or other records associated with the firearm. NCIC 2000 also automates functions that employees previously had to perform manually. For example, the new system supports online validation of records and automatically collects statistics for evaluating the system in terms of usage and benefits.

New databases, such as the Convicted Sexual Offender Registry and the Convicted Person on Supervised Release File, now provide law enforcement officers with instantaneous information about the whereabouts of individuals who have entered the criminal justice system. NCIC 2000 searches all transactions against the new Convicted Sexual Offender Registry. This provides officers with information on convicted sexual offenders under a wide variety of circumstances.

A new feature, with perhaps the most potential, stores and retrieves digital images on records pertaining to people, vehicles, and articles. NCIC 2000 can associate a mugshot, fingerprint, signature, and identifying photographs with a wanted, missing, or unidentified person record. It also can attach one identifying photograph to a vehicle,

---

CTQ

Do you think that increased usage and availability of computerized criminal information for both large and small police departments will lead to a higher number of arrests being made as a result of the automation of criminal justice information?

WEB

For more information on the NCIC, visit our Web site, www.prenhall.com/territo.

boat, vehicle part, or article record. This new capability can help law enforcement officers in many ways, from identifying individuals stopped for traffic violations to finding missing children to returning stolen property to its rightful owners.

In addition, NCIC 2000 has many other new features. Digital pictures can be attached to NCIC files. A suspect's file might include not only a digital mug shot but also a picture of an identifying tattoo. That's much more precise than nebulous text descriptions such as "5′ 10‴" or "blond hair," as was the case with the older NCIC. In addition, text searches on NCIC 2000 are more powerful. For example, a search for someone named "Bill" will also return hits for "Billy" or "William." The new Integrated Automated Fingerprint Identification System (IAFIS) perhaps is an even more potent tool. Unlike the fingerprinting features of NCIC 2000, which would be used primarily in the field, police officers use IAFIS mostly at booking. It checks whether someone who has been arrested has a criminal history in other states. Traditionally at booking, the police would take ink fingerprints and mail the ten prints to the FBI, which would then manually search 41 million prints for a match, a process that took months to complete. Now with IAFIS the FBI's vast files are all digitized and state or local agencies can submit prints to the FBI electronically. Turnaround time on a digital search is less than two hours.

EVOLUTION IN POLICING: COP AND POP

It has been suggested that there have been three eras of policing in American history: the political, the reform, and the community eras.[26] During the political era, between 1840 and 1930, police leaders were often appointed by elected politicians. Their appointments were made not on the basis of law enforcement expertise but for political reward. This system of patronage (or spoils) flourished throughout all levels of government during this era. Unfortunately, more often than not, police corruption and inefficiency were the end product.

This led to the reform era of policing. During this time, from the 1930s to the early 1980s, strong efforts were made by police chiefs such as August Vollmer and O. W. Wilson to disassociate police departments from politics and the political structure. It was largely during this era that police came to view their role as "crime fighters." In addition, during this era the police went to great efforts to maintain impartiality and distance from members of the public.

During the 1980s, police leaders began to reexamine the focus of the police role with regard to members of the community. Some authorities feel that it was a "combination of dissatisfaction with criminal justice and the role of patrol officers, research results, and the trend towards private policing that led to the third era of policing—the community era."[27]

In the community era, terms such as **community-oriented policing (COP)** and **problem-oriented policing (POP)** have been used to describe the changing philosophy. The focus of community-oriented policing is proactive rather than reactive. As noted shortly, COP emphasizes police departments working as partners with members of the community to resolve crime-related problems and to prevent crime where possible:

> Community policing is a new philosophy of policing based on the concept that police officers and private citizens working together in creative ways can help solve contemporary community problems related to crime, fear of crime, social and physical disorder, and neighborhood decay. . . . It shifts the focus of police work from handling random calls to solving community problems.[28]

Table 5.2 further illustrates the differences between traditional policing and policing in the community era. Descriptions of community policing in action is offered in "In the News: Community Policing" and "In the News: Policing Neighborhoods." Figure 5.6 shows a community police officer interacting with a citizen.

CTQ

Do you believe that the increasing amount of personal information being collected by the government for criminal databases poses potential risks to an individual's right to privacy? If so, briefly explain why.

CTQ

Should police officers be primarily "crime fighters" or community-oriented in their approach to policing? Support your answer.

TABLE 5.2 Comparison of Traditional Policing and Community Policing

Question	Traditional Policing	Community Policing
Who are the police?	A government agency principally responsible for law enforcement.	Police are the public; the public are the police; the police officers are those who are paid to give full-time attention to the duties of every citizen.
What is the relationship of the police force to other public-service departments?	Priorities often conflict.	The police are one department among many responsible for improving the quality of life.
What is the role of the police?	Focusing on solving crimes.	A broader problem-solving approach.
How is police efficiency measured?	By detection and arrest rates.	By the absence of crime and disorder.
What are the highest priorities?	Crimes that are high-value (e.g., bank robberies) and those involving violence.	Whatever problems disturb the community most.
What, specifically, do police deal with?	Incidents.	Citizens' problems and concerns.
What determines the effectiveness of police?	Response times.	Public cooperation.
What view do police take of service calls?	Deal with them only if there is no real police work to do.	Vital function and great opportunity.
What is police professionalism?	Swift, effective response to serious crime.	Keeping close to the community.
What kind of intelligence is most important?	Crime intelligence (study of particular crimes or series of crimes).	Criminal intelligence (information about the activities of individuals or groups).
What is the essential nature of police accountability?	Highly centralized; governed by rules, regulations, and policy directives; accountability to the law.	Emphasis on local accountability to community needs.
What is the role of headquarters?	To provide the necessary rules and policy directives.	To preach organizational values.
What is the role of the liaison department?	To keep the "heat" off operational officers so they can get on with the job.	To coordinate an essential channel of communication with the community.
How do the police regard prosecutions?	As an important goal.	As one tool among many.

Source: Malcolm K. Sparrow, *Implementing Community Policing.* Washington, D.C.: U.S. Department of Justice, National Institute of Justice, 1988, pp. 8–9.

FIGURE 5.6

Community policing involves a variety of constructive efforts to build relationships between the police and citizens. In this photo a community police officer is conducting a crime prevention seminar for a group of students.

© Dale Stockton.

A recent National Institute of Justice survey of police chiefs and sheriffs revealed what they felt to be the major benefits of community policing:

- Fewer problems on issues of concern to citizens
- Improved physical environment in neighborhoods
- More positive public attitudes toward law enforcement agencies
- Decreased potential for conflict between citizens and police
- Increased officer/deputy satisfaction
- Reduced crime rates[29]

In the same NIJ survey, agencies practicing community policing reported that they used the following operational practices:

- Permanent neighborhood-based offices or stations
- Designation of "community" or "neighborhood" officers
- Foot patrol as a specific assignment or periodic expectation
- Regularly scheduled meetings with community groups
- Specific training and interagency involvement in problem identification and resolution
- Use of regulatory codes to combat drugs/crime

Community Policing and the Office of the Sheriff

Missing from most of the literature regarding community policing efforts are studies from county sheriffs' offices across the country. This is unfortunate given the fact that of the more than 17,000 law enforcement agencies in the United States, approximately 3,100 are sheriffs' offices. Certainly not all sheriffs' offices are alike. According to one authority there are at least four organizational models for sheriff's officers: a *law enforcement model* handling strictly policing duties; a *civil-judicial model* that deals only with court activities; a *correctional-judicial model* that handles all functions except law enforcement; and a *full-service model* that provides law enforcement, correctional and judicial services.[30] Regardless of the model, the office of the sheriff is an important provider of law enforcement, correctional, and court services in many geographical locations.

Regardless the type of organizational model, the political sheriff is an important figure in contemporary policing. The office of the sheriff is, in all but two states, a local, elected political office. To be re-elected an incumbent sheriff must both win the approval of the citizenry at election time and be available to the public on a routine basis the rest of the time. Sheriffs must be present at social events, speak to service clubs, and appear before civic associations, not only to explain policy, but also to learn firsthand the views of the people they serve. As elected officials, they must be responsive to and incorporate community input into their organizational philosophy. Some have suggested that the office of the sheriff should be considered more of an "open system" than municipal police agencies due to the natural flow of information between the sheriff and the citizenry.[31] Hence, as elected officials sheriffs are somewhat more insulated from local power brokers, yet they must be concerned with the views of their communities on a variety of crime and quality-of-life issues.

It is reasonable to presume that gaining input on these issues from the citizenry affords the sheriff the opportunity to establish policies and procedures that better reflect community needs. Thus, the political nature of the sheriff's office makes it uniquely fertile for community-based policing initiatives.

The results of recent research lend general support to the hypothesis that sheriffs' offices are by their very nature interactive with and accountable to their community.[32] Theoretically, it is within this type of organizational context that community-oriented policing may find the most support. Certainly, it will be necessary to further track the evolution of community-oriented policing in sheriffs' offices as well as in municipal police departments.

Trends in Community Policing

The following describes an overview of the results of a current major study of trends in community policing in the United States.[33]

> **CTQ**
>
> What is unique about the office of the sheriff today? Do you believe that sheriffs' offices would be more or less responsive to community needs when compared to city police agencies? Justify your response.

IN THE NEWS

A HUMAN PERSPECTIVE

COMMUNITY POLICING: THE PERSONAL TOUCH

Officer Joseph Balles, an eight-year veteran of the Madison (Wisconsin) Police Department, attended a neighborhood meeting in the community center where he has his office. Balles had called the meeting himself, circulating fliers through the neighborhood and urging residents to attend. More than 100 of them did.

"I need your help," Balles said in his flier. "The arrival of crack cocaine this year has slowly strangled the families of our neighborhood one by one. If we are to survive, we must drive drugs out of our neighborhood, and out of our lives. . . ."

It is, perhaps, significant that Balles referred to the neighborhood as "our neighborhood." As one of the officers assigned to Madison's Experimental Police District, Balles exemplifies community policing in action.

Balles knows firsthand about the crack problem in his neighborhood. He recently arrested and charged a man with murder after a drug-related killing.

Balles stresses the importance of personal contact with the residents of the community he serves. "I was really impressed with the turnout at our meeting," he said. "The people in this neighborhood, most of them, really want to make it a better place. They know I'm here to help, and they trust me."

"Officer Joe," as he is known, has been walking this beat for the past three years. His tour as a community police officer in Madison's Broadway-Simpson neighborhood is nearly over (officers assigned to community policing agree to serve three terms in one place) and, he says, he has enjoyed it. "Unless I'm promoted (off a beat), I'll sign up again," he says. "I really think I'm making a difference here."

Neighborhood children greet him as he makes his rounds. "Hey, Officer Joe," they shout. "How you making it?" A man stops him, a man who heads a neighborhood group. "You are making a real contribution," the man says. "I know you must hear negative comments from time to time. Pay no attention. Most of the people in this neighborhood are on your side."

Officer Balles's neighborhood on Madison's South Side is no ghetto. There are trees; the streets are clean. Madison is a small city, with a population of around 200,000, not counting the University of Wisconsin. The apartment buildings on the South Side were once desirable housing. They are now low-income properties, and there are signs of neglect. Broken windows go unrepaired; doors sag.

"It doesn't look like a low-income area because of all the trees," Balles says. "And it's pretty clean. But these people have very little money, very little food in some instances. And, more and more, we're starting to see drugs in here. Crack. It's coming from Chicago." He pauses. "We're starting to see the problems of the big city. Chicago is only two hours away, after all."

In New York City's 72nd precinct, by the waterfront of New York Harbor's Upper Bay, Patrolman Luis Sanchez is also finding drugs a problem, but the drug is not crack cocaine. "It's heroin, mostly," Sanchez says, "and our problem is with prostitutes hustling to feed their habit. We get out here at the ramps to the BQE (the elevated Brooklyn-Queens Expressway that arches over the 72nd precinct), where they pick up their johns."

"The worst part of it is," Sanchez says, "these women are sick. Most of them are outpatients at Lutheran Medical Center, right down the street there. And it's confirmed, 65 percent of them are HIV infected. We think the true figure is higher. But the 65 percent is documented."

Sanchez is 30 years old and married. He commutes to his job from his home in Long Island City. He's been with the New York Police Department (NYPD) for four years. He thinks the NYPD move toward community policing is a smart one. He has, perhaps because of his ability to speak Spanish with the majority populations in the 72nd precinct, one of the highest arrest rates in the precinct.

"People tell me things," he says. "I walk my beat; people come up with problems; I act on the information."

"I gave this woman my card," he says. "She almost kissed me. She told me: 'This is the first time in my life I've ever known the name of someone to call if I need help.' I'll tell you, that made me feel great."

Community policing in the 72nd precinct is intended to serve as a model for the rest of NYPD. It is hoped that successes there can be replicated throughout the city. Sanchez is enthusiastic. "If we can get support across the department, this can work," he says. "We're getting support from downtown. That's critical."

Balles and Sanchez work in different worlds. There are 306 uniformed personnel on the entire Madison police force; there are 240 uniformed personnel in New York's 72nd precinct alone. But what these two men are doing is remarkably similar. Each is spending his working hours with the people of the community, listening to the complaints, trying to help solve the problems, and, not incidentally, arresting those who commit crimes.

Source: Reprinted from the *National Institute of Justice Journal* (August 1992), p. 5.

As part of an ongoing partnership between the Bureau of Justice Statistics (BJS) and the Office of Community Oriented Policing Services (COPS), data were collected on the community-policing practices of state and local law enforcement agencies in 1997 and 1999. The Law Enforcement Management and Administrative Statistics (LEMAS) survey was used to assess the impact of community policing on personnel, training, policies, programs, and the use of technology.

A HUMAN PERSPECTIVE

POLICING NEIGHBORHOODS: A REPORT FROM ST. PETERSBURG

INTRODUCTION
Agencies implementing community policing are striving to change how police do their work and what contributions citizens make to policing. Researchers are exploring what policing is like in St. Petersburg, Florida, a city that has implemented community policing. This Research Preview reports findings from the Project on Policing Neighborhoods, sponsored by the National Institute of Justice and the Office of Community Oriented Policing Services.

METHODOLOGY
In 1997, the researchers observed police officers for approximately 240 hours in each of 12 of St. Petersburg's 48 Community Policing Areas (CPAs). These CPAs were selected to represent variation in social distress (determined by the amount of unemployment and poverty and the number of female-headed households), which affects service conditions for police. Field researchers observed 911 officers responsible for answering calls for service, Community Policing Officers (CPOs) free to focus on problem solving, and supervisors assigned to the selected CPAs. Researchers also personally interviewed nearly all St. Petersburg patrol officers ($n = 240$) and their immediate supervisors ($n = 37$). In addition, more than 1,900 randomly selected residents of St. Petersburg were surveyed by telephone.

FINDINGS
Police role. Community policing expands an officer's role beyond just law enforcement. Interviews revealed some ambivalence in officers' perception of their role. Ninety-eight percent of officers agreed that assisting citizens is as important as enforcing the law, but 88 percent also said that enforcing the law is an officer's most important responsibility. Almost all officers agreed that citizen input about neighborhood problems is important, but 25 percent said they have reason to distrust most citizens.

CPOs generally favored views associated with community policing more than did 911 officers. They were much more likely than 911 officers to say that minor disorders were police business. They were far more likely to rank reducing repeat calls for service as an important goal and far less likely to rank handling their call load or making arrests as important goals. Some views were related to officers' length of service. Experienced officers were more likely to expect officers to respond to all minor disorders except family disputes (on which there were no clear differences by length of service). They were less likely to stress the importance of making arrests, issuing citations, and performing drug and gun interdictions and were more likely to view public involvement in neighborhood improvement and reducing fear of crime as important. Contrary to assumptions common to many researchers and practitioners, newer police officers were not the ones with the most positive outlook on community policing.

Allocation of officer time. The researchers found that the St. Petersburg officers they studied spent, on average, between one-fourth and one-third of their time not on specific tasks, but rather on general patrol or personal business. Contrary to widely held beliefs about the reactive nature of police patrol, 911 officers were typically free of dispatcher or supervisor assignments for 5-6 hours of their 8-hour shift. Because of the nature of CPOs' job assignments, virtually all of their time was available for self-directed activities, including officer-initiated encounters with the public, involvement with other government agencies, administrative tasks, general patrol, and personal business.

The proactive nature of patrol work in St. Petersburg is revealed by the rate of officer-initiated encounters with the public. On average, 911 officers initiated approximately 45 percent of their public contacts; CPOs, approximately 66 percent. Dispatch calls, supervisor assignments, and contacts initiated directly by citizens at a scene or by telephone accounted for the balance. Not surprisingly, CPOs spent substantially more time engaged in problem-solving activities than 911 officers (17 percent and 7-10 percent, respectively, depending on the shift). Eighty-three percent of CPOs indicated involvement with a problem-solving project in the past year, as did 57 percent of 911 officers.

Police-citizen interactions. Community policing is generally concerned with solving problems, but also is concerned with enhancing the quality of police-citizen interactions. Researchers found that CPOs tended to spend substantially less time in face-to-face contact with citizens than 911 officers. CPOs had a somewhat lower rate of contact with the public in general, but they also had much lower rates of contact with suspects/disputants and help-seekers while having much higher rates of strictly social contacts.

Community policing promotes greater police-citizen cooperation. The researchers found a relatively high level of such cooperation in everyday police-citizen contacts. The police made a positive response to at least one request from citizens 85 percent of the time. Citizens responded positively to at least one request or demand from police approximately 82 percent of the time.

Citizen perceptions. Under community policing, citizens play two important roles—as consumers of police services and as co-producers of policing itself. Eighty-five percent of the interviewed citizens said they were "very" or "somewhat" satisfied with their neighborhood police services. Black respondents were somewhat less likely to give these responses than whites. Two-thirds of survey respondents rated St. Petersburg police as "excellent" or "good" at working with residents to solve problems. Whites were substantially more likely than blacks to give a strong rating, but blacks were more aware of police-citizen problem-solving efforts and were more likely to report participation in such efforts.

continues

(continued)

Establishing a visible and familiar police presence is important to most police agencies. Approximately one-third of residents surveyed said they had seen the police in the previous 24 hours. Twenty-eight percent of all interviewed residents said they knew police officers who worked in their neighborhoods. The researchers examined the relationship between a resident knowing an officer and offering a favorable rating of the police. Familiarity with neighborhood police was associated with positive ratings of police among blacks and other minorities but did not affect ratings of whites.

CONCLUSION

The research showed that community policing clearly made inroads in the outlook of St. Petersburg officers and that the strength of those effects is related to whether an officer has a specialized community policing assignment or serves as a general patrol officer. There were a number of distinctions that suggest considerable care is warranted concerning how officer responsibilities are constructed if departments are to promote community policing attitudes and behavior. Regardless of job assignments, St. Petersburg patrol officers have substantial self-directed time available for targeted activities. The challenge is to find ways to coordinate and supervise these activities effectively. Citizens of St. Petersburg are relatively satisfied with police services, which compares to responses to surveys in other U.S. cities. Although minority citizens tended to evaluate their police somewhat lower than whites did, they showed a stronger willingness to become involved in problem solving. This represents an excellent opportunity for strengthening police-community relations and improving the quality of life in minority neighborhoods. These and other research results have been used by the St. Petersburg Police Department to develop and implement plans for the future.

Source: This information is based on research conducted by Stephen D. Mastrofski, Ph.D., Professor, Michigan State University; Roger B. Parks, Ph.D., Professor, Indiana University; Albert J. Reiss, Jr., Ph.D., Professor Emeritus, Yale University; and Robert E. Worden, Ph.D., Associate Professor, University at Albany, State University of New York, 1999. The research was sponsored under NIJ grant number 95-1J-CX-0071, with funds from the Office of Community Oriented Policing Services. This and other NIJ publications can be downloaded from the NIJ Web site (http://www.ojp.usdoj.gov/nij).

- State and local law enforcement agencies had nearly 113,000 community policing officers or their equivalents during 1999, compared to about 21,000 in 1997. This included 91,000 local police officers in 1999, up from 16,000 in 1997.
- Sixty-four percent of local police departments, serving 86 percent of all residents, had full-time officers engaged in community-policing activities during 1999, compared to 34 percent of departments serving 62 percent of residents, in 1997.
- In 1999, 87 percent of local police officers were employed by a department that provided community-policing training for some or all new recruits, and 85 percent by a department that provided it for at least some in-service officers.
- In 1999, 63 percent of local police departments, serving 85 percent of all residents, used routine foot and/or bicycle patrol. About half of all officers worked for a department that actively encouraged them to engage in problem-solving projects on their patrol beats.
- As of June 30, 1999, 79 percent of local police departments, serving 96 percent of all residents, had met with community groups within the past year; 40 percent of departments, serving 71 percent of residents, had formed a problem-solving partnership within the past three years.
- During 1999, 92 percent of residents were served by a local police department that provided them with routine access to crime statistics or crime maps, compared to 70 percent in 1997.

WEB

For more information on community policing, **visit our Web site,** www.prenhall.com/territo.

These data reflect the major commitment made by many police agencies to operationalize community policing.

The Problem-Oriented Approach to Policing

While somewhat different than community-oriented policing, "problem-oriented policing" is a method in which the community-oriented philosophy can be put into practice.[34] Frequently, police officers respond to requests for assistance at locations where they or other officers have been summoned for help on prior occasions. In many cities, officers can usually predict when they may be summoned in response to burglaries, assaults, and robberies. "In the News: The Standard Approach" and "In the News: The Problem-Oriented Approach" provide some insight into a fairly typical police response to a robbery associated with prostitution and a nontraditional response.[35]

Reacting to incidents reported by citizens—as in the first "In the News" box—is the standard method for delivering police services today. But there is growing recognition that standard "incident-driven" policing methods do not have a substantial impact on many of the problems that citizens want police to help solve. Equally important, enforcing the law is but one of many ways that police can cope with citizens' problems. Although alternative methods of handling problems have long been available, the police have made relatively little use of them. Or they have been used only sporadically, more often by a special unit or an informal group of innovative officers.

An alternative approach to policing called problem-oriented policing (POP) has been developed to help solve this problem. It grew out of an awareness of the limitations of standard police practices and responses to criminal incidents. Police officers, detectives, and their supervisors can use the problem-oriented approach to identify, analyze, and respond on a routine basis to the underlying circumstances that create the incidents that prompt citizens to call the police. Herman Goldstein, who first used the term "problem-oriented policing" in the late 1970s, details this strategy in his book *Problem-Oriented Policing*.[36]

Problem-oriented policing is the outgrowth of twenty years of research into police operations that converged on three main themes: increased effectiveness by attacking underlying problems that give rise to incidents that consume patrol and detective time; reliance on the expertise and creativity of line officers to study problems carefully and develop innovative solutions; and closer involvement with the public to make sure that the police are addressing the needs of citizens. The strategy called SARA consists of four parts:

- *Scanning*. Instead of relying on broad, law-related concepts—robbery and burglary, for example—officers are encouraged to group individual related incidents that come to their attention as "problems" and define these problems in more precise and therefore useful terms. For example, an incident that typically would be classified simply as a "robbery" might be seen as part of a pattern of prostitution-related robberies committed by transvestites in downtown hotels.
- *Analysis*. Officers working on a well-defined problem then collect information from a variety of public and private sources—not just police data. They use the information to illuminate the underlying nature of the problem and suggest its causes and a variety of options for its resolution.
- *Response*. Working with citizens, businesses, and police and private agencies, officers tailor a program of action suitable to the characteristics of the problem. Solutions may go beyond traditional criminal justice system remedies to include other community agencies or organizations.
- *Assessment*. Finally, the officers evaluate the impact of these efforts to see if the problems were actually solved or alleviated.

The Future of Community-Oriented Policing and Problem Solving (COPPS)

As we have noted, community-oriented policing and its complementary strategy of problem-oriented policing seem to be the trends of the immediate future in American policing. However, some authorities have raised legitimate concerns or questions with regard to these concepts, such as "Do the police have the ability to create 'communities'"[37] and "Is community organizing the proper role for police?"[38] Others have raised the following questions with regard to COPPS:

1. Will chief executives have the innovative drive necessary to change the culture of their department, implement this new concept, flatten the original structure of their departments, and see that other officers' work is properly evaluated?

CTQ

In your opinion, what types of crime problems would best be addressed by applying the strategy known as problem-oriented policing? Support your answer.

IN THE NEWS
A HUMAN PERSPECTIVE

THE STANDARD APPROACH

At 1:32 A.M., a man we will call Fred Snyder dials 911 from a downtown corner phone booth. The dispatcher notes his location and calls the nearest patrol unit. Officer Knox arrives four minutes later.

Snyder says he was beaten and robbed twenty minutes before but didn't see the robber. Under persistent questioning Snyder admits he was with a prostitute he had picked up in a bar. Later, in a hotel room, he discovered the prostitute was actually a man, who then beat Snyder and took his wallet.

Snyder wants to let the whole matter drop. He refuses medical treatment for his injuries. Knox finishes his report and lets Snyder go home. Later that day Knox's report reaches Detective Alexander's desk. She knows from experience that the case will go nowhere, but she calls Snyder at work.

Snyder confirms the report but refuses to cooperate further. Knox and Alexander go on to other cases. Months later, reviewing crime statistics, the city council deplores the difficulty of attracting businesses and people to the downtown area.

---

2. Will departments work with their communities, other city agencies, businesses, elected officials, and the media to sustain COPPS?
3. Can police departments, from top to bottom, become more customer- and value-oriented?
4. Will police executives and supervisors develop the necessary policies and support mechanisms to support COPPS, including recruitment, selection, training, performance appraisals, and reward and promotional systems?
5. Will the police attempt to bring diversity into their ranks, reflecting ever-changing demographics and cultural customs of our society?

Only time will provide the necessary answers that will go a long way to deciding the future success of failure or these trends in policing.[39]

IN THE NEWS
A HUMAN PERSPECTIVE

THE PROBLEM-ORIENTED APPROACH

Midnight-watch patrol officers are tired of taking calls like Snyder's. They and their sergeant, James Hogan, decide to reduce prostitution-related robberies, and Officer James Boswell volunteers to lead the effort.

First, Boswell interviews twenty-eight prostitutes who work the downtown area to learn how they solicit, what happens when they get caught, and why they are not deterred. They work downtown bars, they tell him, because customers are easy to find and police patrols don't spot them soliciting. Arrests, the prostitutes tell Boswell, are just an inconvenience: Judges routinely sentence them to probation, and probation conditions are not enforced.

Based on what he has learned from the interviews and his previous experience, Boswell devises a response. He works with the Alcoholic Beverage Control Board and local bar owners to move the prostitutes into the street. At the request of the police, the commonwealth's attorney agrees to ask the judges to impose stiffer conditions on probation: Convicted prostitutes would be given a map of the city and told to stay out of the downtown area or go to jail for three months.

Boswell then works with the vice unit to make sure that downtown prostitutes are arrested and convicted and that patrol officers know which prostitutes are on probation. Probation violators are sent to jail, and within weeks all but a few of the prostitutes have left downtown.

Then Boswell talks to the prostitutes' customers, most of whom don't know that almost half the prostitutes working the street are actually men, posing as women. He intervenes in street transactions, formally introducing the customers to their male dates. The Navy sets up talks for him with incoming sailors to tell them about the male prostitutes and the associated safety and health risks.

In three months, the number of prostitutes working downtown drops from twenty-eight to six and robbery rates are cut in half. After eighteen months, neither robbery nor prostitution shows signs of returning to its earlier level.

SUMMARY

This chapter served a number of purposes in introducing police operations. In order to better understand why police departments operate the way they do today, we found it useful to provide not only a current profile of police departments but also to discuss how policing evolved in America. For example, we spent some time describing early policing efforts in Boston and New York City. We also provided an overview of smaller police departments in the United States, since the majority of communities are served by this type of agency.

In addition, considerable time was spent in this chapter describing the role and functions of uniformed patrol officers, who constitute the majority of personnel in any law enforcement agency. We briefly discussed some of the activities that are performed by a patrol officer in a typical police department. Later in this section, we discussed how patrol strategies have changed as a result of police research conducted during the last two decades. A section on zero-tolerance enforcement has been added.

One of the most frequently criticized but least understood functions performed by police officers relates to their traffic responsibilities. Therefore, provided some insight in this chapter regarding these important duties. We also discussed both rural and campus policing. The role of the detective or investigator was described, and research conducted by the Rand Corporation and PERF regarding the detective role was discussed in some detail.

We also included an overview of computerized criminal history information, specifically the use of the National Crime Information Center (NCIC and NCIC 2000) by law enforcement agencies. In the final portion of this chapter, we described an evolution occurring in modern-day policing that involves a change in philosophy and operational approaches. We highlighted some of the elements in community-oriented policing (COP) and problem-oriented policing (POP). Also discussed was community policing within the context of an elected sheriff's office. Questions regarding the future of COP and POP were also discussed.

DISCUSSION AND REVIEW

1. Briefly describe the differences and similarities between smaller law enforcement agencies and their urban or suburban counterparts.
2. Briefly discuss the creation of police forces in the United States.
3. List four of Sir Robert Peel's principles for effective policing that still exist in today's law enforcement agencies.
4. Describe the emergence of state police in the United States.
5. Briefly discuss the roles of the FBI and the DEA.
6. What is the role of the field training officer?
7. Describe some of the job-related factors that compel officers to transfer out of the patrol division and into higher management positions.
8. Describe some of the nonpolice functions that officers are asked to perform during the course of their work.
9. List some of the tasks carried out during a preliminary investigation by the first officer on the scene.
10. Discuss some of the findings of the Kansas City Preventive Patrol Experiment as well as some of the patrol alternative strategies utilized since the study.
11. Name four types of nontraditional patrol.
12. Discuss zero-tolerance policing and its relationship to the "broken windows" perspective.
13. How has the role of campus police evolved in the last few decades?
14. Describe the media image of the working detective.

15. What policy recommendations were made based on the Rand Criminal Investigation Study?
16. What was the major difference between PERF's research on criminal investigations and research conducted earlier?
17. Briefly describe the three eras of policing in American history.
18. List some of the community-policing practices described in a survey of chiefs and sheriffs.
19. Discuss problem-oriented policing and the SARA process.
20. Describe why community policing may be very compatible within a sheriff's office.

Chapter Resources

In the Literature

Books

D. BAYLEY, *Policing for the Future.* New York: Oxford University Press, 1944.

W. GELLER, *Police Leadership in America.* New York: Praeger, 1985.

H. GOLDSTEIN, *Problem-Oriented Policing.* New York: McGraw-Hill, 1990.

J. GREENE, *Community Policing: Rhetoric or Reality?* New York: Praeger, 1988.

P. MANNING, *Police Work.* Cambridge, Mass.: MIT Press, 1977.

J. SKOLNICK, *Justice without Trial: Law Enforcement in a Democratic Society.* New York: Wiley, 1986.

M. TONRY AND N. MORRIS, eds., *Modern Policing.* Chicago: University of Chicago Press, 1992.

J. WILSON, *Varieties of Police Behavior.* Cambridge, Mass.: Harvard University Press, 1968.

Articles

J. HARPOLD, "Medical Model for Community Policing," *FBI Law Enforcement Bulletin,* vol. 69 (June 2000), p. 23.

H. KUNTZ, "Battered Women, Reluctant Police," *Washington Post,* February 28, 1988.

R. LANE, "Urban Police and Crime in Nineteenth Century America." In N. Morris and M. Tonry, eds., *Crime and Justice,* Vol. 2. Chicago: University of Chicago Press, 1980.

W. MILLER, "The Good, the Bad, and the Ugly: Policing America," *History Today* vol. 50 (August 2000), p. 29.

B. REAVES, "State and Local Police Departments." Washington D.C.: Bureau of Justice Statistics, 2000.

J. WILSON AND G. KELLING, "Broken Windows: The Police and Neighborhood Safety," *Atlantic Monthly,* vol. 29 (March 1982), pp. 29–38.

Endnotes

1. Bureau of Justice Statistics, "Local Police Departments 1997." Washington, D.C.: U.S. Department of Justice, 1999, p. 1.
2. B. Reaves and M. Hickman, "Local Police Departments, 1999." Washington, D.C.: Bureau of Justice Statistics, U.S. Department of Justice, 2001, pp. iii–20; B. Reaves and M. Hickman, "Sheriff's Offices, 1999." Washington, D.C.: Bureau of Justice Statistics, U.S. Department of Justice, 2001, pp. iii–20.
3. V. Sims, "Issues in Small Town Policing." In International Association of Chiefs of Police, ed., *Managing the Small Law Enforcement Agency.* Dubuque, Iowa: Kendall/Hunt, 1990.
4. For a complete description of the evolution of local, state, and federal police agencies in America, see H. M. Wrobleski and K. M. Hess, *Introduction to Law Enforcement and Criminal Justice,* 6th ed. St. Paul: West, 2001.
5. W. J. Bopp and D. O. Schultz, *A Short History of American Law Enforcement.* Springfield, Ill.: Charles C. Thomas, 1972, pp. 30–31.
6. Ibid., pp. 12, 13.
7. See Wrobleski and Hess, p. 14.
8. V. L. Folley, *American Law Enforcement.* Boston: Allyn & Bacon, 1980, p. 88.
9. For a further discussion of police patrols, see M. S. Lyman, *The Police.* Upper Saddle River, N.J.: Prentice Hall, 2002; G. L. Kirkham and L. A. Wollan, Jr., *Introduction to Law Enforcement.* New York: Harper & Row, 1980; G. Eastman and E. Eastman, eds., *Municipal Police Administration.* Washington D.C.: International City

Management Association, 1982; and S. G. Chapman, ed., *Police Patrol Readings*. Springfield, Ill.: Charles C. Thomas, 1970.

10. G. L. Kelling, T. Pate, D. Dieckman, and C. E. Brown, *The Kansas City Preventive Patrol Experiment*. Washington, D.C.: Police Foundation, 1974.

11. For a complete discussion of the Flint Police Department Foot Patrol Program, see R. C. Trojanowicz et al., *An Evaluation of the Neighborhood Foot Patrol Program in Flint, Michigan*. East Lansing: Michigan State University, School of Criminal Justice, 1985, pp. 1–95.

12. The information regarding directed patrol was adapted from W. G. Gay, T. H. Schell, and S. Schack, *Improving Patrol Productivity*, Vol. 1: *Routine Patrol Prescription Package*. Washington, D.C.: U.S. Department of Justice, National Institute of Law Enforcement and Criminal Justice, July 1977, pp. 1–7.

13. Adapted from L. Sherman, "Police Crackdowns." *NIJ Reports* (Washington, D.C.: U.S. Department of Justice, 1990), p. 3.

14. J. Q. Wilson and G. L. Kelling. "Broken Windows: The Police and Neighborhood Safety," *Atlantic Monthly* (March 1982), pp. 29–38.

15. G. L. Kelling and C. M. Coles, *Fixing Broken Windows*. New York: Free Press, 1996.

16. The information on rural policing was drawn from R. A. Weisheit, D. N. Falcone, and L. E. Edwards, "Rural Crime and Rural Policing." *NIJ Research in Action* (Washington, D.C.: U.S. Department of Justice, 1994), pp. 1–10.

17. Ibid., p. 10.

18. For a more complete discussion of contemporary campus policing, see M. Bromley, "Policing Our Campuses: A National Review of Statutes," *American Journal of Police*, vol. 15, no. 3 (1996), pp. 1–22; and M. Bromley and B. Reaves, "Comparing Campus and City Police Operational Practices," *Journal of Security Administration*, vol. 21, no. 22 (1998), pp. 41–54.

19. B. Reaves and A. Goldberg, *Campus Law Enforcement Agencies, 1995*. Washington, D.C.: U.S. Department of Justice, Bureau of Justice Statistics, 1998, pp. i–iii.

20. This discussion of the detective bureau and the accompanying references were adapted from P. W. Greenwood and J. Petersilia, *The Criminal Investigation Process: A Dialogue on Research Findings*, Vol. 1. Washington, D.C.: U.S. Government Printing Office, 1977, 5–11. Also see B. Smith, *Police Systems in the United States*. New York: Harper & Row, 1960.

21. R. Fosdick, *American Police Systems*. New York: Century, 1921.

22. This summary and the accompanying references were adapted, with permission, from P. W. Greenwood, *The Rand Criminal Investigation Study: Its Findings and Impacts to Date*. Santa Monica, Calif.: Rand Corporation, 1979, pp. 3–7.

23. The review and discussion of the PERF criminal investigation study was adapted with permission from J. E. Eck, *Solving Crimes: The Investigation of Burglary and Robbery*. Washington, D.C.: Police Executive Research Forum, 1983, pp. xii–xxxi.

24. The discussion of computerized criminal information files and the NCIC system was adapted from P.L. Woodard, *Criminal Justice "Hot" Files*. Washington, D.C.: U.S. Department of Justice, Bureau of Justice Statistics, 1986, pp. 1–23.

25. S. L. Hitt, "NCIC 2000," *FBI Law Enforcement Bulletin* (July 2000), pp. 12–15. To ensure the validity of the records, the investigating agency enters the information into the system, and only the agency entering the records can update or clear these entries.

26. G. L. Kelling and M. H. More, "From Political to Reform to Community: The Evolving Strategy of Police." In J. R. Green and S. D. Mastrofski, eds., *Community Policing: Rhetoric or Reality*. New York: Praeger, 1991, pp. 3–25.

27. L. S. Miller and K. M. Hess. *Community Policing Theory and Practice*. St. Paul: West, 1994, p. 12.

28. R. C. Trojanowicz and B. Bucqueroux. *Community Policing: A Contemporary Perspective*. Cincinnati: Anderson, 1990, p. 5.

29. The survey information on COP practices was adapted from National Institute of Justice Research Review, "Community Policing Strategies." Washington, D.C.: U.S. Department of Justice, 1995, pp. 1–6.

30. L. Brown, "The Role of the Sheriff." In A. Kohen, ed., *The Future of Policing*. Beverly Hills, Calif.: Sage, 1978.

31. D. Falcone and L. Wells, "The County Sheriff as a Distinctive Policing Modality," *American Journal of Police*, vol. 15 (1995), pp. 123–149.

32. J. Cochran, M. Bromley, and L. Landis, "Officer Work Orientations, Perceptions of Readiness and Anticipated Effectiveness of an Agency-Wide Community Policing Effort Within a County Sheriff's Office," *Journal of Police and Criminal Psychology*, vol. 14, no. 1 (1999), pp. 43–65.

33. M. Hickman and B. Reaves, *Community Policing in Local Police Departments, 1997 and 1999*. Washington, D.C.: U.S. Department of Justice, Bureau of Justice Statistics, 2000, pp. 1–11.

34. K. Peak and R. Glensor, *Community Policing and Problem Solving*, 2nd ed. Upper Saddle River, N.J.: Prentice Hall, 1999.

35. W. Spelman and J. E. Eck, *Problem-Oriented Policing*. Washington, D.C.: U.S. Department of Justice, 1987, pp. 1–7.

36. H. Goldstein, *Problem-Oriented Policing*. New York: McGraw-Hill, 1990.

37. S. Walker, *The Police in America: An Introduction*, 2nd ed. New York: McGraw-Hill, 1992.

38. D. Bayley, "Community Policing: A Report from the Devil's Advocate." In J. Green and S. Mastrojski, eds., *Community Policing: Rhetoric or Reality?* New York: Praeger, 1988, pp. 225–237.

39. Hickman and Reaves.

6 ISSUES AND TRENDS IN POLICING

Chapter Outline

Professionalism
Law Enforcement Agency Accreditation
  Benefits of Accreditation
Higher Education and Law Enforcement
  The Rationale for Collegiate Standards
  Educational Upgrading: A Second Rationale
Police Misconduct
Employment of Minorities and Women in Policing
  Recruitment of Minorities
  Innovative Minority Recruiting
  Recruitment of Women
  Research on Women on Patrol
  The Current Status of Women in Policing
Officer Health
  Job Stress
  Stress and Female Police Officers
  Alcoholism
  Police Department Drug Testing
  Suicide
  Coping with Health Problems
Police Contact with the Public
Use of Deadly Force
  Managing the Use of Force
  Shooting-Control Techniques
  Research on Use of Force by Police
  Violence-Prone Police Officers
  Evaluating the Use of Pepper Spray as an Alternative to Deadly Force
Police-Prosecutor Cooperation

Private Security and Law Enforcement: Partners for the Future
Technological Trends in Policing
  Computer-Aided Dispatch
  Fingerprint Automation
  Police Use of Laptop Computers
  Future Applications of Computers
  DNA Profiling
  Geographical Information Systems
Police/Citizen Roles in Crime Prevention
  Citizen Responsibility in Crime Prevention
  Neighborhood Watch Programs
  Fear of Crime and Police Response
  Evaluating Crime-Prevention Programs
Crime Prevention Through Environmental Design
  Applications of CPTED
  Combining CPTED and Community-Policing Strategies
  What Police and Residents Can Do
  Specific Crime Prevention Activities
Citizen Involvement in Crime Prevention
  The McGruff Campaign
  The CAT Program
  The Watch Your Car Program
  Campus Crime Prevention
  Community Anti-Drug Efforts
Summary

Key TERMS

campus crime-prevention programs, p. 246
Combat Auto Theft (CAT) program, p. 246
Commission on Accreditation for Law Enforcement Agencies, p. 218
computer-aided dispatch (CAD), p. 234
Crime Prevention Through Environmental Design (CPTED), p. 243
deadly force, p. 230
DNA profiling, p. 238
fingerprint automation, p. 235
geographical information system (GIS), p. 238
International Association of Chiefs of Police (IACP), p. 218
job stress, p. 226
Law Enforcement Critical Life Events Scale, p. 226
McGruff campaign, p. 245
National Organization of Black Law Enforcement Executives (NOBLE), p. 218
National Sheriffs' Association (NSA), p. 218
Neighborhood Watch, p. 240
Police Executive Research Forum (PERF), p. 218
police misconduct, p. 220
shooting-control techniques, p. 232
signs of crime, p. 241

© Dale Stockton.

This chapter focuses on numerous topics that are of paramount concern and interest to criminal justice students, citizens, and police: professionalism in law enforcement; police misconduct; affirmative action and equal employment opportunities in policing; officer health; police use of deadly force; law enforcement's response to violence in America; the emergence of private security in this country and its relationship to public policing; and some specific technological trends that will assist law enforcement in future decades. In this chapter we also discuss crime prevention and the important role played by citizens and the police. Innovative programs are also described.

PROFESSIONALISM

Solutions to whatever ails law enforcement have consistently been sought within the concept of the "professionalization" of policing. Thus, the term *professional* has acquired almost mystical properties in the law enforcement community. Police officers praise a fellow officer's performance by calling it "professional." Well-organized, smoothly run police departments are complimented for their "professionalism." Conduct unbecoming a police officer is criticized as being "unprofessional."

In part, the preoccupation with professionalism among police officers and administrators is directly related to a comparison of salaries, educational requirements, and status in relation to their perceived position in the other professions within the criminal justice system. The police perceive themselves to be near the bottom of the occupational totem pole. In almost any comparison of prestige and income with prosecutors, defense counsels, judges, physicians, psychiatrists, and expert witnesses (usually with earned doctorates), the police officer comes up short.

LAW ENFORCEMENT AGENCY ACCREDITATION

The law enforcement profession has attempted, for the first time, to develop and implement recognized accreditation standards, as has been done in the fields of medicine and law. One such attempt has resulted in the creation of a formal accreditation process for law enforcement agencies to meet agreed-upon standards and a commission to administer the process.

The **Commission on Accreditation for Law Enforcement Agencies** was formed in 1979 to develop a set of law enforcement standards and to administer a voluntary accreditation process.[1] Through accreditation, law enforcement agencies at the state, county, and local level can demonstrate that they meet professional criteria. The accreditation commission, which is composed of twenty-one members, reflects broad representation of state, county, and local law enforcement practitioners, including police chiefs and sheriffs from departments of varying sizes. The commission also includes representatives from the public and private sectors, such as state, county, and city administrations; labor; academia; and the courts.

The commission was formed through the combined efforts of the **International Association of Chiefs of Police (IACP)**, the **National Organization of Black Law Enforcement Executives (NOBLE)**, the **National Sheriffs' Association (NSA)**, and the **Police Executive Research Forum (PERF)**. Executive members of these four groups supervise 80 percent of the law enforcement community in the United States. Originally supported by grants from the U.S. Department of Justice, the commission operates primarily with fees paid by agencies applying for accreditation and encourages financial assistance from foundations and corporations to help defray part of these fees.

The standards are the key element in the accreditation program. In measurable terms, they define policies and procedures essential to providing the highest quality protection to the public and to the individual officer.

Like medical and educational accreditation, law enforcement accreditation is a process of improvement and change. Primarily a management tool, accreditation provides police chiefs and sheriffs with a structure by which they can upgrade the quality of their agencies' service to the public.

Benefits of Accreditation

Accreditation represents a commitment to excellence and professionalism. Accreditation, according to some law enforcement practitioners, provides the following benefits:

- Nationwide recognition of professional excellence
- Community understanding and support
- Employee confidence; esprit
- State and local government officials' confidence
- State-of-the-art, impartial guidelines for evaluation and change, when necessary

---

WEB

For more information on law enforcement accreditation, visit our Web site, www.prenhall.com/territo.

- Proactive management systems; documented policies and procedures
- Liability insurance costs contained or decreased
- Liability litigation deterred
- Coordination with neighboring agencies and other parts of the criminal justice system
- Access to the latest law enforcement practices

Many law enforcement officials believe that an agency, once accredited, can provide its community with accurate budget justifications, reduced possibility of vicarious liability, and better relationships with other criminal justice system representatives.

HIGHER EDUCATION AND LAW ENFORCEMENT

Formal education has traditionally been the path to both self-improvement and increased status in a particular line of work. With the passage of the Omnibus Crime Bill in 1968, public funds were made available to police personnel to pursue a college degree at federal expense—or with a partial federal subsidy. Because many officers and administrators took advantage of this assistance, today's law enforcement personnel are, on the average, much better educated than they were thirty years ago.

The Rationale for Collegiate Standards

Do college graduates make better police officers than people who lack a college education? This question is deceptively simple. What specific criteria, for example, are involved in defining "better"? Higher arrest rates? Fewer citizen complaints? Faster promotion? In a police department with extremely low productivity in terms of arrests and clearance rates, one might expect that the infusion of college-educated officers would lead to increased productivity. If increased productivity were one of the goals of college recruiting, and if the behavior of officers were directed toward this end, then higher arrest and clearance rates certainly would indicate the success of higher educational requirements. However, arrest and clearance rates are often highly inflated and counterproductive. That is, arrests are made in many situations that lend themselves to alternative solutions; other arrests are made based on insufficient evidence; and some crimes are cleared based on dubious criteria. If such arrests and solutions are attributed to the competence of agency personnel—and they often are—then the infusion of college-educated officers might well result in a reduction in arrests and clearance rates (even though such reductions are usually thought of as indicators of poor performance). Similarly, the crime rate might rise or fall depending on the perceived ability of officers to establish community rapport and thus increase crime reporting.

In short, the success of any police program—including the implementation of higher personnel standards—is extremely difficult to assess. The appropriateness of a particular measure of productivity depends on the individual agency and the characteristics of the situation. Hence, efforts to establish the credibility of higher educational standards for the police are plagued by a lack of agreement about what constitutes "good" or "bad" performance.

In some police departments, rewards are based primarily on the ability to make arrests. In other agencies, notoriety may be obtained by becoming involved in a gun battle or making a "big bust" (note that college education contributes little to one's ability to perform either of these endeavors). On the other hand, an officer who properly refers a criminal offender to psychiatric care may go unrecognized or may even be negatively rewarded.

Educational Upgrading: A Second Rationale

Traditional police training programs emphasize the more mechanical aspects of law enforcement. By necessity, these programs deal with subjects such as preservation of crime scenes, proper collection of evidence, motor vehicle codes, and physical and firearms training. Unfortunately, some training academies have not taken the time, and too often do not have the qualified staff, to educate officers about social conflict or human behavior.

CTQ

Why would some police agencies not pursue law enforcement accreditation?

CTQ

If you were the police chief of a department of fifty personnel in a city of 25,000 citizens, what minimum education level would you establish for your new police officers? Justify your response.

WEB

For more information on law enforcement and education, **visit our Web site, www.prenhall.com/ territo**.

CTQ

Should police departments increase the recruitment of college-educated officers? Why or why not?

It is true that police officers perform many mundane tasks such as directing traffic, issuing parking tickets, conducting permit inspections, and driving tow trucks. Such tasks obviously do not require college training. However, many routine tasks are rapidly being turned over to civilian employees and other governmental agencies. Thus, police officers are going back to more essential tasks, which include social control in a period of increasing social turmoil, preservation of our constitutional guarantees, and exercise of broad discretion—sometimes in life-and-death situations. If the tasks performed by police are those normally performed by professionals, and if other professionals normally prepare for their roles by academic study, then the police should do the same.

Thus, the police function, as it relates to conflict resolution and order maintenance in urban society, involves both social work and law enforcement techniques. Whether these techniques are employed at an appropriate time and in an appropriate way can mean the difference between successful and unsuccessful resolution of conflict. Unsuccessful resolution exacts a human cost, whether criminal behavior results or not.

A second rationale for educational upgrading is that college-educated individuals are more able to cope with role conflict, and a college education provides officers with a social perspective and abilities more conducive to conflict resolution. Given the diverse socioeconomic and cultural populations that today's police officers must serve, a higher education seems to be a critical requirement. A PERF study hypothesized a number of advantages for police officers having college educations.[2]

Having a college education provides individuals with a broader base of information for decision making, allows a greater appreciation for the democratic form of government and engenders flexibility in handling ambiguous situations. PERF also notes that college-educated officers should be more flexible in their decision making, be more empathetic toward diverse populations they serve, and be better able to communicate in a less authoritarian manner. (See Figure 6.1).

"In the News: Utah Officers Head Back to School" illustrates how several communities are helping police officers achieve their higher education.

POLICE MISCONDUCT

In our society, authority is conveyed to a public servant from the community with the trust that it will be exercised within parameters of conduct set by its duly elected officials.[3] **Police misconduct** is actions by a public servant that are outside these standards of conduct and are a breach of public trust. There are as many ways to breach public trust as there are laws and regulations to control conduct. If a public official responsible for safeguarding a large amount of funds absconds with those funds, he or she has breached public trust. Similarly, if a public servant negligently operates an official vehicle, public trust is breached. These two actions of misconduct result from different intentions and will be treated differently, one as a major crime of theft and the other as a violation of organizational rules of conduct. Unauthorized disclosure of information, failure to carry out an assigned responsibility, and excessive use of force by a police officer are also breaches of public trust.

Corruption has been a problem of varying degrees among police officers from the beginning of policing. With the widespread availability of illicit drugs, especially cocaine, there is increased opportunity for wrongdoing stimulated by greed or other motives. Millions of dollars in seized drug money has compounded temptations faced by police. These opportunities are not limited to officers assigned to drug enforcement units. Patrol units, which encounter large supplies of drugs and cash and which usually have less oversight than do specialized units, face even greater temptation and certainly greater opportunity. The challenge among police administrators and police officers is to sustain the highest level of integrity when there is daily opportunity for integrity breakdown.

FIGURE 6.1

The importance of having college-educated police officers is recognized by progressive departments. This photo shows the awarding of a college degree to an officer who has just graduated.

© Dale Stockton.

WEB

For more information on police misconduct, **visit our Web site,** www.prenhall.com/territo.

IN THE NEWS

A HUMAN PERSPECTIVE

UTAH OFFICERS HEAD BACK TO SCHOOL
by Julie Slama

More and more Utah law enforcement officers are college-bound as part of a new venture between Salt Lake Community College (SLCC) and a number of Utah police departments. While the idea of officers' pursuing college degrees certainly is not unique, how many of them can say that they attended college classes held at the police station or a police training facility? On any given day, Utah citizens can see officers of all ranks walk into the department with textbooks under their arms.

Law enforcement administrators recognize that the complex demands of the job dictate that officers receive as much training and education as possible. Officers themselves realize the value of learning and understanding the attitudes, views, and perspectives of others. Bringing the college classroom to the officers shows citizens an agency's commitment to law enforcement professionalism and its desire to have educated officers serving the community.

PROGRAM INCEPTION
The partnership between the college and the police departments began when SLCC's criminal justice coordinator and the Sandy City police chief met to discuss the idea of bringing the college's program to the officers. The agency had an on-site classroom equipped with CD-ROMs, TV/VCR units, and other instructional technologies. With this learning environment already in place, the chief realized that very little stood in the way of implementing a program that would give officers an avenue to higher education. Sandy City's officers enthusiastically welcomed the opportunity to attend college. As word of the program's success spread, five other law enforcement agencies—Salt Lake City, South Salt Lake City, Murray, and the West Valley City police departments and the Salt Lake County Sheriff's Department—joined in the venture.

BENEFITS
When many of the officers who have enrolled in SLCC courses joined their agencies, college attendance or an advanced degree was not required. Today, this no longer holds true. In many departments, officers need a college education to get promoted. For example, the Sandy City Police Department requires that officers have an AA or an AS degree to be promoted to sergeant; a BA degree is required for promotion to captain and higher ranks. In the Salt Lake County Sheriff's Department, a bachelor's degree from an accredited college or university is required for the ranks of sergeant, lieutenant, and captain, although service in the current rank can substitute for the required education on a time equivalency basis (30 semester hours or 45 quarter hours equals one year of experience). Some departments add stipends to officers' base salaries for educational achievements; the more college credits an officer has earned the higher the base pay. In other departments, college credits reduce the time it takes for officers to become eligible for promotion, or officers receive better benefits upon retirement if they have attended college.

Along with professional development comes personal achievement. Officers feel gratified knowing they earned a college degree that some thought was beyond their reach. They also set a positive example for others, particularly younger officers and family members.

CONCLUSION
Both officers and departments alike recognize the value of a college education. Many officers themselves now admit that college is a must for a career in law enforcement given the complexity and demands of the job.

Officers need to be able to think, analyze, perform, and make decisions based on more than their street experience. They also need the knowledge, critical thinking, and problem-solving skills that come from a college education. Administrators from Salt Lake Community College and law enforcement are working together to merge the two learning venues to enhance the confidence and abilities of Utah's officers.

Source: J. Slama, "Utah Officers Head Back to School," *FBI Law Enforcement Bulletin* (May 1997), pp. 18–19.

Contributing to this challenge is a new phenomenon: the former drug user as police applicant. The abuse of illicit drugs has become so pervasive in our society that many law enforcement agencies find large numbers of former and current drug users among their police officer applicants. Due to a need to hire more officers from a limited pool of applicants, some agencies are choosing to hire former users.

The task of managing a large urban police department seems never to have been more challenging than it is today. Chiefs and sheriffs are charged to reduce crime despite reduced budgets and a criminal justice system strained to the breaking point. Jails are overcrowded, and in some places, one inmate must be released if a newly convicted criminal is to be incarcerated. Unions press for better benefits, shorter work hours, and more control of tour assignments while being forced to defend officers engaged in corruption and drug abuse against departmental removal actions. The news media is filled with stories of politicians and professionals engaged in massive corruption schemes, some that

CTQ

Should police officers who engage in illegal misconduct be punished more or less severely than their civilian counterparts? Do you agree that ethics course trainings are the best preventative way to deal with police misconduct?

WEB

For more information on police conduct, **visit our Web site,** www.prenhall.com/territo.

reach into the billions of dollars. A department must develop a clear and precise statement of policy, such as the sample that follows, that defines the exact level of priority given to departmental integrity. The following is typical of such a policy.

Sample policy statement

The public demands that the integrity of police officers be above reproach. The dishonesty of any police officer may impair public confidence and cast suspicion upon the entire department. Succumbing to even minor temptations can destroy an officer's effectiveness and contribute to the corruption of others. An officer must avoid any conduct which might compromise his or her own integrity, or that of fellow officers, or of the department.

Just as each officer is responsible to maintain the highest level of personal integrity, the department must develop and foster an environment where honesty will thrive. It is the policy of this police department to place the objective of enhancing and sustaining integrity at the cornerstone of all its policies and operations.

In addition, many police departments have adopted a code of ethics such as the one developed by the International Association of Chiefs of Police (see Figure 6.2).

Many people involved in criminal justice education and the media who are concerned about police brutality and corruption seem to think that ethics courses in police academies and in-service training are the best remedy. However, their recommended solution covers only a tiny part of the overall objective of achieving the highest level of integrity in a police department. Institutional educational programs matter, but it also matters profoundly how the department as a whole is run.

Delattre suggests that it is important for police chiefs and sheriffs to provide leadership in requiring ethical and honest behavior on the part of their officers.[4] An important aspect of this effort is to carefully examine administrative issues such as recruiting, selection, academy, and field training standards. Requiring individual and supervisory accountability for all police activities and having a proactive internal affairs unit are other important components of an overall strategy to reduce unethical and dishonest behavior in a law enforcement agency.

FIGURE 6.2

The Law Enforcement Code of Ethics.

As a law enforcement officer, my fundamental duty is to serve mankind; to safeguard lives and property; to protect the innocent against deception, the weak against oppression or intimidation, and the peaceful against violence or disorder; and to respect the Constitutional rights of all men to liberty, equality, and justice.

I will keep my private life unsullied as an example to all; maintain courageous calm in the face of danger, scorn, or ridicule; develop self-restraint; and be constantly mindful of the welfare of others. Honest in thought and deed in both my personal and official life, I will be exemplary in obeying the laws of the land and the regulations of my department. Whatever I see or hear of a confidential nature or that is confided to me in my official capacity will be kept secret unless revelation is necessary in the performance of my duty.

I will never act officiously or permit personal feelings, prejudices, animosities, or friendships to influence my decisions. With no compromise for crime and with relentless prosecution of criminals, I will enforce the law courteously and appropriately without fear or favor, malice or ill will, never employing unnecessary force or violence and never accepting gratuities.

I recognize the badge of my office as a symbol of public faith, and I accept it as a public trust to be held so long as I am true to the ethics of the police service. I will constantly strive to achieve these objectives and ideals, dedicating myself before God to my chosen profession . . . law enforcement.

Source: International Association of Chiefs of Police.

EMPLOYMENT OF MINORITIES AND WOMEN IN POLICING

The traditional argument for increasing minority recruitment on the police force is that such recruitment increases the effectiveness of the force. Police officers cannot be effective in a hostile environment—an environment where they are unfamiliar with the culture of the community or where they feel alien, frightened, belligerent, or awkward. Citizens will not cooperate with them, will not report crimes, and will not aid in their investigations. One solution to this problem is to assign police officers that have the same ethnic background as the residents. An alternative approach is to provide cross-cultural communication training for all officers in order to provide them with the skills necessary to operate effectively in a variety of neighborhoods.

Recruitment of Minorities

According to Brian Reaves minorities now constitute approximately 20 percent of the local police officers in the United States.[5] One of the difficulties that even well-intentioned police administrators encounter is the lack of sufficient minority applicants to fill assignments. Minority recruitment, although not nearly as difficult as some contend, is not a simple matter. After decades of exclusion, suspicion, and discrimination, a passive "open-door" policy of recruitment is not enough. Peer-group pressure, fear of failure, nonacceptance, and even outright discrimination may work against it. Furthermore, job opportunities for minorities in other fields are often more attractive than those offered by a police department.

In spite of such obstacles, however, minority recruitment can be improved. First, a department can initiate a strong recruitment program. Recruitment left to a civil service board will probably not be successful. Such boards have many other responsibilities, and few have the time or skills needed to attract the kind of candidates police departments require. Thus, the department itself generally assumes the major responsibility.

A commitment to internal equal opportunity is also a key component. Applicants are being asked to commit themselves to a new career, and they need to know that the department recruiting them is dedicated to helping them advance. Many departments have demonstrated such commitment by appointing qualified minority individuals, from both within and outside the department, to high positions. Most of these departments are also taking the important step of removing discrimination from their promotional systems.

Innovative Minority Recruiting

Some researchers have suggested that many communities contain a sufficient number of qualified, well-educated minority members available for police positions. According to one study, law enforcement agencies need to make a more concerted effort to identify and hire college-educated minority police applicants. The following section describes examples of efforts being made in that regard.[6]

The number of college-educated officers, and particularly college-educated minority applicants, can be increased through the implementation of innovative personnel management programs. Personnel processes currently used by most police departments tend to be inflexible and unaccommodating. There is an underlying feeling of cynicism and distrust, rather than an open and optimistic perspective. If an organization seeks to have professional employees, then it must treat applicants and employees in a professional manner. Thus, an initial step is to establish an ideological change concerning personnel processes.

With this philosophical foundation, the department can then establish policies and procedures that enhance personnel hiring and selection processes. This would include such things as eliminating residency requirements, accommodating testing and physical examinations, and working the interviews and selection procedures into the schedules of applicants, instead of vice versa. A highly sought-after candidate will tend to choose an organization that is accommodating, rather than one that is unaccommodating or suspicious.

CTQ

As a police chief, what programs would you implement to hire and retain more minorities and women for your department?

WEB

For more information on minorities and policing, **visit our Web site,** www.prenhall.com/territo

Beyond ideological and procedural changes, new programs may be established that will increase the number of minority applicants and maintain college-level standards. For example, cadet programs are primarily designed to increase the number of college-educated minorities (although nonminorities are also eligible for the program). College-aged students are employed by the department in a nonsworn capacity and are required to attend college full-time. They not only receive a stipend but also have some of their college expenses paid for by the department. When a cadet graduates from college and completes the cadet corps program, he or she attends the police academy to become a sworn officer, with an obligation to work for the department.

Some departments have instituted community service officer (CSO) programs that target minority candidates. Recognizing that requiring a college education may limit the number of minority applicants, the CSO positions were established as an alternate avenue for a person to become a sworn officer. Candidates who apply to be a CSO must have at least a high school education and be admissible to an accredited college or university. In addition, the CSO applicant must meet all other employment criteria for a full-service police officer, as well as go through the same selection process (background investigation, drug tests, physical examination, and so forth).

Once employed, the CSO performs support tasks such as working in a security position or in the jail. In addition, the CSO attends college with expenses paid by the police department. Once the CSO has earned enough college credits for full-service police employment, the officer may go through continued training and be commissioned as a police officer. The most common argument in opposition to programs of these types is expense—and although the programs are desirable, they are simply too costly for the department.

Another change from traditional personnel practices would be to broaden the applicant pool. Essential to this would be to increase the age of employment of new officers. Many police agencies establish thirty-five as the maximum age for employment. Some authorities argue that the rationale for this practice is dated and that police agencies are missing candidates who would benefit the police service. One of the more frequently cited reasons for the "thirty-five-year rule" is physical conditioning. Yet in an era of physical fitness, this argument loses much of its impact. This change would attract people who are seeking a career change or those who retired early from another career, such as the military or public service.

Progressive police executives examine their personnel practices to see if they are meeting the desired ends of attracting and selecting the best possible people to become police officers. Employing simple short-term programs that neither encourage nor select the best possible candidates can create geometrically greater costs over the long term (see Figure 6.3).

Recruitment of Women

Not so many years ago, it was common for police administrators to dismiss the idea that women could adequately perform functions within the exclusive domain of male officers—patrol work, nonfamily crime investigations, and motorcycle patrol. However, legislative, administrative, and judicial action have long since resolved the question of whether women should be permitted to perform these functions, and women have put to rest questions about their ability to handle such tasks. Empirical evidence supports the proposition that carefully selected and carefully trained women are as effective as carefully selected and carefully trained men. And although not all women are suited for police work, neither are all men. This is not to suggest, however, that women have been universally and enthusiastically accepted by their male counterparts—only that their employment and career advancement opportunities have improved immeasurably in the past decade.

FIGURE 6.3

Many police departments are increasing the diversity of their workforce. Today approximately 20 percent of the nation's local police officers are minority group members.

© Dale Stockton.

Research on Women on Patrol

Following the introduction of women into patrol functions as police officers in the 1970s, several studies have been conducted on gender differences and police performance. More specifically, the notion of whether female officers are as capable as male officers at performing the required duties of patrol has been examined at length. The first and perhaps the most thorough study concerning the effectiveness of women on patrol was conducted in Washington, D.C., in 1973 by Bloch and Anderson. At the time, the Washington, D.C., police department was integrating policewomen into patrol duty. The study was designed to evaluate the female officers' effectiveness in patrol compared to their male counterparts.

This study found that men and women perform patrol work in a similar manner. They responded to similar calls and handled violent citizens with similar results, and citizens reported equal amounts of respect, acceptability, and capability with regard to female and male officers. In fact, there were no reported incidents that cast doubt on whether women had the ability to perform patrol work satisfactorily.[7]

Several subsequent studies also used objective measures of the performance of female police officers, such as supervisor performance ratings and reviews of police complaint files. The findings of these studies indicated that female and male officers have many similarities and differences, but overall concluded that women can perform the job of patrol officer as well as men.[8]

The Current Status of Women in Policing

Several years ago a document entitled "Report on the Status of Women in Policing" was published by the Police Foundation. The results of the research published in this study reveal that a variety of strategies, including affirmative action and evolving law, has led to a growth in the number of women in policing in America. Some authorities suggest that both the police and the public have gained by the increase in the number of women on today's police forces.[9] Specifically, in the years following the 1972 amendments to the Civil Rights Act, significant progress was made by women in policing.

With regard to increasing the number of women in policing there are several potential policies for police agencies to consider during the next decade, including implementing affirmative action policies for hiring and altering promotion policies to eliminate criteria irrelevant to identifying surprising ability or potential. In addition, increasing the number of women in recruitment, training, and other high-visibility assignments was recommended. Finally, it is important to have and enforce sexual harassment policies.

According to a recent study by the International Association of Chiefs of Police, women now make up nearly 12 percent of the total number of police officers.[10] While this represents an overall improvement, women still are faced with difficulties in the police work setting (see Figure 6.4).

OFFICER HEALTH

As a result of some of the unique factors associated with their job, police officers often feel isolated from other parts of society. Police officers are taught early in their academy training to be suspicious of nonpolice people and to be overly cautious and aware of the potential for danger. Likewise, the authority that law enforcement in our society represents often makes officers the target of citizens who have legitimate grievances (such as poor housing and unemployment),

WEB

For more information on women and policing, visit our Web site, www.prenhall.com/territo.

CTQ

What administrative strategies would you find most useful for increasing the recruitment of women officers?

FIGURE 6.4

The number of female officers who have advanced through the ranks has increased substantially over the last 25 years. Today several large cities have female police chiefs.

© Dale Stockton.

yet the officers are not empowered to address those problems. Individual officers may, with some justification, be depicted in the media as brutal, corrupt, or bigoted. Many law enforcement officers, however, feel they are all unjustly labeled when such events occur. Consequently, further isolation from society in general may result, wherein the police develop their own subculture. As Jerome Skolnick stated, "Set apart from the conventional world, the policeman experiences an exceptionally strong tendency to find his social identity within his occupational milieu."[11]

Historically, business and industry in the United States have been slow to identify and provide for the needs of workers. Largely because of labor unions, however, the U.S. worker has attained a variety of benefits, ranging from increased wages to comprehensive medical care to retirement programs. The evolution of mental health compensation as a significant management issue occurred through a combination of union pressures and simple economics. A healthy, well-adjusted worker means increased efficiency and higher production from the corporation. As a consequence, **job stress** "has moved from the nether world of 'emotional problems' and 'personality conflicts' to the corporate balance sheet. . . . Stress is now seen as not only troublesome but expensive."[12]

Police work is highly stressful. It is one of the few occupations in which employees continually face physical dangers and may be asked to put their lives on the line at any time. The police officer is exposed to violence, cruelty, and aggression and must often make critical decisions in high-pressure situations (see Figure 6.5).

Job Stress

Numerous researchers have studied occupational stress in law enforcement. Although these researchers do not group stressors into identical categories, they do follow similar patterns.[13] Thus, most of the stressors can be grouped into four categories: (1) organizational practices and characteristics; (2) criminal justice system practices and characteristics; (3) public practices and characteristics; and (4) police work itself.

The **Law Enforcement Critical Life Events Scale,** developed by Jim Sewell, established a ranking system whereby officers would rate events from most to least stressful. Sewell's research indicated that the events requiring the greatest amount of readjustment were those relating to the categories of violence, threat of violence, personnel matters, and ethical concerns.[14] One of the many stressful events facing police officers is suicide attempts (see "In the News: Officers Stop Suicide Attempt").

WEB

For more information on officer health, **visit our Web site,** www.prenhall.com/territo.

CTQ

What factors do you believe contribute most to officer stress? Which contribute least? Why?

FIGURE 6.5

Police work is an inherently dangerous profession. In this photo police officers pay final tribute to a fellow officer who died in the line of duty.

© Dale Stockton.

IN THE NEWS

A HUMAN PERSPECTIVE

OFFICERS STOP SUICIDE ATTEMPT

Officers Steve Shoemaker and Jerry Bledsoe of the Scott County, Missouri, Sheriff's Office were dispatched to a report of a man attempting to hang himself from a railroad trestle bridge. When the officers arrived at the scene, they located a man standing on the bridge with a rope tied around his neck. The man said his wife left him and took his children; therefore, he felt he had no reason to live. Officers Shoemaker and Bledsoe spent over a hour talking to the man. When it was obvious that he intended to jump, the officers began to maneuver themselves closer, in different directions, making it difficult for the man to watch them. As Officer Shoemaker attracted his attention, Officer Bledsoe leaped to the edge of the bridge, grabbed the man by the arm and held him until Officer Shoemaker could assist him. The officer struggled with the man as they hung from the edge of the bridge and removed the rope from the man's neck. Officer Bledsoe received minor injuries during the incident. Later, the man later told Officer Shoemaker that he fully intended to kill himself. Heroic actions by Officers Shoemaker and Bledsoe saved the man's life.

Source: FBI Law Enforcement Bulletin, vol. 69, no. 5 (May 2000), p. 33.

Stress and Female Police Officers

Several studies have examined both the levels and causes of stress among female police officers. For example, some research indicates that women not only experienced stress similar to that of their male counterparts, but they also had categories of stress that were gender-specific, including negative attitudes of male officers; group blame; negative responses from male citizens; and lack of role models.[15] In other research, stress in female officers was found to be related to dissatisfaction with co-workers.[16] In a study of female officers only, respondents expressed among other things a lack of acceptance by male officers, which led to job stress.[17] Meridith Bowman found little evidence of gender-related stress among female officers in the law enforcement agencies studied.[18] This researcher also found that high levels of stress in both male and female officers were associated with critical incidents such as violent death of a fellow officer and suicide of an officer who was a close friend. Clearly, further research needs to be conducted on the causes of stress in both male and female police officers.

Alcoholism

Alcoholism in government and industry is not only widespread but is also extremely costly—a fact established by many independent researchers. It is estimated that 6.5 million workers in the United States today are alcoholics. Loss of productivity because of alcoholism has been computed at billions of dollars.[19]

Although precise figures are not available, in some departments officials report informally that as many as 25 percent of their officers have serious alcohol problems.[20] These problems manifest themselves in a number of ways: higher than normal absentee rates prior to and immediately before regular days off, complaints of insubordination by supervisors, complaints by citizens of misconduct in the form of verbal and physical abuse, intoxication during regular working hours, involvement in traffic accidents while under the influence of alcohol on and off duty, and reduced overall performance.

It has been suggested that police work is especially conducive to alcoholism. Because police officers frequently work in an environment where social drinking is common, it is relatively easy for them to become social drinkers. The nature of the work and the environment in which it is performed are the stress stimuli. Traditionally, police departments adhered to the "character flaw" theory of alcoholism. This outdated philsosophy called for the denunciation and dismissal of the officer with an alcohol problem. Today police departments attempt to rehabilitate officers, and typically they are separated from the service only after such attempts have failed. Police departments now have a broad mix of employee assistance programs (EAPs) to assist officers with their drink-

WEB

For more information on police stress, **visit our Web site,** www.prenhall.com/territo.

CTQ

What administrative measures do you believe should be taken by police departments to curb alcoholism among officers? Do you agree with the statement that police work is especially conductive to alcoholism, or does that hold true for a number of other high-stress jobs?

WEB

For more information on police alcoholism, **visit our Web site,** www.prenhall.com/territo.

ing problems, including self-assessment checklists, peer counseling, in-house psychologists and those on retainers, and support groups.

There is no single "best way" for a police department to assist an officer with a drinking problem, but some agencies have enjoyed a fair degree of success in their efforts. For example, the Denver Police Department now uses a closed-circuit television system to reach officers who are problem drinkers and encourage them to join an in-house program. The in-house program is designed to persuade the problem drinkers—after they have been sufficiently educated about their problem—to enter the Mercy Hospital Care Unit for recovering alcoholics.

Reports from the Denver Police Department indicate that the department has benefited greatly from its alcohol abuse program. Some of the benefits are as follows:

1. Retention on staff of most officers who suffer from alcoholism
2. Solution of complex and difficult personnel problems
3. Realistic and practical extension of the police agency's program into the entire city government
4. Improved public and community attitudes for officers and their families
5. Elimination of the dangerous and antisocial behavior of officers in the community
6. Full cooperation with rehabilitation efforts from police associations and unions that represent officers
7. Development of a preventive influence on moderate drinkers

Police Department Drug Testing

A significant issue facing police departments in the present time is that of drug use by officers. The personal and legal ramifications are significant for officers, departments, and the communities they serve.[21]

The availability and widespread use of illegal drugs are causes of national alarm today. Reports of drug abuse come from every segment of our society. It should come as no surprise that the police have not been immune to the contagion of drug abuse. Police officers experience stress and trauma in their jobs, and some may turn to drugs as a means of coping. Drug use by police officers is receiving national media attention because of its potential threat to the integrity of law enforcement and the safety of the community.

To learn how police departments are addressing this problem, the National Institute of Justice sponsored a telephone survey of thirty-three major police departments. Twenty-four had drug-testing programs. These departments explained their testing procedures, selection process, and the procedures that were used after a positive test. They also discussed whether treatment programs were available and whether random testing had even been considered. Departments provided information on the types of tests conducted, the administration of the tests, the procedures used to establish chain of custody, and the costs of the tests.

Among other results, the survey found that almost three-quarters of the departments used drug screening of applicants. Virtually all of the departments had written policies for conducting drug tests on officers suspected of using illegal drugs. In addition, almost a quarter of the departments indicated that treatment of officers using drugs, rather than dismissal, would be appropriate in some circumstances. These results show that many police managers are taking steps to make their departments as drug-free as possible.

Further impetus for action has come from the International Association of Chiefs of Police (IACP), which has developed a model drug-testing policy for local police departments to consider in identifying and dealing with the use of illegal drugs by police officers. This policy calls for actions such as testing police applicants and recruits; testing current employees under certain circumstances, such as suspected impairment or allegations of possession or sale of drugs; and requiring officers in certain assignments such as narcotics or vice enforcement units to be tested periodically.

Many police departments already have policies along these lines. The IACP's endorsement of these steps may encourage other departments to take similar action to deal with employee drug abuse.

CTQ

Do you think it is important to have a drug-screening policy for police officers? Why or why not? If you were chief, what would you do with an officer who was found to be using illegal drugs?

Suicide

A considerable number of studies have been conducted with regard to suicide among police officers. Early research suggested several possible reasons for police suicide,[22] including the following: Police work is a male-dominated profession and men have a higher suicide rate; officers have firearms readily available; and officers suffer psychological repercussions from constantly being exposed to death.

Several prior studies report that police suicide rates are relatively high.[23] Other research concluded that police suicide rates were actually lower than national suicide rates.[24] These contradictory findings may be due to the local nature of many of the studies, small sample size and a lack of adequate comparative groups, and inadequate analytic techniques. There is also some concern that some officer suicides may be misclassified in order to save the department and the family embarrassment. Therefore, the actual number of police suicides may be higher than reported.

Recent research has attempted to correct some of the deficiencies noted in prior police suicide research. Using national data, Stack and Kelley found police suicide rates slightly higher than that of an age-matched male peer group.[25] Moreover, they also found that once controls are introduced for socioeconomic variables, being a police officer is not significantly associated with the odds of death by suicide.

During the last decade many police agencies have established employee assistance programs and other mental health components to assist officers in need. Admittedly, it is difficult to determine the actual number of police suicides committed annually and to determine the actual rate of suicide. However, it is critical that police chiefs and sheriffs adopt a proactive preventive approach to deal with the problem of police suicide.

Coping with Health Problems

There are many ways to reduce stress and to cope with health problems on the police force. The following methods and programs have been recommended in past years by the International Association of Chiefs of Police: using efficient preemployment screening; increasing practical training for police on the subject of stress; increasing support from police executives; instituting mandatory alcoholic rehabilitation programs; providing immediate consultation to officers involved in traumatic incidents; providing complete false-arrest and liability insurance; and providing psychological services to police officers and their families. As shown in Figure 6.6, aerobic exercise is a good form of stress relief for police officers.

Whatever the methods, a firm commitment is required from both the individual officer and the department. Any effort to increase effectiveness in coping with stress will be less successful in the absence of close cooperation between these parties.

WEB

For more information on police suicide, **visit our Web site,** www.prenhall.com/territo.

FIGURE 6.6

There are a variety of ways for police officers to reduce stress levels. Jogging is considered an excellent means of reducing stress and enhancing physical well-being.

© Dale Stockton.

POLICE CONTACT WITH THE PUBLIC

For many years there has been a significant level of attention paid to interactions between police and citizens. Over the years the media have reported numerous incidents of negative contact between the police and community members. Incidents that involve allegations of police abuse of authority can have long-term repercussions in any community. It is therefore important to know more about how often and under what circumstances a police contact with a citizen becomes problematic. The Bureau of Justice Statistics has explored these questions in a national survey of citizens in this country. One of the most important findings noted by the Bureau of Justice Statistics is that "most people, of any race, who have a contact with police, most often through a traffic stop, evaluate the stop as having been appropriate."[26] Other findings of this research published in 2001 follow.

About one-fifth of U.S. residents had police contact within the last year, with the primary form of contact being a traffic stop. Most drivers stopped (84 percent) felt the stop was legitimate, and 90 percent felt the police behaved properly. Almost 90 percent of the white drivers and three-quarters of the African American drivers said the officer made a legitimate stop. Less than 1 percent of the police-citizen contacts involved police use of force. The various reasons for police-citizen contacts by percentage are shown in Table 6.1.

USE OF DEADLY FORCE

No aspect of police work elicits more passionate concern or more divided opinion than the use of **deadly force.** Many community groups and minority organizations believe that police killings of civilians are excessive and often unjustifiable.

Few would argue with the idea that police officers have the right to use deadly force to protect their own lives or the lives of innocent people. In many states, however, the law and departmental policies allow officers discretion that goes far beyond the simple edicts of self-defense or the defense of others. Some laws and policies are still modeled after English common law, which allows a police officer to use deadly force to apprehend someone reasonably believed to have committed a felony. The rationale for this formula is based on the fact that, until the early 1800s in both the United States and England, virtually all felonies were punishable by death. A felon was someone who, by his or her act, had forfeited the right to life.[27]

Recommendations that restrict police discretion in the use of deadly force are becoming increasingly common in law enforcement agencies. In addition to humanitarian reasons, there are legal, political, and social reasons for controlling police use of deadly force. Financial liability might also result from the use of deadly force. Deaths occurring from police action often result in substantial judgments against financially hard-pressed cities.

Managing the Use of Force

Police departments, which are ultimately held responsible for the actions of their employees, are required to ensure that their officers have received adequate training and supervision in various means of force that they might employ. The St. Paul (Minnesota)

WEB

For more information on the use of deadly force by police, **visit our Web site, www.prenhall.com/territo.**

TABLE 6.1 Percentage of Citizens with a Police Contact

Motor vehicle stop	52%
Report a crime	19%
Ask for assistance	12%
Report a neighborhood problem	9%
Involved in a traffic accident	8%
Witness to a traffic accident	5%
Witness a crime	3%
Questioned as crime suspect	3%
Attended crime prevention meeting	1%
Served warrant	1%

Source: Bureau of Justice Statistics, 2001.

Police Department designed a research study on the use of force by its employees. Officers were required to identify on a report form both the specific amount of force they have used in a situation and the level of force that they encountered when attempting to take an individual into custody.[28] A similar form is shown in Figure 6.7.

FIGURE 6.7

Form Used When Officers Use Force in Arrest Situations

UNIVERSITY OF SOUTH FLORIDA POLICE DEPARTMENT
USE OF FORCE REPORT

Date of Incident: _____ Time of Incident: _____ Case Number: _____
Subject/Defendant Name: _____ Race: _____ Sex: _____ DOB: _____
Alcohol/Drug Involvement Suspected: ☐YES ☐NO Explain: _____ Hgt: _____ Wgt: _____
Charge(s): _____

Subject/Defendant Level of Resistance:
(may ✓ more than one)
1. ☐ Verbal (words used) _____
   _____

2. ☐ Passive Physical (i.e., sat still, lay on ground) _____

3. ☐ Active Physical (i.e., refused handcuffing, braced/pushed/pulled away) _____

4. ☐ Aggressive Physical (i.e., punched, kicked, bit) _____

5. ☐ Aggravated Physical (i.e., numerous kicks, club, knife, firearm, motor vehicle, other weapon) _____

6. ☐ Attempted to Disarm (i.e., from the front, rear, or side) _____

7. ☐ Officer Disarmed (i.e., OC, baton, handcuffs, firearm) _____

Law Enforcement Weapons/Tools Used: (✓ all that apply)
1. ☐ Personal Weapons (hands, feet, knees)
2. ☐ Handcuffs
3. ☐ BodyGuard System
4. ☐ OC Spray
5. ☐ Baton (extended, closed)
6. ☐ Firearm unholstered
7. ☐ Firearm pointed at suspect (handgun, shotgun)
8. ☐ Firearm discharged (handgun, shotgun)
9. ☐ Other (i.e., ticket book, clipboard, flashlight) _____

Officer's Level of Response: (may ✓ more than one)
1. ☐ Officer's Presence: ☐ Uniformed   ☐ Plain Clothes
                          ☐ Marked Unit   ☐ Unmarked Unit

2. ☐ Verbal Communication (words used, commands given) _____

3. ☐ Physical Control (control points, transporters) _____

4. ☐ OC Spray _____

5. ☐ Takedowns (subject taken to the ground, counter moves) _____

6. ☐ Intermediate Weapons (indicate area struck) _____

7. ☐ Incapacitation (indicate area and type of strike, i.e., side of neck, upper chest) _____

8. ☐ Threat of Deadly Force (i.e., pointed firearm) _____

9. ☐ Deadly Force (describe) _____

INJURIES: (✓ all that apply)

Subject:	Officer:	Subject:	Officer:
Visible Injury:	Visible Injury:	Medical Attention Required:	Medical Attention Required:
☐ None	☐ None	☐ None	☐ None
☐ Redness	☐ Redness	☐ EMT/Paramedic	☐ EMT/Paramedic
☐ Swelling	☐ Swelling	☐ Doctor's Examination	☐ Doctor's Examination
☐ Abrasion	☐ Abrasion	☐ X-Ray	☐ X-Ray
☐ Other _____	☐ Other _____	☐ Stitches	☐ Stitches
		☐ Other _____	☐ Other: _____
Complaint of Pain:	Complaint of Pain:	☐ Hospitalization	☐ Hospitalization
☐ None	☐ None	Fatality:	Fatality:
☐ Minor	☐ Minor	☐ Yes	☐ Yes
☐ Moderate	☐ Moderate	☐ No	☐ No
☐ Intense	☐ Intense		

Officer's Name: _____ Officer's Signature: _____ Date: _____
Supervisor: _____ Date: _____

Source: Courtesy of Chief Pat Johnson, University of South Florida Police Department, Tampa, Florida.

IN THE NEWS

A HUMAN PERSPECTIVE

OFFICER USES DEADLY FORCE TO SAVE LIFE

Waiting at a traffic light while en route to work in the early morning hours, Sergeant Robert Shearer of the Harrisburg, Pennsylvania, Bureau of Police observed two naked men running through the snow-covered street, with one man attempting to assault the other. Sergeant Shearer pulled his personal vehicle onto an adjoining street and, opening his civilian overcoat to reveal his uniform and badge, identified himself as a police officer. The assailant, who had caught the other man and began stabbing him frantically with a large kitchen knife, ignored Sergeant Shearer's repeated commands to drop the knife. Hoping to avoid the use of deadly force, Sergeant Shearer rushed the assailant and knocked him off the critically injured victim. Instead of discontinuing his attack, however, the assailant raised the knife and began advancing toward the victim again. Sergeant Shearer fired one shot, which struck the 6'8", 260-pound assailant but failed to slow his advance. He fired two more shots, which finally stopped the man, who subsequently died in the emergency room of a local hospital. Though critically wounded, the victim, who had come to the aid of his wife and child when the assailant attacked the woman as she prepared to leave for work, made a full recovery.

Source: FBI Law Enforcement Bulletin, vol. 66 (1997), p. 33.

CTQ

Do you believe that the use of deadly force by a police officer is ever justified? If so, under what conditions?

The St. Paul study found that in 11,989 custody situations, officers encountered significant resistance: 1,750 times during the year, or nearly five times per day. Of all those cases, only 1 percent resulted in injuries to suspects that required outpatient medical treatment; five individuals were hospitalized overnight; two died.

This type of validated statistical information may be used in any civil suit where the quality of overall department training is questioned. It can also be presented to community groups as part of any package describing department performance.

Unfortunately there are times that police officers are required to use deadly force. "In the News: Officer Uses Deadly Force to Save Life" illustrates one such occasion.

Shooting-Control Techniques

One of the few areas in which the deadly force research data do seem to offer beleaguered police leaders meaningful guidance is on the question of what **shooting-control techniques** help limit problematic violence.[29] Shooting-control techniques may be policy-oriented, such as written directives that narrow officer discretion, direct accountability up the chain of command for inappropriate officer aggressiveness, and reward systems for officers who resolve situations by less violent means when that option is available. Other shooting-control techniques may relate to equipment such as the availability of modern communications equipment, use of lightweight soft-body armor, and "less-than-lethal" weapons such as stun guns and rubber bullets. Finally, training for officers in violence-reduction techniques and "cultural awareness" can also be useful in reducing the instances of deadly force use.

Big-city departments that have employed a number of these techniques together have produced positive results: fewer controversial shootings by officers, fewer serious injuries of officers, no increase in the crime rate, and no decline in officers' aggressiveness in making arrests.

This and other evidence convinced the U.S. Supreme Court in March 1985 to decide, by a 6–3 vote, that more than half the states' laws and many law enforcement agencies' regulations on police use of deadly force were unconstitutionally permissive. In *Tennessee v. Garner*, for the first time, a national minimum standard was imposed. Although ambiguities remain, the ruling prohibits police from shooting at unarmed, nonviolent, fleeing felony suspects. The Supreme Court heard and rejected the argument that a criminal suspect forfeits his or her right to live by committing a crime and disobeying a lawful police order to surrender. The Court reasoned that there must be a proportionally reasonable balance between the alleged criminal conduct and the governmental response.

Research on Use of Force by Police

While the use of force by police in citizen contacts is relatively infrequent, it is still of critical interest to society at large and to specific communities. Therefore, it is important to examine what is known about police use of force in citizen encounters. The National Institute of Justice sponsored a recent study of the use of force by the police. This national study of 150 police departments included a number of findings.[30] For instance, the police use-of-force rate was about four per every 10,000 responded-to calls for service. The type of force used most often was physical force, in 87 percent of the cases. Chemical force was used in 7 percent of the cases and firearms in about 5 percent.

Violence-Prone Police Officers

Some research suggests that a relatively small proportion of police officers are involved in a substantial number of use-of-force incidents on a repeated basis. For example, in a study of one police agency in the southeast, Lersch and Mieczkowski found that only 7 percent of the officers in that department could be labeled as "chronic offenders" with regard to citizen complaints.[31] Most of these complaints were for violence or harassment on the part of the officers. One way to deal with officers labeled as chronic offenders is for police agencies to track these officers' actions and to impose appropriate discipline at the earliest stage possible.

Evaluating the Use of Pepper Spray as an Alternative to Deadly Force

Violent encounters between police officers and individuals resisting arrest have historically resulted in injury and frequently in complaints about the level of force used by police. In addition to concern over these issues, increased civil liability and court-imposed limitations on the use of deadly force have stimulated the search for safe and effective less-than-lethal (LTL) force alternatives. One widely used option is oleoresin capsicum (OC) aerosol, commonly called pepper spray.

Despite extensive applications in hundreds of police departments, few systematic studies of OC usage and effectiveness have been documented. A National Institute of Justice–sponsored assessment of pepper spray's usefulness focused on the Baltimore County Police Department's use of this LTL.[32]

A summary of key results of this study revealed that pepper spray may not fully subdue individuals appearing to be on drugs; that the rate of assaults on officers continued to decline after OC was introduced; and that use-of-force complaints decreased by 53 percent and there were no complaints regarding the use of OC during the period of the study. While these findings are generally encouraging for police use of pepper spray, more systematic research should be conducted in other locations (see Figure 6.8).

POLICE-PROSECUTOR COOPERATION

Another trend emerging in law enforcement over the last decade is police and prosecutors in many jurisdictions working together as a team throughout every step of the criminal justice process. Their goal in these instances is to achieve the same end—conviction.[33]

Police and prosecutors are mutually pursuing their common goal of protecting society from crime and violence. Police want to make arrests that lead to criminal justice penalties for the guilty and that protect communities from further crimes. Prosecutors want to build strong cases that can succeed in bringing convictions. When relations between the two agencies are not well synchronized, the important efforts of both may be stymied.

Today's professional police officers are skilled in evaluating evidence in the field and establishing probable cause for arrest. To carry the case forward to successful prosecution, however, the prosecutor requires evidence that can meet the court's higher standard of certainty. Better coordination between police and prosecutors in meeting the requirements for evidence can improve the quality of cases and boost conviction rates.

Examples of good police-prosecutor cooperation are evident in jurisdictions across the country. A variety of activities have increased cooperation between agencies and have ultimately convicted more criminals. Several characteristics of these cooperative agencies are top-down commitment by police and prosecution agencies; recognition

---

WEB

For more information on research of the use of force by police, **visit the link to the Police Foundation, a nonprofit organization that also conducts police research, on our Web site, www.prenhall.com/ territo**.

CTQ

Considering previous research findings, do you think the use of pepper spray is an effective alternative to more violent methods for subduing criminals? Why or why not?

WEB

For more information on alternatives to pepper spray use by police, **visit our Web site, www.prenhall.com/ territo**.

FIGURE 6.8

Police departments are searching for various ways to subdue violent criminals without resorting to lethal force. One popular tool used by many agencies today is oleoresin capsicum (OC) spray.

© Dale Stockton.

that one agency cannot be successful without the other; placement of police and prosecution line-personnel offices close to one another; having the same officers work with the same prosecutors over time; and ensuring daily informal contact between police and prosecutors.

PRIVATE SECURITY AND LAW ENFORCEMENT: PARTNERS FOR THE FUTURE

CTQ
What problems do you believe could be associated with private policing? What are some of the benefits?

An important trend in the United States is the desire of public law enforcement and private security to examine their respective and interactive roles. Given the increased demands for service made to police agencies coupled with a constant or decreasing tax support base, the need to review critically which services can best be provided by public law enforcement versus the private security industry is an issue being discussed. Politicians, police managers, and private security executives are faced with the same question: "How can we serve our constituents in the most cost-effective manner, relative to crime control?"[34]

WEB
For more information on private policing, visit our Web site, www.prenhall.com/territo.

Traditionally, society's efforts to prevent and control crime have relied almost exclusively on the police and other parts of the criminal justice system. Less visible are the private security resources of business, industry, and institutions. Today, private security plays a major protective role in the nation's life. It employs more people and expends more dollars for products and services than its public law enforcement counterparts.

TECHNOLOGICAL TRENDS IN POLICING

Numerous technological trends have evolved over the last decade in law enforcement. Five specific innovations of interest are computer-aided dispatch (CAD), fingerprint automation, DNA profiling, use of laptop computers, and the application of geographical information systems (GIS).

Computer-Aided Dispatch

WEB
For more information on computer-aided dispatch, visit our Web site, www.prenhall.com/territo.

The critical tasks of a police radio dispatcher include obtaining accurate information from members of the public who need assistance and efficiently sending an officer to provide the help necessary. Therefore, appropriate management of information by the dispatcher may mean the difference between life and death. In a **computer-aided dispatch (CAD)** system, the police radio dispatcher is assisted by a high-speed digital computer.[35]

IN THE WORKPLACE

DISPATCHER

Responsible for monitoring the location of emergency services personnel from any one or all of the jurisdiction's emergency services departments. Responsible for performing a variety of general support duties related to dispatch activities, including the following: record keeping, typing and filing, monitoring teletype communications, receiving incoming calls for police and emergency assistance, and determining priority and dispatch emergency units as necessary. Minimum qualifications are as follows: high school diploma or equivalent, dispatch experience, knowledge of geographic features and streets within the area served, correct punctuation and grammar usage.

CAD systems also offer greater options for managing service demands. Dispatchers must manage two lists: the backlog of unanswered police calls for service and the list of available police patrol cars in the dispatch area. Too many police dispatchers (with or without a CAD system) will send a police car to an incident in the dispatch area if at least one police car is available there. This policy often depletes all available police resources by assigning them with equal priority to all varieties of calls for service, stacking them only when all cars in a given area are simultaneously busy.

Guided by an intelligent CAD system, dispatchers can deliberately delay more and more low-priority calls when cars become scarce. Then the remaining cars would be available as "insurance" for high-priority calls that might come in. Rather than simply acting as an electronic conveyor belt, this system would assist in the correct prioritization and management of demand for police services.

Advanced CAD systems can also assist dispatchers with important details. It is often no trivial task for the operator to obtain the correct address. The caller is often distressed and unable to enunciate the street name and number, much less give the correct spelling of the street name. In some cities and larger multijurisdictional CAD systems, two or more streets may have the same name. Well-publicized tragedies have occurred when incorrect addresses were typed into CAD systems (see "In the News").

The majority of police calls are of low priority or are noncriminal, but for the 5 or 10 percent that are urgent, police must have correct information and act on it swiftly. An intelligent CAD system would detect an ambiguous address or one that does not exist and could suggest that the operator question the caller to verify the address.

Several currently implemented CAD systems have made major strides in "getting the address right," including the addition of hazardous-address files, which contain information on repeat callers, dangerous situations, and the like.

Fingerprint Automation

A second trend in law enforcement technology has been **fingerprint automation.** As the agency that serves as the central repository of fingerprints in the United States, the FBI

> **CTQ**
> In what ways do you think technological trends affect policing practices in America?

> **WEB**
> For more information on police and technology, **visit our Web site,** www.prenhall.com/territo.

IN THE NEWS

A HUMAN PERSPECTIVE

ADDRESS MISTAKE LEADS TO TRAGEDY

A woman residing in a village just outside Buffalo, New York, was brutally murdered by an intruder after being assured police assistance was on the way. Unfortunately, patrol units were dispatched to a duplicate address within the city of Buffalo, where the same street and number existed. Police were delayed fourteen minutes, during which the break-in and homicide occurred.

IN THE WORKPLACE

FINGERPRINT ANALYST

Responsible for retrieving, evaluating, comparing, documenting, and preserving latent prints. Performs a variety of duties, including the following: visiting crime scenes, recovering prints from all items of physical evidence by utilizing a variety of techniques, photographically documenting evidence and latent print detail, determining if print is of sufficient quality to establish identity, providing expert testimony, and providing training to law enforcement on techniques of latent print development. Minimum qualifications are as follows: high school diploma or equivalent, five years of experience in fingerprint-related field, college can substitute for the required experience on a year-to-year basis.

---

conducted research to find an answer to the ever-increasing problem of accurate, timely fingerprint processing.[36]

In recent years, computer technology has been used as an aid in latent fingerprint work to solve criminal cases. With more and more of FBI Identification Division data placed in computerized files, it is more feasible to let the computer perform tasks too labor-intensive to be performed manually.

In the past, a latent fingerprint specialist would use every approach humanly possible to try to identify latent prints submitted as evidence in a case. But after exhausting all possible suspects or leads without making an identification, the case would be returned to the contributing agency unsolved. Due to the millions of criminal fingerprints on file, attempts to develop additional suspects in a case were impractical.

But with the introduction of the computer, it has become feasible to use new techniques to select logical suspects in cases involving crime-scene latent fingerprints. One program, the Latent Descriptor Index, can perform a computer search of FBI Identification Division automated files through the use of latent fingerprint pattern types, physical description information, and case information. Since it was instituted, the Latent Descriptor Index has solved cases that would not have been solved otherwise.

The Automated Latent System Model provides online searching and matching capability against a database of repeat offenders and criminals categorized by specific crimes. This system works by entering as much of the personal descriptive information, crime information, and fingerprint data as is available into a semiautomatic fingerprint reader terminal. The Automated Latent System Model selects candidates from the database that match the personal and crime descriptive information submitted. Then all possible candidates are compared with the latent fingerprint via the matching algorithm.

"In the News: An IAFIS Success Story" describes a success story using the FBI's Integrated Automated Fingerprint Identification System (IAFIS).

IN THE NEWS

A HUMAN PERSPECTIVE

AN IAFIS SUCCESS STORY

In Massachusetts, the police charged an 18-year-old male with trespassing, underage drinking, and drinking in public. Based on these offenses, his release was imminent. However, using the FBI's Integrated Automated Fingerprint Identification System (IAFIS), law enforcement officers learned of wanted charges for a drug-related murder of another 18-year-old in Greenville, South Carolina. This case shows how IAFIS can raise the capacity of the police to identify wanted persons to the next generation of crime fighting.

Source: *FBI Law Enforcement Bulletin*, vol. 70, no. 9 (September 2001), p. 22.

Police Use of Laptop Computers

The public image of the patrol officer suggests a role other than that of information processor. In fact, however, police departments are information-intensive organizations. Information plays such a vital role that its efficient processing can mean the difference between successful and unsuccessful prosecution of a case.[37]

A great deal of the information processed by a police department comes from the police reports written by patrol officers. Along with dispatch and investigation functions, patrol accounts for the preponderance of all information gathered. The experience of the Los Angeles Police Department (LAPD) is illustrative: Of all reports of any type written in the department, 46 percent are the PIRs (Preliminary Investigative Reports) prepared by patrol officers. A considerable amount of an officer's time—about 15 to 20 percent, by one estimate—is invested in completing the reports, which traditionally have been written by hand. In addition to requiring a great deal of time, handwritten reports may be incomplete or illegible. Errors are made if clerks select the wrong code for entering report information into the database to be used by other criminal justice staff. Delays occur if data are not processed immediately, and the delays in turn prevent timely receipt by detectives and management. Accuracy and thoroughness are essential because of the role of the police report as the initial documentation of what happened at the crime scene. The reports are filled out by the officer who is dispatched to or otherwise arrives at the place where the crime was committed. In the course of dealing with the incident, the officer makes a record of what occurred and submits it to the department. Police reports contain information about suspects, victims, witnesses, property recovered as evidence, the time the crime was committed, and the like. Carefully and completely prepared reports make the work of detectives easier. The same is true for prosecutors, who use police reports to help prepare cases to be filed.

In police agencies nationwide, central office computers are meeting the need to make sense of reported data and to transform them into useful information. Automating data entry is one of the remaining needs. The preparation of police reports is a data entry task that stands close to the "headwaters" of the information stream in a police department. Automating these reports would electronically capture much of the information used in law enforcement.

For these reasons, automating police reports would be a major step toward paperless police operations, in which any piece of information could be retrieved electronically from any point in the criminal justice system.

Future Applications of Computers

The current extent of computerization in law enforcement is difficult to determine with much precision because it is happening faster than published reports can document it. It is probably safe to say that although applications seem to be virtually universal, the anticipated "computer revolution in policing" has not taken place.

New developments are on the horizon, however. The same digital data links that serve mobile data terminals by transmitting characters can also transmit pictures. With the availability of portable facsimile (fax) equipment, scanners, and VCR cameras, transmission to and from the patrol car of all sorts of images (of fingerprints or property, for example) becomes feasible. Among other prospects are patrol vehicles equipped with voice-recognition modules that transmit to dispatch an officer's statement of his or her location or a suspect's license plate number. Robots—in the form of speed-surveillance transceivers located on roadways—can write speeding tickets. Interviews with victims and suspects may be also digitally recorded.

The ability of a police department to function efficiently and effectively is determined to a great extent by its ability to process information. In flowing to its many users, both in the department and elsewhere, information is fed by many sources. The dispatch unit is the "headwaters"; information processing begins when the patrol officer is sent to the scene of a crime. The stream of information grows continuously from police reports until disposition by the court. In the information stream, the police report has a central role, because it is the initial documentation of what happened at the crime scene.

IN THE WORKPLACE

CRIME ANALYST

Responsible for reviewing and analyzing of crime reports, field interview cards, and related criminal data and information daily to identify and evaluate crime series, trends, and patterns. Performs duties including the following: maintaining manual and automated systems for storage and retrieval of crime information, preparing crime data reports and studies, participating in developing applications of the computer system to crime information, and acting as a liaison with local, state, and federal law enforcement to exchange crime information. Minimum qualifications are as follows: valid driver's license; bachelor's degree from an accredited college in criminal justice, public administration, or a related field.

CTQ
Some authorities have suggested that despite the improvements in the use of technology, policing remains primarily a "people" profession. Do you agree? Why or why not?

CTQ
What constitutional concerns might the establishment of a DNA databank composed of samples from nonconvicted offenders have?

WEB
For more information on DNA profiling, visit our Web site, www.prenhall.com/territo.

Along the way, information sharing occurs among and within agencies. A police report is not only shared within the department but also becomes information for use by state agencies and the FBI. In varying degrees, the court system also depends on police reports.

The advent of automation has made it imperative for police departments to streamline information processing and sharing. In fact, the very availability of advanced technology creates the need for it and helps determine its use. The National Institute of Justice has been at the forefront of research efforts to find ways to adapt new technologies to increase the effectiveness and efficiency of the criminal justice system.

The studies described explored such issues as cost, increases in productivity, effects on quality of reports, and the impact of this aspect of automated information processing on both those using the system and on others in the criminal justice network.

Although these experiments did not resolve all the issues, they did much to further our knowledge of the challenges facing police departments as they look for ways to reduce mountains of paperwork.

We may never achieve a truly "paperless police department." But enthusiastic acceptance of laptops by the police officers who used them in these experiments, plus the promise of cost savings, indicate the potential of advanced technologies to further enhance criminal justice system operations.

DNA Profiling

Of all the technological advances introduced to law enforcement within the last twenty-five years, perhaps the one with the greatest impact has been **DNA profiling.** Research in this important area has continued to evolve and to improve this valuable investigative tool. The use of DNA profiling to identify or eliminate potential suspects is now considered by many the equivalent of molecule fingerprints. "In the News: DNA Profiling Advancement" provides a useful example.

Geographical Information Systems

A **geographical information system (GIS)** is a computerized database system that combines map images with other spatially referenced information. It is composed of two types of data files (maps and descriptive data) and also some type of CAD software to display this information in a graphical format. For years in law enforcement, analysis of spatial information has provided valuable clues to help find and apprehend criminals. Traditional pin maps have been around almost as long as police departments. With the advent of computers, these maps have become much easier to create and manipulate, thus providing more valuable information.[38] Additionally, the ability to generate maps quickly and easily by computer has increased the number of potential applications within law enforcement.

IN THE NEWS

A HUMAN PERSPECTIVE

DNA PROFILING ADVANCEMENT

Correctional officer Iran Shuttlesworth was convicted of the kidnapping and first-degree sexual assault of a Milwaukee woman. As they do in many crimes, examiners from the FBI Laboratory had compared the suspect's DNA to that of a semen stain found on the victim's clothing. At the trial, an examiner testified that the FBI had identified Shuttlesworth as the source of the semen stain.

This case represents a major breakthrough for DNA evidence. Although recognized as the genetic blueprint for an individual, in the past, DNA tests could do no more than show that an individual could not be excluded as a possible source of an evidence stain. Sometimes the odds of another person in a given population having the same DNA were astronomical; nevertheless, scientists could not positively link a specific person with a particular evidence stain.

Improved profiling techniques, as well as an unparalleled statistical base, provide the framework for this scientific breakthrough. In a process known as Restriction Fragment Length Polymorphism (RFLP) typing, FBI scientists generate DNA profiles from six sites, or loci, on the DNA molecule. These loci provide enough information to compare with the DNA profiles from evidence stains and declare a match. Experts then compare the matching profile to various population groups and calculate the likelihood of selecting an individual from the population with a similar profile. If that number proves exceedingly rare, the suspect can be named as the source of the evidentiary stain. The ability to do so testifies to the FBI's statistical methods. In addition, improvements in RFLP typing have allowed the FBI to examine six loci in less than two weeks, a process that once took more than three times that long and involved only four sites. Moreover, once DNA testing required relatively large stains with high-quality DNA, and it took weeks to reach a conclusion. Today, however, FBI scientists can type DNA from the back of a postage stamp, the shaft of a hair, and the end of a cigarette in a matter of days. Over a decade of research paved the way for the FBI's ability to match suspects to evidence stains.

Now the equivalent of molecule fingerprints, DNA profiles have indeed proved to be valuable investigative tools. As the FBI Laboratory continues to develop innovative technologies and share its expertise with criminal justice professionals worldwide, it takes great strides in bringing offenders to swift and sure justice, while clearing innocent individuals and protecting crime victims.

Source: "DNA Profiling Advancement," *FBI Law Enforcement Bulletin* (February 1998), p. 24.

There are a number of applications for geographical information systems in law enforcement, such as displaying geographical patterns of crimes; targeting crime-prevention programs based on geographical information; mapping pursuit routes; deploying police personnel effectively; and efficiently evacuating areas in emergencies.

POLICE/CITIZEN ROLES IN CRIME PREVENTION

In the remaining parts of this chapter we discuss the trends that involve citizens and the police working together to prevent crimes.

Citizen Responsibility in Crime Prevention

The idea that crime prevention is the duty of each citizen is not new. In the early days of law enforcement—well over a thousand years ago—the peacekeeping system encouraged the concept of mutual responsibility. Individuals were responsible not only for their own actions, but also for the actions of their neighbors. Citizens who observed a crime were obligated to rouse their neighbors and pursue the criminal. Thus, for the most part, peace was kept not by officials but by the entire community.[39]

With specialization in law enforcement, citizens began to delegate their personal responsibilities to paid officials. Law enforcement became a multifaceted specialty, as citizens relinquished more and more of their crime-prevention activities. But such specialization has its drawbacks: In the absence of citizen assistance, neither staffing, nor improved technology, nor money can enable law enforcement to shoulder the monumental burden of combating crime in America.

One role that citizens can play within the criminal justice system is a preventive one of reducing the circumstances and situations in which crimes are likely to be committed. In recent years, for example, citizens have banded together in programs such as

WEB

For more information on geographical information systems, visit our Web site, www.prenhall.com/territo.

WEB

For more on police use of crime mapping, visit our Web site, www.prenhall.com/territo.

CTQ

How do you think civic responsibility for crime prevention is viewed in your community today?

WEB

For more information on community crime prevention and police, visit our Web site, www.prenhall.com/territo.

neighborhood watch, through which participants combat crime by marking property to make it more secure, increasing surveillance of public areas, and promoting behavior that increases citizen safety (for example, avoiding walking alone after dark).

Essential to the effectiveness of these crime-prevention measures is enhanced willingness on the part of citizens to call the police about suspicious activity. Even when police take no action other than answering a citizen observation of suspicious behavior, police presence can serve as a warning that citizens and police are vigilant to the possibility of crime and are willing to take additional steps, if necessary.

Neighborhood Watch Programs

The maintenance of an ongoing neighborhood watch program requires leadership of citizens and police officials. The following section describes one method that can be utilized to enhance the effectiveness of a neighborhood watch program.[40]

Frequently implemented under community-oriented policing plans, neighborhood watch programs have received much attention over the past ten years. However, experts rarely discuss the steps that lead to their successes. Many police departments have implemented neighborhood watch programs with much success; however, some have difficulty initiating and sustaining the groups. Unfortunately, this proves particularly true in communities that most need assistance. Middle-class communities, with the least to fear, seem to sustain the effort. On the other hand, low-income communities have a difficult time maintaining community-based groups, even in the presence of severe crime rates.[41]

Indeed, developing programs and maintaining community participation in neighborhood watch programs remain difficult leadership challenges. The average life expectancy of a neighborhood watch group is rather short, and the program itself is problematic. The most successful watches recruit new members a few times a year. Ongoing recruitment nurtures the program by involving new, motivated members. These fresh individuals replace those who feel they no longer need to participate because they either have become disenchanted with the program or feel their concerns have been addressed.

Despite the difficulties associated with establishing a successful community program, experts rarely discuss the steps that lead to success. Although police agencies interested in obtaining specific details on starting a group can do so easily, material on broad leadership issues, such as group dynamics and maintenance techniques, remain undeveloped areas. Such information would help organizers facilitate and maintain these successful supporting programs. In short, communities need information on how to start them.

Without citizen trust and cooperation, police officers work in an information vacuum and lack the criminal intelligence needed to perform their basic duties. Identifying the fundamental causes of crime depends, to a great extent, on citizens who make observations and report illegal activity. Police executives are in a position to reward these efforts and take appropriate steps to encourage continued citizen support and cooperation.

The success of a neighborhood watch program directly relates to the department's commitment to establish a strategic plan, train the participants, and encourage open communication within the community. Starting a neighborhood watch program may prove less difficult than maintaining citizen interest and participation. Leaders first must define the group's mission in order to establish direction. Next, by assessing and articulating community needs, they can sustain the program's direction. Finally, they should redirect the members to new goals and objectives once they complete a specific mission. Indeed, citizens who participate in crime prevention programs must have adequate support and opportunities to help implement positive changes in their communities.

Fear of Crime and Police Response

We know that fear of crime results from many causes besides crime itself. Some kinds of people and people in some kinds of neighborhoods probably fear crime more than they

---

CTQ

Why do you think low-income communities have a more difficult time maintaining community-based prevention programs than middle-class communities?

WEB

For more information on neighborhood watches and community policing, **visit our Web site, www.prenhall.com/territo.**

need to, given their low risk of actually becoming victims. What makes them fearful is seeing things they associate with crime.

The **signs of crime** associated with higher levels of fear are both social and physical. The social signs include prostitutes soliciting for customers, drug dealers conducting visible transactions, rowdy teenagers loitering on corners, derelicts panhandling or lying in the street in a stupor, and mentally ill people shouting at the tops of their lungs at unseen enemies. The physical signs include broken windows, garbage littered on sidewalks, abandoned cars, and broken bottles and glass (as indicated by the "broken windows" concept discussed in Chapter 5).

Both physical and social signs of crime indicate disorder in the neighborhood and convey a sense that things are "out of control." Ultimately, disorder may attract such predatory violent crimes as robbery; a neighborhood that cannot control minor incivilities may advertise itself to potential robbers as a neighborhood that cannot control serious crime either. But long before serious crime develops, the residents of disorderly areas suffer fear. Neighborhood businesses suffer loss of patronage due to that fear. Property values may decline. People who have sufficient resources may move elsewhere. The fear of crime is an important problem in itself.

It is tempting to describe disorder as an inner-city problem that is especially concentrated in minority and poor neighborhoods, and unprotected, low-density residential areas as a middle-class suburban problem, but that would be an oversimplification. Although there are some differences of degree, middle-class suburbs often suffer disorder problems at shopping centers and even on some residential street corners. Poor inner-city neighborhoods in many cities are often quite low in density, with many houses empty during the day. Both problems pose a challenge to almost all kinds of police departments. Many have developed a variety of programs to deal with these problems.

These programs share the goal suggested by some experts of "breaking down the barriers" between the police and the public that are created by the low-density, automobile-based lifestyle. Other programs address problems of disorder and the causes of fear of crime. To the extent that these programs are successful, the better quality of life may leave people better off than they were before, even if crime is not reduced. If police can help foster a sense of community in an anonymous, automized residential neighborhood, there are good reasons to believe the neighborhood will be a better place to live.[42]

Several general types of programs have been initiated by police to reduce the fear of crime and the amount of crime itself. These include program efforts such as community-organized neighborhood watch programs, establishing police storefront operations in communities, and reinstating neighborhood foot patrol. Some police agencies have used community newsletters to demonstrate their concern and to attempt to reduce citizen fear to the extent possible. These newsletters serve a variety of purposes for police departments and frequently provide citizens with examples of citizen-oriented crime-prevention programs that are available (see Figure 6.9).

> **CTQ**
>
> What signs of crime can you identify in your community? Do any of these contribute significantly to your fear of crime? Why or why not?

Evaluating Crime-Prevention Programs

Historically, very few crime-prevention programs have been rigorously evaluated in a scientific fashion. Recently, the National Institute of Justice conducted a systematic review of numerous state and local crime-prevention programs funded by the U.S. Department of Justice. A snapshot of some of the key findings of this review are as follows:[43]

- Neighborhood watch programs organized by police are often ineffective in reducing crime. The primary problem found by the evaluations is that the areas with the highest crime rates are often most reluctant to organize.[44]
- Community meetings between the police and public do not prevent crime.[45] However, in his research on Community Policing in Chicago, Skogan did find more promise with meetings in Chicago that were more specifically focused on crime problems in the area.[46]

FIGURE 6.9

A Police Department Community Newsletter

CRIME PREVENTION SERVICES/EDUCATION PROGRAMS

The University of South Florida offers a number of programs intended to reduce the potential for personal injury and loss of property. Presentations on Safety are included in the orientation of incoming students and residence hall students, and are held frequently during fall and spring semesters for the benefit of students, faculty and staff.

Crime Prevention Programs

The University Police Department encourages all students and members of the faculty and staff to be involved in campus crime prevention. Information on safety and security concerns and precautions are provided to students, faculty, and staff members regularly through seminars, films, bulletins, crime alerts, posters, brochures and university staff and student newspapers. In an on-going effort to facilitate this process, University Police officers provide crime prevention programs each semester on the following topics:

- Date/Acquaintance Rape Programs for both Men and Women
- Rape Aggression Defense (RAD) [Self-Defense for Women]
- Personal Safety—Reducing Your Risks
- Drinking and Driving—DUI Information
- Drugs—Health Risks, Liabilities
- Burglary and Theft Prevention
- Operation ID—Engraving
- USF Police Department—Who We Are and What We Do
- Bike Engraving and Theft Prevention
- Cash Handling and Robbery Precautions
- Child Safety Programs
- Violence in the Workplace
- Alcohol Programs

Additional programs are provided by the University to include:

- The Campus Alcohol and Drug Resource Center sponsors National Collegiate Alcohol Awareness Week in the fall and National Collegiate Drug Awareness in the spring.
- Mandatory Orientation programming for all new students includes a session on Campus Safety and another on Wellness issues. Through these programs, student awareness is increased about health and safety issues for their personal life.
- The Health Education Department offers a variety of outreach programming which includes:
  - Introduction to Women's Health
  - Sexually Transmitted Diseases
  - Substance Abuse Awareness
  - Sexuality
  - AIDS Education.

USF's Drug-Free Schools and Community Program

The University of South Florida is committed to providing an orderly and safe environment for all students, faculty and employees. To this end, the University advises all community members that it is unlawful to manufacture, distribute, dispense, possess and/or use illegal drugs on its premises. Any violation may be cause for disciplinary action and criminal prosecution. (Please refer to: **USF, A Drug-Free Workplace and University of South Florida Student Handbook.**)

The use of alcohol beverages by members of the University Community is at all times subject to the alcoholic beverage laws of the State of Florida and USF Alcohol Policy and Guidelines. Specifically, it is unlawful for any person to sell, give, serve or permit to be served alcoholic beverages to a person under 21 years of age or to consume said beverages on licensed premises. It is also unlawful for a person to misrepresent or misstate his or her age or the age of any other person for the purpose of inducing any licensee or his agents or employees to sell, give, serve or deliver any alcoholic beverage to a person under 21 years of age. A violation of the proceeding may be cause for disciplinary action and criminal prosecution.

Drug and Alcohol Counseling

Programs are available to assist students and employees who may be in need of drug or alcohol counseling and treatment or rehabilitation programs. The Counseling Center receives referrals from Housing, the Student Health Services, Campus Alcohol and Drug Resource Center, DUI Counter Attack School, Student Affairs administration, University Police and self-referrals from individuals for alcohol and drug related problems.

The Counseling Center provides psychological assessment and screening, short-term treatment of appropriate cases or referral to other treatment resources as needed. An Employee Assistance Program (EAP) is available in the Counseling Center for faculty or staff who may be experiencing drug or alcohol related difficulties. Supervisors may refer staff members or individuals may independently contact EAP.

Weapons

Florida State Statute 790.06(12) forbids any person from carrying a firearm on a university campus. Firearms are not allowed in USF housing facilities. To assist persons who may desire to have access to firearms for recreational purposes,

Source: Courtesy of Chief Pat Johnson, University of South Florida Police Department, Tampa, Florida.

- Police storefront operations had no impact on crime but did result in more positive citizen evaluations of police.
- The use of police newsletters sent to the public with information regarding crime and prevention issues had no effect on the victimization rates of households receiving them in Newark and Houston.

While current evaluations of many police/community crime-prevention programs suggest that they have little effect on crime reduction, many of these efforts will continue given their relative popularity. The results of these evaluations indicate that efforts to mobilize citizens in community crime prevention needs to be redirected in ways that are more specific in nature and thus more effective.

CRIME PREVENTION THROUGH ENVIRONMENTAL DESIGN

Environmental approaches to crime prevention and security were made popular by Oscar Newman in his book *Defensible Space*. These concepts have been successfully demonstrated in schools and commercial, residential, and transportation areas. They are now being widely adopted by industry because they contribute to productivity. City governments are finding out that it is a lot cheaper to design crime prevention into the way things are done than to hire extra police or to pay for extra protection that really only makes the community like a fortress—instead of a nice place to live.[47]

The conceptual thrust of **Crime Prevention Through Environmental Design (CPTED)** is that proper design and effective use of the physical environment can produce behavioral effects that will reduce the incidence and fear of crime, thereby improving the quality of life. These behavioral effects can be accomplished by reducing the propensity of the physical environment to support criminal behavior.

Environmental design, as used in the CPTED program, is rooted in the design of the person/environment relationship. It embodies several concepts. The term *environment* includes people and their physical and social surroundings. As an example, a design strategy of improved street lighting must be planned and evaluated in terms of the behavior it promotes or deters and the impact of the lighted (and related) areas in terms of all users of the area (offenders, victims, other permanent or casual users). Likewise, any strategies related to the lighting strategy (such as block-watch, 911 emergency service, and police patrol) must be evaluated in the same regard. This reflects the comprehensiveness of the CPTED design approach in focusing on both the proper design and effective use of the physical environment. Additionally, the concept of proper design and effective use emphasizes the desired relationship among strategies to ensure that the desired results are achieved. Improved street lighting alone (a design strategy) is ineffective against crime without the conscious and active support of citizens (in reporting what they see) and of police (in responding and conducting surveillance). Therefore, CPTED involves the effort to effectively integrate design, citizen and community action, and law enforcement strategies to accomplish surveillance consistent with the design and use of the environment.

CTQ

Do you agree with the statement that proper design and effective use of the physical environment can produce behavioral effects that will reduce the incidence and fear of crime? Why or why not?

Applications of CPTED

In some states, principles of the CPTED concept have been applied in a real-world setting. The following represents a review of how CPTED has been put into action in at least one state.[48]

Law enforcement departments and other criminal justice agencies continually work to stem the tide of crime and its impact on victims. Enforcement and prosecution are important, but these efforts must be complemented by a strong prevention component. Communities need training, education, technical assistance, and other programs designed to reduce or eliminate criminal opportunity. In the past, crime prevention often meant little more than hardening the intended target by adding locks, bars, and alarms. The spread of crime, however, has inspired us to seek out more nontraditional approaches to prevention that involve citizens from across the spectrum of our communities.

Florida has been instrumental in developing crime prevention programs and activities. Chief among these are the Convenience Business Security Act and the Safe Neighborhoods Program.

Convenience Stores A study by the Virginia Department of Criminal Justice Services reports that convenience store clerks are employed in the riskiest jobs in the country. In Florida, when the number of convenience store robberies continued to rise, the Gainesville Police Department decided it was time to take a long, hard look at the problem. Its analysis revealed that the number and location of store clerks, lighting levels, cash handling procedures, and other factors significantly affected the rate at which convenience stores were robbed.

Gainesville responded by adopting a series of ordinances that required strong new security steps, including the addition of a second clerk during overnight hours. The result was a dramatic 65 percent reduction in convenience store robberies. Gainesville's success and continuing proliferation of convenience store crimes prompted state officials to enact legislation that requires convenience store owners and operators to take action to prevent crime. A study conducted by the National Association of Convenience Stores has also suggested that adding a second clerk may reduce robberies in already-robbed convenience stores.[49] Following these studies the Florida legislature passed the Convenience Business Security Act, which requires every convenience business to provide employee training, adequate lighting, cash management procedures, unobstructed views, security cameras, or other security measures that will result in a safer environment.

Safe Neighborhoods The Safe Neighborhoods Program, created by the Florida legislature, is designed to reduce opportunities for crime by coordinating planning and crime-prevention activities. The legislation provided planning grants to local communities willing to adopt Safe Neighborhoods Improvement Plans based on crime prevention through environmental design, or CPTED.

Florida's Safe Neighborhoods Program was the first of its kind in the nation. A number of communities formally participated by establishing neighborhood improvement districts by local ordinance and then applying for grants and preparing the required plans. The office of the state attorney general, which administers the program, is now working with these communities as they implement their goals and objectives.

Other communities have recognized the value of the CPTED concept and have sought alternative ways to apply it. Sarasota, for example, used the state's growth-management requirements to achieve similar results. Sarasota recognized that CPTED depends on communities establishing logical and orderly patterns of development, promoting and maintaining stable neighborhoods, and providing adequate public facilities and services. As a result, Sarasota made CPTED a part of its ongoing planning and development processes. Now, planners and designers concerned with the preservation of public health, safety, and general welfare in Sarasota consider how their decisions and actions may create or deter opportunities for crime.

WEB

For more information on safe neighborhoods, **visit our Web site,** www.prenhall.com/territo.

Combining CPTED and Community-Policing Strategies

Crime prevention today benefits from two strategies for protecting neighborhoods from crime and the fear of crime—CPTED and community policing. CPTED programs, through design and management of the physical environment of buildings, residential neighborhoods, and business areas, increase public safety and reduce fear of crime. Community-policing programs, by making police more visible and familiar to the people and with the physical environment of their beats, reinforce these efforts and promote police-citizen partnerships to prevent crime and disorder.[50]

What Police and Residents Can Do

Thus, police agencies, community residents, and local officials all have roles to play in implementing a comprehensive CPTED/community-policing strategy to promote public safety in private neighborhoods, business areas, and public housing.[51] The police can engage in a number of activities that support CPTED and community policing. For example, they can conduct security surveys for residents and inform them of high-risk areas in their neighborhoods. Police can also work closely with urban planners and traffic engineers to review building plans and traffic flow from a security viewpoint. Redesigning traffic flow patterns to help reduce crime has been the subject of evaluations that support these techniques, with results that include reductions in burglary, homicides in Los Angeles, and violent crime in Dayton.[52]

Residents can also play an active role in securing their neighborhoods. For example, they may engage in cleanup programs to remove trash and graffiti, which are physical signs of an apathetic community. Residents may also play an active role by joining neighborhood watch programs or conducting their own patrols to identify neighborhood problems relating to security.

Specific Crime-Prevention Activities

The following activities can be coordinated with local government and citizens to reduce crime in and around facilities.

Security in Parks Parks can be refurbished, lighting can be installed, and opening and closing times can be scheduled to improve security. Adopt-a-park programs can be used to involve residents in cleaning up trash and litter and providing information to police about illegal activities. Recreational events can be scheduled to increase the community's informal social control of these places.

Building Regulations Local governments can be encouraged to use building codes as well as inspection and enforcement powers to increase environmental security. The owners of deteriorated or abandoned buildings can be required to repair, secure, or demolish them. Provisions related to security can also be incorporated into the city building code. These provisions include target-hardening tactics (such as locks, strong doors, and lighting) as well as security standards for the design of the structure and site.

Civil Remedies Civil actions can be used against building owners or tenants to control criminal activity or inappropriate use of property. These actions may include the following: obtaining title to abandoned property by community-improvement associations; using nuisance abatement along with inspections by public works, building, fire, housing, or utility authorities to control criminal behavior or drug use in specific buildings or settings; enforcing liquor laws to control violence and disorderly behavior around bars or liquor stores (especially at closing times); and using antitrespassing laws to control unwanted loitering.

CITIZEN INVOLVEMENT IN CRIME PREVENTION

Citizen-oriented crime-prevention programs continue to provide an effective means to involve a cross-section of society in self-protection. Given the budget constraints faced by many local governments there is neither the human nor fiscal resources to provide the level of community safety desirable. The following sections highlight several citizen-based innovations.

The McGruff Campaign

The **McGruff campaign** ("Take a Bite Out of Crime") was initiated as a collaborative effort on the part of groups such as the Crime Prevention Council and the U.S. Department of Justice. The program encouraged citizens to join in making their communities safer places to live. The campaign uses a "spokesdog" to give helpful crime-prevention tips through a variety of techniques—television ads, posters, newsletters, and brochures. The McGruff figure is easily recognized by children and adults and is strongly identified with the crime-prevention movement.

The CAT Program

A crime-prevention program that involves police and citizen initiative is focused on the problem of car theft, described in an earlier chapter as a crime that plagues many of our towns and cities. The program, initiated in New York, is called **Combat Auto Theft (CAT).** Citizens voluntarily sign a form given to them by the police stating that they do not normally drive between 1 A.M. and 5 A.M. In many jurisdictions, these times are considered peak hours for auto theft.

The car owners are then provided a tamper-resistant CAT decal that is attached prominently to their rear car window. If an officer sees a car bearing the CAT decal driving on the roadway between 1 A.M. and 5 A.M., the police are allowed to make a stop based upon the form originally signed by the lawful car owner. The CAT program is one innovative way to protect autos from being stolen. At present, many other cities are experimenting with the CAT program.

The Watch Your Car Program

A similar program is the Watch Your Car Program. The Motor Vehicle Theft Prevention Act (MVTPA) authorizes the U.S. Attorney General to develop—through the Bureau of Justice Assistance (BJA) in cooperation with the states—a national voluntary motor vehicle theft-prevention program. The national Watch Your Car Program allows owners of motor vehicles to voluntarily display a decal or device, such as a state-issued, customized license plate, on their vehicles to alert police that their vehicles are not normally driven between the hours of 1 A.M. and 5 A.M. Motorists may also choose to display another decal or device to signify that their vehicles are not normally driven in the proximity of international land borders or ports.[53]

The main advantage of the national Watch Your Car Program is that it uses a decal that will eventually become an instantly recognizable icon by police everywhere. It provides for intrastate and interstate enforcement through the checking of vehicles with differing county and/or state license plates. Thus, if a thief steals a vehicle, drives to another city or state, and attempts to operate that vehicle between 1 A.M. and 5 A.M., police in that jurisdiction are authorized to stop the vehicle and check the identity of the driver.

Campus Crime Prevention

College campus communities have been very active over the last decade in developing and implementing **campus crime-prevention programs.** The campus environment is generally vulnerable to both property and personal crimes. Today, proactive crime-prevention programs are found on campuses both large and small. Usually, they involve campus law enforcement officials, students, and college staff members in a variety of efforts such as educational workshops, lighting surveys, operation identification, dorm watch programs, and personal escorts. These programs stress public education and a high degree of campus community participation. Publicity campaigns, including posters and brochures, are often used effectively. "In the News: Gotcha! Campus Crime-Prevention Program Earns High Marks" illustrates a successful college crime prevention program in operation.

CTQ

If you were a campus law enforcement official or administrator, what educational programs would you implement in your college or university to stress community participation in the prevention of campus crime?

Community Anti-Drug Efforts

In response to the illicit drug trade that became especially troublesome in many cities, a remarkable community anti-drug movement has formed, with groups becoming active in some of the most afflicted neighborhoods. Armed only with their courage and imagination, citizens have devised a variety of clever strategies and tactics to reclaim their streets and parks from drug traffickers.

A review of thirteen case studies of grassroots community responses to illegal drugs in their neighborhoods provides some useful information for police and their communities.[54] For example, effective community anti-drug efforts show wide variations in institutional robustness and in the breadth of approach to drug problems. In general, the researchers recommend that citizens be encouraged and helped to address drug problems from a perspective broader than that of drugs alone. In addition, community efforts that provide a comprehensive approach to drugs and crime are more likely to be sus-

IN THE NEWS

A HUMAN PERSPECTIVE

GOTCHA! CAMPUS CRIME-PREVENTION PROGRAM EARNS HIGH MARKS
by T. Utz

College students generally have more on their minds than security and crime prevention. They may leave their valuables unattended or allow strangers access to restricted areas. And, when they do ... Gotcha!

The Towson State University Police Department has worked to decrease crime on campus and to improve the crime prevention awareness and attitudes of the students and faculty with a program called "Gotcha." Under this program, uniformed officers of both the patrol division and the K-9 section search the campus for security or safety violations, such as open or unlocked doors or valuables left unattended. Once found, the officers leave key-shaped "Gotcha" cards at the scene of the infraction.

The cards say: "If this had been an actual 'Rip Off,' you would have been a statistic. Don't give a thief an opportunity to rip you off. Lock it up!" The cards also have spaces for officers to identify the applicable security/safety violation, such as "your door unlocked," "your valuables left in plain view," or "equipment not secured." A blank space allows officers to make additional comments.

Plainclothes officers direct another aspect of the Gotcha Program. They test the university community's security awareness by attempting to get students and faculty to give them access to restricted or secure areas, which have "no trespassing" warnings clearly posted at all entrances. If admitted, the officers identify themselves and discuss how the individual should handle the situation differently in the future. They also explain the importance of security and crime prevention, as well as the campus community's role in each.

Increasing student awareness of the program's goals remains a top priority of the department, because each school year brings a new class of students to the campus. This requires officers to conduct crime prevention and security awareness seminars throughout each school year.

RESULTS
The Gotcha Program has successfully decreased crime on campus. Students and faculty are more security conscious, and their increased interaction with the police has made them more willing to provide information on crimes that do occur. This cooperative effort between the police and the community led to the department's recovery of almost $50,000 in stolen property in one calendar year. In addition, the department's crime prevention section, which sponsors the program, has been honored with the Governor's Annual Crime Prevention Award.

CONCLUSION
The Gotcha Program reflects the Towson State University Police Department's commitment to protect and serve the campus community. It has become a critical tool in the fight against crime on campus. Furthermore, it reminds students and faculty that they are the "key" to successful crime prevention. The "Gotcha" test may be the most important exam students take all year.

Source: T. E. Utz, "Gotcha! Campus Crime Prevention Program Earns High Marks," *FBI Law Enforcement Bulletin*, vol. 12 (1996), p. 17.

---

tained. In addition, these case studies revealed that policymakers should consider carefully the broad scope of help they can provide citizens, which ranges from financial help to granting access to decision makers to providing a meeting room to offering technical assistance on organizing and implementing program activities.

The case studies also suggest that the police play a particularly pivotal role in citizens' assault on drugs. Many citizens initially regard the drug problem as one of obtaining adequate police protection but, in general, partnerships involving citizens, police, and other agencies provide useful strategies to combat drugs. To forge productive relationships between police and citizens, police executives should actively support local patrol officers in working with citizen groups. Police officers should be encouraged to respond to all interested citizens, even those who initially may be rancorous and complain, since these individuals often evolve into hardworking partners with the police.

Since no single community response to drugs can be considered the best, research should continue to identify approaches that work best under specific conditions and in various neighborhood settings. "In the News: Quality of Relationship with the Police" story describes the importance of maintaining a high quality of relationship between police and citizens in anti-drug efforts.

Police are developing many new partnerships in an effort to reduce specific crimes in their communities. "In the News: Realtor-Police Partnership for Safety" describes how the police and real estate agents have formed a partnership to prevent crime in one community.

CTQ
What role can the police play in assisting residents with community anti-drug efforts?

IN THE NEWS

A HUMAN PERSPECTIVE

QUALITY OF RELATIONSHIP WITH THE POLICE
by S. Weingart, F. Hartman, and D. Osborne

The case studies present ample evidence that the police response to citizens' efforts profoundly affects the character and success of the venture. The quality of the relationship between police and citizens is a decisive factor in determining the course and character of the community response to drugs.

EARLY CONFRONTATIONS
With few exceptions, citizen drug fighters complained bitterly about the amount and quality of the police services that they received early on. Drug dealers swamped the neighborhood, many seemed to say, because the police were ineffective in keeping them out. These sentiments led to confrontational meetings between citizens and police in Philadelphia, Denver, Boston, Kansas City, and Washington. For example, in Kansas City, the mayor and a member of the city council called a meeting between the police and black leaders in the wake of the murders of a number of young black women. The meeting, planned as a session for 100 representatives of the black community, became a contentious public forum where angry residents confronted police and city officials.

Unfortunately for the police, demands for better service are one of the earliest and most consistent responses in the citizens' repertoire. The police, if they are to meet the needs of the communities they are charged to serve and protect, must have the professionalism that enables them to see community anger as an opportunity to address problems of drugs and crime. They may find it counterproductive to interpret such anger as a rejection of the role of the police or to take as a personal affront. Anger is rather a reaching out on the part of the community and responsible police departments will see past the heat of confrontation to seize the moment.

BUILDING A RELATIONSHIP
One of the critical features in the development of a productive relationship between police and community is the establishment of contact with a senior police official who is willing to take the citizens' group seriously and to work with it. A single receptive police official can have a profound effect on the development of a community response to drugs. Yet, no department had a formal protocol for dealing with citizen anti-drug groups, or a policing philosophy that encouraged officers to be responsible for promoting and nurturing citizen efforts. The officers developed the relationships not because of their department's philosophy and organization, but despite it.

HAZARDS OF CONVENTIONAL POLICING
Aggressive law enforcement remains a crucial prerequisite to citizen action in many of the most disorganized neighborhoods, but this approach, which involves traditional law enforcement, is often insufficient. The Boston case is a compelling example of what can happen when police employ traditional strategies in their interactions with citizen drug fighters without using community resources to maximum effect.

In Boston's Hill Street neighborhood then Police Commissioner Roache responded to citizen complaints with the traditional response of establishing a three-person special task force to break the back of the drug trade. Here, the priorities of the police drove citizens' behavior: The residents learned how to provide detailed, reliable, and rapidly executed reports to police officers, often dialing into a telephone beeper carried by the patrol sergeant. These measures helped the police dramatically increase the number of arrests. Although the police response was a genuine effort to assist, they retained total control over the planning and execution of the enhanced enforcement effort.

Police officials rated the Hill Street neighborhood as a high priority because of the severity of the problem (drug trafficking, gangs, and violence). They focused less on the nature of the solution (competent partners at the grass roots). In other words, police involvement in Boston derived from an overall law enforcement strategy for the city and the need to respond to problem areas, but to do so in the traditional way. The police response included but was not based on close relations with the residents, shared aspirations for a neighborhood, and personal commitments. (By contrast, the Houston police were heavily involved in the Link Valley anti-drug effort and did not use arrests as a major means to solve problems.) Thus, when the police special task force was transferred from the Boston neighborhood, the community's relationship with the police reverted to the status quo ante, as citizens' former misgivings about the commitment of the police and their trustworthiness reemerged.

The residents might well have asked: How could everyone do the right thing with so little to show for it? The answer may have something to do with the "enforcement-resistant" character of the drug market on Hill Street. But it also implicates the police strategy, which could have more fully exploited the creative solutions that the citizens have the potential to deliver. The Boston cases illustrate the need for law enforcement to leverage, not replace, citizen initiative. When the police use conventional responses, they often assign citizens to narrow and limited roles and thus reduce the likelihood that those citizens will invent novel tactics or participate in innovative partnerships.

Source: S. N. Weingart, F. X. Hartman, and D. Osborne, *Case Studies of Community Anti-Drug Efforts.* Washington, D. C.: U.S. Department of Justice, National Institute of Justice, 1994, pp. 1–15.

IN THE NEWS

A HUMAN PERSPECTIVE

RELATOR-POLICE PARTNERSHIP FOR SAFETY
by Karl Leonard

Recent newspaper stories depict only a few of the increasing numbers of crimes committed against real estate agents nationwide. Real estate agents have daily, one-on-one contact with various individuals—virtual strangers—and put themselves at risk every day. They advertise their availability by displaying a trail of signs, usually adorned with balloons indicating an open house, and remain relatively easy targets to criminals. Personal safety and security remain important issues.

By forming a partnership with local realtors, police departments can help real estate agents identify and possibly prevent crimes against them. To prevent the nationwide trend of violent acts against real estate agents from becoming a local reality, the Chesterfield County, Virginia, Police Department began a joint training venture with area realtors as an extension of their community policing program.

SAFETY ISSUES
In training sessions offered every six months, officers from Chesterfield County's community policing and crime prevention divisions provide valuable safety tips that help realtors thwart possible harmful situations. Police officers instruct realtors how to take precautions when meeting prospective clients and how to protect themselves if an incident occurs. Among the information provided, officers advise realtors to conduct the first meeting with clients at the realty office. This provides the realtor an opportunity to become somewhat acquainted with clients, rather than merely judging them by their outward appearance. Officers also instruct real estate agents to identify clients before a house showing by acquiring an address and telephone number, if possible, and to leave this information with another individual. Officers advise realtors to show homes in pairs when possible, especially at night, and inform another person of their destination and who will accompany them, all while within earshot of the client. These precautions advise prospective customers that other individuals know their names and the realtor's location at all times and that assistance remains available to realtors in emergency situations.

REALTORS HELPING POLICE
In addition to preventing crime by educating realtors, this program also represents a partnership intended to benefit law enforcement officers. Realtors work 7 days a week, all hours of the day, and travel through many subdivisions and housing areas that law enforcement officers may not always get a chance to patrol. Real estate agents can act as extra eyes for the police. Many realtors travel with a cellular telephone and can contact law enforcement officers when observing any unusual activities in their areas. This further assists the police in their efforts in crime prevention as well as in the apprehension of violators.

As in the case in Chesterfield County, Virginia, most states have governing boards that mandate realtor training annually. If approved, this training rewards the realtors as well as satisfies part of their annual training requirements. Almost all populated areas have a local realtor association with which to work. These associations usually have education and public affairs departments that can provide assistance.

Source: K. Leonard, "Realtor-Police Partnership for Safety," *FBI Law Enforcement Bulletin*, vol. 66 (1997), p. 23.

SUMMARY

This chapter has focused on issues deserving of special attention in the last decade: professionalization of the police; police misconduct; affirmative action and equal opportunities in law enforcement; police officer stress and suicide; police use of deadly force and less-than-deadly force; police contact with the public; the emergence of private security in the United States and its interactive role with public law enforcement; and, finally, technological trends designed to assist police agencies now and in the future.

In addition, in this chapter we discussed the history and evolution of crime prevention. Our focus was on the role played by citizens and police as well as some of the innovative programs now being used to prevent crime in our communities. Evaluations of crime-prevention programs and community anti-drug efforts were also included in this chapter.

DISCUSSION AND REVIEW

1. What is the principal motivation for police administrators and officers wanting to achieve the status of professionals?

2. What are the major benefits of attaining accreditation?
3. Why has the widespread availability of illicit drugs increased police corruption?
4. Describe the relationship between higher education and law enforcement today.
5. What arguments are traditionally offered for increasing minority recruitment in the police force?
6. Discuss the results of the Bloch and Anderson study on female officers' effectiveness in patrol.
7. What are the four categories of stress in law enforcement?
8. What benefits do Denver police derive from their alcohol abuse program?
9. What can be done to help police officers reduce stress or learn to cope with it?
10. What are five examples of shooting-control techniques that can be used by police departments to control the use of force by officers?
11. What findings did the St. Paul (Minnesota) Police Department report regarding the use of force by police?
12. What common goals do police and prosecutors share?
13. What was the significance of the U.S. Supreme Court's decision in *Tennessee v. Garner*?
14. Why are police departments considered information-intensive organizations that seemingly will be able to benefit from the use of laptop computers?
15. How does the use of DNA profiling to identify or eliminate potential suspects improve on the traditional method of fingerprint identification?
16. What role did citizens play in crime prevention before the specialization of law enforcement?
17. How can environmental design affect the incidence of crime?
18. What are some of the "signs of crime" associated with higher levels of citizen fear?
19. What are three general types of programs initiated by police that have been initiated to reduce the fear of crime and crime itself?

Chapter Resources

In the Media

Video

CNN Today Video: *Introduction to Criminal Justice,* Vol. 1: segment 4, "Parting the Blue Curtain"
CNN Today Video: *Introduction to Criminal Justice,* Vol. 2: segment 7, "Culture and Violence"
CNN Today Video: *Introduction to Criminal Justice,* Vol. 3: segment 4, "Officer Stopped Verdict"
FHH Custom CJ Video: segment 4, "Suicide and the Police Officer"
FHH Video: *The Tarnished Shield: When Cops Go Bad*
NIJ Crime File Video: *Deadly Force*

Film

Angel Eyes (2001)
The Fugitive (1993)
Training Day (2001)

Television

The District
Law and Order
NYPD Blue

IN THE LITERATURE

Books

H. GOLDSTEIN, *Police Corruption: A Perspective on Its Nature and Control.* Washington, D.C.: Police Foundation, 1975.

J. GREENE AND S. MASTROFSKY, eds., *Community Policing: Rhetoric or Reality?* New York: Praeger, 1988.

Human Rights Watch, *Shielded from Justice: Police Brutality and Accountability in the United States.* Washington, D.C.: Human Rights Watch, 1998.

A. REISS, *Police and the Public.* New Haven, Conn.: Yale University Press, 1971.

C. SHEARING AND P. STENNING, eds., *Private Policing.* Newbury Park, Calif.: Sage, 1987.

J. SKOLNICH AND J. FYFE, *Above the Law: Police and the Excessive Use of Force.* New York: Free Press, 1993.

S. SMITH, G. STEADMAN, T. MINTON, AND M. TOWNSEND, *Criminal Victimization and Perceptions of Community Safety in 12 Cities.* Washington, D.C.: Bureau of Justice Statistics, 1999.

Articles

L. GELHAUS, "Civil Suits against Police Change Domestic Violence Response," *Trial*, vol. 35 (September 1999), p. 103.

D. GRISWOLD, "Complaints against the Police: Predicting Dispositions," *Journal of Criminal Justice*, vol. 22 (1994): 215–224.

W. KING AND B. SANDERS, "Nice Guys Finish Last: A Critical Review of Police Officers Killed in the Line of Duty," *Policing*, vol. 20 (1997), pp. 392–408.

J. MCCORMICK, "On a High-Tech Firing Line: Simulators That Shoot Back are Helping Cops Learn How to Use Deadly Force," *Newsweek*, December 6, 1999.

C. MILLER, "In the Line of Fire: Learning from Assaults on Law Enforcement Officers," *FBI Law Enforcement Bulletin*, vol. 67 (1998), pp. 15–24.

M. VAUGHN, "Police Civil Liability for Abandonment in High-Crime Areas and Other High-Risk Situations," *Journal of Criminal Justice*, vol. 22 (1994), pp. 407–424.

M. VAUGHN, "Police Sexual Violence: Civil Liability under State Tort Law," *Crime and Delinquency*, vol. 45 (1999), pp. 334–357.

CASE

Tennessee v. Garner, 105 S.Ct. 1694 (1985)

ENDNOTES

1. "Accreditation Program for Law Enforcement Agencies" and "Accreditation Program Overview," two brochures published by the Commission on Accreditation for Law Enforcement Agencies, Inc.

2. D. Carter, A. Sapp, and D. Stephens, "Higher Education as a Bona Fide Occupational Qualification (BFOQ) for Police: A Blueprint," *American Journal of Police*, vol. 7, no. 2 (1988), pp. 16–18.

3. *Building and Reducing Drug Corruption in Police Departments.* Washington, D.C.: U.S. Department of Justice, Bureau of Justice Assistance, 1989, pp. 1–10.

4. E. J. Delattre, *Against Brutality and Corruption: Integrity, Wisdom, and Professionalism.* Tallahassee, Fla.: Florida Department of Law Enforcement, 1991.

5. B. Reaves, *Local Police Departments, 1993.* Washington, D.C.: Bureau of Justice Statistics, U.S. Department of Justice, 1996.

6. The information in this section is based on D. L. Carter and A. D. Sapp, *Police Education and Minority Recruitment: The Impact of a College Requirement.* Washington, D.C.: Police Executive Research Forum, 1991.

7. P. B., Bloch, and D. Anderson, *Policewomen on Patrol: Final Report.* Washington, D.C.: Police Foundation, 1974.

8. For a more complete discussion of these current findings, see M. Cuadrado, "Female Police Officers: Gender Bias and Professionalism," *American Journal of Police*, vol. 24 (1995), pp. 149–165; K. M. Lersch, "Exploring Gender Differences in Citizen Allegations of Misconduct: An Analysis of a Municipal Police Department," *Women and Criminal Justice*, vol. 9 (1998), pp. 69–79. Much of this discussion was adapted from M. Healy, "Female Police Officers: A Contemporary Examination of Attitudes of Acceptance." Master's thesis, University of South Florida, Tampa, Fla., 2002.

9. S. E. Martin, *Women on the Move: A Report on the Status of Women in Policing.* Washington, D.C.: Police Foundation, 1989, pp. 1–8.

10. International Association of Chiefs of Police. "The Future of Women in Policing: Mandates for Action," *Police Chief*, vol. 66, no. 3 (1999), pp. 53–56.

11. J. Skolnick, *Justice without Trial: Law Enforcement in a Democratic Society.* New York: Wiley, 1966.

12. K. Slobogin, "Stress," *New York Times Magazine*, November 20, 1977, pp. 48–55.

13. For more discussion on police stress research, see W. H. Kroes, *Society's Victim—the Policeman.* Springfield, Ill: Charles C. Thomas, 1976; W. H. Kroes, B. I. Margolis, and J. J. Hurrell, "Job Stress in Policemen," *Journal of Police Science and Administration*, vol. 2 (1974), pp. 145–156; T. Eisenberg. "Labor-Management Relations and Psychological Stress," *Police*

Chief, vol. 42 (1975), pp. 54–58; M. Reiser, "A Psychologist's View of the Badge," *Police Chief*, vol. 37 (1970): pp. 24–27; M. Reiser, "Some Organizational Stress of Policemen," *Journal of Police Science and Administration*, vol. 2 (1974), pp. 156–165; M. Reiser, "Stress, Distress, and Adaptation of Police Work," *Police Chief*, vol. 43 (1976), pp. 24–27; M. D. Roberts, "Job Stress in Law Enforcement: A Treatment and Prevention Program." In W. H. Kroes and J. J. Hurrell, eds., *Job Stress and the Police Officer: Identifying Stress Reduction Techniques*. Washington, D.C.: U.S. Department of Health, Education, and Welfare, 1975.

14. J. D. Sewell, "The Development of a Critical Life Events Scale for Law Enforcement," *Journal of Police Science and Administration*, vol. 11 (1983), pp. 109–116.

15. J. Wexler and D. Logan, "Sources of Stress among Women Police Officers," *Journal of Police Science and Administration*, vol. 11 (1983), pp. 46–53.

16. N. Norvell, H. Hills, and M. Murrin, "Understanding Female and Male Law Enforcement Officers," *Psychology of Women Quarterly*, vol. 17 (1993), pp. 289–301.

17. J. Daum and C. Johns, "Police Work from a Woman's Perspective," *Police Chief*, vol. 19 (1994), pp. 339–348.

18. M. Bowman, "Female-Specific Police Stress: A Study of the Stressors Experienced by Female Police Officers." Master's thesis, Department of Criminology, University of South Florida, Tampa, Fl. 1999.

19. L. Dishlacoff, "The Drinking Cup." *Police Chief*, vol. 43 (1976), p. 32.

20. J. Hurrell and W. Kroes, "Stress Awareness." In W. Kroes and J. Hurrell, eds., *Job Stress and the Police Officer: Identifying Stress Reduction Techniques*. Washington, D.C.: U.S. Department of Health, Education, and Welfare, 1971, pp. 234–246.

21. J. T. McEwen, B. Manili, and E. Connors, *Employee Drug Testing Policies in Police Departments*. Washington, D.C.: U.S. Department of Justice, 1986, pp. 1–5. (The discussion of police department drug test policies was adapted from this source.)

22. Z. Nelson and W. Smith, "The Law Enforcement Profession: An Incidence of Suicide," *Omega*, vol. 1 (1970), pp. 293–299.

23. For more discussion, see M. F. Heiman, "The Police Suicide," *Journal of Police Science and Administration*, vol. 3 (1975), pp. 267–273; M. Wagner and R. Brzeczek, "Alcoholism and Suicide," *FBI Law Enforcement Bulletin*, vol. 52 (1983), pp. 8–17; G. James, "Police Detective Commits Suicide," *The New York Times*, November 15, 1993, p. B15.

24. J. Dash and M. Reiser. "Suicide among Police in Urban Law Enforcement Agencies," *Journal of Police Science and Administration*, vol. (1978), pp. 18–21.

25. S. Stack and T. Kelley, "Police Suicide: An Analysis," *American Journal of Police*, vol. 13, no. 4 (1994), pp. 73–90.

26. Bureau of Justice Statistics, *Contacts between Police and the Public*. Washington, D.C.: U.S. Department of Justice, 2001, pp. 1–4.

27. K. Milton, J. W. Halleck, J. Lardner, and G. L. Abrecht, *Police Use of Deadly Force*. Washington, D.C.: Police Foundation, 1977, p. 39.

28. R. Lundstrom and C. Mullan, "The Use of Force: One Department's Experience," *FBI Law Enforcement Bulletin* (January 1987), pp. 6–9. (The discussion of the St. Paul [Minnesota] Police Department research on officers' use of force in situations was adapted from this source.)

29. The discussion of shooting-control techniques was adapted from W. Geller, *Deadly Force*. Washington, D.C.: U.S. Department of Justice, National Institute of Justice, 1987, p. 3.

30. K. Adams, G. Alpert, R. Greenfield, M. Henriquez, P. Langan, C. Maxwell, and S. Smith, *Use of Force by Police: Overview of National and Local Data*. Washington, D.C.: National Institute of Justice, Bureau of Justice Statistics, 1999.

31. K. Lersch and T. Mieczkowski, "Who Are the Problem-Prone Officers? An Analysis of Citizen Complaints," *American Journal of Police*, vol. 15 (1996), pp. 23–42.

32. S. M. Edwards, J. Granfield, and J. Onnen, *Evaluation of Pepper Spray*. Washington, DC: National Institute of Justice, 1997, pp. 1–8.

33. *Police-Prosecutor Coordination: The Key to Effective Prosecution*. Washington, D.C.: U.S. Department of Justice, National Institute of Justice, 1990, pp. 1–15. (The discussion regarding the recent trends in police-prosecutor cooperation was adapted from this source.)

34. W. C. Cunningham and T. H. Taylor, *The Growing Role of Private Security*. Washington, D.C.: U.S. Department of Justice, 1984, pp. 1–5. (This discussion was based on the findings of a thirty-month study of private security conducted by Hallcrest Systems, Inc., of McLean, Virginia. The discussion of private security and law enforcement was reprinted with permission from this source).

35. R. C. Larson, "The Future of Police Emergency Response Systems," *National Institute of Justice Reports* (March 1985), pp. 2–6. (The discussion of computer-aided dispatch systems was adapted from this source.)

36. C. D. Neudorfer, "Fingerprint Automation: Progress in the FBI's Identification Division," *FBI Law Enforcement Bulletin* (March 1986), pp. 2–8. (The discussion of fingerprint automation was adapted from this source.)

37. *Toward the Paperless Police Department: The Use of Laptop Computers*. Washington, D.C.: U.S. Department of Justice, National Institute of Justice, 1993. (The discussion of the use of laptop computers by police departments was adapted from this source.)

38. D. Hills, "Calgary, Canada Police Services." Paper presented at the convention of the International Association of Crime Analysts, 1995, San Pedro, Calfornia.

39. J. T. Duncan, *Citizen Crime Prevention Tactics: A Literature Review and Selected Bibliography*. Washington, D.C.: U.S. Government Printing Office, 1980, pp. 2, 3, 21–25. (The historical overview of crime-prevention activities, along with the accompanying references, was adapted from this source.)

40. T. E. Baker, J. P. Baker, and R. Zezza, "Neighborhood Watch: A Leadership Challenge," *FBI Law Enforcement Bulletin* (February 1999), pp. 12–18.

41. D. Rosenbaum, "The Theory of Research behind Neighborhood Watch," *Crime and Delinquency*, vol. 33 (1987), pp. 103–134.

42. L. W. Sherman, *Crime File—Study Guide: Neighborhood Safety*. Washington, D.C.: U.S. Department of Justice, National Institute of Justice, 1987, pp. 2, 3. (The discussion of the causes of the fear of crime was adapted from this source.)

43. L.W. Sherman et al., *Preventing Crime: What Works, What Doesn't, What Is Promising*. Washington, D.C.: National Institute of Justice, 1997.

44. T. Hope, "Community Crime Prevention." In M. Tonry and D. Farrington, eds., *Crime and Justice*, Vol. 19., *Building a Safer Society*. Chicago: University of Chicago Press, 1995.

45. M. Wycoff and W. Skogan, "Community Policing in Madison: Quality Policing from the Inside Out. An Evaluation of Implementation and Impact." Washington, D.C.: National Institute of Justice, 1993.

46. W. Skogan, *Community Policing in Chicago, Year Three*. Chicago: Illinois Criminal Justice Implementation Authority, 1996.

47. T. D. Crowe, *Crime Prevention Through Environmental Design: A Basic Training Manual*. Louisville, Ky.: National Crime Prevention Institute, College of Urban and Public Affairs, University of Louisville, 1990. (The discussion of crime prevention through environmental design was adapted from this source.)

48. R. Butterworth, *Planning for Prevention*. Tallahassee, Fla.: Florida Department of Law Enforcement, 1993, pp. ii–iii.

49. National Association of Convenience Stores, *Report and Recommendations*. Alexandria, Va.: National Association of Convenience Stores, 1991.

50. "Combining CPTED and Community Policing" was adapted from D. Fleissner and F. Heinzelmann, *Crime Prevention Through Environmental Design and Community Policing*." Washington, D.C.: U.S. Department of Justice, National Institute of Justice, 1996, pp 1–4.

51. R. Titus, *Crime Prevention Through Environmental Design at the National Institute of Justice*. Washington, D.C.: U.S. Department of Justice, National Institute of Justice, 1994. (The discussion of what police and residents can do together to prevent crime was adapted from this source.)

52. R. Atlas and W. LaBanc, "The Impact on Crime of Street Closures and Barricades: A Florida Case Study," *Security Journal*, vol. 5 (1994), pp. 140–145. For further discussion on this topic, see J. Lasley, *Using Traffic Barriers to Design Out Crime: A Program Evaluation of LAPD's Operation Cul-De-Sac*. Fullerton: California State University, 1996; O. Newman. *Creating Defensible Space*. Washington, D.C.: U.S. Department of Housing and Urban Development, 1996.

53. The Watch Your Car Program overview was adapted from Bureau of Justice Assistance, *The Watch Your Car Program*. Washington, D.C.: U.S. Department of Justice, 1996, pp. 1–6.

54. This material was adapted from S. N. Weingart, F. X. Hartman, and D. Osborne, *Case Studies of Community Anti-Drug Efforts*. Washington, D.C.: U.S. Department of Justice, National Institute of Justice, 1994, pp. 1–15.

7 THE DYNAMICS OF THE CRIMINAL COURT

Chapter Outline

What Is a Court?
   What Is a Court's Jurisdiction?
The Dual Court System
   The Federal Court System
   State and Local Court Systems
The U.S. Supreme Court
   How Supreme Court Case Law Comes into Being
   State Courts of Last Resort
State and Federal Intermediate Appellate Courts
Federal and State Trial Courts
State and Federal Lower Courts
Specialty Courts
   Drug Courts: A Blend of Treatment and Coercion through Judicial Sanctions
   Military Tribunals in the Age of Terrorism
Court Administrative Personnel
   The Law Clerk
   The Judicial Assistant
   The Bailiff
   The Court Reporter
   The Court Clerk
   The Court Administrator
   The Courthouse Regulars
   Special-Service Court Employees
   The Chief Judge
The Effect of Courtroom Congestion on Case Processing Time
American Criminal Courts
Prosecutors and Defense Lawyers— Adversaries in the Criminal Court
   The Adversarial System
   The Prevalence of Guilty Pleas in the American Criminal Justice System
   The Adversarial Model of the Criminal Trial versus the Reality of Plea Bargaining

The Dynamics of the Criminal Court
The Prosecutor
   The Prosecutor's Specific Function
   Step by Step—The Prosecutor's Role
   The Prosecutor's Public Image
   Division of Prosecutorial Duties
   The Decision to Prosecute
   The Power of Prosecutorial Discretion
   Unethical Procedures and Wrongful Conviction
   The Prosecutor's Constitutional Duty to Disclose Evidence Favorable to the Defendant
   Prosecutorial Diversion
   Adjudication Deferred/Withheld Adjudication
   Too Many Cases, Too Few Prosecutors
The Criminal Defense Lawyer
   The Role of the Criminal Defense Lawyer
   Privately Retained Counsel
Legal Services for the Poor
   The Public-Defender System
   The Assigned-Counsel System
   The Contract System
The Judiciary
   The Selection of Judges
   The Election of Judges
   The Appointment of Judges
   Modified Appointment of Judges
   Which Is the Best System for Selecting Judges?
   Judges at Work
   Female Judges and Justices
Courthouse Culture and the Socialization of Judges
   Job Stress and the Judiciary
The Consequences of Court Congestion, Delay, and Backlog
Summary

Key TERMS

adversary system, p. 280	dual court system, p. 259
appellate court, p. 259	en banc, p. 266
assigned-counsel systems, p. 295	judge, p. 257
bailiff, p. 275	judicial assistant, p. 274
chief judge, p. 266	jurisdiction, p. 257
contract system, p. 296	justice, p. 257
court, p. 256	law clerk, p. 274
court administrator, p. 276	magistrate, p. 257
court clerk, p. 275	pro se, p. 291
court reporter, p. 275	prosecuting attorney, p. 283
defense attorney, p. 290	public defender, p. 293
deferred adjudication, p. 289	writ of *certiorari*, p. 265
de novo, p. 268	writ of *habeas corpus*, p. 266

Courtesy Jerry Driendl/Getty Images, Inc.-Taxi.

Just as American law borrowed heavily from English law, the organization of American courts reflects its English heritage. A common-law tradition was important in shaping the early American court system. During the colonial period, political power was concentrated in the hands of the governors. As appointees of the English king, the governors performed the executive, legislative, and judicial functions. The courts in early colonial times were rather simple institutions.

The structure of these early American courts replicated English courts in form, but not in substance. The complex, numerous, and highly specialized courts of the mother country were ill-suited to meet the needs of a small group of colonists trying to survive on the edge of the wilderness, so the colonists greatly simplified the English procedures.

The county courts stood at the heart of the American colonial government. Besides adjudicating cases, they all performed important administrative functions. Appeals from all courts were taken to the governor and the colonial council. After the American Revolution, a major dispute developed as to whether there should be a federal court system separate from the state system. When the U.S. Constitution was being drafted, the anti-Federalists, who feared a strong government, thought that a new national government threatened both individual liberties and state rights and wanted only a limited federal system. The Federalists, on the other hand, fearing the regional prejudices of the states, believed that lawsuits tried exclusively in state courts would put litigants involved in the suit who were from out of state at a distinct disadvantage. The Federalist forces were successful in creating the federal district courts. The first judicial system was a compromise allaying some of the fears of the anti-Federalists. These courts were empowered to enforce national law along state lines and did not cross state boundaries. The selection process adopted ensured that the judges would be residents of the state.[1]

After the Civil War, the structure of American courts changed in many important ways. Rapid institutionalization produced fundamental changes in all aspects of American life, the law included. Increases in population, the growth of cities, and the rise of industrialization greatly expanded the volume of litigation. Moreover, the types of disputes coming into court changed as well. Not only did the growth of industry and commerce result in disputes over the new wealth, but the concentration of people in cities, many of whom were immigrants, coupled with the pressures of unemployment, created a new set of problems for the courts. States and localities responded with increased volumes of litigation. Glick and Vines cite the incredible complexity of the court system during urbanization in 1931 in Chicago:

> City courts were created to deal with the new type of cases in the urban areas; specialized courts were formed to handle specific classes of cases (small claims court, juvenile court, and family relations court are examples). And more courts were added more often by specifying the court's jurisdiction in terms of a geographical boundary within the city. The result was a sporadic and unplanned growth. Each court was a separate entity; each had a judge and a staff. Such organizational structure meant there was no way to shift cases from an overloaded court to one with little to do. In addition, each court produced political patronage jobs for the city political machines. The development of the courts in Chicago illustrates the confusion, complexity, and administrative problems resulting from this erratic and unplanned growth in American courts. In 1931, Chicago had 556 independent courts; the large majority were justice of the peace courts which handled only minor offenses. Other state and local courts included municipal, circuit, superior, county, probate, juvenile, and criminal courts. Sometimes other courts, such as the rackets courts, were added to deal with special problems. The jurisdiction of these courts was not exclusive; that is, a case could be brought before a variety of courts depending upon the legal or political advantages that each one offered. Factors such as cost, reputation of the judge, court delay, and complexity of court procedures were considered before determining which court to use. For example, the prosecuting attorney in a criminal case could choose a court likely to produce either a harsh or lenient judgment. Other attorneys sought to have their cases entered into courts where procedures were so complex it would entangle and confuse the opposition in legal technicalities. Partisan political considerations were also involved. The justices of the peace . . . competed for fees and therefore often were eager to trade favored decisions for court business.[2]

WHAT IS A COURT?

As was demonstrated in Chapter 1, the criminal justice system refers to all of the various agencies and institutions that are directly involved in the implementation of public policy concerning crime. The criminal justice system primarily consists of three major components: police, courts, and corrections. The **court** plays a pivotal role within the system because after a crime has been committed, any formal action must be funneled through the judiciary. Only by permission of the courts can a person be detained prior to trial; only in the courts can this person be found guilty; only in the courts can a sentence be given that incarcerates this person. To the contrary, of course, the courts may release the suspect prior to trial, find him or her not guilty, or decide to sentence the guilty person to an alternative to prison. The decisions the courts make have significant consequences for the other components of the criminal justice system (see "In the News: Plastic to the Rescue: Bullet-Proof Courts").

The term *court* can refer to a particular person (a judge), a number of people (a judicial assembly), a room or building where a tribunal meets to hear and adjudicate cases, or a session of some judicial assembly. A **judge** is an officer who presides in a court of law; the judge is also the senior officer of the court in criminal litigation. His or her duties are varied. During the trial, the judge rules on questions of evidence and procedure and guides the questioning of witnesses. During a jury trial, the judge instructs the jury members as to which evidence they may properly examine and which they should ignore. In addition, the judge charges the jury by instructing its members on the points of law and evidence they need to consider to reach a verdict in the case. If the defendant waives his or her right to a trial by jury, the judge replaces the jury as the fact finder in the case. In the highest courts (for example, the U.S. Supreme Court), a judge may be called a **justice.** A **magistrate** is another name for a judge usually presiding over a "lower court," who performs a variety of judicial functions, such as signing search warrants or holding bail hearings and other procedures, other than trial or appellate duties. Magistrates may be regular judges acting temporarily in the capacity of magistrate, or they may be elected or appointed to their positions.

What Is a Court's Jurisdiction?

The authority of a court, as established both by the power as well as the legal limits within which it has been authorized by legal statutes to handle certain cases, is referred to as the court's **jurisdiction.** *Jurisdiction* means that the court in which the prosecution is pending must be competent according to its own standards. The court must be vested by local law with the power to punish and try the accused for the offense involved. Jurisdiction is a matter regulated by the statutes of each state.

The jurisdiction each court attains is varied by its history, geography, and subject matter, and where it stands in the hierarchy of the courts surrounding it. The cases a court is authorized to hear typically depend on the nature of the disputes being brought

WEB

For more information on the American Bar Association's standards for criminal justice, **visit our Web site, www.prenhall.com/territo.**

IN THE NEWS

A HUMAN PERSPECTIVE

PLASTIC TO THE RESCUE: BULLET-PROOF COURTS
by D. Lemov

Screening participants and spectators with metal detectors is common practice in many courts, but Milwaukee's have gone a step further: Spectators in most felony courtrooms are separated from the proceedings by a shield of clear, bullet-proof plastic. Although metal detectors also are used in the court building, Presiding Circuit Court Judge Jeffrey Wagner thinks the barriers go one better. "It's another tool to increase security and to help the bailiffs maintain control," he says. "With gang-related trials, for example, where emotions run relatively high, it's better to have a more substantial barrier." The barriers don't come cheap. The county budgets about $20,000 per courtroom, including installation and add-ons such as sound systems. And even with the added safety, the barriers have their detractors. Since the program began in 1987, Presiding Judge Victor Manian has resisted putting one in his courtroom. He says the shield "erects a barrier of mutual mistrust." Milwaukee is one of a number of jurisdictions experimenting with the barriers, and Charles Hannah, a specialist on court security affiliated with the National Sheriffs' Association, is skeptical of the trend. Hannah thinks it's more important to keep weapons out of the courtroom in the first place. But Judge Wagner still believes in the barriers. "It certainly eliminates a lot of worries, especially for the bailiffs," he says.

Source: D. Lemov, "Plastic to the Rescue: Bullet-Proof Courts," *Governing,* December 1995. Reprinted with permission, *Governing* magazine, copyright 1995.

TABLE 7.1 Parallels between the State and Federal Court Systems

	State Court System	Federal Court System
Courts of last resort	Supreme court, court of criminal appeals, supreme court of appeals, supreme judicial court, etc.	U.S. Supreme Court
Intermediate appellate courts	Superior court, district court of appeals, appellate court, supreme court, etc.	U.S. Courts of Appeal
Trial courts (courts of general jurisdiction)	Circuit court, district court, state court, county court, etc.	U.S. District Courts
Lower courts (courts of limited jurisdiction)	Municipal court, small claims court, traffic court, justice of the peace, etc.	U.S. magistrates (e.g., U.S. Customs Court)

before it and on specific political boundaries—city, county, township, parish, circuit—in which it is located. Additionally, some courts are limited only to specific matters such as misdemeanors, juvenile justice, and civil actions; others deal with specific aspects of civil law, such as domestic relations, probate and estates, patents, trademarks, and tort–personal-injury cases. Therefore, a particular court's ultimate jurisdiction is a function of its power. The central question of jurisdiction is, what are the appropriate cases in which a particular court in question has the power to adjudicate? If one knows the answer to that question, one knows the nature of that court's jurisdiction.

Jurisdiction can also be viewed in a three-part simplified hierarchy of limited jurisdiction, general jurisdiction, and appellate jurisdiction. Both federal and state courts have these three-part hierarchical systems (see Table 7.1).

1. *Courts of limited jurisdiction:* These are the lower courts that do not have many powers to extend over the administration of justice. Most often they try misdemeanor rather than felony cases; they are not authorized to hear appeals. Seldom do they keep an exact record of their trial proceedings.

2. *Courts of general jurisdiction:* These courts are the major felony trial courts in the criminal justice system. They have the power and the authority to try and decide major criminal cases. They are a court of original jurisdiction for felonies. They also act as a court of appellate jurisdiction for misdemeanor convictions that initially were adjudicated guilty in a court of limited jurisdiction.

3. *Courts of appellate jurisdiction:* These are the appeals courts in the U.S. judiciary. They are limited in their jurisdictional decision, allowing them to make questions of law arising from both the trial transcript and from appeals courts of general jurisdiction.

It is important to distinguish between trial courts and appellate courts. Both exist at the state and federal levels. Both are involved in making and interpreting laws. However, it is said generally that the trial courts try the *facts* of the case, while the appellate courts are concerned only with the *law* of the case. There are, of course, exceptions to this general rule.

The felony trial courts are the major fact finders in a case. The trial's jury (or the judge, if the case is not tried by a jury) answers one of two basic questions of fact: (1) Is the accused guilty of the crime for which he or she is being tried? To answer this question, the judge or jury determines whether the state failed to present evidence that is sufficiently persuasive to hold the defendant accountable for the crime charged. (2) What is the level of credibility of all the witnesses presented to the court? In making one of these two findings, the judge or jury considers evidence presented by both the defense and the prosecution.

Because the trial judge and jury hear and see the witnesses, it is assumed that they are in a better position than the appellate court to determine which witnesses are credible, which are less credible, and which are not credible at all. Thus, it is argued, some of the judges of the appellate court are never afforded the perspective of the case. Therefore, their functions should be confined exclusively to issues of law.

CTQ

What is the jurisdictional dilemma between the state and federal courts in high-profile cases, and how might it be resolved?

After the judge or jury has made a decision at the trial level, the defendant, if found guilty, may appeal that decision. In a criminal case, the defendant has the right of appeal in both the state and federal court systems, although he or she does not (except in a few specific cases) have the right to appeal to the highest court in the system.

At the appellate level, the defendant usually alleges that certain errors were committed before and during the trial and court proceeding (for example, that the judge admitted into evidence an illegal confession or that the judge allowed exclusion of minority groups from the jury during the jury selection). Because of these alleged legal errors, the defendant argues to the appellate court that he or she should receive a new trial. The appellee (the prosecution at trial), on the other hand, argues in the appellate courts either that the errors alleged did not exist, or if they did, that they did not prejudice the appellant's case, and, therefore, the appellant should not be granted a new trial.

In the appellate courts, cases are heard and determined by judges, not juries. The **appellate court** looks at the trial court record, considers a written brief, and submits it to the attorneys who use these briefs to establish and support their legal arguments. Appellate judges hear oral arguments from the defense and the prosecution regarding alleged errors during the trial and rules on those issues. If the appellate court holds that no errors were committed during the trial, it affirms the lower court's decision. To the contrary, the appellate court may hold that there were errors and that the errors did prejudice the defendant. Such a holding means that the defendant did not receive a fair trial. If the appellate court makes such a ruling, the verdict of the trial court is reversed. An order is then issued to send the case back to the original trial court for a second trial with instructions concerning errors. This holding is referred to as *reversed and remanded*. When the appellate court reverses a case *with prejudice*, the consequence of such a ruling means that no further trials are permitted and the defendant is to be released from incarceration immediately.

In essence, appellate courts are trying the procedures and rulings used during the original trials. This system allows appellate courts to exercise some administrative control over trial courts, thus achieving more uniformity among courts than would exist otherwise. Trial court judges and juries exercise considerable power in criminal justice systems. However, although many cases are not appealed, in cases that are appealed and retried, frequently the lower court reaches the same decision on retrial.[3]

It is common practice to refer to certain courts as *lower courts* or *inferior courts*, and to venerate other courts by calling them *higher courts* or *superior courts*. The former includes courts of limited jurisdiction; the latter include the appellate courts, especially the highest appellate court, the court of last resort. The status of trial courts (courts of general jurisdiction) in this hierarchy is variable; they sometimes are included among the lower courts, sometimes among the higher courts. Such distinctions are largely the result of custom and usage—a reflection of the prestige afforded to the various courts by the legal profession.

THE DUAL COURT SYSTEM

The United States has a **dual court system** consisting of state and federal courts. State crimes are prosecuted in state courts and defined by state statutes. Federal crimes are tried in federal courts and are defined by Congress. Normally, the two systems are autonomous except in the exceptional instances demonstrated shortly.

One such example occurs when a criminal act violates both federal and state statutes. In such a case, the defendant may be tried in a state court, a federal court, or both. The most famous case in point was of the four Los Angeles police officers, one of whom was officer Stacy Koon (Figure 7.1), who were initially acquitted of brutality charges in a California state court for the excessive use of force in arresting Rodney King. Yet afterward, these same officers were tried in a federal court for the exact same event, which was the violation of Rodney King's federal civil rights. The officers were convicted in federal court. (See Figure 7.1.)

Yet generally, federal courts and lower state courts still constitute separate systems. Cases may not be appealed from a state court to a federal court (with the exception that a ruling from the state supreme court may be sent directly to the U.S. Supreme Court). Such appeals are possible only when a federal statutory or constitutional right is

CTQ

What is the dual court system? Why do we have a dual court system in America? Could the drive toward court unification eventually lead to a monolithic court system? Would such a system be effective?

FIGURE 7.1

L.A. police officer Stacy Koon leaves the federal courthouse where he was convicted of using excessive force on Rodney King, a charge for which he earlier had been acquitted in state court.

Courtesy James Cachero/CORBIS.

involved. Yet another way to bridge this gap in American criminal courts is through a writ of *habeas corpus*.

Federal courts only hear cases over which they have jurisdiction. Yet many cases challenged in federal courts are brought by state prisoners. The shift of jurisdiction in federal court is appropriate because the inmates are alleging that federal rights have been violated. Using a writ of *habeas corpus*, allows for such a transcendence from one particular court system into the other.[4]

The Federal Court System

Only the federal courts have jurisdiction to litigate criminal cases committed throughout the entire territory of the United States. This means that the federal courts have jurisdiction over all federal codes and in all fifty states, all U.S. territories, and the District of Columbia. Additionally, federal jurisdiction includes the power to prosecute and punish violations of local codes and ordinances in Guam, the Virgin Islands, the Canal Zone, and the Northern Mariana Islands.

Federal courts are structured along state lines. Thus, they enforce a uniform body of national criminal laws and local customs and justices; as a result, there are important variations among a multitude of federal district courts in the United States in the special applications of the law in a given case. These variations are an indication that the American courts are deeply rooted in local heritage.

The federal court system is a four-part hierarchy. The U.S. magistrate courts are the base; the second level is the U.S. District Courts; the third level is the U.S. Courts of Appeal; and the U.S. Supreme Court is at the top of the hierarchy (see Figure 7.2).

The U.S. Supreme Court is the only federal court specifically mandated by the Constitution. Other federal courts were established by legislative action. Article III, Section 1 of the Constitution states that "the judicial power of the United States shall be vested in one Supreme Court, and in such inferior courts as the Congress may from time to time ordain and establish."

State and Local Court Systems

As stated previously, just as American law borrowed heavily from the English, the organization of American courts also reflects its English heritage. Common-law tradition was important in shaping the early American court system.

No generalizations can be made regarding the jurisdictions, functions, and titles of state and local courts, although there are structural parallels between state court systems and the federal judicial system. The hierarchy in any given state may include two, three,

---

CTQ

What type of restructuring would be most efficient to unify the state court systems?

WEB

For more information, **visit the link to the federal judiciary on our Web site, www.prenhall.com/territo.**

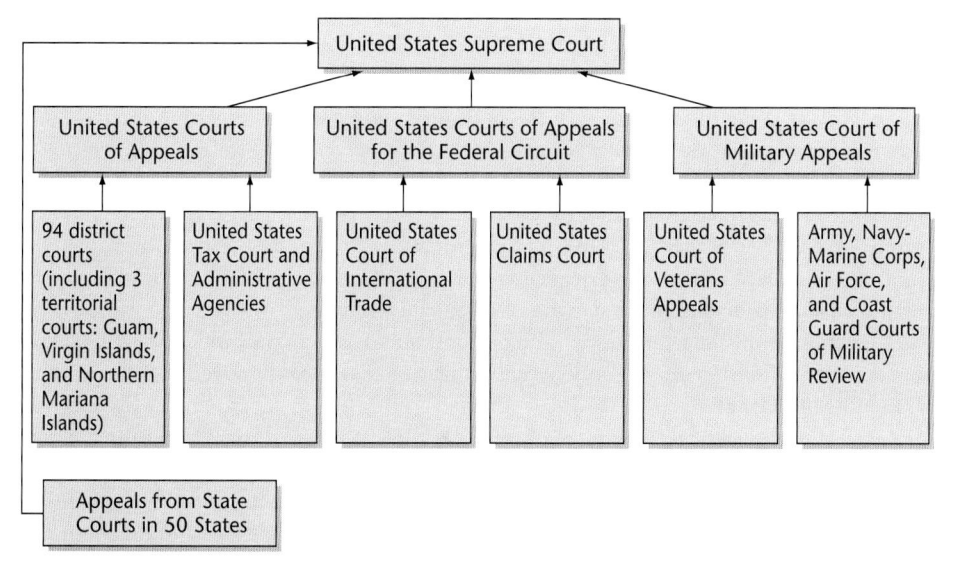

FIGURE 7.2

The Federal Court System

Source: The Administrative Office of the U.S. Courts. Washington, DC: U.S. Government Printing Office, 1991.

TABLE 7.2 Estimated Case Filings in State Courts, 1995

Level of Court	Totals
Trial courts of limited and general jurisdiction[a]	85,800,000
Civil courts[b]	14,800,000
Criminal courts[c]	13,300,000
Juvenile courts	1,900,100
Traffic courts[d]	50,900,000
Intermediate appellate courts	193,000
Courts of last resort[e]	84,710

[a] Data from Indiana, Mississippi, Nevada, and Ohio were not available.
[b] Tort, contract, small claims, domestic relations, and probate.
[c] Felonies, misdemeanors, ordinance violations (other than traffic), and miscellaneous criminal and preliminary hearings in courts of limited jurisdiction.
[d] Some states include parking violations as part of their traffic caseload, but others do not.
[e] Data from Indiana and Nevada were not available.
Source: Brian Ostram and Neil Kouder *Examining the Word of State Courts,* 1995 (Williamsburg VA: National Center for State Courts, 1996).

four, or even more levels of courts. To confound matters further, the nomenclature for courts is rather arbitrary. Consequently, courts are often referred to by title rather than by their jurisdiction or function. "State courts process the vast majority of cases. The courts in a single medium-size state handle more cases than the entire federal system"[5] (see Table 7.2).

American state courts are strikingly decentralized. In only a few states are the court systems completely unified on a statewide basis, funded by the state government, and centrally administered. In the rest of the country, although the state criminal courts operate under the state penal code, they are managed, financed, and staffed by their individual county or city governments. Thus, local politics can be brought to bear on state courts and their local officials. This influence often determines the resources to be allocated to the judiciary.

Such decentralization causes a considerable lack of coordination among state courts, which results in overstaffing in some state courts while others have tremendous case backlogs. Overcrowded courts often are lenient toward offenders, while the overstaffed courts are too severe. Also, the time for processing criminal cases varies widely depending on local traditions.

WEB

For more information about your state court system, **visit the link to the Villanova Law and Policy on our Web site, www.prenhall.com/territo.**

WEB

For more information **visit the link to the National Center for State Courts on our Web site, www.prenhall.com/territo.**

CTQ

What types of cases fall under the jurisdiction of the U.S. Supreme Court?

WEB

For more information about the procedures followed in your state courts, **visit our Web site, www.prenhall.com/territo.**

THE U.S. SUPREME COURT

The U.S. Supreme Court is known also as the "high court" and "highest tribunal" (see Figure 7.3). It is the highest court in the nation. It stands at the apex of the federal judiciary and is truly the court of last resort. The U.S. Supreme Court, often referred to simply as "the Court," consists of nine judges called justices who are appointed by the president, subject to confirmation by the Senate (see Figure 7.4). The president also appoints one member of the Court to act as chief justice. As the chair of the Court, the chief justice has no formal powers of coercion over the other justices, but he or she may apportion caseloads or direct the writing of a judicial decision.

Justices hold their tenure for "life or good behavior," as provided by the Constitution. A justice can be removed only by voluntary retirement or impeachment (see "In the News: Off the Bench?"). The Constitution also denies Congress the authority to reduce the salaries of the justices. The term of the Court is variable. Although statutory law requires that the term begin each year on the first Monday of October, it does not set a closing date. Thus, the Court continues in session as long as it has business to transact. The workload has steadily increased with the expansion of the federal and state judiciaries. Although the Supreme Court gets most of its cases on appeal from these courts, the number of justices on the Court has not changed to meet the growing caseload. Each term, the Court receives approximately five thousand cases or petitions for review. Yet it votes to hear only a small percentage of these cases.

Each year, between 140 and 190 cases of great importance and interest are decided on their merits; about one-half of these decisions are announced in fully published opinions. The Supreme Court historically has refused to hear many times the number of cases that it has agreed to accept.

The appellate jurisdiction of the Court accounts for the overwhelming bulk of its business. The Court reviews cases from lower federal courts and from state tribunals when issues are involved that pertain to the Constitution or to laws of the United States. In addition, the U.S. Supreme Court has ultimate appellate jurisdiction over the federal appeals courts, the state courts of appeals, the District of Columbia court of appeals, and the supreme court of Puerto Rico. The

FIGURE 7.3

The Supreme Court Building in Our Nation's Capital

Courtesy H.D. Seawell/CORBIS.

WEB

The Supreme Court maintains a Web site with a wealth of information on its history, procedures, case filings, and rulings. **Visit the link to the Supreme Court on our Web site, www.prenhall.com/territo.**

FIGURE 7.4

The Nine Justices of the 2003 Supreme Court of the United States

Courtesy Paul Hosefros/New York Times Pictures.

IN THE NEWS

A HUMAN PERSPECTIVE

OFF THE BENCH?

Soon after the John Ashcroft confirmation battle, a Democratic elder statesman sidled up to George W. Bush at a White House gathering. "You know, Mr. President," he said, "you can handle the Russians. You can handle the Iraqis. The one thing you can't handle is one of those Supreme Court Justices quitting on you."

"I hadn't thought of it that way," Bush replied. "But you might be right."

The test could come this summer. Most Supreme Court scholars think two members—Chief Justice William H. Rehnquist, 76, and Sandra Day O'Connor, who is nearly 71 and was the first woman on the court—want to pack up their robes and go. With a Republican in the White House (put there by the Justices, their critics complain), either could sign off knowing a retirement would bear passing ideological resemblance to him- or herself. A rumor shot through the legal community that O'Connor would announce her retirement within a few weeks; that came on top of her widely reported dismay, at an election-night party, over news that Florida had gone for Gore. It was "terrible," she said; her husband explained that she wants to retire but not with a Democrat choosing her successor. She's expressed the same desire to her friends. Another report, even more recent, had Rehnquist pledging to take a chair at the University of Arizona Law School next fall.

The guessing game comes in the wake of the Court's bitter 5–4 decision shutting down the Florida recount and handing the election to Bush—a ruling that left the Court wounded and at war with itself. O'Connor, who voted with the majority, is said to have been especially troubled by the public anger directed at the Court. When a friend praised the Court's ending the election saga, she replied, "Yes, but with a price."

Which leads to part 2 of the game: Who would be tapped to take their places? The answer will determine whether the confirmation process is a mere brawl or a full-scale conflagration. The clash over Attorney General Ashcroft, with 42 Senate Democrats voting no, was cast by both sides as a warm-up for the war over the next high court opening, a slot with lifetime tenure. The Senate's 50-50 split adds still more flammability. Bush continues to say he most admires ultraconservative Justices like Antonin Scalia and Clarence Thomas, but will his resolve melt when he has to face the fire?

"Both sides are set for a pitched battle, and it could be a replay of my experience," says Robert Bork, a conservative whose 1987 nomination to the Court went down in an ugly partisan clash. Bush might get away with naming an unbending conservative to Rehnquist's slot. But one of the toughest tasks of Bush's presidency could be replacing O'Connor—a swing vote on a Court that often rules 5 to 4 and the crucial fifth vote upholding *Roe v. Wade,* since pro-choice groups no longer count on Anthony Kennedy. "Any effort by Bush to appoint a far right-wing justice to replace O'Connor could make the Ashcroft battle look like a walk in the park," says Elliott Minceburg, legal director of People for the American Way, which is already doing opposition research on possible nominees.

Rehnquist's departure would open a broader field of true-blue conservatives. Michael Luttig and J. Harvie Wilkinson III, colleagues on the Fourth Circuit Court of Appeals, know they're in the running and have jousted competitively in recent opinions. Senate Judiciary Committee Chairman Orrin Hatch is said to want the job, and nominating him or another "member of the club" would confound possible foes. But Hatch's age, almost 67, works against him. Replacing Rehnquist has its own hazards: Bush must decide whether to give the chief's gavel to the new appointee or elevate a current justice—triggering another hearing. All the moving parts are at least as hard to juggle if liberals John Paul Stevens or Ruth Bader Ginsburg, for age or health reasons, step down.

Source: Banks, "Off the Bench?" *Time,* February 26, 2001, p. 188. © 2001 TIME, Inc. Reprinted by permission.

Supreme Court has almost absolute power to control its agenda, thus enabling it to be highly selective and to assume jurisdiction only in cases that raise an issue it wishes to consider (see Figure 7.5).

As stated above, a *writ of certiorari* is a request in an appellate proceeding for reexamination of the section of an inferior court. Whether or not to grant the writ is at the discretion of the Supreme Court. However, the Court must grant its jurisdiction in all instances in which (1) a federal court has held an act of Congress to be unconstitutional; (2) a U.S. Court of Appeals has found a state statute to be unconstitutional; (3) a state's highest court of appeals has ruled a federal law to be invalid; and (4) an individual's challenge to a state statute on federal constitutional grounds is upheld by the state supreme court. Over half of the requests for Court time come from losing parties in the U.S. Courts of Appeal; most of the remainder come from disappointed litigants in the state tribunals of last resort.

> **CTQ**
>
> What effect does the Supreme Court's refusal to issue a writ of *certiorari* have on the lower court's decisions?

FIGURE 7.5

Tracing the Course of a Case to the U.S. Supreme Court

Source: National Institute of Justice, Bureau of Justice Statistics, 1994. Washington, DC.

Full Judicial Decision by the U.S Supreme Court (Majority and Dissenting Opinions)

(The Court affirms or reverses lower court decisions. [Exception: The decision is not always a final judicial action. Lower courts may try the case again or, as in civil litigation, the case may be retired.] Note: There is no appeal process beyond the U.S Supreme Court.)

Decision-making Conferences by the Justices

(Four votes govern the acceptance or rejection of a case: [1] a decision and a full opinion; [2] if the case is accepted, there may be a summary decision of a dismissal or affirmation of a lower court decision [per curiam]; [3] if the case is rejected, no explanation [reconsideration is possible]; and [4] a rehearing after an unfavorable decision is possible.

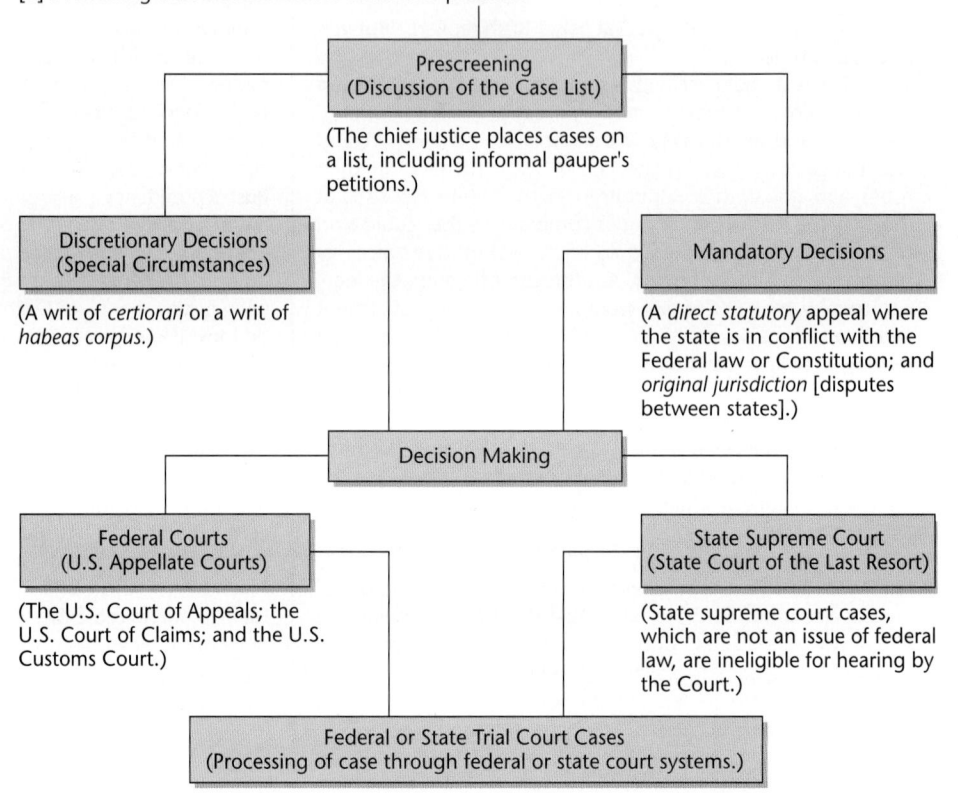

Prescreening (Discussion of the Case List)

(The chief justice places cases on a list, including informal pauper's petitions.)

Discretionary Decisions (Special Circumstances)

(A writ of *certiorari* or a writ of *habeas corpus*.)

Mandatory Decisions

(A *direct statutory* appeal where the state is in conflict with the Federal law or Constitution; and *original jurisdiction* [disputes between states].)

Decision Making

Federal Courts (U.S. Appellate Courts)

(The U.S. Court of Appeals; the U.S. Court of Claims; and the U.S. Customs Court.)

State Supreme Court (State Court of the Last Resort)

(State supreme court cases, which are not an issue of federal law, are ineligible for hearing by the Court.)

Federal or State Trial Court Cases (Processing of case through federal or state court systems.)

CTQ

What is meant when one calls the Supreme Court the court of last resort?

How Supreme Court Case Law Comes into Being

When the Supreme Court rules on a case, usually by majority decision (at least five votes), its rule becomes precedent that must be honored by all lower courts. The use of precedent in the legal system gives the Supreme Court the power of influence to mold the everyday operating procedures of the police, corrections departments, and trial courts.

When the Court hears a case, the chief justice speaks first, usually outlining the facts and issues in the case and expressing his or her tentative vote. The other justices follow with their views in order of descending seniority. The outcome is now provisionally decided, and the majority opinion is assigned by the chief justice or by the senior justice in the majority. Then begins the writing process, for the majority and the dissenters. A justice produces a draft, or reworks one from a law clerk, and circulates it to colleagues. Changes may be requested or offered to pick up or hold a vote. A coalition can come unraveled; a close initial vote may wind up going the other way. So the first audience a justice must please is within the Court, but the final opinions are directed beyond the litigants to guide lower-court judges, sometimes to instruct the nation, occasionally even to address Congress. This overwhelming power of the Supreme Court is manifested in its greatest authority, judicial review (discussed later in this chapter).

TABLE 7.3	Number of Judges on Courts of Last Resort in Different States
Supreme Court	Alabama (9), Alaska (5), Arizona (5), Arkansas (7), California (7), Colorado (7), Connecticut (6), Delaware (5), Florida (7), Georgia (7), Hawaii (5), Idaho (5), Illinois (7), Indiana (5), Iowa (9), Kansas (7), Kentucky (7), Louisiana (7), Michigan (7), Minnesota (9), Mississippi (9), Missouri (7), Montana (7), Nebraska (7), Nevada (5), New Hampshire (5), New Jersey (7), New Mexico (5), North Carolina (7), North Dakota (5), Ohio (7), Oklahoma (9)°, Oregon (7), Pennsylvania (7), Rhode Island (5), South Carolina (5), South Dakota (5), Tennessee (5), Texas (9)°, Utah (5), Vermont (5), Virginia (7), Washington (9), Wisconsin (7), Wyoming (5)
Court of Appeals	Maryland (7), New York (7)
Supreme Judicial Court	Maine (7), Massachusetts (7)
Court of Criminal Appeals	Oklahoma (3),° Texas (9)°
Supreme Court of Appeals	West Virginia (5)

°Two courts of last resort in these states.
Source: U.S. Department of Justice, Bureau of Justice Statistics, *State Court Organizations, 1980* (Washington, D.C.: U.S. Government Printing Office, 1982); Council of State Governments, *Book of the States, 1986–1987* (Lexington, Ky.: Council of State Governments, 1986).

State Courts of Last Resort

Each state has an appellate tribunal that serves as the court of last resort. In New York, Kentucky, and Maryland, the court of last resort is known as the Court of Appeals. In other states, it is called the Supreme Court of Appeals, Supreme Court of Errors, Court of Criminal Appeals, or Supreme Judicial Court. Whatever its title, the court of last resort is the final authority in cases involving issues of state law (see Table 7.3).

In almost all states, the courts of last resort are established by the respective constitutions of the states. Judges most often are elected to the court, usually for longer terms of office than the judges of lesser courts in the state. In most states, a candidate for the state supreme court bench must have practiced law for a specified number of years to become eligible for this position.

Courts of last resort relate to the lower state courts in much the same way that the U.S. Supreme Court relates to the lower federal courts. As the highest judicial body of the sovereign states, these tribunals have discretionary power to decide which cases they will hear. For this purpose, the court uses a **writ of *certiorari***—a writ of review commanding a lower court to "send up the record" of a case for consideration (the U.S. Supreme Court uses the writ of *certiorari* in much the same way, as described earlier).

In states where the court of last resort does not have an intermediate court of appeals (for example, Mississippi), the state supreme court does not have the power to choose which cases will be placed on its docket. It must listen to every case appealed to it. To complicate matters further, Texas and Oklahoma have two courts of last resort, the Supreme Court (civil) and the Courts of Criminal Appeals.

The number of state supreme court justices varies from as few as three in some states to as many as nine (see Table 7.3). Unlike the intermediate courts of appeal, these courts do not use panels in making their decisions. Rather, the entire panel participates and decides in each case. The state supreme courts are the ultimate review board for matters involving interpretations of state law. After a loss at a state supreme court, the only avenue for appeal for a disgruntled litigant is the U.S. Supreme Court, but successful applications are few and must involve important questions of federal law.

STATE AND FEDERAL INTERMEDIATE APPELLATE COURTS

Thirty-six of the most heavily populated states have an intermediate level of appellate courts that correspond to the U.S. Courts of Appeal. As in the federal system, these intermediate courts provide relief for overburdened state supreme courts and serve as courts of last resort for the majority of appeals received from the courts of original jurisdiction.

Some of the names given to intermediate appellate courts are *superior court, appellate court,* and *supreme court.* In some states, courts of appeal may have both original and appellate jurisdiction; in others, jurisdiction may be restricted to particular kinds of cases. Some states assign the defendant the right to appeal, regardless of whether the court wants to hear the case. Following a conviction for a criminal offense, an individual may appeal the decision arrived at by the court.

The U.S. Supreme Court has ruled that convicted defendants who are indigents have a right to a free attorney to represent them in the first automatic appeal of their conviction.[6] In thirty-six states, this appeal is to an intermediate appellate court. However, once an appeal is exhausted unfavorably at the intermediate court, an indigent defendant does not have the right to a free attorney to take his or her case to the Supreme Court.[7]

In most state systems, courts of appeal review the decisions of the trial courts for judicial error. The facts of a case are not questioned, and all of the trial court's decisions on facts are binding on the appellate court. Thus, evidence is not presented to the court of appeals; rather, the review is accomplished from the trial record. An appellate court cannot reverse the factual findings of the trial court unless they are totally erroneous. In states where there is a second level of review, the trial record and the intermediate court's decision are examined. Usually, refusing to hear an appeal of a lower appellate court's ruling is the same as upholding the decision; the case stops there unless a **writ of habeas corpus** is filed separately in federal court on a constitutional issue.

One final model of state appellate courts should be noted. Some states have two final appellate courts: one court makes the final decisions in criminal cases; the other makes final appellate decisions in civil cases.

Much like the states' intermediate courts of appeal, the U.S. Courts of Appeal are designated as lower federal courts. They were established in 1891 to lighten the Supreme Court's caseload from appeals from federal district courts.[8] Until 1948, the U.S. Courts of Appeal were known as the U.S. Circuit Courts of Appeal. They are characterized as intermediate appellate courts because they stand between the U.S. District Courts, the U.S. magistrates, and the specialized federal courts on the one hand and the Supreme Court on the other hand (see "In the News: Judge to Shape Political Scene for 10 Years"). They have the principal responsibility for reviewing judicial decisions in the lower courts.[9]

The number of judges authorized to sit on each federal court of appeal ranges from six (in the First Circuit) to twenty-eight (in the Ninth Circuit). A **chief judge** of each circuit, the most senior judge in terms of service and under age 70, has supervisory responsibilities for the circuit. The U.S. Courts of Appeal have jurisdiction not only to review final decisions of the district courts but also to act on certain legal issues that arise while a lawsuit is still going on in a district court (called *interlocutory appeals*). In addition, the U.S. Courts of Appeal can hear appeals from a host of quasi-judicial tribunals such as the National Labor Relations Board.

U.S. Courts of Appeal are essentially what the name implies; appellate courts only. The courts of appeal hear cases that are appealed from the district courts. In only three instances can a case that has been tried in the lower federal courts bypass the particular court of appeal in its circuit and go directly to the Supreme Court: (1) if the case has been decided by a special three-judge district court; (2) if a federal statute has been held unconstitutional by a U.S. District Court and the United States is a litigant in the case; and (3) if it can be shown that the case is of imperative public importance so as to require immediate settlement.

At least two judges must sit on each federal appeals case, but decisions are normally made by a panel of three. The composition of these groups varies from case to case, with the presiding judge in each court making the assignments. On occasion, when disagreement arises among the judges on an important point of law, the matter may be decided by the full court of that particular U.S. Court of Appeals in an *en banc* decision. **En banc** pronounced "in bank," describes a judicial proceeding wherein the full bench of judges is authorized by the particular court of appeal of the district to hear a specific case.

There are thirteen U.S. Courts of Appeal (including one for the District of Columbia), each with jurisdiction over a particular geographical section of the country—a

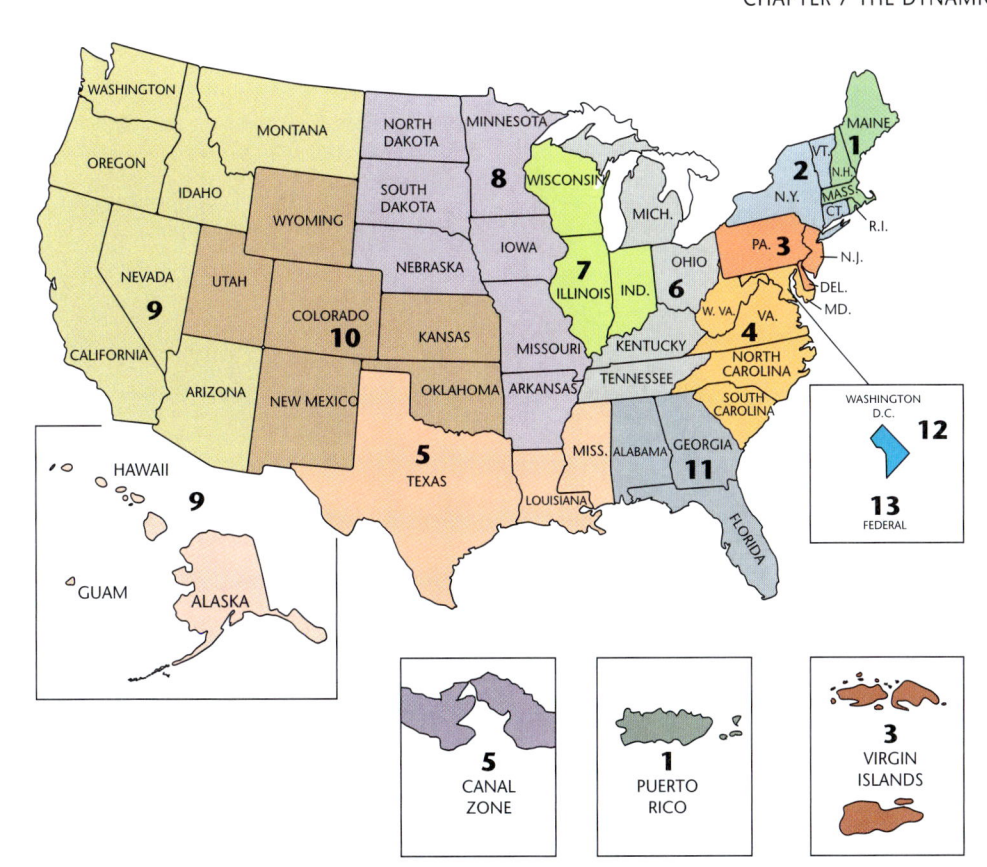

FIGURE 7.6

The Thirteen Federal Judicial Circuits of the U.S. Courts of Appeal

so-called judicial circuit (see Figure 7.6). The thirteen courts of appeal hear an average of 30,000 cases each year involving both criminal and civil matters.[10] More than 100 judgeships are authorized for the U.S. Courts of Appeal.

FEDERAL AND STATE TRIAL COURTS

Trial courts are where criminal cases begin. The trial court conducts arraignments, sets bail, takes pleas, and conducts trials (see Figure 7.7). If the defendant is found guilty (or pleads guilty), the trial court imposes a sentence.

The federal district courts are staffed by district court judges who are nominated by the president and confirmed by the Senate; they serve for life. District court judges possess full judicial powers, including conducting trials, accepting guilty pleas, and imposing sentences.

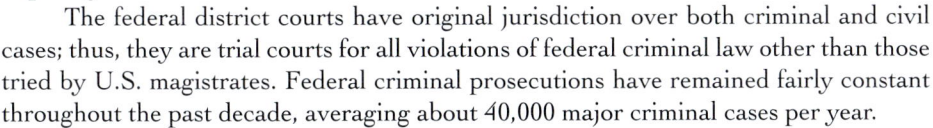

The federal district courts have original jurisdiction over both criminal and civil cases; thus, they are trial courts for all violations of federal criminal law other than those tried by U.S. magistrates. Federal criminal prosecutions have remained fairly constant throughout the past decade, averaging about 40,000 major criminal cases per year.

Like federal district courts, state trial courts are also known as courts of general or original jurisdiction. They are the courts that have original jurisdiction in most criminal cases, and they are the lowest courts of record at the state level. State trial courts are referred to as district courts, circuit courts, superior courts, or courts of common pleas, and they are structured differently from state to state (see Table 7.4). Some systems provide

FIGURE 7.7

One of the dynamics of the criminal courtroom: a defense attorney attempting to persuade the jury during her closing argument that a reasonable doubt exists in this case and therefore her client should be found not guilty.

Courtesy Billy E. Barnes/PhotoEdit.

TABLE 7.4 The State Felony Courts

Circuit Court
Alabama, Arkansas, Florida, Hawaii, Illinois, Indiana,[*] Kentucky, Maryland, Michigan, Mississippi, Missouri, Oregon, South Carolina, South Dakota, Tennessee, Virginia, West Virginia, Wisconsin

Court of Common Pleas
Ohio, Pennsylvania

District Court
Colorado, Idaho, Iowa, Kansas, Louisiana, Minnesota, Montana, Nebraska, Nevada, New Mexico, North Dakota, Oklahoma, Texas, Utah, Wyoming

Superior Court
Alaska, Arizona, California, Connecticut, Delaware, District of Columbia, Georgia, Indiana,[*] Maine, Massachusetts, New Hampshire, New Jersey, North Carolina, Rhode Island, Vermont, Washington

Supreme Court
New York

[*] Concurrent jurisdiction for felonies.
Source: U.S. Department of Justice, U.S. Bureau of Census, *The National Survey of Court Organizations*. Washington, D.C.: U.S. Government Printing Office, 1973.

WEB
For more information, **visit the link to National Center for State Courts on our Web site, www.prenhall.com/territo.**

WEB
For more information on interesting and controversial cases, **visit the link to Court TV on our Web site, www.prenhall.com/territo.**

for separate criminal and civil divisions; a few retain equity or chancery tribunals; and others have special probate and domestic relations courts.

Regardless of how they are structured, however, the trial courts handle the bulk of major litigation under state law. The number of criminal cases processed by these courts is slightly less than 11 million across the nation. In federal courts, however, the number of cases is significantly less. The workload of these courts is reflected in Table 7.5. All important civil litigations originate in these courts, and people accused of criminal offenses—other than petty crimes—are also tried in these courts.

These tribunals also serve as appellate units for cases instituted in courts of limited jurisdiction. However, because such cases are tried *de novo* (as though they had not previously been heard), further appeal normally lies with a higher court. In contrast, in the trial courts of limited jurisdiction, proceedings are typically informal. Cases are processed on a mass basis. Trials are rare, and most are disposed of quickly.

TABLE 7.5 Workload of U.S. Courts, 1985

	Total Cases Filed	Minor Cases Criminal	Minor Cases Civil
U.S. Supreme Court (9 judgeships)	5,006		
U.S. courts of appeal (156 judgeships)	33,360[a]	4,989	23,571
U.S. district courts (575 judgeships)	313,270	39,500	273,670
U.S. magistrates (253 full-time judgeships)[b]	363,687	210,900[c]	152,787

[a] Includes 3,179 appeals from administrative agencies.
[b] There are also 284 part-time U.S. magistrates.
[c] Initial proceedings in criminal cases.
Source: Administrative Office of the United States Courts, *Annual Report of the Director, 1985*. Washington, D.C.: U.S. Government Printing Office, 1985.

STATE AND FEDERAL LOWER COURTS

At the bottom of the state court hierarchy are the lower courts, also known as courts of limited and special jurisdiction. More than 13,000 of these courts are in place across the United States. Typically, the state criminal court system is the focal point for initiating the criminal justice process. They handle all minor criminal offenses such as drunk and disorderly conduct, driving while intoxicated, prostitution, petty theft, traffic offenses, and violations of county and city ordinances. These minor tribunals of local character are identified by titles such as *justice of the peace, magistrate, municipal judge, police,* and *small claims courts*. These courts have various duties and jurisdictions. They are not courts of record, so appeals from them are usually appeals for a completely new trial before the next level of courts in the state system. In some states, justices of the peace and magistrates also conduct preliminary hearings in criminal matters to determine whether accused individuals should be bound over for trial in higher tribunals.

Generally, lower courts are restricted to imposing a maximum fine of $1,000 and a sentence of no more than one year in jail. In some states, however, they are authorized to levy fines as high as $5,000 and sentences of up to five years in prison. The number of trial courts of limited (and sometimes special) jurisdiction varies from none in Idaho, Iowa, and South Dakota, where their function has been assigned to the trial courts, to more than a thousand in New York and Texas.

Historically, the American experience with lower courts has not been reassuring. It was once common practice (and still is in some areas) for laypeople with no formal legal training and little judicial aptitude to preside over lower courts. Considering this background, the following comment of a justice of the peace about defendants brought before him is hardly surprising: "I don't ever remember having one who wasn't guilty. If the sheriff picks up a man for violating the law, he's guilty or he wouldn't bring him in here. Anyway, I don't get anything out of it if they aren't guilty."[11] The following excerpt from *Task Force Report: The Courts*, authored by the President's Commission on Law Enforcement and Administration of Justice, conveys something of the atmosphere that characterizes the functioning of the lower courts:

> An observer in the lower criminal courts ordinarily sees a trial bearing little resemblance to those carried out under traditional notions of due process. There is usually no court reporter unless the defendant can afford to pay one. One result is an informality in the proceedings which would not be tolerated in a felony trial. Rules of evidence are largely ignored. Speed is the watchword. . . . Traditional safeguards honored in felony cases lose their meaning in such proceedings; yet there is still the possibility of lengthy imprisonment or heavy fine.
>
> In some cities, trials are conducted without counsel for either side; the case is prosecuted by a police officer and defended by the accused himself. . . . Short jail sentences of one, two, or three months are commonly imposed on an assembly line basis. . . .[12]

An offender subjected to a process of this kind is not likely to emerge changed for the better. Rather, he or she will return to the streets to begin the cycle again in all of its futility.

Two relatively new parts of the federal judiciary are the U.S. Magistrates, formerly called *U.S. commissioners*, and a variety of specialized courts. U.S. magistrates are federal judges whose powers are limited to trying lesser misdemeanors, setting bail for more serious cases, and assisting district courts in various legal matters. In 1976, the U.S. magistrates' authority was expanded to include issuing search and arrest warrants, reviewing civil rights and *habeas corpus* petitions, and conducting pretrial conferences in both civil and criminal hearings. U.S. magistrates can be either full-time or part-time jurists and are appointed by federal district court judges.[13]

About 300 full-time and 150 part-time magistrates are presently sitting on the bench. These magistrates are appointed to this position by federal district court judges. Full-time magistrates are appointed for eight-year terms, whereas part-time magistrates are appointed for only four years, with reappointment possible for either. Each year, magistrates handle criminal misdemeanor cases involving nearly 100,000 defendants.[14]

CTQ

What are the major problems found in the lower courts, and how might these be remedied?

WEB

To find out more about procedures followed by your state courts, **visit the link to the American Law Source on our Web site,** www.prenhall.com/territo.

SPECIALTY COURTS

Throughout the history of the United States, many states have often resorted to different types of courts to deal with different types of problems. For example, in the 1930s more than thirty different courts served Chicago litigants. Most of the time, a court is established to handle a particular problem that is seemingly unique and requires special attention. In the twenty-first century, two serious problems have arisen that have necessitated the establishment of special types of court: drugs and terrorism.

Drug Courts: A Blend of Treatment and Coercion through Judicial Sanctions

The war on drugs, declared in the 1980s by President Ronald Reagan, was ostensibly undertaken to reduce both the supply of and the demand for illicit substances. As the number of individuals incarcerated for drug-related offenses increased during this decade, it became painfully obvious to policymakers and government officials that the strategy of incarceration, in and of itself, was neither an effective nor efficient mechanism by which to accomplish the goals and objectives that the war on drugs was supposed to achieve.

This strategy of incarceration did not take into account the fact that substance abuse–related criminality and delinquency was a public health problem of epidemic proportion that had a biological, psychological, and sociological basis. Furthermore, the continued use of incarceration as a remedy to the problem of substance abuse–related crime and delinquency failed to recognize that many of the individuals who had been incarcerated for drug-related offenses were, in fact, likely candidates for treatment based on the appropriate use of science-based assessment tools and patient placement criteria.

In the early 1990s, the drug court movement sought to implement a more balanced approach in dealing with the problem of substance abuse as specifically linked to drug-related crime. The thrust of the drug court movement was based upon the observation that the 1980s had produced a series of failed efforts to ameliorate the drug problem through incarceration. It also gave credence to the idea that drug *treatment*, and not just incarceration, might reduce drug-related recidivism for adult and juvenile offenders.

Drug courts do, in effect, represent an alternative to incarceration as a diversion. Although often characterized as a specialized "boutique" or problem-solving court, the drug court realistically has numerous links to other components of the criminal justice and juvenile justice systems. The primary thrust of the drug court is to provide, through intensive judicial oversight and intervention, treatment to adult and juvenile offenders who seek to reclaim their lives from the ravages of drug abuse. Ongoing case management, urinalysis testing, a system of graduated sanctions, the provision of ancillary treatment-related services, and aftercare are also key dimensions associated with the drug court treatment process.

Currently, more than 600 operational drug courts exist in the United States, with another 450 in the planning stages. The federal government, through the U.S. Department of Justice's Office of Justice Programs, has committed more than $56 million to financially support drug courts. The drug court movement has been so effective that it has given rise to a number of other problem-solving courts, including mental health courts, domestic violence courts, DUI courts, and re-entry courts.[15]

When compared with the strategy of incarceration, drug courts are, at least philosophically, designed as a more realistic and cost-effective alternative. The practical question surrounding their operation, however, thus becomes, are drug courts, in fact, more cost-effective, and if so, how much more? Do drug courts really work as well as they were designed to? If not, what are the constraints and limitations surrounding their use?

As noted earlier, from the perspective of a structural overview of the drug courts, a drug court may be defined as "a special court given the responsibility to handle cases involving drug-addicted offenders through an extensive supervision and treatment program."[16] There are several fundamental implications of this definition.

First, the drug court is indeed specialized to the extent that it deals with cases with a specific and narrow focus. It has its own docket and deals only with cases that involve

---

WEB

To read several government reports on drug courts, visit the link to the U.S. Department of Justice on our Web site, www.prenhall.com/territo.

the progress of defendants who have been admitted to the drug court program. Second, supervision is provided not only through the drug court treatment team; the drug court judge is also intimately involved in the overall progress of each individual drug court client. This judicial monitoring process includes the imposition of sanctions if the client's progress is not in compliance with the individualized treatment plan. Third, the pivotal focus of the drug court is treatment, coupled with the use of judicial sanctions for noncompliance. Treatment is the defining characteristic of the drug court program, and provides the rationale for its existence.

Drug court participants, whether adult or juvenile, undergo long-term treatment and counseling, incentives, sanctions, and frequent court appearances for the purposes of judicial case monitoring. A client who successfully completes the drug court program may have his or her charges dismissed, be subject to reduced or set aside sentences, receive penalties of a lesser degree, or any combination of these.

Although drug courts vary from one jurisdiction to the next in terms of their structure, scope, operations, and target populations served, they all share three primary goals: reduction of drug-related recidivism, reduction of substance abuse among drug court participants, and engagement of participants in the treatment and rehabilitation process. Regardless of any specific drug court's structure, the Office of Justice Programs lists a number of characteristics that typify all drug courts:

- Creating a nonadversarial relationship between the defendant and the court
- Identifying defendants in need of treatment and referring them to treatment as soon as possible after arrest
- Providing access to a continuum of treatment and rehabilitative services
- Incorporating drug testing into the treatment process
- Monitoring abstinence through frequent and mandatory drug testing
- Maintaining judicial interaction and supervision of each drug court participant
- Establishing a coordinated strategy to govern drug court responses to the compliance or noncompliance of each participant
- Forging partnerships among drug courts, public agencies, and community-based organizations to generate local support and enhance drug court effectiveness
- Continuing interdisciplinary education to promote effective drug court planning, implementation, and operation
- Monitoring and evaluating program goals and measuring their effectiveness.[17]

There are significant differences between the operations of the drug court and the operations of the traditional criminal court.[18] In the traditional court, the court team consists of the judge, prosecutor, and the defense attorney, who operate within an adversarial environment. The goal of the traditional court is to expedite the processing of cases. The judge exercises a limited role in the supervision of the defendant, although the judge has the discretion to invoke interventions for substance-abuse problems. In the traditional setting, the relapse of the accused may lead to an increased sentence.

In drug court, however, the drug court "team" provides supportive treatment interventions within a nonadversarial court environment. The goal of the drug court is to restore the defendant as a productive, noncriminal member of society. The drug court judge plays a crucial role in monitoring the progress of the defendant in a formalized and structured intervention and treatment process. Finally, a system of graduated sanctions responds to lapses of compliance in drug court program requirements and conditions.

The involvement of the drug court judge is consistent with the philosophy of *therapeutic jurisprudence*, which emphasizes the role of the law as a therapeutic agent. Therapeutic jurisprudence relies on the social sciences to guide its analysis of the law, and represents a departure from the perspective of traditional jurisprudence.

Multidisciplinary in its orientation, therapeutic jurisprudence suggests that society should use the theories, philosophies, and findings of diverse subject areas to shape the framework and development of the law. Instead of being viewed as the dominant perspective, therapeutic jurisprudence is considered a tool for gaining a new and distinct perspective on questions regarding the law and its application. Fundamentally, this approach identifies the potential effects of proposed legal arrangements on therapeutic outcomes, thereby allowing policymakers to make legal policy determinations based on empirical studies and not on uninformed hunches.

Drug courts reflect the growing recognition on the part of judges, prosecutors, and defense attorneys that the traditional methods of incarceration, probation, or supervised parole have *not* stemmed the tide of drug use among criminal and drug-related crimes in the United States.[19] The question now becomes, do drug courts work? A number of research endeavors have offered evidence that, at least on a preliminary basis, supports the efficacy of drug courts. Although drug courts show promise and display the rebirth of rehabilitation,[20] the proliferation of drug courts in the past several years has been extraordinary and has won broad support. In addition, the 2001 Annual Report of the U.S. Office of National Drug Control Policy states that drug courts have been an important step forward in diverting nonviolent offenders with drug problems into treatment and other community resources, leaving the criminal justice system to address violent acts.[21] The annual report of the Office of National Drug Control Policy (ONDCP) further maintains that drug courts provide closer supervision than other treatment programs and substantially reduce drug use and criminal behavior among participants.

The 1999 Florida Drug Control Strategy similarly emphasizes the success of drug courts in the fight against illegal drug abuse, as evidenced by lower recidivism and greater cost savings.[22] Moreover, the report estimates that the average cost of a drug court participant is $1,800 per year, a cost significantly less than the average annual cost of $19,000 per year for one prisoner incarcerated in a nontreatment venue. The outcome is compelling: Through the use of stringent protocols and emphasizing adherence to treatment, drug courts increase the likelihood of successful rehabilitation of participants through a variety of methods such as early, continuous, intensive judicially supervised treatment; mandatory drug testing; and the use of rehabilitative services.[23]

In an analysis of outcomes of two treatment-based drug court programs, it was found that drug court graduates were significantly less likely to be arrested and had fewer arrests during follow-up than members of a control group of offenders who were placed on probation or in alternative forms of treatment. Even more profound was the observation that the rate of arrests declined in direct relationship to the length of drug court involvement. The implication of this finding is striking: The longer the client is engaged in treatment, the less likelihood of recidivism.[24] In a further review of evaluative research involving seven drug court programs, findings demonstrated that drug court participants had fewer days between arrest and involvement in treatment, higher program retention rates, lower recidivism rates, and lower cost per participant when compared with non–drug court participants.[25] An analysis of research regarding drug court operations and their basis in "coerced treatment" found that coercion is the best chance available for increasing the quality of life for substance-abusing offenders; that drug courts have proven especially successful in retaining participants in treatment, thereby reducing substance abuse and criminality; that coerced clients stay in treatment longer; that drug court retention rates exceed retention rates for other public-sector treatment programs; and that drug courts demonstrate that coerced treatment success helps both participants and community resources.[26]

Military Tribunals in the Age of Terrorism

Throughout American history, in times of national crisis, the "perceived enemy" has often been adjudicated in a different kind of American courtroom, which was expeditious and outcome-certain. After September 11, 2001, when American commercial jets were hijacked by terrorists and crashed into the World Trade Center towers in New York City and the Pentagon in Washington, D.C., America became officially engaged in a war against terrorism. All of the pilots were of Middle Eastern descent and pledged allegiance to the al-Qaeda terrorist organization loosely headed by Osama bin Laden. Subsequently, many Americans of Middle Eastern decent became targets of law enforcement and the criminal justice system. Many civil libertarians have reacted sarcastically and angrily to the thousands of detentions of Middle Eastern Islamic men by agencies of the American

---

WEB

The Office of Justice Programs Drug Court Clearinghouse and Technical Assistance Project offers information and sample materials for those interested in drug courts. For more information, **visit the OJP link on our Web site, www.prenhall.com/territo**.

CTQ

What is the best solution for reducing the number of drug cases in the American court system?

criminal justice system. One such critic (a student) remarked that this process seems to be the "rounding up of the usual suspects as long as their names were Mohammed."[27]

For the purposes of this chapter, something much more disturbing happens after the roundup—the trial. These trials have historically been referred to as military tribunals. Attorney General John Ashcroft promised this would be the only due process that suspected terrorists would receive in determining their guilt or innocence with regard to their activities in terrorism (see "In the News: Is Justice Being Kept in the Dark?").

IN THE NEWS

A HUMAN PERSPECTIVE

IS JUSTICE BEING KEPT IN THE DARK? THE MILITARY TRIBUNAL

Mohammed Irshaid has lived in the United States of America for 22 years. Now a civil engineer in New York, the Jordanian-born Irshaid, 41, went to college in Ohio at the University of Toledo; his three children are American citizens, and he was close, he thought, to obtaining his long-cherished green card. As he was sitting in his office on the morning of Nov. 6, he was arrested by federal agents who told him his visa had expired and implied that they had information linking him to a terrorist plot. Irshaid was ashamed to be led away in handcuffs in front of his co-workers; "it was absolutely the most humiliating thing to happen to me in my life," he says.

More humiliation was to follow. He was thrown into a New Jersey cell with nearly three dozen other men, all Muslims, who asked to hold on to their food trays so they could observe the Ramadan fast and eat after sundown. The guard wasn't having any of it. "I don't care about f—ing Ramadan," the turnkey said. The U.S. government never filed any charges against Irshaid. After three weeks, he was finally released. Irshaid says he was so happy he would have jumped for joy, had he not still been shackled and chained in leg irons. "This doesn't change my love of America," he said. "But with all due respect to Mr. Ashcroft, if somebody wants to accuse you of something, they should tell you what it is."

Such stories are becoming uncomfortably commonplace. As innocent Muslim men swept up in the post–September 11 dragnet begin to emerge after being held in custody, often in secret, for weeks and months, they are telling embarrassing and sometimes horrifying tales of official indifference and, occasionally, abuse. Civil libertarians and a growing chorus of op-ed-page Cassandras are warning of a new McCarthyism and accusing Attorney General John Ashcroft of playing a modern-day Torquemada. Ashcroft is not exactly shying from the role of Grand Inquisitor: "people have to make a choice," said the Attorney General. Recently, 86 percent of Americans still think the administration has not gone too far in restricting civil liberties in its response to terrorism. White House officials say that every time the "liberal media" fret about Ashcroft's assaulting civil liberties, the president's approval rating goes up. "Attack us some more," quips one aide. And yet there exists some public ambivalence about the details. Secrecy does not sit well; a majority (58 percent) want trials to be open all or most of the time. Less than half believe that foreigners who are recent immigrants should be subjected to military tribunals. Support for giving more power to the government to fight terrorism has waned since September 11, from 54 percent to 35 percent. Furthermore, some senior officials in the criminal division of the Justice Department as well as the FBI have also privately expressed concerns about going too far. The question is whether the military tribunals turn into kangaroo courts. That seems doubtful: under the scrutiny of a critical and watchful press and Congress, the administration is likely to use the tribunals sparingly and make sure that suspects receive some basic guarantees of a fair trial. The greater risk may be that the heavy-handed tactics could backfire. By rounding up young Muslim men for questioning, or holding them indefinitely on minor immigration charges, the Justice Department may alienate precisely the people they need to blow the whistle on suspicious activity.

The actual impact of the administration's antiterror program turns on the way it is put into practice. In the beginning, White House officials insisted it would be too dangerous and cumbersome to give terrorists normal criminal trials. Judges, lawyers and jurors would be at risk of reprisal; the government would not be able to introduce classified evidence without compromising secret "sources and methods" of gaining intelligence; highly publicized trials could drag on and become circuses. All true. But the president's decree calling for military tribunals was so vague and overly broad that it seemed to sweep aside any semblance of constitutional safeguards. It applies not just to terrorists but those who "harbor them." Does that include landlords and cabdrivers? Only non-citizens could be tried before the tribunals, but some 20 million non-citizens live in the United States. On its face, the president's decree would invite the military to secretly whisk off suspects to a ship or to a distant military base and summarily execute them.

In fact, the precise rules for the tribunals are still being written by the Pentagon. It is more than likely that by the time these rules are put into use, Congress and the career lawyers at Justice will have some moderating input. Pentagon lawyers will be under pressure to build in basic safeguards, like the presumption of innocence, proof beyond a reasonable doubt, public proceedings (with narrow exceptions to avert real security breaches), a unanimous verdict to impose a death sentence, a defendant's right to choose his own counsel and a right of appeal of the highest military court. Indeed, all these are already required by the Uniform Code of Military Justice for ordinary courts-marshal, notes legal analyst Stuart Taylor Jr. The judges may also include not just military officers—who are

(continues)

(continued)

beholden to their commander in chief—but retired federal judges or prominent citizens whose stature and independence are beyond question.

And what if the rules do not offer such safeguards? A terrorist suspect captured abroad, it is true, will have no real recourse. In international law, terrorists, like spies, are "unlawful combatants." They don't even enjoy the basic rights of prisoners of war, who are entitled by the Geneva Convention to be properly fed and housed and not subject to torture. But terror suspects living in the United States will be able to go to a federal court to file a writ of habeas corpus, a protection against arbitrary imprisonment by the state.

The federal courts are likely to throw out any military tribunals that do not offer the "fair and full trial" promised by the Bush administration. So far, according to senior officials, only a small number of suspects now in federal custody are likely to be considered to be tried in a military tribunal—and only then if a strong connection to the al Qaeda network can be firmly established.

The United States aims to capture and try as many al Qaeda leaders as it can dig out of the caves of Afghanistan, at least those who don't die there first. Secretary of Defense Donald Rumsfeld, whose swagger sometimes outdoes even Ashcroft's, made clear that the Pentagon wants Northern Alliance and other Afghan tribesmen to hand over Taliban or al Qaeda operatives arrested abroad. The laws of the European Union and many European countries prevent the extradition of criminal suspects to countries where they could face the death penalty.

According to President Bush's order, the new military tribunals would admit any evidence that is relevant "to a reasonable person." This could include hearsay or other evidence that a criminal court might dismiss. Furthermore, unlike suspects in federal court, those facing the tribunal may not be informed of the charges against them. Critics fear that these tribunals will severely limit defendants' constitutional rights—including the right to an independent attorney, to review evidence, confront their accusers, and protect themselves against self-incrimination. Additionally, Bush's order says trials may be held "at any time and any place." They may be held in secret, inside or outside the United States, on aircraft carriers or naval bases. The Secretary of Defense will appoint a panel of military officers to act as a jury. Finally, it is unclear what standard the military panel will use to establish guilt. And unlike a federal court, which requires a unanimous jury, Bush's court needs only a two-thirds majority to convict—even if the suspect is facing the death penalty. Defendants cannot appeal to any court, but the President himself (and the Secretary of Defense) can review the verdict and make what the order calls a "final decision." Once convicted, sentencing and execution could be carried out in secret.

Source: D. Klaidman et al., "Justice Kept in the Dark," *Newsweek* (December 10, 2001), pp. 37–43. From *Newsweek,* December 10, 2001. © 2001, Newsweek, Inc. Reprinted by permission.

COURT ADMINISTRATIVE PERSONNEL

Employees of the court can generally be classified into four groups: (1) judges and their immediate or confidential staff, all of whom have the duty of confidentiality (these include law clerks, judicial assistants, bailiffs, and court reporters); (2) court clerks and their support staff; (3) administrative personnel; and (4) personnel responsible for special services, such as probation, bail, and victim assistance, and those who may be part of the executive branch attached to the court.

The Law Clerk

Included in the judge's confidential staff are law clerks. In both federal and state court systems, the **law clerk** is a prestigious position, often leading to employment in a desirable law firm. Virtually all law clerks are recent law school graduates. All federal judges have one or two law clerks, and most state judges are provided with clerks, although some district judges may share a limited number of clerks. In general, law clerks are responsible for providing legal research for judges and writing memoranda. Law clerks often take notes for the judge during a hearing and may write the initial drafts of some rulings or opinions.

An intimate relationship exists between judges and their law clerks. Clerks are privy to the judge's thinking about pending cases. Therefore, law clerks are expected to maintain ethical standards close to those of the judge. The relationship between law clerk and judge is so widely accepted that, for example, judges have been required to disqualify themselves when their law clerks have a conflict of interest.[28]

The Judicial Assistant

The second confidential employee is the judge's secretary/receptionist. This position has recently been called **judicial assistant** in some jurisdictions. Many of the duties of the judicial assistant are similar to the duties of any other business assistant, with one very im-

---

WEB

The Washtenaw County (Michigan) Trial Court Web site takes visitors inside the operating procedure of a trial court, including an introduction of the people employed there. For more information, visit their link on our Web site, www.prenhall.com/territo.

IN THE WORKPLACE

JUDICIAL ASSISTANT

Responsible for secretarial and administrative duties to support the judge's fulfillment of judicial and administrative responsibilities. Performs a variety of duties, including the following: researches applicable laws and court decisions; prepares legal memoranda for use in cases before the court; monitors the scheduling of cases for trials, judgments, and hearings; types correspondence and administrative reports; proofreads typed material for accuracy; performs related administrative duties as required. Minimum qualifications are as follows: high school diploma or equivalent; prior administrative experience; typing skills of 75 wpm; excellence in organizational, communication, and personal skills; knowledge of basic grammar; and knowledge of various software applications relative to the position.

portant exception: He or she must be very cautious in giving or receiving *ex parte* (from one party of the lawsuit only) communication. The traditional assistant (personal secretary) is bound by the same obligation of confidentiality as is the judge. The judicial assistant also has to deal with the public and the lawyers on the judge's behalf.

The Bailiff

The third confidential employee is the bailiff, or court deputy. The **bailiff** is charged with the responsibility of maintaining order, security, and decorum of the court. In a large metropolitan court that meets daily, the bailiff is generally a permanent employee. In smaller, rural communities, a bailiff may be appointed by a judge to serve only for the duration of a trial. However, in most urban and rural areas, the bailiff is normally a deputy sheriff.

The duties of the bailiff vary. As a sergeant-at-arms within the courtroom, the bailiff keeps watch over defendants and suppresses disorderly behavior among spectators. The bailiff also summons witnesses when they are called to testify and maintains the legal proprieties pertaining to the actions of jurors and witnesses. When the jury is sequestered on the order of the judge, the bailiff accompanies the jurors and guards to prevent violations of trial secrecy—such as making unauthorized phone calls, reading unedited newspapers, or listening to accounts of the trial on the radio or television. It is also the bailiff's job to see that the jury is suitably housed and fed during the trial.

The Court Reporter

The last confidential employee is the court reporter. **Court reporters** take down a verbatim account of the proceedings in all cases conducted within a court of record. Most of these highly proficient reporters use a stenotype recorder—a mechanical device that types shorthand symbols. At the close of each day in court, or the conclusion of the entire trial, the reporter's notes are transcribed (this is not the case, of course, if the defendant was found not guilty. Usually no transcript would be needed for an appeal since the prosecution is barred from appealing a case by the defendant's constitutional right prohibiting double jeopardy.). Occasionally one is needed if a civil trial arises out of the same proceedings. In most courts, in addition to a base salary, the court reporter is paid by the page for the preparation of the record. Consequently, "it is not rare to find triple spaced, wide margined transcripts."[29]

WEB

For more information, **visit the link to the National Court Reporters Association on our Web site**, www.prenhall.com/territo.

The Court Clerk

The **court clerk** keeps all the records of the court. In federal or appellate court, court clerks are appointed; in lower courts, they are elected. In many areas, the duties of county clerk and court clerk are combined into a single office.

The court clerk has the authority to handle nearly all of the paperwork that accompanies a judicial proceeding. Returns of arrest and search warrants, indictments, informations, all pleadings filed by the prosecutor and defense counsel, instructions to the jury, verdicts, and sentences are filed by the clerk or are transcribed into a permanent court record. Subpoenas for witnesses, notices regarding jury service, and records of all

IN THE WORKPLACE

COURT REPORTER

Responsible for verbatim record of court proceedings to ensure a complete, accurate, and secure legal record. Performs a variety of duties, including the following: produces transcripts, reads back requested portions of records, creates an outline and typewritten log of proceedings, secures and files all exhibits with the clerk's office, edits transcripts, types court orders and dismissals, sets hearings for petitions, prepares paperwork for restraining orders. Minimum qualifications are as follows: high school diploma or equivalent, successful completion of a court reporting program, court reporter certification or equivalent where applicable, and excellent grammar skills.

---

cases filed, dismissed, tried, and appealed are the responsibility of the court clerk. The court clerk is also responsible for docketing cases, collecting fees, overseeing jury selection, and, of course, maintaining court records. Without doubt, these local officials have enormous power. Although there are notable exceptions, most clerks are not trained to manage the local courts.[30] The task of the court clerk is made unnecessarily arduous and complex by the fact that judicial record keeping is a bewildering hodgepodge of diverse procedures. Despite continuing efforts by professional organizations of court clerks, there is little in the way of uniformity or standardization. It is not unusual to find that a particular criminal justice agency (such as a correctional facility) receives more than a dozen different forms for the same document from the various courts within the state, at an annual cost to taxpayers of thousands of dollars.

A vague subdivision of the clerk of the court is the deputy clerk of the court. The deputy clerk of the court can be a member of the judge's confidential staff who provides general information or retrieves files. There are countless types or grades of deputy clerks. In the case of probation, juvenile, or pretrial release, such clerks may be employed by either the judiciary or the executive branch.[31]

The Court Administrator

The relatively new challenging position of court administrator (first established in the 1980s) was mandated at the federal court level by the Ninety-First Congress. The duties of the **court administrator** include exercising administrative control over all nonjudicial activities of the court of appeals in the circuit to which the administrator is appointed; formulating and managing a system of personnel administration; preparing the budget; maintaining a modern accounting system; collecting, compiling, and analyzing statistical data for reports; and other activities relating to the business and administration of the courts. The court administrator—a skilled professional trained in systems analysis, budgeting procedures, the use of computers, and modern techniques of office management and personnel administration—may well prove to be the best hope for bringing efficiency and order to overburdened courts. The function of court administrators is certainly not to usurp the judge's authority. Instead, this key court personnel member's task is to develop the court's organizational structures so that it may be more effective. Although the judge remains the policymaker of the court, he or she still relies on the court administrator to assist in the judicial role to a degree that satisfies the judge. The administrator's job is to recommend and implement innovative procedures of executing policy and to help guide the court along appropriate avenues to improve the administration of justice. Despite the obvious advantages of employing a court administrator as the overall court manager, some courts continue to refuse to respond to the need for well-centralized administration.

Computers have become an important tool in the administration and management of modern courts. The computer can rapidly retrieve necessary data for court functions. Many courts use computer technology in such areas as videotaped testimonies, new court reporting devices, computer-based information systems, and data processing systems for the court's docket and jury management. In 1968, only ten states had state-level

IN THE WORKPLACE

TRIAL COURT ADMINISTRATOR

Responsible for the daily administrative operation of the court's operations; serves as a liaison to other state and county agencies. Performs a variety of duties, including the following: assists in preparing budgets for court facilities and county funded support staff, works with jury commissioners in establishing the proper number of jurors to be called and impaneled, analyzes monthly reports prepared by both the state and the United States Supreme Courts to maintain balance in judicial caseloads, answers complaints, disseminates information concerning trial courts, attends public meetings as the court's representative, maintains personnel records for state judicial employees, and monitors daily criminal dockets. Minimum qualifications are as follows: Bachelor's degree in business or public administration or related field and eight years' experience in court management, including three years of supervisory experience. Knowledge of human resource management, information systems, and facilities management; legislative processes; budgeting rules, regulations, policies, and procedures; auditing and financial management methods; and customer service practices.

---

automated information systems; today, all states employ such systems for at least one element in the field. The following areas are likely to undergo expanded computerization in the future: monitoring the case schedule; preparing documents; indexing cases; maintaining case histories and statistical reporting; notifying witnesses, attorneys, and others of required appearances; and issuing summonses.

Because the position of the court administrator is so new, several aspects of the role are still being debated. Arguments concerning the precise nature of what a true court administrator should center on two topics: qualifications and administrative relations with other agencies.

Courthouse Regulars

Even to the most casual observers, a group of people often in the court referred to as "courthouse regulars" have a special status that others found in the courtroom on any given day do not have.[32] They are not employees; however, they freely issue instructions, such as don't smoke, don't talk, and don't read the newspaper, to temporary visitors to the courthouse. They themselves smoke, talk, and read the newspapers. In addition to these courthouse regulars are professionals whose duty is to be in court, such as lawyers, judges, and court personnel. Others, who do have such a duty, also are in the courthouse. These persons, however, are not considered courthouse regulars; they are ordinary citizens—defendants, friends of defendants, victims, witnesses, and disinterested observers. They sit on hard seats in the rear of the courtroom and may approach the bench through a gate dividing the courtroom only when specifically requested. The Courthouse regulars, on the other hand, enjoy easy access to the front part of the courtroom, freely passing the railing near the judge's bench.

Another indication of the special status of the courthouse regulars is the nature of their casual conversations. Courtrooms are subject to numerous, unpredictable periods of inactivity. During these times, courthouse regulars engage in casual conversations, demonstrating that they know each other well.

As a special kind of courthouse regular, defense attorneys are much more likely to talk to their nominal adversary, the prosecutor, than to pass the time of day with their client. A number of studies have attempted to assess the activities of these officials. They have found a complex network of ongoing social relationships among judges, prosecutors, and defense attorneys who work together on a daily basis. This level of cooperation certainly never was envisioned by the formal adversary model.

Special-Service Court Employees

The category of special-service court employee is a catchall for people who provide various services to the court. They are usually employed by the executive branch, though they function almost exclusively within the courts. A list of special-service positions is potentially

IN THE NEWS

A HUMAN PERSPECTIVE

A DAY IN THE LIFE OF LOIS G. FORER
by L. Forer

A long day on the bench begins at 9:30 in the morning, and frustrations mount as overloaded public defenders arrive late, witnesses cannot be found, and defendants are forgotten at the jail rather than brought to court when they are needed. Cases have to be continued, and judges are asked to decide on bail for men and women they cannot see to talk to and whom the public defender knows nothing about. They are asked to sentence people using only two alternatives: prison or the streets. What is often needed instead is a drug program or hospital plan, but these alternatives are seldom available. Judges must sit through five-hour sanity hearings and decide which team of psychiatrists is correct about a defendant. They are frustrated by jail overcrowding, but they face harsh public and self-criticism if they release anyone who commits another crime. They encounter seemingly unsolvable cases in which there are simply no resources to provide for the needs of defendants. At the end of a day, in which as a judge, I have taken action affecting for good or ill the lives of perhaps 15 or 20 litigants and their families, I am drained. I walk out of the stale-smelling, dusty courtroom into the fresh sunshine of a late spring day and feel as if I were released from prison. I breathe the fresh air, but in my nostrils is the stench of the stifling cell blocks and detention rooms. While I sip my cool drink in the quiet of my garden, I cannot forget the prisoners, with their dry bologna sandwiches and only a drink of water provided at the pleasure of the hot and harried guard.

Source: L. Forer, "View from the Bench: A Judge's Day" *Washington Monthly*, 1975. Reprinted with permission from *The Washington Monthly*. Copyright by Washington Monthly Publishing, LLC, 733 15th St. NW Suite 520, Washington, DC 20005. (202) 393-5155, Web site: www.washington.monthly.com.

---

endless. Some categories that might be generally agreed upon include adult and juvenile probation officers, court interpreters, personnel in charge of pretrial release or bail supervision programs, victim assistance counselors, drug and alcohol abuse program coordinators, case workers, and family counselors. Referees, mediators, and hearing officers, all of whom hold quasi-judicial positions, might also be included in the special services category.[33]

The Chief Judge

Finally, the boss of the administrative side of the courtroom and the person who is ultimately responsible for the administration of the court is the chief judge. Although chief judges historically have been responsible for court administration, they have almost always been ineffective managers. This is primarily because of the unique environment in which the court operates. (See "In the News: A Day in the Life of Lois G. Forer.") Chief judges are not trained for effective management of all court personnel. The skills of a lawyer center on treating each case individually. Most practicing attorneys handle only a few cases at one time. The result is that lawyers who become chief judges are not accustomed to analyzing patterns of case dispositions or managing large dockets. Yet those are essential skills for a manager.

Although the chief judge has general administrative responsibilities with respect to the other judges, he or she is not considered their superior or boss. Particularly when chief judges assume the position by seniority, as they do, there is no guarantee that the person will be interested in personnel management or that he or she will be effective in it. To the contrary, if the judge becomes chief by an election of other judges, there is a better chance that an effective manager will be selected. However, an election could also result in the appointment of a chief judge who will not rock the boat.[34]

THE EFFECT OF COURTROOM CONGESTION ON CASE PROCESSING TIME

The nation's courts handle more than 100 million civil, criminal, and traffic cases each year, resulting in backlogs, delays, and what is sometimes called "assembly-line justice." Of these cases, approximately 13 million are criminal cases and 15 million are civil cases.[35]

These figures seem overwhelming, and they are even more disturbing because of the sharp increase in both civil and criminal litigation in the past few years. For example, in 1987, federal district courts disposed of 29,000 criminal cases; by 1997, the number had increased to about 45,000.[36] In 1990, about 4,400 criminal appeals were heard in federal circuit courts; by 1992, the number had grown to almost 12,000.[37] It is not surprising that the average case takes about six months to go from arrest through trial. Delays are so long that there is actually not much difference in the case processing time (discussed shortly) between cases that go to a jury trial and those handled by a plea bargain.

Analyses of data in one study indicate that in 1992 almost 900,000 adults were convicted of a felony or felonies in state courts. Of those convicted, 54 percent were sentenced to a state prison and 26 percent were sentenced to a local jail.[38] The volume of felony convictions in state courts rose by 34 percent between 1988 and 1992, a growth rate in excess of the arrest growth rate. Of those convicted in 1992, guilty pleas were entered by 92 percent, with only 8 percent convicted after a trial. Fifty-two percent of those convicted were white, and 47 percent were African American.[39]

Case processing time refers to the elapsed time between a defendant's arrest that led to a court sentence and the imposition of that sentence. The period has two major parts: the time between arrest and conviction, and the time between conviction and sentencing.

In a 1997 study undertaken by the National Center for State Courts, the average elapsed time from arrest to conviction was about 5½ months. There was some indication that felony cases disposed by juries took the longest to convict: 6½ months. Average elapsed time from arrest to conviction for other cases was slightly over 5 months for bench trials and about 5½ months for guilty pleas. Convictions for half of all felony cases occurred within 4 months of arrest.[40]

Of all the specified offenses, murder cases had the longest average processing time. Whether by jury, judge, or plea, the average time taken to convict a felon of murder was about 9 months. Depending on the method of conviction, the average time for a rape conviction was between 6 and 8 months; for drug trafficking, between 5½ and almost 8 months; for burglary, between 3½ months and less than 5 months. Frustrated with these delays, the majority of courts in the first decade of the twenty-first century are anxious to resolve the problem of court congestion.[41]

AMERICAN CRIMINAL COURTS

Examine any courtroom in America, from the U.S. Supreme Court to a justice-of-the-peace courtroom above a gasoline station, and you will find one thing in common with almost all of them—they may be elegantly decorated and designed or may have only four walls and a roof, but if that were all they were, they would just be structures. Without anything else, however, these structures would remain uninteresting.

Yet most Americans believe that the American courtroom is one of the most dynamic, electric, and exciting settings that this country has to offer. Why? It is the "players" who are authorized to occupy American courtrooms and practice their profession in them, be they major or minor players; it is also the people who make up the cross-section of the community who sit in the courts and watch these players in action that make a courtroom in which a case is being tried one of the most vital, dynamic places to be. All of these people contribute. They include part-time players: the law clerk, the judicial consultant, the bailiff, the court reporter, the court clerk, the court administrator, and the courtroom regulars as well. But also there are the citizen players. These are the jury, the panel from which jurors are chosen, the spectators, and the press.

The most important players in the courtroom are the trial judge, the prosecutor, and the defense counsel. Together these three players transform a dead structure (the courtroom) into an event so spectacular that it is the base of our American pride and the envy of other nations.

PROSECUTORS AND DEFENSE LAWYERS—ADVERSARIES IN THE CRIMINAL COURT

The image of prosecutors and defense attorneys in popular television programs, movies, and novels gives a somewhat distorted and oversimplified view of the functions these people perform. There are not real-life counterparts to television's popular defense attorneys, such as *The Practice*'s leading characters, who somehow always manage to have their client acquitted ten minutes before the end of the program. However, there are prosecutors like *Law and Order*'s prosecutor Jack McCoy who manage to win most cases and lose only a few.

Our system of justice and the roles played by attorneys tend to mystify the average citizen, who often has great difficulty understanding why or how anyone could defend certain classes of criminals. There is even greater confusion as to why individuals who have obviously committed crimes are sometimes released on technicalities. Moreover, it often appears that prosecutors and defense attorneys are more concerned with winning their cases rather than seeking truth or justice, and that the final outcome of a criminal trial is affected more by the skills, personalities, and theatrics of attorneys than the merits of the case.[42]

In this part of the chapter, we address some of the public's concerns and misconceptions and provide the reader with an overview of the rationale underlying the dynamics of the courtroom in our system of criminal justice. Furthermore, we outline the functions and discretion of the prosecutor and discuss the implications of this discretion. Lastly, we examine the role of the defense attorney and the pros and cons of various legal-assistance programs available to citizens.[43]

The Adversary System

To the layperson, and perhaps even to some social scientists, the role of all lawyers is to see that justice is done. Anyone who has been educated in our legal traditions, however, knows that justice must be done according to law and within the procedures of the **adversary system**.[44]

The adversary system, which is central to the administration of criminal justice, is not the result of abstract thinking about the best way to settle disputes of law and fact. Rather, it is the result of a slow evolution from trial by combat or by champions to a less violent form of testing by argument and evidence. An atmosphere of contention still marks our way to justice, however, and for that reason, the adversary system has received much criticism. One criticism is that the system does not provide the best setting for discovering the facts of a particular case or for resolving legal policy. However, it must be recognized that the presentation of opposing views in vigorous debate as a prelude to decision is a feature also found in the legislative and executive branches of government. By contention—provided it is kept within proper bounds—a dispute is narrowed, and arguments that appear to be correct and logical, but are not, are exposed in the course of debate. Contest spurs each side to greater intellect and imagination so that, in the words of the nineteenth-century statesman Thomas B. Macaulay, "it is certain that no important consideration will altogether escape notice."[45]

Cross-examination has proved to be an effective means to expose not only false testimony but, more frequently, inaccurate testimony. Two adversaries, approaching the facts from entirely different perspectives and functioning within the framework of an orderly set of rules, will uncover more of the truth than investigators seeking to compose a picture of the event. Scientists may quarrel with this technique for discovering facts, because their approach is properly one of discovering absolute truth. But lawyers know that our legal system is a human creation and does not exclusively seek absolute truth. Rather, it is subject to limiting rules directed at higher values and larger purposes than would be a system that guarantees the conviction of every transgressor. Just as we reject, for example, torture and other inhumane techniques, so also we reject certain modes of investigation that, although not inhumane, are incompatible with the values of a free people. Moreover, a human-created system, inevitably finite and fallible, must provide safeguards to account for its fallibility. Because some error is inevitable, the adversary system deliberately chooses to err on the side of the guilty in order to protect the innocent.

Ideally, the neutrality of the judge and jury reflects the historical wisdom of our mode of justice: Parties who bring a matter to the attention of the courts are likely to accept the decision of a neutral tribunal. In the context of a criminal case, this means that the victim and the public must accept the finality of an acquittal or a disposition less

---

WEB

Are you interested in what the American courtrooms of the future might be like? If so, **visit the link to the Maricopa County Court on our Web site, www.prenhall.com/territo**.

harsh than they desired. For the defendant, a neutral tribunal provides assurance of fair treatment and establishes confidence that encourages him or her to stand trial rather than to flee or otherwise seek to subvert the legal process. If found guilty, the defendant must, in theory, then accept the penalty in a spirit conducive to rehabilitation.

Each adversary in a situation must have ample opportunity to present information relevant to the final court decision. The rules of procedure and evidence are designed to protect that opportunity within the bounds of time and the judge or jury's capacity to absorb information—as well as to preclude (so far as is possible) the introduction of material that does not contribute to the rational disposition of a case.

As limited by rules and procedures, the adversary system is also designed to ensure that the goals of finding the facts and treating everyone justly and fairly are not achieved at the expense of human dignity. Common-law legal institutions long ago decided that the system must permit (but not require) the accused to compel the state to establish guilt under the rules of procedure and evidence—even though the accused may privately admit facts that, if shown, would warrant a guilty verdict. Thus, lawyers are often asked to defend a person who has admitted guilt.

Traditionally, guilt is ascertained only at the conclusion of the adversarial trial process. Our purpose is not merely to protect an innocent person from the possibility of an unjust conviction, precious as that objective is, but to preserve the integrity of society itself. The system aims at keeping sound and wholesome the procedures by which society expresses its condemnation on an erring member. The essence of the adversary system is challenge. The survival of our system of criminal justice and the value that it advances depends on constant searching, and creative questioning of official decisions and authority. Lawyers serve this function when they secure the acquittal of defendants, undeserving though they may be, when conviction is sought by methods repugnant to basic values protected by the Constitution. This is the rationale behind the suppression doctrine, an essentially American invention, by which reliable evidence may be excluded from a trial because of the manner in which it was acquired. In sum, the adversary system seeks to accomplish justice by eliciting facts that can be proven under fixed rules of procedure. This policy, evolved largely by judges, is designed to ensure that trials are conducted fairly in both reality and appearance.

CTQ

"The primary adversarial relationship in the courts is not between the plaintiff (prosecutor, or state) and the defendant, but rather between the ideal of justice and the reality of bureaucratic limitations." Explain why you agree or disagree with this statement.

The Prevalence of Guilty Pleas in the American Criminal Justice System

The most common disposition of a felony arrest that is not rejected or dismissed is some form of a guilty plea, according to a Bureau of Justice Statistics special report. The Constitution guarantees the right to trial by jury and protects against self-incrimination; however, for at least sixty years, defendant pleas of guilty, not trial by jury, have been the more common means of criminal case conviction.[46] Although defendants have a right to trial to determine guilt or innocence, many decide to plead guilty to the original or reduced charges. Bureau of Justice Statistics data obtained from prosecutors in a number of urban jurisdictions show that in 1999, 45 of every 100 felony arrests ended in guilty pleas, while only 5 ended in trials (four guilty verdicts and one acquittal). The remaining dispositions (50 of every 100) were rejections and dismissals. Consistent with prior studies, guilty pleas were found to outnumber trials about ten to one.

Recognition of this fact—that the majority of convictions are the result of a guilty plea rather than a guilty verdict—has since the mid-1960s fostered a vigorous national debate over the importance of the criminal court as a cornerstone of the criminal justice system. Since the criminal trial occurs so seldom, we must ask why the criminal court is so important. At the center of this debate is the role the prosecutor plays in obtaining guilty pleas.[47]

The Adversarial Model of the Criminal Trial versus the Reality of Plea Bargaining

What is the fundamental essence that dominates the ethos of all American courtrooms? The source of American pride in the criminal justice system is most often based on the fairness of due process procedures, adversary-system methodology, the extracting of truth and exposing of falsehoods, the dynamic nature of the jury, the presumption of innocence, the requirement of proof for guilt beyond a reasonable doubt, the manner by which the criminal rules of evidence are used so that only the most reliable and truthful evidence is heard by the jury, and the rule of the judge as a neutral and detached administrator of the law. Most Americans believe that these features produce the best form of justice (although not a perfect form) compared to any previous or present justice system in any civilization. This superlative is especially grounded in the American criminal trial process and its adversarial nature, because of the importance of the criminal trial in the criminal justice system; one often refers to the trial as the "balance wheel of the entire process."[48]

> **CTQ**
> Is it true that there is no concern for truth in our adversarial system of justice?

The adversary proceeding is the heart of a criminal trial. This is a formal process conducted in an orderly and specific fashion according to the rules of criminal evidence, the Constitution, and the criminal law. In the adversary process, both the prosecution and the defense follow specific requirements in order to argue the merits of their cases in the most favorable light and in the most persuasive manner before the jury. While it cannot be denied that drama is inherent in adversarial proceedings, the jury trial has proven—over centuries of evolution to its present form—to be a reliable means of uncovering the truth. It accomplishes this by following a formal set of rules for presenting evidence; rules that seek to deny advantage to either the prosecution or the defense. Much of what laypeople might regard as fussy preoccupation with procedural details of interpretations of legal precedent is, in fact, the expression of a painstaking effort to eliminate bias.[49]

Nijboer, referring to the adversary nature of American criminal jurisprudence, calls the jury trial a "sublimated brawl."[50] Smith and Pollack seriously question the generality and validity of the public image of the courtroom as a place where "truth is discovered through. . . trial by combat between two equally armed lawyer-gladiators, with the struggle presided over by the judge (as repository of the wisdom of the community)."[51] Despite criticism, however, the adversary model of courtroom procedure is one of the most cherished legacies of English common law and a symbol of the freedoms guaranteed to American citizens under the U.S. Constitution.

> **WEB**
> The National Center for Victims of Crime take a strong stand with regard to plea bargaining. For more information, **visit the link to the center on our Web site,** www.prenhall.com/territo.

Yet while such accolades are poured on the American criminal court system, it may or may not embody the best way to determine the truth, and may or may not give defendants due process rights, depending on what aspect of the criminal justice system is being glorified. It is only the adversarial nature of criminal court cases and trial procedures is worthy of this recognition and these superlatives.

Unfortunately, the adversarial system's acuity at dispensing justice is a rare occurrence. Indeed, in most cities, the criminal trial is but a minor function in producing criminal verdicts. Instead, the part of the system that produces more than 90 percent of the system's verdicts—plea bargaining—receives no such superlatives and little recognition. Justice is not accomplished because most punishments issued in plea bargains are sentences that are much lower than permitted by the seriousness of the crime. Often, even though several crimes were committed, the defendant is ultimately charged with only one of them.

THE DYNAMICS OF THE CRIMINAL COURT

Let us begin our examination by analyzing two of the three main lawyers in the trial phase of the criminal justice system—the prosecutor and the defense attorney (the third, of course, is the judge). In order to be eligible for these roles, both must first receive a legal education. Although historically a legal education meant many things, including an apprenticeship, in order to receive a legal education today, prosecutors and defense attorneys must initially obtain an undergraduate degree from a university. Subsequently, they must complete three years of law school. After seven years of formal education, a would-be attorney must then pass a state bar examination before a license to practice law in that state is issued. Many young lawyers get their first practical experience in the legal profession by accepting positions as prosecutors or public defenders.

THE PROSECUTOR

In the Western world, a **prosecuting attorney** generally is recognized as the legal representative of the state, with sole responsibility for bringing criminal charges. In the United States, he or she is referred to as a *district attorney, state's attorney,* or *county attorney.* The prosecutor in the American criminal justice system differs markedly from prosecutors in the systems from which our legal institutions originated—Roman law and English common law.

An American prosecutor is a government attorney who instigates the prosecution of an accused person and represents the state at trial. Most often, the prosecutor is an elected public official and, as such, is considered the chief law enforcement agent within a jurisdiction. Normally, the prosecutor determines which cases will be brought to trial and in what manner they will be disposed of. The prosecutor also determines whether the case presented to his or her office by the police is legally sufficient and, if so, in which court it will be pursued. The prosecutor further decides whether the original charges against the accused will be reduced or even dropped. In many jurisdictions, prosecutors assist law enforcement agencies in searches, arrests, and investigations of targeted criminal activity.

Across the nation, about 2,350 prosecutors' offices handle felony cases in state trial courts. A chief prosecutor is the attorney who is primarily responsible for advocating for the public in felony cases and in a variety of misdemeanor cases. State law determines the number of chief prosecutors in a state and whether they are elected or appointed. More than 95 percent of chief prosecutors are elected locally.

During the 1990s, state court prosecutors' offices employed approximately 65,000 total staff, with a median annual office budget of $226,000. The median staff size was eight. In about 70 percent of prosecutors' offices, the chief prosecutor served full-time. Furthermore, half of the offices closed 250 or more felony cases and obtained 180 or more convictions.[52]

The Prosecutor's Specific Function

The prosecutor's function in the criminal justice system is at best unclear. Prosecutors serve the state in a number of different ways. They give counsel to the police department and draft legal opinions on the latest changes in constitutional law to use as a guide to modify future police procedures. More important, a district attorney is the primary representative of the state in court. As the state's chief law investigative officer, the prosecutor draws the line when police conduct infringes upon individual rights. And as an elected official, the prosecutor must reflect community opinion in making decisions on whether to prosecute (see "In the News: An Irresistible Case").

The Advisory Committee on the Prosecution and Defense Functions of the American Bar Association has pointed out that, unlike any of the other major players in the administration of justice, the role of the prosecutor spans the entire criminal justice process.[53] Prosecutors, taking a cue from law enforcement agencies' community policing initiatives, are establishing similar programs aimed at involving members of their communities in the justice system.

Step by Step—the Prosecutor's Role

In almost every major step of the criminal justice system, the prosecutor has an important role:

> *Investigation.* During the investigation phase of the criminal justice process, prosecutors prepare search and arrest warrants and work with police in ensuring that investigative reports are complete. In some circumstances, either through citizen complaints or suspicion of alleged criminal acts, prosecutors initiate their own investigations, which may be independent of police activity.
>
> *Arrest.* Subsequent to arrest, prosecutors screen cases to determine which should be prosecuted and which should be dropped.
>
> *Initial appearance.* During the first court appearance, the prosecutor ensures that all defendants are notified of the charges against them. Additionally, prosecutors

---

WEB

For more information on prosecution, **visit the link to the Bureau of Justice Statistics on our Web site,** www.prenhall.com/territo.

CTQ

Should the prosecutor's office be an elected or an appointed position? Is it possible to separate politics from the prosecutor's office?

WEB

To learn more about current research on prosecutorial issues, **visit the link to the American Prosecutors Research Institute on our Web site,** www.prenhall.com/territo.

WEB

A number of reports on community justice programs are available from the Center for Court Innovation. For more information, **visit the link to the center on our Web site,** www.prenhall.com/territo.

IN THE NEWS

A HUMAN PERSPECTIVE

AN IRRESISTIBLE CASE—A PROSECUTOR IS CHOSEN TO LITIGATE THE OKLAHOMA CITY BOMBING CASE
by P. Annin, A. Murr, and M. Liv

Joe Hartzler always relished the big-time cases. As one of Chicago's hottest federal prosecutors in the 1980s, he put away Puerto Rican terrorists and corrupt public officials, winning over juries with his Boy Scout's demeanor and first-rate legal mind. In 1989, as Hartzler parlayed his success into a job with a prestigious private firm, he visited a doctor about the strange weakness in his legs. The diagnosis was multiple sclerosis, the neurological disease that would eventually rob him of his ability to walk. Hartzler took stock and realized that he missed government service and wanted more time with his family. In 1991 he returned to the United States Attorney's Office, in slower-paced Springfield, Ill., where he could nail bad guys and still coach his son's Little League team.

As Hartzler listened in his car to radio accounts of the Oklahoma City bombing, its enormity sank in. When he heard Attorney General Janet Reno was looking for prosecutors, Hartzler, 44, decided he had one more big case left in him. "Whoever did this should spend some time in hell," he told a local defense attorney. "I just want to accelerate that process." Hartzler got his chance. Reno selected him to head up the eight-member government team which indicted Timothy McVeigh and Terry Nichols, the only two suspects in custody.

Casting is everything in a major trial. So with dozens of attorneys available for the grueling assignment, why Hartzler? Some suggested that a wheelchair-bound prosecutor would appeal to a jury in a case with so many maimed victims. Others saw a malleable personality easily micromanaged by superiors in Washington. Federal officials say they see something else in Hartzler: an attorney with superb trial skills and an even-handed style that will wear well with a jury, especially against the proverb-spouting theatrics of Mike Tigar, Nichols's lawyer. And in a case in which McVeigh's counsel, Stephen Jones, portrayed his client as a misunderstood Persian Gulf veteran victimized by a heavy-handed federal government, Hartzler's all-American persona—he was honored at the White House in May as MS Father of the Year—is attractive to Justice Department officials. "He's a levelheaded guy who's got his priorities right," said one top Reno aide. Deputy Attorney General Jamie Gorelick, who met Hartzler when they worked at a Washington law firm two decades ago, calls him an "incredibly nice guy who'd go over well in the heartland."

Hartzler came to the case with a reputation for pulling together the strands of complex and politically sensitive criminal investigations. In 1985 he prosecuted members of FALN, a Puerto Rican nationalist group that killed five people in a nine-year bombing spree. The collegial Hartzler smoothed over the turf fights that often leave federal agents and prosecutors at each other's throats. "When the eyes of the world are upon you, it takes a special type of person to bring out the best in people," says former Chicago prosecutor Jeremy Margolis.

But is he up to the job? While stress and heat can aggravate MS, medical experts say Hartzler shouldn't have a problem if he takes reasonable precautions. Friends say that Hartzler, who declined to talk to *Newsweek*, was serious about reordering his life. But author Greg Smith, who has known him for 30 years, said he's "always had an ambivalent relationship to the fast track.... The Oklahoma case came along and he saw this as a second chance at the brass ring."

Much of America thinks Hartzler has an open-and-shut case. He knows better. Hartzler decided to cut deals for potentially damning testimony from witnesses like McVeigh's friend Mike Fortier—rather than risk trying to sell a largely circumstantial case to a jury. Hartzler realized that the stakes were high. Springfield defense attorney Brian Otwell spoke with him about the huge expectations. "It's the kind of case you have nightmares about," Otwell remembers telling him. He said that Hartzler agreed. But Joe Hartzler might have lost more sleep had he decided to pass on the case of a lifetime. [Note: Hartzler acquired murder convictions on McVeigh and Nichols, which he sought on all counts.]

Source: P. Annin, A. Murr, and M. Liv, "An Irresistible Case—A Prosecutor Is Chosen to Litigate the Oklahoma City Bombing Case." From *Newsweek*, August 14, 1995. © 1995 Newsweek, Inc. All rights reserved. Reprinted by permission.

---

serve as the government's attorney in minor cases. They also participate in bail decisions. Importantly, prosecutors can also discontinue a prosecution by drafting a *nolle prosequi*. A *nolle prosequi*, also referred to as *nol. pros.*, consists of formally entering into the record the prosecution's declaration that the state is unwilling to prosecute the case. It is an agreement not to proceed further.

Grand jury. The prosecutor is the judge and prosecutor within the grand jury. He or she is the only major legal officer in the room when the citizens determine whether to indict. The prosecutor is the only person who chooses what evidence the grand jury will hear and not hear in order to make their decision.

Preliminary hearing. Prosecutors have two functions at the preliminary hearing: to establish probable cause or to *nol. pros.* cases when appropriate. In jurisdictions where they have no initial appearance but proceed directly to the preliminary hearing, prosecutors have the additional task of giving formal notice of charges and participating in bail decisions.

Information and indictment. The prosecutor prepares the information that establishes probable cause and binds an accused over for trial. In jurisdictions that use indictment rather than information, prosecutors establish probable cause before the grand jury.

Arraignment. In this proceeding, prosecutors arraign particular defendants. They bring an accused person to the court to answer to the matters charged in the information or indictment (see Chapter 9). Prosecutors also participate in plea negotiation during this time. Plea negotiation allows defendants to plead guilty to a reduced charge or charges and can occur at any time between formal charging and the reading of the verdict.

Pretrial motions. As representatives of the state, prosecutors initiate and participate in the argument for any pretrial motions.

Trial. Prosecutors are the government's trial lawyers, and as such, argue to prove the guilt of the accused beyond a reasonable doubt (see Figure 7.8).

Sentencing. Prosecutors make sentencing recommendations to the judge, usually arguing for more rigid punishment. Sometimes, however, they suggest a lenient sentence to the trial judge.

Appeal. Through written and oral debate, prosecutors ensure that convictions were obtained properly and should not be reversed before appellate courts.

Parole. In some jurisdictions, prosecutors make recommendations for or against parole for inmates up for review. In most instances, however, prosecutors typically limit themselves to opposing early release of serious offenders.

Probation and parole revocation hearing. When a probationer or parolee violates a condition of probation or parole, he or she is entitled to a hearing to determine whether probation or parole will be revoked. Prosecutors act as advocates for the state in these hearings.[54] (For a more detailed discussion of probation and parole, see Chapter 13.)

FIGURE 7.8

The prosecutor makes her opening statement to the jury.

Courtesy Jeff Cadge/Getty Images, Inc.-Image Bank.

It is at trial where the prosecutor most fully manifests his or her role as an advocate. This role means that the prosecutor will present his or her side of the case with as much passion, one-sidedness, vigor, and logic that a reasonable interpretation of the facts from an extreme point of view allows. However, there are limits beyond which a prosecutor may not passionately argue the state's case. Although the crime may be insulting and the acts alleged may be insulting to all who become aware of them, prosecutors are not allowed to be insulting.

If the prosecutor is successful at trial, then he or she also represents the state at the sentencing hearing, which often occurs sometime later. In this hearing, the prosecutor will argue the state's position for the appropriate sentence to give to the convicted felon for the judge's consideration. Although normally the state attorney general's office handles any appeals from a felony conviction, there are times when the trial prosecutor, because he or she is so involved with a case, will want to participate in writing appellate briefs and arguing the merits of the appeal before the appellate court.

The Prosecutor's Public Image

The final function of the prosecutor is to maintain a certain media image. As part of the deterrent effort of their office, prosecutors often appear on television with messages to the public at large that people who commit crimes similar to the ones they are prosecuting will be prosecuted vigorously and sentenced sternly. These types of prosecutorial appearances, however, are not the only television appearances made by prosecutors. In other instances, the chief law enforcer appears for the purpose of seeking reelection. Media presentations may also be made by a subordinate who desires his or her boss to be reelected. Fortunately or unfortunately, in the beginning of the twenty-first century, many people are elected due to the frequency of their media exposure and their name recognition rather than because of their qualifications for the office. Hence, prosecutors seem to be making statements on the six o'clock news with far greater regularity than was true twenty years ago.

The political involvement of the prosecutor varies by jurisdiction. In some jurisdictions, prosecutors are required to run with a party designation; other prosecutors are elected on a nonpartisan basis. The powers of prosecutors are formidable, and these men and women are important in their communities. If they are not truly independent and professional, their powers can be misused for political or other improper purposes. Perhaps even more than that of other public officials, the prosecutor's activity is largely open to public gaze—as it should be—and spotlighted by the press.

Division of Prosecutorial Duties

The prosecutor has specific functions in various stages of the criminal justice system. In many state prosecution offices, prosecutorial tasks are divided into either *segmented* or *fluid* prosecutorial functions.

In a segmented office, only a certain number of prosecutors within the office perform duties during one particular stage of the system. For example, in many metropolitan areas, the younger prosecutors fill the prosecutorial role at initial appearances and preliminary hearings. More-senior prosecutors in these systems often determine whether the facts warrant sufficient evidence to bring criminal charges and, if so, what charges will be made. Other prosecutors in segmented offices are in charge of arraignments and pretrial motions. Still another group of attorneys work as the state's trial litigators. These attorneys present the case to a jury and litigate it. Still another group of lawyers handles cases exclusively on appeal.

In fluid offices, some state attorneys handle a case from beginning to end. This system is more conducive to smaller offices, although some extraordinarily large offices also use this system. Prosecutors in fluid offices take a case from its inception; they are involved in its investigation and continue with the case as it is processed through the system. This means that the prosecutors assist in investigation, prepare search or arrest warrants, and often initiate their own investigations. This same prosecutor subsequently will determine who will be arrested, who should be prosecuted, and what crimes have been committed. The prosecutor will also represent the state during the accused's initial appearance; participate in bail decisions; and, most important, make a rather autonomous decision as to whether the case warrants litigation. This means that the prosecutor may choose to discontinue all prosecution action through filing a motion for *nolle prosequi*.

In a fluid office, the same prosecutor will also represent the state at a preliminary hearing. There the prosecutor will call the necessary witnesses to prove probable cause that a crime has been committed and that the defendant committed it. The same prosecutor, if necessary, also will represent the state during grand jury proceedings. There he or she will seek to indict targeted defendants.

The Decision to Prosecute

Deciding whether to prosecute and what the charge will be is the focus of the formal job of the prosecuting attorney. These determinations can legally be made by the prosecutor alone, and the consequences have a great impact, not only on defendants, but also on the other agencies that participate in the administration of justice.

CTQ
Does the prosecutor have too much power over the criminal justice process? What is his or her most powerful tool of controlling the criminal justice process?

As the due process model emphasizes (see Chapter 3), a decision to label a citizen a defendant in a criminal action should be undertaken only with full and serious understanding. There are negative aspects to being arrested, but there are even greater penalties attached to being charged with a crime. Once a suspect becomes a defendant, the entire weight of the criminal justice process is brought to bear on the individual. The state may restrain the person's liberty, and economic burdens are imposed by the requirement that bail be posted and a lawyer hired. There is also the nontangible penalty of damage to the person's reputation; though the public gives lip service to the idea of "innocent until proven guilty," it may also subscribe to the notion that where there's smoke, there's fire.[55]

LANDMARK CASE — United States v. Armstrong

Mr. Armstrong was arrested for a violation of federal drug and firearm laws. He alleged that he had been selected for prosecution because he was African American, and filed a motion for dismissal of the charges and for discovery of government documents regarding the prosecution of similar defendants. The district court granted the discovery motion and dismissed the indictment when the government would not comply with discovery. The court of appeals reversed but then, upon hearing the case *en banc,* affirmed the district court's order of dismissal. The Supreme Court granted *certiorari* and answered the following issue: "Must a criminal defendant bringing a selective-prosecution claim make a credible showing of different treatment of similarly situated persons in order to obtain discovery in support of the claim?"

Chief Justice Rehnquist said yes, they must, and reversed and remanded the lower court's decision. Rehnquist cited the rule that "a criminal defendant bringing a selective-prosecution claim must make a credible showing of different treatment of similarly situated persons in order to obtain discovery in support of the claim. Rehnquist continued, stating that under Federal Rule of Criminal Procedure 16, which controls discovery in a criminal case, a defendant must show some evidence of disparate treatment—similar to the requirement under equal-protection claims. Rehnquist concluded that here Armstrong did not make such a showing. Thus, the district court's dismissal of the case was improper.

Source: *United States v. Armstrong,* 16 S. Ct. 1480 (1996).

The Power of Prosecutorial Discretion

Under American law, criminal litigation generally does not occur until an action is initiated by a prosecutor. The prosecutor has the power of discretion—the power to decide whether to investigate citizens, order arrests, present one-sided arguments to the grand jury, and recommend sentences to the court. It is also the prosecutor's decision whether a charge will be pursued, reduced, plea bargained, or dropped altogether—and these choices are made with little or no statutory or caselaw guidance.[56] The duties of the prosecutor are generally not specifically defined by law—other than by state statutes and constitutions that require the "prosecutor to proceed with litigation against those who transgress the jurisdiction's laws," or by case law that describes the prosecutor's duties in equally general terms (see the Landmark Case *United States v. Armstrong*).

Prosecutorial discretion is normally initiated after arrest. Prosecutors receive a copy of the police reports in their office and screen and evaluate the merit of these reports. In a fluid office, one particular prosecutor will decide whether to go forward with the case. In a segmented office, the decision to go forward is made by committee or by senior members of the staff. The decision whether to go forward to trial is called selective prosecution.

When a case is brought to the attention of a prosecutor, he or she may simply refuse to proceed. Even after charges are filed or a grand jury indictment is in, the process can be stopped by the principle of *nolle prosequi,* the halting of prosecution. A prosecutor may even ask the court to dismiss the charges. The right of the prosecutor not to prosecute further in a case is without higher review; this is true in spite of the fact that sufficient evidence may exist for conviction. This type of decision is singularly the most powerful example of discretionary authority within the criminal justice system.

Although some district attorneys' offices have an internal review of *nol. pros.* decisions within the office, many do not. Only in rare instances does the judiciary intervene in the prosecutor's decision not to prosecute. After all, the state is the victim of every crime. It is the state's right to decide whether to go forward with charges on a crime. Nonetheless, the use of *nol. pros.* in thousands of cases annually has lent itself to obvious

CTQ

Comparing the roles of the police and the prosecutors, who has more discretion, and who has greater potential for abuse of their discretion? Why?

CTQ

Why are public prosecutors considered to be the most dominant figures in the American criminal justice system?

> **CTQ**
>
> What, if any, are some of the judicial restraints put on prosecutorial discretion? What are some of the system factors and case factors that affect the prosecutor's decision making process?

problems. The possibility of favoritism and discrimination, corruption, nepotism, and bribery always exists when discretionary powers are that great and unchecked.

Unethical Procedures and Wrongful Conviction

The large amount of discretion held by the prosecutor creates considerable abuse potential. Discretionary decisions not to prosecute friends or political cronies, or to accept guilty pleas to drastically reduced charges for personal considerations, are always dangerous possibilities. On the other hand, overzealous prosecution, or district attorneys seeking heightened visibility in order to support grand political ambitions, can be another source of difficulty. Administrative decisions such as case scheduling can also be used by prosecutors to harass defendants into pleading guilty. Some forms of abuse may be unconscious. At least one study suggests that some prosecutors tend toward leniency for female defendants, but tend to discriminate against minorities in deciding whether to prosecute.[57]

> **CTQ**
>
> What is "prosecutorial vindictiveness" and what have the courts done to control it?

Although the citizens are the final authority to whom prosecutors must answer, gross misconduct by prosecutors may be addressed by the state supreme court or the state attorney general's office. Short of criminal misconduct, however, most of the options available to either the court or the attorney general are limited. As members of the legal profession, prosecutors are subject to the Code of Professional Responsibility of the American Bar Association (ABA). Serious violations of the code may result in their being disbarred from the practice of law. The ABA standard for Criminal Justice 3-1.1 describes the prosecutor's duty this way: "The duty of the prosecutor is to seek justice, not to merely convict." Hence, a prosecutor is barred by the standards of the legal profession from advocating any fact or position that he or she knows is untrue.[58] One wonders if the sheriff in "In the News: The Frame Game" was in collusion with the prosecutor the whole time.

IN THE NEWS
A HUMAN PERSPECTIVE

THE FRAME GAME
by A. Cohen

It was the kind of crime that breaks a community's heart. Ten-year-old Jeanine Nicarico, home from school with a cold, was taken from her suburban Chicago house in broad daylight, raped and killed. Her badly beaten body was discovered two days later in a wooded area six miles away. The public demanded that the murder be solved, and the police obliged. DuPage County residents slept a little better after police arrested Rolando Cruz, a street tough from a nearby town. Local prosecutors finished the job, presenting a solid case that landed Cruz on Illinois death row.

The only trouble was that Cruz didn't kill Jeanine Nicarico. A sheriff's officer later admitted that he testified inaccurately about a key piece of evidence used at Cruz's trial. Cruz was freed in 1995, after 11 years in jail. Another man—a convicted murderer and rapist whose earlier confession to the murder had been ignored—was linked to the crime by DNA. After an independent investigation, seven prosecutors and law enforcement officials were indicted on charges of fabricating and suppressing evidence to frame Cruz.

The trial of the DuPage Seven, as they are known, began the first week in April, 1999. If found guilty, the prosecutors in the group would be the first in the nation ever convicted of crimes for railroading an innocent man. The charges, which the defendants deny, have caused an uproar in Illinois. The state has freed two men from its death row this year after investigations supported their innocence.

The Illinois cases of errant prosecution bring a new element to the growing national debate about overzealous law enforcement agents, a furor stoked by high-profile police shootings in New York and California, as well as "racial profiling" by New Jersey state troopers. The question is whether law enforcement, amid its extraordinary success in pushing the crime rate down, is showing too little regard for individual rights—especially those of blacks and Hispanics, who are most often targets of alleged misconduct.

UPDATE
After almost eleven hours of deliberation, the five men accused of railroading Rolando Cruz onto death row were acquitted of charges of conspiracy, perjury, obstruction of justice, and official misconduct. The announcement of the verdicts sparked bedlam in the courtroom.

Source: A. Cohen, "The Frame Game," *Time*, March 29, 1999. © 1999 TIME, Inc. Reprinted by permission.

The Prosecutor's Constitutional Duty to Disclose Evidence Favorable to the Defendant

For most of the twentieth century, discussion of corruption and other forms of misconduct in criminal justice have focused on police behavior. Increasingly, however, problems in the legal and judicial sectors have become more visible. Moreover, a variety of criticisms have been aimed at all members of the courtroom work group.

There have been charges of dishonesty—a growing number of judges, lawyers, and prosecutors are being accused of conflicts of interest, defrauding clients, or participating in other misdeeds that reflect contempt for professional ethics. There have been charges of greed—lawyers are being accused of charging fees that go far beyond what is justified by the work involved. And there have been charges of incompetence—various legal practitioners are being cited for costly mistakes and inexcusable errors during trials. In addition to ineffective representation on the part of attorneys, there are cases of misconduct on the part of prosecutors and judges. Prosecutors can take advantage of defendants and compromise their rights by knowingly admitting false testimony and hiding evidence.[59]

Prosecutorial Diversion

A middle ground between a prosecutor dropping a case and going forward with a full criminal trial is *diversion*. The prosecutors who use diversion often believe that the ideals of justice can be better served if they do not seek criminal trial. Traditionally, the accused were diverted by requiring them to join the army, join the Peace Corps, or promise never to come back to town. Today, however, diversion has taken on a much more sophisticated meaning. Often the accused receive psychological, social, and medical help to deal with problems thought to be at the root of their criminal behavior. Likewise, if the accused are first-time offenders, these diversions allow them to escape the label of "criminal." This gives them a better chance to reintegrate into society.

Adjudication Deferred/Withheld Adjudication

For first-and second-time offenders as well as youthful offenders, many prosecutors nationwide have determined that in certain cases, it is in the best interest of society that the adjudication of guilt of such defendants be deferred or withheld. An agreement between the prosecution and defense to receive a **deferred adjudication** is usually the result of a plea bargain. Although it is required that the defendant plead guilty or *nolo contendere* in these cases, the trial judge does not find the defendant at that time. Instead, the judge defers making a finding of guilt on the issue in question. Afterwards, the defendant is usually placed on probation for a specified period of months and is required to perform some type of community service. If the defendant violates a condition of probation during a probationary period, then the court adjudicates him or her guilty and assesses new punishment. However, if the probationary period has expired and the court has not received a violation notice, then the court at a stated future time will enter an order of dismissal for the proceedings against him or her. This order discharges the defendant.

Normally, a dismissal and discharge under either deferred-adjudication or adjudication-withheld programs may not be deemed a conviction for any purpose within American society. The only exception is upon subsequent conviction of the same state's criminal statutes. This particular tool of the prosecutor affords a valued second chance to people who have made a mistake, have learned their lesson, and probably will never recidivate.

Too Many Cases, Too Few Prosecutors

Of the 90 percent of adults convicted of felonies that were reported in the 1990s, 56 percent of them were sent to prison, according to a statewide study.[60] For every felony conviction in most jurisdictions, an additional ten misdemeanor cases were processed. This increase in cases has caused extreme court congestion, delays in trials, and a clogged-up criminal justice system.

CTQ

What is the primary duty of the prosecutor in your opinion? Is it to seek justice, or is it merely to secure a conviction?

WEB

To see the American Bar Association's Ethical Standards for the Prosecution and Defense, visit the ABA link on our Web site, www.prenhall.com/territo.

THE CRIMINAL DEFENSE LAWYER

Most American lawyers either never take a criminal case or do so only on rare occasions. Most lawyers commonly view criminal defense as one of the least desirable fields of specialization. Wice estimates that the total number of lawyers, excluding public defenders, who "accept criminal cases more than occasionally" is approximately 14,000. Another study indicates that no more than 1 percent of all private practitioners in Manhattan and the Bronx consider themselves criminal lawyers.[61]

As stated in Chapter 3, the Sixth Amendment provides that in all felony criminal prosecutions, the accused shall enjoy the right to counsel for his or her defense. Despite this rather unambiguous language, for almost a century and a half after the framing of the Constitution, only people charged with federal crimes punishable by death were guaranteed the right to counsel. However, as stated previously, all of this changed when the Court's most significant decision, *Gideon v. Wainwright*, was decided in 1963. In that case, the Supreme Court extended the right to counsel to all state indigent defendants facing felony trials.

The Role of the Criminal Defense Lawyer

The primary responsibility of the **defense attorney** is to represent a defendant, who has the constitutional right to counsel. The defense attorney is responsible for preparing the case and for selecting the defense strategy. In the criminal justice process, the defense attorney is the counterpart of the prosecuting attorney.

An American placed on trial in an American courtroom has the right to be represented by counsel. This is considered a fundamental liberty in the American criminal justice system. Defendants facing criminal charges need a lawyer to assist them. The procedures and the laws that they must understand require a certain type of expertise that most criminal defendants themselves do not have. A lawyer helps these defendants understand the nature and consequences of the proceedings against them and courtroom operations, and assists them in attacking the prosecution's case while bolstering their own. The American Bar Association suggests that the defense counsel performs a multitude of functions while representing a client throughout a criminal proceeding: representing the accused immediately after arrest to provide advice during interrogation and to ensure constitutional safeguards during pretrial procedures; reviewing police reports and further investigating the details of the offense; interviewing the police, the accused, and the witnesses in seeking out additional evidence on behalf of the accused; discussing the offense with the prosecutor to gain initial insight into the strength of the state's case; representing the accused at bail hearings and during plea negotiations; preparing, filing, and arguing various pretrial motions; preparing the case for trial; participating in jury selection; representing the accused at the trial; providing advice and assistance at sentencing; determining and pursuing an appropriate basis for appeal; and presenting written or oral arguments for appeal.[62]

Because of the extraordinary volume of crime, both private and public defense attorneys (especially in urban areas) face immense caseloads that severely limit the quality of the services they are able to provide. The "sausage factory" character of many urban criminal courts creates strong pressures on defenders to process cases rapidly. And the interpersonal relationships between prosecutors and defenders combine with court pressures to motivate the defense to "keep the assembly line moving." Thus, a strong pressure exists on criminal defendants to plea bargain. This pressure may not come from the prosecutor, but from the defense lawyer. In this way, private and public defenders contribute to a decline in the quality of justice dispensed by the criminal courts.[63]

Defending a criminal client involves both informal and formal procedures. The usual goal of a defense lawyer is to get the best possible result for the client. This result, in light of the circumstances, might be the lowest sentence possible, and that sentence might be a life sentence in prison. On the other hand, the defense counsel's function is to ensure that the accused's safeguards are protected at trial and were protected during investigation and processing through the criminal justice system (see "In the News: What Do Lawyers Want to Know?"). If these rights were not sufficiently protected, the defense lawyer makes various motions to try to correct these inadequacies and at the same

---

CTQ

Do defense attorneys have an obligation to defend a client who they know is guilty of committing the criminal act? Why or why not?

CTQ

Should criminal defense attorneys disclose information given to them by their clients concerning their participation in earlier unsolved crimes?

IN THE NEWS

A HUMAN PERSPECTIVE

WHAT DO LAWYERS WANT TO KNOW?

There are two approaches: some never want to know what their client did. Others, myself included, believe there's no way you can render proper legal advice unless you get from your client every thing he knows, even if that means you can't put your client on the stand. But it also means you won't be surprised later when something incriminating comes out. And you'll be able to consider how things might look incriminating might be explained to look less so.

Source: "What Do Lawyers Want to Know?" *U.S. News & World Report,* March 17, 1997. Copyright 1997 *U.S. News & World Report, L.P.* Reprinted with permission.

---

time essentially make the prosecutor's life miserable with a paper blizzard of motions that will likely take many hours to answer. Motions are often a vehicle by which prosecutors become more lenient in their plea-bargaining discussions.

More than 90 percent of all citizens accused of a crime in the United States cannot afford to retain counsel. They are then given the right to government counsel at no charge to them; or, if they so choose, they may represent themselves. Self-representation is called **pro se.**

The Supreme Court recognizes that the Sixth Amendment does not merely provide a lawyer for the accused. It grants to the accused, personally, the right to make his or her own defense. It is the accused, not counsel, who must be informed of the nature and the cause of the accusation and who must be confronted with witnesses against him or her, said the Court. Hence, the right to counsel also includes the right to act as one's own counsel.[64]

Even a defendant who can afford private counsel is not guaranteed competent or interested legal representation. Many lawyers who station themselves outside municipal courtrooms and offer their services to people brought in by officers have a vested financial interest in encouraging their clients to plead guilty. Few of these types of lawyers are willing or able to conduct extensive investigations on behalf of their clients or to engage in intensive pretrial preparation. The best (that is, the most competent and interested) criminal lawyers are more expensive; there is frequently a direct correlation between the defendant's ability to pay and the quality of representation he or she receives. For indigents, private counsel is not a viable option, and the only avenue for their defense is through public defenders or court-appointed attorneys.

The defense counsel is an attorney as well as an officer of the court. As an attorney, the defense counsel is obligated to uphold the integrity of the legal profession and to observe the requirements of the Model Rules of Professional Conduct in the defense of a client. According to these rules, the duties of the lawyer to the adversary system of justice are as follows: investigating the incident; interviewing the client, police, and other witnesses; discussing the matter with the prosecutor; representing the defendant at the various pretrial procedures (arrest, interrogation, and arraignment); entering into plea negotiations; preparing the case for trial; filing and arguing legal motions with the court; representing the defendant at trial; providing assistance at sentencing; and determining the appropriate basis for appeal. These are some of the major duties of any defense attorney, whether privately employed by the accused, appointed by the court, or serving as a public defender.

Our legal system provides for the adjudication of disputes governed by the rules of substantive, evidentiary, and procedural law. An adversary presentation counters the natural human tendency to judge too swiftly in terms of the familiar instead of that which is not known; the advocate, by his or her zealous preparation of facts and law, enables the tribunal to come to the hearing with an open and neutral mind to render impartial judgments. The duty of a lawyer to his or her client and to the legal system are the same: to represent the client zealously within the boundaries of the law.

> **CTQ**
>
> Should defense attorneys cooperate with prosecutors if it means that it dramatically increases the chance that their clients will go to jail?

Privately Retained Counsel

Almost like athletes, certain individual defense attorneys have developed a reputation that gives them an aura of mystique and a sense of invincibility every time they walk into a courtroom. Most people know the names of Barry Scheck (see Figure 7.9), F. Lee Bailey, Richard "Racehorse" Haynes, and Johnnie Cochran. However, most citizens are dismayed that they cannot afford the likes of these lawyers should they ever get into trouble.

What most citizens do not understand about private criminal defense attorneys is that their relationships toward their clients are often ones of ambivalence. Abram S. Bloomberg has referred to the attorney-client relationship in privately retained counsel as a "confidence game." Bloomberg says the mission of these attorneys is fixing and collecting fees. Once the fee has been acquired by the attorney, his or her function should be clear. Practice tells us, however, that such is often not the case. In one particular case, six attorneys, including James B. Halsted, were co-counseling and defending six clients in a joint criminal trial. All defendants initially pleaded not guilty. The case was delayed almost two years. Yet by the time of the trial, every attorney had been paid sums by their respective clients ranging from $10,000 to $55,000 to defend them in court.

The nature of the evidence in this particular case seemed to weigh heavily for the defense. However, the night before trial, five of these criminal defense lawyers began thinking about their pocketbooks and tight schedules. Then it happened. One by one, each lawyer (having been fully paid) participated in a kind of confidence game with their client, which has been called "bleed 'em and plead 'em" by an anonymous criminal defense lawyer. This tactic involves a series of subtle psychological threats from a defense lawyer, intending to frighten the client. It begins by the lawyer making no promises that an acquittal will come about should the trial begin. The next stage of this game is to show the client the maximum punishment for each count charged. Then the attorney advises the client of the risks of incurring the maximum punishments (when, in fact, the reality of the sentencing guideline procedure in most states does not yield nearly the risk described). This threat, intimidation, and fear tactic has a purpose. Its purpose is to persuade the client to plead guilty to the charges in exchange for some form of plea agreement. People in vulnerable situations (especially when characterized as such by the lawyer paid to represent and protect them) are usually the ones most likely to take the advice and suggestions of someone they trust. Retained attorneys have such a trust.

In the case just described, five guilty pleas came forward; all co-defendants except one pleaded guilty to all of the charges; they received massive fines and protracted probated sentences. The one remaining defendant, whose lawyer recognized he had a solid defense in the case, pleaded not guilty and litigated the case for two weeks. Subsequently, a jury read out fifty-five verdicts of not guilty on every felony charged. From the point of view of the other lawyers, by "bleeding and pleading" their clients guilty, they saved themselves two weeks of work and hours and hours of preparation (which they probably had not yet put into the case). Yet nonetheless, they still received a maximum cost benefit. They were paid their full retainer and attorney fees anyway without wasting time and effort. Their clients' lives, however, were not in a risk-free position. One violation of the conditions of their probation (including the payment of tens of thousands of dollars in restitution) would incarcerate them for a substantial number of years. The practice of "bleed 'em and plead 'em" is too often a reality of the privately retained attorney's career. It is a basic truth in the practice of criminal law that once a criminal attorney has been paid, his or her life just has become much easier. Life becomes wonderful, if the client pleads. From a certain perspective, every consequence that follows is a great benefit to the attorney: time is saved, embarrassment is saved, lack of previous preparation will not be exposed, and one now has two weeks open to either relax or recruit other clients.

FIGURE 7.9

This is criminal defense lawyer Barry Scheck. He is young, brilliant, an expert on DNA evidence, and expensive to hire. Here Mr. Scheck is making a point during the adversarial drama of a criminal trial.

Courtesy Bill Nation/CORBIS.

IN THE NEWS

A HUMAN PERSPECTIVE

PRIVATELY RETAINED COUNSEL

Of an estimated 800,000 practicing lawyers in the United States, only between 10,000 and 20,000 accept criminal cases on a "more than occasional" basis and of these, only 14,000 are employed as public defenders. In the sole contemporary national study of the criminal bar, Paul Wice found that the number and quality of privately retained lawyers varied among cities, with legal, institutional, and political factors accounting for much of the variance. Given the small proportion of lawyers engaged in criminal practice, the questions arise: Who does take criminal cases? What are the qualifications of the practitioners? The average criminal lawyer practices alone, not as a member of a law firm; comes from a middle-class, nonprofessional background; graduated from a lesser law school; and entered private criminal practice after some experience as a public lawyer. Only an estimated 4 percent are women. Wice further found that 38 percent of his sample of private criminal lawyers previously had been prosecutors and that 24 percent had been public defenders, had worked for legal services (civil law work), or had held civil service positions.

Source: Based on Paul Wice, *Criminal Lawyers: An Endangered Species* (Beverly Hills, CA: Sage Press).

On the other hand, the manner in which privately retained attorneys defend their clients is the stuff that the best movies and novels are made of. The quality of these private attorneys' defenses are spectacular (a marvelous example is Johnnie Cochran). Their efforts are stupendous. And their clients owe their life and liberty to these lawyers' intelligence, knowledge, expertise, and wit. In these situations, the right to counsel takes on its most profound significance (see "In the News: Privately Retained Counsel").

Because of the way the U.S. system of justice operates today, criminal defense attorneys face many role conflicts. They are viewed as the prime movers in what is essentially an adversarial process: The prosecution and the defense engage in conflict over the facts of the case at hand, with the prosecutor arguing the case for the state and the defense counsel using all the means at his or her disposal to aid the client.

LEGAL SERVICES FOR THE POOR

About three million offenders are given free legal services annually. Programs providing counsel to offenders who are unable to afford private counsel can be divided into three major categories: public defender systems, assigned-counsel systems, and contract systems (see Figure 7.10). In addition, some jurisdictions use a mixed system, which involves representation by both the public defender and the private bar, law school clinical program, and prepaid legal services (see "In the News: The Cost of Legal Services for the Poor").

The Public-Defender System

Public defender programs may be either statewide or local. Under a statewide system, a chief defender is appointed by either the governor or the judiciary. He or she is charged with providing the system with legal representation for each of the counties in the state. The chief defender usually establishes branch offices staffed by assistants, although contractual arrangements with local law firms may be used by some counties. The local branches are subject to supervisory authority of the chief defender and receive support services from the central office. Local defender agencies are organized by the county or judicial district. Most are government agencies, but some are private nonprofit organizations receiving funding from the local courts or the community.[65]

The public-defender system is more often than not a full-time county, state, or federal government job. A public defender earns a fixed salary and specializes in criminal law representing criminal indigents. The public-defender position is particularly popular in urban areas, and it has become increasingly popular in smaller jurisdictions. Twenty-three states have adopted the public-defender system. The size of the public-defender office

FIGURE 7.10

Criminal Defense Systems in the United States

Source: Bureau of Justice Statistics.

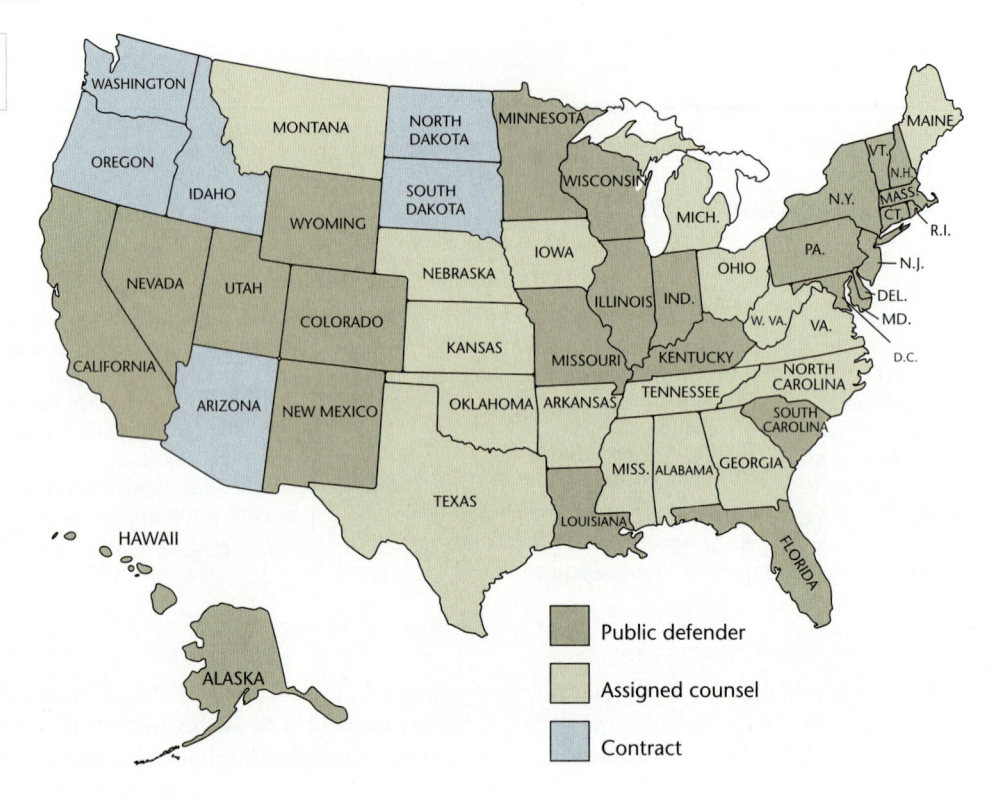

- Public defender
- Assigned counsel
- Contract

IN THE NEWS
A HUMAN PERSPECTIVE

THE COST OF LEGAL SERVICES FOR THE POOR

In 1990, state and local governments spent $1.3 billion to provide legal representation for criminal defendants unable to afford their own—and over 80 percent of all defendants in felony cases depended upon court-appointed attorneys or public defenders to represent them. A series of United States Supreme Court decisions have guaranteed that defendants unable to pay for private criminal defense attorneys will receive adequate representation at all stages of criminal justice processing.

Source: "Pay the Costs of Justice," USA Today (March 30, 1993). Copyright 1993, USA TODAY. Reprinted with permission.

is directly proportional to the constituency to be served. In a rural setting there may be but one public defender, whereas in a major metropolitan setting, there are usually hundreds (see "In the News: The Trials of a Public Defender").

The merits of the public-defender system include the assurance that the indigent receive competent legal counsel. It avoids some of the worst excesses of the assigned-counsel system (such as soliciting money from the families of clients) because most or all are paid constant salaries. Public defenders can handle comparatively large caseloads more efficiently and less expensively than privately appointed attorneys. Critics of the system contend that public defenders are often not completely independent from prosecutors because of their close day-to-day working relationship. Further, their heavy caseloads reduce public defenders' ability to interview their clients properly and to pursue legal research.

Today, public-defender systems exist in most urban areas and are increasingly being adopted by many small and medium-sized jurisdictions. These systems, however, vary widely. In Los Angeles, for example, there are hundreds of public defenders on staff to serve a population of indigent defendants, while in other areas there is only a single such counsel, who is responsible for the criminal caseload of an entire county.

WEB

The National Legal Aid and Defenders Association offers leadership skills to support public-defender services. For more information, **visit the link to the association on our Web site**, www.prenhall.com/territo.

IN THE NEWS

A HUMAN PERSPECTIVE

THE TRIALS OF A PUBLIC DEFENDER

Every day, as he ambles through the cobwebbed halls of the New Orleans criminal court building, public defender Richard Teissier feels he violates his clients' constitutional rights. The Sixth Amendment established, and the landmark *Gideon* Supreme Court case affirmed, the right of poor people to receive legal counsel. At any given moment, Teissier is representing some ninety accused murderers, rapists, and robbers. Yet his office has no money to hire experts or track down witnesses; its law library consists of a set of lawbooks spirited away from a dead judge's chambers.

With so many clients and so few resources, Teissier decided he could not possibly do justice to them all. So he filed suit against himself. He demanded that the court judge his work inadequate and find more money for lawyers. A judge agreed and declared the state's indigent-defense system unconstitutional. "This is a test of whether there is justice in the United States," Teissier says. "If you're only going to pay it lip service, then get rid of *Gideon*."

The typical public defender is underpaid and overwhelmed. When Jacquelyn Robins was appointed New Mexico's state public defender in 1985, there were six lawyers in Albuquerque's Metro court to handle the load of 13,000 misdemeanor cases. Three years later, Robins persuaded state legislators to put up funds for three more lawyers. Even then, lawyers could manage only cursory conferences with clients just thirty minutes before their court appearance. In 1991 Robins again went begging for dollars. When she was accused of having a "management problem," she quit. The move caused such a furor that the governor promised additional funds.

Albuquerque's chief public defender, Kelly Knight, now has sixteen lawyers, but the pace is still grueling. "I'm 34, not married, and I have no children," Knight says. "But I'm really, really burned out." She plans to take a sabbatical next year—whether she is granted one or not.

Source: J. Smolowe, "The Trials of a Public Defender," *Time* (March 29, 1993). © 1993 *TIME*, Inc. Reprinted by permission.

The Assigned-Counsel System

Some jurisdictions prefer the assigned-counsel system to the public-defender system. The **assigned-counsel system** is certainly the oldest and most widely used method of indigent legal representation in the history of American jurisprudence. Lawyers representing indigent criminal defendants under this system handle one case at a time. At the defendant's initial appearance, when the judge is made aware that the defendant is indigent, he or she will refer to a list of attorneys. Throughout the United States in assigned-counsel systems, the list that the judge refers to is usually one of two types. The oldest type includes all the practicing attorneys in the jurisdiction; the other list includes only those lawyers who have volunteered to defend indigents for a set fee. Thus, the lawyer that an indigent defendant receives is initially limited by the scope of the list in front of the judge and secondly by the whimsical discretion of the judge who assigns the case. Often in the assigned-counsel system, the judge will note whether any of the lawyers on the list are present in court and, if so, assign them merely due to the fact they happen to be in the courtroom that day.

The assigned-counsel system has both strengths and weaknesses. It is psychologically beneficial to the client because the defendant sees the traditional lawyer-client relationship preserved. Also, a wide spectrum of the legal community is involved in the process. This method of providing counsel is the most practical and cost-effective for jurisdictions too small to justify a full-time legal aid office. Critics of the system claim that it is subject to abuse because judges may appoint their friends who need the income. Others believe that judges concerned with processing large numbers of cases will appoint attorneys who either encourage their clients to plead guilty or do not raise too many difficulties during the trial. In addition, some critics believe that young and inexperienced—and less competent—attorneys are assigned to counsel work. Lastly, the assigned-counsel system has been criticized because the pleas that defendants are advised to enter may not be in the defendant's best interest, but rather a reflection of the desires of the assigned counsel.

In small jurisdictions, the assigned-counsel system is less expensive in the long run because public funds are needed for only a small number of cases that can be parceled out to a variety of private attorneys. These attorneys are customarily chosen from the local bar association's membership rolls. Under most assigned-counsel systems, however, a list of eligible and willing attorneys is maintained by the court. Lawyers indicate to the court that they want to be placed on the list. Some jurisdictions require attorneys who want to be placed on the list to qualify by experience and/or training before they are assigned. This is more the exception than the rule, however. In either event, the judge is generally responsible for the actual appointment of the defense counsel in a particular case.

The Contract System

Until recently, the types of indigent defense systems were limited to public-defender systems and appointed-counsel systems. Under the new **contract system,** individual attorneys, bar associations, and private law firms contract with the government to provide specific services for a dollar amount. These awards are usually based on competitive bidding. Selection criteria are integrated as part of the final award. Six states (Washington, Oregon, Idaho, North Dakota, South Dakota, and Arizona) use the contract system as their most significant form of indigent representation.

Contract attorneys appear to be at least as effective as assigned counsel and are more cost-effective.[66] Although the contract system is currently used less frequently than either public defenders or assigned counsel, the number of jurisdictions turning to contract attorneys appears to be growing.

The contract system is generally used in counties that also have public-defender offices. These two systems complement each other in instances when a public defender must withdraw from a case due to a conflict of interest with another defendant. If the entire public defender's office has been exposed by the first case, the contract system can take over without damaging the defendant's interests.

THE JUDICIARY

The symbolism and rituals of the judicial process are summarized in the figure of the goddess of justice, Themis, who stands blindfolded with scales suspended in one hand and a sword in the other. The scales signify the weighing of evidence; the sword implies the power and authority of punitive sanction; and the blindfold indicates that justice is oblivious to temptation or bribery.

Courts and the judicial process usually bring to mind a picture of a judge draped in a black robe overseeing a trial. When a judge enters a courtroom, everyone rises and stands quietly until he or she sits behind the elevated bench and raps the gavel to start the proceedings. In courts composed of a number of members, such as the U.S. Supreme Court, it is common for judges to march in together quickly, as if choreographed to take their seats on cue in a flourish of flowing robes. Loud talking or even whispering among court spectators is not permitted.

At the U.S. Supreme Court, severe-looking ushers holding long sticks roam the aisles, and they poke these sticks at individuals who talk too loudly or distract others from focusing on the front of the large courtroom. Called "the Marble Palace," the U.S. Supreme Court building is very ornate, with high ceilings and decorated walls, polished floors, and long benches that resemble pews in a church. Reverence and respect are expected and enforced. Other courtrooms are less magnificent, but the floor plan, furniture arrangement, and the judge raised above everyone else are similar and clearly show who is in charge and what goes on.

As recently as 1980, the majority of Americans would not picture an African American or a woman presiding over a court. However, a significant percentage of members of the American judiciary are female, African American, or both. The traditional perception (not the reality) of judges is of middle-aged white males, perhaps slightly overweight, with graying or white hair. This perception is rapidly changing in the first decade of the 21st century, due in large part to the extraordinary number of minority and female actors who portray judges in popular television shows such as *Law and Order, The Practice, Ally McBeal, Family Law,* and, of course, *Judge Judy.*

The Selection of Judges

In selecting judges, it is necessary to distinguish between formal procedures and requirements (as specified by constitutional or statutory law) and actual practice. The former provide the legal specifications to be allowed in choosing judicial personnel but leave an undefined area in which informal practices develop. State law may call for the popular election of judges, but who runs may be determined by the political parties. Thus, to win a judgeship, the candidate must first secure his or her party's nomination and then campaign on the party ticket. This means that potential state judges normally are embroiled in the same type of partisan politics that are prevalent in the election of legislators, governors, presidents, and other government officials. The system necessarily results in the election of the most politically active candidates, rather than possibly the most competent to serve. In other states, the law may provide for gubernatorial appointments, but the choice of candidates may actually be dictated by political leaders or bar associations.

Until recently, few formal requirements—other than those of age, residency, citizenship, and admission to the bar—were prescribed for judicial selection. Candidates with prior experience on the bench do not necessarily have a better chance of appointment or selection than those without such qualifications.

For example, since the U.S. Supreme Court was established in 1790, a majority of nominees to the Court had no prior judicial careers; the percentage is no higher for the appellate tribunals of most states. Only in the case of the U.S. Courts of Appeal does experience appear to give a candidate a decided advantage; in recent decades, the majority of the nominees to these courts have had extensive experience on the bench before their appointments.

There are various methods for selecting judges, and each has its own advocates and supporting arguments. The selection procedures used in the United States may be grouped into three general categories: elective, appointive, and appointive with modification. The method of election prevails in thirty-three states, with nearly equal numbers of partisan (in which the nominee declares a party affiliation) and nonpartisan elections. Appointments are used in the federal judiciary and in somewhat less than one-fourth of the states. The third method of selection, appointive with modification, sometimes referred to as the Missouri Plan, is a nonpartisan court plan.

The Election of Judges

According to those who support the election of judges, judges should be politically responsible for the conduct of their offices. However, proponents of the appointive system declare the need for judicial candidates to compete with one another for popular favor in partisan or even nonpartisan campaigns. They maintain that the average voter is ill-equipped to assess the technical fitness and judicial aptitude of the individuals who seek judgeships. Further, they contend that judges who are dependent on popular support for their office incur political obligations that may affect their decisions.

Popular election of state court judges is actually not as predominant as statistics suggest. Numerous vacancies on the bench occur through the death, resignation, or retirement of an incumbent before the expression of a term. When this occurs, the governor of a state usually has the power to fill the judgeship for the remainder of the term or until the next election. In other words, governors select a substantial number of judges, even in states that have elective systems. Individuals so appointed have a distinct advantage in later elections, because they enter the elections as incumbents.

Campaigns for American judgeships are generally low-key, low-visibility affairs marked by the absence of controversy. Voter turnout tends to be low. Judges seldom are voted out of office. The electoral sway of the incumbent judge is so powerful that sitting judges seldom are opposed for reelection. Therefore, elected judges do spend some of their time maintaining contact with local voters, to remain visible and to keep close ties to lawyers to ensure against having to wage a costly campaign for reelection.

The Appointment of Judges

The appointment of judges is generally viewed as apolitical in character. However, an examination of the election process in the federal court system should dissolve any illusions about the apolitical character of judicial appointments. When a vacancy occurs on the federal bench, a set procedure is followed: names of nominees are submitted by senators to the attorney general's office, which serves as a clearinghouse

> **CTQ**
>
> What are the benefits and drawbacks of holding judicial elections?

or screening agency for all appointments to the national judiciary. Informal discussions then take place among members of the Department of Justice, White House staff, senators, and party leaders from the state where the vacancy exists. When the choice is narrowed, the Federal Judiciary committee of the American Bar Association is invited to comment on the candidates (this practice was initiated during Eisenhower's administration).

The bar association's committee does not initiate or suggest prospective nominees; it simply makes recommendations on the names submitted by the attorney general. In this capacity, however, the committee exerts its influence by deterring the nomination of individuals it deems unqualified. Simultaneously with the bar committee's review, full field investigation of the potential nominees is conducted by the FBI. At the conclusion of these activities, the attorney general makes a recommendation to the president. By this time the acceptability of a candidate to the senators (of the president's party) has been established. Only rarely does a president submit the name of a judicial nominee over the objection of the official.

Judges are appointed in the states as well. Several different methods are used to appoint and confirm judges, depending on the level of the court's jurisdiction. In some states, the governor simply appoints the judges. However, in others, the judicial recommendation must be confirmed by either (1) the state senate, (2) the governor's council, (3) a special confirmation committee, (4) the executive council elected by the state assembly, or (5) an elected review board.

Modified Appointment of Judges

The modified appointment plan, developed by the American Bar Association and the American Judicature Society, was first adopted in Missouri in 1940. This plan combines restrictive executive selection with popular approval. In Missouri, for example, the governor fills judicial vacancies on the state supreme court and on the circuit courts of Jackson County (Kansas City) and St. Louis County (the intermediate appellate tribunals) from lists submitted by nonpartisan nominating commissions. These commissions are composed of gubernatorial appointees, lawyers selected by the state bar, and the presiding judge of one of the appellate courts. The commission in Jackson County, for example, includes two laypeople, two lawyers elected by members of the local bar association, and the presiding judge of the Kansas City Court of Appeals. After newly appointed judges have served on the bench for one year, their names are submitted on ballots to area voters, who determine whether the judges should be retained in office. A similar referendum is held every six years thereafter for circuit court judges and every twelve years thereafter for appellate justices.

By the 1970s, the Missouri Plan or a comparable form of merit selection of judges had been established in some twenty-eight states.[67] More recently, however, it appears that the Missouri Plan may have been running into some difficulties. In Missouri, where the plan originated in 1940 as a cure for widespread patronage appointments, there have been allegations that the merit selection process once again has become politically influenced. Moreover, studies are beginning to suggest that when comparing the Missouri plan of selection with partisan election systems, the characteristics of the judges selected under the two alternative processes tend to be similar in both background and legal experience. By the latter half of the 1980s, the popularity of the merit system had declined, with the majority of the states choosing judges through partisan (using political parties) or nonpartisan (without political parties) elections.

Which Is the Best System for Selecting Judges?

Experience has demonstrated the difficulty of excluding politics from the selection process—even under a restrictive appointment method. This was shown in Missouri under the nonpartisan court plan during the plan's first twenty-five years: Of the sixty judges appointed during this period, the majority belonged to the same political party as the governor. Charges have been made that governors may attempt to influence the choice of names on the nominee lists through their appointees on the nominating commissions. These allegations have led to proposals to take the appointment of lay members of such commissions out of the governor's hands.

To what degree can the selection process be removed from politics? To deny a governor any voice in the composition of the nominating panel would further strengthen the role of the bar associations in the choice of judicial appointees. For example, Hearnes reported in 1965 that more than half of the members of the Missouri bar believed that the nonpartisan court plan substituted bar politics and gubernatorial politics for the traditional politics of party leaders and political organizations.[68] Few members, however, regarded this development unfavorably, and some suggested removing the element of gubernatorial politics altogether by eliminating the governor's power to appoint part of the nominating panel. If this happened, only bar politics would influence the decision. In the final analysis, any selection method—no matter how it is designed—includes a political decision at some point in the process.

The relationship between the method of selection and the caliber of judges who staff the courts remains more a matter of individual perception than of systematic study. Does the appointive process produce better judges than popular election? Or is the Missouri Plan superior to either appointment or election? The subject has been debated for some time. Proponents of executive selection point to the experience of the federal branch, which has traditionally enjoyed a higher reputation for competency than its state counterparts. How much of this relative superiority can be attributed to the mode of selection is not known, however. The greater benefits of federal judgeships—lifetime tenure, better pay, and higher prestige—are probably much more important factors. It can be assumed that the more attractive a position is made because of money, security, and prestige, the more the position will appeal to people with ability and talent.

Judges at Work

Formal powers of judges extend throughout the criminal court process from arrest to final disposition. The accused face a judge whenever decisions affecting their futures are made. Judges set bail and revoke it. They determine whether there is sufficient probable cause to hold defendants. They rule on pretrial motions. They exclude evidence; they accept pleas of guilty; if there is a trial, they preside. After conviction, they set punishment. Throughout the process, judges are expected to discharge their powers and responsibilities judiciously and without the appearance of impropriety.

Although we tend to think of judges primarily in terms of presiding at trials, their work is much more varied. Much of their work day is spent conducting hearings, accepting pleas, imposing sentences, or working in their office (called *chambers*). In carrying out the responsibility of the office, judges mainly react to the work of prosecutors and defense attorneys.

The pressure in today's criminal justice system means that the ideals surrounding the judge are not always borne out in reality. Trial court judges in the nation's largest cities sometimes find staggering caseloads. Instead of having time to reflect on changing legal questions or to consider the proper sentence for a convicted felon, trial judges must move cases, acting more like administrators in a bureaucracy rather than judicial sages.

WEB

For more information, **visit the link to the American Judges Association on our Web site,** www.prenhall.com/territo.

CTQ

What are some of the various functions undertaken by a criminal court judge during a jury trial?

CTQ

Do rapid trials lead to "less justice"?

Female Judges and Justices

Historically, women were considered neither suitable nor capable to hold judgeships. As a justice of the Wisconsin Supreme Court said in 1875,

> Our profession has essentially and habitually to do with all that is selfish and extortionate, knavish and criminal, coarse and brutal, repulsive and obscene. Nature has tempered women as little for the judicial conflict of the courtroom as for the physical conflicts of the battlefield.[69]

The history of women on the bench in America is long. Wyoming appointed the first female judge in 1870. She was a justice of the peace. The timing of her appointment is interesting, since at that time women had not yet won the right to vote. By 1950, women had token representation. However, it was not until 1979 that every state had at least one female judge. A common explanation for the disparity in judicial selection is the "eligibility pool" theory. This eligibility pool began to change in the mid-1980s, when enrollment in law schools consisted of more female than male law students.

The demographic composition of the judiciary has changed as well. In 1981, Sandra Day O'Connor became the first woman to be nominated and confirmed as a member of the United States Supreme Court. In 1993 she was joined by Ruth Bader Ginsburg. In 1979 female judges organized the National Association of Women Judges.

During his first two years in office, President Clinton appointed more federal judges than any other president in history, and he appointed a higher percentage of women and minorities than his predecessors. Of the 129 judges appointed by Clinton during those first two years, almost 60 percent were women or minorities, compared to 8 percent by Ronald Reagan and 27 percent by Jimmy Carter.[70]

Female judges have noted some of the problems they have faced. At the fourth annual convention of the National Association of Women Judges, women indicated that often they were lonely in their positions and that they were still excluded from some all-male clubs where judges and attorneys meet for social occasions. Some believed that they had little influence in court administration and policymaking and limited influence and power in their bar associations. Some expressed dissatisfaction with what they called tokenism at both the state and federal levels.[71] The women said that they received less glamorous assignments than their male colleagues, "and are subjected to standards that are both stricter and sillier than those applied to men."[72]

COURTHOUSE CULTURE AND THE SOCIALIZATION OF JUDGES

The transition from advocate to arbitrator can be a difficult one. The high regard and prestige of the judiciary accentuates the positive aspects and hides the negative: Problems of isolation or the routineness of judging are difficult to realize without firsthand experience. New judges often are not prepared for the conflict between idealized views of the office and the reality of actual experience. With some final comments on the socialization of "freshman judges," longtime judge Harold R. Medina, in his authorized biography, was quoted as saying, "The job of a federal judge was far different than I perceived it being from the other side of the bench." When considering the comments, it is important to realize that in 1947 Medina left his $100,000 a year practice for a $15,000 federal judgeship in New York. Medina assumed the office feeling that judging was "just what my whole career led me to do." In reality, his transition from a practicing lawyer to a trial judge was not easy.[73]

Rosett and Cressey describe the complex relationship of shared values, attitudes, and informal norms of cooperation that make up what they call a "subculture of justice within the courthouse": Ever wonder what it means to be working as a Supreme Court justice, the most revered judicial slot in the land?

> Even in the adversary world of law, men who work together and understand each other eventually develop shared conceptions of what are acceptable, right and just ways of dealing with specific kinds of offenses, suspects, and defendants. These conceptions form the bases of understanding, agreements, working arrangements and cooperative attitudes. . . . Over time, these shared patterns of belief developed the coherence of a distinct culture, a style of social expression peculiar to the particular courthouse.[74]

Newcomers to the bench undergo a process of on-the-job learning that transforms them into jurists. During this process, judges are exposed to and absorb various aspects of the "courthouse culture" that pertain to organizational goals, preferred means for achieving these goals, role responsibilities, required behavior, and rules for maintaining the court as an organization.[75]

Alpert has identified five stages in the occupational socialization of trial court judges: professional socialization, initiation, resolution, establishment, and commitment. *Professional socialization* occurs prior to judicial selection. This period covers both formal legal training in law school and informal training that occurs in legal practice. It also includes experience in public office (for example, as a prosecutor or city attorney) that may help prepare an individual for the bench. *Initiation* is a period of bewilderment and confidence building. The newcomer learns how to behave in court, manage the docket, make proper rulings, and maintain order in trials and hearings. *Resolution,* which occurs during years one through four in the judicial experience, completes the transformation of the newcomer from advocate to arbiter. The judge reaches a level of comfort in which he or she begins to handle the isolation and the external pressures endemic to the job.

Establishment follows resolution and covers a period of approximately four years. During this time, many judges are susceptible to midcareer crises, as personal and family needs conflict with organizational demands. Judges face the decision of whether to remain on the bench or to seek more lucrative opportunities in nonjudicial pursuits. It is a period of introspection and rumination about the future. *Commitment,* the final stage in the socialization process, is marked by a deep-seated identification with the court, an increase in personal satisfaction, and a growing sense of dedication to a judicial career.[76]

In contrast, speakers on a panel before the annual meeting of the American Political Science Association identified only three phases of judicial socialization. The first, according to Howard, is the *anticipator phase.* This means preparing in advance to be a judge. It is the primary American theory and the primary American practice. Judges are expected to learn how to judge on their way to the bench. They have been expected to acquire the norms, attitudes, and values of the office in becoming eligible for it.

The second phase, *freshmen socialization,* is a short, transitory adjustment to the internal rules, practices, and procedures of the collective organization judges join. The final phase is *occupational socialization.*" This phase is marked by continuous learning and can be both painful and fun. Howard describes the phase as "an adult growing process, when you shift from being a lawyer, an advocate, or some sort of professional into the actual job of judging."[77]

A judge's colleagues are the foremost training agents in the process of judicial socialization. They accomplish this task through formal meetings and seminars and by informal exchanges during the workday. A second major source of information derives from attorneys who appear in their courtrooms; in addition, the influence of people on the judge's staff (law clerks, secretaries, court administrators, and bailiffs) also contribute to this process. These people supply the judge with critical advice on procedural and administrative matters.[78]

When judges seek out knowledgeable people, they may be limited to those within the courthouse or those who enter the judiciary. In a statement made before the annual meeting of the American Political Science Association, newly elected Supreme Court justice Ruth Bader Ginsburg said when she was asked about the transition from professor to judge: "I've been tempted many times to say, 'Oh, what a fascinating issue this is. I would love to call in professor so and so and see what he thinks about it.' That I can't do. I can ask one of my colleagues who shares my ignorance. I can call a law clerk and talk about it, but I can't have a communication outside. That's verboten."[79]

But in the end, the judicial socialization process is largely a matter of self-education in which judges spend a lot of time reading in law libraries, seeking out counsel of knowledgeable people, and learning by doing.

Job Stress and the Judiciary

In Chapter 5, we discussed how stress and anxiety affect the job performance and personal lives of police officers and administrators. In much the same way, occupational and social stresses result from pressures and conflicts experienced by members of the judiciary. One source of job stress for judges is the cases they encounter. For example, consider judges who are confronted regularly with jury trials involving gruesome accounts of violent crimes. The judges must try to act impartially, even though they are bombarded with facts that would upset the average person. Judges have direct, meaningful, and unending daily contact with crisis situations that they cannot escape as long as they remain in their jobs.

Another source of job stress for judges is public image. The public traditionally views judges as people equipped to handle situations and make consequential decisions swiftly and correctly. Hence, judges are expected to move from one emotionally charged situation to the next, while remaining aloof and detached. They are expected to be fair and impartial, regardless of the choices they must make. They must be able to use emotional control and shut off or suppress emotional responses to provocative situations. To meet these demands, a judge may "keep a tight rein on his emotions, and over a period of time isolate his feelings or become uncomfortable in expressing them. This can be analogized to a pressure cooker that has its top spout tightened down so that the steam which builds up cannot escape. Eventually, with the constant buildup of steam, the pressure cooker will explode."[80]

People who decide to seek a career as a judge are sometimes attracted by the rewards of independence; thus they often refuse to admit their dependence upon others, because this dependence is inconsistent with their self-concept. Unless they stay within the confines of their role, they may have feelings of uncertainty about their status as perceived by others. Thus, the job can be a lonely one. This same point has been made about executives with regard to leadership: "I have watched executives curse in desperation the forces which, in moments, vitiated years of their efforts. I have listened to them protest the loneliness of their sometimes opulent offices, and distance from old friends. I have seen them cry out their pent-up fury . . . and disguise their tears with alcohol."[81]

Political pressures are another source of stress for the judiciary. Once, a regrettable situation occurred during a Supreme Court election in California in which Judge Rose Bird, who was up for merit retention, became the target of an ugly political campaign.[82] Judge Bird's decision to reverse an appellate court decision and provide the possible release of a defendant accused of a brutal rape was based on a point of law rather than on her personal feelings about the crime. She could not use her repugnance toward the crime and the criminal as a basis for rewriting the statutes—and political conservatives agreed with her. However, unfair publicity and slanted editorializing put her election in jeopardy. The result was a heavily ideological campaign that had a broader target than a single judge; the campaign was designed to exert pressure on all the judges in the state to conform with reactionary views on matters involving criminal law. In 1987 Judge Bird was removed from office by a recall election.

Stress seems to present itself to judges at every angle of the judicial process, including many of the issues involved in socialization. Stress is described as nonspecific to outside demands. It is the state of being "on duty." Even as judges sleep, they are responding to various demands of the body, the environment and the mind (dreams). Stress is a normal part of life. As demands increase, the body and the mind reorganize continually to cope. Eventually, under chronic conditions of overload, the efficiency of that coping process becomes marginal. The quality of the professional's work is threatened.[83]

The types of stressors inherent in the judicial career are unique. Despite the existence of national and state judicial education programs, most judges enter their career with little guidance or preparation. Even though, as a group, judges are willing to help each other, the new judge is wary of reaching out for help. The demands of the new role in public office are clearly considerable. To go it alone, as still most appear to do, is unnecessarily stressful.

The social isolation attendant upon assuming the bench requires further emotional adaptation, leading to additional stress upon a judge. Judges are the only occupational group required to divest themselves of long-held personal associations at the peak of their career. Social life with members of the local bar, memberships in associations and clubs, and seats on boards have to go or at least be reconsidered.

One stress factor not usually perceived by the public is the financial pressure most judges are under. Our society tends to equate success and income. Most judges maintain good self-respect despite modest pay for people with their capabilities. This does not mean that consciously undertaken cuts in income do not continue for many to be a source of stress. As caseloads keep going up, stress goes higher. For most of the population, the average judicial salary may appear to be comfortable, yet their own self-image places judges more within the ranks of highly paid federal and state executives. Living with such discrepancies produces stress.

Judges get very little feedback or constructive criticism on their daily work. Appellate review and occasional seminars are not frequent enough to provide trial judges with collegial stimulation and support. Constantly being alert to monitor one's own professional behavior is an undue stress if it is not occasionally relieved by objective peer review.

In the case of trial court judges, because there is little control over the types of people that appear before them, judges perceive themselves as anchored to their courtroom, having to face whatever and whomever is put before them. Zimmerman identifies this as one of the most important factors contributing to the exhaustion of judges.[84] When the workload grows steadily, a feeling of incipient dread and helplessness affects even the most conscientious and hardworking judge.

When considering stress, one must consider the types of cases that judges are faced with in the first decade of the twenty-first century. The courts have been deluged with juvenile cases. These cases present an additional stress because the increasingly violent nature of the offenders requires judges to decide whether to try them as adults or to retain their juvenile status and, therefore, reduce the possibilities of sanctions. As one judge put it, "If a judge believes that there is some possibility that the juvenile sanction may rehabilitate the offender, the judge will be inclined to retain the juvenile status of the offender. Sadly, there are not many juvenile sanctions that are effective for serious offenders. Moreover, today's juveniles are committing crimes 'just for the fun of it.' This trend seems to be a disease for which we need to find a cure."

Yet another problem that has caused a great deal of stress for some judges is the issue of pretrial-presentence release. More and more often, incidents are being reported in which judges have released an offender on bail under certain circumstances, only to have the offender commit another, possibly more violent crime while awaiting trial or sentencing. In these cases, judges tend to look "soft" on crime, a title a judge up for reelection does not want to carry.

The introduction of television cameras in the courtroom has added an additional stress to the bench. Television can distort the judicial process by encouraging participants to play to the camera. This is also misleading to the public, because only the most sensational trials are covered at their most sensational moments. This type of coverage suggests that the judicial system progresses at an exciting level every day.

A continuing issue for judges is HIV in the courtroom. A number of ill and infected people pass through the judicial system daily. On a paper on judicial leadership in coping with AIDS, a New York supreme court justice outlines the need for judges to become involved with policymaking efforts for HIV-positive defendants. A study done in New York City shows that 20 percent of the state prison inmates tested positive for HIV. It is important to realize that this study was done at the beginning of the epidemic, and the numbers have probably increased dramatically.[85]

The justice insists that judges must get involved in AIDS policy when the issue involves a litigant with HIV/AIDS who has been improperly denied a right or remedy. The denial or loss is usually irreparable. Attorneys may not vigorously represent, or may refuse to represent, HIV-positive defendants, and if such a defendant is denied access to the courtroom, time is critical. Similarly, if a litigant with AIDS does not receive a fair trial because of bias or hostility, given the pace of the appellate process, he or she probably won't be around for retrial. Finally, if a defendant is sentenced to prison merely because of his or her HIV status, the person usually receives substandard medical care and other deprivations before an appeals court can rectify the situation. The weight of an issue like this poses a great deal of stress for trial judges.[86]

Proposals for sentencing reform have often called for trial judges to provide reasons in writing for decisions made in difficult, complex, or unusual cases. Trial judges are pressured to document the reasons for particular sentences because of the "increase in appellate review and reversal, the heightened criticism by the press and the public, and consequent diminution of the judiciary's role."[87] Robins feels that this pressure is intrinsically threatening and stress-producing because discretion contributes significantly to the self-concept and occupational satisfaction of judges. Further, a judge's rejection of sentencing accountability "is rooted in the recognizably human and pervasive aversion to being criticized, countermanded, and sanctioned."[88] "Viewed publicly, every formalized judicial statement accompanying sentencing is perceived as a justification of action taken and thus invites evaluation and criticism from all sources."

Perhaps the most direct way to understand the stress and anxiety judges experience is to follow a judge through a typical day in court (see "In the News: A Day in the Life of Lois G. Forer").

Considering the amount of stress caused by the issues discussed here, it's time to take a look at one possible solution. The use of sabbaticals has long been accepted in academia and business. The time has come for the granting of sabbaticals in the judicial system. *Sabbatical* denotes a period of rest that occurs at regular intervals. Historically, sabbaticals were considered sources of spiritual, mental, and physical regeneration; economic renewals of resources; and education of people about their faith and their purposes in the world.[89]

Judicial sabbaticals can be used to improve a judge's morale and health. Health is particularly important, since stress can cause a number of problems such as high blood pressure and coronary artery disease.

THE CONSEQUENCES OF COURT CONGESTION, DELAY, AND BACKLOG

Congestion and delay in the courtroom may be the most serious problems facing the courts (see Figure 7.11). These phenomena have engulfed the state and county court systems throughout the nation, with few exceptions. While reformers and patrons acknowledge the existence of these problems, few efforts appear to have any impact on the immediate problems. One criminal defense lawyer was quoted as saying:

> The criminal courts of troubled urban America are failing wretchedly. Like scarecrows put in the fields to frighten the birds of lawlessness, tattered and unmasked from neglect, frightening to no one, they have become roosting places for the crows. To the innocent, to the victims of crime, to the witnesses of crime, to the illiterate, the uneducated, and the poor, many of our big city criminal courts are a sham and a broken promise.[90]

Courtroom overcrowding is a problem that seems inherent to the process. As the number of jail facilities erected increases, the tougher the sentences become that judges hand out. What happens before judgment is passed? Why can't justice move swiftly and accurately?

Everyone agrees that the problems exist, but in many cases, there are large discrepancies as to what these problems are. Technically, delay refers to court conditions that are unavoidable. Delay occurs in well-organized and well-managed courts as well as in poorly administered systems. Congestion, on the other hand, implies administrative mismanagement or lack of management. Despite this distinction, the two terms are used interchangeably throughout the following discussion.

The causes for unnecessary delay in the state court are numerous. First, the focus must be on fundamental causes. Judges have traditionally attempted to keep the judiciary away from politics, including political lobbying for court reform. The result of this separation has been a tremendous amount of underfinancing for the state courts. Chief Justice Overton of Florida noted in 1976 that the cost of running Florida's judicial branch was approximately 0.07 percent of the total state budget.[91] Since then, the population of Florida has increased tremendously. Crime has disproportionately increased, and the amount of civil litigation tying up resources has skyrocketed. Second, one must consider the inner workings of the system and all its players. The lack of properly trained administrators, the inability of the states to employ a proportionately correct number of court personnel for the increasing amount of intake, the lack of modernization and computerization, and the increasing amount of criminal sanctions imposed by Congress and the state legislatures — these are the problems to which we need immediate solutions.

The backlog of cases within which each state court works each day is not lessening; in fact, the amount of case backlog is ever-increasing. To solve this problem, reformers have looked at the root of the backlog, which is congestion. Congestion occurs when the cases to be handled outnumber the means to handle them. To correct the problem of backlog, it is necessary to understand why this backlog occurs. For this, one must consider case processing time, the amount of time from arrest to final disposition (see Chapter 8).

FIGURE 7.11

An overcrowded group of persons charged with a misdemeanor wait for their case to be called. All have been scheduled to have their "day in court" on the same day.

Courtesy Peter Byron/PhotoEdit.

Backlog creates a problem for the reformer in that no two courts move cases along at exactly the same rate. For that matter, no two judges use the same amount of time to properly dispose of a case. The second problem is that case processing time is largely up to the judge who is to rule on the case. The American Bar Association accepts a time frame of six months to a year for a court to reach the final disposition of a case. The Conference of State Court Administrators dictates that no more than six months is needed to properly dispose of a felony case, and a maximum of three months for a misdemeanor.[92]

While all agree that certain case processing time intervals are necessary, all do not agree on which stages of the process should be manipulated or reformed. The Law Enforcement Assistance Administration (LEAA) compiled a court delay reduction program that divided total processing time into three segments: lower-court time, upper-court time, and sentencing time. This was done because the survey recognized that certain aspects of processing are uncontrollable by the courts, such as presentencing investigations. It is difficult to accurately measure processing time using the mean, because certain extremes skew the curve, leading to false assumptions. To remedy this, the LEAA uses the median, which means that half the cases use more time than the median score and half use less.[93]

While court reformers agree that delay is a paramount problem, little has been done to document the consequences that delay generates. The following is a representative assumption concerning the consequences of delay:

> Congestion and delay in courts throughout the country threaten to strangle our system of justice. For as delay increases, the innocent who cannot afford to make bail suffer longer in jail, the guilty who are released pose greater threats to society, and the deterrent value of speedy justice is lost. The resulting pressures to dispose of cases more and more quickly lead to other wrongs; less and less attention is given to each case, great reliance is placed on the disposition of cases through "plea bargaining," and the likelihood of injustice increases.[94]

The consequences of delay are exceedingly important to the litigants, as well as to the whole society. One of the primary goals of the American judicial system is to promote justice. This objective is not fulfilled, however, when trials never take place because of unnecessary delays. In criminal and civil litigation, for example, witnesses may die or move away. Thus, those accused or being sued do not have the opportunity of defending themselves and clearing their name. On the other hand, those initiating suits are not afforded the opportunity of collecting the damages they deserve, and society is unable to protect itself from criminal elements.

There are a number of other important consequences of delay. In both criminal and civil actions, there may be adverse psychological effects on witnesses and litigants alike, who must constantly bear the stigma of criminal accusations. Moreover, accused people must often languish in jail for many months if they cannot afford bail. This has obvious economic, social, and psychological implications for their families as well.

If the defendant is found guilty and has been granted bail, delay threatens the whole of society. After all, the fact that indicted individuals free on bond often commit crimes is well documented. Moreover, delays in prosecuting those guilty of criminal offenses destroy the deterrent effects of the criminal sanction. Excessive time to dispose of a criminal case is said to hinder all purposes of penal law: deterrence, societal protection, and rehabilitation. Delay is also said to contribute to prison overcrowding and riots, to an increase in rates of failure to appear, and finally, and to a lack of citizen respect for the image of justice in the eyes of the community.

Lengthy pretrial detention is believed to be a factor that can pressure an innocent defendant into pleading guilty. For this reason, a number of states have enacted speedy-trial laws premised on the need to protect the defendant's rights. Delay is also seen as hampering society's need for a speedy conviction.[95] This view stresses the harm done to the prosecutor's case. One aspect of this effect is the "deterioration of evidence" hypothesis. As time passes, witnesses forget, move away, or die. Thus, the moving party, either the plaintiff or the prosecutor, presumably has a progressively weaker case. The defense is therefore more likely to receive more concessions in negotiations or complete exoneration through a dismissal or a favorable verdict. As the delay continues, the defendant's bargaining position increases; thus, prosecutors are more likely to accept pleas.

Court delay is seen as contributing to the erosion of the public's confidence in the judicial process. Citizens quickly lose faith in the swiftness and certainty of punishment. Delay can cause witnesses and victims to make many needless trips to the courthouse, wasting their time and again decreasing public faith in the system. Aside from the inconvenience, the delay can create a strain on the available resources. Pretrial detainees, not released and waiting for trial, can clog jail facilities. Commonly, police officers must appear in court on numerous occasions; this is done at the public's expense.

Factors asserted to affect trial court case processing—and therefore delay—can be grouped under two main headings: (1) resource and workload, the staffing of courts and the number and type of actions in the caseload; and (2) administrative, procedural, legal, and managerial aspects of court system case processing. If influencing the quality and type of cases entering the judicial system is problematic, the alternative remedy of focusing on court system resources is deceptively simple: add more judges. A greater number of judges will presumably dispose of a greater number of cases, thereby reducing both pending case backlog and delays in case processing time.

Even more problematic is evaluating whether, and to what extent, case processing time is affected by the workloads of attorneys and court staff. It is often asserted, for example, that a shortage of attorneys specializing in criminal litigation causes delay. Yet the relationship of delay to court workload and resources is complex and needs thorough examination. A number of court systems suffer from an inadequate number of judges, prosecutors, or defense attorneys. The most common and probably the most expensive response to a delay problem is increasing staffing levels. It is not clear, however, if this remedy will produce the desired result in all courts.

SUMMARY

The American judicial system is extremely complex. It is more accurate, in fact, to speak of the American judicial *systems;* there are courts at the federal, state, county, and municipal levels of jurisdiction, all of which make independent decisions. The state operates trial courts, intermediate appellate courts, and courts of last resort (the highest tribunals to which cases can be appealed). This pattern is repeated at the federal level. Federal appellate courts, however, can rule on state cases and have greater power to change state decisions than state courts have to change federal decisions. The U.S. Supreme Court is the court of last resort for all cases involving constitutional issues that are decided in the United States, regardless of whether they are decided initially in federal court or in state trial court.

Our system of criminal justice is based upon the adversary system—the presentation of opposing views in vigorous debate as a prelude to decision making. The system is not designed to discover the ultimate truth in the absolute sense, but rather to protect the people against the abuse of governmental power and to assure that no innocent person is found guilty of a crime he or she did not commit. Cross-examination is used to determine the facts and historically has proven to be the most effective means of exposing false testimony and inaccuracies in testimony. Our system also rejects the practice of torture and other inhumane practices incompatible with the values of free people. In summary, the adversary system seeks to accomplish justice by eliciting provable facts under fixed rules of procedure.

In America, prosecutors represent the executive branch of the government. Their powers are formidable, and they exert considerable influence upon and within the criminal justice system. Their power to institute criminal prosecution vests in them an authority in the administration of criminal justice as large as, if not greater than, the authority of the judge who presides in criminal cases. They may initiate criminal charges, stop the charging process, or request that the court dismiss the charges. Thus, the power within the prosecutor's office in this country is indeed quite formidable.

On the opposing side is the defense counsel. The courts have mandated that counsel be provided at both the state and federal levels in all cases where the defendant is threatened with loss of liberty, whether the accused is charged with a misdemeanor or a felony. Legal assistance may be provided by privately retained counsel, public defenders, counsel assigned by the courts, or counsel under contract. Each alternative has its strengths and weaknesses. For example, hiring a private attorney does not guarantee competent or interested representation. The best criminal lawyers are expensive, and frequently there is a direct correlation between the defendant's ability to pay and the quality of representation received.

Direct supervision of the courts is the responsibility of the judiciary. Judges either are appointed or elected, or attain office on a modified appointment plan (the Missouri Plan). As public officials, they are involved in the political issues and controversies that are an inseparable feature of public life. Coming from a variety of backgrounds and experiences, newcomers to the bench undergo a process of learning that gradually accommodates them to the role of judge. The human side of judging is no more clearly revealed than in the job-related stresses that affect members of the judiciary. This stress seems particularly evident when judges campaign for reelection. Other members of the judicial staff include the bailiff, court clerk, court reporter, chief judge, and court administrator. These members of the judicial team provide expert assistance and counsel, without which the judicial process would barely function. The court administrator, in particular, is beginning to emerge as the focal figure in easing the administrative and management burden, especially for the chief judge.

Court congestion and delay in the courtroom may be the most serious problems facing the courts. These phenomena have engulfed the state and county court systems throughout the nation, with few exceptions. While reformers and patrons acknowledge the existence of these problems, few efforts appear to have any impact on the immediate problems.

DISCUSSION AND REVIEW

1. Why are state supreme courts sometimes called courts of last resort?
2. What are the principal areas of jurisdiction of the U.S. Supreme Court? How does the Court obtain its cases?

3. What is the process by which the nine justices of the U.S. Supreme Court determine which cases they will review, how they vote on each case, and who is chosen to write the opinion?
4. What are the areas of jurisdiction of the U.S. District Courts?
5. What is the normal length of time it takes to process a criminal case between arrest and conviction and between conviction and sentencing?
6. What are the duties and functions of a trial judge?
7. What is the most serious problem facing the courts today?
8. List at least six of the prosecutor's general functions during his or her handling of a case for the state.
9. Compare and contrast the prosecutorial office's tasks in fluid offices versus segmented offices.
10. What are the major functions of the criminal defense attorney? Name at least ten.
11. What is the nature of the public defender system and how does it function?
12. Describe the attorney-client relationship between a defendant and privately retained counsel. What are some of the unforeseen difficulties in hiring privately retained counsel?
13. What is the nature of the contract counsel system and how does it function?
14. What percentage of guilty pleas account for all convictions? What would happen if guilty pleas were not maintained at this rate?
15. What is the nature of the assigned-counsel system and how does it function?
16. What are the duties and functions of a trial judge?
17. What is the judicial function?
18. Discuss the most common reasons for rejection or dismissal of a criminal case.
19. Explain the role of specialty courts in the state court system.
20. Describe the function of the three-tiered federal court system.
21. List some factors that a prosecutor may consider in exercising his or her decision to charge.
22. Describe the three major programs that provide counsel to indigent defendants; identify the problems inherent in each program.
23. Explain how a writ of *certiorari* is issued by the Supreme Court.
24. Why might defendants prefer private attorneys to public counsel?

CHAPTER RESOURCES

IN THE MEDIA

Film

A Time to Kill
The Devil's Advocate
A Few Good Men
The Firm
Night Falls on Manhattan
Murder in the First
Silkwood

The Verdict
To Kill a Mockingbird
Body Heat

Television

Law and Order
The Practice

IN THE LITERATURE

Books

P. FINN AND A. NEWLYN, *Miami's Drug Court*. Washington, D.C.: National Institute of Justice, 1993.

I. JANIS AND L. MANN, *Decision Making*. New York: Free Press, 1977.

Articles

C. ANDERSON, "Court Ruling Will Provide More Legal Sources for the Poor," *Tampa Tribune*, July 24, 1993.

Associated Press, "Courtroom Insults of Jurors Land Prosecutor in Hot Water," *Tampa Tribune*, July 2, 1993.

S. BRILL, "Benching Bad Judges: Should It Be Easier Than It Is to Remove Federal Judges?" *Esquire*, April 10, 1979.

J. BUCHANAN, "Police-Prosecutor Teams: Innovations in Several Jurisdictions," *National Institute of Justice Reports* (May/June 1989).

R. BURKE, "Occupational Stresses and Job Satisfaction," *Journal of Social Psychology*, vol. 100 (1976).

L. FORER, "View from the Bench: A Judge's Day," *Washington Monthly* (February 1975).

L. FULLER, "The Adversary System." In H. J. Berman, ed., *Talks on American Law*. New York: Vantage Books, 1960.

R. GEBELEIN, "The Rebirth of Rehabilitation: Promise and Perils of Drug Courts." U.S. Department of Justice. Papers from the Executive Sessions on Sentencing and Corrections #6 (May 2000).

J. GOLDCAMP, "Judicial Responsibility for Pretrial Release Decision-Making and the Information Role of Pretrial Services," *Federal Probation* 57 (1993).

T. GUEST, "Crackdown on Judges Who Go Astray," *U.S. News & World Report*, February 28, 1983.

"Judging the Judges," *Time*, August 20, 1979.

P. MARCOTTE, "Federalism and the Rise of State Courts," *ABA Journal*, April 1, 1987.

E. POOLE AND R. REGOLI, "The Decision Not to Prosecute in Felony Cases," *Journal of Contemporary Criminal Justice*, vol. 2 (March 1983).

"Supreme Court Justices No Bench Mark of Civility," *USA Today*, May 14, 1991.

Government Publications

Bureau of Justice Assistance. *State Civil RICO Programs*. Washington, D.C.: U.S. Department of Justice, 1992.

National Advisory Committee on Criminal Justice Standards and Goals, *Courts*. Washington, D.C.: U.S. Government Printing Office, 1973.

National District Attorney's Association, *The Presenting Attorneys of the United States*. Chicago: NDAA, 1966, p. 194.

National Institute of Justice. *Miami's Drug Court: A Different Approach*. Washington, D.C.: U.S. Department of Justice, 1993.

C. GASKINS, "Felony Case Processing in State Courts 1986." *Bureau of Justice Statistics Special Report*. Washington, D.C.: U.S. Department of Justice, 1990.

U.S. Department of Justice. *National Institute of Justice Update*. Washington, D.C.: U.S. Government Printing Office, 1995.

CASES

Douglas v. California, 372 U.S. 353 (1963)
Faretta v. California, 422 U.S. 806 (1975)
Gideon v. Wainwright, 372 U.S. 335 (1963)
Ross v. Moffitt, 417 U.S. 600 (1974)
United States v. Armstrong, 16 S.Ct. 1480 (1996)

ENDNOTES

1. D. Neubauer, *America's Courts and the Criminal Justice System*. (Pacific Grove, Calif. Brooks/Cole, 1992.

2. H. Glick and K. Vines, *State Court Systems*. Englewood Cliffs, N.J.: Prentice Hall, 1973.

3. N. Holten and L. Lamar, *The Criminal Courts*. New York: McGraw-Hill, 1991, pp. 294–297.

4. S. Reid, *Criminal Law*. Boston: McGraw-Hill, 1988, p. 216.

5. Neubauer, op. cit., p. 89.

6. *Douglas v. California*, 372 U.S. 353 (1963).

7. *Ross v. Moffitt*, 417 U.S. 600 (1974).

8. Federal courts other than the U.S. Supreme Court often are referred to collectively as *lower federal courts*. U.S. District Courts are included in this category.

9. F. Klein, *Federal and State Court Systems—A Guide*. Cambridge, Mass.: Ballinger, 1977.

10. K. Maguire and A. Pastore, *Sourcebook of Criminal Justice Statistics, 1993*. Washington, D.C.: U.S. Department of Justice, 1994, p. 543.

11. L. Banks, "Crisis in the Courts," *Fortune*, vol. 65 (1961), pp. 86–89.

12. President's Commission on Law Enforcement and Administration, *Task Force Report: The Courts*. Washington, D.C.: U.S. Government Printing Office, 1967, pp. 31–33.

13. Institute of Judicial Administration, *A Guide to Court Systems*. New York: Institute of Judicial Administration, 1971, p. 13.

14. Administrative Office of the United States Courts, *Annual Report of the Director, 1987*. Washington, D.C.: U.S. Government Printing Office, 1988, pp. 389, 393.

15. Drug Courts Program Office, *Looking at a Decade of Drug Courts*. Washington, D.C.: Office of Justice Programs, 2001.

16. Drug Courts Program Office, *Looking at a Decade of Drug Courts*. Washington, D.C.: Office of Justice Programs, 1998.

17. Drug Courts Program Office, *Defining Drug Courts: The Key Components*. Washington, D.C.: Office of Justice Programs, 1997.

18. Substance Abuse and Mental Health Services Administration, "1999 Household Survey Highlights." Available online at http://www.samhsa.gov/hhsurvey/content/highlights.html.

19. P. Hora, W. Schma, and J. Rosenthal, "Therapeutic Jurisprudence and the Drug Treatment Court Movement: Revolutionizing the Criminal Justice System's Response to Drug Abuse and Crime in America," *Notre Dame Law Review*, vol. 74, no. 2 (1999), pp. 456–457.

20. R. Gebelein, "The Rebirth of Rehabilitation: Promise and Perils of Drug Courts." U.S. Department of Justice. Papers from the Executive Sessions on Sentencing and Corrections #6 (May 2000).

21. Office of National Drug Control Policy, *National Drug Control Strategy: 2001 Annual Report*. Washington, D.C.: U.S. Government Printing Office, 2001.

22. Office of Drug Control, *Florida Drug Control Strategy*. Executive Office of the Governor, State of Florida, 1999.

23. Office of National Drug Control Policy, op. cit., p. 27.

24. R. Peters, A. Haas, and M. Murrin, "Predictors of Retention and Arrest in Drug Courts," *National Drug Court Institute Review II*, no. 1 (1999), pp. 33–60.

25. K. Robinson, "Research Update: Reports on Recent Drug Court Research," *National Drug Court Institute Review III*, no. 1 (2000), pp. 121–134.

26. S. Satel, "Drug Treatment: The Case for Coercion," *National Drug Court Institute Review III*, no. 1 (2000), pp. 1–56.

27. Taken from a class lecture by James B. Halsted, University of South Florida, 2002.

28. P. Ozar, J. Kelley, and V. Begue, "Ethical Conduct of State Employees and Administrators—The Search for Standards," *Judicature*, vol. 71 (1988), pp. 223–228.

29. N. Chamelin, V. Fox, and P. Whisenand, *Introduction to Criminal Justice*. Englewood Cliffs, N.J.: Prentice Hall, 1979, p. 278.

30. Neubauer, op. cit., p. 138.

31. Ozar, Kelley, and Begue, op. cit.

32. Neubauer, op. cit., p. 135.

33. Ozar, Kelley, and Begue, op. cit.

34. Neubauer, op. cit.

35. B. Ostrom and N. Kavder, *Examining the Work of State Courts, 1998*. Williamsburg, Va.: National Center for State Courts, 2000.

36. Administrative Office of the United States Courts, *Annual Report to the Director, 1993*. Washington, D.C.: Administrative Office of the United States Courts, 1994.

37. Ibid, p. 552.

38. Bureau of Justice Statistics, *Felony Sentences in State Courts, 1992*. Washington, D.C.: U.S. Department of Justice, 1995, p. 1.

39. Ibid.

40. Ostrom and Kavder, op. cit.

41. National Institute of Justice, *Priority Prosecution of High-Rate Dangerous Offenders*. Washington, D.C.: U.S. Department of Justice, 1991.

42. Readers interested in the topics of lawyer training, bar associations, admission to the bar, and so on may wish to review J. J. Bonsignore et al., *Before the Law*. Boston: Houghton Mifflin, 1977, Chapter 3, pp. 173–218; H. Jacob, *Justice in America: Courts, Lawyers, and the Judicial Process*. Boston: Little, Brown, 1978, Chapter 4, pp. 45–78.

43. This is particularly relevant in the light of the verdicts reached in: *California v. O. J. Simpson, Florida v. William Kennedy Smith*, and *California v. Stacy Kuhn* (the Rodney King case).

44. American Bar Association Project on Standards for Criminal Justice, *Standards Relating to the Administration of Criminal Justice*. Washington, D.C.: American Bar Association, 1974, p. 56.

45. G. Kessel, "Adversarial Experiences in the American Criminal Trial," *Notre Dame Law Review*, vol. 67 (1992), p. 402.

46. W. McDonald, *Plea Bargaining: Critical Issues in Common Practice*. Washington, D.C.: U.S. Government Printing Office, 1985.

47. A. Alschuler, "The Prosecutor's Role in Plea Bargaining," *University of Chicago Law Review*, vol. 76 (1968), p. 53.

48. S. Salzburg, "Lawyers, Clients and the Adversary System," *Mercer Law Review*, vol. 37 (1986), pp. 651–655.

49. G. Kessel, op. cit., p. 407.

50. J. Nijboer, "The American Adversary System in Criminal Cases: Between Ideology and Reality," *Journal of International and Criminal Law* (Spring 1997), p. 74.

51. A. Smith and H. Pollack, *Criminal Justice and Mass Society*. New York: Rinehart & Winston, 1972.

52. Bureau of Justice Statistics, *Prosecutors in State Courts, 1994*. Washington, D.C.: U.S. Government Printing Office, 1996.

53. Advisory Committee on the Prosecution and Defense Functions, *Prosecution Functions and Defense Functions*. New York: American Bar Association, 1970, pp. 17–134.

54. Ibid.

55. G. Cole, "The Decision to Prosecute," *Law and Society Review*, vol. 3 (1983), pp. 331–343.

56. M. Lewis, W. Bundy, and J. Hague, *An Introduction to the Courts and Judicial Process*. Englewood Cliffs, N.J.: Prentice Hall, 1978.

57. C. Spahn, J. Gruhl, and S. Welch, "The Impact on Ethnicity and Gender in the Decision to Reject or Dismiss Charges," *Criminology*, vol. 25 (1997), pp. 175–191.

58. American Bar Association, *Standards for Criminal Justice: Prosecution Functions and Defense Functions* Washington, D.C.: American Bar Association, 1993 pp. 18–19.

59. K. Davis, *Discretionary Justice*. Baton Rouge: Louisiana State University Press, 1969.

60. Ostrom and Kavder, op. cit.

61. P. Wice, *Criminal Lawyers: An Endangered Species*. Beverly Hills, Calif: Sage, 1978.

62. Advisory Committee on the Prosecution and Defense Functions, op. cit.

63. C. Willard, *Criminal Justice on Trial*. Skokie, Ill.: National Textbook Company, 1976, pp. 111–121.

64. *Faretta v. California*, 422 U.S. 806 (1975).

65. Y. Kamisar, W. LaFave, and G. Israel, *Basic Criminal Procedure*, 9th ed. St. Paul, Minn.: West, 1999).

66. P. Houlden and S. Balkin, "Quality and Cost Comparisons of Private Bar Indigent Defense Systems: Contract vs. Ordered Assigned Counsel," *Journal of Criminal Law and Criminology*, vol. 76 (1985), pp. 176–200.

67. J. Lozier, "The Missouri Plan a.k.a. Merit Selection Is the Best Solution for Selecting Michigan Judges," *Michigan Bar Journal* (September 1996), p. 917.

68. W. Hearnes, "Twenty-Five Years under the Missouri Plan," *Journal of the American Judicature Society*, vol. 49 (1965), pp. 100–104.

69. "Women Find Bar to Bench a Far Journey," *The New York Times* October 17, 1982, p. E15. Reprinted with permission from *The New York Times*, all rights reserved.

70. "President's Judicial Appointments Are Divers, But Well in the Mainstream." *The New York Times*, October 17, 1994, p. 11. Reprinted with permission from *The New York Times*, all rights reserved.

71. "Some Problems Shared by Women on the Bench," *The New York Times*, October 17, 1994, p. 11. Reprinted with permission from *The New York Times*, all rights reserved.

72. "Women Find Bar to Bench a Far Journey," op. cit.

73. J. W. Howard, "The Freshman Years," *Judicature*, vol. 69 (1985), pp. 127–146.

74. A. Rosett and D. Cressey, *Justice by Consent: Plea Bargains in the American Courthouse*. (Philadelphia: Lippincott, 1976, pp. 90–91.

75. L. Alpert, *Learning about Trial Judging: The Socialization of State Trial Judges*, ed. A. Cramer. Beverly Hills, Calif.: Sage, 1981.

76. Ibid.

77. Howard, op. cit., p. 134.

78. A. Blumberg, *Criminal Justice: Issues and Ironies*. New York: New View Points, 1972.

79. R. Ginsberg, et al., "On Becoming a Judge: Socialization to the Judicial Role," *Judicature*, vol. 69 (1985), pp. 139–146.

80. Ibid.

81. H. Levinson, *Executive Stress*. New York: Harper & Row, 1970.

82. P. Stultz, *Judging Judges: The Investigation of Rose Bird and the California Supreme Court*. New York: Free Press, 1981.

83. I. Zimmerman, "Stress: What It Does to Judges and How It Can Be Lessened," *Judges' Journal*, vol. 20, no. 3 (1981), pp. 4–9, 48–49.

84. Ibid.

85. Ibid.

86. Ibid.

87. I. Robins, "Has the Time Come for Judicial Sabbaticals?" *Judicature*, vol. 71 (1988), pp. 136–142.

88. Ibid., p. 205

89. Ibid.

90. W. Seymour, *Why Justice Fails*. New York: Morrow, 1973, p. 78.

91. B. Overton, *Report to the Legislature on the State Judiciary*. Tallahassee, Fla., 1976.

92. Neubauer, op. cit., p. 439.

93. Law Enforcement Assistance Administration, *National Survey of Court Organization, 1971: Preliminary Reports*. Washington, D.C.: U.S. Government Printing Office, 1972.

94. J. Jennings, *Evaluation of the Manhattan Criminal Courts Master Calendar Project*. New York: Rand Corporation, 1972.

95. Neubauer, op. cit.

8

PRETRIAL PROCEDURES: BAIL, PRETRIAL HEARINGS, AND PLEA BARGAINING

Chapter OUTLINE

Initiating Prosecution in Misdemeanor Cases
- Pretrial Detention
- The Complaint
- Three Types of Preliminary Hearings

Bail or Jail?
- The Time and the Criteria for the Bail Decision
- Drug Testing to Reduce Pretrial Misconduct

Types and Amounts of Bail
- Commercial Bail
- The Bail Schedule
- State Bail Statutes
- Conditions of Bail
- Alternatives to Bail
- Forfeiture of Bail
- Defects in the Bail System: Commercialization of Bail Bondspeople, Bounty Hunters, and Bail Jumpers

Denial of Bail
- Reforms in the Bail System
- The Effects of Preventive Detention
- May a Convicted Defendant Be Out on Bail While Awaiting an Appeal?

Misdemeanor Trials

Initiating Felony Prosecution

The Preliminary Hearing (the Bindover Hearing)

The Grand Jury
- The Grand Jury Today
- True Bills and Presentments
- The Special Investigative Grand Jury

Formal Felony Charging
- Constitutional Requirements of a Prosecutor's Information
- Showups, Lineups, and Other Pretrial Identification Procedures during the Prearrest, Postarrest, and after the Formal Felony Charging
- Constitutional Requirements and Identification Procedures

The Arraignment

Pretrial Motions
- The Motion to Dismiss
- The Motion for Discovery
- The Motion for a Change of Venue
- The Motion of Intention to Provide Alibi
- The Motion for Severance
- The Motion to Determine Competency
- The Constitutional Right of Being Competent to Stand Trial
- The Motion for a Bill of Particulars

The Suppression Hearing
- The Motion to Suppress
- The Right to a Suppression Hearing

Plea Negotiations
- Justification for Plea Bargaining
- The Prevalence of Guilty Pleas
- Entering a Constitutional Guilty Plea
- The Plea Process
- The Victim and Plea Bargaining

Factors in Plea Negotiations
- Evaluating Plea Bargaining
- How Can a Defendant Successfully Appeal a Guilty Plea?

Pretrial Diversion as an Alternative to Plea Bargaining

Summary

Key Terms

- arraignment, p. 339
- bail, p. 317
- bail bondsperson, p. 318
- change of venue, p. 341
- citation, p. 314
- complaint, p. 314
- forfeiture, p. 318
- grand jury, p. 334
- indictment, p. 336
- initial appearance, p. 316
- motion for discovery, p. 341
- *nolle prosequi*, p. 317
- plea colloquy, p. 346
- presentment, p. 335
- pretrial diversion program, p. 351
- pretrial misconduct, p. 320
- pretrial motion, p. 340
- preventive detention, p. 328
- probable cause, p. 314
- summary trial, p. 317
- true bill, p. 335
- victim-impact statement, p. 348

Courtesy David Young-Wolf/PhotoEdit

However important the criminal trial by jury may be to the novelist or dramatist, it occupies a relatively minor position in the administration of justice in the United States. In any given year, less than 10 percent of suspects apprehended for serious crimes go through the formal steps of a criminal trial. Thus, much of the criminal process is administrative rather than judicial. That is, the process flow is accomplished through negotiation rather than adversarial proceedings.

The fact that this administrative model is inconsistent with the traditional model of litigated criminal prosecution should not be viewed with alarm. Given the enormous number of cases that must be processed, particularly in metropolitan areas, the resources of the criminal justice system would be strained beyond the breaking point if most cases were not dropped or carried to a negotiated conclusion.[1] The administration of justice would not merely be slowed, it would come to a complete halt. In addition, the facts in many criminal cases are not disputed. The suspect either clearly did or clearly did not commit the offense with which he or she is charged. If the facts are beyond dispute, there is no need for a time-consuming, expensive, and laborious criminal trial (Figure 8.1).

FIGURE 8.1

The Criminal Justice System as a Filtering Process

Source: Bureau of Justice Statistics, *The Prosecution of Felony Arrests.*

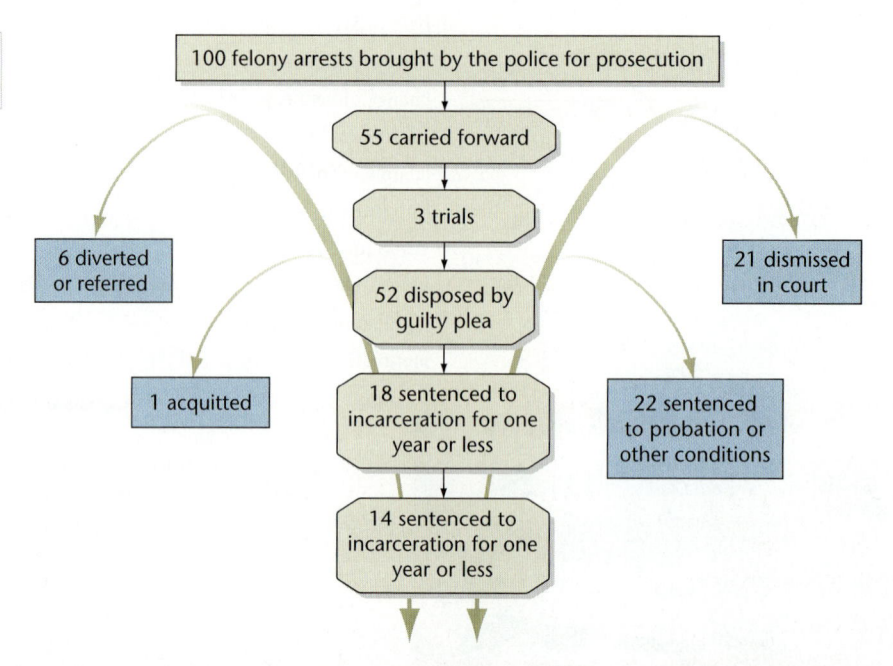

- 100 felony arrests brought by the police for prosecution
- 55 carried forward
- 3 trials
- 52 disposed by guilty plea
- 6 diverted or referred
- 21 dismissed in court
- 1 acquitted
- 18 sentenced to incarceration for one year or less
- 22 sentenced to probation or other conditions
- 14 sentenced to incarceration for one year or less

CTQ

What is case attrition?

INITIATING PROSECUTION IN MISDEMEANOR CASES

A misdemeanor, as we noted in Chapter 2, "The Substantive Criminal Law," is a less serious offense that may be punished by a fine or incarceration in a city or county jail for a period of less than one year. Prosecution for a misdemeanor is usually initiated by the issuance of a complaint. The **complaint** is usually made by a victim of or a witness to the crime; often, the arresting officer is the complaining witness. The purpose of filing a complaint is to determine whether there is probable cause for an arrest warrant. All of the existing evidence, and in a few cases the testimony of the complainant, is presented by the officer to a magistrate to prove that probable cause exists. **Probable cause** means that it is reasonable to believe that a crime was committed and that the defendant committed it. If the magistrate determines that probable cause exists, he or she then will issue an arrest warrant.

In some lesser offenses, where the crime charged is a minor offense punishable in some circumstances by no more than a fine, the police may be permitted to use a citation. A **citation** is an order to appear before a judge at some future date. In all other circumstances, however, a physical arrest must occur (as described in Chapter 3). When the suspect is present, the process continues to the interrogation and booking phases.

After a suspect is arrested, he or she is brought to the police station, detained, and interrogated. Following interrogation, the suspect may be released (for lack of evidence of wrongdoing) or booked. Booking is the administrative record of the arrest. At the time of booking, the accused's name and address, the time and place of the arrest, and the arrest charge are entered into the police log. Booking often includes fingerprinting and photographing the suspect.

Following booking, a suspect may be released in one of six ways (see Table 8.1), or may be confined in jail to await trial. The choice is made based on the suspect's reputation and the seriousness of the offense. If the decision is made not to release the suspect, he or she is placed in pretrial detention. The suspect will await trial incarcerated in the county jail.

Pretrial Detention

The criminal defendant who is not eligible for bail or does not have the financial resources to either (1) post the full amount or (2) pay 10 percent of the bail amount to the bail bondsperson is subject to pretrial detention in the local county jail. To a large extent, jails are in poor condition because few people care about them (jails are discussed in greater detail in Chapter 11). For this reason, a detainee must see a magistrate quickly because the jail has been a trouble spot for the criminal justice system for quite some

TABLE 8.1　Pretrial Release Mechanisms*

Authority	Release Mechanism
Police	*Field citation release* — An arresting officer releases the arrestee on a written promise to appear in court, at or near the actual time and location of the arrest. This procedure is commonly used for misdemeanor charges and is similar to issuing a traffic ticket.
Police	*Station house release* — The determination of an arrestee's eligibility and suitability for release and the actual release of the arrestee are deferred until after he or she has been removed from the scene of an arrest and brought to the station house or police headquarters.
Police/Pretrial	*Jail release* — The determination of an arrestee's eligibility and suitability for citation release and the actual release of the arrestee are deferred until after he or she has been delivered by the arresting department to a jail or other pretrial detention facility for screening, booking, and/or admission.
Pretrial/Court	*Direct release authority by pretrial program* — To streamline the release process and reduce the length of stay in detention, courts may authorize pretrial programs to release defendants without direct judicial involvement. Where court rule delegates such authority, the practice is generally limited to misdemeanor charges, but felony release authority has been granted in some jurisdictions.
Police/Court	*Bail schedule* — An arrestee can post bail at the stationhouse or jail according to accounts specified in a bail schedule. The schedule is a list of all bailable charges and a corresponding dollar amount for each. Schedules may vary widely from jurisdiction to jurisdiction.
Court	*Judicial release* — Arrestees who have not been released by either the police or the jailer and who have not posted bail appear at the hearing before a judge, magistrate, or bail commissioner within a set period of time. In jurisdictions with pretrial release programs, program staff often interview arrestees detained at the jail prior to the first hearing, verify the background information, and present recommendations to the court at arraignment.

*These are techniques which allow an arrested suspect to get out of jail on bail without having to go through a traditional bail hearing in front of a trial judge.

IN THE NEWS

A HUMAN PERSPECTIVE

SUSPECTS CAN BE HELD 48 HOURS WITHOUT WARRANT, DECISION HOLDS

The U.S. Supreme Court ruled that police generally may jail persons arrested without a warrant for up to 48 hours before a judicial hearing has to be held to determine if sufficient cause exists to detain criminal suspects.

The 5-to-4 decision—Justice David H. Souter—set aside a federal court order issued in a civil rights lawsuit brought by Donald Lee McLaughlin in 1987 against Riverside County, Calif., where probable-cause hearings were generally held in 48 hours. Under Riverside County's policy, delays of three or four days were not uncommon if an arrest occurred on or close to weekends and holidays. The federal court ordered county officials to establish a 36-hour deadline during which the judicial proceeding must be held (June 1991).

Source: Reprinted with permission from *Law Enforcement News*, John Jay College of Criminal Justice, June 20, 1991.

---

time. Conditions tend to be poor and rehabilitation nonexistent (see "In the News: Suspects Can Be Held 48 Hours Without Warrant, Decision Holds"). In terms of the number of people affected per year, pretrial custody on misdemeanors in jail account for more incarceration time in the United States than does the actual punishment of imprisonment for misdemeanors after being convicted and sentenced for the commission of these misdemeanors.[2] Because of these considerations, recent efforts have concentrated on improving the standards for bail, rather than on easing its application.

The Complaint

As mentioned, the issuance of a complaint is the basis for proceeding with the prosecution of misdemeanors following arrest. The word *complaint* is somewhat misleading, because it suggests that an action is being taken by the injured party or victim of a crime. Although the victim of the crime may be the complainant, the true plaintiff is actually the people of the state acting through their lawful representative, the district attorney. It is the public prosecutor, therefore, who issues the complaint in a criminal proceeding. The complaint is a written document that identifies the criminal charge, the place and date of the crime's occurrence, and the circumstances surrounding the arrest. The complaint is sworn to and signed under oath by the complainant, usually a police officer, although sometimes a citizen does this.

A complaint is essentially a justification for the arrest of a defendant so that he or she can be arraigned—that is, have the charge formally read aloud to him or her and be allowed to enter a plea. There are four questions a prosecutor must ask to determine if a complaint should be prepared:

1. Has a crime (public offense) been committed?
2. Did a particular individual whose identity is known commit the crime?
3. Is there sufficient legally admissible evidence to ensure a conviction?
4. Are there no adequate alternatives to prosecution available that are preferable to the formal processing of the offender through the criminal justice system?

Unless the answer to all of these questions is yes, a complaint should not be prepared.

The Three Types of Preliminary Hearings

What the legal system has labeled the *initial presentment* of the accused before a judge has been called by many names. In general, the initial presentment of an accused before a judicial officer is referred to as a preliminary hearing. There are many preliminary encounters between a defendant and a judge during a judicial proceeding. Preliminary hearings occur between the suspect's arrest and trial. Generally a preliminary hearing may serve one of three purposes: (1) to determine whether probable cause for arrest and detention exist, (2) to set bail or some other condition for a pretrial release and to assign an indigent defendant an attorney, or (3) to make a probable cause determination as to whether or not to uphold the prosecution's decision to charge the accused. It is important to note that the probable-cause requirement may be satisfied at an earlier stage in the criminal process, thereby limiting the necessity for such a preliminary examination. Thus, when a *grand jury indictment* is obtained prior to an arrest or when an arrest was made pursuant to an *arrest warrant*, the preliminary examination need not be held, since probable cause to detain has already been established.

However, a person who has been arrested without an arrest warrant and has not been indicted has a constitutional right (pursuant to the Fourth Amendment) to a judicial determination. Typically he or she has the right to the first type of preliminary hearing in the form of what is referred to in legal circles a *Gerstein hearing*. The sole purpose of a *Gerstein* hearing is to determine whether probable cause exists for continued detention.[3] This probable-cause determination is required *only* when a significant pretrial restraint on liberty is involved; the restraint must be something other than the condition that the suspect appear for trial. Hence, a *Gerstein* hearing is never given to someone who has taken advantage of pretrial release mechanisms.

The characteristics of a *Gerstein* hearing are as follows: The probable cause to obtain a hearing must be determined within a short period of time following an arrest to avoid any significant restraints on the constitutionally protected liberty of the accused. A forty-eight-hour delay has been held presumptively reasonable, but a delay of more than forty-eight hours is presumptively unreasonable.[4] Separate and distinguishable from a *Gerstein* hearing is the second type of preliminary hearing, usually referred to as an *initial appearance*. Whether or not the defendant's case requires a *Gerstein* hearing, a hearing in which the defendant is brought before the judicial officer within twenty-four to seventy-two hours of the arrest is called an **initial appearance.** At this kind of preliminary hearing, the judicial officer informs the defendant of his or her rights, sets bail under the conditions of pretrial release, and appoints counsel if the defendant is indigent. This hearing is nonadversarial and can be combined with a *Gerstein* hearing when required. At the initial appearance, the accused does not have the right to present a defense.

Generally when legal scholars discuss the initial hearings, they combine all three preliminary hearings. Yet the initial appearance is not a fact-finding or probable-cause hearing. The sufficiency of the arrest warrant is examined at this stage. At this time the magistrate will note for the record whether the accused is represented by counsel. If the accused suggests that he or she is too poor to afford counsel, the magistrate will make an inquiry into the defendant's financial status, often called an indigency hearing. If a finding of indigency is made, the magistrate will require that the accused sign an affidavit swearing to financial impoverishment. This allows the court to appoint a public defender to represent the accused.

Due process requires additional constitutional procedures during the initial appearance. The accused must be given formal notice of the charges against him or her. Such official notice occurs for the first time at the initial appearance. At the same time, the accused is also notified of his or her legal rights, similar to a *Miranda*-type warning (see Chapter 3, "The Law of Criminal Procedure and The Rights of the Criminally Accused"). Also during the initial appearance, bail is determined for those who did not receive a temporary release during the booking phase.

Seldom but not often during the initial appearance (when the magistrate is reviewing minor offenses such as prostitution, or other cases where a simple citation has been issued), the magistrate also conducts a **summary trial** and sentencing. Both are concluded during the initial appearance. In these instances, the defendant needs no further case processing. In rare situations, the magistrate presiding at the initial appearance may determine that the evidence available is insufficient to warrant further criminal processing, similar to a prosecutor's use of **nolle prosequi** (see Chapter 7, "The Dynamics of the Criminal Court"). Thus, the magistrate dismisses the case. The third type of preliminary hearing (a bindover hearing) is discussed fully later in this chapter.

BAIL OR JAIL?

Defendants are not quite like other persons in that there is probable cause to believe that they have committed an offense. This may justify some special level of state supervision. Accused defendants have not been convicted and therefore cannot justly be punished. In addition, defendants know that the state intends to prosecute them, and if the case against them is strong enough, they might have reason to flee rather than stand trial.

The basic purpose of **bail** is to furnish a means for the release of a detained individual while his or her case is pending, provided the accused is ready to give reasonable and sufficient assurance of a willingness to appear in court at the appropriate time. In providing for release on bail, the presumption of innocence goes beyond its well-known place in trial proceedings (that is, the necessity for proof of guilt beyond a reasonable doubt), emphasizing that, in American criminal jurisprudence, guilt is the decision of the court and is not inherent in prosecution.

Bail has a constitutional basis. The Eighth Amendment guarantees that excessive bail shall not be required. Note that this is not a guarantee of the right to bail, but only a prohibition against excessive bail once bail is granted.

The main function of bail is to ensure the presence of the accused at the trial.[5] Bail is usually set by a judicial officer at the initial appearance of the defendant after the arrest. Bail also prevents the infliction of punishment before conviction, thereby giving meaning to the presumption of innocence that underlines the criminal justice system. Release on bail also permits the accused to assist in the preparation of his or her defense. The defendant's presence in the community is necessary to secure and to interview witnesses.

Constitutional issues exist in answering the question of what constitutes excessive bail. The Supreme Court has held that the function of bail is limited to ensuring the presence of the accused at trial. Thus, the bail is excessive if it is higher than the amount reasonably calculated to ensure the presence of the accused.

Once it has been determined that there is probable cause to bind a defendant over for felony trial, it is the function of the lower-court magistrate to again set bail. Bail is a legal procedure for securing temporary liberty following arrest through a written promise to appear in court as required. In support of this promise, it may be necessary to provide cash bail, post a surety bond, or supply evidence of equity in real property, together with the written assurance of another person or persons.

To post bail, an accused is required to give the court some form of monetary surety, most often cash, property, or a bond from a bonding company. In most jurisdictions, individuals arrested for misdemeanors can be released almost immediately by posting bail at the county jail or police station where they are booked. The size of the bail is usually determined by a fixed bail schedule and is relatively small. The so-called schedule of bail contains a list of misdemeanors and the amount of bail required for release. It may also specify a standard amount of bail for release for all misdemeanor offenses not listed in the schedule.

The Time and the Criteria for the Bail Decision

The procedures by which the bail decision is made vary among jurisdictions, but a hearing is required and the defendant is entitled to the benefit of counsel at that hearing. In the federal system, the hearing must take place within twenty-four hours of arrest. In some jurisdictions there are statutes specifying what types of offenses are bailable. In others there are specifications concerning what the magistrate should consider in making the decision. In many cases, however, the magistrate has wide discretion in the bail decision, and there is virtually no check on this decision.

The magistrate has wide latitude in setting the amount of bail. In the federal system, the factors most closely related to the level of bail, in order of importance, are the seriousness of the current charge, the district in which the bail hearing occurs, and the criminal record of the offender.[6]

Drug Testing to Reduce Pretrial Misconduct

The Director of the Administrative Offices for the United States court found that monitoring the use of drugs by defendants on bail reduces not only their use of drugs but also their pretrial misconduct. In Pima and Maricopa Counties in Arizona, a computerized case-tracking system selected a control group and an experimental group of similar defendants on bail. The system included information about prior record, court appearance history, offense, living arrangements, bail decision, failure to appear, and criminal behavior while on bail. The control group received normal supervision; the experimental group received drug monitoring during pretrial release.[7]

No significant differences in failure-to-appear or rearrest rates between the two groups occurred in Pima County, except that members of the monitored group were slightly less likely to get rearrested for the possession of drugs. In Maricopa County, arrest and failure to appear rates were higher in the monitored group than in the control group. On the basis of their findings, the authors concluded: "Systematic drug testing and monitoring in the pretrial setting. . . is not likely to achieve significant or major reductions in pretrial misconduct."[8]

TYPES AND AMOUNTS OF BAIL

The theoretical purpose as well as the guideline of bail is to ensure that the accused appears in court for trial. When determining the amount of bail to fix, the magistrate sometimes is obliged to use this guideline to order an amount of money that he or she believes will guarantee the defendant's presence at future court hearings.

CTQ

Is it possible for an expert to give a scientific opinion on the question of whether or not a particular human being has a proclivity toward future violence?

Commercial Bail

From the nineteenth century until the 1960s, American jurisdictions required money bail. Although pretrial release programs, pretrial detention, and preventive detention supplement it, commercial bail, or bail bonding as a private business, still exists. Judges set the bail amount. Defendants pay a fee to the **bail bondsperson,** usually 10 percent of the bail amount. Bondspeople guarantee to pay a **forfeiture**—the face amount of the bail bond—if defendants do not appear. Fees are bondspeople's livelihood. Suppose a court sets bail at $1,000. If a defendant secures a bail bond for a 10 percent fee, the bondsperson retains the $100 (10 percent of the bail amount). If, on the other hand, a defendant pays $1,000 deposit to the court, the court returns the full amount when the defendant appears.

The Bail Schedule

The bail schedule eliminates disparity in the setting of bail by bail decision makers. It provides judges with a tool that uniformly designs bail criteria while at the same time allows sufficient flexibility to deal with individual situations. Such schedules define the intensity of an accused's bail risk.

Bail amounts usually are somewhat lower for defendants who have lived at the same address for several years, as compared to more transient arrestees; somewhat lower for women than for men; and lower for defendants with college and high school educations than for defendants with no high school education. Holding other factors constant, there is no relationship between the amount of bail imposed and such factors as race, age, drug use, income, employment history, number of dependents supported by the defendant, and past history of jumping bail. As one would expect, the probability of posting bail decreases as the amount of bail increases.

During the postarrest period of detention, the bail amount depends upon the severity of the offense, whether the arrest was made with or without a warrant, and whether the defendant has been arraigned. When an arrest is made on a warrant alleging a public offense, bail should be in the amount specified on the warrant's endorsement by the issuing magistrate. When the arrest is for a misdemeanor, the amount of bail should be fixed by the magistrate at the time of arraignment. Prior to arraignment, bail should be set as fixed in the arrest warrant. If the arrest is made without a warrant, the amount of bail should coincide with the nationwide schedule of bail for misdemeanors[9] (see Figure 8.2).

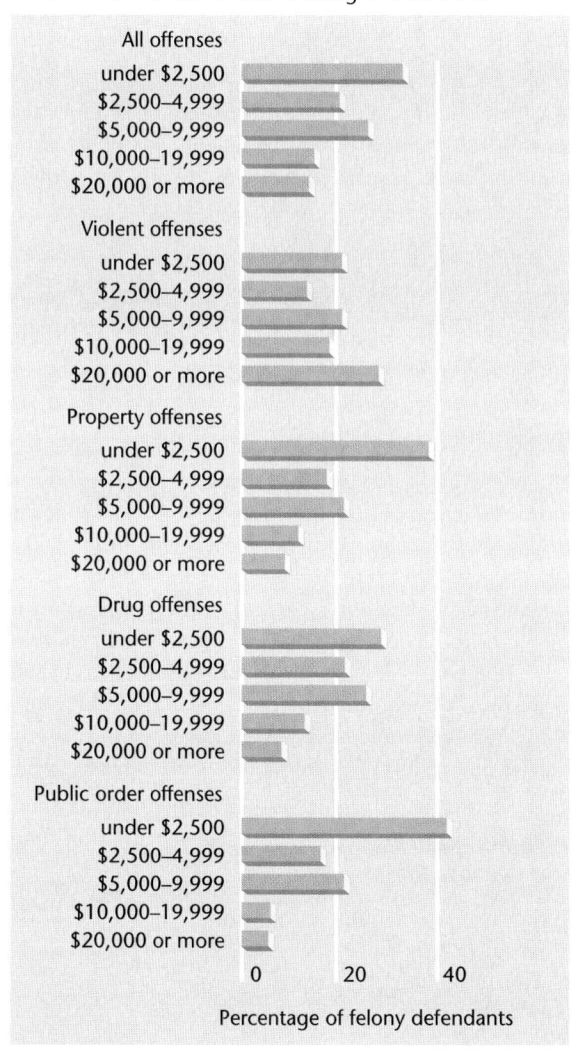

FIGURE 8.2

Bail Amounts for Felony Defendants by Type of Offense

Source: U.S. Department of Justice, Bureau of Justice Statistics, *National Update*, vol. 1.

State Bail Statutes

State bail statutes vary widely, but since the 1970s they have reflected a shift from emphasizing defendants' rights and securing their appearance in court to concentrating on crime control and community safety. A Florida law, for example, implies that the intent of bail statutes enacted by the legislature should give primary consideration to the protection of the community from risk of physical harm to people. Ten state statutes briefly list gross criteria, which means leaving the bail decision to judges as "a matter of sound discretion." Others resemble the federal act and list release conditions in detail. (See "Conditions of Bail" in the next section.)

Whether or not statutes formally prescribe procedures in detail, most judges act similarly in practice. Judges base bail decisions primarily on the seriousness of charges against defendants, a clear and easily applied standard. The strength of the prosecution's case against defendants also carries weight, as does the prior criminal history, or "rap sheet," of defendants. In most localities, judges give little or no weight to community ties or defendants' background and character.[10]

Conditions of Bail

Certain factors have been found to correlate with **pretrial misconduct** (such as arrest for a new crime while out on bail, willful failure to appear for a court date, and violations of the technical conditions of release): (1) The longer the person is out on bail before the trial, the greater the likelihood of some kind of pretrial misconduct; (2) the more extensive the prior criminal record, the greater the likelihood of misconduct; (3) drug use increases the likelihood of misconduct; and (4) the probability of misconduct is higher for minority males and young defendants. Should any pretrial misconduct occur that violates the agreement between the accused and the bail bondsperson (see Figure 8.3) or the judge, then the bondsperson has the right to revoke the surety and the judge will order the accused to be rearrested and placed back in jail again.

Massive jail overcrowding has been an unintended benefit for detainees who cannot afford bail. A desperate situation calls for desperate measures, such as a judge issuing a writ to release detainees who, but for the overcrowded situation, would await their trials incarcerated (see Figure 8.4).

Alternatives to Bail

In recent years various alternatives to bail have gained wide usage in response to two factors: the aforementioned unfairness of bail and the overcrowding of jail facilities that is due largely, in most parts of the country, to the incarceration of people who are unable to post bail or even to pay the bondsperson's fees. Some of these alternatives are as follows:

1. *Release on own recognizance.* Release on personal recognizance involves a personal pledge to appear and is not a particularly new system for release. It is appropriate when a person's ties to the community are sufficient to justify releasing that person on his or her own word. During the bail reform movement of the 1960s, studies showed that release on personal recognizance (usually referred to as "R.O.R.") is a low-risk endeavor if the accused's background is checked for a number of factors. A prime factor to be considered is, of course, the likelihood that the defendant, if found guilty, would receive a substantial sentence. In the authors' jurisdiction, over one-third of people arrested are offered R.O.R., and that includes both those who otherwise would have posted cash or surety bonds and those who would otherwise have had to remain in jail awaiting trial.

2. *Supervised release.* Supervised release places the accused in the custody of another person or organization, including so-called halfway houses. (This system is discussed in much greater detail in Chapter 13.) It is designed to take people who are slightly greater "skip risks" than the ideal R.O.R. candidate and release them under circumstances that tend to ensure their return for court proceedings. These programs typically require the released person to make periodic reports to a counselor and to hold a job.

3. *Release upon summons or notice to appear.* A large and growing number of jurisdictions have implemented systems that apply in misdemeanor situations and

---

WEB

For more information on R.O.R. and pretrial release, **visit the link to the Vera Institute on our Web site,** www.prenhall.com/territo.

FIGURE 8.3

Typical Bail Bond Information Sheet

This sheet lists breaches of the bail agreement that could result in the accused's immediate incarceration to await trial.
Agent: _____

BAIL BOND INFORMATION SHEET

DEFENDANT: _____   POWER NUMBER(S): _____

AS A PRINCIPAL (defendant) AND/OR INDEMNITOR (guarantor) ON A BAIL BOND, YOU MUST BE GIVEN A COPY OF ANY COLLATERAL DOCUMENT THAT YOU SIGN FOR THE BOND.
　　WHEN ALL AGREEMENTS HAVE BEEN FULFILLED AND BOND IS DISCHARGED IN WRITING BY THE COURT, AND WITHOUT LOSS EXPENSE ON THE BOND, YOUR FULL COLLATERAL WILL BE RETURNED TO YOU.
　　BE AWARE COLLATERAL IS AT RISK IF THE PRINCIPAL FAILS TO APPEAR IN COURT OR IF THE PRINCIPAL COMMITS ANY BREACH (VIOLATION) OF AGREEMENT.
　　ANY OF THE FOLLOWING HAPPENINGS IS A BREACH OF AGREEMENT:

1. If principal fails to appear in court;
2. If principal shall depart the jurisdiction of the court without the written consent of the court and the Surety, or its Agent;
3. If principal shall move from one address to another without notifying the Surety, or Agent, in writing prior to said move;
4. If principal shall commit any act which shall constitute reasonable evidence of principal's intention to cause a forfeiture of the bond;
5. If principal shall make any material false statement in the application;
6. If principal shall violate any special restriction or condition of the bond imposed by the Court.

For general information regarding your collateral, contact the agent—name and address at top of this sheet.

　　　　　　　　FOR FURTHER INQUIRY/COMPLAINT, CONTACT:
　　　　　　　　UTAH BAIL BOND REGULATORY BOARD
　　　　　　　　UTAH DEPARTMENT OF INSURANCE
　　　　　　　　546-A LARSON BUILDING
　　　　　　　　SALT LAKE CITY, UT 32399-0300
　　　　　　　　PHONE: 934/488-6488

　　　　　　　　　　　　　　**********

PRINCIPAL/INDEMNITOR ACKNOWLEDGMENT

I/WE HAVE RECEIVED A COPY OF THIS INFORMATION SHEET. I/WE HAVE RECEIVED A COPY OF ALL COLLATERAL DOCUMENTS THAT I/WE SIGNED FOR THIS BOND.

_____　　　　　_____
Signature　　　　　　　　　　　　　　　　　Signature

---

encourage an officer to evaluate factors that make a person very likely to appear in court. Under this system, if these factors are present, the officer has the discretion not to arrest an offender, but instead issue a *summons*, or *notice to appear*, which is analogous to a traffic ticket. This system is available only for those who otherwise would be arrested for misdemeanors. Officers do not have the authority to release accused felons. Some jurisdictions require that the offender be first brought to the station and that a *stationhouse release* be effected; others allow *field citations*, with release on the spot.

　　A number of state systems allow release by the officer on the scene or by the jailer after an examination of residency, employment, family, and so on. Such a system keeps most local residents from having to post bond—a practice

FIGURE 8.4

Re: Extraordinary Pretrial Release Procedures to Relieve Jail Overcrowding

WHEREAS, members of the criminal justice community in this circuit recognize that the proper detention and release of accused defendants prior to trial is a matter of great public concern and community safety; and

WHEREAS, the Hillsborough County jail facilities must operate within mandatory population guidelines set by law; and

WHEREAS, the courts of this circuit seek to comply with jail population guidelines without compromising the safety of the community; and

WHEREAS, a committee consisting of judges, the State Attorney, the Public Defender, and the Sheriff, has reviewed pretrial release procedures and has recommended changes to Administrative Order S-13-89-57; and

Misdemeanor or Ordinance Offenses Charged by Information, or Felony Offenses

All accused offenders who are booked into the county jail pursuant to misdemeanor or ordinance offenses charged by information, or pursuant to felony charges, shall be screened by a classification section of the sheriff's office for possible signature or own-recognizance; the investigation shall include verification of the accused offender's residence and employment. In addition, the classification section shall contact the alleged victim of the crime (in the case of a crime against a person) to receive input from the alleged victim and inform them that the accused offender is being considered for release on his or her own recognizance.

In order to meet the minimum standards for pretrial release, an arrestee must meet the following qualifications:

A. An arrestee must not be charged with a capital life or first-degree felony, or be on active parole or probation.

B. An arrestee must receive at least six points to be considered for release on the arrestee's own recognizance based on the following criteria:

Residence	Points
Current resident 1 year or current resident and 1.5 years at previous address	3
Current resident 6 months or current resident and 1 year at previous address	2
Current resident 4 months or current resident and 6 months at previous address	1
Last 2 years or more in Hillsborough County or Pinellas, Pasco, Polk, Manatee or Sarasota	1

Family Ties	
Lives with spouse and children OR head of household with children	4
Lives with parent(s), spouse, older person, one or more children, or other family relative	3
Lives with non-family friend or has regular contact with family	2

Employment, School, Resources	
Current job 1 year or more and can return to work	4
Current job 1 year or more or retired or homemaker with children	3
Current job 4 months or current and prior job 6 months, or homemaker	2
Current job or receiving unemployment or worker's compensation	1
Currently in school full-time attending regularly	4
Left school within 6 months and employed or attending school part-time	2
Left school within 3 months and unemployed	1

Health	
Poor health and regular visits to doctor	1
Definite knowledge of alcoholism or felony drug use	−1

Prior Record	Units
No convictions	2
Felonies	7 times number
Misdemeanors	2 times number

Any accused offender who is released on his or her own recognizance pursuant to this order, except those released pursuant to a notice to appear, shall receive a notice substantially stating the following:

"You are being released pursuant to administrative order because you have met the criteria for release. You have supplied an address to which all future court process will be sent. As a condition of your release, you must refrain from criminal activity of any kind and you must refrain from any contact with the alleged victim of the crime with which you have been charged except through pretrial discovery pursuant to the Florida Rules of Criminal Procedures. If you violate these conditions, or fail to appear for any of your court dates, your recognizance status will be revoked and you may remain in jail or be required to post a substantial bond until your charges have been disposed."

that keeps the police officer or deputy sheriff from having to leave the patrol zone to engage in the lengthy procedure of booking the defendant as well as eliminating any expense to the defendant. It should be understood that bail reform, including all of the alternatives mentioned here, is attractive to law enforcement not only for altruistic reasons but for practical ones: Bail reform can help to ease the overcrowded conditions of our jails. (For a more detailed discussion of jail overcrowding, see Chapter 11.)

4. *Property bonds.* Other items of value in place of cash, such as land, houses, automobiles, stocks, and so on, are assigned to the court for collateral against trial flight.

5. *Conditional release.* This type of release imposes a set of requirements for the defendant, which might include attending a drug treatment program, staying away from specific people such as potential witnesses or victims, and regular job attendance. Release under supervision is similar to conditional release, but adds the stipulation that the defendant report to an officer or to the court.

6. *Unsecured bond.* This release is based on a court-determined dollar amount of bail. Like the practice of receiving money on credit, it requires no monetary deposit with the court. The defendant signs the agreement. A failure to appear will result in the forfeiture of the bond, which might then be used to seize land, personal property, or bank accounts.

7. *Third-party custody.* This bail bond alternative assigns custody of the defendant to an individual or agency that promises to ensure his or her later appearance in court. Some pretrial release programs allow attorneys to assume this responsibility.

8. *Signature bond.* This type of bond allows the suspect to be released on his or her written promise to appear. Signature bonds involve no particular assessment of the defendant's dangerousness or likelihood to appear in court. They are used only in cases of minor offenses such as traffic and drug violations.

Pretrial release is a common practice. Approximately 85 percent of all state criminal defendants and 82 percent of all federal criminal defendants are released prior to trial. Sixty-three percent of state felony defendants and 60 percent of federal felony defendants are similarly released.[11]

Forfeiture of Bail

If, without sufficient excuse, a defendant fails to appear as required in the bail agreement, or on any other occasion when his or her presence in court is required by law, the court will enter this fact on the record and will declare a forfeiture of bail. Such a defendant becomes a fugitive from justice. If the amount of the bail or deposit exceeds fifty dollars, the bondsperson or depositor must be notified and the defendant is then subject to rearrest by either the bondsperson or the police.

After a forfeiture of bail, the bondsperson or depositor has 180 days in which to adjust the forfeiture in one of three ways: (1) The defendant and the bondsperson or depositor appear in court and provide an acceptable explanation or justification for the defendant's neglect or satisfactorily indicate to the court that the absence was not with the support of the bondsperson or depositor; (2) the bondsperson may appear in court and certify that the defendant is dead or physically unable to appear during the time allowed; and (3) the defendant may be turned over to the court.

Most bail bondspeople carry insurance. This fact, not known by the general public, eliminates the substantial risk most people believe that bail bondspeople have based on the nature of their business. If a client fails to appear and the court demands a bail forfeiture, the insurance company, rather than the bondsperson, covers the costs. This situation presents an extreme irony. Most people think of the bail bondsperson as having a great risk. In truth, the risk is spread out among all bail bondspeople and is covered by an insurance policy.

Finally, in addition to the forfeiture of bail, a defendant's failure to appear in court as required entails other consequences: (1) a capias or bench warrant is issued by the

IN THE WORKPLACE

BAIL BONDSPERSON

Approved and licensed by the insurance commissioner. Responsible for pledging cash or approved securities with the commissioner as security for bail bonds written about a judicial proceeding; receives or is promised money or other things of value. Performs a variety of duties, including the following: assisting in the apprehension and surrender of defendants to the court; executing of bonds. Minimum qualifications are as follows: 18 years old; resident of the state; person of good moral character; no felony convictions; no outstanding bail bond obligations; completion of twenty hours of education in the laws and regulations relating to a bail bondsperson; must score 70 percent or higher on a written bail bond examination.

court authorizing the defendant's arrest; and (2) the defendant becomes eligible for the state to prosecute him or her for a newly committed offense, which in many states is a felony with a maximum sentence of five years in prison and a $5,000 fine.

Defects in the Bail System: Commercialization of Bail Bondspeople, Bounty Hunters, and Bail Jumpers

When an accused person lacks financial resources, the bail system adds a discriminatory element to the administration of criminal justice. In his 1964 review of major findings about the bail systems of New York and Philadelphia, E. Johnson, nationally recognized bail expert, noted that many indigent defendants were unable to furnish bail, especially when bail was set above $1,000. Bail usually was set so high for serious offenses that few defendants in the cases obtained pretrial release. In addition, between 10 and 20 percent of defendants incarcerated pending trial were not convicted. For similar crimes, Johnson noted that jailed offenders were most likely to be convicted and to receive longer sentences than offenders released on bail. Another study found similar results. Why? The indigent defendant is unable to hire a lawyer, locate witnesses, and pay for the investigation necessary to present his or her case adequately, especially when being incarcerated for a pending trial interrupts normal earnings. Even when convicted, the bailed defendant has the advantage of showing evidence of steady employment and good conduct while awaiting trial. Such evidence supports a plea for probation.[12]

Another feature of the bail system that stands on the periphery of the criminal justice system is the bail bondsperson. He or she is a central figure in the bail system and is normally available twenty-four hours a day. Bondspeople are often viewed as the Achilles' heel in the bail system because even though they are private individuals and hence are not bound by law to the courts and the judicial process, they have the power to overrule a judge's decision concerning the release of the defendant when a suspect skips bail by failing to appear on the trial date (a bail jumper). Normally, bondspeople employ bounty hunters to catch bail jumpers. Usually bounty hunters are individuals (often ex-convicts) with an unsavory reputation (see Figure 8.5). They may travel interstate and use criminal methods such as kidnapping and false imprisonment to bring their customers to justice. Studies have demonstrated that some commercial bondspeople corrupt the system by offering kickbacks to judges in exchange for a judge's hesitancy to collect on outstanding sureties. Judicial officials generally agree that bondspeople hold

FIGURE 8.5

A bounty hunter is not always the cliché of a tough ex-con with a scary disposition.

Courtesy Dan Callister/Getty Images, Inc.-Stone Allstock.

the key to the jail in their pockets. They determine for whom they will act as surety—who in their judgment is a good risk. The bad risks, in the bondsperson's judgment, and the ones who are unable to pay the bondsperson's fees, remain in jail. The court is relegated to the relatively unimportant chore of fixing the amount of bail.[13] The step in the criminal justice process when commercial bondspeople, bail jumpers, and bounty hunters are performing their roles is illustrated in the overview of the entire system as represented in Figure 8.6.

Bail critic J. Murphy refers to the arrest and custody power of bondspeople as "a degenerate vestige of a bail relationship between defendant and surety that either perished or never gained footing in this country"[14] (see Figure 8.3). Nevertheless, the courts have consistently upheld this power in cases where fugitives have been taken at gunpoint, handcuffed, shackled to the floor of an automobile, beaten severely, and driven long distances without food or water in order to secure the remission of a misdemeanor bond of a few hundred dollars.

Whenever bail bondspeople are prosecuted for such abuses as fee splitting, bribery, and "fixing" of minor criminal cases, a fine or some other punitive action soothes the public and presumably restores the theoretical purity of the bail system. However, reformers maintain that it is not abuses in the bail system that constitute the problem; it is the system itself.[15] Any reform that leaves the bondsperson with undiminished powers of arrest and custody is an exercise in futility.[16] Murphy argues that the answer lies in adjusting the official retrieval system to increase efficiency without causing a corresponding loss of civil liberties—a move that could encourage the final replacement of bondspeople with police officers, a socially acceptable goal.[17]

Frank Devine's research indicates that the internal structure of the commercial bail system is its greatest defect. Indeed, all common-law countries except the United States have eliminated commercial bail bonding. In England, Australia, Canada, and New Zealand it is a crime to act as a commercial bail bondsperson. Devine argues that the reason for other countries' dissatisfaction with commercialized bail bonding is that it defeats the entire purpose of the bail system. In current practice, most defendants pay a 10 percent fee to the bondsperson, who then secures a bond from an insurance company. The financial risks of forfeiture are transferred to the bondsperson and then to the insurance company. This, according to Devine, eliminates the defendant's financial penalty. The fact that the bondsperson's fee is not returnable under any circumstances further reduces the incentive to appear.[18]

For example, if an accused defendant charged with a serious felony is out on a $10,000 bail and the defendant received bail from a commercial bondsperson, the defendant had to put up only $1,000 of his or her own money. Thus, if the defendant fails to return to court and stand trial (which might be tempting), he or she forfeits little. Therefore, the bondsperson or the insurance company is responsible for the other $9,000 owed the court. Even if the defendant decides to appear for trial, he or she would still forfeit the same $1,000, since that is the bondsperson's fee.

Hence, no matter what decision the defendant makes—to return to trial or to skip bail—he or she is out the same $1,000. Thus no additional financial hardship is imposed on a defendant for failing to return for trial. This contradicts the fundamental assumption of the American bail system. Requiring a defendant to post bail is meant to impose such a potential financial hardship that the defendant will choose to return for trial in order to avoid this hardship.

The 1990s movie *The Fugitive* was an adaptation of a 1960s television series. In the movie, the charming, enigmatic, and charismatic Harrison Ford played the title role (see Figure 8.7). Perhaps this is why many Americans look at fugitives with romantic but ambiguous curiosity.

DENIAL OF BAIL

No right to bail exists in capital cases. The rationale for this exception is that someone accused of a crime for which he or she might receive the death penalty is unlikely to return to court no matter how high the bail. Furthermore, the Supreme Court ruled that

FIGURE 8.6

An Overview of the Criminal Justice System

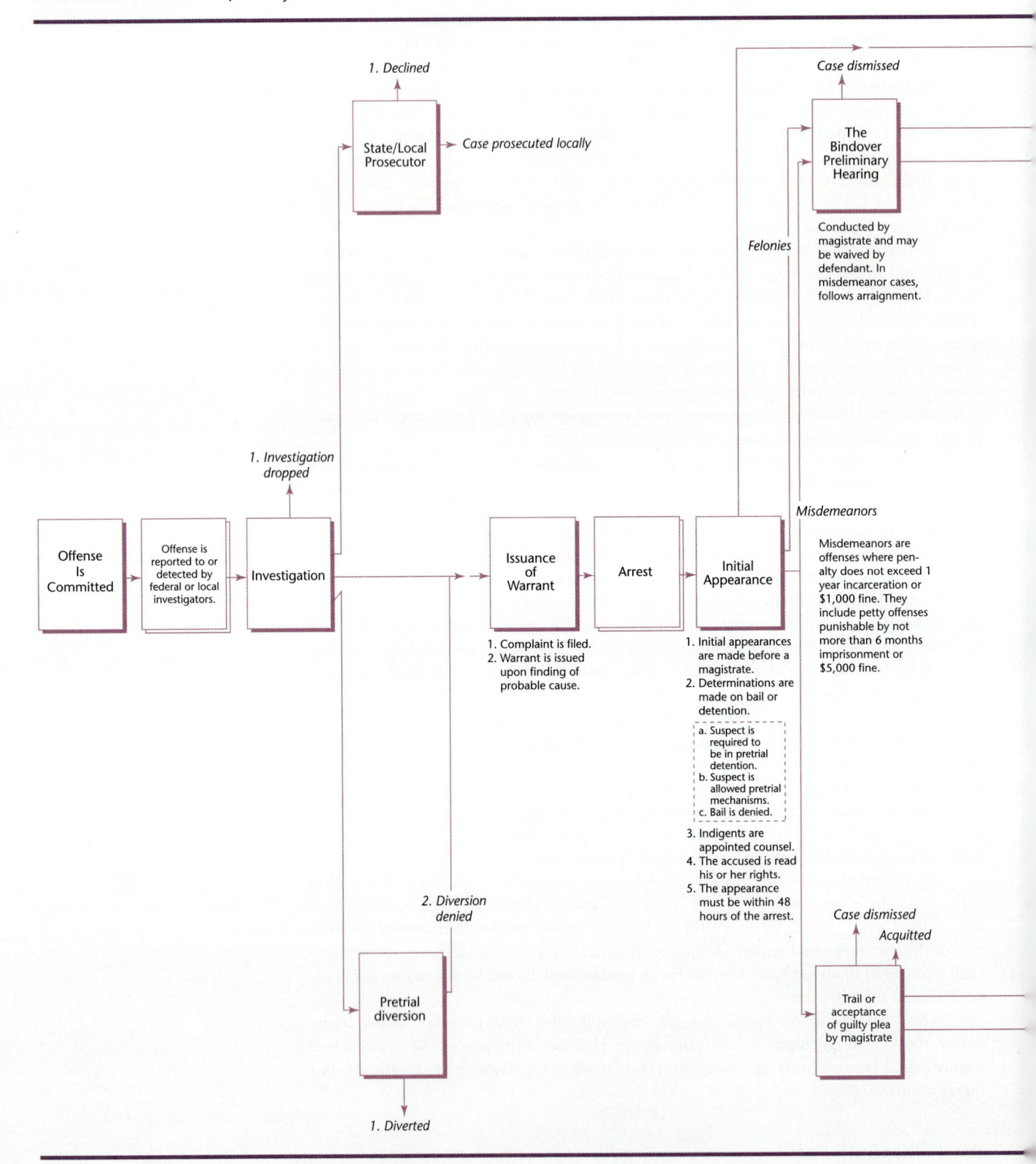

Offense Is Committed → **Offense is reported to or detected by federal or local investigators.** → **Investigation**

From Investigation:
- 1. Investigation dropped
- To State/Local Prosecutor:
  - 1. Declined
  - Case prosecuted locally
- 2. Diversion denied → **Pretrial diversion**
  - 1. Diverted

Issuance of Warrant
1. Complaint is filed.
2. Warrant is issued upon finding of probable cause.

→ **Arrest** → **Initial Appearance**

1. Initial appearances are made before a magistrate.
2. Determinations are made on bail or detention.
   a. Suspect is required to be in pretrial detention.
   b. Suspect is allowed pretrial mechanisms.
   c. Bail is denied.
3. Indigents are appointed counsel.
4. The accused is read his or her rights.
5. The appearance must be within 48 hours of the arrest.

Felonies → **The Bindover Preliminary Hearing**
- Case dismissed

Conducted by magistrate and may be waived by defendant. In misdemeanor cases, follows arraignment.

Misdemeanors: Misdemeanors are offenses where penalty does not exceed 1 year incarceration or $1,000 fine. They include petty offenses punishable by not more than 6 months imprisonment or $5,000 fine.

Trail or acceptance of guilty plea by magistrate
- Case dismissed
- Acquitted

326 CRIME AND JUSTICE IN AMERICA

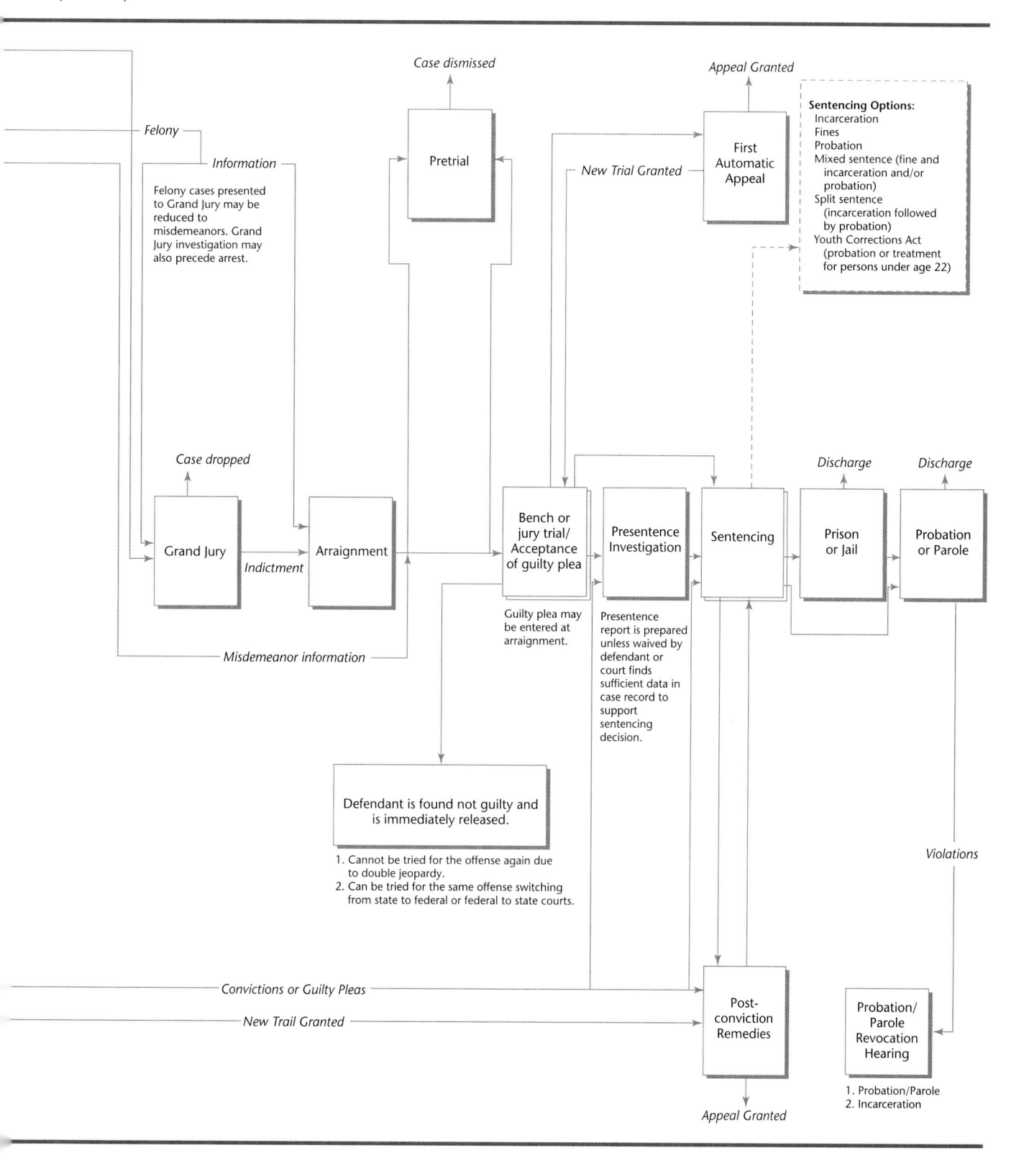

CHAPTER 8 PRETRIAL PROCEDURES: BAIL, PRETRIAL HEARINGS, AND PLEA BARGAINING 327

FIGURE 8.6
(continued)

Felony cases presented to Grand Jury may be reduced to misdemeanors. Grand Jury investigation may also precede arrest.

Sentencing Options:
- Incarceration
- Fines
- Probation
- Mixed sentence (fine and incarceration and/or probation)
- Split sentence (incarceration followed by probation)
- Youth Corrections Act (probation or treatment for persons under age 22)

Guilty plea may be entered at arraignment.

Presentence report is prepared unless waived by defendant or court finds sufficient data in case record to support sentencing decision.

Defendant is found not guilty and is immediately released.
1. Cannot be tried for the offense again due to double jeopardy.
2. Can be tried for the same offense switching from state to federal or federal to state courts.

1. Probation/Parole
2. Incarceration

FIGURE 8.7

Movie star Harrison Ford played Dr. Richard Kimble, an innocent man on the run after being wrongfully convicted of killing his wife. As such, he was considered a "fugitive" from the law.

Courtesy Picture Desk, Inc./Kobal Collection.

the Eighth Amendment prohibition against excessive bail does not give all defendants the right to bail.[19]

The major reason for the denial of bail in this country is preventive detention. Many states and Congress have adopted preventive-detention provisions that permit courts to deny bail to defendants who are allegedly dangerous to society. Preventive detention is justified by one of the following conditions that the prosecutor must prove at the bail hearing: (1) There is a serious risk that the accused will flee; (2) the accused will obstruct justice or threaten to intimidate a prospective witness, juror, or member of the community at large; (3) the offense is of a certain magnitude of violence or is punishable by life imprisonment or death.

In some states, opponents of **preventive detention** argue that the system denies an accused the right to bail and requires courts to make often inaccurate predictions of future dangerousness. Nevertheless, preventative-detention schemes have usually been upheld by the courts in the states as long as they are tied to expedient docket positions for detained defendants. Another factor in this discussion is the Federal Bail Reform Act of 1984, which gave federal courts the authority to detain the arrestee when a judge determines after a hearing that no condition of release would reasonably ensure the appearance of the person and the safety of the community.

At the bail hearing, the defendant has the right to testify, to present other evidence, to have counsel, and to cross-examine witnesses. The court's decision to detain an arrestee must be based on "clear and convincing" evidence. If the detention is ordered, the defendant is entitled to an expedient review of that decision.

The Supreme Court upheld the preventive-detention provision of the act, concluding that pretrial detention is "regulatory, not penal," and that liberty interests implicated are outweighed by the government's overwhelming interest in community safety.[20] (See Figure 8.8 and the Landmark Case *United States v. Salerno*.) However, when preventive detention is anticipated, the Constitution requires that a prompt hearing be afforded. Hearings must be held at the first appearance in front of a judicial officer, or within five days after that appearance if the government seeks a continuance.[21]

Reforms in the Bail System

A National Institute of Justice study concluded that public policy in America is cynical. Today, the balance can be said to have shifted slightly in favor of public safety, whereas in the recent past the interests of the accused were paramount. Reforms in the bail system have responded to public concerns and research findings. How you feel about bail and preventive detention may depend on whether you sympathize more with the point

FIGURE 8.8

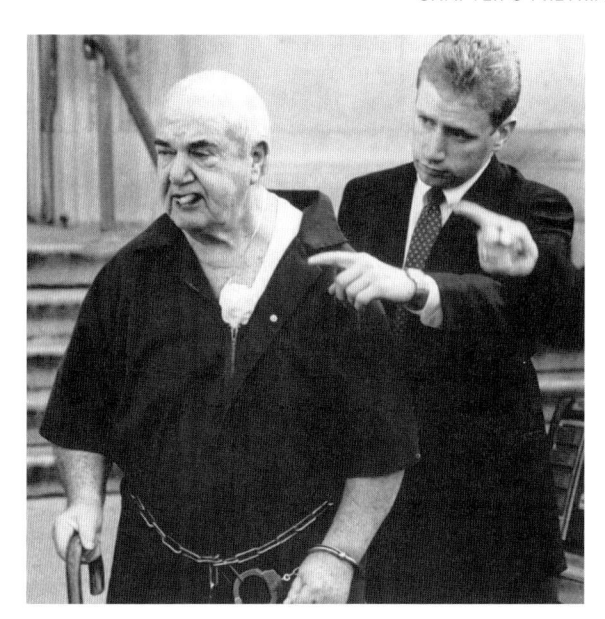

Tony "Fat Boy" Salerno. His case was tantamount to having the effect that the Supreme Court did not consider the Eighth Amendment right "excessive bail should not be imposed" as meaning that the denial of bail was excessive or that this right was a due process right that should be selectively incorporated and made applicable to all of the states under the Fourteenth Amendment's "Due Process" clause.

Courtesy AP/Wide World Photos.

LANDMARK CASE: United States v. Salerno

On March 21, 1986, Anthony Salerno (see Figure 8.8) and co-defendant Vincent Cafaro were charged in a twenty-nine-count indictment alleging various racketeering violations, including gambling, wire fraud, extortion, and conspiracy to commit murder. At their arraignment, the government moved to have them detained on the grounds that no condition of release could ensure community safety. At a detention hearing, the prosecution presented evidence that Salerno was the "boss" of the Genovese crime family and that Cafaro was a "captain." Wiretap evidence indicated that the two men had participated in criminal conspiracies, including murder. The court heard testimony from two witnesses who had personally participated in the murder conspiracies. In rebuttal, Salerno provided character statements, presented evidence that he had a heart condition, and challenged the government's witnesses. Cafaro claimed that the wiretaps had merely recorded "tough talk." The trial court allowed the detention on grounds that the defendants wanted to use their personal freedom to continue their "family" business and "when business as usual involves threats, beatings, and murder, the present danger that such people pose to the community is self-evident."

On appeal, the U.S. Court of Appeals for the Second Circuit agreed with the defendant's claim that the government could not detain suspects simply because they were thought to represent a danger to the community. The circuit court found that the criminal law holds people accountable for their past deeds, not their anticipated future actions. The government appealed this decision to the Supreme Court, which held that the preventive-detention act had a legitimate and compelling regulatory purpose and did not violate the due process clause. Preventive detention was not designed to punish dangerous individuals but to find a solution to the social problem of people committing crimes while on bail; preventing danger to the community is a legitimate societal goal.

The Court also stated that society's need for protection can outweigh an individual's liberty and that, under some circumstances, individuals can be held without bail. The Federal Bail Reform Act provides that only the most serious criminals can be held and mandates careful procedures to ensure that the judgment of future dangerousness is made after careful deliberation. Finally, the Court found that the Eighth Amendment does not limit the setting (or denial) of bail simply to prohibit the defendant's flight to avoid trial and held that considerations of dangerousness are a valid reason to deny pretrial release.

Source: United States v. Salerno, 479 U.S. 1026 (1987).

TABLE 8.2 How the Right to Be Released on Bail is Limited in the States*

Limitation	State
Exclusion of certain crimes from automatic bail eligibility	Colorado, District of Columbia, Florida, Georgia, Michigan, Nebraska, Wisconsin
Definition of the purpose of bail to ensure appearance and safety	Alaska, Arizona, California, Delaware, District of Columbia, Florida, Hawaii, Minnesota, South Carolina, South Dakota, Vermont, Wisconsin
Inclusion of crime-control factors in the release decision	Alabama, California, Florida, Georgia, Minnesota, South Dakota, Wisconsin
Inclusion of release conditions related to crime control	Alaska, Arkansas, Delaware, District of Columbia, Florida, Hawaii, Illinois, Minnesota, New Mexico, North Carolina, South Carolina, Vermont, Washington, Wisconsin
Limitations on the right to bail for those previously convicted	Colorado, District of Columbia, Florida, Georgia, Hawaii, Michigan, New Mexico, Texas, Wisconsin
Revocation of pretrial release when there is evidence that the accused committed a new crime	Arkansas, Colorado, Illinois, Massachusetts, Nevada, New York, Rhode Island, Virginia, Wisconsin
Limitations on the right to bail for crimes alleged to have been committed while on release	Colorado, District of Columbia, Florida, Maryland, Michigan, Nevada, Tennessee, Texas, Utah
Provisions for pretrial detentions to ensure safety	Arizona, California, District of Columbia, Florida, Georgia, Hawaii, Michigan, Wisconsin

*Determining a detainee's eligibility for bail is dependent on a state's statutes concerning eligible crimes and on the willingness to accept the arrestee by the bondspeople, the conditions of bail, certain limitations on the particular suspect, and the definition of the conditions necessary for the revocation of bail.

Source: Bureau of Justice Statistics, *Report to the Nation on Crime and Justice*, 2nd ed. Washington, D.C.: U.S. Government Printing Office.

of view of the public defenders or the prosecutors. One must ask whether the purpose of bail is to protect the accused or prevent crime. What has yet to be discovered is whether bail can serve both purposes (see Table 8.2).

The Effects of Preventive Detention

To better understand the effects of preventive detention, Kennedy and Carlson compared the pretrial experiences of people released in 1983 (before the 1984 Federal Bail Reform Act went into effect) with 1985 cases that were handled under the new law. They found that although the act's preventive-detention provisions significantly affected federal pretrial release and detention practices, the number of defendants released before trial remained relatively stable (76 percent in 1983 and 71 percent in 1985). About 54 percent of all defendants were released on their own recognizance in both 1983 and 1985.[22]

At the same time, the preventive-detention statute did result in a number of changes. Although about 2 percent of all defendants were denied bail outright in 1983, by 1985 the number held without bail rose to 19 percent. The number of defendants making bail remained stable because a higher percentage of defendants in 1985 who were eligible for bail were able to put up the required funds. It is evident that before the act took effect, judges detained the most dangerous defendants by requiring bail amounts they simply could not afford; after 1985, judges relied more on the act's pretrial-detention provisions. Most of those who received preventive detention (40 percent) were charged with drug, immigration, and violent offenses. There was little relationship between social variables, such as race and economic status, and the probability of preventive detention.

In a connected several-year study of four judicial districts involving more than 2,000 defendants, Scott found that (1) more defendants were detained under the Federal

CTQ
What is the purpose of bail versus the purpose of preventive detention?

Bail Reform Act (31 percent compared to 26 percent) than under the prior statute; (2) fewer defendants were detained because of their inability to make surety or cash bail; and (3) the rate of failure to appear was 2.1 percent under the old bail act, compared to 1.8 percent under the new act, while the percentage of defendants who were rearrested for committing new crimes was equally low under both statutes.[23]

The data seem to suggest that judges will use preventive detention, but that its actual effect on the total number of people detained before trial may be marginal. Defendants who are not subject to preventive detention would in the past have been assigned high bail amounts designed to keep them incarcerated before trial. Rather than being a new "get tough" approach, preventive detention continues the judiciary's long-standing practice of detaining defendants it views as dangerous and releasing those who meet its standard of behavior.

May a Convicted Defendant Be Out on Bail While Awaiting Appeal?

Both the United States Code and federal criminal procedure allow a convicted individual to be eligible for bail pending an appeal of a conviction. However, bail will be denied if it appears that the appeal was frivolous or taken solely to delay the imposition of the sentence. Normally the standard for appellate bail is that there must be some justifiable issue upon which the appellate court would take serious consideration in reaching a decision.

MISDEMEANOR TRIALS

If a defendant is charged with a misdemeanor offense, his or her case will go before misdemeanor court. The charging instrument in all misdemeanor trials is the complaint. Misdemeanor courts are known by various names throughout the United States, including, but not limited to *justice of the peace court, county court, lower court,* and *misdemeanor court* (see the discussion on lower courts in Chapter 7, "The Dynamics of the Criminal Courts" for a full discussion).

During the initial appearance in misdemeanor court, the courtroom is usually filled with other charged misdemeanants (see Chapter 7, Figure 7.7). The great majority of those misdemeanants will plead guilty after being read their rights at their initial appearance. Other magistrate courts will set a new time for arraignment and guilty pleas, and a third very small group of those charged in misdemeanor court will contest their charges by trial. In the trial demanded, the defendant usually is not afforded the opportunity to litigate the facts before a jury. Instead, in this lower court, the magistrate (or county judge or misdemeanor judge) serves the role of both the judge and the jury.

A magistrate has summary jurisdiction and because of this is empowered to determine guilt or innocence and can impose minor sentences for petty offenses. However, in many states, the accused can request a jury trial.

Overall, the setting within which misdemeanor justice is administered is not likely to inspire much respect for law or confidence in the impartiality of justice. Ninety percent of the nation's criminal cases are heard in the less prestigious lower courts. These are the courts that process the hundreds of thousands of Americans accused each year of disturbing the peace, shoplifting, being drunk, and driving too fast. Although these cases may individually appear to be minor—almost petty—collectively the work of the lower courts is quite important. Misdemeanor courts are generally referred to as courts of limited jurisdiction.

For decades reformers have pointed out the problems of the lower courts. Only a fraction of the adversary model of criminal justice can be found in these courts. Many defendants are not represented by an attorney. Trials are rare. Jail sentences are imposed, sometimes with lightning speed. Informality, rather than the rules of courtroom procedure, predominates. In short, practices that would be condemned if they occurred in higher courts are commonplace in the lower courts. Is this justice, we might ask? The President's Commission on Law Enforcement and Administration of Justice asked the same question and expressed shock over the conclusions it reached: "No findings of this

Commission are more disquieting than those relating to the conditions of the lower criminal courts."[24]

INITIATING FELONY PROSECUTION

Felony offenses are serious crimes that are punishable by incarceration for a year or more in a state prison, or by death in the case of capital offenses (see Chapter 2, "The Substantive Criminal Law"). Some felony offenses are settled by dismissal or by the entrance of a guilty plea at an early stage in the criminal justice process.

Since a felony is a more serious crime than a misdemeanor, intermediate steps must be taken before the accused can be tried in a felony court. Two different types of objective bodies within the criminal justice system exist to ensure that evidence is sufficient to prove that a crime has taken place and that the accused should be tried on the matter. This proof needs only to be established by the probable-cause standard. The two bodies that make these probable-cause determinations are the bindover preliminary hearing and the grand jury (see Figure 8.6).

Finally, in states that have eliminated the preliminary hearing and grand jury indictment in favor of liberal pretrial depositions, a move is afoot to eliminate even the use of depositions. Depositions have already been eliminated from misdemeanor cases in several states; some studies are examining the possibility and feasibility of eliminating them as well in juvenile justice pretrial procedures and in minor felony charges.

THE PRELIMINARY HEARING (THE BINDOVER HEARING)

In many states, following arrest and initial appearance, a suspect accused of a felony offense is brought before a lower court for a bindover preliminary hearing. A majority of the states employ this hearing rather than the grand jury. A bindover preliminary hearing is conducted before a magistrate (a misdemeanor court judge) and is open to the public.

The nature of this hearing differs from a *Gerstein* hearing or initial appearance in that it is adversarial in nature; the defendant is entitled to counsel and, if indigent, appointed counsel.[25] Both sides must swear witnesses and present evidence. In most jurisdictions, the prosecution must prove that there is competent evidence of each element of the offense for which the accused is detained. Generally, in bindover preliminary hearings, either side may preserve testimony of witnesses who will later be unavailable to testify at trial, as long as the other side had an opportunity to cross-examine.[26]

In some ways, the bindover preliminary hearing resembles a mini-trial, although no jury is involved at this stage. The case is presented before a judge, who evaluates the evidence and initial testimony to determine whether probable cause exists to hold the defendant for trial. Because the burden of proof is on the prosecutor, he or she must present evidence and call witnesses to support the state's case.

The defendant is present at the bindover preliminary hearing, as are attorneys for the defense and prosecution. At this stage only the prosecution needs to present evidence to the bindover preliminary hearing judge (see Figure 8.9). The defendant also has the right to present evidence at the hearing but seldom does so. This procedure affords the defendant an excellent opportunity to discover the substance of the prosecutor's case, information that he or she can use later as part of the defense strategy in felony court. An interesting aspect of a preliminary hearing is that the defendant has the right to waive the hearing if the prosecutor and the judge agree to the waiver. Usually the only time defendants waive the bindover preliminary hearing is when they have decided to plead guilty or fear the adverse publicity that the bindover preliminary hearing might bring upon themselves and their families.

FIGURE 8.9

Sheila McGovern was the preliminary hearing judge in the famous O. J. Simpson murder case.

Courtesy Boston College Law School.

IN THE NEWS

A HUMAN PERSPECTIVE

O. J. SIMPSON'S MOTION TO SUPPRESS A BLOODY GLOVE FOUND ON HIS PREMISES IS OVERRULED

O. J. Simpson's case took a giant setback with the defeat of a defense motion to suppress eleven pieces of evidence collected at the Simpson mansion after the murders of his ex-wife and her friend. Spots of blood were found on Simpson's Bronco and on the driveway leading from the front gate to the mansion's door. Also, a bloody glove was discovered behind Simpson's guest house.

In all, the defense made a motion during the suppression hearing to exclude eleven specific pieces of evidence that were found in O. J. Simpson's estate. Although the evidence was discovered without a search warrant, the following evidence was allowed to be admitted in the preliminary hearing:

- A bloodstained right glove, similar to a left-hand glove found at the murder scene, recovered from behind the guest house.
- A bloodstain on the back fence near the glove.
- A bloodstain discovered on the driver's door of Simpson's Bronco.
- Five bloodstains found on Simpson's mansion grounds, between an entry gate and the front door of the house.
- A blue plastic bag seized behind Simpson's guest house.
- A wooden stick discovered in the front yard.
- A Marlboro cigarette butt taken from the curb in front of the home.

In denying the motion to suppress, the [bindover] preliminary hearing judge noted that the four homicide detectives went to Simpson's home to tell him his ex-wife had been killed and his children were staying at the police station. They claimed that at the time, Simpson was not yet a suspect.

In explaining her decision to deny the defense motion to suppress, the [bindover] preliminary hearing judge reasoned that a sensible homeowner would welcome that kind of behavior—the police rushing into a home under these circumstances without a search warrant to help. The judge also said that law enforcement personnel should not be stuck at the gate because of some hard and fast rule. This ruling denying O. J. Simpson's motion after the suppression hearing resulted in the court admitting into evidence only those items which pertained to the [bindover] preliminary hearing.

Source: "Evidence Admitted," *USA Today*, July 8, 1994, pp. 1–2. Copyright 1994, *USA Today*. Reprinted with permission.

The primary purpose of the bindover preliminary hearing is to protect defendants from unwarranted prosecution. Furthermore, the magistrate will determine the existence of probable cause for which a warrant was issued for the defendant's arrest, and will also inquire into the reasonableness of the arrest and search and the compliance of the executing officer with the requirements of the search warrant. In certain states, the bindover preliminary hearing is the venue for motions to exclude evidence. For example, several years ago such an inquiry was critical to the O. J. Simpson preliminary hearing. Simpson made a motion to suppress in an attempt to have the judge exclude the bloody glove found on his estate recovered by Detective Mark Fuhrman (see "In the News: O. J. Simpson's Motion to Suppress a Bloody Glove Found on His Premises Is Overruled").

During the final stages of the bindover preliminary hearing, the court also reviews the bail that may have been set at the first appearance. At this time, depending on the authority vested in him or her, the bindover preliminary hearing judge may exercise the option to raise or lower the amount of bail.

After evidence is presented by the prosecution, the preliminary hearing judge decides whether there is probable cause to believe that the accused person committed the alleged crimes. If the answer is yes, the defendant is *bound over* for felony trial; if the answer is no, charges are dismissed and the defendant is released from custody. If the former is the case, the prosecutor files an information with the court where the trial will be held. The time allowed for filing varies from jurisdiction to jurisdiction, but fifteen days from the preliminary hearing is a typical period. As mentioned earlier, the right of the prosecutor not to prosecute further, even in the face of evidence that seems sufficient to win the case, demonstrates one of the most significant examples of discretionary authority in the criminal justice system.

THE GRAND JURY

Like the bindover preliminary hearing, the function of the **grand jury** is to investigate criminal charges to determine, or adjudicate, whether a defendant should be brought to felony trial. When performing this function, the grand jury is supposed to act as the community's conscience in determining whether an unjust accusation has been brought against an accused. Often, however, the general public is unaware that another equally important function of grand juries in addition to adjudicating probable cause is to investigate. Investigative grand juries usually are impaneled to investigate organized crime or political corruption.

The grand jury system, which is eight centuries old, developed early in English common law. The concept of a grand jury was brought to the United States by its earliest settlers and later incorporated into the Fifth Amendment of the U.S. Constitution, which states that "no person shall be held to answer for a capital or otherwise infamous charge unless on a presentment or indictment of a grand jury." According to Bloch and Geis, "grand juries were intended to allow the defendant to avoid a public accusation and the trouble and expense of a public trial before establishing the likelihood of his having committed the crime. They were also intended to prevent hasty, oppressive, and malicious prosecutions."[27]

The Fifth Amendment guarantees all citizens the right to indictment by grand jury. However, in 1884, the Supreme Court announced in *Hurtado v. California* that this right was not applicable to the states. Since grand juries are not constitutionally required, the states are split on the manner in which they systematically handle the grand jury function. Most states handle pretrial screening through a preliminary hearing. A substantial minority handle this function by the grand jury (see Figure 8.6), and still a smaller group of states have abolished the grand jury and the preliminary hearing altogether. The size of the American grand jury remains the same as it was in common law. Normally, twenty-three people ("tried and true") are impaneled to protect citizens against unfair accusation.

Every felony processed through federal court is first processed through a grand jury. At the state level, nineteen states have no grand juries. The grand jury sits for a period of time, generally three months, to determine if the evidence presented to them by the prosecutor is sufficient to warrant formal charges against the defendant. The standard of proof is the same here as it is in the bindover preliminary hearing—probable cause.

The grand jury does not seek to determine guilt or innocence; rather it duplicates in many respects the function of the bindover preliminary hearing. The only major difference is that the defendant has no legal right to be present at grand jury deliberations. Thus, the decision to indict or not to indict is made solely on the evidence presented by the prosecuting attorney.

The Grand Jury Today

By the latter part of the twentieth century, grand jury indictments for prosecution were optional in nearly half the states and required for all crimes in only four states (see Figure 8.10.). Today, at least six states limit grand jury indictments to capital crimes only, and Pennsylvania prohibits grand jury indictments altogether.

Grand jury proceedings are secret. The defendant has no right to appear or send witnesses. However, the Supreme Court has held that when the desire for grand jury secrecy conflicts with the witnesses' First Amendment rights, often the latter will prevail.[28] An indictment is not subject to challenge on the grounds that the grand jury acted on the basis of incompetent and inadequate evidence.[29] Furthermore, a grand jury indictment can be based on hearsay evidence. However, some courts attempt to limit the possible abuse of narrowly interpreting the sufficiency of hearsay evidence supporting the indictment.[30] Moreover, an indictment may not be dismissed because the federal court failed to present exculpatory evidence that the grand jury knew about.[31] Finally, within grand jury proceedings no unanimity of vote is required. All that is needed to indict is more than 50 percent of the grand jurors voting for indictment.

FIGURE 8.10

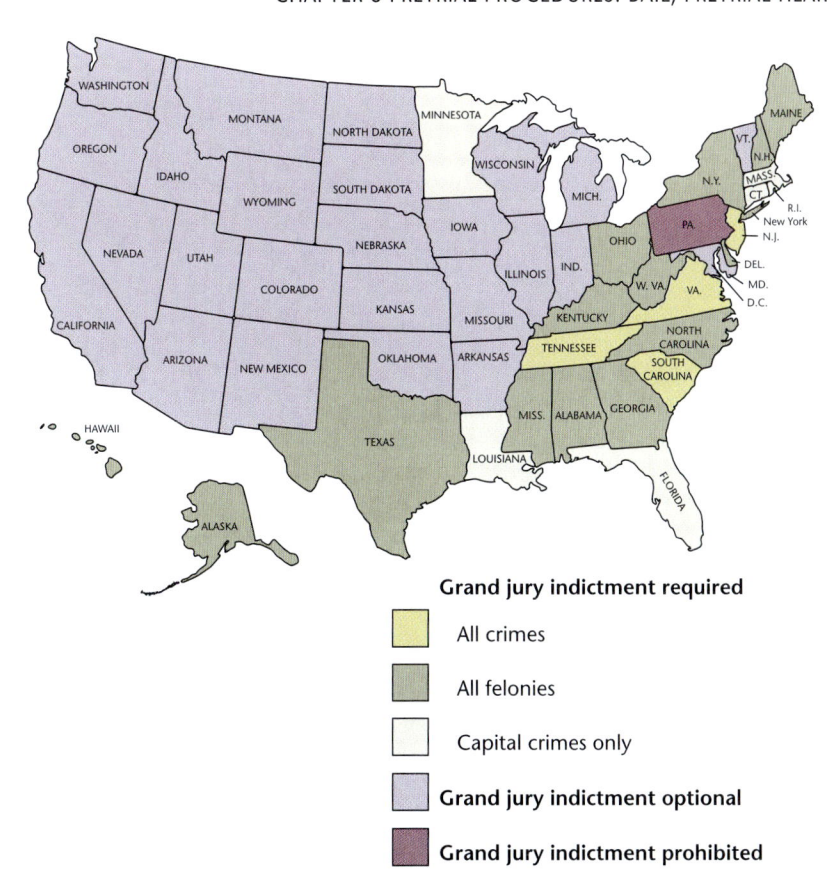

State-by-State Grand Jury Requirements

Source: Marianne Zawitz, *Report to the Nation on Crime and Justice,* 2nd ed. Washington, D.C.: U.S. Government Printing Office.

Grand jury indictment required
- All crimes
- All felonies
- Capital crimes only
- Grand jury indictment optional
- Grand jury indictment prohibited

True Bills and Presentments

Once it hears all the testimony, the grand jury retires to deliberate and votes to determine whether there is a sufficient basis for believing that the crime was committed by the targeted witness. Recall that, unlike trial juries, grand juries are not required to make this determination of proof beyond a reasonable doubt. Rather, they only need to determine whether probable cause exists. Based on such a determination, the grand jury then issues a bill of indictment, referred to as a **true bill.** In the majority of indictments, the grand jury follows the inclination of the prosecutor. If the jury determines that the evidence is insufficient to charge a suspect, it returns a *no bill.* When the grand jury acts on its own to investigate criminal activity, without the prosecutor having called it together, the accusation it may issue is called a **presentment.**

The Special Investigative Grand Jury

An indictment may also originate from a grand jury's own investigation of criminal activity. This represents an extraordinary model of the criminal justice system, as most criminal proceedings begin with an information (see next page). Special or investigative grand juries operate in most cases involving organized crime and political corruption. Citizens often find the similarities amazing between a grand jury and a bindover preliminary hearing and an interrogation at the police station. However, there is an enormous difference in rights afforded in the three different venues (see Table 8.3).

FORMAL FELONY CHARGING

Following preliminary procedures such as the grand jury, the preliminary hearing, or the prosecution's thought and reflection, the Sixth Amendment gives every criminal defendant the right to be formally notified in writing of the charges against him or her. There are three different types of formal written charges generated in felony trials in the American criminal justice system.

CTQ

Does the grand jury play too large a role in the criminal justice system? Is the weight of its special investigative power justified?

CTQ

If the grand jury indicts in almost every case that it hears, then why do we have the grand jury?

TABLE 8.3 Rights Afforded during Police Interrogation or a Preliminary Hearing versus a Grand Jury Proceeding

Rights Afforded during a Police Interrogation or Preliminary Hearing	Rights Afforded during a Grand Jury Proceeding
Must warn the subject that he or she is suspected of committing the crime.	With the aid of subpoena power, the grand jury does *not* have to reveal to the suspect that he or she is indeed a suspect.
Police must have probable cause to arrest.	Grand juries can subpoena target witnesses without any evidence of probable cause.
The suspect can refuse to cooperate in the interrogation and all questioning must cease.	If the suspect refuses to cooperate, he or she can be held in contempt of court.
Competent evidence must be gathered.	Illegal and incompetent evidence may be gathered.
A preliminary hearing gives the accused a detailed notice of the charges.	A grand jury proceeding gives no notice of the charges.
The accused has the right to consult with counsel.	Counsel cannot even be in the same room.
The accused has the right to be present throughout a preliminary hearing.	The accused does *not* have the right to be present.
The accused has the right to confront witnesses against him or her in the preliminary hearing.	The accused has *no right to confrontation*.
The accused has the right to present witnesses in a preliminary hearing.	The accused has *no right* to present witnesses.
The rules of evidence are generally observed in a preliminary hearing.	The rules of evidence are generally not relevant.
The accused has a Fifth Amendment right against self-incrimination that he or she may exercise by never taking the stand in a preliminary hearing.	The accused must take the stand and can remove himself or herself from giving testimony only by pleading the Fifth to every single question.

Source: L. Territo, J. Halsted, and M. Bromley, *Crime and Justice in America*, 4th ed. Minneapolis, Minn.: West, 1995, pp. 387–391.

In many jurisdictions, the charges filed at the initial appearance are likely to originate with the police officer's complaint and may not have been reviewed by the prosecutor before that hearing. The police may file only the minimum charge relevant to the case, or may routinely file every legally possible charge (a process called *creative charging*) and then let the prosecutor determine which charges are most likely to result in a conviction. Understandably, charges filed by the police are often modified by the prosecutor when a more complete review of the case is conducted.

The first type of charge sheet is called a *prosecutor's information*. The prosecutor files an information in which he or she states the formal felony charges against the defendant, articulates the statutes that have been violated, and cites evidence to support the charges. If the defendant has been screened by a grand jury, an **indictment** is issued, which is the second type of formal charging instrument. The indictment, normally drafted by the prosecutor, charges the defendant with a felony in a manner almost identical to the language and style of the information, except that it is signed by the grand jury foreperson rather than the district attorney. The third type of formal charging document is a presentment. A *presentment*, as described earlier, is a written notice of accusation issued by an investigative grand jury. The presentment is based not on the evidence and testimony provided to the grand jury by the prosecution, but rather on the evidence that was acquired by the initiative of the grand jury itself. In actual practice, however, *presentment* and *indictment* are substantially interchangeable terms.

Constitutional Requirements of a Prosecutor's Information

The information is a written accusation prepared by prosecutors in the name of the state charging the person with a commission of a crime. The information is used to charge a person with criminal offenses in cases where a grand jury indictment was not required or has been waived by the accused. In modern practice the information is used more frequently than the indictment.[32]

IN THE NEWS

A HUMAN PERSPECTIVE

SUSAN MCDOUGAL: A COURAGEOUS HUMAN PERSPECTIVE

Susan McDougal, a close friend and financial partner to President and Mrs. Clinton, refused to testify before the independent prosecutor when subpoenaed to do so after her husband and other personal close associates either were convicted or pleaded guilty to the Whitewater investigations. McDougal was aware that these potential witnesses had been sentenced and were talking to the government believing they would receive "sweetheart" sentences if their testimony proved pleasing and truthful to government prosecutors. McDougal instantly recognized the "plea inducement domino game sham" and realized that she was again being played by the elite Federal Special Task Force of U.S. attorneys.

She became certain that these games were an attempt to induce these witnesses to testify to a significant event "X" (which would be devastating to the president's case), whereas McDougal was absolutely certain the event was "not X." Hence, when subpoenaed to testify before the grand jury, she refused out of a sense of high-mindedness, fundamental fairness, and respect for the oath. McDougal knew that if she testified truthfully that "not X" had occurred, she immediately would be charged, convicted, and sentenced to felony perjury based on the testimony of the other witnesses. If Susan McDougal had perjured herself before the grand jury by testifying "X," she would have been freed, as were the other witnesses. McDougal weighed her options and chose not to testify at all, "so I would not be convicted of perjury." She thus remained in a jail cell for contempt of court. Subsequently, she was victorious at her trial and, under tremendous public pressure, released from jail on the contempt citation. As of the writing of this book, the federal government has spent twice as much money investigating Whitewater (an event which occurred a significant number of years before Clinton became president) than it has on investigating the terrorist attacks on the World Trade Center in New York.

Courtesy AFP/CORBIS.

UPDATE

Susan McDougal never reneged. As the Whitewater independent counsel was working on his investigation, he came to realize that all of his threats and intimidations would not persuade McDougal to testify before the grand jury and risk perjury. Subsequently, she was released and never incarcerated again. On his last day in office, President Clinton gave McDougal a pardon, which has the effect of exonerating her from all her alleged criminal activities and taking them off the books as though nothing ever happened.

IN THE WORKPLACE

PRE-LAW UNDERGRADUATE ADVISOR

Responsible to the chair of the academic department within a college or university for class scheduling and career advising for departmental undergraduate students; participates in recruitment, retention, and outcome assessment efforts. Performs a variety of duties, including the following: designing a schedule of courses, coordinating with other university departments in assisting students to meet graduation requirements, serving as the coordinator of the departmental internship program; serving on departmental committees, and coordinating with community colleges regarding articulation agreements and other transfer issues. Minimum qualifications are as follows; master's degree in criminal justice/criminology or a related social science discipline such as political science required; should have undergraduate advising experience; knowledge of computers, university programs and services, and university policies; effective communication skills.

Certain constitutional limitations exist on filing the information. Most states, for example, require prior bindover preliminary hearings before a prosecutor can file an information. However, the bindover preliminary hearing is not a constitutional right.[33] And some states do not require a bindover preliminary hearing or grand jury investigation.

The Constitution requires that the content of the information be specific. Hence, the information must reasonably inform the accused of the charges, so that he or she may have the opportunity to present and prepare a defense. This requirement is generally satisfied if the charges are expressed in words of the statute defining the offense. Frequently, an information also includes the date, time, place, and events of the offense, but generally, these elements are not essential.

The defense has certain obligations to disclose the information. Some states provide that the prosecution is entitled to receive information from the defense prior to the trial. For example, some states require the defendant to give advance notice of alibi defenses (including the names of alibi witnesses). Such requirements do not violate the Fifth Amendment privilege against self-incrimination.[34] Yet if the state is entitled to discovery information from the defense, the defense must be entitled to reciprocal discovery from the state or the due process clause will be violated.

Showups, Lineups, and Other Pretrial Identification Procedures during the Prearrest, Postarrest, and after the Formal Felony Charging

Certain identification procedures that attempt to link the accused with the crime have been constitutionally scrutinized. As stated previously, the police have the authority to order a suspect to go to the police station and require his or her participation in a certain number of identification procedures. In order for the results of these identification procedures to be admitted into a court, the judge first must be satisfied that these procedures have met constitutional standards of due process by not being "unduly suggestive."

One such procedure is a *showup*. This generally takes place shortly after a crime has been committed, when the victim is a witness. The victim is taken to the police station and then confronted with a suspect. In a showup, the victim is not offered an array of individuals in which the suspect is included, as is the case with a lineup. Rather, a showup is a one-on-one confrontation. Usually this procedure is presented in the context of questioning the victim: "Is he or she the one?"

Showups have had constitutional problems. As a result, police and the courts have tended to favor the use of lineups instead. A *lineup* is a procedure wherein the suspect is placed together with several other people. With some jurisdictional variations, the following guidelines for conducting lineups have been suggested by law enforcement agencies:

- All people in the lineup should be of the same general age and race and have similar physical characteristics. The clothing worn by each should be similar.
- Statements by people in the lineup should not be requested unless a witness suggests it. If statements are made, all participants should repeat the same words. However, because many states prohibit a defendant from being forced to say anything during the lineup, investigators should first consult with local prosecutors.
- Front and profile color photographs of the lineup should be taken and developed as soon as possible.
- A witness should be prevented from seeing the defendant in custody prior to the lineup. Witnesses should not be shown a photograph of the defendant before the lineup.
- If more than one person is to view a lineup, they should do so independently.
- No actions should be taken by investigators or statements made to witnesses to suggest that a suspect is standing in any particular place.
- Before entering the lineup room, the witness should be given a form on which the identification can be made. There should be at least six people in the lineup.
- If the suspect's attorney is present, he or she should be allowed to make suggestions concerning the suggestiveness of the lineup and not to tip off witnesses.

- Before the lineup, the witness should give a detailed description of the perpetrator and the description should be put in writing.
- If possible, law enforcement officers should not be used in lineups. A suspect has no right to refuse a lineup.[35]

Constitutional Requirements and Identification Procedures

The police use a variety of identification procedures to verify that a suspect taken into custody in fact perpetrated the crime. These procedures have the dual function of solving crimes and providing evidence for trial. Three important constitutional provisions are considered in connection with identification procedures: the privilege against self-incrimination, the right to counsel, and the due process clause.

These types of identification procedures do not violate a defendant's privilege against self-incrimination to compel him or her to stand in a lineup, to utter specific words when asked to do so, or to wear a certain item of clothing. These are held to be "testimonial" and thus not within the privilege.[36]

The Sixth Amendment requires that a lawyer be present during certain identification proceedings to ensure the fairness of the ultimate trial process.[37] However, the function of the lawyer is not always clear. Many jurisdictions allow the attorney to participate only to the extent of observing the proceedings.

The Supreme Court has made an unusual distinction about when the lawyer can and cannot be present during lineups. The right to counsel, according to Supreme Court cases, attaches only after the initiation of an adversary criminal proceeding against the accused, such as the filing of an indictment or a prosecutor's information. Thus, there is no right to assistance of counsel at police lineups conducted before the accused is indicted or otherwise formally charged with the crime.[38]

However, the burning issue becomes the question of what exactly constitutes an adversarial criminal proceeding or confrontation.[39] This may not require an arraignment or the like. Some courts have held that if the accused is taken into custody under an arrest warrant, this is tantamount to a "formal charge" (because it is issued by a magistrate showing probable cause). Some states, by statute, have determined that the issuance of the arrest warrant is the initiation of adversary judicial proceedings under *Kirby v. Illinois*.[40] Some states, under appropriate state constitutional provisions, wholly reject the *Kirby* postindictment stage restriction and require counsel at all lineups.[41] However, the Supreme Court is extremely explicit that a police lineup or face-to-face confrontation conducted after the accused has been formally charged with the crime is considered a "critical stage of the proceedings," and the accused has a right to have counsel present. If the lineup is conducted "pre-adversarial stage" in the process, *Kirby* states that the defendant does not have the right to have an attorney present.

Furthermore, failure to provide counsel precludes the admissibility of evidence of the confrontation or lineup, but does not automatically exclude the testimony of witnesses who were able to identify the accused at the lineup. If the witness can identify the accused at the trial—without having to rely on the earlier lineup identification—the in-court identification will be valid.[42]

Quite apart from the right to counsel, a pretrial confrontation for identification purposes may be so unreliable as to infringe upon the defendant's right to due process of law.[43] In determining the constitutionality of identification procedures, the courts consider all the circumstances leading up to the identification. A due process violation will be found only when in the light of such circumstances, the procedure was such as to give rise to a likelihood that the identification was unreliable. Generally, an unreliable lineup is one that is unduly suggestive. However, even an unnecessarily suggestive identification procedure, such as a photo showup, will not violate due process if the identification is found to be reliable.[44]

THE ARRAIGNMENT

Normally, the arraignment takes place after an indictment or information is filed following a grand jury session or a preliminary hearing. At the **arraignment,** the judge informs the defendant of the charges against him or her. The judge also appoints counsel if counsel has not

FIGURE 8.11

An incarcerated defendant standing before a judge at an arraignment prepares to make a plea to the charges he faces as read to him by the judge.

Courtesy Michael Newman/PhotoEdit.

yet been retained by the defendant. The accused has a constitutional right at this stage of the process to be informed of the nature and the cause of the accusations against him or her. The judge accomplishes this by reading the formal charging document—the complaint, the information, or the indictment—to the accused. The judge must ensure that the accused understands the charges. After the charges are read and explained, the defendant is asked to enter a plea (see Figure 8.11). If the plea is not guilty, a trial date is set.

If the defendant pleads not guilty, this places the burden on the state to move forward with the case. After a plea of not guilty, the state is required to prove beyond a reasonable doubt all the charges against the defendant.

At this time, the defendant is notified of his or her rights by the judge. Next a judicial determination is made of the defendant's competency to stand trial, or such a determination is ordered. If counsel still has not been appointed and if the defendant is indigent, the counsel will be appointed as soon as possible. Sometimes at this stage, the counsel for the defense asks for trial by judge, but most often, the request is for a trial by jury.

PRETRIAL MOTIONS

It is fairly standard for defense attorneys to make pretrial motions even before a plea is entered. A **pretrial motion** is an application made to the court or to the judge prior to trial requesting an order or ruling in favor of the applicant.

In some jurisdictions, pretrial motions may be filed any time prior to trial, including the day of trial. However, in other jurisdictions, the judge requires the pretrial motions to be filed prior to the date of trial. The burden of proof in a pretrial motion lies with the defense attorney, if he or she is the one who made the motion. If the prosecutor makes the motion, then the burden of proof is on the prosecutor. Making a pretrial motion is advantageous in many ways for the accused: (1) It forces the prosecutor to disclose evidence that might lead him or her to an early plea bargain; (2) the motion forces the prosecutor to make available discoveries before the trial and allows the defendant to better prepare his or her case; (3) pretrial motions act as a discovery tool; (4) pretrial motions allow the defense attorney to learn which witnesses will testify for the state; and (5) pretrial motions allow the defendant to see his or her attorney in action.

The Motion to Dismiss

A common pretrial motion is to dismiss the indictment or information. This *motion to dismiss* often alleges that the government's allegation assumes the truth thereof, does not allege a crime, or is not in correct form. This motion often alleges that the undisputed facts in the case do not establish a simple case of guilt against the defendant. A motion to dismiss may also be upheld if it is based on the fact that the defendant has been granted immunity.

The motion to dismiss the charges on double jeopardy is based on the Fifth Amendment of the U.S. Constitution. The Supreme Court has guaranteed that an accused will not suffer multiple prosecution for the same offense or multiple punishments for the same crime. Hence, if a defendant has been previously tried for a crime for which he or she is now standing charged, the present action violates the Fifth Amendment's double jeopardy clause. A motion to dismiss based on the statute of limitations, on the other hand, asserts that the state failed to try the accused within the statutorily prescribed period of time after the offense was committed.

The Motion for Discovery

Another effective pretrial motion is one requesting the state to reveal information or evidence that the prosecution has gathered against the defendant. This is called a **motion for discovery** or a motion for a bill of particulars. If the motion for a bill of particulars is upheld by the court, the prosecutor will be ordered to clarify the charges by adding the necessary facts to the original indictment or by adding information in the form of an amendment. This will better allow the defendant to understand the nature of the charges against him or her.

The motion for discovery is made prior to trial. It is a request to examine the evidentiary documents, the list of witnesses, and the physical evidence in the possession of the prosecution. Furthermore, the Supreme Court has held that when a prosecutor fails to disclose evidence favorable to the accused upon request, the state violates the accused's due process rights.[45]

The Motion for a Change of Venue

Typically, criminal cases are tried in the county (or district, in federal cases) in which the crime was committed. However, the defense may make a motion for a **change of venue** if there has been excessive pretrial publicity about the case or if there is reason to believe that substantial prejudice exists that would deny the defendant a fair trial (see the Landmark Case *Travis v. United States*). If the trial judge agrees, the trial is moved to another county or district. The prosecution frequently objects to a motion for a change of venue because of the difficulty and expense in transporting staff and witnesses to another city.

For example, as a result of the court-authorized change-of-venue motion made by the defense in the state trial of the four Los Angeles police officers charged with assaulting Rodney King, the trial was moved from Los Angeles to the predominately white suburb of Simi Valley. The defense argued that they would be unable to obtain an impartial jury in Los Angeles, where the case had received so much attention and racial tensions were running high. The prosecution, objecting unsuccessfully to the motion, argued that the change of venue was unnecessary and would not likely produce a jury representative of the racial composition of Los Angeles. In the subsequent federal trial of the same officers on charges that they had violated King's civil rights, the defense also requested a change of venue. This time, the judge denied the request and the trial was held in Los Angeles.

The Motion of Intention to Provide Alibi

If the defense plans to present a defense of alibi, it must file a *motion of intention to provide alibi*. The motion must place the defendant in a location different from the crime scene at the time of the crime in such a way that it would have been impossible for him or her to be the guilty party. The names and addresses of witnesses to the defendant's location at the time of the crime must be disclosed to the prosecutor before the trial. Although the states vary greatly in how early a motion of alibi must be filed before the beginning of a trial, federal rules require disclosure of alibi witnesses at least ten days before trial.[46]

The Motion for Severance

Many legal actions involve multiple charges against the defendant. The accused may have been arrested for a number of different crimes resulting from a single incident. For example, the theft of a bus followed by the destruction of property and the bus itself, resisting arrest, and assaulting a police officer, involves several crimes. The accused may then be charged for multiple crimes for the same offense.

> ## LANDMARK CASE — Travis v. United States
>
> Travis was convicted of making and filing a false non-Communist affidavit required by the National Labor Relations Act. Travis executed this affidavit as a union officer in Colorado, from where he mailed it to Washington, D.C. Travis contended that the venue in this action was improperly laid in Colorado, since the crime of making and filing the affidavit was completed and filed in Washington, D.C. The prosecution contended that the venue was properly defined in federal law in the district of Colorado. The issue before the Supreme Court was whether the Constitution requires that criminal trials be held in the districts in which the offenses were committed. The courts said that yes, they do. Justice Douglas stated that Article III of the Constitution states that criminal trials shall be held in the state where the said crimes shall have been committed (where it was filed, in Washington, D.C.). This safeguard is reinforced by the Sixth Amendment's mandate of trial by jury of the state where the crime was committed.
>
> Source: *Travis v. United States*, 364 U.S. 631 (1961).

For the sake of expediency, the prosecution may want to consolidate these multiple charges into a single case. The defense, however, may feel that different tactics are required in dealing with the charge. Thus, the *motion for severance of charges* requests that each specific charge be tried in a separate manner. Similarly, often more than one person is charged with participation in the same crime. For example, there may be four co-defendants in a rape case. There are times when it is in the best interest of one or more of the accused to be tried in separate proceedings. For example, one defendant may wish to have a trial by jury, another may wish to blame the other defendants, and a third may want a trial by judge. Thus the motion for severance of defendants calls for one or more of the accused to be tried at separate proceedings. The joining of co-defendants may have negative consequences for them because when defendants are joined in the same trial, there is a greater tendency for convictions of both individuals. Furthermore, when charges are joined, the jurors may confuse the evidence among the various charges and make more negative inferences about the characters of the defendants.

The Motion to Determine Competency

Another pretrial motion is the *motion to determine competency* of the accused to stand trial. If the defendant is mentally disturbed, he or she may be declared incompetent to stand trial. This motion is predicated upon the theory that a mentally ill person cannot be held responsible for criminal acts. Should a defendant be found incompetent to stand trial, the defendant will be institutionalized until becoming competent to stand trial.

The Constitutional Right of Being Competent to Stand Trial

Before determining the right of competency to stand trial, it is first necessary to distinguish between competency and sanity. Competency to stand trial must be carefully distinguished from the insanity defense, although both rest on the defendant's abnormality. Insanity is a defense against a criminal charge. A defendant acquitted by reason of insanity may not be retried or convicted, although he or she may be hospitalized under some circumstances. Incompetency to stand trial depends on the defendant's mental condition at the time of the trial. Incompetency is not a defense, but rather a bar on trial.

The basis of the incompetency claim is the notion under the due process clause of the Constitution that the defendant may not be tried, convicted, or sentenced if, as a result of mental disease or defect, he or she is unable to understand the nature of the proceeding being brought against him or her, or to assist counsel in the preparation of the case. In order to determine competency under the due process clause, which prevents a defendant from being declared incompetent without notice and a hearing, many jurisdictions grant a right to a jury determination of competence. If evidence of a defendant's incompetency appears to the trial judge, the judge has a constitutional obligation to conduct further inquiry and determine whether the defendant is competent. The burden of proof is on the defendant to prove by a preponderance of the evidence that he or she is not competent to stand trial. Such a burden does not violate due process. Finally, a finding by a judge or a jury that the defendant is incompetent to stand trial has the effect of suspending criminal proceedings, and invariably results in the commitment of the defendant into psychiatric hospitalization until such time as the defendant regains competence. But the defendant cannot be hospitalized indefinitely or for a long period of time simply because he or she was found incompetent; this can only be done if independent "civil commitment" proceedings are begun and result in commitment.[47]

If the accused is restored to legal competency, he or she may be tried for the offense originally charged. Another motion available to the defense is the motion to suppress pretrial identification of the accused. This motion is designed to determine whether the pretrial identification procedures employed by the police in having an eyewitness identify an accused violated the constitutional rights of the accused to have a fair lineup.

The Motion for a Bill of Particulars

A *motion for a bill of particulars* is a written statement that specifies additional facts other than the charges contained in the information in the indictment. As a motion by the defense, it requests more details from the prosecution. The motion is not made for the purpose of discovering evidence or for learning exactly how much the prosecution knows, and is not designed to suggest an insufficient indictment. Rather, a motion for a bill of particulars asks for details about what the prosecution claims in order to give the accused a fair notice of what must be defended.

THE SUPPRESSION HEARING

The Motion to Suppress

A *motion to suppress* is a request by the defense to have certain evidence excluded from the consideration of the jury. Typically, it is filed to prohibit evidence that was obtained by an alleged illegal search or seizure or wiretap, or to challenge the validity of the confession.

When the defense makes a motion to suppress evidence gained through an unlawful search and seizure, it alleges that the evidence was obtained in violation of the defendant's Fourth Amendment rights and therefore cannot be used against him or her in a criminal trial.[48] Upon this motion by the defense, the court will hold a pretrial evidentiary hearing. During the hearing, testimony is taken by the trial judge regarding the procedures used by the police in obtaining the challenged evidence. If the evidence was obtained by a warrantless search or seizure, the burden of proof is on the government. If the evidence was obtained by a search warrant, the burden of proof to establish the validity of the search rests on the defense. The conflicting evidence that almost always results from this hearing is resolved by how much credibility the judge gives the various witnesses, the police officers' testimony, and usually the defendant's testimony. A determination of credibility is the sole decision of the judge.

When the defense makes a motion to suppress a confession, admission, or other statements the accused made to the police, the defendant again is relying on the Constitution. The Fifth Amendment entitles a defendant to a determination by the court of whether a confession is voluntary prior to the confession being made known to a jury. This type of suppression hearing can involve a number of related inquiries, including whether the defendant was advised that he or she had the right to remain silent and the right to counsel, or whether he or she was coerced into making a statement.

As was the case with a motion to suppress a search, a motion to suppress a confession is done before the judge alone in an evidentiary hearing called a suppression hearing. A suppression hearing is a pretrial hearing, outside of the jury's view, wherein the defendant attempts to prohibit the introduction of harmful evidence against him or her based on the alleged fact that the police acquired the evidence in question in violation of the accused's Fourth, Fifth, or Sixth Amendment rights. Hence, the accused argues as in

Mapp v. Ohio that the evidence should be excluded from the jury's consideration whenever they determine and judge the accused's guilt or innocence.

If the defendant is successful in the suppression hearing, the judge orders the items determined to be illegally seized, or the evidence of a confession the bench determined to be unconstitutionally acquired, to be excluded from evidence. The rule allowing the judge to make such an order is the exclusionary rule.

Making pretrial motions is advantageous in many ways for the accused. Such motions force the prosecutor to disclose evidence that may lead him or her to consider an early plea bargain. They also force the prosecutor to make certain decisions before the final preparation of the case, and they also act as a discovery tool that allows the defense attorney to learn which witnesses are going to testify for the state. Finally, pretrial motions allow the defendant to see his or her attorney in action. This gives the defendant an opportunity to gain more confidence in the lawyer.

The Right to a Suppression Hearing

The defendant has a right to a suppression hearing outside the jury's presence, at which time a judge decides whether evidence or a confession is admissible.[49] If the judge decides that the evidence or confession is admissible, the jury may consider it. The defendant may present to the jury much of the same evidence presented at the suppression hearing in an attempt to persuade the jury not to believe the confession.[50] Finally, the defendant has no right to a specific finding of fact on each factual question.[51] However, the defendant does have a right to testify at the suppression hearing; any such testimony may not be used against the defendant at trial on the issue of guilt.[52] The government also bears the burden of establishing admissibility of evidence of a confession by a preponderance of the evidence.[53]

PLEA NEGOTIATIONS

Prosecutors are legally empowered to negotiate with defendants and their attorneys (see Figure 8.12). Generally, plea bargaining is a defendant's agreement to plead guilty to a criminal charge, with a rational expectation of receiving some consideration from the prosecutor for doing so. Often defendants will plead guilty without a plea bargain and expect to receive some benefit nonetheless. These negotiations are likely to be much more informal during the pretrial period than at a later stage when the court becomes officially involved in the trial. Plea negotiation fulfills various purposes, the most important of which are (1) improving the administrative efficiency of the courts, (2) lowering the costs of prosecution, and (3) permitting the prosecution to devote additional time to more important and more serious cases.[54]

More accurately, plea bargaining refers only to guilty pleas in exchange for concessions made by the government. Express or implicit bargaining prevails in most jurisdictions. In *express bargaining*, prosecutors, defendants, defense lawyers, and sometimes trial judges meet face-to-face to work out specific concessions (see Figure 8.12). *Implicit bargaining* involves no direct meetings. Instead, local practice, sometimes called the going rate for guilty pleas, determines concessions. The going rates vary from one community to another, are products of the individual courthouse and community, and are not primarily shaped by state or national considerations. In one jurisdiction, an armed robber may receive eight years after a trial and five years if he pleads; in another, the comparable figures may be seven and four, or ten and eight, and so on.[55]

In implicit bargaining, defense attorneys can fairly assume that if their clients plead guilty to "normal" crimes, they will receive concessions in line with the going rate.

FIGURE 8.12

Two attorneys in court negotiating a plea in the judge's presence.

Courtesy PhotoEdit.

According to one Detroit judge familiar with the practice, "The system operates in terms of defense attorney and defendants' expectations—what is widely known as a rate. It's an expectation model."[56]

Concessions in negotiations usually take three forms. The first form is *charge bargaining,* wherein prosecutors drop some charges and/or file charges less serious than the facts justify in exchange for a defendant's guilty plea. For example, a defendant who has committed a first-degree murder carrying a mandatory life term might plead guilty to second-degree murder with a term of twenty years to life. The plea to second-degree murder gives the judge discretion to sentence the defendant to less than life imprisonment. The second form of negotiation is *sentence bargaining.* In this type, defendants plead guilty to charges actually warranted by the facts in the case, but with the understanding that the judge will grant, or at least the prosecutor will request, a lenient sentence, such as probation. The third type of negotiation is a *slow plea.* Under this type of negotiation, defendants go to trial, but the trials are short and superficial. The government and defense agree to set aside the rules of evidence, and they stipulate, or agree, not to argue over guilt; conviction becomes a foregone conclusion.

As mentioned earlier, prosecutors prefer to pursue cases that have a good chance for conviction. Thus, because many major crimes include the elements of lesser crimes (such as murder and manslaughter), prosecutors with shaky cases may accept a guilty plea to "lesser included offenses" to save the time, money, and risk of a trial for a major crime.

They may also offer various incentives to the accused to elicit information about other offenders or to induce them to give testimony that will help the prosecution. One such incentive is an offer to accept a plea of guilty to a lesser charge (called a reduction in charge); another is immunity from further prosecution on the incidental charge. Thus, as a result of plea bargaining, a number of misdemeanor convictions began as felony charges; drunken driving may be reduced to "reckless driving," or statutory rape to "contributing to the delinquency of a minor."

The defendant and counsel may also attempt to bargain for a reduction in sentence. It has been estimated that more than 90 percent of criminal convictions result in negotiated guilty pleas. Even in serious felony cases, many jurisdictions encounter four times as many bargains as requests to litigate the cases in trial.

Justification for Plea Bargaining

As early as the 1920s, the legal profession was united in its opposition to plea bargaining. Roscoe Pound, Raymond Moley, and others associated with the crime surveys of the period stressed the opportunities for political influence as a factor in the administration of criminal justice. As late as the 1980s, criminal trials were conducted in the military, under the Uniform Code of Military Justice, without plea bargaining. This practice was illegal. Today, under nonmilitary criminal codes, under the pressures generated by crime in an urban society and the reality of bargaining, a shift has occurred so that professional groups are primarily interested in procedures that will allow for the review of guilty pleas and for other safeguards. Plea bargaining is now justified on the grounds that it individualizes justice and that it is administratively necessary.

The Prevalence of Guilty Pleas

The most common disposition of a felony arrest not rejected or dismissed is a guilty plea, according to a Bureau of Justice Statistics special report. The Constitution guarantees the right to trial by jury and protects against self-incrimination—but for at least sixty years defendants' pleas of guilty, not trials by jury, have been the more common means of criminal case conviction.[57] Although defendants have a right to a trial to determine guilt or innocence, many decide to plead guilty to the original or reduced charges. Bureau of Justice Statistics data obtained from prosecutors in a number of urban jurisdictions show that 45 of every 100 felony arrests ended in guilty pleas, while only five ended in trials (four guilty verdicts and one acquittal). The remaining dispositions (50 of every 100) were rejections and dismissals. Consistent with prior studies, guilty pleas outnumbered trials by about ten to one.[58]

CTQ

Research has shown that plea bargaining is key in the ability of players in the criminal justice system to manage their caseloads. If it were eliminated, what would happen to the functioning of the system, as well as to criminal justice in America, besides the extraordinary financial strain and the strain on efficient administration of the criminal justice system?

CTQ

What are the legal issues in plea bargaining?

CTQ

Should a criminal be allowed to bargain for a reduced sentence in exchange for a guilty plea?

Recognition of this fact—that most convictions are the result of guilty pleas rather than guilty verdicts—has since the mid-1960s fostered a vigorous national debate over the nature and propriety of the guilty-plea process. At the center of this debate is the role of the prosecutor, who actively engages in obtaining guilty pleas in 90 percent of the cases.

Entering a Constitutional Guilty Plea

The Supreme Court has outlined various requirements for a guilty plea to be constitutional. The trial judge must address the defendant personally in open court and on the record to determine whether the plea is indeed voluntary and intelligent.[59] Specifically, the judge must be sure that the defendant knows and understands the following six concepts: (1) the nature of the charge to which he or she has pleaded[60]—a plea would be considered involuntary if the defendant had not formed the intent essential for the crime; (2) the maximum penalty possible for the offense and the mandatory minimum penalty; (3) the fact that he or she has a right to plead not guilty; (4) the fact that by pleading guilty, the defendant waives his or her right to a trial; (5) the applicable sentencing guidelines;[61] and (6) the possibility that the court may order the defendant to make restitution to the victim of the offense.

The judge must be satisfied that the plea was both voluntary and intelligent. This requirement is not constitutionally mandated for taking guilty pleas in state cases, although some states in their own rules require the showing of a factual basis to support the idea. Ironically, an admission of guilt is not necessary to constitute a factual basis, nor is it a prerequisite of an imposition of a criminal penalty. In *North Carolina v. Alfred*,[62] the defendant did not admit his guilt in open court, but the Supreme Court stated that as long as the state introduces strong evidence of the defendant's guilt, then the defendant's voluntary plea appears to be an intelligent choice among the alternatives. A guilty plea is transformed to a guilty verdict shortly thereafter by the criminal court judge presiding over the case.

Often there is a conversation between the judge and the defendant for the judge to determine whether the defendant is factually guilty. This conversation is often referred to as the **plea colloquy.** If the judge is satisfied, he or she may deliver a sentence at that time or schedule a sentencing hearing. If the judge is not satisfied, he or she can refuse to consider the guilty plea and enter a plea of not guilty for the defendant in the record, set a trial date, and demand that the defendant stand trial.

The Supreme Court has ruled that "when a guilty plea rests in any significance on the promise or an agreement of the prosecutor, so it can be considered to be part of the inducement or consideration, such a promise must be fulfilled"[63] (see the Landmark Case *United States v. Ammidown*). Hence, when a guilty plea is given to a judge, the judge is mandated to ask a series of questions to ensure that the method by which the plea bargain was reached adheres to the principles dictated by the Court. Around the courthouse, this series of questions is referred to as the "copping out ceremony."

The Plea Process

Many pleas to reduced charges are not the result of negotiations between the prosecutor and defense counsel, but rather reflect a decision on the part of the prosecutor that the appropriate conviction charge should be a less serious crime than the initial arrest or court charges. Often such decisions are made at screening or in the early pre-bindover stages of felony case processing, before the prosecutor has any opportunity to talk with defense counsel. The reduction of a felony charge to a misdemeanor, for example, most often reflects the prosecutor's decision not to carry certain types of cases forward to the felony court, rather than being the result of a negotiated plea.

Rather than view the plea process from a total system perspective, most studies have focused on the guilty plea process only in the felony court. But even after cases have been bound over to the felony court, the nature of the plea process is more varied than is indicated by the notion of a prosecutor and defense attorney negotiating charge reductions.

Some view the idea of inducements by prosecutors to encourage guilty pleas as a violation of both the Fifth and Sixth Amendments, while others view the very same inducements as excessive leniency that violates the constitutional protection of domestic

---

CTQ

Do most criminals, including those who are innocent, "cop a plea" to a charge because the reduction of the charge is so significant that they can't afford not to due to the risk involved?

CTQ

In 2002–2003, criminal justice research revealed a shockingly large number of inmates who later were conclusively proven innocent (usually by DNA evidence) but who nonetheless often had confessed and even more often had pleaded guilty to crimes they did not commit. What policy implications do these revelations suggest about the whole plea-bargaining process in the American criminal justice system? What practical remedies do you believe can be taken to correct these unconscionable situations?

LANDMARK CASE — United States v. Ammidown

Ammidown was charged with first-degree murder and conspiracy to commit murder. He confessed that he had arranged to have his wife murdered but the plan was never carried out. Later, however, he arranged with Richard Lee to abduct his wife and to threaten her life, in an effort to extort money from her family. Lee did abduct Mrs. Ammidown and then raped and killed her. Ammidown did not confess to the actual murder of his wife. Prior to the trial, the U.S. Attorney made an agreement with Ammidown whereby he would plead guilty to second-degree murder, and the first-degree murder charge would be dismissed. In return for dismissing first-degree charges, Ammidown would agree to testify in a grand jury proceeding and in the trial of Lee, whom the prosecutor believed was involved in another murder.

The trial judge refused to approve the agreement. He stated that because the crime was so heinous and major and the evidence was so strong, the public interest would not be served by allowing a judgment of second-degree murder.

The issue before the federal court was whether a trial judge could reject an agreement made by the prosecutor that allowed the defendant to plead guilty to a lesser crime. The judge thought that the defendant should be tried for a more serious crime. The court held that no, the judge could not in fact make such a judgment, stating that in an overwhelming number of cases, the trial judge should accept the determination of the prosecutor concerning the agreement with the defendants. The court said that the prosecutor has the best position to evaluate the staff resources available in his or her office, the number of cases that must be tried, and how to best allocate the available resources. Furthermore, when a prosecutor abuses discretion in the making of a deal, it is an extreme trespass in the sentencing power of the judge to overturn the plea bargain.

Source: United States v. Ammidown, 497 F.2d 615 (D.C. Cir. 1973).

---

tranquility. Victims often see plea bargaining as a practice that further removes them from the criminal justice system. Others see it as an "under-the-table" procedure that serves primarily to undermine respect for the criminal justice system.

It is important to clarify that this chapter focuses directly on the prevalence of pleas, and not on the process of plea negotiation or "plea bargaining" per se. It has been discovered previously that even in jurisdictions where the process of plea negotiation is terminated, approximately 80 percent of all convictions are obtained by means of pleas rather than trial verdicts. (See "In the News: For a Guilty Plea and 650 Million.")

The prosecutor can affect the defendant's probability of conviction if tried by deciding how to allocate his or her trial resources; similarly, the prosecutor can affect sentencing differentials between pleas and trial by making sentencing recommendations to the judge. Consequently, the ratio of pleas to trials indicates how defendants' individual decisions, taken collectively, are made in light of the probabilities confronting them.

The Victim and Plea Bargaining

Related to the issue of the prosecutor's exercise of discretion, discussed in Chapter 7, "The Dynamics of the Criminal Court," is the proper role of the victim in influencing plea bargaining. Often defense attorneys criticize prosecutors for treating victims' interests as paramount and oppose the practice of seeking approval for the proposed plea from a victim or family member. Some suggest that the system today is too "victim driven." Others maintain that the victim plays an almost secondary role in the process.

In reality, the victim is *not* "empowered" at the *pretrial stage of the criminal process.* Statutes do not require that the prosecutor defer to the victim's wishes, and there are no legal consequences for ignoring the victim in a plea bargaining decision. Even the

CTQ
Should the judge participate in the court's plea bargaining, since 90 percent of the cases brought before the court are disposed of in that manner?

CTQ
Will the now allowable and required participation of victims during plea bargaining offer them an even more important sense of their own significance and a sense of well-being?

IN THE NEWS
A HUMAN PERSPECTIVE

FOR A GUILTY PLEA AND $650 MILLION
by J. Greenwald

Christmas was just around the corner, but the videotaped tidings that Frederick Joseph handed out to the TV networks last Wednesday evening were not exactly festive. Looking tired and tense, the silver-haired chief executive officer of Drexel Burnham Lambert discussed the settlement that Drexel had reached that day with federal prosecutors to end the largest probe ever of a U.S. securities firm. Declaring that the long-awaited agreement "makes sense from a business and human point of view," Joseph, 51, tried to be upbeat. The deal, he said, would leave the firm "in a very strong financial position, and allows us to refocus our energies on running the business successfully."

In fact, the agreement was a stunning about-face by the most influential, go-go investment-banking house of the 1980s. After maintaining for two years that Drexel had done nothing wrong, a shaken board of directors voted 16 to 6 to accept the stiff terms proposed by Rudolph Giuliani, U.S. Attorney for the Southern District of New York. The deal calls for Drexel to plead guilty to six felony counts involving mail, wire, and securities fraud and to pay a record $650 million in penalties. Some $300 million of the fine would go to the government, which has spent an estimated $10 million prosecuting the case so far, and $350 million would be set aside to compensate the victims of Drexel's wrongdoing.

In return, Giuliani agreed to drop his stated plan to bring racketeering charges that could have crippled Drexel, the fifth-largest U.S. securities firm. Before the deal can be completed, however, Giuliani stipulated, a 184-page civil complaint that the Securities and Exchange Commission brought against Drexel in September must be settled by January 10. The SEC could conceivably ask for a larger pool of money to compensate victims who range from ordinary stockholders to Drexel's clients. Even so, Giuliani declared Drexel's fines and concessions "appropriate punishment." He added, "You do not put corporations in prison."

During the nearly two years that the government spent preparing its case, Drexel defiantly declared its innocence and launched a major advertising campaign extolling the civic virtues of its junk bonds. Joseph claims that the two-year federal probe cost Drexel $1.5 million in legal and advertising fees. Since November, the firm has bargained for an agreement that, as chairman Robert Linton put it, "would not make us look like a bunch of thieves."

But the blows kept furiously raining down, and Joseph's smile began to fade. When the board voted that Monday, Giuliani had already turned three close Milken (CEO of Drexel) associates into government witnesses by granting them immunity from prosecution. The knockout power of an indictment under the 1970 Racketeer Influenced and Corrupt Organizations Act was also greatly feared. Charges under RICO, developed to prosecute the Mafia and other organized criminals, would allow Giuliani to tie up much of Drexel's $2.3 billion of capital—including the fortunes of the firm's 1,700 employee stockholders—throughout a lengthy trial.

But the government's big prize was Drexel, which must now face life as a confessed felon. Said Congressman Edward Markey, a Massachusetts Democrat who heads a House subcommittee that covers finance: "We now know that the single most financially successful Wall Street firm of the 1980s in large measure built its fortune on the foundation of criminality."

Source: J. Greenwald, "Let's Make a Deal," *Time*, January 2, 1989. © 1989 TIME, Inc. Reprinted by permission.

American Bar Association Model Uniform Victims of Crime Act only suggests that the prosecutor "confer" with the victim.[64] (See Figure 8.13.)

Victims are certainly not in a position to veto a plea bargain. Most of the work of the victims' rights movement in the justice system is devoted to securing financial compensation from the state and some restitution when possible from the defendant. Currently, the victim has the greatest influence at the sentencing stage. Before the court imposes a sentence, the victim often has the right to offer a **victim-impact statement** after a guilty determination. This statement is presented by anyone who was negatively affected by the crime, including the actual victim and his or her family members. They are given the opportunity to come forward and tell about every conceivable effect that the crime has had on their lives, jobs, and emotional and psychological health, as well as their entire being.

There is no question that the prosecutor should consider the impact that a plea bargain may have on the victim or the victim's family. Some victims' groups even suggest that the victim's family should have statutory authority to approve or disapprove any plea bargain between the prosecutor and defense attorney in criminal homicide cases. Given the volume of plea bargains in the plea process, it appears unreasonable that state statutes have been passed affording victims greater participation.

As we have mentioned, more than 90 percent of all criminal cases are generally disposed of without a trial. Plea bargaining is an inevitable result and essential to the smooth functioning of the criminal process. If that is so, then it must be conducted fairly, and as George Fletcher, a noted legal scholar at Columbia Law School, indicates, "with due consideration of the victim whose complaint initiates the action."[65]

FACTORS IN PLEA NEGOTIATION

According to Mather, the following variables are most frequently identified as having a significant influence on case disposition: caseload of the prosecutor, strength or weakness of the case, type of defense attorney, personal characteristics of the defendant (such as age, race, prior record, bail status), and the type of crime.[66] What is not clear from research is the relative importance of these factors in determining case disposition; nor is it clear how these factors are weighted when seen from the different perspectives of the principals in the negotiations: the prosecutor, the defense counsel, and the defendant.

Mather's findings on the factors that influence the prosecutor's decision to plea bargain were expanded in his seminal study, which was conducted several years ago. Of course, the prosecutor was never required to participate in the plea negotiation and make plea bargains. Indeed, some cases by their very nature are such that the prosecution would never consider a plea bargain due to the severity of the crime. "In the News: Hauling Butts into Court" appears to be an excellent example of such a nonnegotiable case.

FIGURE 8.13

An unidentified crime victim (left) participates in a plea negotiation outside of the courtroom with the prosecutor.

Courtesy Paul Conklin/PhotoEdit.

IN THE NEWS

A HUMAN PERSPECTIVE

HAULING BUTTS INTO COURT
by M. Lavelle

The road to a criminal case began with a theatrical congressional hearing in 1994, where six CEOs testified under oath that their products were not addictive. Anti-tobacco members of Congress immediately asked the Justice Department to investigate possible perjury charges. Such charges were explored, but the chances that perjury will form the basis of the case have diminished, in part because it would require proving not only that CEOs didn't tell the truth, but that they were consciously lying.

Instead, the Justice Department appears to be focusing on allegedly false statements that industry officials made to the Food and Drug Administration and the Office of the Surgeon General. The first break in the investigation came when a California biotechnology company, DNA Plant Technology, admitted to authorities that it had helped one firm—later revealed to be Brown & Williamson—develop a super-high-nicotine tobacco plant code-named Y-1. In pleading guilty to a misdemeanor export violation, DNAP agreed to provide testimony that could explain Brown & Williamson's drive to produce high-nicotine leaf.

In addition, prosecutors are close to striking a wide-ranging immunity deal with the smallest of the five major tobacco companies, Liggett Group Inc., in which officials of the company would be protected from prosecution if they testify against other companies about industry-wide strategies on scientific research, legal defense, and dealings with federal officials.

More evidence for criminal charges is being sought in the voluminous documents on the industry's use of nicotine that have just been made public, especially those just uncovered in a megatrial against tobacco underway in Minnesota brought by state Attorney General Hubert H. Humphrey III and Blue Cross Blue Shield of Minnesota. Asked in a videotaped deposition about his company's use of nicotine, a retired Philip Morris vice president for science and research, Thomas Osdene—author of a 1980 memo saying "the thing we sell most is nicotine"—took the Fifth Amendment against self-incrimination 135 times. Sources say Osdene's lawyers have asked the Justice Department for immunity from prosecution—a sign that he, too, may be willing to help them build their case.

Source: M. Lavelle, "Hauling Butts into Court," *U.S. News & World Report*, March 9, 1988. Copyright 1998 U.S. News & World Report, L.P. Reprinted with permission.

U.S. Department of Justice attorneys judged the following eleven factors most relevant in deciding whether to bargain a case:

- The defendant's willingness to cooperate in the investigation or prosecution of any other defendants
- The defendant's history with respect to criminal activity
- The nature and seriousness of the offenses charged
- The defendant's remorse or contrition and willingness to assume responsibility for his or her conduct
- The desirability of prompt, certain disposition in the case
- The likelihood of obtaining a conviction at trial
- The probable effect on the witnesses
- The probable sentence or other consequences if the defendant is convicted
- Public interest in having the case tried rather than disposed of by a guilty plea
- The expense of the trial or appeal
- The need to avoid delay in the disposition of other pending cases[67]

Finally, it should be noted that for a defendant, the best sentencing results are almost always a consequence of the plea bargain. (See Figure 8.14.)

Evaluating Plea Bargaining

The guilty plea occurs in up to 90 percent of felony cases before state and federal courts. Although often explained in terms of the heavy caseloads being processed through the system, plea bargaining can be in the interests of all participants: The prosecutor secures a guilty plea and does not have to go to trial; the defense attorney is able to use time more efficiently; the judge moves the caseload; and the defendant receives a sentence that is less than the law could impose. With the decisions of the Supreme Court and the increased public awareness of plea bargaining, it can be expected that the practice will continue and will be increasingly legitimized.

How Can a Defendant Successfully Appeal a Guilty Plea?

A defendant may not collaterally attack his or her guilty plea after sentencing if it represents a "voluntary and intelligent choice" among known alternatives. The Supreme Court has held that after sentencing, defendants generally do not have the right to attack

FIGURE 8.14

Conviction by Guilty Plea, Bench Trial, or Trial by Jury: A Comparison of Prison Sentences

U.S. Department of Justice, Bureau of Justice Statistics.

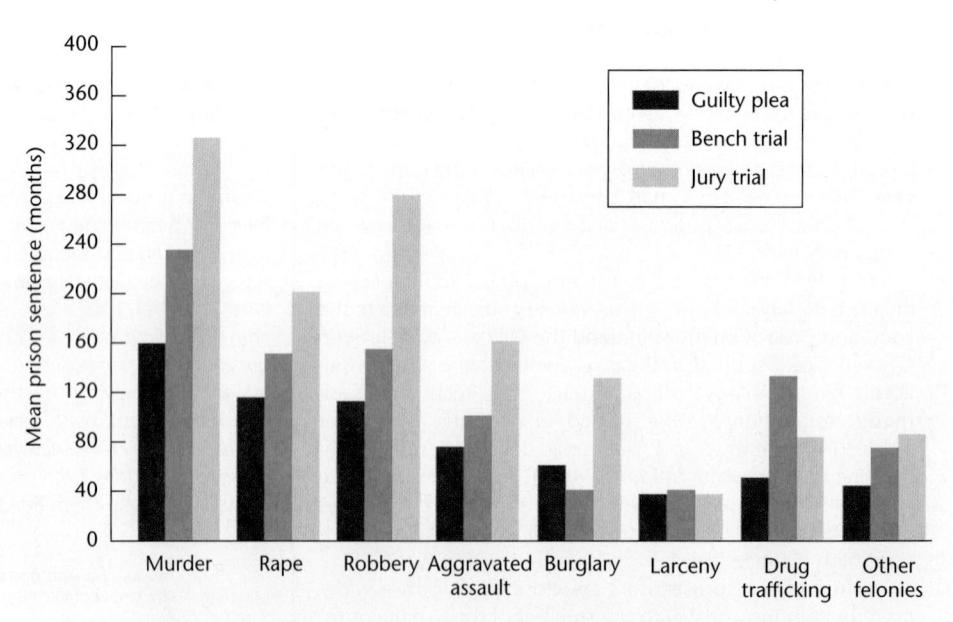

Although it appears it is in the offender's interest to plead guilty for most crimes, there is not enough information in this graph to support such a conclusion. What else would you need to know?

IN THE WORKPLACE

VICTIM/WITNESS COORDINATOR

Responsible for coordinating necessary hearings, legal arrangements, and communications with crime victims and witnesses. Performs a variety of duties, including the following: notifying victims of trials, court hearings, and case dispositions; informing victims about the criminal justice process; responding to service requests of victims; assisting victims in restitution matters; tracking cases, maintaining records; reporting progression of cases; maintaining a current list of victims' addresses for parole hearing and release notifications; assisting in preparing victims and witnesses to testify in court; providing a list of legal counselors to victims; and conducting criminal history investigation of witnesses. Minimum qualifications are as follows: equivalent of an associate degree in counseling or a related field; one year work experience in law, law enforcement, social work, or criminal justice; ability to pass a full background check; interpersonal communication skills; knowledge of criminal justice process; ability to draft legal documents.

their pleas on the grounds of prior constitutional violations. The Court indicated that by pleading guilty, a defendant presumably has balanced the likelihood of success and the advantages of a guilty plea against the strength of the state's case going to trial. A guilty plea cannot be attacked simply because the defendant miscalculated his chances or the strength of the case against him or her.[68]

However, there are a few exceptions to this general rule. Some states have special provisions guaranteeing judicial review of certain constitutional claims even after a guilty plea. For example, in some states, the defendant may plead guilty and then appeal the denial of his or her motion to suppress.[69] Another exception is that a defendant can attack his or her guilty plea by showing that the court that took the plea lacked the jurisdiction to do so.[70] A third exception is one in which a defendant may successfully attack the guilty plea on the grounds that his or her counsel failed to provide advice about the claims that he could assert. Finally, the fourth exception is the failure of the prosecutor to abide by the agreement on a good faith basis.

PRETRIAL DIVERSION AS AN ALTERNATIVE TO PLEA BARGAINING

An alternative to plea bargaining in the overcrowded prison situation is pretrial diversion. Pretrial diversion programs were first established in the late 1960s and early 1970s, when it became apparent that a viable alternative to the highly stigmatized criminal sentence was needed. In **pretrial diversion programs,** formal criminal proceedings against an accused are suspended while that person participates in a community treatment program under court supervision. Diversion helps the offender avoid the stigma of a criminal conviction and enables the justice system to reduce costs and alleviate prison overcrowding. Normally, an accused will not be allowed to participate in a pretrial diversion unless the prosecutor, judge, and often the probation officer agree that he or she is a good candidate for the program. The accused's successful completion of the program will allow him or her to avoid prosecution and often have the case dismissed.

During the diversion period, the accused is monitored by the diversion staff's personnel to assess his or her continued suitability to the program. Often these programs include alcohol and drug rehabilitative counseling, job training, and family counseling. After the accused participates in the program, charges may be dismissed entirely. If the program needs to be continued and if staff members are unsure of their client's progress, the trial may be postponed. If the accused fails to participate in the program, however, he or she will be processed through normal court channels. Pretrial diversion reduces court congestion and often gives a first offender a second chance to turn his or her life around. Some critics suggest it is the last arena for the rehabilitative process in the criminal justice system that has the opportunity to become truly effective. (For a more detailed discussion of pretrial diversion programs, see Chapter 13.)

SUMMARY

Since the due process revolution of the 1960s, the Supreme Court has recognized that constitutional rights begin only after the suspect has been arrested or subjected to a custodial interrogation. This pretrial period is the time when many important decisions are made about what will happen to the defendant. If a grand jury proceeding or preliminary hearing results in sufficient evidence to produce probable cause that the defendant committed the felony, then the defendant will be arraigned. At arraignment, the defendant is read the charges against him or her and informed of his or her constitutional rights, particularly the right to representation of counsel. Next, the arraignment judge places the accused in confinement, frees the accused on bail, or releases the accused on his or her own recognizance. At this stage, the defendant will be given an opportunity to enter a plea to the charges. Prior to to the trial, many pretrial motions by the defense counsel are made on the defendant's behalf in order to dismiss charges or to exclude evidence before trial begins.

The two critical issues that most significantly affect an accused during the pretrial period both involve discretion of the two central agencies in the criminal justice system. The first of these involves the discretion of the judge. Every defendant makes a motion for pretrial release. A defendant who is detained in jail generally suffers adverse consequences from the experience, but the defendant's individual plight has to be weighed against the possibility that release will result in further danger to society or the possibility of escape. The second act of discretion is performed by the district attorney's office, in the area of plea negotiation. Since the criminal justice system is so overcrowded, it lacks the resources to criminally litigate even 10 percent of those accused of a crime. As a consequence, the practice of plea negotiation, despite its critics and detractors, is essential and is the most common element in the administrative disposition of the largest percentage of criminal cases processed through the American criminal justice system.

DISCUSSION AND REVIEW

1. Discuss at least five forms of pretrial release mechanisms.
2. What is a bail schedule and how does it work? What is a conditions-of-bail form, and what are the consequences of breaching those conditions?
3. What are some of the major inequities of the bail system?
4. Why are some arrested Americans sent to jail and stay there until their trial, while others remain free until their trial?
5. Explain Devine's argument that the internal structure of the commercial bail bond system is its greatest fault.
6. What are the identification procedures used to link an accused person with a crime?
7. What is preventive detention, and why do some people think it is inconsistent with the presumption of innocence?
8. What is pretrial diversion?
9. Are there any disadvantages for the defendant in the bindover preliminary hearing? What are the advantages for the prosecution?
10. What are the major functions and responsibilities of the grand jury?
11. What are the formal ways in which one can be charged with a felony in jurisdictions throughout the United States?
12. What are pretrial motions, and how are they advantageous to the accused?
13. Name at least four different pretrial motions and the effect of each motion on the ultimate outcome of the defendant's case.
14. What is the plea process and how is it carried out?
15. What are pretrial procedures and why are they important to the criminal justice process?
16. What are the five main factors of plea negotiation described by Mather?

17. What is the relationship of a bail jumper and a bounty hunter?
18. What is pretrial diversion? How does it work?
19. What are the possible roles of the prosecution, defense attorney, judge, and victim in the plea bargaining process?
20. What is plea bargaining? What are its effects on the operation of the criminal justice system? What impact does it have on the defendant?
21. What is the bindover preliminary hearing? How does it differ from the grand jury indictment process?
22. Do defendants have a legal right to bail, according to the Constitution?
23. How do the procedures following arrest for misdemeanors and felonies differ?

CHAPTER RESOURCES

IN THE MEDIA

Video

A&E American Justice Series
CNN Today Videos: *Introduction to CJ Today*, Vol. 2: segment "Jail and Bail"
FFH Video: *Pretrial Process*
FHH CJ Custom Video: *Plea Bargaining* and *Dealing with Justice*

NIJ Crime Mob Video
NIJ Videos: *Introduction to CJ*, Vol. 2: segment 9, "Grand Jury"

Film

. . . *And Justice For All* (1979)
Inherit the Wind (1960)

IN THE LITERATURE

Books

F. ALLEN, *The Judicial Question for Penal Justice: The Warren Court and the Criminal Cases*. Champaign, Ill.: University of Illinois Law Foundation, 1975.

AMERICAN CIVIL LIBERTIES UNION, *Secret Detention of the Chicago Police*. New York: Free Press, 1969.

N. BASES AND W. MCDONALD, *Preventive Detention in the District of Columbia: The First Ten Months*. New York: Vera Institute of Justice, 1974.

B. BURTON, *Bail Enforcer: The Advanced Bounty Hunter*. Boulder, Colo.: Paladin Press, 1990.

W. CHAMBLISS, *Crime and the Legal Process*. New York: McGraw-Hill, 1969.

J. CREAMER, *The Law of Arrest, Search and Seizure*, 3d ed. New York: Holt, Rinehart & Winston, 1980.

D. D. EMMERSON, *Grand Jury Reform: A Review of Key Issues*. Washington, D.C.: National Institute of Justice, 1983.

J. EISENSTEIN AND H. JACOB, *Felony Justice: An Organizational Analysis of Criminal Courts*. Boston: Little, Brown, 1977.

J. FRANKEL AND B. NAFTALIS, *The Grand Jury: An Institution on Trial*. New York: McGraw-Hill, 1975.

G. FISHER, "Plea Bargaining's Triumph," *Yale Law Journal*, vol. 105, no. 5 (March 2000), p. 857.

M. HEUMANN, *Plea Bargaining: The Experiences of Prosecutors, Judges, and Defense Attorneys*. Chicago: University of Chicago Press, 1991.

E. JOHNSON, *Crime, Correction, and Society*. Homewood, Ill.: Dorsey Press, 1964.

J. HEWETT, *Public Defender: Lawyer for the People*. New York: Longstar Books, 1991.

Y. KAMISAR, W. LAFAVE, AND G. ISRAEL, *Basic Criminal Procedure*, 7th ed. St. Paul, Minn.: West, 1993.

S. KENNEDY AND K. CARLSON, *Pretrial Release and Detention: The Bail Reform Act of 1984*. Washington, D.C: Bureau of Justice Statistics, 1988.

H. KERPER, *Introduction to the Criminal Justice System*. St. Paul, Minn.: West, 1972.

W. LAFAVE AND G. ISRAEL, *Criminal Procedure*. St. Paul, Minn.: West, 1985.

M. LEVIN, *Urban Politics and the Criminal Courts*. Chicago: University of Chicago Press, 1977.

F. MILLER, *Prosecution: The Decision to Charge a Suspect with a Crime*. New York: Hill & Wang, 1970.

N. MORRIS AND M. MILLER, *Predictions of Dangerousness in the Criminal Law*. Washington, D.C.: National Institute of Justice, 1987.

N. MORRIS, *The Future of Imprisonment*. Chicago: University of Chicago Press, 1974.

National Lawyers Guild, *Before Federal Grand Juries*, 3rd ed. St. Paul, Minn.: West, 1985.

President's Commission on Law Enforcement and Administration of Justice, *The Challenge of Crime in a Free Society*. Washington, D.C.: U.S. Government Printing Office, 1967.

A. Rosett and D. Cressey, *Justice by Consent*. Philadelphia: Lippincott, 1976.

Articles

C. Albonette, "Criminality, Prosecutorial Screening and Uncertainty: Toward a Theory of Decision Making in Felony Case Prosecution," *Criminology*, vol. 24 (1986).

"Booming Business for Bounty Hunters," *USA Today*, March 28, 1994, p. 10A.

M. Feeley, "The Effects of a Heavy Caseload." Paper presented at the annual meeting of the American Political Science Association, San Francisco, September 1975.

J. Grace, "The Things Kids Say," *Time*, September 14, 1998.

J. Halsted, "The American Grand Jury—Due Process or Right to Regress?" *Criminal Justice Policy Review*, vol. 2, no. 2 (1987).

D. A. Henry and B. D. Beaudin "Bail Bondsmen," *American Jails*, vol. 4 (1990), pp. 8–16.

B. Herman, "Think about Plea Bargaining." In P. Nardulli, ed., *The Study of Criminal Courts*. Cambridge, Mass.: Ballinger, 1979.

J. Keeney and B. Walsh, "The American Bar Association's Grand Jury Principles: A Critique from a Federal Criminal Justice Perspective," *Idaho Law Review*, vol. 14 (1978).

M. Lehtinen and G. Smith, "The Relative Effectiveness of Public Defenders and Private Attorneys: A Comparison." *Legal Aid Briefcase*, vol. 34 (1974).

M. Lemanick, "In the Showdown at Rocky Flats, Rockwell and Uncle Sam Face the Grand Jury That Won't Go Away." *Time*, January 25, 1993.

D. Lynch, "The Improprieties of Plea Agreements." *Law and Social Inquiry*, vol. 19 (1994).

L. Mather, "Some Determinants of Case Disposition: Decision Making by the Public Defenders in Los Angeles," *Law and Society Review*, vol. 81 (1996).

D. Newman, "Pleading Guilty for Considerations: A Study of Bargain Justice," *Journal of Criminal Law, Criminology, and Police Science*, vol. 46 (1956).

"Plea Offer Not Binding When It's Withdrawn." *The New York Times*, June 12, 1984, p. 12.

J. Rivers, "When Men Hunt Man: The Rights and Duties of the Bounty Hunter in the American Criminal Justice System," *Houston Law Review*, vol. 33 (1966), pp. 731–793.

J. Striden, "Plea Bargaining in the Shadow of the Guidelines," *California Law Review*, vol. 8 (1993).

"Technicality May Free Three," (Orlando) *Sun-Sentinel*, February 28, 1992.

"Technologic: Video Was a Hit with Cops," *Law Enforcement News*, vol. 15, no. 301 (1989).

F. Ungeheuer, "Let's Make a Deal: For a Guilty Plea and $650 Million, Drexel Hopes to Get a Clean Slate," *Time*, January 8, 1989, pp. 84–87.

P. Wald, "Right to Bail Revisited: A Decade of Promise without Fulfillment." In S. S. Nagel, ed., *The Rights of the Accused*. Beverly Hills, Calif.: Sage, 1972.

J. Wheatley, "Plea Bargaining—A Case for Its Continuance," *Massachusetts Law Quarterly*, vol. 59 (1974).

Government Publications

H. Sturz, *National Conference of Bail and Criminal Justice*. Washington, D.C.: U.S. Government Printing Office, 1965.

Task Force Report: The Courts. Washington, D.C.: U.S. Government Printing Office, 1967.

United States Attorney's Manual, 1985, Sec. 9–11.

U.S. Department of Justice, *The Prevalence of Guilty Pleas*. Washington, D.C.: Bureau of Justice Statistics, 1984.

U.S. Department of Justice, *Principles of Federal Prosecution*. Washington, D.C.: U.S. Government Printing Office, 1980.

Federal Rules of Criminal Procedure, 5, 1(a), 6(d)(2), 6(e)(5).

Hearings on Preventive Detention Before the Subcommittee on Constitutional Rights of the Senate Committee on the Judiciary, 91st Cong., 2d Sess. (1970) (statement of Senator Sam Ervin).

National Advisory Commission on Criminal Justice Standards and Goals, *Courts*. Washington, D.C.: U.S. Government Printing Office, 1973.

National District Attorneys Association, *National Prosecution Standards*. Chicago: National District Attorneys Association, 1977.

National Institute of Justice, *Predictions of Dangerousness in the Criminal Law*, March 1987.

STATUTE

18 U.S.C. 360

CASES

Barber v. Arkansas, 429 F.2d 20 (8th Cir. 1970)
Barefoot v. Estelle, 463 U.S. 880 (1983)
Blair v. United States, 250 U.S. 273 (1919)
Costello v. United States, 350 U.S. 359, 397 (1956)
Curry v. Illinois, 406 U.S. 682 (1972)
Dunaway v. New York, 442 U.S. 200 (1979)
Hamilton v. Alabama, 368 U.S. 52 (1961)
Hurtado v. California, 110 U.S. 516 (1884)
Miranda v. Arizona, 384 U.S. 436 (1966)
United States v. Mundujano, 425 U.S. 564 (1974)
United States v. Procter and Gamble Co., 356 U.S. 677 (1958)
United States v. Thompson, 251 U.S. 407 (1920)
Warden v. Hayden, 387 U.S. 436 (1967)

ENDNOTES

1. D. A. Henry, "Pretrial Services: Today and Yesterday," *Federal Probation* (June 1991), p. 4.
2. P. Kunsa and Andobe, "The Relationship of Pretrial Custody to the Outcome of the Trial," *Criminology Law Quarterly*, vol. 17 (1975), pp. 391–400.
3. *Gerstein v. Pugh*, 420 U.S. 103 (1975).
4. *Riverside County v. McLaughlin*, 500 U.S. 44 (1991).
5. *Stack v. Boyle*, 342 U.S. 1 (1951).
6. M. Toborg, *Pretrial Release: A National Evaluation of Practices and Outcomes*. Washington, D.C.: National Institute of Justice, 1982.
7. K. Segebarth, *Pretrial Services and Practices in the 1990s*. Washington, D.C.: Pretrial Resource Center, 1991, p. 3.
8. Ibid.
9. Bureau of Justice Assistance, *Pretrial Service Programs*. Washington, D.C.: U.S. Government Printing Office, 1990, p. 3.
10. Toborg, op. cit.
11. Hall, op. cit., pp. 32–33.
12. E. Johnson, *Crime, Corrections and Society*. Homewood, Ill.: Dorsey Press, 1964.
13. W. Burger, "Address at the American Bar Association Annual Conference," *The New York Times*, August 11, 1970, p. 1.
14. J. Murphy, *Arrest by Police Computer*. Lexington, Mass.: Lexington Books, 1975, p. 40.
15. W. H. Thomas, *Bail Reform in America*. Berkeley: University of California Press, 1976.
16. Murphy, op. cit.
17. Ibid.
18. F. Devine, *Commercial Bail Bonding: A Comparison of Common Law Alternatives*. New York: Praeger, 1991.
19. *Murphy v. Hunt*, 455 U.S. 478 (1982).
20. *United States v. Salerno*, 479 U.S. 1026 (1987).
21. *United States v. Montalvo-Murillo*, 495 U.S. 711 (1990).
22. S. Kennedy and K. Carlson, "The Denial of Bail: Pretrial Miscarriage," *Criminal Justice Research Bulletin*, vol. 3, no. 6 (1987).
23. T. Scott, "Pretrial Detention under the Bail Reform Act of 1984," *American Criminal Law Review*, vol. 21 (1989), p. 19.
24. D. Neubauer, *American Courts in the Criminal Justice System*, 3rd ed. Pacific Grove, Calif.: Brooks-Cole, 1988, p. 399.
25. *Coleman v. Alabama*, 399 U.S. 1 (1970).
26. *Ohio v. Roberts*, 448 U.S. 56 (1980).
27. H. A. Bloch and G. Geis, *Man, Crime, and Society*. New York: Random House, 1962, p. 481.
28. *Butterworth v. Smith*, 494 U.S. 624 (1990).
29. *United States v. Calandra*, 414 U.S. 338 (1974).
30. *United States v. Estepa*, 471 F.2d 1132 (2d Cir. 1972).
31. *United States v. Williams*, 504 U.S. 36 (1992).
32. Federal Rules of Criminal Procedure, 7(a).
33. *Gerstein v. Pugh*, op. cit.
34. *Williams v. Florida*, 399 U.S. 220 (1977).
35. *Kirby v. Illinois*, 406 U.S. 682 (1972).
36. *United States v. Wade*, 388 U.S. 218 (1967).
37. Ibid.
38. *Kirby v. Illinois*, op. cit.
39. *Moore v. Illinois*, 434 U.S. 220 (1977).
40. *Kirby v. Illinois*, op. cit.
41. *Blue v. Alaska*, 558 P.2d 636 (Alaska 1977).
42. *Gilbert v. California*, 388 U.S. 267 (1967).
43. *Stobalt v. Denno*, 388 U.S. 293 (1967).
44. *Manson v. Brathwaite*, 432 U.S. 98 (1977).
45. *Brady v. Maryland*, 373 U.S. 83 (1963).
46. Federal Rules of Criminal Procedure, 16(b)(1)(a)–(c)
47. *Jackson v. Indiana*, 406 U.S. 715 (1972).
48. *Mapp v. Ohio*, 367 U.S. 643 (1961).
49. *Jackson v. Denno*, 378 U.S. 368 (1964).
50. *Lego v. Twomey*, 404 U.S. 477 (1972).
51. *La Vallee v. Delle Rose*, 410 U.S. 690 (1973).
52. *Simmons v. United States*, 390 U.S. 377 (1968).
53. *Lego v. Twomey*, op. cit.
54. *Santobello v. New York*, 404 U.S. 257 (1971).
55. D. Smith, "The Plea Bargaining Controversy," *Journal of Criminal Law and Criminology*, vol. 77 (1986), pp. 949–967.
56. Ibid.
57. A. Alschuler, "Prosecution's Role in Plea Bargaining," *University of Chicago Law Review*, vol. 36 (1968), pp. 50–112.
58. Bureau of Justice Statistics Special Report, *The Prevalence of Guilty Pleas*, December 1984.
59. *McCarthy v. United States*, 394 U.S. 459 (1969).
60. *Henderson v. Morgan*, 426 U.S. 637 (1976).
61. Federal Rules of Criminal Procedure, 11(c)(1).
62. *North Carolina v. Alfred*, 400 U.S. 25 (1970).
63. *Ricketts v. Adamson*, 483 U.S. 1 (1987).
64. National Victims Constitutional Amendment Network News page at http://www.NVCAN.org/news.htm. Accessed April 25, 2003.
65. G. Fletcher, *With Justice for Some—Victims' Rights in Criminal Trials*. New York: Addison-Wesley, 1995.
66. L. Mather, *Plea Bargaining or Trial?* Lexington, Mass. Lexington Books, 1979.
67. W. McDonald, *Plea Bargaining: Critical Issues and Common Practices*. Washington, D.C.: U.S. Government Printing Office, 1985).
68. *Tollett v. Henderson*, 411 U.S. 258 (1973).
69. *Lefkowitz v. Newsome*, 420 U.S. 283 (1975).
70. *Blackledge v. Perry*, 417 U.S. 21 (1974).

9 THE CRIMINAL TRIAL

Chapter Outline

- **The Question of Guilt Disposed of by the Criminal Trial**
- **The Philosophical Foundations of the Criminal Trial**
  - The Defendant Is Presumed Innocent
  - The State Has the Burden of Proof
  - The State Must Prove the Defendant Guilty beyond a Reasonable Doubt
- **The Criminal Trial's First Step—Impaneling a Fair and Impartial Jury**
  - The Press in the Courtroom
  - The Problem of Pretrial Publicity
  - The Social and Political Baggage Juries Bring to Trial
  - The Jury Selection Process
- **The Rules of Evidence**
  - Requirements for Admissible Evidence—It Must Be Relevant, Material, and Competent
  - Testimonial Evidence
  - Real Evidence
  - Opinion Evidence Offered by an Expert Witness
  - A Limitation—Evidence of Privileged or Confidential Communications
  - Another Limitation—Hearsay Evidence
  - Some Exceptions to the Hearsay Rule
- **The Procedural Order of a Criminal Trial**
- **Opening Statements**
- **Presentation of the State's Evidence**
- **Presentation of the Defense's Case**
- **The Affirmative Defenses**
  - The Defense of Infancy
  - The Insanity Defense
  - Self-Defense
  - The Defense of Ignorance or Mistake of Fact
  - The Defense of Protection of Property
  - The Defense of the Use of Force to Effect an Arrest
  - The Battered-Spouse Defense
- **Rebuttal and Surrebuttal**
- **Closing Arguments**
- **The Trial Judge's Charge to the Jury**
- **The Jury's Deliberations**
- **The Jury's Verdict**
  - A Hung Jury
  - Polling the Jury
  - Jury Nullification
  - Postverdict Motions
- **Summary**

Key TERMS

adversary proceeding, p. 357
challenge for cause, p. 364
circumstantial evidence, p. 366
direct evidence, p. 366
factual guilt, p. 358
hearsay, p. 371
jury consultants, p. 366
legal guilt, p. 358

M'Naghten test of insanity, p. 378
peremptory challenge, p. 364
preponderance of evidence, p. 359
real evidence, p. 366
reasonable doubt, p. 359
testimonial evidence, p. 366
venire, p. 363
voir dire, p. 363

Courtesy of Getty Images, Inc.-Stone Allstock.

The **adversary proceeding** is the heart of a criminal trial. This is a formal process conducted in an orderly and specific fashion according to the rules of criminal evidence, the Constitution, and the criminal law. In the adversary process, both the prosecution and the defense follow specific requirements in order to argue the merits of their cases in the most favorable light and in the most persuasive manner before the jury (see Figure 9.1). While it cannot be denied that drama is inherent in adversarial proceedings, the jury trial has proven—over centuries of evolution to its present form—to be a reliable means of uncovering the truth. It accomplishes this by following a formal set of rules for presenting evidence, rules that seek to deny advantage to either the prosecution or the defense. Much of what laypeople might regard as a fussy preoccupation with procedural details or interpretations of legal precedent is, in fact, the expression of a painstaking effort to eliminate bias.

Smith and Pollack seriously question the generality and validity of the public image of the courtroom as a place where "truth is discovered through . . . trial by combat between two equally armed lawyer-gladiators, with the struggle presided over by the judge (as repository of the wisdom of the community)."[1] Despite criticism, however, the adversary model of courtroom procedure is one of the most cherished legacies of English common law and a symbol of the freedoms guaranteed to American citizens under the U.S. Constitution.

FIGURE 9.1

The cross-examination of a witness after she has previously testified to direct questions is at the core of the adversarial system, by which the advocate's examinations afford a better probability of rendering the truth than does any other court tribunal in the world.

Courtesy of John Neubauer/PhotoEdit.

WEB

For more information on famous legal cases, **visit our Web site, www.prenhall.com/territo.**

WEB

For more information on significant features of the criminal trial, **visit our Web site, www.prenhall.com/territo.**

CTQ

Should prosecutors have more or less control over the life, liberty, and property of defendants than they presently have, which is more than any other public officer?

WEB

For more information on the operating procedures and personnel of criminal courts, **visit the link to the Thirteenth Judicial Circuit serving Hillsborough County, Florida, on our Web site, www.prenhall.com/territo.**

CTQ

If a defendant waives his or her right to a jury trial, what type of trial takes place?

WEB

For more information on the only trial ever conducted on the assassination of President John F. Kennedy, **visit our Web site, www.prenhall.com/territo.**

The criminal trial has been referred to as the "balance wheel of the entire process,"[2]; referring to the adversary nature of American criminal jurisprudence, the jury trial has been called a "sublimated brawl."[3]

THE QUESTION OF GUILT DISPOSED OF BY THE CRIMINAL TRIAL

The criminal trial serves several formal purposes. It is a symbol of justice. If all goes as it should, a criminal trial shows that crime does not convict the innocent but rather punishes the guilty. In the criminal trial the innocent person receives vindication, and the criminal justice system effectively distributes justice. Unpopular trial outcomes can teach the opposite. The trial then becomes a negative symbol, proving that the wicked prevail; crime pays; and power, privilege, and clever lawyers can determine who gets convicted and who goes free. Such unfavorable lessons lead to contempt for criminal justice institutions and processes. For good or ill, the trial teaches a public, visible, and potent lesson about the integrity, fairness, and effectiveness of the criminal justice process.

Criminal trials are elaborate fact-finding proceedings. According to strict rules, they ferret out the facts that prove legal guilt. **Legal guilt** means the government has proven the defendant's guilt and criminal responsibility beyond a reasonable doubt throughout the course of a constitutionally fair trial that resulted in a jury verdict of guilty. **Factual guilt** is when a jury believes beyond a reasonable doubt that the evidence gathered by police from their investigations, as well as other evidence admitted at trial, has revealed that the defendant did commit the facts of the crime; but due to the lack of an analysis of the surrounding circumstances of the crime that might excuse or justify the act, proof of factual guilt alone can never guarantee criminal responsibility and thus a legally guilty verdict. Criminal trials ensure that the fact-finding processes are fair and conducted according to due process of law. Rules governing changes of venue, jury selection, obtaining and presenting evidence, speedy trial, and proof beyond a reasonable doubt attempt to ensure accurate fact-finding regarding legal guilt.

THE PHILOSOPHICAL FOUNDATIONS OF THE CRIMINAL TRIAL

Of all the steps of the criminal process, the trial attracts the most public attention. Every year books, movies, and television dramas use courtroom encounters as a method of entertainment. Trials of well-known people receive extensive national press coverage. Some of these—the William Kennedy Smith and O.J. Simpson trials come quickly to mind—become the center of a ritual drama of good and evil. Even local murder trials are the subject of many newspaper stories and the topic of local conversation.

This public interest is partially a reflection of the key role the trial plays in American criminal law. Almost half of the Bill of Rights guarantees deal with criminal procedure, specifically referring to the trial stage. To Anglo-American criminal jurists, the trial serves as the ultimate forum for vindication of the innocence of the accused.

This public interest combined with the centrality of the trial to American law would seemingly make the trial the prime ingredient in the criminal courts. Yet roughly 90 percent of all felony cases (and a much higher percentage of misdemeanor offenses) are disposed of by a guilty plea. Thus in a very fundamental sense, a trial represents a deviant case. But at the same time, few cases that are disposed of at trial have a major impact on the operations of the whole criminal justice system. Trials are the balance wheel of the process. Although the criminal trial is supported by a great number of philosophical propositions that give the trial the high status it enjoys, three major philosophical foundations seem to be the most significant: (1) the defendant is presumed innocent, (2) the state has the burden of proof, and (3) the state must prove the guilt of the defendant beyond a reasonable doubt.

The Defendant Is Presumed Innocent

In the U.S. criminal justice system, the defendant is presumed innocent. The presumption of innocence is an important principle. It means that the prosecution has the responsibility of proving every element of the crime(s) required for conviction and that the defendant does not have to prove innocence. The defendant can do nothing and still be acquitted if the government does not prove its case. Despite the importance of the presumption, former Attorney General Edwin Meese said, "If a person is innocent of a crime, then he is not a suspect." To that statement, Lawrence Tribe, a noted Harvard law professor and scholar of constitutional law, replied, "Mere accusation does not transform one into a criminal. Civilized society could not long survive if Mr. Meese's views became prevalent."[4]

The presumption of innocence is essential in ensuring a fair trial to those who are going to trial for alleged criminal offenses. (Even then, innocent people are sometimes convicted.) Most judges instruct the jury on this presumption, although the U.S. Supreme Court has held that it is not constitutionally required that an instruction on the presumption of innocence be given. But, according to the Court, one of the determinations made on appeal is whether the defendant had a fair trial without an instruction on the presumption. If not, the case will be reversed for failure to give instruction.[5]

The State Has the Burden of Proof

All prosecutorial evidence in a criminal trial must present a standard of proof that is higher than in any other trial in the American system of justice. As stated before, the standard of proof is "guilt beyond a reasonable doubt." No defendant may be convicted in this country during the adjudicatory stage of the criminal process without the prosecution meeting this burden of proof. The **reasonable doubt** standard of proof is the fundamental legal principle of the American criminal justice system. It is viewed as the essential instrument for lessening the risk of conviction based on factual errors. The U.S. Supreme Court has announced in many decisions that it is better to release a hundred guilty people than to convict someone who is innocent.

Civil law, on the other hand, has a standard of proof called the **preponderance of evidence.** This is a much lower standard than "beyond a reasonable doubt." The level of certainty derived by a jury from the weight of the evidence presented to them at trial, to meet the "preponderance of evidence" standard must be slightly greater (50.001%) than the weight of the evidence presented by the other side. This is the burden of proof in civil trials, in pretrial motions, in suppression hearings, and in other instances during criminal trials. However, in a criminal trial under the "beyond a reasonable doubt" standard, if the prosecution only produces more-compelling evidence than the defense, then the jury must find the defendant not guilty.

The State Must Prove the Defendant Guilty beyond a Reasonable Doubt

The formal purpose of this highly popularized sparring is to determine whether the defendant has been proven guilty of the crime charged according to a long-entrenched standard of proof beyond a reasonable doubt. In criminal cases, prosecutors must prove their case to the degree that it is completely consistent with the guilt of the defendant and inconsistent with any other plausible conclusion. All evidence the state presents serves

---

WEB

For more information on the O. J. Simpson trial and to view some of the evidence, **visit our Web site, www.prenhall.com/territo**.

CTQ

Does the jury trial live up to its exalted reputation of maintaining the defendant's presumption of innocence?

WEB

For more information on the American Civil Liberties Union and the constitutional questions they raise, **visit our Web site, www.prenhall.com/territo**.

CTQ

Why is there a higher standard of proof in a criminal trial than for a civil trial?

CTQ

"The burden of proof in a criminal trial to show that the defendant is guilty beyond a reasonable doubt by the government is at the heart of the adversarial system of criminal justice." Explain the meaning of this statement.

that purpose, or at least formally is supposed to serve it. The state must find, arrange, present, and support the case against defendants. The defense has no obligation to aid the state in its case. Defendants, in other words, do not need to prove their innocence. They are, to use the well-worn phrase, "innocent until proven guilty." Therefore, the defense's role in criminal trials is essentially reactive: to cast doubt on the prosecution's case, not to create a case on its own.[6]

According to the Supreme Court, the Constitution requires the "reasonable doubt" standard. The standard's role in the American scheme of criminal procedure is vital, because it reduces the risk of mistakenly convicting innocent people.[7] The Court decided that criminal defendants have at risk such vital interests—loss of property, liberty, and sometimes life, as well as the stigma attached to conviction—that reasonable doubt about guilt should prevent such consequences from befalling a citizen of a free society. Placing a heavy burden on the prosecution, it is believed, reduces the margin of error in criminal convictions. The "reasonable doubt" standard also commands the respect and confidence of the community in applications of the criminal law. A lesser standard of proof reduces the law's moral force and leaves citizens uncertain about the capacity of courts to condemn guilty defendants and vindicate innocent people.[8]

In trying to help jurors come to a decision, courts have struggled to define proof beyond a reasonable doubt. Here are some common definitions various courts have offered: A certainty of about 9.0 on a scale of 10 is a reasonable doubt that would cause prudent people to hesitate before acting in a matter of importance to themselves; a doubt based on reason and common sense; not frivolous or fanciful doubt; substantial doubt; and finally, persuasion to a moral certainty. Certainly, judging from the lack of precision among these standards, it becomes clear that the legal term *beyond a reasonable doubt* is more a metaphor than an easily defined concept.

THE CRIMINAL TRIAL'S FIRST STEP—IMPANELING A FAIR AND IMPARTIAL JURY

The right to a fair and impartial jury is required by the concept of due process and the Sixth Amendment. This right operates to ensure that a defendant is tried only by an impartial jury. Under the U.S. Constitution, a defendant has a right to a jury or trier of fact that is free from unfair influences. Throughout the years, the Supreme Court has determined that unfair prejudices can arise in several ways. For example, in the case of *Estelle v. Williams*,[9] the Court determined that the defendant was unfairly prejudiced since he was tried while wearing prison clothing. The Court went on to say that if the defendant makes a timely objection to standing trial in prison clothing, it is unconstitutional for the state to compel him to do so.[10] Another example came in 1965, when the Court proclaimed that the defendant's due process rights were violated when the prosecution's witnesses had a constant and intimate association with the jurors. In this case, two sheriffs, who were also prosecution witnesses, were simultaneously running errands for the jury.[11]

Due process is also violated when the criminal trial is conducted in a manner that interferes with the jury's ability to give the evidence reasonable consideration. This happened in a case where local media were televising and broadcasting parts of a trial in a manner that might influence the jury apart from the existing notoriety of the trial.[12] However, the state may constitutionally permit the televising of a criminal proceeding over the defendant's objections as long as the televising does not prejudice the jury.[13]

The Press in the Courtroom

Often overlooked, because they do not have an official role in courtroom proceedings, are spectators and the press. At any given trial, both spectators and media representatives may be present in large numbers. Spectators include members of the families of both victim and defendant, friends of both sides, and curious onlookers—some of whom are avocational court watchers.

Newswriters, TV reporters, and other members of the press are apt to be present at "spectacular" trials (those involving some especially gruesome aspect or famous personality) and at those in which there is a great deal of community interest. The right of

WEB

For more information on the jury selection process, **visit our Web site, www.prenhall.com/territo**.

reporters and spectators to be present at a criminal trial is supported by the Sixth Amendment's insistence upon a public trial.

Press reports at all stages of a criminal investigation and trial often create problems for the justice system. Significant pretrial publicity about a case may make it difficult to find jurors who have not already formed an opinion as to the guilt or innocence of the defendant. News reports from the courtroom may influence or confuse nonsequestered jurors (the jurors who are allowed to go home after their day in court) who hear them, especially when they contain information brought to the bench, but not heard by the jury.

In 1976, the U.S. Supreme Court ruled that trial court judges could not legitimately issue gag orders, preventing the pretrial publication of information about a criminal case,[14] as long as the defendant's right to a fair trial and an impartial jury could be ensured by traditional means. These means include (1) a change of venue, whereby the trial is moved to another jurisdiction less likely to have been exposed to the publicity; (2) trial postponement, which would allow for memories to fade and emotions to cool; and (3) jury selection and screening to eliminate biased people from the jury pool. In 1986 the Court extended press access to preliminary hearings, which, it said, are "sufficiently like a trial to require public access."[15] In 1993, the Court effectively applied that requirement to all territories under U.S. control.[16]

Today, members of the press as well as video, television, and still cameras are allowed into most state courtrooms. Thirty-three states allow cameras in most trials, while fifteen states substantially restrict the use of cameras.[17] Two states (Mississippi and South Dakota) and the District of Columbia completely prohibit cameras at trial and appellate hearings.[18]

The U.S Supreme Court has been far less favorably disposed to television coverage than have most courts. In 1981, a Florida defendant appealed his burglary conviction to the Supreme Court, arguing that the presence of television cameras at his trial had turned the court into a circus for attorneys and made the proceedings more a sideshow than a trial. The Supreme Court, recognizing that television cameras have a distracting effect upon many people, agreed. In the words of the court, "Trial courts must be especially vigilant to guard against any impairment of the defendant's right to a verdict based solely upon the evidence and the relevant law."[19]

The Judicial Conference of the United States, the primary policymaking arm of the federal courts, seems to agree with the justices. A three-year pilot project that allowed television cameras into six U.S. District Courts and two appeals courts on an experimental basis closed on December 31, 1994, when the conference voted to end the project. The conference terminated the experiment, ruling that neither still nor video cameras would be allowed into federal courtrooms in the future. Conference members expressed concerns that cameras were a distracting influence and were having a "negative impact on jurors and witnesses"[20] by exposing them to possible harm by revealing their identities. Hence, under current policy, television and radio coverage of federal criminal and civil proceedings at both the trial and appellate level is effectively banned. Changes, however, may soon be in the works.

The Problem of Pretrial Publicity

Another way to deny a defendant his or her right to a fair and impartial jury is the existence of pretrial publicity that is so pervasive that it would require the trial to change cities (venue) in order for the defendant to obtain a fair trial or retrial. This violation is always present if a trial is held before a jury that was familiar with the material facts of the case and that had formed an opinion as to the defendant's guilt before the trial.[21] However, due process is satisfied, according to the Supreme Court, if the judge asks all those sitting to be selected as jurors, whether they were exposed to pretrial publicity, and if so, whether it would affect their impartiality and ability to hear the case with an open mind. The Supreme Court went on to say that the judge does not have to ask about the specific source or context of the pretrial information.[22] Earlier, the Court had stated that a new trial is required if the defendant was denied a change of venue and then was tried before a jury drawn from people who had seen an interview in which the defendant confessed.[23]

Finally, a defendant is entitled to an unbiased jury. This means that he or she is entitled to a jury derived from a fair cross-section of the community. Clearly, a defendant's

WEB

For more information on cameras in the courtroom, **visit our Web site,** www.prenhall.com/territo.

CTQ

The Sixth Amendment guarantees a jury drawn from a cross-section of the defendant's geographical area; yet, recent studies have shown that juries come from the low end of the social, economic, and intellectual spectrum of society. Does this satisfy the right to a fair and impartial jury of one's peers?

CTQ

What are the pros and cons of the jury trial versus a bench trial?

CTQ

Describe the necessary conditions for a defendant to receive a fair and impartial trial by jury in the age of technology.

right to a trial by jury includes, as stated previously, the right to a fair and impartial jury. Often, in sensational cases, "fair" and "impartial" become problematic terms because of the community's exposure to pretrial publicity. For this reason, the best jurors are ones who have no knowledge of the case or preconceived notions about the defendant or the witnesses that will be called. Yet massive pretrial publicity exposes potential jurors to all of these possibilities, making finding a fair and impartial jury an almost impossible task. During the 1990s, the problem of pretrial publicity was evident in the search for unbiased juries for the trials of William Kennedy Smith, O. J. Simpson, and Timothy McVeigh.[24] Even more problematic today is the challenge of finding a jury that will base its verdict on the facts, rather than on how it feels the public will react to the verdict.

The Social and Political Baggage Juries Bring to Trial

The law and constitutional framework of the jury do not explain how the jury actually operates. The nineteenth-century French commentator on American government Alexis de Tocqueville wrote that "the jury is, above all, a political institution, and it must be regarded in this light in order to be understood."[25] De Tocqueville's observation is no less true today than it was more than 150 years ago. Jurors try hard to make their decisions based entirely on the facts and their rational assessment of them. In clear-cut cases where the evidence and arguments of lawyers lead only to one result—either guilty or not guilty—this is probably what they do. But in cases that can go either way, extralegal influences enter the jury room and impinge on jurors' deliberations and decisions.[26]

Research has shown that jurors try hard to get at the truth. Their reliance on extralegal considerations is subconscious. Jurors operate according to a liberation hypothesis, say Harry Kalven and Hans Zeisel in their classic study of the jury. According to Kalven and Zeisel, determining the truth and making value judgments are intertwined.[27] In close cases, the jurors' value judgments unconsciously affect their finding of the facts. In all cases, but particularly in close cases, the facts are ambiguous, thus open to a number of interpretations. The trial process heightens the possibility of reading the facts in at least two starkly contrasting ways. The prosecution argues strongly for that which supports conviction; defense counsel argues equally strongly for that which supports acquittal. The ambiguities in the evidence, the adversary process, and the closeness of the case "liberate" jurors to decide cases according to their own values. They resolve doubts in favor of their sentiments.[28]

Furthermore, personal prejudice may determine the sentiments of jurors. But most frequently their sentiments reflect the values of their communities, which they represent in the jury room. These values range across a broad spectrum:

- Conservative and liberal views concerning the crime problem and the value of punishment
- Values and positions regarding gender, race, and ethnicity
- Conflicts in moral standards
- Beliefs about law and social problems such as self-defense, euthanasia, police power, drug use, the homeless, and the environment

For these reasons, a truly impartial jury can never be an absolute reality in American courtrooms.

The Jury Selection Process

The first step in initiating a litigated criminal trial is for the prosecution and defense to select a jury. Several issues are presented during this process. The first issue is whether the defendant has a right to be tried by jury. The second issue is the efficacy of the selection of the jury and the questioning of the jury by the lawyers. In a litigated criminal trial, a significant trial strategy used by both the prosecution and the defense is the various manners by which they interact with potential juror members

---

CTQ
In what ways may negative pretrial publicity damage the objective outcome of a criminal trial?

CTQ
What do you think is the greatest concern for jury selection when the objective is to impound a fair and impartial jury so that the defendant will have the best opportunity to receive a just verdict?

CTQ
Given the roles of the defense counsel and the prosecution, is the deliberate seeking of biased jurors either legal or ethical?

FIGURE 9.2

Jury Size for Felony and Misdemeanor Trials

Source: U.S. Department of Justice, Bureau of Justice Statistics, *Report to the Nation on Crime and Justice,* 2nd ed. Washington, D.C.: U.S. Government Printing Office.

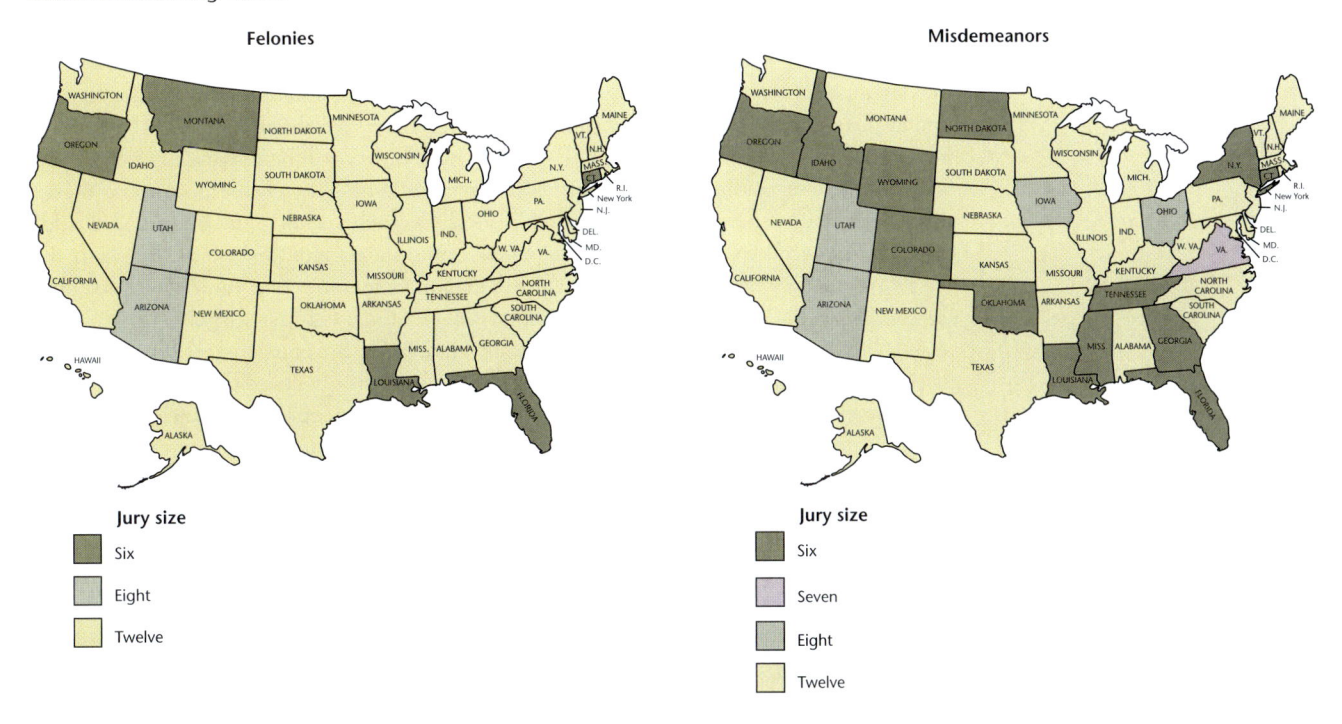

Felonies

Jury size
- Six
- Eight
- Twelve

Misdemeanors

Jury size
- Six
- Seven
- Eight
- Twelve

in order to select a final jury for the case. Issues that arise in the selection of the jury include the following:

1. How many jurors can constitutionally sit on a case?
2. Can a jury be selected by scientific means?
3. Can certain jury members be excluded due to race or any other minority status?

Eligible voters, taxpayers, or vehicle registration rolls comprise the list from which a group of potential jurors, called the jury panel or **venire,** is selected. Ideally, the venire (sometimes called the *array*) should represent a cross-section of the community. The mandated size of the jury varies from state to state, as shown in Figure 9.2, although all states require twelve-member juries in capital cases and six states permit juries of fewer than twelve in felony cases. For the venire to be constitutional, the original selection must both be randomly and scientifically made from an up-to-date list of all adult citizens. Such a group must meet the qualifications for jury duty as set by statute in the jurisdiction of the court. (In federal cases, the members of the jury are drawn from the entire jurisdiction of the district court trying the case).

The members of the venire are sometimes questioned in open court to determine their general qualifications for jury duty. The names of the prospective jurors are randomly selected from the members of the venire who remain after exemption questioning. A fairly common procedure is to write the names on slips of paper and place the slips into a revolving drum; the court clerk then draws names out one by one. As a juror's name is read, he or she takes a place in the jury box and is questioned by both the defense counsel and the prosecutor in the so-called voir dire. The **voir dire** (usually translated as "to speak the truth") is a predictable question-and-answer session among prospective members of the jury, the prosecutor, the defense counsel, and the trial judge, in order to determine whether each juror is suitable to sit and to judge the case without bias or prejudice. The potential jurors also receive written questions about their knowledge of the case and whether that knowledge might affect their ability to hear the evidence impartially (see Figure 9.3). They also are asked about their acquaintance with the participants in the trial (the defendant, judge, attorneys, and witnesses) as a possible source of bias in their judgment of the evidence, and they are asked whether they have already formed an opinion of the facts or issues involved in the case.

If the jurors answer any of these questions in a manner that demonstrates that they cannot sit as an unbiased juror, they may be **challenged for cause** by the prosecution, the defense lawyer, or the trial judge. These challenges, unlimited in number, are for particular jurors who have given information to the court saying that they cannot be fair and impartial triers of fact in this particular case. These jurors will be dismissed by the judge from the case immediately. Prospective jurors may be questioned on almost any matter that bears on that person's ability or willingness to reach an impartial decision. In addition, the judge may exercise an option to examine the potential jurors. (Note that dismissal from a jury panel in one case does not exclude a member of a venire from selection for service on another trial jury during the respective term of jury duty.)

> **CTQ**
> Explain the jury selection process. Is the process fundamentally fair? Is it really "jury selection" or "jury nonselection"? Why?

After both sides have made all of their challenges for cause, each side is then allowed a specified number of **peremptory challenges**—requests to the court to exclude a prospective juror without reason. For example, the prosecutor may decide that he or she does not want a woman under age 45 or a man over age 50 on the jury; the defense attorney may feel uneasy about a potential juror on the basis of his or her facial expression, clothing, or demeanor. These reasons, whatever they are, do not have to be justified—or even stated—to the court.

Most criminal lawyers generally have a "feel" for what makes a good juror for the defense or the prosecution. This intuition is normally based on what is believed to be the conservative or liberal leanings of the prospective juror, the juror's capacity for fairness, or the juror's possible bias in favor of whichever side the criminal lawyer happens to be on.

> **CTQ**
> Describe how the voir dire process is different between challenges for cause and peremptory challenges.

A due process remedy exists in all instances where an impartial and fair jury cannot be successfully chosen from the venire; this remedy, the change-of-venue motion, requests that the case be moved to a different location where an impartial jury can be selected. Either the prosecution, the defense, or the judge may request a change of venue. The validity of this motion is ultimately up to the wide discretion of the trial judge. However, only in rare instances will his or her decision not to change venue be overturned by the appellate court.

The voir dire can be crucially important to the strategy of both the criminal defense lawyer and the prosecutor during a criminal proceeding. Lawyers also take this opportunity to present disguised arguments supporting their cases before the jury. Furthermore, voir dire also facilitates a bond between the lawyer and the potential jurors. One defense counsel summed up the significance of voir dire as follows:

> There is much more to a voir dire than the simple process of questioning and selecting jurors. In addition to the gamesplay and the psychology, a voir dire is an opportunity for the attorneys to educate the jury about theories of their case. It is also an opportunity to plant the seeds of doubt that they hope will produce a favorable verdict. It is a chance to predispose jurors to be receptive to the attorney's case.[29]

The voir dire examination of potential jurors continues until the required number of jurors has been selected. The trial jury is selected from the jury panel (the specific number of jurors varies from state to state, but normally a jury has twelve members—see Chapter 3 for more information). One or two *alternate jurors* are also chosen; they sit through the entire trial and are available to replace a regular jury member should he or she be forced to withdraw due to illness or disqualification. Alternate jurors do not, however, participate in the deliberations of the jury unless one of the original jurors is unable to continue in the proceedings. After the jurors have been selected, the whole panel is then sworn in. Shortly thereafter, or at the beginning of their deliberations, one of the members is chosen as foreperson.

FIGURE 9.3

Typical Jury Questionnaire

PANEL: JUROR NUMBER

To facilitate the jury selection process, the court requires that you provide the information requested below under penalty of perjury. The completed questionnaire will be a public record and open to public inspection. If you feel that any question requires an answer which is too sensitive (personal or private) to be included in a public record, you have the right to request a private hearing rather than filling out the answer in writing. If you prefer to have a private hearing for a sensitive question, write "P" (for "private") in the spaced provided for the answer.

QUALIFICATIONS

I am able to read and understand English.	Yes	No
I am now serving as a grand juror in a court in this state.	Yes	No
I am a citizen of the United States.	Yes	No
I am under a court appointed conservatorship.	Yes	No
I am eighteen years of age or older.	Yes	No
I am a law enforcement officer.	Yes	No
I am a resident of Hillsborough County.	Yes	No
I have been convicted of a felony.	Yes	No

If so, answer yes unless you have received a full pardon.

1. Marital Status: Married   Single   Divorced   Widowed

2. Education: Completed Degrees: _____ Highest grade level: _____

3. Occupation: _____ Previous Occupation: _____

4. Information regarding spouse or other adults with whom you reside:
   Occupation: _____ Previous Occupation: _____
   Employer: _____ Previous Employer: _____

5. Information about your children or stepchildren:
   [ ] I have no children or stepchildren

AGE	SEX	OCCUPATION	AGE	SEX	OCCUPATION
___	___	_____	___	___	_____
___	___	_____	___	___	_____
___	___	_____	___	___	_____

6. Military Service: Branch _____
   Highest Rank _____
   Specialty _____
   Did you have any involvement with the military criminal justice system?
   If yes, explain.

7. Prior jury service: (For each case, without disclosing the results, indicate yes or no, did the case end in a verdict?)

YEAR	TYPE OF CASE	YES/NO	YEAR	TYPE OF CASE	YES/NO
___	_____	___	___	_____	___
___	_____	___	___	_____	___

8. In what area of Hillsborough County do you live (neighborhood)?

9. Have you, a close friend or relative ever been employed by a law enforcement agency (federal, state, or local)? If yes, what agency?

10. Have you, a close friend or relative ever been a victim of crime? If yes, state the nature of the crime(s).

11. Have you, a close friend or relative ever been arrested for a crime (including driving under the influence)? If yes, state the nature of the crime(s).

12. Except as revealed in question 10 or 11 above, have you, a close friend or relative ever been witness to a crime? If yes, state the nature of the crime(s).

I hereby declare under penalty of perjury that the foregoing is true and correct.
Executed in Hillsborough County, Florida

Date _____   Signature _____

Scientific Jury Selection Scientific jury selection is the application of tools and techniques that have long been familiar in social science research—questionnaires, interviews, attitude scales, public-opinion surveys, and careful sampling procedures—to determine the best type of juror who probably would vote for a particular side in a particular case. Data obtained from field research are analyzed to identify key variables that may affect the jury's decision-making process.

During the 1970s, scientific jury selection attracted a great deal of interest from both the mass media and the legal community. But once the glare of publicity dimmed, skepticism about the success of the method and a concern for ethical issues focused professional interest on the technical details (sampling procedures, questionnaires, and behavior checklists for observing prospective jurors). According to Ellison and Buckhout, one of the factors that limited enthusiasm for this approach to jury selection was cost.

The Use of Jury Consultants The jury selection process is also complicated by the use of **jury consultants.** These specialists are social scientists used by trial lawyers—defense attorneys in particular—to help decide which jurors would most likely vote for their side. Jury consultants were used in the William Kennedy Smith case (acquittal in seventy-seven minutes), the Menendez brothers' trial (hung jury), and the Lorena Bobbitt trial (temporary insanity), among other high-profile cases. After significant preparation before a trial, the consultant observes the responses and body language of jury pool members and analyzes the answers to the detailed questionnaires that the consultant drafted and gave to the jury before trial regarding each potential juror's background. These form part of the basis for the consultant's recommendation to the attorney on which jury members to select. Jury consultants also use computers and mock trials to profile the ideal juror.

Some experts suggest that jury consultants should be barred from the justice system because they allow wealthy defendants, such as O. J. Simpson, to hand-pick a very sympathetic jury who would be predisposed to acquit. Certainly, no court is going to order the state to pay for a trial consultant for indigent or middle-class defendants, and the government ordinarily does not have funds for such purposes.

The Relationship between Quality Jury Selection and the Outcome of the Trial Modern legal scholars propose that the present U.S criminal trial process is inadequate because it is too complicated and requires an inordinate amount of time. Furthermore, the accuracy of the jury verdict is often questioned by the public, and serious questions remain regarding the use of the unanimous verdict and peremptory challenges. The past decade has seen serious criticisms of the jury system by legal professions, the press, and the public.

THE RULES OF EVIDENCE

The rules of evidence govern the presentation of evidence at a trial in much the same way that the rules of a game govern the conduct of the players. Continuing with this analogy, the judge acts as the impartial referee or umpire. Evidence consists of legal proofs presented to the court in the form of witnesses, records, documents, objects, and other means, for the purpose of influencing the opinions of the judge or jury toward the case of the prosecution or the defense.

The four kinds of evidence are real evidence, testimonial evidence, direct evidence and circumstantial evidence. **Real evidence** refers to objects of any kind (weapons, clothing, fingerprints, and so on). Real evidence must be the original evidence or objects. Reasonable facsimiles such as photographs, reproductions, or duplicates that are necessitated by practical considerations may also be introduced as real evidence. Interestingly, though, this is not as clear-cut as it seems (see "In the News: DNA Detectives"). **Testimonial evidence** consists of the statements of competent, sworn witnesses. All real evidence must be accompanied by testimonial evidence. Next, there is **direct evidence,** which refers to the observations of eyewitnesses. Finally, **circumstantial evidence** comprises information that tends to prove or disprove a point by inference. Circumstantial evidence proves a subsidiary fact from which the existence of the ultimate fact in a criminal trial—guilt or innocence—may ultimately be inferred by the jury.

CTQ
Why is the phenomenon of jury science not significant for most criminal defendants?

CTQ
Does the fact that the rich can hire a jury consultant and the poor cannot violate the equal protection clause of the Fourteenth Amendment, which provides that no citizen should be at an advantage or disadvantage based upon poverty or wealth?

WEB
For more information on scientific jury selection, visit the links to the jury consultant firms Trial Behavior Consulting and Jury Solutions on our Web site, www.prenhall.com/territo.

CTQ
How does our jury system serve or not serve individual rights and public order needs, and especially render respected justice?

CTQ
What is the relationship between the structured rules of evidence and the real facts of the case?

CTQ
As you read on, explain the difference between testimonial evidence and real evidence, between lay witnesses and expert witnesses, and between direct and circumstantial evidence.

WEB
For more information on evidence, visit our Web site, www.prenhall.com/territo.

IN THE NEWS

A HUMAN PERSPECTIVE

DNA DETECTIVES
by J. Kluger

In October, 1998, a 24-year-old woman who had been comatose for more than three years gave birth to a baby girl. It was only a few days before the delivery that the staff at the woman's nursing home in Lawrence, MA, even discovered that she was pregnant. Under the circumstances, the pregnancy had to have been the result of rape; yet the woman was uniquely unable to name her assailant. If she couldn't speak, however, the blood of her daughter could. Shortly after the baby's birth, the police drew a sample of the infant's blood, then took voluntary samples from male relatives of the woman, as well as from nursing-home personnel and others who might have had access to her. Comparing the men's DNA with the baby's, they figured, could lead them to the rapist.

Over the past decade, DNA profiling has become almost as important a part of crime fighting as fingerprinting. But even as technology pushes forensic science forward, the Constitution has held it back. The Fourth Amendment guarantees citizens protection from unreasonable searches and seizures, and although the Founding Fathers didn't contemplate strands of DNA when drafting the Bill of Rights, what search could be more invasive than an assay of our very genes?

The power of DNA technology expanded exponentially last fall when the FBI activated its new Combined DNA Index system. A database containing the gene prints of 250,000 convicted felons—as well as 4,600 DNA samples left behind at the scene of unsolved crimes—the system acts as sort of investigatory intranet through which law enforcement officials can surf when trying to match a known criminal to a crime.

This kind of investigatory yin and yang is keeping opponents of DNA fingerprinting mollified—but for how long? Now that the gene genie is out of the bottle, there may be little that can be done to stuff it back in. Scientists in the U.S. and England already speak dreamily of moving beyond testing general genetic evidence alone, expanding their work to sample other—more richly encoded—areas of the genome. Kevin Sullivan of England's Forensic Science Service predicts that within a decade researchers may be able to use DNA analysis to draw a sort of genetic police sketch of a suspect's appearance, including build, facial shape, and even inherited physical defects.

The most complex traits, of course, would be the ones even the best detectives would have a hard time seeing: personality traits. If temperament is at least partly determined by genetic hard-wiring, somewhere in the vast tangle of human DNA there must be strands that influence behavior—including criminal behavior.

The problem is, if you could locate such genes, what would you do with that knowledge? Should you incarcerate people for crimes they haven't yet committed but are genetically predisposed to commit? Is it possible to fix such miswired genes, and if so, should you try? The possibility of mucking about with such fundamental genetic coding gives a lot of people existential shivers—and it should. "This is the kind of technology that would flourish in an Orwellian society," says social critic Bereano.

For now there's nothing to suggest that things are nearly so dire; DNA fingerprinting has been used for years, and so far it is only wrongdoers who have real cause to wish it hadn't. But when it comes to scientific advances, human beings have often been a slapdash species—racing out ahead with a new technology before fully appreciating its power. If DNA fingerprinting should get into the wrong hands, society's law-abiding members may find they have more in common with its lawbreakers than they ever dreamed possible.

Source: J. Kluger, "DNA Detectives," *Time*, January 11, 1999. © 1999 TIME, Inc. Reprinted by permission.

Requirements for Admissible Evidence—It Must Be Relevant, Material, and Competent

To be accepted by the court, evidence must be relevant, material, and competent. *Relevant evidence* directly pertains to the issue in question. That is, evidence is relevant not only when it tends to prove or disprove a fact at issue, but also when it establishes facts from which further inferences can be drawn. Whether the defendant "did it" is not relevant to his or her successful prosecution. The only thing that is relevant is the prosecution's ability to produce admissible evidence to prove the defendant's guilt beyond a reasonable doubt. Sometimes this is problematic, especially when dealing with the human factor.

Relevancy often is confused with the concept of materiality of evidence. *Material evidence* relates to the crime charged or has a legitimate and effective bearing on the decision of the case. Evidence is sometimes held to be inadmissible because it does not tend to prove the specific issue (is immaterial). Thus certain evidence may be logically relevant, but not necessarily material. For example, material evidence in a murder case includes evidence that suggests motive, although motive is not an element of the offense.

Competent evidence is evidence supplied by a competent witness, obtained by investigators in a legal and constitutional manner, or does not violate any of the constitutional

CTQ

Under what circumstances can evidence be inadmissible?

protections of the defendant. Certain evidence, such as privileged and hearsay evidence (discussed later), is not considered competent evidence.

Very young children and people who are mentally retarded or mentally disturbed may be considered incompetent witnesses by the court. Competency, however, is a complex and controversial issue. Just how old must children be before they can distinguish between right and wrong, or can understand the meaning of what they have seen or heard? If a witness has been institutionalized or treated for mental illness, is this incontrovertible proof that the witness is incapable of giving reliable and competent testimony on a specific question?

Competency also concerns the constitutionality of the admissibility of certain evidence. Evidence is incompetent when it is privileged, as the next section explains. Evidence based on hearsay is also considered incompetent evidence. Whether evidence is competent is a matter for the trial judge to decide; determining what weight the evidence receives is the exclusive province of the jury.

> **CTQ**
> When an adversary presents testimonial evidence through a witness, should the jury receive a judicial instruction that eyewitness testimony is inherently unreliable, and the jury should consider such evidence with caution before basing any conclusions upon it?

> **WEB**
> For more information on factual case evidence of forensic solved crimes, visit our Web site, www.prenhall.com/territo.

Testimonial Evidence

Witnesses may present testimonial evidence. They may be called by the prosecution or by the defense, and they are sworn in before they are permitted to testify. If they do not tell the truth, they may be prosecuted for the crime of perjury. There are several types of witnesses.

The testimony of a *victim-witness* is a preferred type of testimonial evidence by the prosecution because juries often give this type of testimony the most weight during deliberations. In many cases, prosecutors drop charges if victims will not agree to testify against the accused. *Eyewitnesses* are individuals who saw part of or all of the commission of the crime being tried before them. They are prime candidates for being called to testify in criminal cases, although some psychologists question the use of eyewitnesses, finding evidence that jurors sometimes place too much weight on this type of testimony.[30]

Generally witnesses must testify only in regards to perceptible facts, and not about their personal opinions. However, in some instances witnesses are allowed to offer their opinion. This is usually limited to two types of questions: (1) whether the witness believed the individual on trial was drunk, and (2) whether the individual driving the car was speeding. All witnesses, both expert and lay alike, are never permitted to testify to the ultimate question of fact in a criminal case: the guilt or innocence of the defendant.

Real Evidence

Real evidence is evidence that is real to the senses, is tangible, and may be brought into the courtroom and passed around to the jury for their personal inspection, in contrast to evidence presented by the testimony of other people. Examples of real evidence include the weapon used in the crime, blood samples, hair samples, and clothing. In the most famous criminal case in the last decade, the O. J. Simpson case, the murder weapon, a knife (or knives), was not found and thus could not be presented at trial. But the bloody glove found at the crime scene, and its companion glove found at O. J. Simpson's estate, were also introduced as real evidence. These tangible pieces of property are examples of

IN THE WORKPLACE

COURT INTERPRETERS AND TRANSLATORS

Responsible for providing high-quality simultaneous and consecutive interpreting for defendants, witnesses, litigants, and others according to law. Perform a variety of duties, including the following: interpret in-court proceedings, trials, omnibus hearings, arraignments, traffic court, motions, and all hearings for non-English-speaking parties; review daily docket to determine which courts and proceedings will require an interpreter; maintain statistics as to the number of interpreting contacts; provide draft translations of forms in working language; and assist in coordination and development of continuing-education programs for staff and certified interpreters. Minimum qualifications are as follows: one year of professional interpreting experience, college-level vocabulary in both languages, ability to communicate complex information.

different types of real evidence that seemingly bolstered the prosecution's case, at least until prosecutor Chris Darden asked Simpson to try on the gloves.

As Simpson struggled to do so, he quipped, "They don't fit." Many argued that this demonstration, which caught the prosecution by surprise, weakened the case against the defendant. Defense attorney Johnnie Cochran used the demonstration as one theme in his closing arguments, repeating often, "If it does not fit, you must acquit." Furthermore, blood samples found at the home of O. J. Simpson's former wife Nicole Simpson (the "crime scene"), in O. J. Simpson's car, and at his home are still other examples of real evidence from the Simpson case. To be admissable in court, real evidence (photographic evidence, too) must be introduced by the testimony of a witness that the real evidence is authentic and has not been disturbed by the chain of custody (see Figure 9.4). Moreover, the prosecution had admitted into evidence a sample of O. J. Simpson's blood as well as samples from the two victims. All three of these samples are considered real evidence, even though the defense attorneys challenged their authenticity.

Opinion Evidence Offered by an Expert Witness

A cardinal rule of evidence restricts laypeople (non-expert witnesses) to giving testimony based only on direct evidence; that is, what they have seen, heard, smelled, tasted, or touched. Therefore a layperson's opinions, speculations, or conclusions are not admissible in courts of law. Exceptions to this rule cover certain situations in which an opinion can be supported by the observation of facts that fall within the realm of common experience. Thus, a witness's opinion that a defendant was drunk or was speeding in his car may be accepted by the court on the basis of the additional testimonial of the witness; that the witness smelled alcohol on the defendant's breath, heard the defendant use slurred speech, saw him or her down several drinks in rapid succession, or observed the defendant walking with an unsteady gait.

Unlike eyewitnesses or alibi witnesses, expert witnesses usually do not have to have any firsthand knowledge of the crime, nor are they restricted by the rules of evidence from expressing their opinions. In fact, expert witnesses are summoned for the specific purpose of expressing opinions as evidence. The court can accept any person as an expert witness whose credentials establish a personal expertise in a particular field or discipline. Fingerprint specialists, handwriting specialists, crime lab technicians, or criminal investigators may act as expert witnesses. Psychiatrists and psychologists may be asked to give their expert opinion on the mental status of the defendant; a ballistics specialist may testify regarding his or her opinion about the identification of a murder weapon; an art dealer may be asked to appraise the value of a stolen painting introduced as evidence. Even merchants, artisans, and skilled workers (electricians, plumbers, locksmiths), whose long experience in their field qualifies them as experts among their peers, may be called in specific cases.

Specialists must first be qualified by the court to act as expert witnesses. The side that calls the expert—the prosecution or the defense—must convince the court that the witness is, in fact, an expert and is therefore capable of expressing a valid and reliable opinion. A witness is deemed an expert by virtue of special knowledge, skill, experience, training, or publication in the pertinent field about which the witness is to testify. Opposing counsel may shorten the inquiry considerably by agreeing that the witness is acceptable as a qualified expert. This is often done when the expert's credentials are well known to both sides. In some instances, the opposing counsel may object to qualifying the witness and may attempt, through cross-examination, to disqualify the individual as an expert. If the witness is discredited, the judge will rule that the witness cannot testify as an expert in the trial.

As a consequence, a certain cynicism seems to prevail among litigation attorneys concerning expert witnesses, they believe that some expert witnesses will testify for the

FIGURE 9.4

Trial witnesses not only testify to what they perceived but also are used to identify real, documented evidence taken from the crime scene as well as photographs that the witnesses took of the crime scene.

Courtesy of AP/Wide World Photos.

CTQ

Does new technology and scientific evidence, such as video and hyperspecialized cameras, DNA, and computers, dramatically affect the trustworthiness that jurors give such evidence in criminal trials, in much the same way that the advent of the fingerprint did?

CTQ

Since expert witnesses can cost the criminal defendant up to $20,000 for their testimony, does not the availability of expert witnesses to the rich and their nonavailability to the poor discriminate in criminal trials?

WEB

For more information on victim-witnesses, **visit the link to the prosecutor's office of Golden, Colorado, on our Web site, www.prenhall.com/territo.**

CTQ

Since expert witnesses are known to testify for both sides, is it fair to say that their testimony is available to the highest bidder?

FIGURE 9.5

Psychotherapist-Patient Privilege
Source: Fl. Stat. Ch. 3.129 (1996).

---

(1) For purposes of this section:
   (a) A "psychotherapist" is:
      1. A person authorized to practice medicine in any state or nation, or reasonably believed by the patient so to be, who is engaged in the diagnosis or treatment of a mental or emotional condition, including alcoholism and other drug addiction: or
      2. A person licensed or certified as a psychologist under the laws of any state or nation, who is engaged primarily in the diagnosis or treatment of a mental or emotional condition, including alcoholism and other drug addiction.
   (b) A "patient" is a person who consults, or is interviewed by, a psychotherapist for purposes of diagnosis or treatment of a mental or emotional condition, including alcoholism and other drug addiction.
   (c) A communication between psychotherapist and patient is "confidential" if it is not intended to be disclosed to third persons other than:
      1. Those persons present to further the interest of the patient in the consultation, examination, or interview.
      2. Those persons necessary for the transmission of the communication.
      3. Those persons who are participating in the diagnosis and treatment under the direction of the psychotherapist.
(2) A patient has a privilege to refuse to disclose, and to prevent any other person from disclosing, confidential communications or records made for the purpose of diagnosis or treatment of his mental or emotional condition, including alcoholism and other drug addiction, between himself and his psychotherapist, or persons who are participating in the diagnosis or treatment under the direction of the psychotherapist. This privilege includes any diagnosis made, and advice given, by the psychotherapists in the course of that relationship.

---

highest bidder. This implies that they are not testifying as to what they believe is true in a case, but rather they are simply testifying in the manner most favorable to the side that has paid them. Indeed, the word *prostitute* is used in certain circles in the same sentence as *expert witness* in conversations among trial attorneys. This is not to say, however, that there are not hundreds or even thousands of expert witnesses in this country who are ethical and dedicated, and will testify for a client only if they believe that their testimony is accurate, truthful, and honest.

A Limitation—Evidence of Privileged or Confidential Communications

The distinction between privileged and confidential communications is often unclear to laypeople. *Privileged communications* are communications between people that are protected by law (such as between attorney and client or between priest and penitent). The person receiving the communication cannot be compelled to divulge the contents of the communication unless the person making the statement waives his or her legal right to secrecy. Also, communications between husband and wife are privileged; in some states, however, a person may be permitted to testify for his or her spouse. Figure 9.5 illustrates a typical statutory privilege. Privileged statements can also occur between police informers and police, physicians and psychotherapists and their patients, and newspaper reporters and their anonymous sources. If the state in which these conversations transpire has passed a statute making the communication privileged, then the communication is indeed a privileged one.

Confidentiality (which applies to a statement given in a personal and private moment) refers to an ethical obligation on the part of a professional person to safeguard the privacy of communications made to him or her by another within the context of a professional relationship. The communication is not legally privileged, however; a professional person can be forced to reveal these communications during a criminal trial when he or she takes the witness stand. All privileged conversations are also confidential. Communications among friends, parents and children, and colleagues have no legal protection in the courts unless they are recognized as privileged communications as well. A marriage counselor, for example, is bound by the ethics of the professional relationship to maintain the confidentiality of statements made by the client. Nevertheless, such statements do not constitute privileged communications. Thus, the counselor could be ordered to reveal the confidential statements or risk a citation for contempt of court.

CTQ

Is it socially worthwhile to allow all of these privileged communications to exist within our society, knowing that if they were revealed, many more people would be convicted?

TABLE 9.1	Hearsay Testimony and the Hearsay Rule
Hearsay Testimony	**The Hearsay Rule**
All testimony and all statements that were uttered outside the courtroom by a third person and were heard by a witness who subsequently enters the courtroom, takes the stand, and testifies as to what he or she heard the third person say constitute hearsay testimony in a criminal trial.	The hearsay rule defines hearsay as evidence of a statement made out of court and made as an assertion to show the truth of the matters asserted therein, thus resting on the value of the credibility of the out-of-court asserter. Hence, unlike hearsay testimony, the hearsay rule excludes only out-of-court statements that are offered to prove the truth of the matters asserted.

Another Limitation—Hearsay Evidence

Another type of evidence the rules of evidence excludes in the criminal trial is hearsay testimony. **Hearsay** testimony is knowledge or information that a witness has acquired secondhand (that is, facts that he or she hears from someone else and then repeats as testimony). The Supreme Court views hearsay evidence as a denial of the defendant's Sixth Amendment right to confront witnesses against him or her. This is because there is no opportunity to establish the truth of the hearsay evidence since it is impossible to cross-examine the actual witness who originally asserted it. Because of this, for over a hundred years, the United States has used the hearsay rule, which excludes all hearsay testimony from a jury's consideration unless the testimony falls within one of the specified exceptions. Table 9.1 compares and contrasts hearsay rule and exceptions to the hearsay rule.

CTQ

Most of us base a majority of our significant opinions in life on hearsay evidence. Therefore, is it just to have hearsay evidence inadmissible in a criminal trial?

CTQ

If you could create exceptions to the hearsay rule, what would they be?

Some Exceptions to the Hearsay Rule

The law of evidence in American courtrooms has carved out certain exceptions to the hearsay rule, in spite of the fact that opposing counsel does not have a right to challenge the credibility of the original declaration. These exceptions arose because they were considered a type of hearsay that was inherently reliable and profoundly trustworthy. Hence they have become admissible as evidence as exceptions to the hearsay rule. There are twenty-five recognized exceptions to the hearsay rule in American courtrooms[31] (see Table 9.2). Because the Constitution provides safeguards against self-incrimination, the

TABLE 9.2	Twenty-five Legally Recognized Exceptions to the Hearsay Rule
Present sense impression	Learned treatises
Excited utterance	Reputation concerning personal or family history
Then-existing mental, emotional, or physical condition	Reputation concerning boundaries or general history
Statements for purposes of medical diagnosis or treatment	Reputation as to character
Recorded recollection	Judgment of previous conviction
Records of regularly conducted activity	Judgment as to personal, family, or general history, or boundaries
Absence of an entry in records kept in accordance with a rigid standard of record keeping	Former testimony of a witness
Public records and reports	Statement made under belief of impending death
Records of vital statistics	Statement against interest
Marriage, baptismal, and similar certificates	Statement of personal or family history
Family records	Other exceptions to the hearsay rule are seldom but sometimes recognized if they strictly adhere to the following requirements: (a) the declarant is out of court, (b) the hearsay is inherently reliable, and (c) the hearsay is remarkably trustworthy.
Records of documents affecting an interest in property	
Statements in ancient documents	
Market reports and commercial publications	

Source: Fed. R. Evid. 803.

defendant is not required to take the witness stand. Yet a defendant's confession may be presented by a law enforcement officer who testifies that he or she heard the defendant state outside the courtroom that he or she had committed the crime. The prosecution has an extremely strong interest in admitting this type of hearsay as evidence for the jury's consideration.

The defense counsel is equally concerned with keeping the confession out of evidence. If the defendant is incriminated by his or her own statements, it is obviously difficult to obtain a verdict of not guilty. In any event, the judge carefully examines the circumstances under which a confession is made (such as whether it was given voluntarily and without coercion) before the judge allows the confession to be read to the jury.

The admissibility of a *dying declaration* is another exception to the hearsay rule. This exception is based on the belief that a person aware of impending death has no motive to lie. Most courts limit dying declarations to be admitted into evidence only in homicide cases. Special requirements must be met in order for this type of evidence to be admitted. The dying declaration must be that of the victim and not a third person; the victim's death must have been imminent at the time the declaration was made; witnesses who testify about the statement must have the mental clarity required of any other witnesses; and the statement must pertain to the circumstances surrounding the killing of the victim. Thus, deathbed declarations must include evidence of the declarer's knowledge of impending death. In many cases involving deathbed statements, the witness to the statement is a police officer or detective.

One of the most controversial issues surrounding the hearsay rule in the first decade of the twenty-first century involves the testimony of the victim during a child sexual molestation criminal trial. Traditionally, the child victim was required to testify when the defendant was present in the courtroom. For years, under the rule of hearsay evidence, it was believed that any other way to introduce the child's testimony would be a violation of not only the hearsay rule, but also of the defendant's right to confront all witnesses testifying against him or her. This requirement has caused many problems because it was believed, especially due to the defendant's courtroom presence, that the child victim often froze in fear while testifying on the witness stand as the defendant glared at him or her, and the child often recanted his or her testimony.

In response, some legislators and trial judges (in absence of legislation) have experimented with new procedures designed to create an atmosphere less traumatizing for the child, but at the same time, preserve the defendant's constitutional rights. An example is allowing the child to testify via closed-circuit television. This type of testimony appears to deny the defendant his or her Sixth Amendment right to confront witnesses face-to-face, as demonstrated in the Landmark Case *Coy v. Iowa*.

THE PROCEDURAL ORDER OF A CRIMINAL TRIAL

A criminal trial is a complex and intricate proceeding that begins as soon as the jury is sworn in. The only real decision that must be made before the trial formally begins is the judge's decision whether to *sequester* the jurors. Sequestration of jury members is a process by which the judge removes all jurors and alternates from possible outside influences. Normally, they are sequestered in hotel rooms and escorted by bailiffs to ensure they are not exposed to any publicity about the trial. Sequestration is seldom used in criminal trials.

Once the sequestration issue is resolved, the formal procedures of the criminal trial can begin. These procedures have developed into a series of at least ten steps:

1. Jury selection, the impaneling of the jury, and administration of oath to the jurors
2. Opening statements made by both sides (facts only)
3. The presentation of the state's case through the presentation of various forms of evidence
4. The presentation of the defense's case through the presentation of various forms of evidence, an affirmative defense, and the presentation of evidence that the government has failed to meet its burden of proof

---

CTQ If the philosophical basis for allowing certain exceptions to the hearsay rule is the trustworthiness and reliability of this particular hearsay evidence, is it an objective standard?

CTQ Why do most courts believe that a person who is about to die is likely to tell the truth? Do you believe this?

CTQ Is not the terror of a child having to face the molesting defendant in court justification enough to allow out-of-court testimony by the child victim to come in as hearsay, rather than to victimize the child again through the trauma of the courtroom experience?

LANDMARK CASE

Coy v. Iowa

Coy was charged with molesting two girls. At trial, pursuant to enabling legislation, the courtroom was petitioned to hide Coy from the view of the girls when they testified. Coy was convicted and the Iowa Supreme Court affirmed. The U.S. Supreme Court accepted review. The issue before the Court was whether a defendant may be hidden from the view of minor witnesses testifying against him or her. Justice Scalia said no, declaring that a defendant may not be hidden from the view of a minor witness against him or her. The Constitution guarantees a criminal defendant the right to confront his or her accusers. This concept dates back to antiquity, at least as far as Roman law, and was incorporated in Anglo-Saxon law even before the right to a trial by jury evolved. The reason for this is clear. The phrase "Look me in the eye and say that" reflects the understanding that a false accuser may have difficulty with perjury in the face of the person that he or she accuses, and the accused has the right to permit the fact-finder to view the accuser in this light. The Court went on to state that to hide the defendant nullifies this right, even if the accused and accuser are in the same room. Here, the statute permits courts to hide the defendant in all molestation cases. While special circumstances may exist at times that will permit such a practice, a broad rule such as that applied here is not permissible.

Source: Coy v. Iowa, 108 S.Ct. 2798 (1988).

---

5. Rebuttal evidence (state)
6. Surrebuttal evidence (defense)
7. Closing arguments by attorneys from both sides
8. The judge's charge to the jury (instructions on the law applicable to the case at hand)
9. The jury's deliberations, which occur in total privacy, followed by an announcement of its decision, called a verdict, in open court
10. A sentencing hearing followed by formal sentencing of the defendant by the trial judge

The formal processes of the criminal felony trial are conducted in a specific and orderly fashion in accordance with rules of criminal law, procedure, and evidence. Unlike what transpires in popular television programs involving lawyers—where witnesses are often asked leading and prejudicial questions and where judges go far beyond their supervisory role—the modern criminal trial is a complicated and often time-consuming technical affair.

When presenting a case, the prosecutor reveals direct testimony, physical evidence, and possibly a confession, if available, in order to persuade the jury that the evidence demonstrates that the accused is guilty beyond a reasonable doubt. The defense attorney, on the other hand, rebuts the government's case with contrary evidence, and makes certain that the rights of the criminal defendant afforded under the federal and state constitutions are considered during all phases of the trial, as well as asserting affirmative defenses that are available to the defendant. The defense lawyer also uses his or her skill to negate the state's case by vigorous cross-examination of the state's evidence and witnesses in order to discredit the evidence and impeach witnesses. Perhaps the state's witnesses have changed their statements from the time they gave them to the police; perhaps their memory is faulty; perhaps their background is unsavory; and so on. Furthermore, the defense counsel determines whether an appeal is appropriate if the client is found guilty. From the beginning of the process to its completion, the criminal trial judge is responsible for promoting an orderly and fair administration of the criminal trial (see Figure 9.6).

> **CTQ**
>
> Should there be any differences in the arrangement of steps in the criminal trial, other than the ones that are listed here that have been that way for a century?

> **CTQ**
>
> Should the formal process of the litigated felony case be more flexible and allow for experimentation to seek a more reliable way of ascertaining the truth?

FIGURE 9.6

One of the criminal trial judge's primary responsibilities is to rule on motions and objections made by the adversarial attorneys during the trial.

Courtesy of John Neubauer/PhotoEdit.

CTQ

What dangers lie in the defense attorney's disputing a prosecutor's opening statement when the defense gives his or her opening statement?

CTQ

Since most of the prosecution witnesses in a criminal trial are paid a salary by the state (e.g., the police), which also is the same entity that is prosecuting the defendant, is their testimony reliable?

CTQ

If during the cross-examination of a state's witness, he or she is caught in a lie, should the state subsequently prosecute him or her for perjury?

OPENING STATEMENTS

After the jury is impaneled, the trial opens with a reading of the indictment or information. Then the prosecution presents its opening statement. (The order in which the defense and prosecution present their cases varies from state to state, but each state follows a legally established procedure. Generally, the prosecution goes first.) The prosecutor addresses the jury and explains the charge, describes the crime the defendant is alleged to have committed, and draws a general picture of what the state intends to prove beyond a reasonable doubt. The purpose of the opening statement is to provide the members of the jury—who lack familiarity with legal matters and procedures of criminal investigation—with an outline of the major objectives of the prosecution's case, the evidence it plans to present, the witnesses it intends to summon, and what it will seek to prove through the testimony of those witnesses. With the opening statement, the prosecutor tries to show the jury a finished jigsaw puzzle of the case. The prosecutor also explains the nature of each of the pieces of the puzzle and how they fit together to produce a whole picture that, it will be argued, must lead to a guilty verdict. The idea is to make it easier for jurors to grasp the meaning and significance of evidence and testimony and to keep them from becoming confused by the complexities of the case.

The prosecutor may not refer to evidence that is known to be inadmissible and also may not comment on the defendant's prior criminal record, if one exists. Should the prosecutor make such remarks in the opening statement, it could result in either a mistrial or a reversal of a conviction upon appeal.

Once the prosecutor concludes with the opening statement, the defense can either follow with its opening statement or defer that presentation until later in the case. In the opening statement, the defense attorney usually describes how he or she plans to expose the weaknesses or inadequacies of the prosecution's case and to present evidence that demonstrates to the jury that the defendant is not guilty beyond a reasonable doubt. In no state is the defense compelled to make an opening statement.

PRESENTATION OF THE STATE'S EVIDENCE

After opening statements are concluded, the prosecution calls its first witness. The witness takes an oath or affirmation to tell the truth. The prosecutor then begins the presentation of testimonial evidence by direct examination of the witness—a question-and-answer procedure designed to elicit information from the witness about the case. This is called *direct examination*.

Prosecution witnesses are required to respond directly to the question asked, and attempts to avoid the direct thrust of the question or to volunteer additional information beyond the question's scope are not allowed. The basic reason for requiring direct responsiveness is that a witness, if given freedom to do so, might blurt out material that is legally objectionable, and if highly prejudicial, might constitute a mistrial or result in reversible error. These procedural restrictions upon offering testimony are designed, insofar as possible, to ensure that objectionable material is not heard by the jury.

Generally speaking, the most important witness for the prosecution is the victim. Throughout the history of American criminal trials, the cases that may have most dramatically proved this axiom true were the two trials constituting the separate state and federal prosecutions of the same acts of misconduct by four members of the Los Angeles Police Department, which have been called the Rodney King cases by the media. In the state trial, the prosecution made a fatal error, it did not put Rodney King on the stand. The prosecutor explained that he believed that the famous videotape of King's being severely beaten by the defendants (the police officers) would be the best evidence. Yet the officers were acquitted by an all-white suburban jury. Subsequently, in the federal trial, more conventional wisdom prevailed and King testified. After a change of venue to downtown Los Angeles, the federal prosecution secured a jury conviction against the officers by convicting them of violating King's civil rights by using excessive force to secure his arrest.

When the prosecutor finishes with the presentation of its witness, the defense attorney has the option to conduct a cross-examination of these witnesses. *Cross-examination* is designed to test a witness's powers of observation and recollection, truthfulness, and possible bias against the cross-examiner's side or, in general, the believability of the witness's original testimony. On cross-examination, the witness can be asked only about topics on which he or she testified during direct examination. But on cross-examination, opposing counsel is permitted to ask leading questions (questions that suggest the answers). Sometimes a skillful cross-examiner attempts to confuse, fluster, anger, or frighten the witness, causing him or her to lose self-control and composure and thus lose credibility in the eyes of the jurors.

During the cross-examination of prosecution witnesses, the defense lawyer has two goals in mind. One is to diminish the perceptual or relevant effectiveness of a particular witness's testimony against the defendant. This is normally done by showing that what the witness had to say is either wrong, mistaken, false, or irrelevant. The second goal of the defense lawyer's cross-examination is to impeach the credibility of the prosecution's witness. This cross-examination technique involves an inquiry of the witness that is distinct from the question of guilt or innocence of the accused. If the impeachment of the credibility of a witness is successful, this shows that a witness is less believable than he or she might appear to be. Generally, there are ten legally recognized methods to impeach the credibility of a prosecution (or for that matter, a defense) witness:

1. Other witnesses' testimony is contrary to what the prosecution witness has said on the stand.
2. The witness has no knowledge of the facts.
3. The witness's senses were so dulled by sleep or drink that his or her perceptions are questionable.
4. The witness has a poor character and reputation for truthfulness.
5. The witness has a bias about the outcome of the case (for example, he or she is a relative of the victim).
6. The witness has a vested interest in the case (for example, he or she will stand to gain financially from a conviction).
7. The witness has made prior statements that are inconsistent with those he or she made on the stand.
8. The witness has had a valid felony conviction(s).
9. The witness has committed acts that reflect poorly on his or her honesty (such as cheating on college exams or income taxes).
10. The witness has a poor reputation in the general community for truthfulness.[32]

Upon completion of cross-examination by the defense counsel, the prosecutor may then conduct a *redirect examination* to clarify some point or issue raised during the cross-examination. Afterwards, the defense counsel may carry out a recross-examination. These examinations are restricted to matters dealt with in the immediately preceding examination.

Subsequently, additional witnesses are called by the prosecution. Approximately the same processes and procedures outlined previously are followed again with each of them. The prosecution presents all of its witnesses before any witnesses are called by the defense. After the last witness for the prosecution has testified and the prosecution has introduced all of the state's other forms of evidence (real, documentary, photographic, scientific, and opinion), then the prosecution rests its case.

IN THE WORKPLACE

PARALEGAL

Responsible for performing activities related to legal research and discovery under direction of attorneys. Performs a variety of duties, including the following: research legal information, summarize depositions, perform court filings, respond to citizen complaints and inquiries, assist in providing education and training in court procedures and policies, and assist attorneys in complying with court rules for filing briefs. Minimum qualifications are as follows: high school diploma or equivalent, certificate of completion or a degree from an approved paralegal program, one year of relevant legal experience, excellent verbal/written skills, interpretation skills, knowledge of court procedures and interpretation.

PRESENTATION OF THE DEFENSE'S CASE

The presentation of the case for the defense is similar to that of the prosecution. The defense counsel calls witnesses and directly examines them; then turns them over to the prosecution for cross-examination. Also the defense may submit relevant real, documentary, photographic, scientific, and opinion evidence. The defense, however, has the choice not to introduce evidence at criminal trial. This strategy is used most often when it seems plain to the defense team that the government has failed to meet its burden of proof to demonstrate the guilt of the client. (see Figure 9.7.)

Several options are available to defense counsel when contemplating what trial strategy will provide the most effective defense for his or her client:

1. The defendant is not required by law to present witnesses; instead, the defense can be based entirely on the evidence and testimony presented by the state.
2. The defendant is not required to give personal testimony. A defendant's refusal to take the stand cannot be called to the attention of the jury by either the prosecutor or the judge. If he or she does choose to take the witness stand, a defendant faces the same hazards of cross-examination as any other witness.
3. The defense lawyer is not obligated to prove the innocence of the client, but merely to show that the state has failed to prove guilt beyond a reasonable doubt.
4. The defense can present an affirmative defense.

Defendants have certain rights during the presentation of their defense. First, they have the right under the Sixth Amendment to call any witness they may choose to testify for them, including their own co-defendant.[33] Under the Sixth Amendment, they also have several additional trial rights, as presented in Chapter 3.

If the defendant has a special defense in the case, such as an alibi or one of the affirmative defenses (discussed shortly), he or she has the burden of going forward and proving the defense. For example, if the defendant claims to have been insane at the time of the crime and the defense produces an expert witness who testifies that the defendant was indeed insane, but the witness is not qualified as an expert according to the judge, then the threshold of the admissability of the defendant's affirmative defense necessary to place the insanity defense as an issue before the jury has not been properly met. Hence, the judge will later instruct the jury to ignore the possibility that the defendant may have been insane at the time of the crime. When the testimony of the last defense witness is completed and all of the defense's other real and documentary evidence has been introduced, the defense rests its case.

FIGURE 9.7

Famous criminal defense lawyer and Harvard law professor Alan Dershowitz huddles with O. J. Simpson's other attorneys in an attempt to create the trial strategy that will have the greatest impact on rendering a favorable verdict for their client. Simpson never took the stand at his criminal trial.

Courtesy of Sam Mircovich/CORBIS.

WEB

For more information on statistics on defendants, **visit the link to the Bureau of Justice Statistics on our Web site, www.prenhall.com/territo.**

CTQ

Is it ever wise for the defense not to present a case, but rather to close and base its theory of a case on the argument that the prosecution has failed to meet the burden of proof (beyond a reasonable doubt) required to convict?

IN THE WORKPLACE

PUBLIC DEFENDER

Responsible for representing indigent people charged with criminal-law and mental-health violations, directing all legal administrative functions of public-health violations, and directing all legal and administrative functions of the public defender's office. Performs a variety of duties, including the following: plan, organize, and supervise the office of the public defender; hire and coordinate the work of all staff; prepare and monitor budgets; review, coordinate, and assign cases; serve as lead attorney on cases with courtwide impact; negotiate pleas with the state attorney's office; and maintain law library. Minimum qualifications are as follows: graduation from an accredited law school, several years of felony trial experience, professional supervisory experience.

THE AFFIRMATIVE DEFENSES

American criminal jurisprudence recognizes that, although someone may have in fact committed the crime he or she is charged with, this does not necessarily mean the defendant is guilty of the charge. As discussed in Chapter 2, the state also must prove the five general elements of every crime: (1) that the defendant had criminal intent, (2) that he or she committed the criminal act, (3) that the act and the intent coincided in time, (4) that there were no attendant circumstances (such as self-defense) that negate criminal liability, and (5) that a result was caused by the criminal act.

Both the common law as well as American statutes have recognized that a certain number of *affirmative defenses* are justified. If these defenses are shown to be true by a preponderance of the evidence by the jury, then the jury verdict must render as a matter of law that a particular affirmative defense negates the criminal responsibility of the accused. This finding of fact ensures that the defendant will be found not guilty of the crime charged (even though the accused admitted the perpetration of the criminal act). Some defendants have achieved national stature by asserting these defenses (see Figure 9.8). Generally, these affirmative defenses are limited in number. That is, the defense cannot make up an affirmative defense for the purposes of the specific case at trial.

Other affirmative defenses are emerging, some of which have taken root in certain states. For example, the battered-woman defense is recognized in some states as an affirmative defense. Other defenses, such as mercy killing, no matter how emotionally appealing they might be, have not been recognized in any state to negate criminal liability of the defendant who kills out of love for his or her victim. The following are selective examples of some of the affirmative defenses used by criminal defendants in American courtrooms.

The Defense of Infancy

In common law, one of several different presumptions is applied regarding a child's capacity to commit crime. Under common law and the majority of states, the defense of *infancy* is available to a child under age 7 because the child is presumed conclusively to be unable to form criminal intent and therefore cannot be held criminally responsible for the acts that constitute the crime. A child between ages 7 and 14 is likewise presumed incapable of forming criminal intent, but this presumption is rebuttable. In other words, the prosecution can obtain a conviction by introducing evidence sufficient to establish that the child defendant knew what he or she was doing. Examples include evidence of the child's intent to conceal the commission of the crime, to bribe a witness, or to accuse others of committing the crime. At age 14 and older, children can be treated as adults.

Both under the common law and in modern statutes, it is the child's age at the time of the commission of the crime (rather than at the time of trial) that determines whether he or she will be prosecuted. Similarly, it is the chronological age—rather than the "mental age"—of the child that is the determining factor. All American jurisdictions have legislation that confers upon juvenile courts exclusive jurisdiction over children of certain ages that are alleged to have committed crimes. (See Chapter 14 for a complete discussion of the juvenile justice system.)

The Insanity Defense

Many reasons for the *insanity* defense have been offered, most turning on the strong and widespread sentiment that a person should not be punished for what he or she cannot help doing.[34] If a criminal act is part of an illness, it seems unjust to punish a person for what the illness caused the person to do. Put another way, the criminal law exists to inhibit and to punish wrong choices by people; if there was no freedom of choice, there should be no punishment.

CTQ

Since the core of an affirmative defense is the defendant's admission that he or she in fact committed the acts that constitute the crime, isn't this tantamount to the defendant getting off on a legal technicality?

CTQ

Would there ever be a case in which the defense attorney would not want to put the defendant on the stand during an affirmative defense, since the defendant admitted to committing the act that he or she is charged with committing?

CTQ

Is it fair that the burden of proof of most affirmative defenses is on the defendant, rather than requiring the prosecution to prove that the affirmative defense does not exist beyond a reasonable doubt?

CTQ

At what age do you think a child is too young to possibly be held criminally responsible for his or her acts?

FIGURE 9.8

Televised image of Andrea Yates during a hearing to determine her competency to stand trial for the murder of her five children. Yates claimed that she was innocent by reason of insanity.

Courtesy of AP/Wide World Photos.

There is no medical definition of insanity. Insanity is a legal term that varies with the question to be decided. Is an individual so insane that he or she should be civilly committed? Is the defendant so insane that he or she cannot be tried for an alleged crime? Reflection will reveal that different legal standards should apply to the answer of each of these questions.

The American Law Institute, in drafting its Model Penal Code, made this point: "The problem is to discriminate between the cases where a punitive-correctional disposition is appropriate and those in which a medical-custodial disposition is the only kind that the law should allow."[35] Yet in some sensational cases, the defense of insanity is successful (Figure 9.9).

How frequently is the defense of insanity successfully pleaded? Of one million criminal cases disposed of each year in state and federal courts, fewer than 0.1 percent involve insanity pleas, and only one in four of these pleas leads to acquittals. The majority of these involve misdemeanor cases.[36] The defense of insanity is, thus, an extremely rare plea; it generally is advanced only in serious cases and where there is no other reasonably valid defense. A common misconception is that the insanity defense is a piece of legal chicanery by which many people—particularly the wealthy—routinely escape punishment.

While the defense of insanity is not exclusively presented in murder trials, it is most often used as a defense to this charge. One reason for this is that, under recent case law, a person found not guilty by reason of insanity may be held in a mental hospital longer than if he or she had been convicted and sentenced to the maximum prison term. This provides a strong disincentive to use the plea except in extreme cases, particularly cases where capital punishment may be a possibility. The insanity defense is recognized in the federal system and in all states except Idaho and Montana. Eight states provide another related defense, "guilty but mentally ill."

The Legal Definition of Insanity The basic **M'Naghten test of insanity** was taken from English law—in particular, from the M'Naghten case in 1843—and is the definition used by the majority of states:

> To establish a defense on the grounds of insanity, it must be clearly proven that, at the time of the committing of the act, the party accused was laboring under such a defect of reason from disease of the mind as not to know the nature and quality of the act he was doing; or, if he did know it, that he did not know he was doing what was wrong.[37]

Other tests have attempted to challenge the M'Naghten's authority, although not successfully.

The insanity defense tests that have evolved in the federal system reflect most of the different practices of the various states (see Table 9.3). Until 1984, the federal tests of insanity were all "judge-made" law. But during that year, Congress provided for such a defense but did not define it. The present federal law, spreading to a number of states, is found in the Comprehensive Crime Control Act of 1984, which accepts the thrust of recommendations made after John W. Hinckley, Jr., tried to assassinate Ronald Reagan. Hinckley stood trial for attempted murder and pleaded insanity, claiming that the basis for insanity was his belief that he had a secret connection to actress Jodie Foster. On the other hand, the American Bar Association and the American Psychiatric Association provide a new test for the defense of insanity: It is an affirmative defense to a prosecution under any federal statue that, at the time of the commission of the acts constituting the offense, the defendant, as a result of a severe mental disease or defect, was unable to appreciate the nature and quality of the wrongfulness of his acts. In this test it is the defendant who has the burden of providing the defense of insanity by clear and convincing evidence.

Other experts recommend even greater restrictions on the insanity defense than does the Comprehensive Crime Control Act of 1984. Some even suggest that there should be no insanity defense at all. This position has been advocated by a number of judges, psychiatrists, and commentators. It is also the recommendation of the American Medical Association in its post-Hinckley reconsideration of this defense.

FIGURE 9.9

Lorena Bobbitt cut off her husband's penis as he slept, then she threw it out in the snow. She faced twenty years in prison for "malicious wounding." The defense claimed that Ms. Bobbitt was not guilty due to a "brief period of insanity" brought on by her husband's raping her, which was the culminating act of years of physical abuse she had endured from his relentless physical assaults. Her doctors testified that she had been raped just minutes before cutting off the penis, which, combined with her long history of physical abuse, caused Ms. Bobbitt to suffer from a severe, longstanding mental illness. This resulted in "a psychotic breakdown which caused her to be unable to control her impulses"—the legal definition of insanity in her state. Hence, the affirmative defense of insanity in this case is not being legally held to be responsible for cutting off her husband's penis.

Courtesy of AP/Wide World Photos.

CTQ

Some states have required that the defendant prove by clear and convincing evidence that he or she was insane in order for the insanity defense to work, rather than the traditional practice of requiring the state to prove that the defendant was not insane beyond a reasonable doubt. Is this new requirement just?

CTQ

In what ways do changes and developments in the insanity defense reflect the shifting conception of how to balance individual rights with the need to punish wrongdoers?

TABLE 9.3 Conflicting Insanity Defense Standards Used in Various Criminal Jurisdictions in the United States

Test	Legal Standard of Mental Illness	Final Burden of Proof	Who Bears the Burden of Proof
M'Naghten	"Didn't know what he was doing or didn't know it was wrong"	Varies from proof by a balance of probabilities on the defense to proof beyond a reasonable doubt on the prosecutor	Prosecutor
Irresistible impulse	"Could not control his conduct"	Beyond a reasonable doubt	Prosecutor
Durham rule	"The criminal act was caused by his mental illness"	Beyond a reasonable doubt	Prosecutor
Substantial capacity	"Lacks substantial capacity to appreciate the wrongfulness of his conduct or to control it"	Beyond a reasonable doubt	Prosecutor
Current federal law	"Lacks capacity to appreciate the wrongfulness of his conduct"	Clear and convincing evidence	Defense

Source: N. Morris, *Crime Study Guide: Insanity Defense.* Washington, D.C.: National Institute of Justice.

Self-Defense

Generally, a person is privileged to use such force as reasonably *appears necessary* to defend himself or herself against an apparent threat of unlawful immediate violence from another. This privilege is called the *right of self-defense*. In all cases where the defendant claims to have acted in self-defense, the following four elements must be established. First, the defendant must believe that the force used was necessary for his or her own protection, and this belief must have been reasonable (that is, a reasonable person in the same or similar circumstances would have formed the same belief). Sometimes an honest and reasonable belief is enough. The defense is still available even though it turns out that the belief was understandably wrong and there was in fact no actual need for the use of force and self-defense.

Second, the defendant must have reasonably believed that the threat of harm was *imminent*—that is, that it would be inflicted immediately if he or she did not act in self-defense. Thus, it is necessary to consider whether the threatening person was actually present, and, if so, whether the person appeared to be willing and able to injure the defendant.

Third, the threatened harm must have been *unlawful*. This raises the issues of whether force can be used to resist an unlawful arrest and whether one who is the initial aggressor in the altercation can claim the defense at all.

Fourth, *the force the defendant used* must have been *reasonable*. In other words, it must have been no more than appeared necessary under the circumstances to prevent the victim from inflicting harm. (See the Landmark Cases *State v. Realina* and *People v. Goetz.*)

American courts have placed special limits on *deadly force* used in self-defense. This is force used with the intent to cause death or serious bodily injury, or that is known by its user to create a substantial risk of death or serious bodily injury.[38] Although there is no prohibition against the use of deadly force in self-defense, there are some special limits on when it may be used.

All courts agree that deadly force may be used in self-defense only if the defendant reasonably believed that the other person was about to inflict death or great bodily injury and that the deadly force that the defendant used was necessary to prevent the harm. Still, certain limitations have been placed on the doctrine of self-defense by American courts. One is that the initial aggressor doesn't have available to him or her the right of self-defense; another is that self-defense is not available to one who escalates the amount of force used in retaliation to defend the original blow or attack. The rationale for this limitation is that the victim, in defending himself or herself against the aggressor, ordinarily is using lawful force. As discussed previously, self-defense is available in response to threats of *lawful* harm.

WEB

For more information on the insanity defense, visit our Web site, www.prenhall.com/territo.

CTQ

Are the four elements of self-defense too rigid in applying the defense, and should they be more relaxed?

CTQ

Do you think the concept of self-defense should be extended to using defensive threats?

CTQ

Are the two limitations on self-defense valid, when someone is in fear of his or her life or serious bodily harm? When such is the case, should there be no limitations on when one should defend oneself?

LANDMARK CASE — State v. Realina

In Hawaii, defendant Realina was involved in several verbal altercations with Mr. Hardisty over Realina's visits to Hardisty's wife, during which Hardisty threatened Realina with body injury. Realina was driving when he noticed that Hardisty was following him. Fearing a violent altercation, Realina drove to the police station. Hardisty approached Realina's car, threatening to kill him, and grabbed him by the shirt in an effort to prevent him from leaving. Realina found a knife in his car and got out with it in his hand. Hardisty ran toward the police station, with Realina chasing him. Realina was ordered by the police officers to drop the knife, and he immediately complied. He was arrested and charged with "terroristic threatening." He contended at trial that he was justified in chasing Hardisty because he acted in self-defense. At issue in the case was whether a person can be held criminally responsible for using force toward another in the reasonable belief that he or she was acting in self-defense. The Hawaii appellate court refused the petition, saying a person will not be held criminally liable for using or threatening to use force on, or toward another if the person believed the force was immediately necessary for the purpose of protecting himself or herself against the use of unlawful force. The court articulated that the doctrine of "self-defense" includes both the actual force to protect oneself from injury and the use of threatened force. They said that it was clear due to the past relationship between the parties that it was reasonable for Realina to be fearful of bodily injury from Hardisty. Therefore, Realina's actions in threatening to use a knife were justified pursuant to defending himself, and he could not be held criminally responsible.

Source: State v. Realina, 1 Haw. 167, 616 P.2d 229 (Haw. Ct. App. 1980).

There are, however, two situations in which the initial aggressor may regain the right to act in self-defense. The first is if the victim responds to the aggressor's use of nondeadly force with deadly force. In such instances, the aggressor can use whatever force is reasonably necessary (including deadly force) to repel the attack. The rationale used by the courts in this exception is that since nondeadly force cannot be met with deadly force, the victim has been threatened with unlawful harm. The other exception is when the aggressor withdraws from the fray first, but must then continue to defend himself or herself after being chased and continuously physically threatened by the other combatant.

LANDMARK CASE — People v. Goetz

In a New York subway, Bernhard Goetz shot and wounded several youths who he believed were trying to harass and rob him. The prosecutor instructed the grand jury that the defense of justification was available if Goetz reasonably used deadly force. Goetz successfully moved to dismiss the indictment for attempted murder on the basis that the self-defense justification was available if he subjectively believed that his life was in danger. The prosecution appealed the dismissal by the grand jury. At issue is whether a person is justified in using force against another if he or she reasonably believes such force is necessary to defend himself or herself. The New York appellate court said yes. This is an objective test, said the court, and is not available when the person acts solely under a subjective belief that he or she is in danger. In this case, Goetz acted out of past experience with muggers and not based on the circumstances presented. The test is an objective one, and hence the indictment was proper, reversing the decision that sent Goetz into trial.

Source: People v. Goetz, 506 N.Y.S.2d 18, 497 N.E.2d 41 (1986).

LANDMARK CASE — People v. Vogel

Vogel was told by his wife that she was going to divorce him and marry Earl Heck. She said she had married Heck and was living with him. Based on this, Vogel remarried, believing that he was divorced. He was arrested for bigamy. He unsuccessfully made a motion to admit evidence of his good faith belief that he was divorced. He was convicted and appealed. The issue before the California Supreme Court was whether a person who remarries under the good-faith belief that he or she was single is still guilty of bigamy. The court held that he was not, and stated that when Vogel remarried under the reasonable bona fide belief that he was single, he was not guilty of bigamy. The crime of bigamy requires knowledge of multiple marriages as an essential element of the crime. Therefore, his mistake of fact was an absolute defense to the case, and the decision was reversed.

Source: People v. Vogel, 46 Cal. 2d 798 (1986) (en banc)

The Defense of Ignorance or Mistake of Fact

Generally, *ignorance or mistake of fact* surrounding the commission of the crime is an affirmative defense that will prevent criminal liability if the defendant lacked the knowledge of the true facts of the situation. A basic principle of criminal law is that the defendant cannot be convicted where it is shown that he or she did not have the necessary mental state. Here, simple ignorance (that is, the defendant never thought about the matter), not affirmative mistake (that is, the defendant thought about the matter but reached the wrong conclusion), negates the essential mental state for a valid defense. Traditionally, the mistake of fact must be reasonable; that is, one that a reasonable person would also have made under the circumstances. However, many courts have not required a showing of reasonableness where the mistake is offered to negate the existence of the specific intent required for guilt. (See the Landmark Case *People v. Vogel*).

The Defense of Protection of Property

The right to use force in the protection of one's property is much more limited than the right to use force for the protection of one's person. However, unlike the limitations on the use of deadly force, nondeadly force may be used to protect both real and personal property and one's possessions if it appears reasonably necessary to prevent or terminate an unlawful intrusion into or interference with property.

There are limited instances where one may use deadly force in defense of a dwelling. Under common law, the courts viewed even the use of deadly force in defense of one's dwelling to be legal if it reasonably appeared necessary to prevent a forcible entry into the dwelling and a warning was first given to the intruder to desist and not enter. However, modern courts have limited the use of deadly force in the defense of one's dwelling. The general rule of law is that the use of deadly force in such an instance is permissible only (1) if the defendant reasonably believed that the intruder intended to commit a felony and (2) if there was a great likelihood that the intruder would harm someone in the dwelling because he or she was perceived to be dangerous. Some courts have adopted an even narrower view by recognizing that the use of deadly force to protect a dwelling is reasonable only if it is used for thwarting the felony and if the intruder is dangerous. (See the Landmark Case *State v. Mitcheson*.)

Special problems are encountered any time a property owner uses mechanical devices such as spring guns to protect his or her property through the use of force. Traditionally, a killing or injury inflicted by a mechanical device is never justifiable. Rarely, the law ties the use of such devices to a very restricted right to the use of deadly force in the defense of a dwelling. However, the Model Penal Code suggests that a mechanical device designed or known to cause death or serious bodily harm is never permissible.[39]

CTQ

How is this defense of ignorance or mistake of fact reconciled to the legal cliché "ignorance of the law is no excuse"?

LANDMARK CASE — State v. Mitcheson

Mitcheson's father purchased a vehicle from Herrera, and a conflict concerning the terms of the sale subsequently arose. On several occasions, Mitcheson and Herrera had heated arguments, and several attempts at physical injury were undertaken. Mitcheson was engaged in a card game one day at his sister's house when Herrera and a friend entered the premises and ignored demands to leave. Mitcheson shot and killed Herrera during the commotion. He was tried for second-degree murder and contended he was justified in using force to protect his habitat from invasion. Mitcheson was convicted and appealed his conviction, contending that the refusal to instruct on defense of habitat was reversible error.

The issue before the Utah Supreme Court was whether Mitcheson was justified in using deadly force against another in protecting his habitat. The court said, in direct contradiction to the overwhelming majority of other states, yes. This justification for the use of force dates back to common-law concepts of the sanctity of the home. The rationale is to preserve the peace and good order of society. Therefore, the justification should be interpreted broadly enough to include not only the defendant's actual place of residence, but also whatever dwelling he is peacefully occupying as a substitute home. The defense of dwelling was allowed and the case was reversed.

Source: State v. Mitcheson, 560 P.2d 1120 (1977).

CTQ

Can you make an argument for the fact that many Americans believe that whenever one finds an intruder in one's home, one has the right to use deadly force against the intruder?

CTQ

In the last thirty years, police shooting suspects have been the cause of many urban riots and loss of life, infliction of personal injury, and millions of dollars in property damage to the entire community. Does this counterbalance the officer's right to use deadly force to effect an arrest in terms of the overall social good?

FIGURE 9.10

The arrest of suspect Rodney King by the Los Angeles police was caught on videotape, which revealed six officers wielding their batons at a seemingly defenseless King. At trial the officers defended their actions, claiming that the law allows them as much force as necessary to subdue an arrestee and that King was still resisting.

Courtesy of Dan Levine/TimePix.

The Defense of the Use of Force to Effect an Arrest

While both private citizens and police officers generally have a right to use force to effect an arrest, the availability of this specific defense usually arises in the context of police activity. The defense of the use of force to effect an arrest is an affirmative defense that justifies an officer's use of whatever amount of nondeadly force that reasonably appears necessary to use in order to make the full custodial arrest (bringing the suspect into physical submission) for a felony or a misdemeanor. However, the use of deadly force traditionally has been limited only to situations where the officer reasonably believes that the suspect committed a felony or is an escaping felon and is presently dangerous. Thus, if an officer can apprehend a misdemeanor suspect only by using a gun (or other deadly instrument), the officer must forgo the arrest and let the suspect escape.

Modern statutes and case law have limited the use of deadly force to effect an arrest only to "dangerous felonies." The courts have reasoned that there are far more felonies today than there were at common law. Other courts reject the traditional distinction between arrests for felonies and misdemeanors. These courts hold that the use of deadly force to effect an arrest is permissible only if the officer is unable to apprehend a fleeing felon and has reason to believe that the suspect has committed a dangerous felony—that is, one involving physical harm to others, such as murder, manslaughter, kidnapping, rape, or robbery.

Similarly, the Model Penal Code legalizes the use of deadly force to effect an arrest if its use is limited only to situations where the crime for which the arrest is being made involves the use of threatened or deadly force, or if there is a substantial risk that the suspect would cause death or serious bodily injury if the arrest were delayed. Of course, an officer who meets resistance in attempting to arrest a suspect has the right to use force (including deadly force) in his or her own self-defense. However, the affirmative defense issue here is one of self-defense for the officer. This affirmative defense should be carefully distinguished from the use of force (deadly or nondeadly) to effect an arrest.

In any case, police officers are entitled to use force to make an arrest as long as they reasonably believe that the suspect has committed a felony and that the force used was necessary for the arrest. (See Figure 9.10.) The officer has this affirmative defense even if that belief turns out to be wrong. Again, reasonable appearances, not the ultimate

LANDMARK CASE — Tennessee v. Garner

Garner was shot and killed by a Tennessee police officer while fleeing the scene of a felony. The officer saw that Garner was unarmed, yet shot him to prevent his escape. Garner's father sued, contending that the use of deadly force by a police officer in this type of situation, where the fleeing victim is unarmed, is unconstitutional. The trial court entered a judgment in favor of the state of Tennessee, holding that the statute allowing such force was constitutional. The U.S. Supreme Court then ruled, answering no to the the question of whether deadly force may be used to prevent an escape of an unarmed, nonviolent felon. It held that deadly force may not be used unless (1) it is necessary to prevent escape, and (2) the officer harbors a good-faith belief that the suspect poses a significant threat of death or serious injury to the officer or others. Both of these requirements must be met, the Court went on to say, and the case was of constitutional significance because an arrest is in fact a seizure, which as an unreasonable procedure is protected by the Fourth Amendment. The Court said "the seizure in the case of the non-violent felon occurs when he is ordered to stop and relinquish himself to police. Use of deadly force when that order is ignored goes beyond the constitutional bounds of reasonable force unless deadly force has been threatened." Thus, the statute allowing for such force was unconstitutional.

Source: Tennessee v. Garner, 471 U.S. 1 (1985).

---

truth, control this defense of the use of force to effect an arrest. (See the Landmark Case *Tennessee v. Garner.*)

The Battered-Spouse Defense

The battered-spouse defense presents interesting legal issues when a defendant claims a long history of physical abuse. In such cases, the defendant must have been attacked by the victim and endured a long episode of physical abuse. Usually, under this defense, the use of force appears to be unreasonable, since most defendants appear to have the option of leaving their attacker rather than killing the person (thousands of battered women *do* leave their abusive spouses rather than being killed by them). However, even though the threat of immediate harm (which is a traditional necessary element of self-defense) is not apparent in the home at the time the crime is committed, the legal theory of the battered-spouse defense, according to some courts, is reasonable. These cases insist that the actions of a battered woman, or sometimes a battered child, must be evaluated in light of the battered person's physical and psychological characteristics.[40] These courts have further stated that a battered woman's specific experiences, and perhaps the disadvantaged position that women have occupied in society, are relevant to determining her level of apprehensiveness when she killed her spouse.

When determining whether the battered-spouse defense is relevant to the case as a form of self-defense, juries may be instructed to determine whether the spouse actually believed, although it may have been an unreasonable belief, that her life was in imminent danger and that killing the attacker immediately would be her only means to survive. Under this approach, certain attacks by a battered spouse may be determined to have been reasonable responses (self-defense) to the battering spouse's brutal conduct. (See the Landmark Case *People v. Humphrey.*)

The rationale of the defendant spouse's point of view that supports the affirmative defense of the battered-spouse defense has been applied in some instances when battered children have killed their parents—some apparently for financial gain, like the Menendez brothers.

> **CTQ**
> Since the battered-spouse defense is based on the concept of self-defense, does not the fact that when the defendant was killed, there was no immediate threat to her life negate the legal principle upon which the defense is based?

> **CTQ**
> Many argue that battered children and spouses can just flee from the threat posed by their abusers. If this is so, why are they allowed to use these defenses?

LANDMARK CASE: People v. Humphrey

Humphrey killed her abusive boyfriend and was charged with murder. She claimed that it was in self-defense, and presented expert testimony at trial on battered-woman syndrome. To prove that the killing was in self-defense, Humphrey was required to show that she actually and reasonably believed in the need to defend herself. The trial court instructed the jury that they could consider the evidence in deciding whether the defendant actually believed it was necessary to kill in self-defense, but not in deciding whether that belief was reasonable. The jury found Humphrey guilty of voluntary manslaughter. Humphrey appealed, claiming that the jury instructions given were improper. The California Supreme Court had to answer the issue of whether the right to kill in self-defense exists if the defendant reasonably believes in the existence of imminent harm, evaluated objectively from the standpoint of a reasonable person *in the defendant's position*—that is, a person who is a reasonable person and also a battered woman. The court said yes. Therefore, the Court held that the jury instructions were prejudicially erroneous because evidence of battered-woman syndrome might have helped the jury understand the circumstances in which the defendant found herself at the time of the killing, and was relevant to the reasonableness of her belief. The court concluded that the jury, not the expert, should determine whether the defendant's actions were objectively reasonable from a battered spouse's point of view.

Source: *People v. Humphrey*, 56 Cal. Rptr. 2d 142 (1996).

Other affirmative defenses have their own particular rules and limitations (see Table 9.4). What must be remembered is that although sometimes a new affirmative defense is allowed in some jurisdictions (such as the battered-spouse defense and the battered-child defense), criminal defendants are almost always limited to only affirmative defenses articulated by the law of the state in which the crime was committed.

TABLE 9.4 Traditional and Nontraditional Affirmative Defenses

Traditional Affirmative Defenses	Innovative Defenses
Self-defense	Abuse defense
Defense of others	Premenstrual syndrome
Defense of home or property	Other biological defenses
Necessity	Black rage
Consent	Urban survival syndrome
Resisting unlawful arrest	The twinkie defense
Duress	Road rage
Age	Airport rage
Mistake	
Involuntary intoxication	
Unconsciousness	
Provocation	
Insanity	
Diminished capacity	

REBUTTAL AND SURREBUTTAL

At the conclusion of the defense's case, the prosecution is given an opportunity for *rebuttal*. That is, it may summon additional witnesses to buttress its case, which may have been weakened by evidence and testimony presented by the defense. Testimony offered in rebuttal must be limited to matters covered in the defense's case.

Often rebuttal witnesses are used by the prosecution in an attempt to introduce evidence that it forgot to present or overlooked in the state's case in chief (the state's initial presentation of all of its evidence followed by the statement "The state rests"). As such, this evidence does *not* rebut the evidence offered by the defense. However, evidence introduced as rebuttal evidence to support the prosecution's original case rather than to rebut the evidence offered by the defense is inadmissible.

In addition, if the prosecutor chooses to conduct a rebuttal, the defense may summon *surrebuttal* witnesses to bolster its case. Defense surrebuttal witnesses are likewise limited to testifying only about matters covered in the testimony of the prosecution rebuttal witnesses.

CTQ

Presently, under the rules of evidence, the prosecution does not have to advise the defense of the availability or the existence of any of their rebuttal witnesses. Is this nondisclosure essentially consistent with a fair trial?

CLOSING ARGUMENTS

Before attorneys give their closing arguments to a jury, they have already made a series of motions before the judge outside of the jury's hearing. These motions usually contain the attorneys' proposed instructions that they believe the jury should receive from the judge concerning which laws are appropriate to the specific case at trial. By the time of closing arguments, the judge will have ruled on what law he or she considers proper and the ones that will be instructed to the jury.

Most trial attorneys consider the *closing arguments* the prime opportunity to practice their craft as a criminal lawyer. Closing arguments, or summations, challenge the defense counsel and the prosecutor to summarize evidence and testimony and the applicable law to persuade the jury to accept their interpretation of the case. Normally, the state, which has the burden of proof in a case, argues first and the defense argues second. Under the theory that the state has the burden of proof, some jurisdictions allow the prosecution then to rebut the defense arguments. In other states, closing arguments from the defense lawyer are the last words spoken from the attorneys on the case. The closing arguments are the opposing lawyers' last opportunity to articulate clearly their theories of the defendant's guilt or innocence based on the evidence and the law.

At one time, the summation (closing arguments) was a theatrical display of forensic eloquence, as the opposing attorneys sought to influence the emotions of the jury. Hence, the old adage for trial lawyers: If the law is against you, pound the facts; if the facts are against you, pound the law; if both the law and the facts are against you, pound the table. At present, table pounding is considered in poor taste by most judges, and excessive flamboyance on the part of either counsel is apt to draw a rebuke from the bench.

THE TRIAL JUDGE'S CHARGE TO THE JURY

When all of the evidence has been presented and both sides have rested their cases, it is the responsibility of the judge to instruct, or charge the jury. As already noted, it is the prerogative of the jury to decide the facts, but the court must instruct the members of the jury on the aspects of the law that apply to the case. In instructing the jury, the judge must clearly explain the law arising from the evidence. The judge also instructs the jury on the possible verdicts, the law of the rules of evidence that manifested themselves in the case, and the meaning of the "reasonable doubt" standard. Furthermore, the judge will instruct the jury on the elements of the alleged crime(s), and the fact that each and every element must be proven beyond a reasonable doubt or the jury must find the defendant not guilty. The judge further instructs the jurors to review all the evidence thoroughly and tells them the procedures they should use during their deliberations.

CTQ

Practicing criminal trial lawyers generally agree that the most important part of their case is their closing argument. Why do you think they consistently believe this to be the case?

THE JURY'S DELIBERATIONS

After receiving their instructions, the jurors retire to the jury room to begin their deliberations in an effort to arrive at a verdict. The conduct of jurors and the procedures governing jury deliberations are established by local statutes and court rules. Generally, such rules restrict the members of the jury from communicating with anyone except the bailiff or the judge during their deliberations. Most jurisdictions do not allow the jury to separate once deliberations have begun. If it appears that jury deliberations might continue for more than several hours, arrangements may have to be made to sequester the jury in an adjacent hotel or motel.

CTQ: What is the major problem with the judge's instruction to the jury, and the fact that the judge is not present during jury deliberations?

THE JURY'S VERDICT

A unanimous verdict in criminal cases has been a basic requirement of common law since the fourteenth century, and remains federal case law. The U.S. Supreme Court upheld this requirement in both the nineteenth and twentieth centuries, and most states have endorsed this position in their provisions for jury trials. However, in 1972, the Court held that Louisiana's use of 9–3 verdicts in major criminal cases was constitutional;[41] a similar decision was made in 1972 regarding Oregon's use of 10–2 verdicts in serious criminal cases[42] (see a more complete explanation of this legal point in Chapter 3). More recently, the Court dealt with the issue of less-than-unanimous verdicts in cases involving juries with fewer than twelve members. In 1979, the Court held that where the jury consists of only six members and it renders[43] a 5–1 vote for conviction, the vote is invalid and violates the Sixth Amendment. The jury's verdict can be any of the following: (1) guilty of the crime charged, (2) not guilty of the crime charged, (3) guilty of the lesser included offense of the crime charged, (4) not guilty by reason of insanity, or (5) a hung jury.

CTQ: Should the jury have a written copy of the judge's instructions during their deliberations so they can refer to what the law actually states?

A Hung Jury

If a jury is hopelessly deadlocked and cannot render a unanimous verdict after prolonged deliberations, it may return to the courtroom, where the judge will instruct the members to go back to the jury room for a final effort to arrive at a verdict. The judge usually sets a specific time period for this to be done. If all reasonable methods are exhausted without reaching unanimity—resulting in a *hung jury*—the judge dismisses the jury, declares a mistrial, and schedules a retrial of the case with a new jury. Sometimes after a hung jury, the prosecution decides not to retry the case.

CTQ: Presently, jurors are prohibited from discussing with attorneys the manner in which they deliberated, even though attorneys believe it would be most helpful to know this information. Should attorneys be given access to jurors to discuss the full nature of their deliberations?

Polling the Jury

When the jury returns a verdict, the defense counsel or the prosecutor may request that the jurors be polled. Each juror is asked individually by the court clerk or the judge if the verdict announced is his or her verdict. The rationale for this procedure is to determine whether each juror is voting freely according to the dictates of conscience or is responding to pressure from fellow jurors. If polling discloses a less-than-unanimous verdict where one is required by law, the jury may be instructed to return to the jury room and continue its deliberations, or it may be dismissed and a mistrial declared. A mistrial places the defendant in the same position as if no trial had occurred, and proceedings may be reinstated against the defendant. However, if the verdict is not guilty, the defendant is discharged and free to go his or her own way.

CTQ: As we enter the twenty-first century, how can we make the jury system more workable?

Jury Nullification

One of the little-known procedures in criminal trials is *jury nullification*, which occurs in one of two ways. The first is when juries do not follow the court's interpretation of the law in every instance or otherwise "nullify" or suspend the force of strict legal procedure. For a jury nullification to occur, the jurors may have disregarded what they were told about the law or certain aspects of evidence because they considered the application of certain laws to be unjust.

CTQ: Some people argue that the way to eliminate a hung jury is to allow nonunanimous verdicts. Do you agree with this assessment?

Yet jury nullification is a two-fold process. When a verdict of guilty is returned by a jury and, in the judge's opinion the verdict represents an erroneous decision, the judge has the power to refuse to abide by the jury's verdict and may direct the jury to acquit the accused. This is another form of jury nullification. At other times the judge may tell the jury to "arrest" its verdict and enter a judgment of acquittal. However, a trial judge does not have the authority to direct a jury to convict and enter a judgment arresting (i.e., holding in abeyance) a verdict of guilty. Finally, the judge can nullify the jury verdict by finding the defendant guilty of a lesser included offense.

Although jury nullification in legal circumstances has always meant the judge's exercise of his or her prerogative to change a jury verdict in favor of the defendant, the term now seems to have taken on a colloquial meaning expressing just its opposite. Many laypeople consider jury nullification an event that occurs only when the jury nullifies the law by acquitting a defendant who may be guilty according to an instruction given by the court. In other words, according to this particular notion, the jury acquits in spite of the evidence rather than because of it.[44]

CTQ

What can we do to correct the two aspects of jury nullification? Should they be corrected?

Postverdict Motions

If the jury returns a guilty verdict, the defense may make a *motion for a judgment of acquittal*. The motion may be made before the case goes to the jury and probably is more appropriately done at that time. The motion is based on the argument that the evidence is not sufficient to support a guilty verdict. The court may be more likely to grant that motion before the jury has returned a verdict, particularly in a close case.

The more common motion made by the defense after a guilty verdict is a motion for a new trial. This motion may be made on several specific grounds or on general grounds—that is, a new trial is in the interest of justice. Court rules or statutes may enumerate specific grounds on which this motion may be based. But assuming that even after all the various defense motions, the guilty verdict still stands, some serious economic, social, and political consequences to a defendant convicted of a felony then follow (see "In the News: How Serious Is a Felony Conviction? It Depends on What State You Are In").

CTQ

Should the judge have the power to enter a verdict of not guilty after a jury of one's peers has found the defendant guilty beyond a reasonable doubt?

IN THE NEWS

A HUMAN PERSPECTIVE

HOW SERIOUS IS A FELONY CONVICTION? IT DEPENDS ON WHAT STATE YOU ARE IN

In addition to the sentence which is imposed upon a convicted felon, numerous civil disabilities often are imposed. These disabilities, which adversely affect an offender not only during his or her incarceration but also after release, include denial of such privileges as voting, holding public office, possession of a firearm, and maintaining family relations. In some states, persons convicted of serious crimes are declared civilly dead, which means that all rights and privileges of the convicted offender (including the right to contract and to sue and be sued) are forfeited.

Scholars surveyed the fifty states and the District of Columbia statutes, case laws, and attorneys general in a review of the specific privileges and rights that felons might lose after conviction. Their major findings were as follows:

1. Eleven states permanently disenfranchise the felon from state and federal elections, both during and after confinement in prison.
2. In sixteen states courts may terminate parenting rights on the conviction or incarceration of a parent.
3. Twenty-eight states permit divorce for conviction or imprisonment of a felony.
4. Six states permanently bar convicted felons from public employment in their home states.
5. Convicted felons may not hold public office in nineteen states.
6. Thirty-one states forbid "violent" felons from possessing firearms.
7. In thirty-one states convicted felons are permanently barred from jury duty.
8. Eight states require felons to register as former offenders.
9. Four states continue the practice of civil death.

Source: "How Serious Is a Felony Conviction? It Depends on What State You Are In," *The New York Times,* March 5, 1992. Reprinted with permission of *The New York Times.*

Summary

Compared with the total volume of cases entering the criminal justice system, relatively few cases are disposed of by a criminal trial. Nevertheless, the criminal trial is an indispensable feature of our system. The accused is brought to trial under the presumption of innocence; it is the task of the prosecution to prove beyond a reasonable doubt that the defendant is guilty of the crime with which he or she is charged. The burden of proof, however, during the conservative 1980s and 1990s, has shifted somewhat. For example, should the defendant plead insanity in many courts, the burden of proof is on the defendant to prove either by clear and convincing evidence or by a preponderance of the evidence that he or she was insane when the crime was committed.

The adversary concept of criminal justice is most clearly exhibited at trial. The prosecutor uses the authority and the resources of the state in an attempt to gather enough evidence to convince the court and a jury of the guilt of the defendant. The defense counsel attacks weaknesses of the prosecution's case, seeks to impeach the testimony of state's witnesses, questions the validity and reliability of the prosecution's evidence, and is alert to any tactics of the opposing counsel that may violate the constitutional rights of his or her client.

An extremely important aspect of the trial is the selection of the people to serve on the jury. Jurors are chosen by a procedure called voir dire, which allows both lawyers to ask prospective jurors a multitude of questions and assigns the prosecution and the defense a number of challenges for cause (a stated reason or reasons why a particular person is unfit to serve on a jury) and peremptory challenges (challenges for which no reason need be given, except in the case of discrimination based on race). In recent years, there have been noteworthy attempts to use the methods of the social scientist to pick jurors who may be inclined to favor the defendant. This process of scientific jury selection has been attacked as "jury stacking" but also has been defended as a guarantor of fairness. Whatever its defects or merits, however, the expenses involved will probably keep it from becoming a routine procedure in criminal trials.

Trials are governed by the rules of criminal procedure and the rules of evidence that have evolved over many years and have been articulated by judges and criminal statutes. These rules are enforced by the trial judge who, during the trial, acts as a decision maker, arbitrator, and referee as to what the proper procedure will be and how the case will move forward. The jury can discern the facts of a case based only on competent, reliable, and relevant evidence presented to it by both sides. A series of rules has evolved concerning the inadmissibility of evidence that might somehow be relevant to the case but has been excluded based on its nature as either hearsay, confidential, opinion, or privileged evidence.

The order of the criminal trial may vary somewhat from one jurisdiction to another, but it generally conforms to a standard pattern. After the reading of the formal charges against the defendant, the prosecution presents its case by making an opening statement and then introducing evidence and witnesses whose testimony is subject to cross-examination by the defense. At the conclusion of the prosecution's case, the defense presents its case, including evidence and testimony. Often the defendant asserts his or her defense by attacking the state's case as failing to meet its burden of proof and thus resting, declaring that there was no wrongdoing. The defendant may also admit that he or she is guilty of the crime charged but is not criminally responsible for the act under an affirmative defense. Examples include the defense of infancy, the battered-spouse defense, the defense of insanity, self-defense, and the defense of mistake of fact. The defense may call the defendant to testify on his or her own behalf or may choose not to do so. Following the presentation of evidence, both counsel present closing arguments to the jury. Next, the judge instructs the jury on the specific law applicable to the particular case. Finally, the jury is sequestered and deliberates until it subsequently announces its verdict in open court. Sometimes the jury is hopelessly deadlocked in a case and cannot reach a unanimous verdict. This is called a hung jury, which causes a mistrial, requiring that the entire process be reinitiated. If a verdict is reached, often the lawyers poll the jury. This procedure requires each individual juror to stand up and convey his or her verdict to the open court. Jury nullification occurs when the trial judge lessens the jury's verdict and finds the defendant not guilty or guilty of a lesser included offense as a matter of law. Hence, a judge can indeed change or nullify a jury verdict, but only in favor of the defendant.

DISCUSSION AND REVIEW

1. How is the question of guilt disposed of by a criminal trial?
2. How does excessive pretrial publicity endanger a defendant's Sixth Amendment right to a fair and impartial jury?
3. What is the significance of counsel's opening statement?
4. What are affirmative defenses and how are they used as procedures in a criminal trial to determine guilt or innocence of the defendant?
5. Discuss the distinctions among real, testimonial, and circumstantial evidence.
6. How does competent evidence differ from relevant evidence? From material evidence? How is the competency of a witness established?
7. Distinguish between privileged communications and confidential communications. Which types of confidential communications are protected by law?
8. How does the "beyond a reasonable doubt" standard of proof differ from the "preponderance of evidence" standard?
9. What do the terms "presumption of innocence" and "proof beyond a reasonable doubt" mean? How do they operate in a criminal trial?
10. Distinguish between direct examination and cross-examination. What limitations are imposed on cross-examination?
11. What are some of the major rights of the defendant with respect to the admissibility of evidence and testimony in a criminal trial?
12. What are the legal definitions of insanity, and what happens to those found not guilty by reason of insanity?
13. Distinguish between incompetency and insanity. Why is the insanity defense so controversial if it is used so sparingly in criminal trials?
14. What is the significance of the M'Naghten rule?
15. What are the elements of self-defense?
16. Compare and contrast the following terms: *jury deliberation, jury nullification, charging the jury,* and *jury verdict*.
17. Describe the formal steps in a trial. Can we do anything to make the trial process more just or efficient?
18. What are challenges for cause? How do they affect the makeup of a jury?
19. Why are the jury instructions considered so important, and why are they so often the subject of appellate review?
20. What is the role of the jury in the criminal trial, and how does it differ from the role of the judge?
21. Describe the stages in the jury selection process.
22. What is jury nullification? Is it possible to control its effects in criminal trials?
23. Discuss the role of expert witnesses in the criminal trial.

CHAPTER RESOURCES

IN THE MEDIA

Video

A&E American Justice Video: *Why O. J. Simpson Won*

ABC News/Prentice Hall Video: *Color of Justice*

ABC News/Prentice Hall Video: *William Kennedy Smith Rape Trial*

CNN Today Video: *Criminology*, Vol. 4: segment 1, "The Insanity Defense"

Court TV Video: *The Greatest Trials of All Time — Sam Sheppard*

Court TV Video: Michigan v. Kevorkian: *Dr. Death or Angel of Mercy?*

Court TV Video: Vermont v. Grace

FAH Court's CJ videos

Insight Media Video: *The Anatomy of a Trial*

Insight Media Video: *Criminal Trial Procedure*

Insight Media Video: *Evidence*

Insight Media Video: *Eyewitnesses*

Insight Media Video: *Fact or Fiction*

Insight Media Video: *Going to Court*

Insight Media Video: *The Great Crimes and Trials of the Twentieth Century*

Insight Media Video: *Landmark American Trials*

Insight Media Video: *The O. J. Simpson Trial*

Insight Media Video: *The Rodney King Case: What a Jury Saw in California v. Powell*

Insight Media Video: *Trial by Jury*

Insight Media Video: *You Are the Jury*

NIJ Crime File videos

NIJ videos

PBS Video: *The State of Florida versus Ted Bundy*

Film

A Few Good Men (1992)

The Juror (1996)

A Time to Kill (1996)

The Verdict (1982)

Television

Law and Order

The Practice

IN THE LITERATURE

Books

J. ABRAMSON, *We, the Jury: The Jury System and the Ideal of Democracy*. New York: Basic Books, 1994.

J. BELLKNAP, *The Invisible Woman: Gender, Crime, and Justice*. Belmont, Calif.: Wadsworth, 2001.

S. BRILL, ed. *Trial by Jury: The Tactics, Deals, and Decisions That Determined the Outcome of Seventeen of the Decade's Biggest Legal Cases*. Englewood Cliffs, N.J.: Simon & Schuster, 1990.

L. CAPLAN, *The Insanity Defense and the Trial of John W. Hinckley, Jr."* Boston: Godine, 1984.

L. CHIASSON, *The Press on Trial: Crimes and Trials as Media Events*. Westport, Conn.: Praeger, 1997.

W. FREEMAN, *The Constitutional Right to a Fair and Speedy Criminal Trial*. New York: Quorum Books, 1989.

T. GARDNER AND T. ANDERSON, *Criminal Evidence: Principles and Cases*. Belmont, Calif.: Wadsworth, 2001.

R. GILES AND R. SNYDER, eds. *Covering the Courts: Free Press, Fair Trials, and Journalistic Performance*. New Brunswick, N.J.: Transaction, 1999.

R. GOLDFARB, *T.V. or Not T.V.: Television, Justice, and the Courts*. New York: New York University Press, 1998.

L. GREENFIELD AND T. SNELL, "Women Offenders." Washington, D.C.: Bureau of Justice Statistics, 1999. NCJ 175688.

V. HANS AND N. VIDMAR, *Judging the Jury*. New York: Plenum Press, 1986.

D. HEILVRONER, *Rough Justice: Days and Nights of a Young D.A.* New York: Pantheon, 1989.

M. KURLAND, *How to Try a Murder: The Handbook for Armchair Lawyers*. New York: Macmillan General Reference, 1998.

E. LOFTUS, AND K. KETCHAM, *Witness for the Defense*. New York: St. Martin's Press, 1991.

C. MANN, *Unequal Justice: A Question of Color*. Bloomington: Indiana University Press, 1993.

L. MCINTYRE, *The Public Defender: The Practice of Law in the Shadows of Repute*. Chicago: University of Chicago Press, 1987.

K. MILLER AND M. RADELET, *Executing the Mentally Ill: The Criminal Justice System and the Case of Alvin Ford.* Newbery Park, Calif.: Sage, 1993.

L. MORRIS, *The Brothel Boy and Other Parables of the Law.* New York: Oxford University Press, 1992.

G. MUNSTERMAN, P. HANNAFORD, AND G. WHITEHEAD, eds., *Jury Trial Innovations.* Williamsburg, Va.: National Center for State Courts, 1997.

National Institute of Justice, *Eyewitness Evidence: A Guide for Law Enforcement.* Washington, D.C.: U.S. Department of Justice, 1999.

R. SATTER, *Doing Justice: A Trial Judge at Work.* New York: Simon & Schuster, 1990.

R. SIMON, *The Jury and the Defense of Insanity,* 2nd ed. Boston: Little, Brown, 1998.

R. SIMON AND J. LANDIS, *The Crimes Women Commit, the Punishments They Receive.* New York: Lexington Books, 1991.

S. WALKER, C. STOHN, AND M. DELONE, *The Color of Justice,* 2nd ed. Belmont, Calif.: Wadsworth, 2000.

Articles

J. BACKSTRAND, D. GIBBONS, AND J. JONES, "Who Is in Jail: An Examination of the Rapid Hypothesis," *Journal of Crime and Delinquency,* vol. 38 (1992), pp. 219–220.

R. BOATRIGHT, "The 21st Century American Jury: Reflections from the CANTIGNY Conference," *Judicature,* vol. 83 (2000), pp. 288–297.

R. BONNIE, N. POYTHRESS, S. HOGE, AND J. MONAHAN, "Decision Making and Criminal Defense: An Empirical Study of Insanity Pleas and the Impact of Doubted Client Confidence," *Journal of Criminal Law and Criminology,* vol. 87 (1996), pp. 48–76.

D. BRODY, "Balancing Jury Secrecy and the Rule of Law: Second Circuit's Guide to Nullifying Jurors," *Justice System Journal,* vol. 20 (1998), pp. 113–120.

L. CAO, A. ADAMS, AND V. JENSEN, "A Tale of a Black Subculture and Violence Thesis: Research Methods," *Criminology,* vol. 34 (1997), pp. 367–379.

J. DUNAWAY, F. COLLINS, V. BURTON, AND T. EVANS, "The Myth of Social Class and Crime Revisited: An Examination of Class and Adult Criminality," *Criminology,* vol. 38 (2000), pp. 589–613.

H. FAHRINGER, "The Peremptory Challenge: An Endangered Species?" *Criminal Law Bulletin,* Vol. 84 (1995), pp. 400–463.

J. HILLWIZE, "Religion-Based Peremptory Challenges Are Unconstitutional," *Trial Magazine,* vol. 35 (1999), p. 15.

T. HOGAN, G. MISE, AND K. CLARK, "How to Improve the American Jury," *World and I,* vol. 13 (1998), p. 64.

I. HOROWITZ AND T. WILGING, "Changing Views on Jury Power: The Nullification Debate 1787–1998," *Journal of Law and Human Behavior,* vol. 15 (1991), p. 165.

P. JENKINS AND B. DAVIDSON, "Battered Women and the Criminal Justice System: Analysis of Gender Stereotypes," *Behavioral Sciences and the Law,* vol. 8 (1990), pp. 161–170.

L. KROHMAN, "Constituting Power and Sexual Assault Cases: Prosecutorial Strategies for Victim Management," *Journal of Social Problems,* vol. 45 (1998), pp. 393–427.

G. LAFREY AND K. RUSSEL, "The Argument for Studying Race and Crime," *Journal of Criminal Justice Education,* vol. 4 (1993), pp. 273–289.

K. VERNETTE, "Letting Focus Groups Work for You," *Trial,* vol. 35 (1999), p. 74.

N. WONDERS, "Women's Work? A Contradictory Implication of the Courses on Women and the Criminal Justice System," *Journal of Criminal Justice Education,* vol. 4 (1993), pp. 79–100.

E. ZAKARIA, "The Role of Juries and the Justice System," *Contemporary View,* vol. 274 (1999), p. 277.

CASES

Apodaca v. Oregon, 406 U.S. 404 (1972)
Burch v. Louisiana, 446 U.S. 130 (1979)
Caribbean International News Corp. v. Puerto Rico, 508 U.S. 147 (1993)
Chandler v. Florida, 449 U.S. 560 (1981)
Estelle v. Williams, 425 U.S. 501 (1976)
Estes v. Texas, 381 U.S. 532 (1965)
Irvin v. Dowd, 366 U.S. 717 (1961)
Johnson v. Louisiana, 409 U.S. 1085 (1972)
Kentucky v. Whorton, 441 U.S. 786 (1979)
M'Naghten case, 8 Eng. Rep. 718 (1843)
Mu'Min v. Virginia, 500 U.S. 415 (1991)
Nebraska Press Association v. Stuart, 427 U.S. 539 (1976)
People v. Goetz, 506 N.Y.S.2d 18, 497 N.E.2d 41 (1986)
People v. Humphrey, 56 Cal. Rptr. 2d 142 (1996)
People v. Vogel, 46 Cal. 2d 798 (1986) (en banc)
Press Enterprise Company v. Superior Capital Court of California, 478 U.S. 1 (1986)
Rideau v. Louisiana, 373 U.S. 723 (1963)
State v. Leidholm, 334 N.W.2d 811 (N.D. 1983)
State v. Mitcheson, 560 P.2d 1120 (1977)
State v. Norman, 378 S.E. 8 (N.C. 1989)
State v. Realina, 1 Haw. 167, 616 P.2d 229 (Haw. Ct. App. 1980)
Tennessee v. Garner, 471 U.S. 1 (1985)
Turner v. Louisiana, 379 U.S. 466 (1965)
Washington v. Texas, 388 U.S. 14 (1967)

STATUTES

Fed. R. Evid. 607–609, 803, 805
Fla. Stat. ch. 3.129 (1998)

Model Penal Code §§ 3.06(5), 3.11(2)

ENDNOTES

1. A. Smith and H. Pollack, *Criminal Justice in a Mass Society*. New York: Holt, Rinehart, & Winston, 1972, p. 137.

2. J. Frank, *Courts on Trial: Myth and Reality in American Justice*. Princeton N.J.: Princeton University Press, 1949.

3. L. Thora, "The Adversary System." in Bearman, ed., *Talk of American Law*. New York: Vintage Books, 1960, pp. 30–43.

4. *American Bar Association Journal*, vol. 71 (December 1985), p. 35.

5. *Kentucky v. Whorton*, 441 U.S. 786 (1979).

6. H. Black, *Black's Law Dictionary*, 5th abridged ed. St. Paul, Minn.: West, 1983), p. 635.

7. Y. Kamisar, W. LaFave, and G. Israel, *Basic Criminal Procedure*. St. Paul, Minn.: West, 2002.

8. *Estelle v. Williams*, 425 U.S. 501 (1976).

9. Ibid.

10. *Turner v. Louisiana*, 379 U.S. 466 (1965).

11. *Estes v. Texas*, 381 U.S. 532 (1965).

12. *Chandler v. Florida*, 449 U.S. 560 (1981).

13. *Estelle v. Williams*, op. cit.

14. *Nebraska Press Association v. Stuart*, 427 U.S. 539 (1976).

15. *Press Enterprise Co. v. Superior Capital Court of California*, 478 U.S. 1 (1986).

16. *Caribbean International News Corp. v. Puerto Rico*, 508 U.S. 147 (1993).

17. D. Couchon, "Federal Courts, Cameraless," *USA Today*, March 10, 1993, p. A2.

18. Ibid.

19. *Chandler v. Florida*, op. cit.

20. "Judicial Conference Rejects Cameras in Federal Courts," *Criminal Justice Newsletter*, September 1994, vol. 15, p. 6.

21. *Irvin v. Dowd*, 366 U.S. 717 (1961).

22. *Mu'Min v. Virginia*, 500 U.S. 415 (1991).

23. *Rideau v. Louisiana*, 373 U.S. 723 (1963).

24. All of these cases were tried in the 1990s: William Kennedy Smith, great-nephew of President John Fitzgerald Kennedy, was tried in Florida for raping an acquaintance. He used the media to degrade the reputation of the acquaintance and was acquitted. In O. J. Simpson's case, which was also called the case of the century, his lawyers successfully used the media to present their defense of incompetency and racism in the Los Angeles Police Department. The Rodney King case involved four white officers mercilessly beating King to effect an arrest under the watchful eye of a video camera for the whole nation to see. The officers were acquitted in their first trial but were retried in federal court and were convicted. After the first trial, massive rioting broke out in Los Angeles. Timothy McVeigh was convicted of the Oklahoma City bombing. His case was moved to Denver because of massive pretrial publicity, and he received the death sentence.

25. A. de Tocqueville, *Democracy in America*, ed. J. Mayer, trans. G. Lawrence. Garden City, N.Y.: Doubleday, 1969, p. 506.

26. J. Levine, *Juries and Politics*. Pacific Grove, Calif.: Brooks/Cole, 1992, p. 14.

27. H. Kalven and H. Zeisel, *The American Jury*. Chicago: University of Chicago Press, 1969.

28. K. Kleine, *The American Jury*. Chicago: University of Chicago Press, 1960.

29. S. Phillips, *No Heroes, No Villains: The Story of a Murder Trial*. New York: Vintage Books, 1978.

30. E. Loftus, *Eyewitness Testimony*. Cambridge, Mass.: Harvard University Press, 1979.

31. Fed. R. Evid. 805.

32. Fed. R. Evid. 607–609.

33. *Washington v. Texas*, 388 U.S. 14 (1967).

34. N. Morris, *Madness in the Criminal Law*. Chicago: University of Chicago Press, 1990.

35. American Law Institute, *Model Penal Code: Official Draft and Explanatory Notes*. Philadelphia: American Law Institute, 1985.

36. E. Silver, C. Cirincione, and H. Steadman, "Demythologizing Inaccurate Perceptions of the Insanity Defense," *Law and Human Behavior*, vol. 18 (1994), pp. 63–70.

37. *M'Naghten* case, 8 Eng. Rep. 718 (1843).

38. Model Penal Code § 3.11 (2).
39. Model Penal Code § 3.06(5).
40. *State v. Norman*, 378 S.E. 8 (N.C. 1989); *State v. Leidholm*, 334 N.W.2d 811 (N.D. 1983).
41. *Johnson v. Louisiana*, 409 U.S. 1085 (1972).
42. *Apodaca v. Oregon*, 406 U.S. 404 (1972).
43. *Burch v. Louisiana*, 446 U.S. 130 (1979).
44. L. Fleischer, "Does Jury Nullification Subvert the Rule of Law? Yes," *New York Law Journal*, June 25, 1997, p. 121.

10

SENTENCING, APPEALS, AND THE DEATH PENALTY

Chapter Outline

Theories of Punishment in the American Criminal Justice System
- The Effects of Prison Overcrowding on Judicial Sentencing
- Retribution
- Deterrence
- Incapacitation
- Rehabilitation/Treatment
- Reintegration

Sentencing
- The Sentencing Hearing
- The Victim-Impact Statement
- What Is Necessary for a Judge to Impose a Constitutional Sentence?

Sentencing Structures
- Determinate or Flat-Time Sentences
- Presumptive Sentences
- Indeterminate Sentences
- Mandatory Minimum Sentences

Enhancement Statutes—Two Punishments for One Crime
- Habitual-Criminal Statutes
- Hate Crimes
- The New Sentencing Structures of the Twenty-First Century

Traditional Sentencing Disparities
- Sentencing Guidelines—An Attempt to Resolve the Problem of Sentencing Disparities
- Gain Time, Good Time, and Actual Time Served

The Appeal Process
- Postconviction Relief—A Hidden Form of Appeal
- Discretionary Review—The Privileged Appeal
- Can a Convicted Defendant Appeal a Harsh Sentence?
- Clemency

The Death Penalty
- The Death Penalty and the Supreme Court
- The Role of the Jury in Capital Cases
- Supreme Court Limitations
- The Current Situation
- Public Attitudes toward the Death Sentence

Death Penalty Appeals

The Capital Punishment Debate
- The Argument That Capital Punishment Acts as a Deterrent
- The Retribution Argument
- The Arbitrariness Argument: The Role of Race and Gender
- The Danger-of-Mistake Argument
- The Incapacitation Argument

Minor Issues in the Capital Punishment Debate
- The Cost-Efficiency Argument
- The Community Protection Argument
- The Appeal-to-Public-Opinion Argument
- The Cruel-and-Unusual-Punishment Argument
- The Brutalization Argument

Summary

Key Terms

appellate review, p. 417
bifurcated trial, p. 402
clemency, p. 420
determinate or flat-time sentences, p. 408
deterrence, p. 399
discretionary review, p. 419
enhancement statutes, p. 410
general deterrence, p. 399
habeas corpus, p. 419
hate crimes, p. 413
incapacitation, p. 400
retribution, p. 398
retribution argument, p. 431
reversible error, p. 418
sentencing, p. 395
sentencing disparity, p. 413
specific deterrence, p. 399

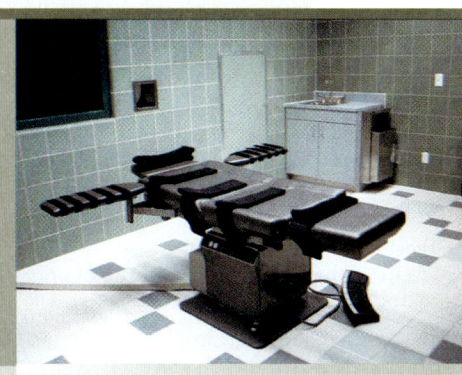

Courtesy of Chuck Robinson/AP Wide World Photos

After the conviction of the defendant during the criminal trial, the court's business with the defendant is not complete. Once a defendant has been proven guilty beyond a reasonable doubt, the trial court has an additional obligation. In a separate hearing, the court must adjudicate an appropriate sentence for the defendant. The American criminal justice system's value of "justice" demands that guilty people must be punished for the crimes for which they have been convicted. The sentencing phase in the criminal justice system has brought some of the strongest and most controversial issues to the American public's consciousness. Cries of outrage from both conservatives and liberals inundate the criminal justice system, blasting the manner by which we punish convicted offenders. On one end of the spectrum are protests that the sentences are too harsh; at the other end, critics charge that guilty people are not being punished severely enough for heinous crimes they have committed.

The traditional roles of the criminal justice system have been to apprehend, convict, and punish offenders. **Sentencing** is a process by which judges impose punishment on people convicted of crimes. These punishments range from probation to the death penalty. Other sentences include fines, community service, and incarceration in jail or prison.

WEB

For more information on sentencing, **visit the link to the U.S. Sentencing Commission on our Web site,** www.prenhall.com/territo

WEB

For up-to-date information on sentencing reports, **visit the link to the Bureau of Justice Statistics on our Web site,** www.prenhall.com/territo

CTQ

Which of the goals of criminal sentencing do you think individual-rights advocates would most likely find attractive? Which ones would crime-control advocates find attractive? Why?

Historically, punishments have involved a full range of effects. Defendants have been sentenced to hard labor, branded, whipped, tortured, and killed. Although many changes have occurred in our society in the last century, the orientation of the criminal justice system is still primarily punitive. Based on the historical systems that have shaped our ideas of law and justice, it is difficult to see how it could have been otherwise; and it is almost impossible to imagine any fundamental changes in the administration of justice without sweeping changes in the basic nature of our society and culture. At the same time, it must be emphasized that punishment for the sake of vengeance alone never has enjoyed unqualified support in this country. However, exceptions to this general rule are on the upswing. In certain states, correctional statutes offer retribution by the state as the sole purpose for a guilty person's incarceration. Recently, one thing can be said for certain about sentencing and its consequences: There has been a dramatic rise in state and federal prison populations (see Figure 10.1).

THEORIES OF PUNISHMENT IN THE AMERICAN CRIMINAL JUSTICE SYSTEM

Punishment is familiar to us in all aspects of life. We are acquainted with its use in the family and in the school; we employ punishment of various kinds with our pets, our children, and with one another; we believe that we understand the operation of punishment, and we can generally foresee its effects when it is employed. Through the use of positive sanctions (such as rewards or reinforcements), groups and societies seek to encourage conformity to various norms; by means of negative sanctions (punishments), attempts are made to discourage deviant behavior.

Reward and punishment, two of the principal techniques or processes for affecting behavior, have been familiar to the philosopher—or indeed to any person with an inquisitive mind—since time immemorial. The notion that people seek to maximize pleasure and avoid pain or discomfort was already ancient when it found its way into Jeremy Bentham's hedonistic calculus. Similar ideas have been expressed by the ancient Greek and Roman philosophers, such as Marcus Aurelius, and in the theories of modern psychiatrists and psychologists, such as Freud's pleasure principle and B. F. Skinner's views on reinforcement. However, these ideas did little more than restate the idea in a more sophisticated form.[1]

The use of punishment to deal with norm violators is traditionally justified by one of five rationales:

1. *Retribution:* "You're going to get what's coming to you."
2. *Deterrence:* "We're going to punish you so that you won't do it again." And a variation: "We're going to punish you so that others won't do the same thing."

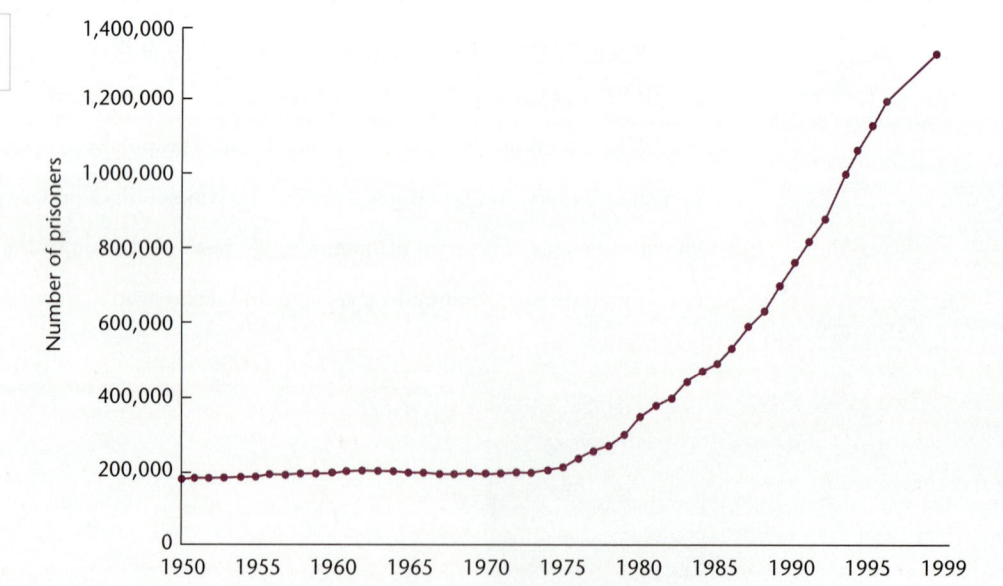

FIGURE 10.1

Growing Prison Population

Source: Bureau of Justice Statistics, U.S. Department of Justice, *Prisoners in 1999.* Washington, D.C.: U.S. Government Printing Office, 2000.

3. *Incapacitation:* "As long as we have you locked up, you won't be out doing something to us."
4. *Rehabilitation:* "We will rehabilitate you so that you can know the errors of your previous way, perhaps learn a skill or trade, and be returned successfully to society, without the allure to repeat your criminality."
5. *Reintegration.* "We will assist you after conviction to successfully integrate yourself as an active member of society, by way of halfway houses or other institutions of reintegration."

It must be emphasized that theories espousing what their respective proponents believe to be the authentic purpose of punishment normally are competing theories. It would be impossible to integrate successfully all of these purposes into a penal philosophy that would provide a philosophical undergirding in modern American jails and prisons in their present state. This is because of the phenomenon of prison overcrowding and the lack of prison personnel, as will be shown later.

Furthermore, it may not even be a philosophy of punishment that provides the philosophical foundation that supports the complex procedures, rules, and regulations governing American corrections today. Instead, the dominant influence of massive prison overcrowding is most responsible for present-day policies that shape the American correctional system.

The Effects of Prison Overcrowding on Judicial Sentencing

The courts have held that aspects of prison life are dictated by the need for security and discipline, thus giving custodial authorities significant discretion in regulating inmate comforts. At the same time, federal courts have monitored the conditions of confinement. Important federal cases have held that offenders who are sent to prison should not have extra punishments or barbaric punishments imposed upon them.

The U.S. Supreme Court concluded in *Rhodes v. Chapman* that overcrowding can be a factor when combined with other conditions, and declared that circumstances of incarceration violate the Constitution.[2] The Court went on to say that prison overcrowding itself is not unconstitutional. Thus, the federal courts have imposed upon corrections administrations a duty to protect inmates from conditions of confinement that are severe and that de facto add to punitive measures that compound the original sentence given in court. Overcrowding causes prisons to function as warehouses. When prisons function as warehouses, they fail to provide the staff, time, and opportunity for meaningful rehabilitation of offenders.

The overcrowding of prisons requires that inmates sentenced for a significant length of time not serve their full sentence. Thus, they are released early so that other convicted felons may take their place. Also, due to the phenomenon of plea bargaining (see Chapter 8, "Pretrial Procedures: Bail, Pretrial Hearings, and Plea Bargaining") at trial, they receive reduced sentences. These combined factors invalidate the incapacitation theory of punishment, because prisoners are incapacitated for such a relatively short time. Furthermore, overcrowded prisons eliminate a speedy, severe, and certain punishment, which is the foundation of the deterrent theory of punishment.

Indeed, the only theory of punishment that overcrowded prisons and warehousing seem to support is the retribution theory. Overcrowded prisons become hostile and dangerous places where the inmate, in addition to the punishment of incarceration, faces dangers from prison gangs, drugs, assault and battery, and sodomy. Those who support the retribution theory of punishment often are delighted at the consequences of these overcrowded situations because they further escalate the punishment that convicted offenders receive. However, a person subjected to these conditions often comes out of prison more dangerous than when he or she went in. Within five years, three out of four ex-convicts will commit a new crime.[3]

Prisons that are dramatically overcrowded, and thus are required by state statutes to implement programs that grant extremely early releases to most of their prisoners, are the most visible manifestation of the corrections component of the American criminal justice system. Critics of the penal institution consider the prison a monument

CTQ

Do you believe that too many people are now being sentenced to prison? Would the current "get tough" approach create an extremely large pool of ex-offenders who are at risk for further crimes?

TABLE 10.1 Types of Sentences Imposed by Conviction Offense

	Prison	Jail	Probation
All Offenses	38%	31%	31%
Violent Offenses	57	22	21
Murder	92	3	5
Rape	63	16	21
Robbery	73	14	13
Aggravated Assault	42	30	28
Other	38	34	27
Drug Offenses	35	37	28
Drug Possession	29	41	30
Drug Trafficking	39	33	27
Property Offenses	34	28	38
Burglary	45	26	29
Larceny	31	32	37
Fraud	26	24	50
Weapons Offenses	40	27	37

Source: D. Levin, P. Langan, and J. Brown, *State Court Sentencing of Convicted Felons, 1996.* Washington, D.C.: Bureau of Justice Statistics, U.S. Department of Justice, 2000.

to society's failure to devise more effective and humane methods for dealing with criminals. This viewpoint deserves careful consideration, but it is only a part of the story. The righteous indignation directed against prisons is misdirected, especially by critics who fail to offer realistic alternatives for coping with the problems that prisons must handle.[4]

More than 85 percent of the 2,200,000 prisoners in state and federal prisons are violent or repeat offenders (see Table 10.1). A recent Justice Department report stated that repeat offenders should not be released early, because this would lead to more crime.[5]

These consequences have had a direct influence on the sentences of American courts and judges. Specifically, a policy supporting sentencing in the cases of nonviolent first offenders would mean releasing more hardened criminals early. And it would cost $100 billion to build enough prisons to hold those first offenders and hardened criminals as well.[6] Clearly, such a policy is unworkable. Alternative sentencing offers us relief from hardened crooks and higher prison bills without higher crime. It costs $25,000 a year to lock a prisoner away, but only $5,000 to keep a prisoner under close supervision at home.

Retribution

The first theory of punishment—**retribution**—is rooted in tradition and buttressed by common sense. The philosophy supporting it can be found in Western civilization's oldest written records. In the Bible, the Judeo-Christian tradition instructs its followers that "when one man strikes another and kills him he shall be put to death," and "an eye for an eye, tooth for a tooth, hand for a hand, foot for a foot, burning for burning, wound for wound. . . ." Retribution—which means "something for recompense"—is a rather primitive (one hesitates to call it *natural*) human reaction: People who get hurt want to hurt back.

Retribution means that punishment is inflicted on a person who has infringed upon the rights and the safety of others. Normally, this theory of punishment insists that the severity of the penalty should be equivalent to the seriousness of the crime. It is not difficult, therefore, to understand why this justification for punishment ("the law of just deserts") has received a good deal of popular support throughout the ages.

The retribution theory of punishment is the one most commonly shared by citizens in a democracy. Most people have felt both the need for revenge and the pleasure that

---

CTQ

Should vengeance be accepted as a rationale for punishment?

CTQ

Most scholars agree that sentencing based on justice evaluates the weight of a criminal act, not the needs of the defendant or the community. Is this a fair measure to determine a sentencing philosophy?

WEB

For more information on the National Association of Sentencing Advocates, **visit our Web site,** www.prenhall.com/territo.

revenge gives them when someone who has wronged them is punished. However, one of the major evolutions of the American criminal justice system is that revenge must be taken out of the hands of the individual. Since the state is the instrument of the community's collective rage, all vigilante acts in this country are criminal in nature. It will be shown later that sometimes the state's failing to act as an adequate agent of revenge has caused frustrated individuals to take the law into their own hands in response. Some believe that such actions are, if not legal, morally correct.

Although certain states have instituted sentencing policies supported only by the philosophy of retribution, such a sentiment is not a consensus in the United States. Indeed, retribution as the only principle of punishment leaves with Americans who hold to this theory a profound ethical dilemma that also confronts our democratic society. A society based on individual rights and civil liberties seems to be inconsistent with a state that merely wants to get even. Such a system seems to contradict basic fundamental libertarian ideals. But with overcrowded prison systems, rising crime rates, and a general fear of being victimized by crime among the populace, libertarian, democratic ideals often take a backseat to humanity's more primitive instinct for vengeance.

Deterrence

In broadest terms, **general deterrence** is a theory of punishment that seeks to discourage would-be offenders from committing the same crimes for which a defendant has been convicted. **Specific deterrence** is designed to prevent the convicted offender from engaging in future criminal acts. Therefore, the most widely held justification for the punishment of individual offenders is to reduce the crime rate. **Deterrence** is supported as a theory of punishment primarily because this is its alleged most profound consequence. This is why a sentencing philosophy like deterrence, which aims in part at reducing the crime rate, is so attractive. The theory of deterrence was developed by reformers in the nineteenth century who were disturbed by the theory of retribution. Furthermore, they argued, by punishing the offender severely, the state demonstrates its determination to control crime. Hence, general deterrence, by the threat of arrest, conviction, and imprisonment, can be thought of as the power of the criminal law and the agencies of the criminal justice system to deter potential offenders from committing crimes (for example, Michael Fay was caned for vandalism in Singapore [see Figure 10.2]).

The three components of assuring a deterrence theory of punishment are speed, severity, and certainty of punishment. These components now have become almost philosophical, since their implementation is almost a practical impossibility. In one major urban area, the state attorney's office processes 195,000 criminal cases a year. This same metropolitan area has fewer than thirty courtrooms assigned to process the cases, fewer than two hundred prosecuting attorneys to bring the cases forward by the state, and fewer than 150 public defenders to assist defendants in their criminal trials.[7] These numbers alone indicate that speed, certainty, and severity must give way to delay, compromise, plea bargaining, and a system in which the state refuses to prosecute 30 percent of the cases brought to it by the police.

However, the existence of overcrowded courtrooms within the American criminal justice system *negates* the possibility of the philosophical principles that, in a perfect world, would make deterrence a viable theory of punishment. The reality of the number of cases processed through the judiciary and the department of corrections, however, severely frustrates any possibilities that general deterrence will be a profound accomplishment.

> **CTQ**
>
> How is the principle of willful wrongdoing central to the idea of retribution, and what does it connote for criminal sentencing in America?

> **CTQ**
>
> Is justice served when a punishment is designed to prevent future law violations, even though there is an overwhelming likelihood that the person may never again violate the law?

> **CTQ**
>
> Which is more important to achieve in criminal sentencing, general deterrence or specific deterrence? Defend your answer with specific examples.

FIGURE 10.2

American Michael Fey vandalized property in Singapore, and as a result he was whacked nine times with a large cane. Effective or cruel and unusual punishment?

Courtesy of Tan Ah Soon/AP/Wide World Photos.

Incapacitation

The third theory of punishment, **incapacitation,** is justified on the grounds that as long as an offender is being held in confinement, he or she is not free to commit more crimes. This rationale is regarded by both supporters and critics of the punitive approach as the most plausible argument in favor of punishment. In everyday language this theory of punishment is known as "lock 'em up and throw away the key."

Incapacitation as a theory of punishment presumes a fact that is false: that within a given jurisdiction, the actual number of serious criminal offenders is a stable or fixed number. In reality, the serious-offender population is growing in every jurisdiction in the United States. This is particularly true in large-population states where the community of criminals grows every day as new citizens move into the state, searching for new criminal opportunities. Furthermore, with the advent of incredibly widespread drug usage among all areas of the population and the attendant crimes (robbery, burglary, larceny, assault and battery, murder, prostitution) that accompany the lifestyles of those addicted to drugs, the criminal population can no longer be considered a small, finite, and fixed segment of the general population within a given jurisdiction. Nonetheless, many practitioners in the criminal justice system continue, unfortunately, to hold the theory that there are a certain small percentage of criminals in the system, and if we would just build enough prisons to lock them up for a long time, we would eliminate the crime problem. Nothing frustrates the solution of a complex problem more than the proposal of a simple solution that is based on false premises and, most important, gives misguided hope.

Another stumbling block facing proponents of the incapacitation theory of punishment is the fact that those who are incapacitated do not stay in confinement; they are eventually released from prison or training school. Their subsequent behavior inevitably reflects the consequences of their experience during confinement. Researchers, for example, contend that confinement of criminality-prone delinquents has the effect of increasing, rather than decreasing, the commitment to a criminal career.[8] Their argument is not directed toward the ineffectiveness of incapacitation but toward the adverse results of confinement in existing correctional institutions. Furthermore, with the advent of good time, gain time, early outs, furloughs, and parole, most prisoners serve only 30 percent of their sentence.[9]

Therefore, like other theories of punishment, incapacitation is undermined by the phenomenon of prison overcrowding. Because of the lack of space to incarcerate the number of prisoners sentenced and the need to release old prisoners to ensure that new prisoners at least serve some time for their crimes, the chances of success for the incapacitation theory of punishment, when combined with the realities of prison overcrowding, the cost of building new prisons, and the unavailability of tax money to build new prisons, are undermined.

Rehabilitation/Treatment

Treatment, according to the general dictionary definition, connotes the manner in which a person or thing is handled, used, or processed. In the context of mental health, the goal of treatment or therapy is to help an individual who has been diagnosed as emotionally disturbed or mentally ill to attain some level of improved functioning.

The idea of *rehabilitation* in corrections began as a matter of moral redemption of the offender. It was gradually co-opted by psychiatry, however, and transformed into a problem for psychotherapy. The goal of correctional treatment was to change the personality of the criminal to improve social behavior and personal adjustment. This was a praiseworthy objective; unfortunately, it had to be pursued within a system whose practitioners and representatives are responsible for defending society, which takes precedence over the rehabilitation of offenders. Consider the issue of incarceration. When rehabilitation was the predominant goal in criminal treatment programs, vocational and psychological training were introduced into prisons. This rehabilitative outlook shaped even the vocabulary of criminal punishment. Prisons were often called *correctional institutions;* those for young adults were often called *reformatories.*

Certainly, there are cases where prisoners return from prison to society and lead extraordinarily successful lives. The question is, however, have they been rehabilitated? Those involved with the famous Watergate scandal in the early 1970s were released from prison and went on the lecture circuits, making hundreds of thousands of dollars per year. One of the most fascinating examples occurred when Michael Milken, one of America's most famous white-collar criminals, was released from prison. Milken would seem to be certainly rehabilitated, based on his subsequent employment as an adjunct professor of finance at UCLA. Yet the question is, has he really been rehabilitated? Or, instead, has he remained the same, but are America's best and brightest eager to learn the secrets of how he became a multimillionaire through his highly intelligent perpetration of white-collar crimes?

Reintegration

The newest correctional philosophy for punishing offenders is called *reintegration* into the free community. This extension of the rehabilitative philosophy attempts to compensate for the weakness of that approach while at the same time adopting more acceptable ideas. Those who advocate reintegration believe that the causes of crime and the functions of corrective efforts are two highways that fail to intersect. These theorists believe that the offender needs help, but at the same time they suggest that criminal behavior is often the result of the offender's failure to integrate properly into society.

This aspect of the reintegration theory separates it from rehabilitation. Whereas rehabilitation attempts to treat the offender as an isolated entity, looking for a medical cause and cure for his or her behavior, the reintegrative model realizes that society and the individual are inseparable and thereby emphasizes particular aspects of the offender's environment as critical.

Under the reintegration theory of punishment, the criminal justice system has implemented halfway houses and social agencies that assist offenders when they are released from prison; the primary emphasis is placed on the offenders' becoming future viable citizens. Proponents of this theory of punishment believe that contact and interaction with the positive rather than the negative elements of society are what is necessary for overall treatment of the offender. This theory has won some acceptance in recent years and seems to enjoy increasing support.[10]

As the phenomenon of prison overcrowding has undermined the possibilities of the serious implementation of the other three theories of punishment, prison overcrowding likewise discourages the possibility that a prison system can be based on rehabilitation in America during the beginning of the twenty-first century. For example, in Parchman, Mississippi, the state penitentiary does not employ a single psychologist or psychiatrist. Furthermore, the general sentiment among most American correctional officers is that the function of the corrections system is not to rehabilitate but to "warehouse."

This theory is complemented by the "N.W." theory of punishment. Because prison overcrowding totally undermines all of the traditional theories of punishment, those who work there—prison guards and even wardens—sense the futility of making something positive out of an inmate's incarceration time. Hence, a new theory of punishment is being touted by these professionals in the field as "N.W.," an inside acronym that means "nothing works."[11] The warehousing function of the correctional system means that the prisoners are simply stored in their allocated space until the time of their release. Lack of resources, overcrowding, untrained personnel, and a correctional budget that is consumed mainly by the construction of new prisons has made warehousing the central reality of the American correctional process. Warehousing necessarily defeats the rehabilitative goal, and thereby eliminates any possibility of employing a meaningful rehabilitative theory of punishment in overcrowded American prisons and jails.

SENTENCING

The practical procedures involved in sentencing a convicted defendant reflect a blend of policies and procedures that derive from legislative, judicial, and administrative authorities.[12] At the moment a judge sentences a convicted defendant to serve some form of punishment, the reality of the situation for the defendant is that the sentence is actually imposed. The judge, in making a decision concerning what sentence to impose, to some extent should incorporate all of the American theories of punishment—retribution, deterrence, incapacitation, rehabilitation, and reintegration. In doing so, some judges also

WEB

For information on the Coalition for Sentencing Reforms, **visit our Web site, www.prenhall.com/territo**.

IN THE NEWS
A HUMAN PERSPECTIVE

JUDGE SENTENCES MAN TO MARRY

An Ohio judge sentenced a 26-year-old man accused of domestic violence to marry a woman he allegedly attacked. "I believe the bonds of marriage might make an abuser think a little bit more before resorting to physical force," Hamilton County Municipal Judge Albert Mestemaker said. The National Organization for Women condemned the ruling, saying it gave Scott Hancock a "hunting license." Hancock, who pleaded no contest to a domestic violence charge on Thursday, was sentenced to nine months probation on the condition that he marry his girlfriend, with whom he reportedly lives. He also was ordered to support the couple's child, seek family counseling and enter an alcohol treatment program.

Source: "Judge Sentences Man to Marry," *St. Petersburg (Fla.) Times,* July 15, 1995, p. 9A. Copyright *St. Petersburg Times,* 1995. Reprinted with permission.

---

become quite innovative (see "In the News: Judge Sentences Man to Marry"). However, the judge is required to follow the statutory alternatives that restrict judicial sentencing that appear in the penal code. For example, the judge cannot go over the authorized punishment of ten years if that is the maximum statutory punishment for strong-armed robbery. Likewise, if the judge chooses to be lenient, and there is a statutory imposition disallowing leniency (such as sentencing guidelines or mandatory minimum sentences), the judge is limited on the extent of leniency that can be shown in the sentence.

But can the judge in effect incarcerate two human beings for the crime of one? That is the sentencing dilemma more and more judges are experiencing when they are faced with a sentencing decision regarding a convicted pregnant mother or a convicted mother with small children (see "In the News: Can You Jail Mom without Punishing the Kids?").

The sentencing of offenders convicted of serious felonies or capital crimes where the death penalty may be imposed requires a **bifurcated trial.** After the jury returns a verdict of guilty, a separate hearing is held on a different day, usually before the trial judge alone. The judge will hear aggravating and mitigating factors about the convicted defendant in order to determine a just punishment.

At sentencing, the judge will consider mitigating and aggravating circumstances and then make a sentencing decision. In some jurisdictions, the trial jury makes the sentence recommendation, whereas a separate jury is selected in others. In either case, the judge is not bound by the jury's recommendation.

In all other felony cases, before the sentencing stage of the criminal justice process can even begin, the defendant has to either have pleaded guilty to, or have been found guilty of, a criminal offense. The court must then decide an appropriate disposition for the individual—a decision that is often complex and difficult for the judge. In earlier times, the imposition of sentences was cut-and-dried. Specific punishments for specific offenses were laid down by the law, and once a verdict of guilty was returned, the judge merely ordered the appropriate sentence to be carried out. The attention was on the offense, not the offender. However, this situation has changed as a consequence of societal reaction to crimes and criminals. Hence, the sentencing hearing has become an integral part of the criminal justice system.

The Sentencing Hearing

Except in lower-court sentencing of minor misdemeanors and ordinance violations, where offenders may be sentenced immediately upon conviction, felony sentencing typically occurs at a sentencing hearing, often scheduled for three to six weeks after conviction. At this hearing, the offender is given an opportunity to deny, explain, or add to information contained in the presentence report. In addition, the prosecutor may submit a written statement or make an oral recommendation regarding the sentence. In many plea agreements, the prosecutor may agree to support a reduced sentence or concurrent sentence, or to make no recommendation about the sentence at all.

A HUMAN PERSPECTIVE

CAN YOU JAIL MOM WITHOUT PUNISHING THE KIDS?

April Rivera, a four-year-old from Miami, is singing the theme to *Barney* with her mother. "I love you. You love me," she chirps. "We're a happy family." Even a purple dinosaur, however, can tell this isn't quite true. April's mom Regla Sanchez, 26, is inmate No. 162850 at the Hernando Correctional Institution, 320 miles away from Brooksville, Fla., and April is looking at an image of her mother on a computer screen. This virtual family is part of a new pilot program, Reading Family Ties, run by the Florida Department of Corrections in an effort to help incarcerated mothers and their kids bond. But when her mom disappears from the screen, April's face crumples. "It's hard," says Isabel Strausser, the program's Miami coordinator. "A lot of times kids cry and beg me to let their mothers go."

Florida is attempting to address a disturbing national phenomenon: the explosion in the number of mothers in prison. The population of women in U.S. prisons has risen 650% in the past two decades. Of the more than 149,000 female inmates currently in local jails and federal penitentiaries, 70% have at least one child under 18. Since these mothers are often the sole provider for their children, the impact on their kids can be devastating. They get shuttled off to live with relatives or sent to foster homes. Studies show that kids with incarcerated mothers are more likely to refuse to eat, wet their beds and do poorly in school. "Not enough attention is being paid to the trauma on these kids," says Ann Jacobs, executive director of the New York City–based Women's Prison Association.

Contacts between incarcerated mothers and their children are fraught with difficulties. Prisons are often located in remote rural locales, inaccessible to poor families without cars. And in-person visits can take an emotional toll on young children. They must endure invasive body searches just like adults. Then there's the frightening clang of doors slamming shut. Once inside the noisy visiting rooms, kids must shout at the top of their lungs. In most state and federal prisons, children are allowed to hug and kiss their moms, but in many jails in which women are awaiting trial and sentencing, contact is forbidden. A pane of thick glass separates the mother and child, which can be yet another trauma. Gail Smith, executive director of Chicago Legal Advocacy for Incarcerated Mothers, described an infant's wrenching visit. "When he saw his mother come out, his little hand went to the glass," Smith says. "But when he realized he couldn't touch her, he just started screaming."

Much of the increase in the rate of female incarceration is a direct result of harsh mandatory-sentencing laws that impose minimum jail sentences for all drug offenses. Many of these drug offenders are women, frequently poor African Americans and Hispanics, who wind up in prisons built for hard-core male felons, not pregnant and parenting women. "These kids are innocent victims of their parents' misconduct," says David Steinhart, co-author of the 1993 book *Why Punish the Children?*

Of course, prisons are for punishment, a part of which is losing the ability to raise kids in the outside world. What's more, in cases where the mother has been physically or emotionally abusive, kids may need to be kept away for their own good. Still, the question is whether society can legitimately punish women for their crimes without punishing their children's lives. The fate of these children has great consequences for society. Half of the 1.5 million kids with an incarcerated parent will commit a crime before they turn 18. "We're creating a new crop that gets bigger and bigger each generation," says Anne Holt, a consultant for Florida's Department of Corrections.

The problem of parenting in prison often begins with childbirth. The number of babies born to mothers in prison is rising. (Most of these women are pregnant when they arrive; conjugal visits, as a rule, are not allowed.) They generally give birth at the nearest hospital. But since prisons are often far from hospitals and expectant mothers must clear various security hurdles, women inmates are at greater risk of delivering their babies before they can make it to the hospital. A scathing report by Amnesty International helped draw public attention to the sometimes harsh treatment of pregnant inmates, such as shackling them during labor—a practice that has since been outlawed in the state of Illinois.

After childbirth, the treatment is often no better. Most states make no special arrangements for the care of newborns in prison. After delivery, mothers and babies are typically separated—sometimes within hours. The infant is sent to live with a family member or goes straight to foster care. New York, Nebraska and Washington State are exceptions; prisons in these states have nurseries in which infants are allowed to live with their mothers for a year to 18 months. But this raises another difficult question: Is it really better for an infant to be raised in prison, just to be near the mother? No one has studied the long-term effect on kids who spend their early months behind bars, though some initial research suggests that babies don't develop as well there because they don't get the kind of attention and stimulation they need. There are also concerns about children's safety in prisons, which are often not adequately childproof, and about the availability of adequate medical care. Then there are the potential long-term psychological effects. "Our concern is that kids will think prison is normal," says Bobbi Costa, executive director of Families and Friends of Violent Crime Victims in Washington State. "We have to be concerned for our younger generation and what values they are developing."

Some states are dealing with the proliferation of mothers in prison by looking for alternative sentencing solutions. California sentences some nonviolent female drug offenders to Family Foundation, a community-based residential drug-treatment program. In Santa Fe Springs, California, female inmates live in what resembles a converted school building with their children up to age six. "You're not just another number where you're not getting any help," says Sarah Ambrosini, 29, who lives there with her two young sons, ages four months and 16 months. The program is expensive, averaging $40,000 a year per inmate, compared with $25,000 in a regular prison. But since families stay together, fewer kids wind up in foster care. Also, follow-up studies show inmates in the program have a lower recidivism rate. Says Sterling O'Ran, an administrator for California's Department of Corrections: "We've been able to get them hooked on their kids instead of drugs." Many prison moms would like the same opportunity.

Source: T. Drummond, "Mothers in Prison," *Time,* November 6, 2000, pp. 106–108. © 2000 TIME, Inc., reprinted by permission.

IN THE WORKPLACE

U.S. MARSHAL

Responsible for protecting federal courts and ensuring effective operation of the judicial system. Performs a variety of duties, including the following: maintaining court security, transporting and processing prisoners, conducting body searches, producing prisoners in court, maintaining custody of prisoners throughout the court proceedings, protecting sequestered juries, protecting court facilities and personnel, executing civil and criminal processes, and enforcing court orders. Minimum qualifications are as follows: U.S. citizen between ages 21 and 36; excellent physical condition; bachelor's degree or three years of law enforcement experience; valid driver's license; must pass a written test, interview, and background investigation; must complete academy training program.

The Structure and Procedures Used in the Sentencing Hearing For less serious offenses, particularly when the case is not tried before a jury, the judge may pronounce a sentence immediately upon finding the defendant guilty or upon accepting a guilty plea. Sentencing also may be immediate when the judge has no option but to assess the statutory penalty.

However, in most cases, sentencing may be set for a future date but not involve any special investigations, with the judge taking recommendations from the defense and prosecution. However, the trend is toward having a separate sentencing hearing. After the trial verdict, the judge sets a formal date for a sentencing hearing, leaving sufficient time to conduct an appropriate presentence investigation.

Constitutional Rights Afforded during a Sentencing Hearing During a sentencing hearing, because the sentencing procedure is deemed a critical stage of the criminal prosecution, a defendant is entitled to a lawyer, either retained or appointed, to render effective assistance at the hearing.[13] Furthermore, at the hearing, the defendant has rights under the confrontation clause of the Sixth Amendment, but they are less strictly applied in the sentencing proceeding than in the trial itself. Indeed, this is particularly true for hearsay statements, where the judge need only consider whether the out-of-court hearsay statement has a basis for trustworthiness.[14]

There are certain rights that are not present during a sentencing hearing that are present during the trial. For example, the defendant has no right to confront or cross-examine witnesses who have supplied adverse information to the court regarding sentencing. Even in a capital case, the sentencing procedure has a purpose different from the trial and confrontation rights are less weighty.[15]

However, the judge, in passing a sentence, is required by the due process clause to consider numerous factors beyond the record of the trial itself, and also may consider the conduct of the defendant at trial in a negative way. The following examples illustrate this right. In a landmark case, a trial judge took into account her belief that the defendant committed perjury while testifying at trial.[16] Such a factor would be important when determining whether the defendant was likely to be rehabilitated after trial. Also, the trial judge may consider the defendant's refusal to assist officials in their investigation of a criminal conspiracy in which the defendant was a confessed participant.[17] However, if the judge goes beyond the record and uses erroneous information in passing a sentence, the convicted defendant's due process rights have been violated, thereby voiding the sentence.[18]

The Effect of the Presentence Report in the Sentence Imposition Although sentencing is the judge's responsibility, the presentence report has become an important ingredient in the judicial mix. Although the primary purpose of the presentence report is to help the judge select the appropriate sentence for the offender, it also assists in the classification of probationers, prisoners, and parolees with respect to treatment planning and risk assessment. Usually a probation officer investigates the convicted person's background, criminal record, job status, and mental condition in order to suggest a sentence that is in the interests of both the person and society. In some states, however, probation officers

IN THE WORKPLACE

PROBATION OFFICER WRITING PRESENTENCING REPORTS

Responsible for conducting investigations, providing sentencing recommendations to the court, and supervising offenders. Performs a variety of duties, including the following: conducts investigations and prepares presentence reports for offenders, which requires interviewing, investigating the offense, prior record, and financial status, contacting law enforcement agencies, attorneys, victims, and so on; determines course of action at closure of presentence report; supervises offenders; and maintains a detailed written record of case activity. Minimum qualifications are as follows: bachelor's degree from an accredited college; one to three years of specialized experience; must submit to pre-employment drug testing and background investigation.

present only factual material to the judge and make no sentencing recommendation. The probation officer may weigh hearsay as well as firsthand information.

The presentence report helps to ease the strain of decision making on judges by shifting partial responsibility to the probation department. Because many sentencing alternatives are open to them, they often rely on the report for guidance.

After studying sentencing decisions in California, Carter and Wilkins found a high correlation (96 percent) between the recommendation for probation in the presentence report and the court's disposition of sentencing the defendant to probation in all cases.[19] When the probation officer recommended incarceration, there was a slight weakening of this relationship, an indication that the officers were more punitive than the judges.

The Victim-Impact Statement

The national victim/witness rights movement called for several modifications in the criminal trial. One of these was the inclusion of the *victim-impact statement* during the sentencing hearing. Generally, the victim-impact statement is a written document. It describes the personal tragedies and suffering of either the victim's survivors or the crime victim himself or herself. Judges are expected to listen to and give due consideration to these statements before arriving at an appropriate sentence for the defendant. Approximately twenty states now have laws mandating this type of involvement in sentencing. Fifty states "allow for some type of submission of a victim impact statement either at the time of sentencing or included in the pre-sentence investigation reports" made by the court officers.[20] Often the courts allow the victim or the relatives of the victim to give in-court testimony during the sentencing hearing.

There is no guarantee that victim-impact statements directly affect judges' decisions by causing them to render harsher sentences. One study found instead that, "these statements did not produce sentencing decisions that reflected more clearly the effects of crime on victims. Nor did we find much evidence that—with or without victim-impact statements—sentencing decisions were influenced by our measures of the effects of crime on victims, once the charge and the defendant's prior record were taken into account."[21]

What Is Necessary for a Judge to Impose a Constitutional Sentence?

The trial judge is given great discretion in many jurisdictions in determining sentences, and when the sentence is within statutory limits, it is generally not reviewed upon appeal unless the sentencing statute so provides. The discretion is not, however, completely unbridled; some constitutional limitations are present (see the Landmark Case *Williams v. New York*).

The Eighth Amendment to the Constitution provides that "cruel and unusual punishments shall not be inflicted." However, if the sentence is within the statutory authorization, the courts are reluctant to apply the Eighth Amendment restriction—even in cases in which the sentence seems quite heavy for the nature of the offense.

One example of this is sentences that appear to be extremely lengthy. In 1983, the Supreme Court announced that the length of the prison sentence cannot be grossly

CTQ
How do the elements contained in the presentence report reflect our assumption about the causes of criminal behavior?

CTQ
How does a presentence investigation report to the judge affect the sentencing decision? How does determinate sentencing affect the importance of the influence of the presentence investigation?

CTQ
Discuss the role of the presentence investigation report on the process of judicial sentencing. What value do you consider appropriate for the judge to place on the report?

CTQ
Would you be in favor of a constitutional amendment setting forth victims' rights as a criminal proceeding? If so, what kind of rights would this involve?

CTQ
Presently, victim-impact evidence is not permitted in death penalty cases; do you believe this is appropriate?

LANDMARK CASE — Williams v. New York

Williams was found guilty of murder in the first degree. The jury recommended life imprisonment. The judge, after considering information in the presentence investigation, imposed the death sentence. Williams appealed, alleging that the judge's consideration of information obtained outside the courtroom, from people whom Williams had not been permitted to confront or cross-examine, violated his due process rights under the Fourteenth Amendment. The U.S. Supreme Court had to determine the issue of whether a sentencing judge should exercise narrow or wide discretion in the sources and types of evidence he or she uses to help in determining the kind and extent of punishment to be imposed within the limits fixed by law. The Court concluded that the sentencing judge can exercise a wide discretion in the sources and types of evidence so used. Specifically, in this case, the defendant had no right to cross-examine or interrogate the witness who was the source of the judge's information.

Source: Williams v. New York, 337 U.S. 241 (1949).

---

disproportionate to the severity of the crime.[22] In this case, a life sentence without the possibility of parole for a seventh nonviolent felony was considered "grossly disproportionate."

But a substantially different approach applies sentence decisions of legislatures and sentencing courts, and successful challenges to the length of a sentence alone are rare. In 1980, the Supreme Court upheld a life sentence, with the possibility of parole, for multiple nonviolent offenses.[23] The Constitution protects defendants from receiving unconstitutional sentences. Throughout the years, there have been three separate situations where the Supreme Court has determined that certain types of sentences were unconstitutional.

First, the Court has said that when the nature of the sentence is shocking, because it is grossly disproportionate to the nature of the minor crime or offense, the sentence must be struck down.[24] Here, the lower court imposed a sentence of twelve years of hard labor for falsifying records; the Supreme Court declared this sentence unconstitutional. However, on the other hand, the Court upheld a mandatory life sentence for possession of a certain quantity of drugs. The Court held that the sentence was not cruel and unusual even though the statute allowed no consideration of mitigating factors.[25]

Second, the Supreme Court has scrutinized the imposition of the death penalty for crimes other than murder. In 1977, the Supreme Court declared the imposition of the death penalty for rape unconstitutional, because the penalty was disproportionate to the crime.[26] The third type of unconstitutional sentences is punishment of so-called status crimes. The Court announced that the Eighth Amendment is violated by statutes that make it a crime to have a particular status (e.g., being an alcoholic, a drug addict, or a pedophile). However, courts have concluded that it is not a violation of this amendment to make activities criminal if related to a certain status. The primary case of this matter was decided by the Supreme Court, which ruled that it is unconstitutional to convict a person of the offense of being addicted to narcotics.[27]

Third, the equal-protection clause protects criminal defendants in sentencing hearings by restricting the types of sentences that may be imposed. This claim is normally raised in connection with a sentence of imprisonment with a fine, or a probation condition requiring the payment of money. The Court has held that it is a violation of the Fourth Amendment to limit punishments to a payment of fines if the defendant has no means to pay the debt. Instead, the defendant shall be given an optional sentence of imprisonment if the fines cannot be paid.[28] Likewise, a court may not revoke probation and imprison a defendant for failure to pay a fine. Before the probation may be revoked, the court must demonstrate that the defendant had the means to pay the fine, but did not do so, or that there was no other alternative form of punishment available.[29]

Finally, the due process clause also affords convicted defendants certain rights during the sentencing stage. This clause states that a defendant may not be punished for appealing a conviction. For defendants who appeal a conviction and are retried and convicted a second time, the sentence may not be harsher than that which was originally imposed, unless the harsher sentence was based on conduct of the defendant that occurred after the original sentencing proceeding.[30]

Thus, the imposition of sentencing by a trial court after a defendant has been convicted involves many nuances: relaxed rules of evidence, certain constitutional rights, certain rights of victims, and the right of the judge to make a decision based on a presentence investigation, which is composed almost entirely of hearsay. The rules for this type of hearing are clearly much more relaxed than the strict rules of evidence and procedure used in the criminal trial itself.

SENTENCING STRUCTURES

The sentencing structure in a criminal case is the statutory limits by which a judge must impose a sentence. These structures differ widely and tend to give great, moderate, or little discretion to a judge when imposing a sentence. Some sentencing structures allow a range for a particular crime from probation to fifty years' imprisonment. The judge has the discretion to determine where a particular case lies within that range. Others, as in Texas, classify crimes as to the degree of felony seriousness that they possess. For example, a third-degree felony carries with it a maximum five-year sentence, a second-degree felony carries a fifteen-year sentence, and a first-degree felony carries a thirty-year sentence. Again, the judge's discretion in sentencing can be significantly curtailed by the advent of sentencing guidelines, mandatory minimum sentences, and *enhancement statutes*, which provide a structure for determining an increased amount of time added onto the sentence of a convicted defendant. In every instance, this sentence will be more severe (enhancement statutes will be discussed later in the chapter). However, the advent of sentencing enhancement statutes has considerably narrowed the trial judge's discretion in the type and amount of sentence he or she can impose on a convicted felon. (See "In the News: Sentencing Study Shows Wrong Convicts in American Prisons.")

IN THE NEWS

A HUMAN PERSPECTIVE

SENTENCING STUDY SHOWS WRONG CONVICTS IN AMERICAN PRISONS
by D. Cauchon

The Justice Department's long-awaited report on mandatory minimum sentences, released in February 1994, found that low-level, nonviolent drug offenders account for 21.2% of the federal prison population. These small-time drug offenders are serving longer prison terms than robbers, rapists and kidnappers, the report said. Critics of mandatory minimums hailed the 106-page report as proof that prisons are being filled with the wrong people.

"American taxpayers are footing the bill for nonviolent, low-level drug offenders to sit in prison uselessly for five or ten years," said Julie Stewart, president of Families Against Mandatory Minimums. She said immediate action should be taken to lower the sentences of these 16,316 prisoners. But former Bush Justice Department official Paul McNulty said the report exaggerates the number of "nonviolent, low-level" offenders. He said many took part in serious criminal activity that do not always show up in court or arrest records. "The report reflects the lack of accountability in the system as much as the harmless nature of the offenders," he said.

The Justice Department's own conclusions were cautious. It said that long mandatory sentences for low-level drug offenders do not deter crime any better than short sentences. It also said it costs $20,000 a year to keep a prisoner. "Some might argue that these resources could be used more efficiently to promote other criminal justice needs, such as providing more money for additional police," the report said.

"Opposing mandatory minimums would have been too bold a step for this administration, but the evidence is there in their own report," Stewart said.

Source: D. Cauchon, "Sentencing Study Treads Cautiously," *USA Today,* March 10, 1993, p. 3A. Copyright 1993 *USA Today.* Reprinted with permission.

Determinate or Flat-Time Sentences

If a legislature fixes the length of a sentence by statute (for example, a term of fifteen years for armed robbery), the sentence is called a **determinate** or **flat-time sentence**. Thus, neither the trial judge nor administrative agencies (such as the parole board or the department of corrections) are permitted any discretion in assigning such sentences. Although allowing judges no discretion in imposing sentences for convictions of certain crimes was the intent of legislatures when they passed determinate or flat-time sentences, many judges have found a technique that lets them actually exercise their judicial discretion by creating sentences like assigning a convicted person to five years (required by a flat-time sentence) and then placing him or her on probation for those five years. The treatment varies from state to state. But how can an innocent defendant, found guilty, escape the inflexible length of these flat-time, determinate sentences? And what if the defendant finally proves his or her innocence? Is the state monetarily liable for wrongful incarceration? DNA evidence is forcing these moral situations on the state (see "In the News: After the Exoneration").

> **CTQ**
> Would convicted offenders be more likely to favor determinate or indeterminate sentences? Why?

Presumptive Sentences

A *presumptive sentence* is a sentence of incarceration for a fixed period of time where there is no possibility of the sentence's being reduced by parole or probation. These sentences have become popular in the last decade, particularly in states that are concerned with the death penalty. For example, in the case of a person convicted of a first-degree murder, a presumptive sentence requires that the convicted person shall be punished by death or imprisonment for the remainder of his or her natural life, without the benefit of probation, parole, or any other reduction. The presumptive sentence is much like the determinate or flat-time sentence structure but with two major differences: (1) It specifically eliminates in its language the possibility of parole, and (2) it is often more directed toward convicts who will spend the remainder of their life in prison without the possibility of parole.

> **CTQ**
> Do you believe that these additional new forms of punishment compounding the original sentence given in the trial court will have a deterrent influence on the crime rate?

IN THE NEWS
A HUMAN PERSPECTIVE

AFTER THE EXONERATION

One unlucky evening in 1984, Ricky Daye was riding in a Buick with a broken taillight in San Diego. The police pulled the car over and thought they recognized Daye from a WANTED sketch. He was arrested and five months later convicted of the brutal rape and kidnapping of a young San Diego mother. Daye spent 10 years in California prisons, insisting all the time that he was innocent. Finally, in 1994, a DNA test showed he could not have been the culprit, and he was freed.

A happy ending? Not entirely. For months afterward, strangers who recognized Daye from TV talk shows would corner him in Kmarts and gas stations and ask, "You got paid at least, right?" Yet six years later, Daye, 42, has not received a cent. He sued the city of San Diego, its police and its prosecutors for millions of dollars. But last year a jury declined to award any damages.

Despite the wonderful clarity of DNA evidence, which has exonerated more than 80 Americans of crimes for which they had been imprisoned, two-thirds have never been given any compensation for their lost years. In a country in which some slip-and-fall claims win millions of dollars, it is startling to realize that decades wrongly spent in maximum-security prisons are typically worth nothing. "In America, when someone is wronged, we pay them," says Adele Bernhard, a Pace University law professor. "It may not be a perfect system, but that's what we do. Why don't we do that here?"

In 36 states, according to Bernhard, no laws explicitly provide for compensating the wrongly imprisoned, while other laws protect police and prosecutors from lawsuits. The reasoning is that public servants could not do their job if they constantly had to fear being sued. As long as officials do not jail the wrong person intentionally (and they almost never do), they are not to blame—and in our justice system, someone has to be blamed before anyone pays. Even in the 14 states that do have laws to compensate victims of courtroom mistakes, the caps on these awards are often miserly. For those coming out of federal prisons, damages cannot exceed $5,000.

Source: Amanda Ripley, "After the Exoneration," *Time*, December, 11 2000, p. 96. Reprinted with permission from *Time*, all rights reserved.

Indeterminate Sentences

For most of the twentieth century, American jurisdictions have had *indeterminate sentencing*, in which criminal statutes generally authorize judges to impose sentences from within a wide range. Probation to five years is a common range; probation to twenty-five years is not unknown. The difference between determinate and indeterminate sentencing is that in the former, the judge is required to impose a sentence of a fixed number of years, whereas in the latter, the judge sentences the offender for an indefinite period with only the minimum and maximum being fixed.

In daily court business, trial judges often lack sufficient time to consider all of the crucial elements of an offense and the special characteristics of the offender before imposing a sentence. Some judges tend to standardize their decision making by announcing sentences to fit certain categories of crimes without paying too much attention to the particular offender. This is especially true in cases involving minor violations. Although individuals convicted of minor offenses are good candidates for reform, they frequently are sentenced immediately after being found guilty or when they enter a guilty plea. And if counsel requests a presentence report before the sentence is imposed, a defendant may have to remain in jail during the delay, a price many defendants are not willing to pay.

CTQ
Would a person who favors indeterminate sentences over determinate sentences be likely to believe in deterrence, retribution, or incapacitation as being the main goal of punishment? Why?

Mandatory Minimum Sentences

In another effort to limit judicial discretion in sentencing, various state legislations have developed *mandatory minimum sentences*. These new sentences require the incarceration of all offenders convicted of specific crimes, without the possibility of the sentence being shortened or reduced to probation or some other community sentence (such as a fine). In other words, all people found guilty of that crime must do some fixed amount of time in prison.

Most states now employ some form of mandatory sentencing. Some make offenders convicted of certain offenses, such as drug trafficking or handgun crimes, ineligible for probation; some exclude recidivists, while others bar offenders from being considered for parole.

Mandatory minimum sentencing legislation may impose indeterminate minimum/maximum terms or a single determinate prison sentence. Mandatory minimum prison sentences are most often provided for murder and multiple convictions for such crimes as rape, drug violations, and robbery. On the one hand, mandatory sentencing generally limits the judge's discretionary power to impose any disposition but that authorized by the legislature; as a result, it destroys the idea of the individualized sentence, impeding rehabilitation efforts by the courts. On the other hand, mandatory sentencing provides equal treatment for all offenders who commit the same serious crime, regardless of age or gender.

WEB
For more information on mandatory minimum sentencing, **visit the link to Families against Mandatory Minimums on our Web site,** www.prenhall.com/territo.

ENHANCEMENT STATUTES—TWO PUNISHMENTS FOR ONE CRIME

In America's forty-year war on drugs and crime, the legislature became fed up with the vast disparity in the sentences convicted felons were receiving from trial judges versus the amount of time convicts actually served in prison to satisfy the sentences imposed on them. Due to massive prison overcrowding in state correctional facilities, a federal court order was established allowing every inmate in every state prison a minimum amount of square feet to live in (less than the minimum would be a violation of the "cruel and unusual punishment" clause of the Eighth Amendment). For every violation of the minimum-square-foot rule, the supervising federal court could fine the correctional institutions tens of thousands of dollars per day (a separate fine for each inmate in a correctional institution that was not afforded the minimum square footage to live in). Hundreds of inmates were being sentenced to correctional facilities that were already full or probably already in violation of the federal court order.

Correctional institution officials determined that room had to be made to house new violent convicts without violating the federal court order. It became clear that the only way to accomplish such a goal would be to provide early releases to inmates presently incarcerated in state correctional facilities in order to make room for the newly convicted inmates.

CTQ
Although crime-control advocates applaud determinate and mandatory sentencing structures, critics fear they will swell prison populations, costing taxpayers additional billions of dollars and taking away from other needs such as higher education, health care, and social security. Which of the two opposing positions do you support? Why?

WEB
For more information on Citizens for Independent Courts, **visit our Web site,** www.prenhall.com/territo.

The amount of time a current inmate would receive in order to achieve an early release became a formula worked out by the Correctional Administration. Days were to be subtracted from the length of the sentence an inmate was given by the judge in criminal court by using various formulas that gave inmates a significant reduction in their original sentence. These formulas take into account (1) the type of crime committed, (2) good-time days acquired, (3) gain-time days acquired, and (4) provisional credits given to certain inmates by the governor to alleviate extreme overcrowding.

The consequence of these procedures was that in almost every state, inmates serving fixed sentences would end up having to serve only 20 to 25% of their actual sentences. This radical cycle of extraordinary early releases reached its peak between the mid-1980s and mid-1990s.[31]

State legislators angered with this situation drafted new laws designed to prevent early release, especially for certain crimes. These new laws are called **enhancement statutes.** Examples of such statutes would be the Habitual Felons Act, RICO, the Career Criminal Act, mandatory minimum sentences for trafficking in narcotics, perpetuating crimes in a violent manner, three-strikes laws (see Figure 10.3), hate-crime laws, and 10-20-Life for using a gun during the commission of a crime. Enhancement statutes are designed to get tough with chronic and persistent offenders and keep them off the streets for an extended period of time.

The central features of enhancement statutes are (1) that they add severe penalties (twenty to twenty-five years) on to the penalty for committing the original crime, and (2) those receiving enhancement-statute punishments are not entitled to features such as early release, gain time, and provisional credits. In sentencing-guideline states, enhancement statutes provide the amount of punishment by calculating that amount outside of the sentencing guidelines, thereby making them immune to the internal reduction nature inherent to these guidelines. The ultimate consequence of enhancement statutes is that they ensure that the inmate undergoes a significantly long period of incarceration; this period is a flat-time sentence that cannot be affected by early-release procedures (see the Landmark Case *United States v. Rodriguez-Moreno*). Thus, the legislators got what they wanted with the implementation of enhancement statutes. The convict will serve almost the same sentence that the judge imposed. Remember, enhancement statutes attach only to a few select crimes. Inmates convicted of other crimes have their prison time reduced by the traditional methods (good time, gain time, provisional credits).

State legislators may like the consequences of trying, convicting, and sentencing a defendant on an enhancement statute, but trial judges definitely do not. This is because the law controlling what kind of sentence a judge can give a defendant convicted under an enhancement statute is already fixed (for example, twenty-five years). The judge therefore is deprived of the power of sentencing such a defendant to fifteen to twenty-four years, even if the case merits it. Trial judges are forced to give a deliberate flat-time sentence that they have no judicial discretion to modify. Furthermore, once a defendant is sentenced to a flat-term number of years under an enhancement statute, due to the "mandatory minimum" feature, the defendant is not subject to early-release mechanisms. Therefore, the defendant will serve the entire sentence, with no exceptions.

Judges know that legislators have totally castrated the judicial discretion powers in every instance where they are faced with sentencing defendants convicted under enhancement statutes. To the trial judge, these rigid consequences seem to indicate a shift in the balance of power. Judicial discretion in sentencing, always an exclusive right of the judiciary, has now become functionally transformed; the amount and nature of sentences has already been predetermined by a different branch of government—the state legislature.

Another popular type of enhancement statute is called "three strikes and you're out." Although popular, this type of statute seemingly could lend itself to offend one's notion of justice. Civil libertarians fear that these statutes may be used in an indiscriminate fashion to punish petty offenders, or to pressure defendants to plea bargain or testify against others (see "In the News: Three Strikes and You're Out").

FIGURE 10.3

Violations in States' Three-Strikes Laws

Source: Adapted from J. Clark, J. Austin, and D. Henry, "'Three Strikes and You're Out': A Review of State Legislation," *NIJ Research in Brief* (September 2001), Exhibits 9 and 10.

Between 1994 and 1995, twenty-four states adopted so-called three-strikes laws. This figure shows that there are significant differences among the states in offenses included, number of strikes required, and in the meaning of the term "out."

State	Major Offenses Included	Strikes Needed	Meaning of "Out"
Arkansas	Murder, kidnapping, robbery, rape	Two	At least 40 years in prison; no parole
California	Any felony if one prior conviction for one of 27 felonies	Two	Twice the usual term for offense involved
	Any felony if two prior convictions for one of 27 felonies	Three	Indeterminate life with no parole eligibility for 25 years
Colorado	Any Class 1 or 2 felony, or any Class 3 if violent	Three	Life in prison with no parole eligibility for 40 years
Connecticut	Murder, arson, kidnapping, robbery, aggravated sexual assault	Two / Three	Up to 40 years in prison / Up to life in prison
Florida	Any forcible felony, aggravated child abuse, lewd or indecent conduct	Three	Up to life in prison
Georgia	Murder, armed robbery, rape, kidnapping, aggravated sodomy	Two	Life without parole
	Any felony	Four	Maximum sentence for charge
Indiana	Murder, rape, child molestation, robbery, drug dealing	Three	Life without parole
Kansas	Any felony against a person	Two	Double term listed in guideline
	Any felony against a person	Three	Triple term listed in guideline
Louisiana	Murder, rape, kidnapping, drug offense punishable by more than 5 yrs.	Three	Life in prison; no parole
Maryland	Murder, rape, burglary, kidnapping, carjacking, use of firearm in felony	Four	Life in prison; no parole
Montana	Deliberate homicide, sexual intercourse without consent	Two	Life in prison; no parole
	Aggravated assault, kidnapping, robbery	Three	Same
Nevada	Murder, robbery, kidnapping, arson	Three	Up to life without parole
New Jersey	Murder, robbery, carjacking	Three	Life in prison; no parole
New Mexico	Murder, kidnapping, criminal sexual penetration	Three	Life in prison; parole eligibility after 30 years
N. Carolina	47 violent felonies	Three	Life in prison; no parole
N. Dakota	Any Class A, B, or C felony	Two	Up to life in prison
Pennsylvania	Murder, rape, arson, kidnapping, robbery	Two	Up to 10 years in prison
	Same offenses	Three	Up to 25 years in prison
S. Carolina	Murder rape, armed robbery, drug trafficking, embezzlement	Two	Life in prison; no parole
Tennessee	Murder and aggravated violent felonies	Two or Three	Life in prison; no parole if prior time served
Utah	Any first- or second-degree felony	Three	Up to life in prison
Vermont	Murder, arson causing death, kidnapping, lewd contact with a child	Three	Up to life in prison
Virginia	Murder, kidnapping, carjacking, sexual assault	Three	Life in prison; no parole
Washington	List of 51 offenses, including murder, arson, and promoting prostitution	Three	Life in prison; no parole
Wisconsin	Murder, abuse of child, sexual assaults, arson, burglary	Three	Life in prison; no parole

LANDMARK CASE

United States v. Rodriguez-Moreno

During a drug transaction in Houston, a New York drug dealer stole thirty kilograms of a Texas distributor's cocaine. The distributor hired Rodriguez-Moreno and the other defendants to find the dealer and to hold captive the middleman in the transaction, Avendano. Rodriguez-Moreno and his co-defendants were tried jointly and charged with conspiring to kidnap Avendano, kidnapping Avendano, and using a firearm in relation to the kidnapping, in violation of federal law. Rodriguez-Moreno moved to dismiss for lack of venue, contending that venue was proper only in Maryland, where the government had proved that he actually used the gun. He was convicted under the enhancement statute of using the gun while perpetrating the crime. The Supreme Court ruled that venue in a prosecution for using or carrying a firearm during and in relation to any crime that violates federal law is proper in any district in which the crime was committed, even if the firearm was carried only in a single district.

Source: United States v. Rodriguez-Moreno, 526 U.S. 275 (1999).

Habitual-Criminal Statutes

Habitual-criminal statutes are another form of enhancement statutes that explode the maximum sentence available to a defendant who has been convicted of and served time for multiple felony offenses. If such a person is subsequently convicted of one additional felony, regardless of severity, he or she will face the habitual-criminal statute as an added punishment (twenty to twenty-five years). Such a defendant will be tried for the felony, as well as under the habitual-criminal statute. If convicted, the defendant will be sentenced both for the felony and under the enhancement statute.

CTQ
Discuss the constitutional implications of habitual-criminal laws.

IN THE NEWS

A HUMAN PERSPECTIVE

THREE STRIKES AND YOU'RE OUT

At the time, it seemed to many people like a good idea. In the wake of several brutal murders by former convicts California enacted the toughest "three strikes" law in the nation. Any criminal with a serious or violent prior felony would automatically have his sentence doubled for a second conviction and, on a third felony conviction, would be put away for 25 years to life. But the 1994 statute, endorsed by 72% of California voters in a ballot initiative, had troubling consequences. The courts became clogged with the three-strikes cases on nonviolent criminals. (One man got 25 years to life for shoplifting two packs of cigarettes; another for stealing a slice of pizza.) Prisons overflowed, and incarceration costs skyrocketed.

The justices agreed. It would be unconstitutional, they declared unanimously, for the law to limit a trial judge's discretion to reduce a three-strike sentence "in furtherance of justice." Prosecutors are allowed to plea-bargain under the law—and so, if they choose, disregard prior convictions. If judges were not allowed to do likewise, the balance of power among the legislative, executive and judicial branches would be skewed. "The legal system has long recognized that rigid application of the law can produce injustice," said Paul Boland, president of the California Judges Association, applauding the ruling. Many of the 18,000 prisoners convicted under the law may now appeal their sentences.

But the court's action, which reinterprets the law, rather than strikes it down, provoked outrage from victim advocates and some politicians. "Those who repeatedly assault our citizens, terrorize our elderly and prey upon our children must pay a severe price," declared Governor Pete Wilson, who pledged to try to overturn the decision either in the legislature or through another ballot initiative. One possibility: make the law even more rigid and remove the discretion of both prosecutors and judges.

But that would further raise the price of three strikes. A Rand Corp. researcher who determined that California faces an annual increase in prison costs of $5.5 billion under the law also analyzed four social programs and found three of them far more effective in reducing crime. "If you're going to spend a million dollars, you prevent three times as much crime if you put it into parent training than if you put it into building more cells," said Peter Greenwood, the study's director.

Source: M. Horn, "Three Strikes and You're Out," *Time,* July 1, 1996, p. 52. © 1996 TIME, Inc. Reprinted by permission.

LANDMARK CASE: Apprendi v. New Jersey

Apprendi fired shots into the home of an African-American family. When he was arrested he stated that he did not want the family in the neighborhood because of their race. He was indicted on twenty-three counts, none of which referred to the New Jersey hate-crime statute or alleged that Apprendi acted with a racially motivated purpose. After an evidentiary hearing on the issue of Apprendi's motive for the shooting, the judge concluded that the crime was motivated by racial bias and he was sentenced to twelve years, to run consecutively with his other sentences. Apprendi appealed. The Supreme Court took the case and held that any fact that increases the penalty for a crime beyond the statutory minimum, other than the fact of a prior conviction, must be submitted to a jury and proved beyond a reasonable doubt (which did not happen in this case). Therefore, the case was sent back to the jury to determine whether the actions of the defendant constituted a hate crime. If the jury determined beyond a reasonable doubt that this act was indeed racially motivated (a hate crime), an additional twelve years could be added onto the sentence, and the enhancement would be constitutional.

Source: Apprendi v. New Jersey, 120 S.Ct. 2348 (2000).

Hate Crimes

Hate crimes activate another form of sentence enhancement (see the Landmark Case *Apprendi v. New Jersey*). Hate crimes are offenses attached to enhancement statutes if the crime is motivated by hatred against the victim because of his or her race, ethnicity, religion, sexual orientation, handicap, or national origin.

The New Sentencing Structures of the Twenty-First Century

The traditional American definition of punishment—"in the United States, the only form of punishment recognized is incarceration"—has expanded into additional arenas. In these cases, punishment not only is incarceration but is also compounded by punishing the offenders with civil commitment and humiliation This triple punishment of incarceration, commitment, and humiliation is particularly new to the American scene. A particular focus of humiliation seems to be criminals who are classified as pedophiles or violent sex offenders. Many laws attempt to punish these offenders in multiple ways, but all can be categorized under the general legal topic of "Megan's Laws." The double and triple punishment of applying Megan's Laws is embodied in two examples (see "In the News: Do 'Megan's Laws' Make a Difference?" and "In the News: A New Scarlet Letter;" and "In the News: State of Florida Publicizes Identity of Probationers").

TRADITIONAL SENTENCING DISPARITIES

Sentencing disparity occurs when offenders who commit the same or similar crimes under similar circumstances with similar backgrounds receive significantly different sentences. Sentencing disparities have been a major issue in American criminal justice. At the heart of this issue is the American notion of the meaning of justice. Historically, justice has meant that there is fundamental fairness in those procedures by which a defendant is tried, convicted, and sentenced, and that people with similar criminal histories who commit similar crimes should receive similar sanctions for their crimes.

With disparities in sentencing, the ideal of American justice has been tarnished. Prisoners who compare their sentences with those of other inmates noticeably and correctly feel that they have been victims of injustice. And furthermore, those who study the criminal justice system who have noticed sentencing disparity have questioned

---

WEB
For more information on hate-crime statutes, **visit the link to the Anti-Defamation League on our Web site,** www.prenhall.com/territo

WEB
For more information on federal sentencing reform, **visit our Web site,** www.prenhall.com/territo.

WEB
For more information about Megan's Laws, **visit our Web site,** www.prenhall.com/territo.

WEB
For more information on sex offender registries, **visit our Web site,** www.prenhall.com/territo.

CTQ
Many jurists believe that a certain amount of discretion in sentencing is inevitable. Is this true, and should we accept it as an inevitable process of sentencing?

IN THE NEWS
A HUMAN PERSPECTIVE

DO MEGAN'S LAWS MAKE A DIFFERENCE?

When Scott Lee Stoller, a convicted child molester, left prison in 1996, Seattle police notified his neighbors with a community meeting and a flier that called him "a high risk to reoffend." But that August, Stoller drove 10 minutes across Lake Washington to Redmond, where parents hadn't been warned of his violent past, and molested two girls, ages 5 and 6. "I don't count on notification to protect anybody," says Robert Hales, a Redmond detective who helped arrest Stoller. "But at least the public is aware that these individuals are living in their neighborhoods."

Washington State was the first in the country to pass a law requiring that communities be notified when a sex offender moves nearby. These laws—now known as "Megan's laws" after the New Jersey girl raped and murdered by her neighbor in 1994—got a big boost in the Supreme Court last week, when it refused to hear arguments that such civil actions constitute double jeopardy, or two punishments for the same crime.

But even if these laws are constitutional, a more basic question remains: Do they deter offenders? Evidence from Washington State's eight-year experience with the law suggests that community notification has little, if any, impact on the likelihood that a convicted sex criminal will strike again. According to a 1995 state study, in the period before the "Megan's law," 22 percent of sex offenders who had been arrested went out again and committed sex crimes. After the law went into effect, the number hardly budges: It was 19 percent.

Officials say that notification is mostly useful as a way to educate the public. Robert Schilling, a Seattle detective who has run hundreds of community meetings, says he uses them to make a louder point, "I always say, 'This person is not our biggest worry. Your biggest worry is the person you don't know about yet.'" By raising the profile of sex crimes, notification laws have put pressure on police to apprehend suspects and the justice system to mete out tougher punishment.

But heightened awareness can also lead to increased fear and suspicion. Sandra Yudilevich, the nurse who examined Stoller's most recent victims, wonders about the long-term consequences of injection of such worry into children's lives: "It's an unknown quantity. I can foresee problems, particularly in homes where protectiveness is really overdone."

Polls bear out changing attitudes about safety: About half of Washington parents, for example, say they're less likely than before the law was passed to leave their kids alone—even with a baby sitter. Roxanne Lieb, an expert on notification laws at the Washington Institute for Public Policy, calls it a rare sight to see younger children walking home from school alone or even waiting for the bus.

Such fear of strangers may be misplaced. Skeptics of notification point out that fewer than 10 percent of sex criminals are strangers to their victims. The most common category of abuse is within the family. Some even argue that Megan's laws could have an adverse affect, silencing victims of incest for fear that those molesting them—their parents or siblings—will become pariahs. This is a particular concept in Louisiana, which is the only state that requires sex offenders to notify the community themselves. Judges have even required offenders to wear special clothing or sandwich boards announcing their past crimes.

One common effect of such disclosure is to make communities rise up against individual offenders. Even in Washington State, where police publicly vow to protect the right of past offenders to be left alone, more than 30 acts of vigilantism have been recorded since the notification law took effect. Most dramatically, in 1993, arsonists burned down the home to which a paroled child rapist was supposed to be released.

Many offenders' daily lives are affected, too. One recently released child molester bought a boat with his wife but was rejected by dozens of different docks in the Seattle area before finding one that would lease him space. Kevin, who asked to be identified by first name only, says he supports community notification because "the best indicator of future behavior is past behavior." But he noted that even intense scrutiny is often not enough to stop many offenders: "No external factor is going to keep me from reoffending—not the program, not my wife, not God. Only me."

Source: Joshua Shenk, "Do 'Megan's Laws' Make a Difference? Pariah Status May Not Deter Sex Offenders," *U.S. News & World Report,* March 9, 1998, p. 27. Copyright 1998 U.S. News & World Report, L. P. Reprinted with permission.

---

whether even-handed justice is being administered in American courtrooms (see Figure 10.4).

There are three major reasons that traditional sentencing disparities exist in the American criminal justice system. One is the structure of indeterminate sentencing, which allows judges great discretion in the severity of the sentence to be imposed. Second, certain judges in certain jurisdictions have the discretionary power to make a wide range of sentencing decisions for those committing identical crimes. And finally, since 90 percent of criminal cases in America are processed by plea bargaining, prosecutors can essentially affect the sentence, basing it not on the crime the offender has committed but rather on the bargaining powers and the negotiating skills of the offender and the attorney who are participating in the plea bargain negotiation.

IN THE NEWS

A HUMAN PERSPECTIVE

A NEW SCARLET LETTER

Gabriel Trevino did a bad, bad thing. Three years ago, at age 31, he fondled a 14-year-old daughter of a friend. For this "slipup," as he calls it, he pleaded no contest and took five years' probation rather than risk a two-20-year prison term. Now he thinks prison would have been preferable. These days, people drive by his modest bungalow house, then back up to read the 18-in. by 24-in. sign posted by the little white birdhouse. DANGER, it says, REGISTERED SEX OFFENDER LIVES HERE.

Sitting by the front window in his darkened living room in Corpus Christi, Texas, last week, Trevino was at once defiant and near tears as he talked about this public mortification. "I made a mistake, and I'm paying for it," he said. But, he wondered, why should his wife and two stepdaughters pay too? "I can't even go out and cut my yard. I just stay in the house . . . I was doing good in therapy. How is this helping me?"

The answer is simple, says state District Judge J. Manuel Banales, who on May 18 ordered Trevino and 13 other "high risk" offenders on probation to post the signs in their yards. "It will keep people like you, sir, honest," he told Trevino last week after denying a request to rescind the order. "Your neighbors will watch you and make sure you're not taking another child into your home." Hours later, Banales ordered yet another sex offender—No. 15—to put up a sign on release from jail.

In the past decade, all 50 states have passed so-called Megan's laws, requiring sex offenders to alert the community to their presence. Twenty-eight states run Internet sites listing such criminals. In the mid-1990s, judges in Texas, Louisiana, Florida, and Oregon began ordering individual sex offenders to post signs outside their homes. But Banales—who also mandated bumper stickers and even temporary placards for traveling in someone else's car—drew national attention by applying his ruling to so many at one time. His move sparked a debate on the rights of these offenders and the merits of the public shaming. "We don't brand people in America," argues Gerald Rogen, president of the Coastal Bend Criminal Defense Lawyers Association (see "In the News: State of Florida Publicizes Indentity of Probationers"). "And we damn sure don't punish the offender's family as well as the offender."

Source: Cathy Booth Thomas, "A New Scarlet Letter," *Time,* June 11, 2001. Reprinted with permission from *Time,* all rights reserved.

Differences in the sentencing tendencies of judges fascinate social scientists. The disparities may be ascribed to a number of factors: the conflicting goals of criminal justice, the fact that judges are products of different backgrounds and have different social values, the administrative pressures on judges, and the influence of community values. Each of these factors affects, to some extent, the judge's exercise of discretion in sentencing. In addition, a judge's perception of these factors depends on his or her own attitudes toward the law, toward a particular crime, or toward a certain type of offender.

Sentencing Guidelines—An Attempt to Resolve the Problem of Sentencing Disparities

Another kind of sentencing structure that state and federal legislatures are passing in the beginning of the twenty-first century is *sentencing guidelines.* Sentencing guidelines are

IN THE NEWS

A HUMAN PERSPECTIVE

STATE OF FLORIDA PUBLICIZES IDENTITY OF PROBATIONERS

The Florida Department of Corrections requires that all probationers, even though their crimes were not serious enough to merit incarceration, experience a new public form of punishment. In the state, all probationers are forced to come to the probation office to be photographed by their probation officer; consequently, the Florida Department of Corrections Web site posts the photograph and name of each probationer, his or her crime(s), address, driver's license number, and other personal information for any and all to see and use. The Web site allows visitors to search for probationers by name, description, or address. Therefore, visitors can conduct a search for probationers living in their neighborhoods.

Source: Florida Department of Corrections Web site, http://www.dc.state.fl.us.

FIGURE 10.4

"Fetch me the law for the rich, will you?" © Punch/Rothco

CTQ

Should we have judicial discretion in sentencing, or should judges be able to exercise unlimited discretion?

CTQ

Explain how the limitations on judicial discretion under sentencing guidelines have increased the prosecution's discretionary authority on the sentencing decision.

developed empirically by examining past judicial decisions within a jurisdiction. The advent of sentencing guidelines represents the frustration of legislatures with sentencing disparities; guidelines are an attempt to develop an instrument to indicate what most judges usually do in a particular type of case. Guidelines are designed to constrain the discretion of judges and direct the judge to the specific action he or she should take in a given circumstance.

Federal sentencing guidelines were introduced as a new type of sentencing structure derived from studies, committees, and legislative think tanks who intended to reduce judicial discretion in meting out punishments and ensure equal justice in sentencing applied throughout the states. The federal government adopted sentencing guidelines on November 1, 1987, hoping that uniformity would be imposed in all federal sentences. The most profound change resulting from sentencing guidelines is that they limit judges' discretion as to the nature of the sentence they are to impose on a convicted criminal.

It probably comes as no surprise that the principal opponents of sentencing guidelines are judges themselves. Most judges feel that their discretion has been taken away, and the guidelines negate their ability in extraordinary cases either to severely punish a deserving convict or to grant extreme leniency in cases where it is appropriate. Indeed, this discretion for the most part is gone. Ironically, the sentencing guidelines themselves are also corrupted by the omnipresent problem of prison overcrowding because of good time, gain time, and actual time served. See Table 10.2 and the next section.

Gain Time, Good Time, and Actual Time Served

Good time is a system in which days are subtracted from a prisoners sentence, in exchange for good behavior or participation in various types of treatment, educational, or vocational programs. Most correctional officials consider these sentence reduction policies necessary to maintain institutional order. They are often used to relieve prison overcrowding. The amount of good time that can be earned varies among states. Some states allow five days a month to count for good time; others allow only forty-five days a year to count for good time. Most often the number of good-time days are either written into statutes or stipulated by the department of corrections.

Due to variations in sentencing structures and prison release laws among the states, it is difficult to compare the amount of time served in prison with the actual length of sentences imposed by the trial judge. Some criminals serve 83 percent of the sentence; others only serve 18.5 percent of the sentence (see Figure 10.5).

TABLE 10.2 Sentencing Guidelines and Sentencing Disparities

Offense	Severity	Maximum Possible	Sentence Imposed under Sentencing Guidelines	Time Actually Served Due to Five Gain-Time Provisions
Attempted murder	First-degree felony	30 years	10 years	3 years
Rape (sexual battery)	First-degree felony	30 years	4 years	14½ months
Armed robbery	First-degree felony	30 years	3 years	10 months
Possession of more than 400 grams of cocaine with intent to distribute	First-degree felony	30 years	4 years	14½ months
Trafficking in excess of 400 grams of cocaine	First-degree felony	30 years	15 years (mandatory minimum sentence)	12 years (with one gain-time provision)

Source: L. Territo, J. Halsted, and M. Bromley, *Crime and Justice in America: A Human Perspective*, 4th ed. Minneapolis, Minn.: West, 1995.

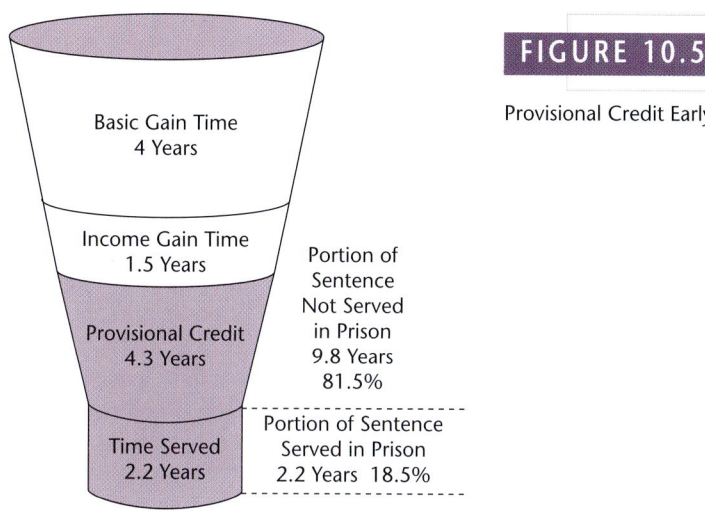

FIGURE 10.5

Provisional Credit Early Release System

- Basic Gain Time: 4 Years
- Income Gain Time: 1.5 Years
- Provisional Credit: 4.3 Years
- Time Served: 2.2 Years

Portion of Sentence Not Served in Prison: 9.8 Years, 81.5%

Portion of Sentence Served in Prison: 2.2 Years, 18.5%

THE APPEAL PROCESS

Defendants who have been convicted and sentenced in criminal court have a right to appeal their conviction. In most jurisdictions, a direct criminal appeal to an appellate court exists as a matter of right for all convicted defendants. This means that a defendant has an automatic right to appeal a conviction based on errors that may have occurred during the trial proceedings (see the Landmark Case *Chapman v. California*).

During **appellate review,** the appellate court analyzes the trial court's transcripts and the lawyers' appellate briefs to determine whether the defendant received a fair trial in accordance with the rights guaranteed by the federal or state constitution, the rules of criminal procedure, and the substantive criminal law. Appellate review acts as a shield for individuals caught up in the process of criminal trial, incarceration, or supervision in the community. The power of the state is great, and citizens must be protected against the capricious and arbitrary exercise of such power. The right to appeal the guilty verdict in a criminal trial is one of the most important aspects of due process. Although it is not spelled out in the Bill of Rights, appellate review embodies certain constitutional guarantees.

The burden of proof on appeal is on the defendant to prove that the conviction should be reversed. Most Americans are unaware that a defendant who has had a successful appeal is not released from incarceration. Rather, the defendant is more often ordered to stand a new trial, and the trial judge who made the error in the original trial

LANDMARK CASE: Chapman v. California

Chapman and others were arrested for kidnapping, robbery, and murder. At trial, none of the defendants testified. The prosecution emphasized the fact that Chapman failed to testify, and all defendants were convicted. Chapman appealed his conviction, based on these grounds. While the case was on appeal, the U.S. Supreme Court held that it was a deprivation of a defendant's rights for the prosecution to comment on his failure to testify. Chapman contended that because the error was constitutional, it was subject to reversible error. The California Supreme Court held the error to be harmless (that is, the error was not sufficient to warrant reversal, modification, or retrial). The U.S. Supreme Court granted review.

The Court considered the issue of whether a constitutional error may be held harmless where it is shown to be harmless beyond a reasonable doubt. The Court said yes. In this case, by commenting on the defendant's failure to testify, the prosecution suggested that this was an admission of guilt. Thus, this case was subject to reversible error and was reversed and remanded.

Source: Chapman v. California, 386 U.S. 18 (1967).

CTQ

Douglas v. California[32] gave indigent defendants the right to free counsel on their first automatic appeal, yet *Ross v. Moffitt*[33] did not give them a free lawyer to the court of last resort in their state or to the U.S. Supreme Court. Can you explain the discrepancy in the philosophy supporting the conclusion of these two cases? Do you believe that these cases render fair justice?

---

is admonished to correct the mistake in the new trial. Appellate courts generally confine their review of convictions to legal issues, as distinct from factual issues. While appellate courts review the legal sufficiency of evidence, they do not attempt to second-guess the factual determinations of trial judges and juries. Rather, appellate courts review such procedural issues as denial of fair trial, denial of counsel, admission of illegal evidence, and improper jury instructions. Appellate courts focus on errors or consequences, often overlooking so-called harmless errors.

Essentially, an appeal of a criminal conviction is based on assignment of errors that were made during the criminal trial itself. These errors will be judged by the appeals court as either harmless or reversible. For example, in a case where a judge allowed the admission of hearsay evidence against a defendant but the prosecution had additional evidence that overwhelmingly proved the defendant guilty, the appeals court would rule that although there was error in the court below, that error did not constitute reversible error. Instead, it was harmless error if the appellate court concludes that during the defendant's trial the error was harmless (that is, had the error not occurred, the result still would have been the same); in this case, the appellant is not afforded a new trial.

Some errors, however, are reversible. For example, when a defendant is not given the opportunity to have counsel at the trial, this is an automatic and **reversible error.** Any time an involuntary confession is admitted against a defendant in a trial, an automatic reversal is required. (However, this precedent has been overruled by a 1991 Supreme Court decision.) In a new trial, the defendant is to be tried without the use of the illegal evidence.

Appeals at criminal trials are not automatic because the defendant must take significant procedural steps after he or she has been convicted in order to preserve or "perfect" the appeal. For example, the court must be given notice within a specific time; an affidavit of errors must allege the mistakes or defects at trial; and a proper brief and motion to appeal must be made to the appellate court, specifically articulating the basis of the appeal (see Figure 10.6).

Finally, defendants have a right to their first automatic appeal in the American criminal justice system. They have the right to have a free attorney in their first automatic appeal in the system.[34] Yet indigent defendants do not have the right to have an attorney assist them in their appeal to the court of last resort—the Supreme Court.[35]

In the 1960s, a series of appellate decisions were made in favor of the incarcerated offender. These decisions had diverse effects on the criminal justice system. On the pos-

FIGURE 10.6

The Florida Supreme Court Justices enter a courtroom to hear an appeal on a defendant's sentence of death by electrocution.

Courtesy of Reuters NewMedia Inc./CORBIS.

itive side, the protections of the Fourth, Fifth, Sixth, and Eighth Amendments were extended to incarcerated offenders through a series of appeals that were based on the due process and equal-protection clauses of the Fourteenth Amendment. The success of such appeals has encouraged more and more defendants to go the appeal route, and the result has been an increase in the appeal rate in some jurisdictions. Less than 20 percent of all appeals in federal courts are for criminal matters.[36]

Postconviction Relief—A Hidden Form of Appeal

A person who has been convicted of a crime, has exhausted all normal appellate remedies, and is confined to prison may still challenge his or her conviction, sentence, or conditions of confinement by filing a petition for a writ of *habeas corpus*. ***Habeas corpus*** is an ancient common-law device that permits judges to review the legality of someone's confinement. The writ is purely procedural; it gives only the right to a hearing. It has no bearing on the substance of the issue or the charge.

In modern American criminal procedure, *habeas corpus* has become a way for prisoners who have exhausted all other avenues of appeal to obtain judicial review. A federal prisoner petitions the appropriate federal district court for *habeas corpus* relief. Under most state statutes, state prisoners may file *habeas corpus* petitions or other similar petitions for postconviction relief with the appropriate state courts.

Under federal law, a state prisoner may petition a federal district court for *habeas corpus* relief if he or she wishes to raise federal constitutional issues, for example, denial of the Sixth Amendment right to have effective counsel (see the Landmark Case *Schlup v. Delo*). The power of federal courts to issue a writ of *habeas corpus* in state cases can be traced to an act of Congress adopted just after the Civil War.

Discretionary Review—The Privileged Appeal

Federal law and the laws of almost every state provide those convicted of crimes a limited right to appeal their convictions to higher tribunals. When convictions are upheld on appeal, defendants may petition higher appellate courts for further review. This appellate process is called **discretionary review.** Such review is available at the discretion of the higher court. The Supreme Court receives thousands of petitions each year from defendants whose convictions have been affirmed by the U.S. Courts of Appeals or the highest appellate tribunals of the states. Naturally, the Supreme Court is able to review only a small percentage of the cases that present important issues of law.

Can a Convicted Defendant Appeal a Harsh Sentence?

Only fifteen states have some system by which defendants may ask for review of their sentences; in other states the prosecution may seek a change of what they believe to be

CTQ

Presently, the Supreme Court has denied indigent defendants the right to an attorney to assist them in filing a *habeas corpus* petition, even though *habeas corpus* is the oldest form of due process protection in the Anglo-American system. Is this denial of the right to an attorney to help a defendant with this petition consistent with your notion of justice? Why or why not?

CTQ

Why do you think the Supreme Court takes so few criminal cases on appeal each year?

LANDMARK CASE — Schlup v. Delo

Schlup was a Caucasian defendant convicted and sentenced to death for the murder of an African-American inmate. Schlup filed a petition for a federal writ of *habeas corpus*, asserting that his trial counsel was ineffective. After the federal district court and court of appeals denied his petition, Schlup petitioned to the U.S. Supreme Court, which granted review. The Court considered the issue of whether a *habeas corpus* petitioner must show that a constitutional violation probably exists and has resulted in the conviction of one who is actually innocent. The Court answered yes. To establish this, the petitioner must show that it is more likely than not that no reasonable juror would have convicted him or her in light of the new evidence. In this case, the defendant was able to establish ineffective counsel due to the attorney's failure to interview a known and easily accessible witness to the crime.

Source: *Schlup v. Delo*, 513 U.S. 298 (1995).

---

lenient sentences. In the states authorizing sentencing review, two methods are used. In seven states, a special panel of trial judges is convened to review the propriety of a sentence in individual cases.[37] On hearing an appeal, the panel may increase or decrease the original sentence. In the other eight review states, requests may be brought to a regular appellate court.[38] In all fifteen states, reformers have sought to require trial judges to provide written explanations for each sentence they impose. Review has not been available in many jurisdictions because of fears of increased litigation,[39] concern that appellate judges are less qualified than trial judges to determine appropriate sentences, and the belief that sentencing is a matter of judicial discretion rather than a matter of law. On the other hand, the American Bar Association (through its Committee on Minimum Standards for Criminal Justice) maintains that "judicial review should be available for all sentences imposed in cases where provision is made for review of the convictions."[40]

CTQ: Should it be constitutionally required that all states allow prisoners to appeal a harsh sentence? Why or why not?

Clemency

Clemency by the governor is a form of appeal of a harsh sentence based on the sovereign's power to grant mercy. The governor's power to grant clemency never has been exercised to any substantial extent in the United States, especially when compared to the number of times it was exercised by former Texas governor Ann Richards during the 1990s. Richards especially granted clemency to defendants convicted of homicide when the victim was a spouse abuser (see "In the News: Texas Considers Clemency to Look at Cases Related to Abuse").

THE DEATH PENALTY

The use of the death penalty has declined dramatically throughout the industrial Western world since the nineteenth century. Nearly every European nation either has formally abolished the death penalty for criminal acts or has abandoned its practice.

WEB: For information on the death penalty, visit our Web site, www.prenhall.com/territo.

The death penalty has been around as long as civilization. Some of the best-known executions—such as those of Socrates and Jesus—took place thousands of years ago. One of the earliest written codes of law—the Babylonian Code of Hammurabi, which was carved on a stone column more than four thousand years ago (see Chapter 2), provided for death as an appropriate response to crime. Capital punishment became more dominant in civilization's philosophy of punishment in the Middle Ages under the direction of the church.[41]

WEB: A more profound site on death sentences can be found at our Web site, www.prenhall.com/territo.

The majority of those executed in the United States during the nineteenth and early twentieth century were African-Americans. In fact, many states had slave codes that applied only to blacks. For example, in the 1830s, Virginia had seventy capital crimes for African Americans and only five for Caucasians; in 1848, Virginia enacted a law requiring death for African Americans convicted of any crime punishable by three years or more in prison. In 1816, Georgia required death for African Americans who raped or attempted to rape Caucasians, but imposed a two-year sentence on Caucasians convicted of rape of an African American.[42]

IN THE NEWS

A HUMAN PERSPECTIVE

TEXAS CONSIDERS CLEMENCY TO LOOK AT CASES RELATED TO ABUSE

With a ceremonial flourish by its former governor Ann Richards, Texas joined the growing list of states that contemplate freeing battered women and children who kill their abusers. The resolution directs the Texas Board of Pardons and Paroles to investigate murder cases directly related to battered women and abused children. But Richards said she's not going to make the same mistakes some other governors might have made. Said Chuck McDonald, spokesman for Richards: "We don't want to do just a blanket thing, which is where some people got into trouble in the past." Maryland Governor William Donald Schaefer freed eight women. Critics said Schaefer may have released women who didn't deserve it. Also, Joyce Danna—one of four female prisoners whose release Schaefer is weighing—was resentenced Thursday to life. The judge said that was the right penalty for premeditated murder. Danna said she killed her husband because he had abused her.

Absolving battered women of their crimes has gained momentum with growing recognition of domestic violence as a national problem. Statistics indicate a woman is beaten every 18 seconds in the USA. Every year 800 to 1,200 women kill the men who abused them. Texas officials estimate there could be as many as 250 individuals convicted in cases involving family violence, and more than 650,000 Texas women are estimated to be abused by their husbands or boyfriends on a regular basis.

Still, she said, the clemency veto may have been a blessing in disguise: Texas learned from the experience of Ohio and Maryland. The Texas resolution says prosecutors, judges, police and victims' families must be consulted before a decision is made to grant a woman clemency.

UPDATE

This clemency policy was aggressively pursued by Governor Richards, especially in her attempts to absolve battered women of their crimes. However, after the early 1990s, Richards failed to win reelection. She was defeated in the gubernatorial election by George W. Bush (now President George W. Bush). Under Bush's eight-year administration, the practice of granting clemency to abused women who killed their husbands all but stopped.

Source: M. Puente, "Texas Considers Clemency to Look at Cases Related to Abuse," *USA Today,* May 17, 1991, p. 4A. Copyright 1991, *USA TODAY.* Reprinted with permission.

Throughout the nineteenth century, it was common to be arrested, tried, convicted, and executed on the same day. Many executions were carried out by lynch mobs. In fact, the Bureau of the Census cited more than one documented lynching per month for many years until it stopped keeping such data in the mid-1950s.[43] Many times, mentally retarded, insane, and young people were victims of this practice.

Yet the nineteenth century also saw some changes. In 1847, the Territory of Michigan became the first English-speaking jurisdiction in the world to abolish the death penalty for all crimes except treason. By the early twentieth century, Wisconsin, Rhode Island, Maine, Minnesota, and North Dakota had all followed Michigan's lead and abolished capital punishment.[44]

As an answer to the cruelty and expense of the gallows, which was the prevalent means of execution in early American history, the electric chair was introduced around the turn of the century. At the Ohio Penitentiary, an inmate electrician named Charles Justice built one of the first electric chairs in the country (see Figure 10.7). Upon being released on parole, he killed a policeman. On October 27, 1911, ironically, Justice paid for his crime in the very chair he had constructed.[45] In 1930, the Justice Department began keeping records of those executed. According to these records, 3,829 people were executed under the state civil authorities from 1930 to 1967.[46]

The gas chamber was introduced in 1938 in California as a means to a cleaner execution (see Figure 10.8). This development occurred during a decade in which there were more executions than any other period in recent U.S. history (see Figure 10.10). This peak was reached in the United States in 1935, when 199 inmates were executed, the highest recorded figure in any single year. Anywhere from 50 to 89 percent of those executed each year for the next three decades were African American, although blacks comprised only 11 percent of America's entire population.[47] Twenty percent of all executions carried out during this period took place in the southern states for the crime of rape.[48] Executions steadily declined from their peak in 1935 until 1967, when they ceased altogether pending the resolution of various legal challenges to the death penalty.

FIGURE 10.7

The Electric Chair

Courtesy of Mark Foley/AP/Wide World Photos.

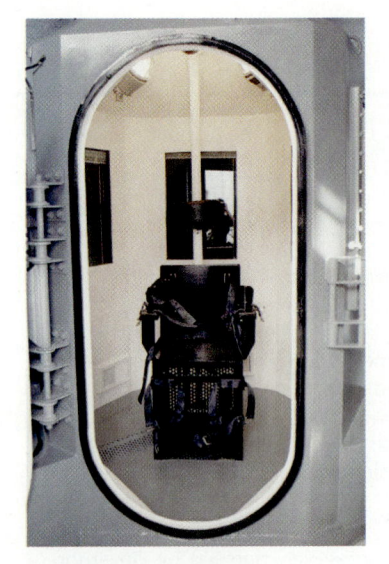

FIGURE 10.8

The Gas Chamber
Courtesy of AP/Wide World Photos.

WEB

If you want to have a visual experience of the death penalty, **visit the link to Court TV's information on the death penalty on our Web site, www.prenhall.com/territo.**

CTQ

Explain the difference between the Supreme Court rulings in the cases of *Furman v. Georgia* (1972) and *Gregg v. Georgia* (1976).

During the 1960s, American public opinion concerning the merits of having a death penalty was at an all-time low. In 1968, for example, only 38 percent of Americans approved of capital punishment.[49] Then, in 1972, the U.S. Supreme Court heard the landmark case *Furman v. Georgia*.[50] On June 29, 1972, the Supreme Court ruled 5–4 that the death penalty, as imposed under existing laws, "constituted cruel and unusual punishment in violation of the Eighth and Fourteenth Amendments." It is important to understand that the justices concentrated their objections on the manner in which the death penalty laws were applied, finding the result so "harsh, freakish, and arbitrary" as to be constitutionally unacceptable. In other words, the Supreme Court did not hold that the death penalty in and of itself was unconstitutional, but rather the way the death penalty was being applied.

To make the nationwide impact of their decision unmistakable, the justices overturned the death sentences of more than six hundred people who were then on death row in states throughout the country. This ruling, coupled with the low approval rating of capital punishment in 1968, as well as the declining number of executions, all suggested the demise of capital punishment. Did we as a nation miss the mark twenty years ago that signaled the end of the death penalty, or have conditions in America changed over the years to make the imposition of death sentences necessary?

The ruling in *Furman v. Georgia* did not abolish capital punishment per se; it simply ruled out the uncontrolled, unguided exercise of it. The states then responded by drawing up new capital punishment laws, which took one of two basic forms. The first form made the death penalty mandatory for certain specified crimes upon conviction. Twenty-one states followed this form in their revisions. The second form was a two-stage trial process in which juries would first decide guilt or innocence and then, upon weighing aggravating and mitigating circumstances, would recommend either imprisonment or death.

Aggravating circumstances in death penalty cases would be such factors as whether the defendant had an extensive prior record, whether he or she murdered in the course of another felony, whether the crime was "heinous, atrocious, or cruel," whether the defendant was incarcerated at the time of the murder (that is, killed a fellow inmate), whether the victim was a police officer, whether there were multiple victims, or whether it was a murder for hire.

Examples of *mitigating factors* in death penalty cases would be if the defendant was very young, the product of an abusive family, or under the influence of a vicious accomplice. If, upon weighing factors like these, the jury found that the scale tipped toward the aggravating factors, then the death penalty would be imposed.[51]

Contrary to the expectations of many observers, *Furman* did not resolve the death penalty controversy. In *Gregg v. Georgia* (1976), four years after *Furman*, the Supreme Court opened the door to a revival of capital punishment. The *Gregg* Court held that various state capital punishment laws enacted in response to *Furman* had sufficiently reduced the randomness permitted by the previous statutes. The Court concluded that the "new" death penalty statutes complied with constitutional requirements, and consequently it permitted the states to resume executions. The state statutes approved by the Court differed from prior penal codes. These new death penalty codes were different from the old ones in that (1) they permitted the imposition of capital punishment only for murder; (2) the death penalty applied only if the specific circumstances surrounding the killing were identical to the grounds authorized by the state statute that made the killing eligible for the death penalty; and (3) the statute established reasonably specific criteria that must be shown to apply if capital punishment was to be imposed.

In *Gregg v. Georgia,* the Supreme Court asserted that the state is authorized to issue a death decision as long as the jury considers aggravating or mitigating circumstances. The problem under the old law was that these circumstances were not considered. The new Georgia statute is a constitutional example that includes the following aggravating conditions: (1) the defendant had a prior conviction for a capital felony or a substantial history of criminal convictions for serious assaults; (2) the murder was committed during the course of a rape, an armed robbery, a kidnapping, a burglary, or an arson; (3) the defendant created a great risk of death to more than one person; (4) the defendant killed for profit; (5) the victim was a judicial officer or a prosecutor killed during the exercise of his or her official duty; (6) the victim was a police officer, corrections employee, or firefighter who was engaged in the performance of his or her duties; (7) the defendant directed another person to kill as an agent; (8) the murder was committed in a wantonly vile or inhumane manner because it involved torture, depravity of the mind, or aggravated battery; (9) the defendant was a prison escapee; or (10) the murder was committed in an attempt to avoid arrest.[52]

The Death Penalty and the Supreme Court

The death penalty is not cruel and unusual punishment under all circumstances. The Court has explicitly stated that capital punishment is permissible for adults under statutes meeting the following requirements: (1) The judge or jury is permitted to consider both aggravating and mitigating factors (about the crime and background of the defendant) relevant to sentencing; and (2) there is a review procedure to ensure against imposition of the death sentence for discriminatory reasons.[53]

The Supreme Court has held that these strict constitutional requirements, first outlined in *Gregg*, are not satisfied when the trial judge imposes a death sentence on the basis of information in a presentence investigation report that is not disclosed to the defendant or his or her counsel or made part of the record to be reviewed on appeal.[54] Furthermore, the Court held that death penalties imposed pursuant to statutes that permit overbroad discretion, and under which the penalty is selectively and capriciously applied, violate the Eighth and Fourteenth Amendments.[55]

The Role of the Jury in Capital Cases

The jury must be given flexibility in reaching its verdict, according to the Supreme Court. Thus, if the jury is not allowed to consider a lesser included offense when deciding on a verdict, the imposition of the death penalty is unconstitutional.[56] A jury's verdict is not final; it can be reviewed by the state supreme court or the U.S. Supreme Court. However, the prosecution cannot tell the jury of this legal fact because the Supreme Court stated that to do so would diminish the jury's "awesome responsibility" of imposing the death penalty.[57] In some states, the jury's role in death penalty cases (a verdict of death or life imprisonment) is only advisory to the judge. In these states, the judge must make the final determination of whether the defendant will receive life or death. In *Harris v. Alabama*, the Court stated that the state is not required to define the weight that a judge must give to an advisory jury's recommendation.[58]

Supreme Court Limitations

Since *Gregg v. Georgia*, the Supreme Court has made several rulings that have shaped the use of capital punishment in the United States. Among the first of these was *Coker v. Georgia* (1977), in which the Court abolished the death penalty for rape on the grounds that it was inconsistent with contemporary standards and values, because the magnitude of the penalty was greater than the magnitude of the victimization.[59] Thus, the Court, in effect, said that the imposition of the death penalty for anything short of taking another human life was unconstitutional. Only the loss of life could possibly mandate the taking of life.

Within the decade following *Coker*, the Court declared that the Eighth Amendment prohibits states from imposing the death penalty on a prisoner who is insane[60] (that is, if the prisoner was sane when he or she committed the crime, but became insane after being sentenced and imprisoned). However, in *Penry v. Lynaugh* the Court indicated that the Eighth Amendment does not prohibit the execution of a murderer who is mentally retarded but competent to stand trial and not insane.[61]

In 1989, the Court ruled on a case involving the use of the death penalty on minor defendants. In *Stanford v. Kentucky*, the Court declared that it was not cruel and unusual punishment to impose the death penalty on murderers who were age 16 or older at the time they committed the murder, because there is no national consensus forbidding such executions.[62] However, in *Thompson v. Oklahoma*, the Court stated that the execution of murderers younger than age 16 at the time of the crime might be forbidden.[63]

WEB

For a view of the death penalty from an ethical perspective, **visit our Web site, www.prenhall.com/territo.**

CTQ

The movement toward abolition of the death penalty in the United States is encouraged by the fact that so many other nations have abandoned it. Should we model our own system of punishment on those of other nations, or is our criminal problem so unique that it requires the use of capital punishment?

WEB

For more information on mental retardation and the death penalty, **visit the link to the American Association of Mental Retardation on our Web site, www.prenhall.com/territo.**

WEB

For up-to-date statistics on juveniles and the death penalty, found in a report by Professor Victor Streibs, **visit our Web site, www.prenhall.com/territo.**

FIGURE 10.9

Number of Persons on Death Row, 1968–2000

Sources: Bureau of Justice Statistics; NAACP Legal Defense and Education Fund, Inc.

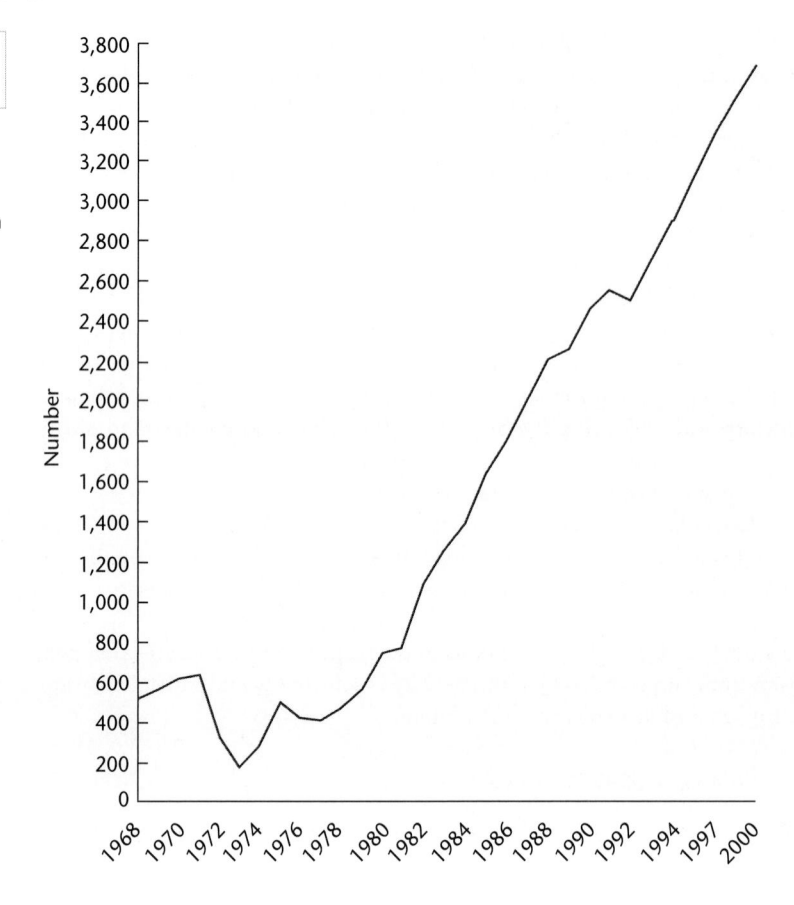

Competency to Stand Trial at the Time of Execution Competency to stand trial depends on the defendant's mental condition at the time of the trial. This is distinguished from insanity, which refers to the defendant's mental condition at the time of the crime. Insanity is a defense; incompetency is a bar to trial. Just as a defendant cannot be tried if unable to understand the nature of the proceedings, a defendant may not be executed if incapable of understanding the nature and the purpose of the punishment.

The Current Situation

The United States is now in transition between enacting the death penalty in the abstract and actually administering the punishment in a manner consistent with society's mores and with its constitutional requirements. The United States is one of the last Western countries with capital punishment (see Figure 10.9).

Over the past decade, an average of at least one country a year has abolished the death penalty, according to Amnesty International. Today, seventy-three countries have abolished the death penalty for all crimes. Another thirteen have abolished the punishment for all but exceptional offenses, such as wartime crimes. Still another twenty-two countries and territories may be considered abolitionist in practice because they no longer carry out executions. Ninety-five countries—more than 47 percent of all countries in the world—have abolished the death penalty in law or practice.[64]

The first prisoner executed in the post-*Gregg* era, Gary Gilmore, demanded that the Utah authorities execute him in 1977. The momentum, though negligible at first, eventually increased. There were no executions in 1978, followed by two in 1979, none in 1980, one in 1981, and two in 1982. The rate more than doubled in 1983 to five. Then in 1984, partially due to the Supreme Court's efforts to accelerate the appeals process and diminish federal oversight, the number of executions increased to twenty-one.

The number of inmates on a particular state's death row is not necessarily positively correlated with the number of executions in that state. For example, 607 inmates

FIGURE 10.10

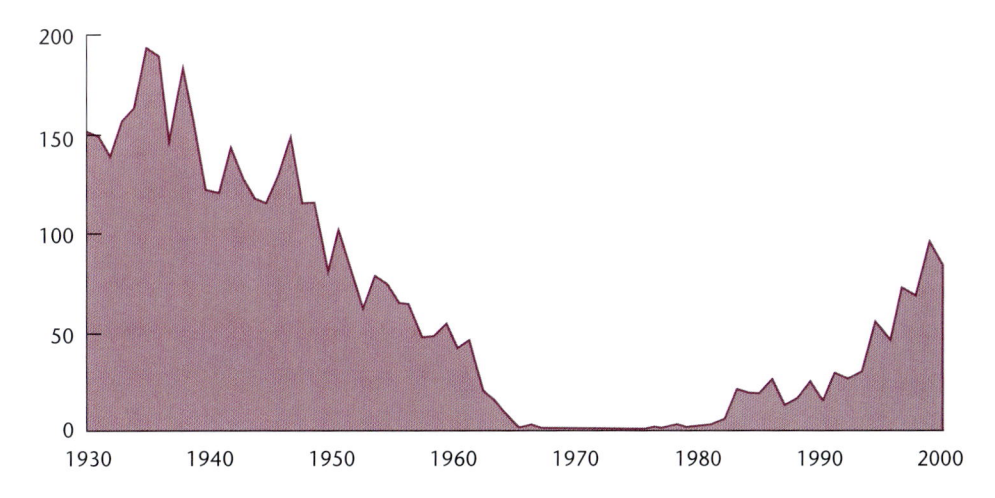

Number of Prisoners Executed at Year End, 1930–2000

Source: Capital Punishment 2001. Washington, D.C.: Bureau of Justice Statistics, U.S. Department of Justice, 2002.

are currently on death row in California, but since 1976, the state has executed only ten inmates (see Table 10.3). Therefore, only 1.6 percent of inmates who have been placed on death row in California have been executed. However, in Missouri, there is a positive correlation between inmates on death row and the number of executions; since 1976, 43 percent of inmates on death row have been executed in Missouri (see Figure 10.10).

The total number of death row inmates as of January 1, 2002, was 3,711. Of those on death row, 46 percent are white, 43 percent are black, 9 percent are Hispanic, and 2 percent are of other ethnicities.[65] Of those inhabitants, 3,656 are men, comprising 98.5 percent of the death row population, with women representing the other 1.5 percent.[66] Notorious child killer Susan Smith, who knowingly committed a heinous crime in the murder of her two sons, was granted a sentence of life rather than death, is a well-publicized example of a woman on death row. More than 90 percent of those on death row were too poor to hire private counsel and had court-appointed attorneys.[67]

Texas ranks as having one of the most humane death rows, allowing inmates 110 hours each week for visitation and exercise, and Ohio ranks as having one of the worst, allowing only two hours a week for out-of-cell indoor exercise.[68] Alaska, the District of Columbia, Hawaii, Iowa, Maine, Massachusetts, Michigan, Minnesota, North Dakota, Rhode Island, Vermont, West Virginia, and Wisconsin are all jurisdictions with no death penalty. All other states have laws providing for capital punishment (see Figure 10.11).

Southern states have the highest percentage of inmates on death row (54 percent), compared to 25 percent in the West, 14 percent in the Midwest, and just over 7 percent in the Northeast. Texas leads the nation in the number of inmates on death row and the number of people executed each year. According to the Bureau of Justice Statistics, prisoners sentenced to death between 1977 and 2000 waited an average of ten years on death row before being executed.[69]

America is poised at a crossroads in the death penalty controversy. In the long term, it appears to be following the trend of the Western world toward abolition. This conclusion can be demonstrated by the relatively low execution rates and the long-term decline in the death penalty's use. On the other hand, the high numbers on death row and the short-term increase in executions may signal a return to the execution rates of the 1950s, if not the 1930s.

The Supreme Court consistently has upheld certain forms of execution in the United States. Electrocution, hanging, shooting, lethal gas, and lethal injection (see Figure 10.13) have been held as constitutional methods of execution. Yet in 1999, the Supreme Court agreed to review the constitutionality of Florida's electric chair. This issue became moot after the Florida legislature joined other states by allowing condemned prisoners to choose between two humane methods of execution approved by the Supreme Court (in Florida, death row inmates have the choice of the electric chair or lethal injection).

WEB

For information on women and the death penalty, **visit our Web site, www.prenhall.com/territo.**

WEB

For a virtual tour of death row, **visit our Web site, www.prenhall.com/territo.**

TABLE 10.3 Capital Punishment, 1976–2002*

State	Inmates on Death Row	Number Executed since 1976	Methods of Execution
Alabama	188	23	Electrocution
Alaska	No death penalty		
Arizona	128	22	Gas, injection
Arkansas	40	24	Injection, electrocution
California	607	10	Gas, injection
Colorado	6	1	Injection
Connecticut	7	0	Injection
Delaware	19	19	Hanging, injection
District of Columbia	No death penalty		
Florida	386	51	Injection, electrocution
Georgia	127	28	Injection
Hawaii	No death penalty		
Idaho	21	1	Injection, firing squad
Illinois	173	12	Injection
Indiana	39	9	Injection
Iowa	No death penalty		
Kansas	4	0	Injection
Kentucky	41	2	Electrocution, injection
Louisiana	93	26	Injection
Maine	No death penalty		
Maryland	15	3	Gas, injection
Massachusetts	No death penalty		
Michigan	No death penalty		
Minnesota	No death penalty		
Mississippi	68	4	Injection
Missouri	75	56	Injection, gas
Montana	6	2	Injection
Nebraska	7	3	Electrocution
Nevada	88	9	Injection
New Hampshire	0	0	Hanging, injection
New Jersey	18	0	Injection
New Mexico	4	1	Injection
New York	6	0	Injection
North Carolina	226	21	Injection
North Dakota	No death penalty		
Ohio	204	3	Injection
Oklahoma	120	50	Injection
Oregon	30	2	Injection
Pennsylvania	247	3	Injection
Rhode Island	No death penalty		
South Carolina	76	25	Electrocution, injection
South Dakota	5	0	Injection
Tennessee	104	1	Electrocution, injection
Texas	455	262	Injection
Utah	11	6	Firing squad, injection
Vermont	No death penalty		
Virginia	29	83	Electrocution, Injection
Washington	15	4	Hanging, injection
West Virginia	No death penalty		
Wisconsin	No death penalty		
Wyoming	2	1	Injection, gas
Federal jurisdictions	24	2	Depends upon state of conviction
U.S. military	7	0	Lethal injection

*As of January 1, 2002

Sources: Death Penalty Information Center; NAACP Legal Defense and Educational Fund, Inc. http://www.deathpenaltyinfo.org.

FIGURE 10.11

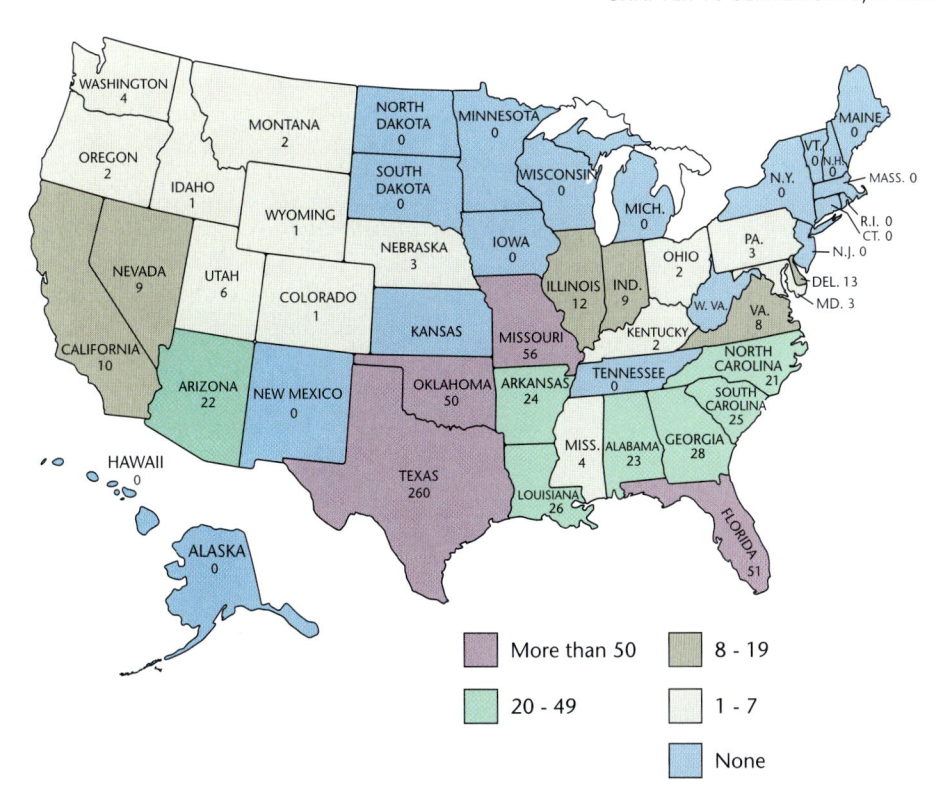

U.S. Executions, 1976–2000, by State

Source: Death Penalty Information Center, data as of January 1, 2002.

FIGURE 10.12

A gurney upon which condemned prisoners lie, are strapped, and are administered a lethal injection into their veins.

Courtesy of AFP/CORBIS.

What remains at issue is whether the electric chair is cruel and unusual punishment. Electrocution, thought to be instantaneous, was a great problem in 1989 in Florida. In 1989, a malfunction in the electric chair caused sparks to fly and Jesse Tafero's mask to catch on fire before he was finally pronounced dead.

In response to the controversy surrounding the use of the electric chair, most states now use lethal injection (see Figure 10.12). Advocates of this method assert that lethal injection causes instantaneous death, as prisoners simply lapse into unconsciousness, thus making it the most humane form of execution, as it avoids torture and pain. This process has been graphically depicted in several movies, including *Dead Man Walking*, *Last Dance*, and *True Crime*. Lethal injection was first used on December 7, 1982, when Charles Brooks, Jr., was put to death in Huntsville, Texas. Brooks was given a dose of barbiturates and potassium chloride, which paralyzed him, stopped his breathing, and ensured his death. By the middle of the 1980s, the debate over the humanity of lethal injection had subsided, and the new focus was on the brutal nature of electrocution, which climaxed in the aforementioned brutal 1989 Tafero execution in Florida.

Public Attitudes toward the Death Sentence

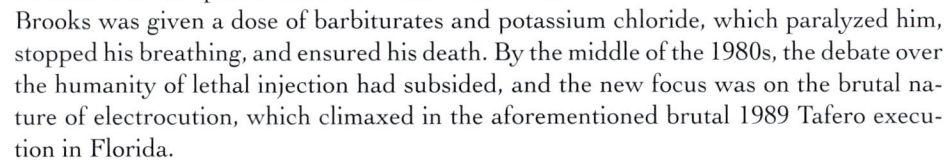

Support for the death sentence has risen steadily since the mid-1960s, when only 42 percent of Americans polled favored capital punishment for murder. By 1980, two-thirds of those polled supported it; by 1994 the number reached 77 percent[70] (see Figure 10.13).

The dramatic increase of support for capital punishment has several important dimensions. Public support has clear racial overtones. Capital punishment is most favored among people who do not know how it works in practice; they support capital punishment because of how they believe it should operate, not how it is actually administered.

CTQ

Which method of execution do you consider the most humane? Which method do you consider the most cruel and unusual?

FIGURE 10.13

Prisoners under Sentence of Death, by Region

Source: *Capital Punishment 1998.* Washington, D.C.: Bureau of Justice Statistics, U.S. Department of Justice, 2000.

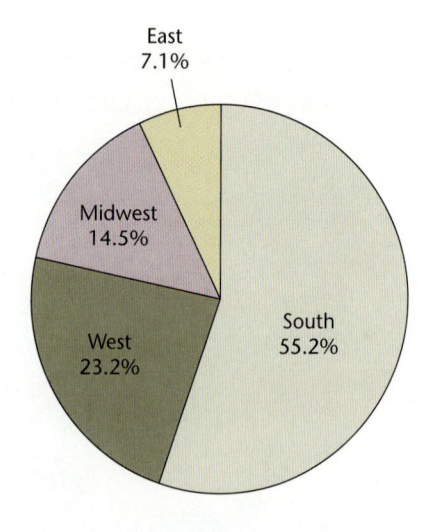

- East 7.1%
- Midwest 14.5%
- South 55.2%
- West 23.2%

CTQ

Can you explain why public opinion was so negative toward the death penalty thirty years ago and is so overwhelmingly in favor of it now? What happened to change all of this?

When all the facts and circumstances about its actual operation become known, however, support weakens among most groups. MacArthur, for example, found that 75 percent of those surveyed believe the death penalty has a deterrent effect.[71] However, if they were convinced that abolition of the death penalty would not increase the murder rate, support for the death penalty would drop from 70 to 55 percent. Furthermore, Flanagan and Maguire studied public opinion in New York and found that 72 percent of the respondents favored the death penalty, but that 62 percent would be willing to support a plan that sentenced a convicted murderer to torture.[72]

DEATH PENALTY APPEALS

Earlier in this chapter, in our discussion of appeals, we looked at *habeas corpus*, which means "you have the body," in depth. Filing a writ of *habeas corpus* is a method used frequently by prisoners who question the legality of their confinement. The writ does not question the issue of guilt or innocence, but asserts that some due process right is being violated or has been violated. The writ of *habeas corpus* is often called the *Great Writ of Liberty*, or the Great Writ, so called by Sir William Blackstone, a great English jurist, because it was used to release individuals from illegal confinement (see "In the News: 9–0 Ruling Will Speed Pace of Executions").

In 1988, Chief Justice Rehnquist appointed a committee, chaired by retired Justice Lewis F. Powell, Jr., to study the issue of *habeas corpus* proceedings in capital cases. That committee issued its report in 1989, recommending that changes be implemented. The committee noted that the current system fosters "piecemeal and repetitive litigation of claims," with some inmates filing multiple *habeas corpus* appeals in federal courts. The committee stated this goal of its proposal:

> Capital cases should be subject to one complete and fair course of collateral review in the state and federal system, free from the time pressure of impending execution, and with the assistance of competent counsel for the defendant. When this review has concluded, litigation should end.[73]

Chief Justice Rehnquist, arguing for placing limits on *habeas corpus* appeals, has encountered some negative reaction from federal judges. In April 1991, the Supreme Court placed some limits on *habeas corpus* appeals. In *McCleskey v. Zant*, the six justices in the majority said that the abuse of *habeas corpus* promotes "disrespect for the finality of convictions" and thus "disparages the entire criminal justice system."[74]

One issue to keep in mind as you analyze your position on death penalty appeals is the issue of counsel. Capital defendants are entitled to appointed competent counsel at state trial and first appeals. In 1989, however, the Supreme Court ruled that capital defendants are not entitled to appointed counsel in state appeals after they are unsuccessful in their first appeal. Many states do make provisions for counsel, however, and the

A HUMAN PERSPECTIVE

9–0 RULING WILL SPEED PACE OF EXECUTIONS

In a ruling likely to speed the pace of executions, the Supreme Court upheld a key part of Congress' crackdown on death row inmates and other prisoners who file numerous appeals in federal court. By a unanimous vote Friday, the justices rejected a Georgia inmate's argument that the law unconstitutionally usurps the court's power. Even worse for more than 3,000 other death row inmates across the nation, Chief Justice William Rehnquist indicated that the court is likely to follow Congress' lead in tightening restrictions on state prisoners' ability to seek help from federal courts.

This decision was not well received by all, as might be expected. A *Criminal Justice Newsletter* editorial proclaimed that "The Court Abuses the Great Writ." In referring to the facts of the *McCleskey* case, the editorial criticized the Court's ruling that the evidence on the appeal in question should have been brought in McCleskey's previous appeal, noting that the evidence was uncovered by counsel "only after years of demands and denials."

Sources: "9–0 Ruling Will Speed Pace of Executions," *St. Petersburg (Fla.) Times*, June 29, 1996, p. 1. Reprinted with permission of The Associated Press. "Judges Challenge Rehnquist on Death Row Appeal Report," *Criminal Justice Newsletter*, November 15, 1989.

Powell committee recommended in the case of *Murray v. Giarrantano* that the gap for appointed counsel should be filled.[75]

THE CAPITAL PUNISHMENT DEBATE

There are five major issues in the capital punishment debate: the role capital punishment plays in deterrence; society's need for retribution; the possibility that death sentences will be imposed arbitrarily; the danger that mistakes will be made; and the role capital punishment plays in incapacitation.

When looking at this issue, one must always deal with two basic values: the value of punishment and the value and sacredness of human life. In considering punishment, both the supporters and opponents of the death penalty feel that punishment is necessary and beneficial, but they differ on its exact objectives. While the supporters of capital punishment primarily emphasize retribution and deterrence as the goals of punishment, the opponents of capital punishment see incapacitation and rehabilitation, to some extent, as the goals of punishment. Thus, the way one views punishment and its objectives will dramatically affect one's stand on the issue. On the other hand, when dealing with the value of human life, both the proponents and opponents of capital punishment see themselves as defenders of human life, and their opponents as insensitive to the respect and sacredness that human life deserves.

Abolitionists feel that executions are simply needless killings, the result of invalid and unsound reasoning, and thus show no respect for life. Supporters of capital punishment feel that in order to show respect for the victims of murder, the only appropriate punishment is death itself. Abolitionists counter by arguing that the primary way of showing respect for life is to avoid killing a human being. While executions may be legal, that does not necessarily mean they are moral. And as "In the News: Death Sentences Being Overturned in 2 of 3 Appeals" indicates, the entire legal procedure that should guarantee that whenever the death penalty is imposed, it is imposed on a guilty defendant, seems to be dramatically flawed.

The Argument That Capital Punishment Acts as a Deterrent

A major purpose of criminal punishment is to deter future criminal conduct. The deterrence theory assumes that a rational person will avoid criminal behavior because the perceived certainty of receiving the punishment outweighs the potential benefits of the illegal conduct. Although the accuracy of many of the assumptions behind the deterrence approach are themselves disputable, the deterrent value of a particularly severe punishment, the death penalty, is important in the current controversy.

CTQ

When you compare and contrast the value of punishment for those who deserve it for a wicked crime versus the value of the sacredness of life, which is more important in your morality scheme?

CTQ

Many death sentence appeals are being overturned and people are being released because they are found innocent after spending years in prison on death row. Is that reason alone enough to eliminate the practice of the death penalty?

CTQ

In your opinion, does capital punishment serve as a deterrent?

IN THE NEWS

A HUMAN PERSPECTIVE

DEATH SENTENCES BEING OVERTURNED IN 2 OF 3 APPEALS

The most far-reaching study of the death penalty in the United States has found that two out of three convictions were overturned on appeal, mostly because of serious errors by incompetent defense lawyers or overzealous police officers and prosecutors who withheld evidence.

The study, an examination of appeals in all capital cases from the time the Supreme Court reinstated the death penalty, in [1976], to 1995, also found that 75 percent of the people whose death sentences were set aside were later given lesser sentences after retrials, in plea bargains or by order of a judge. An additional 7 percent were found not guilty on retrial. Eighteen percent were given the death penalty on retrial, but many of these had their convictions overturned again in the appeals process.

The study is based on a search of state and federal court records. It was conducted by a team of lawyers and criminologists at Columbia University led by James S. Liebman, a professor of law who has served as a defense lawyer in a number of death penalty trials and appeals. The report is likely to intensify an already gathering debate about the death penalty, which has been provoked by the release of some death row inmates after new DNA technology helped exonerate them. Concerns about the death penalty were heightened by the decision in March by Gov. George Ryan of Illinois, a Republican, to declare a moratorium on executions in his state after 13 men on death row there were cleared by new evidence.

While some death penalty supporters have argued that Illinois is an aberration and produces less reliable death sentences than other states, the Columbia study found that the rate of serious error detected by court reviews in Illinois capital cases was 66 percent, slightly below the national average of 68 percent.

Support for the death penalty is overwhelming, but recent Gallup polls have shown it slipping, from a peak of 80 percent in 1994, to 66 percent, its lowest point since 1978, when it was 68 percent.

Even many death penalty supporters have expressed serious concerns about its fairness. The historically conservative New Hampshire Legislature voted to abolish the death penalty, though the bill was vetoed by the state's Democratic Governor, Jeanne Shaheen.

The debate even made a surprise entrance into the presidential race [of 2000], where [then] Gov. George Bush, an outspoken supporter of the death penalty, postponed the execution of a convicted killer to allow DNA testing. It was the first stay that Mr. Bush had granted, after presiding over 131 executions, the most of any governor since the death penalty was reinstated.

A spokesman for [then] Governor Bush, Ari Fleischer, said that "Some people will use this study to call for the abolition of the death penalty." But, Fleischer said, the finding of so many errors in the appeals process "shows that there is an extra level of vigilance and caution in death penalty cases, appropriately so."

As for the study's finding that of the death row inmates whose sentences were set aside on appeal 75 percent were later given lesser sentences and 7 percent were found not guilty, Mr. Fleischer said, "This shows that 93 percent are still found guilty" of some crime. "It's not an error about their innocence. It's just a question of appropriate punishment," he said.

The study had its origin in a request in 1991 by Senator Joseph F. Biden Jr., Democrat to Delaware, then chairman of the Senate Judiciary Committee, to Professor Liebman to calculate the frequency with which federal judges found errors in appeals of death penalty cases and then set aside the sentence.

The high national rate of serious errors leading to verdicts being set aside in cases stands in sharp contrast to the error rate found in other criminal cases, which is estimated to be below 10 percent, several legal experts said. The rate of error found in appeals in death penalty cases ranged from 100 percent in three states—Kentucky, Maryland and Tennessee—and 91 percent in Mississippi, to 18 percent in Virginia, by far the lowest of any of the 34 states with the death penalty, raising questions about whether Virginia's court system is unusually fair or works to make it harder to detect errors. In fact, 24 of the 26 states with the death penalty where there have been fully completed appeals had an error rate of 52 percent or higher, the report said.

Source: F. Butterfield, "Death Sentences Being Overturned in 2 of 3 Cases," *The New York Times,* June 12, 2000. Reprinted with permission of *The New York Times.*

CTQ

In your own life, has the threat of future punishment deterred you from committing a potential criminal act? At some point in time, the majority of people would say that this threat has had that effect. If this is true, then why doesn't the death penalty deter future would-be killers?

The deterrence achieved by using the death penalty must be examined in the context of the entire criminal justice system. For the death penalty to deter first-degree (or capital) murders, the killer must know of the penalty's application to the crime and must believe that the certainty of punishment is sufficient enough to create an unacceptable risk. Without such awareness, the killer will probably not be deterred. An additional factor is that a punishment's deterrent value must be judged in the context of alternatives. If a lesser penalty achieves the same or greater level of deterrence, no deterrent justification supports the enhanced punishment.

Possibly because deterrence is ingrained in our lives—for example, as children we were punished for violating family rules—a majority of the public supports the death penalty because they consider it an effective deterrent. Supporters contend that death sentences and executions heighten the risk of punishment in a potential killer's mind. By threatening to take the killer's life, society "ups the ante" of killing another person.

Studies of the deterrent effect of the death penalty have been conducted for several years, with varying results. These studies have focused on comparing three statistics: (1) homicide rates in states that have a death penalty versus those states that do not; (2) murder rates in a given area both before and after an execution; and (3) crime rates in general, as well as murder rates in a particular jurisdiction before and after the abolition of capital punishment. All of these studies have failed to produce any credible evidence that the death penalty deters homicide.[76]

As opponents of the death penalty argue, first, most of these studies have failed to produce evidence that the death penalty deters murders more effectively than the threat of protracted imprisonment. Second, the actual probability that a murderer will receive a death sentence is quite low and the risk of being executed even smaller—about 1 per 1,000 convicted homicide defendants were sentenced to death in 1984.[77] Even when the certainty of punishment is higher, many killers might refuse to believe they will be apprehended, let alone executed. Third, the assumption of a rationally functioning human being, on which deterrence theories are based, may not be valid for many killers.

The deterrence issue, important as it is, will not be resolved by statistical studies. Both supporters and opponents agree that the deterrent value of the death penalty is unproven. Furthermore, the practical limits on studies of this type, as well as the complexity of the problem, will probably prevent any definitive "scientific" resolution of the deterrence issue in the future.

The Retribution Argument

The central justification for capital punishment is the need for society to express sufficient condemnation for heinous murders by retribution. Supporters of the death penalty contend that the only proper societal response to the most vile murders is the most severe sanction possible. Thus, society should literally interpret the "eye for an eye" principle; when an individual takes a life, society's moral balance will remain upset until the killer's life is also taken. In *Furman*, however, the Supreme Court stated that while retribution was no longer the dominant objective of capital punishment, "neither is it a forbidden objective nor one inconsistent with our respect for the dignity of men."

Although death penalty opponents agree that some form of punishment, even a harsh one, should be imposed on offenders, they disagree with the assumption that society can express its outrage with a vile crime only by inflicting a mortal punishment. Opponents to the **retribution argument** further claim that society's goal of greater morality, is actually defeated when its expression of outrage for the taking of one life is the taking of another life. Indeed, opponents argue that the state's act is, in some respects, more calculated and cold blooded than that of many murderers.

The Arbitrariness Argument: The Role of Race and Gender

A most significant argument against capital punishment is that discrimination is employed in its use. Capital punishment may discriminate against men: Women account for 13 percent of all murder arrests, yet only 1.9 percent of death sentences imposed are on women.[78] On a larger scale, the death penalty seems to discriminate against African Americans. However, many supporters of the death penalty claim that racial discrimination in capital cases was corrected after the Supreme Court's ruling in *Furman v. Georgia*, since the purpose of the ruling was to eliminate racial disparity in a system that was "arbitrary and capricious" and "pregnant with discrimination." But after studying exactly this issue, Bowers and Pierce concluded, to the contrary, that "differential treatment by race of offender and victim has been shown to persist post-*Furman* to a degree comparable in magnitude and pattern to the pre-*Furman* period."[79] A 2000 study by the Justice Department concluded that pervasive disparities are found in the federal death penalty (see "In the News: Pervasive Disparities Found in the Federal Death Penalty").

CTQ

If you are in favor of the death penalty, what is your opinion about the fact that only 1 out of every 1,000 people convicted of murder receives the death penalty? Do you believe this part of the system needs to be fixed? Why?

WEB

For a variety of perspectives about race and the death penalty, go to the link to the ABA's Focus on Law Studies on **our Web site, www.prenhall.com/territo**.

WEB

For more information on minorities and the death penalty, **visit our Web site, www.prenhall.com/territo**.

IN THE NEWS

A HUMAN PERSPECTIVE

PERVASIVE DISPARITIES FOUND IN THE FEDERAL DEATH PENALTY

In the first comprehensive review of the federal death penalty since it was reinstated in 1988, the Justice Department has found significant racial and geographical disparities, say officials who have seen the report. In 75 percent of the cases in which a federal prosecutor sought the death penalty in the last five years, the defendant has been a member of a minority group, and in more than half of the cases, an African-American, according to the report.

Reflecting a lack of geographical uniformity in the application of federal capital punishment, the Justice Department has found that a handful of the 93 United States attorneys account for about 40 percent of the cases sent to the Justice Department for review, according to officials.

On the other hand, about 20 United States attorneys did not file a single death penalty case since 1995. Since there are more than 40 crimes for which the federal death penalty is a potential punishment, the lack of cases from those jurisdictions raised the question of the uniform application of death penalty prosecutions.

The report is expected to increase calls for a moratorium on the federal death penalty. The American Bar Association, which does not take a position for or against the death penalty, sent a letter to former President Clinton on May 2, 2000, asking him to impose an executive moratorium pending a thorough review of the federal capital punishment system.

After the Supreme Court declared in 1972 that the death penalty, as it was then being applied, was unconstitutional, states quickly adopted laws that the Court upheld.

In 1988, Congress adopted what became known as the "drug kingpin statute," which permitted a death penalty against an individual found guilty of committing a murder as part of a larger drug-running enterprise. In 1994, Congress enacted the Federal Death Penalty Act, which greatly expanded the crimes for which a defendant could be executed. They range from murder of the president to large-scale drug trafficking even when no one is killed and include drive-by murders, sexual abuse resulting in death, murder during a bank robbery, carjacking and destruction of an airplane, train or motor vehicle resulting in death.

The report also shows that United States attorneys who have most frequently recommended seeking the death penalty are from states with a high number of executions, including Virginia, Texas, and Missouri. In 80 percent of the cases submitted by United States attorneys for review, the defendant was an ethnic minority. But officials said that former Attorney General Reno's review of the process has reduced the apparent racial bias. In the 682 cases she reviewed in which the defendant was white, she authorized the death penalty 38 percent of the time; when the defendant was black, she authorized the death penalty 25 percent of the time.

Source: R. Bonner and M. Lacey, "Pervasive Disparities Found in the Federal Death Penalty," *The New York Times,* September 12, 2000. Reprinted with permission of *The New York Times.*

WEB

Visit the link to the National Coalition to Abolish the Death Penalty, on our Web site, www.prenhall.com/territo.

CTQ

Do you think that the fact that only 14 percent of Americans are African American and yet 43 percent of the people on death row are African American signals any bias with regard to race in the death penalty? Why or why not?

Essentially, the thesis of the arbitrariness argument used by the abolitionists is that the system that determines who will or will not receive the death penalty after being convicted of murder (as stated earlier, only 1 out of 1,000 convicted homicide defendants receive the death penalty) is an arbitrary and capricious system. A system characterized by arbitrariness has no basis in logic, has no order to it and is constantly changing for no particular reasonable purpose.

While African Americans make up approximately 14 percent of the entire population, around 43 percent of all condemned prisoners are African American. Moreover, the bias becomes more blatant when looking at the race of the victims of those condemned prisoner (see Figure 10.14). In Florida, African American offenders convicted of killing Caucasian victims are eight times more likely to be sentenced to death than someone (Caucasian or African American) who killed an African American victim.[80] Nationwide, they are about four times more likely to be sentenced to death. In fact, prior to 1991, the last white American executed for killing an African American was in 1944. One thousand executions and nearly half a century later, Donald Gaskins was executed in September 1991 in South Carolina. Gaskins was Caucasian and his victim, Rudolph Taylor, was African American. (See "In the News: A Life for a Life—The Truck Dragging Hate Crime".)

One of the most recent studies on the matter of racial discrimination, the Baldus Study, compared 294 pre-*Furman* capital cases with 594 post-*Furman* capital cases in Georgia. Baldus and his associates found that prior to *Furman,* "defendants who were black or whose victims were white received more punitive sentences than other equally

FIGURE 10.14

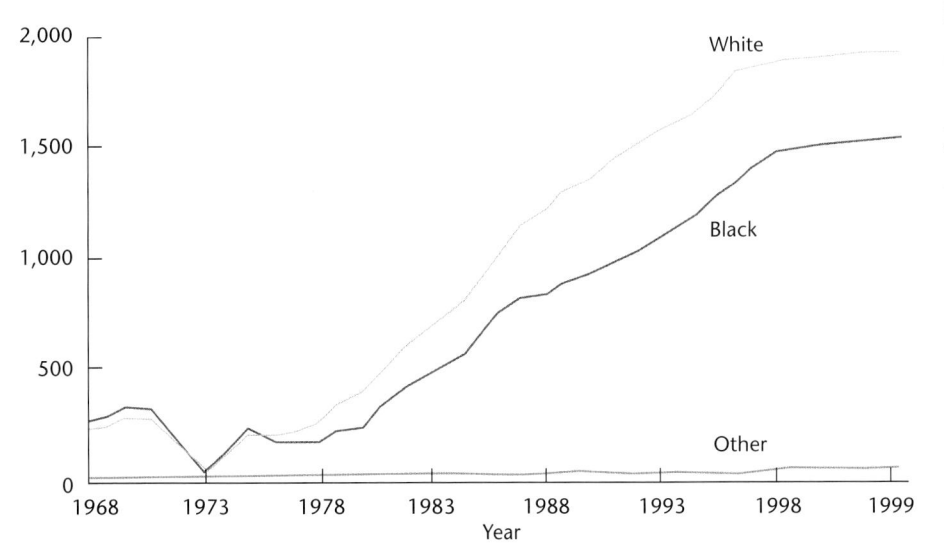

Prisoners on Death Row by Race, 1968–1999

Source: Capital Punishment 1999. Washington, D.C.: Bureau of Justice Statistics, 2000.

Prisoners on death row by race, 1968-1999

IN THE NEWS

A HUMAN PERSPECTIVE

A LIFE FOR A LIFE—THE TRUCK DRAGGING HATE CRIME

If the barbaric dragging death of James Byrd Jr. were a movie—and at times it seemed like pure John Grisham—this was the scene that would have been certain to make it into the trailers. As a scowling John William King, 24, was led out of the Jasper County courthouse in shackles by Texas Rangers last week, reporters asked him if he had any message for the grieving Byrd family. It was a moment when, just briefly, repentance appeared possible. "Yeah," King sneered. He then invited the Byrds to perform a lewd sexual act.

There's a reason King's story feels like a legal thriller: its plot line is melodramatic and painfully one-dimensional. The murder of Byrd is as horrific a crime as can be imagined—chaining a man to a truck and dragging him three miles until he dies of his injuries. And the protagonist is a dime-store white supremacist, spouting anti-black and anti-Semitic dogma and spewing hatred to the bitter.

If ever a crime cried out for grave punishment, it's this one. King and his two friends were driving a 1982 Ford pickup in the early-morning hours last June. They spotted Byrd, 49, an unemployed vacuum-cleaner salesman, walking home from a party on a lonely stretch of Highway 96 and offered him a ride. They drove him to a deserted corner of the backwoods and, after a struggle, chained him to the truck by his ankles. Then they dragged him for three miles along a rural road outside Jasper. Byrd was alive for the first two miles, a pathologist testified at trial, and deliberately twisted his body from side to side, trying to keep his head from hitting the pavement. He may have been conscious at the time of his death, when his head was finally torn off by a concrete drainage culvert. Lawmen later found Byrd's head and upper torso, including his right arm, shoulder and neck, in a ditch about a mile away from the rest of his body.

Byrd's murder was a heinous crime against a man and his family, but it was also something larger. Lynching is the iconic Old South crime, used to punish slave insurrections. Lynch mobs traditionally hanged their victim from a rope tossed over a tree limb. But dragging deaths were not uncommon, first from horses, later from cars and trucks. Lynching was at once a brutal act of vigilante injustice and a larger statement—a warning to blacks to remain subservient.

The early signs from the courtroom were encouraging. The government put on a powerful case—a far cry from the days when Southern prosecutors found ways to lose—or not to bring—race cases like this one.

Jasper's black community hoped for the best but braced for the worst. "Even if you know something is right and that you should get a certain verdict, sometimes you don't get it," says Unav Wade, owner of a beauty salon on the courthouse square. "If it's between races, most likely the white person wins."

But this time the white person lost badly. The jury took only 2½ hours to return the toughest verdict possible, capital murder. Jurors then listened to two days of penalty-phase testimony. Ronald King arrived in court in a wheelchair, with an oxygen tube, needed because of his emphysema. Although some in the courtroom were visibly moved by this frail father's appeal, the jury unanimously voted for the death penalty.

Source: A. Cohen, "A Life for a Life," *Time,* March 8, 1999. © 1999 TIME, Inc. Reprinted by permission.

culpable defendants."[81] The post-*Furman* findings showed a racial disparity in the race of the victim, as did the pre-*Furman* findings; however, there was no statistical significance in racial disparity in the race of the defendant. The post-*Furman* findings indicate that "after *Furman*, there was a decline statewide in the level of discrimination against black defendants that was so prominent in pre-*Furman* Georgia. Such discrimination persists at reduced levels in rural areas, but it is masked in statewide statistics."[82]

As a result of their study, Baldus and his associates concluded that "the principal post-trial source of race-of-victim discrimination is the prosecutorial decision to seek a death sentence." Thus, according to Baldus and his associates, racial discrimination is still alive and well in post-*Furman* capital punishment. The Supreme Court, however, precluded this argument from coming forward as an attack on capital punishment in *McCleskey v. Kemp*.[83] In that case, the U.S. District Court held that statistical data are "incapable of producing evidence on whether racial factors play a part in the imposition of the death penalty in a particular case."[84]

The Danger-of-Mistake Argument

The second major argument against capital punishment is "the danger-of-mistake" argument. This argument reasons that since the death penalty's unique character is its finality and irrevocability, a judgment can never be reversed. Unlike a prison term, which can be commuted at any time, the death penalty, once executed, cannot be recalled. Thus, the irrevocability of the punishment heightens the dangers associated with wrongful convictions.

Opponents of the death penalty argue that the possibility of executing an innocent person necessitates abolishing the penalty. They contend that the likelihood of executing someone who does not deserve to die—that is, one whose crime does not fall within the definition of capital murder—is quite high. And though the person might be guilty of a serious crime, imposing the death penalty in this case would be wrong. The less probable, though more morally unacceptable scenario, is that a state might execute someone who did not commit the crime. Opponents argue that the possibility of executing even one innocent person warrants rejecting the penalty (see "In the News: The Wrong Men on Death Row").

Thomas Jefferson believed that capital punishment was immoral primarily because of the possibility of mistake. He said, "I shall ask for the abolition of the punishment of death, until I have the infallibility of human judgment demonstrated to me."[85] Dolinko explains the argument:

> The unavoidable imperfections of all human fact-finding and decision-making procedures ensure that if any crime is punishable by death, sooner or later some innocent people will be mistakenly convicted of that crime and executed. The possibility—indeed, over enough time, the certainty—of erroneous executions makes capital punishment inherently immoral.[86]

In 1987, Bedau and Radelet published a work in the *Stanford Law Review* that was the result of 25 years of research.[87] In this study, they looked at all crimes that potentially carried the sentence of death. They found that in the twentieth century alone, 350 people had been wrongly convicted. Their work has been criticized because they define innocence quite narrowly, excluding cases in which a conviction might have been reversed solely because of what were generally due process errors.

They also exclude cases in which a defendant was convicted of homicide, but later was determined to have acted in self-defense or out of insanity. Instead, all but a few cases they present involve miscarriages of justice in which the wrong person was convicted of the crime.[88] Thus, in all 350 cases, either the defendant was legally and physically uninvolved in the crime, or the defendant was convicted of a crime that never took place. In fact, one defendant was tried on a charge of first-degree murder five times for the same crime between 1945 and 1958. Four times he was found guilty and sentenced to death, only to have the Pennsylvania Supreme Court finally rule that his long ordeal was a "near tragedy of errors."[89] Out of these 350 wrongful convictions, 139 defendants were sentenced to die and 23 were executed.

DNA and the Death Penalty The advances of DNA technology have lessened the degree of capital punishment by mistake, as was seen previously. Yet historically the states

IN THE NEWS

A HUMAN PERSPECTIVE

THE WRONG MEN ON DEATH ROW
by J. Shapiro

After years of debate, most Americans now believe the death penalty is an appropriate punishment for the most repulsive murders. But that support is rooted in an underlying assumption: that the right person is being executed. The most recent list by an anti–death penalty group shows that 74 men have been exonerated and freed from death row over the past 25 years—a figure so stark it's causing even some supporters of capital punishment to rethink whether the death penalty can work fairly. Among them is Gerald Kogan, who recently stepped down as chief justice of Florida's Supreme Court. "If one innocent person is executed along the way, then we can no longer justify capital punishment," he says.

For every seven executions, one other prisoner on death row has been found innocent. And there's concern even more mistaken convictions will follow as record numbers of inmates fill death rows, pressure builds for speedy executions, and fewer attorneys defend prisoners facing execution.

Executions have been rare since the death penalty was reinstated in 1976. But the pace is picking up. There are now 3,517 prisoners on death row in the 38 capital punishment states—an all-time high and a tripling since 1982. The 74 executions in 1997—the most since 1955—represented a 60 percent spike from the year before. Citing bad lawyering and mistaken convictions, the American Bar Association last year called for a death-penalty moratorium. This month, Illinois legislators will vote on such a ban. That state, more than any other, is grappling with the problem: It has exonerated almost as many men (nine) on death row as it has executed (eleven).

Leonel Herrera died by lethal injection in Texas in 1993 even though another man confessed to the murder. The U.S. Supreme Court ruled that, with his court appeals exhausted, an extraordinary amount of proof was required to stop his execution. Governors, the court noted, can still grant clemency in such cases. But what was once common is now so politically risky that only about one death row inmate a year wins such freedom.

A study found three factors common among wrongful capital convictions. One third involve perjured testimony, often from jailhouse snitches claiming to have heard a defendant's prison confession. One of every seven cases, Bedau and Radalet found, involves faulty eyewitness identifications, and a seventh involve false confessions, like Gauger's.

The falsely convicted is almost always an outsider—often from a minority group. In Illinois, six of the nine dismissed from death row were black or Hispanic men accused of murder, rape, or both of white victims. But the number one reason people are falsely convicted is poor legal representation. Many states cap fees for court-appointed attorneys, which makes it tougher for indigents to get competent lawyers. And it's been harder for inmates to find lawyers to handle appeals since Congress in 1996 stopped funding legal aid centers in 20 states.

DNA profiling, perhaps more than any other development, has exposed the fallibility of the legal system. In the past decade, 56 wrongfully convicted people have won release because of DNA testing, 10 of them from death row. Attorneys Barry Scheck and Peter Neufeld, with the help of their students at New York's Cardozo School of Law, have freed 35 of those. But their Innocence Project has been hobbled by the fact that, in 70 percent of the cases they pursued, police had already discarded semen, hair, or other evidence needed for testing. [See Table 10.4.]

Source: J. Shapiro, "The Wrong Men on Death Row," *U.S. News & World Report,* November 9, 1998. Copyright 1998. *U.S. News & World Report,* L. P. Reprinted with permission.

---

have been reluctant to use DNA evidence due to the presumed fact that the accused has already received a fair trial. Yet DNA yields a higher degree of certainty and if there is a match, there is little doubt that the system is executing the right person. Others say that DNA testing can conclusively demonstrate that so many previous people before were wrongfully convicted. However, even in the president's home state of Texas, a change in attitude about the urgency to use DNA evidence in capital cases seems to be coming out (see "In the News: Texas Lawmakers Seek Wide DNA Testing").

Finally, supporters of capital punishment, for the most part, argue that the current administration of the death penalty contains adequate safeguards to protect against miscarriages of justice. They cite the numerous levels of review and the scrutiny given to each death sentence. In addition, some supporters claim that the slight possibility of executing an innocent person must be accepted as the price of maintaining a credible criminal justice system.

The Incapacitation Argument

A final issue surrounding capital punishment is incapacitation. Incapacitation refers to society's need to prevent a criminal from committing or having the opportunity to commit another crime. Capital punishment can be a total source of effectiveness in implementing the methodology of incapacitation. Clearly, an executed inmate never has a chance to commit additional crimes.

WEB

For more viewpoints of death penalty advocates, **visit our Web site, www.prenhall.com/territo**.

TABLE 10.4 Number of Prisoners Freed from Death Row between 1977 and 2001

By State				By Race	
Florida	21	Alabama	3	Black	43
Illinois	13	Indiana	2	White	42
Oklahoma	7	Massachusetts	2	Latino	11
Texas	7	Missouri	2	Native American	1
Georgia	6	Ohio	2	Other	1
Louisiana	5	Idaho	1		
Arizona	5	Maryland	1		
New Mexico	4	Mississippi	1		
California	3	Nebraska	1		
N. Carolina	3	Nevada	1		
Pennsylvania	3	Washington	1		
S. Carolina	3	Virginia	1		

Source: Death Penalty Information Center. Retrieved September 4, 2001 from http://www.deathpenaltyinfo.org.

In response to the proponents' arguments that incapacitation completely eliminates the defendant's chance to reintegrate into society, the abolitionists argue that sentencing a defendant to "life without the possibility of parole" will also prevent the offender from committing future crimes. Wright argues that the system of capital punishment is infrequent, hardly swift, and certainly not sure.[90] She argues that life without parole would eliminate these problems and guarantee that society will be permanently protected from the offender. Wright goes on to explain that appeals and stays of execution undermine public faith in the criminal justice system. Because the punishment of life without the possibility of parole does not involve the finality of capital punishment, repeated appeal opportunities are not as imperative. Wright argues that life without the possibility of parole offers an alternative that clearly demonstrates commitment to both nonviolence and the basic sanctity of life:

> As Americans attempt to control violent crime, life without parole offers an additional weapon for criminal justice systems' arsenals, whose big gun of

IN THE NEWS

A HUMAN PERSPECTIVE

TEXAS LAWMAKERS SEEK WIDE DNA TESTING
by J. Yardley

With increasing national security and criticism focused on capital punishment in Texas, two prominent state senators, one a Democrat and the other a Republican, called for a new law that would allow post-conviction DNA testing as a safeguard against executing an innocent person. The proposed legislation mirrors laws in New York and Illinois and comes after [then] Gov. George Bush granted a 30-day reprieve last week for Ricky Nolen McGinn shortly before his scheduled execution.

Mr. McGinn was convicted of raping and killing his 12-year-old stepdaughter in 1993, but on June 1, Mr. Bush, citing concerns that adequate tests on DNA evidence had not been performed, granted the reprieve to allow for new DNA tests.

State Senator Rodney Ellis, Democrat of Houston, announced a package of bills for the legislative session that includes a bill that would allow convicted people, with some restrictions, to petition the trial court for DNA testing as part of their appeals.

Heretofore, defense lawyers in Texas often unsuccessfully seek DNA testing as a means of establishing innocence.

In a signal of bipartisanship, State Senator David Shibley, Republican of Waco, appeared with Mr. Ellis at a news conference to endorse the DNA proposal and predicted swift action in the Legislature next year. Mr. Shibley also supported a proposal by Mr. Ellis to create an "innocence commission," much like one established in Illinois, that would review select death penalty cases and make recommendations for improving the Texas death penalty system.

Governor Bush [now President Bush] had presided over 131 executions, easily the most of any governor, and he often expressed his unflinching belief in the fairness of the Texas system. Yet, his 30-day reprieve for Mr. McGinn was the first he had granted.

Source: J. Yardley, "Texas Lawmakers Seek Wide DNA Testing," *The New York Times,* June 9, 2000. Reprinted with permission of *The New York Times.*

capital punishment shows a marked tendency to misfire or shoot blanks. Americans are recognizing that alternatives to capital punishment are needed to control the increasing number of violent murders. Life without parole is an alternative that seems capable of accruing several important philosophical and practical advantages.[91]

The abolitionists argue that life without the possibility of parole offers an alternative to capital punishment that would punish murderers exactly as jurors and the general public expect them to be punished, a much surer sanction actually than the death penalty. Wright explains that capital punishment is sometimes viewed as necessary to deter murderers, protect society, and provide retribution. Life imprisonment, without the possibility of parole, on the other hand, offers an alternative that accomplishes these tasks without the moral cost of taking lives. Capital punishment is disrespectful of the sanctity of human life, but so is paroling the murderers who have shown the ultimate disrespect for human life.

MINOR ISSUES IN THE CAPITAL PUNISHMENT DEBATE

Five minor issues frequently encountered in the death penalty debate are the arguments of cost efficiency, community protection, the appeal to public opinion, cruel and unusual punishment, and the brutalization effect.

The Cost-Efficiency Argument

To do that which is most cost-efficient is to perform and reach the desired goal with the least amount of financial outlay. The debate about the cost of the death penalty has curious origins. Some popular sentiment supports the death penalty on the notion of cost efficiency; it is less costly to execute prisoners than to maintain them in prison for life terms. Abolitionists, by contrast, have sought to demonstrate that executions in the modern United States are more costly than are long prison terms, chiefly because of the cost of special legal processing.

A substantial study has come forward examining comparative costs of life imprisonment versus execution. The research is abundantly clear. Every available quantitative study for this argument demonstrates conclusively that because of the additional appeals and other procedural safeguards (such as jury selection) that are constitutionally required in a capital case, the death penalty costs taxpayers substantially more than life in prison.[92] For example, Florida taxpayers paid most of the cost—an estimated $6 million to $7 million—of making Ted Bundy pay for his crimes.

A national study conducted by the *Miami Herald* in 1988 found that the cost of life in prison (forty years) is approximately $515,964, while the cost of each execution is at least $3,178,623, or approximately six times the cost of life imprisonment.[93] A similar study also conducted in 1988 in Sacramento, California, reported that "it currently costs the State of California at least $15 million per execution to operate its capital punishment system, and that California taxpayers would save $90 million per year by abolishing the death penalty."[94] Furthermore, another study showed that the commutation of the death sentences of fifteen Arkansas prisoners saved the state an estimated $1.5 million.[95]

The Community Protection Argument

The alternative to the death penalty—severe commitment for long periods, for life without the possibility of parole in many states—makes it unlikely that capital punishment decreases crime through incapacitation. Thus, the second minor argument—the community protection argument—that the death penalty permanently incapacitates offenders is without much merit.

Ironically, a murderer's release into the community is not as devastating as one might believe. The President's Commission on Law Enforcement and Administration of Justice concluded that paroled murderers have the lowest recidivism rate of any recidivism of all classes of offenders.[96]

Furthermore, the small number of candidates for execution under any conceivable regime of capital punishment means that executions cannot be regarded as a way of reducing the incidence of violent crimes in the United States. Violent crimes number in the millions, prison populations in the hundreds of thousands. Executions, even at their twentieth-century peak, were under 200 per year. Hence the issue of the death penalty is largely a symbolic one in the crime-control debate, but it is fundamentally important nonetheless.[97]

The Appeal-to-Public-Opinion Argument

Another minor argument in the capital punishment debate is the appeal to public opinion. In the 1970s, California voters overwhelmingly petitioned to reinstate the death penalty in California, and the amendment was approved by a substantial number of votes. Furthermore, in the United States, every poll ever conducted on the matter since 1981 has found most Americans (approximately 80 percent) in favor of the death penalty.[98]

If appeal to public opinion is a valid argument, then the institution of slavery would possibly never had been removed. Indeed, Henry David Thoreau expressed a concern of those who engage in serious ethical argument. He refused to pay a poll tax to support a war, stating in effect that when one man is more right than all of his neighbors he makes a majority of one. Will Durant warned time and time again that America's greatest danger was the tyranny of the majority.

The Cruel-and-Unusual-Punishment Argument

Critics who oppose capital punishment often support their position by pointing out the extreme uncivilized brutality of American execution. They further point out that the brutality is escalating. The fourth minor issue is the cruel and unusual punishment argument.

As mentioned earlier, another alarming issue that has entered the capital punishment debate is what types of people should be eligible for execution. In three remarkable cases in the 1980s, the Supreme Court faced the issues of whether the insane, the mentally retarded, and juveniles could be executed constitutionally. The Supreme Court held that the insane could not be executed (*Ford v. Wainwright*[99]), the mentally retarded could be executed (*Penry v. Lynaugh*[100]), and juveniles under age 16 could not be executed (*Thompson v. Oklahoma*[101]). The issue of executing mentally retarded people is being revisited by the Court.

Ironically, shortly after the Court issued its opinion in *Thompson v. Oklahoma*, the rioting and massacres in Tiananmen Square in the Republic of China were in process. Certainly, the brutal Red Chinese Army executed thousands summarily after the riots. However, the Chinese government refused to execute anyone under age 16. Such, they suggested, was too uncivilized. This argument seems to have little merit with the majority of the present sitting members, because capital punishment per se thus far has been ruled not to be cruel and unusual punishment.

The Brutalization Argument

Another minor argument for the abolitionists is what they call the brutalization effect. In recent years, there have been calls to make executions more accessible; some have suggested that we even televise them.[102] The belief here is that the greater the publicity, the greater deterrent of future killers. Yet at the same time, modern research has cast doubts on the claim that highly publicized executions would deter crime.[103] Scholars such as Bailey and Peterson in their studies in 1990, 1991, 1994, and 1998 suggest that extensive execution publicity will have no deterrent effect on homicide rates.[104] To the contrary, Bowers explains that the effect most likely to occur, but only on a small subgroup of the population who are on the fringe of insanity, is that execution is imaginative and suggestive and therefore it is proper for people in this subgroup to kill those who disgrace, betray, or dishonor them.[105] Cochran, Chamlin, and Seth encountered this brutalization effect when they studied the influence of well-publicized executions in Oklahoma: After the execution, murders of strangers actually increased by one per month.[106]

SUMMARY

Sentencing is perhaps the most important phase of the criminal justice process for the criminal defendant as well as for the public at large. It is at this stage that the disposition of the criminal offender is decided. In earlier periods of American history, offenders were subject to retaliation by physical abuse as punishment for wrongdoing. Contemporary criminal justice is still punitive in its orientation, but its punitive procedures are justified on several theoretical grounds, including retribution, deterrence, and incapacitation.

Until recent years, the goals of rehabilitation and reintegration also were part of the punitive decision. However, with the advent of the new conservatism and the brutal reality of warehousing as the predominant correctional procedure from the 1970s through the beginning of the twenty-first century, tremendous popular support has grown for the position that retribution ("the law of just deserts") is the most important objective of sentencing.

Traditional sentences include fines, probation, and imprisonment. Probation is the most common choice. The sentencing structure itself has been riddled with disparity and problems. Also, due to massive prison overcrowding, citizens have become frustrated with the criminal courts' convicting defendants and sentencing them to long terms in prison, only to find that they have served but a fraction of the sentence that was imposed on them. In response, legislators, in one of the most radical changes in state legislations, enacted enhancement statutes. The effect of these statutes is to require the judge to render an extraordinarily high sentence, often when a defendant has violated a minor crime; but as the result of that crime, the original sentence is enhanced (often from ten to twenty-five years). These enhancements have become common household names: three-strikes, 10-20-Life, habitual-criminal, and trafficking. Enhanced sentences are almost universally disliked by trial judges, because they have no choice but to impose the statute in spite of mitigating factors. Of greatest importance for the judges' disdain is that enhancement statutes almost nullify judicial discretion.

One of the most significant features of sentencing is its tripod structure, involving the legislature, a judge, and a correctional agency. The actions of each of these parties affect the type and length of sentence imposed on the offender. The system often results in sentence disparity, in which the courts seek to fit the sentence to the individual offender rather than to the crime.

Regardless of an accused's sentence, certain appeals are granted based on the defendant's sentence, as well as postconviction remedies. Historically, only on rare occasions have sentences imposed by the court been overturned for being excessive. Recently, however, under the sentencing guidelines, if trial judges choose to go outside the guidelines when sentencing defendants, their sentences are subject to automatic review by appellate courts and are often reversed.

The most serious sentence imposed by American criminal courts is the death penalty. Once thought no longer to be part of American law, the death penalty is gaining popularity at an astonishing rate. Over 80 percent of Americans support the death penalty. Yet for the state to take a life, such action must be theoretically justified. The justification for capital punishment has been hotly debated. Proponents argue that capital punishment acts as a deterrent for the individual as well as for other potential murderers. Furthermore, capital punishment, they say, is the only satisfactory retribution that society can gain for such a heinous act as premeditated murder. Opponents argue that sentences are imposed arbitrarily, often based on the race of the victim. They also point out that there are many instances in American history where the death penalty has mistakenly been imposed. Such a mistake, these opponents argue, justifies the elimination of the death penalty altogether. Finally, they point out that all of the empirical studies on the subject have failed to prove that the death penalty acts as a deterrent. In fact, they argue, it may even have a brutalizing effect. Other minor issues in the capital punishment debate have also come forward, including the cost of capital punishment and the execution of special populations.

DISCUSSION AND REVIEW

1. Explain incapacitation as a theory of punishment and how it affects the crime rate.
2. What is the rehabilitation/treatment philosophy of punishment? Give examples of how this level of punishment acts to reintegrate the offender into society.

3. Should vengeance be accepted as a rationale for punishment?
4. Discuss reintegration as a theory of punishment.
5. How do sentencing structures influence judges' discretion?
6. Discuss the role of presentence investigation reports in the process of judicial sentencing. How much weight should judges place on the information in these reports?
7. What are habitual-criminal statutes used for? How has the Supreme Court acted to limit their use?
8. What are the most important factors regarding sentencing decisions?
9. What effect does the phenomenon of prison overcrowding have on the validity of the theoretical justifications for punishment in the American criminal justice system?
10. Explain the retribution theory of punishment and cite examples of how it has been escalating in popularity as a justification for correctional punishment.
11. Does capital punishment deter crime?
12. How do we distinguish between general and specific deterrence?
13. What are Megan's Laws? To whom are they applied?
14. What is the distinction between a presumptive sentence and flat time? Compare and contrast an indeterminate sentence with a mandatory minimum sentence.
15. How does the Supreme Court interpret "cruel and unusual punishment"?
16. What is a bifurcated trial?
17. How are sentencing guidelines developed empirically for a particular jurisdiction? What is the relationship between offender scores and offense scores in arriving at an appropriate sentence?
18. What is appellate review?
19. What are sentencing guidelines and how do they function as a matter of practice? How has legislators' frustration about sentencing guidelines caused them to pass certain sentencing structures such as habitual-offender statutes and mandatory minimum statutes?
20. What is the relationship between time sentenced and actual time served?
21. What is the significance of the rulings by the Supreme Court in *Furman v. Georgia* and *Gregg v. Georgia*?
22. Examine the five major issues in the capital punishment debate.
23. What are the three necessary components of the punishment theory of deterrence?

CHAPTER RESOURCES

IN THE MEDIA

Video

A&E American Justice Videos
ABC News/Prentice Hall Video: *Capital Punishment: Judgment at Midnight*
ABC News/Prentice Hall Video: *Crime and Punishment*
ABC News/Prentice Hall Video: *Three Strikes: Is It Working?*
ABC News/Prentice Hall Video: *Victim Impact Statements*
ABC News/Prentice Hall Video: *Why Not Wilbert Rideau?*
CNN Today Video: *Introduction to Criminal Justice*
FAH Court CJ Videos
Insight Media Video: *Criminal Justice: From Murder to Execution*
Insight Media Video: *The Death Penalty*

Film

An Innocent Man (1989)
The Chamber (1996)
Criminal Justice (1990)
Dead Man Walking (1995)
Double Jeopardy (1999)
Just Cause (1995)
The Shawshank Redemption (1994)
True Crime (1998)

IN THE LITERATURE

Books

J. AUSTIN AND J. IRWIN, 2001. *It's about Time: America's Imprisonment Binge.* Belmont, Calif.: Wadsworth, 2001.

H. BEDAU, ed., *The Death Penalty in America,* 3rd ed. London: Oxford Press, 1982.

H. BEDAU AND C. PIERCE eds., *Capital Punishment in the United States.* New York: AMS Press, 1976.

W. BOWERS, G. PIERCE, AND J. MCDEVITT, *Legal Homicide: Death as Punishment in America, 1864–1982.* Boston: Northeastern University Press, 1984.

J. CAULKINS, C. RANDALL, W. SCHWABE, AND J. CHISEA, *Mandatory Drug Sentences: Throwing Away the Key or the Taxpayers' Money?* Santa Monica, Calif.: Rand, 1997.

R. JOHNSON, *Condemned to Die: Life under Sentence of Death.* Prospect Heights, Ill: Waveland Press, 1989.

R. PATERNOSTER, *Capital Punishment in America.* New York: Lexington, 1991.

Articles

N. ALONZE AND C. JOHNSON, "Probing Limits of the Female Advantage in Criminal Processing: Pretrial Diversion of Drug Offenders in an Urban County," *Justice System,* vol. 21 (2000), pp. 239–259.

K. DOYLE, "No Defense," *U.S. Catholic,* vol. 64 (1999), p. 18.

P. GLYNN, "Conscience and the Public Square," *Brookings Review,* vol. 17 (1999), p. 24.

S. GRANT, "A Dialogue of the Deaf? New International Attitudes and the Death Penalty in America," *Criminal Justice Ethics,* vol. 17 (1998), p. 19.

M. HIGGINS, "Is Capital Punishment for Killers Only?" *ABA Journal* vol. 83 (August 1997), pp. 30–31.

P. KAMPERT, "Ex-Junk Bond Kingpin Milken Now a Big Hit in Business Class," *Chicago Tribune,* September 15, 1993, p. 1.

K. KEMPF-LEONARD AND L. SAMPLE, "Disparity Based on Sex: Is Gender-Specific Treatment Warranted?" *Justice Quarterly,* vol. 17 (2000), pp. 89–128.

M. MALES, D. MACALLAIR, AND K. TAQI-EDDIN, "Striking Out: The Failure of California's 'Three Strikes and You're Out' Law," *Stanford Law and Policy Review* (Fall 1999).

W. MANNING AND J. RHODEN-TRADER, "Rethinking the Death Penalty," *Corrections Today,* vol. 62 (2000), p. 22.

J. MARQUART AND J. SORENSEN, "Institutional and Postrelease Behavior of *Furman*-Committed Inmates in Texas," *Criminology,* vol. 26 (November 1988), pp. 677–693.

C. MOOREHEAD, Tinkering with death. *World Press Review,* vol. 42 (1995), p. 38.

Government Publications

J. CLARK, J. AUSTIN AND D. HENRY, "'Three Strikes and You're Out:' A Review of State Legislation," *NIJ Research in Brief* (September 2001), Exhibits 9 and 10.

P. DITTON AND D. WILSON, *Truth in Sentencing in State Prisons.* Washington, D.C.: Bureau of Justice Statistics, 1999.

Z. FLANAGAN AND K. MAGUIRE, *Sourcebook on Criminal Justice Statistics 1991.* Washington, D.C.: U.S. Department of Justice, 1992.

P. LANGAN AND M. CONNIFF, "Recidivism of Felons on Probation, 1986–1989." Special Report. Washington, D.C.: U.S. Department of Justice, 1992.

D. LEVIN, P. LANGAN, AND J. BROWN, *State Court Sentencing of Convicted Felons, 1996.* Washington, D.C.: U.S. Department of Justice, 2000

R. SINGER, "Crime File: Sentencing." Washington, D.C.: National Institute of Justice, 1987.

U.S. Department of Justice, "Justice Department Reaches Agreement with Georgia County Jail." Press Release. August 21, 1997.

Georgia Code, 26-1101, 1311, 1902, 2001, 3301 (1972)

Apprendi v. New Jersey, 120 S.Ct. 2348 (2000)
Bearden v. Georgia, 461 U.S. 660 (1983)
Beck v. Alabama, 447 U.S. 625 (1980)
Caldwell v. Mississippi, 472 U.S. 320 (1985)
Castello v. Wainwright, 397 F.Supp. 20 (MD FLA 1975)
Chapman v. California, 386 U.S. 18 (1967)
Coker v. Georgia, 433 U.S. 584 (1977)
Douglas v. California, 372 U.S. 353 (1963)
Ford v. Wainwright, 477 U.S. 399 (1986)
Furman v. Georgia, 408 U.S. 238 (1972)
Gardner v. Florida, 430 U.S. 349 (1977)
Gregg v. Georgia, 428 U.S. 153 (1976)

Harmelin v. Michigan, 501 U.S. 957 (1991)
Harris v. Alabama, 513 U.S. 504 (1995)
Lockett v. Ohio, 438 U.S. 586 (1978)
McCleskey v. Kemp, 481 U.S. 278 (1987)
Mempha v. Rhay, 389 U.S. 128 (1967)
Murray v. Giarrantano, 492 U.S. 1 (1989)
North Carolina v. Pearce, 395 U.S. 711 (1969)
Penry v. Lynaugh, 492 U.S. 302 (1989)
Rhodes v. Chapman, 452 U.S. 337 (1981)
Roberts v. United States, 445 U.S. 552 (1980)
Robinson v. California, 370 U.S. 660 (1962)
Ross v. Moffitt, 417 U.S. 600 (1974)

Rummel v. Estelle, 445 U.S. 263 (1980)
Schlup v. Delo, 513 U.S. 298 (1995)
Solem v. Helm, 463 U.S. 277 (1983)
Stanford v. Kentucky, 492 U.S. 361 (1989)
Tate v. Short, 401 U.S. 395 (1971)
Thompson v. Oklahoma, 487 U.S. 815 (1988)

Townsend v. Burke, 334 U.S. 736 (1948)
United States v. Grayson, 438 U.S. 41 (1978)
United States v. Rodriguez-Moreno, 526 U.S. 275 (1999)
Weems v. United States, 217 U.S. 349 (1910)
Williams v. New York, 337 U.S. 241 (1949)
Williams v. Oklahoma, 358 U.S. 576 (1959)

ENDNOTES

1. B. Smith and H. Vetter, *Theoretical Approaches to Personality*. Englewood Cliffs, N.J.: Prentice-Hall, 1982.
2. *Rhodes v. Chapman*, 452 U.S. 337 (1981).
3. S. Ekland-Olsen et al., *Justice under Pressure: A Comparison of Recidivism Patterns among Four Successive Employee Cohorts*. New York: Springer-Verlag, 1993, p. 146.
4. S. Skouron, "Prison Crowding, the Dimensions of the Problem and Strategies of Population Control." In J. Scott and T. Hirschi, eds., *Controversial Issues in Crime and Justice*. Newbury Park, Calif.: Sage, 1998, p. 190.
5. P. Langan and M. Conniff, "Recidivism of Felons on Probation, 1986–1989." Special Report. Washington, D.C.: U.S. Department of Justice, 1992.
6. U.S. Department of Justice, "Justice Department Reaches Agreement with Georgia County Jail." Press Release. August 21, 1997.
7. Thirteenth Judicial Circuit State Attorney's Office, which serves Tampa and the rest of the population in Hillsborough County, Florida. Figures presented to Dr. Halsted and his students by State Attorney Mark Ober, in a class presentation on June 30, 2001.
8. A. Vachss and Y. Bakal, *The Life-Style Violent Juvenile*. Lexington, Mass.: Lexington, 1979.
9. S. Levitt, "The Effect of Prison Population Size on Crime Rates," *Quarterly Journal on Economics*, vol. 81 (May 1996), p. 317.
10. R. Pursley, *Introduction to Criminal Justice*, 4th ed. New York: Macmillan, 1987.
11. Patrick Arvonio, former assistant warden of the Rahway State Penitentiary. Information presented to Dr. Halsted and his students, 2001.
12. S. Reid, *Crime and Criminology*. New York: Holt, Rinehart & Winston, 1982.
13. *Mempha v. Rhay*, 389 U.S. 128 (1967).
14. *Williams v. Oklahoma*, 358 U.S. 576 (1959).
15. *Williams v. New York*, 337 U.S. 241 (1949).
16. *United States v. Grayson*, 438 U.S. 41 (1978).
17. *Roberts v. United States*, 445 U.S. 552 (1980).
18. *Townsend v. Burke*, 334 U.S. 736 (1948).
19. R. Carter and L. Wilkins, "Some Factors in Sentencing Policy," *Journal of Criminal Law, Criminology, and Police Science*, vol. 58 (1967), p. 503.
20. R. Davis and B. Smith, "The Effects of Victim Impact Statements on Sentencing Decisions: A Test in an Urban Setting," *Justice Quarterly*, vol. 11 (1999), pp. 453–469.
21. E. Erez and P. Tontodonato, "The Effects of Victim Participation in Sentencing Outcomes," *Criminology*, vol. 28 (1990), pp. 451–474.
22. *Solem v. Helm*, 463 U.S. 277 (1983).
23. *Rummel v. Estelle*, 445 U.S. 263 (1980).
24. *Weems v. United States*, 217 U.S. 349 (1910).
25. *Harmelin v. Michigan*, 501 U.S. 957 (1991).
26. *Coker v. Georgia*, 433 U.S. 584 (1977).
27. *Robinson v. California*, 370 U.S. 660 (1962).
28. *Tate v. Short*, 401 U.S. 395 (1971).
29. *Bearden v. Georgia*, 461 U.S. 660 (1983).
30. *North Carolina v. Pearce*, 395 U.S. 711 (1969).
31. P. Ditton and D. Wilson, *Truth in Sentencing in State Prisons*. Washington, D.C.: Bureau of Justice Statistics, 1999.
32. *Douglas v. California*, 372 U.S. 353 (1963).
33. *Ross v. Moffitt*, 417 U.S. 600 (1974).
34. *Douglas v. California*, op. cit.
35. *Ross v. Moffitt*, op. cit.
36. D. Neubauer, *America's Courts and the Criminal Justice System*, 7th ed. Belmont, Calif.: Wadsworth, 2002, p. 458.
37. J. Inciardi, *Criminal Justice*, 7th ed. New York: Harcourt, 2002, p. 465.
38. M. Frankel, *Criminal Sentences: Law without Order*. New York: Hill & Wang, 1973.
39. P. Kratcoski and D. Walker, *Criminal Justice in America: Process and Issues*. Glenview, Ill.: Scott, Foresman, 1978.
40. American Bar Association, *Standards Relating to Sentencing Alternatives and Procedures*. New York: Institute of Judicial Administration, 1968, p. 7.
41. D. Kaplan et al., "The Incorrigibles: They Rape and Molest. They Defy Treatment. How Can Society Protect Itself?" *Newsweek*, January 18, 1993, pp. 48–50.
42. D. Newman and P. Anderson, *Introduction to Criminal Justice*. New York: Random House, 1989.
43. H. Bedau, *Death Is Different: Studies in the Morality, Law, and Politics of Capital Punishment*. Boston: Northeastern University Press, 1987.
44. Amnesty International, *The United States of America: The Death Penalty*. London: Amnesty International, 1987.
45. D. Magee, *Slow Coming Dark*. New York: Pilgrim, 1980.
46. Amnesty International, *The United States of America: The Death Penalty* (London: Amnesty International, 1987).
47. Ibid.
48. H. Bedau, *The Case against the Death Penalty*. New York: American Civil Liberties Union, 1984.
49. Ibid.

50. *Furman v. Georgia*, 408 U.S. 238 (1972).
51. D. Drehle, "Death Penalty: A Failure of Execution," *Miami Herald*, July 10, 1988.
52. Cauchon, op. cit.
53. *Gregg v. Georgia*, 428 U.S. 153 (1976); *Lockett v. Ohio*, 438 U.S. 586 (1978)
54. *Gardner v. Florida*, 430 U.S. 349 (1977)
55. *Furman v. Georgia*, op. cit.
56. *Beck v. Alabama*, 447 U.S. 625 (1980).
57. *Caldwell v. Mississippi*, 472 U.S. 320 (1985).
58. *Harris v. Alabama*, 513 U.S. 504 (1995).
59. *Coker v. Georgia*, op. cit.
60. *Ford v. Wainwright*, 477 U.S. 399 (1986).
61. *Penry v. Lynaugh*, 492 U.S. 302 (1989).
62. *Stanford v. Kentucky*, 492 U.S. 361 (1989).
63. *Thompson v. Oklahoma*, 487 U.S. 815 (1988).
64. Amnesty International USA, *Annual Report 2000: The Death Penalty: An Affront to Our Humanity*. Washington, D.C.: Amnesty International, 2000.
65. Death Penalty Information Center. http://www.deathpenaltyinfo.org.
66. NAACP, "Death Row USA." http://www.deathpenaltyinfo.org.
67. NEAA Legal Defense Fund 1993. http://www.deathpenaltyinfo.org.
68. K. Haas and J. Inciardi, eds., *Challenging Capital Punishment*. Newbury Park, Calif.: Sage, 1988.
69. Bureau of Justice Statistics, http://www.ojp.usdoj.gov/bjs/abstract/cp00.htm.
70. W. Bowers, M. VanDuise, and P. Duzan, "A New Look at Public Opinion on Capital Punishment: What Citizens and Legislators Prefer," *American Journal of Criminal Law*, vol. 22 (1994), p. 97.
71. J. MacArthur, "The Death Penalty and the Decline of Liberalism," *John Marshall Law Review*, vol. 30 (Winter 1997).
72. Z. Flanagan and K. Maguire, *Sourcebook on Criminal Justice Statistics 1991*. Washington, D.C.: U.S. Department of Justice, 1992.
73. Georgia Code, 26-1101, 1311, 1902, 2001, 3301 (1972).
74. *McCleskey v. Zant*, 111 S.Ct. 145 (1987).
75. *Murray v. Giarrantano*, 492 U.S. 1 (1989).
76. H. Bedau and C. Pierce, eds., *Capital Punishment in the United States*. New York: AMS Press, 1976.
77. J. Dilulio, "Abolish the Death Penalty, Officially," *The Wall Street Journal*, December 15, 1977, p. A23.
78. Inciardi, p. 450.
79. W. Bowers and G. Pierce, "Deterrence or Brutalization: What Is the Effect of Executions?" *Crime and Delinquency*, vol. 26, no. 4 (1980), pp. 453–484.
80. M. Radelet, "Racial Characteristics and the Imposition of the Death Penalty," *American Sociological Review*, vol. 46 (1991), pp. 918–927.
81. D. Baldus, G. Woodworth, and C. Pulaski, *Equal Justice and the Death Penalty: An Empirical Analysis*. Boston: Northeastern University Press, 1990.
82. Ibid., p. 160.
83. *McCleskey v. Kemp*, 481 U.S. 278 (1987).
84. Ibid.
85. D. Dolinko, "How to Criticize the Death Penalty," *Journal of Criminal Law and Criminology*, vol. 77 (1986), pp. 553–601.
86. Ibid., p. 585.
87. H. Bedau and M. Radelet, "Miscarriages of Justice in Potential Capital Cases," *Stanford Law Review*, vol. 40, no. 1 (November 1987), pp. 21–197.
88. Ibid.
89. Ibid.
90. J. Wright, "Life without Parole: An Alternative to Death or Not Much of a Life at All?" *Vanderbilt Law Review*, vol. 43, no. 2 (March 1990), pp. 529–568.
91. Wright, p. 555.
92. M. Gray, "The Cost of Taking a Life," *University of California–Davis Law Review*, vol. 18 (1985).
93. Drehle, op. cit.
94. D. Hook and L. Kahn, *Death in the Balance: The Debate over Capital Punishment*. Lexington, Mass.: D. C. Heath, 1989.
95. Bedau, *The Case against the Death Penalty*.
96. President's Commission on Law Enforcement and Administration of Justice, *The Courts*. Washington, D.C.: U.S. Government Printing Office, 1967.
97. R. Singer, "Crime File: Sentencing." Washington, D.C.: National Institute of Justice, 1987.
98. J. Finckenaur, "Public Support for the Death Penalty: Retribution as Just Deserts or Retribution as Revenge?" *Justice Quarterly*, vol. 5 (March 1988), pp. 81–100.
99. *Ford v. Wainwright*, op. cit.
100. *Penry v. Lynaugh*, op. cit.
101. *Thompson v. Oklahoma*, op. cit.
102. H. Bedau, "American Populism and the Death Penalty: Witness at an Execution," *Howard Journal of Criminal Justice*, vol. 33 (1994), pp. 289–304.
103. W. Bailey and R. Peterson, "Murder, Capital Punishment, and Deterrence: A Review of the Evidence and an Examination of Police Killings," *Journal of Social Issues*, vol. 50 (1994), pp. 53–74.
104. Ibid.
105. W. Bowers, "The Effect of Executions Is Brutalization, Not Deterrence." In K. Haas and J. Inciardi, eds., *Challenging Capital Punishment: Legal and Social Science Approaches*. Newbury Park, Calif.: Sage, 1998, pp. 49–89.
106. J. Cochran, M. Chamlin, and M. Seth, "Deterrence or Brutalization? An Impact Assessment of Oklahoma's Return to Capital Punishment," *Criminology*, vol. 32 (1994), pp. 107–134.

11 JAILS AND DETENTION

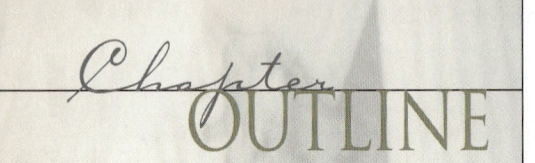

Chapter Outline

A Brief History of Jails
The Purpose of Jails
Jail Crowding
  Looking at the Local Justice System
  How System Decision Makers Can Affect Jail Crowding
Direct Supervision
  Personnel Issues
  Effective Management
  Improved Staff Morale
  Reduced Sick Leave
  Improved Working Conditions
  Staffing Level
  Safe Working Environment
Special-Management Inmates
  Physically Ill Inmates
  Alcoholics
  Inmates with Disabilities
  Aggressive and Assaultive Inmates
  Vulnerable Inmates

  Mentally Ill Inmates
  Drug Addicts
  Sex Offenders
Suicide in Jail
  Precipitating Factors of Suicidal Behavior
  Identifying the Suicidal Inmate
  Key Components of a Suicide Prevention Program
Treatment Programs
Jail Security
  Counts
  Shakedowns
  Frisks
  Tool Control
  Key Control
  Cutlery Control
  Narcotics Control
  Visitation Control
Summary

Key TERMS

alcoholics, p. 456
combination facility, p. 446
contact visit, p. 469
count, p. 466
cutlery control, p. 468
direct-supervision jail, p. 452
frisks, p. 467
jail crowding, p. 450
jail security, p. 466
key control, p. 467
narcotics control, p. 469

pretrial detention facility, p. 446
sentenced facility, p. 446
sex offenders, p. 458
shakedown, p. 467
special-management inmates, p. 455
"The State of Prisons," p. 447
tool control, p. 467
treatment programs, p. 464
visitation control, p. 469
Walnut Street Jail, p. 447

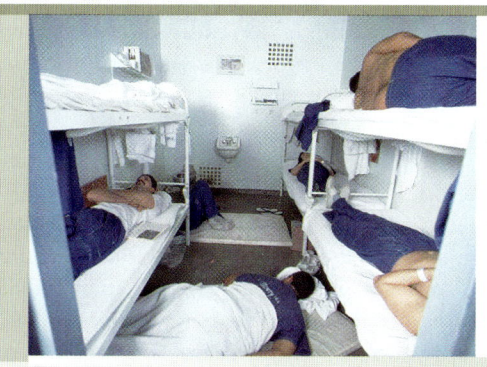

Courtesy of Mark Richards/PhotoEdit.

It is not at all uncommon for laypeople—or, for that matter, people in the criminal justice system—to use the terms *jail* and *prison* as if they were the same entity. Nothing could be further from the truth. For example, jails are usually operated by a local unit of government, while prisons are operated by the state. Jails hold pretrial detainees and sentenced petty offenders—usually misdemeanants. In prisons, inmates are there principally for confinement for felonies of which they have been convicted. In jails, the population changes frequently, perhaps as much as 70 percent within seventy-two hours, while in prison the population is relatively steady. Jails are located in population centers. Historically, prisons have been located in rural areas. Jails tend to have a smaller population than prisons, which conversely tend to have a larger population than jails. Jails also have limited inmate programs, while prisons have diverse inmate programs. Jails have traditionally been ignored by scholars and researchers; prisons have received considerable attention from them.

There are three types of jails in the United States—pretrial detention facilities, sentenced facilities, and combination facilities. The **pretrial detention facility** is used solely to confine people awaiting trial. The **sentenced facility** is where convicted people serve their sentences; inmates in these facilities are usually misdemeanants, although a few such facilities may house felons with short sentences. If operated by a city or county, a sentenced facility is called a city or county farm, a city or county prison, or a city or county correctional facility. To some observers, these facilities are not jails because they contain no pretrial detainees and some of the inmates are serving long sentences. Thus, it can be said that although they technically meet the definition of a jail, sentenced facilities are actually correctional facilities. A **combination facility** houses pretrial detainees and some convicted people, usually misdemeanants—although again, in a few states, felons serving shorter sentences may be housed there. The combination facility is the most common type of jail.

In this chapter we will start by providing the reader with a brief history of jails, beginning with the early period in English history. We will then discuss the purpose of modern jails and the problem of jail overcrowding and its accompanying facets, which can be administratively problematic if not addressed. For example, jail crowding has obviously become endemic in the United States, but administrative solutions are available to mitigate the problem.

The concept of the direct-supervision jail as compared to the traditional jail will also be discussed, along with some of the major personnel issues associated with this form of jail administration. We will also introduce the high-liability area of dealing with special-management inmates: the physically ill, inmates with disabilities, vulnerable inmates, mentally ill inmates, drug addicts, sex offenders, and suicidal inmates. We will also be discussing the various treatment programs offered in jails, such as detoxification, education enhancement, traditional counseling, group counseling, therapeutic community, and community referral.

Jail security is also an area of major concern to jail administrators because the escape of a prisoner, especially a murderer, can result in more murders being committed. A classic example of this is the escape of serial murderer Theodore Robert Bundy from a Colorado jail. He was suspected of having been involved in as many as a hundred murders of young women around the United States. After he escaped from the Colorado jail, he went to Florida and within less than two months he had killed three more women and severely injured three others.

All jails have basically the same components of jail security and involve the following areas: counts, shakedowns, frisks, tool control, key control, cutlery control, narcotics control, and visitation control. These too will be discussed in considerable detail in this chapter.

A BRIEF HISTORY OF JAILS

The word *jail* comes from the Old English word *gaol* (also pronounced "jail").[1] In 1166, King Henry II of England initiated the Assize or Constitution of Clarendon. This law established the first jails, which were locally administered and operated. Jails housed the "misfits" of society. Early jail populations consisted of paupers, drunkards, prostitutes, thieves, robbers, orphaned children, and debtors, as well as people who did not agree with the powerful Church of England.[2]

The "shire-reeves," now known as sheriffs, controlled jails in their individual shires or localities. Each sheriff was responsible for establishing a jail. The individual type of jails carried over to colonial America and continues today. Similarly, today, politics influences the development and operation of U.S. jails. Sheriffs are elected officers, and they bring their own philosophies and staffs to their administrations.

Early English jails held wrongdoers who were accused of violating the law. These violators were held in jails until court convened and determined the actual punishment. Early jails operated on a fee system. Prisoners had to pay fees to the sheriffs and the jailkeepers.

Jail inmates provided cheap labor. Workhouses, such as Bridewell in 1557, used inmates to work for merchants. Corruption was commonplace; food, sanitation, and medical care were substandard. Conditions in jails were appalling. In 1724, an inmate

---

CTQ

What characteristics of prisons make them different from other institutions?

WEB

For current statistics on the American jail system on a regional level, **visit our Web site, www.prenhall.com/territo.**

CTQ

How do modern prisons differ from those in the past?

described London's Newgate Jail as a "terrible stinking dark and dismal place" where prisoners endured "great miseries and hardships."[3] In colonial America, jails continued to be financed by the fee system. Conditions were bad. Many jails held all types of offenders together in dormitories, regardless of gender, age, or type of offense.

Because of the miserable conditions of jails, several reform efforts arose. In 1777, John Howard, a sheriff of Bedfordshire, England, wrote **"The State of Prisons."** This essay urged prison and jail reform, including improved sanitation, abolition of fees, humane treatment, good character and morals of jailers, and systematic inspections. As a result of Howard's efforts, Parliament enacted reforms.

In Philadelphia in 1787, the humane Quaker influence resulted in the formation of the Philadelphia Society for Alleviating the Miseries of Public Prisons (now known as the Pennsylvania Prison Society). Believing that jail conditions needed improvement, these citizen volunteers visited jails, bringing food and clothing and providing education and religious instruction.

Also in Philadelphia, in 1790, an institution known as the "first, true correctional institution in America" opened. This was the **Walnut Street Jail.** Due to the Quaker influence and the ideas of William Penn, the Walnut Street Jail initiated more humane treatment of inmates. Through their efforts, the public and politicians became aware of the bad conditions in jails, and in many cases, conditions improved. Based on their influence, the Walnut Street Jail separated the more serious prisoners from others; it also separated other prisoners by the seriousness of their offenses and by their gender. Prior to this, inmates were all housed together: men, women, and children without any consideration for type of offense. Prisoners engaged in productive labor, and male inmates, were paid a daily wage to offset the cost of incarceration. Many prisons were modeled after the concepts of the Walnut Street Jail.[4]

Since the creation of these early jails, they have had a sketchy but interesting history. Various types of inmate facilities were established, ranging from sheriffs' homes to barns and small houses. States did not take an interest in jails, and sheriffs were reluctant to share information. In 1880, the U.S. Census Bureau started compiling information about jails. The bureau obtained information concerning race, ethnicity, gender, and age every ten years. In 1923, this information was combined into "jail statistics."

In 1923, federal prison inspector Joseph Fishman, in the *Crucible of Crime*, described jail conditions as "horrible" in the 1,500 jails he observed. Recent research indicates that with some exceptions, jail conditions have not changed significantly since Fishman's observations.[5]

THE PURPOSE OF JAILS

Jails serve three main functions. First, jails enhance public safety by segregating people who have been deemed a criminal threat to other people and property, then ensure that those charged with crimes appear at trial. Second, jails are expected to effect some measure of positive behavioral and attitudinal change—rehabilitation. Third, they serve as a form of punishment.

Jails typically have the following functions:

- Receive individuals pending arraignment and hold them awaiting trial, conviction, or sentencing
- Readmit probation, parole, and bail bond violators and absconders
- Temporarily detain juveniles pending transfer to juvenile authorities
- Hold people who are mentally ill pending their movement to appropriate health facilities
- Hold individuals for the military, for protective custody, for contempt, and for the courts as witnesses
- Release convicted inmates to the community upon completion of sentence
- Transfer inmates to federal, state, and other authorities
- House inmates for federal, state, and other authorities because of crowding of their facilities

- Relinquish custody of temporary detainees to juvenile and medical authorities
- Sometimes operate community-based programs as alternatives to incarceration[6]

Many jails in the United States are quite old and, in general, it is fair to say that an old facility is more likely than a new facility to have deficiencies. Unrenovated, uncared-for, mismanaged, or misoperated jails present problems for the jailers, and people confined in them are frequently in danger. Such facilities—with their noxious odors, dirty lavatories, and dirty floors and walls—are offensive to the eye and nose. In addition, some jails are fire hazards; some have inadequate lighting, ventilation, and bedding; and some are vermin-infested and overcrowded.

To a great extent, however, the physical conditions of jail are affected more by the professional competency and philosophy of the sheriff or the jail director than by the age of the facility. The following true case illustrates this point and also shows that even some well-intentioned plans can take some interesting and unanticipated turns.

As frequently happens every four years, there was a hotly contested sheriff's race between two men who were remarkably different in many personal and professional respects. Prior to being elected, the incumbent sheriff had very little formal education and no prior administrative experience or professional training to administer the county jail. His opponent had a master's degree in criminology and broad-ranging experience in criminal justice. The incumbent was defeated, and when the newly elected sheriff took office, one of his first tasks was to conduct a systematic inspection of all parts of the sheriff's office facilities, which included the county jail.

Upon his inspection of the county jail, which was only fifteen years old, the new sheriff was shocked at its general state of disrepair and poor sanitary conditions. Puzzled at the obvious long-term neglect of the facility, the sheriff started questioning some of the jail personnel about it. He learned from them that the former sheriff placed his highest priority on the law enforcement component of the agency and almost no importance on the jail. The former sheriff also believed that inmates were criminals, and that the jail should be as unpleasant a place as possible in order to discourage them from ever wanting to return to it. As a result, the following conditions existed:

- No part of the facility had been painted since it opened.
- Approximately 25 percent of all the lights in the cell block area were burned out; in addition, the cell block area was painted black.
- The showers would not drain properly because they were plugged up with hair, and as a result inmates frequently had to stand in at least three inches of dirty water while showering.
- No cleaning material was provided to clean the commodes in the cell block area, which not only were stained with human waste but also emitted a very unpleasant odor.
- The jail was overrun by roaches, mice, rats, and other vermin.
- The kitchen area, including the stove, had not been cleaned in years.
- The front lobby where people waited to either conduct business at the jail or visit inmates contained couches that were so decrepit and damaged that visitors risked being impaled by the springs if they sat on one of them.

Interestingly, these conditions existed in a state that was alleged to have had very strict state-controlled jail inspections, and yet the facility was always given a satisfactory rating.

The new sheriff felt that such conditions were intolerable, not only for those who were confined in jail but also for his employees who had to work there, a consideration the former sheriff seemed to overlook. Thus, a massive housecleaning effort and repairs were undertaken by the county maintenance department at the request of the new sheriff. In addition, an exterminator was employed to eliminate all of the roaches, mice, rats, and other vermin, and some decent furniture was purchased, at cost, for the lobby area of the jail.

A couple of months after the cleanup and repairs were underway, anonymous phone calls were made to the local newspapers and TV stations and complaints were lodged that the sheriff was spending the taxpayers' dollars to convert the county jail into a "luxury hotel" for criminals. Media representatives contacted the sheriff and requested access to the jail to see if in fact it was as elegant and luxurious as some callers had described. There was some speculation these anonymous phone calls may have been made by some supporters of the former sheriff who were not particularly happy with the defeat of their candidate. The sheriff agreed, but was concerned that the media might present a distorted or inaccurate picture of what he wanted to accomplish. Nevertheless, the doors were opened and representatives of both the local newspapers and TV station were invited in. When they arrived, all employees, jail inmates, and visitors were encouraged to speak freely and openly to the media representatives.

When some of the jail visitors who had witnessed the changes were interviewed, their comments were quite favorable. One of them commented that it was unpleasant enough just having to come to the jail to visit a loved one, but when the place looked like a dungeon, as it previously had, the experience was even more unpleasant. The attorneys who were waiting to see their clients were also quite pleased with the changes. The visitation rooms where they talked to their clients no longer had broken tables, ripped-up floor tiles, broken acoustical tiles, and half the lights burned out. One attorney commented that the facility now gave the impression that "it was being administered by a professional administrator, and not the Marquis de Sade."

The response from the jail officers was also quite positive, and many commented that it was much more pleasant to come to work in a facility that "looked clean and smelled clean." They also appreciated the special attention that the new sheriff had shown them and the jail, and they had a renewed sense of pride in their work.

The last group of people to be interviewed were the inmates themselves. This brought to light one of the most startling and unexpected consequences of the changes to the facility. Since at that point only half of the cell blocks had been repainted, or had the lights and plumbing repaired, the media was exposed to a vivid "before and after" contrast. The first set of cell blocks visited had been repainted light green, the burned-out lights had been replaced, and all of the plumbing had been repaired. As the media representatives walked along the catwalk, they stopped to interview some of the inmates. In some cases, the inmates even called out to the media representatives and requested to talk to them. Both inmates and media representatives had access to each other, but the inmates were not permitted out of their cells. The inmates were questioned about their confinement and asked if they had any complaints about the facility. Although there were some minor complaints about needing more access to a telephone and the usual protestations of innocence, practically none of the inmates had serious complaints.

The second set of cell blocks visited were still in the original state of disrepair, but had basically the same classification of inmates as the previous cell blocks visited. As the heavy steel door to the cell block area was opened, the contrast in lighting and odor was startling. The media group entered and were immediately met with complaints about the food, abuse by jail officers, limited recreational opportunities, poor mail service, and so forth. These complaints were made even though there was no difference between any of the cell blocks in terms of the quality of food, jail officers, recreational opportunities, or mail service. The only real differences between these cell blocks were the ones made by the renovations. Interestingly, the jail officers also reported far more disciplinary problems in the unrepaired and unpainted cell blocks than in the newly renovated ones.

The cost of these changes was negligible to the taxpayers since all of the work was done by the county maintenance department as part of its regular responsibilities. When all of these facts were accurately reported by the media, the criticism subsided.[7]

JAIL CROWDING

The words *jail* and *crowding* seem inseparable these days. The reality of more prisoners than available beds creates a dilemma for local justice officials. Crowded jails may compromise public safety because of the lack of space to confine those who pose serious threats to the living community. Lawsuits challenging the crowded conditions may constrain the community's ability to incarcerate.[8]

WEB

For more information on the modern American jail system, visit our Web site, www.prenhall.com/territo.

CTQ

Do politics ever play a role in the administration of regional correctional facilities? If so, do you think this is a drawback, or can it ever be advantageous for either the inmates or the community into which some will be released?

For the local sheriff or jail administrator, **jail crowding** creates increased prisoner and staff tensions, increased wear and tear of facility and equipment, lawsuits, budgetary problems from overtime staffing, and an inability to meet program and service standards. Less frequently recognized are the problems that crowding creates for other justice system officials:

- Judges, prosecutors, probation and parole officers, and other officials often find crowding a severe constraint in cases where jailing offenders appears necessary but space is unavailable.
- Prosecutors, public defenders, and pretrial services officers find their functions impaired by delayed access to inmates caused by the difficulty of processing large numbers of offenders.
- Court functions overall may suffer when crowding affects the movements of inmates to and from scheduled appearances.

Too often, however, agencies outside jail management are not fully involved in efforts to cope with the problem. And many jurisdictions that do address the symptoms of jail crowding nevertheless leave the underlying causes unaddressed. Other jurisdictions, however, view jail crowding as a problem that demands the cooperative involvement of all key figures in the local justice system.

Looking at the Local Justice System

Virtually every decision made in the local justice system involves the exercise of discretion, and these decisions can and often do affect the jail population. Jurisdictions that use a systemwide approach to jail crowding see the local justice system as a screening mechanism that can be modified to enhance the use of scarce jail space. These jurisdictions develop case-processing flowcharts to understand the details of their case-handling process from the initial contact to final disposition. Flowcharts illustrate the stages of the legal process, specify the points at which decision makers' actions affect the jail population, and identify opportunities to alleviate crowding.

Understanding the local flow of cases can help policymakers identify program and process changes to reduce crowding. Program changes frequently involve eliminating the jailing of people whom a community deems inappropriate for criminal justice processing, such as the mentally ill. Process changes improve system efficiency by eliminating case-handling "catch points" that unnecessarily prolong the confinement of people who might eventually be released through bail, probation, or transfer to the state prison.

Reducing length of confinement often becomes the first focus of population reduction, because efficiency measures are generally less costly and more readily implemented than new programs. Local analysis often reveals that the primary underlying cause of crowding is excessive length of confinement due to inefficient case processing.

How System Decision Makers Can Affect Jail Crowding

System studies in a number of jurisdictions have suggested, as one judge said, "a lot of little ways" to halt or reverse jail population increases without releasing serious offenders. The following are highlights of just a few of the "little ways" at different parts of the system.

Law Enforcement Decisions surrounding local arrest practices—whether to arrest, transport to jail or stationhouse, book, or detain for bail setting—are critical determinants of jail population size. Law enforcement practices both before and after arrest can be modified to reduce jail admissions. Jurisdictions such as San Diego County, California, and Frederick County (Winchester), Virginia, use perhaps the most common form of prearrest diversion through short-term "sobering up" facilities for public inebriates.

San Diego has been successful in reducing crowding through the use of a privately operated detoxification reception program, where inebriates must remain for a minimum of four hours. Though in a largely rural area, the Winchester, Virginia, detoxification program, operated by the division of court services, has also diverted a large number of people from jail.

CTQ
What can be done to ensure that the professional competency and philosophy of the sheriff are consistent with good jail management?

CTQ
What explanations might be given for the increased use of incarceration during the past two decades?

WEB
For more information on jail crowding, **visit our Web site, www.prenhall.com/territo.**

WEB
For more information and examples of local jail systems, visit our Web site, **www.prenhall.com/territo.**

Similar prearrest diversion programs are in effect for those involved in nonviolent family disputes[9] and for homeless people in a number of jurisdictions throughout the United States.

Jail Administrators Elected sheriffs or appointed jail executives are often viewed as the managers who are most affected but have the least control in dealing with jail crowding, admissions, and length of confinement. Nonetheless, jail administrators can help reduce crowding by ensuring ready access for pretrial release screening and bail review.

Quick access to detainees tends to be a common characteristic of successful programs to reduce jail crowding. For example, the sheriff in Mecklenburg County (Charlotte), North Carolina, allows pretrial services staff to be present during the jail admissions process, which gives them access to defendants and speeds decision making.

In some other jurisdictions, jail administrators are delegated authority to release defendants pretrial or divert drunk drivers to treatment centers. Other administrators help develop nonjail pretrial release and sentencing options or cooperate with other jurisdictions to alleviate crowding on a multicounty basis.

Prosecutors Prosecutors face more case-handling decisions than any other officials. This gives them an especially important role in containing the jail population growth. Early case screening by prosecutors reduces unnecessary length of confinement by eliminating or downgrading weak cases as soon as possible. Assistant prosecutors in Milwaukee County, Wisconsin, review arrests around the clock by examining police records and conducting meetings between complainants and suspects. This practice enables Milwaukee prosecutors to decide on the appropriate charge within twenty-four to thirty-six hours after arrest.

Prosecutor cooperation is essential for alternatives in arrest, pretrial confinement, and sentencing. Prosecutor participation and leadership are essential to the effectiveness of task forces dealing with jail crowding. Since the prosecutor "owns" cases on behalf of the state, other are rarely willing to propose case-handling changes without the prosecutor's support.

Pretrial Services Providing background information on defendants, release recommendations, and other pretrial assurance can be an important component of solutions to crowding. Pretrial services can often help merely by adjusting the staff schedules to ensure timely screening and interviews for the maximum number of defendants.

In Mecklenburg County, North Carolina, for example, pretrial services and magistrate bail setting are available twenty-four hours a day, seven days a week. In Kentucky, pretrial staff are on call twenty-four hours a day to interview people who have been arrested, notify judges by phone of the prisoner's qualifications for release, and supervise the release process if nonfinancial bail is authorized.

Limited release authority is delegated to pretrial services staff in an increasing number of jurisdictions. In San Mateo County (Redwood City), California, pretrial staff are authorized to release misdemeanor suspects prior to their first court appearance. Seattle, Washington, is experimenting with delegated release on certain felony charges.

Judiciary Judges make more decisions affecting the jail population than anyone else; this often makes them leaders in seeking jail-crowding solutions. Judges can issue summonses instead of arrest warrants; provide guidelines authorizing direct release by police, jail, and pretrial staff; and provide for the setting of bail outside normal court hours. Evaluators of the four-year Jail Overcrowding Reduction Project of the former Law Enforcement Assistance Administration found that the project's more successful sites were those with strong judicial leadership.

Many courts provide twenty-four-hour bail-setting magistrates. The King County (Seattle), Washington, District Court has a "three-tier" release policy that reduces court time, jail admissions, and length of confinement. The court-established guidelines specify the charges for which pretrial services staff may (1) release without consulting the court, (2) release after phoning a duty judge, or (3) make recommendations to the court in the most serious felony cases.

Reducing court delay is crucial to the effective use of jail space. Bexar County, Texas, seeks to eliminate "dead time" by having the court administrator work with a jail case coordinator to identify cases in need of special attention and processing steps that can be shortened. Each judge receives a weekly list of prisoners awaiting indictment, trial, sentencing, or revocation in his or her court. One result is a 50 percent time saving in disposing of misdemeanor charges and thus a significant cut in overall length of confinement.

Defense   The National Criminal Justice Institute's field test on early representation by defense counsel found that early screening for indigency, defender appointment, and defendant contact can decrease length of confinement and thus yield substantial savings of jails spaces.[10]

In Mecklenburg County, pretrial conferences between defense and prosecution have helped identify, eliminate, or downgrade marginal cases and facilitate plea negotiation. Both sides can thus budget staff time efficiently and lessen pretrial confinement. In St. Louis, Missouri, efforts to reduce staggering defender caseloads by appointing private attorneys in felony cases have also reduced disposition time, stimulated bail review, and resulted in shorter pretrial confinement.

Probation and Parole   Not only do probation and parole agencies provide nonjail alternatives for sentencing, they can also enhance case-processing efficiency by streamlining presentence investigation (PSI) procedures and expediting revocation decisions. All of this helps reduce the length of confinement.

In Brevard County, Florida, the jail population oversight committee spotlighted PSI delays and worked with probation and parole officers to reduce PSI preparation time from ninety days to thirty to thirty-five days for jail cases. The county also reduced to twenty-four hours the time required for decisions on probation revocation, thus decreasing the use of jail beds for people on probation "hold" orders.

Outside the Local Level   State legislation, court rules, executive orders, and other external factors can affect jail population. Guidelines on diversion, bail policy, appointment of legal counsel, sentencing practices, and jail operation all can affect the range of solutions available.

Other outside factors that need to be considered in local planning for jail use include local demographics, availability of state and federal resources, public opinion and media coverage of criminal justice issues, activities of local civic groups and community organizations, and political campaigns and referendums.

Outside the System   Organizations outside the justice system can be instrumental in alleviating shortages of jail space by providing emergency shelter, detoxification, and treatment facilities for the mentally disturbed, public inebriates, and drunk drivers. Many jurisdictions use local mental health centers to provide prompt mental health assessments, diversion, and outpatient treatment. Private agencies in several jurisdictions provide temporary shelter for juveniles, pretrial supervision, and community-service placements.

DIRECT SUPERVISION

Jails with direct supervision stand in sharp contrast to traditional jails. As shown in Figure 11.1, a **direct-supervision jail** differs from the conventional approach because the officer is stationed inside the housing unit. This encourages direct interaction between staff and inmates to prevent negative inmate behavior, and groups inmates into living units of approximately fifty cells that can be efficiently managed by one officer. Rather than separating staff from inmates by security barriers, as is usual, this approach places officers in direct contact with prisoners at all times. It combines principles of human behavioral theory and facility design to create detention environments that maximize the officer's effectiveness.[11]

While some aspects of the two-pod designs are similar (cells clustered around a dayroom, for example), the differences are dramatic. The furnishings and fixtures found

CTQ

What steps can a jail administrator take to ensure successful facility and inmate management?

in the direct-supervision housing pod are usually of normal, commercial grade. Staff assigned to the units work among inmates twenty-four hours a day.

For many people, direct supervision appears to fly in the face of conventional wisdom. They believe that lessons learned in operating traditional linear jails do not provide much support for this new concept. "What can be gained," they ask, "by exposing officers to continuous contact with prisoners and equipping the facilities with furnishings and fixtures not designed to resist abusive behavior?" Managers of direct-supervision jails respond that officers are placed in inmate housing precisely in order to increase staff and inmate safety, and that it is unnecessary and perhaps counterproductive to pay a high price for secure, vandal-proof fixtures and furnishings when officers are in a position to supervise inmate behavior continuously.

This response does not win many immediate converts. More and more jail managers, however, *are* convinced after seeing the direct-supervision concept in action. Although direct-supervision inmate management concepts and principles will prove effective in almost every environment, they can be implemented more feasibly in a facility specifically designed for this purpose.

To identify potential cost savings of "new-generation" jails, the National Institute of Justice (NIJ) sent a questionnaire to twelve local jurisdictions. The survey questions concerned operating and capital costs of each facility and requested specific data to substantiate respondents' observations. Nine of the jurisdictions surveyed were operating direct-supervision facilities and three were under construction. Of the nine direct-supervision institutions, four were designed for that purpose, three were originally designed for remote surveillance and then converted to direct supervision, and two were designed to accommodate either direct supervision or remote surveillance. The questionnaire yielded many similar, if not identical, responses from the jurisdictions surveyed that may prove useful to decision makers exploring cost-effective alternatives to traditional jail management and design.

FIGURE 11.1

A jail officer is interacting with an inmate in a direct-supervision jail. Such jails encourage direct contact between jail personnel and inmates in an effort to prevent negative behavior on the part of inmates.

Courtesy of Mike Davies, Orange County Corrections Department, Orlando, Fla.

WEB

For more information on direct-supervision jails, **visit our Web site.** www.prenhall.com/territo

Personnel Issues

Personnel costs represent the greatest expense for local jails, and managing personnel is usually their most critical concern. Personnel expenditures account for approximately 70 percent of a jail's annual operating costs. In a survey of 2,500 local jails, the National Sheriffs' Association discovered that personnel issues were the number one management concern. When cost savings are being considered, therefore, their potential impact on personnel must receive the highest priority.

IN THE WORKPLACE

JAIL OFFICER/DETENTION DEPUTY

Assigned to the jail and responsible for the safety and security of inmates, civil and criminal processes, and transporting inmates. Performs a variety of duties, including the following: jail security, court services, training personnel, internal affairs, supervise trustees in performance of routine custodial work, transport prisoners as assigned.

Minimum qualifications are as follows: Age 21, free of felony convictions, U.S. citizen, valid driver's license and no more than three moving traffic violations, high school diploma or equivalent; or equivalent combination of knowledge, skills, and training.

Effective Management

Administrators of nine operating facilities in the NIJ survey agreed unanimously that direct-supervision inmate management is an effective technique. However, several pointed out that increased management attention and staff training were required.

One administrator stated that it takes a great deal of management time to encourage teamwork and to remove the feeling of isolation that staff may have when assigned alone to a housing unit. But another manager reported that direct supervision contributed to the effectiveness of his management by reducing conflicts between staff and inmates and by allowing for closer inmate supervision. One went so far as to say, "It is the most positive trend in jail administration that I have ever encountered in my professional career."

> **CTQ**
> What factors contribute to effective management outcomes on the parts of staff and administrators who work in direct-supervision jails?

Improved Staff Morale

While all respondents operating direct-supervision jails reported that staff morale was improved, few were able to quantify this observation in terms of cost savings. When the respondents were asked to substantiate their claims that direct supervision had a positive impact on staff morale, they cited the following:

- Improvement in staff attitudes
- Decrease in staff tension
- Reduced use of sick leave
- Improved treatment of inmates by staff
- Decreased number of staff–inmate conflicts
- Improved institutional cleanliness and orderliness
- Reduction in employee misconduct and confrontation with management

Compared to the conventional approach, direct-supervision jails assign an officer much greater responsibility for inmate behavior. Rather than remaining inside a locked work station, an officer actively supervises all inmates in the housing unit, rather than merely observing them. Many officers noted that staff members' morale improved when they were granted the new authority to be in charge of activity in the housing unit.

Reduced Sick Leave

Sick leave is an indicator that can be quantified. All but one of the responding direct-supervision jail administrators indicated that the use of sick leave had declined since the introduction of direct supervision. The only exception was a jurisdiction (Pima County, Ariz.) in which staff were obliged to work regularly scheduled overtime for eighteen months with only one day off per week.

A study of the Manhattan House of Detention conducted by the National Institute of Corrections several years ago revealed that sick leave was significantly less than the average for the city's other four houses of detention. This difference amounted to an annual cost avoidance of 1,810 staff days, which was equal to eight full-time positions or approximately $250,000 in overtime expenditures (if overtime had been used to fill the vacancies).

There is no absolutely conclusive way to determine why these staff members did not use as much sick leave as staff in traditional detention environments. Nevertheless, improved working conditions and job enrichment are characteristic of new-generation jails, strongly implying that they may result in lower sick leave rates.

> **CTQ**
> Is it fair to conclude that reduced sick leave is entirely attributed to direct-supervision management techniques, or are there additional factors?

Improved Working Conditions

The growing demand by the private sector for trainable employees means that jails will face increasing competition in their efforts to hire and train new personnel. A jail that can offer safe, clean, and orderly working conditions, as well as opportunities for fulfillment and career advancement, will be in a good position to compete for qualified employees.

Staffing Level

Perhaps the most important question about the new-generation jails is whether they require more staff than more traditional jails. The answer, of course, varies to the degree that jail staffing patterns vary. The direct-supervision facility in Dade County, Florida, for example, houses 1,000 inmates yet has a staff only half the size of that needed to operate the county's older linear jail, which houses approximately 1,300 inmates. On the other hand, several facilities surveyed have relatively high staffing ratios, where there are fewer than forty-eight cells in a housing unit.

Housing unit staffing is the best area in which to identify the staffing benefits of direct supervision. A wide variety of settings over the past decade have consistently demonstrated that one officer can effectively supervise approximately fifty inmates, and several institutions have assigned more than fifty inmates to a housing unit with satisfactory results.

Texas is an example of a state where specific staffing ratios are contained in jail standards, requiring one housing-area officer for every forty-eight inmates. In other jurisdiction, higher ratios are acceptable. Jail administrators making such decisions will have to determine whether housing-area staffing ratios of one officer to forty-eight or sixty-four inmates are suitable for the circumstances in their jurisdiction.

Managers of direct-supervision jails often cite staff efficiency as a ready example of improvement over traditional jail facilities. Because conventional jails separate staff from inmates, officers are virtually unable to actively supervise behavior. The addition of more staff positions has little positive impact since officers are simply observing inmate behavior. Hence, adding more staff to traditional jails with management problems or overcrowding often fails to improve conditions.

In contrast, the direct-supervision jail may operate efficiently under a variety of adverse conditions with a fixed number of personnel. The efficiency of fewer staff is possible because personnel are in constant contact with the inmate population, thereby allowing staff to control the situation at all times.

Safe Working Environment

Personnel safety is an important determinant of the quality of a work environment. All new-generation jails reported fewer incidents of violence. Pennsylvania's Bucks County, for example, reported that fighting dropped by at least 50 percent; the use of disciplinary segregation has diminished by 30 percent. New Jersey's Middlesex County reported that in the first eighteen months of operation with direct supervision, it has had no incidents of inmate–officer or inmate–inmate violence. Colorado's Larimar County reported, "Much less violence; we are in charge for a change!"

SPECIAL-MANAGEMENT INMATES

Jails, like the general community, have a population made up of a wide variety of people. Unfortunately, the urban jail has become a place where the **special-management inmates** seems to gravitate. These inmates pose serious management problems and require special attention in order to provide for the safety of other inmates, the safety of the staff, and the general security of the facility.[12]

Years ago, jail managers questioned whether they should divert resources and space for the special populations. The question now appears to be *how* to provide for the special-management inmates. A recent study of lawsuits filed against prisons and jails found that the most frequent issues for litigation were physical security (21 percent) and medical treatment (17 percent). Both of these issues reflect the importance of the treatment of the special-management inmate.

Among this category of inmates are the physically ill, including those infected with HIV/AIDS, tuberculosis (TB), hepatitis B and C, syphilis, gonorrhea, and other sexually transmitted diseases. Also included are alcoholics, disabled inmates, aggressive and assaultive inmates, vulnerable inmates, the mentally ill, drug addicts, sex offenders, and suicidal inmates. Such prisoners often require professional attention, and although jail

---

CTQ

In what areas are new-generation jails traditionally viewed as requiring more staffing? In what areas do they not require more staffing? How does the varying degree of staffing affect the level of efficiency at which personnel operate?

CTQ

What can be done to convince governmental officials and the public that direct-supervision jails are the most cost-effective and do not "coddle" criminals?

CTQ

What are some of the management problems associated with special offender populations, such as those who are elderly or disabled or have contracted HIV/AIDS?

WEB

For more information on special-management inmates, **visit our Web site, www.prenhall.com/territo.**

CTQ

What steps do jail officials take in the management and containment of physically ill inmates? Why is there such a disproportionately large number of physically ill inmates in comparison to the general population?

FIGURE 11.2

A medical evaluation being conducted on an inmate. Jails often have many inmates with special medical needs. Thus it is important from a medical, ethical, and legal standpoint for jails to provide adequate medical care.

Courtesy of Charles Rex Arbogast/AP/Wide World Photos.

officers are not expected to serve as physicians, psychiatrists, or psychologists, they do need to have some knowledge of the problems involved in supervising various types of special prisoners.

Physically Ill Inmates

Infectious diseases are an increasing concern to jail staff, medical staff, and jail administrators.[13] "Inmate populations contain disproportionate numbers of people of low socioeconomic status, individuals with problems of substance abuse, and individuals with generally high-risk and unhealthy lifestyles and poor access to medical care. As in the community beyond the walls of prisons and jails, such groups are much more susceptible to a range of infectious and sexually transmitted diseases."[14]

For example, the appearance of multidrug-resistant tuberculosis (MDR-TB) has greatly increased the threat of the disease's spread in a jail's closely confined population. As with other special-management populations, intake screening, identification, and proper placement are critical for physically ill inmates (see Figure 11.2). Inmates with symptoms of tuberculosis (night sweats, weight loss, and persistent coughs) should be placed in medical isolation areas for further testing and treatment. It is recommended that all inmates who have been in custody for several days have a skin test and in some cases have a chest x-ray. Inmates who have flulike symptoms should be tested for hepatitis B. If the results are positive, such inmates must be isolated and put on a regimen of bed rest and fluids.[15]

Alcoholics

Alcoholics are the type of special-management prisoner seen most often by jailers. The familiar symptoms of intoxication include shakiness, staggering, thick speech, and a blank, glassy-eyed look. However, because other conditions can produce the same symptoms, it is a mistake to assume that everyone who exhibits them is intoxicated. Multiple sclerosis (MS), for example, sometimes causes a person to stagger; people with MS have been arrested for public intoxication despite protests that they have had nothing to drink.

The symptoms of a head injury can also be confused with the effects of excessive drinking. A person who has been hit over the head or who strikes his or her head in a fall may appear to be intoxicated. Such a person should receive immediate medical attention. Someone in a diabetic coma may resemble a drinker who has passed out; if the diabetes goes untreated, the person may die. Thus, even when jailers are virtually certain they are dealing with a simple case of intoxication, they should make sure the prisoner is checked regularly. A person who has consumed a large amount of alcohol might first show typical signs of intoxication but might later lapse into deep unconsciousness and die.

Inmates with Disabilities

Title II of the Americans with Disabilities Act requires state and local government agencies to provide equal access for people with disabilities to programs, services, and activities. (See Figures 11.3 and 11.4.) This has serious implications for jails and jail programs considered by administrators: (1) Do policies and procedures exclude inmates with disabilities from participation in programs? (2) Do physical barriers exist that limit the inmates' participating in programs and activities? (3) Do communication problems limit the inmates' involvement in programs, services, and activities?

Aggressive and Assaultive Inmates

Aggressive and assaultive inmates must be separated for the protection of the other inmates and must be managed with additional security concerns to provide for staff protection. (See Figures 11.5 through 11.7.)

Vulnerable Inmates

Some inmates, because of their small size, feminine or youthful appearance, or history of child molestation, may require extra protection from the general inmate population.

FIGURE 11.3

This prisoner transport van is used when an inmate who is wheelchair bound is taken into custody or there is a need to transport such an individual to a medical facility or to court.

Courtesy of Lt. Richard E. Hohl, Jr., Polk County Sheriff's Office, Bartow, Fla.

FIGURE 11.4

This photo depicts a wheelchair ramp specifically constructed to assist in the easy movement of wheelchair bound inmates from one part of the jail to another.

Courtesy of Mike Davies, Orange County Corrections Department, Orlando, Fla.

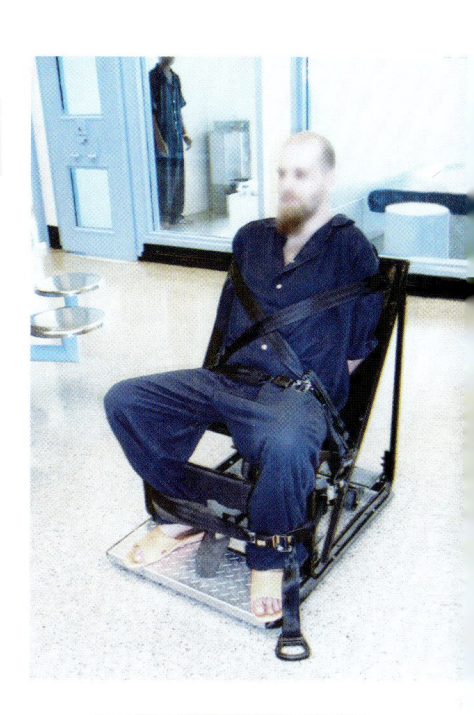

FIGURE 11.5

A restraint chair may be used when necessary on individuals who become violent during booking or after being housed in the jail. It should be used only to restrain individuals who may be a danger to themselves or others, never for punishment. When the inmates calm down, they are removed from the restraint chair.

Courtesy of Mike Davies, Orange County Corrections Department, Orlando, Fla.

Mentally Ill Inmates

Mental illnesses that are least understood are likely to be the most frightening. The behavior of a mentally disturbed person is often strange and alarming. The term *mental illness* is also misleading because it covers such a wide range of complicated emotional disorders that may involve physical, mental, and behavioral disturbances. A disorder may be relatively mild and difficult to detect, and it may not seriously handicap the individual. At the other extreme, the condition may be so obvious and serious that the person requires constant care and may even present a danger to himself or herself and others. It is quite clear that jails have now become, by default, dumping grounds for the mentally ill (see "In the News: By Default, Jails Become Mental Institutions").

Drug Addicts

When long-term drug users are brought to jail, they may appear normal and be difficult to recognize as addicts. Nevertheless, cautious jailers should watch for signs of drug intoxication and withdrawal and examine prisoners for needle marks and scars over the blood vessels of the arms and legs. Weight loss and loss of appetite are also signs of drug addiction.

Jail personnel should observe prisoners closely to prevent them from obtaining unauthorized drugs. Jailers are responsible for keeping the addict safe from self-imposed injuries during drug withdrawal to assist with the medical aspects of the process. The jail physician is responsible for the addicted prisoner's medial care, although most of the care is actually given by the jail staff. If a prisoner becomes seriously ill during withdrawal, the physician may recommend a short period of controlled hospitalization.

CTQ

Why are inmates suffering from mental illnesses often the most difficult for jail personnel to manage? In what ways can the behavior of the mentally ill confuse jail officials and delay the diagnosis of a disorder?

458　CRIME AND JUSTICE IN AMERICA

FIGURE 11.6

When violent and aggressive inmates refuse to leave their jail cells, specially trained extraction teams are used to overpower, control, restrain, and extract them from their cells.

Courtesy of Mike Davies, Orange County Corrections Department, Orlando, Fla.

FIGURE 11.7

A "time out" cell in a direct-supervision jail used to temporarily house and isolate aggressive, violent, and assaultive inmates. This is done to remove them from the general population for the protection of the other inmates, themselves, and jail personnel.

Courtesy of Pierce County Sheriff's Department, Corrections Bureau, Tacoma, Washington.

Sex Offenders

The jailer is likely to see a wide variety of **sex offenders,** including people accused of indecent exposure, window peeping, child molestation, and rape. Despite popular belief, these offenders are quite different from one another, and each presents unique problems. Not all of them require the same degree of supervision or segregation. For example, a prisoner charged with molesting a child usually poses no sexual threat to adults, but he (or rarely, she) may have to be protected from other prisoners. Anger toward child molesters and other sexual criminals is often very intense among other inmates. In general, most sex offenders are passive people who pose no major problems in a jail setting; only a few are violent or dangerous. However, because some such offenders become depressed and suicidal, close observation is required.

WEB

For more information on suicide in jails and suicide prevention in jails, **visit our Web site, www.prenhall.com/territo.**

SUICIDE IN JAIL

For those who work in jails, suicide is an issue of great concern, not only because someone entrusted to their care and prosecution might kill himself or herself, but also because of the inevitable litigation against the jail that would ensue.

A HUMAN PERSPECTIVE

BY DEFAULT, JAILS BECOME MENTAL INSTITUTIONS
by Fox Butterfield

Michael H. had not had a shave or haircut in months when he was found one recent morning sleeping on the floor of St. Paul's Episcopal Church in suburban Lancaster, next to empty cans of tuna and soup from the church pantry.

There was little to suggest that he had once been a prosperous college graduate with a wife and two children—until he developed schizophrenia, lost his job and, without insurance, could no longer afford the drugs needed to control his mental illness. Charged with illegal entry and burglary, Michael H. was taken to the Los Angeles County Jail. The jail, by default, is the nation's largest mental institution. On an average day, it holds 1,500 to 1,700 inmates who are severely mentally ill, most of them detained on minor charges, essentially for being public nuisances.

The situation in the jail, scathingly criticized as unconstitutional by the United States Justice Department last fall, is the most visible evidence that jails and prisons have become the nation's new mental hospitals.

On any day, almost 200,000 people behind bars—more than 1 in 10 of the total—are known to suffer from schizophrenia, manic depression or major depression, the three most severe mental illnesses. The rate is four times that in the general population. And there is evidence, particularly with juveniles, that the numbers in jail are growing.

Some of these people have committed serious, violent crimes. But many more are homeless people like Michael H., charged with minor crimes that are byproducts of their illnesses. Others are picked up with no charges at all, in what police call mercy arrests, simply for acting strange.

They include adults like Helen Rose Akanni, a woman with paranoid schizophrenia who was mistakenly charged with drunken driving and held for a week before a psychiatrist saw her. They include teen-agers like Jason E., a manic-depressive whose violence gives his father the choice of having him jailed or endangering his family.

"Part of mental illness in America now is that you are going to get arrested," said Laurie M. Flynn, executive director of the National Alliance for the Mentally ill, an advocacy group of relatives and friends of people with mental disorders.

What experts call the criminalization of the mentally ill has grown as an issue as the nation's inmate population has exploded and as corrections officials and families of the emotionally disturbed have become alarmed by the problems posed by having the mentally ill behind bars.

But the trend began in the 1960s, with the mass closings of public mental hospitals. At the time, new antipsychotic drugs made medicating patients in the community seem a humane alternative to long-term hospitalization. States also seized the chance to slash hospital budgets. From a high of 559,000 in 1955, the number of patients in state institutions dropped to 69,000 in 1995.

But the drugs work only when they are taken—and when they work, patients are tempted to stop, because of the unpleasant side effects. As states lagged in opening a promised network of clinics and halfway houses to monitor patients, obtaining treatment became harder. Health insurers restricted coverage, for-profit hospitals turned away the psychotic, and new laws made it more difficult to commit disturbed people. Thousands began to fall through the cracks.

Coincidentally, with voters willing to spend freely to fight rising crime rates, states were building more jails and prisons. Jails become the only institutions left open to the mentally ill 24 hours a day.

Homelessness was the most public sign of the problem. But for growing numbers of people, the price of mental illness was arrest.

Ms. Akanni, for example, became upset when she could not find her 2-year-old daughter; the girl had fallen asleep under a bed. To calm herself, Ms. Akanni went for a drive, but she got into an accident. When she gave her name as the Lord God Almighty, an officer arrested her for drunken driving. A week passed before a psychiatrist saw her and she was able to explain that she had a 2-year-old, at home, alone.

When Ms. Akanni was released, she was arrested again, for abandoning her child. The girl had survived by eating garbage.

"The inmates we see in jail today are the same people I used to see in psychiatric hospitals," said Dr. Eugene Kunzman, the former medical director of the mental health program at the Los Angeles jail.

In many states, so many public hospitals have closed, or the laws regulating admission to hospitals have been made so tight, that sometimes the only way to get care is to be arrested. Resources are especially scarce for juveniles.

In Dallas, social workers advised Jason E.'s family to have him jailed to get treatment. He had assaulted both parents and his brother, and hospitals were too expensive or refused him because he was violent. Jason's father rejected the advice and kept him at home—only to be warned that he could be charged with endangering his other son.

"It's tragic," said Judge Hal Gaither of the Dallas County Juvenile Court. "If you are a young person and mentally ill, you have to get arrested to receive treatment."

Though some people do benefit from regular medication while in jail, other suffer as the stress deepens their depression, intensifies delusions or leads to a psychotic break. Suicide is a risk: 95 percent of those who commit suicide in jail or prison have a diagnosed mental disorder, a study in the *American Journal of Psychiatry* found.

Locking up the mentally ill also has high costs for the nation's crowded prisons and jails. Because judges are often reluctant to grant bail to the mentally ill, and because they need special treatment, they tend to stay in jail much longer than other inmates.

On Rikers Island, New York City's jail, where 15 percent of new inmates have serious mental disorders, the average stay for all inmates is 42 days, but it is 215 days for the mentally ill, said Dr. Arthur Lynch, the official in the New York City Health and Hospitals Corp. who oversees treatment in the jail.

continues

BY DEFAULT, JAILS BECOME MENTAL INSTITUTIONS (continued)

Jails and prisons often find themselves unprepared to deal with the mentally ill. Guards may not know, for example, how to respond to disturbed inmates who simply are not capable of standing in an orderly line for meals; a common result is that the inmates are put in solitary confinement.

"We are doing the best we can, but it is definitely frustrating for the officers," said Gayle Ray, the county sheriff for Nashville, where 142 inmates on antipsychotic medication—8.6 percent of her jail system's 1,630 inmates—are housed on one floor of the Criminal Justice Center. "Jails were not designed to be mental hospitals, and what's happening is a real passing of the buck to another part of the system."

Advocates for the mentally ill say the clock is being turned back to the 19th century, when it was common in the United States to confine people with mental illnesses in jails. Mental hospitals, or asylums, grew out of a crusade in the 1840s by Dorothea Dix, the Boston reformer, who warned that "insane persons" were being confined in "cages, closets, cellars, stalls, pens: chained, naked, beaten with rods and lashed into obedience."

"Criminalization," said Dr. E. Fuller Torrey, a leading researcher of schizophrenia in Washington, D.C., "has been both a personal disaster for the mentally ill, and an institutional disaster for the criminal justice system."

SPECIAL INMATE PROBLEMS AT THE LOS ANGELES COUNTY JAIL

In Los Angeles, an average of 1,000 new offenders a day are brought to the county jail system, seven separate jails spread across 4,000 square miles housing a total of 22,000 inmates. It is a logistical nightmare.

When the Justice Department investigated the jail last year, this was the screening procedure it found: On entering, each prisoner was issued a sheet and towel and was shown an informational video. Among other questions, the video asked new arrivals to tell jailers if they had a mental health problem.

Many of the sickest new arrivals said they did not, because they were in denial. Others did not respond because they had been to the jail before. They knew that if they did, they would be issued yellow jumpsuits, which made them easy targets for guards or other inmates. They might be locked up 23 hours a day in dirty isolation cells. And any medication they had would be confiscated until a jail psychiatrist saw them—which could take weeks.

"Unconstitutional conditions exist at the Los Angeles County Jail," the report by the Justice Department's Civil Rights Division concluded, "including a deliberate indifference to the inmates' serious mental health needs."

The study, prompted by relatives of people who had been jailed, was the first federal review of the predicament of the mentally ill in jail. It produced a case study of the forces that draw the mentally ill into jails, and of the problems that they pose for jails and that jails pose for them.

"The problem I see is that the whole concept of treatment of the mentally ill in jails is an oxymoron," says David Myer, who directs the Los Angeles Mental Health Department's programs in the jail. "Jail is a horrible place. It isn't good for people who are well. For someone who is mentally ill, it is terrible."

The troubles begin with the fact that the county jail is a jail, not a hospital. It is run by the sheriff's department to keep discipline among its large population and to process inmates for court.

In addition, most deputies have little training in dealing with the emotionally disturbed, said Anita Dunsay, a recently retired clinical psychologist who worked in the jail.

"The deputies tend to be fresh graduates of the sheriff's academy, and baby-sitting isn't what they joined up for, so they easily get angry at the mentally ill," she said.

One result, the Justice Department charged, was that even though 1,700 inmates a day got some form of treatment, many more had mental illnesses that were going undetected. This was particularly true of those who were quietly depressed or had personality or anxiety disorders, illnesses for which California law does not mandate care.

The report also charged that record-keeping was so haphazard that some mentally ill inmates were lost in the system, while many illnesses were misdiagnosed and patients were given the wrong medication.

On a tour of the Central Jail three months after the report's release, mentally ill inmates in yellow jumpsuits could be seen meeting with a psychiatrist on a street bench in a busy corridor. A stench from the jail's blocked sewer caused people to cover their noses and mouths. Cells reserved for the mentally ill were so crowded that some men had to sleep on the floor. Some babbled; others complained that they could not sleep because of rats in their quarters.

The physical conditions improved dramatically in January, when the sheriff's department, under threat of a Justice Department lawsuit, moved most of the mentally disturbed inmates to the county's new Twin Towers jail. There, inmates are housed in clean, modern, one- and two-man cells.

The screening process was also updated: deputies now directly ask new arrivals if they are on medication. Already the number identifying themselves as mentally ill has increased, and Myer said he expected it would eventually climb by 50 percent.

"The moral of the story," Myer said, "is that if you want to get something done you need to bring the power of the federal government in and threaten to take over your jail."

But even as the Los Angeles jail moves toward, in effect, creating its own mental hospital, there are still problems inherent in dealing with the mentally ill in any jail. Inmates, said Kunzman, the former medical director, are seldom in jail long enough to stabilize them on the right medication, to offer them adequate therapy or to plan for their care after release. And so far the changes at the Los Angeles County Jail affect mainly physical conditions, not treatment, said Marianne Baptista, an administrator at Set Up on Second, a mental health agency in Santa Monica whose caseworkers often search the jail for missing clients. "On our end, nothing's changed," she said.

Her agency's clients still often disappear into the jail after being arrested, without any notification to the clinic. "More often than not, once in jail, their medications are taken away from them or they are given something different, and then their symptoms come out again," she said. "Being in jail may make them more crazy."

continues

That cycle can cause long-term physical damage, said Kay Redfield Jamison, a professor of psychiatry at Johns Hopkins School of Medicine. "Every relapse you have increases the odds that your brain is being damaged and that you will have another relapse faster, just like with heart attacks," she said.

Without the state hospitals, experts say, a revolving door has been created, in which mentally ill people cycle from clinics to homelessness to jail.

In Los Angeles, more than 70 percent of the severely mentally ill homeless have been arrested at least once, according to a report prepared for the Los Angeles County Board of Supervisors by Carla Jacobs, a board member of the National Alliance for the Mentally Ill. Many mentally ill people do manage to get treatment and do not end up in jail, of course, especially those with higher incomes. But the magnitude of the problem is suggested by a survey by the National Alliance for the Mentally Ill of families with a seriously mentally ill member; 40 percent of the ill individuals had been arrested.

On an average day, said Linda A. Teplin, a professor of psychiatry at Northwestern University Medical School, 9 percent of men and 18.5 percent of women in local jails—about 56,000 people—are severely mentally ill. An estimated 10 percent of all inmates in state and federal prisons, or 122,000 people, are severely mentally ill, said Allen J. Beck of the Justice Department's Bureau of Justice Statistics.

And about 20 percent of juveniles in criminal justice facilities, or 20,000 people, are that ill, said Joseph Cocozza, director of the GAINS Center, a research organization in Delmar, N.Y. It was Professor Teplin's research that first demonstrated the mentally ill are arrested much more often than people in the general population. But the problem, she said, is not police callousness. "The police arrest the mentally ill because they have no other alternative," she said.

She recalled riding with the police in a Midwestern city one night when they received a call about a crazy man on a bus. The man, named Charlie, was both schizophrenic and a drunk. They took him to a detoxification center, where he fell asleep. But the detox center recognized him and insisted he was crazy, not drunk, so the police sent him to a hospital. At the hospital the doctors also knew Charlie. Regarding him as difficult, they said he was an alcoholic to avoid admitting him.

Finally, the police arrested Charlie, Professor Teplin said. It was a cold night and they did not want him to freeze to death. He was charged with disorderly conduct.

THE DELINQUENT: YOUNG, MENTALLY ILL AND BOUND FOR JAIL

The 16-year-old girl suffered from delusions and hallucinations. The diagnosis was "psychotic, not otherwise specified." Her father was in prison for sexually abusing her sister. Her mother was an alcoholic. Not surprisingly, the girl began skipping school. She got pregnant. She assaulted her mother.

Before most state hospitals were closed, the girl would probably have been committed to a state psychiatric hospital. But in Texas, where she lives, the juvenile court declared her a delinquent and sent her to the state's juvenile justice agency, the Texas Youth Commission. The commission sent her to its Corsicana Residential Treatment Center for seriously emotionally disturbed youths.

The girl personifies the problems facing many young people with mental disorders, said Linda Reyes, a psychologist and assistant deputy executive director of the TYC. "Unless you are wealthy and can afford private doctors, you have to get arrested to get treatment," she said.

Even so, the commission is limited in what it can do. The girl refuses to take antipsychotic medication, and because Corsicana is not a hospital, its staff cannot make her take it. She is not making progress—she walks around naked and urinates on the floor—but by law, when her term expires, she must be released.

Incarcerating mentally ill adolescents is "tragic and absurd," Dr. Reyes said. "The system we have created is totally ineffective. It doesn't rehabilitate the kids. And it doesn't even take care of public safety, because when she is sent home, she will just get picked up again."

Of the 4,791 juveniles in the Texas agency's custody, 22 percent suffer from schizophrenia, manic depression or major depression. The national figure is similar: an estimated 20 percent of incarcerated juveniles are seriously emotionally disturbed.

When other psychiatric disorders are included, the percentages rise sharply. A recent survey by the California Youth Authority found that 35 percent of boys in its custody and 73 percent of girls need treatment, said its director, Francisco Alarcon.

One reason for the higher percentage of young people with mental illness in jail, specialists say, is that many states have cut budgets for adolescent psychiatric hospitals even more than those for adults.

"I had a 15-year-old girl who was hallucinating and psychotic," said Cathy Brock, a supervisor at the Letot Center in Dallas for runaway children. "And a staff member from Mental Health and Mental Retardation agreed she needed hospitalization. But then she said they were over budget for the year—so couldn't I find an offense that would get her arrested, like an assault?"

The Dallas County Juvenile Department has as large a budget for psychiatric hospitalization, $6.6 million this year, as the county's mental health department.

As a result, Ms. Brock said, "When I have a kid who is severely mentally ill and has been arrested, and the family has no resources, I will do everything I can to make sure that kid gets adjudicated." But urging judges and families to convict children, she said, "presents all kinds of ethical binds."

Another reason these young people are incarcerated disproportionately is that they act out their illnesses more than adults, usually in aggressive and impulsive ways that can get them arrested, said the president of the National Mental Health Association, Michael Faenza.

There is evidence that the number of disturbed young people being arrested is increasing. At Corsicana, Dr. Reyes said, the proportion of juveniles on antipsychotic drugs has doubled to 80 percent since 1990.

continues

BY DEFAULT, JAILS BECOME MENTAL INSTITUTIONS (continued)

But it is unclear whether this trend indicates more mental illness, or reflects tougher sentencing laws that are driving greater numbers of young people behind bars. Torrey, the schizophrenia expert, said he does not believe that social conditions like the breakdown of the family and bad parenting cause young people to become mentally ill. "What we are seeing," he said, "is the breakdown of the public mental health system."

THE ASYLUM: WELL-MEANING PLAN TO CLOSE HOSPITALS

For a growing number of the mentally ill, it has come to this, said Dr. Michael Pawel, executive director of the August Aichhorn Center for emotionally disturbed juvenile offenders in Manhattan: "Jail has become the place where, when you have to go there, they have to take you in."

As thousands of the mentally ill end up behind bars, no one has estimated the cost of shifting so many of the mentally ill from one kind of institution, hospitals, to another, jails and prisons. At New York state's rate of $30,000 a year per inmate, the annual cost to prisons alone would be $3.7 billion, not counting the extra expenses of treating the mentally ill. But because of the price exacted on the mentally ill themselves, some therapists and mental health advocates are reconsidering what they did in helping to close state hospitals.

"I was not wrong that antipsychotic medications were good," said Dr. Richard Lamb, a professor of psychiatry at the University of Southern California School of Medicine. Lamb worked in a state hospital in the 1960's and was among those pushing for treating people outside hospitals. "But I was wrong about discharging so many people with severe problems."

Part of the premise, he recalled, was that governments would build places in communities where discharged patients could continue to take their drugs and get therapy. But, largely for economic reasons, this was never done.

Now, Lamb said he realizes, "Some people just need more structured care."

Thinking over what seemed at the time like a wonderful reform, he likened himself to the British colonel in *The Bridge on the River Kwai*. The colonel built a bridge for his Japanese captors because the idea was so magnificent. "What have I done?" he asked himself.

Source: F. Butterfield, *The New York Times,* March 5, 1998. Reprinted with permission of *The New York Times.*

Precipitating Factors of Suicidal Behavior

The precipitating factors of suicidal behavior in jails are well established.[16] It has been theorized that there are two primary causes for jail suicide: First, jail environments are conducive to suicidal behavior; second, the inmates are facing a crisis situation. From the inmate's perspective, certain unique features of the jail environment enhance suicidal behavior: fear of the unknown, distrust of an authoritarian environment, lack of apparent control over the future, isolation from family and significant others, shame of incarceration, and dehumanizing aspects of incarceration. In addition, certain factors are often found in inmates facing a crisis situation that could predispose them to suicide: recent excessive drinking and/or use of drugs, recent loss of stabilizing resources, severe guilt or shame over alleged offenses, and current mental illness and/or prior histories of suicidal behavior. These factors become exacerbated during the first twenty-four hours of incarceration, when the majority of jail suicides occur.[17] Inmates attempting suicide are often under the influence of alcohol and/or drugs and have been placed in isolation. In addition, many jail suicide victims are young and generally are arrested for nonviolent alcohol-related offenses.[18]

Identifying the Suicidal Inmate

The potentially suicidal inmate first must be identified before any suicide watch or suicide precaution procedures are put into effect. The screening device discussed here is used by the Jail Mental Health Services Custody Division of the Los Angeles Sheriff's Department. Each item checked off is counted as one; asterisked items are doubled. If the resulting score is ten or higher, a mental health referral is in order, and psychiatric hospitalization should be considered.[19] The screening device includes the following items:

1. Suicide-risk assessment
2. Relationships with family/friends
3. Significant losses
4. Worry about problems

5. Suicide of family member or significant other
6. Psychiatric history
7. Drug or alcohol history
8. Shocking crime
9. Verbalization of suicidal ideation
10. Past suicide attempts
11. Signs of depression
12. Expressions of embarrassment or shame
13. Strange behavior or comments
14. Under the influence*
15. Appearance of being incoherent, withdrawn, or mentally ill*
16. No prior arrests*
17. Violence of recent suicide attempt, if any*
18. Detailed and feasible suicide plan*

FIGURE 11.8

At booking, arrestees are given both a medical and a suicide risk screening to identify those who may have special medical or mental problems. Failure to do proper screening and when necessary to follow up with appropriate remedial action can result in the death of an inmate and lawsuits by family members.

Courtesy of Lt. Richard E. Hohl, Jr., Polk County Sheriff's Office, Bartow, Fla.

Key Components of a Suicide Prevention Program

The proper training of jail personnel and the use of mental health specialists in the screening and aftercare of suicidal inmates and for the reevaluation of jail directives can go a long way toward reducing the rate of jail suicide. The following list represents the key components of a suicide prevention program.

1. *Identification.* The receiving screening form should contain observation and interview items related to the inmate's potential suicide risk (see Figure 11.8).
2. *Training.* All staff members who work with inmates should be trained to recognize verbal and behavioral cues that indicate potential suicide. The plan should include initial and subsequent training.
3. *Assessment.* This should be conducted by a qualified mental health professional who designates the inmate's level of suicide risk.
4. *Monitoring.* The plan should specify the facility's procedures for monitoring an inmate who has been identified as potentially suicidal. Regular, documented supervision should be maintained (see Figure 11.9).
5. *Housing.* A suicidal inmate should not be housed or left alone. An appropriate level of observation must be maintained. If a sufficiently large staff is not available to constantly supervise the potential suicidal inmate, the inmate should not be isolated. Rather, he or she should be housed with another resident or in

FIGURE 11.9

High-risk inmates such as those with potentially serious medical problems or suicidal tendencies are sometimes placed in cells equipped with TV cameras and monitored full time by jail personnel. Such close monitoring allows for rapid response if needed.

Courtesy of Mike Davies, Orange County Corrections Department, Orlando, Fla.

a dormitory and checked every ten to fifteen minutes. An inmate assessed as being a high suicide risk should always be observed on a continuing, uninterrupted basis or transferred to an appropriate health care facility. However, if a decision is made to isolate the inmate, the cell should be as suicide-proof as possible (for example, without protrusions of any kind that would enable the inmate to hang himself or herself. Such a cell should also allow complete visibility into it as well as have a TV camera with a monitor under constant observation; see Figure 11.10).

6. *Referral.* The plan should specify the procedures for referring potentially suicidal inmates and attempted suicides to mental health care providers or facilities.
7. *Communication.* Procedures should exist for communication between health care and correctional personnel regarding the status of the inmate.
8. *Intervention.* The plan should address how to handle a suicide in progress, including appropriate first-aid measures.
9. *Notification.* Procedures should be in place for notifying jail administrators, outside authorities, and family members of potential, attempted, or completed suicides.
10. *Reporting.* Procedures for documenting the identification and monitoring of potential or attempted suicides should be detailed, as should procedures for reporting a completed suicide.
11. *Review.* The plan should specify the procedures for medical and administrative review if a suicide or a serious suicide attempt (as defined by the suicide plan) does occur.
12. *Critical incident debriefing.* Responding to and/or observing a suicide in progress can be extremely stressful for staff and inmates. The plan should specify the procedures for offering critical debriefing to all affected personnel and inmates.[20]

TREATMENT PROGRAMS

Treatment programs for convicted jail inmates involve a variety of options. **Treatment programs** generally follow the reintegration model of treatment—how to return the offender to the community not as an "ex-con," but as a responsible, productive citizen who can use community resources to help with problems. Offenders need a means of support, and many jail programs can start the process.[21]

Classification helps to identify inmates' problem areas, such as substance abuse. Jail officers make referrals to qualified personnel, such as substance abuse counselors or mental health personnel, who can start a treatment plan. Treatment plans include participation in educational, vocational, substance abuse, religious, or social/life skills programs.

Treatment combats "prisonization," a socialization process in which the inmate not only learns the rules of the jail, but also the informal values, customs, and culture of the jail inmate population, including survival skills and how to cope with jail life.

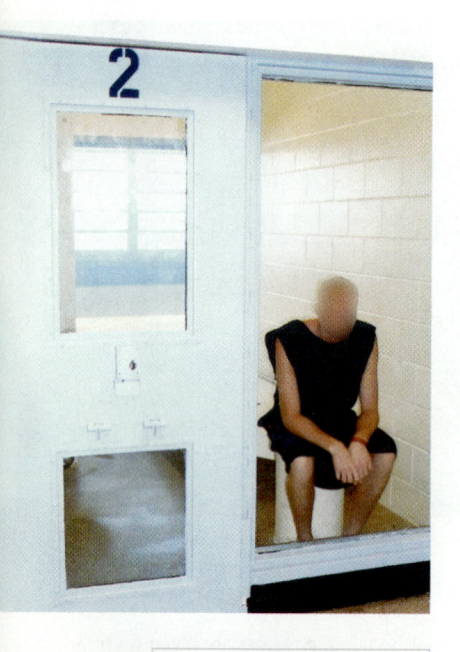

FIGURE 11.10

A specially designed cell to house potentially suicidal inmates. It has no protrusions of any kind (e.g., hooks for hanging clothing, extended shower nozzles) that would enable an inmate to hang himself or herself, and it allows complete visibility by jail personnel. Since clothing can sometimes be used as devices for hanging, inmates are typically given paper dignity garments to wear in these cells.

Courtesy of Mike Davies, Orange County Corrections Department, Orlando, Fla.

CTQ
What should be done to ensure that jail personnel are trained to adequately handle special-management inmates?

IN THE WORKPLACE

INTAKE AND SCREENING OFFICER

Receives and books all new inmates, controlling access into and out of the intake area. This operation includes securing all property and clothing of inmates, reviewing all committal documents, conducting medical screening, taking emergency information, fingerprinting, photographing, and searching inmates for contraband; also responsible for handling violent inmates. Minimum qualifications are as follows: age 18, U.S. citizen, high school diploma or equivalent, must pass a physical examination, and no felony convictions.

TABLE 11.1 Treatment Programs Offered to Inmates

Service	Number of Jails Offering the Service	Average Number per Day of Inmates Receiving the Service
Detoxification	67	1,152
Education	102	3,028
Counseling: individual	83	1,330
Counseling: group	107	2,776
Therapeutic community	41	1,622
Community referrals	96	891

Source: C. T. Camp and G. M. Camp, *The Corrections Yearbook, 1995: Jail Systems.* South Salem, N.Y.: Criminal Justice Institute, 1995, pp. 72–76. Reprinted with permission.

Table 11.1 shows some of the services offered, as described in a survey of 121 jails. An estimated 73 percent of U.S. jails classify inmates to ascertain appropriate constructive/rehabilitative programming. To supplement paid treatment staff, many jails use volunteers from the community who tutor, teach, help with substance abuse programs, or help inmates who are close to release link up with services in the community. The availability, size, number, and staffing of programs depends on commitment from the jails' administration and funds allotted or obtained by federal or state grants or from other sources.

The following is an overview of jail treatment services and programs:

- *Self-help substance abuse programs:* Groups such as Alcoholics Anonymous (AA), Narcotics Anonymous (NA), and Gamblers Anonymous conduct sessions in jails and show inmates positive ways to deal with problems through others who also have had trouble with alcohol, drugs, and gambling. These twelve-step groups work closely with the substance abuse staff. (See Figure 11.11.)

- *Therapy:* Family therapy involves marriage counseling and improvement of parent–child relationships, and serves to strengthen ties with the family. Group therapy involves a trained therapist (psychiatrist, clinical psychologist, or other professional) who works with a small inmate group. Problems and solutions are explored; social skills are improved.

- *Counseling:* Counseling in jail involves developing a rapport or relationship between the inmate and counselor (vocational or mental health counselor) so problems can be solved through mutual consent.

- *Educational programs:* A general equivalency diploma (GED) program allows inmates to obtain a high school equivalency diploma; adult basic education (ABE) assists inmates who have less than a sixth-grade education.

FIGURE 11.11

Self-help substance abuse programs such as Alcoholics Anonymous (AA), Narcotics Anonymous (NA), and Gamblers Anonymous teach inmates positive ways to deal with such problems.

Courtesy of Lt. Richard A. Hohl, Jr., Polk County Sheriff's Office, Bartow, Fla.

IN THE WORKPLACE

JAIL COUNSELOR

Responsible for professional counseling work providing rehabilitation services to adult offenders incarcerated in jail or a correctional facility. Performs a variety of duties, including the following: conducts individual counseling sessions with assigned inmates, develops treatment programs based on counseling sessions, assesses inmate progress toward resocialization and compliance with treatment program recommendations, participates in case conferences regarding treatment alternatives, makes referrals for drug/alcohol treatment and educational programs. Minimum qualifications are as follows: High school diploma or equivalent, age 21.

FIGURE 11.12

Recreational programs and facilities are important to inmate morale and to release tension. Such programs allow inmates to use their free time constructively; improve their physical and mental health; and develop self-esteem, morale, and sportsmanship.

Courtesy of Lt. Richard A. Hohl, Jr., Polk County Sheriff's Office, Bartow, Fla.

- *Religious programs:* Many jails have a full-time chaplain or a clergy member from the community to provide for the needs of inmates with various faiths through worship services, counseling, and family contacts.
- *Therapeutic communities:* Therapeutic communities treat offenders' problems by making a housing unit/cell block an experiment in social living; inmates have to learn to live with one another, use proper social skills, and deal with problems such as criminal thinking or substance abuse.

A varied recreation program can aid rehabilitation for inmates as well as reduce tension in the jail. Physical recreation includes basketball, volleyball, aerobics, and other activities (see Figure 11.12). Other recreations include games, television, radio, and a leisure library with books and popular magazines. These allow inmates to use their free time constructively, to improve their physical and mental health, and to develop self-esteem, morale, and sportsmanship.

The following are two examples of recent, innovative programs:

- *Jails Anonymous (JA):* This program is modeled after the philosophy of Alcoholics Anonymous and Narcotics Anonymous and their twelve steps. Inmates in Jails Anonymous learn to deal with addiction to criminal behavior.[22]
- *Jail Substance Abuse Program (JSAP):* A three-phase program based in the Washington County (Maryland) Detention Center, JSAP emphasizes life skills, education, aftercare on release, and transition back to the community.

JAIL SECURITY

In the real world of jail administration, **jail security** is given marked priority over rehabilitation. Although the two goals are often mentioned in the same breath, there is little question that security comes first. In most institutions, virtually all other activities and functions are subordinated to security. The reason is quite simple; no jail administrator has ever been fired nor has any sheriff been defeated for re-election for failing to rehabilitate an inmate, but many have been dismissed or lost a bid for re-election following prisoner escapes or disturbances.[23] Some of the common security techniques and procedures used throughout the nation are counts, shakedowns, frisks, tool control, key control, cutlery control, narcotics control, and visitation control.

Counts

During a **count,** institutional activities are temporarily halted and all inmates are counted. It is hoped that the total will equal the number of people who are supposed to

---

CTQ

Why are treatment programs in jails cost-effective if they work?

CTQ

Why is jail security given a higher priority than rehabilitation among jail administrators?

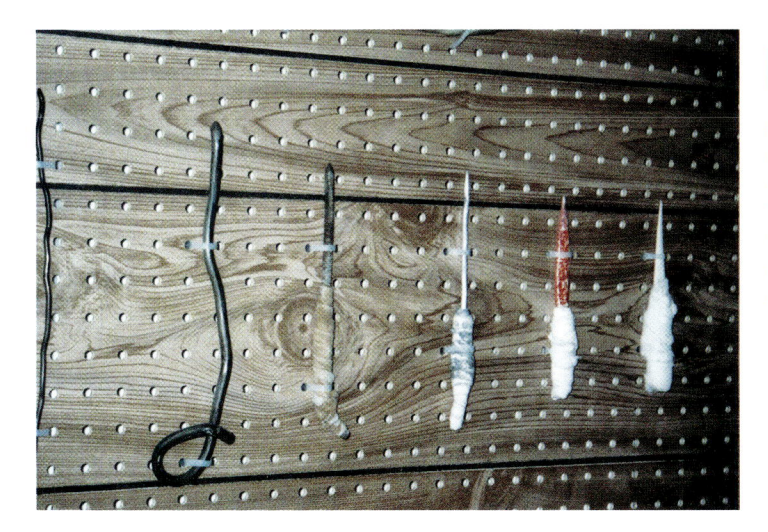

FIGURE 11.13

Jail inmates can form weapons from an assortment of objects never intended for such use. The weapons depicted here are often used to assault jail personnel and other inmates. A "shakedown," a thorough search of the jail cells, is commonly employed to detect and remove such weapons.

Courtesy of Lt. Richard A. Hohl, Jr., Polk County Sheriff's Office, Bartow, Fla.

be in confinement. If it does not, at least one recount is taken, and an attempt is made to identify and locate the missing inmate or inmates. If the count still comes up short, escape procedures are implemented. In the event an escape does occur, the schedule of routine counts provides some knowledge of the time frame within which the escape took place.

Shakedowns

A **shakedown** is a thorough search of a jail or any part thereof for contraband (anything an inmate possesses in violation of institutional rules and regulations, see Figure 11.13). The definition of contraband varies from jail to jail, but weapons, alcohol, and narcotics not prescribed or approved by the jail physician are always prohibited. Prisoners often employ ingenious methods to conceal contraband and to modify available objects for use as weapons or tools for escape.

Frisks

A **frisk** is a "pat search" of an inmate; officers run their hands along the outside of the inmate's clothing to detect concealed contraband. The frequency of frisks depends on the security classification of the inmate and the areas to or from which the inmate is coming or going. For example, if a maximum-security prisoner is leaving an area where there are usually tools (potential weapons), a frisk would be an appropriate, if not a mandatory, security procedure. Some jails use metal detectors instead of, or in addition to, standard frisking.

Tool Control

Tool control is a system of accounting for all tools available in a jail. Tight control is essential because tools can be—and often are—used as weapons or as an aid in escape. Because proper tool control requires up-to-date inventory surveys, all tools should be stored in secure places and be fully accounted for at the end of each workday.

One of the best methods of ensuring adequate tool control is the use of a "shadow board" for tool storage (see Figure 11.14). The outline of each tool is painted on the board so that a toolcrib operator can tell at the end of the day if tools are missing. When tools are checked out, a receipt is completed and attached to the board in place of the tool to ensure accountability.

Key Control

Despite its obvious importance, **key control** is too often less than effective in many jails. There is often no central control system such as that shown in Figure 11.15, and those that do exist may be ineffective because of the casual attitudes of jail officers. Control is particularly difficult in jails that have a different key for every door. A jailer who carries both cell keys and keys to cell blocks risks assault from prisoners attempting to escape.

468 CRIME AND JUSTICE IN AMERICA

FIGURE 11.14

A shadow board used for tool control. The outline of the tool is painted onto the board so that a tool control operator can tell at the end of the day whether any tools are missing.

Courtesy of Lt. Richard A. Hohl, Jr., Polk County Sheriff's Office, Bartow, Fla.

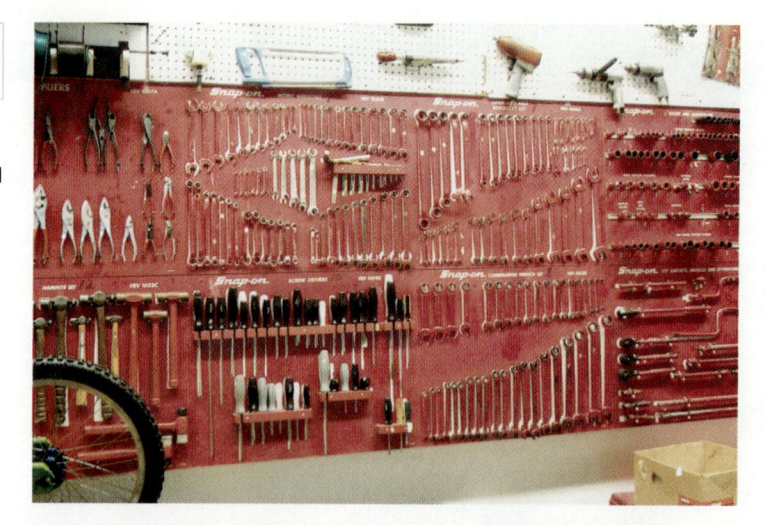

FIGURE 11.15

A key control cabinet designed to store keys when not in use. Too often jails do not have central control systems, and those that do exist may be ineffective because of carelessness by jail officers.

Courtesy of Lt. Richard A. Hohl, Jr., Polk County Sheriff's Office, Bartow, Fla.

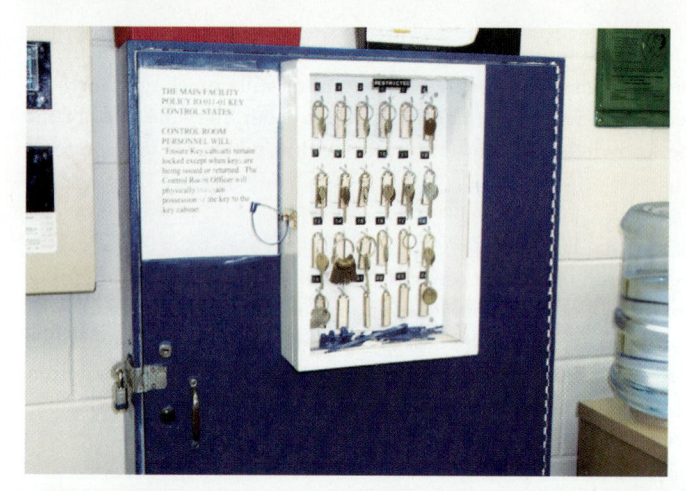

FIGURE 11.16

A shadow board for kitchen utensil control. Such items, especially knives, must be tightly controlled. If any item is missing the area must be searched promptly.

Courtesy of Lt. Richard A. Hohl, Jr., Polk County Sheriff's Office, Bartow, Fla.

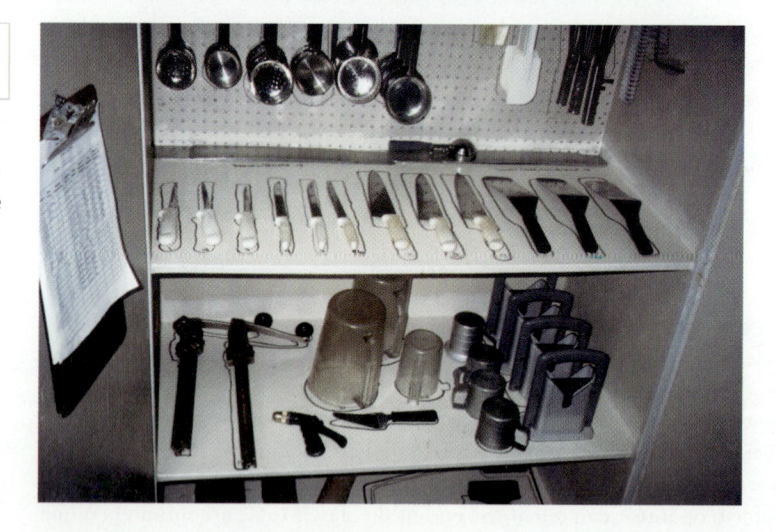

Once prisoners have the keys to their cell block, it is a simple matter for them to get to and open the door leading out of the jail.

Cutlery Control

Cutlery control is a system of accounting for all eating utensils used in a jail. Normally, kitchen equipment such as butcher knives and other potentially dangerous items is monitored under an institution's tool-control program (see Figure 11.16). But special measures are needed to ensure that the cutlery used at meals is not "borrowed" and used for illegal purposes. A table knife is an obvious weapon, and a fork or a spoon that has been sharpened at one end can be equally dangerous.

When inmates eat in communal dining halls, cutlery control is rather standard. When the inmates enter the dining room, they are each handed utensils for that meal. At the end of the meal, as the inmates leave via a main exit, they must deposit into a large receptacle under the observation of an officer the same number and type of utensils they were initially issued. If an inmate fails to do this, he or she is detained in the dining hall. After inmates have deposited their used cutlery as required, the silverware is again counted before it is taken back into the kitchen for washing. If any cutlery is missing at this point, a search or shakedown is conducted to recover the missing items.

When inmates eat in their cells, a common practice in many jails, officers must again be careful to supervise the dispensation and return of silverware. If anything is missing, a search of the area involved should be started promptly. The silverware should also be counted again when it is returned to the kitchen; there is always the possibility that inmates who have access to the silverware will pilfer one or more items during the transit from the cells to the kitchen. Why not use plastic utensils? Because plastic items are difficult to clean properly (given the equipment in most jail kitchens), and it would be extremely expensive and inconvenient to replace utensils after each meal.

Narcotics Control

Narcotics control is a major problem in many jails, particularly in metropolitan areas, because of the high number of addicts confined on criminal charges. This situation creates an immediate and substantial demand for illicit drugs. Again, good control procedures start with an accurate and up-to-date survey of inventory. All narcotics should be stored securely in an area not readily accessible to inmates. Medication prescribed for inmates should be prepared by qualified medical personnel, not by jail officers. In most jails, medication is dispensed in the cell block because too many problems are involved in moving prisoners to and from an infirmary. Medication should be dispensed personally by an officer, and inmates should be required to swallow the medication in the presence of that officer. A guard should check under the tongue to ensure that the medicine has been consumed and not "saved" for purposes of hoarding or sale within the institution. Certain types of medication can be dissolved in water first to get around this problem. Jail personnel also have to be alert to the possibility that drugs might be mailed or smuggled into the jail.

Visitation Control

Any time people from the outside come into or go out of a jail, a threat is posed to the security of the institution. This is especially true today because of narcotics smuggling. Thus, **visitation control**—the control of visiting procedures and facilities—requires careful attention on the part of the prison administrator.

A common form of visitation control is the enclosed booth with a Plexiglas or bullet-resistant glass front. Inmates sit in the booth and communicate with their visitors via voice-activated telephone. Some jails use a less structured arrangement and allow inmates to sit across a table from the visitors (with or without a screen between them). A third visitation mode is an informal, quasi–living room setting—sofas, easy chairs, coffee tables—with few, if any, physical barriers. Another type of visit, one that is currently a source of controversy in some jurisdictions, is the **contact visit.** In such visits, the inmate and his or her spouse are allowed to kiss hello and good-bye and to hold hands during the visit. The purpose of this approach is to make visits as normal as possible.

A key to maintaining proper security during visits is the careful screening of inmates. For example, a maximum-security prisoner who poses an imminent escape risk or is otherwise considered dangerous should be allowed to visit only in the booth arrangement. On the other hand, a minimum-security prisoner who has demonstrated his or her trustworthiness should be allowed to visit in a more relaxed atmosphere. Under any visiting format, however, officers should be present and alert to any sign of trouble or any attempt to pass contraband. For example, one inventive young woman who visited her boyfriend at a county jail in Florida left a felt-tip pen and some writing paper for him after each visit. The pen was always checked by correctional personnel before it was turned over to the prisoner, and each time it appeared to be nothing more than a pen. In fact it was a pen, but it was also used as a container to smuggle marijuana into the jail. Before each visit, the woman would remove the pen's plastic top and take out the ink cartridge. She would then stuff the pen with enough marijuana for two cigarettes. She then added black paper on top of the marijuana to block the view of any one who might remove the top of the pen for inspection. The scheme was discovered only because another inmate informed correctional personnel. The next time the girlfriend visited she was searched and the marijuana was found. The woman was arrested for attempting to smuggle drugs into the jail. To further ensure security, many jails frisk inmates after visits before returning them to their housing or work areas; some jails even perform a complete strip search of every inmate.[24]

Summary

Jails are the intake point of our entire criminal justice system and are the most prevalent type of correctional institution. They are primarily a function of local government and are as diverse in size, physical condition, and efficiency as the units of government that operate them. The three types of jails are pretrial detention facilities for people awaiting trial, sentenced facilities for people serving sentences, and combination facilities for pretrial detentions and some convicted people.

Many jails in the United States are quite old and in need of extensive repair. In addition, many pose health hazards because of noxious odors, dirty facilities, and vermin. Many jail facilities also contain fire hazards that endanger both inmates and correctional staff. In all fairness, however, it must be noted that many jails are clean and well-maintained. Often, the major difference between a poorly run jail and one that is well-maintained is the attitude, philosophy, and priorities of the local sheriff or jail administrator.

Some consequences of jail crowding are well known: increased victimization and fear, decreased public confidence that dangerous people can be locked up, lawsuits, court-imposed limits on the number of prisoners, and damage to facilities and equipment. Crowding increases both tension in the institution and the strain on correctional budgets.

Officials in a growing number of jurisdictions have concluded that if each part of the local justice system does what it can to ease crowding, the sum of all these solutions has a notable cumulative effect. Thus, the separate decisions of law enforcement, judicial prosecution, defense, pretrial services, probation, corrections, and other officials can interact to influence the number of jail admissions and the length of confinement.

Direct-supervision jails encourage direct interaction between staff and inmates to prevent negative inmate behavior, and groups inmates into living units that can effectively be managed by one officer. Rather than separating staff from inmates by security barriers, as is usual, the new approach places officers in direct contact with prisoners at all times. This new concept combines the principles of human behavior and facility design to create detention environments that facilitate the officers' effectiveness.

Special-management inmates that present problems for the jailer include the physically ill, alcoholics, disabled inmates, aggressive and assaultive inmates, vulnerable inmates, the mentally ill, drug addicts, sex offenders, and suicidal inmates. Jail personnel must be properly trained to recognize and supervise such prisoners, and, when necessary, to provide them with special care.

When hard choices must be made between security and rehabilitation in the jail, security is always given priority. This is not surprising, considering that jail administrators can be fired and sheriffs defeated at election time if a dangerous or infamous prisoner escapes. To ensure the integrity of prison security, several measures are employed: counts; shakedowns, which involve a thorough search of a jail or any part thereof for contraband; regular frisking of inmates, especially when they are moved from one part of the jail to another; tool control; key control; cutlery control; narcotics control; and visitation control.

In spite of the bleak picture often presented of American jails, evidence suggests that the quality of jail personnel and jail facilities have steadily improved over the past fifteen years. This occurred in part because of public pressure about jail crowding, unsanitary conditions, poor health care, and physical abuse. Other improvements will occur because the states are now taking a more active role in requiring minimum qualifications and providing training for jail personnel. Finally, there is reason to believe that the chief administrators of our local jails—whether they are sheriffs or civilian administrators—are better educated, better trained, and generally more professional than their predecessors.

DISCUSSION AND REVIEW

1. What are the differences between jails and prisons?
2. What three types of jails are there in the United States?
3. What role did the Quakers play in the early prison system?
4. What are the three main functions of jails?
5. What type of impact does jail crowding have on the various components of the criminal justice system?
6. How do system decision makers affect jail crowding?
7. How do direct-supervision jails differ from conventional jails?
8. What personnel issues arise in direct-supervision jails?
9. What types of jail inmates are considered special-management inmates?
10. What does the following statement mean? "By default, jails have become mental institutions."
11. What are the precipitating factors of suicidal behavior?
12. What are the key components of a suicide prevention program?
13. What treatment programs are available for jail inmates?
14. What are the major components of self-help substance abuse programs?
15. What are the major features of therapy programs in jails?
16. What are the major features of educational programs in jails?
17. Why is jail security given a higher priority than rehabilitation?
18. What is the purpose of a count?
19. What are shakedowns?
20. What is the most basic rule of key control?

CHAPTER RESOURCES

IN THE MEDIA

Video

A&E American Justice Series Video: *Cruel and Unusual*
CNN Today Video: *Introduction to Criminal Justice*, Vol. 2: segment 15, "Prison Guard Abuse"
FHH Video: *Diverting the Mentally Ill from Jail*
FHH Video: *The Second City: Inside the World's Largest Jail*
NIJ Video: *Prison Crowding*

Film

An Innocent Man (1989)
Criminal Justice (1990)
Dead Man Walking (1995)
Double Jeopardy (1999)
Just Cause (1995)
The Last Castle (2001)
The Shawshank Redemption (1994)
True Crime (1999)

IN THE LITERATURE

Books

J. DILULIO, *Governing Prisons*. New York: Free Press, 1987.

R. GOLDFARB, *Jails: The Ultimate Ghetto of the Criminal Justice System*. Garden City, N.Y.: Doubleday, 1976.

L. GOODSTEIN AND D. MACKENZIE, eds., *The American Prison: Issues in Research and Policy*. New York: Plenum Press, 1989.

J. IRWIN, *The Jail: Managing the Underclass in American Society*. Berkeley: University of California Press, 1985.

J. JACOBS, *Stateville*. Chicago: University of Chicago Press, 1977.

R. JOHNSON, *Hard Time: Understanding and Reforming the Prison*, 2nd ed. Belmont, Calif.: Wadsworth, 1996.

K. KAUFFMAN, *Prison Officers and Their World*. Cambridge, Mass.: Harvard University Press, 1988.

K. KERLE, *American Jails: Looking to the Future*. Boston: Butterworth-Heinemann, 1998.

E. MONKKONEN, *Crime and Justice in American History: Prisons and Jails*. New York: K.G. Saur, 1992.

J. M. MOYNAHAN and E. K. STEWART, *The American Jail: Its Development and Growth*. Chicago: Nelson-Hall, 1980.

J. THOMPSON and L. MAYS, eds., *American Jails: Public Policy Issues*. Chicago: Nelson-Hall, 1991.

Articles

K. ADAMS, "The Bull Market in Corrections," *Prison Journal*, vol. 76 (December 1996).

P. FINN, "No Frills Prisons and Jails: A Movement in Flux," *Federal Probation*, vol. 60 (1996), pp. 35–49.

L. HAYES, "Suicide in Adult Correctional Facilities: Key Ingredients to Prevention and Overcoming the Obstacles," *Journal of Law, Medicine & Ethics*, vol. 27, no. 3 (Fall 1999), p. 260.

M. TONRY, "Why Are U.S. Incarceration Rates So High?" *Crime and Delinquency*, vol. 45 (1999), pp. 419–438.

ENDNOTES

1. G. Cornelius, *Jails in America: An Overview of Issues*. Lanham, Md.: American Correctional Association: 1996. The discussion of the history of jails in the United States was adapted with permission from this source, pp. 2–4.

2. D. Champion, *Corrections in the United States: A Contemporary Perspective*. Upper Saddle River, N.J.: Prentice Hall, 1998.

3. V. Fox and J. Stinchcomb, *Introduction to Corrections*, 4th ed. Upper Saddle River, N.J.: Prentice Hall, 1994.

4. Champion, op. cit.

5. Ibid.

6. D. K. Gillard and A. J. Beck, "Prison and Jail Inmates, 1995," *Bureau of Justice Statistics Bulletin* (August 1996), p. 9.

7. L. Territo, "Planning and Implementing Change in Jails." In C.R. Swanson, ed., *Jail Management*. Athens: Institute of Government, University of Georgia, 1983, pp. 11–25.

8. A. Hall, *Systemwide Strategies to Alleviate Jail Crowding*. National Institute of Justice, U.S. Department of Justice, January 1998.

9. Research in violent family disputes indicates that arrest is the preferred police response. This research, now being replicated under NIJ sponsorship, was reported in Lawrence W. Sherman and Richard A. Berck, *Minneapolis Domestic Violence Experiment*. Washington, D.C.: Police Foundation, 1984. NCJ 98905.

10. E. J. Fazio, Jr., executive summary of the Early Representation by Defense Counsel evaluation. Available in microfiche, NCJ 97595.

11. W. R. Nelson, *Cost Savings in New Generation Jails: The Direct Supervision Approach*. Washington, D.C.: National Institute of Justice, 1988, pp. 2–4. The discussion of direct supervision was obtained and modified from this source.

12. W. T. Wood, "Special Management Inmate in Mulnomah County," *American Jails*, vol. 9, no. 5 (1995), pp. 22–26.

13. Ibid.

14. T. M. Hammett and L. Harrold, *Tuberculosis in Correctional Facilities*. Washington, D.C.: U.S. Department of Justice, 1994.

15. Wood, pp. 24, 25.

16. J. R. Rowan and L. M. Hayes, *Training Curriculum on Suicide Detention and Prevention in Jails and Lockups*, 2nd ed. Mansfield, Mass: National Center on Institutions and Alternatives, 1995.

17. L. M. Hayes, "National Study of Jail Suicides: Seven Years Later," *Psychiatric Quarterly*, vol. 60, no. 1 (1989), pp. 7–29.

18. L. M. Hayes, "Prison Suicide: An Interview and a Guide to Prevention," *Prison Journal*, vol. 75, no. 4 (December 1995), pp. 431–456.

19. E. E. Kunzman, "Preventing Suicides in Jail." *Corrections Today* (October 1995), p. 90.

20. *Standards for Health Services in Jails*. Chicago: National Commission on Correctional Health Care, 1996, pp. 66–67.

21. Cornelius, pp. 45–48. The discussion of treatment programs in jail was adapted with permission from this source.

22. J. Rushall, "12 Steps to a Crime Free Life," *American Jails*, vol. 1, no. 1 (March–April 1995), pp. 42–44.

23. E. E. Miller, *Jail Management*. Lexington, Mass.: Lexington, 1978.

24. Miller, op. cit.

12 CORRECTIONAL INSTITUTIONS

Chapter Outline

- **Historical Perspective**
- **Maximum-Security Prisons**
  - The History of Administrative Segregation
  - New Maximum-Security Prisons
- **Medium-Security Prisons**
- **Minimum-Security Prisons**
- **Reception and Classification Centers**
- **Prison Overcrowding**
  - Alternative Approaches to Relieving Prison Crowding
- **Riots and Disturbances in Correctional Institutions**
  - Inmate Groups Prone to Causing Problems
- **Gangs in Prison**
  - Becoming a Gang Member
  - Leaving the Gang
- **Institutional Programs and Services**
  - Educational Programs
  - Prison Work Programs
  - Recreational Programs
  - Treatment Programs
  - Religious Programs
- **Elderly Male Prisoners**
- **Sexuality in Prison**
- **HIV and AIDS in Prisons**
  - Prevention
- **Women in Prison**
  - Early Punishments and Places of Confinement
  - Reformatories for Women
  - Women's Prisons Today
  - Women's Criminal Activity
  - Women's Adaptation to Imprisonment
  - The Nature and Amount of Homosexuality
  - Programs for Women
  - Sexual Contact between Staff and Inmates
- **Private Prisons**
  - Arguments for Privatization
  - Arguments against Privatization
- **Summary**

Key TERMS

AIDS, p. 500
Aryan Brotherhood, p. 492
Auburn system, p. 477
Black Guerilla Family, p. 492
El Rukns, p. 492
gallows, p. 476
general equivalency diploma (GED) programs, p. 495
Great Law of Pennsylvania, p. 476
Latin Disciples, p. 492
Latin Kings, p. 492
maxi-maxi prisons, p. 480
maximum-security prisons, p. 477
medium-security prisons, p. 485
Mexican Mafia, p. 492
minimum-security prisons, p. 486
Nuestra Familia, p. 492
peer tutoring, p. 495
Pennsylvania system, p. 477
pillory, p. 476
prison work programs, p. 496
prisonization, p. 505
reception and classification centers, p. 486
stocks, p. 476
Texas Syndicate, p. 492
Vice Lords, p. 492

Courtesy of A. Ramey/PhotoEdit.

In this chapter we will first discuss the development of correctional institutions in the United States, starting in the late 1600s and proceeding through the nineteenth century. This should provide the reader with a historical framework to understand how we got to where we are today. We then move into the twentieth century and discuss maximum-, medium-, and minimum-security institutions. All three classifications may be used (and usually are) within the same institution: what may be considered maximum security in one state may be considered medium security in another. In general, however, the terms refer to the relative degree of security. We will also devote considerable attention to a fourth classification; the maxi-maxi prison, designed for the most hardcore violent prisoner. In addition, we will discuss the growing problem of prison overcrowding and some alternatives to relieving it. Within this context we will discuss the inmate groups most prone to causing problems (antisocial inmates, racial/ethnic minorities, and racial/revolutionary organizations). In addition, we discuss the growing problem of prison gangs, discussing how one becomes a gang member and the difficulties associated with leaving a gang.

The quality and quantity of institutional programs and services provided in prisons may profoundly affect the inmate's ability to make a transition back into the free world as well as learn life skills that will reduce the possibility of the individual becoming a repeat offender. In this chapter we will discuss some of the major types of institutional programs and services provided in prisons.

The problem of elderly prisoners has rapidly increased over the past decade, due in part to longer and tougher sentences. We will examine the types of crimes elderly prisoners are most likely commit and the administrative and medical problems associated with the housing of such prisoners.

Sexuality in prisons and its associated health problems will also be addressed. The number of HIV- and AIDS-infected prisoners is addressed in a variety of ways by prison officials, but there is some disagreement as to just exactly how these problems should be handled (for example, whether to issue condoms or to isolate infected inmates).

The topic of women in prison will also be discussed; we will trace the early history of punishment and places of confinement for women and the movement in the modern era, starting with reformatories for women in the 1930s. We will also discuss the ways in which women wind up in prison and how they adapt to prison life once they are there.

Lastly we will touch on the use of private prisons as an alternative to government- and state-run prisons.

HISTORICAL PERSPECTIVE

Institutionalization as a primary means of enforcing customs, mores, or laws is a relatively modern practice. In earlier times, restitution, exile, and a variety of corporal and capital punishments—many of them unspeakably barbarous—were used (see Fig. 12.1). Confinement was used only for detention.[1]

The North American colonists brought with them the harsh penal codes and practices of their homelands. In Pennsylvania, founded by William Penn, initial attempts were made to find alternatives to the brutality of British penal practice. Penn knew the nature of confinement well because he had spent six months in Newgate Prison in London for his religious convictions. In the **Great Law of Pennsylvania,** enacted in 1682, Penn eliminated to a large extent the **stocks, pillories,** branding irons, and **gallows.** The Great Law directed "that every county within the province of Pennsylvania and territories thereunto belonging shall . . . build or cause to be built in the most convenient place in each respective county a sufficient house for restraint, labor, and punishment of all such persons as shall be thereunto committed by laws."[2] In time, Penn's jails, like those in other parts of the New World, became places where the untried, the mentally ill, the promiscuous, debtors, and various petty offenders were confined indiscriminately.

In 1787, when the Constitutional Convention was meeting in Philadelphia, social and political thought generally was influenced by the Enlightenment principle of the dignity of man. In that year, the Philadelphia Society for Alleviating the Miseries of Public Prisons was organized. The society believed that the sole purpose of punishment was to prevent crime and that punishment should not destroy the offender. The members of the society, many of them influential citizens, worked hard to create a new penology in Pennsylvania, a penology that largely eliminated capital and corporal punishment as the principal sanctions for major crimes. The penitentiary was created as a substitute for these punishments.

In the first three decades of the nineteenth century, citizens in New York, Pennsylvania, New Jersey, Massachusetts, and Connecticut were busy planning and building monumental penitentiaries. These were not cheap installations built from the crumbs of the public treasury. In fact, the Eastern State Penitentiary in Philadelphia was the most expensive building constructed in the New World up to that time. States were proud of these physical plants. Moreover, they saw in them an almost utopian

CTQ

Do you believe that if any of the early punishments were meted out to inmates today, it would serve as a deterrent to them and others in committing future crimes?

FIGURE 12.1

The pillory at a public jail. This device was used as punishment for minor misdemeanors such as not attending church on Sunday, nagging one's husband, or beating one's wife with a stick thicker than a thumb.

Courtesy of Colonial Williamsburg Foundation.

ideal. They were to become stabilizers of society, laboratories committed to the improvement of all humanity.[3]

At the time these new penitentiaries were planned and constructed, practitioners and theorists believed that criminal behavior was primarily caused by three factors. The first factor was environment. Report after report pointed out the harmful effects of family, home, and other aspects of environment on the offender's behavior. The second factor was the offender's lack of aptitude at work skills, a problem that led to indolence and a life of crime. The third factor was seen as the felon's ignorance of right and wrong because of a lack of knowledge of the Scriptures.

The social planners of the first quarter of the nineteenth century designed prisons and programs to create an experience for the offender in which (1) there would be no injurious influences, (2) the offender would learn the value of labor and work skills, and (3) the offender would have the opportunity to learn about the Scriptures and the principles of right and wrong. Various states pursued these goals in one of two ways. The **Pennsylvania system** was based on solitary confinement, accompanied by bench labor within the offender's cell. The offender was denied all contact with the outside world except through religious tracts and visits from specially selected, exemplary citizens. The prison was painstakingly designed to make this kind of solitary experience possible. The walls between cells were thick, and the cells themselves were large, each equipped with plumbing and running water. Each cell contained a workbench and tools and a small, walled area for solitary exercise. The institution was designed magnificently to eliminate external influences and to provide work and the opportunity for penitence, introspection, and religious learning.[4]

New York's **Auburn system** pursued the same goals by a different method. As in the Pennsylvania system, offenders were isolated from the outside world and were permitted virtually no external contact. However, convicts were confined to their small cells only on the Sabbath and during nonworking hours. During working hours, inmates labored in factory-like shops. The "contaminating effect" of the congregate work situation was eliminated by a rule of silence: Inmates were not allowed to communicate in any way with one another or the jailers.

The relative merits of these two systems were debated vigorously for half a century. The Auburn system ultimately prevailed in the United States because it was less expensive and because it lent itself more easily to the production methods of the Industrial Revolution. But both systems were disappointments almost from the beginning. The solitude of the Pennsylvania system sometimes drove inmates to insanity. And the rule of silence in the Auburn system became increasingly unenforceable, despite regular use of the lash and a variety of other harsh and brutal punishments.

As instruments of reform, prisons were an early failure. But they did have notable advantages. They rendered obsolete a myriad of inhumane punishments, and their ability to separate and hold offenders gave the public a sense of security. Imprisonment was also thought to deter people from crime. But imprisonment had disadvantages, too; for example, many prison "graduates" come back. The prison experience often further reduced the offender's capacity to live successfully in freedom. Nevertheless, prisons have persisted, partly because our nation could neither turn back to the barbarism of an earlier time nor find a satisfactory alternative. For nearly two centuries, American penologists have sought a way out of this dilemma.

MAXIMUM-SECURITY PRISONS

For the first century after penitentiaries were created, most prisons built were **maximum-security prisons**—facilities characterized by high-walled perimeters, internal security, and operating procedures that curtailed movement and maximized control. The early zealots who dreamed of institutions that would not only reform the offender but would also cleanse society itself were replaced by a disillusioned and pragmatic leadership that saw confinement as a valid end in itself. Moreover, the new felons were seen as outsiders—Irish, Germans, and blacks; they did not talk or act like "Americans." The prison became a dumping ground where foreigners and blacks who could not adjust

CTQ

What was the effect of the progressive reform movement in the 1800s? How did this movement change penal practices in America, and has its impact been negated in modern times?

WEB

For more information on the history of prisons in America, **visit our Web site, www.prenhall.com/territo.**

CTQ

Which prison system do you think was most effective in terms of deterrence and rehabilitation: the Auburn system or the Pennsylvania system?

IN THE WORKPLACE

CORRECTIONAL OFFICER

Responsible for maintaining security within a correctional facility, also responsible for the custody, control, care, job training, work performance, and physical restraint, when necessary, of inmates in the facility. Performs a variety of duties, including the following: supervise inmate meals, visits, recreational programs, and other congregate activities; escort inmates within and outside the facility; verify identification of and number of inmates in designated areas; and demonstrate proficiency in use of firearms. Minimum qualifications are as follows: age 19, U.S. citizen, high school diploma or its equivalent, must pass a basic recruit training course.

---

could be held outside the mainstream of society. The new prisons, built in the most remote areas of the country, became asylums—not only for the hardened criminal but also for the inept and unskilled "un-American." Although the rhetoric of reformation persisted, prisons in reality were all about detention.

From 1830 to 1900, most prisons built in the United States reflected the ultimate goal of security. Their principal features were high walls, rigid internal security, cagelike cells, sweatshops, a bare minimum of recreation, and little else. Prisoners were kept in, the public was kept out; that was all that was expected or attempted. Many of these prisons were constructed well and built to last, and they form the backbone of our present-day correctional system.

It is nearly impossible to describe the "typical" maximum-security prison that exists today. The largest such prison confines more than four thousand inmates; another holds fewer than sixty. Some contain massive, undifferentiated cell blocks, each housing as many as five hundred prisoners. Others are built in small modules that house fewer than sixteen inmates each. The industries in some prisons are archaic sweatshops; in others, they are large, modern factories. Many facilities have no space inside for recreation and only a minimum of such space outside; others have superlative gymnasiums, recreation yards, and auditoriums. Some are dark, dingy, and depressing dungeons; others are windowed and sunny. An early-warning system in one prison consisted of cowbells strung along chicken wire to a masonry wall; other facilities have closed-circuit television and electronic sensors to monitor corridors and fences.

Despite these differences, maximum-security institutions share the aim of maintaining the fullest possible supervision, control, and surveillance of inmates. As a result, the architecture of such institutions and the work and recreational programs they provide are largely dictated by security considerations. Buildings and policies restrict the inmates' movements and minimize their control over the environment. The prisons are usually surrounded by a masonry wall or a double fence with towers staffed by armed guards. Inside, prisoners live in windowless cells, not rooms. Doors that might afford privacy are replaced by grills of tool-resistant steel. Toilets are unscreened, and showers are supervised. And the overriding concern with inmate control is not limited to the prison's physical structure. All activity—including dining—is weighed in terms of its relationships to custody. Prisoners often sit on fixed, backless stools and eat without forks and knives at tables devoid of condiments. In spite of such control, however, contraband and weapons still find their way into many American prisons.

The History of Administrative Segregation

Prison authorities are increasingly placing more-disruptive inmates in "administrative segregation," "maximum security," "control," or "lockup" housing units.[5] These units are unique in granting prison administrators total physical control over all aspects of the inmates' behavior. Inmates assigned to such housing areas spend twenty-two to twenty-three hours a day in their single, high-security barren cells with minimal (if any) access to educational, religious, or other self-help programs. Access to small, self-contained razor-wired recreation and exercise "cages" is available on a very limited basis, with no

---

CTQ

What style of management would you use if you were a warden of a large maximum-security prison? Why? How would those tactics differ from those used in a medium-security prison?

CTQ

Can American prisons better achieve the correctional goal of deterrence with their current punitive outlook? Should confinement in prison become more harsh and cruel in order to deter future criminality?

IN THE WORKPLACE

WARDEN

Responsible for planning, implementing, and managing staff; maintaining operational security; developing and analyzing financial reports; preparing, recommending, and administering the budget; developing, reviewing, recommending, and implementing institutional goals; developing policy in security procedures; posting orders and emergency plans; conducting audits of security procedures; ensuring compliance with institution policies. Minimum qualifications are as follows: five years' experience in the correctional field with one year at the deputy warden or next-lowest level; bachelor's degree in a related field preferred; experience maintaining security control and custody of adult inmates through direct supervision and coordination of inmate programs.

---

more than two or three inmates at a time allowed out in the yard. In general, these facilities represent the bottom end of a state's prison system.[6]

The concept of administrative segregation grew out of the practice of solitary confinement, which prison administrators began using in the nineteenth century along with other methods (such as flogging, water torture, and shackling of prisoners to cell walls) to punish particularly troublesome prisoners. By the turn of the century, prison authorities had eliminated most of the other, crueler forms of punishment, but continued to temporarily confine prisoners in "solitary" or the "hole" as the principal form of punishment for rule breaking. In his 1940 study of a "prison community," Clemmer described solitary confinement:

> The twenty-four solitary cells are in a small building known as the yard office... "solitary" is set off by itself and is heavily barred and isolated. The cells themselves contain no furniture. The one window is small, and the iron bars of the door have another wooden door which keeps the light from entering. The cells are cold in winter and hot in summer. The inmate is given one blanket and must sleep on a wood slab raised about two inches from the cement flooring. One piece of bread and a necessary amount of water is allowed each day.[7]

During the first half of the twentieth century, all walled prisons had solitaries or holes. Some, such as the tin sweat boxes in southern work camps or the "dungeon" in San Quentin, were extremely cruel places. The cells studied by Clemmer at the Illinois Menard maximum-security prison were about average. During this time, many prisons also had cells set aside for the segregation of prisoners—those who persistently broke the rules, were openly homosexual, or needed protection from others—whom the administration believed could not be allowed to circulate freely among other prisoners. Unlike solitary confinement, inmates could be held in segregation for long periods of time, sometimes for years.

By the 1950s, the old system of social order among the prison population that was based on a convict code and a few prisoner leaders was breaking down, and new problems of disorder among prisoners developed. Consequently, states began developing new forms of administrative segregation to control an increasingly disruptive inmate population. Many states that had adopted the rehabilitative philosophy of penology—such as California, Illinois, New York, New Jersey, Wisconsin, Washington, and Minnesota—were able to control inmate behavior for a few years (1950–1955) through the indeterminate sentencing system. Using the margins of sentencing discretion contained in the indeterminate sentencing system, along with systems of good-time credits inmates could earn to reduce their prison terms, prison officials and parole boards threatened prisoners with longer stays if they did not conform in prison. However, a small percentage of prisoners were not responsive to either these sentencing incentives or the threat of being placed in the hole. In particular, youthful leaders of well-organized street gangs who had received lengthy prison terms for violent crimes began to assume a greater presence in maximum-security prisons. Prison administrators then expanded the use of administrative segregation to manage this growing and difficult-to-manage population.

By 1970, California had established so-called high-security adjustment centers at its major maximum-security prisons of San Quentin, Folsom, and Soledad.[8] In Illinois, special program units, or SPUs, were established at Joliet, Stateville, and Pontiac prisons in 1972. Other states soon followed these states in their efforts to isolate and control the most disruptive or potentially disruptive segments of the inmate population.

When these first adjustment centers failed to reduce the turmoil and violence, more sections of several prisons were converted into new segregation units (such as "segregated housing units" and "management control units"). By 1980, for example, California had more than two-thousand prisoners in some form of lockup, representing nearly 10 percent of the entire prison population.[9]

New Maximum-Security Prisons

The apparent failure of administrative segregation units to pacify prisoners and restore order to the prisons during the 1970s and early 1980s did not cause penologists to abandon the policy of concentrating troublesome prisoners in the permanent lockup units. What they have done instead is construct new **maxi-maxi prisons** in which they have attempted to eliminate the features believed to have caused the breakdown of order.

In fact, this goal was first attempted some decades earlier by the Federal Bureau of Prisons (FBP) when it took over Alcatraz Island, the site of an old army prison, and opened a small, maximum-security federal prison in 1934 (see Figure 12.2). Alcatraz was intended to house the most "desperate criminals" (such as "Machine Gun" Kelly and Al Capone) and the bureau's most troublesome prisoners. By the early 1960s, federal officials, particularly the attorney general, Robert Kennedy, considered the "Rock," which housed only 275 prisoners, an expensive failure and closed it in 1963. Its prisoners were dispersed among the other federal prisons, mostly Atlanta and Leavenworth, the two most secure prisons next to Alcatraz.

Federal Prison at Marion, Illinois As Alcatraz was being shut down, the FBP was constructing a new, small prison at Marion, Illinois, as an experiment in behavior modification. The facility at Marion was actually to become the first of the modern supermax facilities in the United States (see Figure 12.3). In 1978, prompted by the need to deal with the most violent and disruptive inmates, the federal system decided to "concentrate" these inmates in one place and to designate this Level VI (most secure) facility. Marion was chosen because it was more suitable for high-security operations than other federal prisons. All federal inmates unable to adapt to other prisons were transferred there for disciplinary reasons, as were some from various state systems. The main facility has inmates who exhibit extreme antisocial behavior, are serious escape risks, or have lengthy, complex sentences.[10]

CTQ

Do you believe that maxi-maxi prisons constitute cruel and unusual punishment?

FIGURE 12.2

Aerial view of the federal prison at Alcatraz in San Francisco Bay. This prison was closed in 1963 after serving for thirty years as a prison of last resort for the most violent and persistent offenders and inmates from other institutions who were involved in escapes, escape attempts, riots, protests, work stoppages, and assaults on staff.

Courtesy of Cindy Charles/PhotoEdit.

Initially, the prison operated as a standard maximum-security facility. By 1983, however, increasing violence (inmate murders and assaults and the murder of two correctional officers) and other incidents (work stoppages and prison takeover attempts) brought about the initiation of a regimen that rigidly controlled inmates.[11]

Marion is a self-contained complex of reinforced concrete buildings surrounded by a double-reinforced fence; it is overseen by eight armed towers, electronic detection devices, and perimeter patrols.[12] The facility is organized into nine units: three general-population units, two transfer units, a protective-custody unit, a disciplinary unit, a special-housing unit, and a control unit. Seven of the units contain sixty-eight cells divided into four cell houses of seventeen cells each. The special unit houses seven inmates and the control unit houses fifty-eight.

This stratified housing system is designed to give inmates an active incentive to conform to the high-security program. Newly admitted inmates are placed in one of three general-population units. Their daily routine includes an average of two hours per day out of their cells.[13] They can make phone calls, receive mail, and are permitted noncontact visits. Each inmate has a TV used mainly as a closed-circuit system to provide religious, educational, and self-improvement programs.

The progressive program allows inmates to work themselves out of the institution by demonstrating nondangerous, responsible behavior thorough compliance with prison rules. After a year in a general-population unit with no infractions, they can be transferred to the intermediate pretransfer unit, where inmates are trained for work in UNICOR prison industries, have increased out-of-cell time, and eat together. Six months of good behavior in this unit can lead to a transfer to the pretransfer unit, where inmates either work a daily seven-hour schedule at the UNICOR plant, are employed as barbers, or serve as unit orderlies. They also eat in the prison's dining hall and are allowed out of their cells during the day. Inmates are given the chance to show that they can behave responsibly with fewer restrictions. After another infraction-free six months they are eligible for transfer to a less highly controlled institution. All transfers are at the discretion of the administration of the prison.

Most inmates eventually conform to the behavior requirements of this program and are transferred out. The average length of stay in the prison is 35.6 months.

There are four confinement units at Marion. The administrative/disciplinary confinement unit and the protective custody (PC) unit normally hold inmates for short periods either for disciplinary purposes, while on holdover status, or for protective purposes. Inmates held for disciplinary purposes are denied certain privileges available to the general population. For example, all those under administrative confinement have radios but are denied TVs, while those in disciplinary segregation have neither.

The control unit is reserved for the most dangerous, assaultive inmates at Marion. Inmates are placed here, for a given period of time, only after they have displayed an inability to control their behavior. The unit classification committee imposes this punishment after a full due process hearing and on the approval of an executive review board panel. This panel interviews these inmates monthly and approves all transfers from this unit. While these inmates have access to the same programs as those in the general population, their recreation is limited to seven hours per week and all showers and other activities are done in isolation.

The special PC unit provides high security for inmates requiring special protection. Most of these inmates have committed high-profile offenses that had extensive media coverage (such as spies) and are likely to be at special risk. They are always separated from the rest of the population. Placement in and removal from this unit requires the approval of the director of the Bureau of Prisons (BOP). Conditions on this unit are less restrictive than in the control unit (for example, inmates have the same amount of recreation time as those in the general population).

Federal Prison at Florence, Colorado In 1994 the federal government built a new facility to replace Marion. This facility is located in Florence, Colorado. "In the News: Inside the New Alcatraz" describes the cell conditions, features, and details of the new facility.

FIGURE 12.3

The new U.S. supermax penitentiary at Florence, Colorado. The perimeter security contains fourteen rolls of razor wire and six guard towers. Such security measures are typical of maximum security prisons at both the federal and state levels.

Courtesy of AP/Wide World Photos.

IN THE NEWS
A HUMAN PERSPECTIVE

INSIDE THE NEW ALCATRAZ
by Peter Annin

Driving up the main road you pass a work camp, a medium security facility and a maximum security facility, all part of the big federal corrections complex outside of Florence, Colorado. Then you come to the place that is, literally and figuratively, the end of the line, the new Alcatraz, the toughest federal penitentiary in America. This is the Administrative Maximum Facility, also known as ADX. Inmates call it "The Big One" or the "Hellhole of the Rockies."

Since it opened in 1994, ADX has held the unique mission of confining "the worst of the worst"—400-plus inmates from all across the federal prison system, men so dangerous no other pen can hold them. Some, like terrorist Ramzi Yousef, mastermind of the [1993] World Trade Center bombing, were sent to ADX because authorities feared their supporters might try to rescue them: among other security features, the prison is specifically designed to thwart an attack from the outside. Other cons were transferred there because they killed or assaulted guards or inmates. The cells look like they were designed for Hannibal Lecter. All furniture is concrete, to prevent occupants from making weapons out of bed frames or other metal parts, and each cell has a special vestibule where the inmate is shackled, hands behind his back, when he is being taken elsewhere in the prison. Solitary confinement is the norm: 40 percent of the cons stay in their cells 22 hours a day, and another 33 percent, the hardest of the hardcore, are locked down 23 hours a day. They get out only for an hour of exercise—which they take all alone, in a room that looks like an undersize racquetball court. "It's not a prison where you have to worry about getting raped," one visitor says.

The triangular main building is like something out of M.C. Escher—full of angles and obstructions that aren't quite what they seem. The entry is underground, through a heavily guarded tunnel. Cells have slit windows that show only a sliver of sky. That makes it hard for inmates or visitors to tell precisely where they are within the prison building, which complicates planning rescues or escapes. But it also makes ADX one of the most psychologically debilitating places on earth. "Lock yourself in your bathroom for the next four years and tell me how it affects your mind," says Raymond Luc Levasseur, a veteran of the '70's radical underground who is serving 45 years for a series of bombings. "It begins to erode the five senses. It's dehumanizing."

Who's who at ADX is usually a secret—another security precaution. But the names of high-profile inmates sometimes leak out. *Newsweek* has learned that Oklahoma City bomber Timothy McVeigh and Ted Kaczynski, the Unabomber, share the same cellblock (and round-the-clock video surveillance) with Ramzi Yousef. Terry Nichols, McVeigh's accomplice, may be transferred to the prison soon. Gang leader Luis Felipe, head of New York's Latin Kings, is already there. Felipe, who was convicted of ordering at least six murders while serving time in a New York state prison, is prohibited from having any visitors other than his lawyer, Lawrence Feitell. According to Feitell, Felipe has broken down from the stress of his isolation. He has difficulty sleeping and eating and suffers from shakes or tremors, Feitell said; Prozac hasn't helped. "He falls into fits of weeping. He's written letters to the judge begging for some form of human contact," Feitell says. "The kind of mind it would take to create a place like that is beyond me."

The credit belongs to Norman Carlson. Director of the U.S. Bureau of Prisons unit since 1987, Carlson says ADX is a direct response to the sharp increase in "violent and predatory" inmates during the 1970's and 80's, particularly at the federal pen in Marion, Ill. Twenty inmates were murdered in 18 years at Marion—and on Oct. 22, 1983, two guards were stabbed to death by "two members of the Aryan Brotherhood who were just trying to outdo each other," Carlson says. The whole prison went on permanent 23-hour lockdown and the "supermax" concept was born. Following the Fed's example, more than 30 states now have supermax pens.

This trend disturbs prison-rights activists, who argue that supermax prisons are a form of "cruel and unusual" punishment prohibited by the Constitution. "There has always been solitary confinement in this country," says Jamie Fellner of Human Rights Watch. "The difference is the length of time. We're not talking about putting someone in the hole for 15 days. We're talking about 15 years or life." But the federal courts have upheld the practice of 23-hour lockdowns, and that means ADX and the supermax concept are here to stay. Says architect John Quest, who designed the brick-and-concrete structure: "This building shows that prisons don't have to be ugly to be secure." The view from inside isn't nearly so pretty.

Source: P. Annin, "Inside the New Alcatraz," *Newsweek*, July 13, 1998. © 1998 Newsweek, Inc. All rights reserved. Reprinted by permission.

Following the lead of the Federal Bureau of Prisons, several states have built or converted facilities (or are in the process of doing so) to handle their most dangerous inmates. These jurisdictions justify the operation of supermax facilities because staff and inmates in other facilities are safer by having these inmates removed. As with Florence, inmates can, by conforming to prison rules, work their way out of these facilities too.[14]

California has become the leader in construction of supermax prisons. It has built four new maxi-maxi prisons with a total capacity of 12,000. Other such prisons have been constructed in Nevada, New Mexico, Texas, and Minnesota, with many more planned for other states and cities with major jails (including Los Angeles, New York, and Philadelphia).

The four California maxi-maxi facilities have some common design features. All have "units" or "pods" that cluster around a central control center from which heavily armed guards look down on the units twenty-four hours a day. The cells have fully sealed front doors to restrict the throwing of objects by inmates. Each unit typically has a small day room and adjacent exercise yard.

The Pelican Bay facility, the last of the four to open, is located in an extremely remote area of northern California. Built in 1990 at a cost of $278 million, it was designed to hold 2,080 maximum-security inmates, but it is already overcrowded with an inmate population of 3,250. Within the prison itself, the segregated housing unit has a capacity of 1,056 prisoners:

> Pelican Bay is entirely automated and designed so that inmates have virtually no face-to-face contact with guards or other inmates. For 22½ hours a day, inmates are confined to their windowless cells, built of solid blocks of concrete and stainless steel so that they won't have access to materials they could fashion into weapons. They don't work in prison industries; they don't have access to recreation; they don't mingle with other inmates. They aren't even allowed to smoke because matches are considered a security risk. Inmates eat all meals in their cells and leave only for brief showers and 90 minutes of daily exercise. They shower alone and exercise alone in miniature yards of barren patches of cement enclosed by 20 feet high cement walls covered with metal screens. The doors to their cells are opened and closed electronically by a guard in a control booth....
>
> There are virtually no bars in the facility; the cell doors are made of perforated sheets of stainless steel with slots for food trays. Nor are there guards with keys on their belts walking the tiers. Instead, the guards are locked away in glass-enclosed control booths and communicate with prisoners through a speaker system....
>
> The SHU (Segregated Housing Unit) has its own infirmary; its own law library (where prisoners are kept in secure rooms and slipped law books through slots); and its own room for parole hearings. Inmates can spend years without stepping outside the Unit.[15]

California's former governor George Deukmejian dedicated the prison on June 14th, 1990:

> "California now possesses a state-of-the-art prison that will serve as a model for the rest of the nation . . . Pelican Bay symbolizes our philosophy that the best way to reduce crime is to put convicted criminals behind bars." The governor then remarked that the annual cost of keeping a convicted felon in prison is $20,000, compared with the $430,000 that it costs society when a career criminal is at work on the street.[16]

Pelican Bay is the most completely isolated prison since the early penitentiaries in Pennsylvania. Since 60 percent of the inmates housed at Pelican Bay are from the Los Angeles area, which is 900 miles away with no available air transportation, regular visits from inmates' families are extremely unlikely. But California is not the only state constructing such units. Oklahoma's new "high-max" unit was described in this way:

> Inmates housed in the "high-max" security unit will live 23 hours a day in their cells, with the other hour spent in a small concrete recreation area with 20-foot walls. The space is topped by a metal gate.
>
> Theoretically, an inmate could move into the new cellhouse and never again set foot outdoors. The unit's first residents will be the 114 men on death row. The cellhouse also contains a new execution chamber.
>
> That's how the staff designed it. For about 45 days, workers representing a cross-section of the penitentiary's staff developed plans for the new unit with architects. Guards in the control room of each squad can eavesdrop

on or talk to inmates in any cell at the touch of a button. And the monitoring device should reduce the number of attacks on prisoners, nip conspiracies in the bud, and protect officers.

A corridor behind each cell run will allow officials to work on or shut off water and power to each individual cell.[17]

Finally, here is a description of New York's new supermax, as reported in *The New York Times*:

> The New York prison Southport Correctional Facility has the same mission: to take the worst prisoners. They will include those who have dealt drugs behind bars, attacked guards, even murdered inmates. At Southport, they are being kept isolated, shackled at the waist and wrists when allowed out of their 6 by 10 foot cells, and made to spend their daily recreation hour in newly built cages.[18]

Minnesota Correctional Facility at Oak Park Heights The maxi-maxi prison at Oak Park Heights, Minnesota, is one of the most up-to-date, state-of-the-art installations built to date. This all-male facility was developed on the premise that the quality of the prison environment is determined by management, available resources, and the physical facility, rather than by the nature of the offenses committed by its population.[19]

Designated and conceived specifically to stabilize the inmate population at other Minnesota facilities, the Oak Park Heights facility houses inmates who are chronic management problems, extremely predatory, or high risks for escape. Despite this highly volatile population, the objective remains to create as normal an environment as possible, keeping in mind the need for maximum security. Security is designed to protect the public from these offenders and to provide a safe environment for both staff and inmates.

Community protection is accomplished by a combination of external and internal security measures, but unlike other high-security facilities, the institution does not have a system of external towers or an expensive electronic system. Instead, security is maintained by a system of two fences with coils or razor wire between them and a pit to serve as a vehicle trap. Further, there is an alarm device atop one of the fences to serve as a warning. However, it is doubtful that an inmate would ever reach the fence. To climb the double fences, an escapee would first have to get out of his room or living area and onto the institution's common green, scale one of the walls of the three-story buildings surrounding the green, and cross an open area of approximately 100 yards. It is estimated that it would take an inmate fifty seconds longer to get out of this institution than to get through the federal government's tightest security system.

The institution's four-hundred-plus inmates are housed in eight separate units of fifty-two inmates each. This division of the population into relatively small, manageable, and compatible groups improves security, safety, and control, and provides a better climate for communication and interaction between staff and residents. Moreover, because each housing unit has its own work program and outdoor recreational facilities, the units can be opened separately—although it is not planned that they will be. The housing units themselves are broken down into smaller units of six or seven rooms, each with its own activity area. This provides a defensible space, where staff and inmates can feel a sense of security and control.

A common green large enough for a football field and several baseball fields is located in a central area accessible to all housing units. This area also contains a town center that serves as a congregation area for leisure-time activities and provides access to the visiting area. Because of the central location of the green, the staff can allow residents from all or some of the housing units to move freely from one unit to another.

The facility has one special unit designed to handle the most severe disciplinary cases. Following the model of older maximum-security facilities, this unit is under the supervision of staff specially trained to manage difficult inmates. Unit inmates are allowed to leave their rooms only on a controlled basis. In general, however, the management of inmates in the Oak Park Heights facility does not depend on segregation and sophisticated electronic devices; rather, it is based on programming.

The institution operates a full-day program (sixteen hours) that encompasses both leisure time and working hours and furnishes a full range of program options for inmates. This programming includes industrial work, education, group therapy, and chemical dependency counseling. Although it is not a major focus of the institution, education is available to inmates through both traditional and computer-based approaches.

A major concern of the facility is to enable the offender to earn a legitimate living and to develop a realistic view of the world of "paid work." Inmates experience real work situations such as getting a job, earning wages, and assuming responsibility for on-the-job conduct. They are exposed to hiring and firing, productivity standards, job variety, job progression, and discipline in the workplace.[20]

Industries include microfilming, commercial sewing, production of office and educational supplies (folders, notebooks, and so on), bookbinding, and general shop. Evening activities include sex-offender groups, education, chemical dependency groups, recreation, religion, and organized leisure.

This full-participation program is designed to prepare the inmate for a transfer to one of Minnesota's other adult facilities and to improve his ability to succeed upon returning to the community. Nevertheless, it is recognized that some inmates will not participate in any of the programs available. For such inmates, the facility provides the needed supervision and control to ensure that they do not interfere with or obstruct other inmates who want to take advantage of program options.

MEDIUM-SECURITY PRISONS

Since the early twentieth century, developments in the behavioral sciences, increasing emphasis on education, the dominance of the work ethic, and changes in technology have led to modified treatment methods in corrections. Parole and probation have increased, and institutions have been set up to handle special inmate populations. Pretrial holding centers, or jails, are now separate from facilities that receive convicted felons, and different levels of security have been developed: maxi-maxi, maximum, medium, and minimum. Most of the correctional security in the last fifty years has been medium security.

Today, **medium-security prisons** embody most of the ideals and characteristics of early attempts to reform offenders. It is in these facilities that the most intensive correctional and rehabilitative efforts are conducted. Inmates are exposed to a variety of programs designed to help them become useful members of society. The predominant consideration is still security, however, and inmates are confined where they can be observed and controlled. All facilities have perimeter security, in the form of either masonry walls or double cyclone fences. Electronic sensors may also be used. Perimeter towers are staffed by armed guards and equipped with spotlights.

Internal security is usually maintained by locks, bars, and concrete walls; clear separation of activities; defined movement both indoors and outdoors; tight scheduling; head counts; visual observation; and electronic monitoring. Housing areas, rooms for medical and dental treatment, schoolrooms, recreation and entertainment facilities, counseling offices, vocational training and industrial shops, administrative offices, and maintenance facilities are usually clearly separated. Some activities are located in individual compounds complete with their own fences and sally ports. Barred gates and guard posts control the flow of traffic between areas. Central control stations track movement at all times. Inmate circulation is restricted to certain corridors or outdoor walks, with certain areas designated out of bounds. Closed-circuit television and alarm networks are used extensively. Doors are made of steel (and kept locked), and all external windows, and some internal ones, are barred. Bars or concrete walls line all corridors and surrounding control points.

Housing units in medium-security institutions vary from crowded dormitories to private rooms with furniture. Dormitories may house as many as eighty inmates or as few as sixteen. Some individual cells have grilled fronts and doors. Variations among medium-security institutions are not as extreme as those among maximum-security facilities, perhaps because the former were developed in a shorter period of time.

WEB

For more information on maximum-security prisons, **visit our Web site,** www.prenhall.com/territo.

In recent years, campus-type medium-security facilities have been designed to eliminate the cramped, oppressive atmosphere found in most prisons. Buildings are separated by meandering pathways and modulated ground surfaces to break the monotony. Attractive residences house small groups of inmates in single rooms. The schools, vocational education buildings, gymnasiums, and athletic fields at these facilities compare favorably with the best community colleges. Nevertheless, adequate external and internal security are provided to protect the public.

MINIMUM-SECURITY PRISONS

Minimum-security prisons range from large drug rehabilitation centers to small farm, road, and forestry camps in rural America. The facilities are diverse, but generally they are relatively open; they house inmates who are considered nonviolent and at low risk for escape.

Most, but not all, minimum-security facilities serve the economic needs of society and institution. Cotton is picked, lumber is cut, livestock is raised, roads are built, forest fires are fought, and parks and public buildings are maintained. Remote facilities have major deficiencies, however. They seldom provide education or services (other than work), and the predominantly rural labor bears no relationship to work skills needed for urban life. The prisoners are separated from their real world almost as much as if they were in a penitentiary.

One unusual minimum-security correctional center—a branch of the Illinois State Penitentiary—was opened in 1973 at Vienna, Illinois. Although large, the facility almost seems to have the environment of a nonpenal institution. Buildings resemble garden apartments built around a "town square" complete with churches, schools, and a library. Paths lead to "neighborhoods" where "homes" provide private rooms in small clusters. Extensive indoor and outdoor recreation is provided, and the academic, commercial, and vocational education facilities equal or surpass those of many technical high schools.

CTQ
Do you believe that minimum-security correctional centers are too soft on criminals?

RECEPTION AND CLASSIFICATION CENTERS

The function of **reception and classification centers** is to examine new inmates and assign them to appropriate institutions. In earlier times, before there were state correctional systems and central departments of corrections, each prison was a separate entity, usually managed by a board that reported directly to the governor of the state. If a state had more than one institution, either geography or a judge determined where an offender would go. As the number and variety of institutions increased, however, classification systems and agencies for central control evolved. Eventually, the need for reception and classification centers became obvious.

Not all of these centers operate as distinct and separate facilities, however. In most states, the reception and classification function is performed in an existing institution—usually a maximum-security facility. Thus, most new prisoners start their correctional experience in the most confining, most severe, and most depressing part of the system. After a period of observation, testing, and interviewing, an assignment is made that supposedly reflects the best marriage between the inmate's needs and the system's resources.

IN THE WORKPLACE

HOUSING UNIT OFFICER

Responsible for overseeing whereabouts of all inmates within a designated housing unit. Performs a variety of duties, including the following: maintaining logbooks on inmate movement; monitoring inmate intercoms; sorting and distributing mail; assigning cells to inmates; monitoring inmates on suicide watch; and routing maintenance requests and inmate laundry. Minimum qualifications are as follows: age 18, U.S. citizen, high school diploma or equivalent.

Security in reception and classification centers is based on the premise that "a new fish is an unknown fish." Nowhere on the current correctional scene are there more bars, more barbed wire, more electronic surveillance devices, more clanging iron doors, and less activity and personal space. All of this is justified on the grounds that the nature of the resident is unknown and that his or her stay will be short.

A notable exception to this type of security exists at the Reception and Medical Center at Lake Butler, Florida. This campus-style facility has several widely separated buildings on a fifty-two-acre site enclosed in a double cyclone fence with two towers. Inmates circulate freely between the classification building, gymnasium, dining room, clinic, canteen, craft shops, visiting area, and dormitories. Three-quarters of the inmates are assigned to medium-security units scattered around campus. One-quarter are housed in a maximum-security building.

Inmates not specifically occupied by the demands of the classification process at Lake Butler are encouraged to take part in recreational and self-improvement activities. Visits are allowed in an open-air patio and an indoor visiting facility (ordinarily used only during inclement weather). The relationships among staff and inmates are casual, and movement is not regimented. Morale is high, and escapes are rare. However, overcrowding has become a problem in recent years.

Diagnostic processes in reception centers range from a medical examination and a single inmate-caseworker interview (without privacy) to a full battery of tests, interviews, and psychiatric and medical examinations (supplemented by an orientation program). The process can take from three to six weeks.

PRISON OVERCROWDING

Overcrowded prisons may be the most urgent problem facing the criminal justice system today (see Figure 12.4). The number of prisoners in the United States has increased continuously since the early 1970s, and the rate of incarceration (the number of prisoners per capita) has doubled since 1970. In 2002 more than two million inmates were incarcerated in American prisons and 250,000 people were in jails.

The current situation of prison crowding in the United States stems from the steady growth in prison populations that began in the early 1970s. Until that time, there was a broad consensus that the primary purpose of imprisonment was correction, that is, rehabilitation of the offender. But evaluation of a wide variety of techniques presumed to be rehabilitative failed to show that any were particularly effective. These results shattered the old consensus and led to a new consensus that changing human behavior was extremely difficult. There was no agreement, however, on what to do next.

During the rehabilitation era, parole authorities were empowered to decide when a particular prisoner was rehabilitated and ready for release, which made for an efficient way to accommodate increases in the inflow of prisoners. Any release of prisoners involves some degree of risk, and so marginal shifts in that risk are barely perceptible—especially in view of the considerable difficulty of estimating future criminality. Thus, when prisons become too crowded, the parole board could become somewhat more liberal in deciding whether an inmate was a good candidate for release. In this way, parole provided an important "safety valve" for adjusting prison populations to their available capacity.

The mid-1970s saw a major reaction to this "indeterminate" sentencing system. Since efforts at inmate rehabilitation services were not shown to be effective, it was argued that judgment about a prisoner's state of rehabilitation should no longer influence the length of time served. There came a general shift toward more determinate sentences, set by the judge at the time of sentencing but often within the guidelines established by a legislature or a sentencing commission. The true sentence, as reflected in the time actually served, became more explicit and

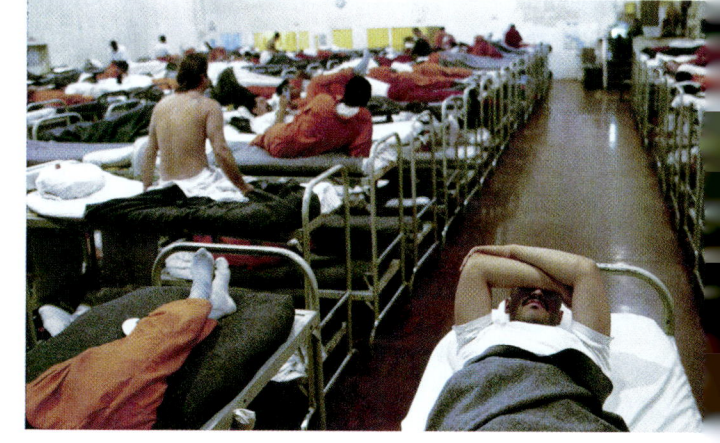

FIGURE 12.4

Prison overcrowding is one of the most severe problems facing correction officials today. Areas within prisons that were not designed to accommodate inmates, such as this gym at a California state prison, are often used for such purposes when there is not enough space in traditional housing units.

Courtesy of Steve Lehman/Corbis/SABA Press Photos, Inc.

more public, and pressure grew to increase sentences in response to the public's concern over rising crime rates in the 1970s.

The changing age composition of the U.S. population has exacerbated the crowding problem. The number of people in their mid-twenties, the ages at which people are most likely to be sent to prison, has grown steadily over the last twenty years. That increase reflects the population growth associated with the postwar baby boom, which started in 1947 and peaked in 1961. Thus, even if there had been no change in the fraction of each age group represented in prison, the larger number of people in the most prison-prone ages would still have crowded the prisons. This situation, together with the increasing severity of sentences, has created the current dramatic increase in prison population.

Alternative Approaches to Relieving Prison Crowding

There are three basic approaches to relieving prison overcrowding: (1) providing more capacity, (2) diverting convicted people to sentences other than prison (the "front-door" approach), and (3) shortening the time served in prison by those who do go there (the "back-door" approach).

Additional prison capacity would permit the same number of prisoners (or more) to be kept, but under more acceptable conditions. Providing the additional capacity costs money, however. Construction costs typically range between $50,000 and $75,000 per bed. Additional money is needed each year—about $10,000 to $15,000 per prisoner—to maintain, guard, and manage prisoners.

Many who argue against providing additional capacity are concerned that the prison population will simply expand to fill the available capacity. One study seemed to show by statistical evidence that this would happen; further studies, however, pointed out errors in those initial studies. It is still possible, of course, that there could be such an effect (even though the initial study failed to demonstrate it). Indeed, some judges are known to restrain their sentencing when they know that prisons are filled. However, during the 1960s, when prison populations were well below the available capacity, there was no pressure on judges to send more people to prison in order to fill that available capacity. Thus, the issue is far from simple.

The "front-door" approach involves finding alternatives to prison for those whom a judge might want to send there. "Front-door" solutions are not intended for the most serious offenders—for those who commit heinous crimes or who represent a serious continuing risk to the community. They are, however, a possibility for marginal offenders who might otherwise be candidates for probation had they not already had one or more prior sentences to probation; these offenders warrant something more severe than probation. The problem is to develop an array of alternatives so the judge, the victim, and the community can be satisfied that the level of punishment is appropriate; the alternatives most often considered are some combination of intensive probation, restitution, community work, and residence in a group home under tight surveillance but with the right to go to work during the day.

The "back-door" approach involves shortening the time served by imprisoned offenders. Indeed, this form is traditionally used by parole boards to regulate prison populations. Parole boards hold the key to the "back door" by their authority to release prisoners who have served an appropriate minimum sentence but less than their maximum term. Some states have adopted emergency release laws under which some prisoners' eligibility for release is advanced, and some prisoners are released, once the prison population reaches a designated level.

The problem of prison crowding is one of the most vexing dilemmas facing the criminal justice system today. There is widespread agreement that people who commit serious crimes must receive punishment, and that recidivists must be punished more severely. There is also agreement that the objectives of prison for punishment and crime control (through general deterrence, rehabilitation, and incapacitation) are appropriate, but there is some disagreement as to how effectively they are achieved. There may also be general agreement in how convicted offenders should be ranked in terms of those most and least deserving of prison. But there is still a significant difference of opinion over who ought to be imprisoned and for how long.

IN THE WORKPLACE

CENTRAL CONTROL OFFICER

Responsible for controlling and monitoring all movement within the controlled part of the detention facility, as part of a team of at least two officers. Operates a state-of-the-art computer that controls security doors, cameras, and intercoms. Also responsible for monitoring the fire control system and all radio communication within the detention facility. Minimum qualifications are as follows: age 18, U.S. citizen, high school diploma or equivalent.

RIOTS AND DISTURBANCES IN CORRECTIONAL INSTITUTIONS

The prison riot as a phenomenon can be viewed in a number of ways. To a behavioral scientist, a riot might be seen as a form of communication or expression, one used after less drastic means have proved unsuccessful. To the revolutionary, a riot may be a form of social protest and a tool for radical change. To the media, a riot is a rare opportunity to portray real-life drama that rivals the best of fiction. To the correction administrator, it is a challenge to authority, an insurrection that threatens the delicate balance of power in an institution and the lives of those who live and work there.[21]

But riots and disturbances in prisons are not a new phenomenon in the United States, and recent decades have seen a continuation of these destructive, violent events (see Figure 12.5). Prison violence seems to run in cycles, and the contagious nature of major prison disturbances is an ongoing concern nationwide. The first major wave occurred during 1952 and 1953, when at least twenty-five different institutions had to quell revolts among their inmates, with incidents that resulted in many injuries, millions of dollars of damage, and the destruction of major facilities and equipment. After a period of relative calm, a new cycle of riots began in Oregon in 1968 and spread across the country. The Attica riot in 1971 and the New Mexico riot in Santa Fe Penitentiary in 1980 resulted in loss of life, great human suffering, and major property damage. Following is a brief summary of some of the more recent prison riots.

- *Kirkland Correctional Institution (Kirkland) — South Carolina.* The Kirkland facility was generally well managed at the time of the disturbance of April 1, 1986, and so was the riot's resolution. The riot began in a housing unit holding the prison's most violent and disruptive inmates. Inmates seized control of this unit, scaled the fence around it, and then used construction tools left on the grounds to release seven-hundred general-population inmates. The riot command post functioned smoothly, resolving the disturbance in six hours.
- *U.S. Penitentiary (Atlanta) — Georgia.* On November 10, 1987, the U.S. State Department announced that Cuba had agreed to reinstate a 1984 accord that would permit the repatriation of up to 2,500 Cuban nationals. Included would be Cubans who had fled in the 1980 Mariel boatlift but who, once released on "immigration parole," had been convicted of a crime and were now detained in one of two federal prisons. Three days after the announcement, the detainees seized control of the U.S. Penitentiary in Atlanta (part of the Bureau of Prisons, U.S. Department of Justice). Their principal demand was that they not be repatriated to Cuba. The uprising lasted eleven days, involved more than a hundred hostages, and required protracted negotiations to resolve.

FIGURE 12.5

One of the bloodiest riots in American history occurred in 1971 at the New York State Penitentiary at Attica, lasting four days. Forty-three inmates and guards were killed, and property worth millions of dollars was damaged. Inmates constructed tents as temporary living quarters in the jail's courtyard.

Courtesy of AP/Wide World Photos.

CTQ

Why should prison officials even concern themselves about prison overcrowding?

WEB

For more information about prison overcrowding, **visit our Web site,** www.prenhall.com/territo.

- *Mack Alford Correctional Center (Mack Alford)—Oklahoma.* The riot that occurred at this medium-security institution between May 13 and May 15, 1988, was preceded by a six-hour period during which black and white inmates milled about in crowds, expressing antagonism toward each other and toward authorities. Despite attempts to defuse the situation, a corrections official was taken hostage late in the evening, marking the start of the riot. Over a two-hour period, inmates seized seven more hostages and took over two-thirds of the prison. No substantive issues were raised during the three-day disturbance, which was eventually resolved through a combination of negotiation, exhaustion on the part of the inmates, and defection by inmates who no longer wanted to participate.
- *Coxsackie Correctional Facility (Coxsackie)—New York.* Coxsackie houses primarily maximum-security inmates; the institution's Special Housing Unit (SHU) is for inmates segregated to serve disciplinary terms for serious violations of the rules. For approximately fourteen hours on August 1–2, 1988, thirty-two SHU inmates held several officers hostage and destroyed much of the SHU facility. The riot began when an inmate assaulted an officer in the exercise yard; the five officers working in the SHU that day were not regularly assigned to this unit, so they were not as familiar with procedures as those who worked there routinely. Staff from the facility and the central office established communications with the inmates almost immediately after the SHU was overtaken and remained in contact during the time it took negotiators to bring about resolution.
- *Idaho State Correctional Institution (ISCI)—Idaho.* ISCI houses medium-custody inmates as well as close-custody inmates (those who are dangerous and difficult to manage), inmates in administrative segregation and detention, and those awaiting execution. On September 28, 1988, inmates in a close-custody housing unit refused to return to their cells after having been observed drinking a homemade alcoholic beverage. They then used an unsecured table to break into the unit's control center. The riot was eventually brought under control by an ultimatum and riot squad deployment.
- *Pennsylvania State Correctional Institution at Camp Hill (Camp Hill)—Pennsylvania.* Since 1975 Camp Hill had been an adult correctional facility, housing minimum- and medium-security inmates. On October 25, 1989, inmates returning from an exercise yard in the late afternoon overwhelmed correctional staff and seized eight hostages. The riot ended through negotiations, and inmates were confined to cells. The next day the superintendent met with the inmates to discuss their grievances. In a development unknown to him, many of the cells to which the inmates had been confined were not secure, permitting the start of a second riot later that same day. Five more hostages were taken. Negotiations were again attempted, but the riot finally ended when state police forcibly entered the compound.
- *Federal Correctional Institution (Talladega)—Alabama.* Changes prompted by the 1987 Cuban detainee riots in the U.S. Penitentiary at Atlanta, Georgia, and at the Federal Detention Center in Oakdale, Louisiana, were put to the test four years later when Cuban detainees rioted at Talladega between August 21 and August 30, 1991. After hostages had been held for ten days, prison administrators concluded that their health and safety were at increasing risk and prospects for a negotiated settlement were dim. A carefully planned and rehearsed assault, maximizing the element of surprise, ended the incident without serious injuries to the hostages or detainees.
- *Southern Ohio Correctional Facility (Lucasville)—Ohio.* Easter Sunday 1993 saw the beginning of an eleven-day rebellion of the 1,800 inmates at Southern Ohio Correctional Facility in Lucasville, Ohio—one of the country's toughest maximum-security prisons. The riot ended with nine inmates and one correctional officer dead. The officer had been hanged.[22]
- *California State Prison (Pelican Bay)—California.* In February 2000, a riot between two-hundred black and Hispanic prisoners left one inmate dead and fifteen others wounded.

WEB

For more information on the history of prison riots, **visit our Web site,** www.prenhall.com/territo.

CTQ

Do you believe that if prisoners were given fewer rights, kept under tight control, and worked longer hours, riots would still occur?

Inmate Groups Prone to Causing Problems

Antisocial Inmates   Some inmates are sociopaths, angry at society and lacking what are considered normal societal values. They are prone to wanton destruction of property and injury to others. Frequently scheming to overthrow authority, as represented in prison society by the administration, they go to great lengths to identify and exploit security breaches. They become astute students of every aspect of the physical plant, as well as institutional operations. Since they spend twenty-four hours each day for years in the institution, their knowledge of security procedures and weaknesses can easily exceed that of administrative staff. Such inmates are a significant concern.

Inmates with Mental Problems   A significant number of inmates can be diagnosed as psychopaths or as having other serious mental health conditions. Some commonly accepted characteristics of the psychopath are an inability to develop meaningful interpersonal relationships, absence of a conscience, a need for immediate gratification, low frustration levels, and an inability to learn from experience. These inmates are frequently hard to understand and manage, especially by correctional staff who have not had appropriate training in the mental health area.

Racial/Ethnic Minorities   Racial/ethnic minority groups are grossly overrepresented in the nation's prisons, as compared to society at large. As a result, minority inmates often view themselves as political prisoners, victimized by an unjust society. Racial and ethnic lines are frequently even more firmly drawn in correctional institutions than in the community. Racial identity therefore may lead to the formation of prison gangs (discussed later in this chapter) and other special inmate groups competing for power and control, sometimes resulting in violence and disturbances.

Radical/Revolutionary Organizations   The antisocial attitudes of many inmates, as well as the tendency of many of them to view themselves as political prisoners, have made them an easy, high-priority target for recruitment by revolutionary organizations. Evidence suggests that some of these organizations have attempted to infiltrate and influence existing prison gangs. These efforts appear to involve training gang members in terrorist tactics and gaining sympathy for political philosophies. Acts of terrorism have become more frequent inside correctional institutions and have on occasion reached outside as well. Certainly not the least serious example of this was a plot several years ago to kidnap the children of California correctional officers.

GANGS IN PRISON

Several years ago, one of the most comprehensive studies ever undertaken on prison gangs was completed.[23] In an effort to collect the most current data, the researchers contacted all state prisons and the Federal Bureau of Prisons, with 94 percent of the agencies contacted responding. The following are some of the findings of the study.

Becoming a Gang Member

Most frequently, membership in a prison gang (see Figure 12.6) is a result of either past association with current gang members or general acceptance of current gang values. Acceptance by most or all of the current gang members is generally required for gang membership.

Ethnicity and geography are the two most significant criteria among gang members. Membership is based first on race and is usually connected with beliefs about racial superiority. Second, prior affiliation or association with members in a close-to-home location can strongly influence membership. Next in importance is the sharing of strong beliefs, political and/or religious. Finally, sharing a lifestyle influences membership. The factors most often associated with membership in prison gangs, therefore, are the following:

- Racial solidarity
- Geographical proximity
- Political biases

CTQ

Which of the inmate groups identified and discussed as prone to causing problems would you believe to be the most difficult for prison officials to control?

FIGURE 12.6

Membership in a prison gang often results either from past association with gangs before incarceration or because of values shared with the other gang members in prison. This inmate, a convicted murderer, was a member of the notorious CRIP gang before he was incarcerated. He is flashing a gang sign.

Courtesy of Mark Richards/PhotoEdit.

- Religious beliefs
- Motorcycle machismo

Examples of prison gangs include the following:

- **Aryan Brotherhood** and Avengers
- **Black Guerilla Family**
- **El Rukns** and Moorish Science Temple
- **Latin Disciples**
- **Latin Kings**
- **Mexican Mafia**
- **Nuestra Familia** (Our Family)
- **Texas Syndicate**
- **Vice Lords**

A prison gang often reflects more than one defining feature. For example, the Black Guerilla Family is both political and radical. The Aryan Brotherhood is both motorcycle-oriented and white supremacist. The Mexican Mafia is both racial and geographic. The Texas Syndicate was started by Texas-born Mexican-American inmates at San Quentin Prison in California in 1975 because they believed they needed protection from other California prison gangs. By 1976 it had five-hundred members and had spread to other California prisons. At that time it not only protected them against other gangs but was also actively involved in such illegal activities as drug trafficking, extortion, and contract murder.

The prospective member's acceptance of the gang's values plays a significant role. In addition, being a "stand-up convict," having an imposing physical presence, and demonstrating an inclination toward violence all play a part in the process. The existing gang appears to view its power and prestige as being enhanced when it is able to attract such individuals. In return, the prospective members seek the personal prestige, power, and protection that the gang affords.

Beyond this, information about the actual recruitment of new members is sketchy. An examination of forty-seven prison gangs' practices, as reported by prison officials in the agencies surveyed in the Camps' study, revealed that in only three instances was more than a little information known about the recruitment process. And in those three—the Aryan Brotherhood (Missouri), the Aryan Brotherhood (Kentucky), and the Avengers (West Virginia)—even this information was minimal.

The use of violence as an initiation—either murdering or drawing blood of another inmate or staff member—clearly sets these prison gangs apart from other gangs. Two reasons appear to be the basis for the commission of such violent acts. On one hand, the gang may promote the "hit" to assure itself that the prospective gang member is really "solid" while at the same time carrying out its own affairs. That is, the new member proves himself and, at the same time, the person to be killed or assaulted is "taken care of"—and the gang's business gets taken care of through this process. A second reason why violence may be associated with becoming a gang member is that some prisoners who aspire to be members of a particular gang may commit violent acts to draw attention to themselves, hoping that will put them in favor with the gang and lead to membership. Some prisoners' predisposition to violence is so great that determining whether a particular act of violence is directly attributable to the gang's initiation practices is made all the more difficult.

Classes of Membership In most gangs, membership carries with it all the rights and privileges. There are generally no levels or degrees of membership reported other than in eight gangs, six of which are motorcycle-oriented. The two non-motorcycle-related gangs are the Aryan Brotherhood (Missouri) and the Aryan Warriors (Nevada). In these two prison gangs, a three-class membership system ranges from prospect to probate to an elite level of membership. The general lack of classes of membership does not imply a lack of hierarchical ranking of members. Leaders, whether using titles or not, were distinguishable from their fellow member followers. Physical prowess, seniority, commission of violent acts, and leadership qualities elevate a member through the gang hierarchy.

Knowledge of Other Members Almost without exception, members of a particular gang know who else is a member. For gangs that wear colors, membership in a particular gang is obvious not only to prisoners but also to staff. Secrecy, at least in terms of membership identity, is second to public recognition of gang affiliation. For prison gangs in which membership is secret to nonmembers and, in particular, to staff, the identity of fellow members is not a secret. The only exception to this occurs when the size of the gang prohibits each member from knowing who else is a member, as is the case within California prisons and in the federal prison system where it is one reported that it is now the practice of the Nuestra Familia to limit the extent to which one member is able to identify other members.

Structure of the Gang: Leadership Leadership and direction for the gang is provided by a single, strong leader in twelve instances; in another five cases, a strong leader shares these powers with a committee or council. In eleven gangs, the leadership and direction is derived from a committee or council without the benefit of a single strong leader; in three gangs, neither a single leader nor a council was present, in which case the gang functions in a relatively leaderless manner. The role of the leader tends to come to the individual who most embodies the gang's values. Longevity of membership is also a factor.

Hierarchy Knowledge of the organizational structure and hierarchical pattern is limited. Internal documents specific to various gangs have been discovered. Some of these documents display elaborate roles, relationships, and function. The degree to which these patterns actually exist is difficult to determine. Only six states (Arizona, Missouri, Nevada, Pennsylvania, Texas, and West Virginia) reported specific awareness of one or more gang hierarchical structures.

Longevity of Current Leadership A prison gang leader's tenure appears to be relatively short, a fact that may be influenced by the institution's ability to transfer prisoners between institutions and across state lines and by other factors, including internal dissatisfaction with the leader's performance. Information on only twenty-four gangs was obtained on this variable. The longest periods of reported leadership tenure were ten to fifteen years for the El Rukns (Illinois) and eleven years for both the Prison Motorcycle Brotherhood (Iowa) and the Vice Lords (Iowa). In descending order of longevity, the Aryan Warriors (Nevada) had ten years of the same leadership, while the Mexican Mafia (Arizona) reported nine years. The mean number of years was 4.2 years, while the median was 2 years.

Replacement of Leader The succession of leaders in the gang occurs as a result of one of two equally likely methods. Either the strongest of the remaining members takes over by the force of his personality, as was the case in eleven gangs, or, through a meeting of the minds of the membership of its elite, agreement is reached on the choice of a new leader, as was the case in nine gangs. In some instances, a vote is taken. In most instances, the actual method of succession is just not known.

Moving Up in Rank The likelihood of moving up in the ranks within the gang or reaching a higher rung of the ladder is increased when a member demonstrates his physical prowess by violent aggressive acts against those who oppose the gang's will. Often, the observed behavior appears bizarre. In other instances, seniority in terms of length of time in the gang is the vehicle for moving up in the ranks. The element of survival plays a role in these cases.

Operation of the Gang: Prescribed Behavior for Members For twenty-five of the gangs on which information was obtained for this variable, a prescribed pattern of behavior was identifiable. The essential elements are present in all twenty-five of these gangs. Loyalty to the gang and allegiance to its members is accompanied by a code of secrecy and an outwardly cooperative attitude toward prison authorities, who in reality are resented. This posture reflects the gang member's basic position, which is placing himself where he can dominate and control others and, in particular, run the prison rackets—primarily the drug traffic within the institution. To intimidate and be feared by other inmates and staff is the model role for all gang members.

Maintaining Order, Loyalty, and Obedience   The most frequently used tactics to maintain order, loyalty, and obedience are fear, intimidation, threats of violence, and violence itself directed against those outside the gang and against members who have turned against the gang. Within the gang, strict adherence to the gang's code of behavior and the peer pressure that is exerted on all members by other members appear to be a significant force in maintaining gang solidarity.

Without exception, violence or the threat of violence is the most prevalent and powerful factor in the maintenance of the gang. It is expressed in a total disregard for human life. The sanctions imposed by the government for killing another inmate are of no consequence to the gang member who is a "true believer." Being uncontrolled by the rules, laws, and sanctions that influence most other people's behavior, the gang member operates not only outside the law but also outside the consequences of violating the law. The gang member maintains order by controlling others with his uncontrollable behavior. Psychologically amoral and psychopathically oriented, the gang member is not deterred by legitimate formal sanction.

Gang Values   While there are some minor variations in emphasis, all gangs share some common values that can be expressed in terms of power and prestige. These are measured by their ability to control other inmates and specific activities within the institution. Money, drugs, and property represent tangible symbols of the ability to exercise control and to dominate others. Prestige comes from the acquisition of power and is also expressed in terms of the premium placed on "ganghood"—the sense of belonging that is reflected in the macho image projected and by tattoos, attire, and symbols. These indicators reflect the value that is placed on dominating and controlling other inmates and the prison environment.

Noncriminal Activities   One of the distinguishing characteristics of the prison gang is the virtual absence of any noncriminal, nondeviant activities. Gang members engage in institutional pastimes—weightlifting being one of the more notable—but in general all of their activities are criminal or deviant in nature. The pursuit of ganghood is analogous to the lifestyle of the career criminal. The gang member is completely immersed in being a career prison gangster, leaving little time and less inclination for other asocial behavior.

Leaving the Gang

In nearly two-thirds of the prison gangs on which information was reported, membership is perceived as a lifetime commitment to the gang. Leaving the gang is an act of betrayal, and, in many cases, the consequences are harsh. Twenty-three gangs fall into the lifelong category, where the only reputed way out is natural death or murder. In reality, the consequences do not seem to be as brutal. Gang members at all levels frequently leave the gang when they leave prison without suffering these consequences. Others seek safety in a protective-custody unit rather than face the possible consequences for their defection. Some gang members, including those in high leadership positions, exchange information about gang members and gang activities for favorable treatment from law enforcement or correctional agencies. Even these "rollovers" are sometimes able to remain in the general population of the prison by virtue of their prior status within the gang, but most "rollovers" seek and receive a high degree of protection from possible harm at the hands of other inmates.

CTQ

Is it possible for prison officials to eliminate the influence of gangs in prisons?

INSTITUTIONAL PROGRAMS AND SERVICES

Educational Programs

Of the prison programs available for inmates, education is probably the most important, as (1) academic skills (reading, writing, and math) are fundamental to achieving success in the labor force, and (2) a large proportion of the inmate population is deficient in these skills.[24] Almost all correctional institutions offer some type of educational programming (see Figure 12.7). The range of programs available is usually related to the institution's size, security level, location, and the characteristics of its inmates.[25] One study found that 304,727 inmates, constituting about 26 percent of the prison population, participated in education programs in 1996.[26] According to Steve Steurer, director of the Correctional Educational Association, "If the number of eligible inmates enrolled in these programs seems small, it may be because the correctional budget has been cut dramatically in the last few years."[27] Steurer contends that most inmates would enroll in correctional education programs if they were available. Twenty-six out of 43 jurisdictions reported that they had waiting lists for inmates wanting to enroll in classes.[28] Nearly half of all inmates participate in academic education during their prison stay, and about one-third are involved in vocational training.[29]

FIGURE 12.7

Education is one of the most important prison programs for inmates. Here three young Hispanic women work in a computer class to develop skills that will help them gain access to employment when they are released.

Courtesy of A. Ramey/PhotoEdit.

Adult Basic Education and Literacy Programs Adult basic education (ABE) programs for inmates have been the mainstays of correctional education. They stress literacy and mathematical skills, science, and social science as a foundation for further education and training.[30]

Literacy programs are not always distinguishable from ABE efforts because they sometimes have similar components. Basic literacy programs focus on providing basic skills to low-level readers and nonreaders. These programs vary, but they are usually personalized in their approach to learning.

One-on-one **peer tutoring,** in which inmates tutor other inmates, and volunteer tutoring often supplement classroom work when funds are scarce or to reach inmates who will not attend school.[31] Community volunteers have also assisted in inmate basic literacy programs. They have the added advantage of providing inmates with free-world contacts. An estimated two-thousand volunteers from national organizations, including Literacy Volunteers of America, currently provide tutoring in local and state adult and juvenile facilities. Many local organizations, such as religious groups, also furnish tutors to assist inmates.[32]

GED Programs Although programs vary from state to state, most **general equivalency diploma (GED) programs** focus on further development of reading, language

CTQ

Are so many prison inmates deficient in academic skills because they lacked the motivation to develop these skills before they were in prison, or are their deficiencies the result of environmental factors beyond their control?

IN THE WORKPLACE

CORRECTIONAL COUNSELOR

Responsible for professional counseling work providing rehabilitation services to audit offenders incarcerated in jail or a correctional facility. Performs a variety of duties, including the following: conducts individual counseling sessions with assigned inmates, develops treatment programs based on counseling sessions, assesses inmate progress toward resocialization and compliance with treatment program recommendations, participates in case conferences regarding treatment alternatives. Minimum qualifications are as follows: age 21, high school diploma or equivalent.

arts, composition, and mathematical skills. This provides an opportunity for inmates to use their time in prison to remediate their educational deficits and become more employable upon release.[33]

Life Skills Programs A major factor in the incarceration of most offenders is their inability to function effectively in society.[34] For many, this may be due to deficiencies in basic academic skills; for others, however, a lack of basic life skills may also be a major contributing factor.

The basic *life skills programs* offered in prisons include the following topics:

- *Consumer skills,* such as money management, comparative shopping, understanding labels and bills, using credit, and shopping for food, housing, clothing, and transportation.
- *The use of community resources,* such as using the telephone, obtaining help from social service agencies, interpreting postal forms, using the library, and finding child care.
- *Health and safety skills,* such as reading warnings, using prescription drugs, practicing first aid, and maintaining a balanced diet.
- *Parenting and family skills* (sometimes included under health skills), such as child-rearing practices, understanding child and spouse abuse and the things that lead to them, and finding alternative ways to settle conflicts.
- *Civic skills,* such as passing a driver's test, registering to vote, interpreting legal forms, filling out tax forms, and understanding the Bill of Rights.
- *Employability/job search skills,* such as career/job awareness, the use of classified ads, writing business letters and résumés, filling out applications, interview techniques, and appropriate behaviors on the job.[35]

Vocational Education Programs The work histories of most inmates show that they have usually been employed at low-paying, low-status jobs with high and fast turnover rates or have never been employed. *Vocational education programs* are thought to be the best vehicles for breaking the cycle of recidivism.[36] These programs are aimed at providing inmates with contemporary marketable skills relating to specific jobs on the outside.

Prison Work Programs

Prison work programs for inmates consists of two general types of jobs: those that maintain the institution (preparing meals, cleaning the dormitories) and those that are industrial or productive in nature. Work in prison serves several functions: It keeps the prison running, keeps inmates busy, saves the state money, produces goods and services used by other institutions and governmental agencies, and teaches a useful skill. These purposes make work a necessary and important part of any prison's work program.

In the United States, inmates have traditionally been occupied in work either related to the maintenance or sustenance of the institution or in item-producing industries. The rest of this section discusses prison maintenance work programs and those that help the community.

Prison Maintenance Programs Correctional facilities require a variety of maintenance tasks and services to function. While civilians could be employed to do this work, inmates have traditionally done it because they are an available and less costly source of labor. Such work also occupies their time, which reduces problems associated with idleness. These jobs include janitorial work; maintenance and repair of the physical plant and equipment; food preparation and service; nonconfidential clerical and stenographic work; repair, laundering, and cleaning of clothing; working as medical and dental assistants; landscaping; power plant operation; teaching; and serving as orderlies. Inmates may also perform domestic, maintenance, and other functions at the warden's house, assistant warden's house, and correctional officers' quarters.

The scarcity of prison industry jobs and other work and programming tends to result in overassignment of inmates to these activities. The result is that two, three, or even more people may be working at a job that would normally only need one person.

Agricultural, Forestry, and Road Work Activities   The employment of inmates in agricultural, forestry, and road work activities has long been a part of the prison system, especially in southern institutions. This work includes picking cotton, cutting lumber, harvesting crops, building roads, fighting fires, raising livestock, and maintaining parks and state buildings.

Recreational Programs

Recreational activities form an important part of prison programming and have a number of benefits essential to successful prison management. Recreational and leisure-time programs encourage inmates to make constructive use of their free time, offering movies, games, sports, social activities, arts and hobby crafts, wellness programs, and other group and individual activities. They address inmates' interests from the youngest to the oldest, and they reflect gender differences. The expected objectives of a complete recreational program are to (1) keep inmates constructively occupied and reduce idleness; (2) provide for the physical, emotional, and social well-being of inmates; (3) encourage and assist inmates in adopting healthy daily lifestyle traits through participation in physical fitness and health education programs; and (4) reduce the need for inmate medical treatment.

Tougher sentencing laws have resulted in inmates serving longer sentences, which has led to a reexamination of prison recreation. With a growing population serving determinate sentences, programs must be designed to meet the needs of male and female inmates. Further, the graying of the inmate population has resulted in the need for leisure programs specifically aimed at chronic-care, nonambulatory inmates with a variety of medical restrictions. Women and men are different, and recreational programs must reflect these differences. A general model for today's inmate leisure activities is built around four dimensions: social, physical, psychological, and health promotion and disease prevention. These programs also provide a means for developing social and interpersonal skills.

> **CTQ**
>
> Do you believe that incarcerated repeat offenders should be required to do hard manual labor as punishment for their repeat offenses, or should they be given the opportunity to develop job skills for when they are eventually released?

Treatment Programs

Mental health, cognitive and behavioral modification, and drug treatment programs represent the major forms of treatment available to inmates.

Mental Health Programs   The courts have made no distinction between the right to health care and the right to mental care for psychiatric or psychological impairments.[37] Thus, courts see deliberate indifference to serious psychological needs of inmates as unconstitutional. Court rulings have provided some guidance how this standard is to be defined. Conditions such as acute depression, nervous collapse, and paranoia are considered sufficiently dramatic to represent serious medical needs. Nevertheless, the "courts continue to rely heavily on [the] . . . judgment [of mental health professionals] to determine whether care is adequate and defer to those judgments except in the most gross circumstances"—that is, when failure to respond to special needs produces unnecessary suffering.[38] The basic components of a correctional mental health treatment system include the following:

- A systematic program for screening and evaluating inmates to identify those needing treatment
- Treatment programs that entail more than segregation and close supervision of inmate clients
- Sufficient numbers of appropriately trained mental health professionals
- Maintenance of accurate, complete, and confidential records of the treatment process
- Avoidance of medication in dangerous amounts, by dangerous methods, or without appropriate supervision and evaluation

- A separate program for identifying, treating, and supervising inmates with suicidal tendencies[39]

Treatment for the Seriously Mentally Ill Major mental illnesses, which can include schizophrenia, major depression, bipolar disorder, and other psychoses, are seriously disabling and chronic in nature. These brain disorders often have their origin in biochemical or neurological abnormalities. Sometimes mental illness also is caused by head injury. The brains of mentally ill individuals function differently from those of others.[40]

The two main treatment methods for serious illness are medication and placement in a therapeutic environment. Through the classification process, mentally ill inmates can be identified and recommended for medication, treatment, counseling, or placement in special mental health units. Often, mentally ill inmates receive treatment in separate units or a hospital. Because of the often disruptive behaviors caused by mental illness, separate mental health units are desirable. Although most prison systems have established specialized programs and units for mentally ill inmates who exhibit severe symptoms, lack of space often results in inmates with less severe symptoms being returned too quickly to the general population.[41]

Standard correctional discipline practices seldom work when applied to seriously mentally ill inmates with behavior problems. Training of correctional officers and the establishment of a continuum of care for mentally ill inmates will result in less institutional disruption and more humane treatment for individuals with serious brain disorders.[42]

Drug Treatment Another aspect of prison medical care is treatment for substance abusers, especially drug offenders. It has been estimated that more than 80 percent of all inmates have serious substance abuse problems; however, only one in ten have received treatment for their drug abuse since admission to prison.[43] The likelihood of an inmate receiving substance abuse treatment increases the longer he or she remains in prison, and thus the proportion of inmates who will receive treatment prior to release will undoubtedly increase.

CTQ

Should nonviolent drug abusers be confined to prison, or do you believe that other less punitive and less expensive alternatives should be employed?

Religious Programs

Although churches have historically provided asylum for accused individuals and religion has often tempered the treatment of criminals, the most direct influence of religion has been through the work of chaplains.[44] In the United States, as prisons developed, chaplains visited offenders or became regular members of the prison staff. They were the earliest paid noncustodial staff and provided education and counseling in addition to religious programs.[45]

Chaplains counsel inmates either individually or in a group setting, and these sessions may focus on religious as well as secular concerns. Inmates who seek help in dealing with their problems from prison counselors, particularly mental health professionals, are more likely to be seen as "crazy" by their fellow inmates because of the common view that anyone seeking this kind of help must be severely disturbed. In contrast, going to a counseling session with a chaplain is not seen as visiting the "shrink" because of the religious context in which these sessions are held. Also, chaplains may refer inmates to receive other types of treatment. The important role played by chaplains in inmate treatment has led some states to recognize them as integral members of treatment teams.

ELDERLY MALE PRISONERS

The proportion of prisoners in the nation's institution who are elderly is rapidly increasing, in part due to the tougher long-term sentences inherent in the current "get tough on crime" stance, but also in part due to the general aging of the general population in America (see Figure 12.8). At least one in ten (about 125,000 inmates) are now age 50 or older.[46] The rate of increase in the number of older inmates (age 50 or older) in Florida already exceeds that of younger offenders.

Elderly male prisoners are more likely to have committed crimes such as homicide, manslaughter, and sexual offenses. They are less likely to be imprisoned for robbery and burglary. Because of their significantly longer sentences, elderly inmates may be concentrated in prisons well beyond their proportions in the civilian population, which will pose problems for them as well as prison administrators. First, they will have health problems and will need preventive health care programs that, if not provided, could be a source of considerable litigation costs. At the very least, they will suffer from depression and differing nutritional needs (less protein, fewer calories, and more soft food and fiber). Because taste sensations decline with aging, the elderly will request food richer in seasonings and will have a decrease in gastric acid and increase in gas production and constipation. Special diets will be needed.

In addition, growing old in prison means having to avoid exploitation and violence by younger inmates,[47] having to adjust new personal needs to prison life, and not having suitable programs (recreational, educational, or housing). Vulnerability to victimization, frailty, and isolation from outside relatives and friends will take their toll, as will fear of death, hopelessness, and being unable to cope when released.

Health care costs will increase significantly for hypertension, diabetes, stroke, cancer, and emphysema. Glasses, dentures, kidney dialysis, and heart surgery will also be required. It has been estimated that by 2005, health care costs for elderly inmates will increase fourteenfold.[48] Many prisons will become geriatric centers,[49] and special staff as well as staff training will be necessary to meet the needs of this special problem segment of the nation's offenders.[50]

SEXUALITY IN PRISONS

The value structure of the lower-class subcultures found in prison, regardless of their ethnic background, places extreme emphasis on maintaining and safeguarding the male inmate's manhood and manliness—his machismo. Moral considerations hold lesser weight in this perspective. The primary result of this role maintenance is an extreme dichotomy of sexual script. Homosexuals and vulnerable, heterosexual "kids" are categorized as female or feminine, and are encouraged or forced to adopt feminized roles and behaviors. The "marked" men who succumb to this sexual pressure are tolerated, since by conforming to the role of the woman they protect (and enhance) the masculine image of the man with whom they have sex.[51]

A further characteristic of this pattern is the distinction drawn between the dominant partner (the "inserter") and the submissive partner (the "insertee"). As long as a participant maintains a dominant role by either performing anal penetration on another inmate or by being orally copulated by another inmate, there is no social sanction against him. In these sexual roles, his basic masculine image remains intact, even though he has participated in a sexual act with another male. To the dominant partner's way of thinking, he is still "all" man. This type of convict—the jocker, stud, or "straight who uses," as he is commonly referred to in prison jargon—is often viewed by prison officials and correctional officers as homosexual, since he is engaging in homosexual acts. However, from the perspective of the submissive homosexual or the heterosexual youngster with whom he engages in sex, however, the dominant partner is viewed as heterosexual (or straight "trade"). For both partners in the sexual act, the dominant partner is seen as maintaining a masculine identity. The jocker's sexual behavior, therefore, can be viewed as *situational* homosexuality. He attempts to replicate the sexual role outside prison, treating his sexual partner as a surrogate female.

What develops is an ambiguity of labels. The jocker sees himself as either heterosexual or bisexual, his submissive partner sees him as heterosexual, and the prison guards consider him homosexual. Because of his ambiguity, when we refer to an inmate's sexual orientation we are using the inmate's own subjective self-definition and stance.

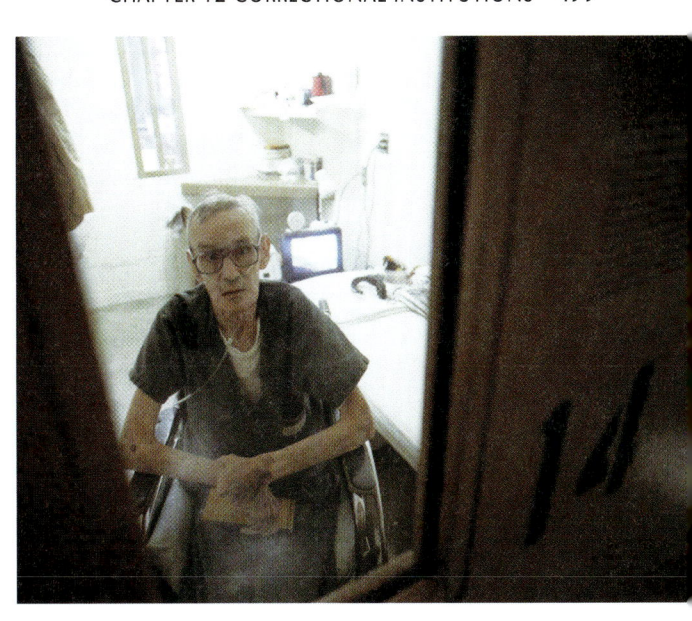

FIGURE 12.8

A 70-year-old convicted sex offender looks out the window of his cell. Like many others, he has numerous health problems and will likely die in prison. This highlights the public health costs associated with elderly prisoners throughout the country.

Courtesy of Sean Cayton/The Image Works.

CTQ

What else would you do administratively to deal with the problems of elderly male prisoners?

Because of the more dominant convict's need to maintain, and often prove, his masculinity, there develops a pattern of sexual aggression and a convict sexual code that defines how sex in prison operates. This code tolerates both the homosexuals and the "kids," as long as they accept the scripts dictated to them by convict subculture. Those homosexuals and "punks" who attempt to challenge this role specification are often even further victimized, although if an inmate "shows some heart" or holds his own," he is often not "hit upon" or "turned out" (forced to have sex against his will). On the other hand, some convicts view men who challenge the convict as conquests.

Tattooing is another statement of manhood. Some inmates are excellent tattoo artists and earn good money tattooing other inmates. Most of the tattoos are quite garish and gruesome. They often include heavily muscled and bearded Vikings, spider webs on the elbows, profane slogans, names of hometowns or barrios in large letters across the shoulders and back or stomach, skulls and crossbones, and decapitated heads dripping blood.

CTQ

How can prison officials best protect inmates from sexual exploitation?

HIV AND AIDS IN PRISON

AIDS is a communicable disease that occurs when the human immune defenses are broken down by the HIV virus and the body becomes unable to combat infections. The virus is transmitted by bodily fluids through sexual contact and by contaminated blood primarily through needle sharing related to intravenous drug use. HIV is difficult to transmit, and scientific evidence shows that it is not passed through casual contact.[52]

The AIDS problem in the United States has of course reached prisons, particularly through offenders with histories of injecting drugs, sharing needles, and engaging in unprotected sexual activities (see Figure 12.9).[53] The overall number, as well as the ethnic, gender, age, and risk-factor distribution of HIV-infected people is relatively well known. Criminal justice officials use a variety of surveys and data analysis to assess the extent of the incarcerated HIV population in different correctional systems and jurisdictions. The sum of these efforts provides a pretty clear picture of how HIV-positive inmates are generally housed together, although not in a particular correctional facility.[54] States with the highest prevalence of HIV in the free-world population have an even higher prevalence in correctional facilities, varying from 14 percent in New York to around 3.5 percent in Florida and 2.4 percent in Texas and California. HIV prevalence in correctional settings reflects the trend in the general population toward increasing rates of infection among women and people of color. Nationwide drug-related arrests and sentencing policies have a notable effect on the number of HIV-positive inmates and on the treatment environment. Because of mandatory sentencing for drug offenses in some states, individuals with HIV infection became concentrated within the prison system. Many of the same factors that put many people at risk for drug-related arrests also put them at risk for HIV infection.

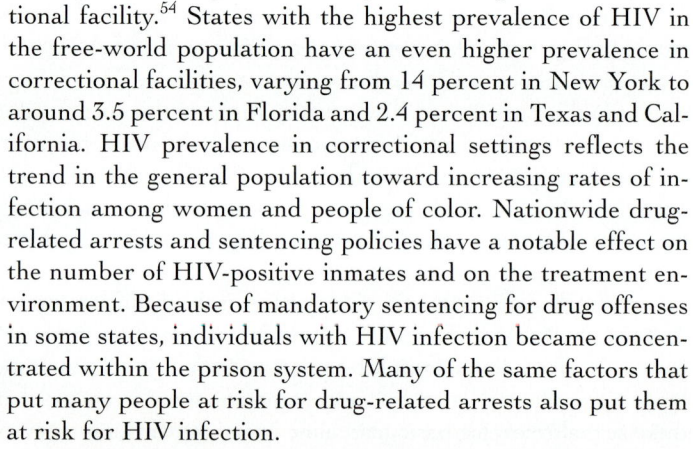

Some states have observed a leveling off of HIV prevalence in their correctional systems in recent years. These may be due to the growing use of alternative sentencing practices in some states, such as community service for a relatively minor drug offense. As a result, some HIV-positive individuals can get care outside the correctional system.[55]

FIGURE 12.9

The AIDS problem in the United States has reached prisons primarily through offenders with histories of injecting drugs, sharing needles, and engaging in unprotected sexual activities. This inmate is infected with the AIDS virus.

Courtesy of A. Ramey/PhotoEdit.

Prevention

Preventing the spread of AIDS is difficult because there is a long incubation period between the time one is infected with HIV and the first outward symptoms. Thus carriers may engage in unsafe drug use and sexual activities without knowing that they are infecting others. Although the overwhelming number of infected offenders received HIV before they were incarcerated, transmission within the institution remains a problem.

In most prisons, educational programs now inform staff and inmates about the disease and the ways in which it is spread. Several observers have suggested that condoms be made available to prisoners so that if they do engage in sexual activity, their behavior will be protected.[56] Advocates of condom distribution assert that sexual behavior is a fact of life in many institutions and that officials should give inmates access to these devices as a means of protecting them from disease. They point to desperate attempts by inmates who "are fashioning makeshift condoms of trash can liners, bread wrappers and other plastic bags," in an attempt to protect their health.[57]

Critics of condom distribution note that sexual activity is prohibited within institutions and that many states have statutes that criminalize homosexual behavior. They argue that this step would imply tacit approval of such conduct by correctional administrators. They are also concerned about how the public might react, and fear that the inmates might use condoms to make weapons or hide contraband.[58]

Jurisdictions that have chosen to distribute condoms report few problems. New York City has not experienced any cases in which inmates used condoms to make weapons or conceal contraband.[59] Inmates received condoms from medical personnel who must dispense AIDS information and counseling about safer sex along with prophylactic devices.[60]

Another facet of prevention has been the testing of all residents and new inmates for the presence of HIV antibodies. Opponents of systemwide testing argue that there is no evidence of higher transmission rates in prisons than in the free community, and thus there is no reason to screen. Further, because it is allegedly impossible to keep test results confidential, infected individuals will be stigmatized while incarcerated and will be discriminated against in connection with insurance, housing, and employment upon release. Finally, policies have been developed to ensure that correctional personnel do not become infected while handling blood or body fluids in the course of their duties. The use of protective covering avoids some needle injuries, and the care and handling of diseased bodies have all become standard operating procedures.[61]

WOMEN IN PRISON

The history of women's institutions reflects the history of women. Because women have long been thought to hold a special place in society, deviant women have been treated differently than both their law-abiding sisters and their male counterparts. In short, female offenders have been perceived as not wholly feminine but definitely not as masculine either. In fact, "from the very beginning, women in prison were treated differently from men who were considered more morally depraved and corrupt and in need of special, closer forms of control and confinement."[62] Some have described these women as "lost," and indeed in both physical surroundings and attitudes toward their redemption, female prisoners have been either brutalized or ignored for the greater part of this country's history.[63] In recent years, some prisons have started treating women inmates in similar ways as male inmates (see Figure. 12.10).

Early Punishments and Places of Confinement

Early English law made it very clear that women and men possessed different rights under the law. Some behavior, such as adultery, was not considered criminal when committed by men or was punished much less severely. For other crimes, however, women may have been punished less often or less severely than men who committed the identical activity.[64] The social order was a male hierarchy; women convicted of several public-order crimes were punished, as were women who were too vocal or too critical of men, and women who were not monogamous. Men who let their wives dominate them or who allowed themselves to be "cuckolded" were also punished:

> Men, for example, might be subjected to a "cuckold's court" or forced to ride backward on a donkey for allowing their wives to cuckold or dominate them. They might also provoke community sanction for overstepping the bounds of appropriate patriarchal domination, when, for example, they beat their wives to excess. It is important to note that it was only when a man grossly

CTQ

Should inmates who have been identified as HIV-positive or as having AIDS be isolated from the general prison population and kept together, or should they be kept in with the general prison population?

WEB

For more information on homosexuality in prisons, **visit our Web site, www.prenhall.com/ territo**.

WEB

For more information on HIV and AIDS in prisons, **visit our Web site, www.prenhall.com/territo**.

CTQ

Do you believe that all inmates should be given condoms on request?

WEB

For more information about women in prison, **visit our Web site, www.prenhall.com/territo**.

FIGURE 12.10

Women inmates at the Maricopa County, Arizona, prison leave the jail for a work detail. This was probably the first female chain gang in American history. The women, who had been in "lock down" for prison rule infractions, were earning their reintegration with other prisoners by working for 30 days in chains.

Courtesy of Agence France Presse/CORBIS.

overstepped the bounds of appropriate chastisement by mutilation or by nearly killing his wife that he might be sanctioned by the community through the performance of a misrule or a charivari.[65]

Women who violated the social order were subject to the dunking stool or more serious punishments.

> The *brank* was an iron cage placed over the head, and most examples incorporated a spike or pointed wheel that was inserted into the offender's mouth in order to "pin the tongue and silence the noisiest brawler." This spiked cage was intended to punish women found to be quarrelsome or not under the proper control of their husbands.[66]

Thus, women were firmly under the control of men, and their behavior judged against the male model of female submissiveness. First her father, and then her husband, had almost total legal control over a woman. Punishment could be imposed whenever the wife or daughter was considered disobedient or unchaste. Women were sent to monasteries when out of control, and husbands turned their errant wives over to bridewells or poorhouses.[67]

Wives had some legal recourse against brutal or improvident husbands, but very little. Thus, if a woman was married to a man who did not give her money to buy food, there was little she could do to provide for herself and her children. Consequently, many imprisoned women were confined for theft or begging. Many succumbed to the only other way females could obtain money: prostitution. Female criminals, when sentenced to bridewells, often received substantially longer sentences than men.[68]

Even when incarcerated, women did not escape their female duties. Women in poorhouses and bridewells were expected to do the cooking and cleaning, spinning, and sewing required for the institution.[69] Other uses of incarcerated women involved their sexual role. The following describes what awaited women who were transported to Australia in the early 1800s:

> In 1812, the Committee on Transportation observed that women were ". . . indiscriminately given to such of the inhabitants as demanded them, and were in general received as prostitutes than as servants . . . " The British government transported women for the purpose of preventing unrest among the free and convict population by providing convict Women as sexual commodities."[70]

Descriptions of early places of confinement for women indicate that there was little regard for their safety or health. Before separation of the sexes in Europe and the United States, men and women were housed together in large rooms where the strong preyed upon the weak and each individual's life was made bearable only by the resources each received from family members or could acquire by begging, bartering, or stealing from other prisoners. After the separation of the sexes, women's lives in prison were only marginally better.

Freedman describes early institutions for women as overcrowded and filthy. In the 1820s, a Philadelphia jail had seven women in a cellar with only two blankets among them; an Albany jail placed fifteen women in one room. Freedman also describes the New York City Tombs jail as having forty-two cells to hold seventy women in 1838.[71] In the early 1800s incarcerated women were found only in jails, because prisons were built solely for male prisoners at that time.[72] In 1825, separate quarters for women were built at a Baltimore prison, and in 1835, officials at Ossining State Penitentiary (Sing-Sing) built a separate unit for women.[73]

Reformatories for Women

The pressure exerted by female reformers for the separation of female prisoners from men, control over women's prisons by female staff and management, and provision of different women's care finally led to the establishment of completely separate institutions:

Male prejudices, male exploitation, and male-dominated institutions, the reformers believed, denied justice to female criminals. Thus, they reasoned, if male influences were removed by placing the female criminal in the hands of her sisters, virtue might be restored. Female officers would provide the salutary influences of education, religion, and love to redeem the female criminal class.[74]

In the 1800s, the female reformers were finally successful in their drive to establish separate women's institutions, run by women. In the 1870s, separate institutions in Indiana and Massachusetts were built, which employed female staff. In 1881, the New York House of Refuge for female misdemeanants was created, and in 1900, Bedford Hills was built.[75] Houses of refuge were designated for young women (as young as 12 or 15) who had been convicted of minor crimes, such as "petit larceny, habitual drunkenness, or being a common prostitute, of frequenting disorderly houses or houses of prostitution or of any misdemeanor," and who were "not insane or mentally or physically incapable of being substantially benefited" by the discipline found there.

Four factors contributed to the women's prison movement: first, an apparent increase in female criminality during the 1860s, from prostitution and abortion associated with the Civil War; second, women's Civil War social service experience; third, the development of the charity organization movement and of a prison reform movement that emphasized the investigation of criminality and the reformatory ideal; and fourth, an embryonic feminist analysis of women's place in U.S. society.[76]

Ironically, the first completely separate institution for women, run by women, did not follow the reformatory ideal. In 1874, the Female Prison and Reformatory Institution for Girls and Women was opened in Indiana. Here, the reformatory concept was only partially followed. The institution received only felons; it did not follow the cottage system.[77] In fact, the first prisons for women in Indiana and Massachusetts were described as castlelike—"grim, dark 'bastille-like' structure(s)."[78] However, the women in Indiana did have separate rooms and wore gingham dresses instead of prison uniforms.

The Massachusetts prison, opened after a long delay, had three-hundred individual cells and two fifty-bed dormitories. Run by a woman with an entirely female staff, this institution, like others, was under the authority of a man:

> At first, men maintained ultimate authority over the Indiana and Massachusetts prisons, and male physicians served in New York and Indiana. Their presence contradicted the theory that women's problems, whether medical or emotional, could best be treated by members of the same sex. Other men worked at each institution, not only to calm fears that inmates would overrun their too-gentle female keepers, but also to perform engineering, firefighting, and carpentry tasks for which there were few women available.[79]

It was a struggle to retain female supervisors once they were in place. For instance, Freedman writes that Clara Barton was superintendent of Framingham for nine months in order to prevent the governor from appointing a man in 1882.[80] Low pay, uncomfortable living conditions, and questionable status made qualified women difficult to find and keep.[81]

Female reformers of the late 1800s who argued for reformatories for women agreed that women would be useful in the care and treatment of female prisoners. Brockway, for instance, advocated using women to supervise women because of their "sisterly care, counsel and sympathy." He advocated the use of reformatories for women, which could provide a "family life, where they shall receive intellectual, moral, domestic, and industrial training, under the influence, example and sympathy of refined and virtuous women."[82] Brockway had himself dealt with female prisoners and had developed his idea of grading and limited freedom with female prisoners in a House of Shelter and the Detroit House of Correction from 1865 to 1869. He later implemented these ideas at Elmira with male prisoners.[83]

Those who were given reformatory terms were carefully chosen. Generally, they were young, relatively unhardened, guilty of only misdemeanors, or victims of difficult circumstances. Most were under age 25, white, and native-born. Two-thirds had been married at some time, but were widowed, divorced, or separated. Most had no prior convictions, and their crimes were minor: More than half had been incarcerated for drunkenness and prostitution.[84] Rafter writes that some of the women sent to Albion were there not for prostitution but because "exasperated mothers or embarrassed husbands" charged them with sexual misconduct.[85] It is instructive to note that these "new" penal institutions were being used to control women's behavior in much the same way as some of the earliest English prisons. In short, prisoners were usually young, women serving short sentences for having been convicted of various moral offenses.[86]

Women in reformatories were younger than those in custodial institutions. Rafter reports that half the women in custodial institutions were between ages 31 and 50, whereas reformatory (Albion) women were between ages 15 and 30.[87]

The institutions offered domestic training and very little else. Academic classes were underfunded; industrial training was opposed by civilian industry; and only a small number of women could get jobs in skilled trades.[88] Many women were trained in the "domestic services": in Massachusetts, an indenture law was passed in 1879, and 1,500 women went into service in family homes.[89] Rafter writes: "Albion provided trained, inexpensive household help. It was the institution's policy to 'place our girls in the home of a woman who will take a motherly interest in them.'"[90] One-quarter of the prisoners were paroled directly to live in domestic positions. In fact, parole revocation usually occurred because of sexual misconduct or "sauciness" to employers.

Women incarcerated in early reformatories were not serious criminals and did not often pose a security risk for the staff, but those who did found that punishment in a women's reformatory was the same as in any prison. "Dungeons," rooms with no ventilation or light, were available for those who attacked officers, destroyed property, or threatened safety.[91] Some serious disturbances occurred in 1888 in Framingham, Massachusetts, and in 1899 in Hudson, New York.[92] These disturbances may have been caused by inefficient security and overcrowding. A more prevalent problem, according to early discipline reports, might have been homosexuality between the races. Because of this "unnatural attraction," staff wanted to segregate the races in Bedford Hills and other institutions.[93]

Overall, the interaction between female staff and female prisoners was one of mutual dependency. Freedman writes that the prisoners transferred their dependency needs to the female staff members. The staff became surrogate mothers to their female dependents. The staff, in turn, needed the prisoners, because they were the only appropriate outlet for female professionals' training and energy.[94] Women who studied female prisoners were outcasts from the male profession of medicine and science.[95] Some institutions, such as Bedford Hills, became centers of research on female criminality. Interestingly, these female researchers pointed out factors in crime causation, such as poor family lives and temptation, years ahead of their "discovery" by male criminologists—yet this earlier work has been largely ignored.

Women's Prisons Today

Something dramatic started happening in women's prisons in the 1980s: During that decade, the number of women in U.S. prisons jumped dramatically. In 1980, there were just over 12,000 women in U.S. state and federal prisons. By 1997, that number had increased to almost 80,000. Thus, in about a decade and a half, the number of women incarcerated in the nation's prisons had increased sixfold.[96]

This astonishing increase should not be seen simply as a reflection of the increase in male incarceration during the same period. Women's "share" of total imprisonment has more than doubled in the past three decades, from 3 percent in 1970 to 6.4 percent in 1997.

The rate of increase in the number of women in prison also has outpaced that of men; since 1985, the number of female inmates has increased by an average of 11.1 percent annually, higher than the 7.6 percent average increase in male inmates. In 1996 alone, the number of women in prison grew at a rate nearly double that of men (9.5 percent, compared to 4.8 percent for men).

Similar patterns have been seen in adult jails: Women constituted 7 percent of the population in the mid-1980s, but today they account for 11 percent of the population. Likewise, the rate of increase in incarceration of women in local jails since 1985 has been 9.9 percent, compared to 6.4 percent for men.

Finally, the rate of women's imprisonment is at a historic high, increasing from a low of six sentenced female inmates per 100,000 U.S. women in 1925 to 54 per 100,000 in 1997. In 1997, California led the nation with 11,076 women in prison, followed by Texas with 10,549, New York with 3,584, and Florida with 3,404.

The correctional establishment, long used to forgetting about women, was taken almost completely by surprise when this change started. Initially, female inmates were housed virtually anywhere (remodeled hospitals, abandoned training schools, and covered motels) as jurisdictions struggled to cope with the soaring increase in women's imprisonment. Increasingly, though, states have begun to open new units and facilities to house female inmates. Between 1930 and 1950, the United States opened approximately two to three facilities for women each decade, but during the 1980s alone, more than 34 percent were opened. By 1990, the nation had seventy-one women-only facilities; in 1995, the number of women's facilities had jumped to 104—an increase of 46 percent.

Women's Criminal Activity

Is the dramatic increase in women's imprisonment a response to a women's crime problem spiraling out of control? Empirical indicators give little evidence of this. For example, the total number of arrests of adult women, which might be seen as a measure of women's criminal activity, increased by 31.4 percent between 1987 and 1996, while the number of women in prison increased by 159 percent.

And despite media images of hyperviolent female offenders, the proportion of women doing time in state prisons for violent offenses has been declining steadily from about half (48.9 percent) in 1979 to just over a quarter (27.6) in 1997. In states such as California, which runs the two largest women's prisons in the nation, the decline is even sharper. In 1992, 16 percent of the women admitted to the California prison system were incarcerated for violent crimes, compared to 37.2 percent in 1982.

A recent study by the Bureau of Justice Statistics (BJS) indicates that growth in the number of violent offenders has been the major factor for population growth in men's prisons, but in the women's prison population, "drug offenders were the largest source of growth." One explanation, then, is that the "war on drugs" has become a largely unannounced war on women. In 1979, one in ten women in prison was doing time for drugs. Today, drug offenders account for more than a third of the women's prison population (37.4 percent). Finally, while the intent of "get tough" policies was to rid society of drug dealers and so-called drug kingpins, more than a third (35.9 percent) of the women serving time for drug offenses in state prisons are there on charges of possession.[97]

Women's Adaptation to Imprisonment

Inmate adaptations to prison vary from facility to facility, depending on such factors as institutional and administrative programs, personal philosophy, and inmate characteristics. These adaptations can be grouped under the concept of **prisonization,** which describes the degree to which inmates participate in and adopt the prison subculture. Research related to the adaptation of women has been criticized for focusing principally on homosexuality and for tending to assume that the variables involved in the men's prison subcultures are applicable to women's prisons.[98] The lack of applicability of the variables is likely a result of the different social roles played by men and women and the manner in which these roles influence adaptive reactions to prison.[99]

Involvement in Pseudofamilies Based on a study of the Women's Federal Reformatory in West Virginia, Giallombardo concluded that women in prison developed links with each other as "family" networks and in homosexual marriages.[100] Referred to as *pseudofamilies,* these groups tended to satisfy the social, psychological, and physiological needs related to the cultural roles women were expected to play. Women participating in these "families" adopted a variety of roles. Within these primary "family"

> **CTQ**
>
> Do you believe that the types of crimes women commit today are different from the ones that they might commit in the future, and will they more closely resemble those committed by men?

groups, women formed strong bonds and had little need to identify with the larger inmate subculture. This bonding has been interpreted as an adaptation to the way in which women in general society sustain themselves emotionally. These family-type groupings involved close emotional relationships not usually found in men's prisons.[101]

The Nature and Amount of Homosexuality

In women's prisons, homosexual relations are generally noncoercive and involve close emotional ties. These liaisons range from "marriage" to "dating" to "tricking" (indiscriminate sexual activity, perhaps for economic gain). The form of the relationships also varies, with some pairs involving a "male" and "female" role and others making no such distinction. In pairs with role differentiation, the woman assuming the male role often takes on the characteristics ascribed to it (for example, she is domineering and dresses and grooms more like a man). Several studies have examined various aspects of female inmates' homosexual activities.[102] They report levels of participation in homosexual behavior ranging from about 20 percent to more than 85 percent. Most women engaging in it were younger, were more likely to be black, and had had their first homosexual encounters outside prison.[103]

Most recent studies suggest a much lower incidence of homosexuality than reported earlier. This difference, according to Pollock-Byrnemay, may be related to "the almost prurient curiosity of so many [early] researchers in the females' sexual identity and activity."[104]

CTQ — How do female homosexuals in prison differ from male homosexuals in prison?

Programs for Women

Programs for women in prison fall into five major categories. The first is maintenance—activities such as clerical work in administration, food service for inmates and staff, and general cleaning and maintenance work around the grounds. The second category is education. As is true of men in prison, most female prisoners need remedial education, although a few could take advantage of college programs if any were offered. The third category of programs is vocational training; ordinarily, in prisons for women, these programs fall into sex-typed categories, such as cosmetology and office skills. The fourth category is designed to rehabilitate the prisoner through personal growth or individual change, for example, group therapy, transactional analysis, or Alcoholics Anonymous. The fifth category is medical care. Arguably not a program at all but a needed service, medical care is included here because it is usually placed under the treatment branch of institutional management.

Sexual Contact between Staff and Inmates

With the advent of correctional administrators integrating male staff into women's facilities, there has been a dramatic increase in prosecutions of staff for sexual assault as well as lawsuits by female inmates claiming a violation of their Eighth Amendment rights by failure to protect them from sexual assaults. Clearly, care in selection, training, and supervision of staff is essential in dealing with such claims and avoiding potential liability. Besides considerations of professionalism, an additional incentive for staff to avoid such sexual contact has been the enactment of statutes in some states that make even consensual sexual contact with an inmate by an employee of the Department of Corrections a violation of the law. For example, a statute passed in Michigan several years ago makes such contact a misdemeanor punishable by up to two years of imprisonment. Such a law makes the argument that a female inmate enticed a male correctional officer a moot issue.[105]

CTQ — If only female correctional officers were permitted to supervise female prisoners, would that eliminate or reduce sexual contact between staff and inmates?

PRIVATE PRISONS

Practitioners, activists, policymakers, and scholars have been searching for ways to revive America's ailing correctional complex. In the 1960s and early 1980s, one popular answer was to stop building secure institutions and to deinstitutionalize offenders—"Tear down the walls!" In the 1980s, amid the ongoing search for meaningful alternatives to incarceration, proposals were made to give the private sector a significant role in the administration, finance, and construction of correctional facilities and programs—"Sell the walls!"

By the beginning of 1987, three states had enacted laws authorizing privately operated state correction facilities, while more than a dozen were actively considering the

FIGURE 12.11

A Houston, Texas, processing center facility administered by the Corrections Corporation of America, a private firm contracted by the state.

Courtesy of Brett Coomer/AP/Wide World Photos.

option. In 1985, Corrections Corporation of America (CCA), a leader among the twenty or so firms that have entered the "prison market," made a bid to take over the entire Tennessee prison system. Though this bid was unsuccessful, CCA now operates several correctional facilities, among them a Federal Bureau of Prisons halfway house, two facilities for the detention of illegal aliens, and a 370-bed maximum-security jail in Bay County, Florida. On January 6, 1986, U.S. Corrections Corporation opened a 300-bed private state prison, a minimum-security facility in Marion, Kentucky, for inmates who are within three years of meeting the parole board.

More than three dozen states now contract with private firms for at least one correctional service or program (see Figure 12.11). The most frequent contracts involve medical and mental health services, community treatment centers, construction, remedial education, drug treatment, college courses, staff training, vocational training, and counseling.

Today more than two million people are behind bars in the United States. Thus, one of the main reasons being suggested for privatization is to deal with this increasing population while at the same time attempting to reduce costs and maintain the quality of service.

The following represent some of the arguments for and against privatization. The section titled "Arguments for Privatization" was written by Charles W. Thomas, a professor of criminology at the Center for Studies in Criminology and Law at the University of Florida; The section titled "Arguments against Privatization" was written by Stephen Ingley, executive director of the American Correctional Association.

Arguments for Privatization

Powerful groups such as the American Federation of State County and Municipal Employees, the American Jail Association, and the National Sheriffs' Association were vehemently opposed to privatization even before its appeal began to explode during the late 1980s. Although their lobbying often reflected nothing more than an interest in preserving the monopoly government agencies enjoyed before privatization arrived on the scene, some of their concerns have received careful attention by everyone in corrections. Their major arguments claim that privatization is unconstitutional, and that private firms cannot deliver promised decreases in correctional costs without reducing the quality of services.

Perhaps because I teach correctional law, I remained unpersuaded by claims that the sky would fall if "privateers" began operating jails and prisons. Even if one were to ignore the less-than-exemplary history of corrections in the United States, one cannot read the facts of recent cases such as *Madrid v. Gomez*—the already infamous Pelican Bay State Prison case—without losing some faith in the value of the status quo. Instead, I thought that privatization deserved the same skeptical treatment public agencies often receive. I also felt that the outcome of the privatization debate should be shaped by hard evidence rather than the rhetorical talents of debaters.

WEB

For more information on the privatization of prisons, **visit our Web site, www.prenhall.com/territo**.

CTQ

Will we ever reach the point where most prisons in the United States are run by private organizations?

Favoring evidence over rhetoric put people like me in an awkward situation in the mid-1980s because little solid data was available. Early developments regarding the private management of local, state, and federal facilities in jurisdictions such as Kentucky, New Mexico, Tennessee, and Texas were positive but too anecdotal to provide a foundation for meaningful generalizations. Today the situation is dramatically different. Since 1990, the capacity of private jails and prisons in operation or under construction has risen from 15,300 to 81,872—an increase of 435 percent. Not one of the more than 100 contract awards has been challenged successfully on legal grounds. Private firms now are responsible for the full-scale operation of virtually every type of adult facility, including both large facilities and facilities housing inmates with maximum-security classifications. Furthermore, of the seventeen firms that have received contracts, some either are or soon will be responsible for more inmates than all but the largest correctional systems. Today, for example, Corrections Corporation of America is operating or constructing facilities with system-rated capacities of 39,580. Only six state systems have larger inmate populations.

Of course, variables such as diversity, growth, and size do not offer direct evidence of cost-effectiveness. However, we now have the benefit of a large body of cost and performance audits, as well as national and international academic research. Evidence has shown a clear pattern of increased frequency of accreditation by the American Correctional Association, decreases in the volume and success of prison-conditions litigation, lower frequencies of escapes and serious disturbances, improvements in programs aimed at reducing recidivism, "customer satisfaction" as reflected by an impressive record of contract renewals, and substantial decreases in both construction and operating costs.

This does not mean that privatization is a magical panacea. It is not. It doesn't mean that privatization initiatives never will fail. Some do. And it doesn't mean that public agencies are inherently less cost-effective than the private sector. However, it does mean that evidence beyond a reasonable doubt has proven that privatization is a viable alternative to a business-as-usual approach in corrections.

To be sure, the appeal of the politics of self-interest persists for those who fear—perhaps correctly—that fair competitions between alternative providers of correctional services will find them holding the short end of the proverbial stick. Change will be painful for those who are not committed to subordinating their special interests to the public interest or who doubt their ability to compete successfully with the private sector. However, the winds of fundamental change in corrections continue to blow strongly—much as they previously did when they reached a broad array of other public-service areas. Privatization focuses our attention on the caliber of services and the cost at which these services are provided. It allows no favored treatment for service providers based merely on their public or private status. It is a reality that has arrived, and it will not be undone by impotent political rhetoric.

Arguments against Privatization

Over the past several years, our nation has engaged in an ongoing dialogue concerning the role of government in our lives and the effectiveness of government versus private operations. Through this discourse, we have begun to see what some might describe as a trend toward privatization. We have observed a tendency toward moving operational control of what was once considered a government duty into the hands of private industry, with the often unfounded belief that the private sector can do a better, less expensive job. Unfortunately, privatization is yet another example of our culture's eagerness for the "quick fix" to issues and problems our country faces. In most instances, this results in reactionary "throw the baby out with the bath water," Band-Aid nonsolutions, and privatization of correctional operations is one of them.

Publications such as *Punishment for Profit: Private Prisons/Public Concerns* by David Schichor (1995) provide evidence of nineteenth-century American correctional history and document the private sector's failure in the area of inmate management. We must ask ourselves if today is any different. Does the private sector operate a better, more cost-effective correctional institution? It is true that private correctional corporations can offer cheaper benefits by replacing government benefits packages with stock options in the company. This is inexpensive for the company, for the only cost is the printing of the stock certificate. Of course, the employee's potential golden years of retirement become subject to the profitability and/or failure of one company—a position I would not wish upon anyone. It also is true that, in some instances, private corrections firms can save time and money because they are not directly accountable to the public. For instance, a government agency often is required to bid on a particular purchase, while a private corporation may be able to avoid this process.

But even when they are armed with these less-than-desirable savings vehicles, there is nothing to suggest that private corporations operate better, more cost-effective correctional facilities. This is evidenced in the August 1996 report from the United States General Accounting Office, titled *Private and Public Prisons: Studies Comparing Operational Costs and/or Quality of Service*. This report, which looks at five studies that have been conducted since 1991, states that "... we could not conclude whether privatization saved money. Similarly, regarding quality of service ... one study (New Mexico) reported equivocal findings, and the other study (Tennessee) reported no difference between the compared private and public facilities."

There is no evidence that private corrections can solve a correctional institution's fiscal or managerial problems, and this is reason enough not to jump "governmental ship." But it's not the only reason. When people say that they support the privatization of jails, they also say and/or acknowledge a great deal more. They affirm that one of the most important jobs in this country—restricting the freedoms of American citizens—should be taken away from the government and placed in the hands of a corporation whose sole purpose is to generate profits for shareholders. They affirm that profit is an acceptable motive for incarceration and often accept that more inmates equals more profits. They agree that private, for-profit, and often publicly held corporations should be granted the authority to use force, including deadly force. They may be under the mistaken and unfortunate impression that all of their liability has been contracted away from them. And they accept that there will be less public accountability, as is evidenced in recent events in Texas. Specifically, the Associated Press (November 6. 1996—Houston) reported numerous escapes and riots, as well as the inability of Texas authorities to prosecute escapees because those from private facilities do not meet "... the offense of escape under Texas law." Private correctional firms often fail to inform the state as to who is being incarcerated in their facilities and for what offenses.

In addition to considering these ethical and technical arguments, answering the question, "What roles should government play in our lives?" is difficult. Although I do not purport to have answered this question, I am confident that maintaining public order and safety clearly falls within the scope of governmental oversight. (If I'm wrong, perhaps we should consider privatizing the United States Armed Forces?)

The grass is not greener on the privatized side. Providing a better correctional tomorrow is a promise that private corrections should not make, for it is one they cannot keep. When you get right down to it, corrections is an expensive, complicated, and dangerous job. It's also a social necessity. Instead of looking for the privatization Band-Aid, we should equip our correctional agencies with the resources they need to carry out their inarguable governmental duty—to protect and to serve.[106]

> **CTQ**
>
> Which of the two arguments presented do you believe is more persuasive in the privatization of jail debate?

SUMMARY

The North American colonists brought with them the harsh penal codes of their homelands. Not until the late 1600s did William Penn take the initial steps that would eventually lead to more humane penal practices and eliminate capital and corporal punishment as sanctions for major crimes.

The monumental penitentiaries still common today in the United States got their start in the first three decades of the nineteenth century. The social planners who designed these prisons had three goals in mind: to remove bad influences; to teach the offender the value of labor and work skills; and to teach the offender about the Scriptures and the principles of right and wrong. The two systems that emerged for meeting these goals were the Pennsylvania system, which was based on solitary confinement, with bench labor within the offender's cell, and the Auburn system, which housed inmates in small cells but confined them only during nonworking hours and on the Sabbath. During working hours, inmates labored in factory like shops. The Auburn system ultimately prevailed in the United States.

Today, the major classifications of correctional institutions are maxi-maxi, maximum security, medium security, and minimum security. Maxi-maxi institutions house hardcore, violent, and incorrigible prisoners. Most have high perimeter security, high internal security, and operating regulations that curtail movement and maximize control. Maximum-security institutions employ full supervision, control, and surveillance of inmates. Medium-security institutions, on the other hand, embody most of the ideals and characteristics of early attempts to reform offenders. Although the top priority in such facilities is still security, intensive rehabilitative efforts are made.

Reception and classification centers are relatively recent additions to the correctional scene. Some are part of larger facilities, and some are completely separate. Most are maximum-security facilities because the propensity of new inmates for escape or violence is generally unknown. The diagnostic procedures in reception centers include medical examinations, psychological testing, and interviews by caseworkers.

Overcrowded prisons may be one of the most urgent problems facing the criminal justice system today. Basically three approaches may be used for dealing with overcrowding: providing more capacity, diverting convicted people to sentences other than prison, and shortening the time served by those who go there.

Riots and disturbances in correctional institutions are a constant and recurring problem. The prison riot can be viewed in a number of ways: to behavioral scientists, a riot may be a form of communication or expression used after less drastic means have proven unsuccessful; to the revolutionary, a riot may be a form of social protest and a tool for radical change; to the media, it's a rare opportunity to portray real-life drama that rivals the best of fiction. To the correctional administrator, however, a prison riot is a challenge to authority and an insurrection that threatens the delicate balance of power in an institution, as well as the lives of those who live and work there.

The phenomenon of prison gangs has become a sensational part of public awareness. These groups are normally clandestine and exclusive; their purposes range from mutual caretaking of members to large profit-making criminal enterprises. Prison gangs are often organized along racial or ethnic lines and deal principally in extortion, drugs, homosexual prostitution, gambling, and protection. Almost without exception, administrators say that gangs are responsible for the majority of drug trafficking in institutions.

Prisons can do much to assist the inmate in making a successful transition into the free world and reduce the possibility of becoming a repeat offender. The various institutional programs and services include educational programs, prison work programs, recreational programs, treatment programs, and religious programs.

The proportion of elderly prisoners in the nation's institutions is rapidly increasing, due to tougher long-term sentences and the aging of the general population in America. Elderly inmates are most likely to have committed crimes such as homicide, manslaughter, and sexual offenses, and are less likely to be in prison for robbery and burglary. Because of the significantly longer sentences, elderly inmates may be concentrated in prisons well beyond their proportion in the civilian population, which will pose problems for them as well as for prison administrators.

Homosexuality is a fact of life in every men's prison in the United States. Typically, there is a convict sexual code that distinguishes dominant partners and submissive partners. One of the hazards associated with homosexuality in prisons is the potential for contracting HIV and AIDS. In most prisons, educational programs inform staff and inmates about the disease and the ways in which it is spread.

Because women have long been thought to hold a special place in society, deviant women have been treated differently not only from their more law-abiding sisters but also their male counterparts. This is reflected in the kinds of violations for which women have traditionally been institutionalized, as well as the administration of the institutions they are confined in. However, a number of factors contributed to the women's prison movement: an apparent rise in female criminality during the 1860s; women's Civil War social service experience; the development of the charity organization and prison reform movements; and an embryonic feminist analysis of women's place in U.S. society.

In the 1980s, the number of women in U.S. prisons jumped dramatically. In 1980 there were just over 12,000 women in U.S. state and federal prisons. By 1997 the number had increased to almost 80,000. In about a decade and a half the number of women incarcerated in the nation's prisons had increased sixfold.

With the advent of correctional administrators integrating male staff into women's facilities there has been a dramatic increase in prosecutions and lawsuits involving sexual assaults on female inmates. Clear care in the selection, training, and supervision of staff is essential in dealing with such claims and avoiding potential liability.

The United States has more people in jail or prison than any other industrialized nation. This has precipitated a serious overcrowding problem, with federal and state prisons currently operating well beyond capacity. Conventional efforts appear unable to cope with the increasing shortage of beds or with inadequate rehabilitation services. One of the bold solutions recommended is to privatize correctional institutions. In this chapter we have discussed the pros and cons of privatization.

DISCUSSION AND REVIEW

1. What were the major features of the Great Law of Pennsylvania?
2. What are the basic differences between the Pennsylvania system of corrections and the Auburn system?
3. Why is it nearly impossible to describe the "typical" maximum-security facility?
4. What is the derivation of the concept of administrative segregation?
5. What was the first modern supermax facility in the United States, and how could its average population be described?
6. What is the philosophy behind the Minnesota correctional facility at Oak Park Heights?
7. What are the major characteristics of medium-security prisons?
8. Describe a typical minimum-security prison.
9. What is the major purpose of a reception and classification center?
10. Three are basically three approaches to dealing with prison overcrowding. What are they, and how does each work?
11. The prison riot as a phenomenon is viewed in a number of ways. What are some of these ways?
12. Which types of inmate groups are prone to causing problems?
13. How does one become a gang member in prison?
14. What factors are most associated with membership in prison gangs?
15. What types of subjects are stressed in adult basic education and literacy programs?
16. What areas do most general equivalency diploma (GED) programs focus on?
17. What types of crimes are elderly inmates most likely to have committed?
18. What types of additional administrative problems result from dealing with elderly male prisoners?
19. In what ways is the heterosexual convict image of machismo chronically overplayed?
20. Four factors contributed to the women's prison movement. What were they?
21. What were the results of a Bureau of Justice Statistics study of the type of male offenders being incarcerated as opposed to female offenders being incarcerated?

CHAPTER RESOURCES

IN THE MEDIA

Video

CNN Today Video: *Corrections*, Vol. 1: segment 3, "Women behind Bars"

CNN Today Video: *Corrections*, Vol. 1: segment 8, "Life.... and Death"

CNN Today Video: *Introduction to Criminal Justice*, Vol. 3: segment 12, "Parole Housing"

Court TV Video: *Maximum Security*

FHH Custom Video: *Prison Security*

FHH Custom Video: *The History of Corrections*

FHH Video: *Life after Prison: Success on the Outside*

NIJ Video: *Prison Crowding*

NIJ Video: *Private Prisons*

Film

American Me (1992)
The Big House (1930)
Birdman of Alcatraz (1962)
Brubaker (1980)
Chained Heat (1983)
Cool Hand Luke (1967)
Escape from Alcatraz (1979)
The Green Mile (1999)
The Longest Yard (1974)
The Rock (1996)
The Shawshank Redemption (1994)

IN THE LITERATURE

Books

P. BAUNACH, *Mothers in Prison*. New Brunswick, N.J.: Transaction Books, 1985.

C. BLINN, ed., *Maternal Ties: A Selection of Programs for Female Offenders*. Lanham, Md.: American Correctional Association, 1997.

M. BRALY, *False Starts: A Memoir of San Quentin and Other Prisons*. New York: Penguin Books, 1976.

R. BURNS AND M. MANCHINI, *I Am a Fugitive from a Georgia Chain Gang!* Athens: University of Georgia Press, 1997.

D. BURTON-ROSE et al., eds., *The Celling of America: An Inside Look at the U.S. Prison Industry*. Monroe, Maine: Common Courage Press, 1998.

J. DILULIO, *Governing Prisons*. New York: Free Press, 1987.

P. EARLEY, *The Hot House: Life inside Leavenworth Prison*. New York: Bantam Books, 1992.

J. GONDLES, *Female Offenders: Meeting the Needs of a Neglected Population*. Latham, Md.: American Correctional Association, 1992.

L. GOODSTEIN AND D. L. MACKENZIE, eds., *The American Prison: Issues in Research and Policy*. New York: Plenum Press, 1989.

V. HASSINE, *Life without Parole: Living in Prison Today*, 2nd ed. Los Angeles: Roxbury, 1999.

J. JACOBS, *B. Stateville*. Chicago: University of Chicago Press, 1977.

R. JOHNSON, *Hard Time: Understanding and Reforming the Prison*, 2nd ed. Belmont, Calif.: Wadsworth, 1996.

K. KAUFFMAN, *Prison Officers and Their World*. Cambridge, Mass.: Harvard University Press, 1988.

D. LOCKWOOD, *Prison Sexual Violence*. New York: Elsevier, 1980.

S. MARTIN AND S. EKLAND-OLSON, *Texas Prisons: The Walls Came Tumbling Down*. Austin: Texas Monthly Press, 1987.

N. MORRIS, *The Future of Imprisonment*. Chicago: University of Chicago Press, 1974.

J. PETERSILIA, ed., *Community Corrections: Probation, Parole, and Intermediate Sanctions*. New York: Oxford University Press, 1997.

N. RAFTER, *Partial Justice: Women in State Prisons, 1800–1935*. Boston: Northeastern University Press, 1985.

D. SCHICHOR, *Punishment for Profit: Private Prisons/Public Concerns*. Thousand Oaks, Calif.: Sage, 1995.

K. WATTERSON, *Women in Prison: Inside the Concrete Womb*. Boston: Northeastern University Press, 1996.

R. A. WRIGHT, *In Defense of Prisons*. Westport, Conn.: Greenwood Press, 1994.

H. ZEHR, ed., *Doing Life: Reflections of Men and Women Serving Life Sentences*. Intercourse, Pa.: Good Books, 1996.

L. ZIMMER, *Women Guarding Men*. Chicago: University of Chicago Press, 1986.

F. E. ZIMRING AND G. HAWKINS, *The Scale of Imprisonment*. Chicago: University of Chicago Press, 1991.

Articles

M. CHESNEY-LIND, "Vengeful Equity: Sentencing Women to Prison." In *The Female Offender: Girls, Women and Crime*. Thousand Oaks, Calif.: Sage, 1997, pp. 1–27.

B. CROUCH, "Looking Back to See the Future of Corrections," *Prison Journal* vol. 76 (1996), p. 468.

S. Donohue and A. Greloch, "Keeping It Simple," *Corrections Today*, vol. 59 (1997), p. 90.

H. Sands and A. Hohnson, "Visitation in Absentia: New Technology Allows Inmates to Receive Visitors without Leaving Cells," *Corrections Today*, vol. 59 (1997), p. 96.

I. Soonachan, "The Future of Corrections: Technological Developments Are Turning Science Fiction into Science Fact," *Corrections Today*, vol. 62 (2000), pp. 64–66.

W. Toller and B. Tsagaris, "Managing Institutional Gangs": A Practical Approach Combining Security and Human Services," *Corrections Today*, vol. 58 (1996), p. 110.

ENDNOTES

1. National Advisory Commission on Criminal Justice Standards and Goals, *Corrections*. Washington, D.C.: U.S. Government Printing Office, 1973, pp. 341–349. Portions of this chapter were adapted from this source.

2. R. Dunn and M. Dunn, eds., *The Papers of William Penn, Vol. 2, 1680–1684*. Philadelphia: University of Pennsylvania Press, 1982, p. 206.

3. D. Rothman, *The Discovery of Institutions: Social Order and Disorder in the New Republic*. Boston: Little, Brown, 1971, Chapters 3–4.

4. H. Barnes, *The Story of Punishment*. Montclair, N.J.: Smith, Patterson, 1972, Chapter 6.

5. J. Irwin and J. Austin, *It's about Time: America's Imprisonment Binge*. Belmont, Calif.: Wadsworth, 1994. This discussion of administrative segregation was taken with permission from this source, and much of the information is based on the experience of these two authors. James Austin was an employee of the Illinois Department of Corrections from 1970 to 1974, and John Irwin was an inmate in the California Department of Corrections from 1952 to 1957. Since then, both authors have been involved in many studies of prisons and jails and have served as expert witnesses for both plaintiffs and defendants in numerous court cases involving the Illinois, Florida, Texas, Nevada, New Mexico, and California prison systems, and the New Orleans, Philadelphia, Seattle, San Diego, San Francisco, Chicago, and New York City jail systems.

6. In ongoing lawsuits in California (*Wright v. Enomoto, Toussaint v. McCarthy*) involving administrative segregation, the federal court adopted the term *lockup* to designate all forms of administrative segregation except protective custody. This was because the California Department of Corrections continued to develop new "units" that they claimed were different from older ones and therefore not subject to the earlier court rulings.

7. D. Clemmer, *The Prison Community*. New York: Holt, Rinehart, and Winston, 1958; originally published in 1940.

8. When they first began expansion, prison administrators usually presented the new policies as nonpunitive and planned new segregation units so they would not be as cruel as solitary confinement. In California, where segregation has been used more than in any other state, initial expansion of segregation units was justified with a therapeutic rationale. In 1956, California prison administrators requested and received funds from the state legislature to construct new housing units or to convert existing units to sections called *adjustment centers*, which were intended to hold prisoners who were not responding to the rehabilitative programs. According to the original plan, these prisoners would receive more intensive rehabilitative strategies, such as counseling and therapy. The adjustment centers were built, but no special rehabilitative programs were introduced.

9. By 1992, at least 15,578 prisoners were locked up in administrative segregation units. This figure was obtained by adding the 13,356 listed in the Justice Department's *Corrections Yearbook* (1992) to the 2,322 that were in California's "special security" units and not listed in the yearbook. The California figure was obtained from the Offender Information Services Branch of the California Department of Corrections. Alabama and Missouri clump segregation and protective custody together and were not included. The number in federal prison segregation units was also not available.

10. I. J. Silverman and M. Vega, *Corrections: A Comprehensive View*. St. Paul, Minn.: West, 1996, pp. 367–368. The discussion of the Marion, Illinois, federal supermax security facility, along with references, was adapted with permission from this source.

11. R. Hold and R. Phillips, "Marion: Separating Fact from Fiction," *Federal Prison Journal*, vol. 2, no. 1 (1991), pp. 29–35.

12. Ibid.

13. P. Millard, "Inside Marion: Warden Gary Hennan Talks about BOP's Most Secure Prison," *Corrections Today* (July 1988), pp. 92–94, 96–98.

14. F. X. Clines, "A Futuristic Prison Awaits the Hard Core," *The New York Times*, October 17, 1994, pp. A1, A12.

15. Ibid.

16. *Corrections Digest*, June 27, 1990, p. 7.

17. *The Sunday Oklahoma*, February 24, 1991.

18. *The New York Times*, February 20, 1991.

19. D. A. Ward and A. K. Schmidt, "Last-Resort Prisons for Habitual and Dangerous Offenders: Some Second Thoughts about Alcatraz." In D. A. Ward and K. F. Schoen, eds., *Confinement in Maximum Security*. Lexington, Mass.: Lexington, 1981.

20. D. A. Ward and K. F. Schoen, eds., *Confinement in Maximum Security*. Lexington, Mass.: Lexington, 1981.

21. J. D. Henderson, *Causes, Preventive Measures, and Methods of Controlling Riots and Disturbances in Correctional Institutions*. Laurel, Md.: American Correctional Association, 1990, pp. 8–13, 14–17. Copyright 1990 by the American Correctional Association, 1990. Used with permission from source.

22. B. Useem, C. G. Camp, G. M. Camp, and R. Dugan, *Resolution of Prison Riots*. National Institute of Justice

Research and Brief, October 1995. The summary of prison riots was taken from this source.

23. G. M. Camp and C. G. Camp, *Prison Gangs: Their Extent, Nature and Impact on Prisons.* Washington, D.C.: U.S. Government Printing Office, 1985. The discussion of prison gangs was adapted from this source.

24. I. J. Silverman, *Corrections: A Comprehensive Overview.* Belmont, Calif.: Wadsworth, 2001, pp. 380–435.

25. "Good Time Survey," *Corrections Compendium*, vol. 22, no. 1 (1997), pp. 3–16.

26. Ibid.

27. J. Lillis, "Education in U.S. Prisons: Part I," *Corrections Compendium*, vol. 29, no. 3 (1994), pp. 5–6.

28. "Good Time Survey," op. cit.

29. Ibid.

30. Ibid.

31. Ibid.

32. A. Tracey, "Literacy: Volunteers Share a Belief in Rehabilitative Effect of Education," *Corrections Today* (August 1990), pp. 102–109.

33. "Good Time Survey," op. cit.

34. E. Shelton, "The Implementation of a Life Coping Skills Program within a Correctional Setting," *Journal of Correctional Education*, vol. 36 (1985), pp. 41–45.

35. D. Bellorado, *Making Literacy Programs Work, Vol. 1, A Practical Guide for Correctional Educators.* Washington, D.C.: National Institute of Corrections, 1986, p. 96.

36. B. Simms, J. Farley, and J. Littlefield, *Colleges with Fences: a Handbook for Improving Corrections Education Programs.* Columbus, Ohio: National Center for Research in Vocational Education, 1987.

37. Branham, L. S., and Krantz, S., *Cases and Materials on the Law of Sentencing, Corrections, and Prisoners' Rights*, 5th ed. St. Paul, Minn.: West, 1997.

38. C. Mayer, "Survey of Case Law Establishing Constitutional Minima for the Provision of Mental Health Services to Psychiatrically Involved Inmates," *New England Journal on Civil and Criminal Confinement*, vol. 15, no. 2 (1989), pp. 243–275.

39. F. Cohen, *Legal Issues and the Mentally Disordered Prisoner.* Washington, D.C.: National Institute of Corrections, November 1998.

40. S. Morris, M. Steadman, and B. Veysey, "Mental Health Services in United States Jails: A Survey of Innovative Practices," *Criminal Justice and Behavior*, Vol. 42, no. 2 (March 1997), pp. 3–19.

41. Ibid.

42. Ibid.

43. A. Beck and D. Gilliard, *Prisoners in 1994.* Washington, D.C.: U.S. Department of Justice, August 1995.

44. F. Kuether, "Religion and the Chaplain." In P. Tappan, ed., *Contemporary Correction.* New York: McGraw-Hill, 1951.

45. C. Johnson, Director of Instruction, Windham School District, Texas Department of Criminal Justice. Personal communication.

46. S. Bradley, "Graying of Inmate Population Spurs Correction Challenges," *On the Line,* vol. 13 (March 1990).

47. R. Dugger, "The Gain of American Prisons," *Corrections Today*, vol. 50 (June 1988), p. 1.

48. Bradley, op. cit.

49. P. Zimbardo, *Transforming California Prisons into Expensive Old Age Homes for Felons.* San Francisco: Center on Juvenile Criminal Justice, 1994.

50. H. E. Allen and C. E. Simonsen, *Corrections in America.* Upper Saddle River, N.J.: Simon & Schuster, 1998.

51. W. S. Wooden and J. Parker, *Men behind Bars: Sexual Exploitation in Prison.* New York: Plenum Press, 1982.

52. T. R. Clear and G. F. Cole, *American Corrections.* Belmont, Calif.: Wadsworth, 1997.

53. Allen and Simonsen, op. cit.

54. R. B. Greifinger, "Management of the HIV Positive Prisoner," *World Health*, CME, 1999.

55. Ibid.

56. Clear and Cole, op. cit.

57. "Condoms for Inmates at Issue in Philadelphia, San Francisco," *Criminal Justice Newsletter*, July 1, 1988, p. 5.

58. T. M. Hammett, *AIDS in Correctional Facilities: Issues and Options*, 3rd ed. Washington, D.C.: National Institute of Justice, April 1988, p. 92

59. Ibid.

60. "Condoms for Inmates," op. cit.

61. Clear and Cole, op. cit.

62. R. P. Dobash, R. E. Dobash, and S. Gutteridge, *The Imprisonment of Women.* New York: Basil Blackwell, 1986.

63. J. M. Pollock-Byrne, *Women, Prison, and Crime.* Pacific Grove, Calif.: Brooks/Cole, 1990, pp. 36–55, 84–106. Copyright 1990 by Wadsworth Publishing. The discussion of women in prison was adapted with permission from this source.

64. Ibid., p. 17.

65. Ibid., p. 18.

66. Ibid., p. 19.

67. Ibid., pp. 22–23.

68. J. Fox, "Women's Prison Policy, Prisoner Activism and the Impact of the Contemporary Feminist Movement: A Case Study," *Prison Journal*, vol. 63, no. 2 (1984), pp. 12–26.

69. Dobash, Dobash, and Gutteridge, pp. 24–25.

70. Ibid., p. 33.

71. E. Freedman, *Their Sisters' Keepers: Women's Prison Reform in America, 1830–1930.* Ann Arbor: University of Michigan Press, 1981, p. 16.

72. K. Strickland. *Correctional Institutions for Women in the United States.* Lexington, Mass.: Lexington, 1976, p. 40.

73. Ibid., p. 40.

74. E. Freedman, "Their Sisters' Keepers: A Historical Perspective of Female Correctional Institutions in America, 1870–1900," *Feminist Studies*, vol. 2 (1974), pp. 77–95.

75. Ibid., p. 80.
76. Ibid., p. 82.
77. N. Rafter, *Partial Justice: State Prisons and Their Inmates, 1800–1935.* Boston: Northeastern University Press, 1985.
78. Freedman, 1981, p. 70.
79. Ibid., p. 71.
80. Ibid., p. 74.
81. Ibid., p. 75.
82. Rafter, op. cit., p. 26.
83. Strickland, op. cit., p. 41.
84. Freedman, 1981, pp. 78–79.
85. Rafter, op. cit., p. 117.
86. Freedman, 1981, p. 82.
87. Rafter, op. cit., p. 126.
88. Freedman, 1981, p. 99.
89. Ibid., p. 92.
90. Rafter, op. cit., p. 124.
91. Freedman, 1981, p. 99.
92. Ibid., p. 100.
93. Ibid., p. 140.
94. Ibid., p. 105.
95. Ibid., p. 121.
96. M. Chesney-Lind, "Women in Prison: From Partial Justice to Vengeful Equity," *Correction* (December 1998), pp. 66–72.
97. In 1979, 26 percent of women doing time in state prisons for drug offenses were incarcerated solely for possession.
98. R. Giallombardo, *Society of Women: A Study of a Women's Prison.* New York: Wiley, 1966.
99. Ibid.; E. Heffernan, *Making It in Prison: The Square, the Cool, the Life.* New York: Wiley, 1972; S. Ansay. Personal communication, January 1994.
100. Giallombardo, op. cit.
101. Silverman and Vega, op. cit.
102. S. Halleck and M. Herski, "Homosexual Behavior in an Institution of Adolescent Girls," *American Journal of Orthopsychiatry,* vol. 32 (1962), pp. 991–917; P. A. Ward and G. Kassebaum, *Women's Prison: Sex and Social Structure.* Chicago: Aldine-Atherton, 1965; Giallombardo, op. cit.; C. Nelson, "A Study of Homosexuality among Women Inmates at State Prisons." Ph.D. dissertation, Temple University, Philadelphia, Pa., 1974; A. Propper, "Importation and Deprivation Perspectives on Homosexuality in Correctional Institutions: An Empirical Test of Their Relative Efficacy." Ph.D. dissertation, University of Michigan, Ann Arbor, Mich., 1976.
103. Silverman and Vega, op. cit, p. 256.
104. Pollock-Byrne, op. cit.
105. M. V. Ochten. "Legal Issues and the Female Offender." in *Female Offender.* Lanham, Md.: American Correctional Association, 1993, pp. 31–36.
106. The arguments presented for and against privatization of prisons were originally published in *Point/Counter.* Lanham, Md.: American Correctional Association, 1998, pp. 26–27.

13 PROBATION, PAROLE, AND COMMUNITY CORRECTIONS

Chapter Outline

Probation
  The Suspended Sentence: Birthplace of Probation
  John Augustus: Father of Probation
  Imposing Probation
  Restructuring Probation as an Intermediate Sanction
  Intensive-Supervision Probation (ISP) Programs
  Revocation of Probation
Innovations in Probation
  House Arrest
  Advantages of House Arrest
  Electronically Monitored Home Confinement
  Disadvantages of House Arrest
Parole
  Origins of the American System of Parole
  Modern Parole
  Enhancing Parole Prediction
Innovations in Parole
  Shock Incarceration Programs
  Community Correctional Centers
  Halfway Houses
  Work Release
  Educational Release
  Furloughs
Community Service
  Objectives of Community Service
  Types of Programs
  Issues in Community Service
Summary

Key TERMS

community service, p. 537	parole board, p. 529
control programs, p. 521	Penal Servitude Act, p. 527
educational release, p. 537	presentence reports, p. 520
electronic monitoring, p. 524	probation, p. 518
furloughs, p. 537	programmed contact devices, p. 524
halfway house, p. 536	Salient Factor Score, p. 532
house arrest, p. 523	selective incapacitation, p. 533
intensive-supervision probation (ISP), p. 521	shock incarceration programs, p. 535
	suspended sentence, p. 518
parole, p. 526	work release programs, p. 537

Courtesy of A. Ramey/PhotoEdit.

Most offenders sent away to prison return, sooner or later, to free society. But imprisonment may not only fail to rehabilitate many offenders, it may also exacerbate their criminal tendencies. Criminal justice authorities, therefore, have long sought realistic, workable alternatives to confinement. In recent years, the emphasis has been on involving offenders in programs and facilities based within the community. Such programs allow society to provide offenders with only the amount of supervision they require. And because crime has its roots in the community, it is reasonable that the community assume some responsibility for dealing with offenders. This approach also minimizes the problem of reintegration.

In this chapter, we will discuss in part the two methods most often used as alternatives to imprisonment: probation and parole. The public's fear of crime has created an increased demand for incarceration; consequently, more felons are being imprisoned than ever before. On the other hand, however, since prison overcrowding has become such an enormous problem, the courts are increasingly using probation as one method of dealing with the problem. In addition to discussing traditional probation, we will also discuss a second type of probation program that is emerging in almost every state: intensive-supervision probation. This form of probation, which imposes more stringent conditions on probation, results in more frequent monitoring and offers expanded services for the offender. We will examine the effect of such programs in three states: Massachusetts, New Jersey, and California.

In addition, there have been some interesting innovations in probation in the past decade, including house arrest. We will examine the advantages and disadvantages of house arrest, including the use of electronic monitoring in home confinement, which seems to have captured the imagination of the judiciary. However, the program is not without its critics. We will also discuss parole, which is not an alternative to confinement the same way that probation is. The reader will learn that parole is actually a form of conditional release for someone already serving a prison term. One of the major challenges facing parole authorities today is to select individuals who will most likely succeed on parole. In order to remove some of the subjectivity involved in making these decisions, the U.S parole commission has developed the Salient Factor Score (an objective scale based on empirical research), which is used as a guide to predict recidivism.

In addition to the more traditional components of parole, we will discuss innovations in parole. These include shock incarceration programs (also known as boot camps). These programs have enjoyed considerable popular support in recent years. We will also be discussing community correctional centers, which can be used for a variety of purposes, including detention, treatment, holding, and prerelease. Some of the more common types of community correctional centers include halfway houses, work release programs, educational release programs, and furloughs.

Lastly, we will discuss the reemergence of the concepts of restitution and community service as alternatives to incarceration and present the views of some proponents and opponents of this concept. Within this context we will discuss the objectives of community service along with specific types of programs.

PROBATION

Probation is intended as a combination of treatment and punishment. An offender is actually serving time on probation but is also supposed to be treated in the context of community-based supervision (see Figure 13.1). Ideally, probationers receive counseling and guidance to ensure that they adjust to free society. But probation is also punitive because restrictions are placed on the probationer. (Many authorities deny the punitive aspects of probation and claim that their policies are strictly rehabilitative.)

Liberal and conservative critics of the criminal justice system agree that placing an offender on probation without using private community services is equal to doing nothing. Such action is neither treatment nor punishment. As one criminal court judge observed, "The offender continues with his life style ... If he is a wealthy doctor, he continues with his practice; if he is an unemployed youth, he continues to be unemployed. Probation is a meaningless ritual; it is a sop to the conscience of the court."[1] A major problem in probation is the built-in role conflict experienced by probation officers. Are they police officers or counselors? Is their responsibility primarily surveillance, or should they be active agents of social change? Many of the other difficulties that plague probation officers—high staff turnover, low morale, and burnout—stem from this basic conflict. There are also critical problems in trying to evaluate the effectiveness of probation as an alternative to confinement. However, some innovative and experimental approaches have been proposed to augment traditional probation programs in an attempt to deal with these problems.

The Suspended Sentence: Birthplace of Probation

Probation is derived from the **suspended sentence,** handed down indirectly from our judicial past. Both a suspended sentence and probation are a form of mitigating punishment through judicial procedures. Their earliest antecedent is the *right of sanctuary,* which is frequently cited in the Bible; holy places and certain cities were traditionally set aside as places of sanctuary for those who had committed a crime. The practice of right of sanctuary was written into Mosaic law. To escape the vengeance of a victim's family, a killer could go to a sanctuary and find refuge. In the Middle Ages, many churches offered sanctuary to people hiding from harsh secular laws. The practice of sanctuary disappeared in England in the seventeenth century; the tradition of the "benefit clergy" took its place. This practice, originally reserved for clerics, was eventually extended to those who could pass the "Psalm 51" test, which required the ability of the

---

CTQ

What is meant by the contention that probation is a combination of treatment and punishment? Can such a combination be expected to work?

FIGURE 13.1

One responsibility of probation officers is to monitor the activities and progress of their probationers by making unannounced visits to their homes, places of employment, or—as shown in this photo—schools.

Courtesy of A. Ramey/PhotoEdit.

offender to read the verse beginning "Have mercy upon me . . . " The result was a form of suspended sentence that allowed offenders to move about in society without undue fear of retribution.

The suspended sentence differs from probation, even though the terms are sometimes used interchangeably. The suspended sentence does not require supervision and usually does not specify a particular set of goals for the offender. It is merely a form of quasi-freedom that can be revoked at the discretion of the court. The practice of suspended sentence, like the right of sanctuary, has outlived its usefulness in the United States and has generally been replaced by supervised probation.

John Augustus: Father of Probation

A nineteenth-century Boston cobbler named John Augustus is regarded as the father of probation. Augustus spent much of his leisure time in the courts and was distressed that common drunks were forced to remain in jail because they had no money to pay their fines. A humane, sympathetic man, he convinced authorities to allow him to pay offenders' fines; after their release, he provided offenders with friendly counsel and supervision. From 1841 to 1848, Augustus bailed out nearly two thousand men, women, and children. Barnes and Teeters describe his approach: "His method was to bail out the offender after conviction, to utilize this favor as an entering wedge to the convict's confidence and friendship, and through such evidence or friendliness as helping the offender to obtain a job and aiding his family in various ways, to drive the wedge home. When the defendant was later brought into court for sentence, Augustus would report on his progress toward reformation, and the judge would usually fine the convict one cent and costs, instead of committing him to an institution."[2]

Augustus's efforts encouraged the state of Massachusetts to pass the first probation statute in 1878. Five more states followed suit before the turn of the century. In 1899, with the creation of the first juvenile court, probation was established as a legitimate alternative to penal confinement. The need to supervise troubled youths and to keep them out of adult prisons provided strong motivation toward developing probation in the United States.

Imposing Probation

Probation can be implemented in three ways. First, the law may allow the trial judge to suspend the execution of the sentence and to place the offender on conditional probation. Second, a state statute may require sentencing but may permit suspension. Finally, sentencing and probation may be left to the discretion of the trial judge. If a probationer violates the conditions of probation, the trial judge usually orders the execution of the sentence originally imposed. If the judge has suspended the sentence, a probation violation might result in a stiffer prison sentence than would have been imposed earlier.

Probation without Adjudication Once the court has decided to grant probation, the sentencing judge must decide whether the offender should be adjudicated guilty and labeled

WEB

For more information on the suspended sentence, **visit our Web site, www.prenhall.com/territo**.

IN THE WORKPLACE

PROBATION OFFICER

Responsible for performing professional work and investigating, assessing, supervising, counseling, and/or classifying offenders. Performs a variety of duties, including the following: evaluates offender's progress and recommends intensity of supervision based on observations from time of conviction through period of adjustment after release from an institution; assists offenders in securing jobs; maintains contact with employers; counsels and refers offenders to specialized treatment services; records offender restitution payments. Minimum qualifications are as follows: graduation from a four-year college or university with major coursework in criminal justice or related field; experience in correctional work with adults or juveniles.

a convicted felon or whether he or she should be placed on probation without adjudication. This decision is outlined by Murcheck:

> Although adjudication of guilt may provide certain safeguards to society such as: requiring criminal registration, serving notice to prosecuting employers that the applicant has been convicted of a criminal offense, preventing the offender from voting, holding public office, serving on a jury and perhaps making it more difficult to obtain firearms, it appears to provide very little appreciable effect in providing protection to society. However, it does, in fact, seriously hamper the offender's chances of rehabilitation.
>
> The withholding of adjudication of guilt, on the other hand, is consistent with the philosophical concepts of probation, which combine community-based treatment with the full utilization of available community resources as a viable alternative to imprisonment and the accompanying degradation and stigma associated with it.[3]

Presentence Investigation Reports   To determine which offenders are good candidates for probation, sentencing judges rely heavily on **presentence reports.** Information secured in presentence investigations can be used at almost every stage in the criminal justice process: by the courts in deciding the appropriate sentence, by the prison classification team in assigning custody level and treatment, by the parole board in determining when an offender is ready to be returned to the community, by probation and parole officers in helping offenders readjust to free society, and by correctional researchers in identifying the characteristics of successful probation.[4] The primary purpose of presentence investigations is not to determine the guilt or innocence of defendants but rather to give insights into their personalities and lives.

Some type of presentence investigation report should be made in every case. Objectivity is essential in the preparation of this document; probation officers must see things as they are, not as they would wish them to be. Under our adversary system of justice, the district attorney and the defense counsel are committed to particular points of view, but the preparer of the presentence investigation report is free to include all facts pertinent to the case. The report should include a description of the offense, including statements of codefendants; the defendant's own version of the offense; prior record; family and marital history; description of the neighborhood in which the defendant was reared; and facts about the defendant's education, religion, interests, mental and physical health, employment history, and military service. Optional information might include the attitude of the defendant toward arresting officers, the amount of bond, and the attitude of arresting officers.

The evaluative summary is the most difficult and important part of the presentence report; it separates professional probation officers from fact-gathering clerks. Probation officers need considerable analytic skills and an understanding of human behavior to interpret the facts in a presentence report and to make a meaningful recommendation to the court. Many judges ask these officers to recommend sentencing alternatives or, if the defendant is placed on probation, to recommend a plan of treatment.

Conditions of Probation and Parole   Although probation is usually managed by the courts, and parole is usually managed by an executive department of government, the conditions of both alternatives are simple. These conditions are generally fixed jointly by the legislature, the court, and the probation and parole departments. Some general regulations—such as requirements that probationers live law-abiding lives, that they not leave the state without the court's consent, that they report periodically to their probation or parole officer, and that they pay court costs—may be fixed by statute; no allowances are made for discretion by the trial court or the parole board. However, unique conditions may be applied in individual cases. For example, probationers may be required either to stay home or leave home, to support their parents, to get a steady job working days, to make restitution to their victims, or to attend church regularly.

Some conditions of probation and parole have been unfair and unrealistic. When this occurs, a probation officer may choose to enforce the conditions selectively, thereby

---

CTQ
Are there any disadvantages of probation without adjudication?

WEB
For more information on imposing probation, visit our Web site, www.prenhall.com/territo.

WEB
For more information on presentence reports, visit our Web site, www.prenhall.com/territo.

muting their effect in the interest of common-sense justice. The concerned probation officer should ask: "Are these rules reasonable?" "Are they effective?" "Do they serve the best interest of the individual and the community?"

Restructuring Probation as an Intermediate Sanction

Limited prison and jail resources make it impossible to incarcerate all convicted offenders. One solution is to restructure probation to include a range of increasingly incapacitating community-based **control programs** for offenders who pose a significant threat to public safety. A wide range of intensive community-based sentencing alternatives have been developed by legislators, judges, and correctional administrators.

The main impetus for this development has been prison overcrowding. In many states, probation departments have designed and implemented community-based programs for offenders who would otherwise be sentenced to prison or jail. Almost every state has developed one or more such programs, which include intensive-supervision probation, house arrest, day reporting centers, and electronic monitoring. Federal probation agencies have embraced intensive supervision for specific categories of offenders (such as drug and white-collar offenders).[5]

Intensive-Supervision Probation (ISP) Programs

Compared with traditional probation, **intensive-supervision probation (ISP)** imposes more stringent conditions, stricter and more frequent monitoring, and, often, expanded services for the offender.[6]

ISP usually requires offenders to pay victims restitution, hold a job or perform community service, submit to unscheduled drug and alcohol testing, and pay part of the cost of their supervision. Caseloads of supervising officers normally range from thirty to fifty probationers. Under traditional probation, where caseloads of 150 to 200 are common, supervision sometimes amounts to little more than probationers mailing a monthly card to the probation officer.[7]

Between 1980 and 1990, every state implemented some form of ISP. A growing number of jurisdictions use ISP to provide rigorous supervision of high-risk probationers in the community, with the aim of reducing the risk to public safety posed by such offenders. Responding to the needs of state and local jurisdictions, the National Institute of Justice (NIJ) began to evaluate ISP in the mid-1980s and continues to study a variety of such programs around the nation, some of which apply the concept to select parolees and defendants on pretrial release as well.

Massachusetts Courts Project An NIJ grant awarded to researchers at Lowell University evaluated the impact of ISP as implemented in thirteen Massachusetts courts. ISP usually targeted a subgroup of probationers classified as being at high risk for recidivism in the near future. Probation officers developed specific intervention strategies based on identified needs (such as drug abuse), contacted each probationer at least ten times a month, verified employment twice a month, and rigorously monitored and enforced probation conditions.[8]

Findings of this study point to the need to combine surveillance and control strategies with offender treatment if ISP is to be successful in reducing recidivism. The researchers note the difficulty of generating community support for funding offender treatment programs. Soliciting support for improved surveillance technologies is much easier, they say.

ISP in New Jersey An NIJ-funded evaluation conducted by the Institute for Criminological Research of Rutgers University reached encouraging conclusions about a New Jersey ISP program. Under the state's program, relatively low-risk felons who had been sentenced and committed to prison were resentenced to intensive supervision in the community by a specially created panel of judges appointed by the state's chief justice. The offenders were released into the ISP program after serving three or four months of their prison terms. The program was designed to deliver appropriate punishment at less cost and with less use of prison resources; its goal was also to deter future offenses.[9] Participants who failed to abide by the program rules, which included face-to-face contacts,

WEB

For more information on probation and parole, **visit our Web site,** www.prenhall.com/territo.

WEB

For more information on probation and intermediate sanctions, **visit our Web site,** www.prenhall.com/territo.

curfew checks, urinalysis tests, and at least sixteen hours of community service each month, were immediately returned to prison.

The NIJ study compared New Jersey's ISP felons with a random sample of 500 other felons who had been sentenced to prison for ISP-eligible offenses, served their full terms, and been released on regular parole. Of the 500 in the sample, a total of 132 closely matched the ISP felons in terms of offense, prior convictions, employment status, drug history, and demographic factors such as age, sex, and race. This subset of the random sample served as the control group for many aspects of the evaluation. The fact that only 132 felons matched the ISP group shows that the ISP program was indeed selective and excluded offenders with prior violent offenses or long criminal careers.

The ISP group served an average of 109 days in prison, whereas the comparison group served 308 days. Thus, ISP saved about 200 prison-bed days per participant. This translated to a cost savings per offender of approximately $7,000 for the combined period of incarceration and ISP. Arrest records at the end of two years showed that 25 percent of offenders of the ISP group, in comparison to 35 percent of the 132 closely matched offenders in the control group, had new arrests.

The researchers concluded that New Jersey's ISP program was cost-effective compared with ordinary terms of imprisonment and parole and that it improved the use of prison space without increasing recidivism.

ISP in Three California Counties The Bureau of Justice Assistance (BJA) funded an ISP demonstration project in fourteen sites in nine states. NIJ selected three counties in California (Contra Costa, Los Angeles, and Ventura) for an initial evaluation by the Rand Corporation. The goal of the ISP project was to improve the success of probation. In each jurisdiction, caseloads were small. Together, the three programs involved a total of 488 high-risk probationers, who were required to participate in work, submit to random drug and alcohol testing, and perform community service.[10] Despite receiving more intense supervision (as measured by increased contacts, monitoring, and drug tests), ISP offenders did not have lower recidivism rates (as measured through official record data) than their counterparts on routine probation. ISP offenders consistently incurred more technical violations than did the routine probationers, although statistical analysis did not reveal a relationship between technical violations and new arrests. Participation in available employment, educational, and treatment programs was low.

A follow-up after one year found that about a third of the offenders in the ISP program had no technical violations or new arrests; another third had committed technical violations only; the remainder had been arrested.

Researchers concluded that one reason for the relatively high failure rates in the three California counties was that ISP participants had been sentenced for more serious crimes and were at higher risk of recidivism than offenders who had participated in previously evaluated ISP programs at other sites.[11]

Revocation of Probation

There are no uniform criteria for revoking probation throughout the country—not even among judges in the same district courts. Conditions of probation should be realistic, and they should be applied fairly. Unrealistic conditions frustrate the offender and may lead to further violations. For example, it is pointless to fine a probationer if severe financial problems caused the original violation. Similarly, compulsory church attendance might create resentment on the part of the probationer. Thus, conditions of probation should be guidelines to help the person on probation lead a law-abiding life—not rigid vows of obedience that only the most disciplined can endure.

When probationers violate the conditions of their probation, care must be taken to determine whether the violation is the result of unrealistic probation rules or the attitude of the probationer.[12] The probation officer must ask, "To what extent is this violation a reflection of deep-seated hostility?" and "To what extent is this behavior symptomatic of a person trying to find himself or herself?" Revocation of probation is justified only when probationers defy the courts or when they become a threat to the community. In cases in-

---

CTQ
Would you add any additional conditions to intensive supervision to make it more effective?

WEB
For more information on intensive-supervision probation (ISP) programs, **visit our Web site,** www.prenhall.com/territo.

volving restitution, if a probationer is sentenced to prison, the crime victim loses out. No violation should result in automatic revocation. Probation officers should ask themselves how they would respond to the probationer's acts if he or she were not on probation. For example, we do not sentence people to prison for losing or quitting their jobs. Thus, all violations should be judged in light of the probationer's total adjustment to society.

The probation officer today is also expected to provide a variety of human services to the probationer. That is, the officer is expected to perform as a social caseworker. The influence of social work has had a profound effect on the development of probation services. In the past, an overemphasis on casework and the medical model—which conceived of the criminal offender as a "sick" person—resulted in a narrow focus on the relationship between the probationer and the probation officer. This led, in turn, to a tendency to overlook the connection between crime and contributing factors such as poverty, racism, unemployment, poor health, substandard housing, and poor education.

One drawback in the model of the probation officer as a caseworker, however, is that officers may have to assume functions not related to probation. Placement in foster homes, operation of shelters, alcoholism, drug addiction, and mental illness may be more properly handled by community mental health agencies. No one probation officer has the background required to deal with all the problems of probationers. Yet probation officers are accountable for probationers who get into trouble again. The first question asked by the court in this situation is usually, "When did you last see your client?" As a result, probation officers tend to overextend themselves to prevent or justify client failures. For many officers, the role conflict of "cop or counselor" is a major source of job stress.

INNOVATIONS IN PROBATION

House Arrest

House arrest is a sentence imposed by the court in which offenders are legally ordered to remain confined in their own residences. They are usually allowed to leave their residences only for medical reasons and employment. They may also be required to perform community service or to pay victim restitution or probation supervision fees.[13] While the goal of house arrest—to restrict freedom—is easily understood, the mechanisms used to confine offenders to their homes vary considerably. Typically, offenders participating in intensive-supervision probation programs are required to be in their residences during the evening hours and on weekends.

In some instances, curfews are added to the offender's court-ordered parole or probation conditions. While curfews permit individual freedom in the community except for particular hours, more-intrusive home-incarceration programs restrict the offenders' freedom in all but court-approved limited activities.

Advantages of House Arrest

Social Benefits Most advocates of house arrest believe that the program is socially cost-effective. A defendant who had a job before being convicted can keep it during and after house arrest. By preventing the breakup of family and family networks, house arrest can also prevent psychological and physical disruptions that may have lasting effects on the offender, his or her spouse and children, and even the next generation.

Furthermore, house arrest has none of the corrupting or stigmatizing effects associated with prison. This is a particular advantage for first-time offenders, who may not yet be committed to a life of crime. They will not come under the influence of career criminals or be exposed to the physical or sexual assaults of prison inmates. Keeping offenders from the criminogenic effects of prison was one of the major reasons Oregon and Kentucky officials devised house arrest programs for drunken drivers.

Most of the operating house arrest programs view these considerations as an important advantage. While prisons are not designed to scar inmates psychologically, many believe that it happens. Avoiding this psychological damage is a desirable social goal, especially for young, inexperienced, or first-time offenders. A sentence that would make such emotional scars less likely or less common without compromising public safety would surely be preferred.

WEB

For more information on house arrest, visit our Web site, www.prenhall.com/territo.

Responsiveness to Local and Offender Needs House arrest is flexible. It can be used as sole sanction or as part of a package of sentencing conditions. It can be used at almost any point in the criminal justice process—as a diversion before an offender experiences any jail time, after a short term in jail, after a prison term (usually joined with work release), or as a condition for probation or parole.

House arrest can also be used to cover particular times of the day or particular types of offenders. This is an attractive option for controlling offenders who are situationally dangerous. The drunk driver, the alcoholic who becomes assaultive in a bar, and the addict may all be likely candidates for house arrest. House arrest also has potential applications for offenders with special needs—such as the terminally ill, the mentally retarded, people with AIDS whose needs cannot be met in jail, and elderly offenders.

Implementation Ease and Timeliness The need to reduce prison crowding is immediate, and jurisdictions are looking for alternatives that can be developed quickly. Because house arrest requires no new facilities and can use existing probation personnel, it is one of the easiest programs to implement (particularly if no electronic monitoring devices are used.). House arrest programs, for the most part, do not require legislative changes and can be set up by administrative decisions. The conditions of house arrest are usually easy to communicate, which also facilitates implementation.

Policymakers also like the notion that the offender can be removed from the community quickly at the first sign of misbehavior. Because house arrestees are usually on some type of suspended jail or prison sentence, the suspension can be revoked quickly and the offenders incarcerated if they fail to meet house arrest requirements. The suspended sentence status makes the process of revocation much simpler and faster than if the offender were simply on probation or parole.

Cost-Effectiveness The surge of interest in house arrest programs is due primarily to their financial appeal. House arrest (particularly without electronic monitoring) is thought to be highly cost-effective. If the offender under house arrest were instead in prison, then not only would the state have to pay the yearly cost of housing the offender, but there would also be added pressure to build new prisons.

Electronically Monitored Home Confinement

When **electronic monitoring** equipment is used, house arrest is not as cost-effective. The equipment is currently quite expensive. For instance, Kentucky spent $32,000 for twenty electronic devices, and Albuquerque, New Mexico, paid $100,000 for its first twenty-five monitor/bracelet sets. However, manufacturers argue that such figures are misleading since they reflect high startup costs that will decline as usage increases. Manufacturers also say that it is misleading to look only at the system's direct costs. Most house arrest programs require the offender to make restitution payments and pay probation supervision fees. Moreover, offenders can continue to support their families, saving the state possible welfare expenditures.

Electronic monitoring equipment receives information about monitored offenders and transmits the information over telephone lines to a computer at the monitoring agency. There are two basic types of equipment—continuously signaling devices that constantly monitor the presence of an offender at a particular location, and **programmed contact devices** that contact the offender periodically to verify his or her presence.

A continuously signaling device has three major parts: a transmitter, a receiver-dialer, and a central computer. The transmitter, which is attached to the offender, sends out a continuous signal. The receiver-dialer, located in the offender's home and attached to the telephone, detects the signals sent by the transmitter. It reports to the central computer when it stops receiving the signal and again when the signal begins. A central computer at the monitoring agency receives these reports from the receiver-dialer over the telephone lines, compares them with the offender's curfew schedule, and alerts correctional officials about any unauthorized absences. The computer also stores information about each offender's routine entries and exits so that a report can be prepared.

CTQ
Do you believe probation should be abolished for all but the most minor offenses?

WEB
For more information on electronic monitoring, **visit our Web site,** www.prenhall.com/territo.

Programmed contact devices, on the other hand, use a computer programmed to telephone the offender during the monitored hours, either randomly or at specified times. The computer prepares a report on the results of the call.

Most but not all programs attempt to verify that the offender is indeed the person responding to the computer's call. Programmed contact devices can do this in several ways. One is to use voice verification technology. Another is to require the offender to wear a wristwatch device programmed to provide a unique number that appears when a special button on the watch device is pressed into a touch-tone telephone in response to the computer's call. A third system requires a black plastic module to be strapped to the offender's arm or leg. When the computer calls, the module is inserted into a verifier box connected to the telephone. A fourth system uses visual verification at the telephone site.[14]

Disadvantages of House Arrest

Nonviolent and low-risk offenders are prime candidates for house arrest; these offenders are least likely to have been sentenced to prison in the first place. As judges become more familiar with house arrest, they may use it for offenders who, because of jail crowding, might otherwise have been sentenced to routine probation with nominal supervision. Alternatively, house arrest may be used as an "add-on" to the sentence the judge would normally have imposed, thus lengthening the total time the offender is under criminal sanction.

In the long run, increased control of convicted offenders with house arrest programs is a realistic possibility, but it cuts both ways. If we begin to regard homes as potential prisons, capacity is, for all practical purposes, unlimited. Yet such a possibility has widespread social implications. Several years ago, the head of the American Civil Liberties Union's National Prison Project said: "We should be looking for ways to place fewer controls on minor offenders, not more. If these devices are used as alternatives to jail, then maybe there's no problem with them. If you're sending the same people to jail and putting people who otherwise would be on probation on them, it's a misuse. We're cautiously concerned."

House Arrest May Not Punish the Crime Some critics of house arrest are concerned that a sentence of house arrest is not sufficiently severe to constitute an appropriate punishment for many crimes. Because many states use house arrest programs as punishment in lieu of prison, critics argue that the result is a depreciation of the seriousness with which crimes are treated. For example, Mothers Against Drunk Driving (MADD) has been particularly critical of house arrest for drunk drivers and sees such sentencing as a step backward for efforts to stiffen penalties for this offense. The lessened severity of punishment, in theory, may reduce the criminal law's deterrent effects. In addition, critics could argue, because some offenders will commit new offenses while on house arrest, the crime-prevention effects that prison sentences achieve by incapacitation will not take place.

House Arrest Focuses Primarily on Offender Surveillance Some critics worry that house arrest, particularly if implemented with electronic devices, will strike the final blow to the rehabilitative ideal. As probation officers focus more heavily on surveillance of offenders, human contact is reduced and the potential for helping offenders is diminished. Most probation officers monitoring house arrest participants admit that they have little time for counseling. Although the research evidence is not optimistic about the rehabilitative effects of probation officers' efforts, many believe it is important that humane efforts be made to reform offenders.

On the other hand, while counseling is reduced in most house arrest programs, employment or enrollment in school is often required of the offender. Having a job or a high school diploma may do more than counseling to reduce the long-term prospects of recidivism.

Other critics argue that because it is a program of personal surveillance, house arrest is intrusive and potentially illegal. The objection is to the state's presence in an individual's home, long regarded as the one place where privacy is guaranteed and government intrusion is restricted by law. The use of electronic devices raises the fear that we may be headed toward the type of society described by George Orwell in his novel *1984*, where citizens' language and movement are strictly monitored and used as tools of government oppression.

But house arrest, with or without electronics, is quite different from the scenario described in *1984*. House arrest is used as a criminal sentence and is imposed on offenders only after they have been legally convicted—and it is imposed with the full consent of the participant. Indeed, its intent is to be used as an alternative to incarceration. Surely a prison cell is more intrusive than any house arrest program.

There have been no formal challenges to date concerning the legality of house arrest. But legal analyses prepared by officials in Utah and Florida conclude that house arrest, with or without electronic monitoring, will withstand constitutional challenges as long as it is imposed to protect society or rehabilitate the offender and the conditions set forth are clear, reasonable, and constitutional.

Class and Income Bias May Enter into Participant Selection Administrators are extremely cautious in selecting participants. Most programs limit participation to offenders convicted of property crimes who have minor criminal records and no history of drug abuse. Such strict screening makes it difficult to identify eligible offenders, and those who are eligible tend disproportionately to be white-collar offenders.

American Civil Liberties Union officials say that the programs also discriminate against the young and the poor because, to qualify for most house arrest programs, a person generally needs to be able to pay a supervision fee, typically $15 to $50 a month. If electronic monitors are used, the fee is higher, and the offender needs to have a home and a telephone. People without these resources may have no alternative but prison. Hence, there are concerns about equal access to such programs. To offset such concerns, some programs have instituted sliding-scale fee schedules, and a few others provide telephones for offenders who do not have them.

House Arrest Compromises Public Safety Some critics seriously question whether house arrest programs can adequately protect the public. Regardless of stringency, most advocates admit that house arrest cannot guarantee crime-free living on the subject's part, since the sanction relies for the most part on the offender's willingness to comply. Can a criminal really be trusted to refrain from further crime if allowed to remain in his or her home?

To date, both recidivism and escape rates for house arrest participants are quite low. Generally less than 25 percent of participants fail to complete the programs successfully. But the low rates result, in part, from such programs' selection of good risks. Eligibility requirements often exclude drug addicts and violent offenders. Profiles of house arrestees show that most have been convicted of relatively minor offenses. Such offenders have lower-than-normal recidivism rates, with or without the house arrest program. Without a controlled scientific experiment, it is impossible to know whether house arrest programs themselves or the characteristics of participants account for the initial successes. As house arrest sentencing becomes more widespread and is extended to other types of offenders, the public safety question will undoubtedly resurface.

CTQ
Does house arrest have the same deterrence effect on recidivism as imprisonment?

PAROLE

Origins of the American System of Parole

Parole—from the French *parol*, meaning "word of honor"—was a means of releasing prisoners of war who promised not to resume arms in a current conflict. Modern parole, the conditional release of convicts prior to the expiration of their sentence, has a number of antecedents.[15]

Transportation to America In colonial America of the early seventeenth century, labor shortages were met by the immigration from England of children—the indentured poor and delinquents—and pardoned criminals. In the beginning, no specific conditions were imposed upon those who received these pardons. However, after a number of those pardoned evaded transportation and returned to England prior to the expiration of their term, it was found necessary to impose certain restrictions. Around 1655, the form of pardons was amended to include specific conditions and provide for the nullification of the pardon if the recipient failed to abide by the conditions imposed.

During the early days of transportation, the government paid a fee to contractors for each prisoner transported. Subsequently, this was changed, and the contractor was given "property in service"—custody of the prisoner until the expiration of the full term. Once prisoners were delivered to the contractor, the government took no further interest in their welfare or behavior unless they violated the conditions of their pardon by returning to England before their sentences expired.

When pardoned felons arrived in the colonies, their services were sold to the highest bidder. The contractor then transferred the "property in service" agreement to the new master, and the felon was no longer referred to as a criminal but became an indentured servant. This process of indentured service bears a similarity to the procedure followed today by parole boards. Like the criminal indentured servant, a prisoner released on parole agrees in writing to accept certain conditions. A release form is signed by the prisoner and the parole board, and some of the conditions imposed on parolees today are similar to those that were included in the indenture agreement.[16] The termination of the Revolutionary War ended this transportation to America, and England then sent its convicts to Australia until 1879.[17]

Maconochie and Norfolk Island   Erikkson refers to 1840 as the year in which "one of the most remarkable experiments in the history of penology was initiated."[18] In that year, Alexander Maconochie (1787–1860) became superintendent of the British penal colony on Norfolk Island, about 930 miles northeast of Sydney, Australia (see Figure 13.2). He set out a philosophy of punishment based on reforming the individual criminal: The convict was to be punished for the past and trained for the future. Since the amount of time needed to instill self-discipline and train a criminal could not be estimated in advance of sentencing, Maconochie advocated sentences that were open-ended, what is known today as an indeterminate sentence. He set up a system of marks to be earned by each inmate based on good behavior; a sentence could not be terminated until a certain number of marks had been achieved.

Norfolk housed the most dangerous felons, and riots occurred both before Maconochie's arrival and after he left the island. His system, however, brought tranquility to the colony. Convicts passed through three stages on the way to release, each with an increasing amount of personal liberty; misbehavior moved an offender back to an earlier stage. Maconochie was relieved of his position in 1844 and returned to England, where he campaigned for penal reforms as a writer and speaker. One of those influenced by him was Walter Crofton.

Crofton and the Irish System   In 1853, the British Parliament enacted the **Penal Servitude Act,** which enabled prisoners to be released—paroled—on a "ticket of leave" and supervised by the police. That same year, Sir Walter Crofton (1815–1897) was commissioned

FIGURE 13.2

A colored lithograph by J. Glen Wilson of the landing place at Sydney Bay, Norfolk Island. Here in June 1826 Major Turton came ashore with soldiers and convicts to reestablish a penal settlement on the island.

Courtesy of Topham Picturepoint/The Image Works.

to investigate conditions in the Irish prison system. Crofton was familiar with the work of Alexander Maconochie, and their views on the reformation of criminals were similar. The Irish system that Crofton established was based on Maconochie's work at Norfolk Island and consisted of four stages. The first stage involved solitary confinement for nine months; during the first three months, the inmate was on reduced rations and was allowed no labor whatsoever. It was reasoned that after three months of forced idleness, even the laziest prisoner would long for something to do. He would then be given full rations, instructed in useful skills, and exposed to religious influences.

In the second stage, the convict was placed in a special prison to work with other inmates, during which time he could earn marks to qualify for a transfer to the third stage. Stage three involved transportation to an open institution where the convict, by demonstrating signs of reformation, could earn release on a ticket of leave.

In the fourth stage, men who had earned tickets of leave were conditionally released in rural districts, supervised by the police; those residing in Dublin, however, were supervised by a civilian employee who had the title of Inspector of Released Prisoners. He worked cooperatively with the police, but it was his responsibility to secure employment for men with tickets of leave. He required them to report at stated intervals, visited their homes every two weeks, and verified their employment—he was in fact the forerunner of a modern parole officer.

> **CTQ**
> Would you be in favor of implementing any features of the system developed by Maconochie and Crofton in today's correctional facilities?

Developments in the United States A modified version of the Irish system was adopted in England, and Crofton's work was widely publicized in the United States. American supporters of the Irish system, however, did not believe that the adoption of the ticket of leave would ever be accepted in the United States. Their attitude was apparently based on the belief that it would be un-American to place any individual under the supervision of the police, yet they did not believe that any other form of supervision would be effective. A letter written by Crofton in 1847, in reply to an inquiry sent to him by the secretary of the New York Prison Association, stressed that the police of Ireland were permitted to delegate competent individuals in the community to act as custodians for men with tickets of leave, and he suggested a similar procedure for the United States. These principles were the first implemented in the Elmira Reformatory.[19]

Elmira Reformatory In 1869, a reformatory was authorized for Elmira, New York, to receive male offenders between ages 16 and 30 (see Figure 13.3). The following year, the first convention of the American Prison Association met in Cincinnati. A paper based on the Irish system that considered the idea of an indeterminate sentence and the possibilities of a system of parole was presented by noted Michigan penologist Zebulon R. Brockway. The prison reformers meeting in Cincinnati urged New York to adopt Brockway's proposal at Elmira; when the Elmira Reformatory opened in 1876, Brockway was appointed superintendent.

Brockway drafted a statute directing that young first offenders be sent to Elmira under an indeterminate sentence not to exceed the maximum term already in place for nonreformatory offenders. The actual release date was set by the Board of Managers based on institutional behavior: "After the inmate accumulated a certain number of marks based on institutional conduct and progress in academic or vocational training, and if the investigation of his assurances of employment were positive, he could be released."[20] Frederick Wines, a colleague of Brockway, described the principles on which the Elmira system was based, a clear manifestation of the so-called positivist school, which is the application of scientific techniques to the study of crime and criminals:

> ... criminals can be reformed; that reformation is the right of the convict and the duty of the state; that every prisoner must be individualized and given special treatment adapted to develop him to the point in which he is weak—physical, intellectual, or moral culture, in combination, but in varying propositions, according to the diagnosis of each case; that the time must be given for the reformatory process to take effect, before allowing him to be sent away, uncured; that his cure is always facilitated by his cooperation, and often impossible without it.[21]

FIGURE 13.3

Cell block in a maximum security prison.

Courtesy of CORBIS.

Inmate cooperation at Elmira was fostered by corporal punishment and the use of a classification scheme, according to which privileges were dispensed. Upon being admitted to Elmira, each inmate was placed in the second grade (of classification). Six months of good conduct meant promotion to the first grade; misbehavior could result in being placed in the third grade, from which the inmate would have to work his way back up. Continued good behavior in the first grade resulted in release—American's first parole system.

Paroled inmates remained under the jurisdiction of the reformatory authorities for an additional six months, during which the parolee was required to report on the first day of every month to his appointed guardian (from which modern-day parole officers evolved) and provide an account of his situation and conduct. It was believed that a longer period under supervision would be discouraged to the average parolee. "Inmates were released conditionally, subject to return if the Board believed there was actual or potential reversion to criminal behavior."[22]

However, no real attention was given to the training of prisoners toward their future adjustment in the community. Both prison administrators and inmates soon accepted the idea that, reformed or unreformed, allowance of time for good behavior was automatic, and release at the earliest possible date was a right rather than a privilege. After release, supervision was either nonexistent or totally inadequate.

The Elmira system was copied by reformatories in other states, such as the Massachusetts Reformatory at Concord, and made applicable to all or part of the prison population in states such as Pennsylvania, Michigan, and Illinois.[23] Ohio and California had parole release statutes in place before the turn of the twentieth century.[24]

In 1907, New York extended indeterminate sentencing and parole release to all first offenders except those convicted of murder. By 1922, parole was used in forty-four states, and by 1939, only three states (Florida, Mississippi, and Virginia) did not have provisions for parole. (According to the South Carolina parole board, however, that state did not begin to use parole until 1941.)

Modern Parole

Parole Selection Prisoners seeking to be released on parole must follow a procedure of recommendation and review to determine their readiness. Review and selection are subject to the decision-making authority of a **parole board,** which generally includes representatives from the prison, the state department of corrections, and other professionals qualified to assess an inmate's eligibility for parole.

Most parole boards assign cases to individual board members, who review the cases in detail and then make recommendations to the full board when it meets. The recommendations of board members are usually accepted, but sometimes the full board asks for more details. Some states even send parole board members into the prisons to interview inmates and institutional staff; other states convene their entire board at individual institutions on a regular schedule. If inmates do not meet board criteria, their sentences are

IN THE WORKPLACE

PAROLE OFFICER

Responsible for performing routine casework involving parole investigations and supervision of parolees. Work involves interviewing offenders in order to prepare appropriate reports. Works under moderate supervision with limited latitude for the use of initiative and independent judgment. Performs a variety of duties, including the following: informs local law enforcement of pre-parole plans and counsels with parolee's family to prepare them for parolee's release; schedules and conducts interviews; prepares pre-parole summaries; delivers parole decisions to offenders; consults with social agencies to secure aid for parolees; assists law enforcement in the apprehension of parole violators. Minimum qualifications are as follows: graduation from a four-year college or university with major coursework in criminal justice or related field; experience in correctional work with adults or juveniles.

continued and they are "flopped." If parole is granted, the inmate is prepared to be turned over to the adult parole authority for the period of supervision determined by the parole board.

A major problem with parole decisions is that offenders often do not know the criteria they are expected to meet and the reasons that parole might be denied. Porter comments on this aspect of the decision-making process:

> "It is an essential element of justice that the role and processes for measuring parole readiness be made known to the inmate. This knowledge can greatly facilitate the earnest inmate toward his own rehabilitation. It is just as important for an inmate to know the rules and basis of the judgment upon which he will be granted or denied parole as it was important for him to know the basis of the charge against him and the evidence upon which he was convicted. One can imagine nothing more cruel, inhuman, and frustrating than serving a prison term without knowledge of what will be measured and the rules determining whether one is ready for release. . . . Justice can never be a product of unreasoned judgment."[25]

Correctional staff should also be told the "rules of the game" so they can guide inmates toward desirable behavior.

Four inmates at the Indiana State Penitentiary have described three aspects of parole decisions that candidates resent. First, most parole boards emphasize candidates' prior record:

> What is so frustrating to men is that they keep getting rejected for parole because of their "past record" when there is obviously nothing they can do about it. It cannot be changed, it cannot be expunged. It therefore generates a feeling of helplessness and frustration, especially in men who take seriously what they are told about rehabilitation and perfect institutional records. These men cannot understand the rationale behind parole denials based on past records especially if the major goal of the correctional system is rehabilitation and if they tried to take advantage of every rehabilitation program offered by the institution. The men know that merely serving another two or five years is not going to further the "rehabilitation" process.[26]

Second, many parole boards believe that their principal responsibility is to protect society, not to rehabilitate the offender. With this attitude, boards are reluctant to release offenders who are considered poor risks. Rather, they prefer to let such offenders serve their full sentences and return to the community without supervision. This practice may reduce the recidivism rate for offenders on parole, but it may not affect nonparoled inmates' chances for successful reintegration. For some, the wait might be positive: The sheer passage of time seems to mature some people. For most inmates, however, the longer they remain in prison, the more likely they are to absorb the values, techniques, and rationalizations of the criminal subculture. Finally, inmates believe that parole boards are more responsive to public opinion and political pressure than to the record and behavior of the individual applicant. This feeling adds to cynicism about the entire parole process.

The third aspect of parole that has come under attack is the inmate's inability to appeal an unfavorable decision. Parole decisions are often subject to question, especially when an inmate is not told why he or she was denied parole. Further parole selection must include self-regulating and internal appeal procedures. If such procedures are not provided, case after case will be sent to court, and the U.S. Supreme Court will eventually step in and establish rules and procedures based on the Fourteenth Amendment, which deals with issues involving due process. Some states have seen the handwriting on the wall and have started to formalize selection criteria and to develop appeal procedures.

Conditions of Parole Many of the first parole procedures imposed unreasonable restrictions on the released offender. Too often the rules were simply a convenient pretext for returning the parolee to prison—which was often done if the parolee caused even the

---

CTQ

Would it be better for prisoner morale if those who realistically will not be considered for parole not be regularly scheduled for parole hearings?

CTQ

Why should a prisoner's past record be considered at his or her parole hearing?

FIGURE 13.4

Statement of Parole Agreement

The members of the parole board agree that you have earned the opportunity of parole and eventual release from your present conviction. The board is therefore ordering a parole release in your case.

Parole status has a twofold meaning: First, it is a trust status in which the parole board accepts your word that you will do your best to abide by the conditions of parole set down in your case; Second, by state law, the Adult Parole Authority has the legal duty to enforce the conditions of parole event to the extent of arrest and return to the institution.

The following conditions of parole apply to your parole release:
- Upon release from the institution, report as instructed to your parole officer (or any other person designated), and thereafter report as often as directed.
- Secure written permission of the Adult Parole Authority before leaving the [said] state.
- Obey all municipal ordinances and state and federal laws, and at all times conduct yourself as a responsible, law-abiding citizen.
- Never purchase, own, possess, or have under your control a deadly weapon or firearm.
- Follow all instructions given by your parole officer or other officials of the Adult Parole Authority.

If you have any problems with the conditions or instructions of your parole, you may request a meeting with your parole officer's supervisor. The request should state your reasons for the conference, and it should be in writing if possible.

Special conditions.

I have read, or have had read to me, the foregoing conditions of my parole. I fully understand them and I agree to observe and abide by them.

Witness _____ Date _____

Parole Candidate _____

slightest trouble for the parole officer. As recently as twenty years ago, it was not uncommon for the conditions of parole to require the parolee to "only associate with persons of good reputation." Rules of this type gave the parole officer great discretionary power. Offenders knew that their parole could be revoked for a technical violation at almost any time—a situation that did not often engender a newfound respect for the law. The parolee's attitude was often, "If I'm going to get busted for a technical violation, I might as well do something really wrong." Today, however, the rules of parole are much more reasonable and realistic (see Figure 13.4).

Enhancing Parole Prediction

Criminal justice officials increasingly use statistical methods to predict whether an individual will commit future crimes. These methods sometimes take the form of sentencing and parole guidelines that classify people into groups on the basis of their likely future behavior. Individuals in high-risk groups generally receive longer prison sentences or are held in prison longer before parole release.[27]

Sentencing and parole decisions generally involve consideration of two matters: the seriousness of the offense and the characteristics of the offender. Most people believe that both should be taken into account; it is difficult to imagine a system in which differences among offenders are totally ignored (for example, a system in which first offenders and habitual offenders are treated identically).

In this context, predicting criminality means attempting to assess the likelihood that a convicted offender will commit another offense when released into the community. Researchers distinguish between the generic definition of recidivism—simply the act of reoffending—and recidivism rates, which tell us the percentage of any group of offenders that is likely to commit a new offense within a specified period.

There is no standard approach to calculating recidivism rates. In any given jurisdiction, the calculation depends on what kind of behavior is to be counted—arrests, violation or parole conditions, convictions, incarcerations—and on the length of time parolees are followed. Generally, the broader the definition of reoffending or the longer the follow-up period, the higher the reported rate of recidivism will be. For example, if recidivism is measured by any arrest within two years, the frequency of recidivism will be higher than if the recidivism is measured by a new conviction for a serious crime within the same time period. If the reoffending is looked at for twelve months, the recidivism rates will be lower than if the follow-up period were twenty-four months.

The Salient Factor Score The experience of the U.S. Parole Commission illustrates how predictions of recidivism are used in the criminal justice system. Several years ago the commission developed an objective scale, based on empirical research, that can be used to assess a prisoner's likelihood of recidivism. This scale, called the **Salient Factor Score,** is similar to the actuarial tables used by insurance companies. For example, because people in one category of life insurance applicants—nonsmokers—are likely to live longer than those in another category—smokers—life insurance companies generally require higher premiums from smokers, whose average life expectancy is lower. So it is with the Salient Factor Score: Members of groups having a higher likelihood of reoffending are likely to be held in prison longer.

The U.S. Parole Commission's Salient Factor Score contains six items:

- The offender's prior criminal convictions
- The offender's prior criminal commitments for longer than thirty days
- The offender's age at the time of the new offense
- How long the offender was at liberty since the last commitment
- Whether the prisoner was on probation, parole, or escape status at the time of the most recent offense
- Whether the prisoner has a record of heroin dependence

These items, individually and collectively, have been demonstrated to indicate a likelihood of recidivism. For each item with a favorable response, the offender receives a fixed number of points. The points scored on each of the six items are added together to produce a total score that can range from 0 to 10. The higher the total score, the lower the predicted likelihood of recidivism. By taking these scores into account when deciding when to release prisoners on parole, the Parole Commission can release low-risk offenders sooner than high-risk prisoners.

The Salient Factor Score and the seriousness of the offender's offense are combined in a grid that can serve as a guideline for the range of total time to be served. The examiner establishes the seriousness of the offense and identifies the horizontal "offense severity" row that applies to the prisoner. Then the examiner calculates the prisoner's Salient Factor Score and finds the vertical column that applies to the score. The cell where the applicable row and column intersect shows the presumptive time to be served by the prisoner. An example of the grid for an offender who has committed an offense of Category Five severity is shown in Table 13.1. This example shows that an offender with a very low Salient Factor Score may serve two or three times as long for the same offense as an offender with a very high Salient Factor Score.

The period of confinement set by the guidelines is *presumptive* (that is, the guidelines have legal authority, and a sentence consistent with them must be imposed or an explanation must be provided if it is not). The commission may depart from the guidelines if it finds aggravating or mitigating factors that are not already reflected in the guidelines, but it must provide specific reasons in writing for such a departure. In this way, the commission can try to be consistent and even-handed while taking unique individual circumstances into account.

How well does the Salient Factor Score predict recidivism? Using one standard definition of recidivism (any new commitment of sixty days or more, including a return to prison for parole violation within a two-year follow-up period), research has shown that federal prisoners with the highest Salient Factor Score (a score of 10–8) had a recidivism rate of 12 percent. Offenders with the lowest Salient Factor Score (a score of

TABLE 13.1 Guidelines for Decision Making: Customary Total Time to Be Served Before Release (Including Jail Time)

Offense Characteristics: Severity of Offense Behavior	Offender Characteristics: Parole Prognosis (Salient Factor)			
	VERY GOOD (10–8)	GOOD (7–6)	FAIR (5–4)	POOR (3–0)
	GUIDELINE RANGE			
Category five	24–36 Months	36–48 Months	48–60 Months	60–72 Months

Adapted from Peter Hoffman, *Predicting Criminality* (Washington, D.C.: U.S. Department of Justice, National Institute of Justice).

3–0) had a recidivism rate of 49 percent, more than four times as high (Table 13.2). As noted, different research studies have used different definitions of recidivism and different follow-up periods. Regardless of the definition of recidivism or the follow-up period used, the Salient Factor Score has shown clear differences in recidivism rates between categories. Yet within a given category, like perfect prediction is possible.

Other Prediction Efforts How do these results compare with other efforts to predict recidivism? The imperfect quality of the Salient Factor Score's predictive power is shared by alternative prediction methods used by others who have conducted research in this area. The criminal justice research community has devoted considerable effort to improving the predictive power of such devices, but the effort has not been notably successful.

Selective incapacitation, a sentencing strategy also based on prediction, has received substantial attention in recent years. The goal is to learn how to identify high-rate offenders in advance, before they commit many offenses. If these offenders can be accurately identified and incarcerated, the crimes they would have committed will not occur, and other offenders who present less risk of recidivism can be incarcerated for shorter periods or not at all. A major research report from the Rand Corporation has given impetus to selective incapacitation efforts.[28]

Researchers found substantial variations in the rates of crime among offenders. The researchers questioned more than two thousand inmates in state prisons in California, Michigan, and Texas about their past criminal conduct. Some admitted to having committed one or two crimes per year; a small proportion said they had committed hundreds per year. The following factors were associated with the differences between high-rate and low-rate recidivists:

- Prior conviction for the same charge
- Incarcerated for more than half of the preceding two years

CTQ

Do you believe that the Salient Factor Score is an accurate and fair device for predicting recidivism?

TABLE 13.2 Salient Factor Score

Salient Factor Score Category	Recidivism Rate
Category A (Scores of 10–8)	12%
Category B (Scores of 7–6)	25%
Category C (Scores of 5–4)	39%
Category D (Scores of 3–0)	49%

- Served time in the state juvenile facility
- Drug use as a juvenile
- Employed for less than half of the preceding two years

The Rand Corporation study is unusual because it is based on prisoners' admissions of the crimes they committed. Most recidivism research, by contrast, is based on arrests or convictions, and because many crimes do not result in arrests and fewer result in convictions, a less complete picture is available.

Although the study by the Rand Corporation did demonstrate that offenders' rates of committing crimes vary dramatically, it cannot yet serve as the basis for actual decision making. First, some of the information required for the predictions is not routinely and reliably available to judges and other officials. Second, because the Rand scale was developed on the basis of information about prisoners, it is not known how it would operate when applied to all convicted people (many of whom have never been prisoners). Third, the research was based on past, not future, criminality. Predictions must deal with future behavior. It is yet to be seen whether prediction devices can be developed that will identify highly active recidivists with even modest accuracy.

The primary alternative to using statistical approaches in predicting recidivism is to rely on the clinical judgments of clinicians. It is plausible to speculate that clinical judgments coupled with statistical predictions may provide better predictions than either alone. This combined approach is used by the U.S. Parole Commission. As noted earlier, its hearing examiners may override the decisions indicated by the Salient Factor Score when they can set forth substantial research evidence that documents whether combined clinical and statistical judgments actually improve predictive accuracy over that obtained by statistical approaches alone.

Critiques and Justifications Critics of the use of predictions of future crime as the basis for parole and sentencing decisions have raised a number of ethical objections. They argue that prediction methods are far from perfect and that many of those who are classified as poor risks will not in fact commit additional crimes. Further, they argue that it is unfair to increase a person's current punishment because of what he or she might do in the future.

Critics also question the legitimacy of relying on certain kinds of information in making predictions. Most people would agree that neither race nor sex should be used as a basis for increasing sentence lengths, even if this information were shown to be statistically related to recidivism rates. Similarly, critics argue, "status items" such as employment and marital status should not be considered in predicting future crime, even though they have been shown to have predictive power. Because low-income people are especially likely to score poorly on these status items, critics argue that using them constitutes a form of class and income bias. In addition, these items of information are not related to the offender's prior criminal record, are not illegal in themselves, and may in some cases not be within the offender's control. For example, even if unemployed or unmarried offenders were found to have higher recidivism rates, would it be fair to punish them with longer sentences than those received by employed or married offenders who have committed the same offense?

Advocates of the use of criminological predictions agree that certain items may be ethically inappropriate to use even if they prove to be predictive (just as some law enforcement techniques, such as coerced confessions, are legally impermissible notwithstanding their effectiveness). But they point out the best predictive items tend to concern prior criminal record, and valid prediction devices have been developed that do not use race, education, employment, or marital status.

Advocates also argue that while most judges and parole officials may not officially or publically take an offender's "dangerousness" into account, they do it subjectively and based on their own intuition. There seems to be a general agreement that statistical prediction devices, even if imperfect, are more reliable than intuition. In addition, if the prediction device applies to all sentencing or parole decisions, it constitutes a single consistent set of standards and is therefore fairer than a system in which each judge or parole examiner applies his or her own idiosyncratic or intuitive standards.

Advocates of criminological prediction acknowledge that statistical methods are far from perfect and that a significant number of offenders who will not commit new offenses will be misclassified. But they argue that the offenders have made themselves vulnerable in the first place by committing the crimes for which they have been convicted. They maintain that a balance must be struck between the rights of the offenders and the right of the community to be protected from further crimes by the offenders.

Proponents of prediction point out that its use is advocated only for those who are convicted, and then only within the range of what would otherwise constitute fair punishment for the offense. That is, advocates of prediction generally agree that the seriousness of the offense should set the upper and lower boundaries of what constitutes "just" punishment. Within these outer limits, they argue, it is both desirable and ethically appropriate to use predictive considerations to attempt to protect society, at least temporarily, by giving prison terms to those most likely to commit additional offenses.

INNOVATIONS IN PAROLE

Shock Incarceration Programs

Since their inception in 1983, **shock incarceration programs** (also known as boot camps) have enjoyed considerable popular support (see Figure 13.5). Like other intermediate sanctions, the programs are intended to alleviate prison crowding and to reduce recidivism. But because they are additionally perceived as being "tough" on crime, they have been enthusiastically embraced as a viable correctional option.[29]

As the name suggests, boot camp programs are modeled after military boot camp training. Participation in military drill and ceremonies, physical training, and hard labor is mandatory. Inmates begin their day before dawn and are involved in structured activities until "lights out" approximately sixteen hours later.

The military-style regimen is generally supplemented with rehabilitative programming such as drug treatment/education or academic education, although the emphasis placed on such programming varies. In New York, for example, the program is structured as a therapeutic community. Rehabilitative programming therefore plays a central role in the program.

As the boot program concept was developed over the years, however, rehabilitative programs have come to play a more prominent role in the day-to-day routine. The earliest boot camp model devoted very little time to such programming. Many of those pioneering programs have since been enhanced with additional therapeutic services. Programs developed in recent years seem to place a greater emphasis on rehabilitative programs from the outset.

By and large, boot camp programs have been designed for young, male offenders convicted of nonviolent offenses. Eligibility and suitability criteria were developed to restrict participation to this type of offender. For example, in a shock incarceration program completed a few years ago, it was determined that the majority of programs (61.5 percent) allowed participation only of individuals convicted of nonviolent offenses. Fifty percent of the programs further restricted participation of individuals serving their felony sentence as an adult. Minimum and maximum age limits were also the norm. The minimum age limit generally fell somewhere between ages 16 and 18, while the maximum age limit most commonly ranged between ages 23 and 25 (although two programs allowed offenders older than 30 to participate, and five programs had not established a maximum age limit). Female offenders were permitted to participate in roughly 50 percent of the states, although the number of beds available to female inmates was generally limited.

Community Correctional Centers

The essential element in successful community-based corrections is the coordination of activities and services for all offenders. Most programs function as separate entities

FIGURE 13.5

Shock incarceration programs (also known as boot camps) are intended to reduce recidivism. These programs are modeled after military boot comp training and are designed for young male offenders convicted on nonviolent offenses. Physical training and hard labor are stressed. Here, a correctional officer expresses displeasure at what an inmate has done or failed to do.

Courtesy of Olga Shalygin/AP/Wide World Photos.

CTQ

What do you believe are the advantages and disadvantages of shock incarceration programs?

WEB

For more information on parole innovations, **visit our Web site,** www.prenhall.com/territo.

under community branches of government. However, some community-based facilities approach and integrate the community correctional center. Such centers are generally open institutions located in the community and use community resources to provide services. The centers can be used for a variety of purposes, including detention, treatment, holding, and prerelease. The following represents some of the common types of community correctional centers and re-entry programs.

Halfway Houses

A **halfway house** is a community correction facility that provides a residence for convicted offenders who do not require the secure custody of a prison; it is also a transitional setting for prisoners being released from a correctional institution (see Figure 13.6). Such facilities may be operated by private for-profit or not-for-profit contractors or public agencies.[30] Their primary purpose is to provide a transitional living arrangement between the environment found in typical state and federal correctional institutions and totally independent living in the community. Some provide room, board, and help with employment; others provide an even broader array of social services, including remedial education, individual group counseling, and other types of life skills training. However, it is important to note that virtually every halfway house in the nation faces three major obstacles.

The first major problem is location. Many times halfway houses are situated in larger, older homes in well-established neighborhoods. The typical neighborhood response, "not in my back yard!," is known as the "NIMBY" syndrome.

The difficulty of finding a suitable location is understandable. Often community input is not sought, and residents are simply informed that a halfway house is to be opened in their neighborhood. The residents reasonably express fears about having criminals living in their midst. They have images of convicted offenders preying on the community's weak and defenseless. Therefore, halfway houses' staff members and managers have two options: (1) They can do a thorough job of informing community residents of their intentions (perhaps by including some of the neighborhood opinion leaders on an advisory board) in order to garner their support, or (2) they can choose another location, such as an old motel in a commercial district away from residential neighborhoods. The second option is often chosen, not because of the suitability of the locale, but because there is less resistance to such a choice.

The second major obstacle facing halfway house operators is staffing. In some ways halfway houses are fortunate in that they can attract energetic young people for staff positions. Some are recent college graduates (sometimes married couples) who may actually live at the halfway house with the residents. The inducement is a place to live, a salary, and close

FIGURE 13.6

The halfway house is a community correction facility that provides a residence for convicted offenders who do not require the secure custody of a prison. In this photo two residents of a halfway house are having a meal.

Courtesy of AP/Wide World Photos.

IN THE WORKPLACE

HALFWAY HOUSE SUPERVISOR

Responsible for developing policies and treatment programs and supervising staff in a halfway house facility for recovering substance abusers. Performs a variety of duties, including the following: supervises halfway house staff and operations to ensure the effectiveness of overall treatment programs; assesses each potential client to determine the appropriateness of placement; develops program policies, procedures, house rules, and sanctions for comprehensive daily operation; coordinates and manages all staff conferences to establish individual treatment goal and aftercare programs for each client. Minimum qualifications are as follows: bachelor's degree with a major in social work, education, psychology, or rehabilitation; four years' experience in rehabilitation or vocational counseling, three years of which should have been in a residential treatment facility.

contact with offenders who are in need of help. The drawback to these kinds of positions is that they require high emotional investments and, as a result, there is a tremendous amount of staff burnout. After a year or two of working in these positions, most staff members are ready to move on to other things. An additional problem with staffing is pay. The pay issue is related to the problem of budget considerations.

Third, halfway houses often depend on a number of public and private funding sources. This is a double-edged sword. On the other hand, the loss of one source of funding probably will not undermine operation. On the other hand, most halfway houses do not have reliable funding sources they can count on year in and year out. Program managers are always scrambling to pull together bits and pieces from a number of funding sources in order to put together the annual budget. The "softer" the funding sources (for example, grant-funded positions), the more uncertainty about whether staff positions will be continued from one year to the next. This causes great uncertainty among staff members, and it works against the long-range planning process.

Now that we have addressed the impediments facing halfway houses, let us move to some of their specific programming efforts. In particular, we will focus on work release, educational release, and other reentry programs such as furloughs.

Work Release

Halfway houses provide a transitional residential placement where offenders can continue their jobs or reenter the workforce. **Work release programs** can be operated out of both jails and prisons, but the halfway house's less restrictive environment makes this almost an ideal location for work release clients. Residents can work jobs, typically during the day, and return to the halfway house in the evening for treatment or additional job training or simply to eat and sleep. Clients have structure and support, while at the same time they experience a growing sense of freedom. They are not simply turned loose to fend for themselves.

In addition to providing an alternative to incarceration, the halfway house provides another benefit to the taxpayers and the criminal justice system. Most halfway house residents are required to pay part of their support from the money they earn. If they have families, they may also be required to support their families. Halfway house advocates see this as a win-win situation. The offenders are benefiting from not being incarcerated, and the public is benefiting from improved job and social skills, lower treatment costs, and hopefully reduced recidivism.

Educational Release

Educational release raises many of the same concerns as work release. A problem for many offenders is their lack of education. In order to ensure their future employability and a smooth transition back into society (for parolees), education must be stressed. Although education and job training are offered in many correctional institutions, programs may be limited in scope and size. In other words, not all inmates may be eligible, certain courses of study may not be large enough to meet inmate demand, and some educational programs may simply not be offered. Therefore, halfway house residents may be able to take advantage of certificate or degree programs offered at community colleges and universities. The goal is not simply to have a better educated ex-offender, but to have one whose education prepares him or her for a crime-free life.

Furloughs

Often we associate **furloughs** with short-term release from prison. However, furlough programs can operate with and through halfway houses as well. Furloughs typically involve short periods of release from custody without supervision. This allows the offender to return home for a few days in order to reestablish family ties. Again, the primary purpose is reintegration, and furloughs can be granted for individuals in secure custody (jail or prison) or residents of halfway houses.

COMMUNITY SERVICE

Community service is another area of community corrections that has seen enormous growth since the late 1970s. Like fines and restitution, community service has its roots in primitive legal codes and in notions such as restorative justice. In its modern form it

---

CTQ

What recommendations would you make to deal with the three problems facing halfway houses?

CTQ

What are the major features of work release programs and educational release programs? Which do you think is more effective?

CTQ

What can be done to ensure that halfway house residents receive a proper education so that they are employable when they are released from the facility?

has been seen as an alternative to incarceration. Community service programs seem especially appropriate for crimes such as spray-painting graffiti or other forms of vandalism (see Figure 13.7).

Objectives of Community Service

Community service is aimed at securing benefits for the community and for the offender as well. The offender provides a service to the community—helping to clean up graffiti, for example. But the offender gains something from community service as well. In fact, the offender seems to receive at least two major benefits. First, the offender is held accountable for the offense, which should help the person take responsibility for his or her actions in the future. Second, the offender benefits from not being incarcerated and from not incurring a financial cost—such as fines, forfeitures, or restitution payments—that may be difficult to repay.

CTQ: Why are community service programs sometimes not a realistic and viable alternative to incarceration?

Types of Programs

In cases that do not seem to warrant incarceration, the judge may order the offender to participate in projects that should provide some community assistance. In some ways, like diversion programs, community service projects are only limited by our imagination. For instance, offenders may be ordered to clean up graffiti, to work in community parks and recreation programs, or to clean up government offices. On occasion offenders are ordered to wash government vehicles such as police cars or fire trucks as part of their obligation. Normally, this is done in conjunction with standard probation, and as one of the specific probation conditions. These efforts may be administered by a probation officer or some other government official, such as a parks and recreation supervisor.

Other community service programs may require offenders to work in hospital emergency rooms (especially for those convicted of drunk driving) or facilities such as clinics, libraries, senior citizen centers, and schools. The objective is for the offender to develop a degree of accountability to the community and to see that the community has been harmed by his or her criminal action.

Issues in Community Service

Community service efforts would seem to be the least controversial community corrections programs imaginable, but this is not the case. In fact, there seem to be three issues that plague community service endeavors. First, ensuring offender accountability presents many problems. Although offenders may appear for their assignments, this does not necessarily mean the jobs are meaningful to them or that they learn any particular lesson as a result of having fulfilled the court order.

Second is the question of supervision of offenders involved in community service projects. Simply because a judge has ordered an offender to perform a certain number of hours does not mean that the person will complete the duties assigned or even show up when ordered to. Someone has to assume the responsibility for holding the offender accountable, and too often this falls upon the overworked probation officers.

Third, and perhaps the most severe community service criticism, deals with punishment. Many members of the general public do not believe that community service is "real" punishment; thus these projects may suffer from a lack of legitimacy because of this lack of credibility.

FIGURE 13.7

Convicted offenders sentenced to community service are pictured here shoveling ice and snow from a driveway and sidewalk.

Courtesy of James Nubile/The Image Works.

SUMMARY

In this chapter we have examined some traditional alternatives to confinement, as well as some of the newer ones. Certainly one of the older and more common alternatives is probation, which can be implemented in three ways. First, the law may allow the trial judge to suspend the execution of sentence and to place the offender on conditional probation. Second, a state statute may require sentencing but may permit suspension. Third, sentencing and probation may be left to the discretion of the trial judge.

In order to determine which offenders are good candidates for probation, sentencing judges rely heavily upon presentence investigation (PSI) reports. The primary purpose of the PSI is not to determine the guilt or innocence of the defendants, but rather to give insight into their personalities and lives.

One of the most interesting innovations in probation during the past decade has been the concept of house arrest. Those in favor of it believe house arrest is socially cost-effective because if the offender has a job before he or she is convicted, the person may keep it during house arrest. By preventing the breakup of the family and family networks, house arrest can also prevent psychological and physical disruptions that may have lifelong effects on the offender, his or her spouse and children, and even the next generation. House arrest is advantageous because it is also flexible and uses a sole sanction as part of the package of sentencing. It can be used at almost any point in the criminal justice process—as a diversion before the offender experiences any jail time, after a short term in jail, after a prison term (usually joined with a work release program), or as a condition for probation or parole. In addition, house arrest helps reduce prison crowding. Because house arrest requires no new facilities and can use existing probation personnel, it is one of the easiest programs to implement.

Some critics of house arrest argue that a sentence of house arrest is not sufficiently severe to constitute an appropriate punishment for many crimes. Others argue that house arrest, particularly if implemented with electronic devices, will start the final blow to the rehabilitative ideal. Some have argued that programs discriminate against the young and the poor because to qualify for most house arrest programs, a person must generally pay a supervision fee every month. Electronic monitors are used for which the offender needs to have a home and a telephone. Other critics have questioned whether house arrest can adequately protect the public, recognizing that it is sometimes difficult to keep criminals from committing further crimes if they are allowed to remain free in their homes.

Parole is conditional, supervised release of offenders from correctional institutions after they have served part of their sentences. Most incarcerated felons released from prison each year enter parole. Parole differs from probation because it implies that the offender has served time. Administratively, parole is a function of the executive branch of government, whereas probation is a judicial act of the court.

Considerable research has been conducted to improve the ability to predict which offenders are good candidates for parole. One of these is the Salient Factor Score, which was developed several years ago by the U.S. Parole Commission to assess prisoners' likelihood of recidivism. This scale is similar to the actuarial tables developed by insurance companies.

A number of other alternative forms of incarceration have been developed in recent years. For example, shock incarceration programs (also known as boot camps) have been around since 1983, and have enjoyed considerable popular support. By and large, boot camp programs are designed for young male offenders who have committed nonviolent offenses. Community correctional centers are another alternative means of sentencing. Halfway houses provide a residence for convicted offenders, do not require for the secure custody of a prisoner, and work as a transitional setting for prisoners being released from a correctional institution.

Lastly, we discussed restitution and community service. These two alternatives to incarceration have seen enormous growth since the 1970s. Some types of community service programs include ordering offenders to clean up graffiti, to work in community parks or recreation programs, to clean up government offices, and to wash government vehicles such as police cars or fire trucks. Other community service programs may include requiring offenders to work in emergency rooms or facilities such as clinics, libraries, senior citizen centers, and schools.

Discussion and Review

1. How does a suspended sentence differ from probation?
2. What does it mean when probation is imposed without adjudication?
3. What is a presentence investigation?
4. What are the basic differences between traditional probation and intensive-supervision probation?
5. What are the advantages of house arrest?
6. What are the disadvantages of house arrest?
7. What types of individuals were transported to colonial America to compensate for a labor shortage?
8. What is the goal of selective incapacitation as a sentencing strategy?
9. How is the RAND Corporation study unusual as compared to other studies?
10. What are shock incarceration programs modeled after? What are they designed for?
11. What is the essential element in successful community-based corrections?
12. What philosophy did Alexander Maconochie espouse relating to the punishment of individual criminals?
13. What are some of the major problems in parole decisions?
14. Sentencing or parole decisions generally involve consideration of two matters. What are they?
15. The U.S. Parole Commission's Salient Factor Score contains six items. What are they?
16. What are the three major obstacles faced by virtually every halfway house in the nation?
17. What are the objectives of community service?
18. What are furloughs?
19. What are the objectives of community service, and what are some examples of community service programs imposed by judges as part of the sentencing?
20. What three issues plague community service endeavors?

Chapter Resources

IN THE MEDIA

Video

CNN Today Video: *Corrections: Female Boot Camp*, Vol. 1: segment 3.

CNN Today Video: *Criminology: Restorative Justice*, Vol. 4: segment 9.

CNN Today Video: *Introduction to Criminal Justice: House Arrest*, Vol. 2: segment 13.

CNN Today Video: *Introduction to Criminal Justice: Parole Housing*, Vol. 3: segment 12.

NIJ Video: *Probation*, Vol. 2.

NIJ Video: *Restitution and Community Service*.

IN THE LITERATURE

Books

J. BYRNE, A. LURIGIO, AND M. MAHONEY, *Smart Sentencing: The Emergence of Intermediate Sanctions*. Newbury Park, CA: Sage, 1992.

G. COLE, B. MAHONEY, M. THORTON, AND R. HANSON, *The Practices and Attitudes of Trial Court Judges Regarding Fines as a Criminal Sanction*. Washington D.C.: U.S. Government Printing Office, 1987.

J. DILULIO, *Governing Prison: A Comparative Study of Correctional Management*. New York: Free Press, 1997.

D. DUFFEE, *Corrections, Practice and Policy*. New York: Random House, 1989.

B. FLETCHER, L. DIXON, AND D. MOON, *Women Prisoners: A Forgotten Population.* Westport, Conn.: Praeger, 1995.

N. MORRIS AND M. TONRY, *Between Prison and Probation: Intermediate Punishments in a Rational Sentencing System.* New York: Oxford University Press, 1990.

J. PETERSILIA AND S. TURNER, *Intensive Supervision for High-Risk Probationers.* Santa Monica, Calif.: Rand Corporation, 1990.

H. TOCH, *Living in Prison.* New York: Free Press, 1977.

Articles

R. GAGLIARDO, "Parole-Centered Counseling: Motivating Inmates by Addressing Their Primary Concerns," *Corrections Today,* vol. 26 (August 2000), p. 16.

P. GENDREAU, T. LITTLE, AND C. GOGGIN, "An Analysis of the Predictors of Adult Offender Recidivism: What Works?" *Criminology,* vol. 34 (1996), pp. 575–607.

J. KADEN, "Therapy for Convicted Sex Offenders: Pursuing Rehabilitation without Incarceration," *Journal of Law and Criminology,* vol. 89 (1998), p. 347.

R. LAWRENCE, "Reexamining Community Corrections Models," *Crime and Delinquency,* vol. 37 (1991), pp. 449–464.

B. MCKAY AND B. PARIS, "Forging a Police-Probation Alliance," *FBI Law Enforcement Bulletin,* vol. 67 (1998), p. 27.

R. MERCER, M. BROOKS, AND P. BRYANT, "Global Positioning Satellite System: Tracking Offenders in Real Time," *Corrections Today,* vol. 62 (2000), pp. 76–79.

ENDNOTES

1. K. Krajick, "Probation: The Original Community Program." *Corrections,* vol. 6 (1980), p. 7.

2. H. E. Barnes and N. K. Teeters, *New Horizons in Criminology.* Englewood Cliffs, N.J.: Prentice-Hall, 1969, p. 554.

3. P. Murchek, "Probations with Adjudication." Paper delivered at the 18th annual Southern Conference on Correction, Tallahassee, Fla. February 25–27, 1973, p. 27.

4. R. M. Carter and L. T. Wilkins, *Probation, Parole, and Community Corrections.* New York: Wiley, 1976

5. J. M. Byrne, *Probation.* Washington, D.C.: U.S. Department of Justice, National Institute of Justice, 1988. The discussion of restructuring probation as an intermediate sanction was adapted from this source.

6. V. B. Gowdy, *Intermediate Sanctions.* Washington, D.C.: U.S. Department of Justice, National Institute of Justice, 1988. The discussion of intensive supervision probation programs was adapted from this source.

7. J. Petersilia, J. Peterson, and S. Turner, "Intensive Probation and Parole: Research Findings and Policy Implications." Draft report to the National Institute of Justice, January 1972.

8. U.S. Department of Justice, Office of Justice Programs, "A Survey of Intermediate Sanctions." September 1990, p. 10.

9. F. S. Pearson, "New Jersey's Intensive Supervision Program." Unpublished report to the National Institute of Justice, June 1988.

10. U.S. Department of Justice, National Institute of Justice, "Searching for Answers—Annual Evaluation Report on Drugs and Crime." July 1992, p. 75.

11. Ibid.

12. E. C. DiCerbo, "When Should Probation Be Revoked?" *Federal Probation,* vol. 30 (1966), pp. 11–17.

13. J. Petersilia, *House Arrest.* Washington D.C.: U.S. Department of Justice, National Institute of Justice, 1988. The discussion of innovations in probation was adapted from this source.

14. A. K. Schmidt, *Electronic Monitoring of Offenders Increases.* Washington, D.C.: U.S. Department of Justice, National Institute of Justice, January/February, 1989, p. 2.

15. H. Abadinsky, *Probation and Parole: Theory and Practice.* Englewood Cliffs, N.J.: Prentice Hall, 1991, p. 71. The discussion of the origins of the American system of parole was taken with permission from this source.

16. *Parole Officer's Manual.* Albany: New York State Division of Parole, 1993.

17. R. Hughes, *The Fatal Shore: The Epic of Australia's Founding.* New York: Knopf, 1987.

18. R. Erikkson, *The Reformers: An Historical Survey of Pioneer Experiments in the Treatment of Criminals.* New York: Elsevier, 1976, p. 81.

19. *Parole Officer's Manual,* op. cit.

20. *1982–83 Annual Report.* Albany: New York State Division of Parole, 1984, p. 6.

21. F. H. Wines, *Punishment and Reformation: A Study of the Penitentiary System.* New York: Crowell, 1975, p. 230.

22. *1982–83 Annual Report,* op. cit.

23. Wines, op. cit.

24. R. G. Zevitz and S. R. Takata, "Paroling Prisoners Sentenced to County Jail: An Analysis of 75 Years of Misdemeanor Parole Legislation," *Journal of Criminal Justice,* vol. 11 (1988), pp. 61–68.

25. E. M. Porter. "Criteria for Parole Selection." Proceedings of the American Correctional Association. New York: American Correctional Association, 1968, p. 227.

26. H. J. Griswold, M. Misenheimer, A. Powers, and E. Tromanhauser, *An Eye for an Eye.* New York: Holt, Rinehart & Winston, 1970.

27. P. Hoffman, *Predicting Criminality.* Washington, D.C.: U.S. Department of Justice, National Institute of Justice, 1987, p. 2.

28. P. W. Greenwood with A. Abrahamse, *Selective Incapacitation.* Report to the National Institute of Justice. Santa Monica, Calif.: Rand Corporation, 1982.

29. D. L. MacKinzie and C. Souryal, "Multisite Evaluation of Shock Incarceration." Final report presented to the National Institute of Justice, November 1994.

30. G. L. Mays and L. T. Winfree, *Contemporary Corrections.* Belmont, CA: Wadsworth, 1998, pp. 282–285, 292–293. The discussion of community correctional centers is taken with permission from this source.

14 JUVENILE JUSTICE

Chapter Outline

The Creation of Delinquency
Development of the Juvenile Court
  The First Juvenile Courts: 1899–1967
  Where We Are Today
Language of the Courts
  Teen Courts
Prevention and Diversion
  The Police
  Intake and the Courts
  Programs outside the Juvenile Justice System
Educational Programs
  Drug Abuse Resistance Education (DARE)
  Education in the Law
Handling Juveniles in the System
  Dependent and Abused Children
  Delinquent Children
  Police Contact
  Juvenile Intake
  Removing Juveniles from Adult Jails
Juvenile Detention Centers
  Research on Juveniles in Detention
Deinstitutionalization of Status Offenders
Postadjudication Dispositions
  Juvenile Restitution Programs
  Community-Based Programs
  Residential Programs
  Wilderness Programs
  Nonresidential Programs
Long-Term Institutional Facilities
Evaluating Juvenile Boot Camps
Community Supervision
  Juvenile Probation
  Juvenile Aftercare
  The Quality of Supervision
  Revocation

Runaway Missing Children
  Characteristics of the Runaway
  The System's Response to Runaway Youth
Juvenile Curfews
  Representative Curfew Programs
Serious and Violent Juvenile Offenders
  SVJ Offenders—A Distinct Group
  Predictors of SVJ Offending
  Interventions to Prevent SVJ Offending
Crime in Schools
  Nonfatal Student Victimization—Student Reports
  Violence and Crime at School—Public School Principal/Disciplinarian Reports
  School Environment
  The School Resource Officer (SRO)
The Secret Service Safe School Initiative
  Background
  Method
  Incident Characteristics
  Preliminary Findings
  Implications
Youth Gangs
  Scope of the Problem
  Why Do Youth Join Gangs?
  Conclusion
Children Who Kill Their Parents
  Youths at Risk
Juvenile Justice in the New Century
  Objectives of an Effective Juvenile Justice System
  Elements of an Effective Juvenile Justice System
Summary

Key TERMS

aftercare, p. 560
delinquent, p. 544
dependent children, p. 551
disposition, p. 555
diversion, p. 548
deinstitutionalization of status offenders (DSO), p. 556
intake, p. 554
Juvenile Justice and Delinquency Prevention (JJDP) Act, p. 555
juvenile, p. 543

juvenile justice system, p. 557
juvenile probation, p. 560
matricide, p. 573
parens patriae, p. 543
patricide, p. 573
restitution, p. 557
runaways, p. 561
school resource officer (SRO), p. 569
status offenses, p. 551
serious and violent juvenile (SVJ), p. 564

Courtesy of Bill Aron/PhotoEdit

According to the 2001 *Uniform Crime Report* (UCR), law enforcement agencies in the United States made an estimated 1.3 million arrests of people under age 18. The Federal Bureau of Investigation (FBI) reported that **juveniles** accounted for 17 percent of all arrests and 27.5 percent of all index offense arrests. Law enforcement arrested juveniles under age 18 for offenses of larceny-theft more often than for any other offenses, whereas adults were most often arrested for drug abuse violations.

The juvenile offender is generally handled in a system distinct from the rest of the criminal justice system. Until recently, the courts that dealt with juvenile cases had few of the features generally associated with a judicial tribunal. The orientation of the courts was toward treatment; there was relatively little concern for determining guilt or innocence of the juvenile through traditional court procedures. Under the guiding philosophy called ***parens patriae***, judges were expected to act as "kind and loving parents" and to do whatever they could to direct juvenile offenders toward socially acceptable conduct. The approach was designed to spare the youngster the punishment and stigma of criminality.

Some critics point out that, although the original objectives of this approach were laudable in theory, they simply could not be achieved in practice. Thus, the juvenile court was doomed to failure because it assumed responsibilities that far exceeded its resources: It tried to take the place of a failed educational system, a poor home environment, or the collapse of informal social control formerly carried out by the neighborhood.

Other critics are concerned with the inability of the juvenile justice system to deal with the increasing numbers of juveniles who commit serious felony offenses such as murder, rape, robbery, aggravated assault, and arson. Some juvenile court authorities maintain that the juvenile court is no longer relevant to today's juvenile criminals, especially those charged with violent crimes. When one encounters a hulking 15-year-old in juvenile detention who is charged with forcible rape and homicide and learns that this is the "child" named in the juvenile court petition—the juvenile court equivalent of indictment—it is difficult to believe that this is the kind of client the founders of the juvenile justice system had in mind. And it does not help much that the terms *delinquent* and *criminal* are widely used as though they were synonymous.

The juvenile courts now appear to be moving in a new direction (for reasons we explore later in this chapter). An increased emphasis on due process safeguards for the accused juvenile is helping to shape the juvenile court into something resembling a "junior criminal court." At the same time, in response to public demands for community protection, growing numbers of juveniles are being placed under the jurisdiction of the adult criminal justice system; many groups believe that the juvenile justice system can no longer handle serious youthful offenders.

THE CREATION OF DELINQUENCY

Delinquency is a relatively new concept. Throughout the Middle Ages, and even as late as the seventeenth century, youths engaged in behavior that today would probably result in their adjudication as **delinquent**—and their parents would probably be charged with contributing to the delinquency of minors. As soon as they could talk, many children used obscene language, drank without restriction in taverns and at home, had sexual experiences freely or under duress, rarely attended school—and when they did, they carried arms and fought duels.[1] Today, however, most people feel that this kind of behavior should be curbed among juveniles.

This change in attitude toward youthful behavior resulted from a change in the conception of childhood and children. In the late sixteenth and early seventeenth centuries, it was widely believed that children require distinctive preparation to become productive members of the community. This view influenced the development of schools, whose function was to assist parents in providing both intellectual and moral training. If children were to attend school, the period of childhood had to be extended, a circumstance that justified restricting children's behavior on the grounds that they were too immature or too naive to engage in certain behaviors. Initially, this conception of childhood influenced mostly the middle class: Lower-class and minority children were not affected until the nineteenth or early twentieth century.

During the early 1800s, institutions for children called *houses of refuge* were established to combat the negative influences of inadequate families and disorganized communities. Designed to serve as family substitutes, these facilities supplied the discipline, affection, and training that parents were not able, or available, to provide.

Although these child-saving institutions were thought by reformers to hold great promise for changing the behavior of wayward youth, they became—in reality—places to house the youthful misfits of society. In light of the discipline, regimen, and living conditions that characterized these institutions, it is not surprising that they did little to change the conduct of their charges. (Punishment included increased workloads, loss of play periods, a diet of bread and water, solitary confinement, wearing a ball and chain, and whippings.) By 1850, these institutions were not producing children who would become upstanding members of the community, but instead were turning out children who—at best—thought, marched, and otherwise behaved like robots.

But other conditions overshadowed these negative results, making the need for child-saving facilities even more critical. The latter part of the nineteenth century brought rapid urban growth, an influx of immigrants, and a marked increase in social instability.[2] Immigrants who arrived in the United States were generally poor and lived in deteriorated areas with high rates of crime and delinquency. Their patterns of behavior—sexual, marital, and linguistic—were viewed as deviant, thus providing a rationale for treating them as inferior and as threats to the social order. Further, the theories of Charles Darwin, as applied to social life, provided justification for regarding immigrants as biologically inferior.

Out of these views on the immigrant community emerged two major themes that had important implications for the continued institutionalization of children. One focused on the "disruptive" conditions of life in industrial urban slums; the second, heavily influenced by Darwin's ideas, attributed crime to biological factors. If crime could be ascribed to social conditions such as poverty and family instability, then these factors could possibly be changed—or at least their more adverse influences could be mitigated—by subjecting affected people to countervailing influences. Thus, despite the contention by some authorities that crime is rooted in biological factors, human behavior was still considered susceptible to environmental influence. Nevertheless, these two themes underscored the need for institutions designed to counter adverse biological and social influences.

During this same era, groups of middle-class women became preoccupied with the so-called child-saving movement. Appalled by the depraved conditions of life in urban slums, these women sought to establish institutions to reverse negative influences and give youngsters a chance to become conventional members of society. At this point, an interesting paradox existed: While it was recognized that the houses of refuge had failed to meet their objectives as "superparents," they were still seen as the only substitute for a natural home providing the education, discipline, and benign environment needed to counteract adverse biological and social factors. This issue was resolved by blaming the failure of these institutions on the methods they employed rather than on the objectives themselves. This view required that new institutions be built.

The new facilities thus established were called *industrial schools* and *reformatories*. Industrial schools, which replaced the houses of refuge, were organized along the cottage or family system. Reformatories, originally intended to replace prisons, came to be used as institutions for youthful offenders convicted of crimes (their philosophy and programs were consistent with the views of the day on how youths should be handled).

Both the reformatory and the industrial school failed miserably. Although their objectives were sound, the methods employed were, in most cases, no better than those employed by the houses of refuge. Discipline was repressive and ranged from benevolent despotism to tyrannical cruelty.[3] Floggings were common but were among the less cruel punishments inflicted on youngsters. The regimen was rigid: Mass formations and military drills were emphasized. The main program of reform involved long hours of tedious work. At industrial schools, the principal work was farm labor, which was of doubtful value to youngsters who returned to the city. In essence, these facilities differed from houses of refuge only in name and location.

The failure of these institutions after a century of experimentation with various juvenile facilities may be surprising, but a valuable lesson was learned; our experiences in the nineteenth century demonstrated the futility of trying to use institutions as a method of social control in periods of rapid social and ideological change. These early facilities provided only a temporary means of incapacitating dangerous offenders; they were not up to the task of socializing or redirecting youthful criminals. Almost a century has passed since we first tried to devise urban institutions to provide justice and opportunity and to offset the problems faced by children in a pluralistic society. Unfortunately, time seems to have done little to improve our ability to deal with the situation, and we are far from encouraged about the future.

Despite the ineffectiveness of nineteenth-century methods of dealing with children, childhood had been recognized by the close of the century as a status distinct from adulthood—one that afforded its occupants exemptions from certain kinds of behavior expected of adults. Children were acknowledged as a distinct group that required not

CTQ

In your opinion, which has the greater influence with respect to juvenile delinquency: biology or environment? Justify your response.

TABLE 14.1 Juvenile Justice Developments: 1646 to the Present

System (Period)	Major Developments	Influences	Child–State Relationship	Parent–State Relationship	Parent–Child Relationship
Puritan (1646–1824)	Massachusetts Stubborn Child Law (1646)	Christian view of child as evil; economically marginal agrarian society	Law provides symbolic standard of maturity; support for family as economic unit	Parents considered responsible for and capable of controlling child	Child considered both property and spiritual responsibility of parents
Refuge (1824–1899)	Institutionalization of deviants; New York House of Refuge established (1824) for delinquent and dependent children	Enlightenment; immigration and industrialization	Child seen as helpless, in need of state intervention	Parents supplanted as state assumes responsibility for correcting deviant socialization	Family considered to be a major cause of juvenile delinquency
Juvenile court (1899–1960)	Establishment of separate legal system for juveniles—Illinois Juvenile Court Act (1899)	Reformism and rehabilitative ideology; increased immigration, urbanization, large-scale industrialization	Juvenile court institutionalizes legal irresponsibility of child	*Parens patriae* doctrine gives legal foundation for state intervention in family	Further abrogation of parents' rights and responsibilities
Juvenile rights (1960–present)	Increased "legalization" of juvenile law—*Gault* decision (1966); Juvenile Justice and Delinquency Prevention Act (1974) calls for deinstitutionalization of status offenders	Criticism of juvenile justice system on humane grounds; civil rights movements by disadvantaged groups	Movement to define and protect rights as well as provide services to children	Reassertion of responsibility of parents and community for welfare and behavior of children	Attention given to children's claims against parents; earlier emancipation of children

Source: Adapted from U.S. Department of Justice, *Reports of the National Juvenile Assessment, Centers: A Preliminary National Assessment of the Status Offender and the Juvenile Justice System.* Washington, D.C.: U.S. Government Printing Office.

TABLE 14.2 Antecedents of the Juvenile Court

1825	New York House of Refuge was opened, followed by houses in Boston (1826), Philadelphia (1828), and New Orleans (1855).
1831	Illinois passed a law that allowed penalties for certain offenses committed by minors to differ from the penalties imposed on adults.
1841	John Augustus inaugurated probation and became the nation's first probation officer.
1854	State industrial school for girls was opened in Lancaster, Massachusetts (first cottage-type institution).
1858	State industrial school for boys in Lancaster, Ohio, adopted a cottage-type system.
1863	Children's Aid Society was founded in Boston. Members of the organization attended police and superior court hearings, supervised youngsters selected for probation, and did the investigation on which probation selection was based.
1869	A law was enacted in Massachusetts to direct the State Board of Charities to send agents to court hearings that involved children. The agents made recommendations to the court that frequently involved probation and the placement of youngsters with suitable families.
1870	Separate hearings for juveniles were required in Suffolk County, Massachusetts. New York followed by requiring separate trials, dockets, and records for children; Rhode Island made similar provisions in 1891.
1899	In April, Illinois adopted legislation creating a first juvenile court in Cook County (Chicago). In May, Colorado established a juvenile court.

only different correctional facilities but also regulations and laws to protect them against exploitation by our economic system. The recognition of these needs helped bring about the establishment of the juvenile court. (See Table 14.1 for a summary of developments in juvenile justice from 1646 to the present. Table 14.2 lists various stages in the creation of the juvenile court.)

DEVELOPMENT OF THE JUVENILE COURT

The first juvenile court was created in Chicago, Illinois, in 1899. In many respects, this court represented the dawn of a new era for our legal system. Previously, our court processes had the objectives of retribution and deterrence, and they gave little attention to individual differences. By the turn of the century, however, teachings and research in the new area of social science began to impact the legal system. It was recognized that differences existed between offenders, regardless of whether they had committed the same offense. This recognition implied that differences in physical and mental conditions, as well as in environmental influences, should be taken into account in judicial decisions. The result was the birth of *individualized justice.*

To put the concept of individualized justice into operation, the courts had to examine a wide variety of psychological and social factors that had nothing to do with guilt or innocence in a strict legal sense. Consideration was given to the economic, social, cultural, and emotional factors that shape the individual and to data regarding the offender's education, career, family, employment record, and community environment. The purpose of this diagnosis was to provide information that could be used to determine the type of treatment needed by the offender.

The First Juvenile Courts: 1899–1967

The establishment (by statute) of the first juvenile court in Illinois in 1899 marked the beginning of an era of "social jurisprudence."[4] Although the juvenile court was a bona fide court, its procedures were dramatically different from adult court proceedings. The court's major objective was to help the wayward child become a productive member of the community. The determination of guilt or innocence, using standard rules of evidence, was not of primary importance. Instead, the purpose of the court hearing was to determine "What is he, how has he become what he is, and what had best be done in his interest and in the interest of the state to save him from a downward career."[5] In other words, court procedures were to be more diagnostic than legal in nature, giving major consideration to the information obtained on the youngster's environment, heredity, and physical and mental condition.[6]

The aim of the Illinois juvenile court was prevention and rehabilitation, not punishment. Any youngsters who violated the law were called juvenile delinquents, not criminals; this term implied that the juveniles were wayward children in need of assistance from the court, their new "superparent." The juvenile court judges were to assume a parental role in an atmosphere less threatening than that of the adult criminal court—reviewing the behavior of youngsters, disciplining them when appropriate, and devising a course of action to prevent further delinquent behavior. To aid in these tasks, the court hired psychologists, psychiatrists, and social workers to prepare comprehensive reports on youngsters' backgrounds and psychological characteristics. The goals and methods of the juvenile court remained essentially unchanged until 1967.

Where We Are Today

Given the basic commitment to rehabilitation rather than punishment, juvenile courts developed along the lines of social casework. Hearings were conducted in an informal atmosphere, and testimony and background data were introduced without regard to rules of evidence. In addition, the juvenile was denied many of the rights guaranteed by due process—including representation by counsel, confrontation with one's accuser, cross-examination, and the right to invoke the privilege against self-incrimination.

In *Kent v. United States* (1966), Justice Abe Fortas of the U.S. Supreme Court expressed concern that the guiding philosophy of the juvenile court—*parens patriae*—had not been realized. Youngsters were getting the worst of both worlds: they were denied the rights accorded adults, and they did not receive the care and treatment promised under the *parens patriae* doctrine.

The *Kent* decision raised many issues and paved the way for the Supreme Court to come to grips with these problems in the *Gault* decision (In re *Gault*, 1967). Gerald Gault,

IN THE WORKPLACE

JUVENILE JUDGE

Responsible for hearing all juvenile court matters, including delinquency and detention cases. Performs a variety of duties, including the following: conducts juvenile court proceedings; issues orders, findings, decisions, and warrants; maintains professional competence in the law; maintains and ensures order and decorum in juvenile proceedings; and affords every person a right to be heard according to the law. Judges are appointed and must meet minimum qualifications. The qualifications vary by jurisdiction.

CTQ

Should we return to the historical philosophy of *parens patriae* for juveniles, or should we continue to grant them due process protections during the juvenile adjudication process?

WEB

For more information on the language of the courts, **visit our Web site, www.prenhall.com/territo.**

CTQ

Should diversion be used in all offenses involving juveniles? Why or why not?

WEB

For more information on prevention and diversion, **visit our Web site, www.prenhall.com/territo.**

---

a 15-year-old, was sentenced to confinement for the "remainder of his minority" (six years) for an offense that carried a maximum adult penalty of only two months. During hearings, Gault was deprived of most of the procedural rights afforded his adult counterparts. His appeal was heard by the U.S. Supreme Court on the following issues: right to notice of the charge, right to counsel, right to confrontation and cross-examination of witnesses, privilege against self-incrimination, right to a transcript of the proceedings, and right to an appellate review.

As a result of *Kent*, *Gault*, and subsequent decisions (such as In re *Winship* [1970]), the juvenile court process now has two distinct phases: an adjudication phase, which accords juveniles the same due process rights as adults, with the exception of a jury trial; and a disposition phase, in which, following a determination of guilt, a treatment or rehabilitation plan is drawn up.

LANGUAGE OF THE COURTS

The terms used in criminal courts have been changed to apply to juvenile justice. For example, *petition* replaces *complaint*, *summons* replaces *warrant*, *finding of involvement* replaces *conviction*, and *disposition* replaces *sentencing*. The words *child*, *youth*, and *youngster* are used synonymously to denote a person of juvenile court age. Juvenile court laws define a child as any person under a specified age, no matter how mature or sophisticated he or she may seem. The most significant terms used in the juvenile system are defined in Table 14.3.

Teen Courts

In some locations the handling of misdemeanor-type offenses committed by juveniles are given a relatively low priority. These are areas in which the juvenile courts are backlogged with more serious cases of delinquency. One innovation that has been implemented to handle the less serious cases is the *teen courts*. The Office of Juvenile Justice and Delinquency Prevention says that "the teen courts present communities with opportunities to teach young people valuable life and coping skills and promote positive peer influence for youth who are defendants and for volunteer youth who play a variety of roles in the teen court process."[7] In some jurisdictions, adolescent shoplifters such as the one shown in the chapter opening photo might end up in teen court.

PREVENTION AND DIVERSION

The concept of delinquency prevention has probably been with us as long as we have sought to differentiate juveniles from adult offenders. Prevention refers to any attempt to forestall anticipated delinquent behavior.[8] **Diversion,** on the other hand, deals with delinquent behavior that has already occurred; thus, it falls within the province of control. Diversion had antecedents within the child-saving movement. Recall that separate institutions for juveniles and the juvenile court itself were originally developed to divert youth from the harsh and punitive orientation of the adult criminal justice system.

The idea of diversion, as already noted, dates back to the beginning of the juvenile justice system. The following discussion on diversion focuses on the police, the courts, and probation departments. However, many diversion programs are administered by

TABLE 14.3   The Language of Juvenile and Adult Courts

Juvenile Court Term	Adult Court Term
Adjudication: a decision by the judge that a child has committed delinquent acts	*Conviction of guilt*
Adjudicatory hearing: a hearing to determine whether the allegations of a petition are supported by the evidence beyond a reasonable doubt.	*Trial*
Adjustment: the settling of a matter so that parties agree without official intervention by the court.	*Plea bargaining*
Aftercare: the supervision given to a child for a limited period of time after he or she is released from training school but while he or she is still under the control of the juvenile court.	*Parole*
Commitment: a decision by the judge to send a child to training school.	*Sentence to imprisonment*
Delinquent act: an act that if committed by an adult would be called a crime. The term does not include such ambiguities and noncrimes as "being ungovernable," "truancy," "incorrigibility," and "disobedience."	*Crime*
Delinquent child: a child who is found to have committed an act that would be considered a crime if committed by an adult.	*Criminal*
Detention: temporary care of an allegedly delinquent child who requires secure custody in physically restricting facilities pending court disposition or execution of a court order.	*Holding in jail*
Dispositional hearing: a hearing held subsequent to the adjudicatory hearing to determine what order of disposition should be made for a child adjudicated as delinquent.	*Sentencing hearing*
Hearing: the presentation of evidence to the juvenile court judge, his or her consideration of it, and his or her decision on disposition of the case.	*Trial*
Juvenile court: the court that has jurisdiction over children who are alleged to be or found to be delinquent. Juvenile delinquency procedures should not be used for neglected children or for those who need supervision.	*Court of record*
Petition: an application for a court order or some other judicial action. Hence, a "delinquency petition" is an application for the court to act in a matter involving a juvenile apprehended for a delinquent act.	*Accusation or indictment*
Probation: the supervision of a delinquent child after the court hearing but without commitment to training school.	*Probation* (with the same meaning as the juvenile court term)
Residential child care facility: a dwelling (other than a detention or shelter care facility) that is licensed to provide living accommodations, care treatment, and maintenance for children and youth. Such facilities include foster homes, group homes, and halfway houses.	*Halfway house*
Shelter: temporary care of a child in physically unrestricting facilities pending court disposition or execution of a court order for placement. Shelter care is used for dependent and neglected children and minors in need of supervision. Separate shelter care facilities are also used for children apprehended for delinquency who need temporary shelter but not secure detention.	*Jail*
Take into custody: the act of the police in securing the physical custody of a child engaged in delinquency. The term is used to avoid the stigma of the word *arrest*.	*Arrest*

schools, juvenile welfare boards, recreation programs and other community agencies, or special organizations established for that purpose.

The Police

As the law enforcement agents of our social system, the police must often make discretionary judgments as to how a juvenile should be handled. In fact, police discretion accounts for as much as 90 percent of all diversion. Patrol officers have always had to decide whether to ignore an incident, to handle a juvenile informally, or to take him or her into custody for further processing. Promoted by the availability of funds and frustration with existing community programs, some police departments have established and operated diversion programs. Some departments operate youth service bureaus, even though such programs were originally intended to be independent of the juvenile justice system.

Intake and the Courts

Intake workers—who are usually probation officers, juvenile court personnel, or state youth service counselors—are in a strategic position to reduce the penetration of juveniles further into the juvenile justice system. *Penetration* is a term used to characterize a youngster's contacts with the formal agencies of the system. Intake workers can warn and release juveniles, refer them to outside programs, place them on informal probation, or file a petition with the juvenile court. Pressures on juvenile court intake units have led them to develop their own diversion programs to minimize penetration.

Programs outside the Juvenile Justice System

Diversion programs that operate outside the juvenile justice system are in the best position to fulfill the goals of diversion. That is, they can provide a juvenile with assistance without the stigma of involvement in programs associated with official agencies of social control. These programs are sponsored by a variety of community organizations, including departments of children's services, welfare departments, mental health departments, religious organizations, and nonprofit organizations established to provide services to children and young people.

EDUCATIONAL PROGRAMS

Drug Abuse Resistance Education (DARE)

Drug Abuse Resistance Education (DARE) is a comprehensive educational program designed to prevent substance abuse and violence by educating children about the threats and consequences associated with such activities.[9] The DARE curriculum focuses on building self-esteem, taking responsibility for one's behavior, resisting peer pressure, and making responsible decisions (see Figure 14.1). The DARE curriculum was developed by educators to be presented to schoolchildren by specially trained, uniformed police officers. Since its implementation, the core curriculum has undergone continuous review and improvement, incorporating contemporary teaching methods to educate children in the prevention of drug abuse, violence involvement, and gang affiliation. Building on the original DARE concept of 1983, the curriculum has expanded to cover the entire span of a child's school years.

Community Policing and DARE The DARE program requires the integrated effort of police, schools, and parents. One of these groups alone is unlikely to succeed in directing a child's behavior toward a constructive, responsible end; furthermore, law enforcement probably has the least influence of the three. However, through programs like DARE, law enforcement officers can reinforce the positive efforts of parents and schools. Such reinforcement is enhanced when the police department is "driven" by the partnership and problem-based orientation of community policing. Combining a community policing mission with an educational initiative, DARE can prove beneficial. The DARE program is intended to foster the close and prolonged contact with the community that is fundamental to community policing. Removing the DARE officer from the patrol car allows him or her to interact closely with school administrators, teachers, parents, community members, and young people over an extended period of time.

WEB
For more information on intake and the courts, **visit our Web site, www.prenhall.com/territo.**

WEB
For more information on DARE, **visit our Web site, www.prenhall.com/territo.**

CTQ
What factors do you believe to be responsible behind the criticism that the DARE program is not effective in reducing future student drug use?

FIGURE 14.1

Drug education programs for youths are popular today. Here one student is receiving her certificate of completion for one of these courses.
© Dale Stockton

Criticism of DARE Despite its popularity and the fact that it is the nation's best-funded substance abuse prevention program, DARE is not without its critics. Evaluations of DARE have generally found the program useful in that it raises the level of the student's awareness of substance abuse. However, these same evaluations have found that DARE is not effective in reducing student drug use.[10] The DARE curriculum and its instructional delivery system may need to be changed, based upon its recognized shortcomings.

Education in the Law

Another program that has been established to help young people recognize that they have a stake in their future if they are to become law-abiding, responsible citizens has been developed by the federal Office of Juvenile Justice and Delinquency Prevention (OJJDP).[11]

OJJDP's approach was built on a belief that teaching students about the law through active, personal engagement could give them a deeper understanding of the law. By bringing alive the concepts of statutes that often strike youths as arbitrary or merely prohibitive, OJJDP hoped to link legal and constitutional matters to everyday life. To do so, the program uses Law-Related Education (LRE), a curriculum for elementary through high school students. Issues such as drugs and respect for property and life are emphasized.

Creativity and adaptability are two distinguishing characteristics of LRE. No single format or lesson plan dominates the approach. LRE strategies may be inserted as a course, or as part of existing courses; as a full curriculum, kindergarten through twelfth grade; as a special event for all students on a day set aside to study law and the Constitution; as a series of courses offering special opportunities for students interested in public service; or as a nonacademic program in training and reform school settings.

LRE programs teach objective facts but communicate them through the immediacy of group process. Mock trials, role playing, debates, writing of persuasive briefs, police ride-alongs, home security audits, case studies, and legislative assemblies are just a few of the activities used to teach students about justice concepts. The retention rate may be tested objectively, depending on the context, but as with all good education, the less tangible by-products may turn out to be the most cherished: a greater sense of civic virtue, an increased understanding of the legal and constitutional struggles of others, increased respect for law officers and authority figures, the experience of resolving disputes, and an increase in law-abiding behavior.

Another benefit teachers observe in LRE students is pride in being in a high-profile, high-status curriculum, a general attitude that may affect citizen behavior positively but is not easily quantified. Nevertheless, improvements in attitudes and behavior are measurable to some extent. An early OJJDP-sponsored evaluation of LRE at a number of sites found that LRE inspired more understanding of the law and respect for it, and that around half the students were less willing to resolve conflicts through violence or to associate with delinquent peers. "In the News: Teaching Youths about the Law" describes how one police department is teaching youths about the law.

HANDLING JUVENILES IN THE SYSTEM

Dependent and Abused Children

As noted earlier, youngsters who break laws are not the only concern of juvenile authorities. Some children need the protection of the state just to fulfill the most basic needs of life. Such youngsters—referred to as **dependent children**—often come to the attention of the juvenile or family court because their parents have died and they cannot receive adequate support from other family members. In other cases, children have to be taken away from parents or relatives because they have failed to meet the legal standard of care for the child.

Abused children (as they are referred to by the juvenile court) usually become the concern of authorities as a result of reports from neighbors, friends, or relatives. For example, children may be subjected to sexual or physical abuse—the typical circumstances of the battered child. Even when they are severely abused, children tend to remain loyal to their parents; thus, abuse is seldom reported by the children themselves.

Delinquent Children

Delinquency itself takes two different patterns. The first type of delinquency includes offenses that would be considered crimes if they were committed by adults. Burglary, larceny, and motor vehicle theft are examples of property crimes that fall into this category. The second category is **status offenses**—violations of statutes that apply exclusively to juveniles. Examples of status offenses are underage alcohol consumption and truancy.

> **WEB**
> For more information on abused and dependent children, **visit the link to the National Council of Juvenile and Family Court Judges on our Web site, www.prenhall.com/ territo.**

> **CTQ**
> How should status offenses be dealt with by the police and the courts?

IN THE NEWS
A HUMAN PERSPECTIVE

TEACHING YOUTHS ABOUT THE LAW
by Larry Murdo

In recent years, police officers in Albany, California, as in other areas of the country, have experienced a frustrating number of confrontational contacts with young people. Often, the acrimonious nature of these contacts is fueled by the youths' general lack of understanding of their rights and responsibilities under the law. In an effort to address this void and the problems it often spawned, the Albany chief of police developed a program to provide area students with practical instruction about the law and the methods that law enforcement officers and the criminal justice system use to uphold it. Since it was introduced in spring 1992, the course has proven to be an effective way to communicate important information to this young and impressionable audience, while cultivating an enhanced understanding of the role police play in society.

THE INSTRUCTION
Constitutional Law/Practical Applications Instruction for Youth is delivered each May to students in the city's public middle and high schools. The chief meets with 8th grade students as they prepare to advance to high school and with high school seniors as they prepare to graduate. By delivering the instruction twice—in slightly modified formats—the program reinforces the principles at pivotal points in the students' lives.

The instruction stresses the balance the law seeks to strike between the rights of individuals as protected by the Constitution and the responsibilities of citizens. The curriculum explains, for example, that no constitutional right exists to resist arrest or defy a court-ordered sanction.

During the free-flowing discussions with the students, it quickly becomes evident that, prior to the classroom instruction, they received most of their information regarding the police or the legal system from television, motion pictures, and other products of the entertainment industry.

The students' lack of a balanced and accurate sense of the law becomes most clear early in the discussion when the youths respond to a series of questions designed to gauge their grasp of practical legal matters. The students rarely articulate informed responses to such questions as:

- If police officers stop a car, can they order all of the passengers out and conduct personal searches? Can officers search the interior of the vehicle? Can they search individual bags or cases within the passenger compartment without a warrant?
- If a police officer stops a citizen in a public place and begins to ask questions, must the citizen respond?
- Can police officers lawfully enter a private residence, without a warrant, to arrest the home-owner or someone else in the home?

The concepts of probable cause and related issues are introduced to students so that they can formulate informed and accurate responses to such questions. While students may not always agree with the laws and judicial rulings presented, most gain a new appreciation for the reasoned approach the law must take to balance maintaining order and protecting personal freedoms.

CONCLUSION
As the most visible component of the criminal justice system, the police always have represented different things to different people. For too many young people, the police have come to represent an oppressive force that views youths contemptuously and treats them unfairly. Unfortunately, this perception becomes understandable given the steady stream of distorted and often-negative messages youths receive about law enforcement via the media and the entertainment industry. These images not only reinforce a negative view of law enforcement, but they also undermine respect for the law, which is essential to the functioning of a free society.

But law enforcement can take steps to correct the misinformation youths receive. By taking the time to discuss practical aspects of constitutional law, as well as the complex role police play to maintain order and ensure individual rights, agencies can help nurture a deeper appreciation for the law among youths. As youths come to see the positive aspects of the laws they are asked to live by, they gain a more balanced view of law enforcement and the roles police play in society.

Source: L. Murdo, "Teaching Youths about the Law," *FBI Law Enforcement Bulletin* (July 1997), p. 19.

Juvenile justice authorities are sharply divided on the issue of who should have jurisdiction over status offenses. Those who wish to leave jurisdiction with the juvenile court argue that today's status offender is tomorrow's adult criminal and that further acts of delinquency cannot be prevented unless such juveniles are discovered. Their opponents emphasize that the social services usually required to deal effectively with the problems of status offenders can be made available without formal adjudication.

Police Contact
The police officer is usually the first representative of societal authority and the criminal justice system to come in contact with a youthful offender. Police contact with juveniles

may result from juvenile involvement in serious offenses, disturbances, or status offenses. A substantial number of contacts occur just because juveniles are out and about—which brings them to the attention of officers on patrol. Because juveniles tend to congregate at shopping malls, street corners, fast-food operations, and the like, they may be the object of complaints requiring police attention.

Police have a variety of alternatives available to them in making dispositions in juvenile cases:[12]

1. *Warn and release.* In the case of a minor offense, a police officer may simply warn a youth not to engage in the same type of behavior again. The youth may be further advised that future violations will result in official action.
2. *Release and report.* The juvenile may be released, but an official report will be prepared detailing the incident.
3. *Release to parents.* A juvenile may be placed in the custody of his or her parents with just a warning or an official report.
4. *Agency referral.* Depending on departmental policies, the availability of appropriate programs, and police awareness of community resources, juveniles may be referred to community-based social service agencies or welfare agencies. Police are in an ideal position to divert youths from the juvenile justice system to community agencies, where they can receive the help they need without the stigma associated with processing by the juvenile court. Typical police referrals are to youth service bureaus, special school programs, boys clubs and YMCAs, community mental health agencies, and drug programs.
5. *Juvenile court referral.* Depending upon the jurisdiction, a police officer can use several methods to bring a juvenile offender to the attention of the juvenile court. Rather than taking a youngster into custody, for example, an officer can issue a citation or make a formal report to juvenile intake or the juvenile court and release the youngster to the custody of parents or guardians. The police may also take a youngster into custody and deliver him or her to juvenile intake or detention.[13]

> **CTQ**
>
> Should the police have many alternatives available to them in disposing of juvenile cases? Why or why not?

Research conducted in Flint, Michigan, further illustrates the various options police officers can use in dealing with juvenile offenders. The research focused on the officers' role in resolving complaints about a group of rowdy juveniles as part of their neighborhood foot patrol program.

In resolving the rowdy-teenager situations, Flint police officers mentioned various actions they took: (1) made a referral to social services, (2) counseled the teenagers, (3) counseled the parents, (4) reassured the complainants, (5) tried to get people to empathize with each other and see each other's side, (6) gave orders, (7) made an arrest, and (8) threatened arrest.[14] The research in Flint also identified five role identity orientations assumed by police officers in dealing with rowdy juvenile encounters: problem solver, peacekeeper and competent law enforcer, authority figure, friend or peer, and knight in shining armor.[15] The following statements by officers in the Flint, Michigan, study illustrate these five role identity orientations and indicate how the officers view their interactions with rowdy juveniles:

Problem Solver and Peacekeeper
I would like my supervisor to picture me as having solved the problem, that is, having quieted the people involved and satisfied the neighbor to the best of my ability and hopefully prevented a recurrence, without any type of arrest or negative police enforcement.

   I could have saved time by just making an arrest, but that wouldn't have solved anything. It was talking to the man, the kids, to the parents—trying to get everybody to see where everybody was coming from.

Competent Law Enforcer
I'll be professional, won't cuss out the kids. Handle [the situation] within the realm of the law. Efficient, won't be blasé, won't play fun games.

I understand the problem. As a police officer I will have to obtain proper evidence to be able to make a case.

Authority Figure
Very authoritative. Possibly intimidating. This is all I have working for me.

I advised them [the teenagers] that they should leave when told, and if necessary we would show them that we were the "baddest gang" in town.

Friend or Peer
I go home at 3:30 every day and watch cartoons. I let them [the teens] understand I'm human with needs. I jog a lot with the kids after work.

I found the head honcho, ring leader, and talked to him man to man. I don't want to talk down to him. I explained the situation he was putting me in.

Knight in Shining Armor
I'm there to save the day. "Don't worry sir, I'll take care of it; I'll talk to the boys and if necessary the parents." [I'm] the perfect public servant because these situations are easy if kids are reasonable. They can call again if the problem recurs.

Even if it can't [I] want the victim to feel something can be done. They start talking about how things used to be here. Before you know it, you make a friend. When you leave: "Hey, he was the greatest cop there ever was!"

Juvenile Intake

Juveniles are often referred by the police to the juvenile court intake unit, which is frequently staffed by probation officers. The primary purpose of **intake** is to determine if youngsters accused of criminal acts or status offenses should be diverted from the juvenile court. Intake officers consider a variety of factors in making this decision. First, they must decide if the juvenile falls within the jurisdiction of the court by virtue of his or her age, the place where the offense took place, and the nature of the offense itself. For example, a juvenile can be beyond a court's jurisdiction if he or she is above juvenile court age, has committed the offense in another jurisdiction, or is involved in behavior considered deviant but not prohibited by law.

In many jurisdictions, intake workers must also ascertain the legal sufficiency of the referred offense and determine if there is sufficient evidence to support the allegations of delinquent conduct. Following this, a decision is made whether to refer the case to the juvenile court. In making this decision, intake workers consider the seriousness and time of day of the alleged offense; the type of neighborhood where the youth lives; and the youth's age, attitude toward authority, involvement in religious activities, prior

IN THE WORKPLACE

JUVENILE INTAKE OFFICER

Responsible for scheduling and attending juvenile proceedings, maintaining juvenile court records, collecting fines, monitoring temporary and final orders to insure compliance, and performing such other tasks as the court may require; notifies parents of the child's detention and advises the child and parents of their rights, including the right to have an attorney present at all proceedings; decides whether to release the child to the parent's custody or place him or her in a licensed juvenile detention center. The intake officer may withhold the filing of a formal delinquency petition or may attempt to make informal adjustment, which may include counseling, curfew, or required attendance at school. The intake office may proceed with formal filing if informal adjustment is not followed. Minimum qualifications are as follows: high school diploma or equivalent, valid driver's license, ability to communicate fluently in English.

court and police contacts, home environment, school record, reaction to sanctions previously imposed, and present interests and activities. In recent years, the intake function has taken on increasing importance because of the dual emphasis on diverting as many youths as possible while at the same time protecting the community.

After an assessment of the legal and social factors associated with the case, the intake worker must decide on an appropriate **disposition:** outright dismissal, informal adjustment, informal probation, consent decrees, or filing of a petition. Complaints are dismissed if the intake worker determines that the alleged violation is not within the jurisdiction of the juvenile court. Informal adjustment involves a decision to close the case after the youngster is warned, or on the provision that the youngster meet certain conditions (such as restitution, private treatment, involvement in a diversion program, or an agreement by the parents to improve supervision). Informal probation generally involves a period of informal supervision during which the youngster is required to fulfill certain requirements such as attending school or obeying his or her parents.

Filing a petition is a step that may be taken by an intake worker. In this case the intake person is requesting formally that the court assume jurisdiction over the juvenile. A consent decree is a midpoint between informal supervision and a formal disposition. It involves a formal order for treatment or supervision to be provided by the court staff or another agency. The decree requires the approval of the judge and the consent of the child and his or her parents. The advantage of this disposition is not only that it eases the caseload of the court, but also that it protects the community while enabling the juvenile to avoid the stigma of formal adjudication. To protect the rights of the juvenile, decrees should not be issued unless (1) there is sufficient evidence that the juvenile committed the alleged offense; (2) they are limited to a period of six months, or at the most a year; and (3) they do not require the juvenile to be removed from the family. In this way, staff members can provide juveniles with supervision or services without requiring them to go through formal adjudication.

Removing Juveniles from Adult Jails

Many of the thousands of young people taken into police custody and referred to the juvenile court each year can be released to parental custody to await court action. However, some—those who have committed serious crimes or who are at risk of becoming victims—are often removed from their homes pending court hearings. The relatively small number of youths arrested for serious crimes need to be placed in secure juvenile detention facilities, and those at risk for victimization need to have a safe place to stay.[16]

Historically, this has often meant placing young people in adult jails or lockups. Yet in these places juveniles are at risk of physical or sexual harm from adult prisoners. To protect them from such harm, some jail officials place the juveniles in solitary confinement, aggravating the psychological effects of jailing and, in some extreme cases, leading to suicide. At the very least, young people in adult facilities are deprived of the educational and other services required in juvenile facilities.

The reasons for using jails to detain juveniles are many. Some communities lock up juvenile arrestees to keep them from getting into further trouble or to deter their peers; others merely want to detain the juveniles long enough to ensure their appearance in court or to find more appropriate placement in other facilities. In rural areas, especially, adequate or secure juvenile facilities may not exist nearby.

In 1974 Congress passed the **Juvenile Justice and Delinquency Prevention (JJDP) Act,** which established the Office of Juvenile Justice and Delinquency Prevention (OJJDP) within the Department of Justice. This office administers formula and discretionary grants to the states and territories to provide technical assistance to help jurisdictions comply with the act's provisions. The act mandates that participating states remove status offenders (such as truants and runaways) and nonoffenders (such as abused and neglected youth) from juvenile detention and correctional facilities.

In addition, the act mandates that when juveniles and adults are detained in the same facilities, the juvenile detainees must be outside the sight and hearing of adult prisoners. In 1980, the act was amended to further require that the states remove all juveniles from adult jails and lockups.

CTQ

Do you think the practice of diverting youth offenders in any way compromises the level of safety in their community? Why or why not?

WEB

For more information on removing juveniles in adult jails, **visit our Web site, www.prenhall.com/territo.**

WEB

For more information on the JJDP Act, **visit our Web site, www.prenhall.com/territo.**

While it has been difficult for all states to come into full compliance with the federal law, OJJDP has remained committed to providing federal direction, coordination, resources, and leadership to help all states ensure that detained juveniles are being held in appropriate facilities.

JUVENILE DETENTION CENTERS

For a variety of reasons, some juvenile offenders are formally detained in juvenile facilities prior to eventual release or court appearance. Variables considered in deciding whether to detain a juvenile offender include the following:

1. The child is alleged to have committed an act that would be a felony if it were committed by an adult.
2. The child is an alleged escapee from a juvenile justice facility or control program.
3. The child is wanted in another jurisdiction for committing a misdemeanor or felony.
4. The child has committed an act of violence.
5. There are reasonable grounds to believe that the child, if not detained, will fail to appear at subsequent hearings.
6. There are reasonable grounds to believe that the child, if not detained, will be a threat to witnesses, victims, or other people.
7. The prior record indicates that the child has committed other acts of delinquency.
8. There is no parent, guardian, or responsible adult relative to whom to release the child.

Research on Juveniles in Detention

One area of interest regarding juveniles who end up in detention centers relates to the various problems they have experienced. Two specific areas of concern are the relationships between juvenile detainees' drug use and crime, and the association between detainees' physical abuse and sexual victimization experiences and their delinquent behavior.

Dembo and associates conducted significant research regarding these issues.[17] Their work involving urinalysis revealed that approximately 40 percent of the youths entering a southeastern detention center had recently used marijuana or cocaine. The researchers also found that juveniles who test positive for marijuana use have higher rates of referral to juvenile court for nondrug property felonies. Although a specific cause-and-effect relationship could not be established, high frequency of marijuana use needs to be regarded as a sign that a youth may need some form of intervention. Cocaine or heroin users usually require special intervention or treatment to reduce the likelihood of continued personally and socially harmful patterns of behavior.

Dembo's research also revealed high rates of physical abuse and sexual victimization among juvenile detainees. A relationship was also found between the detainees' physical and sexual abuse experiences and their use of illicit drugs. Many cases of physical or sexual abuse took place within the youths' households. Again, this information has implications for intensive intervention efforts. Although most juvenile detention centers are not equipped to deal with issues such as drug abuse or physical and sexual abuse, if detention center staff are fully informed, they can make appropriate referrals to other public or private resources for intervention and follow-up.

DEINSTITUTIONALIZATION OF STATUS OFFENDERS

Deinstitutionalization of status offenders (DSO) refers to the removal of youths whose only infractions are *status offenses* (such as running away, incorrigibility, truancy, and curfew violation) from secure institutions and detention facilities. Serious efforts to deinstitutionalize status offenders (youths whose offenses would not be crimes if committed by an adult) began in most states after Congress established the Office of Juvenile Justice and Delinquency Prevention (OJJDP) in 1974 and issued a strong mandate for the removal of these youths from secure confinement.[18]

Several different rationales have been put forth to support a policy of deinstitutionalization. First, and perhaps most common, is the argument that deprivation of liberty for people who have not violated the criminal code is unjust and unwarranted.

Another argument is that decreasing coercive contact between status offenders and the juvenile court will have a positive impact on recidivism. Labeling theorists contend that a juvenile develops a fixed self-image as a delinquent primarily in response to being treated or labeled as a delinquent by people in authority. This result may occur through subtle psychological pressures or through learning delinquent behavior from confinement with delinquents who have committed more serious offenses.

The third argument hinges on costs and priorities within the **juvenile justice system.** According to this argument, it is too expensive to institutionalize juveniles who are not committing crimes and too expensive for the court to continue expending a large portion of its resources on these nonoffenders. Instead, the court should devote its attention to serious and violent offenders and leave the nonoffenders in the hands of the social welfare system.

POSTADJUDICATION DISPOSITIONS

In deciding on a disposition for adjudicated juveniles, judges can exercise considerable discretion and are limited only by available resources and statutory requirements. Examples of the options open to them include probation; warning the youngster; placing the youngster in the custody of his or her parents; levying a fine; ordering restitution; assigning work; placing the youngster in a community-based program such as a foster home, group home, or halfway house; placement in a wilderness camp; or—as a final resort—committing the youngster to a training school. Several of these adjudication options are expanded on in the following sections.

Juvenile Restitution Programs

Restitution is one of the postadjudication alternatives available to juvenile judges. It is defined as repayment by the offender, in money or services, of the losses suffered by the victim or society as a result of the offender's criminal/delinquent act.

One of the most profound changes in juvenile justice during the past decade has been the phenomenal growth in the use of restitution as a sanction for juvenile offenders.[19] Every state and the District of Columbia has at least one of the programs described here. Most offer both community service restitution and financial restitution, while smaller numbers provide for victim-offender mediation or other victim services. Financial restitution and community service restitution are almost equally common; 84 percent of the programs responding to a national survey handle monetary restitution orders, and 90 percent handle community service. Seventy-five percent have both types. Victim service components are offered by 28 percent of these programs; 23 percent offer victim-offender mediation. The oldest financial restitution program identified through the Warner and Burke survey was established in 1945 in Bartow, Florida.

Community-Based Programs

Community-based programs for juveniles developed on two premises: (1) that traditional institutional programs are ineffective at best, and at worst actually reinforce delinquency, and (2) that alternative environments are needed to help youths who do not require institutionalization in order to protect the community.[20] These programs take place in both residential and nonresidential facilities. Residential programs include foster homes, group homes, and halfway houses; nonresidential programs range from those that provide sporadic supervision (such as probation and aftercare) to those that supervise youngsters for all or part of the day.

Residential Programs

Foster homes board neglected, dependent, and delinquent youngsters. Foster parents are paid by the state to provide supervision within the home. Delinquent and status offenders are placed in foster homes when it is believed that unsuitable circumstances in the parental home may have contributed to the problem behavior. Misbehavior by juveniles is sometimes a result of parent-child conflicts, child abuse, the inability or unwillingness of parents to provide appropriate support and supervision, and parental problems—alcoholism, mental illness, or criminal behavior. Foster parents can provide the juvenile with the supervision and support lacking in the real family and can do so in a more sustained manner than a probation officer. Also, this type of placement removes the juvenile from the neighborhood and companions with whom he or she previously engaged in deviant behavior. The foster home is the least expensive alternative to institutionalization.

Group homes, group residences, and group foster homes are all terms used to describe programs that provide residential care for groups of four to twelve youngsters. The residences may be owned or rented by the state, a private agency, or the house parents. Typically, they are operated by a husband and wife assisted by one or more staff members. The objective is to provide a family environment for youngsters who cannot adjust to a one-to-one relationship with foster parents but who can benefit from and adjust to a family environment in the company of their peers.

Halfway houses are small facilities that serve as few as five residents but typically have populations of between ten and twenty-five. Standing somewhere between the community and training schools, these facilities serve youngsters released from an institution as part of a reintegration program, as well as those who come directly from the juvenile court. One of the advantages of these programs is that they provide alternative placement for youngsters who require more supervision than they can receive in nonresidential programs, yet do not require the level of supervision and security provided by training schools.

Wilderness Programs

Some community-based programs for juvenile delinquents have found success in locating their facilities outside urban areas. The following describes one such approach, which has drawn nationwide attention.[21]

Eckerd Family Youth Alternatives, Inc. (EFYA) originated in 1961 as a charitable trust, the Jack and Ruth Eckerd Foundation. The Eckerds founded the first Wilderness Education System camp in 1968 in Brooksville, Florida. The camp was modeled after the successful therapeutic wilderness camping programs begun for Texas youth in 1945. Program highlights include the following: (1) highly structured activities combined with positive adult role models; (2) close group work and peer counseling; (3) a small-group setting that mimics a family and teaches youth appropriate interactions within a family unit; and (4) numerous learning opportunities in which youth learn appropriate responses to varying situations. A second example, the Eckerd Leadership Program (ELP) in Fort Pierce, Florida, is a day treatment program established in 1996 that provides intensive day treatment and aftercare services for youth directly committed from juvenile court as well as stepped down from residential programs.

Nonresidential Programs

Day treatment programs provide supervision for juveniles for all or part of the day, but they do not require that a youngster live at the facility housing the program. Juveniles in these programs require more supervision than can be provided through probation or aftercare, yet they are judged capable of living at home during their involvement. Thus, these youngsters are forced to confront the problems that contributed to their delinquency: school problems, adverse community influences, family difficulties, and work problems. Counseling and group sessions focus on problems that the youngsters encounter in their daily lives. Also, because youths usually live near the program facility, staff members can work closely with the parents to achieve successful home adjustment. Day treatment programs usually cost less than halfway houses because they use community resources and services and do not provide housing, meals, and clothing for their clients.

CTQ

Which of the postadjudication program alternatives do you find most appropriate for first-time juvenile offenders? Which do you find most appropriate for chronic juvenile offenders? Why?

LONG-TERM INSTITUTIONAL FACILITIES

In some instances juveniles may be ordered by the juvenile court to spend time in a secure institution usually called a youth camp or by the more traditional term "training school." According to the Census of Juveniles in Residential Placement, about 33 percent of juveniles in secure institutions were being held for crimes against the person. Approximately seventy larger juvenile institutions across the nation are designed to hold the most serious juvenile offenders.[22] The facilities may hold up to two-hundred juvenile offenders.

EVALUATING JUVENILE BOOT CAMPS

Despite the rapid growth of boot camps for adult offenders throughout the 1990s in the U.S. adult correctional system, the juvenile system did not immediately adopt boot camps because of questions and about their appropriateness for young offenders.[23] But as the population of juvenile offenders increased sharply and caused overcrowding at facilities, correctional officials began to take a hard look at boot camps as a way of preventing less serious juvenile offenders from embarking on a life of crime and institutionalization.

Could the adult model be adapted to the unique correctional needs of juveniles? To find out, the Office of Juvenile Justice and Delinquency Prevention (OJJDP) funded demonstration programs at three sites to develop prototypical camps and aftercare programs for male juveniles.

The agenda for the demonstration programs was ambitious. It mirrored that of adult boot camps in that adjudicated, nonviolent offenders were placed in an environment emphasizing discipline and work, but it also required that treatment and rehabilitation be the ultimate objectives of all boot camp and aftercare activities. More specifically, the programs were to (1) serve as a cost-effective alternative to institutionalization; (2) promote discipline through physical conditioning and teamwork; (3) instill moral values and a work ethic; (4) promote literacy and increase academic achievement; (5) reduce drug and alcohol abuse; (6) encourage participants to become productive, law-abiding citizens; and (7) ensure that offenders are held accountable for their actions.

The evaluation team's observations and data indicated that planning and implementation met the demonstration program's goals, namely: (1) The sites formed active public-private partnerships; (2) first-year boot camp completion rates were high, ranging from 80 percent to 94 percent; (3) youths improved in educational performance, physical fitness, and behavior; (4) youths who graduated from the three-month boot camp and remained in aftercare for at least five months reported positive changes in attitudes and behavior; and (5) estimates of daily costs per youth indicated that the boot camps appeared more cost-effective than state or local correctional facilities.

The evaluations note that some difficulties existed in the programs. For example, two programs were disrupted by high staff turnover, and all struggled to find appropriate and effective disciplinary measures and a clear-cut termination policy. In addition, staff found it difficult to achieve a healthy balance between programming emphasizing military discipline and programming focusing on remedial education and counseling. Finally, the aftercare phase was hampered by high levels of absenteeism and noncompletion. Nearly half of the youths who entered aftercare dropped out, were arrested for new offenses, or were terminated for not complying with the programs' aftercare rules.

More information is needed on why aftercare is hampered by high levels of absenteeism and noncompletion and what can be done to lower those rates. In addition, more information is needed on recidivism over the long term as well as on the costs of other alternatives to incarceration.

CTQ

Should boot camp be used more often as an alternative to institutionalization? Why or why not?

COMMUNITY SUPERVISION

Community supervision of juveniles includes probation and aftercare services. Probation is viewed as a desirable disposition for youths who need some supervision but do not require the level of control supplied by nonresidential day treatment programs or residential community-based programs. Aftercare, in the form of supervision and

IN THE WORKPLACE

JUVENILE PROBATION OFFICER

Responsible for monitoring and documenting behavior of juveniles under the jurisdiction and supervision of the juvenile court. Performs a variety of duties, including the following: manages a juvenile caseload, performs intake and magistrate duties, performs risk/needs assessments and identifies resources available to help children, counsels and advises children, conducts school visits, presents information in court relating to children on probation, investigates and processes probation violations, and monitors aftercare. Minimum qualifications are as follows: four-year degree from an accredited college, valid driver's license.

---

services, is frequently required for juveniles released from training schools or community-based facilities.

Juvenile Probation

Juvenile probation actually preceded the first juvenile court. Probation is a legal status, imposed by the juvenile court, that permits a youth to remain in the community under the guidance and supervision of a probation officer. Probation involves much more than merely giving a youngster another chance; it is also intended to enable the youngster to adjust to the free community. From a variety of standpoints, probation represents the most desirable formal alternative to the juvenile court. While on probation, juveniles are able to (1) live at home and maintain family ties; (2) remain in school or retain their jobs; (3) maintain their involvement in community activities; and (4) avoid the stigma of being removed from their home and placed in a residential program. The alternative also costs less than placing youth in residential programs. Probation is the most frequent disposition used by the juvenile court.

Juvenile Aftercare

Aftercare is the juvenile equivalent of parole after a child is released from an institution. The purpose of aftercare is to assist the juvenile in making the transition from institutional supervision to community life. The term *aftercare* was proposed in an effort to dissociate juvenile programs from the legalistic language and concepts of adult parole.

Historically, juvenile aftercare in the United States can be traced to the system of indenture employed by houses of refuge in the early nineteenth century. The superintendents of these facilities were authorized to bind as apprentices youngsters they believed were reformed. Total control of the children was invested in their guardians, who could supervise boys until age 21, girls until age 18. Within these limits, the employer decided when a youth had earned the right to be discharged. Girls were usually indentured as domestics, and boys were placed on farms, on ships, in stores, or in factories.

The importance of quality aftercare is clear when one considers the impact of institutionalization on youth. Some youngsters become more sophisticated and antisocial as a result of their training school experience; others become dependent and timid. There are also vast differences in the community settings to which these youngsters return. Most juveniles return to their old communities and are therefore exposed to the same conditions (such as peer influences) that originally contributed to their delinquency. And many youngsters must overcome the stigma of confinement in a juvenile institution. Thus, each youngster has specific needs that require the use of all available resources both within and outside the institution.

The advantages of good aftercare more than justify the required investment of time and money. First, aftercare provides a transitional period in which youths can adjust to the community with the assistance and support of a parole officer. The parole officer can help youngsters and their families cope with problems that may have contributed to prior delinquency, readjust to school, or secure employment. A good aftercare program can

---

WEB

For more information on community supervision, **visit the link to the Office of Juvenile Justice and Delinquency Prevention on our Web site, www.prenhall.com/territo.**

WEB

For more information on juvenile probation, **visit our Web site, www.prenhall.com/territo.**

also minimize a youth's length of stay at an institution; authorities are likely to expand the number of early releases if they know that released youths will be supervised by aftercare workers. Another advantage is that it costs less to keep a youth on parole than to retain the youth in a juvenile training school.

The Quality of Supervision

Typically, youths on probation are under the jurisdiction of the juvenile court; as a rule, youths on aftercare are under the jurisdiction of an agency or a state system. Youths on probation are more likely to have less serious and less extensive records than youths involved in aftercare; and youths on aftercare have to readjust to the community after their period of institutionalization. In spite of these differences, however, probation and aftercare are based on many of the same principles and considerations, and they have similar requirements.

The major elements of effective community supervision are surveillance, service, and counseling. Thus, the probation or aftercare worker must perform both police and counseling functions. Counseling requires trust between counselor and client, but the police function—the duty to ferret out client violations—makes the establishment of trust difficult or impossible. In surveillance, the worker is required to maintain contact with the youngster, his or her parents, school, and other people directly concerned with the youth's adjustment to community life. It is the worker's responsibility to determine not only the extent to which the youth is meeting his or her commitments, but also how well the family, school, and others are conforming to their responsibility as agreed upon in the comprehensive plan.

In performing the service function, the worker must assess the extent to which the problems confronting the youth and his or her family may be ameliorated by available community resources—including community mental health centers, state employment agencies, health departments, vocational training programs, drug and alcohol abuse programs, and recreational programs. Based on that assessment, the worker must then develop a plan to use these services effectively for each child and family.

The counseling function is both the most important and most demanding of the aftercare or probation worker's responsibilities. For counseling to be effective, the worker must establish a relationship with a youth based on mutual confidence, trust, and understanding. In the course of individual or group sessions, the youngster, his or her family, and other people directly involved must be helped to confront and comprehend the personal or environmental problems that contribute to delinquency.

Revocation

Probation revocations are generally handled by the juvenile court; the aftercare agency typically has the authority to revoke aftercare. A revocation of aftercare status usually results in the juvenile offender being sent to a secure juvenile facility.

RUNAWAY AND MISSING CHILDREN

Over the years there has been an increase in the public's concern for runaway and other missing children. Accounts of missing children becoming homicide or sexual abuse victims, as well as being involved in street crimes or drug and alcohol abuse, have attracted public attention.[24]

It is useful to consider missing children in terms of four major categories: (1) runaways, (2) stranger or acquaintance abductions, (3) parental kidnappings, and (4) lost or accidentally injured children. In general, when a child is not where he or she is supposed to be, that child is labeled missing. To be labeled missing, however, means that someone cares enough about the child to report the incident. When more about the child's whereabouts is learned, he or she may fall into one of the following categories:

- *Runaways.* **Runaway** children make up the largest category of missing children. Sometimes called "voluntary missings," runaways are usually defined as those who have left their parents or other caretakers without permission. Although their departure may appear voluntary, not all runaways wish to leave their homes.

Instead, they may feel that they are being pushed out because they are troublesome or unemployed. Adolescents who are forced out of their homes or ignored by their families and who find their way to the streets are often called "throwaway children." Children who are allowed to come and go as they please also fall into this category.

- *Abducted children.* Abducted children may be taken by either a family member or a person who is not part of the child's family. Circumstances of family member abduction—often called "parental kidnapping"—include a divorced or separated parent's failing to return a child to the child's guardian or taking the child without the knowledge or permission of the child's guardian. Children abducted by nonfamily members (sometimes called "stranger abductions") are also taken without the knowledge or permission of the child's caretaker.
- *Homeless youth.* Runaways, throwaways, or abducted youth eventually may become homeless, although the term generally applies to the runaway group. It implies that either the family has abandoned the youth completely or the youth has voluntarily chosen to be exiled from the family group.
- *Lost or accidentally injured children.* This category refers to situations in which, for example, a child wanders into the woods, becomes injured or trapped, and is unable to contact others for help. The child's intention was not to run away; rather, the situation occurred in the context of daily childhood activities.

Characteristics of the Runaway

Contemporary U.S. studies have found that in addition to being adventurous, rebellious, and stubborn, the typical runaway is often a victim of a troubled family environment and of multiple abuses. The youth is without employment skills or plans, and by the act of running away becomes vulnerable to the dangers of survival in the unprotected environment of the street. The runaway, denied the opportunity to live in a safe and stable environment, is a youth at risk of physical and emotional injury, of sexual and other criminal exploitation—and even death. Frequently, a pattern of runaways may develop.

Clearly, runaways are often the victims of some sort of abuse, and behind their defensive demeanor, many of them are frightened. Although they have positive potential as members of society, they do not feel important in their families and are not valued by family members or by society. Many of them have been kicked out, forced out, or never allowed into the spotlight of the family or the community.

Running away exacts a high price on the adolescent. Life on the street frequently means learning tactics, often criminal, for survival. This perpetuates further the public's image of the runaway as an outcast of society, rather than as a member of a troubled family.

The System's Response to Runaway Youth

Agencies have responded to runaways in a number of ways:

- *Runaway shelters.* To provide runaways with a safe haven, communities and agencies have established shelters, halfway houses, and crisis centers throughout the country. Some runaways—lonely, terrified, and hungry—come to these places of their own accord, while others are left there by police to await return to their homes or placement elsewhere. Nevertheless, the so-called freedom of life on the streets still has a powerful attraction for many runaways. Some choose not to use the crisis centers at all and instead stay with friends or literally live on the streets. In addition, many runaways who do use or are placed in shelters run from these havens, despite the risks of living on the streets.

    Runaways as a group present critical questions for social service agencies that provide them with food and shelter. Many agencies adhere to conventional policies of returning runaways to their homes. This approach, however, simply allows the chronic runaway to continue in the cycle of leaving home. Many runaways avoid or leave the various agencies set up to keep them. When the runaway's reasons for leaving home are not adequately addressed, the running

CTQ

In your opinion, should the juvenile justice system play a greater role in trying to improve the public's understanding of runaways? Why or why not?

continues. Although many local communities do attempt to help runaways with their problems, a lack of resources may affect these programs.

- *Law enforcement.* Law enforcement personnel also experience obstacles in dealing with runaway youth. Because a runaway cannot be detained, the police officer who brings a runaway to a shelter may, within a few hours, see the same runaway out on the street again. In addition, many police departments may place runaways low on their lists of priorities, particularly in view of the fact that many youths reported as missing or runaway return home of their own accord within a relatively brief period of time.
- *Health and mental health.* Runaways often turn to health clinics and emergency rooms for medical attention. Nurses and physicians, in attending to immediate health concerns, may not be able to inquire about the safety of the youth's living environment. Mental health professionals, who may discover a history of running away during an intake evaluation, may not always connect the running behavior with the youth's psychological problems.

It is clear that immediate efforts at intervention for the youth on the street and the families in crisis deserve the priority attention of existing service and legal agencies. The public health dimensions of the problem as a symptom of deeper conflicts and disturbances, however, require national attention. Congress highlighted this problem and took important steps to resolve it by passing the Missing Children Act in 1982 and, later, the Missing Children Assistance Act of 1984. Establishment of the National Center for Missing and Exploited Children is another example of the federal government's commitment to solving the problem of missing and exploited children.

JUVENILE CURFEWS

Traditionally, the determination of a minor's curfew has been considered a family issue, within the parental purview, rather than a matter to be determined by government.[25] Nevertheless, public curfews have been enacted and enforced throughout the nation's history in reaction to increased juvenile delinquency, decreased parental supervision, and other social trends. Recent increases in juvenile crime and victimization have prompted local communities in many states to once again consider evening curfews (e.g., from 11 P.M. to 6 A.M. on school days and from midnight to 6 A.M. on nonschool days) as a viable means to enhance the safety of the community and its children. Although most curfew ordinances apply to juveniles under age 16, some include 16- and 17-year-olds. This section explores developments in curfew ordinances, legal issues related to curfews, how jurisdictions have responded to legal challenges, the elements of sound community-based curfew programs, and examples of a range of curfew programs and services from seven jurisdictions. Curfew ordinances have gained popularity as a way to curb juvenile crime.

Representative Curfew Programs

Local governments have enacted juvenile curfews pursuant to their general police powers or state statutes specifically authorizing such ordinances. The U.S. Department of Justice reviewed the experiences of seven cities that had enacted their ordinances pursuant to specific authorizing state legislation.[26]

Law enforcement professionals generally view a juvenile curfew ordinance as an effective means to combat late-evening crime. However, curfews are also intended to protect youth from becoming victims of crime. The curfew ordinances described shortly were enacted in the context of a comprehensive, community-based program designed to protect both the community and the juvenile from victimization and to serve as a constructive intervention against developing patterns of delinquency.

Each jurisdiction collected statistical data on juvenile crime and victimization before passing a curfew ordinance. This activity also laid a foundation for formulating a curfew ordinance that addressed the jurisdiction's unique juvenile crime and victimization problems. Although juvenile crime is not restricted to evening hours, the data analysis done by these cities demonstrated that their rates of juvenile crime and victimization were serious enough to warrant a carefully crafted evening curfew program.

> **CTQ**
>
> Do you personally know anyone who as a juvenile was a runaway? What happened to him or her short and long term? Did the system help the youth short or long term?

Each city reviewed its own unique and innovative approach to addressing the problem of juvenile crime and victimization through a curfew ordinance. The approaches demonstrate a range of community partnerships and nonpunitive strategies designed to promote early intervention to prevent the development of delinquent behavior and to address the issues of parental responsibility, discipline, and family dysfunction. The strategies have been credited with helping to prevent juvenile crime and victimization and repeated curfew violations while providing protection and safety to the community.

While the comprehensive, community-based curfew programs implemented by the seven cities employ a variety of strategies, each program includes one or more of the following common elements: creation of a dedicated curfew center to receive juveniles who have been picked up by the police for violating curfew; staffing of curfew centers with social service professionals and community volunteers; intervention, in the form of referrals to social service providers, for the juveniles and their families; and procedures for repeat offenders. Finally, these curfew programs also included recreation and jobs programs; anti-drug and anti-gang programs and hotlines for follow-up services and crisis intervention. The cornerstone of each program is creative community involvement that works to transform the juvenile curfew from a reactive, punitive response to a proactive intervention against the root causes of juvenile delinquency and victimization.

Curfew ordinances are in effect in most the nation's largest cities. While curfews have been challenged in many jurisdictions on a variety of constitutional and other grounds, narrowly crafted ordinances designed to address specifically identified problems appear able to withstand such challenges. Statistical analyses of the impact of curfew ordinances on delinquency and juvenile victimization in many communities continue to be conducted. The information made available by the communities highlighted in this section and by other communities with curfew programs indicates that comprehensive, community-based juvenile curfew programs may help to reduce juvenile delinquency and victimization. It is important for communities that are enforcing or considering curfew ordinances to keep abreast of legal developments, establish a firm foundation for the ordinances, and model the curfew program after community-based efforts in other jurisdictions. Communities that develop and implement curfew ordinances in conjunction with programs and services designed to assist youth and families to solve underlying individual or family problems have an opportunity to enhance positive youth development, prevent delinquency, and reduce the victimization of children.

SERIOUS AND VIOLENT JUVENILE OFFENDERS

Serious and violent juvenile (SVJ) offenders are a troubled and often dangerous population (see Figure 14.2). Although their numbers are small, they are responsible for a disproportionate amount of crime. To know what to do about this difficult problem and to garner the necessary financial, political, and public support to deal with it effectively, policymakers need a solid research foundation. To build this research base, the Office of Juvenile Justice and Delinquency Prevention (OJJDP) convened the Study Group on Serious and Violent Juvenile Offenders. The findings of this distinguished panel of researchers are quite hopeful and compelling. They conclude that it is never too early to begin efforts to prevent SVJ offending, and it is never too late to intervene with known serious and violent juvenile offenders.[27]

SVJ Offenders—A Distinct Group

The first major conclusion of the study group was that the SVJ offender is substantially different from the typical juvenile involved in delinquent conduct. Most SVJ offenders are male and usually display early minor behavior problems that lead to more serious delinquent acts. Generally, three pathways can help explain males' progression to SVJ offending: the authority conflict pathway (before age 12), the overt pathway, and the covert pathway. Those who reach the last step in each pathway usually have gone through the preceding steps. When these youth begin to commit more-serious delinquent acts, they typically also continue to commit less-serious delinquent acts. Most SVJ offenders also tend to have multiple problems such as substance abuse and mental health

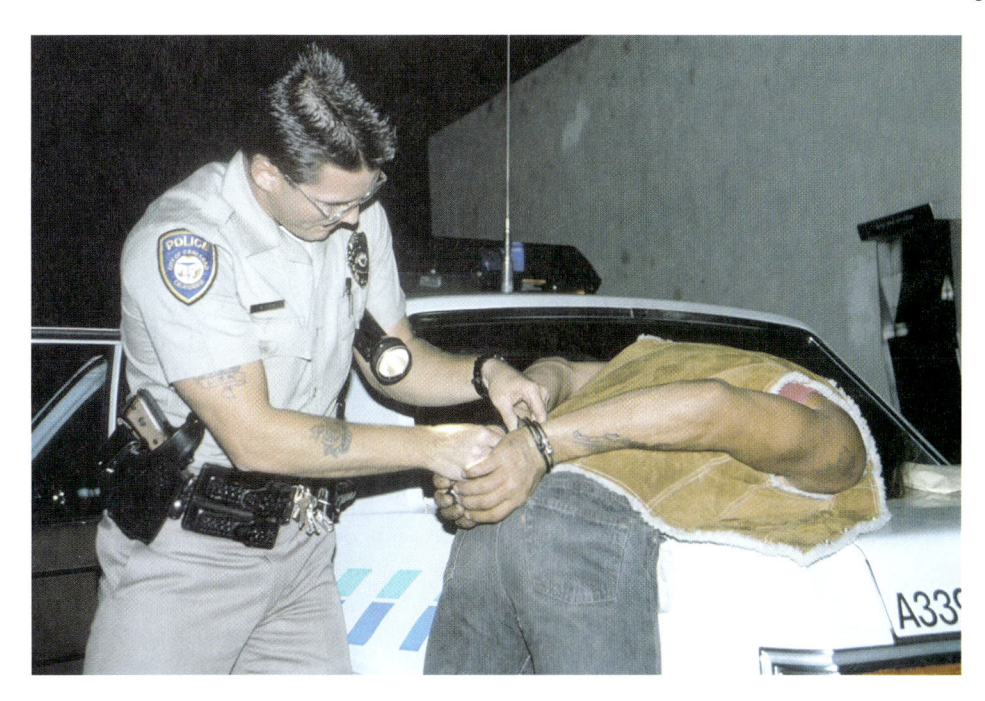

FIGURE 14.2

Serious and violent juvenile offenders (SVJs) present a major problem for the traditional juvenile justice system. This photo shows the arrest of an SVJ.

© Dale Stockton

difficulties in addition to truancy, suspension, expulsion, and dropping out of school. Furthermore, SVJ offenders are disproportionately victims of violence.

Predictors of SVJ Offending

In general, violent behavior results in an interaction of individual, contextual (family, school, and peers), situational, and community factors. The study group report yields further knowledge about the predictors of serious and violent offending and how they can inform and guide the interventions of the juvenile justice system, child welfare system, mental health system, and schools. The importance of predictor variables is underscored by the fact that juveniles with the most risk factors are five to twenty times more likely to engage in subsequent SVJ offending than other youth.

There are many other identified predictors of SVJ offending—for example, persistent precocious behavior problems (such as sexual behavior and experimentation with illegal substances) during the elementary school–age years for children between ages 6 and 11, nonserious delinquent acts, aggression, substance use, low family socioeconomic status, and antisocial parents. For youth between ages 12 and 14, SVJ predictors included weak social ties, antisocial peers, nonserious delinquent behavior, poor school attitude and performance, and psychological conditions such as impulsivity. For adolescents, one predictor was joining delinquent gangs. Rates of SVJ offending increase after joining a gang and decrease after leaving a gang. Perhaps not surprisingly, drug dealing was found to be a predictor of SVJ.

Interventions to Prevent SVJ Offending

Because several factors put children at risk of becoming SVJ offenders, it is unlikely that intervention efforts directed only toward a single source of influence (such as individual, family, school, or peers) will be successful. Multiple-component programs are needed, and priority should given to preventive actions that reduce risk factors in multiple domains. Because many of the risk factors that predict adolescent delinquency and violence also predict substance abuse, school dropout, early sexual involvement, and teen pregnancy, the benefits of such early-intervention programs can be wide ranging.

To be effective, the prevention of SVJ offending must involve (1) effective screening for children who are exposed to adverse circumstances or who exhibit behaviors that place them at high risk of becoming SVJ offenders; (2) access by families, children, and adolescents to early-intervention services and programs; (3) preventive interventions based on public health approaches and implemented within a comprehensive,

CTQ

What is the best way to deal with SVJ offenders? Justify your response.

community-based program that targets risk factors in disadvantaged neighborhoods; (4) integration of services, including those provided by the juvenile justice system, mental health system, medical system, schools, and child protection agencies; and (5) prevention of gang formation and involvement, drug dealing, drug markets, and violent victimization.

CRIME IN SCHOOLS

The string of tragic violent incidents that occurred in recent school years has refocused the American public's attention on school crime and safety. When the first events occurred, it became clear that there was no single source of information about crime and violence in the nation's schools, and former President Clinton called on the Departments of Justice and Education to produce an annual report card on school violence. The departments responded to that request by producing an annual report on school safety to inform educators, parents, and students about the current nature of crime in schools and about programs that schools and school systems have instituted to work toward making schools safer. The following represents a summary of that work.[28]

Schools should be safe and secure places for all students, teachers, and staff members. Recent effort by schools, local authorities, and the state and federal governments have prompted the nation to focus on improving the safety of American schools. It is the hope that all children will be able to go to and from school and be at school without fearing for their safety or the safety of their friends and teachers. Judging progress toward providing safer schools requires establishing good indicators on the current state of school crime and safety and periodically monitoring and updating these indicators.

Nonfatal Student Victimization—Student Reports

In this report, students ages 12 through 18 were victims of about 255,000 incidents of nonfatal serious violent crime at school and about 671,000 incidents away from school. These numbers indicate that when students were away from school they were more likely to be victims of nonfatal serious violent crime—including rape, sexual assault, robbery, and aggravated assault—than when they were at school.

Violence and Crime at School—Public School Principal/Disciplinarian Reports

Ten percent of all public schools reported at least one serious violent crime to the police or a law enforcement representative. Principals' reports of serious violent crimes included murder, rape or other types of sexual battery, suicide, physical attack or fight with a weapon, or robbery (see Figure 14.3). Another 47 percent of public schools reported a less serious violent or nonviolent crime (but not a serious violent one). Crimes in this category include physical attack or fight without a weapon, theft/larceny, and vandalism. The remaining 43 percent of public schools did not report any of these crimes to the police.

Elementary schools were much less likely than either middle or high schools to report any type of crime. They were much more likely to report vandalism. At the middle and high school levels, physical attack or fight without a weapon was generally the most commonly reported crime. Theft or larceny was more common at the high school than the middle school level (6 versus 4 per 1,000 students).

School Environment

- The report noted increases in the percentages of students feeling unsafe while they were at school and while they were going to and from school.
- Approximately 2.1 million students indicated that they avoided one or more places at school for fear of their own safety.

FIGURE 14.3

The presence of weapons in today's schools is a concern in many communities. The semiautomatic handgun in the photo was confiscated before it could be used.

Courtesy of Dwayne Newton/PhotoEdit.

- More than one-quarter of students (28 percent) reported gangs in their schools.
- The percentage of male high school seniors who reported carrying a weapon to school at least one day within the four weeks before the survey was 9 percent. The percentage of female students who reported doing so was 3 percent.
- Although twelfth-graders were less likely to use alcohol at school than at home or at parties, about 8 percent of twelfth-graders had consumed alcohol at school in the past twelve months.

"In the News: School Violence" describes lessons that have been learned from several gruesome acts of school violence that left many dead or seriously injured.

IN THE NEWS

A HUMAN PERSPECTIVE

SCHOOL VIOLENCE
by Steven Band and Joseph Harold

In Pearl, Mississippi, a 16-year-old boy allegedly killed his mother, then went to his high school and shot 9 students, 2 fatally. Three students were killed and 5 others were wounded in a high school in West Paducah, Kentucky; a 14-year-old student pleaded guilty. During a false fire alarm at a middle school in Jonesboro, Arkansas, 4 girls and a teacher were shot to death and 10 individuals were wounded when 2 boys, 11 and 13 years old, allegedly opened fire from the woods. A science teacher was shot to death in front of students at an 8th-grade dance in Edinboro, Pennsylvania; a 14-year-old awaits trial. Two teenagers were killed and more than 20 individuals were hurt when a 15-year-old boy allegedly opened fire at a high school in Springfield, Oregon. The deadliest incident of school violence recently occurred at a high school in Littleton, Colorado, when 2 young male students went on a killing spree and then committed suicide.

These and other incidents of school violence have shocked Americans and created an atmosphere of fear and disbelief in many U.S. communities. How can youngsters commit such vicious attacks? Why are they occurring? What can be done to stop them? As the first responders to these tragic incidents, the law enforcement agencies directly involved face many difficult challenges and previously unthinkable situations. What lessons can the law enforcement community learn from these wanton acts of violence?

First and foremost, all aspects of a community need to work together. School violence is not the sole responsibility of the school system. Law enforcement, local government, civic groups, corporate entities, schools, and parents must form a partnership to combat these violent acts. Schools must prepare for these attacks. Law enforcement must develop response plans for handling such incidents. And communities must work with both to prevent such tragedies from occurring.

PREVENTIVE MEASURES
Law enforcement agencies, schools, and communities can employ preventive measures that may help identify potential at-risk students and defuse violent confrontations. Anonymous reporting programs, school resource officers, zero-tolerance policies, educational programs, effective liaison, and legislative and social reforms constitute some of the ways communities can safeguard their children.

IMPLEMENT ANONYMOUS REPORTING PROGRAMS
In all but one of the six school shootings, the suspects "leaked" their intentions to other students, but the police did not receive this information. At the time of the shootings, none of these schools had a Scholastic Crime Stoppers Program or an anonymous tip line or comment box in place. A tip line or similar program would facilitate the flow of anonymous information from the students to the police and would constitute a definitive preventive effort. To ensure effectiveness, school officials should monitor this tip line or comment box 24 hours a day or at least access it before the school day begins. A good working relationship must exist between school authorities and the police to ensure that the police receive the information in a timely way. If the targeted schools had had an anonymous tip program, the police probably could have caught several of the shooters as they entered their schools.

EMPLOY SCHOOL RESOURCE OFFICERS
In conjunction with a tip program, schools should consider school resource officers (i.e., officers permanently assigned to the school by the police department). These officers can provide positive information quickly, weed out rumors, and develop intelligence regarding potential or planned acts of violence. Besides school resource officers and other officers with school duties, patrol officers should adopt schools in their assigned areas and, whenever possible, have lunch at the school. This gives students an opportunity to develop trust and to talk to police officers in a neutral, nonthreatening atmosphere.

DEVELOP A ZERO-TOLERANCE POLICY
Schools should establish a zero-tolerance policy for students who make threats. Such a policy might include expulsion or suspension of students who threaten to kill or assault others and, if appropriate, quickly provide psychological evaluation or intervention for these students. When adults take threats seriously, students will realize that violence is not a condoned resolution to conflict.

continues

SCHOOL VIOLENCE (continued)

EDUCATE TEACHERS AND PARENTS

The police should train teachers, school counselors, and parents to recognize students at risk of committing violence. While society can prevent or minimize violence, it rarely, if ever, can predict it because of the numerous human variables involved. Therefore, teachers and parents must look for "leakage" in student behavior that may signal the potential for violence. One behavior leakage that was present in all but one of the shootings involved the stated or implied desire to commit a violent act or suicide. Other general warning signs or personal background indicators include:

- a history of violence;
- a close family member who has committed a violent act;
- a history of alcohol or drug abuse;
- a precipitating event, such as a failed romance or the perception of a failed romance, which was the case in several of the school shootings;
- the availability of a weapon or the means to commit violence;
- a recent attempt to commit suicide or an act of violence, as was the case in several of the school shootings;
- a lack of coping skills or strategies to handle personal life crises with no controls to prevent anger or positive ways to release it; and
- no apparent emotional support system.

When teachers, school counselors, or parents see a problem, they should notify school security personnel and the police. Police should meet with parents and teachers to encourage them to seek counseling for youths who exhibit symptoms indicating a need for intervention. However, because many incidents and changes in life can cause changes in student behavior, it becomes difficult to know what is normal student behavior and what constitutes grounds for concern and possible intervention.

Moreover, communities must send positive messages to all of their children that they are valuable and important to the community. Parents and other concerned adults must find ways to sincerely praise children, positively recognize their contributions to the community, and actively show children that they are loved and respected. At the same time, communities should encourage zero tolerance for violence whether committed by children or adults.

EXPLORE LEGISLATIVE AND SOCIAL REFORMS

Law enforcement, schools, and parents can do only so much to prevent school violence. Society must begin to explore ways to combat these vicious attacks. Such initiatives could include legislation that:

- provides for mandatory custody to evaluate any juvenile found in the possession of a firearm or other deadly weapon;
- requires school officials to report to the police any criminal offenses committed at their schools and to furnish blueprints of their facilities to local law enforcement authorities;
- enables law enforcement, schools, juvenile authorities, and other criminal justice agencies to share information for the purpose of criminal investigations or identifying children who may pose a danger to themselves and others; and
- allows courts to try as adults juveniles who commit homicide.

Besides supporting legislative action, communities should develop programs that denounce violence and encourage respect for life and education, along with initiatives that increase individual and parental responsibility and accountability. Communities also should advocate mental health services for individuals who need it, meaningful sanctions for those who demonstrate an unwillingness to conform their behavior to the law, and avenues for obtaining information that may enable behavioral scientists to better identify predictive behavior and thresholds of behavior that require intervention (treatment or sanctions, as appropriate).

CONCLUSION

Many Americans may find the old adage an ounce of prevention is worth a pound of cure difficult to believe. But who would have thought that such horrible acts of school violence could occur in rural areas of the United States? Unfortunately, Americans need to accept that grisly, violent acts can occur anywhere and be committed by almost anyone, even a child.

If a youngster can take a gun to school and pull the trigger, then communities must come together to deal with this problem in a multidisciplinary approach. The phenomenon of school violence is complicated and will take a great deal of wisdom to address properly. Meanwhile, law enforcement agencies must develop comprehensive plans for responding to such attacks, and they must join with their schools and communities to implement prevention programs. Doing so will make American children feel good about themselves, their families, their neighborhoods, and their country.

Source: Adapted from Stephen Band and Joseph Harold, "School Violence–Lessons Learned," *FBI Law Enforcement Bulletin* (September 1999), pp. 9–16.

The School Resource Officer (SRO)

In the aftermath of school violence outbreaks in recent years, the safety of children at school remains an important national issue.[29] Although research continues to show that schools are relatively safe places for children (students were twice as likely to be victims of serious violent crime away from school than at school in 1998), the subject of school safety continues to concern families, school administrators, and communities. The perception of imminent danger in the school environment has become commonplace in many communities, leaving parents, students, and school personnel with, at best, a tenuous sense of security. The **school resource officer (SRO)** concept offers an approach to improving school security and alleviating community fears.

Part Q of Title I of the Omnibus Crime Control and Safe Streets Act of 1968, as amended, defines the SRO as "a career law enforcement officer, with sworn authority, deployed in community-oriented policing, and assigned by the employing police department or agency to work in collaboration with school and community-based organizations." According to the Center for the Prevention of School Violence at North Carolina State University, the SRO concept evolved during the 1950s in Flint, Michigan, where community policing had been implemented and police officers had become involved in schools. The concept flourished during the 1960s and 1970s (predominantly in Florida), then languished in the 1980s, and did not gain momentum nationwide until the mid-1990s.

Today, the concept of what constitutes an SRO varies from one state or local jurisdiction to another, making counting of the number of SROs difficult. Although the number of identified SROs has continued to grow, key issues related to SRO program funding, definition and standardization of SRO roles and responsibilities, and provision of appropriate and adequate training for SROs remain to be addressed.

On September 6, 2000, the Department of Justice announced that the COPS in Schools program of its Office of Community Oriented Policing Services (COPS) would award $68 million in grants to hire 599 SROs in 289 communities across the Nation. These grants enable communities to hire new police officers and encourage working relationships between police and schools, thus bringing the principles and philosophy of community policing directly into the school environment.

Although these community grants provide the funding needed to hire new SROs, the SRO's multifaceted role—as law enforcement officer, counselor, teacher, and liaison between law enforcement, schools, families, and the community—requires training beyond that traditionally offered in police academies. The SROs' focus on youth in schools means that these officers work with a complex population in an environment unfamiliar to most law enforcement officers. To help communities prepare SROs for their unique role, Congress appropriated $5 million in fiscal year (FY) 2000 and an additional $3 million in FY 2001 for the COPS program to provide training and technical assistance.

THE SECRET SERVICE SAFE SCHOOL INITIATIVE

Background

Most official statistics show that rates of school violence have steadily decreased in recent years.[30] As reports from the U.S. Department of Education and others have shown, school is one of the safest places for our nation's children. However, several high-profile shootings in schools over the past decade have resulted in increased fear among students, parents, and educators. The Secret Service Safe School Initiative focuses on a rare but significant component of the problem of school violence—incidents of targeted violence in school. "Targeted violence" is a term developed by the Secret Service to refer to any incident of violence where a known (or knowable) attacker selects a particular target prior to his or her violent attack. The target may be an identified (or identifiable) person, such as a particular classmate or teacher, or it could be a building, such as the school itself.

Other kinds of problems in American schools are far more common than the targeted attacks in schools that have occurred in Jefferson County, Colorado; Jonesboro, Arkansas; West Paducah, Kentucky; and other communities. Moreover, children and adolescents face many other problems in school and out. However, the tremendous impact of each one of these school shootings—on the school, the surrounding community, and the nation—and the increased fear these events have engendered have made it necessary for school officials, parents, and others to consider steps they can take to prevent incidents of targeted violence in their schools.

The Safe School Initiative was developed and implemented as a partnership with the U.S. Department of Education, under the direction of the secretary of education, and in close collaboration with the director of the Department of Education's Safe and Drug-Free Schools Program. In this collaboration, the U.S. Secret Service brought to the problem of school violence its experience in researching, understanding, and preventing targeted violence. The goal of the Safe School Initiative is to provide accurate and useful information to school administrators, educators, law enforcement professionals, and others who have protective and safety responsibilities in schools, to help prevent incidents of targeted violence in school.

Method

For this project, personnel from the Secret Service National Threat Assessment Center (NTAC) studied thirty-seven school shootings, involving forty-one attackers who were current or recent students at the school, and where the attacker(s) chose the school for a particular purpose (and not simply as a site of opportunity). Shootings that were clearly related to gang or drug activity, or to an interpersonal or relationship dispute that just happened to occur at the school, were not included.

For each incident, researchers reviewed primary source materials, such as investigative, school, court, and mental health records and answered several hundred questions about the case. Teams of investigators and social science researchers coded each of the cases, with at least two raters assigned to each case. Each rater independently answered questions about the incident in a codebook, then discussed his or her ratings with the other team member and produced a single "reconciled" scoring for the case. Information gathered about each case included facts about the attacker's development of an idea and plan to harm the target, selection of the target, motivation for the incident, communications about their ideas and intent, acquisition of weapons, and demographic and background information about each attacker.

In addition to file reviews for each case, NTAC personnel have conducted supplemental interviews with ten of the attackers. The purpose of the interviews is to get the attacker's perspective on his decision to engage in a school-based attack. The findings included here are based primarily on the information obtained from review of available files in each case. The information gleaned from interviews is used to illustrate particular aspects of a case.

Incident Characteristics

Contrary to common belief, incidents of targeted violence at school are not a new phenomenon. The earliest case examined occurred in 1974, where a student brought guns and homemade bombs to his school, set off the fire alarm, and shot at janitors and firefighters who responded to the alarm. Since the first case in 1974, NTAC personnel identified thirty-seven incidents, involving forty-one attackers, that meet the study criteria specified earlier. These incidents took place in twenty-six states, with more than one incident occurring in Arkansas, California, Kentucky, Missouri, and Tennessee; all of the incidents were committed by boys or young men. Contrary to the impression given from the attack at Columbine High School in Jefferson County, Colorado, fellow students were not the only targets chosen by the attackers. In more than half of the incidents, the attacker had selected at least one school administrator, faculty member, or staff member as a target. In more than two-thirds of the incidents, the attacker killed one or more students, faculty, or others at the school. Handguns and rifles/shotguns were the primary weapons used. More than half of the attacks occurred in the middle of the school day.

Preliminary Findings

1. Incidents of targeted violence at school are rarely impulsive. The attacks are typically the result of an understandable and often discernible process of thinking and behavior.
2. There is no accurate or useful profile of "the school shooter."
3. Most attackers engaged in some behavior, prior to the incident, that caused others concern or indicated a need for help.

Implications

Students who engaged in targeted violence in school typically did not "just snap." Because information about these attackers' intent and planning was potentially knowable before the incident, some attacks may be preventable. However, because the time span between the attacker's decision to mount an attack and the actual incident may be short, quick efforts to inquire and intervene are necessary. An inquiry should include investigation of, and attention to, grievances and bad feelings about school or potential targets that a student may be experiencing.

The use of profiles is not effective either for identifying students who may pose a risk for targeted violence at school or—once a student has been identified—for assessing the risk that a particular student may pose for school-based targeted violence. The personality and social characteristics of the shooters varied substantially. Knowing that an individual shares characteristics, features, or traits with prior school shooters does not advance the appraisal of risk. Moreover, the use of profiles carries a risk of overidentification—the great majority of students who fit any given profile will not actually pose a risk of targeted violence. Finally, use of profiles will fail to identify some students who in fact pose a risk of violence—but who share few if any characteristics with prior attackers.

An inquiry should focus instead on a student's behaviors and communications to determine if the student appears to be planning or preparing for an attack. A fact-based approach may be more productive in preventing school shootings than a trait-based approach. The ultimate question to answer in an inquiry is whether a student is on a path toward a violent attack, and if so to determine how fast the student is moving and where intervention may be possible.

A significant problem in preventing targeted violence in schools is determining how best to respond to students who are already known to be in trouble or needing assistance, not only to identify students who are plotting an attack. In cases where there is concern about potential targeted violence, an inquiry should include investigation of, and attention to, a student's difficulty coping with major losses or perceived failures, particularly where it may have led to feelings of desperation and hopelessness.

YOUTH GANGS

Despite the recent decline in juvenile crime, our country continues to face a youth gang problem.[31]

Scope of the Problem

Assessing the scope of the youth gang problem in the United States is difficult. No consensus exists on what constitutes a youth gang. Many jurisdictions deny the existence of gangs. Others incorrectly, many experts believe, characterize less serious forms of adolescent law-violating groups as gangs.[32] Some call gangs by other names, such as "crews" or "posses," although some of these are not bona fide gangs; rather, they are specialized groups engaged in predatory crimes or drug trafficking. It appears that communities are likely to label troublesome adolescent groups as gangs if the public perceives them to be a problem.[33] Although youth gang definitions vary, most include the following elements: a self-formed group, united by mutual interests, that controls a particular territory, facility, or enterprise; uses symbols in communications (see Figure 14.4); and is collectively involved in crime.[34]

CTQ

How should school administrators and school resource officers deal with students who are thought to be a potential risk for targeted violence?

CTQ

What factors do you believe contribute most to the reasons why youth join gangs?

WEB

For more information on youth gangs, **visit our Web site,** www.prenhall.com/territo.

FIGURE 14.4

While assessing the scope of the youth gang problem is difficult, there is no denying their presence in many communities. Here youth gang members flash their signs.

Courtesy of A. Ramey/PhotoEdit.

Why Do Youth Join Gangs?

Some authorities view joining youth gangs as consisting of both pulls and pushes.[35] Pulls pertain to the attractiveness of the gang. Gang membership can enhance prestige or status among friends[36] and provide opportunities to be with them.[37] Gangs provide other attractive opportunities such as the chance for excitement.[38] Thus, many youth see themselves as making a rational choice in deciding to join a gang: They see personal advantages to gang membership.[39]

Social, economic, and cultural forces push many adolescents in the direction of gangs. Feeling marginal, adolescents join gangs for social relationships that give them a sense of identity.[40] For some youth, gangs provide a way of solving social adjustment problems, particularly the trials and tribulations of adolescence.[41] In some communities, youth are intensively recruited or coerced into gangs.[42] They seemingly have no choice. A few are virtually born into gangs as a result of neighborhood traditions and their parents' earlier (and perhaps continuing) gang participation or involvement in criminal activity.[43]

Conclusion

Youth gang problems are prevalent across the United States, even in small cities and towns. At the same time, the composition of youth gangs is changing. Smaller, less structured gangs are emerging, and although drug trafficking is generally not an organized activity managed by gangs, drug gangs are more predominant now than in previous decades. The racial/ethnic composition of gangs also is changing, and gangs are becoming more organized.

Gang violence—particularly homicide—has increased, owing mainly to availability and use of more dangerous weapons, especially automatic and semiautomatic handguns. This violence also has been linked to gangs' proclivity to be associated with drug trafficking. New research, however, questions the extent to which gang-related drug sales are a major cause of violence. It appears that most gang violence is related to conflicts with other gangs.

Most gang problems are homegrown. Gang migration appears to contribute little to local gang problems, including drug trafficking, except within geographic regions. There is some discrepancy between research results and investigatory agency reports on youth and adult gang migration and drug trafficking; however, much of this can be explained by the studies' use of different research methods, definitions, and information sources.

Although significant progress is being made in identifying the major risk factors for youth gang involvement, much more information is needed to specify the developmental sequence by which these risk factors operate. This knowledge could be very useful in the development of prevention and intervention programs. Progress also is being made in developing comprehensive programs that combine prevention, social intervention and rehabilitation, and suppression of gang violence. Because of a dearth of program evaluations, however, little is known about the effectiveness of these interventions. An evaluation of OJJDP's five-site program may shed more light on the effectiveness of comprehensive programs.

A key issue in combating youth gangs is providing a uniform definition for them—distinguishing them from troublesome youth groups and adult criminal organizations. Youth gangs and adult criminal organizations have different origins, and they serve unique purposes for participants. Efforts to develop effective long-term interventions must take these differences into account.

CHILDREN WHO KILL THEIR PARENTS

One of the more disturbing crimes in today's society involves children who kill their parents. One noted criminologist, Kathleen Heide, has conducted considerable research into the causes and prevention of this type of crime. Some of her findings are reviewed in the following sections.[44]

Youths at Risk

Analysis of ten years of supplementary homicide report data by the Federal Bureau of Investigation indicated that about sixty-five natural parents were slain by youths under age 18 each year. When this low rate of **matricides** (the killing of one's mother) and **patricides** (the killing of one's father) is examined in light of the problems of predicting violent behavior or dangerousness, the conclusion is inescapable: it is impossible to predict which youths will kill their parents. Some youths, are, however, at a higher risk of slaying a parent. Five factors help target such youths: (1) The youth is raised in a chemically dependent or other dysfunctional family; (2) an ongoing pattern of family violence exists in the home; (3) conditions in the home worsen, and violence escalates; (4) the youth becomes increasingly vulnerable to stressors in the home environment; and (5) a firearm is readily available in the home (see Figure 14.5).

Adolescent parricide offenders typically represent a low risk to society. Most can be reintegrated into society if given effective treatment by mental health professionals

FIGURE 14.5

Children who have killed their parents have been the subject of recent research by Dr. Kathleen Heide. The ready availability of firearms is one of the major factors associated with these homicides.

Courtesy of Barros & Barros/Getty Images Inc.

trained to work with survivors of severe trauma. The real killer in these types of cases is often child maltreatment. The following recommendations are designed to reduce the conditions that cause many children unnecessary physical and emotional harm, and make the killing of a parent seem the only way out to some of them.

- Teach child development and parenting skills to parents and incorporate such information into high school curricula.
- Teach students at elementary and high school levels about various types of child abuse and encourage them to take appropriate action if victimized.
- Educate and insulate children who are being raised in chemically dependent families from potential damage by their parents.
- Provide a supportive network in the schools to guide children through the process of getting help.
- Use the media to educate the public about different types of child abuse and sources of help.

CTQ
What can society do to deal with children who kill their parents?

WEB
For more information on juvenile justice in the twenty-first century, visit our Web site, www.prenhall.com/territo.

JUVENILE JUSTICE IN THE NEW CENTURY

"In the News: A Juvenile Justice System for the Twenty-First Century" provides an example of what we may expect in order to improve the current juvenile justice system.

Objectives of an Effective Juvenile Justice System

An effective juvenile justice system must meet three objectives: (1) hold the juvenile offender accountable; (2) enable the juvenile to become a capable, productive, and responsible citizen; and (3) ensure the safety of the community.[45]

Elements of an Effective Juvenile Justice System

The most effective juvenile justice interventions are swift, certain, consistent, and appropriate. To meet these objectives, an effective juvenile justice system must:[46]

- Include a mechanism for comprehensively assessing a juvenile when he or she first enters the system, in order to determine both the risk to the community and appropriate interventions and sanctions.

IN THE NEWS
A HUMAN PERSPECTIVE

A JUVENILE JUSTICE SYSTEM FOR THE TWENTY-FIRST CENTURY
by Shay Bilchik

It is time to examine how the juvenile justice system can operate more effectively to reduce juvenile crime, particularly violent crime, and meet system goals. The juvenile justice system needs to be revitalized so that it will ensure immediate and appropriate sanctions, provide effective treatment, reverse trends in juvenile violence, and rebuild public confidence in and support for the system

Since the first juvenile court was established in Chicago, IL, in 1899, a variety of strategies have been pursued to address the particular issues posed by juvenile offenders, but results have been mixed. Young people need to know that if they break the law, they will be held accountable. They also need to be put on a path toward responsible adulthood. The Office of Juvenile Justice and Delinquency Prevention (OJJDP) has developed a strategy, set forth in the publication *Comprehensive Strategy for Serious, Violent, and Chronic Juvenile Offenders (Comprehensive Strategy)*, to help communities prevent delinquency and establish a juvenile justice system based on graduated sanctions that combine accountability with increasingly intensive treatment services. The *Comprehensive Strategy* calls for immediate interventions when high-risk or delinquent behavior first occurs.

Source: Shay Bilchik, *A Juvenile Justice System for the Twenty-First Century.* Washington, D.C.: U.S. Department of Justice, Office of Juvenile Justice and Delinquency Prevention, 1998, pp. 1–2.

IN THE WORKPLACE

SCHOOL RESOURCE OFFICER

Responsible for providing guidance and direction to students, parents, and teachers. Performs a variety of duties, including the following: participates as resource person in class discussion; interprets law to students; prevents juvenile delinquency; improves image of police officers, and assists in protection of the school, staff, and students in accordance with the duties of a police officer. Minimum qualifications are as follows: age 21, high school diploma or equivalent, valid driver's license.

- Have the capacity to provide a range of treatment services, from family counseling to outpatient drug treatment to out-of-home care.
- Incorporate increasingly severe sanctions and enhanced treatment services when a juvenile fails to respond to initial interventions or is involved in a particularly serious or violent offense as a first-time offender.

An effective juvenile justice system does not use detention as a sanction, but instead uses detention resources only for preadjudicated juveniles who must be detained, based on their risk of reoffending, harming themselves or others, or failing to appear at future proceedings—factors that can be assessed by applying objective criteria. For adjudicated delinquents, an effective juvenile justice system includes a full range of graduated sanctions that begins with comprehensive risk and needs assessments and includes aftercare for juveniles returning to the community from out-of-home placements. The entire process needs to be complemented by quality case management.

SUMMARY

The juvenile justice system evolved as an attempt to deal constructively with the problems of dependent, neglected, and delinquent youngsters within an informal, nonadversarial setting. The first juvenile courts operated as a blend of the social casework agency and the criminal court. However, the procedural informality of these courts often resulted in the denial to juveniles of rights guaranteed to adults under the Constitution. Thus, in a series of important decisions in the 1960s, the U.S. Supreme Court eventually extended due process and equal protection rights to juveniles. In this chapter we discuss the federal mandate to remove juveniles from adult jails.

The police and the courts make a strong effort to divert as many youths as possible from the juvenile justice system. Once a juvenile is adjudicated delinquent, a variety of postadjudication alternatives are available to the court in the form of residential and nonresidential programs. As many delinquents as possible are handled in community-based correctional programs, but training schools continue to house many adjudicated delinquents. Release from training school may allow a youngster to remain in the community under aftercare supervision, a status that roughly corresponds to parole for adult offenders. The private sector is also becoming involved in juvenile services.

Prevention, diversion, and the use of special education programs for juveniles were highlighted in this chapter. The issues of missing and exploited children will continue to receive a great deal of attention from the juvenile justice system and the public in general. In this chapter we also discussed serious and violent juvenile offenders, and juvenile violence in our schools.

Many cities and even smaller towns are experiencing a resurgence of youth gang violence. Juveniles who participate in gang activity often belong to the category of "lifestyle violent juveniles"—youth born and reared in a subculture that reinforces exploitative aggression. Thus far, the juvenile justice system has been unable to deal effectively with these offenders. Many juveniles who commit violent crimes are shuttled in and out of the system until they become the responsibility of the adult criminal courts. Tactics such as juvenile curfew laws and juvenile boot camps were also reviewed.

Some critics of the current juvenile justice system call for additional reforms that would make the system more closely parallel adult process. Juvenile justice practitioners will continue to examine repeat juvenile justice offenders in relationship to the resources available in the system.

Discussion and Review

1. What were the principal objectives of the child-saving movement? How influential was this movement in the development of the juvenile court?
2. Discuss the concept of individualized justice and the role it played in the emergence of the juvenile court in the United States.
3. Discuss the implications of the *Gault* case for the juvenile justice system.
4. In addition to delinquents, what other types of youngsters are handled by the juvenile courts?
5. How do status offenses differ from crimes?
6. What steps can intake workers take to reduce or prevent juveniles from entering the juvenile justice system?
7. What are the criticisms of Drug Abuse Resistance Education (DARE)?
8. What alternative dispositions are available to the police and intake workers in handling juvenile cases?
9. In the Flint, Michigan, study of police officers and their handling of juvenile encounters, what were five role identity orientations assumed by police officers?
10. What are some of the problems associated with placing juveniles in adult jails or lockups?
11. Describe the postadjudication alternatives available to the court in the disposition of juvenile cases.
12. What does the research on juveniles in detention indicate?
13. It is useful to think of missing children in four major categories. What are the categories?
14. What are the essential elements in effective community supervision of delinquent youngsters?
15. List the common elements of community-based juvenile curfew programs.
16. List and discuss predictors of SVJ offending.
17. Describe nonfatal student school victimizations based on reports from students.
18. Briefly discuss some of the preventive measures used in public schools in an effort to reduce violence.
19. Discuss why some youths join gangs.
20. List Heide's five factors that can be used to target youths who are at a higher risk of slaying a parent.

CHAPTER RESOURCES

IN THE MEDIA

Video

A&E American Justice Videos
ABC Custom Video: *Girls in the Hood*
ABC Custom Video: *Reports of Child Abuse and Neglect* (Show TM39)
ABC News Library Video: *This Week with David Brinkley*
ABC NEWS Video: *Young Criminals, Adult Punishments*
NIJ Crime File Videos: *Juvenile Offenders*

Film

Bad Boys (1983)
Colors (1993, Columbia Pictures)

Television

The Guardian (CBS)

IN THE LITERATURE

Books

T. BERNARD, *The Cycle of Juvenile Justice* New York: Oxford University Press, 1992.

M. CLEMENT, *The Juvenile Justice System: Law and Process*. Boston: Butterworth-Heinemann, 1996.

D. HAWKINS, *Delinquency and Crime: Current Theories*. New York: Cambridge University Press, 1996.

M. JACOBS, *Screwing the System and Making It Work: Juvenile Justice in the No-Fault Society*. Chicago: University of Chicago Press, 1990.

M. KNOX, *Gangsta in the House*. Troy, Mich.: Momento Books, 1995.

B. KRISBERG, AND J. AUSTIN, *Reinventing Juvenile Justice*. 2nd ed. Newbury Park: Calif.: Sage, 1993.

A. PLATT, *The Child Savers: The Invention of Delinquency*. Chicago: University of Chicago Press, 1969.

J. RODRIGUEZ, *East Side Stories: Gang Life in East L.A.* New York: PowerHouse Cultural Entertainment, 1998.

I. SCHWARTZ, *(In) Justice for Juveniles: Rethinking the Best Interest of the Child*. Lexington, Mass.: Lexington Books, 1989.

A. WILLIAMS, *A Kind and Just Parent: The Children on Juvenile Court*. Boston: Beacon Press, 1997.

Articles

B. FIELD, "Abolish the Juvenile Court: Youthfulness, Criminal Responsibility, and Sentencing Policy," *Journal of Criminal Law and Criminology*, vol. 88 (1997), pp. 68–136.

S. MORSE, "Immaturity and Irresponsibility," *Journal of Criminal Law and Criminology*, vol. 88 (1997), pp. 15–67.

S. ROSENBAUM, "Civil Rights Issues in Juvenile Detention and Correctional Systems," *Corrections Today*, vol. 61 (1999), p. 148.

R. SHELDEN, J. HORVATH, AND S. TRACY, "Do Status Offenders Get Worse? Some Clarifications on the Question of Escalation," *Crime and Delinquency*, vol. 35 (April 1989) pp. 202–216.

M. SICKMUND, H. SNYDER, AND E. POE-YAMAGATA, "Juvenile Offenders and Victims: A 1997 Update on Violence. (Washington, D.C.: U.S. Department of Justice, Office of Juvenile Justice and Delinquency Prevention, 1996) p. 33.

ENDNOTES

1. L. T. Empey, *American Delinquency: Its Meaning and Construction*. Homewood, Ill.: Dorsey, 1978.

2. Ibid.

3. N. K. Teeters and J. O. Reineman, *The Challenge of Delinquency*. Englewood Cliffs, N.J.: Prentice Hall, 1950.

4. F. L. Faust and P. J. Brantingham, eds., *Juvenile Justice Philosophy: Readings, Cases, and Comments*. St. Paul, Minn.: West, 1979.

5. Ibid., p. 112.

6. J. C. Mack, "The Juvenile Court." In F. L. Faust and P. J. Brantingham, eds., *Juvenile Justice Philosophy: Readings, Cases, and Comments*. St. Paul, Minn.: West, 1979.

7. T. M. Godwin, *A Guide for Implementing Teen Court Programs*. Washington, D.C.: Office of Juvenile Justice and Delinquency Prevention, 1996.

8. F. W. Ward, "Prevention and Diversion in the United States." In V. L. Stewart, ed., *The Changing Faces of Juvenile Justice*. New York: New York University Press, 1978.

9. The information regarding the DARE program and community policing was adapted from Bureau of Justice

Assistance, *Community Policing and D.A.R.E.* Washington, D.C.: U.S. Department of Justice, 1995, pp. 1–7.

10. For more information regarding the evaluation of DARE, see D. Rossenbaum and G. Manson, "Assessing the Effects of School-Based Drug Education: A Six-Year Multi-Level Analysis of Project DARE," *Journal of Research in Crime and Delinquency,* vol. 35 (1998), pp. 381–412; D. Rossenbaum, R. Flewelling, S. Bailey, C. Ringalt, and D. Wilkinson, "Cops in the Classroom: A Longitudinal Evaluation," *Journal of Research in Crime and Delinquency,* vol. 31 (1994), pp. 3–31.

11. The discussion of the LRE program was derived from *Education in the Law: Promoting Citizenship in the Schools.* Washington, D.C.: U.S. Department of Justice, 1990, pp. 1–3.

12. See also H. Wrobleski and K. Hess, *Introduction to Law Enforcement and Criminal Justice.* Belmont, Calif.: Wadsworth/Thompson Learning, 2000.

13. National Advisory Commission on Standards and Goals, *Report of the Task Force on Juvenile Justice and Delinquency Prevention.* Washington, D.C.: U.S. Government Printing Office, 1976.

14. J. Belknap, M. Morash, and R. Trojanowicz, *Implementing a Community Policing Model for Work with Juveniles—An Exploratory Study.* East Lansing: National Neighborhood Foot Patrol Center, School of Criminal Justice, Michigan State University, 1986.

15. Ibid. pp. 9–12.

16. The discussion regarding the removal of juveniles from adult jails was derived from *OJJDP Helps States Remove Juveniles from Adult Jails and Lockups.* Washington, D.C.: U.S. Department of Justice, 1990, pp. 1, 2.

17. This discussion on research regarding juveniles in detention centers was provided courtesy of Dr. Richard Dembo, University of South Florida. A more complete review of this research appears in the following articles: R. Dembo et al., "Physical Abuse, Sexual Victimization and Illicit Drug Use: A Structural Analysis among High-Risk Adolescents," *Journal of Adolescence,* vol. 10 (1987), pp. 13–33; "Heavy Marijuana Use and Crime among Youths Entering a Juvenile Detention Center," *Journal of Psychoactive Drugs,* vol. 19 (1987), pp. 47–56; "Further Examination of the Association between Heavy Marijuana Use and Crime among Youths Entering a Juvenile Detention Center," *Journal of Psychoactive Drugs,* vol. 19 (1987), pp. 360–373.

18. The majority of the information regarding the impact of deinstitutionalization of status offenders was adapted from A. L. Schneider, *Reports of the National Juvenile Justice Assessment Centers—The Impact of Deinstitutionalization and Recidivism and Secure Confinement on Status Offenders.* Washington, D.C.: U.S. Department of Justice, December 1985, pp. v, vi, 1, 2, 19.

19. The information regarding juvenile restitution programs was adapted and modified from J. S. Warner and V. Burke, eds., *National Directory of Juvenile Restitution Programs, 1987.* Washington, D.C.: U.S. Government Printing Office, 1987, pp. 1, 3, 4, 5, 28, 69, 130.

20. President's Commission on Law Enforcement and Administration of Justice, *Task Force Report: Corrections.* Washington, D.C.: U.S. Government Printing Office, 1967. See also the National Advising Committee on Criminal Justice Standards and Goals, *Report of the Task Force on Juvenile Justice and Delinquency Prevention.* Washington, D.C.: U.S. Government Printing Office, 1973, pp. 19–26.

21. The information regarding the wilderness program was adapted from K. Davanzo, *Eckerd Family Youth Alternatives Annual Report, 1996.*

22. The discussion of long-term institutional facilities was adapted from "Juvenile Offenders in Residential Placement." OJJDP Fact Sheet. Washington, D.C.: U.S. Government Printing Office, March 1999.

23. Adapted from *Boot Camps for Juvenile Offenders: An Implementation Evaluation of Three Demonstration Programs.* Washington, D.C.: U.S. Department of Justice, Office of Justice Programs, 1996, pp. 1–5.

24. Much of this discussion of missing and runaway children was adapted from A. W. Burgess, *Youth at Risk: Understanding Runaway and Exploited Youth.* Washington, D.C.: National Center for Missing and Exploited Children, September 1986, pp. 2, 5, 29, 43, 45. This report was prepared under Cooperative Agreement #86-MC-CS-K003 from the Office of Juvenile Justice Assistance, Research, and Statistics, U.S. Department of Justice.

25. Adapted from *Curfew: An Answer to Juvenile Delinquency and Victimization?* Washington, D.C.: U.S. Department of Justice, Office of Justice Programs, 1996, pp. 1–6.

26. Ibid., pp. 2–6.

27. This information was derived from *Serious and Violent Juvenile Offenders.* Washington, D.C.: U.S. Department of Justice, Office of Juvenile Justice and Delinquency Prevention, 1998, pp. 1–7.

28. The discussion of crime in schools was adapted from *Indicators of School Crime and Safety 1998.* Washington, D.C.: National Center for Educational Statistics and Bureau of Justice Statistics, 1998, pp. 3–7.

29. The information on school resource officers was adapted from C. Girouard, *School Resource Officer Training Program.* Washington, D.C.: Office of Juvenile Justice and Delinquency Prevention, 2001, p. 1.

30. This discussion was adapted from B. Vossekuil, M. Reddy, R. Fein, R. Borum, and W. Modzeleski, *U.S.S.S. Safe School Initiative: An Interim Report on the Prevention of Targeted Violence in Schools.* Washington, D.C.: U.S. Secret Service, National Threat Assessment Center, 2000, pp. 1–16.

31. The discussion of youth gangs was adapted from J. Howell, *Youth Gangs: An Overview.* Washington, D.C.: U.S. Department of Justice, *Office of Juvenile Justice and Delinquency Prevention,* 1998, pp. 1–14.

32. W. B. Miller. *Crime by Youth Gangs and Groups in the United States,* rev. ed. Washington, D.C.: U.S. Department of Justice, 1992 (NCJ 156221).

33. Ibid.

34. G. D. Curry and S. H. Decker, *Confronting Gangs: Crime and Community.* Los Angeles, Calif.: Roxbury, 1998.

35. S. H. Decker and B. Van Winkle, *Life in the Gang: Family, Friends, and Violence.* New York: Cambridge University Press, 1996.

36. W. F. Baccaglini, *Project Youth Gang-Drug Prevention: A Statewide Research Study.* Rensselaer: New York State Division for Youth, 1993.

37. C. Slayton, J. W. Stephens, and D. W. MacKenna, *Kids Speak Out: Opinions, Attitudes, and Characteristics of Fort Worth Gang and Non-Gang Members.* Fort Worth, Texas: Fort Worth Gang Research Project, 1993.

38. S. Pennell, E. Evans, R. Melton, and S. Hinson, *Down for the Set: Describing and Defining Gangs in San Diego.* San Diego: Criminal Justice Research Division, Association of Government, 1994.

39. M. S. Sanchez-Jankowski, *Islands in the Street: Gangs and American Urban Society.* Berkeley: University of California Press, 1991.

40. J. D. Vigil, *Barrio Gangs: Street Life and Identity in Southern California.* Austin: University of Texas Press, 1988.

41. J. D. Vigil and J. M. Long, "Emic and Etic Perspectives on Gang Culture." In C. R. Huff, ed., *Gangs in America.* Newbury Park, Calif.: Sage, 1990, pp. 55–70.

42. J. W. Johnstone, "Recruitment to a Youth Gang," *Youth and Society,* vol. 14 (1983), pp. 281–300.

43. J. W. Moore, *Homeboys: Gangs, Drugs and Prison in the Barrios of Los Angeles.* Philadelphia: Temple University Press, 1978.

44. K. H. Heide, *Why Kids Kill Parents: Child Abuse and Adolescent Homicide.* Newbury Park, Calif.: Sage, 1995.

45. Ibid.

46. Ibid.

15 DRUGS, CRIME, AND THE CRIMINAL JUSTICE SYSTEM

Chapter Outline

What Is Drug Addiction?
  Narcotics
  Depressants
  Psychedelics
  Stimulants
Drug-Facilitated Sexual Assault
  Drugs of Choice
  Other Date-Rape Drugs
Emerging Drug Trends
Reducing the Demand for Illicit Drugs
  Reducing Demand through Treatment
  Reducing Demand through Prevention

Community Collaboration with Law Enforcement
  Antidrug Coalitions and Partnerships
  Drug-Free Workplace Programs
  Faith Community Involvement
  National Service Programs
  Prevention Research
The Arguments for and against the Legalization of Drugs
  Arguments for Legalization
  Arguments against Legalization
Summary

Key Terms

analgesia, p. 583
barbiturates, p. 586
cocaine, p. 589
codeine, p. 583
freebasing, p. 589
gamma hydroxybutyrate (GHB), p. 592
heroin, p. 583
hypnotic, p. 583
ketamine, p. 588
lysergic acid diethylamide (LSD), p. 586
marijuana, p. 586
mescaline (peyote), p. 586
mesolimbic reward system, p. 582
methamphetamine, p. 589
morphine, p. 582
opium, p. 582
phencyclidine (PCP), p. 586
psilocybe mushrooms, p. 586
raves, p. 588
Rohypnol, p. 591

Courtesy of Barbara Peacock/Getty Images, Inc.

We live in a drug-saturated society. The different kinds of drugs available in this country number in the hundreds, the number of drug takers are counted in the millions, and the doses taken every year number in the billions. Some of these drugs are difficult to obtain, whereas others are as handy as the over-the-counter shelves of the local drugstore. Some drugs put you to sleep; others wake you up. If you are underactive, depressed, too relaxed, lethargic, too tired, or not assertive enough, there are drugs available to bring you out of it. There are also drugs for the person who is too active, overanxious, overaggressive, or tense. There are pills, capsules, or liquids for losing or gaining weight, for alleviating pain, or for just feeling good. Want to relax, enjoy others' company, have a party, have some recreation? A range of substances are available with the promise to do just that.

Most of this use of drugs is legitimate use of legitimate substances. There are positive social functions of drugs, and the availability of certain substances provides social and personal benefits and contributions to society. Drugs alleviate both physical and mental illness. They can be life-saving. Both prescribed and self-administered medication can ease pain and enable people to function who otherwise would not be able to do so.

However, much drug use is not legitimate. It is deviant, violates laws, contravenes social norms, and is disapproved of by most people. It presents society with enormous costs and problems. Even medically beneficial drugs can be misused and abused. The litany of drug-related problems and damage to people and society seems endless. Drugs often lead to damaged health, injury, and death. People die of overdoses. Drugs (and drug-alcohol combinations) are the second leading method of suicide. At least half of highway fatalities are alcohol- or drug-related. Four out of five cases of lung cancer are related to smoking. Alcohol consumption is implicated in heart disease, cancer, high blood pressure, and circulatory diseases and about half of murders, suicides, and accidental deaths. Intravenous drug use is the second leading route of AIDS infection. Lives are disrupted and destroyed by drug abuse. Relationships, careers, families, and whole neighborhoods and communities suffer from the ravages of drug and alcohol abuse. The precise direct and indirect economic costs of substance use and abuse in law enforcement, health care, treatment, crime, loss of employment, and lowered productivity are difficult to estimate accurately, but they are enormous.[1]

In this chapter we will discuss the major types of drugs most frequently abused, including narcotics, depressants, psychedelics, and stimulants. We will also discuss the growing problem of drug-facilitated sexual assault. In addition, we will examine the emerging drug trend, especially as it relates to drug use among young people, and we will discuss the various treatment programs that have been used or suggested to deal with the problematic aspects of drugs in American social life. Lastly we will discuss the arguments for and against the legalization of drugs.

WHAT IS DRUG ADDICTION?

Although each drug discussed in this chapter has some idiosyncratic mechanisms of action, virtually all drugs associated with abuse have common effects, either directly or indirectly, on a single pathway deep within the brain, the **mesolimbic reward system.** Activation of this system appears to be a common element in what keeps drug users taking drugs. This is not unique to any one drug; all addictive substances affect this circuit.

Not only does acute drug use modify brain function in critical ways, but prolonged drug use causes pervasive changes in brain function that persist long after the individual stops taking the drug. Significant effects of chronic use have been identified for many drugs at all levels: molecular, cellular, structural, and functional. The addicted brain is distinctly different from the nonaddicted brain, as manifested by changes in brain metabolic activity, receptor availability, gene expression, and responsiveness to environmental cues. Some of these long-lasting brain changes are idiosyncratic to specific drugs, whereas others are common to many different drugs. We can actually see these changes through use of recently developed technologies, such as positron emission tomography. The common brain effects of addicting substances suggest common brain mechanisms underlying all addiction.

The fact that addiction is so clearly tied to changes in brain structure and function is what makes it, fundamentally, a brain disease—a metaphorical switch in the brain to be thrown following prolonged drug use. Initially, drug use is a voluntary behavior, but as that switch is thrown, the individual moves into the state of addiction, characterized by compulsive drug seeking and use.

Understanding that addiction is, at its core, a consequence of fundamental changes in brain function means that a major goal of treatment must be either to reverse or to compensate for those brain changes. This could be accomplished through either medications or behavioral treatments (behavioral treatments alter brain function in other psychobiological disorders). Elucidation of the biology underlying the metaphorical switch is key to the development of more effective treatments, particularly antiaddiction medications.[2]

Narcotics

Drugs that are classified as narcotics are among the most ancient of the psychotropics; their use traces back at least 3,500 years. True narcotics are derivatives of the opium poppy (*Papaver somniferum*), whose sap contains a number of chemically active alkaloids, most notably **morphine.** These naturally occurring compounds can be harvested in the form of **opium,** a concentrate of the opium poppy's resinous sap (see Figure 15.1). This sap can also be subject to chemical processing, which can extract components of the resin

---

WEB

For more information on drug addiction, **visit our Web site,** www.prenhall.com/territo.

CTQ

Do you believe that drug addiction is a brain disease or a matter of individual character flaws and weaknesses? What evidence do you have for your answer?

IN THE WORKPLACE

NARCOTICS OFFICER

Responsible for infiltrating organizations that deal in drugs, seizing the largest quantity of drugs possible, and prosecuting any people involved in the illegal dealing and possession of drugs. Performs a variety of duties relating to the investigation of the sale, trafficking, and use of drugs, including follow-up on drug-related complaints and prescription-related offenses. Minimum qualifications are as follows: age 21, U.S. citizen, no prior convictions, one year field experience, high school diploma or equivalent.

FIGURE 15.1

Opium Poppies. Raw opium is collected by incising the seed capsules left after the petals have fallen. The opium first appears as white droplets, then turns brown before it is harvested.

Courtesy of Dorling Kindersley Media Library.

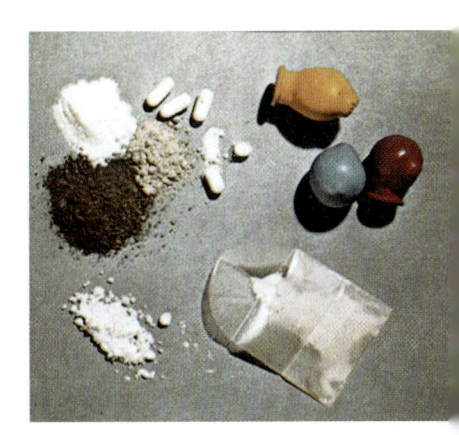

FIGURE 15.2

Heroin. An odorless crystalline powder, usually white but sometimes brown, heroin is usually sold in glassine paper packets, aluminum foil, or capsules. Four to five times stronger than morphine, it is the principal drug of addiction among the opium derivatives. It is sometimes smuggled into the country in balloons hidden in body cavities.

Courtesy of Drug Enforcement Administration.

WEB

For more information on narcotics, visit our Web site, www.prenhall.com/territo.

(like morphine). Also, chemical processing can codify the natural products and make them more powerful.

Heroin, for instance, is much more powerful than opium or morphine and is produced by acidifying morphine with acetic acid (see Figure 15.2). Another popular opiate derivative is **codeine,** which is more powerful than opium but less powerful than morphine or heroin. Products like heroin, which are made from a natural base like opium, are referred to as semisynthetic narcotics.

With current chemical technology it is also possible to produce a purely synthetic narcotic. That is, the narcotic is "built" by chemists from other compounds and thus requires no naturally harvested opium sap. These synthetic narcotics are widely used in medicine and, as a consequence, are also categorized as drugs of abuse. Synthetics notable for their illegal use include Demerol (meperidine), fentanyl, and Dilaudid. Narcotics are almost exclusively consumed by hypodermic injection in the United States, although opium and other narcotics are sometimes taken by mouth or smoked (see Figure 15.3).

The major effects of narcotics are **analgesia** (the elimination of somatic pain or discomfort); an initial sense of euphoria; and a **hypnotic** or soporific (sleep-inducing) effect. Narcotics are considered strongly addictive. They produce *tolerance*, which means that to achieve the same effect or sensation from the drug, the user must escalate the size of the dose. Narcotics also produce *cross-tolerance*, which means that as the user develops a tolerance for one type of opiate (such as heroin), he or she will develop a tolerance to other opiates (such as morphine) as well. Withdrawal from narcotics typically involves moderate to strong psychological discomfort.

FIGURE 15.3

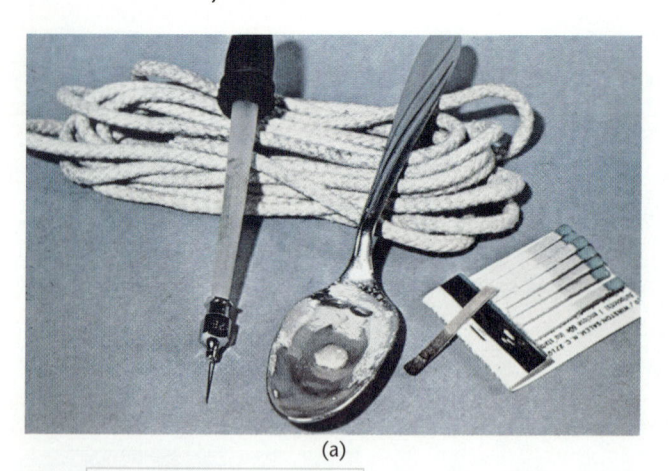

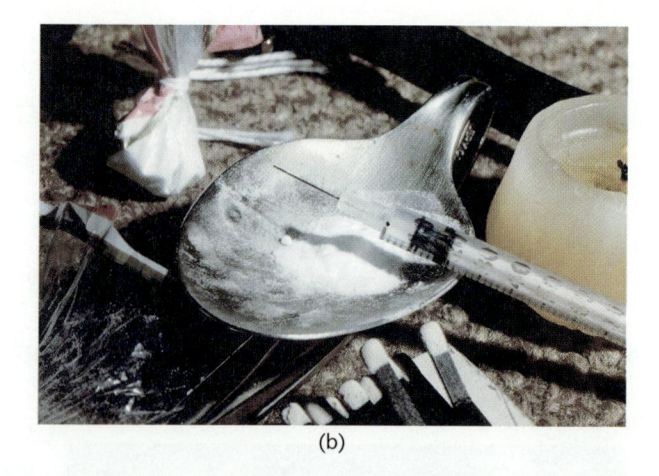

Heroin Addict's Paraphernalia. Typically either a rope or a rag is tied around the arm or leg to make the vein more visible. The heroin is placed in a spoon along with some water, dissolved by heating with matches, and injected intravenously with an eyedropper converted to a hypodermic needle.

(a) Courtesy of Drug Enforcement Administration, (b) Courtesy of SIU/Photo Researchers, Inc.

Heroin is smuggled into the United States in West Coast and northern states and across the Mexican border. Southeast Asian heroin originates from Burma, Laos, and Thailand. It transits California for major markets there and is shipped to the eastern seaboard. Heroin smuggled directly to markets such as New York City and other East Coast ports is also produced in the Middle East, Southwest Asia, and Colombia. Mexican heroin is smuggled across the U.S.-Mexican border principally to markets in the southwest United States. The drug is often transshipped across Africa and Europe. Nigeria, for example, has become a significant transshipment location (see Figure 15.4).

Another powerful narcotic that is presently sold legally but is making its way into the illegal markets is OxyContin. This drug, which is usually prescribed for cancer patients, has pushed aside marijuana, cocaine, and other narcotics as the drug of choice for

FIGURE 15.4

Heroin Trafficking Patterns

Source: Bureau of Justice Statistics, U.S. Department of Justice.

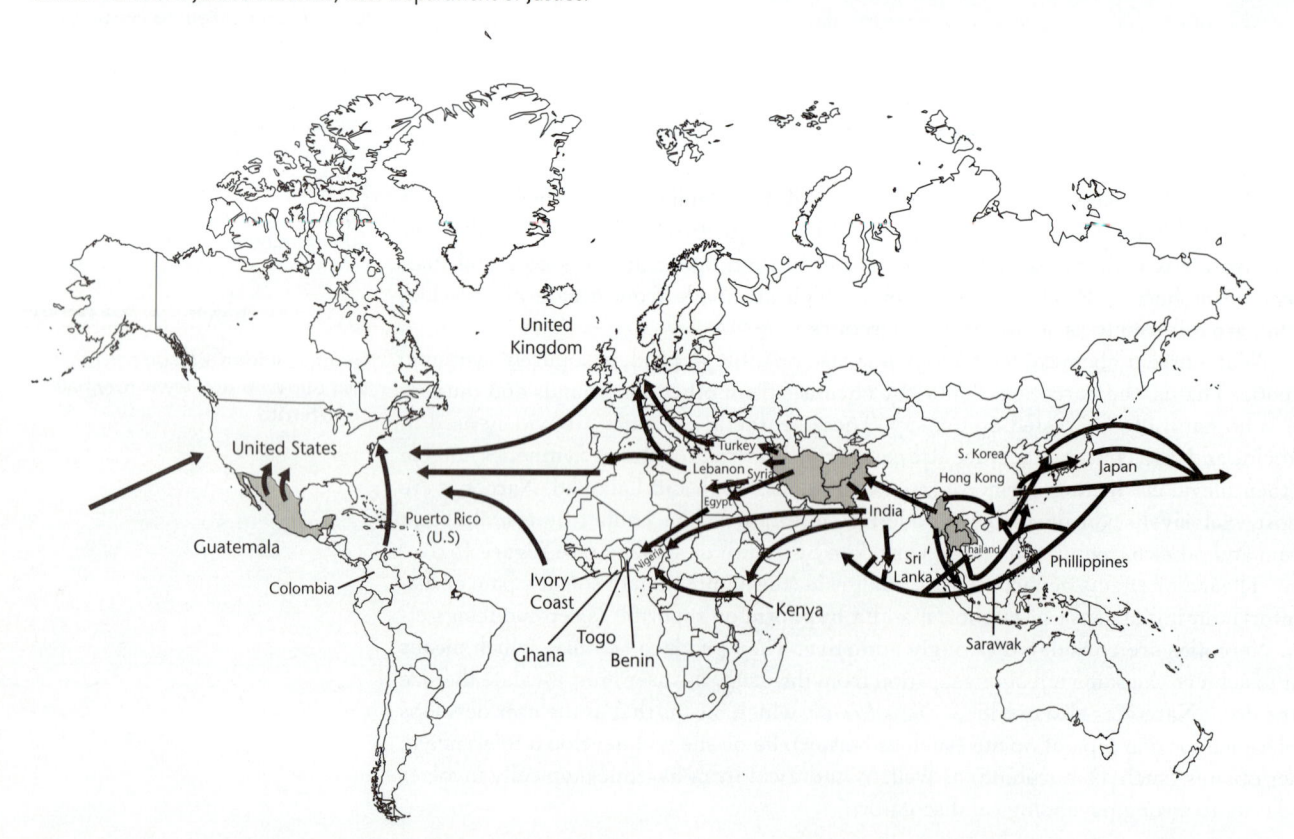

addicts and teenage abusers. The active ingredient in OxyContin is a morphinelike substance called oxycodone, also found in the prescription drugs Percodan and Tylox. But unlike those, which need to be taken in repeated dosages, OxyContin is a time-released formula that is effective for up to twelve hours. Experts say, however, that addicts can achieve an intensely pure high by crushing the pills and snorting or injecting them. A telltale piece of paraphernalia among adolescent users is a pill crusher sold by drugstores to help elderly people swallow their medication.[3] However, in an effort to deal with this growing problem, drug manufacturers have come up with blueprints for a "smart pill" that would make it more difficult to abuse the drug. The new painkiller is designed to destroy its own narcotic ingredients if crushed into powder. "In the News: The Potent Perils of a Miracle Drug" provides information about the extent of this problem at this time.

CTQ

Do you believe that prescription drugs like OxyContin should be more strictly regulated by the government? How will this affect patients with legitimate uses for the drug?

A HUMAN PERSPECTIVE

THE POTENT PERILS OF A MIRACLE DRUG
by Timothy Roche

For a woman dying of cancer, Terry Sanborn didn't seem to suffer. She and her unemployed husband Stephen lived on Medicaid and $512 a month in Social Security in a quiet blue-collar cul-de-sac in tiny Bangor, Maine. But they managed to pay $78,000 in cash for that roomy house at the bottom of Hershey Avenue with a swing set in the backyard. They forked over an additional $17,000 for a Ford Econoline van. Not until drug agents raided the place did neighbors know how they were able to afford it all.

The Sanborns were accused of dealing OxyContin, the morphine-like drug prescribed for Terry's pain. In any given week, her husband reportedly told investigators, the couple supplemented their Social Security by selling drug addicts $8,000 worth of the tiny white tablets that are chewed or smashed to remove the time-release coating, then snorted or injected, generating a high as intoxicating as that of heroin. So popular and addictive is OxyContin these days that it has stirred up a blizzard of a crime wave through the towns of Calais and Bangor, say drug counselors and police investigators. People are using bogus prescriptions to obtain the drug, or they are smuggling the pills across the nearby Canadian border. "Three months ago, we had needles show up outside the middle school," says local drug counselor Carrie McDonald.

Not just in rural Maine: OxyContin is quietly becoming a dangerously popular drug in other pockets of the nation. In the New Orleans suburb of St. Bernard Parish, police say OxyContin abuse is an "epidemic." Officers are making as many arrests for the "killers," as it is known there, as for crack cocaine. The town has had five documented overdoses, but police captain John Doran believed the number may be higher. "We're a suburb, so you see a lot of middle-class families—folks who'd never dream of taking a needleful of heroin," he says. The same is true in Pulaski, Va. (pop. 10,000), where OxyContin has overtaken cocaine and marijuana. Property crime is up 50%, says police chief Eric Montgomery. Four overdoses have been confirmed so far by police, who suspect more than have been reported. More alarming, says U.S. Attorney Bob Crouch, is a recent survey of students in southwestern Virginia indicating that 20% of high school kids and 10% of middle school kids know about OxyContin and how to obtain it.

With abuse of OxyContin on the rise, police in at least three states are reporting a record number of pharmacies being broken into. The homes of people with legitimate OxyContin prescriptions are being robbed in invasions targeting the pills. These patients are often tracked down by relatives who know what is inside their medicine chests or by their small-town neighbors who hear small-town talk about their prescriptions. Thieves are even accosting customers in drugstore parking lots, on a hunch that they might be carrying the sought-after drug, says Bangor authorities. OxyContin rings get prescriptions from sloppy or questionable doctors and use the usual means of forging them, either by photocopying the form or by using a pen to change a prescription for 10 tablets, for example, to 100. The truly inventive ones ask their doctors for another drug, then take the prescription home, soak the ink off with chemicals and write themselves a new prescription.

Not everyone agrees that OxyContin is problematic. Dr. David Haddox, senior medical director for Purdue Pharma, the drug's manufacturer, insists that doctors are not overprescribing. But the company has a lot to lose if the controversy lingers and doctors take their patients off it. Last April the *Wall Street Journal* reported that OxyContin sales increased 95% in one year, generating $600 million in sales for Purdue Pharma. Indeed, the drug, introduced in 1995, has been hailed as a miracle; it eases chronic pain because its dissolvable coating allows a measured dose of the opiate oxycodone to be released into the bloodstream. However, abusers quickly found that by smashing the pills, they can get all the drug's potency in a rush of euphoria.

Facing pressure from prosecutors, investigators and drug counselors, OxyContin's manufacturer has begun working with doctors to minimize forged prescriptions. In Maine the problems have caused a quandary for doctors. In 1999 the legislature passed new medical rules requiring doctors to treat pain more aggressively. Now Maine is the second largest consumer of OxyContin, among all the states, and had 35 deaths from overdoses last year. "We haven't had a drug problem like this in the high schools in Maine until now," says U.S. Attorney Jay McCloskey, who is waging a war against the doctors who so repeatedly write OxyContin prescriptions. "We've had people tell us if a doctor had just asked them to roll up their sleeve for a blood pressure test, they would have seen the trace marks."

Source: Timothy Roche, *Time,* January 12, 2001. © Tribune Media Services, Inc. All Rights Reserved. Reprinted with permission.

FIGURE 15.5

Barbiturates. When taken in large doses, they produce symptoms of impaired coordination and disorientation, including slurred speech and poor reactions to stimuli. Barbiturates produce the most serious addiction and present the most severe dangers during withdrawal or detoxification. When taken in conjunction with alcohol, they are particularly dangerous.

Courtesy of Drug Enforcement Administration.

CTQ

Do you believe that by increasing law enforcement resources, importation of drugs can be eliminated?

CTQ

Why is alcohol considered a drug?

WEB

For more information on barbiturates and depressants, **visit our Web site, www.prenhall.com/territo.**

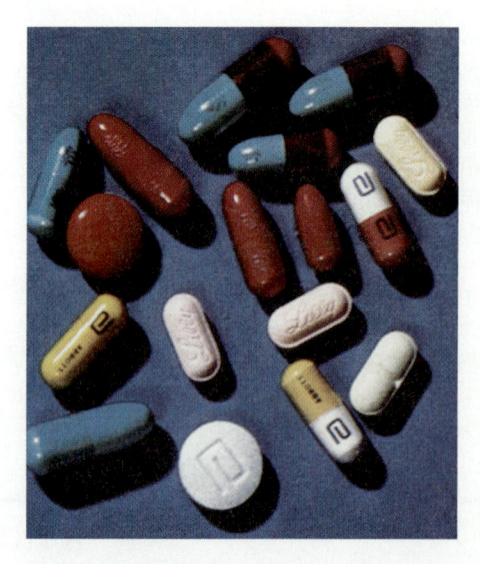

CTQ

Do you believe that marijuana use in the United States is a problem? Why or why not?

Depressants

The depressants are a large class of substances that include most prominently ethyl alcohol, the various barbiturates, mild tranquilizers and antianxiety agents such as Valium, and the synthetic hypnotics such as Doriden. These substances have a variety of medical uses, including sleep induction, anxiety relief, anticonvulsive effects, antispasmodic effects, and muscle relaxation. Taken in large doses, they produce symptoms of impaired coordination and real-time disorientation, including slurred speech and poor reaction to stimuli. The **barbiturates** produce serious addiction and represent the most severe dangers during withdrawal or detoxification (see Figure 15.5.) Most of these compounds are taken by mouth in the form of pills or capsules. It is important to note that the barbiturates and some related compounds can *potentiate* one another. That means that their effects are greatly magnified when taken in combination. Particularly dangerous is the combination of alcohol and barbiturates.

Alcohol is a general depressant and the most prominently represented drug when reviewing levels of use, substances associated with crime, and economic costs. In every category of drugs that are a social problem, alcohol is the most prominent of all psychotropic substances. Along with caffeine and nicotine (both of which are stimulants), it is the only powerful over-the-counter psychotropic legally available in the United States. The costs of alcohol-related problems are twice that of all other drugs combined. Close to 100,000 deaths per year are associated with alcohol use, and about one-quarter of these are traffic accidents involving an alcohol-impaired driver.

Psychedelics

Psychedelics are a large category of drugs whose effects are quite varied. They are generally grouped around the property that they cause significant distortion of sensory input involving the visual, tactile, and auditory modes of perception. Psychedelics are often labeled *hallucinogenic* drugs because of this property. The hallucinogens are also associated with depersonalization, or "out-of-body" effects. Exactly why the psychedelics have these effects is not well understood. It does appear that they act in the higher brain centers where they affect neurotransmission, especially the agents serotonin and L-dopa. Powerful hallucinogens/psychedelics include **lysergic acid diethylamide (LSD)** (see Figure 15.6), dimethyltryptamine (DMT), **mescaline (peyote;** see Figure 15.7), **psilocybe mushrooms** (see figure 15.8), and a series of designer drugs or pharmaceuticals such as **phencyclidine (PCP)** (see Figure 15.9). Generally, **marijuana** (see Figure 15.10) is classified as a psychedelic or hallucinogen, although most authorities agree that its effects are less powerful than the above-mentioned substances and it may be better categorized as a separate substance.[4]

Marijuana is the fourth most frequently consumed psychotropic (after alcohol, caffeine, and nicotine). It is estimated that more than fifty million Americans have tried marijuana, and perhaps twenty million use it on some regular basis.[5,6] There is controversy over the immediate effects associated with marijuana use, but generally it is considered to mildly stimulate, impair to some extent cognitive and motor functions, affect memory and concentration, and increase heart rates. The method of action of marijuana, whose chief active ingredient is tetrahydrocannabinol, is not well understood. It has considerable variability among subjects, and in some people produces relatively severe paranoid reactions. However, several authorities have argued that the behavioral effects of a drug are largely mediated by the psychological and social behavioral consequences of drug consumption and are context sensitive, and that generalizations must be made cautiously.[7,8]

FIGURE 15.6

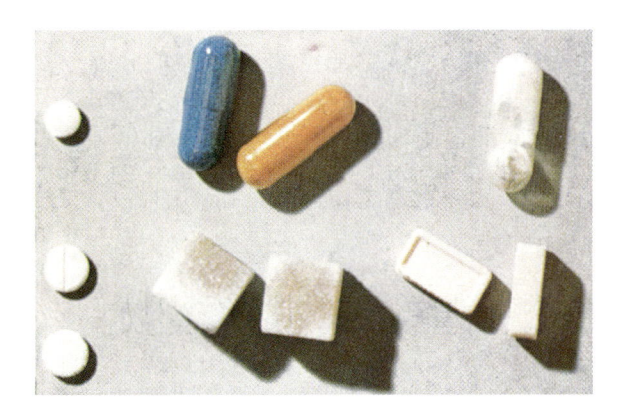

LSD is a semisynthetic compound produced by lysergic acid, a natural substance found in ergot fungus, a disease affecting rye and wheat. A dose of thirty to fifty micrograms (about the size of a pinpoint) will take the user on a "trip" lasting ten to twelve hours.

Courtesy of Drug Enforcement Administration.

FIGURE 15.7

Mescaline (Peyote). Derived from the bottom of the peyote cactus, this hallucinogen has been used by Indians of Central America and the southwest United States for centuries in religious rites. It is generally ground into powder and taken orally. A dose of 350 to 500 milligrams of mescaline produces illusions and hallucinations for five to twelve hours.

Courtesy of Drug Enforcement Administration.

FIGURE 15.8

Psilocybe Mushroom. Psilocybin or psyilocyn, obtained from mushrooms generally grown in Mexico, have historically been used in Indian rites. The effect is similar to mescaline. A dose of four to eight milligrams taken orally produces effects lasting about sixteen hours. Psilocybe mushrooms do not produce physical dependence, but users may develop a tolerance for them.

Courtesy of Drug Enforcement Administration.

FIGURE 15.9

PCP (phencyclidine) is a powerful hallucinogen that is commonly sold as a powder or liquid or is applied to a leafy material such as oregano and smoked.

Courtesy of Drug Enforcement Administration.

FIGURE 15.10

Manicured Marijuana and Seeds. Marijuana, a hallucinogen, is the fourth most frequently consumed psychotropic after alcohol, caffeine, and nicotine. Smoking low doses tends to produce initial restlessness and a sense of well-being. The cigarette on the left is a standard regular cigarette; the ones on the right are marijuana cigarettes, which are typically smaller.

Courtesy of Drug Enforcement Administration.

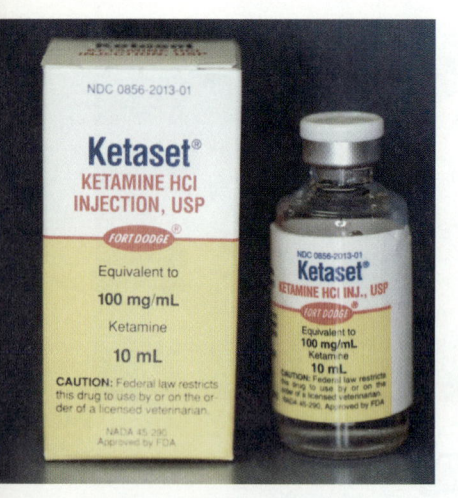

Ketamine Ketamine hydrochloride, a synthetic drug that was developed in the mid-1960s, is an anesthetic agent that has legitimate uses, mostly in veterinary medicine (see Figure 15.11). **Ketamine** was used extensively in the Vietnam War because it is fast-acting and has a relatively short duration, making it a drug of choice for "battlefield medicine." However, it soon became obvious that many humans who were anesthetized with ketamine often became agitated and suffered hallucinations when they awoke. It has since been replaced as an anesthetic for humans by other more efficient agents with fewer side effects.

Ironically, the side effects that made ketamine unpopular and unsafe as a legitimate medical drug have spawned its use in the illegitimate market. On the street, ketamine is called Vitamin K, Kat, Kit, "Special K," or "K." It has been closely associated with the all-night party phenomenon known as a *rave* (discussed shortly), where large crowds of young people listen to music and dance for six to eight hours at a time. Ketamine causes hallucinations, excitement, and delirium similar to those caused by PCP and LSD; however, the effects are not as pronounced or as long in duration. Hallucinations caused by ketamine may last only an hour or two, but the intoxication-like effects of the drug may be noticeable for several hours. Because ketamine is an anesthetic, it may temporarily mask the feeling of pain. Users of ketamine can injure themselves and not know it.

Because ketamine is so difficult to produce, it is not manufactured in clandestine laboratories. Most of the ketamine abused today comes from stolen veterinary stock, and is known by such brand names as Ketalar and Ketaset. The legitimate drug is usually supplied in vials of liquid, although it can be in the form of white powder or pills.

In liquid form, ketamine may be injected into a large muscle. This route allows for a slower absorption and longer duration than the intravenous route. In powder form, ketamine is usually snorted in the same manner as cocaine. Both powder and liquid can be sprayed or sprinkled on vegetable matter and smoked, or mixed with a drink. While it is not known if a person can become physically dependent upon ketamine, tolerance and psychological dependence are direct possibilities with frequent uses.[9]

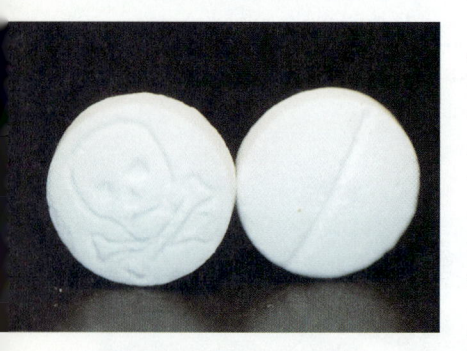

MDMA *Ecstasy*—a bitter white powder that is known as MDMA, short for methylenedioxymethamphetamine—enjoyed a brief period of popularity in the early 1960s, but it was not until the early mid-1980s that Ecstasy gained a regular following in both Europe and the United States in the nightclub and party scene (see Figure 15.12). In recent years the drug's popularity has grown at a rate that has alarmed authorities in the United States, although it is difficult to say exactly how many people are experimenting with the drug. It has become one of the illicit drugs that law enforcement officials consider the most troubling because of their widespread use.

Many users of Ecstasy are drawn by its ability to reduce inhibitions, promote euphoria, produce light hallucinations, and suppress the need to eat or sleep. One pill's effects can last as much as six hours, but users build up a tolerance, and an overdose can cause accelerated heartbeat, high blood pressure, aching muscle cramps, or panic attacks. Many experts consider Ecstasy psychologically addictive and can cause paranoia and psychosis.

The drug is largely manufactured in laboratories in Belgium and the Netherlands, where it is sold for as much as $40 a pill. For the most part, Israeli organized crime syndicates have been implicated as the main source of the distribution of the drug in the United States. This so-called club drug has become increasingly popular among juveniles and is commonly used as a recreational drug at large parties called **raves.**[10] A rave is an all-night party where techno music is played, elaborate lighting is used, and extensive drug use is all part of the scene. Also, the drug use is done secretly out of fear of police and club security. The age range for rave parties is usually between 18 and 30; in some cases, 13- or 14-year-old children have been found attending. Rave parties and drug overdoses from Ecstasy in nightclubs are very common.

Individuals under the influence of MDMA generally sweat a great deal and have a difficulty in standing still. In addition, they may also be seen using Vicks inhalers and may be seen blowing the menthol into each others' faces and eyes. They also smoke menthol cigarettes because of the intense flavor resulting from them. Menthol provides a very

FIGURE 15.11

Ketamine hydrochloride is a synthetic drug that was developed in the mid-1960s. It is an anaesthetic agent closely associated with all-night parties called "raves." Ketamine causes hallucinations, excitement, and delirium similar to LSD and PCP.

Courtesy of Sergeant Christopher McKissick and Detective Tyler Parks, Port Orange, Florida, Police Department.

FIGURE 15.12

Ecstacy pills are street-named "Pirates" because of the skull and crossbones sometimes imprinted on them. Manufactured mainly in Belgium and The Netherlands, Ecstacy has gained a regular following on the nightclub and party scenes in Europe and the United States. It has become increasingly popular among juveniles and is commonly used as a recreational drug at "raves." According to many experts, Ecstacy is psychologically addictive and can result in paranoia and psychosis.

Courtesy of Sergeant Christopher McKissick and Detective Tyler Parks, Port Orange, Florida, Police Department.

intense stimulation. In addition, they may also be seen eating lollipops with gum in them called "Blow-Pops." This is done because the drug results in the grinding of teeth. On occasion female users will be seen with baby pacifiers. Once again, this is an effort to try to control the grinding of the teeth.

Stimulants

The stimulants constitute a sizable segment of the generally used drugs of abuse. Stimulants increase the state of excitement of the central nervous system. They are "mood elevators" insofar as they enhance a sense of self-worth and confidence. Likewise, they allay fatigue, increase alertness, and suppress hunger.

Cocaine   Currently, the single most popular of the stimulants is **cocaine,** an alkaloid salt derived from the plant *Erythroxylum coca* (see Figures 15.13 and 15.14). Cocaine is consumed by intranasal ingestion (snorting), smoking in the base form (as crack, also called **freebasing**), or by injection both intramuscularly as well as intravenously.

Methamphetamine   A second category of stimulants is the amphetamine family, which includes phenmetrazine and crystallized **methamphetamine** (see Figure 15.15). Amphetamine stimulates certain areas of the nervous system and increases blood pressure, heart rate, respiratory and metabolic rates. Appetite is markedly decreased and the senses are hyperalert. The body is in a general state of stress as if it were extremely threatened or expecting a violent fight. This groups of drugs artificially intensifies and prolongs such stimulation, keeping the body in a state of tension for prolonged periods of time. Many sorts of people use amphetamines, including middle-aged businesspeople, housewives, student athletes, and truck drivers. Drivers take them to stay awake on long trips; students take them while cramming for exams; athletes take them for extra energy.

FIGURE 15.13

Cocaine, derived from cocoa leaves, is the most popular stimulant consumed by intranasal ingestion (snorting). The powder is often adulterated to about half its volume with lactose or glucose—in part to maximize the profit from its sale.

Courtesy of Drug Enforcement Administration.

FIGURE 15.14

Rock cocaine/crack is a smokable form of cocaine that provides an immediate "rush." It is relatively inexpensive and very popular among cocaine users. The drug is made by mixing ordinary baking powder and water and heating the solution in a pot. The resulting crack rocks are pure and more concentrated than regular cocaine.

Courtesy of Drug Enforcement Administration.

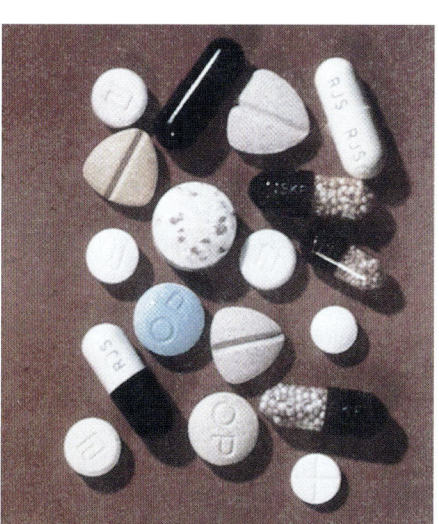

FIGURE 15.15

Amphetamine tablets come in a variety of sizes and shapes, and the drug's street name often corresponds to the color and shape of the pill (e.g., "hearts"). Amphetamines stimulate areas of the central nervous system that control blood pressure, heart rate, and respiratory and metabolic rates, all of which are increased with their use. Many different classes of people take amphetamines in abusive quantities. Some studies indicate that young people are its greatest abusers.

Courtesy of Drug Enforcement Administration.

CTQ

Why do you suppose MDMA/Ecstasy has experienced such a marked increase in popularity among youths and college students?

WEB

For more information on MDMA and other drugs, **visit our Web site,** www.prenhall.com/territo.

Medical use of amphetamines includes control of narcolepsy, appetite control, and control of hyperactivity in children. Phenmetrazine is related chemically to amphetamine; it too is a stimulant and its abuse produces similar effects to amphetamine abuse. It was developed early in 1975 and was approved for marketing as a drug to be used in treatment of hyperactive children. It is prescribed for treatment of mild depression in adults and attention deficit disorders.

Crystal Meth   The more serious drug problem today is posed by crystallized methamphetamine—better known as *crystal meth* and *speed* during the 1960s and 1970s—which was originally taken as pills or injected. A smokable version, known as *ice*, first appeared on the drug market in Hawaii in 1989. It was sold in $50 cellophane packets that contained about $1/10$ gram, good for one or two smokes. Ice owes its special appeal to several factors: A puff of crack cocaine buoys its user for approximately twenty minutes, but the high from smoking ice endures for twelve to twenty-four hours. It does, however, share crack's addictive properties, and it produces similar bouts of severe depression and paranoia as well as convulsions.

Ice can be manufactured in clandestine speed labs, whereas cocaine must be extracted from the leaf of the coca plant, refined, and imported by smugglers at considerable risk. Because it is odorless, ice can be smoked in public virtually without detection (see Figure 15.16).

In its solid form the drug resembles rock candy or a chip of ice. When lighted in a glass pipe, the crystals turn to liquid and produce a potent vapor. When inhaled, it enters the bloodstream directly through the lungs. Ice reverts to its solid state when it cools, thus becoming reusable and highly transportable.

Methcathinone   Called Cat or goob, methcathinone is a psychomotor stimulant with a chemical structure similar to methamphetamine. The effects of methcathinone on the human body are similar. It is reported by users to induce feelings of omnipotence and euphoria, marked by increased energy. Other reported effects include relief from fatigue, increased self-assurance, acute alertness, hyperactivity, talkativeness, a sense of invisibility, confidence, and increased sexual stimulation.

Methcathinone is usually a white or off-white powdered substance, very similar in appearance to methamphetamine. It is usually sold in gram quantities for $75 to $100 and snorted in lines ranging from $1/10$ to $1/4$ of a gram. The most consistently reported side effect—one with a serious implication for law enforcement officers—is extreme paranoia. In one case, a Cat abuser killed himself when he thought he was about to be arrested.

Symptoms of methcathinone intoxication can include profuse sweating, sweaty palms, increased heart rate, restlessness, increased body temperature, and uncontrollable shaking. Officers encountering suspected Cat users should be particularly aware of withdrawal symptoms, which include irritability and argumentativeness. Other withdrawal symptoms include convulsions, hallucinations, and severe depression.[11]

CTQ
Are there any circumstances in which the use of amphetamines is beneficial? Should these substances be more tightly controlled to reduce their availability?

WEB
For more information on amphetamines, visit our Web site, www.prenhall.com/territo.

WEB
For more information on illicit drug use, visit our Web site, www.prenhall.com/territo.

CTQ
Of the various categories of drugs discussed, including narcotics, depressants, psychedelics, and stimulants, which do you believe are most dangerous and present the greatest problem to law enforcement?

FIGURE 15.16

Methamphetamine, better known as "speed," was originally taken as a pill or injected. However, a smokable version known as "ice" has arrived on the drug market in recent years. In its solid form, ice resembles rock candy. Because it is odorless, it can be smoked in public virtually undetected.

Courtesy of Drug Enforcement Administration.

DRUG-FACILITATED SEXUAL ASSAULT

The U.S. Department of Justice estimates that more than 430,000 people in this country are victimized by sexual assault each year, and three out of four victims are acquainted with their attackers. Many of the women who report being raped by an acquaintance also report unusual symptoms such as blackouts and hazy or nonexistent memories surrounding the attacks. The growing popularity of "date-rape drugs" such as Rohypnol, used as tools of submission by sexual offenders, accounts for much of the complexity surrounding these cases.

Congress has responded to the growing use of date-rape drugs by passing the Drug-Induced Rape Prevention and Punishment Act of 1996, an amendment of the Controlled Substance Act. The law imposes a prison term of up to twenty years for anyone convicted of giving any controlled substance to another person without his or her knowledge, with the intention of committing a sexual assault. The law also requires the U.S. Drug Enforcement Administration to consider reclassifying Rohypnol from a Schedule IV (a low potential for abuse relative to the drugs or other substances; a currently accepted medical use in treatment in the United States; abuse may lead to limited physical or psychological dependence) to a Schedule I (a high potential for abuse; no currently accepted medical use in the United States; a lack of accepted safety for use under medical supervision) controlled substance to provide for closer control, and it instructs the U.S. attorney general to create educational materials for law enforcement.

Law enforcement can contribute to the successful prosecution of drug-facilitated sexual assault cases by recognizing the symptoms of drugging, the availability and toxicology of widely used substances, and the range of delivery methods.[12]

Drugs of Choice

The two drugs that are most commonly used by sex offenders to commit their type of crime are Rohypnol and gamma hydroxybutyrate (GHB).

Rohypnol, also known as flunitrazepam, produces a spectrum of effects similar to that of benzodiazepines such as diazepam (Valium), including skeletal muscle relaxation, sedation, and reductions in anxiety (see Figures 15.17a and b). Of these effects, the sedative/hypnotic effects are most important. Rohypnol is considered approximately eight to ten times more potent than Valium. The effect of "high" may last from seven to twelve hours or more after the last dose. With pills or "hits" readily available for prices ranging from $2 to $5, Rohypnol is extremely sought after. Street names include *roofies, R-2s, Roach-2s, trip&fall,* and *mind erasers.* This fast-acting drug can be ground into a powder and easily slipped into food or drink. It can take effect within thirty minutes and symptoms may persist for up to eight hours.[13]

Symptoms of Rohypnol intoxication include sedation, dizziness, visual disturbances, memory impairment, and loss of consciousness and motor coordination.[14] These effects may be compounded, and made potentially lethal, by alcohol. It is traceable in a person's urine for only forty-eight to ninety-six hours after ingestion; in blood, only twelve hours.

The drug is easily obtained on the black market and the Internet or in other countries. A significant amount of Rohypnol makes it to the United States from Mexico and Colombia. The recent notoriety of Rohypnol as a date-rape drug has prompted manufacturers to create a tablet that is more difficult to dissolve in liquid and will turn a drink blue. Unfortunately, the original colorless, dissolvable tablets are still widely available.

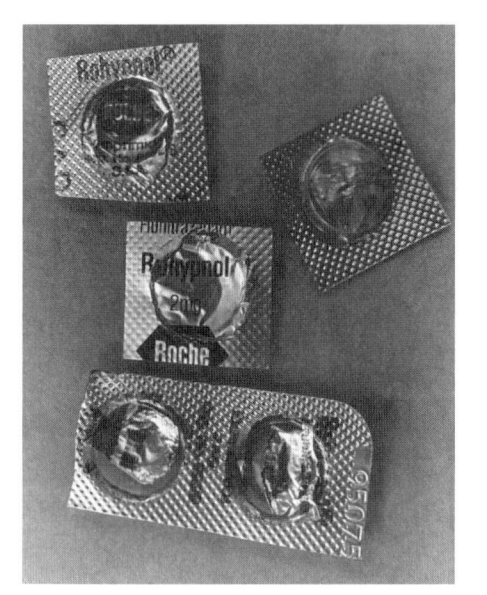

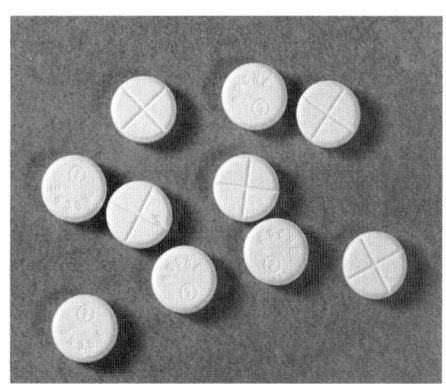

> **CTQ**
>
> How can potential victims of drug-facilitated date rape protect themselves against the seemingly undetectable properties of date-rape drugs?

FIGURE 15.17

Rohypnol Packaging (a) and Rohypnol tablets (b). Rohypnol is commonly used by sex offenders to facilitate their crime. It produces skeletal muscle relaxation, sedation, and reduction in anxiety. It can be slipped into food or drink and can take effect in thirty seconds. It is often used in the commission of date rapes.

Courtesy of Sergeant Christopher McKissick and Detective Tyler Parks, Port Orange, Florida, Police Department.

(a)

(b)

Many victims of drug-induced sexual assault are targeted at parties, clubs, and bars. The college-age population is especially vulnerable to perpetrators of drug-induced sexual assault. The atmosphere of college towns and the lifestyle of college students easily lend themselves to selection by perpetrators. College and university police can play an important role in identifying patterns of assault and educating students as to simple prevention strategies. The following case, which occurred in Prince William County, Virginia, several years ago, illustrates this point:

> Two 15-year-old girls were forcibly raped after unknowingly ingesting Rohypnol. During the trial, prosecutors dubbed this drug the "New Stealth Weapon" on the basis of its odorless and tasteless properties. . . .
>
> Prince William County's investigation revealed that in the late afternoon, the two young girls were taken willingly to an adult's apartment, having been reassured they would be returned home after they saw the apartment. Once at the apartment, they were offered a soft drink. They both drank the Mountain Dew and started to feel "weird," as one victim put it, within about 30 minutes. Neither victim could remember what occurred over the next 9 hours.
>
> The first victim woke up, disoriented, on the couch in the early morning hours. She went to the bathroom and noticed "hickeys" on her neck that had not been present the day before. She could not remember having sexual contact with anyone. She then went to look for the second victim, whom she found asleep on a pull-out bed. Once awakened, she too was disoriented. The second victim noticed a "hickey" on her inner thigh but did not remember engaging in any sexual contact. During the subsequent interviews, the men present in the apartment admitted having sexual intercourse with the victims but said it was consensual.
>
> Three white tablets marked "RH" were recovered from one of the men. These tested positive for Rohypnol. Both victims were seen by a sexual assault nurse examiner. The internal genital findings were consistent with nonconsensual sexual assault.
>
> After a jury trial, the defendant was found guilty of rape, distribution of a Schedule IV drug to a minor, and contributing to the delinquency of a minor. The codefendant was found guilty of contributing to the delinquency of a minor.[15]

Gamma hydroxybutyrate (GHB) (also known as *Gamma-OH, Liquid Ecstasy, Georgia Home Boy,* or *Scoop*) is another central nervous system depressant that is used to perpetrate sexual assaults. It is a clear liquid, slightly thicker than water, and can easily be mixed into food or drinks. As with Rohypnol, GHB ingestion can lead to a variety of symptoms such as intense feelings of relaxation, seizures, loss of consciousness, coma, and even death.[16] GHB is traceable in a person's blood for only four to eight hours and in urine for twelve to fifteen hours.

The Internet abounds with recipes for homemade GHB. The intoxicating effects of the drug have led to its increasing popularity at parties and nightclubs.[17] GHB is often marketed as an antidepressant and a bodybuilding and weight-control supplement.

A party in Detroit was the scene of an incident that resulted in the death of 15-year-old Samantha Reid. Three men at a party slipped GHB into Samantha's soft drink with the intention of raping her. She lapsed into a coma and died the next day, and the three men were convicted of involuntary manslaughter in connection with her death.

Two California men, Steven Haremann and Daniel Bohannon, were convicted of more than fifty counts of rape and sexual assault for drugging women with GHB at raves and nightclubs over a period of two years. After the Los Angeles Sheriff's Department received complaints and had sufficient evidence to obtain a search warrant, the officers uncovered more than two thousand photographs of unconscious, naked women being assaulted and in sexually explicit poses. Many of the victims were un-

---

WEB

For more information on emerging drugs, **visit our Web site,** www.prenhall.com/territo.

CTQ

Why do you think a demand for more synthetic and designer drugs has emerged in the drug market?

aware that they had been violated until they identified themselves in the photographs, and many of the women in the photographs have yet to be identified. Steve Harmann received a seventy-seven-year sentence while Daniel Bohannon was sentenced to nineteen years.

Other Date-Rape Drugs

Rohypnol and GHB are only two substances used to facilitate rape. A host of other depressants and benzodiazapines are available to debilitate sexual assault victims. Valium, Ambien, Temazepam, Flexeril, Xanax, and Benadryl are all drugs that may be legitimately obtained but then appropriated for illicit purposes. For example, five teenage girls who were raped at a party went to the authorities with strong suspicions that they had been drugged. Each victim tested positive for Valium. Two men were later convicted of five counts of rape in connection with the incident.[18]

EMERGING DRUG TRENDS

> **CTQ**
> What can potential victims do to protect themselves against drug-facilitated sexual assaults?

The 1999 *Annual National Household Survey,* conducted by the Substance Abuse and Mental Health Services Administration (SAMHSA), showed that the decline in illicit drug use among young people ages 12 to 17 that began in 1997 continued through 1999. Illicit drug use among the overall population age 12 and older remained flat.[19] According to the trend data in the report, an estimated 9 percent of youths ages 12 to 17 reported current illicit drug use in 1999, meaning they had used an illicit drug during the thirty days before the survey was taken. There had been a significant consistent downward trend over the last three years, from 11.4 percent in 1997 to 9.9 percent in 1998 and 9.0 percent in 1999.

For the first time ever, the survey provides state-by-state estimates of illicit drug, alcohol, and cigarette use by age group, as well as information about the brands of cigarettes that Americans smoke. This new, expanded data on demographic and geographic populations will be a valuable tool for states and community-based organizations to better tailor their programs to their communities. According to this new expanded survey, current drug use varies substantially among states, ranging from a low of 4.7 percent to a high of 10.7 percent for the overall population, and from 8.0 percent to 18.3 percent for youths ages 12 to 17.

Marijuana use for youths ages 12 to 17 has also decreased since 1997 (9.4 percent in 1997, 8.3 percent in 1998, and 7.0 percent in 1999). Among youths ages 12 to 17, the rate for cigarette use was 15.9 percent in 1999, not statistically different than in 1998 (18.2 percent), but significantly lower than the rate in 1997 (19.9 percent). The Marlboro, Newport and Camel brands account for the vast majority of adolescent cigarette smoking, with 54.5 percent of current smokers ages 12 to 17 reporting Marlboro as their usual brand.

In a separate study, the U.S. Department of Health and Human Services (HHS) reported that the number of emergency room visits for drug-related reasons decreased 11 percent for youths ages 12 to 17 from 1998 to 1999. The 1999 Drug Abuse Warning Network (DAWN) records drug-related emergency department episodes, not drug abuse prevalence, and helps provide a fuller picture of drug problems across the country. Overall, there were more than 550,000 drug-related hospital emergency department episodes in the United States in 1989.

Among other national trend data, the National Household Survey also showed that current use of cocaine, inhalants, hallucinogens, and heroin for individuals ages 12 and older was stable, and use of smokeless tobacco decreased significantly from 3.1 percent in 1998 to 2.2 percent in 1999.

Among youths ages 12 to 17, current use of cocaine, heroin, hallucinogens, and inhalants remained stable (see Table 15.1). The survey also showed no significant changes in the percentage of youths who report great risk of using marijuana once a month (30.8 percent in 1998 to 29.0 percent in 1999). Among youths ages 12 to 17, perceived risk of cocaine use decreased significantly from 54.3 percent in 1998 to 49.8 percent in 1999.

The national trends from the National Household Survey are generally consistent with results from other HHS surveys. Both the Monitoring the Future Study and the Youth Risk Behavior Survey have shown a leveling or declining trend in illicit drug,

TABLE 15.1 Percentages of Youths Ages 12 to 17 Reporting Past Use of Illicit Drugs, 1999

Drug	Lifetime	Past Year	Past Month
Any illicit drug*	27.6%	20.3%	10.9%
Marijuana and hashish	18.7	14.4	7.7
Cocaine	2.4	1.6	0.5
Crack	0.6	0.4	0.1
Heroin	0.4	0.3	0.2
Hallucinogens	5.7	3.8	1.1
LSD	3.8	2.4	0.6
PCP	0.9	0.4	0.1
Inhalants	9.1	4.6	1.9
Nonmedical use of any psychotherapeutic	10.9	7.0	2.9
Pain relievers	8.2	5.3	2.2
Tranquilizers	2.5	1.5	0.5
Stimulants	3.9	2.1	0.7
Methamphetamine	1.4	0.7	0.3
Sedatives	0.8	0.5	0.2

*"Any illicit drug" indicates use at least once of marijuana/hashish, cocaine (including crack), heroin, hallucinogens (including PCP and LSD); inhalants, or any perception-type psychotherapeutic used nonmedically.

Source: Substance Abuse and Mental Health Services Administration (SAMHSA), Office of Applied Studies, *National Household Survey on Drug Abuse*, 1999, Washington, DC: U.S. Department of Health and Human Services.

marijuana, and cigarette use among adolescents since 1997, after a period of significant increases in the early 1990s.

The rate of current alcohol use among youths ages 12 to 17 and the general population has remained relatively flat for the past several years. According to national trend data in 1999, 19 percent of youth ages 12 to 17 reported that they drank at least once in the past month, and 52 percent of Americans age 12 and older reported current alcohol use. In 1999, 7.8 percent of youths ages 12 to 17 reported past-month binge drinking and 3.6 percent reported past-month heavy alcohol use.

Among adults ages 18 to 25, the survey found increases in current illicit drug use. The rate increased between 1997 and 1999 (14.7 percent in 1997, 16.1 percent in 1998, and 18.8 percent in 1999). The rates for the age groups 26–34 years old and 35 years and older in 1999 have not changed significantly since 1994.

Dr. Nelba Chavez, administrator of SAMHSA, said, "Our efforts appear to be paying off in the lower levels of drug use among teens, but we must do more to reduce illicit drug use among adults, particularly those age 18 to 25. The need for drug treatment is real and growing. People need to know that treatment can help people get off and stay off drugs."

The National Household Survey provides annual estimates of the prevalence of illicit drug, alcohol, and tobacco use in the United States and monitors the trends in use over time. It is based on a representative sample of the U.S. population age 12 and older, including people living in households and in some group quarters such as dormitories and homeless shelters. The national trends in substance use presented in the 1999 report are based on data from a sample of 13,000 respondents using paper questionnaires similar to those used in prior years.

Over the years, SAMHSA has made improvements in the National Household Survey to provide better and more complete information on substance use. In 1999, a new, interactive, bilingual, computer-assisted questionnaire was introduced. A new sample design was implemented and the sample size was expanded almost fourfold to support the development of both national and state estimates of substance use. This new sample reflects information obtained from nearly 70,000 people. Due to changes in the new methodology, national estimates from the expanded survey cannot be compared to data from prior surveys. The results from the expanded survey, however, will set a new baseline for better year-to-year comparisons for state and national levels.

REDUCING THE DEMAND FOR ILLICIT DRUGS

Reducing Demand through Treatment

The best way to reduce the overall demand for illicit drugs is to reduce the number of chronic, hard-core drug users.[20] To accomplish this, communities, jails, and prisons must provide effective drug treatment. Current treatment capacity, however, falls well below the level of resources needed to address the problems of chronic, hard-core drug use. To increase treatment capacity, state and local officials must more effectively use available federal treatment funds to direct drug users to treatment, and the criminal justice system must use the sanctions at its disposal to provide treatment to as many chronic, hard-core users under their authority as possible.

Managed Care and State Health Care Reform   Managed-care facilities have been able in many cases to (1) reduce per-person costs for substance abuse treatment, (2) increase the percentage of people who receive care, (3) maintain high levels of satisfaction with care, and (4) achieve positive treatment outcomes. States are expanding managed care and are requesting waivers of Medicaid regulation to experiment with numerous strategies for reducing unnecessary and costly care. The Substance Abuse and Mental Health Services Administration will assist states in evaluating the impact of state health care reforms, including managed care, to identify effective strategies for reducing treatment costs and improving treatment outcomes. The Administration encourages states to experiment with managed care so that funds for treatment can be used as efficiently as possible.

Linking Criminal Justice and Treatment   The number of drug-related arrests made each year is staggering. Drug abuse continues to burden the nation's prison system because the majority of federal prisoners are drug offenders as well as criminals. The courts and the correctional system must use their power to convince drug-using offenders to "clean up their act" to the fullest extent possible for the benefit of all citizens. Studies have demonstrated that when drug addicts within the criminal justice system receive effective treatment, they commit fewer crimes; in turn, Americans enjoy safer streets and neighborhoods. The Violent Crime Control and Law Enforcement Act of 1994 (hereafter referred to as the Crime Control Act) formalizes the link between criminal justice and treatment systems and empowers judges to use a valuable range of treatment and punishment options.

WEB

For more information on emerging drug trends, **visit our Web site,** www.prenhall.com/territo.

WEB

For more information on drug treatment, **visit our Web site,** www.prenhall.com/territo.

CTQ

Do you believe that if treatment programs were more readily available to the drug-using population, a subsequent drop in illicit drug use would result?

WEB

For more information on linking criminal justice and treatment, **visit our Web site, www.prenhall.com/territo.**

IN THE WORKPLACE

DRUG COUNSELOR

Responsible for counseling and other services for individuals receiving treatment for problems related to alcohol or drug abuse. Performs a variety of duties, including the following: conducts professional screenings, assessments, and intake referrals with clients; provides effective individual, group, or family case management in the area of addiction services, psychological services, and educational groups with substance abuse clients and family. Minimum qualifications are as follows: high school diploma or equivalent, ability to interview and counsel, ability to interact with chemically dependent people, ability to speak in large groups.

Drug Courts The Crime Control Act authorized $1 billion over six years of the "drug courts" initiative to provide competitive grant assistance to planning, establishing, or improving judicially supervised, integrated sanctions and services for nonviolent offenders. Such programs free up jail and prison space for violent, predatory criminals. To be effective, drug courts and offender management programs must provide integrated services and sanctions that include continuing close supervision; mandatory periodic drug testing, treatment, and aftercare services; and a system of escalating sanctions for those who fail to meet program requirements. This reasonable but tough treatment for drug offenders can help ensure that drug-addicted criminals do not revert to the same criminal activity and continue to pass through the criminal justice system. In addition, the role of structured aftercare in reducing rates of recidivism is becoming increasingly important.

Treatment Research Effective treatment is grounded in solid research. The Treatment, Prevention, and Medical Research Subcommittee, a branch of the White House's Office of National Drug Control Policy (ONDCP), will pursue a range of research priorities, including the following:

- The development of effective recruitment and retention strategies (that is, ways to direct those who need treatment to enter and stay in treatment)
- The enhancement of outcome studies comparing various modalities of treatment
- Rigorous evaluation of behavioral and counseling approaches
- Development, testing, and dissemination of specialized treatment interventions for such populations as adolescents, women, and minorities
- Pharmacological research focusing on the development of new medications for cocaine and heroin addiction
- Investigation of the integration of behavioral and pharmacologic approaches to treatment

Reducing Demand through Prevention

Ultimately it is prevention efforts that will bring about a long-term solution to the nation's drug abuse problem. Prevention is critically important to keeping new users from entering the pipeline to chronic, hard-core drug use and breaking the intergenerational cycle through which many children of addicts become users.

Alcohol Abuse by Minors Alcohol is the single most abused substance in the United States, especially among young people in secondary schools, colleges, and universities. Because underage drinking is frequently a forerunner or companion to illicit drug use, and because it is so harmful to the health and safety of young people, preventive efforts that focus on alcohol abuse by minors must be part of any strategy to reduce the demand for illicit drugs.

Safe and Drug-Free Schools School-based drug prevention programs, such as those supported through the Safe and Drug-Free Schools and Communities Act (SDFSCA), help prevent young people from using drugs. Recently authorized, the SDFSCA has been expanded to address the prevention of violence, to provide better accountability and enhanced coordination and community links, and to improve the targeting of funding to areas in need. The Department of Education also will implement the new Family and Community Endeavor Schools grant program, which will support programs in high-poverty and high-crime areas to improve the academic and social development of at-risk students. The Department of Health and Human Services will implement the Community Schools and Youth Services and Supervision grant program, which will support similar activities in areas of high poverty and juvenile delinquency.

COMMUNITY COLLABORATION WITH LAW ENFORCEMENT

One key initiative at the local level is the Community Oriented Policing Services (COPS) program to put 100,000 new police officers "on the beat." For this initiative, police officers will work to identify drug-use and drug-trafficking trouble spots, coordinate crisis intervention services, and encourage community residents to come forward with information pertinent to criminal investigations and transfer intelligence information to drug enforcement personnel.

One of the programs that law enforcement officers have been involved in for the past ten years is called Drug Abuse Resistance Educations (DARE). "In the News: Truth, DARE, and Consequences" discusses the results of a six-year study.

Antidrug Coalitions and Partnerships

To assist the comprehensive and coordinated antidrug responses at the community level, efforts will focus on achieving a range of goals, including (1) forming partnerships with

WEB

For more information on police involvement in the war against drugs, **visit our Web site**, www.prenhall.com/territo.

IN THE NEWS

A HUMAN PERSPECTIVE

TRUTH, DARE, AND CONSEQUENCES

A six-year study that tracked students who took Drug Abuse Awareness Education classes taught by police officers has concluded that the popular program has little effect in persuading youths to stay away from illegal drugs.

The longitudinal study by Dennis P. Rosenbaum, chairman of the Criminal Justice Department at the University of Illinois at Chicago, tracked 1,800 students starting in the fifth and sixth grades, before they began taking DARE courses. About 1,100 students were still participating in the study six years later, by which time they were in high school.

The study looked at students at 36 schools—24 of them located in Chicago and its suburbs and 12 in rural areas. Each school was paired with another of similar demographics, with one school offering DARE in the spring of 1990, while the other did not.

The study found that DARE had little effect on preventing future drug use as the students got older, and in some cases, may have contributed to the likelihood of their involvement in drugs and alcohol. "The main finding is that levels of drug abuse . . . did not differ as a function of whether students participated in DARE or did not," the report concluded.

The finding backs results gleaned in previous studies in which DARE "has been unable to show consistent preventive effects on drug use, and the observed effects have been small in size and short-lived," the study added.

While DARE was found to have both immediate and short-term impacts of up to two years in several areas, such as resistance skills and attitudes about drugs, the study said that "nearly all of these effects disappeared with the passage of time and did not survive into the critical high school years" when most juvenile drug use begins. The program had the most beneficial effects on urban children, while suburban youngsters reaped the least benefit, the study said, suggesting this might be due to the fact that urban DARE officers spend more time at schools and interact more with students outside the classroom.

"In contrast, DARE officers in suburban schools were quick to move on to another school," the study noted. "In essence, students in urban schools had more opportunity to 'connect' or 'bond' with the DARE officer than did their suburban counterparts, and to see them as part of the school environment."

The study added that DARE was taught to the urban kids beginning in the fifth grade, but not taught to the suburban students until sixth grade.

Ralph Lochridge, a spokesman for DARE in America, the Los Angeles–based organization that provides assistance to DARE programs nationwide, said Rosenbaum's conclusions tend to mirror the findings of prior studies, including some by Rosenbaum himself.

"We don't disagree with the findings at all, in terms of the long-term effectiveness," Lockridge told *Law Enforcement News*. "Our feeling is that it's kind of a no-brainer that you give somebody 17 lessons an anything in the fifth grade, after three or four years, if they don't get any reinforcement, boosters or additional skills training to build on that foundation, their knowledge is going to erode."

The researchers did not consider the entire DARE program, he added, nor did they take into account that the curriculum they examined hasn't been used since 1994. Rosenbaum dismissed those arguments, saying it's time that the public knew the program is not as effective as its advocates claim.

"I feel it's important that we get the truth out about this and that we stop pretending that we're having effects that we're not having on our kids," he told *LEN*. "DARE is a good program in the short run, but it does not have the effects that parents, teachers, or police think it's having."

Source: Reprinted with permission from *Law Enforcement News*, John Jay College of Criminal Justice (CUNY), 555 West 57th St., New York, NY 10019. April 15, 1998.

such coalition-building efforts as the Robert Wood Johnson Foundation's "Fighting Back" initiative and the Community Anti-Drug Coalitions of America, (2) targeting resources and programs toward high-risk youth, and (3) developing effective models for community action.

Drug-Free Workplace Programs
Many drug users in the workplace can be identified and motivated to stop using drugs through employee assistance programs that offer cost-effective prevention and intervention services. To encourage drug-free workplace programs, ONDCP has established a Drug-Free Workplace Working Group composed of representatives from federal agencies to recommend actions providing employers with (1) incentives to adopt drug-free workplace policies and programs, (2) information on model programs shown to be effective, and (3) specific knowledge that can support efforts to establish and maintain drug-free environments.

Faith Community Involvement
The faith community can help prevent drug use and serve as a familiar community advocate against violence. Community partnerships and coalitions are encouraged to work closely with members of the faith community to develop strategies that will reduce alcohol and drug abuse. Specialized technical support and training have been provided to faith community leaders and seminaries to identify federal resources and pertinent information about the relationship between substance abuse and violence.

National Service Programs
The Corporation of National Service is harnessing the energy, enthusiasm, and commitment of young people to provide service to their nation, community, and fellow youth. National Service Programs have resulted in thousands of young people working with local programs that assist high-risk youth to withstand the lure of drug and gang involvement.

Prevention Research
Because of the long-term goal of behavior change, prevention efforts are especially difficult to evaluate. The National Structured Evaluation (NSE), a recently concluded comparative analysis of hundreds of prevention efforts, provides much-needed guidance for prevention practitioners. The findings will be further evaluated, combined with other relevant findings, and shared systematically with local communities. This information dissemination effort is one of the objectives of the National Drug Prevention System (NDPS). The NDPS is building on the knowledge gained in the past several years and is designated to leverage federal resources and promote strong prevention partnerships among federal, state, and local entities. The NDPS unites prevention sectors and serves as a comprehensive system to address the drug-abuse prevention needs of the nation's diverse population.

THE ARGUMENTS FOR AND AGAINST THE LEGALIZATION OF DRUGS

Arguments for Legalization
Historically, the regulation of the use and distribution of drugs has followed a traditional punishment model. The logic of this approach is based on the concept that people will avoid behaviors for which they are punished. Therefore, to reduce or eliminate the use of drugs it is necessary to punish those who engage in this behavior. The establishment of punishment will, furthermore, create a climate of deterrence. Realizing that to engage in drug-related behaviors will incur punishment, citizens will not adopt those behaviors.

However, judging by the degree to which drug use has proliferated within a social environment of serious and sustained criminal sanctions, it has been argued that there is some fundamental flaw in the punitive model. It simply does not appear to work very well. As a result, a number of people interested in the issues of drug abuse have argued that rather than punish the offender by criminal sanctions, policies ought to take a completely different approach. The major vehicle for deterring drug use, in this view, must come from each person's free and rational choice. The fact of criminality is not relevant to this decision. Instead, because people would be effectively educated about the negative aspects of drugs, treatment would be available if they had the desire to stop but found themselves unable to do so. And those who continue to use them and have no desire to stop would suffer whatever consequences befell them. The legalization model offers the following general outline of what a desirable social policy would contain.

The Punitive Model for Regulating Drug Use Has Proved a Historical Failure In spite of many decades of unrelenting criminalization, the level of drug use continues to rise. Therefore, the basic logic of criminalization models is flawed. The concept of deterring drug use by fear and criminal sanctions has had ample time to prove itself, and it has failed.

> **CTQ**
> Are there any steps that you would take to reduce the demand for illicit drugs if you had the power to do so?

Drugs Vary Substantially in Their Effects, Health Consequences, and Addictive Potential Yet drug laws fail to recognize this basic fact. One reason for the failure of criminal sanctions is that it has an incorrect view of the reality of drug use. While it is undoubtedly true that many people have serious debilities associated with their drug use, it is equally true that, as with alcohol, many more people appear to use these substances in a controlled fashion. Drug laws have failed to recognize this reality, and this has contributed to their failure.

The Costs of Criminal Enforcement, Processing, and Confinement of Drug Offenders Are Exceedingly High The aggressive punishment of drug users and sellers consumes scarce criminal justice resources and displaces resources from more serious forms of crime such as violent offenses. This is even more pronounced when, as is true in current practice, a "demand side" enforcement policy is advocated, because there are many more users than sellers, and focusing on users as offenders means inevitably increasing the load on criminal justice facilities at all levels of the system.

Criminalization of Recreational and Limited Use of Drugs Does Not Conform to Many Americans' Moral Values and Breeds Cynicism About the Law Furthermore, drug laws are not uniformly enforced and appear to selectively target the poor, minorities, and "fringe groups" in society. This contributes to alienation and social fragmentation, and detracts from the integrity of the law in the public's mind. The problem is aggravated by the fact that while the use of some powerful substances such as alcohol is condoned or even encouraged, comparable substances such as marijuana are criminalized. This smacks of hypocrisy.

Drug Use Is a Social Health Issue, Not a Crime Issue Drug abuse, like alcoholism, is best treated in a medical, moral, and psychological context. The reduction of drug use will require the provision of treatment services, aftercare services, and the establishment of a generally more healthy and less alienating social environment. Subjecting drug users to a criminal sanction and its concomitant environment will only compound the problem and reduce the likelihood of users stopping on their own.

The Illegality of Drugs Gives Rise to Additional Problems Associated with the Underground Economy Resulting from Illegal Drug Distribution These include violence, political corruption and destabilization, and billions of dollars in unaccounted-for and untaxed income that is funneled into the criminal underworld.

Basic Constitutional Guarantees Are Threatened by Overzealous Enforcement Such guarantees as freedom from illegal search and seizure are threatened in an environment where people are willing to "do anything" to stop the use of illegal drugs, and become willing to cede extraordinary powers to the state to achieve that goal. Furthermore, it does not appear likely that granting these extraordinary powers will achieve the goal of ending drug use in any event.

If Drugs Were Legalized, Crime and the Violence Associated with Drug Use Would Decrease
It is the illegal nature of drug production, trafficking, and use that fuels crime and violence. Turf wars, gang activity, and drug-related crimes are the result of the illegal nature of the drug trade. Users commit crimes to pay for drugs now because they cannot easily obtain them. If drugs were legal, the enormous profits associated with them because of their illegal status would evaporate and, once gone, the black market and criminal activity associated with drugs would also be eliminated.

Arguments against Legalization

It is widely claimed by those advancing the case of legalization that crime is largely committed by drug traffickers protecting their turf. However, it is the experience of many local officers that crime is committed not only because people want to buy drugs but more often because people use drugs. There is no denying the fact that drug use changes behavior and exacerbates criminal activity.[21]

The following represents some of the specific arguments against drug legalization.

Increased Acceptance of Drugs Leads to Increased Levels of Drug Use Our struggle with drug abuse has taught us a sobering lesson: Drug use increases dramatically when society reinforces the acceptability of drug use. In 1962, fewer than 4 million Americans had ever tried illegal drugs; by 1995 almost 74 million had. During the intervening years, many pro-legalization and discrimination proponents actively sought to broaden public acceptance of drug use, and our society saw the number of drug users increase steadily.

In the late 1970s, drug tolerance and leniency reached a peak in the United States. Not surprisingly, drug use among children skyrocketed, reaching a high point in 1979 when one in ten high school seniors was "high" on marijuana every day of the week. Two out of three high school seniors had tried marijuana. In 1979, more than 56 million people had tried illegal drugs; in 1985, that number rose to 66 million.

After a period of aggressive and consistent law enforcement, antidrug education, and a social shift of public opinion away from drugs, the number of regular users of illegal drugs was reduced between 1985 and 1995 (from 23.3 million to 12.8 million). Currently, our nation is seeing an increase in marijuana use among young people, with a doubling of use since 1992. In some measure, this increase is due to diminished perceptions of risk, reductions in the frequency of network news coverage of the dangers of drugs, and an ambivalence about drug use on the part of baby boomer parents. The legalization movement and the growing destigmatization of drugs, along with confusing messages about the beneficial properties of substances like marijuana, can result in further decreases in the perceptions of risk, and a concurrent increase in the drug use.

Increased Drug Availability and Use Will Worsen Our Crime Problem Numerous government reports clearly demonstrate that drug users are more likely to be involved in criminal activities. The preliminary findings in a 1996 National Institute of Justice study that compiled statistics on the levels of drug use among arrestees indicated that a median 68 percent of arrestees test positive for at least one drug arrest, and the same study conducted in 1995 revealed that 31 percent of both male and female arrestees reported that they were under the influence of drugs or alcohol when they committed crimes. That year's report also indicated that 28 percent of inmates arrested for homicides were under the influence of drugs when they committed that crime. In 1986, during the midst of the crack epidemic, violent crime reached a level of 617 violent crimes per 100,000 people. As we experienced a continuing escalation of drug-related violence, this figure rose in 1993 to 746 violent crimes for every 100,000 inhabitants.

In recent years, we have seen a decrease in the violent crime rate in many American communities, attributable, in part, to aggressive law enforcement efforts and the incarceration of criminals. We know that vigorous law enforcement actions aimed at criminal activity, including illegal drug use, can have a material effect on reducing violent crime in our communities.

After making progress against violent crime during the past several years, we should not erode these gains by instituting policies such as legalization, which we know will increase drug use and drug-related crime.

Increased Drug Use Has Terrible Consequences for Our Citizens Drug-related illness, death, and crime are estimated to cost Americans almost $67 billion a year. This figure comes from the combined costs of health care, extra law enforcement, car crashes, crime, and lost productivity due to drug use.

Drug use also affects the productivity of America's workers. Seventy-one percent of all illicit drug users are age 18 or older and employed. In a study conducted by the U.S. Postal Service, the data collected shows that among drug users, absenteeism is 66 percent higher and health benefits use is 84 percent greater in dollar terms when compared with other workers. Disciplinary actions are 90 percent higher for employees who are drug users, as compared to non–drug users.

Public safety is also a critical issue. A National Highway Traffic Safety Administration study conducted several years ago reported that 18 percent of 2,000 fatally injured drivers from seven states had drugs other than alcohol in their system when they died.

Legalization of Dangerous Substances Sends a Conflicting Message to the Youth of America According to the Monitoring the Future Study conducted several years ago by the University of Michigan, today's teens are less likely to consider drug use harmful and risky, more likely to believe that drug use is widespread and tolerated, and feel more pressure to try illegal drugs.

The Partnership for a Drug-Free America reported that the results of a recent survey showed that as young Americans perceive that drugs are dangerous, drug use drops proportionately. Conversely, as young Americans get the message that social disapproval drops, as they hear in the legalization debate, drug use increases.

Legalization of drugs tells our children that adults believe that drugs can be used responsibly. News coverage of individuals smoking marijuana in cannabis clubs tells kids that drug taking can be fun. Within this atmosphere, it is very difficult—if not impossible—to reach children and convince them that doing drugs is bad.[22]

Unsuccessful Experiments Experiences of a number of foreign countries including Great Britain, the Netherlands, Switzerland, and Sweden are often cited to demonstrate that other nations have successfully controlled drug use by providing areas where drug takers can obtain and use drugs. Until the mid-1960s, British physicians were allowed to prescribe heroin to certain cases and classes of addicts. But the British system did not work; addiction levels rose, especially among teenagers, and many addicts chose to boycott the program and continued to get their heroin from pushers.

The Netherlands, despite its controlled program, is having troubles. Under the so-called expediency principle, Dutch prosecutors have wide discretion in prosecuting or ignoring people in possession of small quantities of drugs for personal use. In fact, marijuana and hashish, for instance, are openly sold and consumed in coffeehouses. The Amsterdam Municipal Health Service showed a rise in hard-core addicts several years ago, attributable to a significant rise in local heroin supply, which led to a price drop by as much as 75 percent.

Switzerland has become a magnet for drug users the world over. One thing small European nations have learned is that tolerance about drugs brings a lot of unwelcome visitors. In 1987, Zurich permitted drug use and sales in a part of the city called Platzspitz, dubbed "Needle Park." Five years later the experiment was curtailed after an influx of addicts and increased violence and death. In 1992, Zurich municipal spokesman Andres Ohler told *The New York Times* that the number of regular drug users at the park had swelled from a few hundred in 1987 to 20,000 by 1992.

In Sweden in the late 1960s, there was an increase in the use of hard drugs, which stabilized at a fairly high level at the beginning of the 1970s.[23] A case-finding study in

1979 estimated the number of hard-drug users at between 10,000 and 14,000. Of those, between 7,500 and 10,000 injected; there were 1,500 to 2,000 heroin "mainliners." A 1992 study showed much higher numbers: 14,000 to 20,000 heavy addicts. This study indicated 5,000 heroin users—a significant increase despite large efforts in the field of prevention and medicare. At the same time, it emerged that the recruiting of young users of hard drugs was very modest in the 1980s. In 1979, 37 percent of the heavy addicts were under age 25; in 1992, the proportion was only 10 percent. New addicts were recruited in the late 1970s and early 1980s. After that, drug use declined, although it has recently reappeared on the horizon.

Lately, the Swedish police have noticed a rising demand for synthetic drugs and a new pattern in the consumption of drugs. They have also noticed that a more liberal attitude toward drugs is spreading via international trends and opinions. This requires new procedures and methods in prevention and international action. Cooperation across the borders is facilitated, as always, if the criminalization in vital areas—such as drug enforcement—is harmonized. To put a stop to the increasing drug abuse among young people is on top of the agenda—especially for the police.

By an international comparison, Sweden is adopting a restrictive drug policy. In Sweden the objective has been and still is very clear and unambiguous: a drug-free society. This attempt is based on a lot of vital experiences. In the mid-1960s (from the spring of 1965 until the spring of 1967), a tentative project was initiated with the legal prescription of narcotic drugs, opiates, and central stimulants. The idea was to limit the harmful effects of drug abuse, for both the community and the individual addicts. Abusers were given the choice of care, and their social and medical status would be improved—among other things, because they would not have to commit crimes to finance their abuse. Having free access to drugs, it was assumed that they would eventually tire of using them. These are the same ideas we now hear propagated in different quarters of Europe.[24]

The Swedish experiment included a sociomedical study of the patients involved. It gave a picture of these abusers' situations before and after they received legal drugs. The study showed the following:

- Drug-related crime handled by the police practically disappeared during the period of legalization
- About as many drug users committed crimes during the year they were getting legal drugs as in the years before
- The number of offenses per individual even increased somewhat
- All other types of crime increased—"crimes against the public" as well as traffic offenses and other crimes—both in relative and absolute figures

In time, however, the responsible doctors lost control and the previously favorable attitude in the media turned. The opinion was one of strong repudiation of any type of legalization.[25]

CTQ
Which arguments are more persuasive: those in favor of drug legalization or those opposed to drug legalization?

SUMMARY

In this chapter we have reviewed the major types of drugs that are abused, highlighting their distinctive attributes and effects. These categories of drugs examined include narcotics, depressants, psychedelics, and stimulants. We have also discussed drug-facilitated sexual assault and provided specific information on the two primary drugs used in drug-facilitated sexual assault—Rohypnol and gamma hydroxybutyrate (GHB).

We have also examined in detail the emerging drug trends in the United States, especially as they relate to illicit drug use by young people, and discussed the best ways to reduce overall demand for illicit drugs. In order to accomplish this, communities, jails, and prisons must provide more effective drug treatment. The current drug treatment capacity, however, falls well below the level of resources needed to address the problem of chronic, hard-core drug use. We also have discussed the linking of criminal justice and treatment, the role of drug courts, treatment research, reducing demand through prevention, alcohol abuse by minors, and safe and drug-free schools. Lastly, we discussed the arguments for and against the legalization of drugs.

DISCUSSION AND REVIEW

1. What is drug addiction?
2. What is the mesolimbic reward system?
3. Which narcotic drugs are derived from the opium poppy?
4. What types of drugs fall into the classification of depressants?
5. What are the major effects of narcotics?
6. What medical uses do depressants have?
7. What types of drugs fall into the category of psychedelics?
8. What effects do stimulants have?
9. What kind of people employ amphetamines in abusive quantities?
10. What are the effects of psychedelics?
11. What are the legitimate medical uses of amphetamines?
12. What is MDMA (Ecstasy)? What are some of the behavioral signs that indicate that someone may be under the influence of Ecstasy?
13. What is methcathinone and what are its effects on the body?
14. What illegal drugs are used to facilitate sexual assaults, and what are their physical effects?
15. When laboratories conduct drug-screening tests in order to identify drugs that might have been used in sexual assault, which category of drugs should they screen for?
16. What are the physiological differences between smoking crack cocaine and ice?
17. What are some of the consequences of youth substance abuse?
18. What is the best way to reduce the overall demand for illicit drugs, and how is this best accomplished?
19. What are the arguments in favor of decriminalization of drugs?
20. What are the arguments against drug legalization?

CHAPTER RESOURCES

IN THE MEDIA

Video

Beat the Street
The Cocaine Monkey
Drugs on the Net
Ecstasy: When the Party Is Over
Let's Party
Methamphetamine: Deciding to Live
Rave Clubs: What Every Parent Should Know
Relapse
Stolen Lives: Children of Addicts
Street Drugs

Film

Blow (2001)
Drugstore Cowboy (1989)
Fear and Loathing in Las Vegas (1998)
Go Ask Alice (1972)
Lady Sings the Blues (1972)
Lenny (1974)
The Panic in Needle Park (1971)
Requiem for a Dream (2000)
Rush (1991)
Traffic (2000)
Trainspotting (1996)

Television

America's Most Wanted
Chasing the Dragon
Conflicting Signals
Corey Feldman: The E! True Hollywood Story
ER
Gia
The Oprah Winfrey Show, "High-Class Drug Problem," October 11, 1994
Queer as Folk
The Sopranos

IN THE LITERATURE

Books

J. FRIEDMAN AND M. ALICEA, *Surviving Heroin*. Gainesville: University Press of Florida, 2001.

J. INCIARDI AND D. LOCKWOOD, *Women and Crack-Cocaine*. New York: Macmillan, 1993.

M. LANDRY, *Understanding Drugs of Abuse: The Processes of Addition, Treatment, and Recovery*. Washington, D.C.: American Psychiatric Press, 1994.

J. LANGONE, *Tough Choices: A Book about Substance Abuse*. Boston: Little, Brown, 1995.

T. MILLER, *The Hippies and American Values*. Knoxville: University of Tennessee Press, 1991.

J. PLATT, *Cocaine Addiction*. Cambridge, Mass.: Harvard University Press, 1997.

G. ROSENWALD AND R. OCHBERG, *Storied Lives*. New Haven, Conn.: Yale University Press, 1992.

D. SPUNGEN, *And I Don't Want to Live This Life*. New York: Random House, 1983.

P. STARES, *Global Habit: The Drug Problem in a Borderless World*. Washington, D.C.: Brookings Institution, 1996.

R. STEPHENS, *The Street Addict Role*. Albany: State University of New York Press, 1991.

C. STERK, *Fast Lives: Women Who Use Crack Cocaine*. Philadelphia: Temple University Press, 1999.

Articles

S. AZIZ AND A. SHAH, "Home Environment and Peer Relations of Addicted and Nonaddicted University Students," *Journal of Psychology*, vol. 129, no. 3 (1995), pp. 122–138.

T. D'AUNNO AND T. VAUGHN, "Variations in Methadone Treatment Practices," *Journal of the American Medical Association*, vol. 267, no. 2 (1992), pp. 253–258.

V. DOLE AND H. JOSEPH, "Long-term Outcomes of Patients Treated with Methadone Maintenance," *Annals of the New York Academy of Sciences*, vol. 311, pp. 181–189.

P. EMMELKAMP AND H. HEERES, "Drug Addition and Parental Rearing Style," *International Journal of the Addictions*, vol. 23, pp. 207–216.

R. GRANFIELD AND W. CLOUD, "The Elephant That No One Sees," *Journal of Drug Issues*, vol. 26, pp. 45–61.

P. MORGAN AND K. JOE, "Citizens and Outlaws," *Journal of Drug Issues*, vol. 26, pp. 135–142.

E. PREBLE AND J. CASEY, "Taking Care of Business," *International Journal of the Addictions*, vol. 4, pp. 1–24.

C. STERK-ELIFSON, "Just for Fun? Cocaine Use among Middle-Class Women," *Journal of Drug Issues*, vol. 26, pp. 63–76.

A. SUTTER, "The World of the Righteous Dope Fiend," *Issues in Criminology*, vol. 2, pp. 177–222.

ENDNOTES

1. R. I. Akers, *Drugs, Alcohol, and Society*. Belmont, Calif.: Wadsworth, 1992.

2. A. I. Leshner, *Addiction Is a Brain Disease—And It Matters*. Washington, D.C.: U.S. Department of Justice, National Institute of Justice, October 1998, p. 4.

3. "Prescription Cancer Drug Is Narcotic of Choice," *Law Enforcement News*, February 19, 2001, p. 5.

4. R. Stephens, *Mind-Altering Drugs*. Newbury Park, Calif.: Sage, 1987.

5. J. Inciardi, *The War on Drugs*. Mountain View, Calif.: Mayfield Press, 1986.

6. Stephens, op. cit.

7. N. Zinberg, *Drug, Set, and Setting*. New Haven, Conn.: Yale University Press, 1984.

8. H. S. Becker, "Becoming a Marijuana User," *American Journal of Sociology*, vol. 59 (1953), pp. 235–242.

9. J. S. Farrell, "An Overview of Ketamine Abuse," *Police Chief* (February 1998), p. 47.

10. R. Hernandez, "New Drug Battles, Use of Ecstacy among Young Soars," *The New York Times on the Web*, August 2, 2000.

11. J. McGivney, "Made in America: The New Methcathinone," *Police Chief* (April 1994), pp. 20–21.

12. T. Chapman, "Drug-Facilitated Sexual Assault," *Police Chief* (June 2000), pp. 38–39.

13. U.S. Department of Justice, Bureau of Justice Statistics, "Violence against Women: Estimates from the Design Survey." August 1995.

14. Hoffmann-La Roche, Inc., "Rohypnol Fact Sheet." Drug Enforcement Administration Intelligence Report. July 1995.

15. A. G. Gardiner, Jr., "Rohypnol: The New Stealth Weapon," *Police Chief* (April 1998), p. 37.

16. *Drug Enforcement Administration Fact Sheet (GHB) Training Bulletin.* San Diego, Calif.: FDA Office of Criminal Investigations, August 1998.

17. Executive Office of the President's Office of National Drug Control Policy, "Gamma Hydroxybutyrate (GHB) Fact Sheet." October 1998.

18. Chapman, p. 41.

19. The Office of National Drug Control Policy, *National Drug Control Strategy, 1995.* Washington, D.C. The discussion of the demand for illicit drugs was adapted from this source, p. 22–26.

20. Substance Abuse and Mental Health Services Administration, *Annual Household Survey Results — Youth Drug Use Continues Downward Trend: First Time State-by-State Data Available.* News release, August 31, 2000. The discussion of emerging drug trends has been adapted from this source. A more comprehensive discussion may be found on the World Wide Web at http://www.samhsa.gov.

21. U.S. Department of Justice, *Speaking Out against Drug Legalization.* October 1999.

22. D. Sanders and T. A. Constantine, "A Police Chief's Guide to the Legalization Issue," *Police Chief*, (February 1998), p. 27.

23. L. Nylen, "Legalizing Nonmedical Drug Use: The Swedish Experience." *Police Chief* (February 1998), pp. 32, 34.

24. "Heavy drug abuse" is defined in Sweden as people either injecting drugs or using drugs in some other way daily or virtually every day. Thus, by Swedish standards, a person smoking hashish nearly every day is a heavy drug abuser.

25. Nylen, op. cit.

INDEX

A

Abduction. *See* Kidnapping
Abortion clinics, violence against, 17–18
Abuses of trust, 7
Accreditation issues, police, 218–219
Acquittal, motion for, 387
Actus reus
   criminal responsibility and, 49
   mens rea and, 50
Adelphia Communications case, 8–9
Adequate provocation
   conditions necessary to establish, 55
   defined, 53
Adjudication
   deferred, 289
   probation with, 519–520
Administrative law, 47
Administrative Maximum Facility (ADX), 482
Administrative segregation, 478–480
Adopt-a-park programs, 245
Adult basic education (ABE) programs, 495
Adultery, 73, 75, 501
Adversary proceeding
   criminal trial and, 357–358
   defined, 357
Adversary system, 280–281
Affidavit, defined, 100
Affirmative defenses
   battered-spouse defense, 383–384
   defense of ignorance, 381
   defense of infancy, 377
   defense of protection of property, 381
   defense of use of force to subdue arrestee, 382–383
   insanity defense, 377–378
   introduction to, 377
   self-defense, 379–380
   traditional and nontraditional, 384
African Americans. *See also* Ethnic groups
   conviction rates of, 26–28
   death penalty and, 421, 432
   stereotypes and, 26
Aftercare
   benefits of, 560–561
   defined, 560
Age
   for boot camps, 535
   composition of U.S. population, 488
   of consent, 63
   of male prisoners, 498
   of persons in lineup, 338
Agency rule exception, 120
Aggravated assault/battery
   criminal law and, 40
   defined, 57
   tools of, 59
   victims of, 148–149
   weapons used in, 59, 148

Aguilar/Spinelli test, 108
AIDS
   inmates with, 455, 500
   policy, 303
   prevention of, 500–501
Alcatraz federal penitentiary, 480, 482
Alcohol
   as depressant, 586
   use among youth, 593, 594, 596
Alcoholics/alcoholism
   in jails, 456
   police officers and, 227–228
   self-help programs for, 466
Alcoholics Anonymous, 506
Alfred v. North Carolina, 346
Alibi
   motion of intention to provide, 341
   witnesses, 369
Alimentary canal smuggling, 112
Al-Qaeda group, 18–19
Alternate jurors, 364
American Correctional Association, 508
American Federation of State, County, and Municipal Employees, 507
American Jail Association, 507
American Political Science Association, 301
American Prison Association, 528
Ammidown v. United States, 347
Amphetamines, 589, 590
Analgesia, 583
Anonymous reporting programs, 567
Anti-drug efforts, 246–247
Appeal(s)
   of convictions, 266, 331, 417–419
   death penalty, 428–429
   double jeopardy prohibition and, 133
   federal courts and, 259
   interlocutory, 125, 126, 266
   for parole, 530
   postconviction relief and, 419
   process, 417–419
   prosecutor's role in, 285
   as step in criminal justice process, 24
   Supreme Court and, 262
Appeal-to-public-opinion argument, 438
Appellate court(s)
   decisions of, 258–259
   intermediate, state and federal, 265–267
   judge, 96
   vs. trial courts, 258
Apprendi v. New Jersey, 413
Armstrong v. United States, 287
Arraignment
   criminal justice process and, 24
   defined, 339
   process, 339–340
   prosecutor's role in, 285

Arrest(s)
  clearance and, 202
  constitutional, 99–100
  defense of use of force to effect an, 382–383
  drug courts programs and, 272
  drug-related, 595
  false, 105
  Fourteenth Amendment rights on, 98–99
  landmark cases, 100, 102, 104
  lawful, 111–112
  patrol officers and, 188
  prosecutor's role in, 283
  as a step in criminal justice process, 22
  stops and detentions and, 103–105
  using deadly force for, 102, 104–105
  for violent crimes, 26–27
Arrest warrant
  court ruling on, 315
  defined, 100
  requirements for, 100–102
Arson
  criminal statutes and, 67
  defined, 67
  elements of, 67
  rate of, 150–151
Articles of Confederation, 92, 93
Aryan Brotherhood, 492
Asian Americans. *See* Ethnic groups
Assault
  aggravated, 148–149
  criminal and civil law and, 39–40
  defined, 61–62
  types of, 62
Assigned-counsel system, 295–296
Attendant circumstances, criminal liability and, 50
Attorneys, duties of, 128
Auburn system, 477
Augustus, John, 519
Automated Latent System Model, 236
Automation. *See* Technological trends
Automobile exception, 112–113
Auto theft, 150

B

Babylonian Code of Hammurabi, 420
Bail
  bondsperson, 318, 323–325
  denial of, 325, 328
Bailiff, duties of, 275
Bail issues/system
  alternatives to, 320, 323
  amount of, 319
  bond, 321, 323
  commercial, 318
  conditions of, 320
  defects in, 324–325
  excessive, 134
  forfeiture of, 323–324
  jumpers, 324
  posting, 318
  pretrial detention and, 314–315
  purpose of, 317
  reforms in, 328–329
  right to be released on, 330
  schedule, 319
  statutes, 320
Band-Aid nonsolutions, 508, 509

Barbiturates, 586
Barker v. Wingo, 129
Battered child syndrome, 60
Battered husband syndrome, 61
Battered women, granting clemency to, 421
Battery
  attempted, 62
  elements of, 56
  mens rea of, 56
"Battlefield medicine," 588
Beats, defined, 190
Behavior
  normative, 43
  social sanctions and, 42
Bias crime. *See* Hate crimes
Bifurcated trial, 402
Bigamy, 75
Biker gangs, 45
Bill of Rights
  Constitution and, 92–95
  criminal procedure law and, 91–92
  defined, 91
  selected incorporation of, 97
Bindover hearing. *See* Preliminary hearing
Blackmail. *See* Extortion
"Bleed 'em and plead 'em" practice, 292
Blockbuster test, 134
Booking process, 23
Boot camps
  features of, 535
  for juvenile offenders, 559
Bostick v. Florida, 115
Bounty hunters, 324
Bowers v. Hardwick, 75
Brower v. Inyo County, 104
Burden of proof, 359
Bureau of Justice Assistance (BJA), 246, 522
Bureau of Justice Statistics (BJS), 208, 505
Bureau of Prisons (BOP), 481
Burger Court, 90
Burglary
  criminal statutes and, 66–67
  defined, 66
  elements of, 66
  rate of, 149
Business crimes, 8

C

CAD system, 234–235
California State Prison, 490
Campus
  crime prevention programs, 246, 247
  police, 198–199
Campus Sexual Assault Victims' Bill of Rights, 154
Capital cases
  death penalty appeals and, 428–429
  jury's role in, 423
Capital felony, 49
Capital punishment
  appeal-to-public-opinion argument and, 438
  arbitrariness argument and, 431–432, 434
  brutalization argument and, 438
  community protection argument and, 437–438
  cost-efficiency argument and, 437
  cruel-and-unusual-punishment argument and, 438
  danger of mistake argument and, 434–435
  incapacitation argument and, 435–437

retribution argument and, 431
role in deterrence, 428–431
Carnal knowledge, 63
Carroll v. United States, 112
Case assignment, 201
Case law, *stare decisis* and, 47
Cat (drug), 590
CAT program, 246
Causation, defined, 51
Central control officer, 489
Challenged for cause, defined, 364
Change of venue, defined, 341
Chapman v. California, 418
Charge
bargaining, 345
criminal justice process and, 23
Chicago v. Morales, 134, 135
Chief judge
defined, 266
duties of, 278
Child(ren). *See also* Juvenile offenders
abducted, 562
born in prison, 403
defense of infancy and, 377
delinquent, 551–552
dependent and abused, 551
drug use among, 600, 601
homeless, 562
houses of refuge and, 544, 545
parents killed by, 573–574
runaway and missing, 561–563
shelter for, 549
teaching about law to, 552
testimony of, 372
as victims, 165–167
Child abuse/molestation. *See also* Sex offenses/offenders
defined, 60–61
juvenile justice system and, 551
results of, 167
Chimel v. California, 112
Cigarette smoking, 593
Circumstantial evidence, 366
Citation, defined, 314
Citizen(s)
role in CPTED applications, 244–245
role in crime prevention, 239–240
Civil actions, crime prevention with, 245
Civil law vs. criminal law, 39–41
Civil proceedings exception, 120
Civil trials, 40–41
Clearance rate of index crimes, 146
Clearing the books technique, 152
Clemency, purpose of, 420
Cloning, 12
Closing arguments, 385
Club drug, 588
Cocaine, 589
Codeine, 583
Coker v. Georgia, 423
Combat Auto Theft (CAT) program, 246
Comber v. United States, 56, 57
Combination facility, 446
Combined DNA Index system, 367
Commercial bail issues, 324–325
Commission on Accreditation for Law Enforcement Agencies, 218

Common law
defined, 46
of England, 46–47
substantive criminal law and, 51
Commonwealth v. Matsos, 80
Community-based programs
curfew programs, 564
for juveniles, 557
for preventing school violence, 568
Community correctional centers
educational release program and, 537
features of, 535–536
furlough programs and, 537
halfway houses, 536–537
work release programs and, 537
Community-oriented policing (COP). *See also* Drug Abuse Resistance Education (DARE) program
benefits of, 207
CPTED concept and, 244
crime prevention and, 249
defined, 30, 205
future of, 211–212
neighborhood watch programs and, 240, 242
personal touch, 208
sheriff's office and, 207
vs. traditional, 206
trends in, 207–208, 210
violent crimes and, 30
Community protection argument, 437–438
Community service
defined, 537–538
issues in, 538
objectives of, 538
patrol officers and, 187
types of, 538
Community service officer (CSO), 224
Community supervision
introduction to, 559–560
juvenile aftercare and, 560–561
juvenile probation and, 560
quality of, 561
revocation and, 561
Compensation
for courtroom mistakes, 408
eligibility requirements for, 156
victim, 155
Competency
admissibility of evidence and, 368
motion to determine, 342
to stand trial at time of execution, 424
Competent evidence, 367
Complaint
defined, 314
filing process, 23
preparation of, 316
Comprehensive Crime Control Act of 1984, 378
Computer(s)
bulletin boards, 11
crimes, 77–78
future applications of, 237–238
police use of, 237
role in court administration, 276–277
Computer-aided dispatch (CAD) system, 234–235
Con artist crime, 72, 169
Condom distribution, 501
Confession
constitutional, 124–126

defined, 119
exclusionary rule and, 119–120
Confidentiality issues, 370
Con games, defined, 8
Consensual crimes
  defined, 73
  examples of, 73
  landmark cases, 74
Consent doctrine, 113–115
Constitution
  Bill of Rights and, 92–95
  criminal law and, 47–48
Constitutional arrest, right to, 99–100
Constitutional law, 47
Constitutional right(s)
  of being competent, 342
  during sentencing hearing, 404
Contact visit, defined, 469
Contract system, features of, 296
Controlled Substance Act, 591
Control programs, 521
Convenience store robberies, 244
Conventional crime, 6–7
Conversion, defined, 70
Convicted Sexual Offender Registry, 204
Conviction(s)
  appeal of, 266, 331, 417–419
  by guilty plea, 281, 350
  rates, 27–28
  wrongful, 288, 434
Corporate scandals
  Adelphia Communications Corp, 8–9
  Drexel Burnham Lambert, 348
Corporation of National Service, 598
Correctional institutions. *See* Jail(s); Prison(s)
Correctional officer, duties of, 478
Corrections Corporation of America (CCA), 507
Corruption, police misconduct and, 220–222
Counseling in jails, 465
Counterterrorism, 16–17
Counting of inmates, 466–467
County attorney. *See* Prosecutor(s)
County law enforcement, 183
Court(s)
  administrator, 276–277
  analyst, 136
  bullet-proof, 257
  clerk, 275–276
  courthouse regulars in, 277
  defined, 256
  interpreters, 368
  jurisdiction, 257–258
  of last resort, 265
  mistakes made by, 408
  personnel, 274–278
  reporter, 275–276
  special-service employees in, 277–278
  testimony in, 189
  translators, 368
Courtroom
  compensation for mistakes made in, 408
  media in, 303, 360–361
Court system(s). *See also specific types*
  appellate courts and, 265–267
  court congestion and, 304–306
  dual, 259–261
  history of, 256

introduction to, 255
lower courts and, 269
state vs. federal, 258
Supreme Court and, 262–265
trial courts, 267–268
Coxsackie Correctional Facility, 490
Coy v. Iowa, 373
CPTED concept
  community policing and, 244
  for crime prevention, 243–244
  police's role in, 244–245
Crack cocaine, 29, 589, 590
Crackdowns
  examples of, 194
  patrol strategies and, 193
Crime(s). *See also* Violence
  in American history, 4–5
  analysis, 193
  analyst, 238
  business, 8
  classification of, 6–19, 49
  compensable, 156
  con artist, 72
  costs associated with, 171–172
  defined, 6, 38
  drug use and, 599, 600
  environmental influence and, 545
  fear of, 240
  immigrant community and, 545
  impact of, 5–6, 155
  introduction to, 3–4
  predictions of future, 534–535
  rate, 143–144
  reporting, 21
  Salient Factor Score and, 532–533
  in schools, 566–567
  signs of, 241
  victimization, 25–26
  by women, 505
Crime Control Act of 1984, 378, 595
Crime control model, 92
Crime data
  campus, 154–155
  national, 152, 159–160
  specialist, 146
Crime prevention
  activities, 245
  anti-drug efforts for, 246–247
  campus, 246, 247
  CAT program for, 246
  citizen role in, 239–240
  CPTED applications for, 243–244
  McGruff campaign for, 245
  police's role in, 240–241
  programs, 241, 243
  Watch Your Car Program for, 246
Crime Prevention Through Environmental Design (CPTED), 243–245
Crimes against habitation
  arson, 67, 150–151
  burglary, 66–67, 149
  defined, 66
Crimes against morality
  adultery, 75
  bigamy, 75
  fornication, 75
  historical roots of, 74–75

illicit cohabitation, 75
incest, 75
prostitution, 76–77
sodomy, 75–76
Crimes against persons
battery, 56–61
defined, 6
false imprisonment, 65
hate crimes, 61
kidnapping, 65
landmark cases, 60, 63
rape, 62–64
sexual harassment, 64–65
Crimes against property
burglary, 149
defined, 6
embezzlement, 70–71
extortion, 72
larceny, 68–69, 149–150
obtaining property by false pretense, 71–72
receiving stolen property, 72–73
robbery, 69–70
Criminal court. *See* Court system(s); Trial courts
Criminal infraction, defined, 49
Criminal intent of the crime. *See Mens rea*
Criminal justice educator, 41
Criminal justice process
cost issues, 599
court congestion impact on, 306
steps in, 21–25
Criminal justice system
crime victims' treatment by, 156
defined, 21
degree of certainty used in phases of, 99
guilty pleas in, 281
jail overcrowding and, 450
overview of, 326–327
strengthening diversity in, 28
unresolved victim and, 172
Criminal law
vs. civil law, 39–41
deviant behavior and, 44–45
Criminal liability, 50
Criminally negligent homicide, 56
Criminal procedure, defined, 46
Criminal procedure law
Bill of Rights and, 91–92
constitutional arrest and, 99–107
Constitution's role in, 92–95
defined, 91
double jeopardy prohibition and, 133–134
Eighth Amendment rights and, 134
equal justice and, 135–136
exclusionary rule and, 117–122
Fifth Amendment privilege and, 122–126
Fourteenth Amendment and, 95–97
Fourth Amendment and, 98–99
introduction to, 89–90
search warrant and, 107–117
Sixth Amendment and, 126–133
vs. substantive criminal law, 90–91
substantive due process and, 134–135
Criminal profiles, stereotypes and, 26
Criminal responsibility
defined, 46
principles of, 49–51
Criminal trial
adversary proceeding and, 357–358

affirmative defense, 377–384
appeal at, 417–419
closing arguments, 385
criminal justice process and, 24
fair and impartial jury and, 360–366
foundations of, 358–360
judge's charge to the jury, 385
jury's deliberations, 386
jury's verdict, 386–387
opening statements, 374
vs. plea bargaining, 281–282
presentation of defense case, 376
presentation of state evidence, 374–375
procedures, 372–373
purpose of, 358
rebuttal and surrebuttal, 385
rules of evidence and, 366–372
Crisis intervention counselor, 64
Crofton, Sir Walter, 528
Cross-examination
adversary system and, 280
purpose of, 374–375
of witnesses, 375
Crystal meth, 590
Curfews, 523, 563–564
Cutlery control system, 468–469
Cybercrime, 11–12

D

Danger of mistake argument, 434–435
DARE program, 550–551, 597
Date rape
defined, 63
vs. stranger rape, 64
Date rape drugs
Rohypnol, 591–592
sexual assault and, 590–591
Dating relationships, violence in, 170
Deadly force
for defense of protection of property, 381
defined, 102
pepper spray as an alternative to, 233
shooting-control techniques and, 232
use of, 104–105, 230–233, 379–380
Death penalty
appeals, 428–429
codes, 422–423
controversy about, 422
cost issues, 437
current situation about, 424–425, 427
disparities in, 432
DNA testing for, 434–435
history of, 420–421
imposition of, 406
public attitude toward, 427–428
Supreme Court and, 423, 425
Death row
inmates, 424–426, 432
number of prisoners freed from, 436
wrong men on, 434
Death sentence, overturning of, 430
Defendant. *See also* Bail issues/system
appeal process for, 417–420
appellate court and, 259
clemency to, 420
compulsory process right of, 132–133
court congestion impact on, 306
HIV-positive, 303

minor, 423
preliminary hearing and, 332–333
presumption of innocence of, 359
proving guilt of, 359–360
right to a particular lawyer, 128
right to confront witnesses against, 131–132
right to suppression hearing, 118
self-representation right of, 128
Defense
battered-spouse, 383–384
of ignorance, 381
of infancy, 377
insanity, 378
jail overcrowding and, 452
of protection of property, 381
self-defense, 379–380
of use of force to subdue an arrestee, 382–383
Defense lawyers
educational requirements for, 282
presentation of case by, 376
privately retained, 292–293
prosecutors and, 279–282
rate of, 360
role of, 290–291
Deferred adjudication, 289
Deinstitutionalization of status offenders, 556–557
Delinquency
creation of, 544–546
prevention of, 548–550
Denver Police Department in-house program, 228
Depressants, 586
Designer drugs, 586
Detective(s)
activities of, 200–202
duties of, 199
PERF study on, 203
Rand study on, 202–203
role of, 199–200
Detention centers, 556
Detention deputy, duties of, 453
Determinate sentence, 408
Deterrence theory
capital punishment and, 428–431
components of, 399
Detoxification program, 450
Deviant behavior
defined, 38
examples of, 44–45
normative variations and, 42–43
theories related to, 44
Dickerson v. United States, 125
Dimethyltryptamine (DMT), 586
Direct evidence, 366
Direct-supervision jails. *See* Jail(s)
Disabilities, inmates with, 456
Discretionary review, defined, 419
Discrimination issues, 431–432
Dismissals, double jeopardy prohibition and, 133
Dispatcher, duties of, 235
Disposition(s)
advantages of, 555
postadjudication, 557–558
District attorney. *See* Prosecutor(s)
District court. *See* Trial courts
Disturbances. *See* Riots
Diversion programs, 289
juvenile courts and, 548–550

plea bargaining and, 351
DNA profiling/testing
advancement in, 239
for death penalty, 434–435
use of, 238, 367
Doctrine of selective incorporation, 93–95
Domestic crisis intervention unit, 162
Domestic terrorism, 16–18
Domestic violence
children and, 165–167
defined, 57
handling cases of, 161–163
landmark case, 60
types of, 58, 60–61
victims of, 162–163
Double jeopardy
exceptions to, 133
prohibition against, 133
prosecution and, 134
Drug(s)
addiction, 582
counselor, 595
date rape, 590–593
depressants, 586
hypnotic effect of, 583
legalization of, 598–602
markets, 30
narcotics, 582–585
police corruption and, 220–222
psychedelics, 586–589
psychotropic, 19
smuggling of, 469–470
stimulants, 589–590
testing, 318
Drug abuse
among children, 600
experiments for preventing, 601–602
law enforcement agencies and, 228, 597–598
by youth, 593
Drug Abuse Resistance Education (DARE) program, 550–551, 597
Drug Abuse Warning Network (DAWN), 593
Drug addicts
drug courts and, 596
in jails, 457
narcotics control and, 469
self-help programs for, 465, 466
treatment programs for, 498
Drug courts
benefits of, 596
defined, 270
establishment of, 270
features of, 271
vs. traditional court, 271–272
Drug Enforcement Administration (DEA), 183
Drug-Induced Rape Prevention and Punishment Act of 1996, 591
Drug trafficking
alimentary canal smuggling and, 112
anti-drug efforts and, 246–247
arrests related to, 595
by ethnic groups, 28
of heroin, 584
victim intimidation and, 157–158
by women, 505
youth gangs and, 572–573
Drunk driving
accidents, 168

crackdowns, 194
criteria for getting charged with, 81
house arrest and, 525
landmark cases, 82
Dual court system
defined, 259
federal courts, 260
state and local, 260–262
Due process
basis of incompetency claim and, 342
vs. crime control model, 92
defined, 91
Fourteenth Amendment and, 95–97
identification procedures and, 339
initial appearance and, 317
jury and, 360, 364
sentencing hearing and, 407
substantive, 134
Duncan v. Louisiana, 131
DuPage Seven trial, 288
Dying declaration, admissibility of, 372

E

Ecclesiastical crimes, 74
Eckerd Family Youth Alternatives, Inc. (EFYA), 558
Economic crime
case study, 8–9
corporate scandals in, 8–10
defined, 7
types of, 7–10
Ecstasy, 588–589
Educational programs
DARE program, 550–551
for HIV-positive inmates, 501
LRE program, 551
in prisons, 495–496, 506
Educational release program, 537
Education for police officers, 219–221
Eighth Amendment
bail issues under, 317
cruel and unusual punishment clause under, 134
nonincorporated rights under, 97
rights against excessive bail, 134
sentencing hearing and, 405–406
Electric chair, 421, 427
Electronically monitored equipment, 524–526
Electronic serial number (ESN), 12, 13
Elmira Reformatory, 528–529
Embezzlement
defined, 70
elements of, 70–71
Emergency responders, 16–17
Employment
of minorities, 223–224
of women, 224–225
Enhancement statutes
defined, 410
features of, 410
habitual-criminal statutes and, 412
hate crimes and, 413
Environmental crimes, 82–83
Equal justice, criminal procedure law and, 135–136
Equal-protection clause, 406
Escobedo v. Illinois, 124
Estelle v. Williams, 360
Ethnic groups
conviction rates of, 26–28

drug offenses by, 28
recruitment of, 223–224
role in organized crime, 15–16
stereotypes and, 26
Evidence
admissible, 367–368
circumstantial, 366
evanescent, 117
hearsay testimony and, 371–372
material, 367
motion to suppress, 343–344
opinion, 369–370
presentation of, 374–375
of privileged communications, 370
prosecutor's duty to disclose, 289
real, 366, 368–369
technicians, 201
testimonial, 368
Excessive bail issues, 134
Exclusionary rule
criticism of, 121–122
defined, 117
exceptions to, 118–121
search warrant and, 117–118
Execution
competency to stand trial at time of, 424
cost issues, 437
decline in, 421
methods of, 425–426
by state, 427
Exigent circumstances, 116–117
Express bargaining, 344
Extortion, defined, 72

F

Factual guilt, defined, 358
Faith community, drug use prevention and, 598
False arrests, 105
False imprisonment, 65
False pretense
defined, 71
elements of, 72
Family therapy, 465
FBI agent, 184
FBI Uniform Crime Reports, 144
Federal Bail Reform Act of 1984, 328, 330
Federal Bureau of Prisons (FBP), 480, 482, 507
Federal Correctional Institution, 490
Federal court(s)
appellate courts, 265–267
hierarchical systems, 258, 260–261
lower courts, 269
trial courts, 267–268
Federal law enforcement, 183–184
Federal prison(s)
in California, 482–484
in Florence, Colorado, 481–482
in Marion, Illinois, 480–481
Minnesota correctional facility, 484–485
in New York, 484
in Oklahoma, 483–484
Felony
charging, 335–336
defined, 6, 49
prosecution, 332
seriousness of, 387
Felony murder rule

defined, 53
landmark case, 55
Female judges, 299–300
Female Prison and Reformatory Institution for Girls and Women, 503
Fetal homicide, 52
Field interrogation files, 202
Field training officer (FTO), 179, 184
Fifth Amendment
 double jeopardy prohibition and, 133
 due process, 92
 nonincorporated rights under, 97
 privilege against self-incrimination, 122–124
 substantive due process and, 134
Fingerprint analyst, 236
Fingerprint automation, 235–236
Firearms. *See* Weapons
Flat-time sentence, 408
Flint (Mich.) foot patrol program, 191–192
Floggings, 545
Florence prison facility (Colorado), 482
Florida v. Bostick, 115
Folkways, defined, 42
Follow-up investigations, 201
Forcible rape
 defined, 146
 reasons for not reporting, 146–147
Ford v. Wainwright, 438
Forfeiture
 of bail, 323–324
 defined, 318
Fornication, defined, 75
Foster homes, 557–558
Fourteenth Amendment
 constitutional confession and, 126
 due process and, 95–97
Fourth Amendment
 government conduct and, 106
 privacy issues under, 106–107
 search warrant and, 107–111
 stops and detentions and, 103–104
 unreasonable search and seizures and, 105–106
Fraud, auto theft and, 150
Freebasing, 589
Frisk, defined, 103, 467
Fruit of the poisonous tree doctrine, 118, 119, 120
Furlough programs, 537
Furman v. Georgia, 422, 431

G

Gallows, 476
Gamma hydroxybutyrate (GHB), 592–593
Gangs
 leaving, 494
 membership, 491–493
 structure of, 493
 youth, 571–573
Garner v. Tennessee, 102, 232, 383
Gas chamber, 421, 422
Gates v. Illinois, 108
GED programs, 495, 496
General deterrence, defined, 399
General equivalency diploma (GED) programs, 495, 496
Geographical information system (GIS), 238–239
Georgia Home Boy (drug), 592–593
Gerstein hearing, 316
Gideon v. Wainwright, 95, 127, 290

Goetz v. People, 380
Gomez v. Madrid, 507
Goob (drug), 590
Good-faith exception, 120
Grand jury
 exception, 120
 investigative, 335
 proceeding, 336
 prosecutor and, 284
 requirements for, 334
 review, 23
Great Law of Pennsylvania, 476
Gregg v. Georgia, 422, 423
Group homes, 558
Guilty pleas
 appealing of, 350–351
 conviction by, 350
 entering a constitutional, 346
 prevalence of, 281, 345–346

H

Habeas corpus, 120, 260, 266, 269, 419–420, 428
Habitual-criminal statutes, 412
Hacking
 defined, 10–11
 illegal bulletin boards and, 11
 telephone phreakers and, 11–13
Halfway houses, 397, 401
 defined, 536
 for juveniles, 558
 problems associated with, 536–537
 supervisor, 536
 work release programs and, 537
Hallucinogenic drugs, 586
Handguns. *See* Weapons
Harassment, defined, 78, 80
Harris v. Alabama, 423
Hate crimes
 defined, 61
 enhancement statutes and, 413
 occurrence of, 151
 statistics, 152
 truck dragging, 433
Health issues
 drug use and, 601
 police officers', 225–229
Hearing. *See also specific types*
 probation revocation, 24–25, 285
 sentencing, 402, 405–406
Hearsay rule
 exceptions to, 371–372
 vs. hearsay testimony, 371
Henry v. United States, 123
Heroin, 14–15
 features of, 583
 smuggling of, 584
Higher Education Act of 1992, 154
Highway patrol officer, 183
Hispanics. *See* Ethnic groups
Hit and run crime, 81
HIV-positive inmates, 500
Home Insurance Co. v. People, 68
Homeless children, 562
Homicide(s)
 by children, 573–574
 crime victimization patterns for, 25–26
 decline in, 29–30

defined, 52
involuntary manslaughter, 56
landmark cases, 55, 56, 57
murder, 52–53
vehicular, 81
voluntary manslaughter, 53, 55
youth gangs and, 572–573
Homosexual inmates, 499–500, 506
Hot pursuit exception, 101
Houghton v. Wyoming, 113
House arrest
benefits of, 523–524
cost issues, 524
defined, 523
disadvantages of, 525–526
electronically monitored, 524–525
Houses of refuge, 544, 545
Housing unit officer, 486
Humphrey v. People, 384
Hurtado v. California, 97, 334

I

Idaho Code of Criminal Procedure, 99
Idaho State Correctional Institution (ISCI), 490
Identification procedures, 339
Identity theft, 78, 79
Illegal bulletin boards, 11
Illicit cohabitation, 75
Illicit drugs
decline in use of, 593
drug courts for fighting, 272
health and safety issues and, 601
reducing demand for, 595–596
use of, 594
Illinois State Penitentiary, 486
Illinois v. Gates, 108, 109
Illinois v. Rodriguez, 114
Immigrant community, crime and, 545
Impeachment exception, 120
Implicit bargaining, 344
Imprisonment, false, 65
Incapacitation argument, 435–437
Incapacitation theory, 400
Incest, 73, 75
Independent source doctrine, 119
Indeterminate sentence, 409
Index crimes
clearance rate of, 146
crimes against property, 149–151
hate crimes, 151–152
violent crimes, 145–149
Index offenses, 144
Indiana State Penitentiary, 530
Indictment
criminal justice process and, 24
defined, 336
prosecutor's role in, 285
Industrial schools, 545
Inevitable discovery doctrine, 119
Initial appearance
criminal justice process and, 23
defined, 316
in misdemeanor cases, 316–317
prosecutor's role in, 283–284
Inmates. *See also* Jail security; Prison(s); Women
aggressive, 456
antisocial, 491
costs of maintaining, 483, 522

counting of, 466–467
death row, 424–426, 428, 432
with disabilities, 456
drug addicts as, 457
educational programs for, 495–496
elderly male, 498–499
executed since 1976, 426
in federal prisons, 480–485
high-risk, 463
HIV-positive, 500
homosexual and heterosexual, 499–500
in maximum-security, 467, 469
mentally ill, 457, 491
minority, 491
paroled, 529
physically ill, 456
prison work programs for, 496–497
radical organizations' impact on, 491
recreational programs for, 497
religious programs for, 498
sex offenders as, 458
sexual contact between staff and, 506
special-management, 455–456
suicidal, 462–464
treatment programs for, 464–466, 497–498
vulnerable, 456–457
Insanity defense
chance of success of, 378
insanity definition for, 378
reasons for, 377
standards, conflicting, 379
Insurance fraud, 169
Intake workers, 549–550, 554
Integrated Automated Fingerprint Identification System (IAFIS), 204, 205
Intensive-supervision probation (ISP) programs
in California, 522
introduction to, 521
in Massachusetts, 521
in New Jersey, 521–522
Intent to commit a felony, 53
Intent to inflict great bodily injury, 53
Intent to kill, 53
Internal computer crime, 77
International Association of Chiefs of Police (IACP), 144, 145, 218, 228
International terrorism, 17
Interrogation, rights afforded during, 336
Intimate-partner violence
domestic violence and, 161–163
statistics, 160–161
Violence against Women Act and, 163–164
Investigations
follow-up, 201
NCIC network in, 204–205
postarrest, 23
prearrest, 22
preliminary, 187–188, 200–201
prosecutor's role in, 283
Investigatory stops, defined, 103
Involuntary manslaughter, 56
Islamic fundamentalists, attacks by, 17–19
ISP programs. *See* Intensive-supervision probation (ISP) programs

J

Jail(s). *See also* Inmates
administrators, 451

construction costs, 488
cost of life in, 437, 522
costs of maintaining, 398
counseling in, 465, 466
direct-supervision, 452
history of, 446–447
juvenile offenders in, 555–556
management of, 452–454
as mental institutions, 459–462
officer, 453
personnel issues, 453
physical conditions of, 448–449
private, 508
purpose of, 447–448
reduced sick leave in, 454
staffing ratio in, 455
staff morale, 454
suicide in, 458, 462–464
treatment programs in, 463–466
types of, 446
women in, 403
working conditions in, 454

Jail overcrowding
current situation of, 487–488
defined, 449–450
enhancement statutes and, 409–410
impact of, 397–398
local justice system and, 450
pretrial release and, 321, 322
problems related to, 450
system decision makers and, 450–452
ways to relieve, 488

Jail security
jail administrators and, 446
for personnel, 455
reception centers and, 487
techniques used for, 466–470

Jail Substance Abuse Program (JSAP), 466
Jeanne Clery Disclosure of Campus Sex Policy and Campus Crime Statistics Act, 154
Jeopardy. *See* Double jeopardy

Job stress
judiciary and, 301–304
police officers and, 226–227
ways to reduce, 229

Joyriding, 150

Judge(s)
appointment of, 297–298
charge to jury, 385
on courts of last resort, 265
defined, 257
drug court, 271
election of, 297
female, 299–300
job stress issues for, 301–304
juvenile, 548
public image of, 301–302
role in jail crowding solutions, 451–452
role in sentencing, 401–402, 405–407
selection of, 296–297
socialization of, 300–301
at work, 299

Judicial assistant, 274–275
Judicial review, 95
Judicial sabbaticals, 304
Judiciary. *See also* Court system(s)
appointment of judges for, 297–298
demographic composition of, 300
election of judges for, 297
introduction to, 296
job stress and, 301–304
selection of judges for, 296–297
socialization of judges and, 300–301

Jurisdiction
court, 257–258
defined, 257

Jury
consultants, 365
deliberations, 386
due process and, 360, 364
hung, 386
judge's charge to, 385
media and, 360–361
nullification, 386–387
personal prejudices of, 362
polling, 386
postverdict motions and, 387
pretrial publicity and, 361–362
questionnaire, 365
role in capital cases, 423
selection process, 362–366
size, 363
social baggage of, 362
trial, 130–131
verdict, 386

Justice administration
conviction rates and, 26–28
court congestion impact on, 305–306
crime victimization and, 25–26
criminal profiles and, 26
justice system diversity and, 28

Juvenile courts
current situation of, 547–548
development of, 547
establishment of, 547
language of, 548–549
various stages in, 546

Juvenile intake officer, 554
Juvenile judge, 548
Juvenile Justice and Delinquency Prevention (JJDP) Act, 551, 555, 556, 559

Juvenile justice system
cost issues, 557
development of, 546
juveniles and, 544
programs outside, 550
in twenty-first century, 574–575

Juvenile offenders. *See also* Youth gangs
adult jails and, 555–556
boot camps for, 559
community supervision and, 559–561
curfews for, 563–564
DARE program for, 551
deinstitutionalization of, 556–557
in detention centers, 556
drug abuse by, 588
institutional facilities for, 559
introduction to, 543
juvenile intake and, 554–555
LRE program for, 551
police's role in handling, 552–554
postadjudication dispositions for, 557–558
serious and violent, 564–566

K

Kansas City Preventive Patrol Experiment, 190

Kat (drug), 588
Katz v. United States, 106
Kent v. United States, 547, 548
Ketamine hydrochloride, 588
Key control system, 467–468
Kidnapping
　of children, 562
　defined, 65
Killings. *See* Homicide(s)
King, Rodney, 374, 382
Kirby v. Illinois, 339
Kirkland Correctional Institution, 489
Kuhlman v. Wilson, 124

L

Laptop computers, police use of, 237
Larceny
　criminal statutes and, 69
　defined, 68
　elements of, 68–69
　landmark cases, 68
　rate of, 149–150
Latent Descriptor Index, 236
Law clerk, 274
Law enforcement
　county, 183
　jail overcrowding and, 450–451
　traffic, 188, 194, 196–197
Law enforcement agencies. *See also* Community-oriented policing (COP)
　accreditation, 218–219
　computerization in, 237–238
　county, state and federal, 182–184
　curfew programs by, 563–564
　private security and, 234
　racial profiling by, 189
　role in preventing drug abuse, 597–598
　role in preventing violence, 567
　runaway children and, 563
　rural policing by, 197–198
　smaller, 180–181
Law Enforcement Assistance Administration (LEAA), 305
Law Enforcement Code of Ethics, 222
Law Enforcement Critical Life Events Scale, 226
Law Enforcement Management and Administrative Statistics (LEMAS), 208
Lawful killings, 52
Law of criminal procedure. *See* Criminal procedure law
Law of precedent, 47
Law-Related Education (LRE) program, 551
Lawsuit(s)
　court congestion impact on, 304–306
　domestic violence, 161–163
　filing of, 261
　O. J. Simpson, 41
　processing time, 278–279
　rulings on, 264
　tracing the course of, 264
Legal guilt, defined, 358
Legal services
　assigned-counsel system, 295–296
　contract system, 296
　public defender system and, 293–294
Leon v. United States, 120, 121
Lethal injection, execution by, 425, 426, 427
Life skills programs, 496

Life without parole, 436–437
Lineup procedure
　age of persons in, 338
　defined, 338
　guidelines for conducting, 338–339
Liquid Ecstasy (drug), 592–593
Literacy programs, 495
Loan-sharking, defined, 14
Logic bombs, 78
Long mandatory sentences, 407
Lower courts, 269
LRE program, 551
LSD drug, 586, 587
Lustig v. United States, 117
Lynching, 433
Lysergic acid diethylamide (LSD), 586, 587

M

Mack Alford Correctional Center, 490
Maconochie, Alexander, 527, 528
Madrid v. Gomez, 507
Mafia
　Mexican, 492
　role in organized crime, 13–15
Magistrate
　appointment of, 269
　defined, 257
Mail fraud/theft, 169
Malice aforethought, defined, 53
Malley v. Briggs, 105
Managed-care facilities, 595
Mandatory minimum sentences, 407, 409
Manifest necessity, 133
Mann Act, 76
Manslaughter
　involuntary, 56
　misdemeanor, 56
　nonnegligent, 145
　voluntary, 53, 55
Mapp v. Ohio, 117, 344
Marijuana, 586, 587, 593, 599, 601
Marion prison facility (Illinois), 480–481
Massachusetts v. Sheppard, 120
Material evidence, 367
Matricides, 573
Matsos v. Commonwealth, 80
Maxi-maxi prisons, 480
Maximum-security prisons, 477–478
McCleskey v. Kemp, 434
McCleskey v. Zant, 428
McGruff campaign, 245
MDMA drug, 588–589
Media
　in the courtroom, 360–361
　public trials and, 130
　stress caused by, 302
Medium-security prisons, 485–486
Megan's Laws, 413, 414
Mens rea
　actus reus and, 50
　of arson, 67
　of battery, 56
　of burglary, 66–67
　to crime of false pretense, 72
　criminal responsibility and, 49–50
　of larceny, 69
　of murder, 53

of rape, 62–63
Mentally ill inmates, 457, 461–462, 497–498
Mescaline (peyote), 586, 587
Mesolimbic reward system, 582
Methamphetamine, 589–590
Methcathinone, 590
Mexican Mafia, 492
Military tribunals
  in the age of terrorism, 272–273
  justice process and, 273–274
Milken, Michael, 401
Mind erasers (drug), 591
Minimum-security prisons, 486
Minnesota correctional facility, 484–485
Minor defendants, 423
Minorities. *See* Ethnic groups
Miracle Drug, 585
Miranda rights, 122, 124, 126
Miranda v. Arizona, 122, 123, 200
Miranda warnings, 125
Misdemeanors
  defined, 6, 49
  manslaughter, 56
  prosecution in, 314–317
  trials, 331–332
Missing Children Act, 563
Missing Children Assistance Act, 563
Missouri Plan, 297, 298, 299
Mistake of fact, 381
Mistrials, double jeopardy prohibition and, 133
Mitcheson v. State, 382
M'Naghten test of insanity, 378
Mobile identification number (MIN), 12, 13
Mock trials, 551
Model Rules of Professional Conduct, 291
Modern crimes
  computer crime, 77–78
  identity theft, 78
  stalking, 78–80
Modus operandi, 202
Morales v. Chicago, 134, 135
Morphine, 582
Mothers Against Drunk Driving (MADD), 168, 171, 525
Motion for a bill of particulars, 343
Motion for a change of venue, 341
Motion for a judgment of acquittal, 387
Motion for discovery, 341
Motion for severance, 341–342
Motion of intention to provide alibi, 341
Motion to determine competency, 342
Motion to dismiss, 340–341
Motion to suppress, 343–344
Motor-vehicle theft, 150
Motor Vehicle Theft Prevention Act (MVTPA), 246
Murder
  case study, 54
  defined, 52, 145
  elements of, 52–53
  fetal, 52
  rate of, 146
  related to recklessness, 55
Murray v. Giarrantano, 429

N

Narcotics
  defined, 582
  effects of, 583
  in jails, 469
  types of, 582–583
National Association of Women Judges, 300
National Center for Missing and Exploited Children, 563
National Crime Information Center (NCIC), 183, 204–205
National Crime Victimization Survey (NCVS), 159
National Drug Prevention System (NDPS), 598
National Incident-Based Reporting System (NBRS), 154
National Institute of Justice (NIJ), 228, 453, 521
National Organization for Victim Assistance (NOVA), 171
National Organization of Black Law Enforcement Executives (NOBLE), 218
National Service Programs, 598
National Sheriffs' Association (NSA), 218, 507
National Structural Evaluation (NSE), 598
National Threat Assessment Center (NTAC), 570
"Needle Park," 601
Neighborhood(s)
  policing, 209–210
  signs of crime in, 241
  watch programs, 240
Network fraud, 13
New York Prison Association, 528
NIMBY syndrome, 536
"No knock rule," 101
Nolle prosequi, 284, 287, 317
Nonconsensual sex offenses, 73
Noncrime calls, 187
Nonresidential programs, 558
Norms
  defined, 42
  deviant behavior and, 44–45
  normative variations and, 42–43
  social sanctions and, 42
  social values and law and, 43
  value consensus and value conflict model and, 43
  value divergence model and, 43
North Carolina v. Alfred, 346

O

O. J. Simpson trials, 40, 41, 368–369
Oak Park Heights prison facility (Minnesota), 484–485
Ochoa v. People, 56
Offenders. *See also* Inmates; Juvenile offenders
  community service by, 537–538
  educational release program for, 537
  furlough programs for, 537
  house arrest for, 523–524
  Salient Factor Score and, 532–533
  sentencing disparities and, 413–417
  shock incarceration programs for, 535
  work release programs for, 537
Office of Community Oriented Policing Services (COPS), 208, 569
Office of Juvenile Justice and Delinquency Prevention (OJJDP), 551, 555, 556, 559
Office of National Drug Control Policy (ONDCP), 272, 596
Oklahoma City bombing case, 284
Older people as victims, 168–169
Omnibus Crime Control and Safe Streets Act, 125, 126, 219, 569
Opening statements, 374
Operation Clean Sweep, 194

Opium, 582, 583
Organized crime
  defined, 13
  future of, 15–16
  Mafia's role in, 14–15
  roots of, 13–14
Outlaws, biker gangs and, 45
OxyContin, 585

P

Paralegal, duties of, 375
Parens patriae philosophy, 543, 547
Parks, crime prevention in, 245
Parole
  appeal for, 530
  boards, 529–530
  conditions of, 520–521, 530–531
  criminological predictions and, 534–535
  decision-making process and, 530
  defined, 24
  developments in, 528
  Elmira Reformatory and, 528–529
  innovations in, 535–537
  jail overcrowding and, 488
  justice process and, 24–25
  officer, 529
  origin of, 526–528
  probation and, 452
  prosecutor's role in, 285
  recidivism rates and, 531–532
  Salient Factor Score and, 532–533
  selection of, 529
  selective incapacitation and, 533–534
Partnership for a Drug-Free America, 601
Patricides, 573
Patrol
  bike, 191
  directed, 193
  division, 184–186
  foot, 191–192
  nontraditional, 190–191
  research of women on, 225
  sergeant, 186
Patrol officer
  activities of, 186–189
  duties of, 185–186
Patrol strategies
  crackdowns and, 193
  directed patrol and, 193
  foot patrol and, 191–192
  Kansas City Preventive Patrol Experiment, 190
  nontraditional, 190–191
Patterson v. People, 53, 55
Payton v. New York, 100, 101, 102, 119
Peery v. State, 74
Pelican Bay prison facility, 483
Penal Servitude Act, 527
Penetration, defined, 550
Pennsylvania State Correctional Institution, 490
Pennsylvania system, 477
Penry v. Lynaugh, 423, 438
People v. Goetz, 380
People v. Home Insurance Co., 68
People v. Humphrey, 384
People v. Ochoa, 56
People v. Patterson, 53, 55
People v. Rojas, 72
People v. Vogel, 381

Pepper spray, 233
Peremptory challenges, 364
PERF study, 203
Personal crimes, 7
Petition, filing of, 555
Phencyclidine (PCP), 586
Physical abuse, 383–384
Pillories, 476
Plain-view exception, 115–116
Plea bargaining/negotiations
  vs. criminal trial, 281–282
  defense lawyers and, 290
  evaluation of, 350
  factors in, 350
  guilty pleas and, 345–346
  justification for, 345
  pretrial diversion as an alternative to, 351
  process, 346–347
  prosecutor's role in, 344–345
  victims and, 347–349
Plea colloquy, 346
Police
  arrest warrant and, 100–102
  campus, 198–199
  constitutional arrest and, 100
  contact with public, 230
  crackdowns, 194
  detective role of, 199–202
  on horseback, 192
  juvenile courts and, 549
  misconduct, 220–222
  partnership with, 248, 249
  patrol operations by, 184–186
  prosecutors and, 233–234
  role in anti-drug efforts, 247
  role in CPTED applications, 244–245
  role in crime prevention, 240–241
  role in domestic violence cases, 161–162
  role in handling juveniles, 552–554
  search rights of, 117
  search warrant and, 112
  traffic responsibilities of, 189, 194, 196–197
  use of deadly force by, 230–233
  zero tolerance policing by, 193–194
Police departments
  features of, 178
  local, 179–181
Police Executive Research Forum (PERF), 203, 218
Police officer(s)
  health issues, 225–229
  higher education for, 219–221
  selection and training of, 179–181
  violence prone, 233
Policing
  accreditation issues, 218–219
  crime prevention and, 239–249
  evolution of, 181–184, 205
  minorities and women in, 223–225
  neighborhoods, 209–210
  problem-oriented approach to, 210–211
  professionalism of, 218
  rural, 197–198
  technological trends in, 234–239
  traditional vs. community, 206
  zero tolerance, 193–194
Political pressures, stress caused by, 302
Postarrest investigation, 23
Postconviction remedies, 24

Prearrest investigation, 22
Pre-law undergraduate advisor, 337
Preliminary (bindover) hearing, 23
   nature of, 332–333
   prosecutor's role in, 284
   purpose of, 316
   rights afforded during, 336
Preliminary investigations
   detectives' role in, 200–201
   patrol officers and, 187–188
Preponderance of the evidence
   criminal law and, 40
   defined, 24
   O. J. Simpson case and, 41
   reasonable doubt and, 359
Prescriptions, defined, 42
Presentence report
   effect of, 404–405
   probation and, 405, 520
Presentment, defined, 335
Press. *See* Media
Presumptive sentence, 408
Pretrial detention
   bail and, 314–315
   facility, 446
Pretrial diversion programs, 351
Pretrial misconduct
   bail issues and, 321
   drug testing and, 318
Pretrial motions
   benefits of, 340
   constitutional right of being competent to stand trial, 342–343
   criminal justice process and, 24
   defined, 340
   motion for a bill of particulars, 343
   motion for a change of venue, 341
   motion for discovery, 341
   motion for severance, 341–342
   motion of intention to provide alibi, 341
   motion to determine competency, 342
   motion to dismiss, 340–341
   prosecutor's role in, 285
Pretrial procedures
   arraignment, 339–340
   bail issues, 317–331
   felony charging, 335–336, 338–339
   grand jury, 334–335
   introduction to, 313
   misdemeanor trials, 331–332
   plea negotiations, 344–351
   preliminary hearing, 332–333
   pretrial diversion programs, 351
   pretrial motions, 340–343
   prosecution issues, 314–317, 332
   suppression hearing, 343–344
Pretrial publicity, 361–362
Pretrial release
   jail overcrowding and, 321
   procedures, 322
Pretrial services, 451
Preventive detention
   denial of bail and, 328
   effects of, 330–331
Prison(s). *See also* Jail(s)
   administrative segregation and, 478–480
   AIDS and HIV in, 500–501
   condom distribution in, 501
   educational programs in, 495–496
   furlough programs and, 537
   gangs in, 491–494
   history of, 476–477
   introduction to, 475–476
   maintenance programs, 496–497
   maximum-security, 477–478, 480–485
   medium-security, 485–486
   minimum-security, 486
   private, 506–509
   reception centers at, 486–487
   riots in, 489–491
   sexuality in, 499–500
   supermax, 480–484
   women in, 501–506
   work programs, 496
Privacy issues, 106–107
Private party exception, 120
Private security, 234
Privatization of prisons
   arguments against, 508–509
   arguments for, 507–508
   introduction to, 506–507
Privileged communications, 370
Proactive beats, 190
Proactive crime prevention, 180
Probable cause
   defined, 98, 314
   requirement, 110
Probation
   with adjudication, 519–520
   conditions of, 520–521
   defined, 24
   father of, 519
   imposing, 519
   innovations in, 523–526
   intensive-supervision, 521–522
   introduction to, 517–518
   jail overcrowding and, 452
   juvenile, 560
   origin of, 518–519
   presentence reports and, 520
   purpose of, 518
   restructuring of, 521
   revocations, 522–523, 561
Probation officer
   as caseworker, 523
   duties of, 405, 519
   house arrest and, 525
   juvenile, 560
Probation revocation hearing
   criminal justice process and, 24–25
   prosecutor's role in, 285
Problem-oriented policing (POP)
   defined, 205
   development of, 210–211
   future of, 211–212
Professional auto theft, 150
Professional officer track, 186
Professional police management track, 186
Programmed contact devices, 524–525
Property crimes, 29
Proscriptions, defined, 42
Pro se, defined, 291
Prosecution
   double jeopardy prohibition and, 134
   felony, 332
   in misdemeanor cases, 314–317

Oklahoma City bombing case and, 284
witnesses, 374
Prosecutor(s)
decision to prosecute, 286
defense lawyers and, 279–282
deferred adjudication and, 289
defined, 283
diversion concept, 289
duty to disclose evidence, 289
educational requirements for, 282
functions of, 283, 286
intimidation prevention by, 157–158
jail overcrowding and, 451
opening statements by, 374
police and, 233–234
power of discretion, 287
public image of, 285–286
role of, 283–285, 344–347
unethical procedures by, 288
Prosecutor's information
constitutional requirements for, 336, 338
defined, 336
Prostitution, 76–77, 194
Protective custody (PC) unit, 481
Pseudofamilies, 505–506
Psilocybe mushrooms, 586, 587
Psychedelics
features of, 586
types of, 586–589
Psychotropics
alcohol, 586
dangerous behavior caused by, 19–20
defined, 19
marijuana, 586
narcotics, 582–585
Public defender
duties of, 376
system, 293–294
Public gatherings, 187
Public image
of judges, 301–302
of prosecutors, 285–286
Public safety, house arrest and, 526
Public trial, 130
Punishment. *See also* Capital punishment
cruel and unusual, 134, 136, 438
enhancement statutes and, 409–413
house arrest as, 525
justification for, 396–397
to women, 501–502
Punishment theories
deterrence, 399
incapacitation, 400
rehabilitation, 400–401
reintegration, 401
retribution, 398–399

Q

Quid pro quo sexual harassment, 64
Quota system, 196–197

R

Racial profiling
conviction rates and, 26–28
house arrest and, 526
in New Jersey, 27
stereotypes and, 26
traffic stops and, 189

victims and, 160
Racing, defined, 80
Racist skinheads, 54
Racketeering, biker gangs and, 45
Rand criminal investigation study, 202–203
Rape. *See also* Date rape drugs
consent and, 62
counselor, 157
date, 63–64
defined, 29, 62
forcible, 73, 146
landmark cases, 63
mens rea of, 62–63
reasons for not reporting, 146–147
statutory, 63, 73
Rave (drug), 588
Reactive beats, 190
Real evidence
defined, 366
examples of, 368
Realina v. State, 380
Reasonable doubt
defined, 359
proving defendant guilty beyond, 359–360
Reasonable provocation, 53
Reasonable requirement, 109–110
Rebuttal, 385
Receiving stolen property, 72–73
Reception and classification centers, 486–487
Recidivism rates
drug courts programs and, 272
Salient Factor Score and, 531–533
selective incapacitation and, 533–534
Reckless driving, 81
Recklessness
defined, 53
murder related to, 55
Recreational programs
inmates, 497
rehabilitation, 466
Reformatories
development of, 545
for women, 502–504
Rehabilitation
components of, 400–401
crime and, 5
drug courts programs and, 272
of female inmates, 506
jail overcrowding and, 487
recreational programs for, 466
Rehnquist Court, 90
Reintegration theory, 401
Release
conditional, 323
mechanism, pretrial, 315
supervised, 321
upon summons, 321, 323
Release on own recognizance (R.O.R), 321
Relevant evidence, 367
Religious programs, 466, 498
Repeat Call Address Policing (RECAP)
Experiment, 194
Residential child care facility, 549
Residential programs, 557–558
Resource coordinator, 136
Restitution programs
defined, 156
for juveniles, 557

Restriction Fragment Length Polymorphism (RFLP) typing, 239
Retribution theory
  capital punishment and, 431
  philosophy supporting, 398–399
Reversible error, defined, 418
Reynolds v. State, 55, 56
Rhodes v. Chapman, 397
Right of competency to stand trial, 342–343
Right to counsel, 122–124, 126–128, 291
Riots, 489–491
Road rage, 81–82
Robberies
  convenience store, 244
  criminal statutes and, 70
  defined, 69, 147
  elements of, 69–70
  motivation for, 70
  rate of, 147–148
Rodney King case, 374, 382
Rodriguez-Moreno v. United States, 412
Rodriguez v. Illinois, 114
Rohypnol, 591–592
Rojas v. People, 72
Roofies (drug), 591
Runaway children
  agencies' response to, 562–563
  defined, 561
  features of, 562
Rural policing, 197–198
Russian organized crime (ROC) organizations, 15–16

S

Sabbaticals, judicial, 304
Safe and Drug-Free Schools and Communities Act (SDFSCA), 596
Safe Neighborhoods Program, 244
Salami technique, 78
Salerno v. United States, 97, 328, 330
Salient Factor Score, 532–533
Schlup v. Delo, 420
Scholastic Crime Stoppers Program, 567
School resource officer (SRO), 567, 569–575
Schools
  industrial, 545
  safe and drug-free, 596
School violence
  crime and, 566
  NTAC study and, 570
  prevention of, 567–568, 571
  reports, 566
  school environment role in, 566–567
  Secret Service Safe School Initiative and, 569–570
  SRO role in handling, 569
Scoop (drug), 592–593
Screening officer, 464
Search(es)
  defined, 98
  Fourteenth Amendment rights on, 98–99
  government conduct and, 106
  for illegal drugs, 599
  lawful arrests and, 111–112
  plain-view, 115–116
  police rights for, 117
  privacy issues under, 106–107
  during routine traffic stop, 103
  unreasonable, 105–106
Search warrant
  defined, 107
  exceptions to requirements of, 111–117
  landmark cases, 108, 113, 114
  requirements for, 107–111
Secret service agent, 184
Secret Service Safe School Initiative, 569–570
Security issues. *See also* Jail security
  illicit drug use and, 601
  in parks, 245
Seizure(s)
  defined, 98
  Fourteenth Amendment rights on, 98–99
  unreasonable, 105–106
Selective incapacitation, 533–534
Selective traffic enforcement, 196
Self-defense, right of, 379–380
Self-incrimination, 122–124
Sentence bargaining, 345
Sentenced facility, 446
Sentencing
  advent of tougher, 29–30
  appeal process and, 417–420
  capital punishment debate and, 429–438
  criminal justice process and, 24
  death penalty issues and, 420–429
  defined, 395
  disparities in, 413–417
  enhancement statutes and, 409–413
  guidelines, 415–417
  harsh, 419–420
  hearing, 402
  house arrest as, 524
  indeterminate, 487
  introduction to, 396
  jail overcrowding impact on, 397–398
  judges' role in, 401–402, 405–407
  parole decisions and, 531
  prosecutor's role in, 285
  structures, 407–409
  in twenty-first century, 413
  types of, 398
  victim-impact statement during, 405
Serious and violent juvenile (SVJ) offenders, 564–565
Sex offenses/offenders
  date rape drugs and, 590–593
  in jails, 458
  Megan's Laws and, 414
  neutral, 63
  nonconsensual, 73
Sexual activity
  in prison, 499–500
  between staff and inmates, 506
Sexual assault. *See* Sex offenses/offenders
Sexual harassment
  case study, 65
  defined, 64
  rules related to, 64
Shakedowns, 467
Shelter, defined, 549
Sheppard v. Massachusetts, 120
Sheriff's office
  community policing and, 207
  features of, 179–180
Shock incarceration programs, 535
Shooting-control techniques, 232
Shoplifting. *See* Larceny
Showup procedures, 338

Silver platter doctrine, 117
Simpson, O. J., 40, 41, 368–369
Sixth Amendment
    identification procedures under, 339
    right to counsel and, 126–128
    speedy trial and, 129
    witness's testimony issues under, 131–132
Slow plea, defined, 345
Smith v. California, 74
Snipers
    case study, 20–21
    terrorist crimes by, 19
Social isolation, stress caused by, 302
Socialization
    defined, 42
    deviant behavior and, 44–45
    of judges, 300–301
    normative variations and, 42–43
    social sanctions and, 42
    social values and law and, 43
    value conflict model and, 43
    value consensus model and, 43
    value divergence model and, 43
Sodomy, 73, 75–76
Southern Ohio Correctional Facility, 490
"Special K" (drug), 588
Special-management inmates, 455–456
Special-purpose police, 178
Specialty courts
    drug courts, 270–272
    military tribunals, 272–274
Specific deterrence, 399
Speed (drug), 590
Speedy trial, right to, 129–130
Spiritual redemption, 4–5
Staff(ing)
    at halfway house, 536–537
    morale issues, 454
    ratio in jails, 455
    sexual contact between inmates and, 506
Stalking
    defined, 78
    investigation strategies, 166
    landmark cases, 80
Stanford v. Kentucky, 423
Stare decisis
    case law and, 47
    defined, 46
State court(s)
    appellate courts, 265–267
    case filings in, 261
    decentralization of, 261
    felony courts, 268
    hierarchical systems, 258, 260
    of last resort, 265
    lower courts, 269
    trial courts, 267–268
State law enforcement, 183
State legislator, 49
State trooper, 183
State v. Mitcheson, 382
State v. Peery, 74
State v. Realina, 380
State v. Taft, 82
State v. Tripp, 60
State v. Walden, 63
"Stationhouse Bail issues/system," 23
Status offenses, 551, 556–557

Statutory law, 47
Statutory rape, 63
Stimulants
    features of, 589
    types of, 589–590
Sting operation, 202
Stolen cars. *See* Motor-vehicle theft
Stop-and-frisk exception, 116
Stops and detentions, 103–105
Strict-liability offense, 50
Student Right-to-Know and Campus Security Act, 154
Subscription fraud, 13
Substance Abuse and Mental Health Services
        Administration (SAMHSA), 593, 594
Substantive criminal law
    crimes against habitation, 66–67
    crimes against morality, 74–77
    crimes against persons, 56–65
    crimes against property, 68–73
    vs. criminal procedure law, 90–91
    defined, 46
    elements of, 51–52
    environmental crimes, 82–83
    homicide, 52–56
    major crimes of, 52
    modern crimes, 77–80
    sources of, 46–49
    traffic offenses, 80–82
Suicide
    among police officers, 229
    precipitating factors for, 458, 462
    prevention programs, 463
    screening inmates for, 462–463
Summary trial, 317
Suppression hearing
    motion to suppress and, 343–344
    right to, 118, 344
Supreme Court
    constitutional arrest and, 103–104
    constitutional confession and, 124–126
    death penalty and, 423, 425
    due process and, 95–97
    judicial review by, 95
    privacy issues and, 106–107
    public trials and, 131
    requirements for guilty pleas, 346
    rulings on a case by, 264
    selective incorporation doctrine and, 94–95
    sentencing hearing and, 406
    state, 265
    structure of, 262–263
    tracing the course of case to, 264
Surrebuttal, 385
Suspended sentence, 518–519
SVJ offending
    predictors of, 565
    prevalence of, 565–566
Synthetic drugs, 602

T

Taft v. State, 82
Take into custody concept, 549
Talion law, 155
Tattooing, 500
Technological trends
    CAD system, 234–235
    DNA profiling, 238

fingerprint automation, 235–236
geographical information system, 238–239
laptop computers, 237
Teen courts, 548
Telecommunication crime
defined, 10
types of, 10–13
Telephone phreakers, hacking and, 11–13
Tennessee v. Garner, 102, 232, 383
Terrorist crimes
counterterrorism and, 16–17
defined, 16
domestic, 17
international, 17
military tribunals and, 272–273
by snipers, 19
Terry v. Ohio, 104, 116
Testimonial evidence, 366
Thompson v. Oklahoma, 423, 438
Three-strikes laws
case study, 412
defined, 410
in various states, 411
Time served, actual, 416
Tool control system, 467
Traffic law enforcement
patrol officers and, 188
police's role in, 194, 196–197
quota system and, 196–197
selective traffic enforcement and, 196
Traffic offenses
DUI/DWI, 81
hit and run, 81
racing, 80
reckless driving, 81
road rage, 81–82
vehicular homicide, 81
Traffic stops, racial profiling and, 189
Trap doors, defined, 78
Travis v. United States, 341, 342
Treatment programs
for inmates, 497–498
in jails, 463–466
Trial(s)
bifurcated, 402
mock, 551
prosecutor's role in, 285
of public defender, 295
right of competency to stand, 342–343
Trial courts
administrator, 277
vs. appellate courts, 258
federal and state, 267–268
felony, 258
important players in, 279
prosecution and defense lawyers and, 279–282
workload of, 268
Tripp v. State, 60
Trojan horses, 77–78
True bill, defined, 335
Tuberculosis, inmates with, 456
Tumbling, 13

U

U.S. Constitution. *See* Constitution
U.S. Courts of Appeal, 266
U.S. Marshal, duties of, 404
U.S. Penitentiary, 489

U.S. Supreme Court. *See* Supreme Court
Unabomber, 17
Unemployment rate, homicide rate and, 30
UNICOR prison industries, 481
Uniform Crime Reporting (UCR) program
criticism of, 152–153
features of, 144–145
future of, 153–154
goal of, 144
vs. NCVS, 159
Uniform Crime Victims Reparations Act, 156
Unions, Mafia's role in, 14
United States v. Ammidown, 347
United States v. Armstrong, 287
United States v. Henry, 123
United States v. Leon, 120, 121
United States v. Rodriguez-Moreno, 412
United States v. Salerno, 97, 328, 329
United States v. Watson, 98
United States v. Wilson, 71
Unlawful arrests. *See* Arrest(s)

V

Valium, 591
Value conflict model, 43
Value consensus model, 43
Value divergence model, 43
V-chip, 30
Vehicular homicide, 81
Venire, defined, 363
Verdict
guilty, 387
jury's, 386
Victim-impact statement, 156, 348, 405
Victimization studies
victims and, 158–160
victim surveys and, 160
Victims
advocate, 157
of aggravated assault, 148–149
categories of, 160–169
children as, 165–167
compensation, 155, 408
criminal and civil law and, 41
cycle of violence and, 167–168
of domestic violence, 163
of drunken-driving accidents, 168
government programs for, 155–158
of hate crimes, 61
impact of crime on, 155
intimidation issues, 157–158
older people as, 168–169
plea bargaining and, 347–349
race and, 160
rape, 62–63, 146–147
of sexual assault, 592
victim special-interest groups for, 170–171
of workplace violence, 170
Victim/witness coordinator, 349
Violence. *See also* School violence
against abortion clinics, 17–18
cycle of, 167–168
gangs and, 492, 494, 571–573
illegality of drugs and, 599, 600
intimate-partner, 160–165
sexual and physical, 169–170
V-chip and, 30
victims of, 160

workplace, 170
Violence against Women Act, 163–164
Violent Crime Control and Law Enforcement Act, 151
Violent crimes
  arrest rates for, 26–27
  decline in, 28
  types of, 145–149
Visitation control system, 469
Vitamin K (drug), 588
Vocational educational programs, 496, 506
Vogel v. People, 381
Void-for-vagueness doctrine, 134
Voir dire
  defined, 363
  examination of jurors, 364
Voluntary manslaughter
  defined, 53
  elements of, 53, 55

W

Waiver of prosecution, 148
Walden v. State, 63
Walnut Street Jail, 447
Warden, duties of, 479
Watch Your Car Program, 246
Watson v. United States, 98
Weapons
  in schools, 570–571
  used by children, 573–574
  used by inmates, 467
  used in aggravated assault, 148
  used in murders, 146
Weeks v. United States, 117
Wheat v. United States, 128
White-collar crime
  defined, 7
  embezzlement, 71
  Michael Milken and, 401
Whitewater investigations, 337
Wilderness programs, 558
Williams v. New York, 406
Wilson v. United States, 71

Witness(es)
  competent and incompetent, 367–368
  compulsory process for obtaining, 132–133
  court congestion impact on, 305–306
  cross-examination of, 375
  expert, 369
  intimidation issues, 157–158
  prosecution, 374
  right to confront, 131–132
  testimonial evidence and, 368
Wolf v. Colorado, 117
Women
  confinement for, 502
  criminal activity of, 505
  domestic training for, 504
  in prison, 403, 501, 504–505
  pseudofamilies and, 505–506
  punishment to, 501–502
  recruitment of, 224–225
  reformatories for, 502–504
  stress and, 227
  violence against, 169–170
Workplace violence, 170
World Trade Center
  bombings at, 17
  destruction of, 18–19
Writ of *certiorari*, 263, 265
Wrongful convictions, 288, 434
Wyoming v. Houghton, 113

Y

Youth gangs
  conclusion about, 572–573
  reasons to join, 572
  scope of problems of, 571–572
Youths, alcohol use among, 593, 594, 596

Z

Zero-tolerance policing
  in Pennsylvania, 195
  by police, 193–194
Zero-tolerance policy, 567